SECOND EDITION

APPLIED REGRESSION ANALYSIS and GENERALIZED LINEAR MODELS

For Bonnie and Jesse (again)

SECOND EDITION

APPLIED REGRESSION ANALYSIS and GENERALIZED LINEAR MODELS

John Fox

McMaster University, Hamilton, Ontario, Canada

Los Angeles • London • New Delhi • Singapore

For information:

SAGE Publications, Inc.
2455 Teller Road
Thousand Oaks,
California 91320
E-mail: order@sagepub.com

SAGE Publications Ltd.
1 Oliver's Yard
55 City Road
London EC1Y 1SP
United Kingdom

SAGE Publications India Pvt. Ltd.
B 1/I 1 Mohan Cooperative Industrial Area
Mathura Road, New Delhi 110 044
India

SAGE Publications Asia-Pacific Pte. Ltd.
33 Pekin Street #02-01
Far East Square
Singapore 048763

Printed in the United States of America

Library of Congress Cataloging-in-Publication Data

Fox, John, 1947-
Applied regression analysis and generalized linear models/John Fox. —2nd ed.
    p. cm.
Rev. ed. of: Applied regression analysis, linear models, and related methods. c1997.
Includes bibliographical references and index.
ISBN 978-0-7619-3042-6 (cloth)
    1. Regression analysis. 2. Linear models (Statistics) 3. Social sciences—Statistical methods. I. Fox, John, 1947- Applied regression analysis and generalized linear models. II. Title.

HA31.3.F69 2008
300.1′519536—dc22   2007047617

Printed on acid-free paper

                    11   12   10   9   8   7   6   5   4

Acquisitions Editor:	Vicki Knight
Associate Editor:	Sean Connelly
Editorial Assistant:	Lauren Habib
Production Editor:	Cassandra Margaret Seibel
Copy Editor:	QuADS Prepress (P) Ltd.
Typesetter:	C&M Digitals (P) Ltd.
Proofreader:	Kevin Gleason
Cover Designer:	Candice Harman
Marketing Manager:	Stephanie Adams

Contents

Preface   **xiv**

1 Statistical Models and Social Science   **1**
1.1   Statistical Models and Social Reality   1
1.2   Observation and Experiment   4
1.3   Populations and Samples   8
Exercise   9
Summary   9
Recommended Reading   10

PART I DATA CRAFT   **11**

2 What Is Regression Analysis?   **13**
2.1   Preliminaries   15
2.2   Naive Nonparametric Regression   17
2.3   Local Averaging   21
Exercise   24
Summary   25

3 Examining Data   **26**
3.1   Univariate Displays   28
      3.1.1   Histograms   28
      3.1.2   Nonparametric Density Estimation   30
      3.1.3   Quantile-Comparison Plots   34
      3.1.4   Boxplots   37
3.2   Plotting Bivariate Data   40
3.3   Plotting Multivariate Data   43
      3.3.1   Scatterplot Matrices   44
      3.3.2   Coded Scatterplots   45
      3.3.3   Three-Dimensional Scatterplots   45
      3.3.4   Conditioning Plots   46
Summary   47
Recommended Reading   49

4 Transforming Data **50**

4.1 The Family of Powers and Roots 50

4.2 Transforming Skewness 54

4.3 Transforming Nonlinearity 57

4.4 Transforming Nonconstant Spread 63

4.5 Transforming Proportions 66

4.6 Estimating Transformations as Parameters* 68

Exercises 71

Summary 72

Recommended Reading 72

PART II LINEAR MODELS AND LEAST SQUARES **75**

5 Linear Least-Squares Regression **77**

5.1 Simple Regression 78

    5.1.1 Least-Squares Fit 78

    5.1.2 Simple Correlation 82

5.2 Multiple Regression 86

    5.2.1 Two Explanatory Variables 86

    5.2.2 Several Explanatory Variables 90

    5.2.3 Multiple Correlation 92

    5.2.4 Standardized Regression Coefficients 94

Exercises 96

Summary 98

6 Statistical Inference for Regression **100**

6.1 Simple Regression 100

    6.1.1 The Simple-Regression Model 100

    6.1.2 Properties of the Least-Squares Estimator 102

    6.1.3 Confidence Intervals and Hypothesis Tests 104

6.2 Multiple Regression 105

    6.2.1 The Multiple-Regression Model 105

    6.2.2 Confidence Intervals and Hypothesis Tests 106

6.3 Empirical Versus Structural Relations 110

6.4 Measurement Error in Explanatory Variables* 112

Exercises 115

Summary 118

7 Dummy-Variable Regression **120**

7.1 A Dichotomous Factor 120

7.2 Polytomous Factors 124

    7.2.1 Coefficient Quasi-Variances* 129

7.3 Modeling Interactions 131

    7.3.1 Constructing Interaction Regressors 132

    7.3.2 The Principle of Marginality 135

    7.3.3 Interactions With Polytomous Factors 135

	7.3.4	Interpreting Dummy-Regression Models With Interactions	136
	7.3.5	Hypothesis Tests for Main Effects and Interactions	137
7.4	A Caution Concerning Standardized Coefficients		140
	Exercises		140
	Summary		141

8 Analysis of Variance — **143**

8.1	One-Way Analysis of Variance		143
8.2	Two-Way Analysis of Variance		149
	8.2.1	Patterns of Means in the Two-Way Classification	149
	8.2.2	The Two-Way ANOVA Model	154
	8.2.3	Fitting the Two-Way ANOVA Model to Data	156
	8.2.4	Testing Hypotheses in Two-Way ANOVA	158
	8.2.5	Equal Cell Frequencies	161
	8.2.6	Some Cautionary Remarks	162
8.3	Higher-Way Analysis of Variance		163
	8.3.1	The Three-Way Classification	163
	8.3.2	Higher-Order Classifications	166
	8.3.3	Empty Cells in ANOVA	172
8.4	Analysis of Covariance		173
8.5	Linear Contrasts of Means		176
	Exercises		180
	Summary		185

9 Statistical Theory for Linear Models* — **187**

9.1	Linear Models in Matrix Form		187
	9.1.1	Dummy Regression and Analysis of Variance	188
	9.1.2	Linear Contrasts	191
9.2	Least-Squares Fit		192
9.3	Properties of the Least-Squares Estimator		194
	9.3.1	The Distribution of the Least-Squares Estimator	195
	9.3.2	The Gauss-Markov Theorem	196
	9.3.3	Maximum-Likelihood Estimation	197
9.4	Statistical Inference for Linear Models		198
	9.4.1	Inference for Individual Coefficients	198
	9.4.2	Inference for Several Coefficients	200
	9.4.3	General Linear Hypotheses	202
	9.4.4	Joint Confidence Regions	203
9.5	Multivariate Linear Models		207
9.6	Random Regressors		210
9.7	Specification Error		212
	Exercises		213
	Summary		217
	Recommended Reading		219

10	**The Vector Geometry of Linear Models***	**220**
	10.1 Simple Regression	220
	10.1.1 Variables in Mean-Deviation Form	222
	10.1.2 Degrees of Freedom	224
	10.2 Multiple Regression	226
	10.3 Estimating the Error Variance	231
	10.4 Analysis-of-Variance Models	233
	Exercises	235
	Summary	236
	Recommended Reading	238

PART III LINEAR-MODEL DIAGNOSTICS   **239**

11	**Unusual and Influential Data**	**241**
	11.1 Outliers, Leverage, and Influence	241
	11.2 Assessing Leverage: Hat-Values	244
	11.3 Detecting Outliers: Studentized Residuals	246
	11.3.1 Testing for Outliers in Linear Models	247
	11.3.2 Anscombe's Insurance Analogy	248
	11.4 Measuring Influence	250
	11.4.1 Influence on Standard Errors	252
	11.4.2 Influence on Collinearity	253
	11.5 Numerical Cutoffs for Diagnostic Statistics	254
	11.5.1 Hat-Values	254
	11.5.2 Studentized Residuals	254
	11.5.3 Measures of Influence	255
	11.6 Joint Influence	255
	11.6.1 Added-Variable Plots	255
	11.6.2 Forward Search	259
	11.7 Should Unusual Data Be Discarded?	260
	11.8 Some Statistical Details*	261
	11.8.1 Hat-Values and the Hat-Matrix	261
	11.8.2 The Distribution of the Least-Squares Residuals	262
	11.8.3 Deletion Diagnostics	262
	11.8.4 Added-Variable Plots and Leverage Plots	263
	Exercises	264
	Summary	265
	Recommended Reading	266

12	**Diagnosing Non-Normality, Nonconstant Error Variance, and Nonlinearity**	**267**
	12.1 Non-Normally Distributed Errors	268
	12.1.1 Confidence Envelopes by Simulated Sampling*	271
	12.2 Nonconstant Error Variance	272
	12.2.1 Residual Plots	272
	12.2.2 Weighted-Least-Squares Estimation*	274
	12.2.3 Correcting OLS Standard Errors for Nonconstant Variance*	275
	12.2.4 How Nonconstant Error Variance Affects the OLS Estimator*	276

12.3 Nonlinearity   277
    12.3.1 Component-Plus-Residual Plots   278
    12.3.2 Component-Plus-Residual Plots for Models With Interactions   282
    12.3.3 When Do Component-Plus-Residual Plots Work?   284
12.4 Discrete Data   287
    12.4.1 Testing for Nonlinearity ("Lack of Fit")   287
    12.4.2 Testing for Nonconstant Error Variance   290
12.5 Maximum-Likelihood Methods*   291
    12.5.1 Box-Cox Transformation of Y 292
    12.5.2 Box-Tidwell Transformation of the Xs   294
    12.5.3 Nonconstant Error Variance Revisited   296
12.6 Structural Dimension   298
Exercises   301
Summary   305
Recommended Reading   306

13 Collinearity and Its Purported Remedies   **307**
13.1 Detecting Collinearity   308
    13.1.1 Principal Components*   313
    13.1.2 Generalized Variance Inflation*   322
13.2 Coping With Collinearity: No Quick Fix   323
    13.2.1 Model Respecification   323
    13.2.2 Variable Selection   324
    13.2.3 Biased Estimation   325
    13.2.4 Prior Information About the Regression Coefficients   328
    13.2.5 Some Comparisons   329
Exercises   330
Summary   331

PART IV GENERALIZED LINEAR MODELS   **333**

14 Logit and Probit Models for Categorical Response Variables   **335**
14.1 Models for Dichotomous Data   335
    14.1.1 The Linear-Probability Model   337
    14.1.2 Transformations of π: Logit and Probit Models   339
    14.1.3 An Unobserved-Variable Formulation   343
    14.1.4 Logit and Probit Models for Multiple Regression   344
    14.1.5 Estimating the Linear Logit Model*   352
14.2 Models for Polytomous Data   355
    14.2.1 The Polytomous Logit Model   355
    14.2.2 Nested Dichotomies   361
    14.2.3 Ordered Logit and Probit Models   363
    14.2.4 Comparison of the Three Approaches   368
14.3 Discrete Explanatory Variables and Contingency Tables   370
    14.3.1 The Binomial Logit Model*   372
Exercises   375
Summary   377
Recommended Reading   378

15	**Generalized Linear Models**	**379**
	15.1 The Structure of Generalized Linear Models	379
	15.1.1 Estimating and Testing GLMs	385
	15.2 Generalized Linear Models for Counts	387
	15.2.1 Models for Overdispersed Count Data	391
	15.2.2 Loglinear Models for Contingency Tables	394
	15.3 Statistical Theory for Generalized Linear Models*	402
	15.3.1 Exponential Families	402
	15.3.2 Maximum-Likelihood Estimation of Generalized Linear Models	404
	15.3.3 Hypothesis Tests	408
	15.3.4 Effect Displays	411
	15.4 Diagnostics for Generalized Linear Models	412
	15.4.1 Outlier, Leverage, and Influence Diagnostics	412
	15.4.2 Nonlinearity Diagnostics	415
	Exercises	417
	Summary	421
	Recommended Reading	424

PART V EXTENDING LINEAR AND GENERALIZED LINEAR MODELS — **425**

16	**Time-Series Regression and Generalized Least Squares***	**427**
	16.1 Generalized Least-Squares Estimation	428
	16.2 Serially Correlated Errors	429
	16.2.1 The First-Order Autoregressive Process	430
	16.2.2 Higher-Order Autoregressive Processes	433
	16.2.3 Moving-Average and Autoregressive-Moving-Average Processes	434
	16.2.4 Partial Autocorrelations	436
	16.3 GLS Estimation With Autocorrelated Errors	438
	16.3.1 Empirical GLS Estimation	439
	16.3.2 Maximum-Likelihood Estimation	440
	16.4 Diagnosing Serially Correlated Errors	440
	16.5 Concluding Remarks	444
	Exercises	446
	Summary	449
	Recommended Reading	450

17	**Nonlinear Regression**	**451**
	17.1 Polynomial Regression	452
	17.1.1 A Closer Look at Quadratic Surfaces*	455
	17.2 Piece-Wise Polynomials and Regression Splines	455
	17.3 Transformable Nonlinearity	460
	17.4 Nonlinear Least Squares*	463
	17.4.1 Minimizing the Residual Sum of Squares	464
	17.4.2 An Illustration: U.S. Population Growth	467
	Exercises	469
	Summary	474
	Recommended Reading	475

18 Nonparametric Regression   **476**

   18.1 Nonparametric Simple Regression: Scatterplot Smoothing   476

      18.1.1 Kernel Regression   476

      18.1.2 Local-Polynomial Regression   479

      18.1.3 Smoothing Splines*   495

   18.2 Nonparametric Multiple Regression   496

      18.2.1 Local-Polynomial Multiple Regression   496

      18.2.2 Additive Regression Models   508

   18.3 Generalized Nonparametric Regression   517

      18.3.1 Local Likelihood Estimation*   517

      18.3.2 Generalized Additive Models   519

   Exercises   523

   Summary   526

   Recommended Reading   529

19 Robust Regression*   **530**

   19.1 *M* Estimation   530

      19.1.1 Estimating Location   530

      19.1.2 *M* Estimation in Regression   535

   19.2 Bounded-Influence Regression   539

   19.3 Quantile Regression   540

   19.4 Robust Estimation of Generalized Linear Models   543

   19.5 Concluding Remarks   544

   Exercises   544

   Summary   546

   Recommended Reading   547

20 Missing Data in Regression Models   **548**

   20.1 Missing Data Basics   549

      20.1.1 An Illustration   550

   20.2 Traditional Approaches to Missing Data   552

   20.3 Maximum-Likelihood Estimation for Data Missing at Random*   556

      20.3.1 The EM Algorithm   558

   20.4 Bayesian Multiple Imputation   561

      20.4.1 Inference for Individual Coefficients   563

      20.4.2 Inference for Several Coefficients*   565

      20.4.3 Practical Considerations   567

      20.4.4 Example: A Regression Model for Infant Mortality   568

   20.5 Selection Bias and Censoring   570

      20.5.1 Truncated- and Censored-Normal Distributions   571

      20.5.2 Heckman's Selection-Regression Model   573

      20.5.3 Censored-Regression Models   578

   Exercises   580

   Summary   584

   Recommended Reading   586

21 Bootstrapping Regression Models — **587**

21.1 Bootstrapping Basics — 587

21.2 Bootstrap Confidence Intervals — 594

    21.2.1 Normal-Theory Intervals — 594

    21.2.2 Percentile Intervals — 595

    21.2.3 Improved Bootstrap Intervals — 596

21.3 Bootstrapping Regression Models — 597

21.4 Bootstrap Hypothesis Tests* — 599

21.5 Bootstrapping Complex Sampling Designs — 601

21.6 Concluding Remarks — 602

Exercises — 603

Summary — 605

Recommended Reading — 606

22 Model Selection, Averaging, and Validation — **607**

22.1 Model Selection — 607

    22.1.1 Model Selection Criteria — 608

    22.1.2 An Illustration: Baseball Salaries — 618

    22.1.3 Comments on Model Selection — 620

22.2 Model Averaging* — 622

    22.2.1 Application to the Baseball Salary Data — 624

    22.2.2 Comments on Model Averaging — 624

22.3 Model Validation — 626

    22.3.1 An Illustration: Refugee Appeals — 628

    22.3.2 Comments on Model Validation — 630

Exercises — 630

Summary — 632

Recommended Reading — 634

Appendix A: Notation — **636**

References — **638**

Author Index — **648**

Subject Index — **652**

Data Set Index — **664**

About the Author — **665**

Preface _____

Linear models, their variants, and extensions—the most important of which are *generalized linear models*—are among the most useful and widely used statistical tools for social research. This book aims to provide an accessible, in-depth, modern treatment of regression analysis, linear models, generalized linear models, and closely related methods.

The book should be of interest to students and researchers in the social sciences. Although the specific choice of methods and examples reflects this readership, I expect that the book will prove useful in other disciplines that employ regression models for data analysis and in courses on applied regression and generalized linear models where the subject matter of applications is not of special concern.

I have endeavored to make the text as accessible as possible (but no more accessible than possible—i.e., I have resisted watering down the material unduly). With the exception of four chapters, several sections, and a few shorter passages, the prerequisite for reading the book is a course in basic applied statistics that covers the elements of statistical data analysis and inference. To the extent that I could without doing violence to the material, I have tried to present even relatively advanced topics (such as methods for handling missing data and bootstrapping) in a manner consistent with this prerequisite.

Many topics (e.g., logistic regression in Chapter 14) are introduced with an example that motivates the statistics or (as in the case of bootstrapping, in Chapter 21) by appealing to familiar material. The general mode of presentation is from the specific to the general: Consequently, simple and multiple linear regression are introduced before the general linear model, and linear, logit, and probit models are introduced before generalized linear models, which subsume all the previous topics. One could start with generalized linear models and develop all these other topics as special cases but that would produce a much more abstract and difficult treatment.

The exposition of regression analysis starts (in Chapter 2) with an elementary discussion of nonparametric regression, developing the notion of regression as a conditional average—in the absence of restrictive assumptions about the nature of the relationship between the response and explanatory variables. This approach begins closer to the data than the traditional starting point of linear least-squares regression and should make readers sceptical about glib assumptions of linearity, constant variance, and so on.

More difficult chapters and sections are marked with asterisks. These parts of the text can be omitted without loss of continuity, but they provide greater understanding and depth, along with coverage of some topics that depend on more extensive mathematical or statistical background.

I do not, however, wish to exaggerate the background that is required for this "more difficult" material: All that is necessary is some exposure to matrices, elementary linear algebra, elementary differential calculus, and some basic ideas from probability and mathematical statistics. Appendices to the text provide the background required for understanding the more advanced material.

All chapters include summary information in boxes interspersed with the text and at the end of the chapter, and most conclude with recommendations for additional reading. You will find theoretically focused exercises at the end of most chapters, some extending the material in the text. More difficult, and occasionally challenging, exercises are marked with asterisks. In addition, data-analytic exercises for each chapter are available on the Web site for the book, along with the associated data sets.

What Is New in the Second Edition?

The first edition of this book, published by Sage in 1997 and entitled *Applied Regression, Linear Models, and Related Methods*, originated in my 1984 text *Linear Statistical Models and Related Methods* and my 1991 monograph *Regression Diagnostics*. The title of the 1997 edition reflected a change in organization and emphasis: I thoroughly reworked the book, removing some topics and adding a variety of new material. But even more fundamentally, the book was extensively rewritten. It was a new and different book from my 1984 text.

This second edition also has a (slightly) revised title, making reference to "*generalized* linear models" rather than to "linear models" (and dropping the reference to "related methods" as unnecessary), reflecting another change in emphasis. There is quite a bit of new material, and some of the existing material was reworked and rewritten, but the general level and approach of the book are similar to the first edition, and most of the material in the first edition, especially in Parts I through III (see below), is preserved in the new edition. I was gratified by the reception of the first edition of this book by book reviewers and other readers; although I felt the need to bring the book up to date and to improve it in some respects, I also didn't want to "fix what ain't broke."

Despite some changes and many additions, therefore, this is not an entirely different book. There is, however, a new chapter on generalized linear models, greatly augmenting a very brief section on this topic in the first edition. What were previously sections on time-series regression, nonlinear regression, nonparametric regression, robust regression, and bootstrapping are now separate chapters, many with extended treatments of their topics. There is a wholly new chapter on missing data and a new chapter on model selection, averaging, and validation (incorporating and expanding material on model validation from the previous edition).

Readers of the first edition will also find smaller changes: There is increased emphasis throughout the text on interpreting the results of data analysis, often by graphing quantities derived from statistical models; I redrew almost all of the many graphs in the book using R (see the section below on computing); I replaced many of the examples in the text, often using larger data sets than in the previous edition; and I modernized the statistical terminology—referring, for example, to "response" and "explanatory" variables rather than to "dependent" and "independent" variables.

To make room for the new material without uncontrollably expanding the size of the book, I moved the appendices to the Web site for the book (with the exception of Appendix A on notation), giving me the opportunity to expand their contents considerably (see below). Additionally, I moved data-analytic exercises and data sets from the book to the Web site.

Synopsis

- *Chapter 1* discusses the role of statistical data analysis in social science, expressing the point of view that statistical models are essentially descriptive, not direct (if abstract) representations of social processes. This perspective provides the foundation for the data-analytic focus of the text.

Part I: Data Craft

The first part of the book consists of preliminary material:[1]

- *Chapter 2* introduces the notion of regression analysis as tracing the conditional distribution of a response variable as a function of one or several explanatory variables. This idea is initially explored "nonparametrically," in the absence of a restrictive statistical model for the data (a topic developed more extensively in Chapter 18).
- *Chapter 3* describes a variety of graphical tools for examining data. These methods are useful both as a preliminary to statistical modeling and to assist in the diagnostic checking of a model that has been fit to data (as discussed, e.g., in Part III).
- *Chapter 4* discusses variable transformation as a solution to several sorts of problems commonly encountered in data analysis, including skewness, nonlinearity, and nonconstant spread.

Part II: Linear Models and Least Squares

The second part, on linear models fit by the method of least squares, along with Part III on diagnostics and Part IV on generalized linear models, comprises the heart of the book:

- *Chapter 5* discusses linear least-squares regression. Linear regression is the prototypical linear model, and its direct extension is the subject of Chapters 7 to 10.
- *Chapter 6*, on statistical inference in regression, develops tools for testing hypotheses and constructing confidence intervals that apply generally to linear models. This chapter also introduces the basic methodological distinction between empirical and structural relationships—a distinction central to understanding causal inference in nonexperimental research.
- *Chapter 7* shows how "dummy variables" can be employed to extend the regression model to qualitative explanatory variables (or "factors"). Interactions among explanatory variables are introduced in this context.
- *Chapter 8*, on analysis-of-variance models, deals with linear models in which all the explanatory variables are factors.

---

[1] I believe that it was Michael Friendly of York University who introduced me to the term *data craft*, a term that aptly characterizes the content of this section and, indeed, of the book more generally.

- *Chapter 9** develops the statistical theory of linear models, providing the foundation for much of the material in Chapters 5 to 8 along with some additional, and more general, results.
- *Chapter 10** applies vector geometry to linear models, allowing us literally to visualize the structure and properties of these models. Many topics are revisited from the geometric perspective, and central concepts—such as "degrees of freedom"—are given a natural and compelling interpretation.

Part III: Linear-Model Diagnostics

The third part of the book describes "diagnostic" methods for discovering whether a linear model fit to data adequately represents the data. Methods are also presented for correcting problems that are revealed:

- *Chapter 11* deals with the detection of unusual and influential data in linear models.
- *Chapter 12* describes methods for diagnosing a variety of problems, including non-normally distributed errors, nonconstant error variance, and nonlinearity. Some more advanced material in this chapter shows how the method of maximum likelihood can be employed for selecting transformations.
- *Chapter 13* takes up the problem of collinearity—the difficulties for estimation that ensue when the explanatory variables in a linear model are highly correlated.

Part IV: Generalized Linear Models

The fourth part of the book is devoted to generalized linear models, a grand synthesis that incorporates the linear models described earlier in the text along with many of their most important extensions:

- *Chapter 14* takes up linear-like logit and probit models for qualitative and ordinal categorical response variables. This is an important topic because of the ubiquity of categorical data in the social sciences (and elsewhere).
- *Chapter 15* describes the generalized linear model, showing how it encompasses linear, logit, and probit models along with statistical models (such as Poisson and gamma regression models) not previously encountered in the text. The chapter includes a treatment of diagnostic methods for generalized linear models, extending much of the material in Section III.

Part V: Extending Linear and Generalized Linear Models

The fifth part of the book discusses important extensions of linear and generalized linear models. In selecting topics, I was guided by the proximity of the methods to linear and generalized linear models and by the promise that these methods hold for data analysis in the social sciences. The methods described in this part of the text are given introductory—rather than extensive—treatments. My aim in introducing these relatively advanced topics is to provide (1) enough information so that readers can begin to use these methods in their research and (2) sufficient background to support further work in these areas should readers choose to pursue them. To the extent possible, I have tried to limit the level of difficulty of the exposition, and only Chapter 19 on robust regression is starred in its entirety (because of its essential reliance on basic calculus).

- *Chapter 16* describes time-series regression, where the observations are ordered in time and hence cannot usually be treated as statistically independent. The chapter introduces the method of generalized least squares, which can take account of serially correlated errors in regression.
- *Chapter 17* takes up nonlinear regression models, showing how some nonlinear models can be fit by linear least squares after transforming the model to linearity, while other, fundamentally nonlinear, models require the method of nonlinear least squares. The chapter includes treatments of polynomial regression and regression splines, the latter closely related to the topic of the subsequent chapter.
- *Chapter 18* introduces nonparametric regression analysis, which traces the dependence of the response on the explanatory variables in a regression without assuming a particular functional form for their relationship. This chapter contains a discussion of generalized nonparametric regression, including generalized additive models.
- *Chapter 19* describes methods of robust regression analysis, which are capable of automatically discounting unusual data.
- *Chapter 20* discusses missing data, explaining the potential pitfalls lurking in common approaches to missing data, such as complete-case analysis, and describing more sophisticated methods, such as multiple imputation of missing values. This is an important topic because social-science data sets are often characterized by a large proportion of missing data.
- *Chapter 21* introduces the "bootstrap," a computationally intensive simulation method for constructing confidence intervals and hypothesis tests. In its most common nonparametric form, the bootstrap does not make strong distributional assumptions about the data and it can be made to reflect the manner in which the data were collected (e.g., in complex survey-sampling designs).
- *Chapter 22* describes methods for model selection, model averaging in the face of model uncertainty, and model validation. Automatic methods of model selection and model averaging, I argue, are most useful when a statistical model is to be employed for prediction, less so when the emphasis is on interpretation. Validation is a simple method for drawing honest statistical inferences when—as is commonly the case—the data are employed both to select a statistical model and to estimate its parameters.

Appendices

Several appendices provide background, principally—but not exclusively—for the starred portions of the text. With the exception of Appendix A, which is printed at the back of the book, all the appendices are on the Web site for the book.

- *Appendix A* describes the notational conventions employed in the text.
- *Appendix B* provides a basic introduction to matrices, linear algebra, and vector geometry, developing these topics from first principles. Matrices are used extensively in statistics, including in the starred portions of this book. Vector geometry provides the basis for the material in Chapter 10 on the geometry of linear models.

- *Appendix C* reviews powers and logs and the geometry of lines and planes; introduces elementary differential and integral calculus; and shows how, employing matrices, differential calculus can be extended to several independent variables. Calculus is required for some starred portions of the text—for example, the derivation of least-squares and maximum-likelihood estimators. More generally in statistics, calculus figures prominently in probability theory and in optimization problems.
- *Appendix D* provides an introduction to the elements of probability theory and to basic concepts of statistical estimation and inference, including the essential ideas of Bayesian statistical inference. The background developed in this appendix is required for some of the material on statistical inference in the text and for certain other topics, such as multiple imputation of missing data and model averaging.

Computing

Nearly all the examples in this text employ real data from the social sciences, many of them previously analyzed and published. The online exercises that involve data analysis also almost all use real data drawn from various areas of application. I encourage readers to analyze their own data as well.

The data sets for examples and exercises can be downloaded free of charge via the World Wide Web; point your Web browser at http://www.sagepub.com/fox. If you do not have access to a fast Internet connection, then you can write to me at the Department of Sociology, McMaster University, Hamilton, Ontario, Canada, L8S 4M4, for information about obtaining the data sets (along with other on-line materials) on a CD. Appendices and exercises are distributed as portable document format (PDF) files.

I occasionally comment in passing on computational matters, but the book generally ignores the finer points of statistical computing in favor of methods that are computationally simple. I feel that this approach facilitates learning. Thus, for example, linear least-squares coefficients are obtained by solving the normal equations formed from sums of squares and products of the variables rather than by a more numerically stable method. Once basic techniques are absorbed, the data analyst has recourse to carefully designed programs for statistical computations.

I think that it is a mistake to tie a general discussion of linear and related statistical models too closely to particular software. Any reasonably capable statistical software will do almost everything described in this book. My current personal choice of statistical software, both for research and for teaching, is R—a free, open-source implementation of the S statistical programming language and computing environment (Ihaka & Gentleman, 1996; R Development Core Team, 2006). R is now the dominant statistical software among statisticians; it is used increasingly in the social sciences but is by no means dominant there. I have written a separate book (Fox, 2002) that provides a general introduction to R and that describes its use in applied regression analysis.

To Readers, Students, and Instructors

I have used the material in this book and its predecessors for two types of courses (along with a variety of short courses and lectures):

- I cover the unstarred sections of Chapters 1 to 8 and 11 to 15 in a one-semester (13-week) course for social-science graduate students (at McMaster University in Hamilton, Ontario, Canada) who have had (at least) a one-semester introduction to statistics at the level of Moore (2006). The outline of this course is as follows:

Week	Topic	Reading (Chapter)
1	Introduction to the course and to regression	1, 2
2	Examining and transforming data	3, 4
3	Linear least-squares regression	5
4	Statistical inference for regression	6
5	Dummy-variable regression	7
6	Review: Through dummy regression	
7	Analysis of variance	8
8	Diagnostics I: Unusual and influential data	11
9	Diagnostics II: Nonlinearity and other ills	12
10	Diagnostics III: Collinearity	13
11	Logit and probit models	14
12	Generalized linear models	15
13	Review: From analysis of variance	

- I used the material in the predecessors of Chapters 1 to 15 and the several appendices for a two-semester course for social-science graduate students (at York University in Toronto) with similar statistical preparation. For this second, more intensive, course, background topics (such as linear algebra) were introduced as required and constituted about one fifth of the course. The organization of the course was similar to the first one.

Both courses include some treatment of statistical computing, with more information on programming in the second course. For students with the requisite mathematical and statistical background, it should be possible to cover almost all the text in a reasonably paced two-semester course.

In learning statistics, it is important for the reader to participate actively, both by working though the arguments presented in the book, and—even more importantly—by applying methods to data. Statistical data analysis is a *craft*, and, like any craft, developing proficiency requires effort and practice. Reworking examples is a good place to start, and I have presented illustrations in such a manner as to facilitate reanalysis and further analysis of the data.

Where possible, I have relegated formal "proofs" and derivations to exercises, which nevertheless typically provide some guidance to the reader. I believe that this type of material is best learned constructively. As well, including too much algebraic detail in the body of the text invites readers to lose the statistical forest for the mathematical trees. You can decide for yourself (or your students) whether or not to work the theoretical exercises. It is my experience that some people feel that the process of working through derivations cements their understanding of the statistical material, while others find this activity tedious and pointless. Some of the theoretical exercises, marked with asterisks, are comparatively difficult. (Difficulty is assessed relative to the material in the text, so the threshold is higher in starred sections and chapters.)

In preparing the data-analytic exercises, I have tried to find data sets of some intrinsic interest that embody a variety of characteristics. In many instances, I try to supply some direction in the data-analytic exercises, but—like all real-data analysis—these exercises are fundamentally open-ended. It is therefore important for instructors to set aside time to discuss data-analytic exercises in class, both before and after students tackle them. Although students often miss important features of the data in their initial analyses, this experience—properly approached and integrated—is an unavoidable part of learning the craft of data analysis.

A few exercises, marked with pound-signs (#), are meant for "hand" computation. Hand computation (i.e., with a calculator) is tedious and is practical only for unrealistically small problems, but it sometimes serves to make statistical procedures more concrete (and increases our admiration for our pre-computer-era predecessors). Similarly, despite the emphasis in the text on analyzing real data, a small number of exercises generate simulated data to clarify certain properties of statistical methods.

I struggled with the placement of cross-references to exercises and to other parts of the text, trying brackets [too distracting!], marginal boxes (too imprecise), and finally settling on traditional footnotes.[2] I suggest that you ignore both the cross references and the other footnotes on first reading of the text.[3]

Finally, a word about style: I try to use the first person singular—"I"—when I express opinions. "We" is reserved for you—the reader—and I.

Acknowledgments

Many individuals have helped me in the preparation of this book.

I am grateful to the York University Statistical Consulting Service study group, which read, commented on, and corrected errors in the manuscript during the 2006–2007 academic year: Lisa Fiksenbaum, David Flora, Michael Friendly, Bryn Greer-Wootten, Depeng Jiang, Hugh McCague, Laura Mills, Georges Monette, Mirka Ondrack, Quiang Pu, Nikolai Slobodianik, Tao Sun, and Ye Sun. I also profited from the comments and suggestions of Robert Andersen, Paul Johnston, William Mason, and an anonymous reviewer.

A number of friends and colleagues donated their data for illustrations and exercises—implicitly subjecting their research to scrutiny and criticism.

Several individuals contributed to this book indirectly by helpful comments on its predecessors (Fox, 1984, 1997): Ken Bollen, Gene Denzel, Shirley Dowdy, Michael Friendly, Paul Herzberg, Georges Monette, Doug Rivers, and Robert Stine.

Edward Ng capably assisted in the preparation of some of the figures that appear in the book.

C. Deborah Laughton, Lisa Cuevas, and—most recently—Sean Connelly, my editors at Sage Publications, were patient and supportive throughout the several years that I worked on the two editions of the book.

I am also in debt to Paul Johnson's students at the University of Kansas, to William Mason's students at UCLA, to Georges Monette's students at York University, to participants at the Inter-University Consortium for Political and Social Research Summer Program in Robert Andersen's advanced regression course, and to my students at McMaster University, all of whom were exposed to various versions of the new edition of this text prior to publication, and who

---

[2] Footnotes are a bit awkward, but you don't have to read them.
[3] Footnotes other than cross references generally develop small points and elaborations.

have improved the book through their criticism, suggestions, and—occasionally—informative incomprehension.

If, after all this help and the opportunity to prepare a new edition of the book, deficiencies remain, then I alone am at fault.

John Fox
Toronto, Canada
May 2007

1

Statistical Models and Social Science

The social world is exquisitely complex and rich. From the improbable moment of birth, each of our lives is governed by chance and contingency. The statistical models typically used to analyze social data—and, in particular, the models considered in this book—are, in contrast, ludicrously simple. How can simple statistical models help us to understand a complex social reality? As the statistician George Box famously remarked (e.g., in Box, 1979, p. 202), "All models are wrong but some are useful." Can statistical models be useful in the social sciences?

This is a book on data analysis and statistics, not on the philosophy of the social sciences. I will, therefore, address this question, and related issues, very briefly here. Nevertheless, I feel that it is useful to begin with a consideration of the role of data analysis in the larger process of social research. You need not agree with the point of view that I express in this chapter to make productive use of the statistical tools presented in the remainder of the book, but the emphasis and specific choice of methods in the text partly reflect the ideas in this chapter. You may wish to reread this material after you study the methods described in the sequel.

1.1 Statistical Models and Social Reality

As I said, social reality is complex: Consider how my income is "determined." I am a relatively well paid professor in the sociology department of a Canadian university. That the billiard ball of my life would fall into this particular pocket was, however, hardly predictable 40 years ago, when I was attending a science high school in New York City. My subsequent decision to study sociology at New York's City College (after several other majors), my interest in statistics (the consequence of a course taken without careful consideration in my senior year), my decision to attend graduate school in sociology at the University of Michigan (one of several more or less equally attractive possibilities), and the opportunity and desire to move to Canada (the vote to hire me at the University of Alberta was, I later learned, very close) are all events that could easily have occurred differently.

I do not mean to imply that personal histories are completely capricious, unaffected by social structures of race, ethnicity, class, gender, and so on, just that they are not *in detail* determined by these structures. That social structures—and other sorts of systematic factors—condition, limit, and encourage specific events is clear from each of the illustrations in the previous paragraph and in fact makes sense of the argument for the statistical analysis of social data presented below. To take a particularly gross example: The public high school that I attended admitted its students by competitive examination, but no young women could apply (a policy that has happily changed).

Each of these precarious occurrences clearly affected my income, as have other events—some significant, some small—too numerous and too tedious to mention, even if I were aware of them all. If, for some perverse reason, you were truly interested in my income (and, perhaps, in other matters more private), you could study my biography, and through that study arrive at a detailed (if inevitably incomplete) understanding. It is clearly impossible, however, to pursue this strategy for many individuals or, more to the point, for individuals in general.

Nor is an understanding of income in general inconsequential, because income inequality is an important feature of our society. If such an understanding hinges on a literal description of the process by which each of us receives an income, then the enterprise is clearly hopeless. We might, alternatively, try to capture significant features of the process in general without attempting to predict the outcome for specific individuals. One could draw formal analogies (largely unproductively, I expect, though some have tried) to chaotic physical processes, such as the determination of weather and earthquakes.

Concrete mathematical theories purporting to describe social processes sometimes appear in the social sciences (e.g., in economics and in some areas of psychology), but they are relatively rare.[1] If a theory, like Newton's laws of motion, is mathematically concrete then, to be sure, there are difficulties in applying and testing it; but, with some ingenuity, experiments and observations can be devised to estimate the free parameters of the theory (a gravitational constant, for example), and to assess the fit of the theory to the resulting data.

In the social sciences, *verbal* theories abound. These social theories tend to be vague, elliptical, and highly qualified. Often, they are, at least partially, a codification of "common sense." I believe that vague social theories are potentially useful abstractions for understanding an intrinsically complex social reality, but how can such theories be linked empirically to that reality?

A vague social theory may lead us to expect, for example, that racial prejudice is the partial consequence of an "authoritarian personality," which, in turn, is a product of rigid child rearing. Each of these terms requires elaboration and procedures of assessment or measurement. Other social theories may lead us to expect that higher levels of education should be associated with higher levels of income, perhaps because the value of labor power is enhanced by training; because occupations requiring higher levels of education are of greater functional importance; because those with higher levels of education are in relatively short supply; or because people with high educational attainment are more capable in the first place. In any event, we need to consider how to assess income and education, how to examine their relationship, and what other factors need to be included.[2]

Statistical models of the type considered in this book are grossly *simplified* descriptions of complex social reality. Imagine that we have data from a social survey of a large sample of employed individuals. Imagine further, anticipating the statistical methods described in subsequent chapters, that we regress these individuals' income on a variety of putatively relevant characteristics, such as their level of education, gender, race, region of residence, and so on. We recognize that a model of this sort will fail to account perfectly for individuals' incomes, so our model includes a "residual," meant to capture the component of income unaccounted for by the systematic part of the model, which incorporates the "effects" on income of education, gender, and so forth.

The residuals for our model are likely very large. Even if the residuals were small, however, we would still need to consider the relationships among our social "theory," the statistical model that we have fit to the data, and the social "reality" that we seek to understand. Social reality, along with our methods of observation, produces the data, our theory aims to explain the data and the model to describe them. That, I think, is the key point: Statistical models are almost always fundamentally *descriptive*.

I believe that a statistical model cannot, and is not literally meant to, capture the social process by which incomes are "determined." As I argued above, individuals receive their incomes as a result of their almost unimaginably complex personal histories. No regression model, not even one including a residual, can reproduce this process: It is not as if my income is partly determined by my education, gender, race, and so on, and partly by the detailed trajectory of my life. It is,

---

[1]The methods for fitting nonlinear models described in Chapter 17 are sometimes appropriate to the rare theories in social science that are mathematically concrete.

[2]See Section 1.2.

therefore, not sensible, at the level of real social processes, to relegate chance and contingency to a random term that is simply added to the systematic part of a statistical model. The unfortunate tendency to *reify* statistical models—to forget that they are descriptive summaries, not literal accounts of social processes—can only serve to discredit quantitative data analysis in the social sciences.

Nevertheless, and despite the rich chaos of individuals' lives, social theories imply a structure to income inequality. Statistical models are capable of capturing and describing that structure or at least significant aspects of it. Moreover, social research is often motivated by questions rather than by hypotheses: Has income inequality between men and women changed recently? Is there a relationship between public concern over crime and the level of crime? Data analysis can help to answer these questions, which frequently are of practical—as well as theoretical—concern. Finally, if we proceed carefully, data analysis can assist us in the discovery of social facts that initially escape our hypotheses and questions.

It is, in my view, a paradox that the statistical models that are at the heart of most modern quantitative social science are at once taken too seriously and not seriously enough by many practitioners of social science. On the one hand, social scientists write about simple statistical models as if they were direct representations of the social processes that they purport to describe. On the other hand, there is frequently a failure to attend to the descriptive accuracy of these models.

As a shorthand, reference to the "effect" of education on income is innocuous. That the shorthand often comes to dominate the interpretation of statistical models is reflected, for example, in much of the social science literature that employs structural-equation models (once commonly termed "causal models," a usage that has thankfully declined). There is, I believe, a valid sense in which income is "affected" by education, because the complex real process by which individuals' incomes are determined is partly conditioned by their levels of education, but—as I have argued above—one should not mistake the model for the process.[3]

Although statistical models are very simple in comparison to social reality, they typically incorporate strong claims about the descriptive pattern of data. These claims rarely reflect the substantive social theories, hypotheses, or questions that motivate the use of the statistical models, and they are very often wrong. For example, it is common in social research to assume a priori, and without reflection, that the relationship between two variables, such as income and education, is linear. Now, we may well have good reason to believe that income tends to be *higher* at higher levels of education, but there is no reason to suppose that this relationship is *linear*. Our practice of data analysis should reflect our ignorance as well as our knowledge.

A statistical model is of no practical use if it is an inaccurate description of the data, and we will, therefore, pay close attention to the descriptive accuracy of statistical models. Unhappily, the converse is not true, for a statistical model may be descriptively accurate but of little practical use; it may even be descriptively accurate but substantively misleading. We will explore these issues briefly in the next two sections, which tie the interpretation of statistical models to the manner in which data are collected.

> With few exceptions, statistical data analysis describes the outcomes of real social processes and not the processes themselves. It is therefore important to attend to the descriptive accuracy of statistical models, and to refrain from reifying them.

---

[3]There is the danger here of simply substituting one term ("conditioned by") for another ("affected by"), but the point is deeper than that: Education affects income because the choices and constraints that partly structure individuals' lives change systematically with their level of education. Many highly paid occupations in our society are closed to individuals who lack a university education, for example. To recognize this fact, and to examine its descriptive reflection in a statistical summary, is different from claiming that a university education literally adds an increment to individuals' incomes.

1.2   Observation and Experiment

It is common for (careful) introductory accounts of statistical methods (e.g., Freedman, Pisani, & Purves, 1997; Moore, 2006) to distinguish strongly between observational and experimental data. According to the standard distinction, causal inferences are justified (or, at least, more certain) in experiments, where the explanatory variables (i.e., the possible "causes") are under the direct control of the researcher; causal inferences are especially compelling in a randomized experiment, in which the values of explanatory variables are assigned by some chance mechanism to experimental units. In nonexperimental research, in contrast, the values of the explanatory variables are observed—not assigned—by the researcher, along with the value of the response variable (the "effect"), and causal inferences are not justified (or, at least, are less certain). I believe that this account, although essentially correct, requires qualification and elaboration.

To fix ideas, let us consider the data summarized in Table 1.1, drawn from a paper by Greene and Shaffer (1992) on Canada's refugee determination process. This table shows the outcome of 608 cases, filed in 1990, in which refugee claimants who were turned down by the Immigration and Refugee Board asked the Federal Court of Appeal for leave to appeal the board's determination. In each case, the decision to grant or deny leave to appeal was made by a single judge. It is clear from the table that the 12 judges who heard these cases differed widely in the percentages of cases that they granted leave to appeal. Employing a standard significance test for a contingency table (a chi-square test of independence), Greene and Shaffer calculated that a relationship as strong as the one in the table will occur by chance alone about two times in 100,000. These data became the basis for a court case contesting the fairness of the Canadian refugee determination process.

If the 608 cases had been assigned at random to the judges, then the data would constitute a natural experiment, and we could unambiguously conclude that the large differences among the judges reflect differences in their propensities to grant leave to appeal.[4] The cases were, however, assigned to the judges not randomly but on a rotating basis, with a single judge hearing all of the cases that arrived at the court in a particular week. In defending the current refugee determination process, expert witnesses for the Crown argued that the observed differences among the judges might therefore be due to factors that systematically differentiated the cases that different judges happened to hear.

It is possible, in practice, to "control" statistically for such extraneous "confounding" factors as may explicitly be identified, but it is not, in principle, possible to control for *all* relevant factors, because we can never be certain that all relevant factors have been identified.[5] Nevertheless, I would argue, the data in Table 1.1 establish a prima facie case for systematic differences in the judges' propensities to grant leave to appeal to refugee claimants. Careful researchers control statistically for potentially relevant factors that they can identify; cogent critics demonstrate that an omitted confounding factor accounts for the observed association between judges and decisions or at least argue persuasively that a specific factor *may* be responsible for this association—they do not simply maintain the abstract possibility that such a factor may exist.

What makes an omitted factor "relevant" in this context?[6]

1. The omitted factor must influence the response variable. For example, if the gender of the refugee applicant has no impact on the judges' decisions, then it is irrelevant to control statistically for gender.

---

[4]Even so, this inference is not reasonably construed as a representation of the *cognitive process* by which judges arrive at their determinations. Following the argument in the previous section, it is unlikely that we could ever trace out that process in detail; it is quite possible, for example, that a specific judge would make different decisions faced with the same case on different occasions.

[5]See the further discussion of the refugee data in Section 22.3.

[6]These points are developed more formally in Sections 6.3 and 9.7.

Table 1.1 Percentages of Refugee Claimants in 1990 Who Were Granted or Denied Leave to Appeal a Negative Decision of the Canadian Immigration and Refugee Board, Classified by the Judge Who Heard the Case

| | Leave Granted? | | | |
Judge	Yes	No	Total	Number of cases
Pratte	9	91	100	57
Linden	9	91	100	32
Stone	12	88	100	43
Iacobucci	12	88	100	33
Décary	20	80	100	80
Hugessen	26	74	100	65
Urie	29	71	100	21
MacGuigan	30	70	100	90
Heald	30	70	100	46
Mahoney	34	66	100	44
Marceau	36	64	100	50
Desjardins	49	51	100	47
All judges	25	75	100	608

SOURCE: Adapted from Table 1 in Greene and Shaffer, "Leave to Appeal and Leave to Commence Judicial Review in Canada's Refugee-Determination System: Is the Process Fair?" *International Journal of Refugee Law*, 1992, Vol. 4, No. 1, p. 77, by permission of Oxford University Press.

2. The omitted factor must be related as well to the explanatory variable that is the focus of the research. Even if the judges' decisions are influenced by the gender of the applicants, the relationship between outcome and judge will be unchanged by controlling for gender (e.g., by looking separately at male and female applicants) unless the gender of the applicants is also related to judges—that is, unless the different judges heard cases with substantially different proportions of male and female applicants.

The strength of randomized experimentation derives from the second point: If cases were randomly assigned to judges, then there would be no systematic tendency for them to hear cases with differing proportions of men and women—or, for that matter, with systematic differences of *any* kind.

It is, however, misleading to conclude that causal inferences are completely unambiguous in experimental research, even within the bounds of statistical uncertainty (expressed, for example, in the *p*-value of a statistical test). Although we can unambiguously ascribe an observed difference to an experimental *manipulation*, we cannot unambiguously identify that manipulation with the explanatory variable that is the focus of our research.

In a randomized drug study, for example, in which patients are prescribed a new drug or an inactive placebo, we may establish with virtual certainty that there was greater average improvement among those receiving the drug, but we cannot be sure that this difference is due (or solely due) to the putative active ingredient in the drug. Perhaps the experimenters inadvertently conveyed their enthusiasm for the drug to the patients who received it, influencing the patients' responses; or perhaps the bitter taste of the drug subconsciously convinced these patients of its potency.

Experimenters try to rule out alternative interpretations of this kind by following careful experimental practices, such as "double-blind" delivery of treatments (neither the subject nor

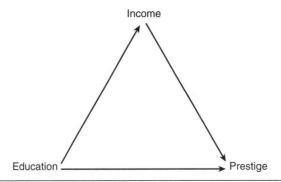

Figure 1.1   Simple "causal model" relating education, income, and prestige of occupations.
Education is a common prior cause of both income and prestige; income intervenes
causally between education and prestige.

the experimenter knows whether the subject is administered the drug or the placebo), and by
holding constant potentially influential factors deemed to be extraneous to the research (the taste,
color, shape, etc., of the drug and placebo are carefully matched). One can never be certain, however, that *all* relevant factors are held constant in this manner. Although the degree of certainty
achieved is typically much greater in a randomized experiment than in an observational study, the
distinction is less clear-cut than it at first appears.

> Causal inferences are most certain—if not completely definitive—in randomized exper-
> iments, but observational data can also be reasonably marshaled as evidence of causa-
> tion. Good experimental practice seeks to avoid confounding experimentally manipulated
> explanatory variables with other factors that can influence the response variable. Sound
> analysis of observational data seeks to control statistically for potentially confounding
> factors.

In subsequent chapters, we will have occasion to examine observational data on the prestige,
educational levels, and income levels of occupations. It will materialize that occupations with
higher levels of education tend to have higher prestige and that occupations with higher levels of
income also tend to have higher prestige. The income and educational levels of occupations are
themselves positively related. As a consequence, when education is controlled statistically, the
relationship between prestige and income grows smaller; likewise, when income is controlled,
the relationship between prestige and education grows smaller. In neither case, however, does the
relationship disappear.

How are we to understand the pattern of statistical associations among the three variables? It
is helpful in this context to entertain an informal "causal model" for the data, as in Figure 1.1.
That is, the educational level of occupations influences (potentially) both their income level and
their prestige, while income potentially influences prestige. The association between prestige
and income is "spurious" (i.e., not causal) to the degree that it is a consequence of the mutual
dependence of these two variables on education; the reduction in this association when education is
controlled represents the removal of the spurious component. In contrast, the causal relationship
between education and prestige is partly mediated by the "intervening variable" income; the
reduction in this association when income is controlled represents the articulation of an "indirect"
effect of education on prestige (i.e., through income).

In the former case, we partly *explain away* the association between income and prestige: Part of the relationship is "really" due to education. In the latter case, we partly *explain* the association between education and prestige: Part of the relationship is mediated by income.

> In analyzing observational data, it is important to distinguish between a factor that is a common prior cause of an explanatory and response variable and a factor that intervenes causally between the two.

Causal interpretation of observational data is always risky, especially—as here—when the data are cross-sectional (i.e., collected at one point in time) rather than longitudinal (where the data are collected over time). Nevertheless, it is usually impossible, impractical, or immoral to collect experimental data in the social sciences, and longitudinal data are often hard to come by.[7] Moreover, the essential difficulty of causal interpretation in non-experimental investigations— due to potentially confounding factors that are left uncontrolled—applies to longitudinal as well as to cross-sectional observational data.

The notion of "cause" and its relationship to statistical data analysis are notoriously difficult ideas. A relatively strict view requires an experimentally manipulable explanatory variable, at least one that is manipulable in principle.[8] This is a particularly sticky point because, in social science, many explanatory variables are intrinsically not subject to direct manipulation, even in principle. Thus, for example, according to the strict view, gender cannot be considered a cause of income, even if it can be shown (perhaps after controlling for other determinants of income) that men and women systematically differ in their incomes, because an individual's gender cannot be changed.[9]

I believe that treating nonmanipulable explanatory variables, such as gender, as potential causes is, at the very least, a useful shorthand. Men earn higher incomes than women be*cause* women are (by one account) concentrated into lower-paying jobs, work fewer hours, are directly discriminated against, and so on (see, e.g., Ornstein, 1983). Explanations of this sort are perfectly reasonable, and are subject to statistical examination; the sense of "cause" here may be weaker than the narrow one, but it is nevertheless useful.

> It is overly restrictive to limit the notion of statistical causation to explanatory variables that are manipulated experimentally, to explanatory variables that are manipulable in principle, or to data that are collected over time.

---

[7]Experiments with human beings also frequently distort the processes that they purport to study: Although it might well be possible, for example, to recruit judges to an experimental study of judicial decision-making, the artificiality of the situation could easily affect their simulated decisions. Even if the study entailed real judicial judgments, the mere act of observation might influence the judges' decisions—they might become more careful, for example.

[8]For clear presentations of this point of view, see, for example, Holland (1986) and Berk (2004).

[9]This statement is, of course, arguable: There are historically many instances in which individuals have changed their gender, for example by disguise, not to mention surgery. Despite some fuzziness, however, I believe that the essential point—that some explanatory variables are not (normally) subject to manipulation—is valid. A more subtle point is that in certain circumstances we could imagine experimentally manipulating the *apparent* gender of an individual, for example, on a job application.

1.3   Populations and Samples

Statistical inference is typically introduced in the context of random sampling from an identifiable population. There are good reasons for stressing this interpretation of inference—not the least of which are its relative concreteness and clarity—but the application of statistical inference is, at least arguably, much broader, and it is certainly broader in practice.

Take, for example, a prototypical experiment, in which subjects are assigned values of the explanatory variables at random: Inferences may properly be made to the hypothetical population of random rearrangements of the subjects, even when these subjects are not sampled from some larger population. If, for example, we find a highly "statistically significant" difference between two experimental groups of subjects in a randomized experiment, then we can be sure, with practical certainty, that the difference was due to the experimental manipulation. The rub here is that our interest almost surely extends *beyond* this specific group of subjects to some larger—often ill-defined—population.

Even when subjects in an experimental or observational investigation are literally sampled at random from a real population, we usually wish to generalize beyond that population. There are exceptions—election polling comes immediately to mind—but our interest is seldom confined to the population that is directly sampled. This point is perhaps clearest when *no* sampling is involved—that is, when we have data on every individual in a real population.

Suppose, for example, that we examine data on population density and crime rates for all large U.S. cities and find only a weak association between the two variables. Suppose further that a standard test of statistical significance indicates that this association is so weak that it easily could have been the product of "chance."[10] Is there any sense in which this information is interpretable? After all, we have before us data on the *entire* population of large U.S. cities at a particular historical juncture.

Because our interest inheres not directly—at least not exclusively—in these *specific* cities, but in the complex social processes by which density and crime are determined, we can reasonably imagine a different outcome. Were we to replay history conceptually, we would not observe precisely the same crime rates and population density statistics, dependent as these are on a myriad of contingent and chancy events; indeed, if the ambit of our conceptual replay of history is sufficiently broad, then the identities of the cities themselves might change. (Imagine, for example, that Henry Hudson had not survived his trip or, if he survived it, that the capital of the United States had remained in New York. Less momentously, imagine that Fred Smith had not gotten drunk and killed a friend in a brawl, reducing the number of homicides in New York by one.) It is, in this context, reasonable to draw statistical inferences to the process that produced the currently existing population. Similar considerations arise in the analysis of historical statistics, for example of time-series data.[11]

Much interesting data in the social sciences—and elsewhere—are collected haphazardly. The data constitute neither a sample drawn at random from a larger population, nor a coherently defined population. Experimental randomization provides a basis for making statistical inferences to the population of rearrangements of a haphazardly selected group of subjects, but that is in itself cold comfort. For example, an educational experiment is conducted with students recruited from a school that is conveniently available. We are interested in drawing conclusions about the efficacy of teaching methods for students in general, however, not just for the students who participated in the study.

---

[10] Cf. the critical discussion of crime and population density in Freedman (1975).

[11] See Chapter 16 for a discussion of regression analysis with time-series data.

Haphazard data are also employed in many observational studies—for example, volunteers are recruited from among university students to study the association between eating disorders and overexercise. Once more, our interest transcends this specific group of volunteers.

To rule out haphazardly collected data would be a terrible waste; it is, instead, prudent to be careful and critical in the interpretation of the data. We should try, for example, to satisfy ourselves that our haphazard group does not differ in presumably important ways from the larger population of interest, or to control for factors thought to be relevant to the phenomena under study.

Statistical inference can speak to the *internal stability* of patterns in haphazardly collected data and—most clearly in experimental data—to causation. *Generalization* from haphazardly collected data to a broader population, however, is inherently a matter of judgment.

> Randomization and good sampling design are desirable in social research, but they are not prerequisites for drawing statistical inferences. Even when randomization or random sampling is employed, we typically want to generalize beyond the strict bounds of statistical inference.

Exercise

Exercise 1.1. Imagine that students in an introductory statistics course complete 20 assignments during two semesters. Each assignment is worth 1% of a student's final grade, and students get credit for assignments that are turned in on time and that show reasonable effort. The instructor of the course is interested in whether doing the homework contributes to learning, and (anticipating material to be taken up in Chapters 5 and 6), she observes a linear, moderately strong, and highly statistically significant relationship between the students' grades on the final exam in the course and the number of homework assignments that they completed. For concreteness, imagine that for each additional assignment completed, the students' grades on average were 1.5% higher (so that, e.g., students completing all of the assignments on average scored 30 points higher than those who completed none of the assignments).

(a) Can this result be taken as evidence that completing homework assignments *causes* higher grades on the final exam? Why or why not?

(b) Is it possible to design an experimental study that could provide more convincing evidence that completing homework assignments causes higher exam grades? If not, why not? If so, how might such an experiment be designed?

(c) Is it possible to marshall stronger observational evidence that completing homework assignments causes higher exam grades? If not, why not? If so, how?

Summary

- With few exceptions, statistical data analysis describes the outcomes of real social processes and not the processes themselves. It is therefore important to attend to the descriptive accuracy of statistical models and to refrain from reifying them.

- Causal inferences are most certain—if not completely definitive—in randomized experiments, but observational data can also be reasonably marshaled as evidence of causation. Good experimental practice seeks to avoid confounding experimentally manipulated explanatory variables with other factors that can influence the response variable. Sound analysis of observational data seeks to control statistically for potentially confounding factors.
- In analyzing observational data, it is important to distinguish between a factor that is a common prior cause of an explanatory and response variable and a factor that intervenes causally between the two.
- It is overly restrictive to limit the notion of statistical causation to explanatory variables that are manipulated experimentally, to explanatory variables that are manipulable in principle, or to data that are collected over time.
- Randomization and good sampling design are desirable in social research, but they are not prerequisites for drawing statistical inferences. Even when randomization or random sampling is employed, we typically want to generalize beyond the strict bounds of statistical inference.

Recommended Reading

- Chance and contingency are recurrent themes in Stephen Gould's fine essays on natural history; see, in particular, Gould (1989). I believe that these themes are relevant to the social sciences as well, and Gould's work has strongly influenced the presentation in Section 1.1.
- The legitimacy of causal inferences in nonexperimental research is a hotly debated topic. Perhaps the most vocal current critic of the use of observational data is David Freedman. See, for example, Freedman's (1987) critique of structural-equation modeling in the social sciences and the commentary that follows it.
- A great deal of recent work on causal inference in statistics has been motivated by "Rubin's causal model." For a summary and many references, see Rubin (2004). A very clear presentation of Rubin's model, followed by interesting commentary, appears in Holland (1986).
- Berk (2004) provides an extended, careful discussion, from a point of view different from mine, of many of the issues raised in this chapter.
- The place of sampling and randomization in statistical investigations has also been widely discussed and debated in the literature on research design. The classic presentation of the issues in Campbell and Stanley (1963) is still worth reading, as is Kish (1987). In statistics, these themes are reflected in the distinction between model-based and design-based inference (see, e.g., Koch & Gillings, 1983) and in the notion of superpopulation inference (see, e.g., Thompson, 1988).
- Achen (1982) argues eloquently for the descriptive interpretation of statistical models, illustrating his argument with effective examples.

PART I

Data Craft

2

What Is
Regression Analysis?

As mentioned in Chapter 1, statistical data analysis is a *craft*, part art (in the sense of a skill developed through practice) and part science (in the sense of systematic, formal knowledge). Introductions to applied statistics typically convey some of the craft of data analysis, but tend to focus on basic concepts and the logic of statistical inference. This and the next two chapters develop some of the elements of statistical data analysis:

- The current chapter introduces regression analysis in a general context, tracing the conditional distribution of a response variable as a function of one or several explanatory variables. There is also some discussion of practical methods for looking at regressions with a minimum of prespecified assumptions about the data.
- Chapter 3 describes graphical methods for looking at data, including methods for examining the distribution of individual variables, relationships between pairs of variables, and relationships among several variables.
- Chapter 4 takes up methods for transforming variables to make them better-behaved—for example, to render the distribution of a variable more symmetric or to make the relationship between two variables more nearly linear.

Figure 2.1 is a *scatterplot* showing the relationship between hourly wages (in dollars) and formal education (in years) for a sample of 14,601 employed Canadians. The line in the plot shows the mean value of wages for each level of education and represents (in one sense) the *regression of wages on education*.[1] Although there are many observations in this scatterplot, few individuals in the sample have education below, say, 5 years, and so the mean wages at low levels of education cannot be precisely estimated from the sample, despite its large overall size. Discounting, therefore, variation in average wages at very low levels of education, it appears as if average wages are relatively flat until about 10 years of education, at which point they rise gradually and steadily with education.

Figure 2.1 raises several issues that we will take up in subsequent chapters:[2] Because of the large number of points in the plot and the discreteness of education (which is represented as number of years completed), the plot is difficult to examine. It is, however, reasonably clear that the distribution of wages at fixed levels of education is positively skewed. One such *conditional distribution* is shown in the histogram in Figure 2.2. The mean is a problematic measure of the center of a skewed distribution, and so basing the regression on the mean is not a good idea for such data. It is also clear that the relationship between hourly wages and education is not linear—that is, not reasonably summarized by a straight line—and so the common reflex to summarize relationships between quantitative variables with lines is also not a good idea here.

Thinking more abstractly, *regression analysis*, broadly construed, traces the distribution of a response variable (denoted by Y)—or some characteristic of this distribution (such as its mean)—as a function of one or more explanatory variables ($X_1, \ldots, X_k$):[3]

---

[1] See Exercise 5.2 for the original statistical meaning of the term "regression."

[2] See, in particular, Chapter 3 on examining data and Chapter 4 on transforming data.

[3] The response variable is often called the *dependent variable*, and the explanatory variables are often called *independent variables*.

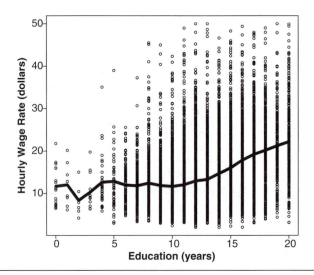

Figure 2.1   A scatterplot showing the relationship between hourly wages (in dollars) and
education (in years) for a sample of 14,601 employed Canadians. The line connects
the mean wages at the various levels of education. The data are drawn from the 1994
Survey of Labour and Income Dynamics (SLID).

$$p(y|x_1, \ldots, x_k) = f(x_1, \ldots, x_k) \qquad (2.1)$$

Here, $p(y|x_1, \ldots, x_k)$ represents the probability (or, for continuous Y, the probability density)
of observing the specific value y of the response variable, *conditional* on a set of specific values
$(x_1, \ldots, x_k)$ of the explanatory variables, and $p(Y|x_1, \ldots, x_k)$ is the *probability distribution* of
Y (or the density function of Y) for these specific values of the Xs.[4] In the relationship between
the response variable wages (Y) and the single explantory variable education (X), for example,
$p(Y|x)$ represents the population distribution of wages for all individuals who share the specific
value x of education (e.g., 12 years). Figure 2.1 is therefore the sample analog of the population
conditional distribution of Y.

The relationship of Y to the Xs is of particular interest when we entertain the possibility that the
Xs affect Y or—more weakly—when we wish to use the Xs to predict the value of Y. Primarily
for convenience of exposition, I will use the term "regression analysis" to refer to those cases
in which both Y and the Xs are quantitative (as opposed to qualitative) variables.[5] This chapter
introduces basic concepts of regression analysis in a very general setting and explores some simple
methods of regression analysis that make very weak assumptions about the structure of the data.

Regression analysis examines the relationship between a quantitative response variable,
Y, and one or more quantitative explanatory variables, $X_1, \ldots, X_k$. Regression analysis
traces the conditional distribution of Y—or some aspect of this distribution, such as its
mean—as a function of the Xs.

---

[4]If the concept of (or notation for) a conditional distribution is unfamiliar, you should consult Appendix D on probability
and estimation. Please keep in mind more generally that background information is located in the appendixes, available
on the Web site for the book.

[5]Later in the book, we will have occasion to consider statistical models in which the explanatory variables (Chapters 7
and 8) and the response variable (Chapter 14) are qualitative/categorical variables. This material is centrally important
because categorical variables are very common in the social sciences.

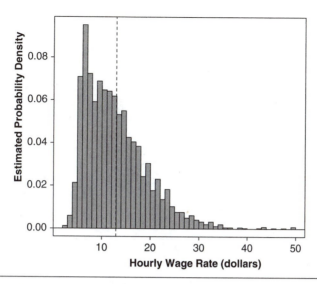

Figure 2.2   The conditional distribution of hourly wages for the 3,384 employed Canadians in the SLID, who had 12 years of education. The vertical axis is scaled as *density*, which means that the total area of the bars of the histogram is 1. Moreover, because each bar of the histogram has a width of 1, the height of the bar also (and coincidentally) represents the proportion of the sample in the corresponding interval of wage rates. The vertical broken line is at the mean wage rate for those with 12 years of education: $12.94.

2.1   Preliminaries

Figure 2.3 illustrates the regression of a continuous Y on a single, discrete X, which takes on several values, labeled $x_1, x_2, \ldots, x_5$. Alternatively, you can think of X as a continuous variable for which $x_1, x_2, \ldots, x_5$ are specific representative values. As illustrated in the figure, the values of X need not be evenly spaced. For concreteness, imagine (as in Figure 2.1) that Y represents wages, that X represents years of formal education, and that the graph shows the conditional distribution $p(Y|x)$ of wages for some of the values of education.

Most discussions of regression analysis begin by assuming that the conditional distribution of the response variable, $p(Y|x_1, \ldots, x_k)$, is a normal distribution; that the variance of Y conditional on the Xs is everywhere the same regardless of the specific values of $x_1, \ldots, x_k$; and that the expected value (the mean) of Y is a linear function of the Xs:

$$\mu \equiv E(Y|x_1, \ldots, x_k) = \alpha + \beta_1 x_1 + \cdots + \beta_k x_k \tag{2.2}$$

This utopian situation is depicted for a single X in Figure 2.4. As we will see,[6] the assumptions of normality, common variance, and linearity, along with independent random sampling, lead to linear least-squares estimation of the model in Equation 2.2. In this chapter, in contrast, we will pursue the notion of regression with as few assumptions as possible.

Figure 2.3 illustrates why we should not be too hasty to make the assumptions of normality, equal variance, and linearity:

- *Skewness*. If the conditional distribution of Y is skewed, as is $p(Y|x_1)$, then the mean will not be a good summary of its center. This is the case as well in Figure 2.1, where the (sample) conditional distributions of wages given education are all positively skewed.

---

[6]Chapters 6 and 9.

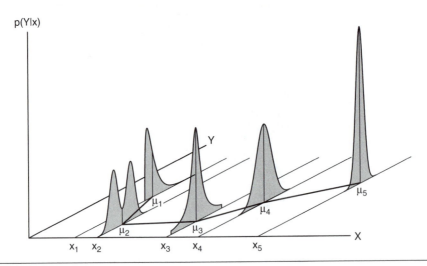

Figure 2.3   Population regression of Y on X. The conditional distribution of Y, $p(Y|x)$, is shown for
each of a few values of X. The distribution of Y at $X=x_1$ is positively skewed; at
$X=x_2$ it is bimodal; at $X=x_3$ it is heavy tailed; at $X=x_4$ it has greater spread than at
$X=x_5$. Note that the conditional means of Y given X, that is, $\mu_1,\ldots,\mu_5$, are not a
linear function of X.

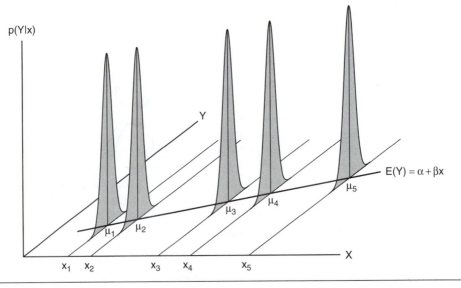

Figure 2.4   Common assumptions in regression analysis: The conditional distributions $p(Y|x)$ are
all normal distributions with the same variance, and the conditional means of Y (here
$\mu_1,\ldots,\mu_5$) are all on a straight line.

- *Multiple modes.* If the conditional distribution of Y is multimodal, as is $p(Y|x_2)$, then it is
  intrinsically unreasonable to summarize its center by a single number.
- *Heavy tails.* If the conditional distribution of Y is substantially non-normal—for example,
  heavy-tailed, as is $p(Y|x_3)$—then the sample mean will not be an efficient estimator of the
  center of the Y-distribution even when this distribution is symmetric.

- *Unequal spread.* If the conditional variance of Y changes with the values of the Xs—compare, for example, $p(Y|x_4)$ and $p(Y|x_5)$—then the efficiency of the usual least-squares estimates may be compromised; moreover, the nature of the dependence of the variance on the Xs may itself be of interest.
- *Nonlinearity.* Although we are often in a position to suppose that the values of Y will increase or decrease with some X, there is almost never good reason to assume a priori that the relationship between Y and X is linear; this problem is compounded when there are several Xs. In Figure 2.3, for example, the conditional means of Y, the μ_i, do not lie on a line in the X, Y plane (as they do in Figure 2.4).

This is not to say, of course, that linear regression analysis or, more generally, linear statistical models are of little practical use. Much of this book is devoted to the exposition of linear models. It is, however, prudent to begin with an appreciation of the limitations of linear models because their effective use in data analysis frequently depends on adapting to these limitations: We may, for example, transform data to make the assumptions of normality, equal variance, and linearity more nearly correct.[7]

There are two additional advantages to approaching regression analysis from a general perspective: First, an appreciation of the practical difficulties of fitting the very general model in Equation 2.1 to data motivates the specification of more restrictive models, such as the usual linear regression model. Second, modern methods of *nonparametric regression*, while not quite as general as the model in Equation 2.1, are emerging as practical alternatives to the more traditional linear models.

The balance of the present chapter is devoted to an initial foray into the territory of nonparametric regression. I will begin by taking a direct or "naive" approach to the problem and then will extend this approach by local averaging. In the process, we will encounter for the first time a number of recurring themes in this book, including the direct examination of data by graphical displays, smoothing to clarify patterns in data, and the detection and treatment of unusual data.[8]

2.2 Naive Nonparametric Regression

Imagine once more that we are interested in the relationship between wages and education. We do not have data for the whole population, but we have a very large sample—say, of 1 million employed Canadians. We could easily display the conditional distribution of income for each of the values of education $(0, 1, 2, \ldots, 25)$ that occur in our data because (I assume) each value of education occurs many times. The example in the previous section, illustrated in Figures 2.1 and 2.2, approaches this situation for some of the more common levels of education.

Although wages is (for practical purposes) a continuous variable, the large quantity of data makes it practical to display its conditional distribution using a histogram with narrow bars (each, say, \$1.00 wide, as in Figure 2.2).[9] If, as is often the case, our interest is in the average or typical value of wages conditional on education, we could—in light of the large size of our data set—estimate these conditional averages very accurately. The distribution of wages given education is likely positively skewed, so it would be better to use conditional medians rather than conditional means as typical values; nevertheless, we will, for simplicity, focus initially on the conditional means, $\overline{Y}|x$.[10]

---

[7]See Chapters 4 and 12.

[8]More sophisticated methods for nonparametric regression are discussed in Chapter 18.

[9]We will explore other approaches to displaying distributions in the next chapter.

[10]We imagine that Figure 2.3 shows the *population* conditional means, $\mu|x$—the values that we now want to *estimate* from our sample.

Imagine now that X, along with Y, is a continuous variable. For example, X is the reported weight in kilograms for each of a sample of individuals, and Y is their measured weight, again in kilograms. We want to use reported weight to predict actual (i.e., measured) weight, and so we are interested in the mean value of Y as a function of X in the population of individuals from among whom the sample was randomly drawn:[11]

$$\mu = E(Y|x) = f(x) \tag{2.3}$$

Even if the sample is large, replicated values of X will be rare because X is continuous.[12] In the absence of replicated Xs, we cannot directly examine the conditional distribution of Y given X, and we cannot directly calculate conditional means. If we indeed have a large sample of individuals at our disposal, however, then we can dissect the range of X into many narrow intervals, or *bins*, of reported weight, each bin containing many observations; within each such bin we can display the conditional distribution of measured weight and estimate the conditional mean of Y with great precision.

> In very large samples, and when the explanatory variables are discrete, it is possible to estimate a regression by directly examining the conditional distribution of Y given the Xs. When the explanatory variables are continuous, we can proceed similarly by dissecting the Xs into a large number of narrow bins.

If, as is more typical, we have only a relatively small sample, then we have to make do with fewer bins, each containing relatively few observations. This situation is illustrated in Figure 2.5, using data on reported and measured weight for each of 101 Canadian women engaged in regular exercise.[13] A partially contrasting example, using the prestige and income levels of 102 Canadian occupations in 1971, is shown in Figure 2.6.[14]

The X-axes in Figures 2.5 and 2.6 are carved into five bins, each bin containing approximately 20 observations (the middle bin contains the extra observations). The nonparametric regression line displayed on each plot is calculated by connecting the points defined by the conditional response variable means $\overline{Y}$ and the explanatory variable means $\overline{X}$ in the five intervals.

---

[11]This is an interesting—and unusual—problem in several respects: First, although it is more reasonable to suppose that actual weight "affects" the report than vice versa, our desire to use the report to predict actual weight (presumably because it is easier to elicit a verbal report than to actually weigh people) motivates treating measured weight as the response variable. Second, this is one of those comparatively rare instances in which a linear-regression equation is a natural specification, since if people are *unbiased* reporters of their weight, we should have $\mu = x$ (i.e., expected reported weight equal to actual weight). Finally, if people are *accurate* as well as unbiased reporters of their weight, then the conditional variance of Y given x should be very small.

[12]No numerical data are literally continuous, of course, since data are always recorded to some finite number of digits. This is why tied values are possible. The philosophical issues surrounding continuity are subtle but essentially irrelevant to us: For practical purposes, a variable is continuous when it takes on many different values.

[13]These data were generously made available to me by Caroline Davis of York University, who used them as part of a larger study; see Davis (1990). The error in the data described below was located by Professor Davis. The 101 women were volunteers for the study, not a true sample from a larger population.

The observant reader will have noticed that there are apparently fewer than 101 points in Figure 2.5: Because both measured and reported weight are given to the nearest kilogram, many points are overplotted (i.e., lie on top of one-another). We will learn to deal with overplotting in Chapter 3.

[14]The Canadian occupational prestige data are described in Fox and Suschnigg (1989). Although there are many more occupations in the Canadian Census, these 102 do not constitute a random sample from the larger population of occupations. Justification for treating the 102 occupations as a sample implicitly rests on the claim that they are "typical" of the population, at least with respect to the relationship between prestige and income—a problematic, if arguable, claim.

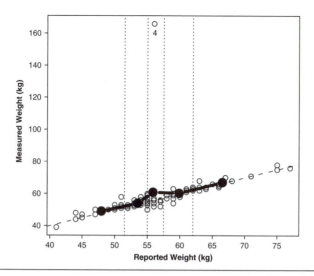

Figure 2.5   Naive nonparametric regression of measured weight on reported weight, each in kilograms. The range of reported weight has been dissected into five bins (separated by broken lines), each containing about 20 observations. The solid line connects the averages of measured weight and reported weight in the five bins, shown as filled circles. The dotted line around which the points cluster is $Y = X$. The fourth observation is an outlier. Because of the very different ranges of measured and reported weight, the scales for the axes are different, and the line $Y = X$ is not at 45 degrees.

Recalling our purpose, which is to estimate the model in Equation 2.3, there are two sources of error in this simple procedure of binning and averaging:

- *Sampling error (variance).* The conditional sample means $\overline{Y}$ will, of course, change if we select a new sample (even if we could retain the same selection of xs). Sampling error is minimized by using a small number of relatively wide bins, each with many observations.
- *Bias.* Let x_i denote the center of the ith bin (here, $i = 1, \ldots, 5$), and suppose that the X-values are evenly spread in the bin. If the population regression curve $f(x)$ is nonlinear within the bin, then the average population value of Y in the bin, say $\overline{\mu}_i$, is usually different from the value of the regression curve at the center of the bin, $\mu_i = f(x_i)$. This situation is illustrated in Figure 2.7. Bias—that is, $\overline{\mu}_i - \mu_i$—is therefore minimized by making the bins as numerous and as narrow as possible.

As is typically the case in statistical estimation, reducing bias and reducing sampling variance work at cross-purposes. Only if we select a very large sample can we have our cake and eat it, too—by constructing a very large number of narrow bins, each with many observations. This situation was, of course, our starting point.

The nonparametric regression lines in Figures 2.5 and 2.6 are also very crude. Although reported weights vary from about 40 to about 80 kg, we have evaluated the regression at only five points in this substantial range; likewise, income values for the 102 occupations vary from about \$600 to about \$26,000. Nevertheless, it is clear from Figure 2.5 that, except for one very discrepant data point (observation 4),[15] the data are very close to the line $Y = X$; and it is clear from Figure 2.6

---

[15]It seems difficult to comprehend how a 166-kg woman could have reported a weight of only 56 kg, but the solution to this mystery is simple: The woman's weight in kilograms and height in centimeters were accidentally switched when the data were entered into the computer.

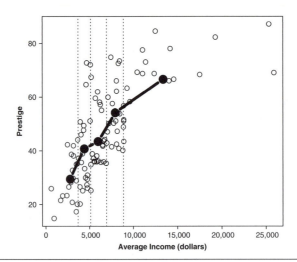

Figure 2.6   Naive nonparametric regression of occupational prestige on average income for 102
Canadian occupations in 1971. The range of income has been dissected into five
bins, each containing about 20 observations. The line connects the average prestige
and income scores in the five bins, shown as filled circles.

that while prestige appears to increase with income, the increase is nonlinear, with prestige values
leveling off at relatively high income.

The opportunity that a very large sample presents to reduce both bias and variance suggests
that naive nonparametric regression is, under very broad conditions, a consistent estimator of
the population regression curve.[16] For, as the sample size gets larger (i.e., as $n \to \infty$), we can
ensure that the intervals grow successively narrower and yet have each contain more data (e.g.,
by employing $\sqrt{n}$ intervals, each containing on average $\sqrt{n}$ observations). In the limit—never, of
course, attained—we have an infinite number of intervals, each of zero width and each containing
an infinite number of observations. In this statistical nirvana, the naive nonparametric regression
and the population regression curve coincide.

It may appear as if naive nonparametric regression—that is, binning and averaging—is a
practical procedure in large data sets or when explanatory variables are discrete. Although this
conclusion is essentially correct, it is instructive—and sobering—to consider what happens when
there is more than one explanatory variable.

Suppose, for example, that we have three discrete explanatory variables, each with 10 values.
There are, then, $10^3 = 1,000$ combinations of values of the three variables, and within each such
combination, there is a conditional distribution of Y [i.e., $p(Y|x_1, x_2, x_3)$]. Even if the Xs are
uniformly and independently distributed—implying equal expected numbers of observations for
each of the 1,000 combinations—we would require a very large sample to calculate the conditional
means of Y with sufficient precision. The situation is even worse when the Xs are continuous,
because dissecting the range of each X into as few as 10 bins might introduce nonnegligible bias
into the estimation.

The problem of dividing the data into too many parts grows exponentially more serious as
the number of Xs increases. Statisticians, therefore, often refer to the intrinsic sparseness of
multivariate data as the "curse of dimensionality." Moreover, the imaginary calculation on which

---

[16]For example, we need to assume that the regression curve $\mu = f(X)$ is reasonably smooth and that the distribution of
Y given x has finite variance (see Manski, 1991, for some details). We should also remember that the reasonableness of
focusing on the mean μ depends on the symmetry—and unimodality—of the conditional distribution of Y.

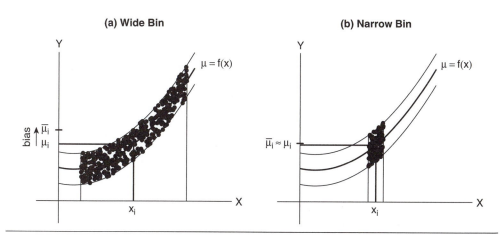

Figure 2.7   When the regression of Y on X is nonlinear in a bin centered at x_i, the average value
of Y in the interval ($\overline{\mu}_i$) can be a biased estimate of the regression curve at the center
of the interval [$\mu_i = f(x_i)$]. This bias will tend to be larger in a wide bin (a) than in a
narrow bin (b).

the consistency of naive nonparametric regression is based—in which the number of explanatory
variables remains the same as the sample size grows—is itself unrealistic because we are apt, in
large samples, to entertain more complex statistical models than in small samples.[17]

2.3 Local Averaging

Let us return to Figure 2.6, showing the naive nonparametric regression of occupational prestige
on income. One problem with this procedure is that we have estimated the regression at only five
points—a consequence of our desire to have relatively stable conditional averages, each based on
a sufficiently large number of observations (here, 20). There is no intrinsic reason, however, why
we should restrict ourselves to partitioning the data by X-values into nonoverlapping bins.

    We can allow X to vary continuously across the range of observed values, calculating the
average value of Y within a moving bin or *window* of fixed width centered at the current focal
value x. Alternatively, we can employ a window of varying width, constructed to accommodate
a fixed number of data values (say, m) that are the nearest X-neighbors to the focal x-value.
The fraction of the data included in each window, $s \equiv m/n$, is called the *span* of the local-
average regression. As a practical matter, of course, we cannot perform these calculations at the
uncountably infinite number of points produced by allowing X to vary continuously, but using
a computer, we can quickly calculate averages at a large number of focal values spanning the
range of X. One attractive procedure, if the sample size n is not very large, is to evaluate the local
average of Y in a window around each of the X-values observed in the data: $x_1, x_2, \ldots, x_n$.

> In smaller samples, local averages of Y can be calculated in a neighborhood surround-
> ing each x-value in the data. In larger samples, we can calculate local averages of Y at
> representative x-values spanning the range of X.

---

[17]I am indebted to Robert Stine, of the University of Pennsylvania, for this insight.

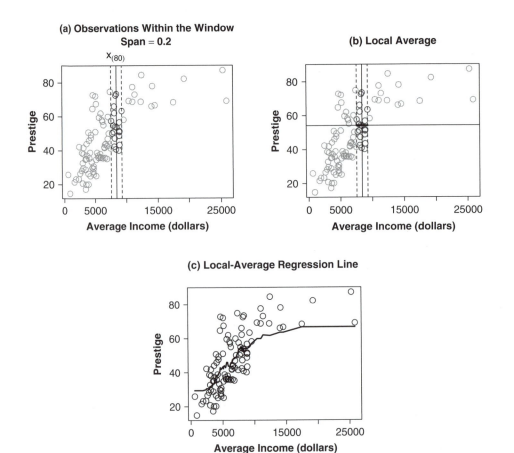

Figure 2.8   Nonparametric regression of occupational prestige on income, using local averages. Each average includes 20 of the 102 observations (i.e., a span of 0.2). Panel (a) shows the window encompassing the 20 nearest neighbors of $x_{(80)}$, the 80th ordered X-value. The mean of the Y-values for these 20 observations is represented by the horizontal line in panel (b). In panel (c), the local-average Y-values for all 102 observations are connected by a line. Note the roughness of the regression line and the flattening of the regression at the far left and right of the plot.

Figure 2.8 illustrates the process of local averaging for the Canadian occupational prestige data, employing $m = 20$ of the 102 observations for each local average, representing a span of $s = 20/102 \approx 0.2$. Figure 2.9 shows the result of applying local averaging to Davis's data on reported and measured weight, again using $m = 20$ obervations for each local average. Three ~ of the procedure are apparent from these examples:

first few local averages are identical to one another, as are the last few, flattening the ~ regression line at extreme X-values.[18] This artificial flattening at the edges of ~lled *boundary bias*.

~he x-values are evenly spaced and that m is 19. Let $x_{(1)}$, $x_{(2)},\ldots,x_{(n)}$ repre-
smallest to largest. Then, the first 19 observations—the Y-values associated with
~ed for the first 10 local averages, making these averages identical to one another. One
~ neighborhoods around each $x_{(i)}$, with the same number of observations below and

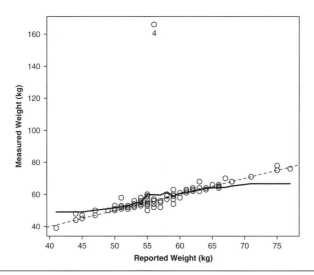

Figure 2.9 Nonparametric regression by local averaging for Davis's data on reported and measured weight. The local averages at each *x*-value are given by the line traced through the plot. Each local average is based on 20 of the 101 observations. Note the impact of the outlying observation on the averages that include it and the flattening of the regression at the lowest and highest reported weights. The broken line is the line of unbiased reporting, $Y = X$.

2. The line connecting the averages tends to be rough because the average "jumps" up or down as observations enter and exit the moving window. (This roughness is more apparent in Figure 2.8, where the relationship between the two variables is weaker, than in Figure 2.9.)

3. Unusual data values, called *outliers*, unduly influence the average when they fall in the window (as is the case for observation 4 in Figure 2.9). In regression analysis, an outlier is a value of Y that is very different from other response variable values associated with similar Xs.

More adequate methods of nonparametric regression are the subject of Chapter 18. Nevertheless, because we will often want to smooth scatterplots in examining data, I anticipate that treatment by applying one such method, called *lowess*, to the two examples.[19] Lowess is in many respects similar to the local-averaging smoother that I just described, except that instead of computing an average Y-value within the neighborhood of a focal x, the lowess smoother computes a fitted value based on a locally weighted least-squares regression, giving more weight to observations in the neighborhood that are close to the focal x than to those relatively far away.[20] The lowess smoother also makes provision for discounting outliers.

As with local averaging, we have to decide how many observations to include in each local regression; this is usually expressed by the span of the lowess smoother—the fraction of the data used to compute each fitted value. As was true of local averaging, larger spans reduce variance but may increase bias; smaller spans can reduce bias but increase variance. Put alternatively, larger spans produce smoother regressions.

---

above the focal $x_{(i)}$; but this procedure implies using smaller and smaller spans as we approach the extreme values $x_{(1)}$ and $x_{(n)}$. For each extreme, for example, the symmetric neighborhood only includes the observation itself.

[19]*Lowess* is an acroynm for *lo*cally *we*ighted *s*catterplot *s*moother and is sometimes rendered as *loess*, for *lo*cal regr*ess*ion.

[20]Weighted least-squares regression is described (in a different context) in Section 12.2.2. The details of local regression are deferred to Chapter 18.

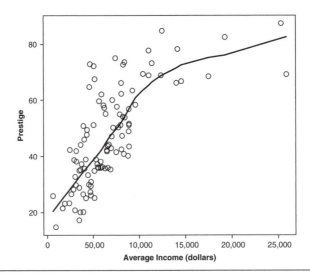

Figure 2.10   Lowess smooth of the relationship between occupational prestige and income. The span of the lowess smoother, 0.6, was determined by visual trial and error.

One way to determine the span is by visual trial and error: Select the smallest span that yields a reasonably smooth result. Applying this procedure to the Canadian occupational prestige data and to Davis's data on reported and measured weight led me to the plots in Figures 2.10 and 2.11. Lowess produces smoother results than local averaging, shows no evidence of boundary bias, and ignores the outlier in the Davis data.

Lowess (locally weighted regression) produces smoother results than local averaging, reduces boundary bias, and can discount outliers. The degree of smoothness is controlled by the span of the lowess smoother: Larger spans yield smoother results.

Exercise

Exercise 2.1.[21] *Figure 2.7 illustrates how, when the relationship between Y and X is nonlinear in an interval, the average value of Y in the interval can be a biased estimate of $E(Y|x)$ at the center of the interval. Imagine that X-values are evenly distributed in an interval centered at x_i, and let $\mu_i \equiv E(Y|x_i)$.

(a) If the relationship between Y and X is linear in the interval, is the average value of Y a biased or an unbiased estimator of μ_i?

(b) Are there any circumstances under which the average Y in the interval is an unbiased estimator of μ_i if the relationship between Y and X is nonlinear in the interval?

(c) What happens when the distribution of X-values in the interval is not uniform?

---

[21]Recall that in addition to the "theoretical" exercises in the text, the Web site for the book includes many data sets and exercises involving data analysis. Relatively difficult exercises are marked with an asterisk (*).

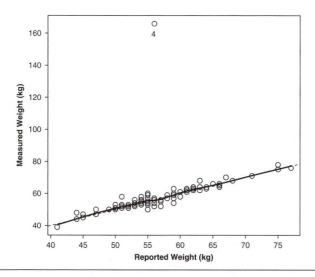

Figure 2.11   Lowess smooth of the relationship between reported and measured weight. The span of the smoother is .3. The broken line is the line of unbiased reporting of weight, $Y = X$.

Summary

- Regression analysis examines the relationship between a quantitative response variable, Y, and one or more quantitative explanatory variables, $X_1, \ldots, X_k$. Regression analysis traces the conditional distribution of Y—or some aspect of this distribution, such as its mean—as a function of the Xs.

- In very large samples, and when the explanatory variables are discrete, it is possible to estimate a regression by directly examining the conditional distribution of Y given the Xs. When the explanatory variables are continuous, we can proceed similarly in large samples by dissecting the Xs into many narrow bins.

- In smaller samples, local averages of Y can be calculated in a neighborhood or window surrounding each x-value. There is a trade-off in local averaging between the bias and the variance of the estimates: Narrow windows reduce bias but, because they include fewer observations, increase variance.

- Lowess (locally weighted regression) produces smoother results than local averaging, reduces boundary bias, and can discount outliers. The degree of smoothness is controlled by the span of the lowess smoother: Larger spans yield smoother lowess regressions.

3

Examining Data

T his chapter, on graphical methods for examining data, and the next, on transformations, represent a digression from the principal focus of the book. Nevertheless, the material here is important to us for two reasons: First, careful data analysis should begin with inspection of the data.[1] You will find in this chapter simple methods for graphing univariate, bivariate, and multivariate data. Second, the techniques for examining and transforming data that are discussed in Chapters 3 and 4 will find direct application to the analysis of data using linear models.[2] Feel free, of course, to pass lightly over topics that are familiar.

To motivate the material in the chapter, and to demonstrate its relevance to the study of linear models, consider the four scatterplots shown in Figure 3.1.[3] The data for these plots, given in Table 3.1, were cleverly contrived by Anscombe (1973) to illustrate the central role of graphical methods in data analysis: Anticipating the material in Chapters 5 and 6, the least-squares regression line and all other common regression "outputs"—such as the correlation coefficient, standard deviation of the residuals, and standard errors of the regression coefficients—are identical in the four data sets.

It is clear, however, that each graph tells a different story about the data. Of course, the data are simply made up, so we have to allow our imagination some latitude:

- In Figure 3.1(a), the least-squares line is a reasonable descriptive summary of the tendency of Y to increase with X.
- In Figure 3.1(b), the linear regression fails to capture the clearly curvilinear relationship between the two variables; we would do much better to fit a quadratic function here,[4] that is, $Y = a + bX + cX^2$.
- In Figure 3.1(c), there is a perfect linear relationship between Y and X for all but one outlying data point. The least-squares line is pulled strongly toward the outlier, distorting the relationship between the two variables for the rest of the data. Perhaps the outlier represents an error in data entry or an observation that differs in some fundamental respect from the others. When we encounter an outlier in real data, we should look for an explanation.[5]
- Finally, in Figure 3.1(d), the values of X are invariant (all are equal to 8), with the exception of one point (which has an X value of 19); the least-squares line would be undefined but for this point—the line necessarily goes through the mean of the 10 Ys that share the value $X = 8$ and through the point for which $X = 19$. Furthermore, if this point were moved,

---

[1] An eminent statistican who has engaged in frequent consulting (and who will remain nameless for fear of embarrassing him) recently told me that his clients routinely extract only about 30% of the information in their data relevant to their research. He attributed this inefficiency largely to failure to examine the data carefully at an early stage in statistical analysis.

[2] See, for example, the treatments of graphical regression "diagnostics" and transformations in Chapters 11 and 12.

[3] See Section 3.2 for a general discussion of scatterplots.

[4] Quadratic and other polynomial regression models are discussed in Section 17.1.

[5] Outlier detection in linear models is taken up in Chapter 11.

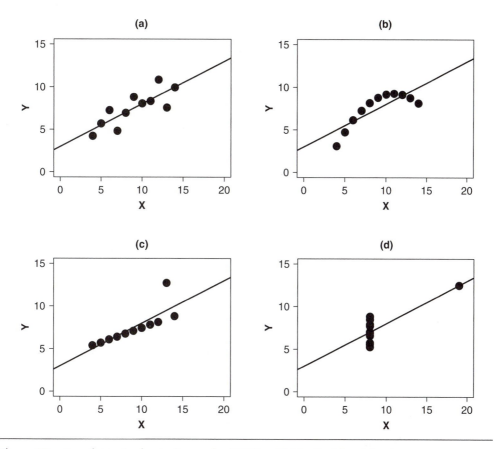

Figure 3.1 Four data sets, due to Anscombe (1973), with identical linear least-squares regressions. In (a), the linear regression is an accurate summary; in (b), the linear regression distorts the curvilinear relationship between *Y* and *X*; in (c), the linear regression is drawn toward an outlier; in (d), the linear regression "chases" the influential observation at the right. The least-squares line is shown on each plot.

   then the regression line would chase it. We are usually uncomfortable having the result of a data analysis depend so centrally on a single influential observation.[6]

The essential point to be derived from Anscombe's "quartet" (so dubbed by Tufte, 1983) is that it is frequently helpful to examine data graphically. Important characteristics of data are often disguised by numerical summaries and—worse—the summaries can be fundamentally misleading. Moreover, directly examining the numerical data is often uninformative: Only in the fourth data set is the problem immediately apparent upon inspection of the numbers.

> Statistical graphs are central to effective data analysis, both in the early stages of an investigation and in statistical modeling.

[6]Influential data are discussed in Chapter 11.

Table 3.1   Four Contrived Regression Data Sets From
                 Anscombe (1973)

$X_{a,b,c}$	Y_a	Y_b	Y_c	X_d	Y_d
10	8.04	9.14	7.46	8	6.58
8	6.95	8.14	6.77	8	5.76
13	7.58	8.74	12.74	8	7.71
9	8.81	8.77	7.11	8	8.84
11	8.33	9.26	7.81	8	8.47
14	9.96	8.10	8.84	8	7.04
6	7.24	6.13	6.08	8	5.25
4	4.26	3.10	5.39	19	12.50
12	10.84	9.13	8.15	8	5.56
7	4.82	7.26	6.42	8	7.91
5	5.68	4.74	5.73	8	6.89

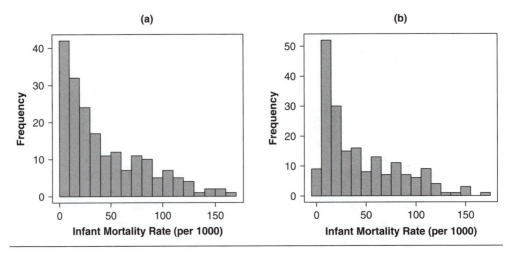

Figure 3.2   Histograms of infant morality for 193 nations. The histograms both use bins of width
                  10; histogram (a) employs bins that start at 0, while (b) employs bins that start at −5.

SOURCE: United Nations (1998).

3.1   Univariate Displays

3.1.1   Histograms

Figure 3.2 shows two *histograms* for the distribution of infant mortality among 193 countries, as reported in 1998 by the United Nations. The infant mortality rate is expressed as number of deaths of children aged less than 1 year per 1,000 live births. I assume that the histogram is a familiar graphical display, so I will offer only a brief description: To construct a histogram for infant mortality, dissect the range of the variable into equal-width intervals (called "bins"); count the number of observations falling in each bin; and display the frequency counts in a bar graph.

Both histograms in Figure 3.2 use bins of width 10; they differ in that the bins in Figure 3.2(a) start at 0 (i.e., 0 to 10, 10 to 20, etc.), while those in Figure 3.2(b) start at −5 (i.e., −5 to 5,

```
    1 | 2: represents 12
     leaf unit: 1
             n: 193

        39      0 | 345555555566666666677777777777888899999
        72      1 | 00012222233334444455556677888899
        95      2 | 0011222333344445555666
       (19)     3 | 0001233445577889999
        79      4 | 012344456889
        67      5 | 11246667888
        56      6 | 01255568
        48      7 | 122347788
        39      8 | 00222456669
        28      9 | 025678
        22     10 | 234677
        16     11 | 023445
        10     12 | 2445
         6     13 | 2
         5     14 | 29

    HI: 153 [Liberia], 154 [Afghanistan), 169 [Sierra Leone]
```

Figure 3.3   Stem-and-leaf display for infant mortality.

5 to 15, etc.).[7] The two histograms for infant mortality are more similar than different—both, for example, show that the distribution of infant mortality is positively skewed—but they do give slightly different impressions of the shape of the distribution.

Figure 3.3 shows an alternative form of histogram, called a *stem-and-leaf display*. The stem-and-leaf plot, introduced by John Tukey (1972, 1977), ingeniously employs the numerical data to form the bars of the histogram. As Tukey suggests, it is simple to construct a stem-and-leaf display by hand to "scratch down" a small data set.

You may be familiar with the stem-and-leaf display. Here is a relatively compressed explanation:

- Each data value is broken between two adjacent digits into a "stem" and a "leaf": In Figure 3.3, the break takes place between the tens and units digits. For example, the infant mortality rate in Albania was 32, which translates into the stem 3 and leaf 2.
- Stems (here, 0, 1, . . . , 14) are constructed to cover the data, implicitly defining a system of bins, each of width 10. Each leaf is placed to the right of its stem, and the leaves on each stem are then sorted into ascending order. We can produce a finer system of bins by dividing each stem into two parts (taking, respectively, leaves 0–4 and 5–9), or five parts (0–1, 2–3, 4–5, 6–7, 8–9); for the infant mortality data, two-part stems would correspond to bins of width 5 and five-part stems to bins of width 2. We could employ still finer bins by dividing stems from leaves between the ones and tenths digits, but, for infant mortality, that would produce a display with almost as many bins as observations. Similarly, a coarser division between the hundreds and tens digits would yield only two stems—0 and 1.
- Unusually large values—*outliers*—are collected on a special "HI" stem and displayed individually. Here, there are three countries with unusually large infant mortality rates. Were there countries with unusually small infant mortality rates, then these would be collected and displayed individually on a "LO" stem.[8]
- The column of *depths* counts in toward the median from both ends of the distribution. The median is the observation at depth $(n + 1)/2$, where (as usual) n is the number of observations. For the infant mortality data, the median is at depth $(193 + 1)/2 = 97$. In

---

[7]Because infant mortality cannot be negative, the contrast between Figures 3.2(a) and (b) is somewhat artificial.
[8]The rule for identifying outliers is explained in Section 3.1.4 on boxplots.

Figure 3.3, there are 39 observations at stem 0, 72 at and below stem 1, and so on; there are five observations (including the outliers) at and above stem 14, six at and above stem 13, and so forth. The count at the stem containing the median is shown in parentheses—here, 19 at stem 3. Note that $95 + 19 + 79 = 193$.

In constructing histograms (including stem-and-leaf displays), we want enough bins to preserve some detail, but not so many that the display is too rough and dominated by sampling variation. Let n^* represent the number of nonoutlying observations. Then, for $n^* \leq 100$, it usually works well to use no more than about $2\sqrt{n^*}$ bins; likewise, for $n^* > 100$, we can use a maximum of about $10 \times \log_{10} n^*$ bins. Of course, in constructing a histogram, we also want bins that start and end at "nice" numbers (e.g., 10 to 20 rather than 9.5843 to 21.0457); in a stem-and-leaf display, we are limited to bins that correspond to breaks between digits of the data values. Computer programs that construct histograms incorporate rules such as these.[9]

For the distribution of infant mortality, $n^* = 193 - 3 = 190$, so we should aim for no more than $10 \times \log_{10}(190) \approx 23$ bins. The stem-and-leaf display in Figure 3.3 uses 15 stems (plus the "HI" stem).

Histograms, including stem-and-leaf displays, are very useful graphs, but they suffer from several problems:

- As we have seen, the visual impression of the data conveyed by a histogram can depend on the arbitrary origin of the bin system.
- Because the bin system dissects the range of the variable into class intervals, the histogram is discontinuous (i.e., rough) even if, as in the case of infant mortality, the variable is continuous.[10]
- The form of the histogram depends on the arbitrary width of the bins.
- Moreover, if we use bins that are narrow enough to capture detail where data are plentiful—usually near the center of the distribution—then they may be too narrow to avoid "noise" where data are sparse—usually in the tails of the distribution.

3.1.2   Nonparametric Density Estimation

Nonparametric density estimation addresses the deficiencies of traditional histograms by averaging and smoothing. As the term implies, "density estimation" can be construed formally as an attempt to estimate the probability density function of a variable based on a sample, but it can also be thought of informally as a descriptive technique for smoothing histograms.

In fact, the histogram—suitably rescaled—is a simple density estimator.[11] Imagine that the origin of the bin system is at x_0, and that each of the m bins has width $2h$; the end points of the

---

[9]More sophisticated rules for the number of bins take into account information beyond n. For example, Freedman and Diaconis (1981) suggest

$$\text{number of bins} \approx \left\lceil \frac{n^{1/3}\left(x_{(n)} - x_{(1)}\right)}{2(Q_3 - Q_1)} \right\rceil$$

where $x_{(n)} - x_{(1)}$ is the range of the data, $Q_3 - Q_1$ is the inter-quartile range, and the "ceiling" brackets indicate rounding *up* to the next integer.

[10]That is, infant mortality rates are continuous for practical purposes in that they can take on many different values. Actually, infant mortality rates are ratios of integers and hence are rational numbers, and the rates in the U.N. data set are rounded to the nearest whole number.

[11]Rescaling is required because a density function encloses a total area of 1. Histograms are typically scaled so that the height of each bar represents frequency (or percent), and thus the heights of the bars sum to the sample size n (or 100). If each bar spans a bin of width $2h$ (anticipating the notation below), then the total area enclosed by the bars is $n \times 2h$. Dividing the height of each bar by $2nh$ therefore produces the requisite density rescaling.

bins are then at $x_0, x_0 + 2h, x_0 + 4h, \ldots, x_0 + 2mh$. An observation X_i falls in the jth bin if (by convention)

$$x_0 + 2(j - 1)h \leq X_i < x_0 + 2jh$$

The histogram estimator of the density at any x value located in the jth bin is based on the number of observations that fall in that bin:

$$\widehat{p}(x) = \frac{\#_{i=1}^n [x_0 + 2(j - 1)h \leq X_i < x_0 + 2jh]}{2nh}$$

where # is the counting operator.

We can dispense with the arbitrary origin x_0 of the bin system by counting locally within a continuously moving window of half-width h centered at x:

$$\widehat{p}(x) = \frac{\#_{i=1}^n (x - h \leq X_i < x + h)}{2nh}$$

In practice, of course, we would use a computer program to evaluate $\widehat{p}(x)$ at a large number of x values covering the range of X. This "naive density estimator" (so named by Silverman, 1986) is equivalent to locally weighted averaging, using a rectangular weight function:

$$\widehat{p}(x) = \frac{1}{nh} \sum_{i=1}^n W\left(\frac{x - X_i}{h}\right) \tag{3.1}$$

where

$$W(z) = \begin{cases} \frac{1}{2} & \text{for } |z| < 1 \\ 0 & \text{otherwise} \end{cases}$$

a formulation that will be useful below when we consider alternative weight functions to smooth the density. Here z is a "stand-in" for the argument to the $W(\cdot)$ weight function—that is, $z = (x - X_i)/h$. The naive estimator is like a histogram that uses bins of width $2h$ but has no fixed origin, and is similar in spirit to the naive nonparametric-regression estimator introduced in Chapter 2.

An illustration, using the U.N. infant mortality data, appears in Figure 3.4, and reveals the principal problem with the naive estimator: Because the estimated density jumps up and down as observations enter and leave the window, the naive density estimator is intrinsically rough.

The rectangular weight function $W(z)$ in Equation 3.1 is defined to enclose an area of $2 \times \frac{1}{2} = 1$, producing a density estimate that (as required) also encloses an area of 1. Any function that has this property—probability density functions are obvious choices—may be used as a weight function, called a *kernel*. Choosing a kernel that is smooth, symmetric, and unimodal smooths out the rough edges of the naive density estimator. This is the essential insight of *kernel density estimation*.

The general kernel density estimator is, then, given by

$$\widehat{p}(x) = \frac{1}{nh} \sum_{i=1}^n K\left(\frac{x - X_i}{h}\right)$$

There are many reasonable choices of the kernel function $K(z)$, including the familiar standard normal density function, $\phi(z)$, which is what I will use here. While the naive density estimator in effect sums suitably scaled rectangles centered at the observations, the more general kernel

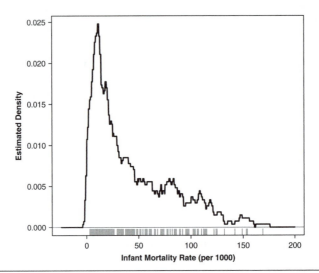

Figure 3.4   Naive density estimator for infant mortality, using a window half-width of $h = 7$. Note the roughness of the estimator. A *rug-plot* (or "one-dimensional scatterplot") appears at the bottom of the graph, showing the location of the data values.

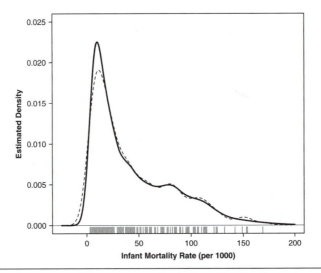

Figure 3.5   Kernel (broken line) and adaptive-kernel (solid line) density estimates for the distribution of infant mortality, using a normal kernel and a window half-width of $h = 7$. Note the relative "lumpiness" of the kernel estimator at the right, where data are sparse.

estimator sums smooth lumps. An example is shown in Figure 3.5, in which the kernel density estimator is given by the broken line.[12]

Selecting the window width for the kernel estimator is primarily a matter of trial and error—we want a value small enough to reveal detail but large enough to suppress random noise. We can,

---

[12]Notice that there is nonzero estimated density in Figure 3.5 below an infant mortality rate of 0. Of course, this does not make sense, and although I will not pursue it here, it is possible to constrain the lower and upper limits of the kernel estimator.

however, look to statistical theory for rough guidance:[13] If the underlying density that we are trying to estimate is normal with standard deviation σ, then (for the normal kernel) estimation is most efficient with the window half-width

$$h = 0.9\sigma n^{-1/5} \tag{3.2}$$

As is intuitively reasonable, the optimal window grows gradually narrower as the sample size is increased, permitting finer detail in large samples than in small ones.[14]

Although we might, by reflex, be tempted to replace the unknown σ in Equation 3.2 with the sample standard deviation S, it is prudent to be more cautious, for if the underlying density is sufficiently non-normal, then the sample standard deviation may be seriously inflated. A common compromise is to use an "adaptive" estimator of spread:

$$A = \min\left(S, \frac{\text{interquartile range}}{1.349} \right) \tag{3.3}$$

The factor 1.349 is the interquartile range of the standard normal distribution, making (interquartile range)/1.349 a robust estimator of σ in the normal setting.

One further caveat: If the underlying density is substantially non-normal—in particular, if it is skewed or multimodal—then basing h on the adaptive estimator A generally produces a window that is too wide. A good procedure, then, is to start with

$$h = 0.9An^{-1/5}$$

and to adjust this value downwards until the resulting density plot becomes too rough. This is the procedure that was used to find the window width in Figure 3.5, where $S = 38.55$ and (interquartile range)/1.349 = (68 − 13)/1.349 = 40.77. Here, the "optimal" window width is $h = 0.9 \times 38.55 \times 197^{-1/5} = 12.061$.

The kernel density estimator usually does a pretty good job, but the window half-width h remains a compromise: We would prefer a narrower window where data are plentiful (to preserve detail) and a wider one where data are sparse (to suppress noise). Because "plentiful" and "sparse" refer implicitly to the underlying density that we are trying to estimate, it is natural to begin with an initial estimate of the density, and to adjust the window half-width on the basis of the initial estimate.[15] The result is the *adaptive-kernel estimator* (not to be confused with the adaptive estimator of spread in Equation 3.3).

1. Calculate an initial density estimate, $\tilde{p}(x)$—for example, by the kernel method.

2. Using the initial estimate, compute local window factors by evaluating the estimated density at the observations:

$$f_i = \left[\frac{\tilde{p}(X_i)}{\tilde{p}} \right]^{-1/2}$$

In this formula, $\tilde{p}$ is the geometric mean of the initial density estimates at the observations—that is,

$$\tilde{p} = \left[\prod_{i=1}^{n} \tilde{p}(X_i) \right]^{1/n}$$

---

[13]See, for example, Silverman (1986, chap. 3) for a detailed discussion of these issues.

[14]If we really knew that the density were normal, then it would be even more efficient to estimate it parametrically by substituting the sample mean $\overline{X}$ and standard deviation S for μ and σ in the formula for the normal density, $p(x) = (2\pi\sigma^2)^{-1/2} \exp[-(x − \mu)^2/2\sigma^2]$.

[15]An alternative is to use a *nearest-neighbor* approach, as in the nonparametric-regression methods discussed in Chapter 2.

(where the operator $\prod$ indicates continued multiplication). As a consequence of this definition, the f_is have a product of 1, and hence a geometric mean of 1, ensuring that the area under the density estimate remains equal to 1.

3. Calculate the adaptive-kernel density estimator using the local window factors to adjust the width of the kernels centered at the observations:

$$\widehat{p}(x) = \frac{1}{nh} \sum_{i=1}^{n} \frac{1}{f_i} K \left(\frac{x - X_i}{f_i h} \right)$$

Applying the adaptive kernel estimator to the infant mortality distribution produces the solid line in Figure 3.5: For this distribution the kernel and adaptive-kernel estimates are very similar, although the adaptive kernel more sharply defines the principal mode of the distribution near 20, and produces a smoother long right tail.

3.1.3   Quantile-Comparison Plots

Quantile-comparison plots are useful for comparing an empirical sample distribution with a theoretical distribution, such as the normal distribution—something that is more commonly of interest for derived quantities such as test statistics or residuals than for observed variables. A strength of the display is that it does not require the use of arbitrary bins or windows.

Let $P(x)$ represent the theoretical *cumulative distribution function* (CDF) with which we want to compare the data; that is, $P(x) = \Pr(X \leq x)$. A simple (but not terribly useful) procedure is to graph the *empirical cumulative distribution function* (ECDF) for the observed data, which is simply the proportion of data below each value of x, as x moves continuously from left to right:

$$\widehat{P}(x) = \frac{\#_{i=1}^{n}(X_i \leq x)}{n}$$

As illustrated in Figure 3.6, however, the ECDF is a "stair-step" function (where each step occurs at an observation, and is of height $1/n$), while the CDF is typically smooth, making the comparison difficult.

The quantile-comparison plot avoids this problem by never constructing the ECDF explicitly:

1. Order the data values from smallest to largest, $X_{(1)}, X_{(2)}, \ldots, X_{(n)}$. The $X_{(i)}$ are called the *order statistics* of the sample.

2. By convention, the cumulative proportion of the data "below" $X_{(i)}$ is given by[16]

$$P_i = \frac{i - \frac{1}{2}}{n}$$

3. Use the inverse of the CDF (that is, the *quantile function*) to find the value z_i corresponding to the cumulative probability P_i; that is,[17]

$$z_i = P^{-1} \left(\frac{i - \frac{1}{2}}{n} \right)$$

---

[16]This definition avoids cumulative proportions of 0 or 1, which would be an embarrassment in step 3 for distributions, like the normal, that never quite reach cumulative probabilities of 0 or 1. In effect, we count half of each observation below its exact value and half above. Another common convention is to use $P_i = \left(i - \frac{1}{3}\right) / \left(n + \frac{1}{3}\right)$.

[17]This operation assumes that the CDF has an inverse—that is, that P is a strictly increasing function (one that never quite levels off). The common continuous probability distributions in statistics—for example, the normal, t-, F-, and χ^2 distributions—all have this property. These and other distributions are reviewed in Appendix D on probability and estimation.

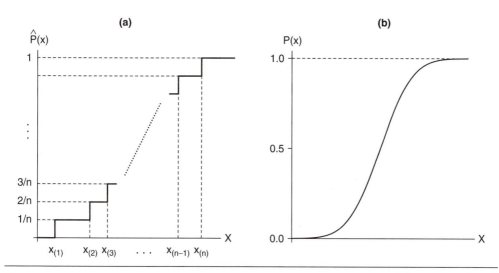

Figure 3.6   A "typical" empirical cumulative distribution function (ECDF) is shown in (a), a "typical" theoretical cumulative distribution function (CDF) in (b). $X_{(1)}, X_{(2)}, \ldots, X_{(n)}$ represent the data values ordered from smallest to largest. Note that the ordered data values are not, in general, equally spaced.

4. Plot the z_i as horizontal coordinates against the $X_{(i)}$ as vertical coordinates. If X is sampled from the distribution P, then $X_{(i)} \approx z_i$. That is, the plot should be approximately linear, with an intercept of 0 and slope of 1. This relationship is only approximate because of sampling error (see point 6). If the distributions are identical except for location, then the plot is approximately linear with a nonzero intercept, $X_{(i)} \approx \mu + z_i$; if the distributions are identical except for scale, then the plot is approximately linear with a slope different from 1, $X_{(i)} \approx \sigma z_i$; finally, if the distributions differ both in location and scale but have the same shape, then $X_{(i)} \approx \mu + \sigma z_i$.

5. It is often helpful to place a comparison line on the plot to facilitate the perception of departures from linearity. The line can be plotted by eye, attending to the central part of the data, or we can draw a line connecting the quartiles. For a normal quantile-comparison plot—comparing the distribution of the data with the standard normal distribution—we can alternatively use the median as a robust estimator of μ and the interquartile range/1.349 as a robust estimator of σ. (The more conventional estimates $\widehat{\mu} = \overline{X}$ and $\widehat{\sigma} = S$ will not work well when the data are substantially non-normal.)

6. We expect some departure from linearity because of sampling variation; it therefore assists interpretation to display the expected degree of sampling error in the plot. The standard error of the order statistic $X_{(i)}$ is

$$\mathrm{SE}(X_{(i)}) = \frac{\widehat{\sigma}}{p(z_i)} \sqrt{\frac{P_i(1 - P_i)}{n}}$$

where $p(z)$ is the probability density function corresponding to the CDF $P(z)$. The values along the fitted line are given by $\widehat{X}_{(i)} = \widehat{\mu} + \widehat{\sigma} z_i$. An approximate 95% confidence "envelope" around the fitted line is, therefore,[18]

---

[18]By the method of construction, the 95% confidence level applies (point-wise) to each $\widehat{X}_{(i)}$, not to the whole envelope: There is a greater probability that *at least one* point strays outside the envelope even if the data are sampled from the

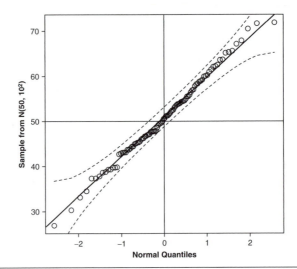

Figure 3.7   Normal quantile-comparison plot for a sample of 100 observations drawn from a normal distribution with mean 50 and standard deviation 10. The fitted line is through the quartiles of the distribution, and the broken lines give a point-wise 95% confidence interval around the fit.

$$\widehat{X}_{(i)} \pm 2 \times \mathrm{SE}(X_{(i)})$$

Figures 3.7 to 3.10 display normal quantile-comparison plots for several illustrative distributions:

- Figure 3.7 plots a sample of $n = 100$ observations from a normal distribution with mean $\mu = 50$ and standard deviation $\sigma = 10$. The plotted points are reasonably linear and stay within the rough 95% confidence envelope.
- Figure 3.8 plots a sample of $n = 100$ observations from the positively skewed chi-square distribution with 2 degrees of freedom. The positive skew of the data is reflected in points that lie *above* the comparison line in both tails of the distribution. (In contrast, the tails of negatively skewed data would lie *below* the comparison line.)
- Figure 3.9 plots a sample of $n = 100$ observations from the heavy-tailed t-distribution with 2 degrees of freedom. In this case, values in the upper tail lie above the corresponding normal quantiles, and values in the lower tail below the corresponding normal quantiles.
- Figure 3.10 shows the normal quantile-comparison plot for the distribution of infant mortality. The positive skew of the distribution is readily apparent. The possibly bimodal character of the data, however, is not easily discerned in this display.

Quantile-comparison plots highlight the tails of distributions. This is important, because the behavior of the tails is often problematic for standard estimation methods like least squares, but it is useful to supplement quantile-comparison plots with other displays—such as histograms or kernel-density estimates—that provide more intuitive representations of distributions. A key point is that there is no reason to limit ourselves to a single picture of a distribution when different pictures bring different aspects of the distribution into relief.

---

comparison distribution. Determining a *simultaneous* 95% confidence envelope would be a formidable task, because the order statistics are not independent.

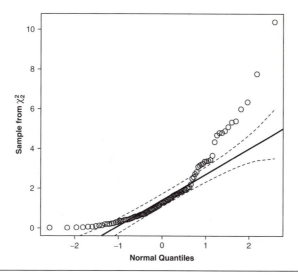

Figure 3.8   Normal quantile-comparison plot for a sample of 100 observations from the positively skewed chi-square distribution with 2 degrees of freedom.

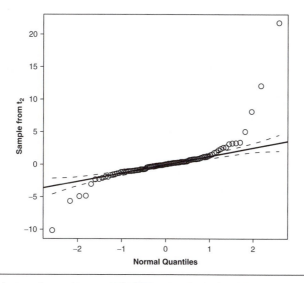

Figure 3.9   Normal quantile-comparison plot for a sample of 100 observations from the heavy-tailed t-distribution with 2 degrees of freedom.

3.1.4   Boxplots

Unlike histograms, density plots, and quantile-comparison plots, *boxplots* (due to Tukey, 1977) present only summary information on center, spread, and skewness, along with individual outlying observations. Boxplots are constructed from the *five-number summary* of a distribution—the minimum, first quartile, median, third quartile, and maximum—and outliers, if they are present. Boxplots, therefore, are useful when we require a compact representation of a distribution (as, for example, in the margins of a scatterplot), when we wish to compare the principal characteristics

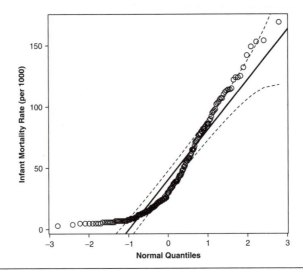

Figure 3.10   Normal quantile-comparison plot for the distribution of infant mortality. Note the positive skew.

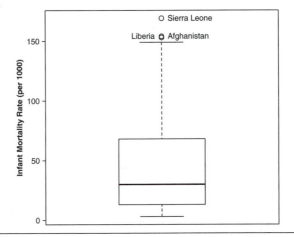

Figure 3.11   Boxplot for infant mortality. The central box is drawn between the hinges; the position of the median is marked in the box; and outlying observations are displayed individually.

of several distributions,[19] or when we want to select a transformation that makes a distribution more symmetric.[20]

An illustrative boxplot for infant mortality appears in Figure 3.11. This plot is constructed according to the following conventions (illustrated in the schematic horizontal boxplot in Figure 3.12):

1. A scale is laid off to accommodate the extremes of the data. The infant mortality data, for example, range between 3 and 169.

---

[19]See Section 3.2.
[20]Transformations to symmetry are discussed in Chapter 4.

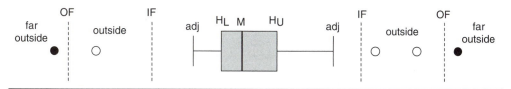

Figure 3.12   Schematic boxplot, showing the median (*M*), hinges (*H$_L$* and *H$_U$*), adjacent values (adj), inner and outer fences (IF and OF), and outside and far-outside observations.

2. The central box is drawn between the *hinges*, which are simply defined first and third quartiles, and therefore encompasses the middle half of the data. The line in the central box represents the median. Recall that the depth of the median is

$$\text{depth}(M) = \frac{n+1}{2}$$

giving the position of the middle observation after the data are ordered from smallest to largest: $X_{(1)}, X_{(2)}, \ldots, X_{(n)}$. When *n* is even, the depth of the median has a fractional part; using "floor" brackets to represent truncation to an integer, we count in from either end to average the two observations at depth $\lfloor (n+1)/2 \rfloor$. For the infant mortality data, $\text{depth}(M) = (193+1)/2 = 97$, and $M = X_{(97)} = 30$.

Likewise, the depth of the hinges is

$$\text{depth}(H) = \frac{\lfloor \text{depth}(M) \rfloor + 1}{2}$$

If depth(*H*) has a fractional part, then, for each hinge, we average the two observations at the adjacent positions, that is, at $\lfloor \text{depth}(H) \rfloor$ and $\lfloor \text{depth}(H) \rfloor + 1$. For the infant mortality distribution, $\text{depth}(H) = (97+1)/2 = 49$. The lower hinge is, therefore, $H_L = X_{(49)} = 13$, and the upper hinge is $H_U = X_{(149)} = 73$. (Counting down 97 observations from the top yields the subscript $197 - 49 + 1 = 149$.)

3. The following rules are used to identify outliers, which are shown individually in the boxplot:

    *   The *hinge-spread* (roughly the interquartile range) is the difference between the hinges:

$$H\text{-spread} = H_U - H_L$$

    *   The lower and upper "inner fences" are located 1.5 hinge-spreads beyond the hinges:

$$IF_L = H_L - 1.5 \times H\text{-spread}$$
$$IF_U = H_U + 1.5 \times H\text{-spread}$$

    Observations beyond the inner fences (but within the outer fences, defined below) are termed "outside" and are represented by open circles. The fences themselves are not shown in the display.

- The "outer fences" are located three hinge-spreads beyond the hinges:[21]

$$OF_L = H_L - 3 \times H\text{-spread}$$
$$OF_U = H_U + 3 \times H\text{-spread}$$

Observations beyond the outer fences are termed "far outside" and are represented by filled circles. There are no far-outside observations in the infant mortality data.
- The "whisker" growing from each end of the central box extends either to the extreme observation on its side of the distribution (as at the low end of the infant mortality data) or to the most extreme nonoutlying observation, called the "adjacent value" (as at the high end of the infant mortality distribution).[22]

The boxplot of infant mortality in Figure 3.11 clearly reveals the skewness of the distribution: The lower whisker is much shorter than the upper whisker; the median is closer to the lower hinge than to the upper hinge; and there are several outside observations at the upper end of the infant mortality distribution, but none at the lower end. The apparent bimodality of the infant mortality data is not captured by the boxplot, however.

> There are many useful univariate displays, including the traditional histogram. The stem-and-leaf plot is a modern variant of the histogram for small data sets, constructed directly from numerical data. Nonparametric density estimation may be employed to smooth a histogram. Quantile comparison plots are useful for comparing data with a theoretical probability distribution. Boxplots summarize some of the most important characteristics of a distribution, including center, spread, skewness, and outliers.

3.2 Plotting Bivariate Data

The *scatterplot*—a direct geometric representation of observations on two quantitative variables (generically, Y and X)—is the most useful of all statistical graphs. The scatterplot is a natural representation of data partly because the media on which we draw plots—paper, computer screens—are intrinsically two dimensional. Scatterplots are as familiar and essentially simple as they are useful; I will therefore limit this presentation to a few points. There are many examples of bivariate scatterplots in this book, including in the preceding chapter.

- In analyzing data, it is convenient to work in a computing environment that permits the interactive identification of observations in a scatterplot.
- Because relationships between variables in the social sciences are often weak, scatterplots can be dominated visually by "noise." It often helps, therefore, to plot a nonparametric regression of Y on X.

---

[21] Here is a rough justification for the fences: In a normal population, the hinge-spread is 1.349 standard deviations, and so $1.5 \times H\text{-spread} = 1.5 \times 1.349 \times \sigma \approx 2\sigma$. The hinges are located $1.349/2 \approx 0.7$ standard deviations above and below the mean. The inner fences are, therefore, approximately at $\mu \pm 2.7\sigma$, and the outer fences at $\mu \pm 4.7\sigma$. From the standard normal table, $\Pr(Z > 2.7) \approx .003$, so we expect slightly less than 1% of the observations beyond the inner fences ($2 \times .003 = .006$); likewise, because $\Pr(Z > 4.7) \approx 1.3 \times 10^{-6}$, we expect less than one observation in 100,000 beyond the outer fences.

[22] All of the folksy terminology—"hinges," "fences," "whiskers," and so on—originates with Tukey (1977).

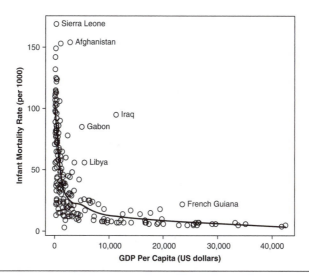

Figure 3.13 Scatterplot for infant mortality and GDP per capita for 193 nations. The line is for a lowess smooth with a span of 1/2. Several nations with high infant mortality for their levels of GDP are identified.

- Scatterplots in which one or both variables are highly skewed are difficult to examine, because the bulk of the data congregate in a small part of the display. Consider, for example, the scatterplot for infant mortality and gross domestic product (GDP) per capita in Figure 3.13. It often helps to "correct" substantial skews prior to examining the relationship between Y and X.[23]
- Scatterplots in which the variables are discrete can also be difficult to examine. An extreme instance of this phenomenon is shown in Figure 3.14, which plots scores on a 10-item vocabulary test against years of education. The data are from 16 of the U.S. General Social Surveys conducted by the National Opinion Research Center between 1974 and 2004, and include in total 21,638 observations. One solution—especially useful when only X is discrete—is to focus on the conditional distribution of Y for each value of X. Boxplots, for example, can be employed to represent the conditional distributions (see Figure 3.16, discussed below). Another solution is to separate overlapping points by adding a small random quantity to the discrete scores. In Figure 3.15, for example, I have added a uniform random variable on the interval $[-0.4, +0.4]$ to each value of vocabulary and education. Paradoxically, the tendency for vocabulary to increase with education is much clearer in the randomly "jittered" display.[24]

> The bivariate scatterplot is a natural graphical display of the relationship between two quantitative variables. Interpretation of a scatterplot can often be assisted by graphing a nonparametric regression, which summarizes the relationship between the two variables. Scatterplots of the relationship between discrete variables can be enhanced by randomly jittering the data.

---

[23] See Chapter 4.
[24] The idea of jittering a scatterplot, as well as the terminology, is due to Cleveland (1994).

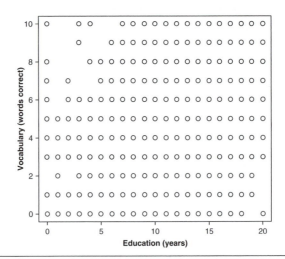

Figure 3.14   Scatterplot of scores on a 10-item vocabulary test versus years of education.
                 Although there are nearly 22,000 observations in the data set, most of the plotted
                 points fall on top of one another.

SOURCE: National Opinion Research Center (2005).

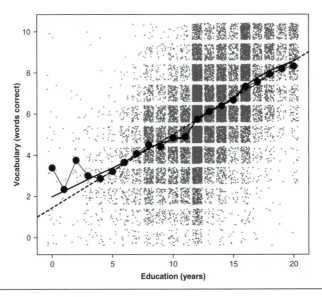

Figure 3.15   Jittered scatterplot for vocabulary score versus years of education. A uniformly
                 distributed random quantity between −0.4 and +0.4 was added to each score for
                 both variables. The heavier solid line is for a lowess fit to the data, with a span of 0.2;
                 the broken line is the linear least-squares fit; the conditional means for vocabulary
                 given education are represented by the dots, connected by the lighter solid line.

As mentioned, when the explanatory variable is discrete, parallel boxplots can be used to display
the conditional distributions of Y. One common case occurs when the explanatory variable is a
qualitative/categorical variable. An example is shown in Figure 3.16, using data collected by Michael
Ornstein (1976) on interlocking directorates among the 248 largest Canadian firms. The response

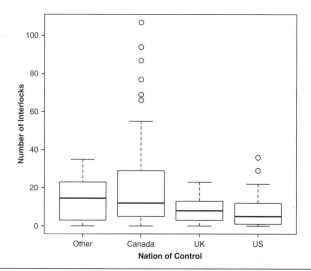

Figure 3.16   Number of interlocking directorate and executive positions by nation of control, for 248 dominant Canadian firms.

SOURCE: Personal communication from Michael Ornstein.

variable in this graph is the number of interlocking directorships and executive positions maintained by each firm with others in the group of 248. The explanatory variable is the nation in which the corporation is controlled, coded as Canada, United Kingdom, United States, and other foreign.

It is apparent from the graph that the average level of interlocking is greater among other-foreign and Canadian corporations than among corporations controlled in the United Kingdom and the United States. It is relatively difficult to discern detail in this display: first, because the conditional distributions of interlocks are positively skewed; and, second, because there is an association between level and spread—variation is also greater among other-foreign and Canadian firms than among U.K. and U.S. firms.[25]

> Parallel boxplots display the relationship between a quantitative response variable and a discrete (categorical or quantitative) explanatory variable.

3.3   Plotting Multivariate Data

Because paper and computer screens are two dimensional, graphical display of multivariate data is intrinsically difficult. Multivariate displays for quantitative data often project the higher-dimensional "point cloud" of the data onto a two-dimensional space. It is, of course, impossible to view a higher-dimensional scatterplot directly (but see the discussion of the three-dimensional case below). The essential trick of effective multidimensional display is to select projections that reveal important characteristics of the data. In certain circumstances, projections can be selected on the basis of a statistical model fit to the data or on the basis of explicitly stated criteria.[26]

---

[25]We will revisit this example in Section 4.4. Because the names of the firms are unavailable, I have not identified the outliers in the plot.

[26]We will apply these powerful ideas in Chapters 11 and 12.

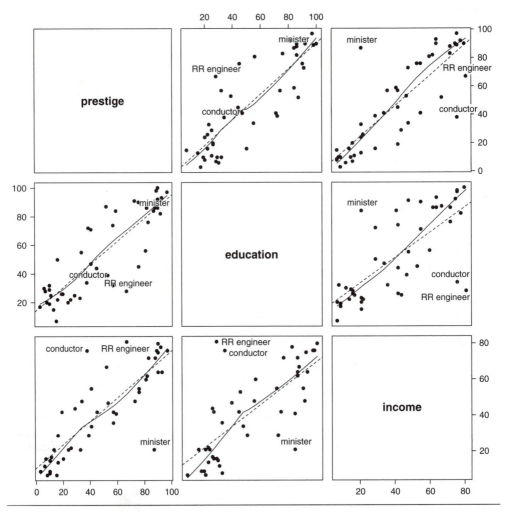

Figure 3.17   Scatterplot matrix for occupational prestige, level of education, and level of income, for 45 U.S. occupations in 1950. The least-squares regression line (broken line) and lowess smooth (for a span of 0.6, solid line) are shown on each plot. Three unusual observations are identified.

SOURCE: Duncan (1961).

3.3.1   Scatterplot Matrices

A simple approach to multivariate data, which does not require a statistical model, is to examine bivariate scatterplots for all pairs of variables. Arraying these plots in a *scatterplot matrix* produces a graphical analog to the correlation matrix.

An illustrative scatterplot matrix, for data on the prestige, education, and income levels of 45 U.S. occupations, appears in Figure 3.17. In this data set, first analyzed by Duncan (1961), "prestige" represents the percentage of respondents in a survey who rated an occupation as "good" or "excellent" in prestige; "education" represents the percentage of incumbents in the occupation in the 1950 U.S. Census who were high-school graduates; and "income" represents the percentage of occupational incumbents who earned incomes in excess of $3500. Duncan's purpose was to use a regression analysis of prestige on income and education to predict the prestige levels of other occupations, for which data on income and education were available, but for which there were no direct prestige ratings.[27]

The variable names on the diagonal of the scatterplot matrix in Figure 3.17 label the rows and columns of the display: For example, the vertical axis for the two plots in the first row of the display is "prestige"; the horizontal axis for the two plots in the second column is "education." Thus, the scatterplot in the first row, second column is for prestige (on the vertical axis) versus education (on the horizontal axis).

It is important to understand an essential limitation of the scatterplot matrix as a device for analyzing multivariate data: By projecting the multidimensional point cloud onto pairs of axes, the plot focuses on the *marginal* relationships between the corresponding pairs of variables. The object of data analysis for several variables, however, is typically to investigate *partial* relationships (between pairs of variables, "controlling" statistically for other variables), not marginal associations. For example, in the Duncan data set, we are more interested in the partial relationship of prestige to education holding income constant than in the marginal relationship between prestige and education ignoring income.

The response variable Y can be related marginally to a particular X, even when there is no partial relationship between the two variables controlling for other Xs. It is also possible for there to be a partial association between Y and an X but no marginal association. Furthermore, if the Xs themselves are nonlinearly related, then the marginal relationship between Y and a specific X can be nonlinear even when their partial relationship is linear.[28]

Despite this intrinsic limitation, scatterplot matrices often uncover interesting features of the data, and this is indeed the case in Figure 3.17, where the display reveals three unusual observations: *Ministers* have relatively low income for their relatively high level of education, and relatively high prestige for their relatively low income; *railroad conductors* and *railroad engineers* have relatively high incomes for their more-or-less average levels of education; *railroad conductors* also have relatively low prestige for their relatively high incomes. This pattern bodes ill for the least-squares linear regression of prestige on income and education.[29]

3.3.2 Coded Scatterplots

Information about a categorical third variable can be entered on a bivariate scatterplot by coding the plotting symbols. The most effective codes use different colors to represent categories, but degrees of fill, distinguishable shapes, and distinguishable letters can also be effective.[30]

Figure 3.18 shows a scatterplot of Davis's data on measured and reported weight.[31] Observations for men are displayed as Ms, for women as Fs. Except for the outlying point (number 12—which, recall, represents an error in the data), the points both for men and for women cluster near the line $Y = X$; it is also clear from the display that most men are heavier than most women, as one would expect, and that, discounting the bad data point, one man (number 21) is quite a bit heavier than everyone else.

3.3.3 Three-Dimensional Scatterplots

Another useful multivariate display, directly applicable to three variables at a time, is the *three-dimensional scatterplot*. Moreover, just as data can be projected onto a judiciously chosen plane

[27]We will return to this regression problem in Chapter 5.

[28]These ideas are explored in Chapter 12.

[29]See the discussion of Duncan's occupational-prestige regression in Chapter 11.

[30]See Spence and Lewandowsky (1990) for a fine review of the literature on graphical perception, including information on coded scatterplots.

[31]Davis's data were introduced in Chapter 2, where only the data for women were presented.

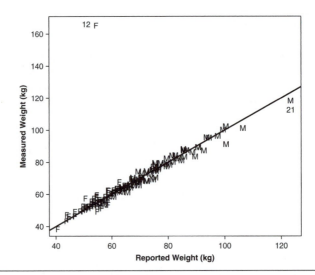

Figure 3.18   Davis's data on measured and reported weight, by gender. Data points for men are
represented by Ms, for women by Fs, and are jittered slightly to reduce overplotting.
The line on the graph is $Y = X$. In the combined data set for men and women, the
outlying observation is number 12.

in a two-dimensional plot, higher-dimensional data can be projected onto a three-dimensional
space, expanding the range of application of three-dimensional scatterplots.[32]

Barring the use of a true stereoscopic display, the three-dimensional scatterplot is an illusion
produced by modern statistical software: The graph represents a projection of a three-dimensional
space onto a two-dimensional computer screen. Nevertheless, motion (e.g., rotation) and the ability
to interact with the display—possibly combined with the effective use of perspective, color, depth
cueing, and other visual devices—can produce a vivid impression of directly examining objects
in three-dimensional space.

It is literally impossible to convey this impression adequately on the static, two-dimensional
page of a book, but Figure 3.19 shows Duncan's prestige data rotated interactively into a revealing orientation: Looking down the cigar-shaped scatter of most of the data, the three unusual
observations stand out very clearly.

3.3.4   Conditioning Plots

Conditioning plots (or *coplots*), described in Cleveland (1993), are another graphical device for
examining multidimensional data. The essential idea of the coplot is to focus on the relationship
between the response variable and a particular explanatory variable, dividing the data into groups
based on the values of other explanatory variables—the *conditioning variables*. If the conditioning
variables are discrete, then this division is straightforward and natural. If a conditioning variable
is continuous, it can be binned: Cleveland suggests using overlapping bins, which are called
"shingles."

An illustrative coplot, for the General Social Survey vocabulary data, is shown in Figure 3.20.
This graph displays the relationship between vocabulary score and education "controlling for"

---

[32]For example, there are three-dimensional versions of the added-variable and component-plus-residual plots discussed
in Chapters 11 and 12. See, for example, Cook and Weisberg (1989).

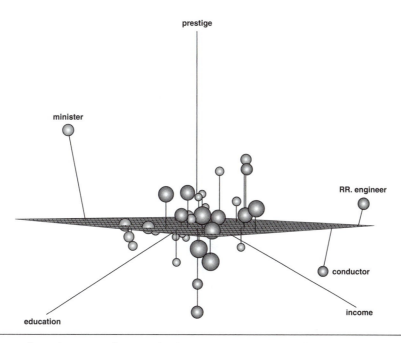

Figure 3.19   Three-dimensional scatterplot for Duncan's occupational prestige data, rotated into an orientation that reveals three unusual observations. From this orientation, the least-squares regression plane, also shown in the plot, is viewed nearly edge on.

gender and the year of the survey. The partial relationships are remarkably similar in the different panels of the coplot; that is, gender and year appear to make little difference to the relationship between vocabulary score and education. The relationships also appear to be very close to linear: In a few panels, the lowess line departs from the linear least-square line at the far left, but data in this region are quite sparse.

Although they can be effective graphs, coplots have limitations: First, if there are more than two, or perhaps three, conditioning variables, it becomes difficult to perceive how the partial relationship between the response and the focal explanatory variable changes with the conditioning variables. Second, because coplots require the division of the data into groups, they are most useful for large data sets, an issue that grows more acute as the number of conditioning variables increases.

> Visualizing multivariate data is intrinsically difficult because we cannot directly examine higher-dimensional scatterplots. Effective displays project the higher-dimensional point cloud onto two or three dimensions; these displays include the scatterplot matrix, the dynamic three-dimensional scatterplot, and the conditioning plot.

Summary _____

- Statistical graphs are central to effective data analysis, both in the early stages of an investigation and in statistical modeling.

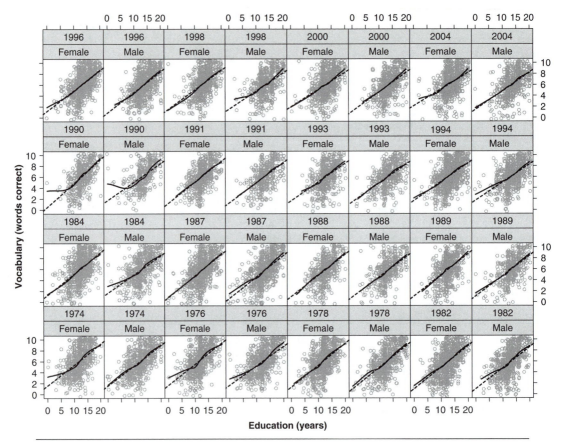

Figure 3.20 Coplot showing the relationship between vocabulary score and education controlling for year and gender. The points in each panel are jittered to reduce over-plotting. The broken line shows the linear least-square fit, while the solid line gives the lowess fit for a span of 0.6.

- There are many useful univariate displays, including the traditional histogram. The stem-and-leaf plot is a modern variant of the histogram for small data sets, constructed directly from numerical data. Nonparametric density estimation may be employed to smooth a histogram. Quantile-comparison plots are useful for comparing data with a theoretical probability distribution. Boxplots summarize some of the most important characteristics of a distribution, including center, spread, skewness, and outliers.
- The bivariate scatterplot is a natural graphical display of the relationship between two quantitative variables. Interpretation of a scatterplot can often be assisted by graphing a nonparametric regression, which summarizes the relationship between the two variables. Scatterplots of the relationship between discrete variables can be enhanced by randomly jittering the data.
- Parallel boxplots display the relationship between a quantitative response variable and a discrete explanatory variable.
- Visualizing multivariate data is intrinsically difficult because we cannot directly examine higher-dimensional scatterplots. Effective displays project the higher-dimensional point

cloud onto two or three dimensions; these displays include the scatterplot matrix, the dynamic three-dimensional scatterplot, and the conditioning plot.

Recommended Reading

The literature—especially the recent literature—on statistical graphics is truly voluminous. I will furnish only the briefest of bibliographies:

- Fox (2000c) presents a brief overview of statistical graphics, including information on the history of the subject. Jacoby (1997, 1998) gives a more extended overview addressed to social scientists.
- Tufte's (1983) influential book on graphical presentation of quantitative information is opinionated but well worth reading. (Tufte has since published several other books on graphics, broadly construed, but I prefer his first book.)
- Modern interest in statistical graphics is the direct result of John Tukey's work on exploratory data analysis; unfortunately, Tukey's idiosyncratic writing style makes his seminal book (Tukey, 1977) difficult to read. Velleman and Hoaglin (1981) provide a more digestible introduction to the topic. There is interesting information on the statistical theory underlying exploratory data analysis in two volumes edited by Hoaglin, Mosteller, and Tukey (1983, 1985).
- Tukey's influence made Bell Labs a center of work on statistical graphics, much of which is described in two accessible and interesting books by William Cleveland (1993, 1994) and in Chambers, Cleveland, Kleiner, and Tukey (1983). Cleveland (1994) is a good place to start.
- Modern statistical graphics is closely associated with advances in statistical computing: The S statistical computing environment (Becker, Chambers, & Wilks, 1988; Chambers, 1998; Chambers & Hastie, 1992), also a product of Bell Labs, is particularly strong in its graphical capabilities. R, a free, open-source implementation of S, was mentioned in the preface. Cook and Weisberg (1994, 1999) use the Lisp-Stat statistical computing environment (Tierney, 1990) to produce an impressive statistical package, called Arc, which incorporates a variety of statistical graphics of particular relevance to regression analysis (including many of the methods described later in this text). Friendly (1991) describes how to construct modern statistical graphs using the SAS/Graph system. Brief presentations of these and other statistical computing environments appear in a book edited by Stine and Fox (1996).
- Atkinson (1985) presents a variety of innovative graphs in support of regression analysis, as do Cook (1998) and Cook and Weisberg (1994, 1999).

4

Transforming Data

"Classical" statistical models, for example, linear least-squares regression, make strong assumptions about the structure of data—assumptions which, more often than not, fail to hold in practice. One solution is to abandon classical methods in favor of more flexible alternatives, such as nonparametric regression analysis. These newer methods are valuable, and I expect that they will be used with increasing frequency, but they are more complex and have their own limitations, as we saw in Chapter 2.[1]

It is, alternatively, often feasible to transform the data so that they conform more closely to the restrictive assumptions of classical statistical models. In addition, and as we will discover in this chapter, transformations can often assist in the examination of data, even in the absence of a statistical model. The chapter introduces two general families of transformations and shows how they can be used to make distributions symmetric, to make the relationship between two variables linear, and to equalize variation across groups.

> Transformations can often facilitate the examination and statistical modeling of data.

4.1 The Family of Powers and Roots

There is literally an infinite variety of functions $f(x)$ that could be used to transform a quantitative variable X. In practice, of course, it helps to be more restrictive, and a particularly useful group of transformations is the "family" of powers and roots:

$$X \to X^p \tag{4.1}$$

where the arrow indicates that we intend to replace X with the transformed variable X^p. If p is negative, then the transformation is an inverse power: For example, $X^{-1} = 1/X$ (i.e., inverse), and $X^{-2} = 1/X^2$ (inverse square). If p is a fraction, then the transformation represents a root: For example, $X^{1/3} = \sqrt[3]{X}$ (cube root) and $X^{-1/2} = 1/\sqrt{X}$ (inverse square root).

For some purposes, it is convenient to define the family of power transformations in a slightly more complex manner, called the *Box-Cox family* of transformations (Box and Cox, 1964):[2]

$$X \to X^{(p)} \equiv \frac{X^p - 1}{p} \tag{4.2}$$

We use the parenthetical superscript (p) to distinguish this definition from the more straightforward one in Equation 4.1. Because $X^{(p)}$ is a linear function of X^p, the two transformations have

---

[1] Also see Chapter 18.

[2] In addition to revealing the relative effect of different power transformations, the Box-Cox formulation is useful for estimating a transformation as a parameter, as in Section 4.6.

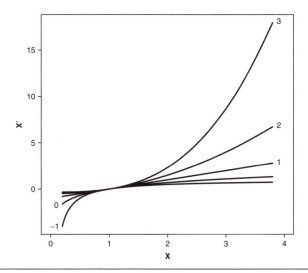

Figure 4.1 The family of power transformations X' of X. The curve labeled p is the transformation $X^{(p)}$, that is, $(X_p-1)/p$; $X^{(0)}$ is $\log_e X$.

the same essential effect on the data, but, as is apparent in Figure 4.1, the definition in Equation 4.2 reveals more transparently the essential unity of the family of powers and roots:[3]

- Dividing by p preserves the direction of X, which otherwise would be reversed when p is negative, as illustrated in the following example:

X	X^{-1}	$\dfrac{X^{-1}}{-1}$	$\dfrac{X^{-1}-1}{-1}$
1	1	-1	0
2	1/2	$-1/2$	1/2
3	1/3	$-1/3$	2/3
4	1/4	$-1/4$	3/4

  Note that subtracting 1 from the numerator does not affect *differences* between adjacent transformed values in the table.
- The transformations $X^{(p)}$ are "matched" above $X = 1$ both in level and in slope: (1) $1^{(p)} = 0$, for all values of p; and (2) each transformation has a slope of 1 at $X = 1$.[4]
- Matching the transformations facilitates comparisons among them and highlights their relative effects. In particular, descending the "ladder" of powers and roots toward $X^{(-1)}$ compresses the large values of X and spreads out the small ones; ascending the ladder of powers and roots toward $X^{(2)}$ has the opposite effect.[5] As p moves further from $p = 1$ (i.e., no transformation) in either direction, the transformation grows more powerful.
- The power transformation X^0 is useless because it changes all values to 1, but we can think of the log (i.e., logarithm) transformation as a kind of "zeroth" power: As p gets very

---

[3] See Exercise 4.1.
[4] *That is, the derivative of $X^{(p)}$ at $X = 1$ is 1; see Exercise 4.2.
[5] The heuristic characterization of the family of powers and roots as a "ladder" follows Tukey (1977).

close to 0, the log function more and more closely approximates $X^{(p)}$.[6] Because the log transformation is so useful, we will, by convention, take $X^{(0)} \equiv \log_e X$, where $e \approx 2.718$ is the base of the natural logarithms.[7]

In practice, it is generally more convenient to use logs to the base 10 or base 2, which are more easily interpreted than logs to the base e: For example, increasing $\log_{10} X$ by 1 is equivalent to multiplying X by 10; increasing $\log_2 X$ by 1 is equivalent to doubling X. Selection of a base for the log transformation is essentially arbitrary and inconsequential, however, because changing bases is equivalent to multiplying by a constant; for example,

$$\log_{10} X = \log_{10} e \times \log_e X \approx 0.4343 \times \log_e X$$

Likewise, because of its relative simplicity, we usually use X^p in applied work in preference to $X^{(p)}$ when $p \neq 0$. Transformations such as log, square root, square, and inverse have a long history of use in data analysis, often without reference to each other; thinking about these transformations as members of a family facilitates their systematic application, as illustrated later in this chapter.

The powers and roots are a particularly useful family of transformations: $X \rightarrow X^p$. When $p = 0$, we employ the log transformation in place of X^0.

The effects of the various power transformations are apparent in Figure 4.1 and in the following simple examples (in which the numbers by the braces give *differences* between adjacent values):

$-1/X$	$\log_2 X$	X	X^2	X^3
-1	0	1	1	1
$\frac{1}{2}$ {	1 {	} 1	} 3	} 7
$-1/2$	1	2	4	8
$\frac{1}{6}$ {	0.59 {	} 1	} 5	}19
$-1/3$	1.59	3	9	27
$\frac{1}{12}$ {	0.41 {	} 1	}7	}37
$-1/4$	2	4	16	64

Power transformations are sensible only when all the values of X are positive. First of all, some of the transformations, such as log and square root, are undefined for negative or zero values. Second, even when they are defined, the power transformations are not monotone—that is, not order preserving—if there are both positive and negative values in the data; for example,

---

[6]*More formally,

$$\lim_{p \to 0} \frac{X^p - 1}{p} = \log_e X$$

[7]Powers and logarithms are reviewed in Appendix C.

X	X^2
−2	4
−1	1
0	0
1	1
2	4

This is not, however, a practical limitation, because we can always add a positive constant (called a "start") to each data value to make all the values positive, calculating the transformation $X \rightarrow (X + s)^p$; in the preceding example,

X	$(X+3)^2$
−2	1
−1	4
0	9
1	16
2	25

It is, finally, worth pointing out that power transformations are effective only when the ratio of the largest data values to the smallest ones is sufficiently large; if, in contrast, this ratio is close to 1, then power transformations are nearly linear and, hence, ineffective. Consider the following example, where the ratio of the largest to the smallest data value is only $2005/2001 = 1.002 \approx 1$:

X	$\log_{10}X$	
2001	3.30125	
1 {		} 0.00021
2002	3.30146	
1 {		} 0.00022
2003	3.30168	
1 {		} 0.00022
2004	3.30190	
1 {		} 0.00021
2005	3.30211	

Using a negative start produces the desired effect:

X	$\log_{10}(X-2000)$	
2001	0	
1 {		} 0.301
2002	0.301	
1 {		} 0.176
2003	0.477	
1 {		} 0.125
2004	0.602	
1 {		} 0.097
2005	0.699	

This strategy should be considered whenever the ratio of the largest to the smallest data value is less than about 5. When the ratio is sufficiently large—either initially or after subtracting a

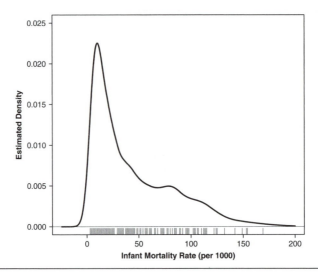

Figure 4.2   Adaptive-kernel density estimate for the distribution of infant mortality rates of 193
nations of the world. The data values are displayed in the rug-plot at the bottom of
the figure.

suitable start—an adequate power transformation can usually be found in the range $-2 \leq p \leq 3$.
We usually select integer values of p or simple fractions such as $\frac{1}{2}$ or $\frac{1}{3}$.

> Power transformations preserve the order of the data only when all values are positive and
> are effective only when the ratio of the largest to the smallest data values is itself large.
> When these conditions do not hold, we can impose them by adding a positive or negative
> start to all the data values.

4.2   Transforming Skewness

Power transformations can make a skewed distribution more symmetric. But why should we
bother?

- Highly skewed distributions are difficult to examine because most of the observations are
  confined to a small part of the range of the data. Recall from the previous chapter, for
  example, the distribution of infant mortality rates, redisplayed in Figure 4.2.[8]
- Apparently outlying values in the direction of the skew are brought in toward the main body
  of the data when the distribution is made more symmetric. In contrast, unusual values in the
  direction opposite to the skew can be hidden prior to transforming the data.
- Some of the most common statistical methods summarize distributions using means. Least-
  squares regression, which traces the mean of Y conditional on X, comes immediately to
  mind.[9] The mean of a skewed distribution is not, however, a good summary of its center.

---

[8] Adapting Figure 3.5.
[9] See Chapter 5.

The following simple example illustrates how a power transformation can eliminate a positive skew:

X	$\log_{10} X$
$9\ \{\begin{matrix} 1 \\ 10 \end{matrix}$	$\begin{matrix} 0 \\ 1 \end{matrix}\ \}\ 1$
$90\ \{\begin{matrix} \ \\ 100 \end{matrix}$	$\begin{matrix} \ \\ 2 \end{matrix}\ \}\ 1$
$900\ \{\begin{matrix} \ \\ 1000 \end{matrix}$	$\begin{matrix} \ \\ 3 \end{matrix}\ \}\ 1$

Descending the ladder of powers to log X makes the distribution more symmetric by pulling in the right tail. Ascending the ladder of powers (toward X^2 and X^3) can, similarly, "correct" a negative skew.

An effective transformation can be selected analytically or by trial and error.[10] Examining the median and the hinges, moreover, can provide some guidance to trial and error. A convenient property of order statistics—including the median and hinges—is that they are preserved under nonlinear monotone transformations of the data, such as powers and roots; that is, if $X' = X^{(p)}$, then $X'_{(i)} = [X_{(i)}]^{(p)}$, and thus median$(X') = [\text{median}(X)]^{(p)}$.[11] This is not the case for the mean and standard deviation.

In a symmetric distribution, the median is midway between the hinges, and consequently, the ratio

$$\frac{\text{Upper hinge} - \text{Median}}{\text{Median} - \text{Lower hinge}}$$

is approximately 1. In contrast, a positive skew is reflected in a ratio that exceeds 1 and a negative skew in a ratio that is smaller than 1. Trial and error can begin, therefore, with a transformation that makes this ratio close to 1.

Some statistical software allows the transformation p to be selected interactively using a "slider," while a graph of the distribution—for example, a density plot—is updated when the value of p changes. This is an especially convenient and effective approach. A static alternative is to show parallel boxplots for various transformations, as in Figure 4.3 for the infant mortality data.

For the distribution of infant mortality rates, we have

Transformation	H_U	Median	H_L	$\dfrac{H_U - \text{Median}}{\text{Median} - H_L}$
X	68	30	13	2.23
$\sqrt{X}$	8.246	5.477	3.605	1.48
$\log_{10} X$	1.833	1.477	1.114	0.98
$-1/\sqrt{X}$	−0.1213	−0.1825	−0.2773	0.65
$-1/X$	−0.01471	−0.03333	−0.07692	0.43

---

[10]See Sections 4.6 and 12.5 for analytic methods for selecting transformations.

[11]There is some slippage here because the median and hinges sometimes require *averaging* adjacent order statistics. The two averaged values are seldom very far apart, however, and therefore the distinction between the median of the transformed values and the transformation of the median is almost always trivial. The same is true for the hinges. The results presented for the example give the median and hinges of the transformed data.

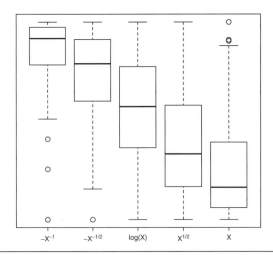

Figure 4.3   Boxplots for various power transformations of infant mortality; because the
distribution of infant mortality is positively skewed, only transformations "down" the
ladder of powers and roots are considered.

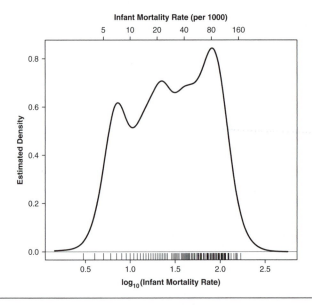

Figure 4.4   Adaptive-kernel density estimate for the distribution of $\log_{10}$ infant mortality. The
window half-width for the adaptive-kernel estimator is $h = 0.1$ (on the $\log_{10}$ infant
mortality scale). A rug-plot of the data values appears at the bottom of the graph and
the original infant mortality scale at the top.

This table and the boxplots in Figure 4.3 suggest the log transformation of infant mortality, and
the result of transforming the data is shown in Figure 4.4. Not only is the distribution much more
symmetric than before, but three modes are clearly resolved (and there is the suggestion of a
fourth); the modes at infant mortality rates of about 7 and 20 were not distinguishable in the
untransformed data.

Note the untransformed scale for infant mortality at the top of the graph: These values, which are equally spaced on the log scale, represent doubling of infant mortality rates. This is, in my experience, an effective device for presenting the results of a statistical analysis in which the familiar scale of a variable is lost through a transformation.

Although it is not the case here, where the log transformation is clearly indicated, we often have a choice between transformations that perform roughly equally well. Although we should try to avoid distorting the data, we may prefer one transformation to another because of interpretability. I have already mentioned that the log transformation has a convenient multiplicative interpretation. In certain contexts, other transformations may have specific substantive meanings. Here are a few common examples: The inverse of the time (say, in hours) required to travel a given distance (a kilometer) is speed (kilometers per hour); the inverse of response latency (say, in milliseconds, as in a psychophysical experiment) is response frequency (responses per 1,000 seconds); the square root of a measure of area (say, in square meters) is a linear measure of size (in meters); and the cube of a linear measure of size (say in centimeters) can be interpreted as a volume (cubic centimeters).

We generally prefer interpretable transformations when variables are measured on familiar and meaningful scales. Conversely, because the rating "scales" that are ubiquitous in social research are not really measurements, there is typically no reason to prefer the original scores to a monotone transformation of them.[12]

> Descending the ladder of powers (e.g., to log X) tends to correct a positive skew; ascending the ladder of powers (e.g., to X^2) tends to correct a negative skew.

4.3 Transforming Nonlinearity

Power transformations can also be used to make many nonlinear relationships more nearly linear. Again, we ask, why bother?

- Linear relationships—expressible in the form $\widehat{Y} = A + BX$—are particularly simple. Recall that this equation specifies that the average value of the response variable Y is a linear function of the explanatory variable X, with intercept A and slope B. Linearity implies that a unit *increase* in X—regardless of the *level* of X—is associated, on average, with a change of B units in Y.[13] Fitting a linear equation to data makes it relatively easy to answer certain questions about the data: If B is positive, for example, then Y tends to increase with X.
- Especially when there are several explanatory variables, the alternative of nonparametric regression may not be feasible because of the sparseness of the data. Even if we can fit a nonparametric regression with several Xs, it may be difficult to visualize the multidimensional result.[14]

---

[12]Rating scales are composed, for example, of items with response categories labeled *strongly agree, agree, disagree, strongly disagree*. A scale is constructed by assigning arbitrary numbers to the categories (e.g., 1–4) and adding or averaging the items. See Coombs, Dawes, and Tversky (1970, Chapters 2 and 3) for an elementary treatment of measurement issues in the social sciences and Duncan (1984) for an interesting account of the history and practice of social measurement. I believe that social scientists should pay more attention to measurement issues (employing, e.g., the methods of item-response theory; e.g., Baker & Kim, 2004). It is unproductive, however, simply to discard rating scales and similar "measurements by fiat" (a felicitous term borrowed from Torgerson, 1958): There is a prima facie reasonableness to many rating scales, and to refuse to use them without adequate substitutes would be foolish.

[13]I use the terms "increase" and "change" loosely here as a shorthand for static comparisons between average values of Y for X-values that differ by one unit: *Literal* change is not necessarily implied.

[14]See, however, the additive regression models discussed in Section 18.2.2, which overcome this deficiency.

- There is a simple and elegant statistical theory for linear models, which we explore in subsequent chapters. If these models are reasonable for the data, then their use is convenient.
- There are certain technical advantages to having linear relationships among the *explanatory* variables in a regression analysis.[15]

The following simple example suggests how a power transformation can serve to straighten a nonlinear relationship: Suppose that $Y = \frac{1}{5}X^2$ (with no residual) and that X takes on successive integer values between 1 and 5:

X	Y
1	0.2
2	0.8
3	1.8
4	3.2
5	5.0

These "data" are graphed in panel (a) of Figure 4.5, where the nonlinearity of the relationship between Y and X is apparent. Because of the manner in which the example was constructed, it is obvious that there are two simple ways to transform the data to achieve linearity:

1. We could replace Y by $Y' = \sqrt{Y}$, in which case $Y' = \sqrt{\frac{1}{5}}X$.

2. We could replace X by $X' = X^2$, in which case $Y = \frac{1}{5}X'$.

In either event, the relationship is rendered perfectly linear, as shown graphically in panels (b) and (c) of Figure 4.5. To achieve an intuitive understanding of this process, imagine that the original plot in panel (a) is drawn on a rubber sheet: Transforming Y "down" the ladder of powers to square root differentially stretches the rubber sheet vertically so that small values are spread out relative to large ones, stretching the curve in (a) into the straight line in (b). Likewise, transforming X "up" the ladder of powers spreads out the large values relative to the small ones, stretching the curve into the straight line in (c).

A power transformation works here because the relationship between Y and X is smooth, monotone (in this instance, strictly increasing), and simple. What I mean by "simple" in this context is that the direction of curvature of the function relating Y to X does not change (i.e., there is no point of inflection). Figure 4.6 seeks to clarify these distinctions: The relationship in panel (a) is simple and monotone; the relationship in panel (b) is monotone but not simple; and the relationship in panel (c) is simple but not monotone. I like to use the term "curvilinear" for cases such as (c), to distinguish nonmonotone from monotone nonlinearity, but this is not standard terminology. In panel (c), no power transformation of Y or X can straighten the relationship between them, but we could capture this relationship with a quadratic model of the form $\hat{Y} = A + B_1 X + B_2 X^2$.[16]

Like transformations to reduce skewness, a transformation to correct nonlinearity can be selected analytically or by guided trial and error.[17] Figure 4.7 introduces Mosteller and Tukey's (1977) "bulging rule" for selecting a transformation: If the "bulge" points *down* and to the *right*, for example, we need to transform Y *down* the ladder of powers or X *up* (or both). This case corresponds to the example in Figure 4.5, and the general justification of the rule follows from

---

[15]This point is developed in Section 12.3.3.

[16]Quadratic and other polynomial regression models are discussed in Section 17.1.

[17]See Sections 4.6 and 12.5 for analytic methods of selecting linearizing transformations.

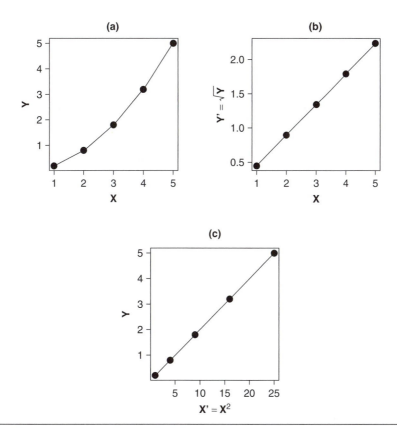

Figure 4.5   How a power transformation of Y or X can make a simple monotone nonlinear relationship linear. Panel (a) shows the relationship $Y = \frac{1}{5}X^2$. In panel (b), Y is replaced by the transformed value $Y' = Y^{1/2}$. In panel (c), X is replaced by the transformed value $X' = X^2$.

the need to stretch an axis differentially to transform the curve into a straight line. Trial and error is simplest with software that provides "sliders" for the power transformations of X and Y, immediately displaying the effect of a change in either power on the scatterplot relating the two variables, but we can in any event examine a series of scatterplots for different transformations.

> Simple monotone nonlinearity can often be corrected by a power transformation of X, of Y, or of both variables. Mosteller and Tukey's bulging rule assists in selecting linearizing transformations.

Now, we reexamine, in the light of this discussion, the relationship between prestige and income for the 102 Canadian occupations first encountered in Chapter 2 and shown in Figure 4.8.[18] The relationship between prestige and income is clearly monotone and nonlinear: Prestige rises with income, but the slope is steeper at the left of the plot, where income is low, than at the right, where it is high. The change in slope appears fairly abrupt rather than smooth, however, and we

---

[18]Repeating Figure 2.10.

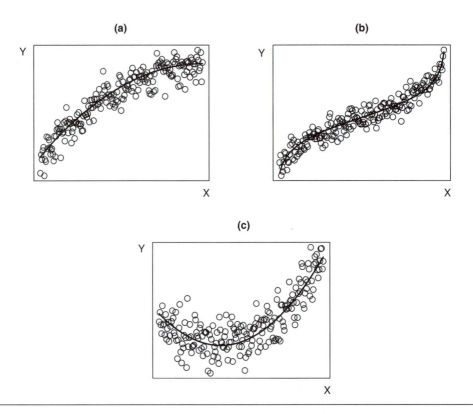

(a) **(b)**

(c)

Figure 4.6   (a) A simple monotone relationship between Y and X; (b) a monotone relationship that is not simple; (c) a relationship that is simple but not monotone. A power transformation of Y or X can straighten (a) but not (b) or (c).

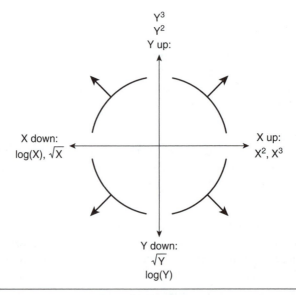

Figure 4.7   Tukey and Mosteller's bulging rule: The direction of the bulge indicates the direction of the power transformation of Y and/or X to straighten the relationship between them.

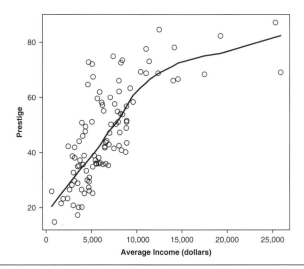

Figure 4.8   The relationship between prestige and income for the Canadian occupational prestige data. The nonparametric regression line on the plot is computed by lowess, with a span of 0.6.

might do better to model the relationship with two straight lines (one for relatively small values of income, one for relatively large ones) than simply to transform prestige or income.[19]

Nevertheless, the bulge points up and to the left, and so we can try transforming prestige up the ladder of powers or income down. Because the income distribution is positively skewed, I prefer to transform income rather than prestige, which is more symmetrically distributed. As shown in Figure 4.9, the cube-root transformation of income works reasonably well here. Some nonlinearity remains, but it is not simple, and the linear regression of prestige on income no longer *grossly* distorts the relationship between the two variables. I would have preferred to use the log transformation, which makes the income distribution more symmetric and which is simpler to interpret, but this transformation "overcorrects" the nonlinearity in the relationship between prestige and income.

For a more extreme, and ultimately more successful, example, consider the relationship between infant mortality and GDP per capita shown in Figure 4.10 and first discussed in Chapter 3.[20] As I pointed out previously, both variables are highly positively skewed and, consequently, most of the data are confined to a small region at the lower left of the plot.

The skewness of infant mortality and income in Figure 4.10 makes the scatterplot difficult to interpret; nevertheless, the nonparametric regression shown on the plot reveals a nonlinear but monotone relationship between infant mortality and income. The bulging rule suggests that infant mortality or income should be transformed down the ladder of powers and roots. In this case, transforming both variables by taking logs makes the relationship nearly linear (as shown in Figure 4.11). Moreover, although several countries still stand out as having relatively high infant mortality for their GDP, others now are revealed to have relatively *low* infant mortality in comparison to countries with similar GDP.

The least-squares regression line in Figure 4.11 has the equation

$$\log_{10} \widehat{\text{Infant mortality}} = 3.06 - 0.493 \times \log_{10} \text{GDP}$$

---

[19]For an alternative interpretation of the relationship between prestige and income, plot the data using different symbols for different types of occupations. (The data set distinguishes among blue-collar, white-collar, and professional and managerial occupations.)

[20]Repeating Figure 3.13. This example is motivated by a discussion of similar data in Leinhardt and Wasserman (1979).

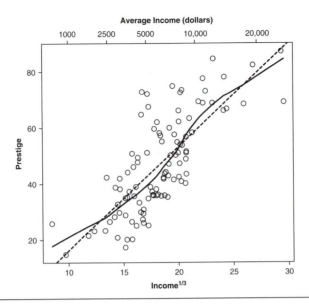

Figure 4.9   Scatterplot of prestige versus income$^{1/3}$. The broken line shows the linear least-squares regression, while the solid line shows the lowess smooth, with a span of 0.6. The original income scale is shown at the top of the graph.

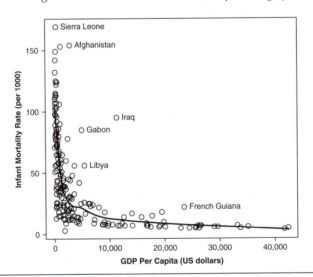

Figure 4.10   Scatterplot for infant mortality and GDP per capita for 193 nations. The line is for a lowess smooth with a span of 1/2. Several nations with high infant mortality for their levels of GDP are identified.

Because both variables are expressed on log scales to the same base, the slope of this relationship has a simple interpretation: A 1% increase in per-capita income is associated, on average, with an approximate 0.49% decline in the infant mortality rate. Economists call this type of coefficient an "elasticity."[21]

---

[21] Increasing X by 1% is equivalent to multiplying it by 1.01, which in turn implies that the log of X increases by $\log_{10} 1.01 = 0.00432$. The corresponding change in log Y is then $B \times 0.00432 = -0.493 \times 0.00432 = -0.00213$.

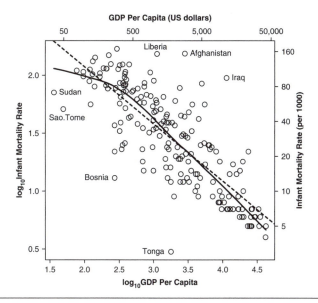

Figure 4.11 Scatterplot of $\log_{10}$ infant mortality rate versus $\log_{10}$ per-capita GDP. The broken line was calculated by linear least-squares linear regression and the solid line by lowess with a span of 1/2. The original scales of the variables appear at the top and to the right.

4.4 Transforming Nonconstant Spread

When a variable has very different degrees of variation in different groups, it becomes difficult to examine the data and to compare differences in level across the groups. We encountered this problem in the preceding chapter, where we compared the distribution of number of interlocking directorships by nation of control, employing Ornstein's data on 248 dominant Canadian corporations, shown in Figure 4.12.[22]

Differences in spread are often systematically related to differences in level: Groups with higher levels tend to have higher spreads. Using the median and hinge-spread as indices of level and spread, respectively, the following table shows that there is indeed an association, if only an imperfect one, between spread and level for Ornstein's data:

Nation of Control	Lower Hinge	Median	Upper Hinge	Hinge Spread
Other	3	14.5	23	20
Canada	5	12.0	29	24
United Kingdom	3	8.0	13	10
United States	1	5.0	12	11

Subtracting 0.00213 from $\log Y$ is equivalent to multiplying Y by $10^{-0.00213} = 0.99511$, that is, decreasing Y by $100 \times (1 - 0.99511) = 0.489 \approx B$. The approximation holds because the log function is nearly linear across the small domain of X-values between $\log 1$ and $\log 1.01$.

[22]Repeating Figure 3.16.

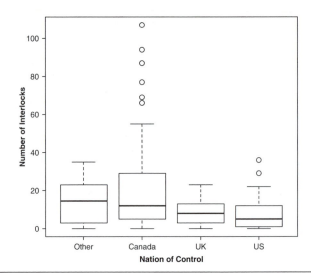

Figure 4.12   Number of interlocking directorate and executive positions by nation of control, for
248 dominant Canadian firms.

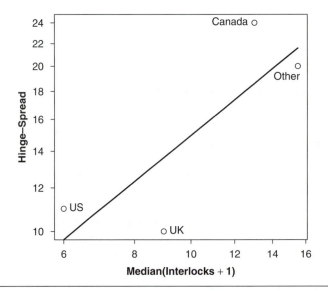

Figure 4.13   Spread (log hinge-spread) versus level [log(median+1)]. The plot is for Ornstein's
interlocking-directorate data, with groups defined by nation of control. The line on
the plot was fit by least squares.

Tukey (1977) suggests graphing the log hinge-spread against the log median, as shown in
Figure 4.13. Because some firms maintained 0 interlocks, I used a start of 1 to construct this
graph—adding 1 to each median but leaving the hinge-spreads unchanged.

The slope of the linear "trend," if any, in the spread-level plot can be used to suggest a spread-
stabilizing power transformation of the data: Express the linear fit as

$$\log \text{ spread} \approx a + b \log \text{ level}$$

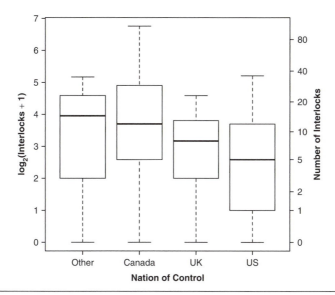

Figure 4.14   Parallel boxplots of number of interlocks by nation of control, transforming
interlocks+1 to the $\log_2$ scale. Compare this plot with Figure 4.12, where number of
interlocks is not transformed. The original scale for number of interlocks is shown at
the right.

Then the corresponding spread-stabilizing transformation uses the power $p = 1 - b$. When spread
is positively related to level (i.e., $b > 0$), therefore, we select a transformation *down* the ladder
of powers and roots.

Starting with this transformation, it is convenient to employ statistical software that connects
a "slider" for the power p to the spread-by-level plot and the parallel boxplots. Changing the
value of p via the slider immediately updates the plots, allowing us to assess the relative effects
of different transformations.

> When there is a positive association between the level of a variable in different groups and
> its spread, the spreads can be made more constant by descending the ladder of powers.
> A negative association between level and spread is less common but can be corrected by
> ascending the ladder of powers.

In Figure 4.13, a line was fit by least squares to the spread-level plot for the interlocking directorate data. The slope of this line, $b = 0.85$, suggests the power transformation $p = 1 - 0.85 =
0.15 \approx 0$. I decided, therefore, to try a log transformation. Figure 4.14 shows the result, employing
logs to the base 2.[23] The spreads of the several groups are now much more similar, and differences
in level are easier to discern. The within-group distributions are more symmetric as well.

The problems of unequal spread and skewness commonly occur together because they often
have a common origin. When, as here, the data represent frequency counts (*number* of interlocks),
the impossibility of obtaining a negative count tends to produce positive skewness, together

---

[23]Recall that increasing $\log_2 X$ by 1 represents doubling X (where, here, X is the number of interlocks plus 1).

```
      1 | 2: represents 12
       leaf unit: 1
               n: 102

      32       0* | 00000000000000111111222233334444
      44       0. | 555566777899
     (8)       1* | 01111333
      50       1. | 5557779
      43       2* | 1344
      39       2. | 57
      37       3* | 01334
      32       3. | 99
               4* |
      30       4. | 678
      27       5* | 224
      24       5. | 67
      22       6* | 3
      21       6. | 789
      18       7* | 024
      15       7. | 5667
      11       8* | 233
               8. |
       8       9* | 012
```

Figure 4.15   Stem-and-leaf display of percentage of women in each of 102 Canadian occupations in 1970. Note how the data "stack up" against both boundaries.

with a tendency for larger levels to be associated with larger spreads. The same is true of other types of variables that are bounded below (e.g., wage and salary income). Likewise, variables that are bounded above but not below (e.g., grades on a very simple exam) tend both to be negatively skewed and to show a negative association between spread and level. In the latter event, a transformation "up" the ladder of powers (e.g., to X^2) usually provides a remedy.[24]

4.5   Transforming Proportions

Power transformations are often unhelpful for proportions because these quantities are bounded below by 0 and above by 1. Of course, if the data values do not approach the two boundaries, then proportions can be handled much like other sorts of data.

Percentages and many sorts of rates (e.g., infant mortality rate per 1,000 live births) are simply rescaled proportions and, therefore, are similarly affected. It is, moreover, common to encounter "disguised" proportions, such as the number of questions correct on an exam of fixed length or the number of affirmative responses to a series of dichotomous attitude questions.

An example, drawn from the Canadian occupational prestige data, is shown in the stem-and-leaf display in Figure 4.15. The distribution is for the percentage of women among the incumbents of each of 102 occupations. There are many occupations with no women or a very small percentage of women, but the distribution is not simply positively skewed, because there are also occupations that are predominantly female. In contrast, relatively few occupations are balanced with respect to their gender composition.

Several transformations are commonly employed for proportions, P, including the following:

- The *logit* transformation,

$$P \rightarrow \text{logit}(P) = \log_e \frac{P}{1-P}$$

---

[24]Plotting log spread against log level to select a spread-stabilizing transformation is quite a general idea. In Section 12.2, for example, we will use a version of the spread-level plot to find a variance-stabilizing transformation in regression analysis.

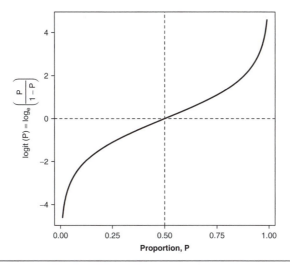

Figure 4.16 The logit transformation $\log_e[P/(1-P)]$ of a proportion P.

The logit transformation is the log of the "odds," $P/(1-P)$. The "trick" of the logit transformation is to remove the upper and lower boundaries of the scale, spreading out the tails of the distribution and making the resulting quantities symmetric about 0; for example,

P	$\dfrac{P}{1-P}$	logit
.01	1/99	−4.59
.05	1/19	−2.94
.1	1/9	−2.20
.3	3/7	−0.85
.5	1	0
.7	7/3	0.85
.9	9/1	2.20
.95	19/1	2.94
.99	99/1	4.59

A graph of the logit transformation, shown in Figure 4.16, reveals that the transformation is nearly linear in its center, between about $P = .2$ and $P = .8$.

- The *probit* transformation,

$$P \rightarrow \text{probit}(P) = \Phi^{-1}(P)$$

where Φ^{-1} is the inverse distribution function (i.e., the quantile function) for the standard normal distribution. Once their scales are equated, the logit and probit transformations are, for practical purposes, indistinguishable: logit $\approx (\pi/\sqrt{3}) \times$ probit.[25]

- The *arcsine-square-root* transformation also has a similar shape:

$$P \rightarrow \sin^{-1}\sqrt{P}$$

---

[25] We will encounter the logit and probit functions again in a different context when we take up the analysis of categorical data in Chapter 14.

Tukey (1977) has embedded these common transformations for proportions into the family of "folded" powers and roots, indexed by the power q, which takes on values between 0 and 1:

$$P \rightarrow P^q - (1 - P)^q$$

When $q = 0$, we take the natural log, producing the logit transformation. Setting $q = 0.14$ yields (to a very close approximation) a multiple of the probit transformation. Setting $q = 0.41$ produces (again, to a close approximation) a multiple of the arcsine-square-root transformation. When $q = 1$, the transformation is just twice the "plurality" (i.e., the difference between P and $\frac{1}{2}$), leaving the shape of the distribution of P unaltered:

$$P \rightarrow P - (1 - P) = 2(P - \tfrac{1}{2})$$

> Power transformations are ineffective for proportions P that simultaneously push the boundaries of 0 and 1 and for other variables (e.g., percentages, rates, disguised proportions) that are bounded both below and above. The folded powers $P \rightarrow P^q - (1 - P)^q$ are often effective in this context; for $q = 0$, we employ the logit transformation, $P \rightarrow \log_e[P/(1 - P)]$.

The logit and probit transformations cannot be applied to proportions of exactly 0 or 1. If, however, we have access to the original counts on which the proportions were based, then we can avoid this embarrassment by employing

$$P' = \frac{F + \frac{1}{2}}{N + 1}$$

in place of P. Here, F is the frequency count in the focal category (e.g., number of women) and N is the total count (total number of occupational incumbents, women plus men). If the original counts are not available, then we can use the expedient of mapping the proportions to an interval that excludes 0 and 1. For example, $P' = .005 + .99 \times P$ maps proportions to the interval [.005, .995].

Employing the latter strategy for the Canadian occupational data produces the distribution for $\text{logit}(P'_{\text{women}})$ that appears in Figure 4.17. Spreading out the tails of the distribution has improved its behavior considerably, although there is still some stacking up of low and high values.

4.6   Estimating Transformations as Parameters* _____

If we lived in a world in which the joint distribution of all quantitative data were multivariate-normal then statistical analysis would be simple indeed: Outliers would be rare, all variables would be symmetrically distributed, all regressions would be linear, and least-squares regression would be a fine method of estimation. Making data as close to multivariate-normal as possible by transformation, therefore, can facilitate their analysis.

If the vector random variable $\mathbf{x} = (X_1, X_2, \ldots, X_p)'$ with population mean vector $\underset{(p \times 1)}{\boldsymbol{\mu}}$ and covariance matrix $\underset{(p \times p)}{\Sigma}$ is multivariate-normal, then its probability density function is[26]

---

[26]See Appendix D on probability and estimation.

```
                        1 | 2: represents 1.2
                       leaf unit: 0.1
                              n: 102

          5      -5* |  22222
          8      -4. |  555
         16      -4* |  44332111
         21      -3. |  98875
         31      -3* |  4432111000
         39      -2. |  98887655
         48      -2* |  443220000
        (10)     -1. |  9888666555
         44      -1* |  331110
         38      -0. |  987666
         32      -0* |  44110
         27       0* |  00122
         22       0. |  577889
         16       1* |  01111
         11       1. |  556
          8       2* |  23
          6       2. |  5
          5       3* |  00014
```

Figure 4.17   Stem-and-leaf display for the logit transformation of proportion of women in each of 102 Canadian occupations. Because some occupations have no women, the proportions were mapped to the interval .005 to .995 prior to calculating the logits.

$$p(\mathbf{x}|\boldsymbol{\mu}, \boldsymbol{\Sigma}) = \frac{1}{(2\pi)^{p/2}\sqrt{\det \boldsymbol{\Sigma}}} \exp\left[-\tfrac{1}{2}(\mathbf{x} - \boldsymbol{\mu})'\boldsymbol{\Sigma}^{-1}(\mathbf{x} - \boldsymbol{\mu})\right]$$

In shorthand, $\mathbf{x} \sim \mathbf{N}_p(\boldsymbol{\mu}, \boldsymbol{\Sigma})$.

For a sample of n observations, $\underset{(n \times p)}{\mathbf{X}}$, we have

$$p(\mathbf{X}|\boldsymbol{\mu}, \boldsymbol{\Sigma}) = \left[\frac{1}{(2\pi)^{p/2}\sqrt{\det \boldsymbol{\Sigma}}}\right]^n \exp\left\{\sum_{i=1}^{n}\left[-\tfrac{1}{2}(\mathbf{x}_i - \boldsymbol{\mu})'\boldsymbol{\Sigma}^{-1}(\mathbf{x}_i - \boldsymbol{\mu})\right]\right\}$$

where $\mathbf{x}_i'$ is the ith row of $\mathbf{X}$. The log-likelihood for the parameters is, therefore,[27]

$$\log_e L(\boldsymbol{\mu}, \boldsymbol{\Sigma}|\mathbf{X}) = -\frac{np}{2}\log_e(2\pi) - \frac{n}{2}\log_e \det \boldsymbol{\Sigma} - \tfrac{1}{2}\sum_{i=1}^{n}\left[(\mathbf{x}_i - \boldsymbol{\mu})'\boldsymbol{\Sigma}^{-1}(\mathbf{x}_i - \boldsymbol{\mu})\right]$$

The maximum-likelihood estimators (MLEs) of the mean and covariance matrix are, then,[28]

$$\widehat{\boldsymbol{\mu}} = \overline{\mathbf{x}} = (\overline{X}_1, \overline{X}_2, \ldots, \overline{X}_p)'$$

$$\widehat{\boldsymbol{\Sigma}} = \{\widehat{\sigma}_{jj'}\} = \left\{\frac{\sum_{i=1}^{n}(X_{ij} - \overline{X}_j)(X_{ij'} - \overline{X}_{j'})}{n}\right\}$$

Now, suppose that $\mathbf{x}$ is not multivariate-normal, but that it can be made so by a power transformation of its elements.[29] It is convenient to use the Box-Cox family of power transformations

---

[27] The likelihood function and maximum-likelihood estimation are described in Appendix D on probability and estimation.

[28] Note that the MLEs of the covariances have n rather than $n - 1$ in the denominator, and consequently will be biased in small samples.

[29] This cannot be strictly correct, because Box-Cox transformations are only applicable when the elements of $\mathbf{x}$ are positive and normal distributions are unbounded, but it can be true to a close-enough approximation. There is no guarantee, however, that $\mathbf{x}$ can be made normal by a power transformation of its elements.

(Equation 4.2) because they are continuous at $p = 0$. Rather than thinking about these powers informally, let us instead consider them as additional parameters,[30] $\boldsymbol{\lambda} \equiv (\lambda_1, \lambda_2, \ldots, \lambda_p)'$, one for each element of $\mathbf{x}$, so that

$$\mathbf{x}^{(\boldsymbol{\lambda})} \equiv \left[x_1^{(\lambda_1)}, x_2^{(\lambda_2)}, \ldots, x_p^{(\lambda_p)} \right]'$$

Then,

$$p(\mathbf{x}|\boldsymbol{\mu}, \Sigma, \boldsymbol{\lambda}) = \frac{1}{(2\pi)^{p/2}\sqrt{\det \Sigma}} \exp\left[-\tfrac{1}{2}(\mathbf{x}^{(\boldsymbol{\lambda})} - \boldsymbol{\mu})'\Sigma^{-1}(\mathbf{x}^{(\boldsymbol{\lambda})} - \boldsymbol{\mu}) \right] \prod_{j=1}^{p} X_j^{\lambda_j - 1} \qquad (4.3)$$

where now $\boldsymbol{\mu} = E\left[\mathbf{x}^{(\boldsymbol{\lambda})}\right]$ and $\Sigma = V\left[\mathbf{x}^{(\boldsymbol{\lambda})}\right]$ are the mean vector and covariance matrix of the transformed variables, and $\prod_{j=1}^{p} X_j^{\lambda_j - 1}$ is the Jacobian of the transformation from $\mathbf{x}^{(\boldsymbol{\lambda})}$ to $\mathbf{x}$.[31]
  The log-likelihood for the model is

$$\log_e L(\boldsymbol{\lambda}, \boldsymbol{\mu}, \Sigma | \mathbf{X}) = -\frac{np}{2}\log_e(2\pi) - \frac{n}{2}\log_e \det \Sigma - \tfrac{1}{2}\sum_{i=1}^{n}\left[(\mathbf{x}_i^{(\boldsymbol{\lambda})} - \boldsymbol{\mu})'\Sigma^{-1}(\mathbf{x}_i^{(\boldsymbol{\lambda})} - \boldsymbol{\mu}) \right]$$

$$+ \sum_{j=1}^{p}(\lambda_j - 1)\sum_{i=1}^{n}\log_e X_{ij}$$

There is no closed-form solution for the MLEs of $\boldsymbol{\lambda}$, $\boldsymbol{\mu}$, and Σ, but we can find the MLEs by numerical methods. Standard errors for the estimated transformations are available in the usual manner from the inverse of the information matrix, and both Wald and likelihood-ratio tests can be formulated for the transformation parameters.

Moreover, because our real interest lies in the transformation parameters $\boldsymbol{\lambda}$, the means $\boldsymbol{\mu}$ and covariances Σ are "nuisance" parameters; indeed, given $\widehat{\boldsymbol{\lambda}}$, the MLEs of $\boldsymbol{\mu}$ and Σ are just the sample mean vector and covariance matrix of $\mathbf{x}^{(\widehat{\boldsymbol{\lambda}})}$. Let us define the *modified Box-Cox family* of transformations as follows:

$$X^{[\lambda]} = \begin{cases} \widetilde{X}^{1-\lambda}\dfrac{X^\lambda - 1}{\lambda} & \text{for } \lambda \neq 0 \\ \widetilde{X}\log_e X & \text{for } \lambda = 0 \end{cases}$$

where

$$\widetilde{X} \equiv \left(\prod_{i=1}^{n} X_i\right)^{1/n}$$

is the *geometric mean* of X. Multiplication by $\widetilde{X}^{1-\lambda}$ is a kind of standardization, equating the scales of different power transformations of X. Let $\mathbf{V}^{[\boldsymbol{\lambda}]}$ represent the sample covariance matrix of

$$\mathbf{x}^{[\boldsymbol{\lambda}]} \equiv \left[x_1^{[\lambda_1]}, x_2^{[\lambda_2]}, \ldots, x_p^{[\lambda_p]} \right]'$$

Velilla (1993) shows that the the MLEs of $\boldsymbol{\lambda}$ in Equation 4.3 are the values that minimize the determinant of $\mathbf{V}^{[\boldsymbol{\lambda}]}$.

---

[30]We will encounter this general approach again in Section 12.5 in the context of the linear regression model.
[31]See Appendix D on probability and estimation.

Applying this approach to the joint distribution of infant mortality and GDP per capita produces the following results:

	$\widehat{\lambda}_j$	$SE(\widehat{\lambda}_j)$	$z_0 = \dfrac{\widehat{\lambda}_j - 1}{SE(\widehat{\lambda}_j)}$	p
Infant mortality	−0.0009	0.0655	−15.28	≪.0001
GDP per capita	0.0456	0.0365	−26.14	≪.0001

The first column in this table gives the the MLE of each transformation parameter; the second column gives the asymptotic standard error of the transformation; the third column gives the Wald statistic for testing the hypothesis H_0: $\lambda_j = 1$ (i.e., that no transformation is required); and the final column gives the two-sided p-value for this test. In this case, evidence for the need to transform the two variables is very strong. Moreover, both estimated transformations are very close to 0—that is, the log transformation. A likelihood-ratio test for the hypothesis H_0: $\lambda_1 = \lambda_2 = 1$ yields the chi-square test statistic $G_0^2 = 680.25$ on 2 degrees of freedom, which is also wildly statistically significant. In contrast, testing the hypothesis that H_0: $\lambda_1 = \lambda_2 = 0$ produces $G_0^2 = 1.649$ on 2 degrees of freedom, for which $p = .44$, supporting the use of the log transformations of infant mortality and GDP. We know from our previous work that these transformations make the distribution of the two variables symmetric and linearize their relationship.

Finally, we can also apply this method to individual variables to attempt to normalize their *univariate* distributions. For the current example, the individual MLEs of the power transformation parameters λ for infant mortality and GDP are similar to those reported above:

	$\widehat{\lambda}$	$SE(\widehat{\lambda})$	$z_0 = \dfrac{\widehat{\lambda} - 1}{SE(\widehat{\lambda})}$	p
Infant mortality	0.0984	0.0786	−11.47	≪.0001
GDP per capita	−0.0115	0.0440	−23.00	≪.0001

> The method of maximum likelihood can be used to estimate normalizing power transformations of variables.

Exercises

Exercise 4.1. Create a graph like Figure 4.1, but for the *ordinary* power transformations $X \to X^p$ for $p = -1, 0, 1, 2, 3$. (When $p = 0$, however, use the log transformation.) Compare your graph to Figure 4.1, and comment on the similarities and differences between the two families of transformations X^p and $X^{(p)}$.

Exercise 4.2. *Show that the derivative of $f(X) = (X^p - 1)/p$ is equal to 1 at $X = 1$ regardless of the value of p.

Exercise 4.3. *We considered starts for transformations informally to ensure that all data values are positive and that the ratio of the largest to the smallest data values is sufficiently large. An alternative is to think of the start as a parameter to be estimated along with the transformation power to make the distribution of the variable as normal as possible. This approach defines a *two-parameter Box-Cox family*:

$$X^{(\alpha, \lambda)} \equiv \frac{(X - \alpha)^{\lambda}}{\lambda}$$

(a) Develop the MLEs of α and λ for the two-parameter Box-Cox family.
(b) Attempt to apply the estimator to data. Do you encounter any obstacles? [*Hint*: Examine the correlation between the parameter estimates $\widehat{\alpha}$ and $\widehat{\lambda}$.]

Summary

- Transformations can often facilitate the examination and statistical modeling of data.
- The powers and roots are a particularly useful family of transformations: $X \to X^p$. When $p = 0$, we employ the log transformation in place of X^0.
- Power transformations preserve the order of the data only when all values are positive and are effective only when the ratio of largest to smallest data values is itself large. When these conditions do not hold, we can impose them by adding a positive or negative start to all the data values.
- Descending the ladder of powers (e.g., to $\log X$) tends to correct a positive skew; ascending the ladder of powers (e.g., to X^2) tends to correct a negative skew.
- Simple monotone nonlinearity can often be corrected by a power transformation of X, of Y, or of both variables. Mosteller and Tukey's bulging rule assists in selecting linearizing transformations.
- When there is a positive association between the level of a variable in different groups and its spread, the spreads can be made more constant by descending the ladder of powers. A negative association between level and spread is less common but can be corrected by ascending the ladder of powers.
- Power transformations are ineffective for proportions, P, that simultaneously push the boundaries of 0 and 1 and for other variables (e.g., percentages, rates, disguised proportions) that are bounded both below and above. The folded powers $P \to P^q - (1 - P)^q$ are often effective in this context; for $q = 0$, we employ the logit transformation, $P \to \log_e[P/(1 - P)]$.
- The method of maximum likelihood can be used to estimate normalizing power transformations of variables.

Recommended Reading

Because examination and transformation of data are closely related topics, most of the readings here were also listed at the end of the previous chapter.

- Tukey's important text on exploratory data analysis (Tukey, 1977) and the companion volume by Mosteller and Tukey (1977) on regression analysis have a great deal of interesting information and many examples. As mentioned in the previous chapter, however, Tukey's writing style is opaque. Velleman and Hoaglin (1981) is easier to digest, but it is not as rich in material on transformations.

- Several papers in a volume edited by Hoaglin, Mosteller, and Tukey (1983) have valuable material on the family of power transformations, including a general paper by Emerson and Stoto, an extended discussion of the spread-versus-level plot in a paper on boxplots by Emerson and Strenio, and a more difficult paper by Emerson on the mathematics of transformations.
- The tools provided by the Lisp-Stat statistical computing environment (described in Tierney, 1990)—including the ability to associate a transformation with a slider and to link different plots—are especially helpful in selecting transformations. Cook and Weisberg (1994, 1999) have developed a system for data analysis and regression based on Lisp-Stat that includes these capabilities. Similar facilities are built into some statistical packages and can be implemented in other statistical computing environments (such as R).

PART II

Linear Models and Least Squares

5

Linear Least-Squares Regression

O n several occasions in the first part of the text, I emphasized the limitations of linear least-squares regression. Despite these limitations, linear least squares lies at the very heart of applied statistics:[1]

- Some data are adequately summarized by linear least-squares regression.
- The effective application of linear regression is considerably expanded through data transformations and techniques for diagnosing problems such as nonlinearity and overly influential data.
- As we will see, the general linear model—a direct extension of linear least-squares regression—is able to accommodate a very broad class of specifications, including, for example, qualitative explanatory variables and polynomial functions of quantitative explanatory variables.
- Linear least-squares regression provides a computational basis for a variety of generalizations, including weighted regression, robust regression, nonparametric regression, and generalized linear models.

Linear least-squares regression, and the closely related topic of linear statistical models, are developed in this chapter and in Chapters 6 through 10:

- The current chapter describes the mechanics of linear least-squares regression. That is, I will explain how the method of least squares can be employed to fit a line to a bivariate scatterplot, a plane to a three-dimensional scatterplot, and a general linear surface to multivariate data (which, of course, cannot be directly visualized).
- Chapter 6 develops general and flexible methods of statistical inference for linear models.
- Chapters 7 and 8 extend linear models to situations in which some or all of the explanatory variables are qualitative and categorical rather than quantitative.
- Chapter 9 casts the linear model in matrix form and describes the statistical theory of linear models more formally and more generally.
- Chapter 10 introduces the vector geometry of linear models, a powerful tool for conceptualizing linear models and least-squares estimation.[2]

---

[1]The extensions of linear least-squares regression mentioned here are the subject of subsequent chapters.

[2]Chapters 9 and 10 are "starred" (i.e., marked with asterisks), and therefore are more difficult; like all starred material in this book, these chapters can be skipped without loss of continuity, although some of the later starred material can depend on earlier starred text.

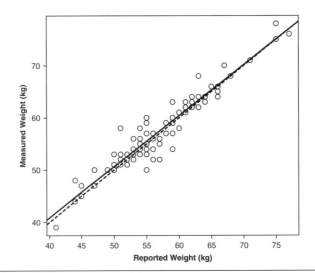

Figure 5.1   Scatterplot of Davis's data on the measured and reported weight of 101 women. The solid line gives the least-squares fit; the broken line is $Y = X$. Because weight is given to the nearest kilogram, both variables are discrete, and some points are overplotted.

5.1   Simple Regression

5.1.1   Least-Squares Fit

Figure 5.1 shows Davis's data, introduced in Chapter 2, on the measured and reported weight in kilograms of 101 women who were engaged in regular exercise.[3] The relationship between measured and reported weight appears to be linear, so it is reasonable to fit a line to the plot. A line will help us determine whether the subjects in Davis's study were accurate and unbiased reporters of their weights; and it can provide a basis for predicting the measured weight of similar women for whom only reported weight is available.

Denoting measured weight by Y and reported weight by X, a line relating the two variables has the equation $Y = A + BX$.[4] It is obvious, however, that no line can pass perfectly through all the data points, despite the strong linear relationship between these two variables. We introduce a *residual*, E, into the regression equation to reflect this fact; writing the regression equation for the ith of the $n = 101$ observations:

$$Y_i = A + BX_i + E_i$$
$$= \widehat{Y}_i + E_i \tag{5.1}$$

where $\widehat{Y}_i = A + BX_i$ is the *fitted value* for observation i. The essential geometry is shown in Figure 5.2, which reveals that the residual

$$E_i = Y_i - \widehat{Y}_i = Y_i - (A + BX_i)$$

is the signed vertical distance between the point and the line—that is, the residual is negative when the point lies below the line and positive when the point is above the line [as is the point (X_i, Y_i) in Figure 5.2].

---

[3]The misrecorded data value that produced an outlier in Figure 2.5 has been corrected.

[4]See Appendix C for a review of the geometry of lines and planes.

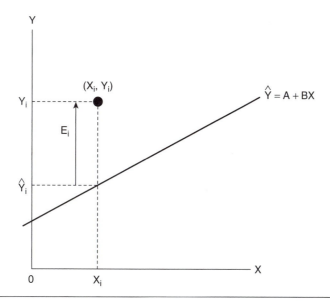

Figure 5.2   Linear regression of Y on X, showing the residual E_i for the ith observation.

A line that fits the data well therefore makes the residuals small, but to determine a line analytically we need to be more precise about what we mean by "small." First of all, we want residuals that are small in magnitude, because large negative residuals are as offensive as large positive ones. For example, simply requiring that the sum of residuals, $\sum_{i=1}^{n} E_i$, be small is futile, because large negative residuals can offset large positive ones.

Indeed, any line through the means of the variables—the point $(\overline{X}, \overline{Y})$—has $\sum E_i = 0$. Such a line satisfies the equation $\overline{Y} = A + B\overline{X}$. Subtracting this equation from Equation 5.1 produces

$$Y_i - \overline{Y} = B(X_i - \overline{X}) + E_i$$

Then, summing over all observations,

$$\sum_{i=1}^{n} E_i = \sum(Y_i - \overline{Y}) - B\sum(X_i - \overline{X}) = 0 - B \times 0 = 0 \qquad (5.2)$$

Two possibilities immediately present themselves: We can employ the unsigned vertical distances between the points and the line, that is, the absolute values of the residuals; or we can employ the squares of the residuals. The first possibility leads to *least-absolute-value* (*LAV*) *regression*:

Find A and B to minimize the sum of the absolute residuals, $\sum |E_i|$.

The second possibility leads to the *least-squares criterion*:

Find A and B to minimize the sum of squared residuals, $\sum E_i^2$.

Squares are more tractable mathematically than absolute values, so we will focus on least squares here, but LAV regression should not be rejected out of hand, because it provides greater resistance to outlying observations.[5]

---

[5]We will return to LAV regression in Chapter 19, which discusses robust regression.

We need to consider the residuals in the aggregate, because it is no trick to produce a 0 residual for an individual point simply by placing the line directly through the point. The least-squares criterion therefore minimizes the *sum* of squared residuals over all observations; that is, we seek the values of A and B that minimize:

$$S(A, B) = \sum_{i=1}^{n} E_i^2 = \sum (Y_i - A - BX_i)^2$$

I have written this expression as a *function $S(A, B)$* of the regression coefficients A and B to emphasize the dependence of the sum of squared residuals on the coefficients: For a fixed set of data $\{X_i, Y_i\}$, each possible choice of values for A and B corresponds to a specific residual sum of squares, $\sum E_i^2$; we want the pair of values for the regression coefficients that makes this sum of squares as small as possible.

*The most direct approach to finding the least-squares coefficients is to take the partial derivatives of the sum-of-squares function with respect to the coefficients:[6]

$$\frac{\partial S(A, B)}{\partial A} = \sum (-1)(2)(Y_i - A - BX_i)$$

$$\frac{\partial S(A, B)}{\partial B} = \sum (-X_i)(2)(Y_i - A - BX_i)$$

Setting the partial derivatives to 0 yields simultaneous linear equations for the least-squares coefficients, A and B.[7]

Simultaneous linear equations for the least-squares coefficients A and B, the so-called *normal equations*[8] for simple regression, are

$$An + B \sum X_i = \sum Y_i$$

$$A \sum X_i + B \sum X_i^2 = \sum X_i Y_i$$

where n is the number of observations. Solving the normal equations produces the least-squares coefficients:

$$A = \overline{Y} - B\overline{X}$$

$$B = \frac{n \sum X_i Y_i - \sum X_i \sum Y_i}{n \sum X_i^2 - (\sum X_i)^2} = \frac{\sum (X_i - \overline{X})(Y_i - \overline{Y})}{\sum (X_i - \overline{X})^2} \tag{5.3}$$

The formula for A implies that the least-squares line passes through the point of means of the two variables. By Equation 5.2, therefore, the least-squares residuals sum to 0. The second normal equation implies that $\sum X_i E_i = 0$, for

$$\sum X_i E_i = \sum X_i (Y_i - A - BX_i) = \sum X_i Y_i - A \sum X_i - B \sum X_i^2 = 0$$

Similarly, $\sum \widehat{Y}_i E_i = 0$.[9] These properties, which will be useful to us below, imply that the least-squares residuals are uncorrelated with both the explanatory variable X and the fitted values $\widehat{Y}$.[10]

---

[6]In Chapter 10, I will derive the least-squares solution by an alternative geometric approach.

[7]As a formal matter, it remains to be shown that the solution of the normal equations *minimizes* the least-squares function $S(A, B)$. See Section 9.2.

[8]The term *normal* here refers not to the normal distribution but to orthogonality (perpendicularity); see Chapter 10 on the vector geometry of regression.

[9]See Exercise 5.1.

[10]See the next section for a definition of correlation.

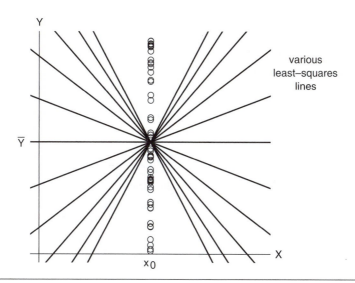

Figure 5.3 When all values of X are the same (x_0), any line through the point $(x_0, \overline{Y})$ is a least-squares line.

It is clear from Equation 5.3 that the least-squares coefficients are uniquely defined as long as the explanatory-variable values are not all identical, for when there is no variation in X, the denominator of B vanishes. This result is intuitively plausible: Only if the explanatory-variable scores are spread out can we hope to fit a (unique) line to the X, Y scatter; if, alternatively, all the X values are the same (say, equal to x_0), then, as is shown in Figure 5.3, any line through the point $(x_0, \overline{Y})$ is a least-squares line.

I will illustrate the least-squares calculations using Davis's data on measured weight (Y) and reported weight (X), for which

$$n = 101$$
$$\overline{Y} = \frac{5780}{101} = 57.238$$
$$\overline{X} = \frac{5731}{101} = 56.743$$
$$\sum(X_i - \overline{X})(Y_i - \overline{Y}) = 4435.9$$
$$\sum(X_i - \overline{X})^2 = 4539.3$$
$$B = \frac{4435.9}{4539.3} = 0.97722$$
$$A = 57.238 - 0.97722 \times 56.743 = 1.7776$$

Thus, the least-squares regression equation is

$$\widehat{\text{Measured weight}} = 1.78 + 0.977 \times \text{Reported weight}$$

Interpretation of the least-squares slope coefficient is straightforward: $B = 0.977$ indicates that a 1-kg increase in reported weight is associated, on average, with just under a 1-kg increase in measured weight. Because the data are not longitudinal, the phrase "a unit increase" here implies not a literal change over time, but rather a notional static comparison between two individuals who differ by 1 kg in their reported weights.

Ordinarily, we may interpret the intercept A as the fitted value associated with $X = 0$, but it is, of course, impossible for an individual to have a reported weight equal to 0. The intercept A is usually of little direct interest, because the fitted value above $X = 0$ is rarely important. Here, however, if individuals' reports are unbiased predictions of their actual weights, then we should have the equation $\widehat{Y} = X$—that is, an intercept of 0 and a slope of 1. The intercept $A = 1.78$ is indeed close to 0, and the slope $B = 0.977$ is close to 1.

> In simple linear regression, the least-squares coefficients are given by $A = \overline{Y} - B\overline{X}$ and $B = \sum(X_i - \overline{X})(Y_i - \overline{Y})/\sum(X_i - \overline{X})^2$. The slope coefficient B represents the average change in Y associated with a one-unit increase in X. The intercept A is the fitted value of Y when $X = 0$.

5.1.2   Simple Correlation

Having calculated the least-squares line, it is of interest to determine how closely the line fits the scatter of points. This is a vague question, which may be answered in a variety of ways. The standard deviation of the residuals, S_E, often called the *standard error of the regression* or the *residual standard error*, provides one sort of answer.[11] Because of estimation considerations, the variance of the residuals is defined using *degrees of freedom* $n - 2$, rather than the sample size n, in the denominator:[12]

$$S_E^2 = \frac{\sum E_i^2}{n - 2}$$

The residual standard error is, therefore,

$$S_E = \sqrt{\frac{\sum E_i^2}{n - 2}}$$

Because it is measured in the units of the response variable, and represents a type of "average" residual, the standard error is simple to interpret. For example, for Davis's regression of measured weight on reported weight, the sum of squared residuals is $\sum E_i^2 = 418.87$, and thus the standard error of the regression is

$$S_E = \sqrt{\frac{418.87}{101 - 2}} = 2.0569 \text{ kg}$$

On average, then, using the least-squares regression line to predict measured weight from reported weight results in an error of about 2 kg, which is small, but perhaps not negligible. Moreover, if the residuals are approximately normally distributed, then about 2/3 of them are in the range ± 2, and about 95% are in the range ± 4. I believe that social scientists overemphasize correlation

---

[11] The term *standard error* is usually used for the estimated standard deviation of the sampling distribution of a statistic, and so the use here to denote the standard deviation of the residuals is potentially misleading. This usage is common, however, and I therefore adopt it.

[12] Estimation is discussed in the next chapter. Also see the discussion in Section 10.3.

(described immediately below) and pay insufficient attention to the standard error of the regression as an index of fit.

In contrast to the standard error of the regression, the *correlation coefficient* provides a *relative* measure of fit: To what degree do our predictions of Y improve when we base these predictions on the linear relationship between Y and X? A relative index of fit requires a baseline—how well can Y be predicted if X is disregarded?

To disregard the explanatory variable is implicitly to fit the equation $\widehat{Y}'_i = A'$, or, equivalently,

$$Y_i = A' + E'_i$$

By ignoring the explanatory variable, we lose our ability to differentiate among the observations; as a result, the fitted values are constant. The constant A' is generally different from the intercept A of the least-squares line, and the residuals E'_i are different from the least-squares residuals E_i.

How should we find the best constant A'? An obvious approach is to employ a least-squares fit—that is, to minimize

$$S(A') = \sum E_i'^2 = \sum (Y_i - A')^2$$

As you may be aware, the value of A' that minimizes this sum of squares is simply the response-variable mean, $\overline{Y}$.[13]

The residuals $E_i = Y_i - \widehat{Y}_i$ from the linear regression of Y on X will mostly be smaller in magnitude than the residuals $E'_i = Y_i - \overline{Y}$, and it is necessarily the case that

$$\sum (Y_i - \widehat{Y}_i)^2 \leq \sum (Y_i - \overline{Y})^2$$

This inequality holds because the "null model," $Y_i = A' + E'_i$, specifying no relationship between Y and X, is a special case of the more general linear regression "model," $Y_i = A + BX_i + E_i$: The two models are the same when $B = 0$.[14] The null model therefore cannot have a smaller sum of squared residuals. After all, the least-squares coefficients A and B are selected precisely to minimize $\sum E_i^2$, so constraining $B = 0$ cannot improve the fit and will usually make it worse.

We call

$$\sum E_i'^2 = \sum (Y_i - \overline{Y})^2$$

the *total sum of squares* for Y, abbreviated TSS, while

$$\sum E_i^2 = \sum (Y_i - \widehat{Y}_i)^2$$

is called the *residual sum of squares*, and is abbreviated RSS. The difference between the two, termed the *regression sum of squares*,

$$\text{RegSS} \equiv \text{TSS} - \text{RSS}$$

gives the reduction in squared error due to the linear regression. The ratio of RegSS to TSS, the proportional reduction in squared error, defines the square of the correlation coefficient:

$$r^2 \equiv \frac{\text{RegSS}}{\text{TSS}}$$

---

[13] See Exercise 5.3.

[14] A formal statistical model for linear regression is introduced in the next chapter.

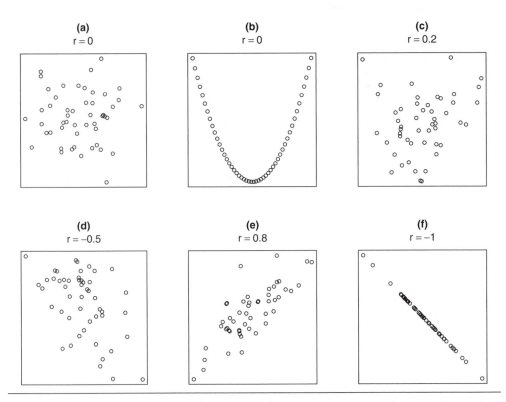

Figure 5.4   Scatterplots illustrating different levels of correlation: $r = 0$ in both (a) and (b); $r = .2$ in (c); $r = -.5$ in (d); $r = .8$ in (e); and $r = -1$ in (f). All the data sets have $n = 50$ observations. Except in panel (b), the data were generated by sampling from bivariate normal distributions.

To find the *correlation coefficient* r, we take the positive square root of r^2 when the simple-regression slope B is positive and the negative square root when B is negative.

Thus, if there is a perfect positive linear relationship between Y and X (i.e., if all of the residuals are 0 and $B > 0$), then $r = 1$. A perfect negative linear relationship corresponds to $r = -1$. If there is no linear relationship between Y and X, then RSS = TSS, RegSS = 0, and $r = 0$. Between these extremes, r gives the direction of the linear relationship between the two variables, and r^2 can be interpreted as the proportion of the total variation of Y that is "captured" by its linear regression on X. Figure 5.4 illustrates several levels of correlation. As is clear in Figure 5.4(b), where $r = 0$, the correlation can be small even when there is a strong *nonlinear* relationship between X and Y.

It is instructive to examine the three sums of squares more closely: Starting with an individual observation, we have the identity

$$Y_i - \overline{Y} = (Y_i - \widehat{Y}_i) + (\widehat{Y}_i - \overline{Y})$$

This equation is interpreted geometrically in Figure 5.5. Squaring both sides of the equation and summing over observations produces

$$\sum (Y_i - \overline{Y})^2 = \sum (Y_i - \widehat{Y}_i)^2 + \sum (\widehat{Y}_i - \overline{Y})^2 + 2 \sum (Y_i - \widehat{Y}_i)(\widehat{Y}_i - \overline{Y})$$

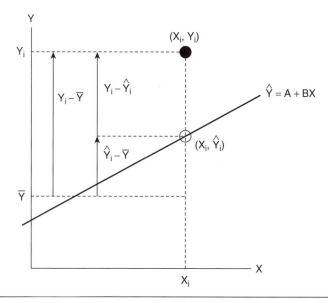

Figure 5.5 Decomposition of the total deviation $Y_i - \overline{Y}$ into components $Y_i - \widehat{Y}_i$ and $\widehat{Y}_i - \overline{Y}$.

The last term in this equation is 0,[15] and thus the regression sum of squares, which I previously defined as the difference TSS − RSS, may also be written directly as

$$\text{RegSS} = \sum (\widehat{Y}_i - \overline{Y})^2$$

This decomposition of total variation into "explained" and "unexplained" components, paralleling the decomposition of each observation into a fitted value and a residual, is typical of linear models. The decomposition is called the *analysis of variance* for the regression: TSS = RegSS + RSS.

Although I have developed the correlation coefficient from the regression of Y on X, it is also possible to define r by analogy with the correlation $\rho = \sigma_{XY}/\sigma_X \sigma_Y$ between two random variables (where σ_{XY} is the covariance of the random variables X and Y, σ_X is the standard deviation of X, and σ_Y is the standard deviation of Y).[16] First defining the *sample covariance* between X and Y,

$$S_{XY} \equiv \frac{\sum (X_i - \overline{X})(Y_i - \overline{Y})}{n - 1}$$

we may then write

$$r = \frac{S_{XY}}{S_X S_Y} = \frac{\sum (X_i - \overline{X})(Y_i - \overline{Y})}{\sqrt{\sum (X_i - \overline{X})^2 \sum (Y_i - \overline{Y})^2}} \tag{5.4}$$

where S_X and S_Y are, respectively, the sample standard deviations of X and Y.[17]

It is immediately apparent from the symmetry of Equation 5.4 that the correlation does not depend on which of the two variables is treated as the response variable. This property of r is

---

[15]See Exercise 5.1 and Section 10.1.

[16]See Appendix D on probability and estimation.

[17]The equivalence of the two formulas for r is established in Section 10.1 on the geometry of simple regression analysis.

surprising in light of the *asymmetry* of the regression equation used to define the sums of squares: Unless there is a perfect correlation between the two variables, the least-squares line for the regression of Y on X differs from the line for the regression of X on Y.[18]

There is another central property, aside from symmetry, that distinguishes the correlation coefficient r from the regression slope B. The slope coefficient B is measured in the units of the response variable per unit of the explanatory variable. For example, if dollars of income are regressed on years of education, then the units of B are dollars/year. The correlation coefficient r, however, is unitless, as can be seen from either of its definitions. As a consequence, a change in scale of Y or X produces a compensating change in B, but does not affect r. If, for example, income is measured in thousands of dollars rather than in dollars, the units of the slope become $1,000$s/year, and the value of the slope decreases by a factor of $1,000$, but r remains the same.

For Davis's regression of measured on reported weight,

$$\text{TSS} = 4753.8$$
$$\text{RSS} = 418.87$$
$$\text{RegSS} = 4334.9$$

Thus,

$$r^2 = \frac{4334.9}{4753.8} = .91188$$

and, because B is positive, $r = +\sqrt{.91188} = .9549$. The linear regression of measured on reported weight, therefore, captures 91% of the variation in measured weight. Equivalently,

$$S_{XY} = \frac{4435.9}{101 - 1} = 44.359$$
$$S_X^2 = \frac{4539.3}{101 - 1} = 45.393$$
$$S_Y^2 = \frac{4753.8}{101 - 1} = 47.538$$
$$r = \frac{44.359}{\sqrt{45.393 \times 47.538}} = .9549$$

5.2 Multiple Regression

5.2.1 Two Explanatory Variables

The linear multiple-regression equation

$$\widehat{Y} = A + B_1 X_1 + B_2 X_2$$

for two explanatory variables, X_1 and X_2, describes a plane in the three-dimensional $\{X_1, X_2, Y\}$ space, as shown in Figure 5.6. As in the case of simple regression, it is unreasonable to expect that the regression plane will pass precisely through every point, so the fitted value for observation i in general differs from the observed value. The residual is the signed vertical distance from the point to the plane:

$$E_i = Y_i - \widehat{Y}_i = Y_i - (A + B_1 X_{i1} + B_2 X_{i2})$$

---

[18]See Exercise 5.2.

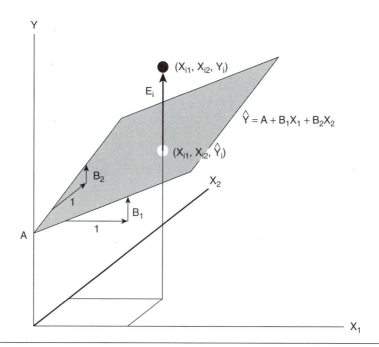

Figure 5.6 The multiple-regression plane, showing the partial slopes B_1 and B_2 and the residual E_i for the ith observation. The white dot in the regression plane represents the fitted value. Compare this graph with Figure 5.2 for simple regression.

To make the plane come as close as possible to the points in the aggregate, we want the values of A, B_1, and B_2 that minimize the sum of squared residuals:

$$S(A, B_1, B_2) = \sum E_i^2 = \sum (Y_i - A - B_1 X_{i1} - B_2 X_{i2})^2$$

*As in simple regression, we can proceed by differentiating the sum-of-squares function with respect to the regression coefficients:

$$\frac{\partial S(A, B_1, B_2)}{\partial A} = \sum (-1)(2)(Y_i - A - B_1 X_{i1} - B_2 X_{i2})$$

$$\frac{\partial S(A, B_1, B_2)}{\partial B_1} = \sum (-X_{i1})(2)(Y_i - A - B_1 X_{i1} - B_2 X_{i2})$$

$$\frac{\partial S(A, B_1, B_2)}{\partial B_2} = \sum (-X_{i2})(2)(Y_i - A - B_1 X_{i1} - B_2 X_{i2})$$

Setting the partial derivatives to 0 and rearranging terms produces the normal equations for the regression coefficients A, B_1, and B_2.

The normal equations for the regression coefficients A, B_1, and B_2 are

$$An + B_1 \sum X_{i1} + B_2 \sum X_{i2} = \sum Y_i$$

$$A \sum X_{i1} + B_1 \sum X_{i1}^2 + B_2 \sum X_{i1} X_{i2} = \sum X_{i1} Y_i$$

$$A \sum X_{i2} + B_1 \sum X_{i2} X_{i1} + B_2 \sum X_{i2}^2 = \sum X_{i2} Y_i \qquad (5.5)$$

Because Equation 5.5 is a system of three linear equations in three unknowns, it usually provides a unique solution for the least-squares regression coefficients A, B_1, and B_2. We can write out the solution explicitly, if somewhat tediously: Dropping the subscript i for observations, and using asterisks to denote variables in mean-deviation form (e.g., $Y^* \equiv Y_i - \overline{Y}$),

$$A = \overline{Y} - B_1 \overline{X}_1 - B_2 \overline{X}_2$$

$$B_1 = \frac{\sum X_1^* Y^* \sum X_2^{*2} - \sum X_2^* Y^* \sum X_1^* X_2^*}{\sum X_1^{*2} \sum X_2^{*2} - (\sum X_1^* X_2^*)^2}$$

$$B_2 = \frac{\sum X_2^* Y^* \sum X_1^{*2} - \sum X_1^* Y^* \sum X_1^* X_2^*}{\sum X_1^{*2} \sum X_2^{*2} - (\sum X_1^* X_2^*)^2} \tag{5.6}$$

The denominator of B_1 and B_2 is nonzero—and, therefore, the least-squares coefficients are uniquely defined—as long as

$$\sum X_1^{*2} \sum X_2^{*2} \neq \left(\sum X_1^* X_2^* \right)^2$$

This condition is satisfied unless X_1 and X_2 are perfectly correlated or unless one of the explanatory variables is invariant.[19] If X_1 and X_2 are perfectly correlated, then they are said to be *collinear*.

To illustrate the computation of multiple-regression coefficients, I will employ Duncan's occupational prestige data, which were introduced in Chapter 3. I will, for the time being, disregard the problems with these data that were revealed by graphical analysis. Recall that Duncan wished to predict the prestige of occupations (Y) from their educational and income levels (X_1 and X_2, respectively). I calculated the following quantities from Duncan's data:

$$n = 45$$

$$\overline{Y} = \frac{2146}{45} = 47.689$$

$$\overline{X}_1 = \frac{2365}{45} = 52.556$$

$$\overline{X}_2 = \frac{1884}{45} = 41.867$$

$$\sum X_1^{*2} = 38,971$$

$$\sum X_2^{*2} = 26,271$$

$$\sum X_1^* X_2^* = 23,182$$

$$\sum X_1^* Y^* = 35,152$$

$$\sum X_2^* Y^* = 28,383$$

Substituting these values into Equation 5.6 produces $A = -6.0647$, $B_1 = 0.54583$, and $B_2 = 0.59873$. The fitted least-squares regression equation is, therefore,

$$\widehat{\text{Prestige}} = -6.065 + 0.5458 \times \text{Education} + 0.5987 \times \text{Income}$$

Although the development of least-squares linear regression for two explanatory variables is very similar to the development for simple regression, there is this important difference in

---

[19]The correlation between X_1 and X_2 is, in the current notation,

$$r_{12} = \frac{\sum X_1^* X_2^*}{\sqrt{\sum X_1^{*2} \sum X_2^{*2}}}$$

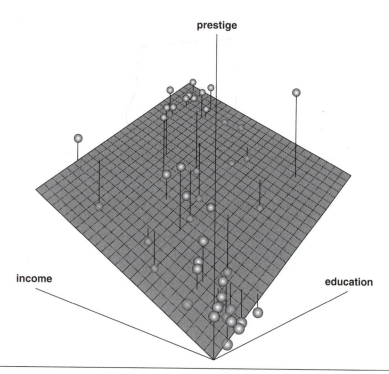

Figure 5.7 The multiple-regression plane in Duncan's regression of prestige on education and income. The two sets of parallel lines on the regression plane represent the partial relationship of prestige to each explanatory variable holding the other explanatory variable at particular values.

interpretation: The slope coefficients for the explanatory variables in multiple regression are *partial* coefficients, while the slope coefficient in simple regression gives the *marginal* relationship between the response variable and a single explanatory variable. That is, each slope in multiple regression represents the "effect" on the response variable of a one-unit increment in the corresponding explanatory variable *holding constant* the value of the other explanatory variable. The simple-regression slope effectively ignores the other explanatory variable.

This interpretation of the multiple-regression slope is apparent in Figure 5.7, which shows the multiple-regression plane for Duncan's regression of prestige on education and income (also see Figure 5.6). Because the regression plane is flat, its slope (B_1) in the direction of education, holding income constant, does not depend on the specific value at which income is fixed. Likewise, the slope in the direction of income, fixing the value of education, is always B_2.

Algebraically, let us fix X_2 to the specific value x_2 and see how $\widehat{Y}$ changes as X_1 is increased by 1, from some specific value x_1 to $x_1 + 1$:

$$[A + B_1(x_1 + 1) + B_2x_2] - (A + B_1x_1 + B_2x_2) = B_1$$

Similarly, increasing X_2 by 1, fixing X_1 produces

$$[A + B_1x_1 + B_2(x_2 + 1)] - (A + B_1x_1 + B_2x_2) = B_2$$

*Because the regression surface

$$\widehat{Y} = A + B_1X_1 + B_2X_2$$

is a plane, precisely the same results follow from differentiating the regression equation with respect to each of X_1 and X_2:

$$\frac{\partial \widehat{Y}}{\partial X_1} = B_1$$

$$\frac{\partial \widehat{Y}}{\partial X_2} = B_2$$

Nothing new is learned here, but differentiation is often a useful approach for understanding *nonlinear* statistical models, for which the regression surface is not flat.[20]

For Duncan's regression, then, a unit increase in education, holding income constant, is associated, on average, with an increase of 0.55 units in prestige (which, recall, is the percentage of respondents rating the prestige of the occupation as good or excellent). A unit increase in income, holding education constant, is associated, on average, with an increase of 0.60 units in prestige. Because Duncan's data are not longitudinal, this language of "increase" or "change" is a shorthand for hypothetical static comparisons (as was the case for the simple regression of measured on reported weight using Davis's data).

The regression intercept, $A = -6.1$, has the following literal interpretation: The fitted value of prestige is -6.1 for a hypothetical occupation with education and income levels both equal to 0. Literal interpretation of the intercept is problematic here, however. Although there are some observations in Duncan's data set with small education and income levels, no occupations have levels of 0. Moreover, the response variable cannot take on negative values.

5.2.2   Several Explanatory Variables

The extension of linear least-squares regression to several explanatory variables is straightforward. For the general case of k explanatory variables, the multiple-regression equation is

$$Y_i = A + B_1 X_{i1} + B_2 X_{i2} + \cdots + B_k X_{ik} + E_i$$
$$= \widehat{Y}_i + E_i$$

It is, of course, not possible to visualize the point cloud of the data directly when $k > 2$, but it is a relatively simple matter to find the values of A and the Bs that minimize the sum of squared residuals:

$$S(A, B_1, B_2, \ldots, B_k) = \sum_{i=1}^{n} [Y_i - (A + B_1 X_{i1} + B_2 X_{i2} + \cdots + B_k X_{ik})]^2$$

Minimization of the sum-of-squares function produces the normal equations for general multiple regression:[21]

$$An + B_1 \sum X_{i1} + B_2 \sum X_{i2} + \cdots + B_k \sum X_{ik} = \sum Y_i$$

$$A \sum X_{i1} + B_1 \sum X_{i1}^2 + B_2 \sum X_{i1} X_{i2} + \cdots + B_k \sum X_{i1} X_{ik} = \sum X_{i1} Y_i$$

$$A \sum X_{i2} + B_1 \sum X_{i2} X_{i1} + B_2 \sum X_{i2}^2 + \cdots + B_k \sum X_{i2} X_{ik} = \sum X_{i2} Y_i$$

$$\vdots \qquad\qquad\qquad\qquad\qquad\qquad\qquad\qquad\qquad\qquad \vdots$$

$$A \sum X_{ik} + B_1 \sum X_{ik} X_{i1} + B_2 \sum X_{ik} X_{i2} + \cdots + B_k \sum X_{ik}^2 = \sum X_{ik} Y_i \qquad (5.7)$$

---

[20]For example, see the discussion of quadratic surfaces in Section 17.1.1.
[21]See Exercise 5.5.

We cannot write out a general solution to the normal equations without specifying the number of explanatory variables k, and even for k as small as 3, an explicit solution would be very complicated.[22] Nevertheless, because the normal equations are linear, and because there are as many equations as unknown regression coefficients $(k + 1)$, there is usually a unique solution for the coefficients $A, B_1, B_2, \ldots, B_k$. Only when one explanatory variable is a perfect linear function of others, or when one or more explanatory variables are invariant, will the normal equations not have a unique solution. Dividing the first normal equation through by n reveals that the least-squares surface passes through the point of means $(\overline{X}_1, \overline{X}_2, \ldots, \overline{X}_k, \overline{Y})$.

> The least-squares coefficients in multiple linear regression are found by solving the normal equations for the intercept A and the slope coefficients $B_1, B_2, \ldots, B_k$. The slope coefficient B_1 represents the average change in Y associated with a one-unit increase in X_1 when the other Xs are held constant.

To illustrate the solution of the normal equations, let us return to the Canadian occupational prestige data, regressing the prestige of the occupations on average education, average income, and the percentage of women in each occupation. Recall that our graphical analysis of the data in Chapter 3 cast doubt on the appropriateness of the linear regression, but I will disregard this problem for now.

The various sums, sums of squares, and sums of products that are required are given in Table 5.1. Notice that the sums of squares and products are very large, especially for income, which is scaled in small units (dollars). Substituting these values into the four normal equations and solving for the regression coefficients produces

$$A = -6.7943$$
$$B_1 = 4.1866$$
$$B_2 = 0.0013136$$
$$B_3 = -0.0089052$$

The fitted regression equation is, therefore,

$$\widehat{\text{Prestige}} = -6.794 + 4.187 \times \text{Education} + 0.001314 \times \text{Income}$$
$$- 0.008905 \times \text{Percent women}$$

In interpreting the regression coefficients, we need to keep in mind the units of each variable. Prestige scores are arbitrarily scaled, and range from a minimum of 14.8 to a maximum of 87.2 for these 102 occupations; the interquartile range of prestige is 24.1 points. Education is measured in years, and hence the impact of education on prestige is considerable—a little more than four points, on average, for each year of education, holding income and gender composition constant. Likewise, despite the small absolute size of its coefficient, the partial effect of income is also fairly large—more than 0.001 points, on average, for an additional dollar of income, or more than 1 point for each $1,000. In contrast, the impact of gender composition, holding education and income constant, is very small—an average decline of about 0.01 points for each 1% increase in the percentage of women in an occupation.

---

[22] As I will show in Section 9.2, however, it is simple to write out a general solution to the normal equations using matrices.

Table 5.1   Sums of Squares (Diagonal), Sums of Products (Off Diagonal), and Sums (Last Row)
for the Canadian Occupational Prestige Data

Variable	Prestige	Education	Income	Percentage of women
Prestige	**253,618.**	55,326.	37,748,108.	131,909.
Education	55,326.	**12,513.**	8,121,410.	32,281.
Income	37,748,108.	8,121,410.	**6,534,383,460.**	14,093,097.
Percentage of women	131,909.	32,281.	14,093,097.	**187,312.**
Sum	4,777.	1,095.	693,386.	2,956.

5.2.3   Multiple Correlation

As in simple regression, the residual standard error in multiple regression measures the "average" size of the residuals. As before, we divide by degrees of freedom, here $n - (k+1) = n - k - 1$, rather than by the sample size n, to calculate the variance of the residuals; thus, the standard error of the regression is

$$S_E = \sqrt{\frac{\sum E_i^2}{n - k - 1}}$$

Heuristically, we "lose" $k + 1$ degrees of freedom by calculating the $k + 1$ regression coefficients, $A, B_1, \ldots, B_k$.[23]

For Duncan's regression of occupational prestige on the income and educational levels of occupations, the standard error is

$$S_E = \sqrt{\frac{7506.7}{45 - 2 - 1}} = 13.37$$

Recall that the response variable here is the percentage of raters classifying the occupation as good or excellent in prestige; an average prediction error of 13 is substantial given Duncan's purpose, which was to use the regression equation to calculate substitute prestige scores for occupations for which direct ratings were unavailable. For the Canadian occupational prestige data, regressing prestige scores on average education, average income, and gender composition, the standard error is

$$S_E = \sqrt{\frac{6033.6}{102 - 3 - 1}} = 7.846$$

which is also a substantial figure.

The sums of squares in multiple regression are defined in the same manner as in simple regression:

$$\text{TSS} = \sum (Y_i - \overline{Y})^2$$

$$\text{RegSS} = \sum (\widehat{Y}_i - \overline{Y})^2$$

$$\text{RSS} = \sum (Y_i - \widehat{Y}_i)^2 = \sum E_i^2$$

---

[23] A deeper understanding of the central concept of degrees of freedom is developed in Chapter 10.

Of course, the fitted values $\widehat{Y}_i$ and residuals E_i now come from the multiple-regression equation. Moreover, we have a similar analysis of variance for the regression:

$$TSS = RegSS + RSS$$

The least-squares residuals are uncorrelated with the fitted values and with each of the Xs.[24]

> The linear regression decomposes the variation in Y into "explained" and "unexplained" components: $TSS = RegSS + RSS$. The least-squares residuals, E, are uncorrelated with the fitted values, $\widehat{Y}$, and with the explanatory variables, $X_1, \ldots, X_k$.

The squared multiple correlation R^2, representing the proportion of variation in the response variable captured by the regression, is defined in terms of the sums of squares:

$$R^2 \equiv \frac{RegSS}{TSS}$$

Because there are now several slope coefficients, potentially with different signs, the *multiple correlation coefficient* is, by convention, the positive square root of R^2. The multiple correlation is also interpretable as the simple correlation between the fitted and observed Y values—that is, $r_{\widehat{Y}Y}$.

> The standard error of the regression, $S_E = \sqrt{\sum E_i^2 / (n - k - 1)}$, gives the "average" size of the regression residuals; the squared multiple correlation, $R^2 = RegSS/TSS$, indicates the proportion of the variation in Y that is captured by its linear regression on the Xs.

For Duncan's regression, we have the following sums of squares:

$$TSS = 43,688.$$
$$RegSS = 36,181.$$
$$RSS = 7506.7$$

The squared multiple correlation,

$$R^2 = \frac{36,181}{43,688} = .8282$$

indicates that more than 80% of the variation in prestige among the 45 occupations is accounted for by the linear regression of prestige on the income and educational levels of the occupations. For the Canadian prestige regression, the sums of squares and R^2 are as follows:

$$TSS = 29,895$$
$$RegSS = 23,862$$
$$RSS = 6033.6$$
$$R^2 = \frac{23,862}{29,895} = .7982$$

---

[24]These and other properties of the least-squares fit are derived in Chapters 9 and 10.

Because the multiple correlation can only rise, never decline, when explanatory variables are added to the regression equation,[25] investigators sometimes penalize the value of R^2 by a "correction" for degrees of freedom. The corrected (or "adjusted") R^2 is defined as

$$\widetilde{R}^2 \equiv 1 - \frac{S_E^2}{S_Y^2} = 1 - \frac{\frac{\text{RSS}}{n-k-1}}{\frac{\text{TSS}}{n-1}}$$

Unless the sample size is very small, however, $\widetilde{R}^2$ will differ little from R^2. For Duncan's regression, for example,

$$\widetilde{R}^2 = 1 - \frac{\frac{7506.7}{45-2-1}}{\frac{43,688}{45-1}} = .8200$$

5.2.4 Standardized Regression Coefficients

Social researchers often wish to compare the coefficients of different explanatory variables in a regression analysis. When the explanatory variables are commensurable (i.e., measured in the same units on the same scale), or when they can be reduced to a common standard, comparison is straightforward. In most instances, however, explanatory variables are not commensurable. Standardized regression coefficients permit a limited assessment of the relative effects of incommensurable explanatory variables.

To place standardized coefficients in perspective, let us first consider an example in which the explanatory variables are measured in the same units. Imagine that the annual dollar income of wage workers is regressed on their years of education, years of labor force experience, and some other explanatory variables, producing the fitted regression equation

$$\widehat{\text{Income}} = A + B_1 \times \text{Education} + B_2 \times \text{Experience} + \cdots$$

Because education and experience are each measured in years, the coefficients B_1 and B_2 are both expressed in dollars/year and, consequently, can be directly compared. If, for example, B_1 is larger than B_2, then (disregarding issues arising from sampling variation) a year's increment in education yields a greater average return in income than a year's increment in labor force experience, holding constant the other factors in the regression equation.

It is, as I have mentioned, much more common for explanatory variables to be measured in different units. In the Canadian occupational prestige regression, for example, the coefficient for education is expressed in points (of prestige) per year; the coefficient for income is expressed in points per dollar; and the coefficient of gender composition in points per percentage of women. I have already pointed out that the income coefficient (0.001314) is much smaller than the education coefficient (4.187) not because income is a much less important determinant of prestige, but because the unit of income (the dollar) is small, while the unit of education (the year) is relatively large. If we were to reexpress income in $1,000s, then we would multiply the income coefficient by 1,000.

By the very meaning of the term, *incommensurable* quantities cannot be directly compared. Still, in certain circumstances, incommensurables can be reduced to a common (e.g., monetary) standard. In most cases, however—as in the prestige regression—there is no obvious basis for this sort of reduction.

In the absence of a theoretically meaningful basis for comparison, an empirical comparison can be made by rescaling regression coefficients according to a measure of explanatory-variable

---

[25] See Exercise 5.6.

spread. We can, for example, multiply each regression coefficient by the interquartile range of the corresponding explanatory variable. For the Canadian prestige data, the interquartile range of education is 4.2025 years; of income, 4081.3 dollars; and of gender composition, 48.610%. When each explanatory variable is manipulated over this range, holding the other explanatory variables constant, the corresponding average changes in prestige are

$$
\begin{array}{lll}
\text{Education:} & 4.2025 \times 4.1866 & = 17.59 \\
\text{Income:} & 4081.3 \times 0.0013136 & = 5.361 \\
\text{Gender:} & 48.610 \times -0.0089052 & = -0.4329
\end{array}
$$

Thus, education has a larger effect than income over the central half of scores observed in the data, and the effect of gender is very small. Note that this conclusion is distinctly circumscribed: For other data, where the variation in education and income may be different, the relative impact of the variables may also differ, even if the regression coefficients are unchanged.

There is really no deep reason for equating the interquartile range of one explanatory variable to that of another, as we have done here implicitly in calculating the relative "effect" of each. Indeed, the following observation should give you pause: If two explanatory variables are commensurable, and if their interquartile ranges differ, then performing this calculation is, in effect, to adopt a rubber ruler. If expressing coefficients relative to a measure of spread potentially distorts their comparison when explanatory variables are commensurable, then why should the procedure magically allow us to compare coefficients that are measured in different units?

It is much more common to standardize regression coefficients using the standard deviations of the explanatory variables rather than their interquartile ranges. Although I will proceed to explain this procedure, keep in mind that the standard deviation is not a good measure of spread when the distributions of the explanatory variables depart considerably from normality. The usual practice standardizes the response variable as well, but this is an inessential element of the computation of standardized coefficients, because the *relative* size of the slope coefficients does not change when Y is rescaled.

Beginning with the fitted multiple-regression equation

$$
Y_i = A + B_1 X_{i1} + \cdots + B_k X_{ik} + E_i
$$

let us eliminate the regression constant A, expressing all the variables in mean-deviation form by subtracting[26]

$$
\overline{Y} = A + B_1 \overline{X}_1 + \cdots + B_k \overline{X}_k
$$

which produces

$$
Y_i - \overline{Y} = B_1(X_{i1} - \overline{X}_1) + \cdots + B_k(X_{ik} - \overline{X}_k) + E_i
$$

Then divide both sides of the equation by the standard deviation of the response variable S_Y; simultaneously multiply and divide the jth term on the right-hand side of the equation by the standard deviation S_j of X_j. These operations serve to standardize each variable in the regression equation:

$$
\frac{Y_i - \overline{Y}}{S_Y} = \left(B_1 \frac{S_1}{S_Y} \right) \frac{X_{i1} - \overline{X}_1}{S_1} + \cdots + \left(B_k \frac{S_k}{S_Y} \right) \frac{X_{ik} - \overline{X}_k}{S_k} + \frac{E_i}{S_Y}
$$

$$
Z_{iY} = B_1^* Z_{i1} + \cdots + B_k^* Z_{ik} + E_i^*
$$

---

[26]Recall that the least-squares regression surface passes through the point of means for the $k + 1$ variables.

In this equation, $Z_{iY} \equiv (Y_i - \overline{Y})/S_Y$ is the standardized response variable, linearly transformed to a mean of 0 and a standard deviation of 1; $Z_{i1}, \ldots, Z_{ik}$ are the explanatory variables, similarly standardized; $E_i^* \equiv E_i/S_Y$ is the transformed residual, which, note, *does not* have a standard deviation of 1; and $B_j^* \equiv B_j(S_j/S_Y)$ is the *standardized partial regression coefficient* for the jth explanatory variable. The standardized coefficient is interpretable as the average change in Y, in standard-deviation units, for a one standard-deviation increase in X_j, holding constant the other explanatory variables.

> By rescaling regression coefficients in relation to a measure of variation—such as the interquartile range or the standard deviation—standardized regression coefficients permit a limited comparison of the relative impact of incommensurable explanatory variables.

For the Canadian prestige regression, we have the following calculations:

$$\begin{array}{lll} \text{Education:} & 4.1866 \times 2.7284/17.204 & = 0.6640 \\ \text{Income:} & 0.0013136 \times 4245.9/17.204 & = 0.3242 \\ \text{Gender:} & -0.0089052 \times 31.725/17.204 & = -0.01642 \end{array}$$

Because both income and gender composition have substantially non-normal distributions, however, the use of standard deviations here is difficult to justify.

I have stressed the restricted extent to which standardization permits the comparison of coefficients for incommensurable explanatory variables. A common misuse of standardized coefficients is to employ them to make comparisons of the effects of the *same* explanatory variable in two or more samples drawn from different populations. If the explanatory variable in question has different spreads in these samples, then spurious differences between coefficients may result, even when *unstandardized* coefficients are similar; on the other hand, differences in unstandardized coefficients can be masked by compensating differences in dispersion.

Exercises

Exercise 5.1. *Prove that the least-squares fit in simple-regression analysis has the following properties:

(a) $\sum \widehat{Y}_i E_i = 0$.

(b) $\sum (Y_i - \widehat{Y}_i)(\widehat{Y}_i - \overline{Y}) = \sum E_i(\widehat{Y}_i - \overline{Y}) = 0$.

Exercise 5.2. *Suppose that the means and standard deviations of Y and X are the same: $\overline{Y} = \overline{X}$ and $S_Y = S_X$.

(a) Show that, under these circumstances,

$$B_{Y|X} = B_{X|Y} = r_{XY}$$

where $B_{Y|X}$ is the least-squares slope for the simple regression of Y on X; $B_{X|Y}$ is the least-squares slope for the simple regression of X on Y; and r_{XY} is the correlation between the two variables. Show that the intercepts are also the same, $A_{Y|X} = A_{X|Y}$.

(b) Why, if $A_{Y|X} = A_{X|Y}$ and $B_{Y|X} = B_{X|Y}$, is the least-squares line for the regression of Y on X different from the line for the regression of X on Y (as long as $r^2 < 1$)?

(c) "Regression toward the mean" (the original sense of the term "regression"): Imagine that X is father's height and Y is son's height for a sample of father-son pairs. Suppose that $S_Y = S_X$, that $\overline{Y} = \overline{X}$, and that the regression of sons' heights on fathers' heights is linear. Finally, suppose that $0 < r_{XY} < 1$ (i.e., fathers' and sons' heights are positively correlated, but not perfectly so). Show that the expected height of a son whose father is shorter than average is also less than average, but to a smaller extent; likewise, the expected height of a son whose father is taller than average is also greater than average, but to a smaller extent. Does this result imply a contradiction—that the standard deviation of son's height is in fact less than that of father's height?

(d) What is the expected height for a father whose son is shorter than average? Of a father whose son is taller than average?

(e) Regression effects in research design: Imagine that educational researchers wish to assess the efficacy of a new program to improve the reading performance of children. To test the program, they recruit a group of children who are reading substantially below grade level; after a year in the program, the researchers observe that the children, on average, have improved their reading performance. Why is this a weak research design? How could it be improved?

Exercise 5.3. *Show that $A' = \overline{Y}$ minimizes the sum of squares

$$S(A') = \sum_{i=1}^{n}(Y_i - A')^2$$

Exercise 5.4. Linear transformation of X and Y:

(a) Suppose that the explanatory-variable values in Davis's regression are transformed according to the equation $X' = X - 10$ and that Y is regressed on X'. Without redoing the regression calculations in detail, find A', B', S'_E, and r'. What happens to these quantities when $X' = 10X$? When $X' = 10(X - 1) = 10X - 10$?

(b) Now suppose that the response variable scores are transformed according to the formula $Y'' = Y + 10$ and that Y'' is regressed on X. Find A'', B'', S''_E, and r''. What happens to these quantities when $Y'' = 5Y$? When $Y'' = 5(Y + 2) = 5Y + 10$?

(c) In general, how are the results of a simple-regression analysis affected by linear transformations of X and Y?

Exercise 5.5. *Derive the normal equations (Equation 5.7) for the least-squares coefficients of the general multiple-regression model with k explanatory variables. [*Hint*: Differentiate the sum-of-squares function $S(A, B_1, \ldots, B_k)$ with respect to the regression coefficients, and set the partial derivatives to 0.]

Exercise 5.6. Why is it the case that the multiple-correlation coefficient R^2 can never get smaller when an explanatory variable is added to the regression equation? (*Hint*: Recall that the regression equation is fit by minimizing the residual sum of squares.)

Exercise 5.7. Consider the general multiple-regression equation

$$Y = A + B_1 X_1 + B_2 X_2 + \cdots + B_k X_k + E$$

An alternative procedure for calculating the least-squares coefficient B_1 is as follows:

1. Regress Y on X_2 through X_k, obtaining residuals $E_{Y|2\ldots k}$.

2. Regress X_1 on X_2 through X_k, obtaining residuals $E_{1|2\ldots k}$.

3. Regress the residuals $E_{Y|2\ldots k}$ on the residuals $E_{1|2\ldots k}$. The slope for this simple regression is the multiple-regression slope for X_1, that is, B_1.

   (a) Apply this procedure to the multiple regression of prestige on education, income, and percentage of women in the Canadian occupational prestige data, confirming that the coefficient for education is properly recovered.

   (b) Note that the intercept for the simple regression in Step 3 is 0. Why is this the case?

   (c) In light of this procedure, is it reasonable to describe B_1 as the "effect of X_1 on Y when the influence of $X_2, \ldots, X_k$ is removed from both X_1 and Y"?

   (d) The procedure in this problem reduces the multiple regression to a series of simple regressions (in Step 3). Can you see any practical application for this procedure? (See the discussion of added-variable plots in Section 11.6.1.)

Exercise 5.8. Partial correlation: The *partial correlation* between X_1 and Y "controlling for" X_2 through X_k is defined as the simple correlation between the residuals $E_{Y|2\ldots k}$ and $E_{1|2\ldots k}$, given in the previous exercise. The partial correlation is denoted $r_{Y1|2\ldots k}$.

(a) Using the Canadian occupational prestige data, calculate the partial correlation between prestige and education controlling for income and percentage women (see the previous exercise).

(b) In light of the interpretation of a partial regression coefficient developed in the previous exercise, why is $r_{Y1|2\ldots k} = 0$ if and only if B_1 (from the multiple regression of Y on X_1 through X_k) is 0?

Exercise 5.9. *Show that in simple-regression analysis, the standardized slope coefficient B^* is equal to the correlation coefficient r. (In general, however, standardized slope coefficients *are not* correlations and can be outside of the range [0, 1].)

Summary

- In simple linear regression, the least-squares coefficients are given by

$$B = \frac{\sum(X_i - \overline{X})(Y_i - \overline{Y})}{\sum(X_i - \overline{X})^2}$$

$$A = \overline{Y} - B\overline{X}$$

  The slope coefficient B represents the average change in Y associated with a one-unit increase in X. The intercept A is the fitted value of Y when $X = 0$.

- The least-squares coefficients in multiple linear regression are found by solving the normal equations for the intercept A and the slope coefficients $B_1, B_2, \ldots, B_k$. The slope coefficient B_1 represents the average change in Y associated with a one-unit increase in X_1 when the other Xs are held constant.

- The least-squares residuals, E, are uncorrelated with the fitted values, $\widehat{Y}$, and with the explanatory variables, $X_1, \ldots, X_k$.
- The linear regression decomposes the variation in Y into "explained" and "unexplained" components: $\text{TSS} = \text{RegSS} + \text{RSS}$. This decomposition is called the analysis of variance for the regression.
- The standard error of the regression, $S_E = \sqrt{\sum E_i^2 / (n - k - 1)}$, gives the "average" size of the regression residuals; the squared multiple correlation, $R^2 = \text{RegSS}/\text{TSS}$, indicates the proportion of the variation in Y that is captured by its linear regression on the Xs.
- By rescaling regression coefficients in relation to a measure of variation—such as the interquartile range or the standard deviation—standardized regression coefficients permit a limited comparison of the relative impact of incommensurable explanatory variables.

6

Statistical Inference for Regression

The previous chapter developed linear least-squares regression as a descriptive technique for fitting a linear surface to data. The subject of the present chapter, in contrast, is statistical inference. I will discuss point estimation of regression coefficients, along with elementary but powerful procedures for constructing confidence intervals and performing hypothesis tests in simple and multiple regression.[1] I will also develop two topics related to inference in regression: the distinction between empirical and structural relationships and the consequences of random measurement error in regression.

6.1 Simple Regression

6.1.1 The Simple-Regression Model

Standard statistical inference in simple regression is based on a *statistical model*, assumed to be descriptive of the population or process that is sampled:

$$Y_i = \alpha + \beta X_i + \varepsilon_i$$

The coefficients α and β are the *population regression parameters*; the central object of simple-regression analysis is to estimate these coefficients. The *error* ε_i represents the aggregated omitted causes of Y (i.e., the causes of Y beyond the explanatory variable X), other explanatory variables that could have been included in the regression model (at least in principle), measurement error in Y, and whatever component of Y is inherently random. A Greek letter, epsilon, is used for the errors because, without knowledge of the values of α and β, the errors are not directly observable. The key assumptions of the simple-regression model concern the behavior of the errors—or, equivalently, of the distribution of Y conditional on X:

- *Linearity.* The expectation of the error—that is, the average value of ε given the value of X—is 0: $E(\varepsilon_i) \equiv E(\varepsilon|x_i) = 0$. Equivalently, the expected value of the response variable is a linear function of the explanatory variable:

$$\mu_i \equiv E(Y_i) \equiv E(Y|x_i) = E(\alpha + \beta x_i + \varepsilon_i)$$
$$= \alpha + \beta x_i + E(\varepsilon_i)$$
$$= \alpha + \beta x_i + 0$$
$$= \alpha + \beta x_i$$

We can remove $\alpha + \beta x_i$ from the expectation operator because α and β are fixed parameters, while the value of X is conditionally fixed to x_i.[2]

---

[1] The focus here is on the procedures themselves: The statistical theory underlying these methods and some extensions are developed in Chapters 9 and 10.

[2] I use a lowercase x here to stress that the value x_i is fixed—either literally, as in experimental research (see below), or by conditioning on the observed value x_i of X_i.

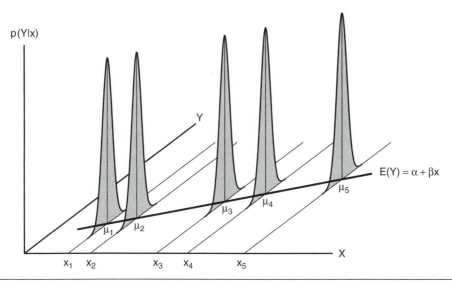

Figure 6.1   The assumptions of linearity, constant variance, and normality in simple regression. The graph shows the conditional population distributions $p(Y|x)$ of Y for several values of the explanatory variable X, labeled $x_1, \ldots, x_5$. The conditional means of Y given x are denoted $\mu_1, \ldots, \mu_5$. (Repeating Figure 2.4)

- *Constant variance.* The variance of the errors is the same regardless of the value of X: $V(\varepsilon|x_i) = \sigma_\varepsilon^2$. Because the distribution of the errors is the same as the distribution of the response variable around the population regression line, constant error variance implies constant conditional variance of Y given X:

$$V(Y|x_i) = E[(Y_i - \mu_i)^2] = E[(Y_i - \alpha - \beta x_i)^2] = E(\varepsilon_i^2) = \sigma_\varepsilon^2$$

Note that because the mean of ε_i is 0, its variance is simply $E(\varepsilon_i^2)$.

- *Normality.* The errors are normally distributed: $\varepsilon_i \sim N(0, \sigma_\varepsilon^2)$. Equivalently, the conditional distribution of the response variable is normal: $Y_i \sim N(\alpha + \beta x_i, \sigma_\varepsilon^2)$. The assumptions of linearity, constant variance, and normality are illustrated in Figure 6.1. It should be abundantly clear from the graph that these assumptions place very strong constraints on the structure of the data.

- *Independence.* The observations are sampled independently: Any pair of errors ε_i and ε_j (or, equivalently, of conditional response-variable values Y_i and Y_j) are independent for $i \neq j$. The assumption of independence needs to be justified by the procedures of data collection. For example, if the data constitute a simple random sample drawn from a large population, then the assumption of independence will be met to a close approximation. In contrast, if the data comprise a time series, then the assumption of independence may be very wrong.[3]

- *Fixed X, or X measured without error and independent of the error.* Depending on the design of a study, the values of the explanatory variable may be fixed in advance of data collection or they may be sampled along with the response variable. Fixed X corresponds almost exclusively to experimental research, in which the value of the explanatory variable is under the direct control of the researcher; if the experiment were replicated, then—at least in principle—the values of X would remain the same. Most social research, however,

---

[3]Chapter 16 discusses regression analysis with time-series data.

is observational, and therefore, X values are sampled, not fixed by design. Under these circumstances, we assume that the explanatory variable is measured without error and that the explanatory variable and the error are independent in the population from which the sample is drawn. That is, the error has the same distribution, $N(0, \sigma_\varepsilon^2)$, for every value of X in the population. This is in an important respect the most problematic of the assumptions underlying least-squares estimation because causal inference in nonexperimental research hinges on this assumption and because the assumption cannot be checked directly from the observed data.[4]

- *X is not invariant.* If the explanatory variable is fixed, then its values cannot all be the same; and if it is random, then there must be variation in X in the population. It is not possible to fit a line to data in which the explanatory variable is invariant.[5]

Standard statistical inference for least-squares simple-regression analysis is based on the statistical model $Y_i = \alpha + \beta x_i + \varepsilon_i$. The key assumptions of the model concern the behavior of the errors ε_i: (1) Linearity, $E(\varepsilon_i) = 0$; (2) constant variance, $V(\varepsilon_i) = \sigma_\varepsilon^2$; (3) normality, $\varepsilon_i \sim N(0, \sigma_\varepsilon^2)$; (4) independence, $\varepsilon_i, \varepsilon_j$ are independent for $i \neq j$; (5) the X values are fixed or, if random, are measured without error and are independent of the errors; and (6) X is not invariant.

6.1.2   Properties of the Least-Squares Estimator

Under the strong assumptions of the simple-regression model, the sample least-squares coefficients A and B have several desirable properties as estimators of the population regression coefficients α and β:[6]

- The least-squares intercept and slope are *linear estimators*, in the sense that they are linear functions of the observations Y_i. For example, for fixed explanatory-variable values x_i,

$$B = \sum_{i=1}^{n} m_i Y_i$$

where

$$m_i = \frac{x_i - \overline{x}}{\sum_{j=1}^{n}(x_j - \overline{x})^2}$$

While unimportant in itself, this property makes it simple to derive the sampling distributions of A and B.

- The sample least-squares coefficients are *unbiased estimators* of the population regression coefficients:

$$E(A) = \alpha$$
$$E(B) = \beta$$

Only the assumption of linearity is required to establish this result.[7]

---

[4] See Sections 1.2, 6.3, and 9.7 for further discussion of causal inference from observational data.

[5] See Figure 5.3 on page 81.

[6] I will simply state and briefly explain these properties here; derivations can be found in the exercises to this chapter and in Chapter 9.

[7] See Exercise 6.1.

- Both A and B have simple sampling variances:

$$V(A) = \frac{\sigma_\varepsilon^2 \sum x_i^2}{n \sum (x_i, -\overline{x})^2}$$

$$V(B) = \frac{\sigma_\varepsilon^2}{\sum (x_i - \overline{x})^2}$$

The assumptions of linearity, constant variance, and independence are employed in the derivation of these formulas.[8]

It is instructive to examine the formula for $V(B)$ more closely to understand the conditions under which least-squares estimation is precise. Rewriting the formula,

$$V(B) = \frac{\sigma_\varepsilon^2}{(n-1)S_X^2}$$

Thus, the sampling variance of the slope estimate will be small when (1) the error variance σ_ε^2 is small, (2) the sample size n is large, and (3) the explanatory-variable values are spread out (i.e., have a large variance, S_X^2). The estimate of the intercept has small sampling variance under similar circumstances and, in addition, when the X values are centered near 0 and, hence, $\sum x_i^2$ is not much larger than $\sum (x_i - \overline{x})^2$.[9]

- Of all the linear unbiased estimators, the least-squares estimators are the most efficient—that is, they have the smallest sampling variance and hence the smallest mean-squared error. This result, called the Gauss-Markov theorem, requires the assumptions of linearity, constant variance, and independence, but not the assumption of normality.[10] Under normality, moreover, the least-squares estimators are the most efficient among *all* unbiased estimators, not just among linear estimators. This is a much more compelling result, because the restriction to linear estimators is merely a matter of convenience. When the error distribution is heavier tailed than normal, for example, the least-squares estimators may be much less efficient than certain robust-regression estimators, which are *not* linear functions of the data.[11]
- Under the full suite of assumptions, the least-squares coefficients A and B are the maximum-likelihood estimators of α and β.[12]
- Under the assumption of normality, the least-squares coefficients are themselves normally distributed. Summing up,

$$A \sim N\left[\alpha, \frac{\sigma_\varepsilon^2 \sum x_i^2}{n \sum (x_i - \overline{x})^2}\right]$$

$$B \sim N\left[\beta, \frac{\sigma_\varepsilon^2}{\sum (x_i - \overline{x})^2}\right] \tag{6.1}$$

---

[8] See Exercise 6.2.

[9] See Exercise 6.3.

[10] The theorem is named after the 19th-century German mathematical genius Carl Friedrich Gauss and the 20th-century Russian mathematician A. A. Markov. Although Gauss worked in the context of measurement error in the physical sciences, much of the general statistical theory of linear models is due to him.

[11] See Chapter 19.

[12] See Exercise 6.5. For an explanation of maximum-likelihood estimation, see Appendix D on probability and estimation.

Even if the errors are not normally distributed, the distributions of A and B are approximately normal, under very broad conditions, with the approximation improving as the sample size grows.[13]

Under the assumptions of the regression model, the least-squares coefficients have certain desirable properties as estimators of the population regression coefficients. The least-squares coefficients are linear functions of the data, and therefore have simple sampling distributions; unbiased estimators of the population regression coefficients; the most efficient unbiased estimators of the population regression coefficients; maximum-likelihood estimators; and normally distributed.

6.1.3   Confidence Intervals and Hypothesis Tests

The distributions of A and B, given in Equation 6.1, cannot be directly employed for statistical inference because the error variance, σ_ε^2, is never known in practice. The variance of the residuals provides an unbiased estimator of σ_ε^2:[14]

$$S_E^2 = \frac{\sum E_i^2}{n - 2}$$

With the estimated error variance in hand, we can estimate the sampling variances of A and B:

$$\widehat{V}(A) = \frac{S_E^2 \sum x_i^2}{n \sum (x_i - \overline{x})^2}$$

$$\widehat{V}(B) = \frac{S_E^2}{\sum (x_i - \overline{x})^2}$$

As in statistical inference for the mean, the added uncertainty induced by estimating the error variance is reflected in the use of the t-distribution, in place of the normal distribution, for confidence intervals and hypothesis tests.

To construct a $100(1 - a)\%$ confidence interval for the slope, we take

$$\beta = B \pm t_{a/2}\text{SE}(B)$$

where $t_{a/2}$ is the critical value of t with $n - 2$ degrees of freedom and a probability of $a/2$ to the right, and $\text{SE}(B)$ is the standard error of B [i.e., the square root of $\widehat{V}(B)$]. For a 95% confidence interval, $t_{.025} \approx 2$, unless n is very small. Similarly, to test the hypothesis, H_0: $\beta = \beta_0$, that the population slope is equal to a specific value (most commonly, the null hypothesis H_0: $\beta = 0$), calculate the test statistic

$$t_0 = \frac{B - \beta_0}{\text{SE}(B)}$$

which is distributed as t with $n - 2$ degrees of freedom under the hypothesis H_0. Confidence intervals and hypothesis tests for α are usually of less interest, but they follow the same pattern.

---

[13] The asymptotic normality of A and B follows from the central-limit theorem, because the least-squares coefficients are linear functions of the Y_is.

[14] See Section 10.3.

> The standard error of the slope coefficient B in simple regression is $\mathrm{SE}(B) = S_E/\sqrt{\sum(x_i - \overline{x})^2}$, which can be used to construct t-tests and t-intervals for β.

For Davis's regression of measured on reported weight (described in the preceding chapter), for example, we have the following results:

$$S_E = \sqrt{\frac{418.87}{101 - 2}} = 2.0569$$

$$\mathrm{SE}(A) = \frac{2.0569 \times \sqrt{329{,}731}}{\sqrt{101 \times 4539.3}} = 1.7444$$

$$\mathrm{SE}(B) = \frac{2.0569}{\sqrt{4539.3}} = 0.030529$$

Because $t_{.025}$ for $101 - 2 = 99$ degrees of freedom is 1.9842, the 95% confidence intervals for α and β are

$$\alpha = 1.7775 \pm 1.9842 \times 1.7444 = 1.777 \pm 3.461$$
$$\beta = 0.97722 \pm 1.9842 \times 0.030529 = 0.9772 \pm 0.0606$$

The estimates of α and β are therefore quite precise. Furthermore, the confidence intervals include the values $\alpha = 0$ and $\beta = 1$, which, recall, imply unbiased prediction of measured weight from reported weight.[15]

6.2 Multiple Regression

Most of the results for multiple-regression analysis parallel those for simple regression.

6.2.1 The Multiple-Regression Model

The statistical model for multiple regression is

$$Y_i = \alpha + \beta_1 x_{i1} + \beta_2 x_{i2} + \cdots + \beta_k x_{ik} + \varepsilon_i$$

The assumptions underlying the model concern the errors, $\varepsilon_i \equiv \varepsilon | x_{i1}, \ldots, x_{ik}$, and are identical to the assumptions in simple regression:

- *Linearity:* $E(\varepsilon_i) = 0$.
- *Constant variance:* $V(\varepsilon_i) = \sigma_\varepsilon^2$.
- *Normality:* $\varepsilon_i \sim N(0, \sigma_\varepsilon^2)$.
- *Independence:* $\varepsilon_i, \varepsilon_j$ are independent for $i \neq j$.
- *Fixed Xs or Xs measured without error and independent of ε.*

In addition, we assume that the Xs are not invariant and that no X is a perfect linear function of the others.[16]

---

[15]There is, however, a subtlety here: To construct separate confidence intervals for α and β is not quite the same as constructing a *joint confidence region* for both coefficients simultaneously. See Section 9.4.4 for a discussion of confidence regions in regression.

[16]We saw in Section 5.2.1 that when explanatory variables in regression are invariant or perfectly collinear, the least-squares coefficients are not uniquely defined.

Under these assumptions (or particular subsets of them), the least-squares estimators A, $B_1, \ldots, B_k$ of $\alpha, \beta_1, \ldots, \beta_k$ are

- linear functions of the data, and hence relatively simple;
- unbiased;
- maximally efficient among unbiased estimators;
- maximum-likelihood estimators;
- normally distributed.

The slope coefficient B_j in multiple regression has sampling variance[17]

$$V(B_j) = \frac{1}{1 - R_j^2} \times \frac{\sigma_\varepsilon^2}{\sum_{i=1}^{n}(x_{ij} - \overline{x}_j)^2}$$

$$= \frac{\sigma_\varepsilon^2}{\sum_{i=1}^{n}(x_{ij} - \widehat{x}_{ij})^2} \qquad (6.2)$$

where R_j^2 is the squared multiple correlation from the regression of X_j on all the other Xs, and the $\widehat{x}_{ij}$ are the fitted values from this auxiliary regression. The second factor in the first line of Equation 6.2 is similar to the sampling variance of the slope in simple regression, although the error variance σ_ε^2 is smaller than before because some of the explanatory variables that were implicitly in the error in simple regression are now incorporated into the systematic part of the model. The first factor—called the *variance-inflation factor*—is new, however. The variance-inflation factor $1/(1 - R_j^2)$ is large when the explanatory variable X_j is strongly correlated with other explanatory variables. The denominator in the second line of Equation 6.2 is the residual sum of squares from the regression of X_j on the other Xs, and it makes a similar point: When the *conditional* variation in X_j given the other Xs is small, the sampling variance of B_j is large.[18]

We saw in Chapter 5 that when one explanatory variable is perfectly collinear with others, the least-squares regression coefficients are not uniquely determined; in this case, the variance-inflation factor is infinite. The variance-inflation factor tells us that strong, though less-than-perfect, collinearity presents a problem for estimation, for although we can calculate least-squares estimates under these circumstances, their sampling variances may be very large. Equation 6.2 reveals that the other sources of imprecision of estimation in multiple regression are the same as in simple regression: large error variance, a small sample, and explanatory variables with little variation.[19]

6.2.2 Confidence Intervals and Hypothesis Tests

Individual Slope Coefficients

Confidence intervals and hypothesis tests for individual coefficients closely follow the pattern of simple-regression analysis: To find the standard error of a slope coefficient, we need to substitute an estimate of the error variance for the unknown σ_ε^2 in Equation 6.2. The variance of the residuals provides an unbiased estimator:

$$S_E^2 = \frac{\sum E_i^2}{n - k - 1}$$

---

[17]Although we are usually less interested in inference about α, it is also possible to find the sampling variance of the intercept A. See Section 9.3.

[18]I am grateful to Georges Monette of York University for pointing this out to me.

[19]Collinearity is discussed further in Chapter 13.

Then, the standard error of B_j is

$$SE(B_j) = \frac{1}{\sqrt{1 - R_j^2}} \times \frac{S_E}{\sqrt{\sum(x_{ij} - \overline{x}_j)^2}}$$

Confidence intervals and tests, based on the t-distribution with $n - k - 1$ degrees of freedom, follow straightforwardly.

> The standard error of the slope coefficient B_j in multiple regression is $SE(B_j) = S_E/\sqrt{(1 - R_j^2)\sum(x_{ij} - \overline{x}_j)^2}$. The coefficient standard error can be used in t-intervals and t-tests for β_j.

For example, for Duncan's regression of occupational prestige on education and income (from the previous chapter), we have

$$S_E^2 = \frac{7506.7}{45 - 2 - 1} = 178.73$$

$$r_{12} = .72451$$

$$SE(B_1) = \frac{1}{\sqrt{1 - .72451^2}} \times \frac{\sqrt{178.73}}{\sqrt{38,971}} = 0.098252$$

$$SE(B_2) = \frac{1}{\sqrt{1 - .72451^2}} \times \frac{\sqrt{178.73}}{\sqrt{26,271}} = 0.11967$$

With only two explanatory variables, $R_1^2 = R_2^2 = r_{12}^2$; this simplicity and symmetry are peculiar to the two-explanatory-variable case. To construct 95% confidence intervals for the slope coefficients, we use $t_{.025} = 2.0181$ from the t-distribution with $45 - 2 - 1 = 42$ degrees of freedom. Then,

Education : $\beta_1 = 0.54583 \pm 2.0181 \times 0.098252 = 0.5459 \pm 0.1983$
Income : $\beta_2 = 0.59873 \pm 2.0181 \times 0.11967 = 0.5987 \pm 0.2415$

Although they are far from 0, these confidence intervals are quite broad, indicating that the estimates of the education and income coefficients are imprecise—as is to be expected in a sample of only 45 occupations.

All Slopes

We can also test the null hypothesis that all the regression slopes are 0:

$$H_0: \beta_1 = \beta_2 = \cdots = \beta_k = 0 \tag{6.3}$$

Testing this global or "omnibus" null hypothesis is not quite the same as testing the k separate hypotheses

$$H_0^{(1)}: \beta_1 = 0; \ H_0^{(2)}: \beta_2 = 0; \ \ldots \ ; \ H_0^{(k)}: \beta_k = 0$$

If the explanatory variables are very highly correlated, for example, we might be able to reject the omnibus hypothesis (Equation 6.3) without being able to reject *any* of the individual hypotheses.

An F-test for the omnibus null hypothesis is given by

$$F_0 = \frac{\text{RegSS}/k}{\text{RSS}/(n - k - 1)}$$

$$= \frac{n - k - 1}{k} \times \frac{R^2}{1 - R^2}$$

Under the omnibus null hypothesis, this test statistic has an F-distribution with k and $n - k - 1$ degrees of freedom. The omnibus F-test follows from the analysis of variance for the regression, and the calculation of the test statistic can be organized in an *analysis-of-variance table*, which shows the partition of total variation into its components:

Source	Sum of Squares	df	Mean Square	F
Regression	RegSS	k	$\dfrac{\text{RegSS}}{k}$	$\dfrac{\text{RegMS}}{\text{RMS}}$
Residuals	RSS	$n-k-1$	$\dfrac{\text{RSS}}{n-k-1}$	
Total	TSS	$n - 1$		

Note that the degrees of freedom (*df*) add in the same manner as the sums of squares and that the *residual mean square*, RMS, is simply the estimated error variance, S_E^2.

It turns out that when the null hypothesis is true, the *regression mean square*, *RegMS*, provides an independent estimate of the error variance, so the ratio of the two mean squares should be close to 1. When, alternatively, the null hypothesis is false, the RegMS estimates the error variance plus a positive quantity that depends on the βs, tending to make the numerator of F_0 larger than the denominator:

$$E(F_0) \approx \frac{E(\text{RegMS})}{E(\text{RMS})} = \frac{\sigma_\varepsilon^2 + \text{positive quantity}}{\sigma_\varepsilon^2} > 1$$

We consequently reject the omnibus null hypothesis for values of F_0 that are sufficiently larger than 1.[20]

> An omnibus F-test for the null hypothesis that all the slopes are 0 can be calculated from the analysis of variance for the regression.

---

[20]The reasoning here is only approximate because the expectation of the ratio of two independent random variables is not the ratio of their expectations. Nevertheless, when the sample size is large, the null distribution of the F-statistic has an expectation very close to 1. See Appendix D on probability and estimation for information about the F-distribution.

For Duncan's regression, we have the following analysis-of-variance table:

Source	Sum of Squares	df	Mean Square	F	p
Regression	36181.	2	18090.	101.2	≪.0001
Residuals	7506.7	42	178.73		
Total	43688.	44			

The p-value for the omnibus null hypothesis—that is, $\Pr(F > 101.2)$ for an F-distribution with 2 and 42 degrees of freedom—is very close to 0.

A Subset of Slopes

It is, finally, possible to test a null hypothesis about a *subset* of the regression slopes

$$H_0: \beta_1 = \beta_2 = \cdots = \beta_q = 0 \tag{6.4}$$

where $1 \leq q \leq k$. Purely for notational convenience, I have specified a hypothesis on the *first* q coefficients; we can, of course, equally easily test a hypothesis for *any* q slopes. The "full" regression model, including all the explanatory variables, can be written as

$$Y_i = \alpha + \beta_1 x_{i1} + \cdots + \beta_q x_{iq} + \beta_{q+1} x_{i,q+1} + \cdots + \beta_k x_{ik} + \varepsilon_i$$

If the null hypothesis is correct, then the first q of the βs are 0, yielding the "null" model

$$Y_i = \alpha + 0 x_{i1} + \cdots + 0 x_{iq} + \beta_{q+1} x_{i,q+1} + \cdots + \beta_k x_{ik} + \varepsilon_i$$
$$= \alpha + \beta_{q+1} x_{i,q+1} + \cdots + \beta_k x_{ik} + \varepsilon_i$$

In effect, then, the null model omits the first q explanatory variables, regressing Y on the remaining $k - q$ explanatory variables.

An F-test of the null hypothesis in Equation 6.4 is based on a comparison of these two models. Let RSS_1 and $RegSS_1$ represent, respectively, the residual and regression sums of squares for the full model; similarly, RSS_0 and $RegSS_0$ are the residual and regression sums of squares for the null model. Because the null model is *nested within* (i.e., is a special case of) the full model, constraining the first q slopes to 0, $RSS_0 \geq RSS_1$. The residual and regression sums of squares in the two models add to the same total sum of squares; it follows that $RegSS_0 \leq RegSS_1$. If the null hypothesis is wrong and (some of) $\beta_1, \ldots, \beta_q$ are nonzero, then the *incremental* (or "*extra*") *sum of squares* due to fitting the additional explanatory variables

$$RSS_0 - RSS_1 = RegSS_1 - RegSS_0$$

should be large.

The F-statistic for testing the null hypothesis in Equation 6.4 is

$$F_0 = \frac{(RegSS_1 - RegSS_0)/q}{RSS_1/(n - k - 1)}$$
$$= \frac{n - k - 1}{q} \times \frac{R_1^2 - R_0^2}{1 - R_1^2}$$

where R_1^2 and R_0^2 are the squared multiple correlations from the full and null models, respectively. Under the null hypothesis, this test statistic has an F-distribution with q and $n - k - 1$ degrees of freedom.

> An F-test for the null hypothesis that a subset of slope coefficients is 0 is based on a comparison of the regression sums of squares for two models: the full regression model and a null model that deletes the explanatory variables in the null hypothesis.

The motivation for testing a subset of coefficients will become clear in the next chapter, which takes up regression models that incorporate qualitative explanatory variables. I will, for the present, illustrate the incremental F-test by applying it to the trivial case in which $q = 1$ (i.e., a single coefficient).

In Duncan's data set, the regression of prestige on income alone produces $\text{RegSS}_0 = 30{,}665$, while the regression of prestige on both income and education produces $\text{RegSS}_1 = 36{,}181$ and $\text{RSS}_1 = 7506.7$. Consequently, the incremental sum of squares due to education is $36{,}181 - 30{,}665 = 5516$. The F-statistic for testing H_0: $\beta_{\text{Education}} = 0$ is, then,

$$F_0 = \frac{5516/1}{7506.7/(45 - 2 - 1)} = 30.86$$

with 1 and 42 degrees of freedom, for which $p < .0001$.

When, as here, $q = 1$, the incremental F-test is equivalent to the t-test obtained by dividing the regression coefficient by its estimated standard error: $F_0 = t_0^2$. For the current example,

$$t_0 = \frac{0.54583}{0.098252} = 5.5554$$

$$t_0^2 = 5.5554^2 = 30.86$$

(which is the same as F_0).

6.3 Empirical Versus Structural Relations

There are two fundamentally different interpretations of regression coefficients, and failure to distinguish clearly between them is the source of much confusion. Borrowing Goldberger's (1973) terminology, we may interpret a regression descriptively, as an *empirical association* among variables, or causally, as a *structural relation* among variables.

I will deal first with empirical associations because the notion is simpler. Suppose that, in a population of interest, the relationship between two variables, Y and X_1, is well described by the simple-regression model:[21]

$$Y = \alpha' + \beta_1' X_1 + \varepsilon'$$

That is to say, the conditional mean of Y is a linear function of X. We do not assume that X_1 necessarily causes Y or, if it does, that the omitted causes of Y, incorporated in ε', are independent of X_1. There is, quite simply, a linear empirical relationship between Y and X_1 in the population. If we proceed to draw a random sample from this population, then the least-squares sample slope B_1' is an unbiased estimator of β_1'.

Suppose, now, that we introduce a second explanatory variable, X_2, and that, in the same sense as before, the population relationship between Y and the two Xs is linear:

$$Y = \alpha + \beta_1 X_1 + \beta_2 X_2 + \varepsilon$$

---

[21]Because this discussion applies to observational data, where the explanatory variables are random, I use uppercase Xs.

That is, the conditional mean of Y is a linear function of X_1 and X_2. The slope β_1 of the population regression plane can, and generally will, differ from β_1', the simple-regression slope (see below). The sample least-squares coefficients for the multiple regression, B_1 and B_2, are unbiased estimators of the corresponding population coefficients, β_1 and β_2.

That the simple-regression slope β_1' differs from the multiple-regression slope β_1 and that, therefore, the sample *simple*-regression coefficient B_1' is a *biased* estimator of the population *multiple*-regression slope β_1 is not problematic, for these are simply empirical relationships, and we do not, in this context, interpret a regression coefficient as the *effect* of an explanatory variable on the response variable. The issue of *specification error*—fitting a false model to the data—does not arise, as long as the linear regression model adequately describes the empirical relationship between the response variable and the explanatory variables in the population. This would not be the case, for example, if the relationship in the population were nonlinear.

The situation is different, however, if we view the regression equation as representing a structural relation—that is, a model of how response-variable scores are determined.[22] Imagine now that response-variable scores are *constructed* according to the multiple-regression model

$$Y = \alpha + \beta_1 X_1 + \beta_2 X_2 + \varepsilon \tag{6.5}$$

where the error ε satisfies the usual regression assumptions; in particular, $E(\varepsilon) = 0$ and ε is independent of X_1 and X_2.

If we use least squares to fit this model to sample data, we obtain unbiased estimators of β_1 and β_2. Suppose, however, that instead we fit the simple-regression model

$$Y = \alpha + \beta_1 X_1 + \varepsilon' \tag{6.6}$$

where, implicitly, the effect of X_2 on Y is absorbed by the error $\varepsilon' \equiv \varepsilon + \beta_2 X_2$ because X_2 is now among the omitted causes of Y. In the event that X_1 and X_2 are correlated, there is a correlation induced between X_1 and ε'. If we proceed to assume wrongly that X_1 and ε' are *uncorrelated*, as we do if we fit the model in Equation 6.6 by least squares, then we make an error of specification. The consequence of this error is that our simple-regression estimator of β_1 is biased: Because X_1 and X_2 are correlated and because X_2 is omitted from the model, part of the effect of X_2 is mistakenly attributed to X_1.

To make the nature of this specification error more precise, let us take the expectation of both sides of Equation 6.5, obtaining

$$\mu_Y = \alpha + \beta_1 \mu_1 + \beta_2 \mu_2 + 0 \tag{6.7}$$

where, for example, μ_Y is the population mean of Y; to obtain Equation 6.7, we use the fact that $E(\varepsilon)$ is 0. Subtracting this equation from Equation 6.5 has the effect of eliminating the constant α and expressing the variables as deviations from their population means:

$$Y - \mu_Y = \beta_1(X_1 - \mu_1) + \beta_2(X_2 - \mu_2) + \varepsilon$$

Next, multiply this equation through by $X_1 - \mu_1$:

$$(X_1 - \mu_1)(Y - \mu_Y) = \beta_1(X_1 - \mu_1)^2 + \beta_2(X_1 - \mu_1)(X_2 - \mu_2) + (X_1 - \mu_1)\varepsilon$$

Taking the expectation of both sides of the equation produces

$$\sigma_{1Y} = \beta_1 \sigma_1^2 + \beta_2 \sigma_{12}$$

---

[22] In the interest of clarity, I am making this distinction more categorically than I believe is justified. I argued in Chapter 1 that it is unreasonable to treat statistical models as literal representations of social processes. Nevertheless, it is useful to distinguish between purely empirical descriptions and descriptions from which we intend to infer causation.

where σ_{1Y} is the covariance between X_1 and Y, σ_1^2 is the variance of X_1, and σ_{12} is the covariance of X_1 and X_2.[23] Solving for β_1, we get

$$\beta_1 = \frac{\sigma_{1Y}}{\sigma_1^2} - \beta_2 \frac{\sigma_{12}}{\sigma_1^2} \qquad (6.8)$$

Recall that the least-squares coefficient for the simple regression of Y on X_1 is $B = S_{1Y}/S_1^2$. The simple regression therefore estimates not β_1 but rather $\sigma_{1Y}/\sigma_1^2 \equiv \beta_1'$. Solving Equation 6.8 for β_1' produces $\beta_1' = \beta_1 +$ bias, where bias $= \beta_2 \sigma_{12}/\sigma_1^2$.

It is instructive to take a closer look at the bias in the simple-regression estimator. For the bias to be nonzero, two conditions must be met: (1) X_2 must be a *relevant* explanatory variable—that is, $\beta_2 \neq 0$; and (2) X_1 and X_2 must be *correlated*—that is, $\sigma_{12} \neq 0$. Moreover, depending on the signs of β_2 and σ_{12}, the bias in the simple-regression estimator may be either positive or negative.

It is important to distinguish between interpreting a regression descriptively, as an empirical association among variables, and structurally, as specifying causal relations among variables. In the latter event, but not in the former, it is sensible to speak of bias produced by omitting an explanatory variable that (1) is a cause of Y, and (2) is correlated with an explanatory variable in the regression equation. Bias in least-squares estimation results from the correlation that is induced between the included explanatory variable and the error by incorporating the omitted explanatory variable in the error.

There is one final subtlety: The proper interpretation of the "bias" in the simple-regression estimator depends on the nature of the causal relationship between X_1 and X_2. Consider the situation depicted in Figure 6.2(a), where X_2 *intervenes* causally between X_1 and Y. Here, the bias term $\beta_2 \sigma_{12}/\sigma_1^2$ is simply the *indirect effect* of X_1 on Y transmitted through X_2, because σ_{12}/σ_1^2 is the population slope for the regression of X_2 on X_1. If, however, as in Figure 6.2(b), X_2 is a *common prior cause* of both X_1 and Y, then the bias term represents a *spurious*—that is, noncausal—component of the empirical association between X_1 and Y. In the latter event, but not in the former, it is critical to control for X_2 in examining the relationship between Y and X_1.[24] An omitted common prior cause that accounts (or partially accounts) for the association between two variables is sometimes called a "lurking variable." It is the always-possible existence of lurking variables that makes it difficult to infer causation from observational data.

6.4 Measurement Error in Explanatory Variables* _____

Variables are rarely—if ever—measured without error.[25] Even relatively straightforward characteristics, such as education, income, height, and weight, are imperfectly measured, especially

---

[23]This result follows from the observation that the expectation of a mean-deviation product is a covariance, and the expectation of a mean-deviation square is a variance (see Appendix D on probability and estimation). $E[(X_1 - \mu_1)\varepsilon] = \sigma_{1\varepsilon}$ is 0 because of the independence of X_1 and the error.

[24]Note that panels (a) and (b) in Figure 6.2 simply exchange the roles of X_1 and X_2.

[25]Indeed, one of the historical sources of statistical theory in the 18th and 19th centuries was the investigation of measurement errors in the physical sciences by great mathematicians like Gauss (mentioned previously) and Pierre Simon Laplace.

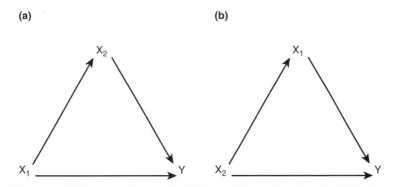

Figure 6.2   Two causal schemes relating a response variable to two explanatory variables: In
(a) X_2 intervenes causally between X_1 and Y, while in (b) X_2 is a common prior cause
of both X_1 and Y. In the second case, but not in the first, it is important to control for
X_2 in examining the effect of X_1 on Y.

when we rely on individuals' verbal reports. Measures of "subjective" characteristics, such as
racial prejudice and conservatism, almost surely have substantial components of error. Measurement error affects not only characteristics of individuals: As you are likely aware, official statistics
relating to crime, the economy, and so on, are also subject to a variety of measurement errors.

The regression model accommodates measurement error in the *response* variable, because
measurement error can be conceptualized as a component of the general error term ε, but the
explanatory variables in regression analysis are assumed to be measured without error. In this
section, I will explain the consequences of violating this assumption. To do so, we will examine
the multiple-regression equation

$$Y = \beta_1 \tau + \beta_2 X_2 + \varepsilon \tag{6.9}$$

To keep the notation as simple as possible, all the variables in Equation 6.9 are expressed as
deviations from their expectations, so the constant term disappears from the regression equation.[26]
One of the explanatory variables, X_2, is measured without error, but the other, τ, is not directly
observable. Instead, we have a fallible *indicator* X_1 of τ:

$$X_1 = \tau + \delta \tag{6.10}$$

where δ represents measurement error.

In addition to the usual assumptions about the regression errors ε, I will assume that the
measurement errors δ are "random" and "well behaved"; in particular,

- $E(\delta) = 0$, so there is no systematic tendency for measurements to be too large or too small.
- The measurement errors δ are uncorrelated with the "true-score" variable τ. This assumption
  could easily be wrong. If, for example, individuals who are lighter than average tend to
  overreport their weights and individuals who are heavier than average tend to underreport
  their weights, then there will be a negative correlation between the measurement errors and
  true weight.
- The measurement errors δ are uncorrelated with the regression errors ε and with the other
  explanatory variable X_2.

---

[26]There is no loss of generality here, because we can always subtract the mean from each variable. See the previous
section.

Because $\tau = X_1 - \delta$, we can rewrite Equation 6.9 as

$$\begin{aligned} Y &= \beta_1(X_1 - \delta) + \beta_2 X_2 + \varepsilon \\ &= \beta_1 X_1 + \beta_2 X_2 + (\varepsilon - \beta_1 \delta) \end{aligned} \tag{6.11}$$

As in the previous section, we can proceed by multiplying Equation 6.11 through by X_1 and X_2 and taking expectations; because all variables are in mean-deviation form, expected products are covariances and expected squares are variances:[27]

$$\begin{aligned} \sigma_{Y1} &= \beta_1 \sigma_1^2 + \beta_2 \sigma_{12} - \beta_1 \sigma_\delta^2 \\ \sigma_{Y2} &= \beta_1 \sigma_{12} + \beta_2 \sigma_2^2 \end{aligned} \tag{6.12}$$

Then, solving for the regression coefficients,

$$\begin{aligned} \beta_1 &= \frac{\sigma_{Y1}\sigma_2^2 - \sigma_{12}\sigma_{Y2}}{\sigma_1^2\sigma_2^2 - \sigma_{12}^2 - \sigma_\delta^2\sigma_2^2} \\ \beta_2 &= \frac{\sigma_{Y2}\sigma_1^2 - \sigma_{12}\sigma_{Y1}}{\sigma_1^2\sigma_2^2 - \sigma_{12}^2} - \frac{\beta_1\sigma_{12}\sigma_\delta^2}{\sigma_1^2\sigma_2^2 - \sigma_{12}^2} \end{aligned} \tag{6.13}$$

Suppose, now, that we (temporarily) ignore the measurement error in X_1, and proceed by least-squares regression of Y on X_1 and X_2. The population analogs of the least-squares regression coefficients are as follows:[28]

$$\begin{aligned} \beta_1' &= \frac{\sigma_{Y1}\sigma_2^2 - \sigma_{12}\sigma_{Y2}}{\sigma_1^2\sigma_2^2 - \sigma_{12}^2} \\ \beta_2' &= \frac{\sigma_{Y2}\sigma_1^2 - \sigma_{12}\sigma_{Y1}}{\sigma_1^2\sigma_2^2 - \sigma_{12}^2} \end{aligned} \tag{6.14}$$

Comparing Equations 6.13 and 6.14 reveals the consequences of ignoring the measurement error in X_1. The denominator of β_1 in Equation 6.13 is necessarily positive, and its component $-\sigma_\delta^2\sigma_2^2$ is necessarily negative. Ignoring this component therefore inflates the denominator of β_1' in Equation 6.14, driving the coefficient β_1' toward 0. Put another way, ignoring measurement error in an explanatory variable tends to *attenuate* its coefficient, which makes intuitive sense.

The effect of measurement error in X_1 on the coefficient of X_2 is even more pernicious. Here, we can write $\beta_2' = \beta_2 + \text{bias}$, where

$$\text{bias} = \frac{\beta_1\sigma_{12}\sigma_\delta^2}{\sigma_1^2\sigma_2^2 - \sigma_{12}^2}$$

The bias term can be positive or negative, toward 0 or away from it. To get a better grasp on the bias in the least-squares *estimand* β_2', imagine that the measurement error variance σ_δ^2 grows larger and larger. Because σ_δ^2 is a component of σ_1^2, this latter quantity also grows larger, but because the measurement errors δ are uncorrelated with variables other than X_1, other variances and covariances are unaffected.[29]

---

[27] See Exercise 6.10.

[28] See Exercise 6.11.

[29] See Exercise 6.12.

Using Equation 6.14,

$$\lim_{\sigma_\delta^2 \to \infty} \beta_2' = \frac{\sigma_{Y2}\sigma_1^2}{\sigma_1^2\sigma_2^2} = \frac{\sigma_{Y2}}{\sigma_2^2}$$

which is the population analog of the least-squares slope for the *simple* regression of Y on X_2 alone. Once more, the result is simple and intuitively plausible: Substantial measurement error in X_1 renders it an ineffective statistical control, driving β_2' toward the marginal relationship between X_2 and Y, and away from the partial relationship between these two variables.[30]

> Measurement error in an explanatory variable tends to attenuate its regression coefficient and to make the variable an imperfect statistical control.

Although there are statistical methods that attempt to estimate regression equations taking account of measurement errors, these methods are beyond the scope of the presentation in this book and, in any event, involve assumptions that are difficult to justify in practice.[31] Perhaps the most important lessons to be drawn from the results of this section are (1) that large measurement errors in the Xs can invalidate a regression analysis; (2) that, therefore, where measurement errors are likely to be substantial, we should not view the results of a regression as definitive; and (3) that it is worthwhile to expend effort to improve the quality of social measurements.

Exercises

Exercise 6.1. *Demonstrate the unbias of the least-squares estimators A and B of α and β in simple regression:

(a) Expressing the least-squares slope B as a linear function of the observations, $B = \sum m_i Y_i$ (as in the text), and using the assumption of linearity, $E(Y_i) = \alpha + \beta x_i$, show that $E(B) = \beta$. [*Hint*: $E(B) = \sum m_i E(Y_i)$.]
(b) Show that A can also be written as a linear function of the Y_is. Then, show that $E(A) = \alpha$.

Exercise 6.2. *Using the assumptions of linearity, constant variance, and independence, along with the fact that A and B can each be expressed as a linear function of the Y_is, derive the sampling variances of A and B in simple regression. [*Hint*: $V(B) = \sum m_i^2 V(Y_i)$.]

Exercise 6.3. Examining the formula for the sampling variance of A in simple regression,

$$V(A) = \frac{\sigma_\varepsilon^2 \sum x_i^2}{n \sum (x_i - \overline{x})^2}$$

why is it intuitively sensible that the variance of A is large when the mean of the xs is far from 0? Illustrate your explanation with a graph.

---

[30]I am grateful to Georges Monette, of York University, for this insight. See Exercise 6.13 for an illustration.

[31]Measurement errors in explanatory variables are often discussed in the context of *structural-equation models*, which are multiple-equation regression models in which the response variable in one equation can appear as an explanatory variable in others. Duncan (1975, Chapters 9 and 10) presents a fine elementary treatment of the topic, part of which I have adapted for the presentation in this section. A more advanced development may be found in Bollen (1989).

Exercise 6.4. The formula for the sampling variance of B in simple regression,

$$V(B) = \frac{\sigma_\varepsilon^2}{\sum(x_i - \bar{x})^2}$$

shows that, to estimate β precisely, it helps to have spread out xs. Explain why this result is intuitively sensible, illustrating your explanation with a graph. What happens to $V(B)$ when there is *no* variation in X?

Exercise 6.5. *Maximum-likelihood estimation of the simple-regression model: Deriving the maximum-likelihood estimators of α and β in simple regression is straightforward. Under the assumptions of the model, the Y_is are independently and normally distributed random variables with expectations $\alpha + \beta x_i$ and common variance σ_ε^2. Show that if these assumptions hold, then the least-squares coefficients A and B are the maximum-likelihood estimators of α and β and that $\widehat{\sigma}_\varepsilon^2 = \sum E_i^2/n$ is the maximum-likelihood estimator of σ_ε^2. Note that the MLE of the error variance is biased. (*Hints:* Because of the assumption of independence, the joint probability density for the Y_is is the product of their marginal probability densities

$$p(y_i) = \frac{1}{\sqrt{2\pi\sigma_\varepsilon^2}} \exp\left[-\frac{(y_i - \alpha - \beta x_i)^2}{2\sigma_\varepsilon^2}\right]$$

Find the log-likelihood function; take the partial derivatives of the log likelihood with respect to the parameters α, β, and σ_ε^2; set these partial derivatives to 0; and solve for the maximum-likelihood estimators.) A more general result is proved in Section 9.3.3

Exercise 6.6. Linear transformation of X and Y in simple regression (continuation of Exercise 5.4):

(a) Suppose that the X values in Davis's regression of measured on reported weight are transformed according to the equation $X' = 10(X - 1)$ and that Y is regressed on X'. Without redoing the regression calculations in detail, find $SE(B')$ and $t_0' = B'/SE(B')$.

(b) Now, suppose that the Y values are transformed according to the equation $Y'' = 5(Y + 2)$ and that Y'' is regressed on X. Find $SE(B'')$ and $t_0'' = B''/SE(B'')$.

(c) In general, how are hypothesis tests and confidence intervals for β affected by linear transformations of X and Y?

Exercise 6.7. Consider the regression model $Y = \alpha + \beta_1 x_1 + \beta_2 x_2 + \varepsilon$. How can the incremental-sum-of-squares approach be used to test the hypothesis that the two population slopes are equal to each other, H_0: $\beta_1 = \beta_2$? [*Hint:* Under H_0, the model becomes $Y = \alpha + \beta x_1 + \beta x_2 + \varepsilon = Y = \alpha + \beta(x_1 + x_2) + \varepsilon$, where β is the common value of β_1 and β_2.] Under what circumstances would a hypothesis of this form be meaningful? (*Hint:* Consider the units of measurement of x_1 and x_2.) Now, test the hypothesis that the "population" regression coefficients for education and income in Duncan's occupational prestige regression are equal to each other. Is this test sensible?

Exercise 6.8. Examples of specification error (also see the discussion in Section 9.7):

(a) Describe a nonexperimental research situation—real or contrived—in which failure to control statistically for an omitted variable induces a correlation between the error and an explanatory variable, producing erroneous conclusions. (For example: An educational researcher discovers that university students who study more get lower grades on average; the researcher concludes that studying has an adverse effect on students' grades.)

(b) Describe an experiment—real or contrived—in which faulty experimental practice induces an explanatory variable to become correlated with the error, compromising the validity of the results produced by the experiment. (For example: In an experimental study of a promising new therapy for depression, doctors administering the treatments tend to use the new therapy with patients for whom more traditional approaches have failed; it is discovered that subjects receiving the new treatment tend to do worse, on average, than those receiving older treatments or a placebo; the researcher concludes that the new treatment is not effective.)

(c) Is it fair to conclude that a researcher is *never* able absolutely to rule out the possibility that an explanatory variable of interest is correlated with the error? Is experimental research no better than observational research in this respect? Explain your answer.

Exercise 6.9. Suppose that the "true" model generating a set of data is $Y = \alpha + \beta_1 X_1 + \varepsilon$, where the error ε conforms to the usual linear-regression assumptions. A researcher fits the model $Y = \alpha + \beta_1 X_1 + \beta_2 X_2 + \varepsilon$, which includes the irrelevant explanatory variable X_2—that is, the true value of β_2 is 0. Had the researcher fit the (correct) simple-regression model, the variance of B_1 would have been $V(B_1) = \sigma_\varepsilon^2 / \sum(X_{i1} - \overline{X}_1)^2$.

(a) Is the model $Y = \alpha + \beta_1 X_1 + \beta_2 X_2 + \varepsilon$ wrong? Is B_1 for this model a biased estimator of β_1?

(b) The variance of B_1 in the multiple-regression model is

$$V(B_1) = \frac{1}{1 - r_{12}^2} \times \frac{\sigma_\varepsilon^2}{\sum(X_{i1} - \overline{X}_1)^2}$$

What, then, is the cost of including the irrelevant explanatory variable X_2? How does this cost compare to that of *failing* to include a relevant explanatory variable?

Exercise 6.10. *Derive Equation 6.12 by multiplying Equation 6.11 through by each of X_1 and X_2. (*Hints:* Both X_1 and X_2 are uncorrelated with the regression error ε. Likewise, X_2 is uncorrelated with the measurement error δ. Show that the covariance of X_1 and δ is simply the measurement error variance σ_δ^2 by multiplying $X_1 = \tau + \delta$ through by δ and taking expectations.)

Exercise 6.11. *Show that the population analogs of the regression coefficients can be written as in Equation 6.14. (*Hint:* Ignore the measurement errors, and derive the population analogs of the normal equations by multiplying the "model" $Y = \beta_1 X_1 + \beta_2 X_2 + \varepsilon$ through by each of X_1 and X_2 and taking expectations.)

Exercise 6.12. *Show that the variance of $X_1 = \tau + \delta$ can be written as the sum of "true-score variance," σ_τ^2, and measurement error variance, σ_δ^2. (*Hint:* Square both sides of Equation 6.10 and take expectations.)

Exercise 6.13. Recall Duncan's regression of occupational prestige on the educational and income levels of occupations. Following Duncan, regress prestige on education and income. Also, perform a simple regression of prestige on income alone. Then add random measurement errors to education. Sample these measurement errors from a normal distribution with mean 0, repeating the exercise for each of the following measurement error variances: $\sigma_\delta^2 = 10^2, 25^2, 50^2, 100^2$. In each case, recompute the regression of prestige on income and education. Then, treating the initial multiple regression as corresponding to $\sigma_\delta^2 = 0$, plot the coefficients of education and income as a function of σ_δ^2. What happens to the education coefficient as measurement error in education grows? What happens to the income coefficient?

Summary

- Standard statistical inference for least-squares regression analysis is based on the statistical model

$$Y_i = \alpha + \beta_1 x_{i1} + \cdots + \beta_k x_{ik} + \varepsilon_i$$

The key assumptions of the model concern the behavior of the errors ε_i:

  1. *Linearity:* $E(\varepsilon_i) = 0$.

  2. *Constant variance:* $V(\varepsilon_i) = \sigma_\varepsilon^2$.

  3. *Normality:* $\varepsilon_i \sim N(0, \sigma_\varepsilon^2)$.

  4. *Independence:* $\varepsilon_i, \varepsilon_j$ are independent for $i \neq j$.

  5. The X values are fixed or, if random, are measured without error and are independent of the errors.

In addition, we assume that the Xs are not invariant, and that no X is a perfect linear function of the others.

- Under these assumptions, or particular subsets of them, the least-squares coefficients have certain desirable properties as estimators of the population regression coefficients. The least-squares coefficients are

  1. linear functions of the data and therefore have simple sampling distributions,

  2. unbiased estimators of the population regression coefficients,

  3. the most efficient unbiased estimators of the population regression coefficients,

  4. maximum-likelihood estimators, and

  5. normally distributed.

- The standard error of the slope coefficient B in simple regression is

$$SE(B) = \frac{S_E}{\sqrt{\sum (x_i - \overline{x})^2}}$$

The standard error of the slope coefficient B_j in multiple regression is

$$SE(B_j) = \frac{1}{\sqrt{1 - R_j^2}} \times \frac{S_E}{\sqrt{\sum (x_{ij} - \overline{x}_j)^2}}$$

In both cases, these standard errors can be used in t-intervals and t-tests for the corresponding population slope coefficients.

- An F-test for the omnibus null hypothesis that all the slopes are 0 can be calculated from the analysis of variance for the regression

$$F_0 = \frac{RegSS/k}{RSS/(n - k - 1)}$$

The omnibus F-statistic has k and $n - k - 1$ degrees of freedom.

- There is an incremental F-test for the null hypothesis that a subset of q slope coefficients is 0. This test is based on a comparison of the regression sums of squares for the full regression model (model 1) and for a null model (model 0) that deletes the explanatory variables in the null hypothesis:

$$F_0 = \frac{(\mathrm{RegSS}_1 - \mathrm{RegSS}_0)/q}{\mathrm{RSS}_1/(n - k - 1)}$$

This F-statistic has q and $n - k - 1$ degrees of freedom.
- It is important to distinguish between interpreting a regression descriptively, as an empirical association among variables, and structurally, as specifying causal relations among variables. In the latter event, but not in the former, it is sensible to speak of bias produced by omitting an explanatory variable that (1) is a cause of Y and (2) is correlated with an explanatory variable in the regression equation. Bias in least-squares estimation results from the correlation that is induced between the included explanatory variable and the error by incorporating the omitted explanatory variable in the error.
- Measurement error in an explanatory variable tends to attenuate its regression coefficient and to make the variable an imperfect statistical control.

7

Dummy-Variable Regression

One of the serious limitations of multiple-regression analysis, as presented in Chapters 5 and 6, is that it accommodates only quantitative response and explanatory variables. In this chapter and the next, I will explain how qualitative explanatory variables, called *factors*, can be incorporated into a linear model.[1]

The current chapter begins with an explanation of how a *dummy-variable regressor* can be coded to represent a *dichotomous* (i.e., two-category) factor. I proceed to show how a set of dummy regressors can be employed to represent a *polytomous* (many-category) factor. I next describe how interactions between quantitative and qualitative explanatory variables can be represented in dummy-regression models and how to summarize models that incorporate interactions. Finally, I explain why it does not make sense to standardize dummy-variable and interaction regressors.

7.1 A Dichotomous Factor

Let us consider the simplest case: one dichotomous factor and one quantitative explanatory variable. As in the two previous chapters, assume that relationships are *additive*—that is, that the partial effect of each explanatory variable is the same regardless of the specific value at which the other explanatory variable is held constant. As well, suppose that the other assumptions of the regression model hold: The errors are independent and normally distributed, with zero means and constant variance.

The general motivation for including a factor in a regression is essentially the same as for including an additional quantitative explanatory variable: (1) to account more fully for the response variable, by making the errors smaller, and (2) even more important, to avoid a biased assessment of the impact of an explanatory variable, as a consequence of omitting another explanatory variable that is related to it.

For concreteness, suppose that we are interested in investigating the relationship between education and income among women and men. Figure 7.1(a) and (b) represents two small (idealized) populations. In both cases, the within-gender regressions of income on education are parallel. Parallel regressions imply additive effects of education and gender on income: Holding education constant, the "effect" of gender is the vertical distance between the two regression lines, which—for parallel lines—is everywhere the same. Likewise, holding gender constant, the "effect" of education is captured by the within-gender education slope, which—for parallel lines—is the same for men and women.[2]

In Figure 7.1(a), the explanatory variables gender and education are unrelated to each other: Women and men have identical distributions of education scores (as can been seen by projecting the points onto the horizontal axis). In this circumstance, if we ignore gender and regress income on education alone, we obtain the same slope as is produced by the separate within-gender

---

[1] Chapter 14 deals with qualitative *response* variables.

[2] I will consider nonparallel within-group regressions in Section 7.3.

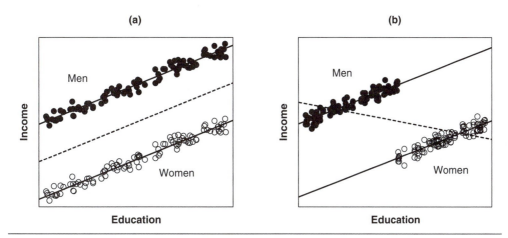

Figure 7.1   Idealized data representing the relationship between income and education for
populations of men (filled circles) and women (open circles). In (a), there is no
relationship between education and gender; in (b), women have a higher average
level of education than men. In both (a) and (b), the within-gender (i.e., partial)
regressions (solid lines) are parallel. In each graph, the overall (i.e., marginal)
regression of income on education (ignoring gender) is given by the broken line.

regressions. Because women have lower incomes than men of equal education, however, by
ignoring gender we inflate the size of the errors.

The situation depicted in Figure 7.1(b) is importantly different. Here, gender and education are
related, and therefore if we regress income on education alone, we arrive at a biased assessment
of the effect of education on income: Because women have a higher average level of education
than men, and because—for a given level of education—women's incomes are lower, on average,
than men's, the overall regression of income on education has a *negative* slope even though the
within-gender regressions have a *positive* slope.[3]

In light of these considerations, we might proceed to partition our sample by gender and perform
separate regressions for women and men. This approach is reasonable, but it has its limitations:
Fitting separate regressions makes it difficult to estimate and test for gender differences in income.
Furthermore, if we can reasonably assume parallel regressions for women and men, we can more
efficiently estimate the common education slope by pooling sample data drawn from both groups.
In particular, if the usual assumptions of the regression model hold, then it is desirable to fit the
common-slope model by least squares.

One way of formulating the common-slope model is

$$Y_i = \alpha + \beta X_i + \gamma D_i + \varepsilon_i \tag{7.1}$$

where D, called a *dummy-variable regressor* or an *indicator variable*, is coded 1 for men and 0
for women:

$$D_i = \begin{cases} 1 & \text{for men} \\ 0 & \text{for women} \end{cases}$$

---

[3]That marginal and partial relationships can differ in sign is called *Simpson's paradox* (Simpson, 1951). Here, the
marginal relationship between income and education is negative, while the partial relationship, controlling for gender, is
positive.

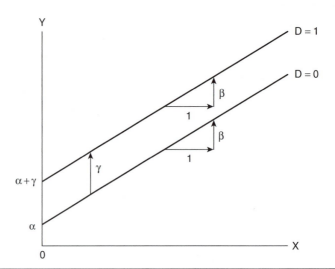

Figure 7.2   The additive dummy-variable regression model. The line labeled $D = 1$ is for men;
the line labeled $D = 0$ is for women.

Thus, for women the model becomes

$$Y_i = \alpha + \beta X_i + \gamma(0) + \varepsilon_i = \alpha + \beta X_i + \varepsilon_i$$

and for men

$$Y_i = \alpha + \beta X_i + \gamma(1) + \varepsilon_i = (\alpha + \gamma) + \beta X_i + \varepsilon_i$$

These regression equations are graphed in Figure 7.2.

This is our initial encounter with an idea that is fundamental to many linear models: the distinction between *explanatory variables* and *regressors.* Here, *gender* is a qualitative explanatory variable (i.e., a factor), with categories *male* and *female.* The dummy variable D is a regressor, representing the factor gender. In contrast, the quantitative explanatory variable *education* and the regressor X are one and the same. Were we to transform education, however, prior to entering it into the regression equation—say, by taking logs—then there would be a distinction between the explanatory variable (education) and the regressor (log education). In subsequent sections of this chapter, it will transpire that an explanatory variable can give rise to several regressors and that some regressors are functions of more than one explanatory variable.

Returning to Equation 7.1 and Figure 7.2, the coefficient γ for the dummy regressor gives the difference in intercepts for the two regression lines. Moreover, because the within-gender regression lines are parallel, γ also represents the constant vertical separation between the lines, and it may, therefore, be interpreted as the expected income advantage accruing to men when education is held constant. If men were *dis*advantaged relative to women with the same level of education, then γ would be *negative.* The coefficient α gives the intercept for women, for whom $D = 0$; and β is the common within-gender education slope.

Figure 7.3 reveals the fundamental geometric "trick" underlying the coding of a dummy regressor: We are, in fact, fitting a regression plane to the data, but the dummy regressor D is defined only at the values 0 and 1. The regression plane intersects the planes $\{X, Y | D = 0\}$ and $\{X, Y | D = 1\}$ in two lines, each with slope β. Because the difference between $D = 0$ and $D = 1$ is one unit, the difference in the Y-intercepts of these two lines is the slope of the plane in the D direction,

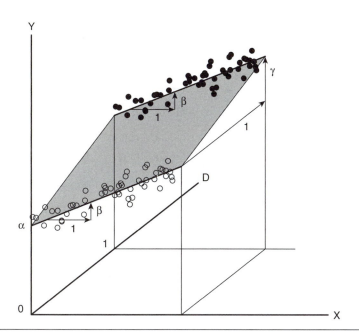

Figure 7.3 The geometric "trick" underlying dummy regression: The linear regression plane is defined only at $D = 0$ and $D = 1$, producing two regression lines with slope β and vertical separation γ. The hollow circles represent women, for whom $D = 0$, and the solid circles men, for whom $D = 1$.

that is γ. Indeed, Figure 7.2 is simply the projection of the two regression lines onto the $\{X, Y\}$ plane.

Essentially similar results are obtained if we instead code D equal to 0 for men and 1 for women, making men the *baseline* (or *reference*) category (see Figure 7.4): The *sign* of γ is reversed, because it now represents the difference in intercepts between women and men (rather than vice versa), but its *magnitude* remains the same. The coefficient α now gives the income intercept for men. It is therefore immaterial which group is coded 1 and which is coded 0, as long as we are careful to interpret the coefficients of the model—for example, the sign of γ—in a manner consistent with the coding scheme that is employed.

To determine whether gender affects income, controlling for education, we can test H_0: $\gamma = 0$, either by a t-test, dividing the estimate of γ by its standard error, or, equivalently, by dropping D from the regression model and formulating an incremental F-test. In either event, the statistical-inference procedures of the previous chapter apply.

Although I have developed dummy-variable regression for a single quantitative regressor, the method can be applied to any number of quantitative explanatory variables, as long as we are willing to assume that the slopes are the same in the two categories of the factor—that is, that the regression surfaces are parallel in the two groups. In general, if we fit the model

$$Y_i = \alpha + \beta_1 X_{i1} + \cdots + \beta_k X_{ik} + \gamma D_i + \varepsilon_i$$

then, for $D = 0$, we have

$$Y_i = \alpha + \beta_1 X_{i1} + \cdots + \beta_k X_{ik} + \varepsilon_i$$

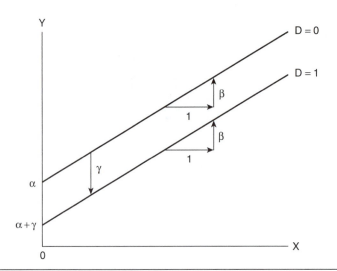

Figure 7.4   The additive dummy-regression model coding $D = 0$ for men and $D = 1$ for women (cf., Figure 7.2).

and, for $D = 1$,

$$Y_i = (\alpha + \gamma) + \beta_1 X_{i1} + \cdots + \beta_k X_{ik} + \varepsilon_i$$

> A dichotomous factor can be entered into a regression equation by formulating a dummy regressor, coded 1 for one category of the factor and 0 for the other category. A model incorporating a dummy regressor represents parallel regression surfaces, with the constant vertical separation between the surfaces given by the coefficient of the dummy regressor.

7.2   Polytomous Factors

The coding method of the previous section generalizes straightforwardly to polytomous factors. By way of illustration, recall (from the previous chapter) the Canadian occupational prestige data. I have classified the occupations into three rough categories: (1) professional and managerial occupations, (2) "white-collar" occupations, and (3) "blue-collar" occupations.[4]

Figure 7.5 shows conditioning plots for the relationship between prestige and each of income and education within occupational types.[5] The partial relationships between prestige and the explanatory variables appear reasonably linear, although there seems to be evidence that the income slope varies across the categories of type of occupation (a possibility that I will pursue in the next section of the chapter). Indeed, this change in slope is an explanation of the nonlinearity in the relationship between prestige and income that we noticed in Chapter 4. These conditioning

---

[4]Although there are 102 occupations in the full data set, several are difficult to classify and consequently were dropped from the analysis. The omitted occupations are athletes, babysitters, farmers, and "newsboys," leaving us with 98 observations.

[5]In the preceding chapter, I also included the gender composition of the occupations as an explanatory variable, but I omit that variable here. Conditioning plots are described in Section 3.3.4.

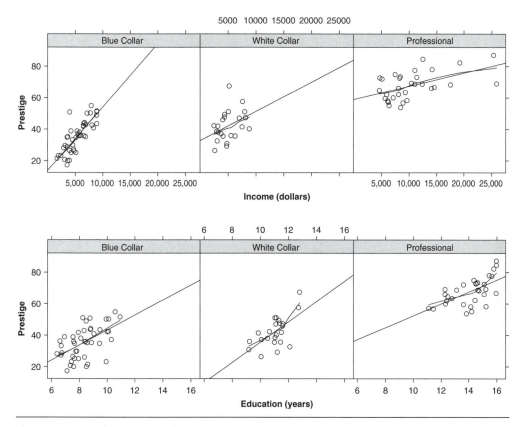

Figure 7.5   Condtioning plots for the relationships between prestige and each of income
(top panel) and education (bottom panel) by type of occupation, for the Canadian
occupational prestige data. Each panel shows the linear least-squares fit and a lowess
smooth with a span of 0.9. The graphs labeled "Professional" are for professional and
managerial occupations.

plots do not tell the whole story, however, because the income and education levels of the occupations are correlated, but they give us a reasonable initial look at the data. Conditioning the plot
for income by level of education (and vice versa) is out of the question here because of the small
size of the data set.

The *three*-category occupational-type factor can be represented in the regression equation by
introducing *two* dummy regressors, employing the following coding scheme:

Category	D_1	D_2	
Professional and managerial	1	0	(7.2)
White collar	0	1	
Blue collar	0	0	

A model for the regression of prestige on income, education, and type of occupation is then

$$Y_i = \alpha + \beta_1 X_{i1} + \beta_2 X_{i2} + \gamma_1 D_{i1} + \gamma_2 D_{i2} + \varepsilon_i \qquad (7.3)$$

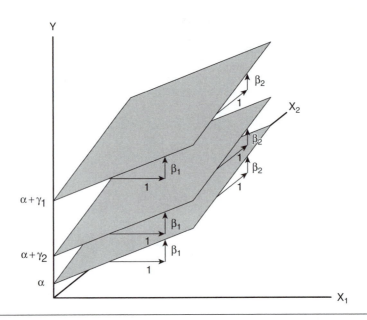

Figure 7.6   The additive dummy-regression model with two quantitative explanatory variables X_1 and X_2 represents parallel planes with potentially different intercepts in the $\{X_1, X_2, Y\}$ space.

where X_1 is income and X_2 is education. This model describes three parallel regression planes, which can differ in their intercepts:

$$\begin{array}{ll} \text{Professional:} & Y_i = (\alpha + \gamma_1) + \beta_1 X_{i1} + \beta_2 X_{i2} + \varepsilon_i \\ \text{White collar:} & Y_i = (\alpha + \gamma_2) + \beta_1 X_{i1} + \beta_2 X_{i2} + \varepsilon_i \\ \text{Blue collar:} & Y_i = \alpha + \beta_1 X_{i1} + \beta_2 X_{i2} + \varepsilon_i \end{array}$$

The coefficient α, therefore, gives the intercept for blue-collar occupations; γ_1 represents the constant vertical difference between the parallel regression planes for professional and blue-collar occupations (fixing the values of education and income); and γ_2 represents the constant vertical distance between the regression planes for white-collar and blue-collar occupations (again, fixing education and income). Assuming, for simplicity, that all coefficients are positive, and that $\gamma_1 > \gamma_2$, the geometry of the model in Equation 7.3 is illustrated in Figure 7.6.

Because blue-collar occupations are coded 0 for both dummy regressors, "blue collar" implicitly serves as the baseline category to which the other occupational-type categories are compared. The choice of a baseline category is essentially arbitrary, for we would fit precisely the same three regression planes regardless of which of the three occupational-type categories is selected for this role. The values (and meaning) of the individual dummy-variable coefficients γ_1 and γ_2 depend, however, on which category is chosen as the baseline.

It is sometimes natural to select a particular category as a basis for comparison—an experiment that includes a "control group" comes immediately to mind. In this instance, the individual dummy-variable coefficients are of interest, because they reflect differences between the "experimental" groups and the control group, holding other explanatory variables constant.

In most applications, however, the choice of a baseline category is entirely arbitrary, as it is for the occupational prestige regression. We are, therefore, most interested in testing the null hypothesis of no effect of occupational type, controlling for education and income,

$$H_0 : \gamma_1 = \gamma_2 = 0 \tag{7.4}$$

but the individual hypotheses H_0: $\gamma_1 = 0$ and H_0: $\gamma_2 = 0$—which test, respectively, for differences between professional and blue-collar occupations and between white-collar and blue-collar occupations—are of less intrinsic interest.[6] The null hypothesis in Equation 7.4 can be tested by the incremental-sum-of-squares approach, dropping the two dummy variables for type of occupation from the model.

I have demonstrated how to model the effects of a three-category factor by coding two dummy regressors. It may seem more natural to treat the three occupational categories symmetrically, coding *three* dummy regressors, rather than arbitrarily selecting one category as the baseline:

Category	D_1	D_2	D_3	
Professional and managerial	1	0	0	(7.5)
White collar	0	1	0	
Blue collar	0	0	1	

Then, for the jth occupational type, we would have

$$Y_i = (\alpha + \gamma_j) + \beta_1 X_{i1} + \beta_2 X_{i2} + \varepsilon_i$$

The problem with this procedure is that there are too many parameters: We have used four parameters ($\alpha, \gamma_1, \gamma_2, \gamma_3$) to represent only three group intercepts. As a consequence, we could not find unique values for these four parameters even if we knew the three population regression lines. Likewise, we cannot calculate unique least-squares estimates for the model because the set of three dummy variables is perfectly collinear; for example, as is apparent from the table in Equation 7.5, $D_3 = 1 - D_1 - D_2$.

In general, then, for a polytomous factor with m categories, we need to code $m - 1$ dummy regressors. One simple scheme is to select the last category as the baseline and to code $D_{ij} = 1$ when observation i falls in category j, and 0 otherwise:

Category	D_1	D_2	$\cdots$	D_{m-1}	
1	1	0	$\cdots$	0	
2	0	1	$\cdots$	0	(7.6)
$\vdots$	$\vdots$	$\vdots$		$\vdots$	
$m-1$	0	0	$\cdots$	1	
m	0	0	$\cdots$	0	

> A polytomous factor can be entered into a regression by coding a set of 0/1 dummy regressors, one fewer than the number of categories of the factor. The "omitted" category, coded 0 for all dummy regressors in the set, serves as a baseline to which the other categories are compared. The model represents parallel regression surfaces, one for each category of the factor.

---

[6]The essential point here is not that the separate hypotheses are of *no* interest but that they are an arbitrary subset of the pairwise differences among the categories. In the present case, where there are three categories, the individual hypotheses represent two of the three pairwise group comparisons. The third comparison, between professional and white-collar occupations, is not *directly* represented in the model, although it is given indirectly by the difference $\gamma_1 - \gamma_2$. See Section 7.2.1 for an elaboration of this point.

When there is more than one factor, and if we assume that the factors have additive effects, we can simply code a set of dummy regressors for each. To test the hypothesis that the effect of a factor is nil, we delete its dummy regressors from the model and compute an incremental F-test of the hypothesis that all the associated coefficients are 0.

Regressing occupational prestige (Y) on income (X_1) and education (X_2) produces the fitted regression equation

$$\widehat{Y} = -7.621 + 0.001241X_1 + 4.292X_2 \qquad R^2 = .81400$$
$$\phantom{\widehat{Y} = } (3.116) \quad (0.000219) \qquad (0.336)$$

As is common practice, I have shown the estimated standard error of each regression coefficient in parentheses beneath the coefficient. The three occupational categories differ considerably in their average levels of prestige:

Category	Number of Cases	Mean Prestige
Professional and managerial	31	67.85
White collar	23	42.24
Blue collar	44	35.53
All occupations	98	47.33

Inserting dummy variables for type of occupation into the regression equation, employing the coding scheme shown in Equation 7.2, produces the following results:

$$\widehat{Y} = -0.6229 + 0.001013X_1 + 3.673X_2 + 6.039D_1 - 2.737D_2$$
$$\phantom{\widehat{Y} = } (5.2275) \quad (0.000221) \qquad (0.641) \quad (3.867) \quad (2.514)$$
$$R^2 = .83486 \tag{7.7}$$

The three fitted regression equations are, therefore,

$$\text{Professional: } \widehat{Y} = 5.416 + 0.001013X_1 + 3.673X_2$$
$$\text{White collar: } \widehat{Y} = -3.360 + 0.001013X_1 + 3.673X_2$$
$$\text{Blue collar: } \widehat{Y} = -0.623 + 0.001013X_1 + 3.673X_2$$

Note that the coefficients for both income and education become slightly smaller when type of occupation is controlled. As well, the dummy-variable coefficients (or, equivalently, the category intercepts) reveal that when education and income levels are held constant statistically, the difference in average prestige between professional and blue-collar occupations declines greatly, from $67.85 - 35.53 = 32.32$ points to 6.04 points. The difference between white-collar and blue-collar occupations is reversed when income and education are held constant, changing from $42.24 - 35.53 = +6.71$ points to -2.74 points. That is, the greater prestige of professional occupations compared with blue-collar occupations appears to be due mostly to differences in education and income between these two classes of occupations. While white-collar occupations have greater prestige, on average, than blue-collar occupations, they have lower prestige than blue-collar occupations of the same educational and income levels.[7]

To test the null hypothesis of no partial effect of type of occupation,

$$H_0 \colon \gamma_1 = \gamma_2 = 0$$

---

[7]These conclusions presuppose that the additive model that we have fit to the data is adequate, which, as we will see in Section 7.3.5, is not the case.

we can calculate the incremental F-statistic

$$
\begin{aligned}
F_0 &= \frac{n-k-1}{q} \times \frac{R_1^2 - R_0^2}{1 - R_1^2} \\
&= \frac{98 - 4 - 1}{2} \times \frac{.83486 - .81400}{1 - .83486} = 5.874
\end{aligned}
\tag{7.8}
$$

with 2 and 93 degrees of freedom, for which $p = .0040$. The occupational-type effect is therefore statistically significant but (examining the coefficient standard errors) not very precisely estimated. The education and income coefficients are several times their respective standard errors, and hence are highly statistically significant.

7.2.1 Coefficient Quasi-Variances*

Consider a dummy-regression model with p quantitative explanatory variables and an m-category factor:

$$
Y_i = \alpha + \beta_1 X_{i1} + \cdots + \beta_p X_{ip} + \gamma_1 D_{i1} + \gamma_2 D_{i2} + \cdots + \gamma_{m-1} D_{i,m-1} + \varepsilon_i
$$

The dummy-variable coefficients $\gamma_1, \gamma_2, \ldots, \gamma_{m-1}$ represent differences (or *contrasts*) between each of the other categories of the factor and the reference category m, holding constant $X_1, \ldots, X_p$. If we are interested in a comparison between any other two categories, we can simply take the difference in their dummy-regressor coefficients. Thus, in the preceding example (letting $C_1 \equiv \widehat{\gamma}_1$ and $C_2 \equiv \widehat{\gamma}_2$),

$$
C_1 - C_2 = 5.416 - (-3.360) = 8.776
$$

is the estimated average difference in prestige between professional and white-collar occupations of equal income and education.

Suppose, however, that we want to know the standard error of $C_1 - C_2$. The standard errors of C_1 and C_2 are available directly in the regression "output" (Equation 7.7), but to compute the standard error of $C_1 - C_2$, we need in addition the estimated sampling covariance of these two coefficients. That is,[8]

$$
\text{SE}(C_1 - C_2) = \sqrt{\widehat{V}(C_1) + \widehat{V}(C_2) - 2 \times \widehat{C}(C_1, C_2)}
$$

where $\widehat{V}(C_j) = \left[\text{SE}(C_j)\right]^2$ is the estimated sampling variance of coefficient C_j, and $\widehat{C}(C_1, C_2)$ is the estimated sampling covariance of C_1 and C_2. For the occupational prestige regression, $\widehat{C}(C_1, C_2) = 6.797$, and so

$$
\text{SE}(C_1 - C_2) = \sqrt{3.867^2 + 2.514^2 - 2 \times 6.797} = 2.771
$$

We can use this standard error in the normal manner for a t-test of the difference between C_1 and C_2.[9] For example, noting that the difference exceeds twice its standard error suggests that it is statistically significant.

---

[8]See Appendix D on probability and estimation. The computation of regression-coefficient covariances is taken up in Chapter 9.

[9]Testing all differences between pairs of factor categories raises an issue of simultaneous inference, however. See the discussion of Scheffé confidence intervals in Section 9.4.4.

Although computer programs for regression analysis typically report the covariance matrix of the regression coefficients if asked to do so, it is not common to include coefficient covariances in published research along with estimated coefficients and standard errors, because with $k + 1$ coefficients in the model, there are $k(k + 1)/2$ variances and covariances among them—a potentially large number. Readers of a research report are therefore put at a disadvantage by the arbitrary choice of a reference category in dummy regression, because they are unable to calculate the standard errors of the differences between all pairs of categories of a factor.

Quasi-variances of dummy-regression coefficients (Firth, 2003; Firth & De Menezes, 2004) speak to this problem. Let $\widetilde{V}(C_j)$ denote the quasi-variance of dummy coefficient C_j. Then,

$$\mathrm{SE}(C_j - C_{j'}) \approx \sqrt{\widetilde{V}(C_j) + \widetilde{V}(C_{j'})}$$

The squared relative error of this approximation for the contrast $C_j - C_{j'}$ is

$$\mathrm{RE}_{jj'} \equiv \frac{\widetilde{V}(C_j - C_{j'})}{\widehat{V}(C_j - C_{j'})} = \frac{\widetilde{V}(C_j) + \widetilde{V}(C_{j'})}{\widehat{V}(C_j) + \widehat{V}(C_{j'}) - 2 \times \widehat{C}(C_j, C_{j'})}$$

The approximation is accurate for this contrast when $\mathrm{RE}_{jj'}$ is close to 1, or, equivalently, when

$$\log(\mathrm{RE}_{jj'}) = \log\left[\widetilde{V}(C_j) + \widetilde{V}(C_{j'})\right] - \log\left[\widehat{V}(C_j) + \widehat{V}(C_{j'}) - 2 \times \widehat{C}(C_j, C_{j'})\right]$$

is close to 0. The quasi-variances $\widetilde{V}(C_j)$ are therefore selected to minimize the sum of squared log relative errors of approximation over all pairwise contrasts, $\sum_{j<j'} \left[\log(\mathrm{RE}_{jj'})\right]^2$. The resulting errors of approximation are typically very small (Firth, 2003; Firth & De Menezes, 2004).

The following table gives dummy-variable coefficients, standard errors, and quasi-variances for type of occupation in the Canadian occupational prestige regression:

Category	C_j	SE(C_j)	$\widetilde{V}(C_j)$
Professional	6.039	3.867	8.155
White collar	−2.737	2.514	−0.4772
Blue collar	0	0	6.797

I have set to 0 the coefficient (and its standard error) for the baseline category, blue collar. The negative quasi-variance for the white-collar coefficient is at first blush disconcerting (after all, ordinary variances cannot be negative), but it is not wrong: The quasi-variances are computed to provide accurate variance approximations for coefficient *differences*; they do not apply directly to the coefficients themselves. For the contrast between professional and white-collar occupations, we have

$$\mathrm{SE}(C_1 - C_2) \approx \sqrt{8.155 - 0.4772} = 2.771$$

Likewise, for the contrast between professional and blue-collar occupations,

$$C_1 - C_3 = 6.039 - 0 = 6.039$$

$$\mathrm{SE}(C_1 - C_3) \approx \sqrt{8.155 + 6.797} = 3.867$$

Note that in this application, the quasi-variance "approximation" to the standard error proves to be exact, and indeed this is necessarily the case when there are just three factor categories, because there are then just three pairwise differences among the categories to capture.[10]

---

[10]For the details of the computation of quasi-variances, see Chapter 15, Exercise 15.11.

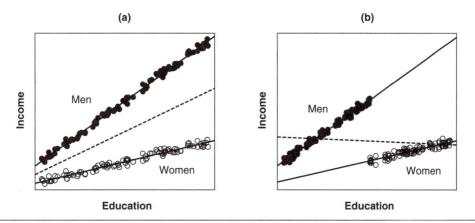

Figure 7.7   Idealized data representing the relationship between income and education
for populations of men (filled circles) and women (open circles). In (a), there is no
relationship between education and gender; in (b), women have a higher average level
of education than men. In both cases, the within-gender regressions (solid lines) are not
parallel—the slope for men is greater than the slope for women—and, consequently,
education and gender interact in affecting income. In each graph, the overall
regression of income on education (ignoring gender) is given by the broken line.

7.3 Modeling Interactions

Two explanatory variables are said to *interact* in determining a response variable when the partial
effect of one depends on the value of the other. The additive models that we have considered
thus far therefore specify the *absence* of interactions. In this section, I will explain how the
dummy-variable regression model can be modified to accommodate interactions between factors
and quantitative explanatory variables.[11]

The treatment of dummy-variable regression in the preceding two sections has assumed parallel
regressions across the several categories of a factor. If these regressions are *not* parallel, then the
factor interacts with one or more of the quantitative explanatory variables. The dummy-regression
model can easily be modified to reflect these interactions.

For simplicity, I return to the contrived example of Section 7.1, examining the regression
of income on gender and education. Consider the hypothetical data shown in Figure 7.7 (and
contrast these examples with those shown in Figure 7.1 on page 121, where the effects of gender
and education are additive). In Figure 7.7(a) [as in Figure 7.1(a)], gender and education are
independent, because women and men have identical education distributions; in Figure 7.7(b)
[as in Figure 7.1(b)], gender and education are related, because women, on average, have higher
levels of education than men.

It is apparent in both Figure 7.7(a) and Figure 7.7(b), however, that the within-gender regressions of income on education are not parallel: In both cases, the slope for men is larger than the
slope for women. Because the effect of education varies by gender, education and gender interact
in affecting income.

It is also the case, incidentally, that the effect of gender varies by education. Because the
regressions are not parallel, the relative income advantage of men changes (indeed, grows) with

---

[11] Interactions between factors are taken up in the next chapter on analysis of variance; interactions between quantitative
explanatory variables are discussed in Section 17.1 on polynomial regression.

education. Interaction, then, is a symmetric concept—that the effect of education varies by gender implies that the effect of gender varies by education (and, of course, vice versa).

The simple examples in Figures 7.1 and 7.7 illustrate an important and frequently misunderstood point: *Interaction* and *correlation* of explanatory variables are empirically and logically distinct phenomena. Two explanatory variables can interact *whether or not* they are related to one another statistically. Interaction refers to the manner in which explanatory variables *combine* to affect a response variable, not to the relationship *between* the explanatory variables themselves.

> Interaction and correlation of explanatory variables are empirically and logically distinct phenomena. Two explanatory variables can interact whether or not they are related to one another statistically. Interaction refers to the manner in which explanatory variables combine to affect a response variable, not to the relationship between the explanatory variables themselves.

7.3.1 Constructing Interaction Regressors

We could model the data in Figure 7.7 by fitting separate regressions of income on education for women and men. As before, however, it is more convenient to fit a combined model, primarily because a combined model facilitates a test of the gender-by-education interaction. Moreover, a properly formulated unified model that permits different intercepts and slopes in the two groups produces the same fit to the data as separate regressions: The full sample is composed of the two groups, and, consequently, the residual sum of squares for the full sample is minimized when the residual sum of squares is minimized in each group.[12]

The following model accommodates different intercepts and slopes for women and men:

$$Y_i = \alpha + \beta X_i + \gamma D_i + \delta(X_i D_i) + \varepsilon_i \tag{7.9}$$

Along with the quantitative regressor X for education and the dummy regressor D for gender, I have introduced the *interaction regressor* XD into the regression equation. The interaction regressor is the *product* of the other two regressors; although XD is therefore a function of X and D, it is not a *linear* function, and perfect collinearity is avoided.[13]

For women, model (7.9) becomes

$$Y_i = \alpha + \beta X_i + \gamma(0) + \delta(X_i \cdot 0) + \varepsilon_i$$
$$= \alpha + \beta X_i + \varepsilon_i$$

and for men

$$Y_i = \alpha + \beta X_i + \gamma(1) + \delta(X_i \cdot 1) + \varepsilon_i$$
$$= (\alpha + \gamma) + (\beta + \delta)X_i + \varepsilon_i$$

---

[12]See Exercise 7.4.

[13]If this procedure seems illegitimate, then think of the interaction regressor as a new variable, say $Z \equiv XD$. The model is linear in X, D, and Z. The "trick" of introducing an interaction regressor is similar to the trick of formulating dummy regressors to capture the effect of a factor: In both cases, there is a distinction between explanatory variables and regressors. Unlike a dummy regressor, however, the interaction regressor is a function of *both* explanatory variables.

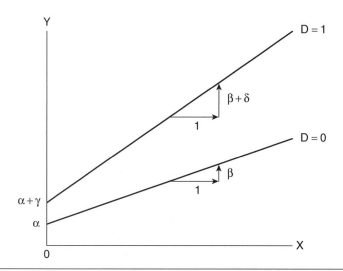

Figure 7.8   The dummy-variable regression model with an interaction regressor. The line labeled $D=1$ is for men; the line labeled $D=0$ is for women.

These regression equations are graphed in Figure 7.8: The parameters α and β are, respectively, the intercept and slope for the regression of income on education among women (the baseline category for gender); γ gives the difference in intercepts between the male and female groups; and δ gives the difference in slopes between the two groups. To test for interaction, therefore, we may simply test the hypothesis H_0: $\delta = 0$.

> Interactions can be incorporated by coding interaction regressors, taking products of dummy regressors with quantitative explanatory variables. The resulting model permits different slopes in different groups—that is, regression surfaces that are not parallel.

In the additive, no-interaction model of Equation 7.1 and Figure 7.2, the dummy-regressor coefficient γ represents the *unique* partial effect of gender (i.e., the expected income difference between men and women of equal education, regardless of the value at which education is fixed), while the slope β represents the *unique* partial effect of education (i.e., the within-gender expected increment in income for a one-unit increase in education, for both women and men). In the interaction model of Equation 7.9 and Figure 7.8, in contrast, γ is no longer interpretable as the unqualified income difference between men and women of equal education.

Because the within-gender regressions are not parallel, the separation between the regression lines changes; here, γ is simply the separation at $X = 0$—that is, above the origin. It is generally no more important to assess the expected income difference between men and women of 0 education than at other educational levels, and therefore the difference-in-intercepts parameter γ is not of special interest in the interaction model. Indeed, in many instances (although not here), the value $X = 0$ may not occur in the data or may be impossible (as, for example, if X is weight). In such cases, γ has no literal interpretation in the interaction model (see Figure 7.9).

Likewise, in the interaction model, β is not the unqualified partial effect of education, but rather the effect of education among women. Although this coefficient *is* of interest, it is not necessarily

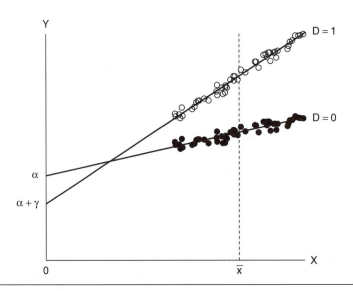

Figure 7.9   Why the difference in intercepts does not represent a meaningful partial effect for a
factor when there is interaction: The difference-in-intercepts parameter γ is *negative*
even though, within the range of the data, the regression line for the group coded
$D = 1$ is *above* the line for the group coded $D = 0$.

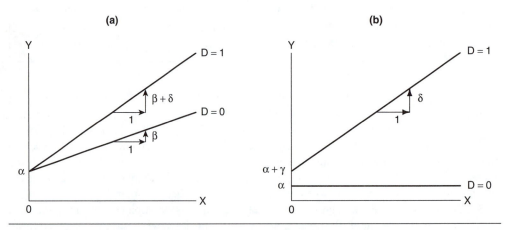

Figure 7.10   Two models that violate the principle of marginality: In (a), the dummy regressor D is
omitted from the model $E(Y) = \alpha + \beta X + \delta\,(XD)$; in (b), the quantitative explanatory
variable X is omitted from the model $E(Y) = \alpha + \gamma D + \delta(XD)$. These models violate
the principle of marginality because they include the term XD, which is a
higher-order relative of both X and D (one of which is omitted from each model).

more important than the effect of education among men ($\beta + \delta$), which does not appear *directly* in the model.

7.3.2 The Principle of Marginality

Following Nelder (1977), we say that the separate partial effects, or *main effects*, of education and gender are *marginal* to the education-by-gender interaction. In general, we neither test nor interpret the main effects of explanatory variables that interact. If, however, we can rule out interaction either on theoretical or on empirical grounds, then we can proceed to test, estimate, and interpret the main effects.

As a corollary to this principle, it does not generally make sense to specify and fit models that include interaction regressors but that omit main effects that are marginal to them. This is not to say that such models—which violate the *principle of marginality*—are uninterpretable: They are, rather, not broadly applicable.

> The principle of marginality specifies that a model including a *high-order term* (such as an interaction) should normally also include the "lower-order relatives" of that term (the main effects that "compose" the interaction).

Suppose, for example, that we fit the model

$$Y_i = \alpha + \beta X_i + \delta(X_i D_i) + \varepsilon_i$$

which omits the dummy regressor D, but includes its "higher-order relative" XD. As shown in Figure 7.10(a), this model describes regression lines for women and men that have the same intercept but (potentially) different slopes, a specification that is peculiar and of no substantive interest. Similarly, the model

$$Y_i = \alpha + \gamma D_i + \delta(X_i D_i) + \varepsilon_i$$

graphed in Figure 7.10(b), constrains the slope for women to 0, which is needlessly restrictive.

7.3.3 Interactions With Polytomous Factors

The method for modeling interactions by forming product regressors is easily extended to polytomous factors, to several factors, and to several quantitative explanatory variables. I will use the Canadian occupational prestige regression to illustrate the application of the method, entertaining the possibility that occupational type interacts both with income (X_1) and with education (X_2):

$$Y_i = \alpha + \beta_1 X_{i1} + \beta_2 X_{i2} + \gamma_1 D_{i1} + \gamma_2 D_{i2}$$
$$+ \delta_{11} X_{i1} D_{i1} + \delta_{12} X_{i1} D_{i2} + \delta_{21} X_{i2} D_{i1} + \delta_{22} X_{i2} D_{i2} + \varepsilon_i \qquad (7.10)$$

Note that we require one interaction regressor for each product of a dummy regressor with a quantitative explanatory variable. The regressors $X_1 D_1$ and $X_1 D_2$ capture the interaction between income and occupational type; $X_2 D_1$ and $X_2 D_2$ capture the interaction between education and occupational type. The model therefore permits different intercepts and slopes for the three types of occupations:

$$\begin{aligned}
\text{Professional: } Y_i &= (\alpha + \gamma_1) + (\beta_1 + \delta_{11})X_{i1} + (\beta_2 + \delta_{21})X_{i2} + \varepsilon_i \\
\text{White collar: } Y_i &= (\alpha + \gamma_2) + (\beta_1 + \delta_{12})X_{i1} + (\beta_2 + \delta_{22})X_{i2} + \varepsilon_i \\
\text{Blue collar: } Y_i &= \alpha + \beta_1 X_{i1} + \beta_2 X_{i2} + \varepsilon_i
\end{aligned}$$

(7.11)

Blue-collar occupations, which are coded 0 for both dummy regressors, serve as the baseline for the intercepts and slopes of the other occupational types. As in the no-interaction model, the choice of baseline category is generally arbitrary, as it is here, and is inconsequential. Fitting the model in Equation 7.10 to the prestige data produces the following results:

$$\begin{aligned}
\widehat{Y}_i = \;\; &2.276 + 0.003522X_1 + 1.713X_2 + 15.35D_1 - 33.54D_2 \\
&(7.057) \;\;\; (0.000556) \;\;\;\;\;\; (0.927) \;\;\;\;\;\; (13.72) \;\;\;\;\; (17.54) \\
&- 0.002903X_1 D_1 - 0.002072X_1 D_2 \\
&\;\;\;\; (0.000599) \;\;\;\;\;\;\;\;\;\; (0.000894) \\
&+ 1.388X_2 D_1 + 4.291X_2 D_2 \\
&\;\;\;\; (1.289) \;\;\;\;\;\;\;\;\;\; (1.757)
\end{aligned}$$

$$R^2 = .8747$$

(7.12)

This example is discussed further in the following section.

7.3.4 Interpreting Dummy-Regression Models With Interactions

It is difficult in dummy-regression models with interactions (and in other complex statistical models) to understand what the model is saying about the data simply by examining the regression coefficients. One approach to interpretation, which works reasonably well in a relatively straightforward model such as Equation 7.12, is to write out the implied regression equation for each group (using Equation 7.11):

$$\begin{aligned}
\text{Professional: } & \widehat{\text{Prestige}} = 17.63 + 0.000619 \times \text{Income} + 3.101 \times \text{Education} \\
\text{White collar: } & \widehat{\text{Prestige}} = -31.26 + 0.001450 \times \text{Income} + 6.004 \times \text{Education} \\
\text{Blue collar: } & \widehat{\text{Prestige}} = 2.276 + 0.003522 \times \text{Income} + 1.713 \times \text{Education}
\end{aligned}$$

(7.13)

From these equations, we can see, for example, that income appears to make much more difference to prestige in blue-collar occupations than in white-collar occupations, and has even less impact on prestige in professional and managerial occupations. Education, in contrast, has the largest impact on prestige among white-collar occupations, and has the smallest effect in blue-collar occupations.

An alternative approach (from Fox, 1987, 2003; Fox & Andersen, 2006) that generalizes readily to more complex models is to examine the high-order terms of the model. In the illustration, the high-order terms are the interactions between income and type and between education and type.

- Focusing in turn on each high-order term, we allow the variables in the term to range over their combinations of values in the data, fixing other variables to typical values. For example, for the interaction between type and income, we let type of occupation take on successively the categories blue collar, white collar, and professional (for which the dummy regressors

D_1 and D_2 are set to the corresponding values given in Equation 7.6), in combination with income values between \$1500 and \$26,000 (the approximate range of income in the Canadian occupational prestige data set); education is fixed to its average value in the data, $\overline{X}_2 = 10.79$.

- We next compute the fitted value of prestige at each combination of values of income and type of occupation. These fitted values are graphed in the "effect display" shown in the upper panel of Figure 7.11; the lower panel of this figure shows a similar effect display for the interaction between education and type of occupation, holding income at its average value. The broken lines in Figure 7.11 give ± 2 standard errors around the fitted values— that is, approximate 95% pointwise confidence intervals for the effects.[14] The nature of the interactions between income and type and between education and type is readily discerned from these graphs.

7.3.5   Hypothesis Tests for Main Effects and Interactions

To test the null hypothesis of no interaction between income and type, H_0: $\delta_{11} = \delta_{12} = 0$, we need to delete the interaction regressors $X_1 D_1$ and $X_1 D_2$ from the full model (Equation 7.10) and calculate an incremental F-test; likewise, to test the null hypothesis of no interaction between education and type, H_0: $\delta_{21} = \delta_{22} = 0$, we delete the interaction regressors $X_2 D_1$ and $X_2 D_2$ from the full model. These tests, and tests for the main effects of income, education, and occupational type, are detailed in Tables 7.1 and 7.2: Table 7.1 gives the regression sums of squares for several models, which, along with the residual sum of squares for the full model, $RSS_1 = 3553$, are the building blocks of the incremental F-tests shown in Table 7.2. Table 7.3 shows the hypothesis tested by each of the incremental F-statistics in Table 7.2.

Although the analysis-of-variance table (Table 7.2) conventionally shows the tests for the main effects of education, income, and type before the education-by-type and income-by-type interactions, the structure of the model makes it sensible to examine the interactions first: Conforming to the principle of marginality, the test for each main effect is computed assuming that the interactions that are higher-order relatives of the main effect are 0 (as shown in Table 7.3). Thus, for example, the test for the income main effect assumes that the income-by-type interaction is absent (i.e., that $\delta_{11} = \delta_{12} = 0$), but not that the education-by-type interaction is absent ($\delta_{21} = \delta_{22} = 0$).[15]

> The principle of marginality serves as a guide to constructing incremental F-tests for the terms in a model that includes interactions.

In this case, then, there is weak evidence of an interaction between education and type of occupation, and much stronger evidence of an income-by-type interaction. Considering the small number of cases, we are squeezing the data quite hard, and it is apparent from the coefficient standard errors (in Equation 7.12) and from the effect displays in Figure 7.11 that the interactions are not precisely estimated. The tests for the main effects of income, education, and type, computed assuming that the higher-order relatives of each such term are absent, are all highly statistically

---

[14]For standard errors of fitted values, see Exercise 9.14.

[15]Tests constructed to conform to the principle of marginality are sometimes called "type-II" tests, terminology introduced by the SAS statistical software package. This terminology, and alternative tests, are described in the next chapter.

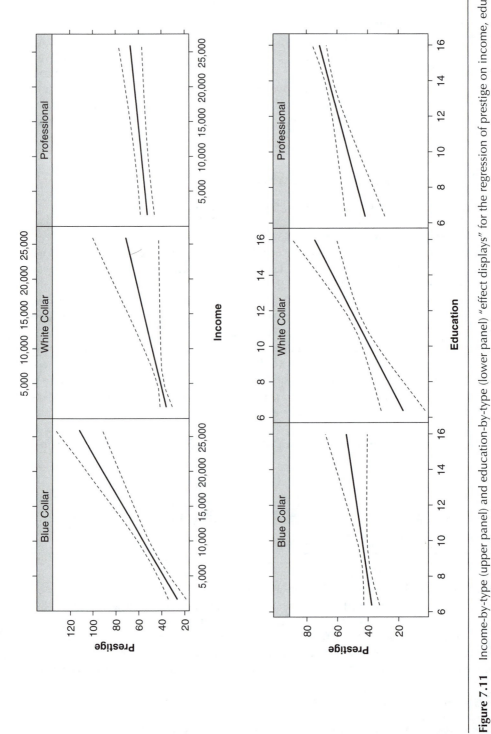

Figure 7.11 Income-by-type (upper panel) and education-by-type (lower panel) "effect displays" for the regression of prestige on income, education, and type of occupation. The solid lines give fitted values under the model, while the broken lines give 95% pointwise confidence intervals around the fit. To compute fitted values in the upper panel, education is set to its average value in the data; in the lower panel, income is set to its average value.

Table 7.1 Regression Sums of Squares for Several Models Fit to the Canadian Occupational Prestige Data

Model	Terms	Parameters	Regression Sum of Squares	df
1	$I, E, T, I \times T, E \times T$	$\alpha, \beta_1, \beta_2, \gamma_1, \gamma_2,$ $\delta_{11}, \delta_{12}, \delta_{21}, \delta_{22}$	24,794.	8
2	$I, E, T, I \times T$	$\alpha, \beta_1, \beta_2, \gamma_1, \gamma_2,$ δ_{11}, δ_{12}	24,556.	6
3	$I, E, T, E \times T$	$\alpha, \beta_1, \beta_2, \gamma_1, \gamma_2,$ δ_{21}, δ_{22}	23,842.	6
4	I, E, T	$\alpha, \beta_1, \beta_2, \gamma_1, \gamma_2$	23,666.	4
5	I, E	α, β_1, β_2	23,074.	2
6	$I, T, I \times T$	$\alpha, \beta_1, \gamma_1, \gamma_2,$ δ_{11}, δ_{12}	23,488.	5
7	$E, T, E \times T$	$\alpha, \beta_2, \gamma_1, \gamma_2,$ δ_{21}, δ_{22}	22,710.	5

NOTE: These sums of squares are the building blocks of incremental F-tests for the main and interaction effects of the explanatory variables. The following code is used for "terms" in the model: I, income; E, education; T, occupational type.

Table 7.2 Analysis-of-Variance Table, Showing Incremental F-Tests for the Terms in the Canadian Occupational Prestige Regression

Source	Models Contrasted	Sum of Squares	df	F	p
Income	3−7	1132.	1	28.35	<.0001
Education	2−6	1068.	1	26.75	<.0001
Type	4−5	592.	2	7.41	<.0011
Income × Type	1−3	952.	2	11.92	<.0001
Education × Type	1−2	238.	2	2.98	.056
Residuals		3553.	89		
Total		28,347.	97		

Table 7.3 Hypotheses Tested by the Incremental F-Tests in Table 7.2

Source	Models Contrasted	Null Hypothesis
Income	3–7	$\beta_1 = 0 \mid \delta_{11} = \delta_{12} = 0$
Education	2–6	$\beta_2 = 0 \mid \delta_{21} = \delta_{22} = 0$
Type	4–5	$\gamma_1 = \gamma_2 = 0 \mid \delta_{11} = \delta_{12} = \delta_{21} = \delta_{22} = 0$
Income ×Type	1–3	$\delta_{11} = \delta_{12} = 0$
Education × Type	1–2	$\delta_{21} = \delta_{22} = 0$

significant. In light of the strong evidence for an interaction between income and type, however, the income and type main effects are not really of interest.[16]

The degrees of freedom for the several sources of variation add to the total degrees of freedom, but—because the regressors in different sets are correlated—the sums of squares do not add to the total sum of squares.[17] What is important here (and more generally) is that sensible hypotheses are tested, not that the sums of squares add to the total sum of squares.

7.4   A Caution Concerning Standardized Coefficients

In Chapter 5, I explained the use—and limitations—of standardized regression coefficients. It is appropriate to sound another cautionary note here: Inexperienced researchers sometimes report standardized coefficients for dummy regressors. As I have explained, an *unstandardized* coefficient for a dummy regressor is interpretable as the expected response-variable difference between a particular category and the baseline category for the dummy-regressor set (controlling, of course, for the other explanatory variables in the model).

If a dummy-regressor coefficient is standardized, then this straightforward interpretation is lost. Furthermore, because a 0/1 dummy regressor cannot be increased by one standard deviation, the usual interpretation of a standardized regression coefficient also does not apply. Standardization is a linear transformation, so many characteristics of the regression model— the value of R^2, for example—do not change, but the standardized coefficient itself is not directly interpretable. These difficulties can be avoided by standardizing only the response variable and *quantitative* explanatory variables in a regression, leaving dummy regressors in 0/1 form.

A similar point applies to interaction regressors. We may legitimately standardize a quantitative explanatory variable *prior* to taking its product with a dummy regressor, but to standardize the interaction regressor itself is not sensible: The interaction regressor cannot change independently of the main-effect regressors that compose it and are marginal to it.

> It is not sensible to standardize dummy regressors or interaction regressors.

Exercises

Exercise 7.1. Suppose that the values -1 and 1 are used for the dummy regressor D in Equation 7.1 instead of 0 and 1. Write out the regression equations for men and women, and explain how the parameters of the model are to be interpreted. Does this alternative coding of the

---

[16]We tested the occupational type main effect in Section 7.2 (Equation 7.8 on page 129), but using an estimate of error variance based on Model 4, which does not contain the interactions. In Table 7.2, the estimated error variance is based on the full model, Model 1. Sound general practice is to use the largest model fit to the data to estimate the error variance even when, as is frequently the case, this model includes effects that are not statistically significant. The largest model necessarily has the smallest residual sum of squares, but it also has the fewest residual degrees of freedom. These two factors tend to offset one another, and it usually makes little difference whether the estimated error variance is based on the full model or on a model that deletes nonsignificant terms. Nevertheless, using the full model ensures an unbiased estimate of the error variance.

[17]See Section 10.2 for a detailed explanation of this phenomenon.

dummy regressor adequately capture the effect of gender? Is it fair to conclude that the dummy-regression model will "work" properly as long as two distinct values of the dummy regressor are employed, one each for women and men? Is there a reason to prefer one coding to another?

Exercise 7.2. Adjusted means (based on Section 7.2): Let $\overline{Y}_1$ represent the ("unadjusted") mean prestige score of professional occupations in the Canadian occupational prestige data, $\overline{Y}_2$ that of white-collar occupations, and $\overline{Y}_3$ that of blue-collar occupations. Differences among the $\overline{Y}_j$ may partly reflect differences among occupational types in their income and education levels. In the dummy-variable regression in Equation 7.7, type-of-occupation differences are "controlled" for income and education, producing the fitted regression equation

$$\widehat{Y} = A + B_1 X_1 + B_2 X_2 + C_1 D_1 + C_2 D_2$$

Consequently, if we fix income and education at particular values—say, $X_1 = x_1$ and $X_2 = x_2$—then the fitted prestige scores for the several occupation types are given by (treating "blue collar" as the baseline type):

$$\begin{aligned}
\widehat{Y}_1 &= (A + C_1) + B_1 x_1 + B_2 x_2 \\
\widehat{Y}_2 &= (A + C_2) + B_1 x_1 + B_2 x_2 \\
\widehat{Y}_3 &= A + B_1 x_1 + B_2 x_2
\end{aligned}$$

(a) Note that the *differences* among the $\widehat{Y}_j$ depend only on the dummy-variable coefficients C_1 and C_2 and not on the values of x_1 and x_2. Why is this so?

(b) When $x_1 = \overline{X}_1$ and $x_2 = \overline{X}_2$, the $\widehat{Y}_j$ are called *adjusted means* and are denoted $\widetilde{Y}_j$. How can the adjusted means $\widetilde{Y}_j$ be interpreted? In what sense is $\widetilde{Y}_j$ an "adjusted" mean?

(c) Locate the "unadjusted" and adjusted means for women and men in each of Figures 7.1(a) and (b) (on page 121). Construct a similar figure in which the difference between adjusted means is *smaller* than the difference in unadjusted means.

(d) Using the results in the text, along with the mean income and education values for the three occupational types, compute adjusted mean prestige scores for each of the three types, controlling for income and education. Compare the adjusted with the unadjusted means for the three types of occupations and comment on the differences, if any, between them.

Exercise 7.3. Can the concept of an adjusted mean, introduced in Exercise 7.2, be extended to a model that includes interactions? If so, show how adjusted means can be found for the data in Figure 7.7(a) and (b) (on page 131).

Exercise 7.4. Verify that the regression equations for each occupational type given in Equation 7.13 (page 136) are identical to the results obtained by regressing prestige on income and education *separately* for each of the three types of occupations. Explain why this is the case.

Summary

- A dichotomous factor can be entered into a regression equation by formulating a dummy regressor, coded 1 for one category of the variable and 0 for the other category. A model incorporating a dummy regressor represents parallel regression surfaces, with the constant separation between the surfaces given by the coefficient of the dummy regressor.
- A polytomous factor can be entered into a regression by coding a set of 0/1 dummy regressors, one fewer than the number of categories of the factor. The "omitted" category, coded

0 for all dummy regressors in the set, serves as a baseline to which the other categories are compared. The model represents parallel regression surfaces, one for each category of the factor.

- Interactions can be incorporated by coding interaction regressors, taking products of dummy regressors with quantitative explanatory variables. The model permits different slopes in different groups—that is, regression surfaces that are not parallel.

- *Interaction* and *correlation* of explanatory variables are empirically and logically distinct phenomena. Two explanatory variables can interact *whether or not* they are related to one another statistically. Interaction refers to the manner in which explanatory variables *combine* to affect a response variable, not to the relationship *between* the explanatory variables themselves

- The principle of marginality specifies that a model including a high-order term (such as an interaction) should normally also include the lower-order relatives of that term (the main effects that "compose" the interaction). The principle of marginality also serves as a guide to constructing incremental F-tests for the terms in a model that includes interactions, and for examining the effects of explanatory variables.

- It is not sensible to standardize dummy regressors or interaction regressors.

8 Analysis of Variance

I introduced the term *analysis of variance* in Chapter 5 to describe the partition of the response-variable sum of squares into "explained" and "unexplained" components, noting that this decomposition applies generally to linear models. For historical reasons, *analysis of variance* (abbreviated *ANOVA*) also refers to procedures for fitting and testing linear models in which the explanatory variables are categorical.[1]

When there is a single factor (also termed a *classification*), these procedures are called *one-way* ANOVA, the subject of the first section of this chapter. Two factors produce *two-way* analysis of variance, three factors, *three-way* ANOVA, and so on. Two-way ANOVA is taken up in Section 8.2, higher-way ANOVA in Section 8.3.

The dummy-variable regression model of the previous chapter incorporates both quantitative and categorical explanatory variables; in Section 8.4 we will examine an alternative formulation of this model called *analysis of covariance* (ANCOVA).

Finally, I will explain how *linear contrasts* can be used to "customize" hypothesis tests in ANOVA.

8.1 One-Way Analysis of Variance

In Chapter 7, we learned how to construct dummy regressors to represent the effects of factors alongside those of quantitative explanatory variables. Suppose, however, that there are *no* quantitative explanatory variables—only a single factor. For example, for a three-category classification we have the model

$$Y_i = \alpha + \gamma_1 D_{i1} + \gamma_2 D_{i2} + \varepsilon_i \tag{8.1}$$

employing the following coding for the dummy regressors:

Group	D_1	D_2
1	1	0
2	0	1
3	0	0

The expectation of the response variable in each *group* (i.e., in each category or *level* of the factor) is the population group mean, denoted μ_j for the jth group. Because the error ε has a mean of 0 under the usual linear-model assumptions, taking the expectation of both sides of the model (Equation 8.1) produces the following relationships between group means and model parameters:

---

[1] The methods and terminology of analysis of variance were introduced by the great British statistician R. A. Fisher (1925). Fisher's many other seminal contributions to statistics include the technique of randomization in experimental design and the method of maximum likelihood.

$$\text{Group 1:} \quad \mu_1 = \alpha + \gamma_1 \times 1 + \gamma_2 \times 0 = \alpha + \gamma_1$$
$$\text{Group 2:} \quad \mu_2 = \alpha + \gamma_1 \times 0 + \gamma_2 \times 1 = \alpha + \gamma_2$$
$$\text{Group 3:} \quad \mu_3 = \alpha + \gamma_1 \times 0 + \gamma_2 \times 0 = \alpha$$

There are three parameters (α, γ_1, and γ_2) and three group means, so we can solve uniquely for the parameters in terms of the group means:

$$\alpha = \mu_3$$
$$\gamma_1 = \mu_1 - \mu_3$$
$$\gamma_2 = \mu_2 - \mu_3$$

It is not surprising that α represents the mean of the baseline category (Group 3), and that γ_1 and γ_2 capture differences between the other group means and the mean of the baseline category.

One-way ANOVA focuses on testing for differences among group means. The omnibus F-statistic for the model (Equation 8.1) tests H_0: $\gamma_1 = \gamma_2 = 0$, which corresponds to H_0: $\mu_1 = \mu_2 = \mu_3$, the null hypothesis of no differences among the population group means. Our consideration of one-way ANOVA might well end here, but for a desire to develop methods that generalize easily to more complex situations in which there are several, potentially interacting, factors.

The first innovation is notational: Because observations are partitioned according to groups, it is convenient to let Y_{ij} denote the ith observation within the jth of m groups. The number of observations in the jth group is n_j, and therefore the total number of observations is $n = \sum_{j=1}^{m} n_j$. As above, $\mu_j \equiv E(Y_{ij})$ represents the population mean in group j.

The one-way ANOVA model is written in the following manner:

$$Y_{ij} = \mu + \alpha_j + \varepsilon_{ij} \tag{8.2}$$

where we would like μ to represent, in some reasonable sense, the general level of the response variable in the population; α_j should represent the effect on the response variable of membership in the jth group; and ε_{ij} is an error variable that follows the usual linear-model assumptions—that is, the ε_{ij} are independent and normally distributed with zero expectations and equal variances.

Upon taking expectations, Equation 8.2 becomes

$$\mu_j = \mu + \alpha_j$$

The parameters of the model are, therefore, underdetermined, for there are $m + 1$ parameters (including μ) but only m population group means. For example, for $m = 3$, we have four parameters but only three equations:

$$\mu_1 = \mu + \alpha_1$$
$$\mu_2 = \mu + \alpha_2$$
$$\mu_3 = \mu + \alpha_3$$

Even if we knew the three population group means, we could not solve uniquely for the parameters.

Because the parameters of the model (Equation 8.2) are themselves underdetermined, they cannot be uniquely estimated. To estimate the model, we would need to code one dummy regressor for each group-effect parameter α_j, and—as we discovered in the previous chapter—the resulting dummy regressors would be perfectly collinear.

One convenient way out of this dilemma is to place a linear restriction on the parameters of the model, of the form

$$w_0 \mu + \sum_{j=1}^{m} w_j \alpha_j = 0$$

where the ws are prespecified constants, not all equal to 0. It turns out that *any* such restriction will do, in the sense that all linear restrictions yield the same F-test for the null hypothesis of no differences in population group means.[2] For example, if we employ the restriction $\alpha_m = 0$, we are, in effect, deleting the parameter for the last category, making it a baseline category. The result is the dummy-coding scheme of the previous chapter. Alternatively, we could use the restriction $\mu = 0$, which is equivalent to deleting the constant term from the linear model, in which case the "effect" parameters and group means are identical: $\alpha_j = \mu_j$—an especially simple solution.

There is, however, an advantage in selecting a restriction that produces easily interpretable parameters and estimates and that generalizes usefully to more complex models. For these reasons, we will impose the constraint

$$\sum_{j=1}^{m} \alpha_j = 0 \tag{8.3}$$

Equation 8.3 is often called a *sigma constraint* or *sum-to-zero constraint*. Employing this restriction to solve for the parameters produces

$$\mu = \frac{\sum \mu_j}{m} \equiv \mu.$$
$$\alpha_j = \mu_j - \mu. \tag{8.4}$$

The dot (in $\mu.$) indicates averaging over the range of a subscript, here over groups. The *grand* or *general mean* $\mu.$, then, is the average of the population group means, while α_j gives the difference between the mean of group j and the grand mean.[3] It is clear that, under the sigma constraint, the hypothesis of no differences in group means

$$H_0: \ \mu_1 = \mu_2 = \cdots = \mu_m$$

is equivalent to the hypothesis that all of the effect parameters are 0:

$$H_0: \ \alpha_1 = \alpha_2 = \cdots = \alpha_m = 0$$

All this is well and good, but how can we estimate the one-way ANOVA model under the sigma constraint? One approach is to code *deviation regressors*, an alternative to the dummy-coding scheme, which (recall) implicitly imposes the constraint $\alpha_m = 0$. We require $m - 1$ deviation regressors, $S_1, S_2, \ldots, S_{m-1}$, the jth of which is coded according to the following rule:[4]

$$S_j = \begin{cases} 1 & \text{for observations in group } j \\ -1 & \text{for observations in group } m \\ 0 & \text{for observations in all other groups} \end{cases}$$

---

[2] See Section 10.4 for an explanation of this surprising result.

[3] There is a subtle distinction between $\mu.$ (the mean of the group means) and the overall (i.e., unconditional) mean of Y in the population. In a real population, $\mu.$ and $E(Y)$ will generally differ if the groups have different numbers of observations. In an infinite or hypothetical population, we can speak of the grand mean but not of the overall (unconditional) mean $E(Y)$.

[4] I use S_j (for "sum-to-zero") to distinguish these from the $(0, 1)$ dummy regressors D_j defined previously.

For example, when $m = 3$,

Group	(α_1) S_1	(α_2) S_2
1	1	0
2	0	1
3	−1	−1

For ease of reference, I have shown in parentheses the parameter associated with each deviation regressor.

Writing out the equations for the group means in terms of the deviation regressors demonstrates how these regressors capture the sigma constraint on the parameters of the model:

$$\text{Group 1:} \quad \mu_1 = \mu + 1 \times \alpha_1 + 0 \times \alpha_2 = \mu + \alpha_1$$
$$\text{Group 2:} \quad \mu_2 = \mu + 0 \times \alpha_1 + 1 \times \alpha_2 = \mu + \alpha_2$$
$$\text{Group 3:} \quad \mu_3 = \mu - 1 \times \alpha_1 - 1 \times \alpha_2 = \mu - \alpha_1 - \alpha_2$$

The equation for the third group incorporates the sigma constraint because $\alpha_3 = -\alpha_1 - \alpha_2$ is equivalent to $\alpha_1 + \alpha_2 + \alpha_3 = 0$.

The null hypothesis of no differences among population group means is tested by the omnibus F-statistic for the deviation-coded model: The omnibus F-statistic tests the hypothesis H_0: $\alpha_1 = \alpha_2 = 0$, which, under the sigma constraint, implies that α_3 is 0 as well.

One-way ANOVA examines the relationship between a quantitative response variable and a factor. The one-way ANOVA model $Y_{ij} = \mu + \alpha_j + \varepsilon_{ij}$ is underdetermined because it uses $m + 1$ parameters to model m group means. This indeterminacy can be removed, however, by placing a restriction on its parameters. Setting one of the α_js to 0 leads to $(0, 1)$ dummy-regressor coding. Constraining the α_js to sum to 0 leads to $(1, 0, -1)$ deviation-regressor coding. The two coding schemes are equivalent in that they provide the same fit to the data, producing the same regression and residual sums of squares, and hence the same F-test for differences among group means.

Although it is often convenient to fit the one-way ANOVA model by least-squares regression, it is also possible to estimate the model and calculate sums of squares directly. The sample mean $\overline{Y}_j$ in group j is the least-squares estimator of the corresponding population mean μ_j. Estimates of μ and the α_j may therefore be written as follows (substituting estimates into Equation 8.4):

$$M \equiv \widehat{\mu} = \frac{\sum \overline{Y}_j}{m} = \overline{Y}.$$
$$A_j \equiv \widehat{\alpha}_j = \overline{Y}_j - \overline{Y}.$$

Furthermore, the fitted Y values are the group means:

$$\widehat{Y}_{ij} = M + A_j = \overline{Y}. + (\overline{Y}_j - \overline{Y}.) = \overline{Y}_j$$

Table 8.1 General One-Way Analysis-of-Variance Table

Source	Sum of Squares	df	Mean Square	F	H_0
Groups	$\sum n_j(\overline{Y}_j - \overline{Y})^2$	$m-1$	$\dfrac{\text{RegSS}}{m-1}$	$\dfrac{\text{RegMS}}{\text{RMS}}$	$\alpha_1 = \cdots = \alpha_m = 0$
Residuals	$\sum\sum(Y_{ij} - \overline{Y}_j)^2$	$n-m$	$\dfrac{\text{RSS}}{n-m}$		$(\mu_1 = \cdots = \mu_m)$
Total	$\sum\sum(Y_{ij} - \overline{Y})^2$	$n-1$			

and the regression and residual sums of squares therefore take particularly simple forms in one-way ANOVA:[5]

$$\text{RegSS} = \sum_{j=1}^{m}\sum_{i=1}^{n_j}(\widehat{Y}_{ij} - \overline{Y})^2 = \sum_{j=1}^{m} n_j(\overline{Y}_j - \overline{Y})^2$$

$$\text{RSS} = \sum_{j=1}^{m}\sum_{i=1}^{n_j}(Y_{ij} - \widehat{Y}_{ij})^2 = \sum\sum(Y_{ij} - \overline{Y}_j)^2$$

This information can be presented in an ANOVA table, as shown in Table 8.1.[6]

I will use Duncan's data on the prestige of 45 U. S. occupations to illustrate one-way ANOVA.[7] Parallel boxplots for prestige in three types of occupations appear in Figure 8.1(a). Prestige, recall, is a percentage, and the data in Figure 8.1(a) push both the lower and upper boundaries of 0% and 100%, suggesting the logit transformation in Figure 8.1(b).[8] The data are better behaved on the logit scale, which eliminates the skew in the blue-collar and professional groups and pulls in all the outlying observations, with the exception of store clerks in the white-collar category.

Means, standard deviations, and frequencies for prestige within occupational types are as follows:

Type of Occupation	Prestige Mean	Standard Deviation	Frequency
Professional and managerial	80.44	14.11	18
White collar	36.67	11.79	6
Blue collar	22.76	18.05	21

Professional occupations therefore have the highest average level of prestige, followed by white-collar and blue-collar occupations. The order of the group means is the same on the logit scale:

---

[5]If the n_j are unequal, as is usually the case in observational research, then the mean of the group means $\overline{Y}.$ generally differs from the overall sample mean $\overline{Y}$ of the response variable, for $\overline{Y} = (\sum\sum Y_{ij})/n = (\sum n_j \overline{Y}_j)/n$, while $\overline{Y}. = (\sum \overline{Y}_j)/m$. (See Footnote 3 for a similar point with respect to population means.)

[6]Although the notation may differ, this ANOVA table corresponds to the usual treatment of one-way ANOVA in introductory statistics texts. It is common to call the regression sum of squares in one-way ANOVA "the between-group sum of squares," and the residual sum of squares "the within-group sum of squares."

[7]Duncan's data were introduced in Chapter 3.

[8]The logit transformation of proportions was introduced in Section 4.5.

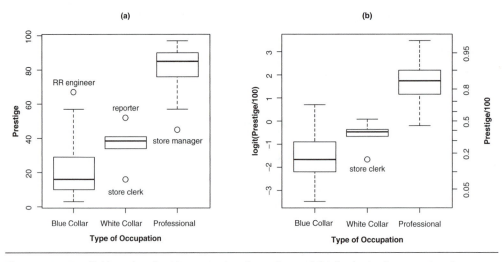

Figure 8.1   Parallel boxplots for (a) occupational prestige and (b) the logit of occupational prestige by type of occupation.

	logit(Prestige/100)	
Type of Occupation	*Mean*	*Standard Deviation*
Professional and managerial	1.6321	0.9089
White collar	−0.5791	0.5791
Blue collar	−1.4821	1.0696

On both scales, the standard deviation is greatest among the blue-collar occupations and smallest among the white-collar occupations, but the differences are not very large, especially considering the small number of observations in the white-collar category.[9]

Using the logit of prestige as the response variable, the one-way ANOVA for the Duncan data is

Source	*Sum of Squares*	*df*	*Mean Square*	*F*	*p*
Groups	95.550	2	47.775	51.98	≪.0001
Residuals	38.604	42	0.919		
Total	134.154	44			

We therefore have very strong evidence against the null hypothesis of no difference in average level of prestige across the occupational types. Occupational types account for nearly three quarters of the variation in the logit of prestige among these occupations ($R^2 = 95.550/134.154 = 0.712$).

---

[9]The assumption of constant error variance implies that the *population* variances should be the same in the several groups. See Section 12.4.2 for further discussions and a test for nonconstant variance in ANOVA.

8.2 Two-Way Analysis of Variance

The inclusion of a second factor permits us to model and test partial relationships, as well as to introduce interactions. Most issues pertaining to ANOVA can be developed for the two-factor "design." Before immersing ourselves in the details of model specification and hypothesis testing for two-way ANOVA, however, it is useful to step back and consider the patterns of relationship that can occur when a quantitative response variable is classified by two factors.

8.2.1 Patterns of Means in the Two-Way Classification

So as not to confuse ourselves with issues of estimation, we will imagine at the outset that we have access to population means. The notation for the two-way classification is shown in the following table:

	C_1	C_2	$\cdots$	C_c	
R_1	μ_{11}	μ_{12}	$\cdots$	μ_{1c}	$\mu_{1\cdot}$
R_2	μ_{21}	μ_{22}	$\cdots$	μ_{2c}	$\mu_{2\cdot}$
$\vdots$	$\vdots$	$\vdots$		$\vdots$	$\vdots$
R_r	μ_{r1}	μ_{r2}	$\cdots$	μ_{rc}	$\mu_{r\cdot}$
	$\mu_{\cdot 1}$	$\mu_{\cdot 2}$	$\cdots$	$\mu_{\cdot c}$	$\mu_{\cdot\cdot}$

The factors, R and C (for "rows" and "columns" of the table of means), have r and c categories, respectively. The factor categories are denoted R_j and C_k.

Within each *cell* of the design—that is, for each combination of categories $\{R_j, C_k\}$ of the two factors—there is a population cell mean μ_{jk} for the response variable. Extending the dot notation introduced in the previous section,

$$\mu_{j\cdot} \equiv \frac{\sum_{k=1}^{c} \mu_{jk}}{c}$$

is the *marginal mean* of the response variable in row j;

$$\mu_{\cdot k} \equiv \frac{\sum_{j=1}^{r} \mu_{jk}}{r}$$

is the marginal mean in column k; and

$$\mu_{\cdot\cdot} \equiv \frac{\sum_j \sum_k \mu_{jk}}{r \times c} = \frac{\sum_j \mu_{j\cdot}}{r} = \frac{\sum_k \mu_{\cdot k}}{c}$$

is the grand mean.

If R and C *do not* interact in determining the response variable, then the partial relationship between each factor and Y does not depend on the category at which the other factor is "held constant." The difference in cell means $\mu_{jk} - \mu_{j'k}$ across two categories of R (i.e., categories R_j and $R_{j'}$) is constant across all the categories of C—that is, this difference is the same for all $k = 1, 2, \ldots, c$. Consequently, the difference in cell means across rows is equal to the corresponding difference in the row marginal means:

$$\mu_{jk} - \mu_{j'k} = \mu_{jk'} - \mu_{j'k'} = \mu_{j\cdot} - \mu_{j'\cdot}. \quad \text{for all } j, j' \text{ and } k, k'$$

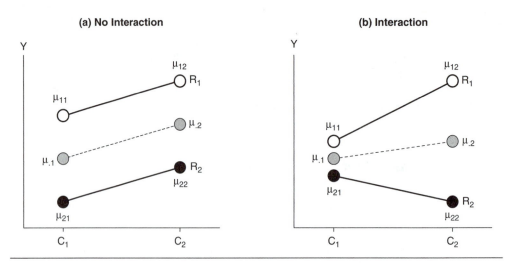

Figure 8.2   Interaction in the two-way classification. In (a), the parallel profiles of means (given by the white and black circles connected by solid lines) indicate that R and C do not interact in affecting Y. The R-effect—that is, the difference between the two profiles—is the same at both C_1 and C_2. Likewise, the C-effect—that is, the rise in the line from C_1 to C_2—is the same for both profiles. In (b), the R-effect differs at the two categories of C, and the C-effect differs at the two categories of R: R and C interact in affecting Y. In both graphs, the column marginal means $\mu_{\cdot1}$ and $\mu_{\cdot2}$ are shown as averages of the cell means in each column (represented by the gray circles connected by broken lines).

This pattern is illustrated in Figure 8.2(a) for the simple case where $r = c = 2$. Interaction—where the row difference $\mu_{1k} - \mu_{2k}$ *changes* across columns $k = 1, 2$—is illustrated in Figure 8.2(b). Note that no interaction implies parallel "profiles" of cell means. Parallel profiles also imply that the column difference $\mu_{j1} - \mu_{j2}$ for categories C_1 and C_2 is constant across rows $j = 1, 2$ and is equal to the difference in column marginal means $\mu_{\cdot1} - \mu_{\cdot2}$. As we discovered in Chapter 7, interaction is a symmetric concept: If R interacts with C, then C interacts with R. When interactions are absent, the partial effect of each factor—the factor's *main effect*—is given by differences in the population marginal means.

Several patterns of relationship in the two-way classification, all showing no interaction, are graphed in Figure 8.3. Plots of means, incidentally, not only serve to clarify the ideas underlying ANOVA, but are also a useful tool for summarizing and presenting data. Indeed, it is very difficult to inspect, understand, and interpret patterns of means in ANOVA *without* plotting the means. In the illustrations, factor C has three levels, which are marked off along the horizontal axis. Because C is a qualitative variable, the order of its categories and the spacing between them are arbitrary.[10] Factor R has two categories. The six cell means are plotted as points, connected by lines (called *profiles*) according to the levels of factor R. The separation between the lines at level C_k (where k is 1, 2, or 3) represents the difference $\mu_{1k} - \mu_{2k}$. As noted above, when there is no interaction, therefore, the separation between the profiles is constant and the profiles themselves are parallel.

---

[10] ANOVA is also useful when the levels of a factor are ordered ("low," "medium," "high," for example) or even discrete and quantitative (e.g., number of bedrooms for apartment dwellers—0, 1, 2, 3, 4), but, in general, I will assume that factors are simply nominal (i.e., qualitative) variables.

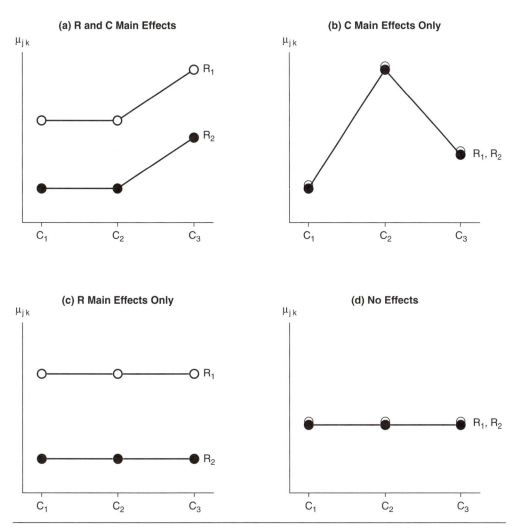

Figure 8.3 Several patterns of relationship in the two-way classification. In all these cases, R and C do not interact. (a) Both R and C main effects. (b) C main effects (R main effects nil). (c) R main effects (C main effects nil). (d) No effects (both R and C main effects nil).

In Figure 8.3(a), both R and C have nonzero main effects. In Figure 8.3(b), the differences $\mu_{1k} - \mu_{2k} = \mu_{1.} - \mu_{2.}$ are 0, and, consequently, the R main effects are nil. In Figure 8.3(c), the C main effects are nil, because the differences $\mu_{jk} - \mu_{jk'} = \mu_{.k} - \mu_{.k'}$ are all 0. Finally, in Figure 8.3(d), both sets of main effects are nil.

Figure 8.4 shows two different patterns of interactions. It is clear from the previous discussion that R and C interact when the profiles of means are not parallel—that is, when the row differences $\mu_{jk} - \mu_{j'k}$ change across the categories of the column factor or, equivalently, when the column differences $\mu_{jk} - \mu_{jk'}$ change across the categories of the row factor. In Figure 8.4(a), the interaction is dramatic: The mean for level R_2 is above the mean for R_1 at levels C_1 and C_3, but at level C_2, the mean for R_1 is substantially above the mean for R_2. Likewise, the means for the three categories of C are ordered differently within R_1 and R_2. Interaction of this sort is sometimes called *disordinal*. In Figure 8.4 (b), in contrast, the profile for R_2 is above that for R_1

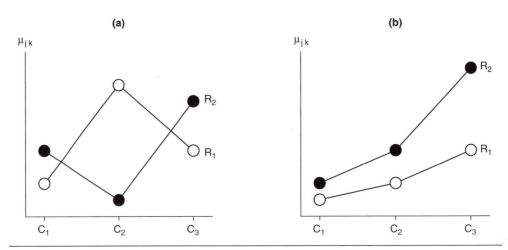

Figure 8.4   Two patterns of interaction in the two-way classification. In (a), the interaction is "disordinal" in that the order of means for one factor changes across the levels of the other factor. In (b), the profiles are not parallel, but the order of means does not change.

across all three categories of C, although the separation between the profiles of means changes. This less dramatic form of interaction can sometimes be transformed away (e.g., by taking logs).

Even when interactions are absent in the population, we cannot expect perfectly parallel profiles of *sample* means: There is, of course, sampling error in sampled data. We have to determine whether departures from parallelism observed in a sample are sufficiently large to be statistically significant or whether they could easily be the product of chance. Moreover, in large samples, we also want to determine whether "statistically significant" interactions are of sufficient magnitude to be of substantive interest. We may well decide to ignore interactions that are statistically significant but trivially small.

In general, however, if we conclude that interactions are present and non-negligible, then we do not interpret the main effects of the factors—after all, to conclude that two variables interact is to deny that they have *separate* effects. This point is a reflection of the principle of marginality, introduced in Chapter 7 in the context of dummy-variable regression: Here, the R and C main effects are marginal to the RC interaction.[11]

> Two factors interact when the profiles of population means are not parallel; when the profiles of means are parallel, the effects of the two factors are additive.

Table 8.2 shows means, standard deviations, and cell frequencies for data from a social-psychological experiment reported by Moore and Krupat (1971).[12] The experiment was designed to determine how the relationship between conformity and social status is influenced by

---

[11] In cases of disordinal interaction, such as in Figure 8.4(a), interpreting main effects is clearly misleading because it makes no sense to average over levels of one factor to examine the effect of the other. In cases such as Figure 8.4(b), however, there may be some sense to examining the marginal means for one factor averaged over levels of the other, despite the interaction.

[12] The data were generously made available by James Moore, Department of Sociology, York University.

Table 8.2   Conformity by Authoritarianism and Partner's
Status, for Moore and Krupat's (1971) Experiment

		Authoritarianism		
Partner's Status		Low	Medium	High
Low	$\overline{Y}_{jk}$	8.900	7.250	12.63
	S_{jk}	2.644	3.948	7.347
	n_{jk}	10	4	8
High	$\overline{Y}_{jk}$	17.40	14.27	11.86
	S_{jk}	4.506	3.952	3.934
	n_{jk}	5	11	7

NOTE: Each cell shows (from top to bottom) the conformity mean and
standard deviation, and the cell frequency.

"authoritarianism." The subjects in the experiment were asked to make perceptual judgments of stimuli that were intrinsically ambiguous. On forming an initial judgment, the subjects were presented with the judgment of another individual (their "partner") who was ostensibly participating in the experiment; the subjects were then asked for a final judgment. In fact, the partner's judgments were manipulated by the experimenters so that subjects were faced with nearly continuous disagreement.

The measure of conformity employed in the study was the number of times in 40 critical trials that subjects altered their judgments in response to disagreement. This measure is a disguised proportion (but because it does not push the boundaries of 0 and 40, I leave the response variable untransformed in the analysis reported below). The 45 university student subjects in the study were randomly assigned to two experimental conditions: In one condition, the partner was described as of relatively high social status (a "physician"); in the other condition, the partner was described as of relatively low status (a "postal clerk").

A standard authoritarianism scale (the "F-scale") was administered to the subjects after the experiment was completed. This procedure was dictated by practical considerations, but it raises the possibility that authoritarianism scores were inadvertently influenced by the experimental manipulation of the partner's status. The authors divided the authoritarianism scores into three categories—low, medium, and high.[13] A chi-square test of independence for the condition-by-authoritarianism frequency table (shown in Table 8.2) produces a p-value of .08, indicating that there is some ground for believing that the status manipulation affected the authoritarianism scores of the subjects.

Because of the conceptual-rigidity component of authoritarianism, Moore and Krupat expected that low-authoritarian subjects would be *more* responsive than are high-authoritarian subjects to the social status of their partner. In other words, authoritarianism and partner's status are expected to interact—in a particular manner—in determining conformity. The cell means, graphed along with the data in Figure 8.5, appear to confirm the experimenters' expectations.

---

[13] Moore and Krupat categorized authoritarianism *separately* within each condition. This approach is not strictly justified, but it serves to produce nearly equal cell frequencies—required by the method of computation employed by the authors—for the six combinations of partner's status and authoritarianism, and yields results similar to those reported here. It may have occurred to you that the dummy-regression procedures of the previous chapter are applicable here and do not require the arbitrary categorization of authoritiarianism. This analysis appears in Section 8.4. Moore and Krupat do report the difference between slopes for the within-condition regressions of conformity on authoritarianism.

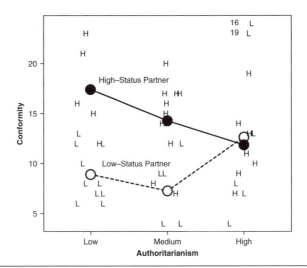

Figure 8.5 The data and cell means for Moore and Krupat's conformity experiment. The black circles connected by solid lines give the means for the high-status partner condition (with the data values represented by Hs); the white circles connected by broken lines give the means for the low-status partner condition (with the data values represented by Ls). The points are jittered horizontally to reduce overplotting. There are two outlying subjects (Numbers 16 and 19) in the bigh-authoritarianism, low-partner status group.

The standard deviation of conformity in one cell (high-authoritarian, low-status partner) is appreciably larger than in the others. Upon inspection of the data, it is clear that the relatively large dispersion in this cell is due to two subjects, Numbers 16 and 19, who have atypically high conformity scores of 24 and 23.[14]

8.2.2 The Two-Way ANOVA Model

Because interpretation of results in two-way ANOVA depends crucially on the presence or absence of interaction, our first concern is to test the null hypothesis of no interaction. Based on the discussion in the previous section, this hypothesis can be expressed in terms of the cell means:

$$H_0: \ \mu_{jk} - \mu_{j'k} = \mu_{jk'} - \mu_{j'k'} \quad \text{for all } j, \ j' \text{ and } k, \ k' \tag{8.5}$$

In words: The row effects are the same within all levels of the column factor. By rearranging the terms in Equation 8.5, we can write the null hypothesis in the following alternative but equivalent manner:

$$H_0: \ \mu_{jk} - \mu_{jk'} = \mu_{j'k} - \mu_{j'k'} \quad \text{for all } j, \ j' \text{ and } k, \ k' \tag{8.6}$$

That is, the column effects are invariant across rows. Once more, we see the symmetry of the concept of interaction.

It is convenient, following the presentation in the previous section, to express hypotheses concerning main effects in terms of the marginal means. Thus, for the row classification we have the null hypothesis

---

[14]See Exercise 8.12.

$$H_0: \quad \mu_{1\cdot} = \mu_{2\cdot} = \cdots = \mu_{r\cdot} \tag{8.7}$$

and for the column classification

$$H_0: \quad \mu_{\cdot 1} = \mu_{\cdot 2} = \cdots = \mu_{\cdot c} \tag{8.8}$$

Formulated in this manner, the main-effect null hypotheses (Equations 8.7 and 8.8) are testable whether interactions are present or absent, but these hypotheses are generally of interest only when the interactions are nil.

The two-way ANOVA model, suitably defined, provides a convenient means for testing the hypotheses concerning interactions and main effects (in Equations 8.5, 8.7, and 8.8). The model is

$$Y_{ijk} = \mu + \alpha_j + \beta_k + \gamma_{jk} + \varepsilon_{ijk} \tag{8.9}$$

where Y_{ijk} is the ith observation in row j, column k of the RC table; μ is the general mean of Y; α_j and β_k are main-effect parameters, for row effects and column effects, respectively; γ_{jk} are interaction parameters; and ε_{ijk} are errors satisfying the usual linear-model assumptions. Taking expectations, Equation 8.9 becomes

$$\mu_{jk} \equiv E(Y_{ijk}) = \mu + \alpha_j + \beta_k + \gamma_{jk} \tag{8.10}$$

Because there are $r \times c$ population cell means and $1 + r + c + (r \times c)$ parameters in Equation 8.10, the parameters of the model are not uniquely determined by the cell means. By reasoning that is familiar from Section 8.1 on one-way ANOVA, the indeterminacy of Equation 8.10 can be overcome by imposing $1 + r + c$ independent "identifying" restrictions on its parameters. Although—from one point of view—any restrictions will do, it is convenient to select restrictions that make it simple to test the hypotheses of interest.

With this purpose in mind, we specify the following sigma constraints on the model parameters:

$$\sum_{j=1}^{r} \alpha_j = 0 \tag{8.11}$$

$$\sum_{k=1}^{c} \beta_k = 0$$

$$\sum_{j=1}^{r} \gamma_{jk} = 0 \quad \text{for all } k = 1, \ldots, c$$

$$\sum_{k=1}^{c} \gamma_{jk} = 0 \quad \text{for all } j = 1, \ldots, r$$

At first glance, it seems as if we have specified too many constraints, for Equation 8.11 defines $1 + 1 + c + r$ restrictions. One of the restrictions on the interactions is redundant, however.[15] In shorthand form, the sigma constraints specify that each set of parameters sums to 0 over each of its coordinates.

---

[15] See Exercise 8.2.

The constraints produce the following solution for model parameters in terms of population cell and marginal means:

$$\mu = \mu_{..}$$
$$\alpha_j = \mu_{j.} - \mu_{..}$$
$$\beta_k = \mu_{.k} - \mu_{..}$$
$$\gamma_{jk} = \mu_{jk} - \mu - \alpha_j - \beta_k$$
$$= \mu_{jk} - \mu_{j.} - \mu_{.k} + \mu_{..} \tag{8.12}$$

The hypothesis of no row main effects (Equation 8.7) is, therefore, equivalent to H_0: all $\alpha_j = 0$, for under this hypothesis

$$\mu_{1.} = \mu_{2.} = \cdots = \mu_{r.} = \mu_{..}$$

Likewise, the hypothesis of no column main effects (Equation 8.8) is equivalent to H_0: all $\beta_k = 0$, because then

$$\mu_{.1} = \mu_{.2} = \cdots = \mu_{.c} = \mu_{..}$$

Finally, it is not difficult to show that the hypothesis of no interactions (given in Equation 8.5 or 8.6) is equivalent to H_0: all $\gamma_{jk} = 0$.[16]

8.2.3   Fitting the Two-Way ANOVA Model to Data

Because the least-squares estimator of μ_{jk} is the sample cell mean

$$\overline{Y}_{jk} = \frac{\sum_{i=1}^{n_{jk}} Y_{ijk}}{n_{jk}}$$

least-squares estimators of the constrained model parameters follow immediately from Equation 8.12:

$$M \equiv \widehat{\mu} = \overline{Y}_{..} = \frac{\sum \sum \overline{Y}_{jk}}{r \times c}$$
$$A_j \equiv \widehat{\alpha}_j = \overline{Y}_{j.} - \overline{Y}_{..} = \frac{\sum_k \overline{Y}_{jk}}{c} - \overline{Y}_{..}$$
$$B_k \equiv \widehat{\beta}_k = \overline{Y}_{.k} - \overline{Y}_{..} = \frac{\sum_j \overline{Y}_{jk}}{r} - \overline{Y}_{..}$$
$$C_{jk} \equiv \widehat{\gamma}_{jk} = \overline{Y}_{jk} - \overline{Y}_{j.} - \overline{Y}_{.k} + \overline{Y}_{..}$$

The residuals are just the deviations of the observations from their cell means because the fitted values are the cell means:

$$E_{ijk} = Y_{ijk} - (M + A_j + B_k + C_{jk})$$
$$= Y_{ijk} - \overline{Y}_{jk}$$

---

[16]See Exercise 8.3.

In testing hypotheses about sets of model parameters, however, we require incremental sums of squares for each set, and there is no general way of calculating these sums of squares directly.[17] As in one-way ANOVA, the restrictions on the two-way ANOVA model can be used to produce deviation-coded regressors. Incremental sums of squares can then be calculated in the usual manner. To illustrate this procedure, we will first examine a two-row × three-column classification. The extension to the general $r \times c$ classification is straightforward and is described subsequently.

In light of the restriction $\alpha_1 + \alpha_2 = 0$ on the row effects of the 2×3 classification, α_2 can be deleted from the model, substituting $-\alpha_1$. Similarly, because $\beta_1 + \beta_2 + \beta_3 = 0$, the column main effect β_3 can be replaced by $-\beta_1 - \beta_2$. More generally, $-\sum_{j=1}^{r-1} \alpha_j$ replaces α_r, and $-\sum_{k=1}^{c-1} \beta_k$ replaces β_c. Because there are, then, $r - 1$ independent α_j parameters and $c - 1$ independent β_k parameters, the degrees of freedom for row and column main effects are, respectively, $r - 1$ and $c - 1$.

The interactions in the 2×3 classification satisfy the following constraints:[18]

$$\gamma_{11} + \gamma_{12} + \gamma_{13} = 0$$
$$\gamma_{21} + \gamma_{22} + \gamma_{23} = 0$$
$$\gamma_{11} + \gamma_{21} = 0$$
$$\gamma_{12} + \gamma_{22} = 0$$
$$\gamma_{13} + \gamma_{23} = 0$$

We can, as a consequence, delete all the interaction parameters except γ_{11} and γ_{12}, substituting for the remaining four parameters in the following manner:

$$\gamma_{13} = -\gamma_{11} - \gamma_{12}$$
$$\gamma_{21} = -\gamma_{11}$$
$$\gamma_{22} = -\gamma_{12}$$
$$\gamma_{23} = -\gamma_{13} = \gamma_{11} + \gamma_{12}$$

More generally, we can write all $r \times c$ interaction parameters in terms of $(r - 1)(c - 1)$ of the γ_{jk}s, and there are, therefore, $(r - 1)(c - 1)$ degrees of freedom for interaction.

These observations lead to the following coding of regressors for the 2×3 classification:

Cell		(α_1)	(β_1)	(β_2)	(γ_{11})	(γ_{12})
Row	Column	R_1	C_1	C_2	$R_1 C_1$	$R_1 C_2$
1	1	1	1	0	1	0
1	2	1	0	1	0	1
1	3	1	−1	−1	−1	−1
2	1	−1	1	0	−1	0
2	2	−1	0	1	0	−1
2	3	−1	−1	−1	1	1

[17] An exception occurs when all the cell frequencies are equal—see Section 8.2.5.
[18] Recall that although there are five such constraints, the fifth follows from the first four—you may want to show this—and there are therefore only four *independent* constraints on the interaction parameters.

That is, for example, according to the third row of this table,

$$\mu_{13} = \mu + \alpha_1 - \beta_1 - \beta_2 - \gamma_{11} - \gamma_{12}$$
$$= \mu + \alpha_1 + \beta_3 + \gamma_{13}$$

as required.

I have constructed these regressors to reflect the constraints on the model, but they can also be coded mechanically by applying these rules:

1. There are $r - 1$ regressors for the row main effects; the jth such regressor, R_j, is coded according to the deviation-coding scheme:

$$R_{ij} = \begin{cases} 1 & \text{if observation } i \text{ is in row } j, \\ -1 & \text{if observation } i \text{ is in row } r \text{ (the last row)}, \\ 0 & \text{if observation } i \text{ is in any other row}. \end{cases}$$

2. There are $c - 1$ regressors for the column main effects; the kth such regressor, C_k, is coded according to the deviation-coding scheme:

$$C_{ik} = \begin{cases} 1 & \text{if observation } i \text{ is in column } k, \\ -1 & \text{if observation } i \text{ is in column } c \text{ (the last column)}, \\ 0 & \text{if observation } i \text{ is in any other column}. \end{cases}$$

3. There are $(r - 1)(c - 1)$ regressors for the RC interactions. These interaction regressors consist of all pairwise products of the $r - 1$ main-effect regressors for rows and $c - 1$ main-effect regressors for columns.

The two-way ANOVA model $Y_{ijk} = \mu + \alpha_j + \beta_k + \gamma_{jk} + \varepsilon_{ijk}$ incorporates the main effects and interactions of two factors. This model is overparametrized, but it may be fit to data by placing suitable restrictions on its parameters. A convenient set of restrictions is provided by sigma constraints, specifying that each set of parameters (α_j, β_k, and γ_{jk}) sums to 0 over each of its coordinates. As in one-way ANOVA, sigma constraints lead to deviation-coded regressors.

8.2.4   Testing Hypotheses in Two-Way ANOVA

I have specified constraints on the two-way ANOVA model so that testing hypotheses about the parameters of the constrained model is equivalent to testing hypotheses about the interactions and main effects of the two factors. Tests for interactions and main effects can be constructed by the incremental-sum-of-squares approach.

For ease of reference, I will write $SS(\alpha, \beta, \gamma)$ to denote the regression sum of squares for the full model, which includes both sets of main effects and the interactions. The regression sums of squares for other models are similarly represented. For example, for the no-interaction model, we have $SS(\alpha, \beta)$; and for the model that omits the column main-effect regressors, we have $SS(\alpha, \gamma)$. This last model violates the principle of marginality because it includes the interaction regressors but omits the column main effects. Nevertheless, as I will explain presently, the model plays a role in constructing the incremental sum of squares for testing the column main effects.

As usual, incremental sums of squares are given by *differences* between the regression sums of squares for alternative models, one of which is "nested" within (i.e., is a special case of) the other. I will use the following notation for incremental sums of squares in ANOVA:[19]

$$SS(\gamma|\alpha, \beta) = SS(\alpha, \beta, \gamma) - SS(\alpha, \beta)$$
$$SS(\alpha|\beta, \gamma) = SS(\alpha, \beta, \gamma) - SS(\beta, \gamma)$$
$$SS(\beta|\alpha, \gamma) = SS(\alpha, \beta, \gamma) - SS(\alpha, \gamma)$$
$$SS(\alpha|\beta) = SS(\alpha, \beta) - SS(\beta)$$
$$SS(\beta|\alpha) = SS(\alpha, \beta) - SS(\alpha)$$

We read $SS(\gamma|\alpha, \beta)$, for example, as "the sum of squares for interaction *after* the main effects" and $SS(\alpha|\beta)$ as "the sum of squares for the row main effects *after* the column main effects and *ignoring* the interactions." The residual sum of squares is

$$\begin{aligned} RSS &= \sum\sum\sum E_i^2 \\ &= \sum\sum\sum (Y_{ijk} - \overline{Y}_{jk})^2 \\ &= TSS - SS(\alpha, \beta, \gamma) \end{aligned}$$

The incremental sum of squares for interaction, $SS(\gamma|\alpha, \beta)$, is appropriate for testing the null hypothesis of no interaction, H_0: all $\gamma_{jk} = 0$. In the presence of interactions, we can use $SS(\alpha|\beta, \gamma)$ and $SS(\beta|\alpha, \gamma)$ to test hypotheses concerning main effects (i.e., differences among row and column marginal means), but—as I have explained—these hypotheses are usually not of interest when the interactions are important.

In the *absence* of interactions, $SS(\alpha|\beta)$ and $SS(\beta|\alpha)$ can be used to test for main effects, but the use of $SS(\alpha|\beta, \gamma)$ and $SS(\beta|\alpha, \gamma)$ is also appropriate. If, however, interactions are *present*, then F-tests based on $SS(\alpha|\beta)$ and $SS(\beta|\alpha)$ *do not* test the main-effect null hypotheses H_0: all $\alpha_j = 0$ and H_0: all $\beta_k = 0$; instead, the interaction parameters become implicated in these tests. These remarks are summarized in Table 8.3.

Certain authors (e.g., Nelder, 1976, 1977) prefer main-effects tests based on $SS(\alpha|\beta)$ and $SS(\beta|\alpha)$ because, if interactions are absent, tests based on these sums of squares follow from the principle of marginality and are more powerful than those based on $SS(\alpha|\beta, \gamma)$ and $SS(\beta|\alpha, \gamma)$. Other authors (e.g., Hocking & Speed, 1975) prefer $SS(\alpha|\beta, \gamma)$ and $SS(\beta|\alpha, \gamma)$ because, in the presence of interactions, tests based on these sums of squares have a straightforward (if usually uninteresting) interpretation. I believe that either approach is reasonable but have a preference for tests that conform to the principle of marginality—here, those based on $SS(\alpha|\beta)$ and $SS(\beta|\alpha)$.[20]

---

[19]You may encounter variations of the SS notation. One common approach (used, e.g., in Searle, 1971) is to include the grand mean μ in the arguments to the sum-of-squares function and to let $R(\cdot)$ denote the "raw" (rather than mean-deviation) sum of squares. Thus, in this scheme, $R(\mu, \alpha, \beta) = \sum\sum\sum \widehat{Y}_{ijk}^2$ is the raw sum of squares for the no-interaction model, while

$$\begin{aligned} R(\alpha, \beta|\mu) &= R(\mu, \alpha, \beta) - R(\mu) \\ &= \sum\sum\sum (\widehat{Y}_{ijk} - \overline{Y})^2 \\ &= SS(\alpha, \beta) \end{aligned}$$

is the mean-deviation explained sum of squares for the same model. (The $\widehat{Y}_{ijk}$ are the least-squares fitted values from the no-interaction model.)

[20]In the SAS statistical computer package, $SS(\alpha|\beta)$ and $SS(\beta|\alpha)$ are called "Type II" sums of squares, while $SS(\alpha|\beta, \gamma)$ and $SS(\beta|\alpha, \gamma)$ are called "Type III" sums of squares. This terminology has become widespread.

The *sequential* sums of squares $SS(\alpha)$, $SS(\beta|\alpha)$, and $SS(\gamma|\alpha, \beta)$ are similarly termed "Type-I" sums of squares. Some researchers are attracted to the sequential sums of squares because they add to the regression sum of squares for the full model, $SS(\alpha, \beta, \gamma)$. This attraction is misguided, however, because $SS(\alpha)$ does not test for row main effects. We should focus on the hypotheses to be tested, not on a superficial property of the sums of squares, such as the fact that they add up in a simple manner.

Table 8.3 Two-Way Analysis of Variance, Showing Alternative Tests for Row and Column Main Effects

Source	df	Sum of Squares	H_0
R	$r-1$	$SS(\alpha|\beta, \gamma)$	all $\alpha_j = 0$ $(\mu_{j.} = \mu_{j'.})$
		$SS(\alpha|\beta)$	all $\alpha_j = 0$ | all $\gamma_{jk} = 0$ $(\mu_{j.} = \mu_{j'.}$ | no interaction$)$
C	$c-1$	$SS(\beta|\alpha, \gamma)$	all $\beta_k = 0$ $(\mu_{\cdot k} = \mu_{\cdot k'})$
		$SS(\beta|\alpha)$	all $\beta_k = 0$ | all $\gamma_{jk} = 0$ $(\mu_{\cdot k} = \mu_{\cdot k'}$ | no interaction$)$
RC	$(r-1)(c-1)$	$SS(\gamma|\alpha, \beta)$	all $\gamma_{jk} = 0$ $(\mu_{jk} - \mu_{j'k} = \mu_{jk'} - \mu_{j'k'})$
Residuals	$n-rc$	$TSS - SS(\alpha, \beta, \gamma)$	
Total	$n-1$	TSS	

NOTE: Each incremental F-test is formulated by dividing an effect mean-square by the residual mean-square (where each mean-square is the corresponding sum of squares divided by its degrees of freedom). The hypothesis tested by each such F-test is expressed both in terms of constrained model parameters and in terms of cell or marginal means.

It is important to understand, however, that while $SS(\alpha)$ and $SS(\beta)$ are useful as building blocks of $SS(\alpha|\beta)$ and $SS(\beta|\alpha)$, it is, in general, *inappropriate* to use $SS(\alpha)$ and $SS(\beta)$ to test hypotheses about the R and C main effects: Each of these sums of squares depends on the other set of main effects (and the interactions, if they are present). A main effect is a *partial* effect, so we need to control for rows in assessing the column main effects, and vice versa.

> Testing hypotheses about the sigma-constrained parameters is equivalent to testing interaction-effect and main-effect hypotheses about cell and marginal means. There are two reasonable procedures for testing main-effect hypotheses in two-way ANOVA: Tests based on $SS(\alpha|\beta, \gamma)$ and $SS(\beta|\alpha, \gamma)$ employ models that violate the principle of marginality, but the tests are valid whether or not interactions are present. Tests based on $SS(\alpha|\beta)$ and $SS(\beta|\alpha)$ conform to the principle of marginality but are valid only if interactions are absent.

For the Moore and Krupat conformity data, factor R is partner's status and factor C is authoritarianism. Sums of squares for various models fit to the data are as follows:

$$SS(\alpha, \beta, \gamma) = 391.44$$
$$SS(\alpha, \beta) = 215.95$$
$$SS(\alpha, \gamma) = 355.42$$
$$SS(\beta, \gamma) = 151.87$$
$$SS(\alpha) = 204.33$$

Table 8.4   Analysis-of-Variance Table for Moore and Krupat's Conformity
                Experiment

Source	SS	df	MS	F	p
Partner's status		1			
$\alpha\|\beta, \gamma$	239.57		239.57	11.43	.002
$\alpha\|\beta$	212.22		212.22	10.12	.003
Authoritarianism		2			
$\beta\|\alpha, \gamma$	36.02		18.01	0.86	.43
$\beta\|\alpha$	11.62		5.81	0.28	.76
Partner's status $\times$ Authoritarianism	175.49	2	87.74	4.18	.02
Residuals	817.76	39	20.97		
Total	1209.2	44			

NOTE: Alternative tests are shown for the partner's status and authoritarianism main
effects.

$$\text{SS}(\beta) = \quad 3.73$$
$$\text{TSS} = 1209.20$$

The ANOVA for the experiment is shown in Table 8.4. The predicted status $\times$ authoritarianism
interaction proves to be statistically significant. A researcher would not normally report both sets
of main-effect sums of squares; in this instance, where the interactions probably are not negligible,
$\text{SS}(\alpha|\beta)$ and $\text{SS}(\beta|\alpha)$ do not test hypotheses about main effects, as I have explained.

8.2.5   Equal Cell Frequencies

Equal cell frequencies simplify—but do not change fundamentally—the procedures of the preceding section. When all the cell frequencies are the same, the deviation regressors for *different* sets of
effects are uncorrelated. Equal-cell-frequencies data are often termed *balanced* or *orthogonal*.[21]

Uncorrelated main-effect and interaction regressors permit a unique decomposition of the
regression sum of squares for the model, $\text{SS}(\alpha, \beta, \gamma)$, into components due to the three sets of
effects. Indeed, for balanced data,

$$\text{SS}(\alpha|\beta, \gamma) = \text{SS}(\alpha|\beta) = \text{SS}(\alpha)$$
$$\text{SS}(\beta|\alpha, \gamma) = \text{SS}(\beta|\alpha) = \text{SS}(\beta)$$
$$\text{SS}(\gamma|\alpha, \beta) = \text{SS}(\gamma)$$

and hence

$$SS(\alpha, \beta, \gamma) = \text{SS}(\alpha) + \text{SS}(\beta) + \text{SS}(\gamma)$$

These results lead to simple direct formulas for the several sums of squares:

$$\text{SS}(\alpha) = n'c \sum_{j=1}^{r}(\overline{Y}_{j\cdot} - \overline{Y}_{\cdot\cdot})^2$$

$$\text{SS}(\beta) = n'r \sum_{k=1}^{c}(\overline{Y}_{\cdot k} - \overline{Y}_{\cdot\cdot})^2$$

---

[21] See Chapter 10, on the geometry of linear models, for an explanation of the term *orthogonal*.

$$SS(\gamma) = n' \sum_{j=1}^{r} \sum_{k=1}^{c} (\overline{Y}_{jk} - \overline{Y}_{j\cdot} - \overline{Y}_{\cdot k} + \overline{Y}_{\cdot\cdot})^2$$

where $n' = n/rc$ is the number of observations in each cell of the RC table.

8.2.6   Some Cautionary Remarks

R. A. Fisher (1925) originally formulated ANOVA for balanced data. Yet, as early as 1934, Fisher's colleague at the Rothamsted Experimental Station in England, Frank Yates, extended ANOVA to unbalanced data. Apart from approximate methods motivated by the desire to reduce the effort of calculation, Yates (1934) suggested two approaches to the two-way classification, naming both for the computational techniques that he developed. The first approach, which he called "the method of weighted squares of means," calculates (using our notation) the main-effect sums of squares $SS(\alpha|\beta, \gamma)$ and $SS(\beta|\alpha, \gamma)$, and the interaction sum of squares $SS(\gamma|\alpha, \beta)$. Yates's second approach, which he called "the method of fitting constants," assumes that interactions are absent and calculates $SS(\alpha|\beta)$ and $SS(\beta|\alpha)$.

Considering the apparent simplicity of the two-way classification and the lucidity of Yates's treatment of it, it is ironic that the analysis of unbalanced data has become the subject of controversy and confusion. While it is not my purpose to present a complete account of the "debate" concerning the proper handling of unbalanced data—and while it is tempting to ignore this debate altogether—there are two reasons for addressing the topic briefly here: (1) You may encounter confused applications of ANOVA or may have occasion to consult other accounts of the method; and (2) computer programs for ANOVA are occasionally misleading or vague in their documentation and output or even incorrect in their calculations (see Francis, 1973).[22]

Much of the confusion about the analysis of unbalanced data has its source in the restrictions—or other techniques—that are used to solve the "overparametrized" (i.e., unrestricted) two-way ANOVA model. Imagine, for example, that we use dummy $(0, 1)$ coding rather than deviation $(-1, 0, 1)$ coding to fit the model to the data.

Let $SS^*(\cdot)$ denote the regression sum of squares for a dummy-coded model. For the full model and the main-effects model, we obtain the same sums of squares as before; that is,

$$SS(\alpha, \beta, \gamma) = SS^*(\alpha, \beta, \gamma)$$
$$SS(\alpha, \beta) = SS^*(\alpha, \beta)$$

Likewise (because they are just the two one-way ANOVAs)

$$SS(\alpha) = SS^*(\alpha)$$
$$SS(\beta) = SS^*(\beta)$$

And because these regression sums of squares are the same, so are the incremental sums of squares that depend on them:

$$SS(\gamma|\alpha, \beta) = SS^*(\gamma|\alpha, \beta)$$
$$SS(\alpha|\beta) = SS^*(\alpha|\beta)$$
$$SS(\beta|\alpha) = SS^*(\beta|\alpha)$$

---

[22]With respect to the second point, it is good practice to test a computer program with known data before trusting it to analyze new data. This advice applies not just to ANOVA calculations, but generally.

In general, however,

$$SS(\alpha, \gamma) \neq SS^*(\alpha, \gamma)$$
$$SS(\beta, \gamma) \neq SS^*(\beta, \gamma)$$

and, consequently (also in general),

$$SS(\alpha|\beta, \gamma) \neq SS^*(\alpha|\beta, \gamma)$$
$$SS(\beta|\alpha, \gamma) \neq SS^*(\beta|\alpha, \gamma)$$

The general lesson to be drawn from these results is that tests that conform to the principle of marginality [here, those based on $SS(\gamma|\alpha, \beta)$, $SS(\alpha|\beta)$, and $SS(\beta|\alpha)$] *do not* depend on the specific restrictions that were employed to identify the model (i.e., remove the indeterminacy in the overparametrized model), while tests that "violate" the principle of marginality [those based on $SS(\alpha|\beta, \gamma)$ and $SS(\beta|\alpha, \gamma)$] *do* depend on the specific restrictions.

I showed that $SS(\alpha|\beta, \gamma)$ and $SS(\beta|\alpha, \gamma)$, based on the sigma constraints, are appropriate for testing hypotheses about main effects in the potential presence of interactions. It follows that $SS^*(\alpha|\beta, \gamma)$ and $SS^*(\beta|\alpha, \gamma)$ *do not* properly test these hypotheses. It is important, in this context, to select constraints that test reasonable hypotheses about cell and marginal means. The SS notation is frequently used carelessly, without attention to the constraints that are employed and to the hypotheses that follow from them.[23]

8.3 Higher-Way Analysis of Variance

The methods of the previous section can be extended to any number of factors. I will consider the three-way classification in some detail before commenting briefly on the general case.

8.3.1 The Three-Way Classification

It is convenient to label the factors in the three-way classification as A, B, and C, with a, b, and c levels, consecutively. A response-variable observation is represented by Y_{ijkm}, where the first subscript gives the index of the observation within its cell. The number of observations sampled in cell $\{j, k, m\}$ is n_{jkm}; and μ_{jkm} is the population mean in this cell. Quantities such as $\mu_{...}$, $\mu_{j..}$, and $\mu_{jk.}$ denote marginal means formed by averaging over the dotted subscripts.

The three-way ANOVA model is

$$
\begin{aligned}
Y_{ijkm} &= \mu_{jkm} + \varepsilon_{ijkm} \\
&= \mu + \alpha_{A(j)} + \alpha_{B(k)} + \alpha_{C(m)} + \alpha_{AB(jk)} \\
&\quad + \alpha_{AC(jm)} + \alpha_{BC(km)} + \alpha_{ABC(jkm)} + \varepsilon_{ijkm}
\end{aligned}
\tag{8.13}
$$

Note that, to avoid the proliferation of symbols, I have introduced a new and easily extended notation for model parameters: The first set of subscripts (e.g., AB) indicates the factors to which a parameter pertains, while the parenthetical subscripts [e.g., (j, k)] index factor categories.

---

[23]Further discussions on the points raised in this section may be found in a variety of sources, including Hocking and Speed (1975), Speed and Hocking (1976), Speed, Hocking, and Hackney (1978), Speed and Monlezun (1979), Searle, Speed, and Henderson (1981), and Steinhorst (1982). Also see Section 9.1.1 and Exercise 9.15.

We make the usual linear-model assumptions about the errors ε_{ijkm} and constrain all sets of parameters to sum to 0 over every coordinate; for example,

$$\sum_{j=1}^{a} \alpha_{A(j)} = 0$$

$$\sum_{j=1}^{a} \alpha_{AB(jk)} = \sum_{k=1}^{b} \alpha_{AB(jk)} = 0 \quad \text{for all } j, k$$

$$\sum_{j=1}^{a} \alpha_{ABC(jkm)} = \sum_{k=1}^{b} \alpha_{ABC(jkm)} = \sum_{m=1}^{c} \alpha_{ABC(jkm)} = 0 \quad \text{for all } j, k, m$$

The sigma constraints for $\alpha_{B(k)}$, $\alpha_{C(m)}$, $\alpha_{AC(jm)}$, and $\alpha_{BC(km)}$ follow similar patterns.

The three-way ANOVA model includes parameters for main effects ($\alpha_{A(j)}$, $\alpha_{B(k)}$, and $\alpha_{C(m)}$), for *two-way interactions* between each pair of factors ($\alpha_{AB(jk)}$, $\alpha_{AC(jm)}$, and $\alpha_{BC(km)}$), and for *three-way interactions* among all three factors ($\alpha_{ABC(jkm)}$). The two-way interactions have the same interpretation as in two-way ANOVA: If, for instance, A and B interact, then the effect of either factor on the response variable varies across the levels of the other factor. Similarly, if the ABC interaction is nonzero, then the joint effect of any pair of factors (say, A and B) varies across the categories of the remaining factor (C).

In formulating models and interpreting effects in three-way ANOVA, we may again appeal to the principle of marginality. Thus, main effects (e.g., of A) are generally not interpreted if they are marginal to non-null interactions (AB, AC, or ABC). Likewise, a *lower-order* inter-action (such as AB) is usually not interpreted if it has a non-null *higher-order relative* (ABC): If the joint effects of A and B are different in different categories of C, then it is not gener-ally sensible to speak of the *unconditional* AB effects, without reference to a specific category of C.

Deviation regressors for main effects in the three-way classification can be coded as before; regressors for interactions are formed by taking all possible products of the main effects that "compose" the interaction. Here, for example, is the coding for $a = 2$, $b = 2$, and $c = 3$:

Cell jkm	A	B	C_1	C_2	AB	AC_1	AC_2	BC_1	BC_2	ABC_1	ABC_2
111	1	1	1	0	1	1	0	1	0	1	0
112	1	1	0	1	1	0	1	0	1	0	1
113	1	1	−1	−1	1	−1	−1	−1	−1	−1	−1
121	1	−1	1	0	−1	1	0	−1	0	−1	0
122	1	−1	0	1	−1	0	1	0	−1	0	−1
123	1	−1	−1	−1	−1	−1	−1	1	1	1	1
211	−1	1	1	0	−1	−1	0	1	0	−1	0
212	−1	1	0	1	−1	0	−1	0	1	0	−1
213	−1	1	−1	−1	−1	1	1	−1	−1	1	1
221	−1	−1	1	0	1	−1	0	−1	0	1	0
222	−1	−1	0	1	1	0	−1	0	−1	0	1
223	−1	−1	−1	−1	1	1	1	1	1	−1	−1

The following points are noteworthy:

- The 12 cell means are expressed in terms of an equal number of independent parameters (including the general mean, μ), underscoring the point that three-way interactions may be required to account for the pattern of cell means. More generally in the three-way classification, there are abc cells and the same number of independent parameters:

$$1 + (a-1) + (b-1) + (c-1) + (a-1)(b-1) + (a-1)(c-1) + (b-1)(c-1)$$
$$+ (a-1)(b-1)(c-1)$$
$$= abc.$$

- The degrees of freedom for a set of effects correspond, as usual, to the number of independent parameters in the set. There are, for example, $a-1$ degrees of freedom for the A main effects; $(a-1)(b-1)$ degrees of freedom for the AB interactions; and $(a-1)(b-1)(c-1)$ degrees of freedom for the ABC interactions.

Solving for the constrained parameters in terms of populations means produces the following results:

$$\mu = \mu \dots$$
$$\alpha_{A(j)} = \mu_{j..} - \mu \dots$$
$$\alpha_{AB(jk)} = \mu_{jk.} - \mu - \alpha_{A(j)} - \alpha_{B(k)}$$
$$= \mu_{jk.} - \mu_{j..} - \mu_{.k.} + \mu \dots$$
$$\alpha_{ABC(jkm)} = \mu_{jkm} - \mu - \alpha_{A(j)} - \alpha_{B(k)} - \alpha_{C(m)} - \alpha_{AB(jk)} - \alpha_{AC(jm)} - \alpha_{BC(km)}$$
$$= \mu_{jkm} - \mu_{jk.} - \mu_{j.m} - \mu_{.km} + \mu_{j..} + \mu_{.k.} + \mu_{..m} - \mu \dots$$

(The patterns for $\alpha_{B(k)}$, $\alpha_{C(m)}$, $\alpha_{AC(jm)}$, and $\alpha_{BC(km)}$ are similar, and are omitted for brevity.) As in two-way ANOVA, therefore, the null hypothesis

$$H_0: \text{ all } \alpha_{A(j)} = 0$$

is equivalent to

$$H_0: \mu_{1..} = \mu_{2..} = \cdots = \mu_{a..}$$

and the hypothesis

$$H_0: \text{ all } \alpha_{AB(jk)} = 0$$

is equivalent to

$$H_0: \mu_{jk.} - \mu_{j'k.} = \mu_{jk'.} - \mu_{j'k'.} \quad \text{for all } j, j' \text{ and } k, k'$$

Likewise, some algebraic manipulation[24] shows that the null hypothesis

$$H_0: \text{ all } \alpha_{ABC(jkm)} = 0$$

is equivalent to

$$H_0: (\mu_{jkm} - \mu_{j'km}) - (\mu_{jk'm} - \mu_{j'k'm})$$
$$= (\mu_{jkm'} - \mu_{j'km'}) - (\mu_{jk'm'} - \mu_{j'k'm'})$$
$$\text{for all } j, j'; k, k'; \text{ and } m, m' \tag{8.14}$$

---

[24] See Exercise 8.4.

Table 8.5   General Three-Way ANOVA Table, Showing Incremental Sums of Squares for Terms Involving Factor A

Source	df	Sum of Squares	H_0
A	$a-1$	SS($A\|B,C,AB,AC,BC,ABC$) SS($A\|B,C,BC$)	$\alpha_A = 0$ $\alpha_A = 0 \mid \alpha_{AB} = \alpha_{AC} = \alpha_{ABC} = 0$
AB	$(a-1)(b-1)$	SS($AB\|A,B,C,AC,BC,ABC$) SS($AB\|A,B,C,AC,BC$)	$\alpha_{AB} = 0$ $\alpha_{AB} = 0 \mid \alpha_{ABC} = 0$
ABC	$(a-1)(b-1)(c-1)$	SS($ABC\|A,B,C,AB,AC,BC$)	$\alpha_{ABC} = 0$
Residuals	$n-abc$	TSS $-$ SS(A,B,C,AB,AC,BC,ABC)	
Total	$n-1$	TSS	

NOTE: Alternative tests are shown for the A main effects and AB interactions.

The second-order differences in Equation 8.14 are equal when the pattern of AB interactions is invariant across categories of factor C—an intuitively reasonable extension of the notion of no interaction to three factors. Rearranging the terms in Equation 8.14 produces similar results for AC and BC, demonstrating that three-way interaction—like two-way interaction—is symmetric in the factors. As in two-way ANOVA, this simple relationship between model parameters and population means depends on the sigma constraints, which were imposed on the overparametrized model in Equation 8.13.

Incremental F-tests can be constructed in the usual manner for the parameters of the three-way ANOVA model. A general ANOVA table, adapting the SS notation of Section 8.2.4 and showing alternative tests for main effects and lower-order interactions, is sketched in Table 8.5. Once more, for compactness, only tests involving factor A are shown. Note that a main-effect hypothesis such as H_0: all $\alpha_{A(j)} = 0$ is of interest even when the BC interactions are present because A is not marginal to BC.

8.3.2   Higher-Order Classifications

Extension of ANOVA to more than three factors is algebraically and computationally straightforward. The general p-way classification can be described by a model containing terms for every combination of factors; the highest-order term, therefore, is for the p-way interactions. If the p-way interactions are nonzero, then the joint effects of any $p-1$ factors vary across the levels of the remaining factor. In general, we can be guided by the principle of marginality in interpreting effects.

Three-way interactions, however, are reasonably complex, and the even greater complexity of higher-order interactions can make their interpretation difficult. Yet, at times, we may expect to observe a high-order interaction of a particular sort, as when a specific *combination* of characteristics predisposes individuals to act in a certain manner.[25] On the other hand, it is common to find that high-order interactions are not statistically significant or that they are negligibly small relative to other effects.

There is, moreover, no rule of data analysis that requires us to fit and test all possible interactions. In working with higher-way classifications, we may limit our consideration

---

[25] An alternative to specifying a high-order interaction would be simply to introduce a dummy regressor, coded 1 for the combination of categories in question and 0 elsewhere.

to effects that are of theoretical interest, or at least to effects that are substantively interpretable. It is fairly common, for example, for researchers to fit models containing only main effects:

$$Y_{ijk...r} = \mu + \alpha_{A(j)} + \alpha_{B(k)} + \cdots + \alpha_{P(r)} + \varepsilon_{ijk...r}$$

This approach, sometimes called *multiple-classification analysis* or *MCA* (Andrews, Morgan, & Sonquist, 1973),[26] is analogous to an additive multiple regression. In a similar spirit, a researcher might entertain models that include only main effects and two-way interactions.

> The ANOVA model and procedures for testing hypotheses about main effects and interactions extend straightforwardly to three-way and higher-way classifications. In each case, the highest-order interaction corresponds to the number of factors in the model. It is not necessary, however, to specify a model that includes all terms through the highest-order interaction.

Cell means for an illustrative four-way classification appear in Figure 8.6, which shows mean vocabulary score in the U.S. General Social Surveys as a function of level of education (less than high school, high school, junior college, bachelor's degree, or graduate degree), age group (five bins, from 18–29 to 60 or more), place of birth (foreign born or native born), and sex.[27] The 18,655 observations in the data set are therefore divided across $5 \times 5 \times 2 \times 2 = 100$ cells. Most cells have a substantial number of observations, but some—especially among the foreign born—are sparse, and although there is some data in every cell, there is, for example, only one foreign-born male, 50–59 years of age, with a junior-college education.

The vertical lines in Figure 8.6 represent ± 2 standard errors around the means; in cells with a very small number of observations, some of these intervals extend beyond the range of the vertical axis (and, indeed, in the cell with only one observation, the interval is infinite). Discounting the means that are highly variable, the pattern of change in mean vocabulary score with education appears quite similar across cells, and education seems to have a much stronger impact on vocabulary score than do the other factors.

Although vocabulary score is discrete, and a disguised proportion, its distribution is reasonably well behaved, and I therefore proceed with a four-way ANOVA, shown in Table 8.6. The tests in this ANOVA table conform to the principle of marginality. Thus, for example, the main-effect sum of squares for education is computed after age, place of birth, sex, and all two- and three-way interactions among these factors, but ignoring all the interactions of which education is a lower-order relative.

One of the important uses of a statistical model is to "smooth" the data, eliminating features of the data that are unimportant.[28] In a large data set, such as this one, even trivial effects can prove to be "statistically significant," and we may wish to ignore such effects in describing

---

[26]The term *multiple-classification analysis* is unfortunate because it is equally descriptive of any ANOVA model fit to the *p*-way classification.

[27]The GSS vocabulary data were introduced in Chapter 3.

[28]Of course, what counts as "unimportant" varies by context, and in some circumstances even a relatively minor feature of the data may prove to be of interest.

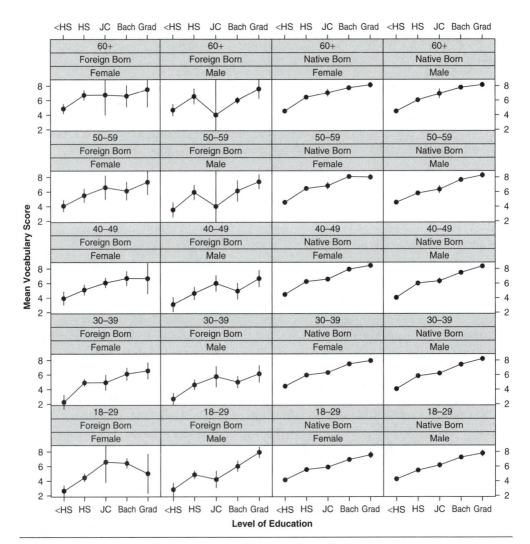

Figure 8.6   Mean vocabularly score by level of education, age group, place of birth, and sex, using data from the U. S. General Social Surveys. The education levels represented are less than high school (<HS), high school (HS), junior college (JC), bachelor's degree (Bach), and graduate degree (Grad). The dots represent the cell means. The vertical line around each dot is ±2 standard errors around the corresponding cell mean. In some cells these intervals extend beyond the end points of the vertical axis, while in other cells the lines are so short that they are not discernible.

the data. Chapter 22 presents methods for selecting a statistical model to summarize data based on considerations other than p-values. Anticipating that discussion, I have settled on a model for the vocabulary data that includes main effects of sex, place of birth, education, and age group, and the two-way interaction between place of birth and age group. This model, with $R^2 = .267$, accounts for almost as much variation in the vocabulary scores as the full model, for which $R^2 = .275$, despite the fact that the former has only 15 coefficients and the latter 100 coefficients!

Table 8.6 Four-Way ANOVA of Vocabulary Score by Sex, Place of Birth, Education, and Age Groups

Source	Sum of Squares	df	Mean Square	F	p
Sex (S)	127	1	127.00	37.58	≪.0001
Place of Birth (B)	1,122	1	1122.00	331.13	≪.0001
Education (E)	20,556	4	5139.00	1516.38	≪.0001
Age Group (A)	1,211	4	302.75	89.31	≪.0001
S×B	3	1	3.00	0.80	.37
S×E	62	4	15.50	4.56	.001
S×A	104	4	26.00	7.66	<.0001
B×E	102	4	25.50	7.50	<.0001
B×A	240	4	60.00	17.73	≪.0001
E×A	103	16	6.44	1.90	.02
S×B×E	37	4	9.25	2.76	.03
S×B×A	18	4	4.50	1.32	.26
S×E×A	74	16	4.63	1.36	.15
B×E×A	110	16	6.87	2.03	.009
S×B×E×A	98	16	6.13	1.81	.024
Residuals	62,917	18,565	3.39		
Total	86,833	18,664			

NOTE: The various sums of squares are computed in conformity with the principle of marginality.

Figure 8.7 shows "effect displays" for the simplified model.[29] In computing each effect, other explanatory variables are held to average values—in the case of factors (and all of the explanatory variables here are factors), to their observed distribution in the data. It is apparent from Figure 8.7 that education is by far the largest influence on vocabulary. The sex main effect, in contrast, is quite small—only a fraction of a word on the 10-word test. Age apparently makes more of a difference to the vocabulary scores of the foreign born than of the native born, and the vocabulary advantage of the native born grows smaller with age.

*Computing the Effect Display**

To compute the effects in Figure 8.7, each variable in a high-order term is allowed to range over its values, while other explanatory variables are set to "average" values. In the case of a factor, we fix the regressors coding the main effects for the factors to their means, which is equivalent to fixing the distribution of the factor to the sample proportions at its various levels; interaction regressors are fixed to the products of the main-effect regressors marginal to the interaction. Effect displays computed in this manner are invariant with respect to the coding of factors, as long as the model obeys the principle of marginality.

Table 8.7 shows the quantities used to compute two of the fitted values in the effect displays in Figure 8.7: (1) the effect of membership in the "graduate degree" category for the main effect of education; and (2) the effect of membership in the combination of categories "foreign born" and "40–49" for the interaction between place of birth and age.

---

[29]Effect displays were introduced in Section 7.3.4.

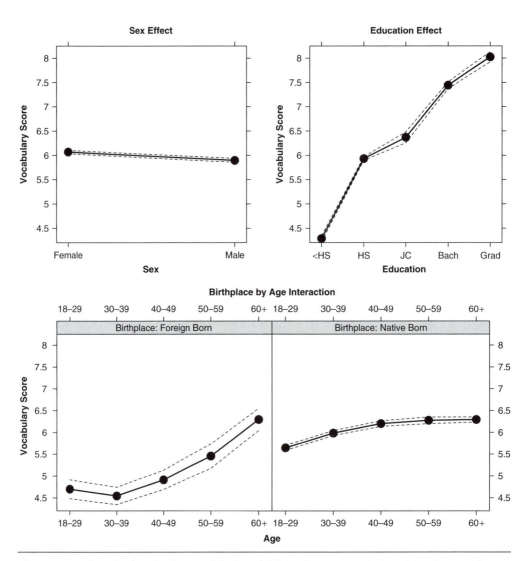

Figure 8.7   Effect displays for the simplified model fit to the GSS vocabulary data, showing the
main effects of sex and education, and the interaction between place of birth and
age—the high-order terms in the model. The broken lines give pointwise 95%
confidence intervals around the estimated effects.

- To calculate the first effect from Table 8.7, we have

$$\widehat{y}_1 = \sum_{j=1}^{15} B_j x_{j1}$$

$$= 6.0350 \times 1 + 0.0861 \times 0.1442 - 2.1247 \times -1.0000$$
$$+ \cdots + 0.0389 \times -0.8649 \times -0.0893$$
$$= 8.0264$$

Table 8.7 Computation of Effects for the Model Including Main Effects of Sex and Education and the Interaction between Place of Birth and Age

Regressor	Coefficient B_j	Regressor Mean, $\overline{X}_j$	Graduate x_{j1}	Foreign, 40–49 x_{j2}
Constant	6.0350	1.0000	1.0000	1.0000
Sex (Male)	0.0861	0.1442	0.1442	0.1442
Education (<HS)	−2.1247	0.1308	−1.0000	0.1308
Education (HS)	−0.4778	0.4669	−1.0000	0.4669
Education (JC)	−0.0431	−0.0102	−1.0000	−0.0102
Education (Bach)	1.0315	0.0817	−1.0000	0.0817
Birthplace (Foreign)	−0.4490	−0.8649	−0.8649	1.0000
Age (18–29)	−0.4585	0.0018	0.0018	0.0000
Age (30–39)	−0.3654	0.0114	0.0114	0.0000
Age (40–49)	−0.0738	−0.0343	−0.0343	1.0000
Age (50–59)	0.2337	−0.0893	−0.0893	0.0000
Foreign × 18–29	−0.0231	—	−0.8649× 0.0018	0.0000
Foreign × 30–39	−0.2704	—	−0.8649× 0.0114	0.0000
Foreign × 40–49	−0.1956	—	−0.8649×−0.0343	1.0000
Foreign × 50–59	0.0389	—	−0.8649×−0.0893	0.0000

NOTE: The column labeled x_{j1} contains the values of the regressors used to compute the effects of membership in the "graduate degree" category of the education factor; the column labeled x_{j2} contains the values of the regressors used to compute the effects of membership in the combination of categories "foreign born" and "40–49" for the interaction of place of birth with age.

Note that in this computation, the regression constant is multiplied by 1 and that because "graduate degree" is the *last* category of education, all the regressors for education take on the value −1 by virtue of the sigma constraint on the coefficients of the education main effect. Other main-effect regressors are set to their mean values, and interaction regressors to the products of the mean values of the main effects composing the interactions.

- Similarly, to compute the second effect,

$$\widehat{y}_2 = \sum_{j=1}^{15} B_j x_{j2}$$
$$= 6.0350 \times 1 + 0.0861 \times 0.1442 + \cdots - 0.0343 \times 1$$
$$+ \cdots - 0.1956 \times 1 + 0.0389 \times 0$$
$$= 4.9129$$

Here, the deviation regressor for place of birth takes on the value 1 (i.e., foreign), as do the regressor for the 40–49 age category and the product regressor for these two categories.

Because the effects are just weighted sums of the regression coefficients, their standard errors can be computed from the coefficient sampling variances and covariances.[30]

---

[30]See Exercise 9.14.

8.3.3   Empty Cells in ANOVA

As the number of factors increases, the number of cells grows at a much faster rate: For p dichotomous factors, for example, the number of cells is 2^p. One consequence of this proliferation is that some combinations of factor categories may not be observed; that is, certain cells in the p-way classification may be empty.

Nevertheless, we can use our deviation-coding approach to estimation and testing in the presence of empty cells as long as the *marginal* frequency tables corresponding to the effects that we entertain contain no empty cells. For example, in a two-way classification with an empty cell, we can safely fit the main-effects model (see below), because the one-way frequency counts for each factor separately contain no 0s. The full model with interactions is not covered by the rule, however, because the two-way table of counts contains a 0 frequency. By extension, the rule *never* covers the p-way interaction when there is a 0 cell in a p-way classification.[31]

To illustrate the difficulties produced by empty cells, I will develop a very simple example for a 2×2 classification with cell frequencies:

	C_1	C_2	*Row marginal*
R_1	n_{11}	n_{12}	$n_{11} + n_{12}$
R_2	n_{21}	0	n_{21}
Column marginal	$n_{11} + n_{21}$	n_{12}	n

That is, the cell frequency n_{22} is 0. Because there are no observations in this cell, we cannot estimate the cell mean μ_{22}. Writing out the other cell means in terms of the sigma-restricted model parameters produces three equations:

$$\mu_{11} = \mu + \alpha_1 + \beta_1 + \gamma_{11}$$
$$\mu_{12} = \mu + \alpha_1 + \beta_2 + \gamma_{12} = \mu + \alpha_1 - \beta_1 - \gamma_{11}$$
$$\mu_{21} = \mu + \alpha_2 + \beta_1 + \gamma_{21} = \mu - \alpha_1 + \beta_1 - \gamma_{11}$$

There are, then, four independent parameters (μ, α_1, β_1, and γ_{11}) but only three population means in observed cells, so the parameters are not uniquely determined by the means.

Now imagine that we can reasonably specify the *absence* of two-way interactions for these data. Then, according to our general rule, we should be able to estimate and test the R and C main effects because there are observations at each level of R and at each level of C. The equations relating cell means to independent parameters become

$$\mu_{11} = \mu + \alpha_1 + \beta_1$$
$$\mu_{12} = \mu + \alpha_1 + \beta_2 = \mu + \alpha_1 - \beta_1$$
$$\mu_{21} = \mu + \alpha_2 + \beta_1 = \mu - \alpha_1 + \beta_1$$

---

[31] It may be possible, however, to estimate and test effects not covered by this simple rule, but determining whether tests are possible and specifying sensible hypotheses to be tested are considerably more complex in this instance. For details see, for example, Searle (1971, pp. 318–324), Hocking and Speed (1975, pp. 711–712), and Speed et al. (1978, pp. 110–111). The advice given in Section 8.2.6 regarding care in the use of computer programs for ANOVA of unbalanced data applies even more urgently when there are empty cells.

Solving for the parameters in terms of the cell means produces[32]

$$\mu = \frac{\mu_{12} + \mu_{21}}{2}$$

$$\alpha_1 = \frac{\mu_{11} - \mu_{21}}{2}$$

$$\beta_1 = \frac{\mu_{11} - \mu_{12}}{2}$$

These results make sense, for, in the *absence* of interaction:

- The cell means μ_{12} and μ_{21} are "balanced" with respect to both sets of main effects, and therefore their average serves as a suitable definition of the grand mean.
- The difference $\mu_{11} - \mu_{21}$ gives the effect of changing R while C is held constant (at level 1), which is a suitable definition of the main effect of R.
- The difference $\mu_{11} - \mu_{12}$ gives the effect of changing C while R is held constant (at level 1), which is a suitable definition of the main effect of C.

8.4 Analysis of Covariance

Analysis of covariance (*ANCOVA*) is a term used to describe linear models that contain both qualitative and quantitative explanatory variables. The method is, therefore, equivalent to dummy-variable regression, discussed in the previous chapter, although the ANCOVA model is parametrized differently from the dummy-regression model.[33] Traditional applications of ANCOVA use an additive model (i.e., without interactions). The traditional additive ANCOVA model is a special case of the more general model that I present here.

In ANCOVA, an ANOVA formulation is used for the main effects and interactions of the qualitative explanatory variables (i.e., the factors), and the quantitative explanatory variables (or *covariates*) are expressed as deviations from their means. Neither of these variations represents an essential change, however, for the ANCOVA model provides the same fit to the data as the dummy-regression model. Moreover, if tests are formulated following the principle of marginality, then precisely the same sums of squares are obtained for the two parametrizations. Nevertheless, the ANCOVA parametrization makes it simple to formulate sensible (if ordinarily uninteresting) tests for lower-order terms in the presence of their higher-order relatives.

I will use Moore and Krupat's study of conformity and authoritarianism to illustrate ANCOVA. When we last encountered these data, both explanatory variables—partner's status and authoritarianism—were treated as factors.[34] Partner's status is dichotomous, but authoritarianism is a quantitative score (the "F-scale"), which was arbitrarily categorized for the two-way ANOVA. Here, I will treat authoritarianism more naturally as a covariate.

A dummy-regression formulation, representing authoritarianism by X, and coding $D = 1$ in the low partner's status group and $D = 0$ in the high partner's status group, produces the following fit to the data (with estimated standard errors in parentheses below the coefficients):

---

[32]The 2×2 classification with one empty cell is especially simple because the number of parameters in the main-effects model is equal to (i.e., no fewer than) the number of observed cell means. This is not generally the case, making a general analysis considerably more complex.

[33]Usage here is not wholly standardized, and the terms *dummy regression* and *analysis of covariance* are often taken as synonymous.

[34]See Section 8.2.

$$\widehat{Y} = 20.79 \ - \ 0.1511X \ - \ 15.53D \ + \ 0.2611(X \times D)$$
$$\quad (3.26) \quad (0.0717) \quad\ (4.40) \quad\ (0.0970)$$
$$R^2 = .2942 \tag{8.15}$$

It makes sense, in this model, to test whether the interaction coefficient is statistically significant (clearly it is), but—as explained in the previous chapter—it is not sensible to construe the coefficients of X and D as "main effects" of authoritarianism and partner's status: The coefficient of X is the authoritarianism slope in the high-status group, while the coefficient of D is the difference in the regression lines for the two groups at an authoritarianism score of $X = 0$.

An ANCOVA model for the Moore and Krupat experiment is

$$Y_{ij} = \mu + \alpha_j + \beta(X_{ij} - \overline{X}) + \gamma_j(X_{ij} - \overline{X}) + \varepsilon_{ij} \tag{8.16}$$

where

- Y_{ij} is the conformity score for subject i in category j of partner's status;
- μ is the general level of conformity;
- α_j is the main effect of membership in group j of partner's status;
- β is the main-effect slope of authoritarianism, X;
- γ_j is the interaction between partner's status and authoritarianism for group j;
- ε_{ij} is the error; and
- the mean authoritarianism score $\overline{X}$ is computed over all the data.

To achieve a concrete understanding of the model in Equation 8.16, let us—as is our usual practice—write out the model separately for each group:

$$\text{Low status:} \quad Y_{i1} = \mu + \alpha_1 + \beta(X_{i1} - \overline{X}) + \gamma_1(X_{i1} - \overline{X}) + \varepsilon_{i1}$$
$$= \mu + \alpha_1 + (\beta + \gamma_1)(X_{i1} - \overline{X}) + \varepsilon_{i1}$$
$$\text{High status:} \quad Y_{i2} = \mu + \alpha_2 + \beta(X_{i2} - \overline{X}) + \gamma_2(X_{i2} - \overline{X}) + \varepsilon_{i2}$$
$$= \mu + \alpha_2 + (\beta + \gamma_2)(X_{i2} - \overline{X}) + \varepsilon_{i2}$$

It is immediately apparent that there are too many parameters: We are fitting one line in each of two groups, which requires four parameters, but there are six parameters in the model—μ, α_1, α_2, β, γ_1, and γ_2.

We require two restrictions, and to provide them we will place sigma constraints on the αs and γs:

$$\alpha_1 + \alpha_2 = 0 \quad \Rightarrow \quad \alpha_2 = -\alpha_1$$
$$\gamma_1 + \gamma_2 = 0 \quad \Rightarrow \quad \gamma_2 = -\gamma_1$$

Under these constraints, the two regression equations become

$$\text{Low status:} \quad Y_{i1} = \mu + \alpha_1 + (\beta + \gamma_1)(X_{i1} - \overline{X}) + \varepsilon_{i1}$$
$$\text{High status:} \quad Y_{i2} = \mu - \alpha_1 + (\beta - \gamma_1)(X_{i2} - \overline{X}) + \varepsilon_{i2}$$

The parameters of the constrained model therefore have the following straightforward interpretations (see Figure 8.8):

- μ is midway between the two regression lines above the mean of the covariate, $\overline{X}$.
- α_1 is half the difference between the two regression lines, again above $\overline{X}$.

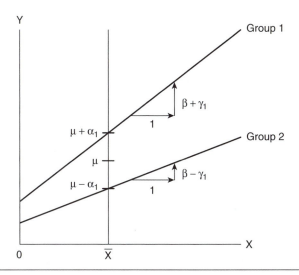

Figure 8.8   The analysis-of-covariance model for two groups, permitting different within-group slopes.

- β is the average of the slopes $\beta + \gamma_1$ and $\beta - \gamma_1$ for the two within-group regression lines.
- γ_1 is half the difference between the slopes of the two regression lines.

Note, in particular, that the constrained parameters α_1 and β are reasonably interpreted as "main effects"—that is, the partial effect of one explanatory variable averaged over the other explanatory variable—even when interactions are present in the model. As usual, however, main effects are likely not of interest when interactions are present.

To fit the model to the data, we need to code a deviation regressor S for partner's status:

Partner's Status	S
Low	1
High	-1

Then we can regress conformity on S, the mean-deviation scores for X, and the product of S and $X - \overline{X}$,

$$Y_{ij} = \mu + \alpha_1 S_{ij} + \beta(X_{ij} - \overline{X}) + \gamma_1[S_{ij}(X_{ij} - \overline{X})] + \varepsilon_{ij}$$

producing the following fit to the Moore and Krupat data:

$$\widehat{Y} = 12.14 - 2.139S - 0.02055(X - \overline{X}) + 0.1306[S(X - \overline{X})]$$
$$\quad\ \ (0.68)\quad (0.681)\quad (0.0485)\qquad\qquad (0.0485)$$
$$R^2 = .2942 \tag{8.17}$$

Because each set of effects has one degree of freedom, incremental F-tests for the main effects and interactions are equivalent to the t-tests produced by dividing each coefficient by its standard error. It is apparent, then, that the partner's status × authoritarianism interaction is statistically significant, as is the status main effect, but the authoritarianism main effect is not. You can verify that the two regression lines derived from the fitted ANCOVA model (Equation 8.17) are the same as those derived from the dummy-regression model (Equation 8.15).[35]

> ANCOVA is an alternative parametrization of the dummy-regression model, employing deviation-coded regressors for factors and expressing covariates as deviations from their means. The ANCOVA model can incorporate interactions among factors and between factors and covariates.

8.5   Linear Contrasts of Means

I have explained how the overparametrized ANOVA model can be fit to data by placing a sufficient number of linear restrictions on the parameters of the model. Different restrictions produce different regressors and hence different parameter estimates, but identical sums of squares—at least for models that conform to the principle of marginality. We have examined in some detail two schemes for coding regressors for a factor: dummy (0, 1) coding and deviation (1, 0, −1) coding. The coefficients for a set of dummy-coded regressors compare each level of a factor with the baseline level, while the coefficients for a set of deviation-coded regressors compare each level (but the last) with the average of the levels.

We do not generally test hypotheses about individual coefficients for dummy-coded or deviation-coded regressors, but we can do so, if we wish. For dummy-coded regressors in one-way ANOVA, a t-test or F-test of H_0: $\alpha_1 = 0$, for example, is equivalent to testing for the difference in means between the first group and the baseline group, H_0: $\mu_1 = \mu_m$. For deviation-coded regressors, testing H_0: $\alpha_1 = 0$ is equivalent to testing for the difference between the mean of the first group and the average of all the group means, H_0: $\mu_1 = \mu_.$.

In this section, I will explain a simple procedure for coding regressors that permits us to test specific hypotheses about *linear contrasts* (also called *linear comparisons*) among group means.[36] Although I will develop this technique for one-way ANOVA, contrast-coded regressors can also be employed for any factor in a two-way or higher-way ANOVA or in an ANCOVA.[37]

For concreteness, let us examine the data in Table 8.8, which are drawn from an experimental study by Friendly and Franklin (1980) of the effects of presentation format on learning and memory.[38] Subjects participating in the experiment read a list of 40 words. Then, after performing a brief distracting task, the subjects were asked to recall as many of the words as possible. This procedure was repeated for five trials. Thirty subjects were randomly assigned to three conditions: In the control or "standard free recall" (*SFR*) condition, the order of presentation of the words on the list was randomized for each of the five trials of the experiment. In the two experimental conditions, recalled words were presented in the order in which they were listed by the subject on the previous trial. In one of these conditions (labeled *B*), the recalled words were presented as a group *before* the forgotten ones, while in the other condition (labeled *M* for *meshed*), the recalled and forgotten words were interspersed. Friendly and Franklin expected that making the order of presentation contingent upon the subject's previous performance would enhance recall. The data recorded in the table are the number of words correctly recalled by each subject for the final trial of the experiment.

---

[35] See Exercise 8.8.

[36] A more general treatment of this topic may be found in Section 9.1.2.

[37] See Exercise 8.11.

[38] I am grateful to Michael Friendly of York University for providing these data.

Table 8.8 Data From Friendly and
Franklin's (1980)
Experiment on the Effects
of Presentation on Recall

	Condition	
SFR	*B*	*M*
39	40	40
25	38	39
37	39	34
25	37	37
29	39	40
39	24	36
21	30	36
39	39	38
24	40	36
25	40	30

NOTE: The data in the table are the number
of words correctly recalled by each subject
on the final trial of the experiment.

Means and standard deviations for Friendly and Franklin's memory data are as follows:

	Experimental Condition		
	SFR	*B*	*M*
Mean	30.30	36.60	36.60
Standard deviation	7.33	5.34	3.03

The mean number of words recalled is higher in the experimental conditions than in the control; the control group also has the largest standard deviation. A jittered scatterplot of the number of words recalled by condition, shown in Figure 8.9(a) reveals a problem with the data: The data are disguised proportions (number correctly recalled of 40 words), and many subjects—particularly in the B and M conditions—are at or near the maximum. This "ceiling effect" produces negatively skewed distributions in the two experimental conditions. Logit-transforming the data helps, as shown in Figure 8.9(b).[39] The means and standard deviations for the transformed data are the following:

	Experimental Condition		
	SFR	*B*	*M*
Mean	1.59	3.31	2.86
Standard deviation	1.46	1.71	1.43

---

[39]Because some subjects recalled all the words correctly, I mapped the proportions to the interval [.005, .995] prior to computing the logits, as explained in Section 4.5.

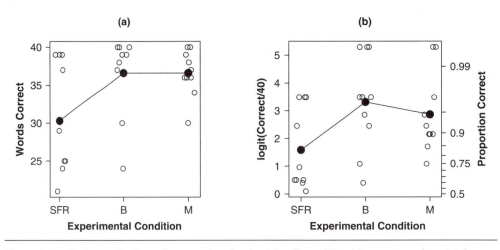

Figure 8.9   Horizontally jittered scatterplots for the Friendly and Franklin memory data: (a) for number of words correct; (b) for the logit of the proportion of words correct.

The logit transformation, therefore, has also made the group standard deviations more similar.

A linear contrast in the group means tests the hypothesis that a particular linear combination of population group means is 0. For the Friendly and Franklin memory experiment, we might wish to test the null hypothesis that the mean for the control group is no different from the average of the means for the experimental groups:[40]

$$H_0\colon \mu_1 = \frac{\mu_2 + \mu_3}{2}$$

and the hypothesis that the means for the two experimental groups are the same:

$$H_0\colon \mu_2 = \mu_3$$

The first hypothesis can be rewritten as

$$H_0\colon 1\mu_1 - \tfrac{1}{2}\mu_2 - \tfrac{1}{2}\mu_3 = 0$$

and the second hypothesis as

$$H_0\colon 0\mu_1 + 1\mu_2 - 1\mu_3 = 0$$

Then, the weights for the group means in these null hypotheses can be used to formulate two linear-contrast regressors, C_1 and C_2:

Group	C_1	C_2
(1) SFR	1	0
(2) B	$-\tfrac{1}{2}$	1
(3) M	$-\tfrac{1}{2}$	-1

---

[40]It would also be reasonable to compare each experimental group with the control group. The comparison could be easily accomplished by using dummy coding, treating the control group as the baseline category.

This simple approach to coding linear contrasts will work as long as the following conditions are satisfied:[41]

1. We need one linear contrast for each degree of freedom. An m-category factor therefore requires $m - 1$ contrasts.

2. Each column of the contrast-coding table must sum to 0.

3. The products of corresponding codes for *different* contrasts must also sum to 0. For the illustration,

$$(1 \times 0) + (-\tfrac{1}{2} \times 1) + (-\tfrac{1}{2} \times -1) = 0$$

When there are equal numbers of observations in the groups, these rules ensure that the contrast regressors are uncorrelated. As a consequence, the regression sum of squares for the ANOVA can be decomposed into components due to the contrasts. When the group frequencies are unequal, the regression sum of squares does not decompose in this simple manner, but properly formulated contrasts are still useful for testing hypotheses about the population group means. Because each contrast has one degree of freedom, we can test it by a t-test (dividing the estimated coefficient for the contrast by its standard error) or—equivalently—by an incremental F-test.

> Linear contrasts permit the researcher to test specific hypotheses about means within the framework of ANOVA. A factor with m categories gives rise to $m - 1$ contrasts, one for each degree of freedom. A simple procedure for constructing contrasts requires that the codes for each contrast sum to 0 and that the products of codes for each pair of contrasts also sum to 0.

For Friendly and Franklin's experiment, the fitted model (working with the logits) is

$$\widehat{Y} = \underset{(0.2804)}{2.5880} - \underset{(0.3966)}{0.9998C_1} + \underset{(0.3434)}{0.2248C_2}$$

$$R^2 = .2008$$

and the ANOVA table is

Source	SS	df	MS	F	p
Groups	16.005	2	8.002	3.39	.049
C_1	14.994	1	14.994	6.35	.018
C_2	1.011	1	1.001	0.43	.52
Residuals	63.696	27	2.359		
Total	79.701	29			

We therefore have evidence that the two experimental conditions promoted higher levels of recall than did the control condition (contrast C_1), but no evidence for the superiority of one experimental treatment relative to the other (contrast C_2). Note that because there are equal numbers of observations in the three groups, the sums of squares for the contrasts add to the sum of squares for groups (i.e., to the regression sum of squares).

---

[41] See Section 9.12 for an explanation of these rules and for a more flexible and general approach to constructing contrasts.

Exercises

Exercise 8.1. *The usual t statistic for testing a difference between the means of two independently sampled groups, under the assumptions of normality and equal group variances, is

$$t_0 = \frac{\overline{Y}_1 - \overline{Y}_2}{\text{SE}(\overline{Y}_1 - \overline{Y}_2)}$$

where

$$\text{SE}(\overline{Y}_1 - \overline{Y}_2) = S\sqrt{\frac{1}{n_1} + \frac{1}{n_2}}$$

$$S^2 = \frac{\sum_{j=1}^{n_1}(Y_{i1} - \overline{Y}_1)^2 + \sum_{j=1}^{n_2}(Y_{i2} - \overline{Y}_2)^2}{n_1 + n_2 - 2}$$

Here, $\overline{Y}_1$ and $\overline{Y}_2$ are the means of the two groups; n_1 and n_2 are the numbers of observations in the groups; and Y_{i1} and Y_{i2} are the observations themselves. Let F_0 be the one-way ANOVA F-statistic for testing the null hypothesis H_0: $\mu_1 = \mu_2$. Prove that $t_0^2 = F_0$ and that, consequently, the two tests are equivalent.

Exercise 8.2. *Show that one of the restrictions on the interaction parameters of the two-way ANOVA model,

$$\sum_{j=1}^{r} \gamma_{jk} = 0 \quad \text{for } k = 1, \ldots, c$$

$$\sum_{k=1}^{c} \gamma_{jk} = 0 \quad \text{for } j = 1, \ldots, r$$

is redundant. [*Hint*: Construct a table of the interaction parameters, labeling the rows $1, 2, \ldots,$ $r - 1, r$ and the columns $1, 2, \ldots, c$. Insert a column for row sums after the last column, and a row for column sums after the last row. At the bottom right corner of the table is the overall sum of the interaction parameters, $\sum_{j=1}^{r} \sum_{k=1}^{c} \gamma_{jk}$. (This table looks much like the table of cell means on page 149, with γs replacing the μs.) Then place a 0 in each entry of the column of row sums, corresponding to the r restrictions $\sum_{k=1}^{c} \gamma_{jk} = 0$. From these restrictions, show that $\sum\sum \gamma_{jk} = 0$, and place this 0 in the lower-right corner. Next, specify 0s for all but the last column sum, $\sum_{j=1}^{r} \gamma_{jk} = 0$, for $k = 1, \ldots, c - 1$. Finally, show that the last column sum, $\sum_{j=1}^{r} \gamma_{jc}$, is necessarily 0.]

Exercise 8.3. *Demonstrate that the hypothesis

$$H_0: \text{ all } \gamma_{jk} = 0$$

for the sigma-constrained two-way ANOVA model is equivalent to the null hypothesis of no interaction stated in terms of the cell means:

$$\mu_{jk} - \mu_{j'k} = \mu_{jk'} - \mu_{j'k'} \quad \text{for all } j, j' \text{ and } k, k'$$

[*Hint*: Write out each of the interaction parameters $\gamma_{jk}, \gamma_{j'k}, \gamma_{jk'}$, and $\gamma_{j'k'}$ in terms of the cell and marginal means (e.g., $\gamma_{jk} = \mu_{jk} - \mu_{j.} - \mu_{.k} + \mu_{..}$). Then show that when the γs are all 0, $\gamma_{jk} - \gamma_{j'k} = \gamma_{jk'} - \gamma_{j'k'}$ (i.e., $0 - 0 = 0 - 0$) implies that $\mu_{jk} - \mu_{j'k} = \mu_{jk'} - \mu_{j'k'}$.]

Exercise 8.4. *Show that in the sigma-constrained three-way ANOVA model, the null hypothesis

$$H_0: \text{ all } \alpha_{ABC(jkm)} = 0$$

is equivalent to the hypothesis given in Equation 8.14 on page 165. (*Hint*: See Exercise 8.3.)

Exercise 8.5. The geometry of effects in three-way ANOVA: Contrived parameter values for a three-way ANOVA model (each set satisfying the sigma constraints) are given in the following tables:

	$\alpha_{A(j)}$	
A_1		A_2
2		-2

	$\alpha_{B(k)}$	
B_1		B_2
-3		3

$\alpha_{C(m)}$		
C_1	C_2	C_3
1	-3	2

$\alpha_{AB(jk)}$	B_1	B_2
A_1	-2	2
A_2	2	-2

$\alpha_{AC(jm)}$	C_1	C_2	C_3
A_1	1	1	-2
A_2	-1	-1	2

$\alpha_{BC(km)}$	C_1	C_2	C_3
B_1	0	3	-3
B_2	0	-3	3

$\alpha_{ABC(jkm)}$	C_1	C_2	C_3
$A_1 B_1$	1	-2	1
$A_1 B_2$	-1	2	-1
$A_2 B_1$	-1	2	-1
$A_2 B_2$	1	-2	1

Use these parameter values to construct population cell means for each of the following models (simply sum the parameters that pertain to each of the 12 cells of the design):

(a) Main effects only,

$$\mu_{jkm} = \mu + \alpha_{A(j)} + \alpha_{B(k)} + \alpha_{C(m)}$$

(b) One two-way interaction,

$$\mu_{jkm} = \mu + \alpha_{A(j)} + \alpha_{B(k)} + \alpha_{C(m)} + \alpha_{AC(jm)}$$

(c) All three two-way interactions,

$$\mu_{jkm} = \mu + \alpha_{A(j)} + \alpha_{B(k)} + \alpha_{C(m)} + \alpha_{AB(jk)} + \alpha_{AC(jm)} + \alpha_{BC(km)}$$

(d) The full model,

$$\mu_{jkm} = \mu + \alpha_{A(j)} + \alpha_{B(k)} + \alpha_{C(m)} + \alpha_{AB(jk)} + \alpha_{AC(jm)} + \alpha_{BC(km)} + \alpha_{ABC(jkm)}$$

For each of these models do the following:

(i) Draw a graph of the cell means, placing factor C on the horizontal axis. Use different lines (solid and broken) or line colors for the levels of factor A, and different symbols (e.g., circle and square) for the levels of factor B. Note that there will be four connected profiles of means on each of these plots, one profile for each combination of categories of A and B across the three levels of C. Attempt to interpret the graphs in terms of the effects that are included in each model.

(ii) Using the table of means generated from each of models (c) and (d), plot (for each model) the six *differences* across the levels of factor B, $\mu_{j1m} - \mu_{j2m}$, by the categories of factors A and C. Can you account for the different patterns of these two graphs in terms of the presence of three-way interactions in the second graph but not in the first?

Exercise 8.6. Adjusted means (continued): The notion of an "adjusted" mean was introduced in Exercises 7.2 and 7.3. Consider the main-effects model for the p-way classification:

$$\mu_{jk...r} \equiv E(Y_{ijk...r}) = \mu + \alpha_{A(j)} + \alpha_{B(k)} + \cdots + \alpha_{P(r)}$$

(a) Show that if we constrain each set of effects to sum to 0, then the population marginal mean for category j of factor A is $\mu_{j...} = \mu + \alpha_{A(j)}$.

(b) Let us define the analogous sample quantity, $\widetilde{Y}_{j...} \equiv M + A_{A(j)}$, to be the *adjusted mean* in category j of factor A. How is this quantity to be interpreted?

(c) Does the definition of the adjusted mean in part (b) depend fundamentally on the constraint that each set of effects sums to 0?

(d) Can the idea of an adjusted mean be extended to ANOVA models that include interactions? (Cf. the discussion of effect displays in this and the preceding chapter.)

Exercise 8.7. ANOVA with equal cell frequencies: In higher-way ANOVA, as in two-way ANOVA, when cell frequencies are equal, the sum of squares for each set of effects can be calculated directly from the parameter estimates for the full model or, equivalently, in terms of cell and marginal means. To get the sum of squares for a particular set of effects, we simply need to square the parameter estimate associated with each cell, sum over all cells, and multiply by the common cell frequency, n'. For example, for a balanced three-way ANOVA,

$$SS(\alpha_{AB}) = n' \sum_{j=1}^{a} \sum_{k=1}^{b} \sum_{m=1}^{c} A_{AB(jk)}^2$$

$$= n'c \sum_{j=1}^{a} \sum_{k=1}^{b} A_{AB(jk)}^2 \qquad .$$

$$= n'c \sum_{j=1}^{a} \sum_{k=1}^{b} (\overline{Y}_{jk\cdot} - \overline{Y}_{j\cdot\cdot} - \overline{Y}_{\cdot k\cdot} + \overline{Y}_{\dots})^2$$

Write out similar expressions for $SS(\alpha_A)$ and $SS(\alpha_{ABC})$ in three-way ANOVA. Show that

$$RSS = (n' - 1) \sum_{j=1}^{a} \sum_{k=1}^{b} \sum_{m=1}^{c} S_{jkm}^2$$

where

$$S_{jkm}^2 = \frac{\sum_{i=1}^{n'} (Y_{ijkm} - \overline{Y}_{jkm})^2}{n' - 1}$$

is the variance in cell j, k, m of the design.

Exercise 8.8. Calculate the fitted regression equation for each group (low and high partner's status) in Moore and Krupat's conformity data using the dummy regression in Equation 8.15 (page 174). Calculate the fitted regression equation for each group using the analysis of covariance in Equation 8.17. Why must the two sets of equations be the same (within rounding error)?

Exercise 8.9. Adjusted means (concluded): The notion of an *adjusted mean* was discussed in Exercises 7.2, 7.3, and 8.6. Now consider the ANCOVA model for two factors, R and C, and two covariates, X_1 and X_2:

$$Y_{ijk} = \mu + \alpha_j + \beta_k + \gamma_{jk} + \delta_1(X_{ijk1} - \overline{X}_1) + \delta_2(X_{ijk2} - \overline{X}) + \varepsilon_{ijk}$$

Note that this formulation of the model permits interactions between the factors but not between the factors and the covariates.

(a) How can the ANCOVA model be used to compute adjusted cell means for the $r \times c$ combinations of levels of the factors R and C?

(b) In computing adjusted means, is anything gained by expressing the covariates as deviations from their respective means rather than as raw scores?

(c) If the interactions between the factors γ_{jk} are deleted from the model, how can we calculate adjusted means for the r categories of R and the c categories of C?

The calculation of adjusted means in additive ANCOVA models is a traditional use of the ANCOVA. Further information on adjusted means can be found in Searle, Speed, and Milliken (1980). Adjusted means are special cases of effect displays, as developed in this and the preceding chapter.

Exercise 8.10. Testing contrasts using group means: Suppose that we wish to test a hypothesis concerning a contrast of group means.

$$H_0: \ c_1\mu_1 + c_2\mu_2 + \cdots + c_m\mu_m = 0$$

where $c_1 + c_2 + \cdots + c_k = 0$. Define the *sample value of the contrast* as

$$C \equiv c_1 \overline{Y}_1 + c_2 \overline{Y}_2 + \cdots + c_m \overline{Y}_m$$

and let

$$C'^2 \equiv \frac{C^2}{\dfrac{c_1^2}{n_1} + \dfrac{c_2^2}{n_2} + \cdots + \dfrac{c_m^2}{n_m}}$$

C'^2 is the sum of squares for the contrast.

- (a) *Show that under the null hypothesis

  - (i) $E(C) = 0$.
  - (ii) $V(C) = \sigma_\varepsilon^2 \left(\dfrac{c_1^2}{n_1} + \dfrac{c_2^2}{n_2} + \cdots + \dfrac{c_m^2}{n_m} \right)$.
  - (iii) $t_0 = C'/S_E$ follows a t-distribution with $n - m$ degrees of freedom. [*Hint:* The $\overline{Y}_j$ are independent, and each is distributed as $N(\mu_j, \sigma_\varepsilon^2/n_j)$.]

- (b) Using Friendly and Franklin's memory data, verify that the test statistics obtained by the method of this exercise [i.e., in (a)(iii)] are the same as those produced by the incremental sum-of-squares approach, used in the text.

Exercise 8.11. *Contrasts in two-way ANOVA: A simple approach to formulating contrasts in two-way (and higher-way) ANOVA is first to specify contrasts separately for each set of main effects, obtaining interaction contrasts by forming all pairwise products of the main-effect contrasts. Then, as long as the main-effect contrasts satisfy the rules, the interaction contrasts will as well. Imagine, for example, a 3×2 classification arising from an experiment in which the first factor consists of a control group (R_1) and two experimental groups (R_2 and R_3). The second factor is, say, gender, with categories male (C_1) and female (C_2). A possible set of main-effect contrasts for this experiment is

	Row contrast	
Group	A_1	A_2
R_1	2	0
R_2	−1	1
R_3	−1	−1

Gender	Column contrast
	B
C_1	1
C_2	−1

The following table shows the full set of main-effect and interaction contrasts for all six cells of the design (with the parameter for each contrast in parentheses):

Cell		(δ_1)	(δ_1)	(β)	(ζ_1)	(ζ_2)
Row	Column	A_1	A_2	B	A_1B	A_2B
1	1	2	0	1	2	0
1	2	2	0	−1	−2	0
2	1	−1	1	1	−1	1
2	2	−1	1	−1	1	−1
3	1	−1	−1	1	−1	−1
3	2	−1	−1	−1	1	1

Note that we use 2 degrees of freedom for condition main effects, 1 degree of freedom for the gender main effect, and 2 degrees of freedom for interaction. Explain the meaning of the following null hypotheses:

(a) H_0: $\zeta_1 = 0$.
(b) H_0: $\zeta_2 = 0$.
(c) H_0: $\delta_1 = 0$.
(d) H_0: $\delta_2 = 0$.
(e) H_0: $\beta = 0$.

Exercise 8.12. Reanalyze Moore and Krupat's conformity data eliminating the two outlying observations, Numbers 16 and 19. Perform *both* a two-way ANOVA, treating authoritarianism as a factor, and an ANCOVA, treating authoritarianism as a covariate.

Summary

- One-way ANOVA examines the relationship between a quantitative response variable and a factor. The one-way ANOVA model,

$$Y_{ij} = \mu + \alpha_j + \varepsilon_{ij}$$

is underdetermined because it uses $m + 1$ parameters to model m group means. This indeterminacy can be removed, however, by placing a restriction on its parameters. Setting one of the α_js to 0 leads to (0, 1) dummy-regressor coding. Constraining the α_js to sum to 0 leads to (1, 0, −1) deviation-regressor coding. The two coding schemes are equivalent in that they provide the same fit to the data, producing the same regression and residual sums of squares.
- The two-way ANOVA model

$$Y_{ijk} = \mu + \alpha_j + \beta_k + \gamma_{jk} + \varepsilon_{ijk}$$

incorporates the main effects and interactions of two factors. The factors interact when the profiles of population cell means are not parallel. The two-way ANOVA model is over-parametrized, but it can be fit to data by placing suitable restrictions on its parameters. A convenient set of restrictions is provided by sigma constraints, specifying that each set of parameters (α_j, β_k, and γ_{jk}) sums to 0 over each of its coordinates. Testing hypotheses about the sigma-constrained parameters is equivalent to testing interaction-effect and main-effect hypotheses about cell and marginal means. There are two reasonable procedures for testing main-effect hypotheses in two-way ANOVA: Tests based on $SS(\alpha|\beta, \gamma)$ and $SS(\beta|\alpha, \gamma)$ employ models that violate the principle of marginality but are valid whether or not interactions are present. Tests based on $SS(\alpha|\beta)$ and $SS(\beta|\alpha)$ conform to the principle of marginality, but are valid only if interactions are absent.

- The ANOVA model and procedures for testing hypotheses about main effects and interactions extend straightforwardly to three-way and higher-way classifications. In each case, the highest-order interaction corresponds to the number of factors in the model. It is not necessary, however, to specify a model that includes all terms through the highest-order interaction. Effect displays for the high-order terms in a model can clarify the interpretation of the model.

- It is possible to fit an ANOVA model to a classification containing empty cells when the marginal frequency tables corresponding to the terms in the model have no empty cells.

- ANCOVA is an alternative parametrization of the dummy-regression model, employing deviation-coded regressors for factors and expressing covariates as deviations from their means. The ANCOVA model can incorporate interactions among factors and between factors and covariates.

- Linear contrasts permit the researcher to test specific hypotheses about means within the framework of ANOVA. A factor with m categories gives rise to $m - 1$ contrasts, one for each degree of freedom. A simple procedure for constructing contrasts requires that the codes for each contrast sum to 0 and that the products of codes for each pair of contrasts also sum to 0.

9 Statistical Theory for Linear Models*

The purpose of this chapter is twofold: to deepen your knowledge of linear models and linear least-squares estimation and to provide a basis for more advanced work in social statistics—in the remainder of this book and more generally. Relying on the mathematical tools of linear algebra and elementary calculus,[1] we will revisit with greater rigor many of the topics treated informally in Chapters 5 to 8, developing the statistical theory on which the methods described in those chapters depend. The next chapter, on the vector geometry of linear models, provides intuitive insight into this statistical theory.

9.1 Linear Models in Matrix Form

The general linear model is given by the equation

$$Y_i = \beta_0 + \beta_1 x_{i1} + \beta_2 x_{i2} + \cdots + \beta_k x_{ik} + \varepsilon_i$$

Note that I have substituted the notationally more convenient β_0 for the regression constant α; I will, for the time being, suppose that the X values are fixed, hence the lowercase x_{ij}.[2]

Collecting the regressors into a row vector, appending a 1 for the constant, and placing the corresponding parameters in a column vector, permits us to rewrite the linear model as

$$Y_i = [1, x_{i1}, x_{i2}, \ldots, x_{ik}] \begin{bmatrix} \beta_0 \\ \beta_1 \\ \beta_2 \\ \vdots \\ \beta_k \end{bmatrix} + \varepsilon_i$$

$$= \underset{(1 \times k+1)}{\mathbf{x}_i'} \underset{(k+1 \times 1)}{\boldsymbol{\beta}} + \varepsilon_i$$

For a sample of n observations, we have n such equations, which can be combined into a single matrix equation:

$$\begin{bmatrix} Y_1 \\ Y_2 \\ \vdots \\ Y_n \end{bmatrix} = \begin{bmatrix} 1 & x_{11} & \cdots & x_{1k} \\ 1 & x_{21} & \cdots & x_{2k} \\ \vdots & \vdots & & \vdots \\ 1 & x_{n1} & \cdots & x_{nk} \end{bmatrix} \begin{bmatrix} \beta_0 \\ \beta_1 \\ \vdots \\ \beta_k \end{bmatrix} + \begin{bmatrix} \varepsilon_1 \\ \varepsilon_2 \\ \vdots \\ \varepsilon_n \end{bmatrix} \tag{9.1}$$

$$\underset{(n \times 1)}{\mathbf{y}} = \underset{(n \times k+1)}{\mathbf{X}} \underset{(k+1 \times 1)}{\boldsymbol{\beta}} + \underset{(n \times 1)}{\boldsymbol{\varepsilon}}$$

---

[1] See Appendices B and C for introductions to linear algebra and calculus.
[2] See Section 9.6 for a discussion of random regressors.

As we will see, with suitable specification of the contents of $\mathbf{X}$, called the *model matrix*, Equation 9.1 serves not only for multiple regression but also for linear models generally.[3]

Because ε is a vector random variable, the assumptions of the linear model can be compactly restated in matrix form. The errors are assumed to be independent and normally distributed with zero expectation and common variance. Thus, ε follows a multivariate-normal distribution with expectation $E(\varepsilon) = \underset{(n \times 1)}{\mathbf{0}}$ and covariance matrix $V(\varepsilon) = E(\varepsilon\varepsilon') = \sigma_\varepsilon^2 \mathbf{I}_n$; in symbols, $\varepsilon \sim N_n(\mathbf{0}, \sigma_\varepsilon^2 \mathbf{I}_n)$. The distribution of $\mathbf{y}$ follows immediately:

$$\mu \equiv E(\mathbf{y}) = E(\mathbf{X}\beta + \varepsilon) = \mathbf{X}\beta + E(\varepsilon) = \mathbf{X}\beta$$
$$V(\mathbf{y}) = E[(\mathbf{y} - \mu)(\mathbf{y} - \mu)'] = E[(\mathbf{y} - \mathbf{X}\beta)(\mathbf{y} - \mathbf{X}\beta)'] \qquad (9.2)$$
$$= E(\varepsilon\varepsilon') = \sigma_\varepsilon^2 \mathbf{I}_n$$

Furthermore, because it is simply a translation of ε to a different expectation, $\mathbf{y}$ is also normally distributed: $\mathbf{y} \sim N_n(\mathbf{X}\beta, \sigma_\varepsilon^2 \mathbf{I}_n)$.

The general linear model can be written in matrix form as $\mathbf{y} = \mathbf{X}\beta + \varepsilon$, where $\mathbf{y}$ is an $n \times 1$ vector of response-variable observations; $\mathbf{X}$ is an $n \times k + 1$ matrix of regressors (called the model matrix), including an initial column of 1s for the constant regressor; β is a $k + 1 \times 1$ vector of parameters to be estimated; and ε is an $n \times 1$ vector of errors. The assumptions of the linear model can be compactly written as $\varepsilon \sim N_n(\mathbf{0}, \sigma_\varepsilon^2 \mathbf{I}_n)$.

9.1.1   Dummy Regression and Analysis of Variance

The model matrices for dummy-regression and analysis-of-variance (ANOVA) models—especially the latter—are strongly patterned. Consider the dummy-regression model

$$Y_i = \alpha + \beta x_i + \gamma d_i + \delta(x_i d_i) + \varepsilon_i$$

where Y is income, x is years of education, and the dummy regressor d is coded 1 for men and 0 for women.[4] In matrix form, this model becomes

$$
\begin{bmatrix} Y_1 \\ \vdots \\ Y_{n_1} \\ \hline Y_{n_1+1} \\ \vdots \\ Y_n \end{bmatrix}
=
\begin{bmatrix} 1 & x_1 & 0 & 0 \\ \vdots & \vdots & \vdots & \vdots \\ 1 & x_{n_1} & 0 & 0 \\ \hline 1 & x_{n_1+1} & 1 & x_{n_1+1} \\ \vdots & \vdots & \vdots & \vdots \\ 1 & x_n & 1 & x_n \end{bmatrix}
\begin{bmatrix} \alpha \\ \beta \\ \gamma \\ \delta \end{bmatrix}
+
\begin{bmatrix} \varepsilon_1 \\ \vdots \\ \varepsilon_{n_1} \\ \hline \varepsilon_{n_1+1} \\ \vdots \\ \varepsilon_n \end{bmatrix}
$$
$$\mathbf{y} = \mathbf{X}\beta + \varepsilon$$

To emphasize the pattern of the model matrix, the n_1 observations for women (for whom d and hence xd are 0) precede the $n - n_1$ observations for men.

---

[3]The model matrix is often called the *design matrix*, a term that is especially appropriate in experimental applications where the explanatory variables, and hence the regressors that compose the $\mathbf{X}$ matrix, derive from the design of the experiment.

[4]This example was discussed in Chapter 7. Here, x and d are treated as fixed; random regressors are considered in Section 9.6.

Now consider the overparametrized one-way ANOVA model[5]

$$Y_{ij} = \mu + \alpha_j + \varepsilon_{ij} \quad \text{for groups } j = 1, \ldots, m.$$

The matrix form of the model is

$$
\begin{bmatrix}
Y_{11} \\
\vdots \\
Y_{n_1,1} \\
\hline
Y_{12} \\
\vdots \\
Y_{n_2,2} \\
\hline
\vdots \\
Y_{1,m-1} \\
\vdots \\
Y_{n_{m-1},m-1} \\
\hline
Y_{1m} \\
\vdots \\
Y_{n_m,m}
\end{bmatrix}
=
\begin{bmatrix}
1 & 1 & 0 & \cdots & 0 & 0 \\
\vdots & \vdots & \vdots & & \vdots & \vdots \\
1 & 1 & 0 & \cdots & 0 & 0 \\
1 & 0 & 1 & \cdots & 0 & 0 \\
\vdots & \vdots & \vdots & & \vdots & \vdots \\
1 & 0 & 1 & \cdots & 0 & 0 \\
\vdots & \vdots & \vdots & & \vdots & \vdots \\
1 & 0 & 0 & \cdots & 1 & 0 \\
\vdots & \vdots & \vdots & & \vdots & \vdots \\
1 & 0 & 0 & \cdots & 1 & 0 \\
1 & 0 & 0 & \cdots & 0 & 1 \\
\vdots & \vdots & \vdots & & \vdots & \vdots \\
1 & 0 & 0 & \cdots & 0 & 1
\end{bmatrix}
\begin{bmatrix}
\mu \\
\alpha_1 \\
\alpha_2 \\
\vdots \\
\alpha_{m-1} \\
\alpha_m
\end{bmatrix}
+
\begin{bmatrix}
\varepsilon_{11} \\
\vdots \\
\varepsilon_{n_1,1} \\
\hline
\varepsilon_{12} \\
\vdots \\
\varepsilon_{n_2,2} \\
\hline
\vdots \\
\varepsilon_{1,m-1} \\
\vdots \\
\varepsilon_{n_{m-1},m-1} \\
\hline
\varepsilon_{1m} \\
\vdots \\
\varepsilon_{n_m,m}
\end{bmatrix}
$$

$$\mathbf{y} = \mathbf{X}\boldsymbol{\beta} + \boldsymbol{\varepsilon}$$

It is apparent that the model matrix is of rank m, one less than the number of columns, because the first column of $\mathbf{X}$ is the sum of the others. One solution is to delete a column, implicitly setting the corresponding parameter to 0. Deleting the last column of the model matrix, for example, sets $\alpha_m = 0$, establishing the last category as the baseline for a dummy-coding scheme.

Alternatively, imposing the sigma constraint $\sum_{j=1}^{m} \alpha_j = 0$ on the parameters leads to the following *full-rank* model matrix $\mathbf{X}_F$, composed of deviation-coded regressors; labeling each column of the matrix with the parameter to which it pertains,

$$
\mathbf{X}_F \atop (n \times m)
=
\begin{bmatrix}
(\mu) & (\alpha_1) & (\alpha_2) & \cdots & (\alpha_{m-1}) \\
1 & 1 & 0 & \cdots & 0 \\
\vdots & \vdots & \vdots & & \vdots \\
1 & 1 & 0 & \cdots & 0 \\
1 & 0 & 1 & \cdots & 0 \\
\vdots & \vdots & \vdots & & \vdots \\
1 & 0 & 1 & \cdots & 0 \\
\vdots & \vdots & \vdots & & \vdots \\
1 & 0 & 0 & \cdots & 1 \\
\vdots & \vdots & \vdots & & \vdots \\
1 & 0 & 0 & \cdots & 1 \\
1 & -1 & -1 & \cdots & -1 \\
\vdots & \vdots & \vdots & & \vdots \\
1 & -1 & -1 & \cdots & -1
\end{bmatrix}
$$

---

[5] See Section 8.1.

There is, then, the following relationship between the group means $\mu = \{\mu_j\}$ and the parameters of the constrained model:

$$
\begin{bmatrix} \mu_1 \\ \mu_2 \\ \vdots \\ \mu_{m-1} \\ \mu_m \end{bmatrix}
=
\begin{bmatrix}
1 & 1 & 0 & \cdots & 0 \\
1 & 0 & 1 & \cdots & 0 \\
\vdots & \vdots & \vdots & & \vdots \\
1 & 0 & 0 & \cdots & 1 \\
1 & -1 & -1 & \cdots & -1
\end{bmatrix}
\begin{bmatrix} \mu \\ \alpha_1 \\ \alpha_2 \\ \vdots \\ \alpha_{m-1} \end{bmatrix}
\tag{9.3}
$$

$$
\underset{(m \times 1)}{\boldsymbol{\mu}} = \underset{(m \times m)}{\mathbf{X}_B} \underset{(m \times 1)}{\boldsymbol{\beta}_F}
$$

In this *parametric equation*, $\mathbf{X}_B$ is the *row basis* of the full-rank model matrix, consisting of the m unique rows of $\mathbf{X}_F$, one for each group; and $\boldsymbol{\beta}_F$ is the parameter vector associated with the full-rank model matrix.

By construction, the $m \times m$ matrix $\mathbf{X}_B$ is of full column rank and hence nonsingular, allowing us to invert $\mathbf{X}_B$ and solve uniquely for the constrained parameters in terms of the cell means: $\boldsymbol{\beta}_F = \mathbf{X}_B^{-1} \boldsymbol{\mu}$. The solution follows a familiar pattern:[6]

$$
\begin{bmatrix} \mu \\ \alpha_1 \\ \alpha_2 \\ \vdots \\ \alpha_{m-1} \end{bmatrix}
=
\begin{bmatrix} \mu. \\ \mu_1 - \mu. \\ \mu_2 - \mu. \\ \vdots \\ \mu_{m-1} - \mu. \end{bmatrix}
$$

Let us next examine a two-way ANOVA model. To make the example manageable, suppose that there are two rows and three columns in the design. Imposing sigma constraints on the main effects and interactions produces the parametric equation:

$$
\begin{bmatrix} \mu_{11} \\ \mu_{12} \\ \mu_{13} \\ \mu_{21} \\ \mu_{22} \\ \mu_{23} \end{bmatrix}
=
\begin{bmatrix}
1 & 1 & 1 & 0 & 1 & 0 \\
1 & 1 & 0 & 1 & 0 & 1 \\
1 & 1 & -1 & -1 & -1 & -1 \\
1 & -1 & 1 & 0 & -1 & 0 \\
1 & -1 & 0 & 1 & 0 & -1 \\
1 & -1 & -1 & -1 & 1 & 1
\end{bmatrix}
\begin{bmatrix} \mu \\ \alpha_1 \\ \beta_1 \\ \beta_2 \\ \gamma_{11} \\ \gamma_{12} \end{bmatrix}
\tag{9.4}
$$

$$
\underset{(6 \times 1)}{\boldsymbol{\mu}} = \underset{(6 \times 6)}{\mathbf{X}_B} \underset{(6 \times 1)}{\boldsymbol{\beta}_F}
$$

As in one-way ANOVA, the row basis of the full-rank model matrix is nonsingular by construction, yielding the following solution for the parameters in terms of the cell means:[7]

$$
\begin{bmatrix} \mu \\ \alpha_1 \\ \beta_1 \\ \beta_2 \\ \gamma_{11} \\ \gamma_{12} \end{bmatrix}
=
\begin{bmatrix}
\mu.. \\
\mu_1. - \mu.. \\
\mu._1 - \mu.. \\
\mu._2 - \mu.. \\
\mu_{11} - \mu_1. - \mu._1 + \mu.. \\
\mu_{12} - \mu_1. - \mu._2 + \mu..
\end{bmatrix}
$$

---

[6] See Exercise 9.1(a) and Section 8.1.
[7] See Exercise 9.1(b) and Section 8.2.2.

> The model matrices for dummy-regression and ANOVA models are strongly patterned. In ANOVA, the relationship between group or cell means and the parameters of the linear model is expressed by the parametric equation $\mu = \mathbf{X}_B \beta_F$, where μ is the vector of means; $\mathbf{X}_B$ is the row basis of the full-rank model matrix; and β_F is the parameter vector associated with the full-rank model matrix. Solving the parametric equation for the parameters yields $\beta_F = \mathbf{X}_B^{-1} \mu$.

9.1.2 Linear Contrasts

The relationship between group means and the parameters of the ANOVA model is given by the parametric equation $\mu = \mathbf{X}_B \beta_F$; thus, as I have explained, the parameters are linear functions of the group means, $\beta_F = \mathbf{X}_B^{-1} \mu$. The full-rank parametrizations of the one-way ANOVA model that we have considered—dummy coding and deviation coding—permit us to test the null hypothesis of no differences among group means, but the individual parameters are not usually of interest. In certain circumstances, however, we can formulate $\mathbf{X}_B$ so that the individual parameters of β_F incorporate interesting contrasts among group means.[8]

In Friendly and Franklin's (1980) memory experiment,[9] for example, subjects attempted to recall words under three experimental conditions:

1. the "standard free recall" (*SFR*) condition, in which words were presented in random order;

2. the "before" (*B*) condition, in which remembered words were presented before those forgotten on the previous trial; and

3. the "meshed" (*M*) condition, in which remembered words were interspersed with forgotten words, but were presented in the order in which they were recalled.

I defined linear contrasts to test two null hypotheses:

1. H_0: $\mu_1 = (\mu_2 + \mu_3)/2$, that the mean of the *SFR* condition does not differ from the average of the means of the other two conditions and

2. H_0: $\mu_2 = \mu_3$, that the means of the *B* and *M* conditions do not differ.

These hypotheses can be written as linear functions of the group means: (1) H_0: $1\mu_1 - \frac{1}{2}\mu_2 - \frac{1}{2}\mu_3 = 0$ and (2) H_0: $0\mu_1 + 1\mu_2 - 1\mu_3 = 0$. Then each hypothesis can be coded in a parameter of the model, employing the following relationship between parameters and group means:[10]

$$\begin{bmatrix} \mu \\ \zeta_1 \\ \zeta_2 \end{bmatrix} = \begin{bmatrix} \frac{1}{3} & \frac{1}{3} & \frac{1}{3} \\ 1 & -\frac{1}{2} & -\frac{1}{2} \\ 0 & 1 & -1 \end{bmatrix} \begin{bmatrix} \mu_1 \\ \mu_2 \\ \mu_3 \end{bmatrix} \tag{9.5}$$

$$\beta_F = \mathbf{X}_B^{-1} \mu$$

---

[8]Linear contrasts were introduced in Section 8.5.

[9]See Section 8.5.

[10]Because it is natural to form hypotheses as linear combinations of means, I start by specifying $\mathbf{X}_B^{-1}$ directly, rather than $\mathbf{X}_B$.

One parameter, μ, is used to code the average of the group means, leaving two parameters to represent differences among the three group means. The hypothesis H_0: $\zeta_1 = 0$ is equivalent to the first null hypothesis; H_0: $\zeta_2 = 0$ is equivalent to the second null hypothesis.

Because the *rows* of $\mathbf{X}_B^{-1}$ in Equation 9.5 are orthogonal, the *columns* of $\mathbf{X}_B$ are orthogonal as well: Each column of $\mathbf{X}_B$ is equal to the corresponding row of $\mathbf{X}_B^{-1}$ divided by the sum of squared entries in that row;[11] thus,

$$\begin{bmatrix} \mu_1 \\ \mu_2 \\ \mu_3 \end{bmatrix} = \begin{bmatrix} 1 & \frac{2}{3} & 0 \\ 1 & -\frac{1}{3} & \frac{1}{2} \\ 1 & -\frac{1}{3} & -\frac{1}{2} \end{bmatrix} \begin{bmatrix} \mu \\ \zeta_1 \\ \zeta_2 \end{bmatrix}$$

$$\boldsymbol{\mu} = \mathbf{X}_B \boldsymbol{\beta}_F$$

The one-to-one correspondence between rows of $\mathbf{X}_B^{-1}$ and columns of $\mathbf{X}_B$ makes it simple to specify the latter matrix directly. Moreover, we can rescale the columns of the row basis for more convenient coding, as shown in Equation 9.6, without altering the hypotheses incorporated in the contrast coefficients: If, for example, $\zeta_1 = 0$, then any multiple of ζ_1 is 0 as well.

$$\mathbf{X}_B = \begin{bmatrix} 1 & 2 & 0 \\ 1 & -1 & 1 \\ 1 & -1 & -1 \end{bmatrix} \tag{9.6}$$

Although it is convenient to define contrasts that are orthogonal in the row basis, it is not necessary to do so. It is always possible to work backward from $\mathbf{X}_B^{-1}$ (which expresses the parameters of the model as linear functions of the population group means) to $\mathbf{X}_B$, as long as the comparisons specified by $\mathbf{X}_B^{-1}$ are linearly independent. Linear independence is required to ensure that $\mathbf{X}_B^{-1}$ is nonsingular.[12]

If there are equal numbers (say n') of observations in the several groups, then an orthogonal model-matrix basis $\mathbf{X}_B$ implies an orthogonal full-rank model matrix $\mathbf{X}_F$—because $\mathbf{X}_F$ is produced by repeating each of the rows of $\mathbf{X}_B$ an equal number (n') of times. The columns of an orthogonal model matrix represent independent sources of variation in the response variable, and therefore a set of orthogonal contrasts partitions the regression sum of squares into one-degree-of-freedom components, each testing a hypothesis of interest. When it is applicable, this is an elegant approach to linear-model analysis. Linear comparisons may well be of interest, however, even if group frequencies are unequal, causing contrasts that are orthogonal in $\mathbf{X}_B$ to be correlated in $\mathbf{X}_F$.[13]

9.2 Least-Squares Fit

To find the least-squares coefficients, we write the fitted linear model as

$$\mathbf{y} = \mathbf{X}\mathbf{b} + \mathbf{e}$$

where $\mathbf{b} = [B_0, B_1, \dots, B_k]'$ is the vector of fitted coefficients, and $\mathbf{e} = [E_1, E_2, \dots, E_n]'$ is the vector of residuals. We seek the coefficient vector $\mathbf{b}$ that minimizes the residual sum of squares, expressed as a function of $\mathbf{b}$:

---

[11] See Exercise 9.2.
[12] See Exercise 9.3.
[13] These conclusions are supported by the vector geometry of linear models, described in Chapter 10.

$$S(\mathbf{b}) = \sum E_i^2 = \mathbf{e}'\mathbf{e} = (\mathbf{y} - \mathbf{Xb})'(\mathbf{y} - \mathbf{Xb})$$
$$= \mathbf{y}'\mathbf{y} - \mathbf{y}'\mathbf{Xb} - \mathbf{b}'\mathbf{X}'\mathbf{y} + \mathbf{b}'\mathbf{X}'\mathbf{Xb}$$
$$= \mathbf{y}'\mathbf{y} - (2\mathbf{y}'\mathbf{X})\mathbf{b} + \mathbf{b}'(\mathbf{X}'\mathbf{X})\mathbf{b} \tag{9.7}$$

Although matrix multiplication is not generally commutative, each product in Equation 9.7 is (1×1); thus, $\mathbf{y}'\mathbf{Xb} = \mathbf{b}'\mathbf{Xy}$, justifying the transition to the last line of the equation.[14]

From the point of view of the coefficient vector $\mathbf{b}$, Equation 9.7 consists of a constant, a linear form in $\mathbf{b}$, and a quadratic form in $\mathbf{b}$. To minimize $S(\mathbf{b})$, we find its vector partial derivative with respect to $\mathbf{b}$:

$$\frac{\partial S(\mathbf{b})}{\partial \mathbf{b}} = \mathbf{0} - 2\mathbf{X}'\mathbf{y} + 2\mathbf{X}'\mathbf{Xb}$$

Setting this derivative to $\mathbf{0}$ produces the matrix form of the normal equations for the linear model:

$$\mathbf{X}'\mathbf{Xb} = \mathbf{X}'\mathbf{y} \tag{9.8}$$

There are $k + 1$ normal equations in the same number of unknown coefficients. If $\mathbf{X}'\mathbf{X}$ is nonsingular—that is, of rank $k + 1$—then we can uniquely solve for the least-squares coefficients:

$$\mathbf{b} = (\mathbf{X}'\mathbf{X})^{-1}\mathbf{X}'\mathbf{y}$$

The rank of $\mathbf{X}'\mathbf{X}$ is equal to the rank of $\mathbf{X}$:

- Because the rank of $\mathbf{X}$ can be no greater than the smaller of n and $k + 1$, for the least-squares coefficients to be unique, we require at least as many observations (n) as there are coefficients in the model ($k + 1$). This requirement is intuitively sensible: We cannot, for example, fit a unique line to a single data point, nor can we fit a unique plane to two data points. In most applications, n greatly exceeds $k + 1$.
- The $k + 1$ columns of $\mathbf{X}$ must be linearly independent. This requirement implies that no regressor can be a perfect linear function of others, and that only the constant regressor can be invariant.[15]

In applications, these requirements are usually met: $\mathbf{X}'\mathbf{X}$, therefore, is generally nonsingular, and the least-squares coefficients are uniquely defined.[16]

The second partial derivative of the sum of squared residuals is

$$\frac{\partial^2 S(\mathbf{b})}{\partial \mathbf{b}\, \partial \mathbf{b}'} = 2\mathbf{X}'\mathbf{X}$$

Because $\mathbf{X}'\mathbf{X}$ is positive-definite when $\mathbf{X}$ is of full rank, the solution $\mathbf{b} = (\mathbf{X}'\mathbf{X})^{-1}\mathbf{X}'\mathbf{y}$ represents a *minimum* of $S(\mathbf{b})$.

If the model matrix $\mathbf{X}$ is of full-column rank, then the least-squares coefficients are given by $\mathbf{b} = (\mathbf{X}'\mathbf{X})^{-1}\mathbf{X}'\mathbf{y}$.

The matrix $\mathbf{X}'\mathbf{X}$ contains sums of squares and products among the regressors (including the constant regressor, $X_0 = 1$); the vector $\mathbf{X}'\mathbf{y}$ contains sums of cross products between the regressors

---

[14]See Exercise 9.4.
[15]If another regressor is invariant, then it is a multiple of the constant regressor, $X_0 = 1$.
[16]We will see in Section 13.1, however, that even when $\mathbf{X}$ is of rank $k + 1$, *near*-collinearity of its columns can cause statistical difficulties.

and the response variable. Forming these matrix products, and expressing the normal equations (Equation 9.8) in scalar format, yields a familiar pattern:[17]

$$B_0 n \quad + B_1 \sum x_{i1} \quad + \cdots + B_k \sum x_{ik} \quad = \sum Y_i$$
$$B_0 \sum x_{i1} + B_1 \sum x_{i1}^2 \quad + \cdots + B_k \sum x_{i1} x_{ik} = \sum x_{i1} Y_i$$
$$\vdots \qquad\qquad\qquad\qquad\qquad\qquad\qquad \vdots$$
$$B_0 \sum x_{ik} + B_1 \sum x_{ik} x_{i1} + \cdots + B_k \sum x_{ik}^2 \quad = \sum x_{ik} Y_i$$

To write an explicit solution to the normal equations in scalar form would be impractical, even for small values of k.

For Duncan's regression of occupational prestige on the income and educational levels of 45 U.S. occupations, the sums of squares and products are as follows:[18]

$$\mathbf{X'X} = \begin{bmatrix} 45 & 1884 & 2365 \\ 1884 & 105,148 & 122,197 \\ 2365 & 122,197 & 163,265 \end{bmatrix}$$

$$\mathbf{X'y} = \begin{bmatrix} 2146 \\ 118,229 \\ 147,936 \end{bmatrix}$$

The inverse of $\mathbf{X'X}$ is

$$(\mathbf{X'X})^{-1} = \begin{bmatrix} 0.1021058996 & -0.0008495732 & -0.0008432006 \\ -0.0008495732 & 0.0000801220 & -0.0000476613 \\ -0.0008432006 & -0.0000476613 & 0.0000540118 \end{bmatrix}$$

and thus the least-squares regression coefficients are

$$\mathbf{b} = (\mathbf{X'X})^{-1}\mathbf{X'y} = \begin{bmatrix} -6.06466 \\ 0.59873 \\ 0.54583 \end{bmatrix}$$

9.3   Properties of the Least-Squares Estimator

In this section, I derive a number of fundamental results concerning the least-squares estimator $\mathbf{b}$ of the linear-model parameter vector β. These results serve several related purposes:

- They establish certain desirable properties of the least-squares estimator that hold under the assumptions of the linear model.
- They furnish a basis for using the least-squares coefficients to make statistical inferences about β.[19]
- They provide a foundation for generalizing the linear model in several directions.[20]

---

[17] See Section 5.2.2.
[18] Cf. the scalar calculations for Duncan's regression, which appear in Section 5.2.1.
[19] See Section 9.4.
[20] See, for example, Section 12.2.2 and Chapters 14 and 15.

9.3.1 The Distribution of the Least-Squares Estimator

With the model matrix $\mathbf{X}$ fixed, the least-squares coefficients $\mathbf{b}$ result from a linear transformation of the response variable; that is, $\mathbf{b}$ is a *linear estimator*:

$$\mathbf{b} = (\mathbf{X}'\mathbf{X})^{-1}\mathbf{X}'\mathbf{y} = \mathbf{M}\mathbf{y}$$

defining $\mathbf{M} \equiv (\mathbf{X}'\mathbf{X})^{-1}\mathbf{X}'$. The expected value of $\mathbf{b}$ is easily established from the expectation of $\mathbf{y}$ (given previously in Equation 9.2 on page 188):

$$E(\mathbf{b}) = E(\mathbf{M}\mathbf{y}) = \mathbf{M}E(\mathbf{y}) = (\mathbf{X}'\mathbf{X})^{-1}\mathbf{X}'(\mathbf{X}\beta) = \beta$$

The least-squares estimator $\mathbf{b}$ is therefore an unbiased estimator of β.

The covariance matrix of the least-squares estimator is similarly derived:

$$V(\mathbf{b}) = \mathbf{M}V(\mathbf{y})\mathbf{M}' = [(\mathbf{X}'\mathbf{X})^{-1}\mathbf{X}']\sigma_\varepsilon^2\mathbf{I}_n[(\mathbf{X}'\mathbf{X})^{-1}\mathbf{X}']'$$

Moving the scalar error variance σ_ε^2 to the front of this expression, and noting that $(\mathbf{X}'\mathbf{X})^{-1}$ is the inverse of a symmetric matrix and is thus itself symmetric, we get

$$V(\mathbf{b}) = \sigma_\varepsilon^2(\mathbf{X}'\mathbf{X})^{-1}\mathbf{X}'\mathbf{X}(\mathbf{X}'\mathbf{X})^{-1} = \sigma_\varepsilon^2(\mathbf{X}'\mathbf{X})^{-1}$$

The sampling variances and covariances of the regression coefficients, therefore, depend only on the model matrix and the variance of the errors.

To derive $E(\mathbf{b})$ and $V(\mathbf{b})$, we do not require the assumption of normality—only the assumptions of linearity [i.e., $E(\mathbf{y}) = \mathbf{X}\beta$], constant variance, and independence [$V(\mathbf{y}) = \sigma_\varepsilon^2\mathbf{I}_n$].[21] If $\mathbf{y}$ is normally distributed, however, then so is $\mathbf{b}$, for—as I have explained—$\mathbf{b}$ results from a linear transformation of $\mathbf{y}$:

$$\mathbf{b} \sim N_{k+1}[\beta, \ \sigma_\varepsilon^2(\mathbf{X}'\mathbf{X})^{-1}]$$

There is a striking parallel, noted by Wonnacott and Wonnacott (1979) and detailed in Table 9.1, between the scalar formulas for least-squares simple regression and the matrix formulas for the general linear model ("multiple regression"). This sort of structural parallel is common in statistical applications when matrix methods are used to generalize a scalar result: Matrix notation is productive precisely because of the generality and simplicity that it achieves.

> Under the full set of assumptions for the linear model, the distribution of the least-squares regression coefficients is
>
> $$\mathbf{b} \sim N_{k+1}[\beta, \ \sigma_\varepsilon^2(\mathbf{x}'\mathbf{x})^{-1}]$$

---

[21] In general, independence of the observations *implies* that the elements of $\mathbf{y}$ are uncorrelated [i.e., that $V(\mathbf{y})$ is diagonal], but the reverse is not the case: The elements of $\mathbf{y}$ *could be* uncorrelated even if the observations are not independent. That is, independence is a stronger condition than uncorrelation. For normally distributed $\mathbf{y}$, however, uncorrelation and independence coincide.

Table 9.1 Comparison Between Simple Regression Using Scalars and Multiple Regression Using Matrices

	Simple Regression	*Multiple Regression*
Model	$Y = \alpha + \beta x + \varepsilon$	$\mathbf{y} = \mathbf{X}\boldsymbol{\beta} + \boldsymbol{\varepsilon}$
Least-squares estimator	$B = \dfrac{\sum x^* Y^*}{\sum x^{*2}}$ $= \left(\sum x^{*2}\right)^{-1} \sum x^* Y^*$	$\mathbf{b} = (\mathbf{X}'\mathbf{X})^{-1}\mathbf{X}'\mathbf{y}$
Sampling variance	$V(B) = \dfrac{\sigma_\varepsilon^2}{\sum x^{*2}} = \sigma_\varepsilon^2 \left(\sum x^{*2}\right)^{-1}$ $= \sigma_\varepsilon^2 \left(\sum x^{*2}\right)^{-1}$	$V(\mathbf{b}) = \sigma_\varepsilon^2 (\mathbf{X}'\mathbf{X})^{-1}$
Distribution	$B \sim N[\beta, \sigma_\varepsilon^2 (\sum x^{*2})^{-1}]$	$\mathbf{b} \sim N_{k+1}[\boldsymbol{\beta}, \sigma_\varepsilon^2 (\mathbf{X}'\mathbf{X})^{-1}]$

NOTE: Subscripts are suppressed in this table; in particular, $x^* \equiv x_i - \bar{x}$ and $Y^* \equiv Y_i - \bar{Y}$.

SOURCE: Adapted from Wonnacott and Wonnacott (1979, Table 12-1), *Econometrics, Second Edition*. Copyright © John Wiley & Sons, Inc. Reprinted by permission of John Wiley & Sons, Inc.

9.3.2   The Gauss-Markov Theorem

One of the primary theoretical justifications for least-squares estimation is the Gauss-Markov theorem, which states that if the errors are independently distributed with zero expectation and constant variance, then the least-squares estimator $\mathbf{b}$ is the most efficient linear unbiased estimator of $\boldsymbol{\beta}$. That is, of all unbiased estimators that are linear functions of the observations, the least-squares estimator has the smallest sampling variance and, hence, the smallest mean-squared error. For this reason, the least-squares estimator is sometimes termed *BLUE*, an acronym for *b*est *l*inear *u*nbiased *e*stimator.[22]

Let $\tilde{\mathbf{b}}$ represent the best linear unbiased estimator of $\boldsymbol{\beta}$. As we know, the least-squares estimator $\mathbf{b}$ is also a linear estimator, $\mathbf{b} = \mathbf{My}$. It is convenient to write $\tilde{\mathbf{b}} = (\mathbf{M} + \mathbf{A})\mathbf{y}$, where $\mathbf{A}$ gives the *difference* between the (as yet undetermined) transformation matrix for the BLUE and that for the least-squares estimator. To show that the BLUE and the least-squares estimator coincide—that is, to establish the Gauss-Markov theorem—we need to demonstrate that $\mathbf{A} = \mathbf{0}$.

Because $\tilde{\mathbf{b}}$ is *unbiased*,

$$\boldsymbol{\beta} = E(\tilde{\mathbf{b}}) = E[(\mathbf{M} + \mathbf{A})\mathbf{y}] = E(\mathbf{My}) + E(\mathbf{Ay})$$
$$= E(\mathbf{b}) + \mathbf{A}E(\mathbf{y}) = \boldsymbol{\beta} + \mathbf{AX}\boldsymbol{\beta}$$

The matrix product $\mathbf{AX}\boldsymbol{\beta}$, then, is $\mathbf{0}$, regardless of the value of $\boldsymbol{\beta}$, and therefore $\mathbf{AX}$ must be $\mathbf{0}$.[23]

I have, to this point, made use of the linearity and unbias of $\tilde{\mathbf{b}}$. Because $\tilde{\mathbf{b}}$ is the *minimum-variance* linear unbiased estimator, the sampling variances of its elements—that is, the diagonal entries of $V(\tilde{\mathbf{b}})$—are as small as possible.[24] The covariance matrix of $\tilde{\mathbf{b}}$ is given by

---

[22] As I explained in Section 6.1.2, the comfort provided by the Gauss-Markov theorem is often an illusion, because the restriction to linear estimators is artificial. Under the additional assumption of normality, however, it is possible to show that the least-squares estimator is maximally efficient among *all* unbiased estimators (see, e.g., Rao, 1973, p. 319). The strategy of proof of the Gauss-Markov theorem employed in this section is borrowed from Wonnacott and Wonnacott (1979, pp. 428–430), where it is used in a slightly different context.

[23] See Exercise 9.7.

[24] It is possible to prove a more general result: The best linear unbiased estimator of $\mathbf{a}'\boldsymbol{\beta}$ (an arbitrary linear combination of regression coefficients) is $\mathbf{a}'\mathbf{b}$, where $\mathbf{b}$ is the least-squares estimator (see, e.g., Seber, 1977, p. 49).

$$V(\widetilde{\mathbf{b}}) = (\mathbf{M} + \mathbf{A})V(\mathbf{y})(\mathbf{M} + \mathbf{A})'$$
$$= (\mathbf{M} + \mathbf{A})\sigma_\varepsilon^2 \mathbf{I}_n (\mathbf{M} + \mathbf{A})'$$
$$= \sigma_\varepsilon^2 (\mathbf{MM}' + \mathbf{MA}' + \mathbf{AM}' + \mathbf{AA}') \qquad (9.9)$$

I have shown that $\mathbf{AX} = \mathbf{0}$; consequently, $\mathbf{AM}'$ and its transpose $\mathbf{MA}'$ are $\mathbf{0}$, for

$$\mathbf{AM}' = \mathbf{AX}(\mathbf{X}'\mathbf{X})^{-1} = \mathbf{0}(\mathbf{X}'\mathbf{X})^{-1} = \mathbf{0}$$

Equation 9.9 becomes

$$V(\widetilde{\mathbf{b}}) = \sigma_\varepsilon^2 (\mathbf{MM}' + \mathbf{AA}')$$

The sampling variance of the coefficient $\widetilde{B}_j$ is the jth diagonal entry of $V(\widetilde{\mathbf{b}})$:[25]

$$V(\widetilde{B}_j) = \sigma_\varepsilon^2 \left(\sum_{i=1}^{n} m_{ji}^2 + \sum_{i=1}^{n} a_{ji}^2 \right)$$

Both sums in this equation are sums of squares and hence cannot be negative; because $V(\widetilde{B}_j)$ is as small as possible, all the a_{ji} must be 0. This argument applies to each coefficient in $\widetilde{\mathbf{b}}$, and so every row of $\mathbf{A}$ must be $\mathbf{0}$, implying that $\mathbf{A} = \mathbf{0}$. Finally,

$$\widetilde{\mathbf{b}} = (\mathbf{M} + \mathbf{0})\mathbf{y} = \mathbf{My} = \mathbf{b}$$

demonstrating that the BLUE is the least-squares estimator.

9.3.3 Maximum-Likelihood Estimation

Under the assumptions of the linear model, the least-squares estimator $\mathbf{b}$ is also the maximum-likelihood estimator of β.[26] This result establishes an additional justification for least squares when the assumptions of the model are reasonable, but even more important, it provides a basis for generalizing the linear model.[27]

As I have explained, under the assumptions of the linear model, $\mathbf{y} \sim N_n(\mathbf{X}\beta, \sigma_\varepsilon^2 \mathbf{I}_n)$. Thus, for the ith observation, $Y_i \sim N(\mathbf{x}_i'\beta, \sigma_\varepsilon^2)$, where $\mathbf{x}_i'$ is the ith row of the model matrix $\mathbf{X}$. In equation form, the probability density for observation i is

$$p(y_i) = \frac{1}{\sigma_\varepsilon \sqrt{2\pi}} \exp\left[-\frac{(y_i - \mathbf{x}_i'\beta)^2}{2\sigma_\varepsilon^2} \right]$$

Because the n observations are independent, their joint probability density is the product of their marginal densities:

$$p(\mathbf{y}) = \frac{1}{\left(\sigma_\varepsilon \sqrt{2\pi}\right)^n} \exp\left[-\frac{\sum (y_i - \mathbf{x}_i'\beta)^2}{2\sigma_\varepsilon^2} \right]$$
$$= \frac{1}{\left(2\pi \sigma_\varepsilon^2\right)^{n/2}} \exp\left[-\frac{(\mathbf{y} - \mathbf{X}\beta)'(\mathbf{y} - \mathbf{X}\beta)}{2\sigma_\varepsilon^2} \right] \qquad (9.10)$$

---

[25] Actually, the variance of the constant $\widetilde{B}_0$ is the *first* diagonal entry of $V(\widetilde{\mathbf{b}})$; the variance of $\widetilde{B}_j$ is therefore the $(j+1)$st entry. To avoid this awkwardness, I will index the covariance matrix of $\widetilde{\mathbf{b}}$ (and later, that of $\mathbf{b}$) from 0 rather than from 1.
[26] The method of maximum likelihood is introduced in Appendix D on probability and estimation.
[27] See, for example, the discussions of transformations in Section 12.5 and of nonlinear least squares in Chapter 17.

Although this equation also follows directly from the multivariate-normal distribution of $\mathbf{y}$, the development from $p(y_i)$ to $p(\mathbf{y})$ will prove helpful when we consider random regressors.[28]

From Equation 9.10, the log likelihood is

$$\log_e L(\beta, \sigma_\varepsilon^2) = -\frac{n}{2} \log_e 2\pi - \frac{n}{2} \log_e \sigma_\varepsilon^2 - \frac{1}{2\sigma_\varepsilon^2}(\mathbf{y} - \mathbf{X}\beta)'(\mathbf{y} - \mathbf{X}\beta) \qquad (9.11)$$

To maximize the likelihood, we require the partial derivatives of Equation 9.11 with respect to the parameters β and σ_ε^2. Differentiation is simplified when we notice that $(\mathbf{y} - \mathbf{X}\beta)'(\mathbf{y} - \mathbf{X}\beta)$ is the sum of squared errors:

$$\frac{\partial \log_e L(\beta, \sigma_\varepsilon^2)}{\partial \beta} = -\frac{1}{2\sigma_\varepsilon^2}(2\mathbf{X}'\mathbf{X}\beta - 2\mathbf{X}'\mathbf{y})$$

$$\frac{\partial \log_e L(\beta, \sigma_\varepsilon^2)}{\partial \sigma_\varepsilon^2} = -\frac{n}{2}\left(\frac{1}{\sigma_\varepsilon^2}\right) + \frac{1}{2\sigma_\varepsilon^4}(\mathbf{y} - \mathbf{X}\beta)'(\mathbf{y} - \mathbf{X}\beta)$$

Setting these partial derivatives to 0 and solving for the maximum-likelihood estimators $\widehat{\beta}$ and $\widehat{\sigma}_\varepsilon^2$ produces

$$\widehat{\beta} = (\mathbf{X}'\mathbf{X})^{-1}\mathbf{X}'\mathbf{y},$$

$$\widehat{\sigma}_\varepsilon^2 = \frac{(\mathbf{y}-\mathbf{X}\widehat{\beta})'(\mathbf{y}-\mathbf{X}\widehat{\beta})}{n} = \frac{\mathbf{e}'\mathbf{e}}{n}$$

The maximum-likelihood estimator $\widehat{\beta}$ is therefore the same as the least-squares estimator $\mathbf{b}$. In fact, this identity is clear directly from Equation 9.10, without formal maximization of the likelihood: The likelihood is large when the negative exponent is small, and the numerator of the exponent contains the sum of squared errors; minimizing the sum of squared residuals, therefore, maximizes the likelihood.

The maximum-likelihood estimator $\widehat{\sigma}_\varepsilon^2$ of the error variance is biased; consequently, we prefer the similar, unbiased estimator $S_E^2 = \mathbf{e}'\mathbf{e}/(n - k - 1)$ to $\widehat{\sigma}_\varepsilon^2$.[29] As n increases, however, the bias of $\widehat{\sigma}_\varepsilon^2$ shrinks toward 0: As a maximum-likelihood estimator, $\widehat{\sigma}_\varepsilon^2$ is consistent.

9.4   Statistical Inference for Linear Models

The results of the previous section, along with some to be established in Chapter 10, provide a basis for statistical inference in linear models.[30] I have already shown that the least-squares coefficients $\mathbf{b}$ have certain desirable properties as point estimators of the parameters β. In this section, I will describe tests for individual coefficients, for several coefficients, and for general linear hypotheses.

9.4.1   Inference for Individual Coefficients

We saw that the least-squares estimator $\mathbf{b}$ follows a normal distribution with expectation β and covariance matrix $\sigma_\varepsilon^2(\mathbf{X}'\mathbf{X})^{-1}$.[31] Consequently, an individual coefficient B_j is normally distributed with expectation β_j and sampling variance $\sigma_\varepsilon^2 v_{jj}$, where v_{jj} is the jth diagonal entry of

---

[28] See Section 9.6.
[29] See Section 10.3 for a derivation of the expectation of S_E^2.
[30] The results of this section justify and extend the procedures for inference described in Chapter 6.
[31] See Section 9.3.1.

$(\mathbf{X}'\mathbf{X})^{-1}.$[32] The ratio $(B_j - \beta_j)/\sigma_\varepsilon \sqrt{v_{jj}}$, therefore, follows the unit-normal distribution $N(0, 1)$; and to test the hypothesis H_0: $\beta_j = \beta_j^{(0)}$, we can calculate the test statistic

$$Z_0 = \frac{B_j - \beta_j^{(0)}}{\sigma_\varepsilon \sqrt{v_{jj}}}$$

comparing the obtained value of the statistic to quantiles of the unit-normal distribution. This result is not of direct practical use, however, because in applications of linear models we do not know σ_ε^2.

Although the error variance is unknown, we have available the unbiased estimator $S_E^2 = \mathbf{e}'\mathbf{e}/(n - k - 1)$. Employing this estimator, we can estimate the covariance matrix of the least-squares coefficients:

$$\widehat{V}(\mathbf{b}) = S_E^2 (\mathbf{X}'\mathbf{X})^{-1} = \frac{\mathbf{e}'\mathbf{e}}{n - k - 1}(\mathbf{X}'\mathbf{X})^{-1}$$

The standard error of the coefficient B_j is, therefore, given by $\mathrm{SE}(B_j) = S_E \sqrt{v_{jj}}$, the square root of the jth diagonal entry of $\widehat{V}(\mathbf{b})$.

It can be shown that $(n - k - 1)S_E^2/\sigma_\varepsilon^2 = \mathbf{e}'\mathbf{e}/\sigma_\varepsilon^2$ follows a chi-square distribution with $n - k - 1$ degrees of freedom.[33] We recently discovered that $(B_j - \beta_j)/\sigma_\varepsilon \sqrt{v_{jj}}$ is distributed as $N(0, 1)$. It can be further established that the estimators B_j and S_E^2 are independent,[34] and so the ratio

$$t = \frac{(B_j - \beta_j)/\sigma_\varepsilon \sqrt{v_{jj}}}{\sqrt{\dfrac{\mathbf{e}'\mathbf{e}/\sigma_\varepsilon^2}{n - k - 1}}} = \frac{B_j - \beta_j}{S_E \sqrt{v_{jj}}}$$

follows a t-distribution with $n - k - 1$ degrees of freedom. Heuristically, in estimating σ_ε with S_E, we must replace the normal distribution with the more spread-out t-distribution to reflect the additional source of variability.

To test the hypothesis H_0: $\beta_j = \beta_j^{(0)}$, therefore, we calculate the test statistic

$$t_0 = \frac{B_j - \beta_j^{(0)}}{\mathrm{SE}(B_j)}$$

comparing the obtained value of t_0 with the quantiles of t_{n-k-1}. Likewise, a $100(1 - a)\%$ confidence interval for β_j is given by

$$\beta_j = B_j \pm t_{a/2, n-k-1}\mathrm{SE}(B_j)$$

where $t_{a/2, n-k-1}$ is the critical value of t_{n-k-1} with a probability of $a/2$ to the right.

For Duncan's occupational prestige regression, for example, the estimated error variance is $S_E^2 = 178.73$, and so the estimated covariance matrix of the regression coefficients is

$$\widehat{V}(\mathbf{b}) = 178.73(\mathbf{X}'\mathbf{X})^{-1}$$

$$= \begin{bmatrix} 18.249387 & -0.151844 & -0.150705 \\ -0.151844 & 0.014320 & -0.008519 \\ -0.150705 & -0.008519 & 0.009653 \end{bmatrix}$$

---

[32] Recall that we index the rows and columns of $(\mathbf{X}'\mathbf{X})^{-1}$ from 0 through k.
[33] See Section 10.3.
[34] See Exercise 9.8.

The standard errors of the regression coefficients are[35]

$$\begin{aligned}
\mathrm{SE}(B_0) &= \sqrt{18.249387} = 4.272 \\
\mathrm{SE}(B_1) &= \sqrt{0.014320} = 0.1197 \\
\mathrm{SE}(B_2) &= \sqrt{0.009653} = 0.09825
\end{aligned}$$

The estimated covariance matrix of the least-squares coefficients is $\widehat{V}(\mathbf{b}) = S_E^2(\mathbf{X}'\mathbf{X})^{-1}$. The standard errors of the regression coefficients are the square-root diagonal entries of this matrix. Under the assumptions of the model, $(B_j - \beta_j)/\mathrm{SE}(B_j) \sim t_{n-k-1}$, providing a basis for hypothesis tests and confidence intervals for individual coefficients.

9.4.2   Inference for Several Coefficients

Although we usually test regression coefficients individually, these tests may not be sufficient, for, in general, the least-squares estimators of different parameters are correlated: The off-diagonal entries of $V(\mathbf{b}) = \sigma_\varepsilon^2(\mathbf{X}'\mathbf{X})^{-1}$, giving the sampling *covariances* of the least-squares coefficients, are 0 only when the regressors themselves are uncorrelated.[36] Furthermore, in certain applications of linear models—such as dummy regression, analysis of variance, and polynomial regression—we are more interested in related sets of coefficients than in the individual members of these sets.

Simultaneous tests for sets of coefficients, taking their intercorrelations into account, can be constructed by the likelihood-ratio principle. Suppose that we fit the model

$$Y = \beta_0 + \beta_1 x_1 + \cdots + \beta_k x_k + \varepsilon \tag{9.12}$$

obtaining the least-squares estimate $\mathbf{b} = [B_0, B_1, \ldots, B_k]'$, along with the maximum-likelihood estimate of the error variance, $\widehat{\sigma}_\varepsilon^2 = \mathbf{e}'\mathbf{e}/n$. We wish to test the null hypothesis that a subset of regression parameters is 0; for convenience, let these coefficients be the first $q \leq k$, so that the null hypothesis is H_0: $\beta_1 = \cdots = \beta_q = 0$. The null hypothesis corresponds to the model

$$\begin{aligned}
Y &= \beta_0 + 0 x_1 + \cdots + 0 x_q + \beta_{q+1} x_{q+1} + \cdots + \beta_k x_k + \varepsilon \\
&= \beta_0 + \beta_{q+1} x_{q+1} + \cdots + \beta_k x_k + \varepsilon
\end{aligned} \tag{9.13}$$

which is a specialization (or restriction) of the more general model (Equation 9.12). Fitting the restricted model (Equation 9.13) by least-squares regression of Y on x_{q+1} through x_k, we obtain $\mathbf{b}_0 = [B_0', 0, \ldots, 0, B_{q+1}', \ldots, B_k']'$, and $\widehat{\sigma}_{\varepsilon_0}^2 = \mathbf{e}_0'\mathbf{e}_0/n$. Note that the coefficients in $\mathbf{b}_0$ generally differ from those in $\mathbf{b}$ (hence the primes), and that $\widehat{\sigma}_\varepsilon^2 \leq \widehat{\sigma}_{\varepsilon_0}^2$, because both models are fit by least squares.

The likelihood for the full model (Equation 9.12), evaluated at the maximum-likelihood estimates, can be obtained from Equation 9.10 (on page 197):[37]

$$L = \left(2\pi e \frac{\mathbf{e}'\mathbf{e}}{n}\right)^{-n/2}$$

---

[35]Cf. the results given in Section 6.2.2.

[36]This point pertains to sampling correlations among the k *slope* coefficients. The regression constant is correlated with the slope coefficients unless all the regressors—save the constant regressor—have means of 0 (i.e., are in mean-deviation form). Expressing the regressors in mean-deviation form, called *centering*, has certain computational advantages (it tends to reduce rounding errors in least-squares calculations), but it does not affect the slope coefficients or the sampling covariances among them.

[37]See Exercise 9.9. The notation here is potentially confusing: $e \approx 2.718$ is the mathematical constant; $\mathbf{e}$ is the vector of residuals.

Likewise, for the restricted model (Equation 9.13), the maximized likelihood is

$$L_0 = \left(2\pi e \frac{\mathbf{e}_0'\mathbf{e}_0}{n} \right)^{-n/2}$$

The likelihood ratio for testing H_0 is, therefore,

$$\frac{L_0}{L_1} = \left(\frac{\mathbf{e}_0'\mathbf{e}_0}{\mathbf{e}'\mathbf{e}} \right)^{-n/2} = \left(\frac{\mathbf{e}'\mathbf{e}}{\mathbf{e}_0'\mathbf{e}_0} \right)^{2/n}$$

Because $\mathbf{e}_0'\mathbf{e}_0 \geq \mathbf{e}'\mathbf{e}$, the likelihood ratio is small when the residual sum of squares for the restricted model is appreciably larger than for the general model—circumstances under which we should doubt the truth of the null hypothesis. A test of H_0 is provided by the generalized likelihood-ratio test statistic, $G_0^2 = -2\log_e(L_0/L_1)$, which is asymptotically distributed as χ_q^2 under the null hypothesis.

It is unnecessary to use this asymptotic result, however, for an exact test can be obtained:[38] As mentioned in the previous section, $\text{RSS}/\sigma_\varepsilon^2 = \mathbf{e}'\mathbf{e}/\sigma_\varepsilon^2$ is distributed as χ^2 with $n - k - 1$ degrees of freedom. By a direct extension of this result, if the null hypothesis is true, then $\text{RSS}_0/\sigma_\varepsilon^2 = \mathbf{e}_0'\mathbf{e}_0/\sigma_\varepsilon^2$ is distributed as χ^2 with $n - (k - q) - 1 = n - k + q - 1$ degrees of freedom. Consequently, the difference $(\text{RSS}_0 - \text{RSS})/\sigma_\varepsilon^2$ has a χ^2 distribution with $(n - k + q - 1) - (n - k - 1) = q$ degrees of freedom, equal to the number of parameters set to 0 in the restricted model. It can be shown that $(\text{RSS}_0 - \text{RSS})/\sigma_\varepsilon^2$ and $\text{RSS}/\sigma_\varepsilon^2$ are independent, and so the ratio

$$F_0 = \frac{(\text{RSS}_0 - \text{RSS})/q}{\text{RSS}/(n - k - 1)}$$

is distributed as F with q and $n - k - 1$ degrees of freedom. This is, of course, the incremental F-statistic.[39]

Although it is sometimes convenient to find an incremental sum of squares by fitting alternative linear models to the data, it is also possible to calculate this quantity directly from the least-squares coefficient vector $\mathbf{b}$ and the matrix $(\mathbf{X}'\mathbf{X})^{-1}$ for the full model: Let $\mathbf{b}_1 = [B_1, \ldots, B_q]'$ represent the coefficients of interest selected from among the entries of $\mathbf{b}$; and let $\mathbf{V}_{11}$ represent the square submatrix consisting of the entries in the q rows and q columns of $(\mathbf{X}'\mathbf{X})^{-1}$ that pertain to the coefficients in $\mathbf{b}_1$.[40] Then it can be shown that the incremental sum of squares $\text{RSS}_0 - \text{RSS}$ is equal to $\mathbf{b}_1'\mathbf{V}_{11}^{-1}\mathbf{b}_1$, and thus the incremental F-statistic can be written $F_0 = \mathbf{b}_1'\mathbf{V}_{11}^{-1}\mathbf{b}_1/qS_E^2$. To test the more general hypothesis $H_0: \boldsymbol{\beta}_1 = \boldsymbol{\beta}_1^{(0)}$ (where $\boldsymbol{\beta}_1^{(0)}$ is not necessarily $\mathbf{0}$), we can compute

$$F_0 = \frac{(\mathbf{b}_1 - \boldsymbol{\beta}_1^{(0)})'\mathbf{V}_{11}^{-1}(\mathbf{b}_1 - \boldsymbol{\beta}_1^{(0)})}{qS_E^2} \tag{9.14}$$

which is distributed as $F_{q,n-k-1}$ under H_0.

Recall that the omnibus F-statistic for the hypothesis $H_0: \beta_1 = \cdots = \beta_k = 0$ is

$$F_0 = \frac{\text{RegSS}/k}{\text{RSS}/(n - k - 1)}$$

---

[38]The F-test that follows is exact when the assumptions of the model hold—including the assumption of normality. Of course, the asymptotically valid likelihood-ratio test also depends on these assumptions.

[39]See Section 6.2.2.

[40]Note the difference between the vector $\mathbf{b}_1$ (used here) and the vector $\mathbf{b}_0$ (used previously): $\mathbf{b}_1$ consists of coefficients extracted from $\mathbf{b}$, which, in turn, results from fitting the *full* model; in contrast, $\mathbf{b}_0$ consists of the coefficients—including those set to 0 in the hypothesis—that result from fitting the *restricted* model.

The denominator of this F-statistic estimates the error variance σ_ε^2, *whether or not* the null hypothesis is true.[41] The expectation of the regression sum of squares, it may be shown,[42] is

$$E(\text{RegSS}) = \beta_1'(\mathbf{X}^{*\prime}\mathbf{X}^*)\beta_1 + k\sigma_\varepsilon^2$$

where $\beta_1 \equiv [\beta_1, \ldots, \beta_k]'$ is the vector of regression coefficients, excluding the constant, and $\mathbf{X}^*_{(n \times k)} \equiv \{x_{ij} - \overline{x}_j\}$ is the matrix of mean-deviation regressors, omitting the constant regressor. When H_0 is true (and $\beta_1 = \mathbf{0}$), the numerator of the F-statistic (as well at its denominator) estimates σ_ε^2; but, when H_0 is false, $E(\text{RegSS}/k) > \sigma_\varepsilon^2$, because $\mathbf{X}^{*\prime}\mathbf{X}^*$ is positive definite, and thus $\beta_1'(\mathbf{X}^{*\prime}\mathbf{X}^*)\beta_1 > 0$ for $\beta_1 \neq \mathbf{0}$. Under these circumstances, we tend to observe numerators that are larger than denominators, and F-statistics that are greater than 1.[43]

An incremental F-test for the hypothesis $H_0: \beta_1 = \cdots = \beta_q = 0$, where $1 \leq q \leq k$, is given by $F_0 = (n - k - 1)(\text{RSS}_0 - \text{RSS})/q\,\text{RSS}$, where RSS is the residual sum of squares for the full model, and RSS_0 is the residual sum of squares for the model that deletes the q regressors in question. Under the null hypothesis, $F_0 \sim F_{q,n-k-1}$. The incremental F-statistic can also be computed directly as $F_0 = \mathbf{b}_1'\mathbf{V}_{11}^{-1}\mathbf{b}_1/q S_E^2$, where $\mathbf{b}_1 = [B_1, \ldots, B_q]'$ contains the coefficients of interest extracted from among the entries of $\mathbf{b}$; and $\mathbf{V}_{11}$ is the square submatrix of $(\mathbf{X}'\mathbf{X})^{-1}$ consisting of the q rows and columns pertaining to the coefficients in $\mathbf{b}_1$.

9.4.3   General Linear Hypotheses

Even more generally, we can test the linear hypothesis

$$H_0: \underset{(q \times k+1)}{\mathbf{L}}\ \underset{(k+1 \times 1)}{\beta} = \underset{(q \times 1)}{\mathbf{c}}$$

where $\mathbf{L}$ and $\mathbf{c}$ contain prespecified constants, and the *hypothesis matrix* $\mathbf{L}$ is of full row rank $q \leq k + 1$. The resulting F-statistic,

$$F_0 = \frac{(\mathbf{Lb} - \mathbf{c})'\,[\mathbf{L}(\mathbf{X}'\mathbf{X})^{-1}\mathbf{L}']^{-1}\,(\mathbf{Lb} - \mathbf{c})}{q S_E^2} \tag{9.15}$$

follows an F-distribution with q and $n - k - 1$ degrees of freedom if H_0 is true.

To understand the structure of Equation 9.15, recall that $\mathbf{b} \sim N_{k+1}[\beta, \sigma_\varepsilon^2(\mathbf{X}'\mathbf{X})^{-1}]$. As a consequence,

$$\mathbf{Lb} \sim N_q[\mathbf{L}\beta, \sigma_\varepsilon^2\mathbf{L}(\mathbf{X}'\mathbf{X})^{-1}\mathbf{L}']$$

Under H_0, $\mathbf{L}\beta = \mathbf{c}$, and thus

$$(\mathbf{Lb} - \mathbf{c})'[\mathbf{L}(\mathbf{X}'\mathbf{X})^{-1}\mathbf{L}']^{-1}(\mathbf{Lb} - \mathbf{c})/\sigma_\varepsilon^2 \sim \chi_q^2$$

---

[41] See Section 10.3.

[42] See Seber (1977, chap. 4).

[43] The expectation of F_0 is not precisely 1 when H_0 is true because the expectation of a ratio of random variables is not necessarily the ratio of their expectations. See Appendix D on probability and estimation.

Equation 9.15 is general enough to encompass all the hypothesis tests that we have considered thus far, along with others. In Duncan's occupational prestige regression, for example, to test the omnibus null hypothesis H_0: $\beta_1 = \beta_2 = 0$, we can take

$$\mathbf{L} = \begin{bmatrix} 0 & 1 & 0 \\ 0 & 0 & 1 \end{bmatrix}$$

and $\mathbf{c} = [0, 0]'$. To test the hypothesis that the education and income coefficients are equal, H_0: $\beta_1 = \beta_2$, which is equivalent to H_0: $\beta_1 - \beta_2 = 0$, we can take $\mathbf{L} = [0, 1, -1]$ and $\mathbf{c} = [0]$.[44]

The F-statistic $F_0 = (\mathbf{Lb} - \mathbf{c})'[\mathbf{L}(\mathbf{X'X})^{-1}\mathbf{L}']^{-1}(\mathbf{Lb} - \mathbf{c})/q S_E^2$ is used to test the general linear hypothesis H_0: $\underset{(q \times k+1)}{\mathbf{L}} \underset{(k+1 \times 1)}{\beta} = \underset{(q \times 1)}{\mathbf{c}}$, where the rank-$q$ hypothesis matrix $\mathbf{L}$ and right-hand-side vector $\mathbf{c}$ contain prespecified constants. Under the hypothesis, $F_0 \sim F_{q,n-k-1}$.

9.4.4 Joint Confidence Regions

The F-test of Equation 9.14 (on page 201) can be inverted to construct a *joint confidence region* for β_1. If H_0: $\beta_1 = \beta_1^{(0)}$ is correct, then

$$\Pr\left[\frac{\left(\mathbf{b}_1 - \beta_1^{(0)}\right)' \mathbf{V}_{11}^{-1} \left(\mathbf{b}_1 - \beta_1^{(0)}\right)}{q S_E^2} \leq F_{a, q, n-k-1} \right] = 1 - a$$

where $F_{a, q, n-k-1}$ is the critical value of F with q and $n - k - 1$ degrees of freedom, corresponding to a right-tail probability of a. The joint confidence region for β_1 is thus

$$\text{all } \beta_1 \text{ for which } \left(\mathbf{b}_1 - \beta_1\right)' \mathbf{V}_{11}^{-1} \left(\mathbf{b}_1 - \beta_1\right) \leq q S_E^2 F_{a, q, n-k-1} \tag{9.16}$$

That is, any parameter vector β_1 that satisfies this inequality is *within* the confidence region and is acceptable as a hypothesis; any parameter vector that does not satisfy the inequality is unacceptable. The boundary of the joint confidence region (obtained when the left-hand side of the inequality in Equation 9.16 equals the right-hand side) is an ellipsoid centered at the estimates $\mathbf{b}_1$ in the q-dimensional space of the parameters β_1.

Like a confidence interval, a joint confidence region is a portion of the parameter space constructed so that, with repeated sampling, a preselected percentage of regions will contain the true parameter values. Unlike a confidence interval, however, which pertains to a *single* coefficient β_j, a joint confidence region encompasses all *combinations* of values for the parameters $\beta_1, \ldots, \beta_q$ that are *simultaneously* acceptable at the specified level of confidence. Indeed, the familiar confidence interval is just a one-dimensional confidence region; and there is a simple

---

[44]Examples of these calculations appear in Exercise 9.10. The hypothesis that two regression coefficients are equal is sensible only if the corresponding explanatory variables are measured on the same scale. This is arguably the case for income and education in Duncan's regression, because both explanatory variables are percentages. Closer scrutiny suggests, however, that these explanatory variables are *not* commensurable: There is no reason to suppose that the percentage of occupational incumbents with at least high school education is on the same scale as the percentage earning in excess of $3500.

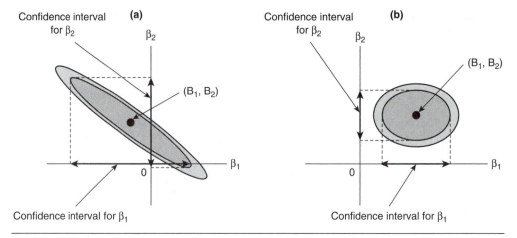

Figure 9.1   Illustrative joint confidence ellipses for the slope coefficients β_1 and β_2 in
multiple-regression analysis. The outer ellipse is drawn at a level of confidence of
95%; the inner ellipse (the confidence-interval generating ellipse) is drawn so that its
perpendicular shadows on the axes are 95% confidence intervals for the individual
βs. In (a), the Xs are positively correlated, producing a joint confidence ellipse that is
negatively tilted. In (b), the Xs are uncorrelated, producing a joint confidence ellipse
with axes parallel to the axes of the parameter space.

relationship between the confidence interval for a single coefficient and the confidence region for
several coefficients (as I will explain shortly).

The essential nature of joint confidence regions is clarified by considering the two-dimensional
case, which can be directly visualized. To keep the mathematics as simple as possible, let us work
with the slope coefficients β_1 and β_2 from the two-explanatory-variable model, $Y_i = \beta_0 + \beta_1 x_{i1} +
\beta_2 x_{i2} + \varepsilon_i$. In this instance, the joint confidence region of Equation 9.16 becomes all (β_1, β_2) for
which

$$[B_1 - \beta_1, B_2 - \beta_2] \begin{bmatrix} \sum x_{i1}^{*2} & \sum x_{i1}^{*} x_{i2}^{*} \\ \sum x_{i1}^{*} x_{i2}^{*} & \sum x_{i2}^{*2} \end{bmatrix} \begin{bmatrix} B_1 - \beta_1 \\ B_2 - \beta_2 \end{bmatrix} \leq 2 S_E^2 F_{a, 2, n-3} \qquad (9.17)$$

where the $x_{ij}^{*} \equiv x_{ij} - \overline{x}_j$ are deviations from the means of X_1 and X_2. The matrix $\mathbf{V}_{11}^{-1}$ contains
mean-deviation sums of squares and products for the explanatory variables;[45] and the boundary
of the confidence region, obtained when the equality holds, is an ellipse centered at (B_1, B_2) in
the $\{\beta_1, \beta_2\}$ plane.

Illustrative joint confidence ellipses are shown in Figure 9.1. When the explanatory variables
are *uncorrelated*, the sum of cross products $\sum x_{i1}^{*} x_{i2}^{*}$ vanishes, and the axes of the confidence
ellipse are parallel to the axes of the parameter space, as in Figure 9.1(b). When the explanatory
variables are *correlated*, in contrast, the ellipse is "tilted," as in Figure 9.1(a).

Specializing (9.16) to a single coefficient produces the confidence *interval* for β_1:

$$\text{all } \beta_1 \text{ for which } (B_1 - \beta_1)^2 \frac{\sum x_{i2}^{*2}}{\sum x_{i1}^{*2} \sum x_{i2}^{*2} - \left(\sum x_{i1}^{*} x_{i2}^{*}\right)^2} \leq S_E^2 F_{a, 1, n-3} \qquad (9.18)$$

---

[45] See Exercise 9.11.

which is written more conventionally as[46]

$$
B_1 - t_{a,\,n-3} \frac{S_E}{\sqrt{\dfrac{\sum x_{i1}^{*2}}{1 - r_{12}^2}}} \leq \beta_1 \leq B_1 + t_{a,\,n-3} \frac{S_E}{\sqrt{\dfrac{\sum x_{i1}^{*2}}{1 - r_{12}^2}}}
$$

The individual confidence intervals for the regression coefficients are very nearly the perpendicular "shadows" (i.e., projections) of the joint confidence ellipse onto the β_1 and β_2 axes. The only slippage here is due to the right-hand-side constant: $2S_E^2 F_{a,\,2,\,n-3}$ for the joint confidence region, and $S_E^2 F_{a,\,1,\,n-3}$ for the confidence interval.

Consider a 95% region and interval, for example. If the residual degrees of freedom $n - 3$ are large, then $2F_{.05,\,2,\,n-3} \approx \chi_{.05,\,2}^2 = 5.99$, while $F_{.05,\,1,\,n-3} \approx \chi_{.05,\,1}^2 = 3.84$. Put another way, using $5.99 S_E^2$ in place of $3.84 S_E^2$ produces individual intervals at approximately the $1 - \Pr(\chi_1^2 > 5.99) = .986$ (rather than .95) level of confidence (but a *joint* 95% confidence region). Likewise, if we construct the joint confidence region using the multiplier 3.84, the resulting smaller ellipse produces shadows that give approximate 95% confidence intervals for *individual* coefficients [and a smaller *joint* level of confidence of $1 - \Pr(\chi_2^2 > 3.84) = .853$]. This *confidence-interval generating ellipse* is shown along with the joint confidence ellipse in Figure 9.1.[47]

Figure 9.1(a) illustrates how correlated regressors can lead to ambiguous inferences: Because the individual confidence intervals include 0, we cannot reject the separate hypotheses that *either* β_1 or β_2 is 0. Because the point $(0, 0)$ is *outside* of the joint confidence region, however, we can reject the hypothesis that *both* β_1 and β_2 are 0. In contrast, in Figure 9.1(b), where the explanatory variables are uncorrelated, there is a close correspondence between inferences based on the separate confidence intervals and those based on the joint confidence region.

Still more generally, the confidence-interval generating ellipse can be projected onto *any* line through the origin of the $\{\beta_1, \beta_2\}$ plane. Each such line represents a specific linear combination of β_1 and β_2, and the shadow of the ellipse gives the corresponding confidence interval for that linear combination of the parameters.[48] This property is illustrated in Figure 9.2 for the linear combination $\beta_1 + \beta_2$; the line representing $\beta_1 + \beta_2$ is drawn through the origin and the point $(1, 1)$, the coefficients of the parameters in the linear combination. Directions in which the ellipse is narrow, therefore, correspond to linear combinations of the parameters that are relatively precisely estimated.

It is illuminating to examine more closely the relationship between the joint confidence region for the regression coefficients and the joint distribution of the X values. I have already remarked that the orientation of the confidence region reflects the correlation of the Xs, but it is possible to be much more precise. Consider the quadratic form $(\mathbf{x} - \bar{\mathbf{x}})' \mathbf{S}_{XX}^{-1} (\mathbf{x} - \bar{\mathbf{x}})$, where $\mathbf{x}$ is a $k \times 1$ vector of explanatory-variable values, $\bar{\mathbf{x}}$ is the vector of means of the Xs, and $\mathbf{S}_{XX}$ is the sample covariance matrix of the Xs. Setting the quadratic form to 1 produces the equation of an ellipsoid—called the *standard data ellipsoid*—centered at the means of the explanatory variables.

---

[46] See Exercise 9.12.

[47] The individual intervals constructed from the larger joint confidence ellipse—called *Scheffé intervals*—can be thought of as incorporating a penalty for examining several coefficients simultaneously. The difference between the Scheffé interval—the shadow of the joint confidence region (for which the multiplier is $kS_E^2 F_{a,\,k,\,n-3}$)—and the individual confidence interval (for which the multiplier is $S_E^2 F_{a,\,1,\,n-3}$) grows larger as the number of coefficients k increases.

[48] See Monette (1990).

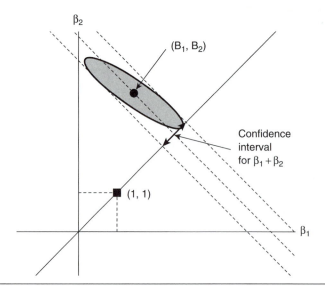

Figure 9.2   To find the 95% confidence interval for the linear combination of coefficients $\beta_1 + \beta_2$, find the perpendicular shadow of the confidence-interval generating ellipse on the line through the origin and the point (1, 1). Note that the regression coefficients (B_1, B_2) and confidence-interval generating ellipse are not the same as in the previous figure.

For two explanatory variables, the standard data *ellipse* has the equation

$$\frac{n-1}{\sum x_{i1}^{*2} \sum x_{i2}^{*2} - \left(\sum x_{i1}^{*} x_{i2}^{*}\right)^{2}} [x_1 - \overline{x}_1, x_2 - \overline{x}_2]$$
$$\times \begin{bmatrix} \sum x_{i2}^{*2} & -\sum x_{i1}^{*} x_{i2}^{*} \\ -\sum x_{i1}^{*} x_{i2}^{*} & \sum x_{i1}^{*2} \end{bmatrix} \begin{bmatrix} x_1 - \overline{x}_1 \\ x_2 - \overline{x}_2 \end{bmatrix} = 1 \qquad (9.19)$$

representing an ellipse whose horizontal shadow is twice the standard deviation of X_1, and whose vertical shadow is twice the standard deviation of X_2. These properties are illustrated in Figure 9.3, which also shows scatterplots for highly correlated and uncorrelated Xs. The major axis of the data ellipse has a positive slope when the Xs are positively correlated, as in Figure 9.3(a).

This representation of the data is most compelling when the explanatory variables are normally distributed. In this case, the means and covariance matrix of the Xs are sufficient statistics for their joint distribution; and the standard data ellipsoid estimates a constant-density contour of the joint distribution. Even when—as is typical—the explanatory variables are *not* multivariate normal, however, the standard ellipsoid is informative because of the role of the means, variances, and covariance of the Xs in the least-squares fit.

The joint confidence ellipse (Equation 9.17 on page 204) for the slope coefficients and the standard data ellipse (Equation 9.19) of the Xs are, except for a constant scale factor and their respective centers, inverses of each other—that is, the confidence ellipse is (apart from its size and location) the 90° rotation of the data ellipse. In particular, if the data ellipse is positively tilted, reflecting a *positive* correlation between the Xs, then the confidence ellipse is negatively tilted, reflecting *negatively* correlated coefficient estimates. Likewise, directions in which the

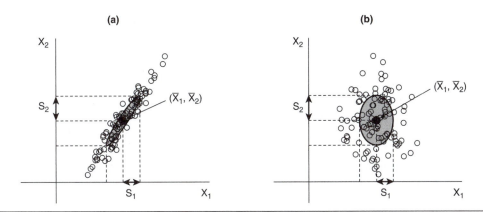

Figure 9.3 Scatterplot and standard data ellipse for (a) two highly correlated regressors and (b) two uncorrelated regressors, X_1 and X_2. In each panel, the standard ellipse is centered at the point of means $(\overline{X}_1, \overline{X}_2)$; its shadows on the axes give the standard deviations of the two variables. (The standard deviations are the half-widths of the shadows.) The data in these figures (along with data on Y) gave rise to the joint confidence ellipses in Figure 9.1. In each case, the confidence ellipse is the rescaled and translated 90° rotation of the data ellipse.

SOURCE: Adapted from Monette (1990, fig. 5.7A), in *Modern Methods of Data Analysis*, copyright © 1990 by Sage Publications, Inc. Reprinted with permission of Sage Publications, Inc.

data ellipse is relatively *thick*, reflecting a substantial amount of data, are directions in which the confidence ellipse is relatively *thin*, reflecting substantial information about the corresponding linear combination of regression coefficients. Thus, when the Xs are strongly positively correlated (and assuming, for simplicity, that the standard deviations of X_1 and X_2 are similar), there is a great deal of information about $\beta_1 + \beta_2$ but little about $\beta_1 - \beta_2$ (as in Figure 9.2).[49]

> The joint confidence region for the q parameters $\boldsymbol{\beta}_1$, given by $\left(\mathbf{b}_1 - \boldsymbol{\beta}_1\right)' \mathbf{V}_{11}^{-1} \left(\mathbf{b}_1 - \boldsymbol{\beta}_1\right) \le q S_E^2 F_{a, q, n-k-1}$, represents the combinations of values of these parameters that are jointly acceptable at the $1 - a$ level of confidence. The boundary of the joint confidence region is an ellipsoid in the q-dimensional parameter space, reflecting the correlational structure and dispersion of the Xs.

9.5 Multivariate Linear Models

The *multivariate linear model* accommodates two or more *response* variables. The theory of multivariate linear models is developed very briefly in this section. Much more extensive treatments may be found in the recommended reading for this chapter.[50]

Specification, estimation, and testing of multivariate linear models largely parallel univariate linear models. The multivariate general linear model is

$$\underset{(n \times m)}{\mathbf{Y}} = \underset{(n \times k+1)}{\mathbf{X}} \underset{(k+1 \times m)}{\mathbf{B}} + \underset{(n \times m)}{\mathbf{E}}$$

---

[49]See Exercise 9.13.

[50]Some applications of multivariate linear models are given in the data analysis exercises for the chapter.

where $\mathbf{Y}$ is a matrix of n observations on m response variables; $\mathbf{X}$ is a model matrix with columns for $k + 1$ regressors, including an initial column for the regression constant; $\mathbf{B}$ is a matrix of regression coefficients, one column for each response variable; and $\mathbf{E}$ is a matrix of errors.[51] The contents of the model matrix are exactly as in the univariate linear model, and may contain, therefore, dummy regressors representing factors, interaction regressors, and so on.

The assumptions of the multivariate linear model concern the behavior of the errors: Let ε_i' represent the ith row of $\mathbf{E}$. Then $\varepsilon_i' \sim \mathbf{N}_m(\mathbf{0}, \mathbf{\Sigma})$, where $\mathbf{\Sigma}$ is a nonsingular error-covariance matrix, constant across observations; ε_i' and $\varepsilon_{i'}'$ are independent for $i \neq i'$; and $\mathbf{X}$ is fixed or independent of $\mathbf{E}$.[52]

The maximum-likelihood estimator of $\mathbf{B}$ in the multivariate linear model is equivalent to equation-by-equation least squares for the individual responses:[53]

$$\widehat{\mathbf{B}} = (\mathbf{X}'\mathbf{X})^{-1}\mathbf{X}'\mathbf{Y}$$

Procedures for statistical inference in the multivariate linear model, however, take account of the fact that there are several, generally correlated, responses.

Paralleling the decomposition of the total sum of squares into regression and residual sums of squares in the univariate linear model, there is in the multivariate linear model a decomposition of the total *sum-of-squares-and-cross-products* (*SSP*) matrix into regression and residual SSP matrices. We have

$$\underset{(m \times m)}{\mathbf{SSP}_T} = \mathbf{Y}'\mathbf{Y} - n\bar{\mathbf{y}}\,\bar{\mathbf{y}}'$$
$$= \widehat{\mathbf{E}}'\widehat{\mathbf{E}} + \left(\widehat{\mathbf{Y}}'\widehat{\mathbf{Y}} - n\bar{\mathbf{y}}\,\bar{\mathbf{y}}'\right)$$
$$= \mathbf{SSP}_R + \mathbf{SSP}_{\text{Reg}}$$

where $\bar{\mathbf{y}}$ is the $(m \times 1)$ vector of means for the response variables, $\widehat{\mathbf{Y}} \equiv \mathbf{X}\widehat{\mathbf{B}}$ is the matrix of fitted values, and $\widehat{\mathbf{E}} \equiv \mathbf{Y} - \widehat{\mathbf{Y}}$ is the matrix of residuals.

Many hypothesis tests of interest can be formulated by taking differences in $\mathbf{SSP}_{\text{Reg}}$ (or, equivalently, $\mathbf{SSP}_R$) for nested models. Let $\mathbf{SSP}_H$ represent the incremental SSP matrix for a hypothesis. Multivariate tests for the hypothesis are based on the m eigenvalues L_j of $\mathbf{SSP}_H \mathbf{SSP}_R^{-1}$ (the hypothesis SSP matrix "divided by" the residual SSP matrix), that is, the values of L for which[54]

$$\det(\mathbf{SSP}_H \mathbf{SSP}_R^{-1} - L\mathbf{I}_m) = 0.$$

The several commonly employed multivariate test statistics are functions of these eigenvalues:

$$\text{Pillai-Bartlett Trace, } T_{PB} = \sum_{j=1}^{m} \frac{L_j}{1 - L_j}$$
$$\text{Hotelling-Lawley Trace, } T_{HL} = \sum_{j=1}^{m} L_j$$
$$\text{Wilks's Lambda, } \Lambda = \prod_{j=1}^{m} \frac{1}{1 + L_j}$$
$$\text{Roy's Maximum Root, } L_1$$

(9.20)

---

[51] A typographical note: $\mathbf{B}$ and $\mathbf{E}$ are, respectively, the upper-case Greek letters Beta and Epsilon. Because these are indistinguishable from the corresponding Roman letters B and E, I will denote the estimated regression coefficients as $\widehat{\mathbf{B}}$ and the residuals as $\widehat{\mathbf{E}}$.

[52] We can write more compactly that $\text{vec}(\mathbf{E}) \sim \mathbf{N}_{nm}(\mathbf{0}, \mathbf{I}_n \otimes \mathbf{\Sigma})$. Here, $\text{vec}(\mathbf{E})$ ravels the error matrix row-wise into a vector, and $\otimes$ is the Kronecker-product operator (see Appendix B on matrices, linear algebra, and vector geometry).

[53] See Exercise 9.16.

[54] Eigenvalues and determinants are described in Appendix B on matrices, linear algebra, and vector geometry.

There are F approximations to the null distributions of these test statistics. For example, for Wilks's Lambda, let s represent the degrees of freedom for the term that we are testing (i.e., the number of columns of the model matrix $\mathbf{X}$ pertaining to the term). Define

$$r \equiv n - k - 1 - \frac{m - s + 1}{2}$$

$$u \equiv \frac{ms - 2}{4}$$

$$t \equiv \begin{cases} \dfrac{\sqrt{m^2 s^2 - 4}}{m^2 + s^2 - 5} & \text{for } m^2 + s^2 - 5 > 0 \\[2ex] 0 & \text{otherwise} \end{cases} \tag{9.21}$$

Rao (1973, p. 556) shows that under the null hypothesis,

$$F_0 \equiv \frac{1 - \Lambda^{1/t}}{\Lambda^{1/t}} \times \frac{rt - 2u}{ms} \tag{9.22}$$

follows an approximate F-distribution with ms and $rt - 2u$ degrees of freedom, and that this result is exact if $\min(m, s) \leq 2$ (a circumstance under which all four test statistics are equivalent).

Even more generally, suppose that we want to test the linear hypothesis

$$H_0: \underset{(q \times k+1)}{\mathbf{L}} \underset{(k+1 \times m)}{\mathbf{B}} = \underset{(q \times m)}{\mathbf{C}} \tag{9.23}$$

where $\mathbf{L}$ is a hypothesis matrix of full-row rank $q \leq k + 1$, and the right-hand-side matrix $\mathbf{C}$ consists of constants (usually zeroes). Then the SSP matrix for the hypothesis is

$$\mathbf{SSP}_H = \left(\widehat{\mathbf{B}}' \mathbf{L}' - \mathbf{C}' \right) \left[\mathbf{L}(\mathbf{X}'\mathbf{X})^{-1}\mathbf{L}' \right]^{-1} \left(\mathbf{L}\widehat{\mathbf{B}} - \mathbf{C} \right)$$

and the various test statistics are based on the $p \equiv \min(q, m)$ nonzero eigenvalues of $\mathbf{SSP}_H \mathbf{SSP}_R^{-1}$ (and the formulas in Equations 9.20, 9.21, and 9.22 are adjusted by substituting p for m).

When a multivariate response arises because a variable is measured on different occasions, or under different circumstances (but for the same individuals), it is also of interest to formulate hypotheses concerning comparisons among the responses. This situation, called a *repeated-measures design*, can be handled by linearly transforming the responses using a suitable model matrix, for example, extending the linear hypothesis in Equation 9.23 to

$$H_0: \underset{(q \times k+1)}{\mathbf{L}} \underset{(k+1 \times m)}{\mathbf{B}} \underset{(m \times v)}{\mathbf{P}} = \underset{(q \times v)}{\mathbf{C}}$$

Here, the matrix $\mathbf{P}$ provides contrasts in the responses (see, e.g., Hand & Taylor, 1987, or O'Brien & Kaiser, 1985). The SSP matrix for the hypothesis is

$$\underset{(q \times q)}{\mathbf{SSP}_H} = \left(\mathbf{P}' \widehat{\mathbf{B}}' \mathbf{L}' - \mathbf{C}' \right) \left[\mathbf{L}(\mathbf{X}'\mathbf{X})^{-1}\mathbf{L}' \right]^{-1} \left(\mathbf{L}\widehat{\mathbf{B}}\mathbf{P} - \mathbf{C} \right)$$

and test statistics are based on the $p \equiv \min(q, v)$ nonzero eigenvalues of $\mathbf{SSP}_H (\mathbf{P}'\mathbf{SSP}_R\mathbf{P})^{-1}$.

The multivariate linear model accommodates several response variables:

$$\mathbf{Y} = \mathbf{XB} + \mathbf{E}$$

(Continued)

> (Continued)
>
> Under the assumption that the rows ε_i' of the error matrix $\mathbf{E}$ are independent and multi-variately normally distributed with mean $\mathbf{0}$ and common nonsingular covariance matrix $\boldsymbol{\Sigma}$, the maximum-likelihood estimators of the regression coefficients are given by
>
> $$\widehat{\mathbf{B}} = (\mathbf{X}'\mathbf{X})^{-1}\mathbf{X}'\mathbf{Y}$$
>
> Hypothesis tests for the multivariate linear model closely parallel those for the univariate linear model, with sum-of-squares-and-products (SSP) matrices in the multivariate case generalizing the role of sums of squares in the univariate case. Several commonly employed test statistics are based on the eigenvalues of $\mathbf{SSP}_H\mathbf{SSP}_R^{-1}$, where $\mathbf{SSP}_H$ is the SSP matrix for a hypothesis, and $\mathbf{SSP}_R$ is the residual SSP matrix.

9.6   Random Regressors

The theory of linear models developed in this chapter has proceeded from the premise that the model matrix $\mathbf{X}$ is *fixed*. If we repeat a study, we expect the response-variable observations $\mathbf{y}$ to change, but if $\mathbf{X}$ is fixed, then the explanatory-variable values are constant across replications of the study. This situation is realistically descriptive of an experiment, where the explanatory variables are manipulated by the researcher. Most research in the social sciences, however, is observational rather than experimental; and in an observational study (e.g., survey research), we would typically obtain different explanatory-variable values on replication of the study. In observational research, therefore, $\mathbf{X}$ is *random* rather than fixed.

It is remarkable that the statistical theory of linear models applies even when $\mathbf{X}$ is random, as long as certain assumptions are met. For fixed explanatory variables, the assumptions underlying the model take the form $\varepsilon \sim N_n(\mathbf{0}, \sigma_\varepsilon^2 \mathbf{I}_n)$. That is, the distribution of the error is the same for all observed combinations of explanatory-variable values represented by the distinct rows of the model matrix. When $\mathbf{X}$ is random, we need to assume that this property holds for *all possible* combinations of explanatory-variable values in the population that is sampled: That is, $\mathbf{X}$ and ε are assumed to be independent, and thus the *conditional* distribution of the error for a sample of explanatory variable values $\varepsilon|\mathbf{X}_0$ is $N_n(\mathbf{0}, \sigma_\varepsilon^2 \mathbf{I}_n)$, regardless of the *particular* sample $\mathbf{X}_0 = \{x_{ij}\}$ that is chosen.

Because $\mathbf{X}$ is random, it has some (multivariate) probability distribution. It is not necessary to make assumptions about this distribution, however, beyond (1) requiring that $\mathbf{X}$ is measured without error, and that $\mathbf{X}$ and ε are independent (as just explained); (2) assuming that the distribution of $\mathbf{X}$ does not depend on the parameters β and σ_ε^2 of the linear model; and (3) stipulating that the covariance matrix of the Xs is nonsingular (i.e., that no X is invariant or a perfect linear function of the others in the population). In particular, we need *not* assume that the *regressors* (as opposed to the *errors*) are normally distributed. This is fortunate, for many regressors are highly non-normal—dummy regressors and polynomial regressors come immediately to mind, not to mention many quantitative explanatory variables.

It would be unnecessarily tedious to recapitulate the entire argument of this chapter, but I will show that some key results hold, under the new assumptions, when the explanatory variables are random. The other results of the chapter can be established for random regressors in a similar manner.

For a particular sample of X values, $\mathbf{X}_0$, the conditional distribution of $\mathbf{y}$ is

$$E(\mathbf{y}|\mathbf{X}_0) = E\left[(\mathbf{X}\boldsymbol{\beta} + \boldsymbol{\varepsilon})|\mathbf{X}_0\right] = \mathbf{X}_0\boldsymbol{\beta} + E(\boldsymbol{\varepsilon}|\mathbf{X}_0)$$
$$= \mathbf{X}_0\boldsymbol{\beta}$$

Consequently, the conditional expectation of the least-squares estimator is

$$E(\mathbf{b}|\mathbf{X}_0) = E\left[(\mathbf{X}'\mathbf{X})^{-1}\mathbf{X}'\mathbf{y}|\mathbf{X}_0\right] = (\mathbf{X}_0'\mathbf{X}_0)^{-1}\mathbf{X}_0'E(\mathbf{y}|\mathbf{X}_0)$$
$$= (\mathbf{X}_0'\mathbf{X}_0)^{-1}\mathbf{X}_0'\mathbf{X}_0\boldsymbol{\beta} = \boldsymbol{\beta}$$

Because we can repeat this argument for *any* value of $\mathbf{X}$, the least-squares estimator $\mathbf{b}$ is conditionally unbiased for any and every such value; it is therefore *unconditionally* unbiased as well, $E(\mathbf{b}) = \boldsymbol{\beta}$.

Suppose now that we use the procedures of the previous section to perform statistical inference for $\boldsymbol{\beta}$. For concreteness, imagine that we calculate a p-value for the omnibus null hypothesis H_0: $\beta_1 = \cdots = \beta_k = 0$. Because $\boldsymbol{\varepsilon}|\mathbf{X}_0 \sim N_n(\mathbf{0}, \sigma_\varepsilon^2\mathbf{I}_n)$, as was required when we treated $\mathbf{X}$ as fixed, the p-value obtained is correct for $\mathbf{X} = \mathbf{X}_0$ (i.e., for the sample at hand). There is, however, nothing special about a particular $\mathbf{X}_0$: The error vector $\boldsymbol{\varepsilon}$ is independent of $\mathbf{X}$, and so the distribution of $\boldsymbol{\varepsilon}$ is $N_n(\mathbf{0}, \sigma_\varepsilon^2\mathbf{I}_n)$ for any and every value of $\mathbf{X}$. The p-value, therefore, is *unconditionally* valid.

Finally, I will show that the maximum-likelihood estimators of $\boldsymbol{\beta}$ and σ_ε^2 are unchanged when $\mathbf{X}$ is random, as long as the new assumptions hold: When $\mathbf{X}$ is random, sampled observations consist not just of response-variable values $(Y_1, \ldots, Y_n)$ but also of explanatory-variable values $(\mathbf{x}_1', \ldots, \mathbf{x}_n')$. The observations themselves are denoted $[Y_1, \mathbf{x}_1'], \ldots, [Y_n, \mathbf{x}_n']$. Because these observations are sampled independently, their joint probability density is the product of their marginal densities:

$$p(\mathbf{y}, \mathbf{X}) \equiv p\left([y_1, \mathbf{x}_1'], \ldots, [y_n, \mathbf{x}_n']\right) = p(y_1, \mathbf{x}_1') \times \cdots \times p(y_n, \mathbf{x}_n')$$

Now, the probability density $p(y_i, \mathbf{x}_i')$ for observation i can be written as $p(y_i|\mathbf{x}_i')p(\mathbf{x}_i')$. According to the linear model, the conditional distribution of Y_i given $\mathbf{x}_i'$ is normal:

$$p(y_i|\mathbf{x}_i') = \frac{1}{\sigma_\varepsilon\sqrt{2\pi}}\exp\left[-\frac{(y_i - \mathbf{x}_i'\boldsymbol{\beta})^2}{2\sigma_\varepsilon^2}\right]$$

Thus, the joint probability density for all observations becomes

$$p(\mathbf{y}, \mathbf{X}) = \prod_{i=1}^{n} p(\mathbf{x}_i')\frac{1}{\sigma_\varepsilon\sqrt{2\pi}}\exp\left[-\frac{(y_i - \mathbf{x}_i'\boldsymbol{\beta})^2}{2\sigma_\varepsilon^2}\right]$$
$$= \left[\prod_{i=1}^{n} p(\mathbf{x}_i')\right]\frac{1}{(2\pi\sigma_\varepsilon^2)^{n/2}}\exp\left[-\frac{(\mathbf{y} - \mathbf{X}\boldsymbol{\beta})'(\mathbf{y} - \mathbf{X}\boldsymbol{\beta})}{2\sigma_\varepsilon^2}\right]$$
$$= p(\mathbf{X})p(\mathbf{y}|\mathbf{X})$$

As long as $p(\mathbf{X})$ does not depend on the parameters $\boldsymbol{\beta}$ and σ_ε^2, we can ignore the joint density of the Xs in maximizing $p(\mathbf{y}, \mathbf{X})$ with respect to the parameters. Consequently, the maximum-likelihood estimator of $\boldsymbol{\beta}$ is the least-squares estimator, as was the case for fixed $\mathbf{X}$.[55]

---

[55]Cf. Section 9.3.3.

> The statistical theory of linear models, formulated under the supposition that the model matrix $\mathbf{X}$ is fixed with respect to repeated sampling, is also valid when $\mathbf{X}$ is random, as long as three additional requirements are satisfied: (1) the model matrix $\mathbf{X}$ and the errors ε are independent; (2) the distribution of $\mathbf{X}$, which is otherwise unconstrained, does not depend on the parameters β and σ_ε^2 of the linear model; and (3) the covariance matrix of the Xs is nonsingular.

9.7 Specification Error

To generalize our treatment of misspecified structural relationships,[56] it is convenient to work with probability limits.[57] Suppose that the response variable Y is determined by the model

$$\mathbf{y}^* = \mathbf{X}^*\beta + \varepsilon = \mathbf{X}_1^*\beta_1 + \mathbf{X}_2^*\beta_2 + \varepsilon$$

where the error ε behaves according to the usual assumptions. I have, for convenience, expressed each variable as deviations from its expectation [e.g., $\mathbf{y}^* \equiv \{Y_i - E(Y)\}$], and have partitioned the model matrix into two sets of regressors; the parameter vector is partitioned in the same manner.[58]

Imagine that we ignore $\mathbf{X}_2^*$, so that $\mathbf{y}^* = \mathbf{X}_1^*\beta_1 + \widetilde{\varepsilon}$, where $\widetilde{\varepsilon} \equiv \mathbf{X}_2^*\beta_2 + \varepsilon$. The least-squares estimator for β_1 in the model that omits $\mathbf{X}_2^*$ is

$$\begin{aligned}
\mathbf{b}_1 &= (\mathbf{X}_1^{*\prime}\mathbf{X}_1^*)^{-1}\mathbf{X}_1^{*\prime}\mathbf{y}^* \\
&= \left(\frac{1}{n}\mathbf{X}_1^{*\prime}\mathbf{X}_1^*\right)^{-1}\frac{1}{n}\mathbf{X}_1^{*\prime}\mathbf{y}^* \\
&= \left(\frac{1}{n}\mathbf{X}_1^{*\prime}\mathbf{X}_1^*\right)^{-1}\frac{1}{n}\mathbf{X}_1^{*\prime}(\mathbf{X}_1^*\beta_1 + \mathbf{X}_2^*\beta_2 + \varepsilon) \\
&= \beta_1 + \left(\frac{1}{n}\mathbf{X}_1^{*\prime}\mathbf{X}_1^*\right)^{-1}\frac{1}{n}\mathbf{X}_1^{*\prime}\mathbf{X}_2^*\beta_2 + \left(\frac{1}{n}\mathbf{X}_1^{*\prime}\mathbf{X}_1^*\right)^{-1}\frac{1}{n}\mathbf{X}_1^{*\prime}\varepsilon
\end{aligned}$$

Taking probability limits produces

$$\begin{aligned}
\text{plim } \mathbf{b}_1 &= \beta_1 + \Sigma_{11}^{-1}\Sigma_{12}\beta_2 + \Sigma_{11}^{-1}\sigma_{1\varepsilon} \\
&= \beta_1 + \Sigma_{11}^{-1}\Sigma_{12}\beta_2
\end{aligned}$$

where

- $\Sigma_{11} \equiv \text{plim}(1/n)\mathbf{X}_1^{*\prime}\mathbf{X}_1^*$ is the population covariance matrix for $\mathbf{X}_1$;
- $\Sigma_{12} \equiv \text{plim}(1/n)\mathbf{X}_1^{*\prime}\mathbf{X}_2^*$ is the matrix of population covariances between $\mathbf{X}_1$ and $\mathbf{X}_2$; and
- $\sigma_{1\varepsilon} \equiv \text{plim}(1/n)\mathbf{X}_1^{*\prime}\varepsilon$ is the vector of population covariances between $\mathbf{X}_1$ and ε, which is $\mathbf{0}$ by the assumed independence of the error and the explanatory variables.

The asymptotic (or population) covariance of $\mathbf{X}_1$ and $\widetilde{\varepsilon}$ is not generally $\mathbf{0}$, however, as is readily established:

$$\begin{aligned}
\text{plim } \frac{1}{n}\mathbf{X}_1^{*\prime}\widetilde{\varepsilon} &= \text{plim } \frac{1}{n}\mathbf{X}_1^{*\prime}\left(\mathbf{X}_2^*\beta_2 + \varepsilon\right) \\
&= \Sigma_{12}\beta_2 + \sigma_{1\varepsilon} = \Sigma_{12}\beta_2
\end{aligned}$$

---

[56]See Section 6.3.

[57]Probability limits are introduced in Appendix D.

[58]Expressing the variables as deviations from their expectations eliminates the constant β_0.

The estimator $\mathbf{b}_1$, therefore, is consistent if Σ_{12} is $\mathbf{0}$—that is, if the excluded regressors in $\mathbf{X}_2$ are uncorrelated with the included regressors in $\mathbf{X}_1$. In this case, incorporating $\mathbf{X}_2^*$ in the error does not induce a correlation between $\mathbf{X}_1^*$ and the compound error $\widetilde{\varepsilon}$. The estimated coefficients $\mathbf{b}_1$ are also consistent if $\beta_2 = \mathbf{0}$: Excluding *irrelevant* regressors is unproblematic.[59]

> The omission of regressors from a linear model causes the coefficients of the included regressors to be inconsistent, unless (1) the omitted regressors are uncorrelated with the included regressors or (2) the omitted regressors have coefficients of 0, and hence are irrelevant.

Exercises

Exercise 9.1. *Solving the parametric equations in one-way and two-way ANOVA:

(a) Show that the parametric equation (Equation 9.3, page 190) in one-way ANOVA has the general solution

$$\begin{bmatrix} \mu \\ \alpha_1 \\ \alpha_2 \\ \vdots \\ \alpha_{m-1} \end{bmatrix} = \begin{bmatrix} \mu_{\cdot} \\ \mu_1 - \mu_{\cdot} \\ \mu_2 - \mu_{\cdot} \\ \vdots \\ \mu_{m-1} - \mu_{\cdot} \end{bmatrix}$$

(b) Show that the parametric equation (Equation 9.4, page 190) in two-way ANOVA, with two rows and three columns, has the solution

$$\begin{bmatrix} \mu \\ \alpha_1 \\ \beta_1 \\ \beta_2 \\ \gamma_{11} \\ \gamma_{12} \end{bmatrix} = \begin{bmatrix} \mu_{\cdot\cdot} \\ \mu_{1\cdot} - \mu_{\cdot\cdot} \\ \mu_{\cdot 1} - \mu_{\cdot\cdot} \\ \mu_{\cdot 2} - \mu_{\cdot\cdot} \\ \mu_{11} - \mu_{1\cdot} - \mu_{\cdot 1} + \mu_{\cdot\cdot} \\ \mu_{12} - \mu_{1\cdot} - \mu_{\cdot 2} + \mu_{\cdot\cdot} \end{bmatrix}$$

Exercise 9.2. *Orthogonal contrasts (see Section 9.1.2): Consider the equation $\beta_F = \mathbf{X}_B^{-1}\mu$ relating the parameters β_F of the full-rank ANOVA model to the cell means μ. Suppose that $\mathbf{X}_B^{-1}$ is constructed so that its rows are orthogonal. Show that the columns of the row basis $\mathbf{X}_B$ of the model matrix are also orthogonal, and further that each column of $\mathbf{X}_B$ is equal to the corresponding row of $\mathbf{X}_B^{-1}$ divided by the sum of squared entries in that row. (*Hint:* Multiply $\mathbf{X}_B^{-1}$ by its transpose.)

Exercise 9.3. Nonorthogonal contrasts: Imagine that we want to compare each of three groups in a one-way ANOVA with a fourth (control) group. We know that coding three dummy regressors, treating Group 4 as the baseline category, will accomplish this purpose. Starting with the equation

---

[59]*Including* irrelevant regressors also does not cause the least-squares estimator to become inconsistent; after all, if the assumptions of the model hold, then $\mathbf{b}$ is a consistent estimator of β even if some of the elements of β are 0. (Recall, however, Exercise 6.9.)

$$\begin{bmatrix} \mu \\ \gamma_1 \\ \gamma_2 \\ \gamma_3 \end{bmatrix} = \begin{bmatrix} 0 & 0 & 0 & 1 \\ 1 & 0 & 0 & -1 \\ 0 & 1 & 0 & -1 \\ 0 & 0 & 1 & -1 \end{bmatrix} \begin{bmatrix} \mu_1 \\ \mu_2 \\ \mu_3 \\ \mu_4 \end{bmatrix}$$

show that the row basis $\mathbf{X}_B = \left(\mathbf{X}_B^{-1} \right)^{-1}$ of the model matrix is equivalent to dummy coding.

Exercise 9.4. Verify that each of the terms in the sum-of-squares function (see Equation 9.7 on page 193)

$$S(\mathbf{b}) = \mathbf{y}'\mathbf{y} - \mathbf{y}'\mathbf{X}\mathbf{b} - \mathbf{b}'\mathbf{X}'\mathbf{y} + \mathbf{b}'\mathbf{X}'\mathbf{X}\mathbf{b}$$

is (1×1), justifying writing

$$S(\mathbf{b}) = \mathbf{y}'\mathbf{y} - (2\mathbf{y}'\mathbf{X})\mathbf{b} + \mathbf{b}'(\mathbf{X}'\mathbf{X})\mathbf{b}$$

Exercise 9.5. Standardized regression coefficients: Standardized regression coefficients were introduced in Section 5.2.4.

(a) *Show that the standardized coefficients can be computed as $\mathbf{b}^* = \mathbf{R}_{XX}^{-1}\mathbf{r}_{Xy}$, where $\mathbf{R}_{XX}$ is the correlation matrix of the explanatory variables, and $\mathbf{r}_{Xy}$ is the vector of correlations between the explanatory variables and the response variable. [*Hints*: Let $\underset{(n \times k)}{\mathbf{Z}_X} \equiv \{(X_{ij} - \overline{X}_j)/S_j\}$ contain the standardized explanatory variables, and let $\underset{(n \times 1)}{\mathbf{z}_y} \equiv \{(Y_i - \overline{Y})/S_Y\}$ contain the standardized response variable. The regression equation for the standardized variables in matrix form is $\mathbf{z}_y = \mathbf{Z}_X\mathbf{b}^* + \mathbf{e}^*$. Multiply both sides of this equation by $\mathbf{Z}_X'/(n - 1)$.]

(b) The correlation matrix in Table 9.2 is taken from Blau and Duncan's (1967) work on social stratification. Using these correlations, along with the results in part (a), find the standardized coefficients for the regression of current occupational status on father's education, father's occupational status, respondent's education, and the status of the respondent's first job. Why is the slope for father's education so small? Is it reasonable to conclude that father's education is unimportant as a cause of respondent's occupational status (recall Section 6.3)?

(c) *Prove that the squared multiple correlation for the regression of Y on $X_1, \ldots, X_k$ can be written as

$$R^2 = B_1^* r_{r1} + \cdots + B_k^* r_{rk} = \mathbf{r}_{yX}'\mathbf{b}^*$$

[*Hint*: Multiply $\mathbf{z}_y = \mathbf{Z}_X\mathbf{b}^* + \mathbf{e}^*$ through by $\mathbf{z}_y'/(n - 1)$.] Use this result to calculate the multiple correlation for Blau and Duncan's regression.

Exercise 9.6. Using the general result $V(\mathbf{b}) = \sigma_\varepsilon^2(\mathbf{X}'\mathbf{X})^{-1}$, show that the sampling variances of A and B in simple-regression analysis are

$$V(A) = \frac{\sigma_\varepsilon^2 \sum X_i^2}{n \sum (X_i - \overline{X})^2}$$

$$V(B) = \frac{\sigma_\varepsilon^2}{\sum (X_i - \overline{X})^2}$$

Table 9.2 Correlations for Blau and Duncan's Stratification Data, $n \simeq 20{,}700$: $X_1 =$ Father's Education; $X_2 =$ Father's Occupational Status; $X_3 =$ Respondent's Education; $X_2 =$ Status of Respondent's First Job; $Y =$ Respondent's Current Occupational Status

	X_1	X_2	X_3	X_4	Y
X_1	1.000				
X_2	.516	1.000			
X_3	.453	.438	1.000		
X_4	.332	.417	.538	1.000	
Y	.322	.405	.596	.541	1.000

SOURCE: Blau and Duncan (1967, p. 169).

Exercise 9.7. *A crucial step in the proof of the Gauss-Markov theorem (Section 9.3.2) uses the fact that the matrix product $\mathbf{AX}$ must be $\mathbf{0}$ because $\mathbf{AX}\beta = \mathbf{0}$. Why is this the case? [*Hint*: The key here is that $\mathbf{AX}\beta = \mathbf{0}$ regardless of the value of β. Consider, for example, $\beta = [1, 0, \ldots, 0]'$ (i.e., one possible value of β). Show that this implies that the first row of $\mathbf{AX}$ is $\mathbf{0}$. Then consider $\beta = [0, 1, \ldots, 0]'$, and so on.]

Exercise 9.8. *For the statistic

$$t = \frac{B_j - \beta_j}{S_E \sqrt{v_{jj}}}$$

to have a t-distribution, the estimators B_j and S_E must be independent. [Here, v_{jj} is the jth diagonal entry of $(\mathbf{X'X})^{-1}$.] The coefficient B_j is the jth element of $\mathbf{b}$, and $S_E = \sqrt{\mathbf{e'e}/(n-k-1)}$ is a function of the residuals $\mathbf{e}$. Because both $\mathbf{b}$ and $\mathbf{e}$ are normally distributed, it suffices to prove that their covariance is $\mathbf{0}$. Demonstrate that this is the case. [*Hint*: Use $C(\mathbf{e}, \mathbf{b}) = E[\mathbf{e}(\mathbf{b} - \beta)']$, and begin by showing that $\mathbf{b} - \beta = (\mathbf{X'X})^{-1}\mathbf{X'}\varepsilon$.]

Exercise 9.9. *Using Equation 9.10 (page 197), show that the maximized likelihood for the linear model can be written as

$$L = \left(2\pi e \frac{\mathbf{e'e}}{n}\right)^{-n/2}$$

Exercise 9.10. Using Duncan's regression of occupational prestige on income and education, and performing the necessary calculations, verify that the omnibus null hypothesis H_0: $\beta_1 = \beta_2 = 0$ can be tested as a general linear hypothesis, using the hypothesis matrix

$$\mathbf{L} = \begin{bmatrix} 0 & 1 & 0 \\ 0 & 0 & 1 \end{bmatrix}$$

and right-hand-side vector $\mathbf{c} = [0, 0]'$. Then verify that the H_0: $\beta_1 = \beta_2$ can be tested using $\mathbf{L} = [0, 1, -1]$ and $\mathbf{c} = [0]$. (Cf. Exercise 6.7.)

Exercise 9.11. *Consider the model $Y_i = \beta_0 + \beta_1 x_{i1} + \beta_2 x_{i2} + \varepsilon_i$. Show that the matrix $\mathbf{V}_{11}^{-1}$ (see Equation 9.14 on page 201) for the slope coefficients β_1 and β_2 contains mean-deviation sums of squares and products for the explanatory variables; that is,

$$\mathbf{V}_{11}^{-1} = \begin{bmatrix} \sum x_{i1}^{*2} & \sum x_{i1}^* x_{i2}^* \\ \sum x_{i1}^* x_{i2}^* & \sum x_{i2}^{*2} \end{bmatrix}$$

Now show, more generally, for the model $Y_i = \beta_0 + \beta_1 x_{i1} + \cdots + \beta_k x_{ik} + \varepsilon_i$, that the matrix $\mathbf{V}_{11}^{-1}$ for the slope coefficients $\beta_1, \ldots, \beta_k$ contains mean-deviation sums of squares and products for the explanatory variables.

Exercise 9.12. *Show that Equation 9.18 (page 204) for the confidence interval for β_1 can be written in the more conventional form

$$B_1 - t_{a,\,n-3} \frac{S_E}{\sqrt{\dfrac{\sum x_{i1}^{*2}}{1 - r_{12}^2}}} \leq \beta_1 \leq B_1 + t_{a,\,n-3} \frac{S_E}{\sqrt{\dfrac{\sum x_{i1}^{*2}}{1 - r_{12}^2}}}$$

Exercise 9.13. Using Figure 9.2 (on page 206), show how the confidence-interval generating ellipse can be used to derive a confidence interval for the *difference* of the parameters $\beta_1 - \beta_2$. Compare the confidence interval for this linear combination with that for $\beta_1 + \beta_2$. Which combination of parameters is estimated more precisely? Why? What would happen if the regressors X_1 and X_2 were *negatively* correlated?

Exercise 9.14. Prediction: One use of a fitted regression equation is to *predict* response-variable values for particular "future" combinations of explanatory-variable scores. Suppose, therefore, that we fit the model $\mathbf{y} = \mathbf{X}\boldsymbol{\beta} + \boldsymbol{\varepsilon}$, obtaining the least-squares estimate $\mathbf{b}$ of $\boldsymbol{\beta}$. Let $\mathbf{x}_0' = [1, x_{01}, \ldots, x_{0k}]$ represent a set of explanatory-variable scores for which a prediction is desired, and let Y_0 be the (generally unknown, or not-yet known) corresponding value of Y. The explanatory-variable vector $\mathbf{x}_0'$ does not necessarily correspond to an observation in the sample for which the model was fit.

(a) *If we use $\widehat{Y}_0 = \mathbf{x}_0'\mathbf{b}$ to estimate $E(Y_0)$, then the error in estimation is $\delta \equiv \widehat{Y}_0 - E(Y_0)$. Show that if the model is correct, then $E(\delta) = 0$ [i.e., $\widehat{Y}_0$ is an unbiased estimator of $E(Y_0)$] and that $V(\delta) = \sigma_\varepsilon^2 \mathbf{x}_0'(\mathbf{X}'\mathbf{X})^{-1}\mathbf{x}_0$.

(b) *We may be interested not in estimating the *expected* value of Y_0 but in predicting or forecasting the *actual* value $Y_0 = \mathbf{x}_0'\boldsymbol{\beta} + \varepsilon_0$ that will be observed. The error in the forecast is then

$$D \equiv \widehat{Y}_0 - Y_0 = \mathbf{x}_0'\mathbf{b} - (\mathbf{x}_0'\boldsymbol{\beta} + \varepsilon_0) = \mathbf{x}_0'(\mathbf{b} - \boldsymbol{\beta}) - \varepsilon_0$$

Show that $E(D) = 0$ and that $V(D) = \sigma_\varepsilon^2[1 + \mathbf{x}_0'(\mathbf{X}'\mathbf{X})^{-1}\mathbf{x}_0]$. Why is the variance of the forecast error D greater than the variance of δ found in part (a)?

(c) Use the results in parts (a) and (b), along with the Canadian occupational prestige regression (see Section 5.2.2), to predict the prestige score for an occupation with an average income of \$12,000, an average education of 13 years, and 50% women. Place a 90% confidence interval around the prediction assuming (i) that you wish to estimate $E(Y_0)$, and (ii) that you wish to forecast an actual Y_0 score. (Because σ_ε^2 is not known, you will need to use S_E^2 and the t-distribution.)

(d) Suppose that the methods of this problem are used to forecast a value of Y for a combination of Xs very different from the X values in the data to which the model was fit. For example, calculate the estimated variance of the forecast error for an occupation with an average income of \$50,000, an average education of 0 years, and 100% women. Is the estimated variance of the forecast error large or small? Does the variance of the forecast error adequately capture the uncertainty in using the regression equation to predict Y in this circumstance?

Exercise 9.15. Suppose that the model matrix for the two-way ANOVA model

$$Y_{ijk} = \mu + \alpha_j + \beta_k + \gamma_{jk} + \varepsilon_{ijk}$$

is reduced to full rank by imposing the following constraints (for $r = 2$ rows and $c = 3$ columns):

$$\alpha_2 = 0$$
$$\beta_3 = 0$$
$$\gamma_{21} = \gamma_{22} = \gamma_{13} = \gamma_{23} = 0$$

These constraints imply dummy-variable (0/1) coding of the full-rank model matrix.

(a) Write out the row basis of the full-rank model matrix under these constraints.
(b) Solve for the parameters of the constrained model in terms of the cell means. What is the nature of the hypotheses H_0: all $\alpha_j = 0$ and H_0: all $\beta_k = 0$ for this parametrization of the model? Are these hypotheses generally sensible?
(c) Let $SS^*(\alpha, \beta, \gamma)$ represent the regression sum of squares for the full model, calculated under the constraints defined above; let $SS^*(\alpha, \beta)$ represent the regression sum of squares for the model that deletes the interaction regressors; and so on. Using the Moore and Krupat data (discussed in Section 8.2), confirm that

$$SS^*(\alpha|\beta) = SS(\alpha|\beta)$$
$$SS^*(\beta|\alpha) = SS(\beta|\alpha)$$
$$SS^*(\gamma|\alpha, \beta) = SS(\gamma|\alpha, \beta)$$

but that

$$SS^*(\alpha|\beta, \gamma) \neq SS(\alpha|\beta, \gamma)$$
$$SS^*(\beta|\alpha, \gamma) \neq SS(\beta|\alpha, \gamma)$$

where $SS(\cdot)$ and $SS(\cdot|\cdot)$ give regression and incremental sums of squares under the usual sigma constraints and deviation-coded $(1, 0, -1)$ regressors.
(d) Analyze the Moore and Krupat data using one or more computer programs available to you. How do the programs calculate sums of squares in two-way ANOVA? Does the documentation accompanying the programs clearly explain how the sums of squares are computed?

Exercise 9.16. * Show that the equation-by-equation least-squares estimator $\widehat{\mathbf{B}} = (\mathbf{X}'\mathbf{X})^{-1}\mathbf{X}'\mathbf{Y}$ is the maximum-likelihood estimator of the regression coefficients $\mathbf{B}$ in the multivariate general linear model $\mathbf{Y} = \mathbf{XB} + \mathbf{E}$, where the model matrix $\mathbf{X}$ is fixed, and the distribution of the errors is $\varepsilon_i \sim \mathbf{N}_m(\mathbf{0}, \boldsymbol{\Sigma})$, with ε_i and $\varepsilon_{i'}$ independent for $i \neq i'$. Show that the MLE of the error-covariance matrix is $\frac{1}{n}\widehat{\mathbf{E}}'\widehat{\mathbf{E}}$, where $\widehat{\mathbf{E}} = \mathbf{Y} - \mathbf{X}\widehat{\mathbf{B}}$.

Summary

- The general linear model can be written in matrix form as $\mathbf{y} = \mathbf{X}\boldsymbol{\beta} + \boldsymbol{\varepsilon}$, where $\mathbf{y}$ is an $n \times 1$ vector of response-variable observations; $\mathbf{X}$ is an $n \times k + 1$ matrix of regressors (called the model matrix), including an initial column of 1s for the constant regressor; $\boldsymbol{\beta}$ is a $k + 1 \times 1$ vector of parameters to be estimated; and $\boldsymbol{\varepsilon}$ is an $n \times 1$ vector of errors. The assumptions of the linear model can be compactly written as $\boldsymbol{\varepsilon} \sim \mathbf{N}_n(\mathbf{0}, \sigma_\varepsilon^2 \mathbf{I}_n)$.

- The model matrices for dummy-regression and ANOVA models are strongly patterned. In ANOVA, the relationship between group or cell means and the parameters of the linear model is expressed by the parametric equation $\boldsymbol{\mu} = \mathbf{X}_B \boldsymbol{\beta}_F$, where $\boldsymbol{\mu}$ is the vector of means; $\mathbf{X}_B$ is the row basis of the full-rank model matrix; and $\boldsymbol{\beta}_F$ is the parameter vector associated with the full-rank model matrix. Solving the parametric equation for the parameters yields $\boldsymbol{\beta}_F = \mathbf{X}_B^{-1}\boldsymbol{\mu}$. Linear contrasts are regressors that are coded to incorporate specific hypotheses about the group means in the parameters of the model.

- If the model matrix $\mathbf{X}$ is of full-column rank, then the least-squares coefficients are given by $\mathbf{b} = (\mathbf{X}'\mathbf{X})^{-1}\mathbf{X}'\mathbf{y}$. Under the full set of assumptions for the linear model, $\mathbf{b} \sim N_{k+1}[\boldsymbol{\beta}, \sigma_\varepsilon^2(\mathbf{X}'\mathbf{X})^{-1}]$. The least-squares estimator is also the most efficient unbiased estimator of $\boldsymbol{\beta}$ and the maximum-likelihood estimator of $\boldsymbol{\beta}$.

- The estimated covariance matrix of the least-squares coefficients is $\widehat{V}(\mathbf{b}) = S_E^2(\mathbf{X}'\mathbf{X})^{-1}$. The standard errors of the regression coefficients are the square-root diagonal entries of this matrix. Under the assumptions of the model, $(B_j - \beta_j)/\mathrm{SE}(B_j) \sim t_{n-k-1}$, providing a basis for hypothesis tests and confidence intervals for individual coefficients.

- An incremental F-test for the hypothesis H_0: $\beta_1 = \cdots = \beta_q = 0$, where $1 \leq q \leq k$, is given by

$$F_0 = \frac{(\mathrm{RSS}_0 - \mathrm{RSS})/q}{\mathrm{RSS}/(n - k - 1)}$$

where RSS is the residual sum of squares for the full model, and RSS_0 is the residual sum of squares for the model that deletes the q regressors in question. Under the null hypothesis, $F_0 \sim F_{q,\,n-k-1}$. The incremental F-statistic can also be computed directly as $F_0 = \mathbf{b}_1' \mathbf{V}_{11}^{-1} \mathbf{b}_1 / q S_E^2$, where $\mathbf{b}_1 = [B_1, \ldots, B_q]'$ contains the coefficients of interest extracted from among the entries of $\mathbf{b}$, and $\mathbf{V}_{11}$ is the square submatrix of $(\mathbf{X}'\mathbf{X})^{-1}$ consisting of the q rows and columns pertaining to the coefficients in $\mathbf{b}_1$.

- The F-statistic

$$F_0 = \frac{(\mathbf{Lb} - \mathbf{c})'[\mathbf{L}(\mathbf{X}'\mathbf{X})^{-1}\mathbf{L}']^{-1}(\mathbf{Lb} - \mathbf{c})}{q S_E^2}$$

is used to test the general linear hypothesis H_0: $\underset{(q \times k+1)}{\mathbf{L}} \underset{(k+1 \times 1)}{\boldsymbol{\beta}} = \underset{(q \times 1)}{\mathbf{c}}$, where the rank-$q$ hypothesis matrix $\mathbf{L}$ and right-hand-side vector $\mathbf{c}$ contain prespecified constants. Under the hypothesis, $F_0 \sim F_{q,\,n-k-1}$.

- The joint confidence region for the q parameters $\boldsymbol{\beta}_1$, given by

$$\text{all } \boldsymbol{\beta}_1 \text{ for which } (\mathbf{b}_1 - \boldsymbol{\beta}_1)'\mathbf{V}_{11}^{-1}(\mathbf{b}_1 - \boldsymbol{\beta}_1) \leq q S_E^2 F_{a,\,q,\,n-k-1}$$

represents the combinations of values of these parameters that are jointly acceptable at the $1 - a$ level of confidence. The boundary of the joint confidence region is an ellipsoid in the q-dimensional parameter space, reflecting the correlational structure and dispersion of the Xs.

- The multivariate linear model accommodates several response variables:

$$\mathbf{Y} = \mathbf{XB} + \mathbf{E}$$

Under the assumption that the rows $\boldsymbol{\varepsilon}_i'$ of the error matrix $\mathbf{E}$ are independent and multivariately normally distributed with mean $\mathbf{0}$ and common nonsingular covariance matrix $\boldsymbol{\Sigma}$, the maximum-likelihood estimators of the regression coefficients are given by

$$\widehat{\mathbf{B}} = (\mathbf{X}'\mathbf{X})^{-1}\mathbf{X}'\mathbf{Y}$$

Hypothesis tests for the multivariate linear model closely parallel those for the univariate linear model, with sum-of-squares-and-products (SSP) matrices in the multivariate case generalizing the role of sums of squares in the univariate case. Several commonly employed test statistics are based on the eigenvalues of $\mathbf{SSP}_H \mathbf{SSP}_R^{-1}$, where $\mathbf{SSP}_H$ is the SSP matrix for a hypothesis, and $\mathbf{SSP}_R$ is the residual SSP matrix.

- The statistical theory of linear models, formulated under the supposition that the model matrix $\mathbf{X}$ is fixed with respect to repeated sampling, is also valid when $\mathbf{X}$ is random, as long as three additional requirements are satisfied:

  1. the model matrix $\mathbf{X}$ is measured without error and is independent of the errors ε;

  2. the distribution of $\mathbf{X}$, which is otherwise unconstrained, does not depend on the parameters β and σ_ε^2 of the linear model; and

  3. the covariance matrix of the Xs is nonsingular.

- The omission of regressors from a linear model causes the coefficients of the included regressors to be inconsistent, unless

  1. the omitted regressors are uncorrelated with the included regressors or

  2. the omitted regressors have coefficients of 0, and hence are irrelevant.

Recommended Reading

There are many texts that treat the theory of linear models more abstractly, more formally, and with greater generality than I have in this chapter.

- Seber (1977) is a reasonably accessible text that develops in a statistically more sophisticated manner most of the topics discussed in the last five chapters. Seber also pays more attention to issues of computation and develops some topics that I do not.
- Searle (1971) presents a very general treatment of linear models, including a much broader selection of ANOVA models, stressing the analysis of unbalanced data. Searle directly analyzes model matrices of less than full rank, an approach that—in my opinion—makes the subject more complex than it needs to be. Despite its relative difficulty, however, the presentation is of exceptionally high quality.
- Hocking (1985) and Searle (1987) cover much the same ground as Searle (1971), but stress the use of "cell-means" models, avoiding some of the complications of overparametrized models for ANOVA. These books also contain a very general presentation of the theory of linear statistical models.
- A fine and accessible paper by Monette (1990) develops in more detail the geometric representation of regression analysis using ellipses (a topic that is usually treated only in difficult sources).
- There are many general texts on multivariate statistical methods. Krzanowski (1988) and Morrison (2005) provide wide-ranging and accessible introductions to the subject, including to the mulivariate linear model. The statistical theory of multivariate linear models is developed in detail by Anderson (2003) and Rao (1973).

10

The Vector Geometry of Linear Models*

As is clear from the previous chapter, linear algebra is the algebra of linear models. Vector geometry provides a spatial representation of linear algebra and therefore furnishes a powerful tool for understanding linear models. The geometric understanding of linear models is venerable: Fisher's development of the central notion of degrees of freedom in linear models was closely tied to vector geometry, for example.

Few points in this book are developed exclusively in geometric terms. The reader who takes the time to master the geometry of linear models, however, will find the effort worthwhile: Certain ideas—including degrees of freedom—are most simply developed or understood from the geometric perspective.[1]

The chapter begins by describing the geometric vector representation of simple and multiple regression. Then, this vector representation is employed to explain the connection between degrees of freedom and unbiased estimation of the error variance in linear models. Finally, vector geometry is used to illuminate the essential nature of overparametrized analysis-of-variance (ANOVA) models.

10.1 Simple Regression

We can write the simple-regression model in vector form in the following manner:

$$\mathbf{y} = \alpha \mathbf{1}_n + \beta \mathbf{x} + \varepsilon \tag{10.1}$$

where $\mathbf{y} \equiv [Y_1, Y_2, \ldots, Y_n]'$, $\mathbf{x} \equiv [x_1, x_2, \ldots, x_n]'$, $\varepsilon \equiv [\varepsilon_1, \varepsilon_2, \ldots, \varepsilon_n]'$, and $\mathbf{1}_n \equiv [1, 1, \ldots, 1]'$; α and β are the population regression coefficients.[2] As before, we will assume that $\varepsilon \sim N_n(\mathbf{0}, \sigma^2 \mathbf{I}_n)$. The fitted regression equation is, similarly,

$$\mathbf{y} = A \mathbf{1}_n + B \mathbf{x} + \mathbf{e} \tag{10.2}$$

where $\mathbf{e} \equiv [E_1, E_2, \ldots, E_n]'$ is the vector of residuals, and A and B are the least-squares regression coefficients. From Equation 10.1, we have

$$E(\mathbf{y}) = \alpha \mathbf{1}_n + \beta \mathbf{x}$$

Analogously, from Equation 10.2,

$$\widehat{\mathbf{y}} = A \mathbf{1}_n + B \mathbf{x}$$

We are familiar with a seemingly natural geometric representation of $\{X, Y\}$ data—the scatterplot—in which the axes of a two-dimensional coordinate space are defined by the variables X and Y and where the observations are represented as points in the space according to

---

[1] The basic vector geometry on which this chapter depends is developed in Appendix B.

[2] Note that the X-values are treated as fixed. As in the previous chapter, the development of the vector geometry of linear models is simpler for fixed X, but the results apply as well when X is random.

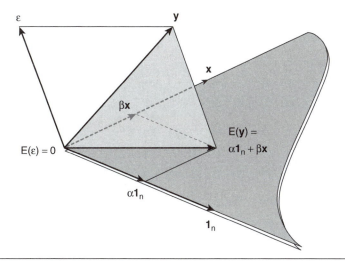

Figure 10.1   The vector geometry of the simple-regression model, showing the three-dimensional subspace spanned by the vectors **x**, **y**, and $\mathbf{1}_n$. Because the expected error is **0**, the expected-Y vector, $E(\mathbf{y})$, lies in the plane spanned by $\mathbf{1}_n$ and **x**.

their $\{x_i, Y_i\}$ coordinates. The scatterplot is a valuable data-analytic tool as well as a device for thinking about regression analysis.

I will now exchange the familiar roles of variables and observations, defining an n-dimensional coordinate space for which the *axes* are given by the *observations* and in which the *variables* are plotted as *vectors*. Of course, because there are generally many more than three observations, it is not possible to visualize the full vector space of the observations.[3] Our interest, however, often inheres in two- and three-dimensional subspaces of this larger n-dimensional vector space. In these instances, as we will see presently, visual representation is both possible and illuminating. Moreover, the geometry of higher-dimensional subspaces can be grasped by analogy to the two- and three-dimensional cases.

The two-dimensional *variable space* (i.e., in which the variables define the axes) and the n-dimensional *observation space* (in which the observations define the axes) each contains a complete representation of the ($n \times 2$) data matrix [**x**, **y**]. The formal duality of these spaces means that properties of the data, or of models meant to describe them, have equivalent representations in both spaces. Sometimes, however, the geometric representation of a property will be easier to understand in one space or the other.

The simple-regression model of Equation 10.1 is shown geometrically in Figure 10.1. The subspace depicted in this figure is of dimension 3 and is spanned by the vectors **x**, **y**, and $\mathbf{1}_n$. Because **y** is a vector random variable that varies from sample to sample, the vector diagram necessarily represents a *particular* sample. The other vectors shown in the diagram clearly lie in the subspace spanned by **x**, **y**, and $\mathbf{1}_n$: $E(\mathbf{y})$ is a linear combination of **x** and $\mathbf{1}_n$ (and thus lies in the $\{\mathbf{1}_n, \mathbf{x}\}$ plane); and the error vector ε is $\mathbf{y} - \alpha\mathbf{1}_n - \beta\mathbf{x}$. Although ε is nonzero in this sample, on average, over many samples, $E(\varepsilon) = \mathbf{0}$.

Figure 10.2 represents the least-squares simple regression of Y on X, for the same data as shown in Figure 10.1. The peculiar geometry of Figure 10.2 requires some explanation: We know that the fitted values $\widehat{\mathbf{y}}$ are a linear combination of $\mathbf{1}_n$ and **x** and hence lie in the $\{\mathbf{1}_n, \mathbf{x}\}$ plane. The residual vector $\mathbf{e} = \mathbf{y} - \widehat{\mathbf{y}}$ has length $\|\mathbf{e}\| = \sqrt{\sum E_i^2}$—that is, the square root of the residual sum of

---

[3] See Exercise 10.1 for a scaled-down example, however.

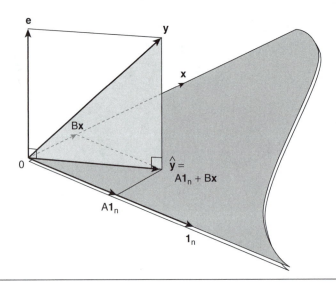

Figure 10.2   The vector geometry of least-squares fit in simple regression. Minimizing the residual sum of squares is equivalent to making the **e** vector as short as possible. The $\widehat{\mathbf{y}}$ vector is, therefore, the orthogonal projection of **y** onto the $\{\mathbf{1}_n, \mathbf{x}\}$ plane.

squares. The least-squares criterion interpreted geometrically, therefore, specifies that **e** must be as short as possible. Because the length of **e** is the distance between **y** and $\widehat{\mathbf{y}}$, this length is minimized by taking $\widehat{\mathbf{y}}$ as the orthogonal projection of **y** onto the $\{\mathbf{1}_n, \mathbf{x}\}$ plane, as shown in the diagram.

> Variables, such as X and Y in simple regression, can be treated as vectors—**x** and **y**—in the n-dimensional space whose axes are given by the observations. Written in vector form, the simple-regression model is $\mathbf{y} = \alpha\mathbf{1}_n + \beta\mathbf{x} + \varepsilon$. The least-squares regression, $\mathbf{y} = A\mathbf{1}_n + B\mathbf{x} + \mathbf{e}$, is found by projecting **y** orthogonally onto the plane spanned by $\mathbf{1}_n$ and **x**, thus minimizing the sum of squared residuals, $\|\mathbf{e}\|^2$.

10.1.1   Variables in Mean-Deviation Form

We can simplify the vector representation for simple regression by eliminating the constant regressor $\mathbf{1}_n$ and, with it, the intercept coefficient A. This simplification is worthwhile for two reasons:

1. Our diagram is reduced from three to two dimensions. When we turn to multiple regression—introducing a second explanatory variable—eliminating the constant allows us to work with a three-dimensional rather than a four-dimensional subspace.

2. The ANOVA for the regression appears in the vector diagram when the constant is eliminated, as I will shortly explain.

To get rid of A, recall that $\overline{Y} = A + B\overline{x}$; subtracting this equation from the fitted model $Y_i = A + Bx_i + E_i$ produces

$$Y_i - \overline{Y} = B(x_i - \overline{x}) + E_i$$

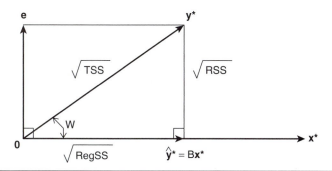

Figure 10.3   The vector geometry of least-squares fit in simple regression for variables in mean-deviation form. The analysis of variance for the regression follows from the Pythagorean theorem. The correlation between X and Y is the cosine of the angle W separating the $\mathbf{x}^*$ and $\mathbf{y}^*$ vectors.

Expressing the variables in mean-deviation form eliminates the regression constant. Defining $\mathbf{y}^* \equiv \{Y_i - \overline{Y}\}$ and $\mathbf{x}^* \equiv \{x_i - \overline{x}\}$, the vector form of the fitted regression model becomes

$$\mathbf{y}^* = B\mathbf{x}^* + \mathbf{e} \tag{10.3}$$

The vector diagram corresponding to Equation 10.3 is shown in Figure 10.3. By the same argument as before,[4] $\widehat{\mathbf{y}}^* \equiv \{\widehat{Y}_i - \overline{Y}\}$ is a multiple of $\mathbf{x}^*$, and the length of $\mathbf{e}$ is minimized by taking $\widehat{\mathbf{y}}^*$ as the orthogonal projection of $\mathbf{y}^*$ onto $\mathbf{x}^*$. Thus,

$$B = \frac{\mathbf{x}^* \cdot \mathbf{y}^*}{||\mathbf{x}^*||^2} = \frac{\sum(x_i - \overline{x})(Y_i - \overline{Y})}{\sum(x_i - \overline{x})^2}$$

which is the familiar formula for the least-squares slope in simple regression.[5]

Sums of squares appear on the vector diagram as the squared lengths of vectors. I have already remarked that

$$\text{RSS} = \sum E_i^2 = ||\mathbf{e}||^2$$

Similarly,

$$\text{TSS} = \sum(Y_i - \overline{Y})^2 = ||\mathbf{y}^*||^2$$

and

$$\text{RegSS} = \sum(\widehat{Y}_i - \overline{Y})^2 = ||\widehat{\mathbf{y}}^*||^2$$

The ANOVA for the regression, $\text{TSS} = \text{RegSS} + \text{RSS}$, follows from the Pythagorean theorem.

The correlation coefficient is

$$r = \sqrt{\frac{\text{RegSS}}{\text{TSS}}} = \frac{||\widehat{\mathbf{y}}^*||}{||\mathbf{y}^*||}$$

---

[4]The mean deviations for the fitted values are $\{\widehat{Y}_i - \overline{Y}\}$ because the mean of the fitted values is the same as the mean of Y. See Exercise 10.2.

[5]See Section 5.1.

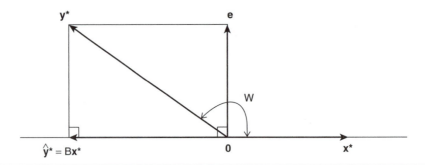

Figure 10.4   The vector geometry of least-squares fit for a negative relationship between X and Y. Here B is negative, so $\widehat{\mathbf{y}} = B\mathbf{x}$ points in the direction opposite to $\mathbf{x}$.

The vectors $\widehat{\mathbf{y}}^*$ and $\mathbf{y}^*$ are, respectively, the adjacent side and hypotenuse for the angle W in the right triangle whose vertices are given by the tips of $\mathbf{0}$, $\mathbf{y}^*$, and $\widehat{\mathbf{y}}^*$. Thus, $r = \cos W$: The correlation between two variables (here, X and Y) is the cosine of the angle separating their mean-deviation vectors. When this angle is 0, one variable is a perfect linear function of the other, and $r = \cos 0 = 1$. When the vectors are orthogonal, $r = \cos 90° = 0$. We will see shortly that when two variables are *negatively* correlated, $90° < W \leq 180°$.[6] The correlation $r = \cos W$ can be written directly as[7]

$$r = \frac{\mathbf{x}^* \cdot \mathbf{y}^*}{||\mathbf{x}^*||\,||\mathbf{y}^*||} = \frac{\sum (x_i - \overline{x})(Y_i - \overline{Y})}{\sqrt{\sum (x_i - \overline{x})^2 \sum (Y_i - \overline{Y})^2}} \tag{10.4}$$

Figure 10.4 illustrates an inverse relationship between X and Y. All the conclusions that we based on Figure 10.3 still hold. Because B is now negative, $\widehat{\mathbf{y}}^* = B\mathbf{x}^*$ is a negative multiple of the $\mathbf{x}^*$ vector, pointing in the *opposite* direction from $\mathbf{x}^*$. The correlation is still the cosine of W, but now we need to take the *negative* root of $\sqrt{||\widehat{\mathbf{y}}^*||^2/||\mathbf{y}^*||^2}$ if we wish to define r in terms of vector lengths; Equation 10.4 produces the proper sign because $\mathbf{x}^* \cdot \mathbf{y}^*$ is negative.

> Writing X and Y in mean-deviation form, as the vectors $\mathbf{x}^*$ and $\mathbf{y}^*$, eliminates the constant term and thus permits representation of the fitted regression in two (rather than three) dimensions: $\mathbf{y}^* = B\mathbf{x}^* + \mathbf{e}$. The ANOVA for the regression, TSS = RegSS + RSS, is represented geometrically as $||\mathbf{y}^*||^2 = ||\widehat{\mathbf{y}}^*||^2 + ||\mathbf{e}||^2$. The correlation between X and Y is the cosine of the angle separating the vectors $\mathbf{x}^*$ and $\mathbf{y}^*$.

10.1.2   Degrees of Freedom

The vector representation of simple regression helps clarify the concept of degrees of freedom. In general, sums of squares for linear models are the squared lengths of variable vectors. The

---

[6]We need only consider angles between 0° and 180° for we can always examine the *smaller* of the two angles separating $\mathbf{x}^*$ and $\mathbf{y}^*$. Because $\cos W = \cos(360° - W)$, this convention is of no consequence.

[7]This is the alternative formula for the correlation coefficient presented in Section 5.1 (Equation 5.4 on page 85). The vector representation of simple regression, therefore, demonstrates the equivalence of the two formulas for r—the direct formula and the definition in terms of sums of squares.

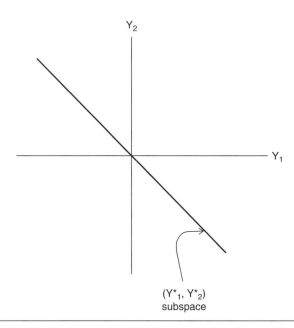

Figure 10.5 When $n = 2$, the mean-deviation vector $\mathbf{y}^* = [Y_1 - \overline{Y}, Y_2 - \overline{Y}]'$ is confined to a one-dimensional subspace (i.e., a line) of the two-dimensional observation space.

degrees of freedom associated with a sum of squares represent the dimension of the subspace to which the corresponding vector is confined.

- Consider, first, the vector $\mathbf{y}$ in Figure 10.2 (page 222): This vector can be located anywhere in the n-dimensional observation space. The *uncorrected* sum of squares $\sum Y_i^2 = ||\mathbf{y}||^2$, therefore, has n degrees of freedom.
- When we convert Y to mean-deviation form (as in Figure 10.3 on page 223), we confine the $\mathbf{y}^*$ vector to an $(n - 1)$-dimensional subspace, "losing" 1 degree of freedom in the process. This is easily seen for vectors in two-dimensional space: Let $\mathbf{y} = [Y_1, Y_2]'$, and $\mathbf{y}^* = [Y_1 - \overline{Y}, Y_2 - \overline{Y}]'$. Then, because $\overline{Y} = (Y_1 + Y_2)/2$, we can write

$$\mathbf{y}^* = [Y_1^*, -Y_1^*]' = \left[Y_1 - \frac{Y_1 + Y_2}{2}, Y_2 - \frac{Y_1 + Y_2}{2}\right]' = \left[\frac{Y_1 - Y_2}{2}, \frac{Y_2 - Y_1}{2}\right]'$$

Thus, all vectors $\mathbf{y}^*$ lie on a line through the origin, as shown in Figure 10.5: The subspace of all vectors $\mathbf{y}^*$ is one dimensional. Algebraically, by subtracting the mean from each of its coordinates, we have imposed a linear restriction on $\mathbf{y}^*$, ensuring that its entries sum to zero, $\sum(Y_i - \overline{Y}) = 0$; among the n values of $Y_i - \overline{Y}$, only $n - 1$ are linearly independent. The total sum of squares TSS $= ||\mathbf{y}^*||^2 = \sum(Y_i - \overline{Y})^2$, therefore, has $n - 1$ degrees of freedom.

We can extend this reasoning to the residual and regression sums of squares:

- In Figure 10.3, $\widehat{\mathbf{y}}^*$ is a multiple of $\mathbf{x}^*$. The vector $\mathbf{x}^*$, in turn, is fixed, and spans a one-dimensional subspace. Because $\widehat{\mathbf{y}}^*$ necessarily lies somewhere in this one-dimensional subspace, RegSS $= ||\widehat{\mathbf{y}}^*||^2$ has 1 degree of freedom.
- The degrees of freedom for the residual sum of squares can be determined from either Figure 10.2 or Figure 10.3. In Figure 10.2, $\mathbf{y}$ lies somewhere in the n-dimensional observation

space. The vectors $\mathbf{x}$ and $\mathbf{1}_n$ are fixed and together span a subspace of dimension 2 within the larger observation space. The location of the residual vector $\mathbf{e}$ depends on $\mathbf{y}$, but, in any event, $\mathbf{e}$ is orthogonal to the plane spanned by $\mathbf{x}$ and $\mathbf{1}_n$. Consequently, $\mathbf{e}$ lies in a subspace of dimension $n - 2$ (the orthogonal complement of the subspace spanned by $\mathbf{x}$ and $\mathbf{1}_n$), and RSS $= ||\mathbf{e}||^2$ has $n - 2$ degrees of freedom. Algebraically, the least-squares residuals $\mathbf{e}$ satisfy two independent linear restrictions—$\sum E_i = 0$ (i.e., $\mathbf{e} \cdot \mathbf{1}_n = 0$) and $\sum E_i x_i = 0$ (i.e., $\mathbf{e} \cdot \mathbf{x} = 0$)—accounting for the "loss" of 2 degrees of freedom.[8]

- Alternatively, referring to Figure 10.3, $\mathbf{y}^*$ lies in the $(n - 1)$-dimensional subspace of mean deviations; the residual vector $\mathbf{e}$ is orthogonal to $\mathbf{x}^*$, both of which also lie in the $(n - 1)$-dimensional mean-deviation subspace; hence, RSS has $(n - 1) - 1 = n - 2$ degrees of freedom.

> Degrees of freedom in simple regression correspond to the dimensions of subspaces to which variable vectors associated with sums of squares are confined: (1) The $\mathbf{y}^*$ vector lies in the $(n-1)$-dimensional subspace of mean deviations but is otherwise unconstrained; TSS, therefore, has $n - 1$ degrees of freedom. (2) The $\widehat{\mathbf{y}}^*$ vector lies somewhere along the one-dimensional subspace spanned by $\mathbf{x}^*$; RegSS, therefore, has 1 degree of freedom. (3) The $\mathbf{e}$ vector lies in the $(n - 1)$-dimensional subspace of mean deviations and is constrained to be orthogonal to $\mathbf{x}^*$; RSS, therefore, has $(n - 1) - 1 = n - 2$ degrees of freedom.

10.2 Multiple Regression

To develop the vector geometry of multiple regression, I will work primarily with the two-explanatory-variable model: Virtually all important points can be developed for this case; and by expressing the variables in mean-deviation form (eliminating the constant regressor), the subspace of interest is confined to three dimensions and consequently can be visualized.

Consider, then, the fitted model

$$\mathbf{y} = A\mathbf{1}_n + B_1\mathbf{x}_1 + B_2\mathbf{x}_2 + \mathbf{e} \tag{10.5}$$

where $\mathbf{y}$ is, as before, the vector of response-variable observations; $\mathbf{x}_1$ and $\mathbf{x}_2$ are explanatory-variable vectors; $\mathbf{e}$ is the vector of residuals; and $\mathbf{1}_n$ is a vector of 1s. The least-squares regression coefficients are A, B_1, and B_2. From each observation of Equation 10.5, let us subtract $\overline{Y} = A + B_1\overline{x}_1 + B_2\overline{x}_2$, obtaining

$$\mathbf{y}^* = B_1\mathbf{x}_1^* + B_2\mathbf{x}_2^* + \mathbf{e} \tag{10.6}$$

In Equation 10.6, $\mathbf{y}^*$, $\mathbf{x}_1^*$, and $\mathbf{x}_2^*$ are vectors of mean deviations.

Figure 10.6(a) shows the three-dimensional vector diagram for the fitted model of Equation 10.6, while Figure 10.6(b) depicts the explanatory-variable plane. The fitted values $\widehat{\mathbf{y}}^* = B_1\mathbf{x}_1^* + B_2\mathbf{x}_2^*$ are a linear combination of the regressors, and the vector $\widehat{\mathbf{y}}^*$, therefore, lies in the $\{\mathbf{x}_1^*, \mathbf{x}_2^*\}$ plane. By familiar reasoning, the least-squares criterion implies that the residual vector $\mathbf{e}$ is orthogonal to the explanatory-variable plane and, consequently, that $\widehat{\mathbf{y}}^*$ is the orthogonal projection of $\mathbf{y}^*$ onto this plane.

---

[8]It is also the case that $\sum E_i \widehat{Y}_i = \mathbf{e} \cdot \widehat{\mathbf{y}} = 0$, but this constraint follows from the other two. See Exercise 10.3.

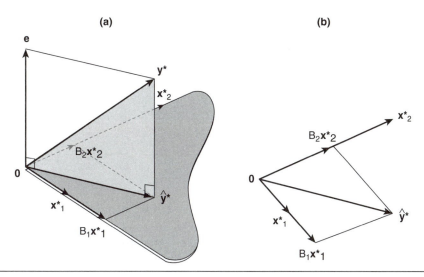

Figure 10.6 The vector geometry of least-squares fit in multiple regression, with the variables in mean-deviation form. The vectors $\mathbf{y}^*$, $\mathbf{x}_1^*$, and $\mathbf{x}_2^*$ span a three-dimensional subspace, shown in (a). The fitted-Y vector, $\widehat{\mathbf{y}}^*$, is the orthogonal projection of $\mathbf{y}^*$ onto the plane spanned by $\mathbf{x}_1^*$ and $\mathbf{x}_2^*$. The $\{\mathbf{x}_1^*, \mathbf{x}_2^*\}$ plane is shown in (b).

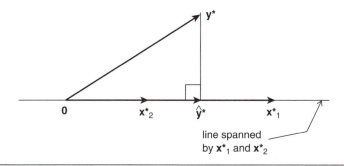

Figure 10.7 When the explanatory variables are perfectly collinear, $\mathbf{x}_1^*$ and $\mathbf{x}_2^*$ span a line rather than a plane. The $\widehat{\mathbf{y}}^*$ vector can still be found by projecting $\mathbf{y}^*$ orthogonally onto this line, but the regression coefficients B_1 and B_2, expressing $\widehat{\mathbf{y}}^*$ as a linear combination of $\mathbf{x}_1^*$ and $\mathbf{x}_2^*$, are not unique.

The regression coefficients B_1 and B_2 are uniquely defined as long as $\mathbf{x}_1^*$ and $\mathbf{x}_2^*$ are not collinear. This is the geometric version of the requirement that the explanatory variables may not be perfectly correlated. If the regressors are collinear, then they span a *line* rather than a plane; although we can still find the fitted values by orthogonally projecting $\mathbf{y}^*$ onto this line, as shown in Figure 10.7, we cannot express $\widehat{\mathbf{y}}^*$ *uniquely* as a linear combination of $\mathbf{x}_1^*$ and $\mathbf{x}_2^*$.

The ANOVA for the multiple-regression model appears in the plane spanned by $\mathbf{y}^*$ and $\widehat{\mathbf{y}}^*$, as illustrated in Figure 10.8. The residual vector also lies in this plane (because $\mathbf{e} = \mathbf{y}^* - \widehat{\mathbf{y}}^*$), while the regressor plane $\{\mathbf{x}_1^*, \mathbf{x}_2^*\}$ is perpendicular to it. As in simple-regression analysis, TSS $= \|\mathbf{y}^*\|^2$, RegSS $= \|\widehat{\mathbf{y}}^*\|^2$, and RSS $= \|\mathbf{e}\|^2$. The identity TSS $=$ RegSS $+$ RSS follows from the Pythagorean theorem.

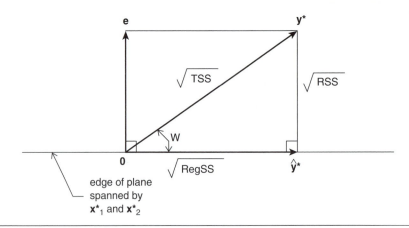

Figure 10.8   The analysis of variance for multiple regression appears in the plane spanned by $\mathbf{y}^*$ and $\widehat{\mathbf{y}}^*$. The multiple correlation is the cosine of the angle W separating $\mathbf{y}^*$ and $\widehat{\mathbf{y}}^*$.

It is also clear from Figure 10.8 that $R = \sqrt{\mathrm{RegSS}/\mathrm{TSS}} = \cos W$. Thus, the *multiple* correlation is the *simple* correlation between the observed and fitted response-variable values, Y and $\widehat{Y}$. If there is a *perfect* linear relationship between Y and the explanatory variables, then $\mathbf{y}^*$ lies in the regressor plane, $\mathbf{y}^* = \widehat{\mathbf{y}}^*$, $\mathbf{e} = \mathbf{0}$, $W = 0°$, and $R = 1$; if, at the other extreme, there is *no* linear relationship between Y and the explanatory variables, then $\mathbf{y}^* = \mathbf{e}$, $\widehat{\mathbf{y}}^* = \mathbf{0}$, $W = 90°$, and $R = 0$.

> The fitted multiple-regression model for two explanatory variables is written in vector form as $\mathbf{y} = A\mathbf{1}_n + B_1\mathbf{x}_1 + B_2\mathbf{x}_2 + \mathbf{e}$. Putting Y and the Xs in mean-deviation form eliminates the constant, $\mathbf{y}^* = B_1\mathbf{x}_1^* + B_2\mathbf{x}_2^* + \mathbf{e}$, and permits a representation in three (rather than four) dimensions. The fitted values, $\widehat{\mathbf{y}}^* = B_1\mathbf{x}_1^* + B_2\mathbf{x}_2^*$, are found by projecting $\mathbf{y}^*$ orthogonally onto the plane spanned by $\mathbf{x}_1^*$ and $\mathbf{x}_2^*$. The ANOVA for the regression, which is essentially the same as in simple regression, appears in the plane spanned by $\mathbf{y}^*$ and $\widehat{\mathbf{y}}^*$. The multiple correlation R is the cosine of the angle separating $\mathbf{y}^*$ and $\widehat{\mathbf{y}}^*$ and, consequently, is the simple correlation between the observed and fitted Y values.

Figure 10.9 shows the vector geometry of the incremental F-test for the hypothesis H_0: $\beta_1 = 0$ in a model with k explanatory variables. RegSS—the regression sum of squares from the full model, where Y is regressed on all the Xs—is decomposed into two orthogonal components: RegSS_0 (for the regression of Y on $X_2, \ldots, X_k$) and the incremental sum of squares $\mathrm{RegSS} - \mathrm{RegSS}_0$.

The vector representation of regression analysis also helps clarify the relationship between simple and multiple regression. Figure 10.10(a) is drawn for two positively correlated regressors. The fitted response-variable vector is, from our previous work, the orthogonal projection of $\mathbf{y}^*$ onto the $\{\mathbf{x}_1^*, \mathbf{x}_2^*\}$ plane. To find the multiple-regression coefficient B_1, we project $\widehat{\mathbf{y}}^*$ parallel to $\mathbf{x}_2^*$, locating $B_1\mathbf{x}_1^*$, as shown in Figure 10.10(b), which depicts the regressor plane. The coefficient B_2 is located similarly.

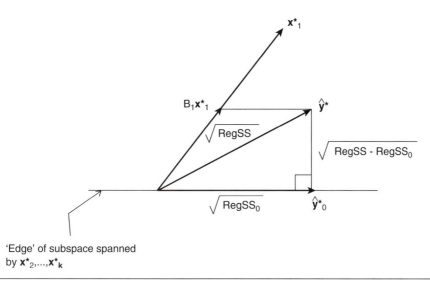

Figure 10.9   The incremental sum of squares for the hypothesis $H_0: \beta_1 = 0$. The vector $\widehat{\mathbf{y}}_0^*$ is for the regression of Y on $X_2, \ldots, X_k$ (i.e., excluding X_1), while the vector $\widehat{\mathbf{y}}^*$ is for the regression of Y on all the Xs, including X_1.

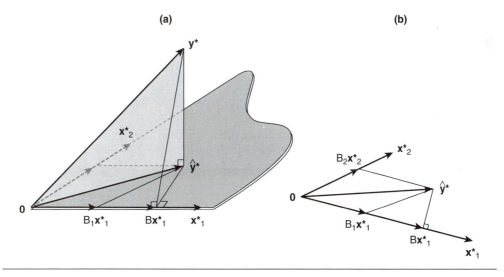

Figure 10.10   When the Xs are correlated (here positively), the slope B for the simple regression of Y on X_1 alone generally differs from the slope B_1 in the multiple regression of Y on both X_1 and X_2. The least-squares fit is in (a), the regressor plane in (b).

To find the slope coefficient B for the *simple* regression of Y on X_1, we need to project $\mathbf{y}^*$ onto $\mathbf{x}_1^*$ *alone*, obtaining $B\mathbf{x}_1^*$; this result also appears in Figure 10.10(a). Because $\mathbf{x}_1^* \cdot \mathbf{y}^* = \mathbf{x}_1^* \cdot \widehat{\mathbf{y}}^*$,[9] the vector $B_1\mathbf{x}_1^*$ is also the orthogonal projection of $\widehat{\mathbf{y}}^*$ onto $\mathbf{x}_1^*$, as shown in Figure 10.10(a) and (b). In this instance, projecting $\widehat{\mathbf{y}}^*$ perpendicular to $\mathbf{x}_1^*$ (simple regression) rather than parallel to $\mathbf{x}_2^*$ (multiple regression) causes the simple-regression slope B to exceed the multiple-regression slope B_1.

The situation changes fundamentally if the explanatory variables X_1 and X_2 are *uncorrelated*, as illustrated in Figure 10.11(a) and (b). Here, $B = B_1$. Another advantage of orthogonal regressors is revealed in Figure 10.11(b): There is a unique partition of the regression sum of squares into components due to each of the two regressors. We have[10]

$$\mathrm{RegSS} = \widehat{\mathbf{y}}^* \cdot \widehat{\mathbf{y}}^* = B_1^2 \mathbf{x}_1^* \cdot \mathbf{x}_1^* + B_2^2 \mathbf{x}_2^* \cdot \mathbf{x}_2^*$$

In contrast, when the regressors are *correlated*, as in Figure 10.10(b), no such partition is possible, for then

$$\mathrm{RegSS} = \widehat{\mathbf{y}}^* \cdot \widehat{\mathbf{y}}^* = B_1^2 \mathbf{x}_1^* \cdot \mathbf{x}_1^* + B_2^2 \mathbf{x}_2^* \cdot \mathbf{x}_2^* + 2B_1 B_2 \mathbf{x}_1^* \cdot \mathbf{x}_2^* \qquad (10.7)$$

The last term in Equation 10.7 can be positive or negative, depending on the signs of the regression coefficients and of the correlation between X_1 and X_2.[11]

> When the explanatory variables in multiple regression are orthogonal (uncorrelated), the regression sum of squares can be partitioned into components due to each explanatory variable: $\|\widehat{\mathbf{y}}^*\|^2 = B_1^2\|\mathbf{x}_1^*\|^2 + B_2^2\|\mathbf{x}_2^*\|^2$. When the explanatory variables are correlated, however, no such partition is possible.

As in simple regression, degrees of freedom in multiple regression correspond to the dimension of subspaces of the observation space. Because the $\mathbf{y}^*$ vector, as a vector of mean deviations, is confined to a subspace of dimension $n - 1$, there are $n - 1$ degrees of freedom for TSS $= \|\mathbf{y}^*\|^2$. The fitted-value vector $\widehat{\mathbf{y}}^*$ necessarily lies in the fixed $\{\mathbf{x}_1^*, \mathbf{x}_2^*\}$ plane, which is a subspace of dimension 2; thus, RegSS $= \|\widehat{\mathbf{y}}^*\|^2$ has 2 degrees of freedom. Finally, the residual vector $\mathbf{e}$ is orthogonal to the explanatory-variable plane, and, therefore, RSS $= \|\mathbf{e}\|^2$ has $(n - 1) - 2 = n - 3$ degrees of freedom.

More generally, k noncollinear regressors in mean-deviation form generate a subspace of dimension k. The fitted response-variable vector $\widehat{\mathbf{y}}^*$ is the orthogonal projection of $\mathbf{y}^*$ onto this subspace, and, therefore, RegSS has k degrees of freedom. Likewise, because $\mathbf{e}$ is orthogonal to the k-dimensional regressor subspace, RSS has $(n - 1) - k = n - k - 1$ degrees of freedom.

> As in simple regression, degrees of freedom in multiple regression follow from the dimensionality of the subspaces to which the $\mathbf{y}^*$, $\widehat{\mathbf{y}}^*$, and $\mathbf{e}$ vectors are confined.

---

[9] See Exercise 10.5.

[10] See Exercise 10.6.

[11] Some researchers seek to interpret $2B_1 B_2 \mathbf{x}_1^* \cdot \mathbf{x}_2^*$ as the variation in Y due to the "overlap" between the correlated explanatory variables X_1 and X_2. That this interpretation is nonsense follows from the observation that the overlap can be negative.

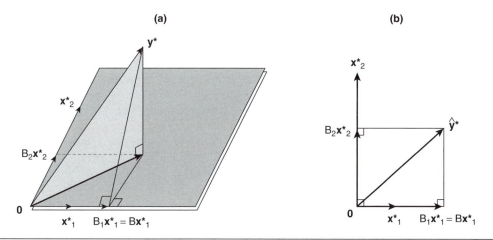

(a)

(b)

Figure 10.11   When the Xs are uncorrelated, the simple-regression slope B and the multiple-regression slope B_1 are the same. The least-squares fit is in (a), the regressor plane in (b).

10.3 Estimating the Error Variance

The connection between degrees of freedom and unbiased variance estimation is subtle but yields *relatively* simply to the geometric point of view. This section uses the vector geometry of regression to show that $S_E^2 = \sum E_i^2/(n-k-1)$ is an unbiased estimator of the error variance, σ_ε^2.

Even when the errors in a linear model are independent and normally distributed with zero means and constant variance, $\varepsilon \sim N_n(\mathbf{0}, \sigma_\varepsilon^2 \mathbf{I}_n)$, the least-squares residuals are correlated and generally have different variances, $\mathbf{e} \sim N_n(\mathbf{0}, \sigma_\varepsilon^2 \mathbf{Q})$. The matrix $\mathbf{Q} \equiv \mathbf{I}_n - \mathbf{X}(\mathbf{X}'\mathbf{X})^{-1}\mathbf{X}'$ is nondiagonal, singular, and of rank $n-k-1$.[12]

Following Putter (1967), we can transform the least-squares residuals into an independent and identically distributed set by selecting an orthonormal basis for the error subspace, defining transformed residuals in the following manner:

$$\underset{(n-k-1\times 1)}{\mathbf{z}} \equiv \underset{(n-k-1\times n)}{\mathbf{G}} \underset{(n\times 1)}{\mathbf{e}}$$

The transformation matrix $\mathbf{G}$ is selected so that it is orthonormal and orthogonal to $\mathbf{X}$:

$$\mathbf{G}\mathbf{G}' = \mathbf{I}_{n-k-1}$$

$$\mathbf{G}\mathbf{X} = \underset{(n-k-1\times k+1)}{\mathbf{0}}$$

The transformed residuals then have the following properties:[13]

$$\mathbf{z} = \mathbf{G}\mathbf{y}$$
$$E(\mathbf{z}) = \mathbf{0}$$
$$V(\mathbf{z}) = \sigma_\varepsilon^2 \mathbf{I}_{n-k-1}$$

If the elements of ε are independent and normally distributed with constant variance, then so are the elements of $\mathbf{z}$. There are, however, n of the former and $n-k-1$ of the latter. Furthermore, the

---

[12] See Exercise 10.10.
[13] See Exercise 10.11.

transformation matrix $\mathbf{G}$ (and hence $\mathbf{z}$) is not unique—there are infinitely many ways of selecting an orthonormal basis for the error subspace.[14]

Transforming $\mathbf{e}$ to $\mathbf{z}$ suggests a simple method for deriving an estimator of the error variance σ_ε^2. The entries of $\mathbf{z}$ have zero expectations and common variance σ_ε^2, so

$$E(\mathbf{z}'\mathbf{z}) = \sum_{i=1}^{n-k-1} E(Z_i^2) = (n - k - 1)\sigma_\varepsilon^2$$

Thus, an unbiased estimator of the error variance is given by

$$S_E^2 \equiv \frac{\mathbf{z}'\mathbf{z}}{n - k - 1}$$

Moreover, because the Z_i are independent and normally distributed,

$$\frac{\mathbf{z}'\mathbf{z}}{\sigma_\varepsilon^2} = \frac{(n - k - 1)S_E^2}{\sigma_\varepsilon^2} \sim \chi_{n-k-1}^2$$

The estimator S_E^2 can be computed *without* finding transformed residuals, for the length of the least-squares residual vector $\mathbf{e}$ is the same as the length of the vector of transformed residuals $\mathbf{z}$; that is, $\sqrt{\mathbf{e}'\mathbf{e}} = \sqrt{\mathbf{z}'\mathbf{z}}$. This result follows from the observation that $\mathbf{e}$ and $\mathbf{z}$ are the *same* vector represented according to alternative bases: (1) $\mathbf{e}$ gives the coordinates of the residuals relative to the natural basis of the n-dimensional observation space; (2) $\mathbf{z}$ gives the coordinates of the residuals relative to an arbitrary orthonormal basis for the $(n - k - 1)$-dimensional error subspace. A vector does not change its length when the basis changes, and, therefore,

$$S_E^2 = \frac{\mathbf{z}'\mathbf{z}}{n - k - 1} = \frac{\mathbf{e}'\mathbf{e}}{n - k - 1}$$

which is our usual estimator of the error variance.

Heuristically, although $\mathbf{e}$ contains n elements, there are, as I have explained, $k + 1$ linear dependencies among them. In calculating an unbiased estimator of the error variance, we need to divide by the residual degrees of freedom rather than by the number of observations.

An unbiased estimator of the error variance σ_ε^2 can be derived by transforming the n correlated residuals $\mathbf{e}$ to $n - k - 1$ independently and identically distributed residuals $\mathbf{z}$, employing an orthonormal basis $\mathbf{G}$ for the $(n - k - 1)$-dimensional error subspace: $\mathbf{z} = \mathbf{G}\mathbf{e}$. If the errors are independent and normally distributed, with zero means and common variance σ_ε^2, then so are the elements of $\mathbf{z}$. Thus, $\mathbf{z}'\mathbf{z}/(n - k - 1)$ is an unbiased estimator of the error variance; and because $\mathbf{z}$ and $\mathbf{e}$ are the same vector represented according to alternative bases, $\mathbf{z}'\mathbf{z}/(n - k - 1) = \mathbf{e}'\mathbf{e}/(n - k - 1)$, which is our usual estimator of error variance, S_E^2.

---

[14]The transformed residuals are useful not only for exploring properties of least-squares estimation, but also in diagnosing certain linear-model problems (see, e.g., Putter, 1967; Theil, 1971, chap. 5).

10.4 Analysis-of-Variance Models

Recall the overparametrized one-way ANOVA model[15]

$$Y_{ij} = \mu + \alpha_j + \varepsilon_{ij} \quad \text{for } i = 1, \ldots, n_j; \, j = 1, \ldots, m$$

The $\mathbf{X}$ matrix for this model (with parameters labeling the columns) is

$$\mathbf{X}_{(n \times m+1)} = \begin{bmatrix} (\mu) & (\alpha_1) & (\alpha_2) & \cdots & (\alpha_{m-1}) & (\alpha_m) \\ 1 & 1 & 0 & \cdots & 0 & 0 \\ \vdots & \vdots & \vdots & & \vdots & \vdots \\ 1 & 1 & 0 & \cdots & 0 & 0 \\ 1 & 0 & 1 & \cdots & 0 & 0 \\ \vdots & \vdots & \vdots & & \vdots & \vdots \\ 1 & 0 & 1 & \cdots & 0 & 0 \\ \vdots & \vdots & \vdots & & \vdots & \vdots \\ 1 & 0 & 0 & \cdots & 1 & 0 \\ \vdots & \vdots & \vdots & & \vdots & \vdots \\ 1 & 0 & 0 & \cdots & 1 & 0 \\ 1 & 0 & 0 & \cdots & 0 & 1 \\ \vdots & \vdots & \vdots & & \vdots & \vdots \\ 1 & 0 & 0 & \cdots & 0 & 1 \end{bmatrix}$$

The $m + 1$ columns of the model matrix span a subspace of dimension m. We can project the response-variable vector $\mathbf{y}$ onto this subspace, locating the fitted-value vector $\widehat{\mathbf{y}}$. Because they are collinear, the columns of $\mathbf{X}$ do not provide a basis for the subspace that they span, and, consequently, the individual parameter estimates are not uniquely determined. This situation is illustrated in Figure 10.12 for $m = 2$. Even in the absence of uniquely determined parameters, however, we have no trouble calculating the regression sum of squares for the model because we can find $\widehat{\mathbf{y}}$ by picking an arbitrary basis for the column space of $\mathbf{X}$. The dummy-coding and deviation-coding schemes of Chapter 8 select alternative bases for the column space of the model matrix: Dummy coding simply deletes the last column to provide a basis for the column space of $\mathbf{X}$; deviation coding constructs a new basis for the column space of $\mathbf{X}$.

> In the overparametrized one-way ANOVA model, $Y_{ij} = \mu + \alpha_j + \varepsilon_{ij}$, the $m + 1$ columns of the model matrix $\mathbf{X}$ are collinear and span a subspace of dimension m. We can, however, still find $\widehat{\mathbf{y}}$ for the model by projecting $\mathbf{y}$ orthogonally onto this subspace, most simply by selecting an arbitrary basis for the column space of the model matrix. Conceived in this light, dummy coding and deviation coding are two techniques for constructing a basis for the column space of $\mathbf{X}$.

Let us turn next to the overparametrized two-way ANOVA model:[16]

$$Y_{ijk} = \mu + \alpha_j + \beta_k + \gamma_{jk} + \varepsilon_{ijk} \quad \text{for } i = 1, \ldots, n_{jk}; \, j = 1, \ldots, r; \, k = 1, \ldots, c$$

---

[15]See Section 8.1.
[16]See Section 8.2.

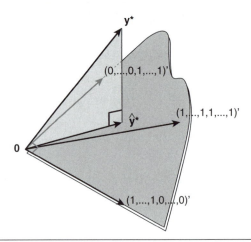

Figure 10.12   The vector geometry of least-squares fit for the overparametrized one-way ANOVA model when there are two groups. The $m+1 = 3$ columns of the model matrix are collinear and span a subspace of dimension $m = 2$.

We will consider the simplest case, where $j = k = 2$. It suffices to examine the parametric equation for the model, relating the four cell means μ_{jk} to the nine parameters of the model:

$$
\begin{bmatrix} \mu_{11} \\ \mu_{12} \\ \mu_{21} \\ \mu_{22} \end{bmatrix} = \left[\begin{array}{c|cc|cc|cccc} 1 & 1 & 0 & 1 & 0 & 1 & 0 & 0 & 0 \\ 1 & 1 & 0 & 0 & 1 & 0 & 1 & 0 & 0 \\ 1 & 0 & 1 & 1 & 0 & 0 & 0 & 1 & 0 \\ 1 & 0 & 1 & 0 & 1 & 0 & 0 & 0 & 1 \end{array} \right] \begin{bmatrix} \mu \\ \hline \alpha_1 \\ \alpha_2 \\ \hline \beta_1 \\ \beta_2 \\ \hline \gamma_{11} \\ \gamma_{12} \\ \gamma_{21} \\ \gamma_{22} \end{bmatrix}
$$

$$\mu = \mathbf{X}_B \beta$$

Note that the four columns in $\mathbf{X}_B$ representing the interactions are linearly independent, and hence the corresponding columns of $\mathbf{X}$ span the *full* column space of the model matrix. The subspaces spanned by the main effects, each consisting of two linearly independent columns, lie in the space spanned by the interaction regressors—the main-effect subspaces are literally *marginal to* (i.e., contained in) the interaction subspace. Finally, the constant regressor is marginal both to the interaction subspace and to each of the main-effect subspaces: The constant regressor is simply the sum of the interaction regressors or of either set of main-effect regressors. Understood in this light, the deviation-coding method of Chapter 8 selects a convenient full-rank basis for the model matrix.

In the overparametrized two-way ANOVA model, $Y_{ijk} = \mu + \alpha_j + \beta_k + \gamma_{jk} + \varepsilon_{ijk}$, the interaction regressors provide a basis for the full column space of the model matrix. The model-matrix columns for the two sets of main effects are therefore marginal to (i.e., subspaces of) the interaction space. The column for the constant regressor is marginal to the main-effect subspaces as well as to the interactions.

Exercises

Exercise 10.1. Here is a very small (contrived) data set with two variables and two observations:

	Variables	
Observations	X	Y
1	1	2
2	3	5

Construct a scatterplot for the two observations in the $\{X, Y\}$ variable space; then construct a vector diagram showing **x** and **y** in the observation space.

Exercise 10.2. Show that the average fitted value, $\overline{\widehat{Y}}$, is the same as the average response-variable value, $\overline{Y}$. [*Hint*: Form the sum, $\sum Y_i = \sum (\widehat{Y}_i + E_i)$.]

Exercise 10.3. *Show that the constraints $\mathbf{e} \cdot \mathbf{x} = 0$ and $\mathbf{e} \cdot \mathbf{1}_n = 0$ imply that $\mathbf{e} \cdot \widehat{\mathbf{y}} = 0$. (*Hint*: $\widehat{\mathbf{y}}$ lies in the plane spanned by **x** and $\mathbf{1}_n$.)

Exercise 10.4. Using Duncan's occupational prestige data (discussed, e.g., in Chapter 5), construct the geometric vector representation for the regression of prestige on education, showing the $\mathbf{x}^*$, $\mathbf{y}^*$, $\widehat{\mathbf{y}}^*$, and **e** vectors drawn to scale. Find the angle between $\mathbf{x}^*$ and $\mathbf{y}^*$.

Exercise 10.5. Prove that $\mathbf{x}_1^* \cdot \mathbf{y}^* = \mathbf{x}_1^* \cdot \widehat{\mathbf{y}}^*$. (*Hint*: $\mathbf{y}^* = \widehat{\mathbf{y}}^* + \mathbf{e}$, and **e** is orthogonal to $\mathbf{x}_1^*$.)

Exercise 10.6. Show that when X_1 and X_2 are uncorrelated, the regression sum of squares can be written as

$$\text{RegSS} = \widehat{\mathbf{y}}^* \cdot \widehat{\mathbf{y}}^* = B_1^2 \mathbf{x}_1^* \cdot \mathbf{x}_1^* + B_2^2 \mathbf{x}_2^* \cdot \mathbf{x}_2^*$$

(*Hint*: Use $\widehat{\mathbf{y}}^* = B_1 \mathbf{x}_1^* + B_2 \mathbf{x}_2^*$.)

Exercise 10.7. Exercise 10.4 (continued): Using Duncan's occupational prestige data, construct the geometric representation for the regression of prestige Y on income X_1 and education X_2. Draw separate graphs for (a) the $\{\mathbf{x}_1^*, \mathbf{x}_2^*\}$ plane, showing the $\widehat{\mathbf{y}}^*$ vector, B_1, and B_2; and (b) the $\{\mathbf{y}^*, \widehat{\mathbf{y}}^*\}$ plane, showing **e**. Draw all vectors to scale. (*Hint*: Calculate the correlation between X_1 and X_2 to find the angle between $\mathbf{x}_1^*$ and $\mathbf{x}_2^*$.)

Exercise 10.8. Nearly collinear regressors: Construct the geometric vector representation of a regression with two explanatory variables in mean-deviation form, $\widehat{\mathbf{y}}^* = B_1 \mathbf{x}_1^* + B_2 \mathbf{x}_2^*$, distinguishing between two cases: (a) X_1 and X_2 are highly correlated, so that the angle separating the $\mathbf{x}_1^*$ and $\mathbf{x}_2^*$ vectors is small; and (b) X_1 and X_2 are uncorrelated, so that the $\mathbf{x}_1^*$ and $\mathbf{x}_2^*$ vectors are orthogonal. By examining the regressor plane, show that slight changes in the position of the $\widehat{\mathbf{y}}^*$ vector (due, e.g., to sampling fluctuations) can cause dramatic changes in the regression coefficients B_1 and B_2 in case (a) but not in case (b). The problem of collinearity is discussed further in Chapter 13.

Exercise 10.9. Partial correlation (see Exercise 5.8):

(a) Illustrate how the partial correlation $r_{Y1|2}$ can be represented using geometric vectors. Draw the vectors $\mathbf{y}^*$, $\mathbf{x}_1^*$, and $\mathbf{x}_2^*$, and define $\mathbf{e}_1 \equiv \{E_{i1|2}\}$ and $\mathbf{e}_Y \equiv \{E_{iY|2}\}$ (where i is the subscript for observations).

(b) *Use the vector diagram in part (a) to show that the incremental F-test for the hypothesis H_0: $\beta_1 = 0$ can be written as

$$F_0 = \frac{(n - k - 1)r_{Y1|2}^2}{1 - r_{Y1|2}^2}$$

Recalling part (b) of Exercise 5.8, why is this result intuitively plausible?

Exercise 10.10. *Show that the matrix $Q = I_n - X(X'X)^{-1}X'$ (see Section 10.3) is non-diagonal, singular, and of rank $n - k - 1$. (*Hints*: Verify that the rows of Q satisfy the $k + 1$ constraints implied by $QX = 0$. If Q is singular and diagonal, then some of its diagonal entries must be 0; show that this is not generally the case.)

Exercise 10.11. *Prove that when the least-squares residuals are transformed according to the equation $z = Ge$, where the $n - k - 1 \times n$ transformation matrix G is orthonormal and orthogonal to X, the transformed residuals z have the following properties: $z = Gy$, $E(z) = 0$, and $V(z) = \sigma_\varepsilon^2 I_{n-k-1}$. (See Section 10.3.)

Exercise 10.12. Exercise 9.15 (continued): Let SS$(\cdot)$ give sums of squares for the two-way ANOVA model

$$Y_{ijk} = \mu + \alpha_j + \beta_k + \gamma_{jk} + \varepsilon_{ijk}$$

using deviation-coded regressors (i.e., employing sigma constraints to reduce the model matrix to full rank); and let SS*$(\cdot)$ give sums of squares for the same model using dummy-coded regressors. Working with the model for $r = 2$ rows and $c = 3$ columns, use the geometric vector representation of the model to explain why

$$SS^*(\alpha|\beta) = SS(\alpha|\beta)$$
$$SS^*(\beta|\alpha) = SS(\beta|\alpha)$$
$$SS^*(\gamma|\alpha, \beta) = SS(\gamma|\alpha, \beta)$$

but that, in general,

$$SS^*(\alpha|\beta, \gamma) \neq SS(\alpha|\beta, \gamma)$$
$$SS^*(\beta|\alpha, \gamma) \neq SS(\beta|\alpha, \gamma)$$

[*Hints*: Show that (i) the subspaces spanned by the deviation and dummy regressors for each of the two sets of main effects are the same; (ii) the subspaces spanned by the deviation and dummy regressors for the full set of effects (main effects and interactions) are the same; but (iii) the subspaces spanned by the deviation and dummy interaction regressors are *different*.]

Summary _____

- Variables, such as X and Y in simple regression, can be treated as vectors—x and y—in the n-dimensional space whose axes are given by the observations. Written in vector form, the simple-regression model is $y = \alpha 1_n + \beta x + \varepsilon$. The least-squares regression, $y = A1_n + Bx + e$, is found by projecting y orthogonally onto the plane spanned by 1_n and x, thus minimizing the sum of squared residuals $||e||^2$.

- Writing X and Y in mean-deviation form, as the vectors $\mathbf{x}^*$ and $\mathbf{y}^*$, eliminates the constant term and thus permits representation of the fitted regression in two (rather than three) dimensions: $\mathbf{y}^* = B\mathbf{x}^* + \mathbf{e}$. The ANOVA for the regression, TSS $=$ RegSS $+$ RSS, is represented geometrically as $||\mathbf{y}^*||^2 = ||\widehat{\mathbf{y}}^*||^2 + ||\mathbf{e}||^2$. The correlation between X and Y is the cosine of the angle separating the vectors $\mathbf{x}^*$ and $\mathbf{y}^*$.

- Degrees of freedom in simple regression correspond to the dimensions of subspaces to which variable vectors associated with sums of squares are confined:
  - The $\mathbf{y}^*$ vector lies in the $(n-1)$-dimensional subspace of mean deviations but is otherwise unconstrained; TSS $= ||\mathbf{y}^*||^2$, therefore, has $n-1$ degrees of freedom.
  - The $\widehat{\mathbf{y}}^*$ vector lies somewhere along the one-dimensional subspace spanned by $\mathbf{x}^*$; RegSS $= ||\widehat{\mathbf{y}}^*||^2$, therefore, has 1 degree of freedom.
  - The $\mathbf{e}$ vector lies in the $(n-1)$-dimensional subspace of mean deviations, and is constrained to be orthogonal to $\mathbf{x}^*$; RSS $= ||\mathbf{e}||^2$, therefore, has $(n-1)-1 = n-2$ degrees of freedom.

- The fitted multiple-regression model for two explanatory variables is written in vector form as $\mathbf{y} = A\mathbf{1}_n + B_1\mathbf{x}_1 + B_2\mathbf{x}_2 + \mathbf{e}$. Putting Y and the Xs in mean-deviation form eliminates the constant, $\mathbf{y}^* = B_1\mathbf{x}_1^* + B_2\mathbf{x}_2^* + \mathbf{e}$, and permits a representation in three (rather than four) dimensions. The fitted values, $\widehat{\mathbf{y}}^* = B_1\mathbf{x}_1^* + B_2\mathbf{x}_2^*$, are found by projecting $\mathbf{y}^*$ orthogonally onto the plane spanned by $\mathbf{x}_1^*$ and $\mathbf{x}_2^*$. The ANOVA for the regression, which is essentially the same as in simple regression, appears in the plane spanned by $\mathbf{y}^*$ and $\widehat{\mathbf{y}}^*$. The multiple correlation R is the cosine of the angle separating $\mathbf{y}^*$ and $\widehat{\mathbf{y}}^*$, and, consequently, is the simple correlation between the observed and fitted Y-values.

- When the explanatory variables in multiple regression are orthogonal (uncorrelated), the regression sum of squares can be partitioned into components due to each explanatory variable: $||\widehat{\mathbf{y}}^*||^2 = B_1^2||\mathbf{x}_1^*||^2 + B_2^2||\mathbf{x}_2^*||^2$. When the explanatory variables are correlated, however, no such partition is possible.

- As in simple regression, degrees of freedom in multiple regression follow from the dimensionality of the subspaces to which the various vectors are confined:
  - The $\mathbf{y}^*$ vector lies in the $(n-1)$-dimensional subspace of mean deviations; TSS, therefore, has $n-1$ degrees of freedom.
  - The $\widehat{\mathbf{y}}^*$ vector lies somewhere in the plane spanned by $\mathbf{x}_1^*$ and $\mathbf{x}_2^*$; RegSS, therefore, has 2 degrees of freedom. More generally, k explanatory variables $\mathbf{x}_1^*, \mathbf{x}_2^*, \ldots, \mathbf{x}_k^*$ span a subspace of dimension k, and $\widehat{\mathbf{y}}^*$ is the orthogonal projection of $\mathbf{y}^*$ onto this subspace; thus, RegSS has k degrees of freedom.
  - The $\mathbf{e}$ vector is constrained to be orthogonal to the two-dimensional subspace spanned by $\mathbf{x}_1^*$ and $\mathbf{x}_2^*$; RSS, therefore, has $(n-1)-2 = n-3$ degrees of freedom. More generally, $\mathbf{e}$ is orthogonal to the k-dimensional subspace spanned by $\mathbf{x}_1^*, \mathbf{x}_2^*, \ldots, \mathbf{x}_k^*$, and so RSS has $(n-1)-k = n-k-1$ degrees of freedom.

- An unbiased estimator of the error variance σ_ε^2 can be derived by transforming the n correlated residuals $\mathbf{e}$ to $n-k-1$ independently and identically distributed residuals $\mathbf{z}$, employing an orthonormal basis $\mathbf{G}$ for the $(n-k-1)$-dimensional error subspace: $\mathbf{z} = \mathbf{Ge}$. If the errors are independent and normally distributed, with zero means and common variance σ_ε^2, then so are the elements of $\mathbf{z}$. Thus, $\mathbf{z}'\mathbf{z}/(n-k-1)$ is an unbiased estimator of the error variance; and because $\mathbf{z}$ and $\mathbf{e}$ are the same vector represented according to alternative bases, $\mathbf{z}'\mathbf{z}/(n-k-1) = \mathbf{e}'\mathbf{e}/(n-k-1)$, which is our usual estimator of error variance, S_E^2.

- In the overparametrized one-way ANOVA model, $Y_{ij} = \mu + \alpha_j + \varepsilon_{ij}$, the $m+1$ columns of the model matrix $\mathbf{X}$ are collinear and span a subspace of dimension m. We can, however, still find $\widehat{\mathbf{y}}$ for the model by projecting $\mathbf{y}$ orthogonally onto this subspace, most simply by selecting an arbitrary basis for the column space of the model matrix. Conceived in this light, dummy coding and deviation coding are two techniques for constructing a basis for the column space of **X**.

- In the overparametrized two-way ANOVA model, $Y_{ijk} = \mu + \alpha_j + \beta_k + \gamma_{jk} + \varepsilon_{ijk}$, the interaction regressors provide a basis for the full column space of the model matrix. The model-matrix columns for the two sets of main effects are therefore marginal to (i.e., subspaces of) the interaction space. The column for the constant regressor is marginal to the main-effect subspaces as well as to the interactions.

Recommended Reading

- There are several advanced texts that treat linear models from a strongly geometric perspective, including Dempster (1969) and Stone (1987). Both these books describe multivariate (i.e., multiple response-variable) generalizations of linear models, and both demand substantial mathematical sophistication. Also see Christensen (1996).
- In a text on matrix algebra, vector geometry, and associated mathematical topics, Green and Carroll (1976) focus on the geometric properties of linear models and related multivariate methods. The pace of the presentation is relatively leisurely, and the strongly geometric orientation provides insight into both the mathematics and the statistics.
- Wonnacott and Wonnacott (1979) invoke vector geometry to explain a variety of statistical topics, including some not covered in the present text—such as instrumental-variables estimation and structural-equation models.

PART III

Linear-Model Diagnostics

11

Unusual and Influential Data

As we have seen, linear statistical models—particularly linear regression analysis—make strong assumptions about the structure of data, assumptions that often do not hold in applications. The method of least squares, which is typically used to fit linear models to data, is very sensitive to the structure of the data and can be markedly influenced by one or a few unusual observations.

We could abandon linear models and least-squares estimation in favor of nonparametric regression and robust estimation.[1] A less drastic response is also possible, however: We can adapt and extend the methods for examining and transforming data described in Chapters 3 and 4 to diagnose problems with a linear model that has been fit to data and—often—to suggest solutions.

I will pursue this strategy in this and the next two chapters:

- The current chapter deals with unusual and influential data.
- Chapter 12 takes up a variety of problems, including nonlinearity, nonconstant error variance, and non-normality.
- Collinearity is the subject of Chapter 13.

Taken together, the diagnostic and corrective methods described in these chapters greatly extend the practical application of linear models. These methods are often the difference between a crude, mechanical data analysis and a careful, nuanced analysis that accurately describes the data and therefore supports meaningful interpretation of them.

Another point worth making at the outset is that many problems can be anticipated and dealt with through careful examination of the data *prior* to building a regression model. Consequently, if you use the methods for examining and transforming data discussed in Chapters 3 and 4, you will be less likely to encounter the difficulties detailed in the current part of the text on "post-fit" linear-model diagnostics.

11.1 Outliers, Leverage, and Influence

Unusual data are problematic in linear models fit by least squares because they can unduly influence the results of the analysis and because their presence may be a signal that the model fails to capture important characteristics of the data. Some central distinctions are illustrated in Figure 11.1 for the simple-regression model $Y = \alpha + \beta X + \varepsilon$.

In simple regression, an *outlier* is an observation whose response-variable value is *conditionally* unusual *given* the value of the explanatory variable. In contrast, a *univariate* outlier is a value of Y or X that is *unconditionally* unusual; such a value may or may not be a regression outlier.

Regression outliers appear in Figure 11.1(a) and (b). In Figure 11.1(a), the outlying observation has an X value that is at the center of the X-distribution; as a consequence, deleting the outlier

---

[1] Methods for nonparametric regression were introduced informally in Chapter 2 and will be described in more detail in Chapter 18. Robust regression is the subject of Chapter 19.

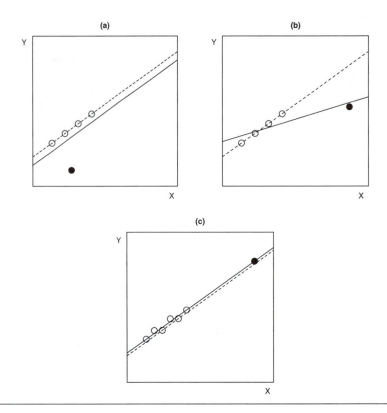

Figure 11.1   Leverage and influence in simple regression. In each graph, the solid line gives the least-squares regression for all the data, while the broken line gives the least-squares regression with the unusual data point (the black circle) omitted. (a) An outlier near the mean of X has low leverage and little influence on the regression coefficients. (b) An outlier far from the mean of X has high leverage and substantial influence on the regression coefficients. (c) A high-leverage observation in line with the rest of the data does not influence the regression coefficients. In panel (c), the two regression lines are separated slightly for visual effect but are, in fact, coincident.

has little impact on the least-squares fit, leaving the slope B unchanged and affecting the intercept A only slightly. In Figure 11.1(b), however, the outlier has an unusually large X value, and thus its deletion markedly affects both the slope and the intercept.[2] Because of its unusual X value, the outlying last observation in Figure 11.1(b) exerts strong *leverage* on the regression coefficients, while the outlying middle observation in Figure 11.1(a) is at a low-leverage point. The combination of high leverage with a regression outlier therefore produces substantial *influence* on the regression coefficients. In Figure 11.1(c), the right-most observation has no influence on the regression coefficients even though it is a high-leverage point, because this observation is in line with the rest of the data—it is not a regression outlier.

The following heuristic formula helps to distinguish among the three concepts of influence, leverage, and discrepancy ("outlyingness"):

$$\text{Influence on coefficients} = \text{Leverage} \times \text{Discrepancy}$$

---

[2]When, as here, an observation is far away from and out of line with the rest of data, it is difficult to know what to make of it: Perhaps the relationship between Y and X in Figure 11.1(b) is nonlinear.

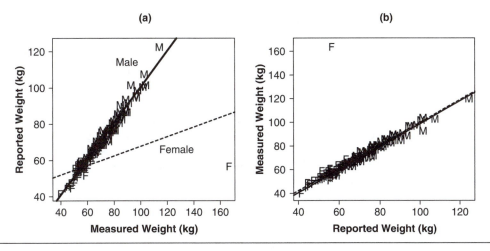

Figure 11.2 Regressions for Davis's data on reported and measured weight for women (F) and men (M). Panel (a) shows the least-squares linear regression line for each group (the solid line for men, the broken line for women) for the regression of reported on measured weight. The outlying observation has a large impact on the fitted line for women. Panel (b) shows the fitted regression lines for the regression of measured on reported weight; here, the outlying observation makes little difference to the fit, and the least-squares lines for men and women are nearly the same.

A simple and transparent example, with real data from Davis (1990), appears in Figure 11.2. These data record the measured and reported weight of 183 male and female subjects who engage in programs of regular physical exercise.[3] Davis's data can be treated in two ways:

- We could regress reported weight (RW) on measured weight (MW), a dummy variable for sex (F, coded 1 for women and 0 for men), and an interaction regressor (formed as the product $MW \times F$). This specification follows from the reasonable assumption that measured weight, and possibly sex, can affect reported weight. The results are as follows (with coefficient standard errors in parentheses):

$$\widehat{RW} = \underset{(3.28)}{1.36} + \underset{(0.043)}{0.990MW} + \underset{(3.9)}{40.0F} - \underset{(0.056)}{0.725(MW \times F)}$$

$$R^2 = 0.89 \quad S_E = 4.66$$

Were these results taken seriously, we would conclude that men are unbiased reporters of their weights (because $A = 1.36 \approx 0$ and $B_1 = 0.990 \approx 1$), while women tend to overreport their weights if they are relatively light and underreport if they are relatively heavy (the intercept for women is $1.36 + 40.0 = 41.4$ and the slope is $0.990 - 0.725 = 0.265$). Figure 11.2(a), however, makes it clear that the differential results for women and men are due to one female subject whose reported weight is about average (for women) but whose measured

---

[3]Davis's data were introduced in Chapter 2.

weight is extremely large. Recall that this subject's measured weight in kilograms and height in centimeters were erroneously switched. Correcting the data produces the regression

$$\widehat{RW} = 1.36 \quad + 0.990MW + 1.98F - 0.0567(MW \times F)$$
$$\quad\quad (1.58) \quad\;\; (0.021) \quad\quad (2.45) \quad\;\; (0.0385)$$

$$R^2 = 0.97 \quad S_E = 2.24$$

which suggests that both women and men are unbiased reporters of their weight.

- We could (as in our previous analysis of Davis's data) treat measured weight as the response variable, regressing it on reported weight, sex, and their interaction—reflecting a desire to use reported weight as a predictor of measured weight. For the *uncorrected* data,

$$\widehat{MW} = 1.79 \quad + 0.969RW + 2.07F - 0.00953(RW \times F)$$
$$\quad\quad (5.92) \quad\;\; (0.076) \quad\quad (9.30) \quad\;\; (0.147)$$

$$R^2 = 0.70 \quad S_E = 8.45$$

The outlier does not have much impact on the coefficients for this regression (both the dummy-variable coefficient and the interaction coefficient are small) precisely because the value of RW for the outlying observation is near $\overline{RW}$ for women [see Figure 11.2(b)]. There is, however, a marked effect on the multiple correlation and regression standard error: For the corrected data, $R^2 = 0.97$ and $S_E = 2.25$.

> Unusual data are problematic in linear models fit by least squares because they can substantially influence the results of the analysis and because they may indicate that the model fails to capture important features of the data. It is useful to distinguish among high-leverage observations, regression outliers, and influential observations. Influence on the regression coefficients is the product of leverage and outlyingness.

11.2 Assessing Leverage: Hat-Values

The so-called *hat-value* h_i is a common measure of leverage in regression. These values are so named because it is possible to express the fitted values $\widehat{Y}_j$ ("Y-hat") in terms of the observed values Y_i:

$$\widehat{Y}_j = h_{1j}Y_1 + h_{2j}Y_2 + \cdots + h_{jj}Y_j + \cdots + h_{nj}Y_n = \sum_{i=1}^{n} h_{ij}Y_i$$

Thus, the weight h_{ij} captures the contribution of observation Y_i to the fitted value $\widehat{Y}_j$: If h_{ij} is large, then the ith observation can have a considerable impact on the jth fitted value. It can be shown that $h_{ii} = \sum_{j=1}^{n} h_{ij}^2$, and so the hat-value $h_i \equiv h_{ii}$ summarizes the potential influence (the leverage) of Y_i on *all* the fitted values. The hat-values are bounded between $1/n$ and 1 (i.e., $1/n \leq h_i \leq 1$), and the average hat-value is $\overline{h} = (k + 1)/n$ (where k is the number of regressors in the model, excluding the constant).[4]

---

[4]For derivations of this and other properties of leverage, outlier, and influence diagnostics, see Section 11.8.

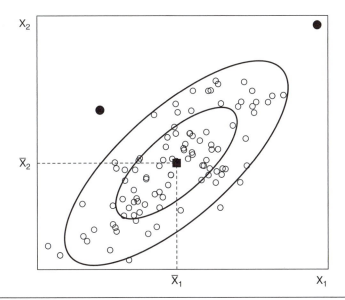

Figure 11.3   Elliptical contours of constant leverage (constant hat-values h_i) for $k = 2$ explanatory variables. Two high-leverage points appear, both represented by black circles. One point has unusually large values for each of X_1 and X_2, but the other is unusual only in combining a moderately large value of X_2 with a moderately small value of X_1. The centroid (point of means) is marked by the black square. (The contours of constant leverage are proportional to the standard data ellipse, introduced in Chapter 9).

In simple-regression analysis, the hat-values measure distance from the mean of X:[5]

$$h_i = \frac{1}{n} + \frac{(X_i - \overline{X})^2}{\sum_{j=1}^{n}(X_j - \overline{X})^2}$$

In multiple regression, h_i measures distance from the centroid (point of means) of the Xs, taking into account the correlational and variational structure of the Xs, as illustrated for $k = 2$ explanatory variables in Figure 11.3. *Multivariate* outliers in the X-space are thus high-leverage observations. The response-variable values are not at all involved in determining leverage.

For Davis's regression of reported weight on measured weight, the largest hat-value by far belongs to the 12th subject, whose measured weight was wrongly recorded as 166 kg: $h_{12} = 0.714$. This quantity is many times the average hat-value, $\overline{h} = (3 + 1)/183 = 0.0219$.

Figure 11.4(a) shows an *index plot* of hat-values from Duncan's regression of the prestige of 45 occupations on their income and education levels (i.e., a scatterplot of hat-values vs. the observation indices).[6] The horizontal lines in this graph are drawn at twice and three times the average hat-values, $\overline{h} = (2 + 1)/45 = 0.06667$.[7] Figure 11.4(b) shows a scatterplot for the explanatory variables education and income: *Railroad engineers* and *conductors* have high leverage by virtue of their relatively high income for their moderately low level of education, while *ministers* have high leverage because their level of income is relatively low given their moderately high level of education.

---

[5] See Exercise 11.1. Note that the sum in the denominator is over the subscript j because the subscript i is already in use.

[6] Duncan's regression was introduced in Chapter 5.

[7] See Section 11.5 on numerical cutoffs for diagnostic statistics.

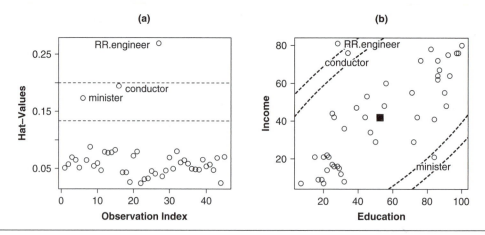

Figure 11.4   (a) An index plot of hat-values for Duncan's occupational prestige regression, with
horizontal lines at $2 \times \bar{h}$ and $3 \times \bar{h}$. (b) A scatterplot of education by income, with
contours of constant leverage at $2 \times \bar{h}$ and $3 \times \bar{h}$ given by the broken lines. (Note that
the ellipses extend beyond the boundaries of the graph.) The centroid is marked by
the black square.

> Observations with unusual combinations of explanatory-variable values have high *leverage*
> in a least-squares regression. The hat-values h_i provide a measure of leverage. The average
> hat-value is $\bar{h} = (k + 1)/n$.

11.3   Detecting Outliers: Studentized Residuals

To identify an outlying observation, we need an index of the unusualness of Y given the Xs.
Discrepant observations usually have large residuals, but it turns out that even if the errors ε_i have
equal variances (as assumed in the general linear model), the residuals E_i do not:

$$V(E_i) = \sigma_\varepsilon^2 (1 - h_i)$$

High-leverage observations, therefore, tend to have small residuals—an intuitively sensible result
because these observations can pull the regression surface toward them.

Although we can form a *standardized residual* by calculating

$$E_i' \equiv \frac{E_i}{S_E \sqrt{1 - h_i}}$$

this measure is slightly inconvenient because its numerator and denominator are not independent,
preventing E_i' from following a t-distribution: When $|E_i|$ is large, the standard error of the
regression, $S_E = \sqrt{\sum E_i^2 / (n - k - 1)}$, which contains E_i^2, tends to be large as well.

Suppose, however, that we refit the model deleting the ith observation, obtaining an estimate
$S_{E(-i)}$ of σ_ε that is based on the *remaining $n - 1$ observations*. Then the *studentized residual*

$$E_i^* \equiv \frac{E_i}{S_{E(-i)}\sqrt{1 - h_i}} \tag{11.1}$$

has an independent numerator and denominator and follows a t-distribution with $n - k - 2$ degrees of freedom.

An alternative, but equivalent, procedure for defining the studentized residuals employs a "mean-shift" outlier model:

$$Y_j = \alpha + \beta_1 X_{j1} + \cdots + \beta_k X_{jk} + \gamma D_j + \varepsilon_j \qquad (11.2)$$

where D is a dummy regressor set to 1 for observation i and 0 for all other observations:

$$D_j = \begin{cases} 1 & \text{for } j = i \\ 0 & \text{otherwise} \end{cases}$$

Thus,

$$E(Y_i) = \alpha + \beta_1 X_{i1} + \cdots + \beta_k X_{ik} + \gamma$$
$$E(Y_j) = \alpha + \beta_1 X_{j1} + \cdots + \beta_k X_{jk} \quad \text{for } j \neq i$$

It would be natural to specify the model in Equation 11.2 if, *before examining the data*, we suspected that observation i differed from the others. Then, to test H_0: $\gamma = 0$ (i.e., the null hypothesis that the ith observation is *not* an outlier), we can calculate $t_0 = \widehat{\gamma}/\text{SE}(\widehat{\gamma})$. This test statistic is distributed as t_{n-k-2} under H_0 and (it turns out) is the studentized residual E_i^* of Equation 11.1.

Hoaglin and Welsch (1978) arrive at the studentized residuals by successively omitting each observation, calculating its residual based on the regression coefficients obtained for the remaining sample, and dividing the resulting residual by its standard error. Finally, Beckman and Trussell (1974) demonstrate the following simple relationship between studentized and standardized residuals:

$$E_i^* = E_i' \sqrt{\frac{n - k - 2}{n - k - 1 - E_i'^2}} \qquad (11.3)$$

If n is large, then the factor under the square root in Equation 11.3 is close to 1, and the distinction between standardized and studentized residuals essentially disappears.[8] Moreover, for large n, the hat-values are generally small, and thus it is usually the case that

$$E_i^* \approx E_i' \approx \frac{E_i}{S_E}$$

Equation 11.3 also implies that E_i^* is a monotone function of E_i', and thus the rank order of the studentized and standardized residuals is the same.

11.3.1 Testing for Outliers in Linear Models

Because in most applications we do not suspect a *particular* observation in advance, but rather want to look for *any* outliers that may occur in the data, we can, in effect, refit the mean-shift model n times,[9] once for each observation, producing studentized residuals $E_1^*, E_2^*, \ldots, E_n^*$.

---

[8]Here, as elsewhere in statistics, terminology is not wholly standard: E_i^* is sometimes called a *deleted studentized residual*, an *externally studentized residual*, or even a standardized residual; likewise, E_i' is sometimes called an *internally studentized residual*, or simply a studentized residual. It is therefore helpful, especially in small samples, to determine exactly what is being calculated by a computer program.

[9]It is not necessary *literally* to perform n auxiliary regressions. Equation 11.3, for example, permits the computation of studentized residuals with little effort.

Usually, our interest then focuses on the largest absolute E_i^*, denoted E_{max}^*. Because we have picked the biggest of n test statistics, however, it is not legitimate simply to use t_{n-k-2} to find a p-value for E_{max}^*: For example, even if our model is wholly adequate, and disregarding for the moment the dependence among the E_i^*s, we would expect to obtain about 5% of E_i^*s beyond $t_{.025} \approx \pm 2$, about 1% beyond $t_{.005} \approx \pm 2.6$, and so forth.

One solution to this problem of simultaneous inference is to perform a *Bonferroni adjustment* to the p-value for the *largest absolute E_i^**.[10] The Bonferroni test requires either a special t-table or, even more conveniently, a computer program that returns accurate p-values for values of t far into the tail of the t-distribution. In the latter event, suppose that $p' = Pr(t_{n-k-2} > E_{max}^*)$. Then the Bonferroni p-value for testing the statistical significance of E_{max}^* is $p = 2np'$. The factor 2 reflects the two-tail character of the test: We want to detect large negative as well as large positive outliers.

Beckman and Cook (1983) show that the Bonferroni adjustment is usually exact in testing the largest studentized residual. Note that a much larger E_{max}^* is required for a statistically significant result than would be the case for an ordinary individual t-test.

In Davis's regression of reported weight on measured weight, the largest studentized residual by far belongs to the incorrectly coded 12th observation, with $E_{12}^* = -24.3$. Here, $n - k - 2 = 183 - 3 - 2 = 178$, and $Pr(t_{178} > 24.3) \approx 10^{-58}$. The Bonferroni p-value for the outlier test is thus $p \approx 2 \times 183 \times 10^{-58} \approx 4 \times 10^{-56}$, an unambiguous result.

Put alternatively, the 5% critical value for E_{max}^* in this regression is the value of t_{178} with probability $.025/183 = 0.0001366$ to the right. That is, $E_{max}^* = t_{178, .0001366} = 3.714$; this critical value contrasts with $t_{178, .025} = 1.973$, which would be appropriate for testing an *individual* studentized residual identified in advance of inspecting the data.

For Duncan's occupational prestige regression, the largest studentized residual belongs to *ministers*, with $E_{minister}^* = 3.135$. The associated Bonferroni p-value is $2 \times 45 \times Pr(t_{45-2-2} > 3.135) = .143$, showing that it is not terribly unusual to observe a studentized residual this big in a sample of 45 observations.

11.3.2 Anscombe's Insurance Analogy

Thus far, I have treated the identification (and, implicitly, the potential correction, removal, or accommodation) of outliers as a hypothesis-testing problem. Although this is by far the most common procedure in practice, a more reasonable (if subtle) general approach is to assess the potential costs and benefits for estimation of discarding an unusual observation.

Imagine, for the moment, that the observation with the largest E_i^* is simply an unusual data point but one generated by the assumed statistical model:

$$Y_i = \alpha + \beta_1 X_{i1} + \cdots + \beta_k X_{ik} + \varepsilon_i$$

with independent errors ε_i that are each distributed as $N(0, \sigma_\varepsilon^2)$. To discard an observation under these circumstances would *decrease* the efficiency of estimation, because when the model— including the assumption of normality—is correct, the least-squares estimators are maximally efficient among all unbiased estimators of the regression coefficients.

If, however, the observation in question does not belong with the rest (e.g., because the mean-shift model applies), then to eliminate it may make estimation more efficient. Anscombe (1960) developed this insight by drawing an analogy to insurance: To obtain *protection* against "bad"

---

[10]See Appendix D on probability and estimation for a discussion of Bonferroni inequalities and their role in simultaneous inference. A graphical alternative to testing for outliers is to construct a quantile-comparison plot for the studentized residuals, comparing the sample distribution of these quantities with the t-distribution for $n - k - 2$ degrees of freedom. See the discussion of non-normality in the next chapter.

data, one purchases a *policy* of outlier rejection, a policy paid for by a small *premium* in efficiency when the policy inadvertently rejects "good" data.[11]

Let q denote the desired premium, say 0.05—that is, a 5% increase in estimator mean-squared error if the model holds for all of the data. Let z represent the unit-normal deviate corresponding to a tail probability of $q(n - k - 1)/n$. Following the procedure derived by Anscombe and Tukey (1963), compute $m = 1.4 + 0.85z$ and then find

$$E'_q = m \left(1 - \frac{m^2 - 2}{4(n - k - 1)} \right) \sqrt{\frac{n - k - 1}{n}} \qquad (11.4)$$

The largest absolute *standardized* residual can be compared with E'_q to determine whether the corresponding observation should be rejected as an outlier. This cutoff can be translated to the studentized-residual scale using Equation 11.3:

$$E^*_q = E'_q \sqrt{\frac{n - k - 2}{n - k - 1 - E'^2_q}} \qquad (11.5)$$

In a real application, of course, we should inquire about discrepant observations rather than simply throwing them away.[12]

For example, for Davis's regression of reported on measured weight, $n = 183$ and $k = 3$; so, for the premium $q = 0.05$, we have

$$\frac{q(n - k - 1)}{n} = \frac{0.05(183 - 3 - 1)}{183} = 0.0489$$

From the quantile function of the standard-normal distribution, $z = 1.66$, from which $m = 1.4 + 0.85 \times 1.66 = 2.81$. Then, using Equation 11.4, $E'_q = 2.76$, and using Equation 11.5, $E^*_q = 2.81$. Because $E^*_{max} = |E^*_{12}| = 24.3$ is much larger than E^*_q, the 12th observation is identified as an outlier.

In Duncan's occupational prestige regression, $n = 45$ and $k = 2$. Thus, with premium $q = 0.05$,

$$\frac{q(n - k - 1)}{n} = \frac{0.05(45 - 2 - 1)}{45} = 0.0467$$

The corresponding unit-normal deviate is $z = 1.68$, yielding $m = 1.4 + 0.85 \times 1.68 = 2.83$, $E'_q = 2.63$, and $E^*_q = 2.85 < |E^*_{minister}| = 3.135$, suggesting that *ministers* be rejected as an outlier.

A regression *outlier* is an observation with an unusual response-variable value given its combination of explanatory-variable values. The studentized residuals E^*_i can be used to identify outliers, through graphical examination, a Bonferroni test for the largest absolute E^*_i, or Anscombe's insurance analogy. If the model is correct (and there are no true outliers), then each studentized residual follows a t-distribution with $n - k - 2$ degrees of freedom.

---

[11] An alternative is to employ a robust estimator, which is somewhat less efficient than least squares when the model is correct but much more efficient when outliers are present. See Chapter 19.

[12] See the discussion in Section 11.7.

11.4 Measuring Influence

As noted previously, influence on the regression coefficients combines leverage and discrepancy. The most direct measure of influence simply expresses the impact on each coefficient of deleting each observation in turn:

$$D_{ij} = B_j - B_{j(-i)} \quad \text{for } i = 1, \ldots, n \text{ and } j = 0, 1, \ldots, k$$

where the B_j are the least-squares coefficients calculated for all the data, and the $B_{j(-i)}$ are the least-squares coefficients calculated with the ith observation omitted. (So as not to complicate the notation here, I denote the least-squares intercept A as B_0.) To assist in interpretation, it is useful to scale the D_{ij} by (deleted) coefficient standard errors:

$$D_{ij}^* = \frac{D_{ij}}{\text{SE}_{(-i)}(B_j)}$$

Following Belsley, Kuh, and Welsch (1980), the D_{ij} are often termed DFBETA$_{ij}$, and the D_{ij}^* are called DFBETAS$_{ij}$.

   One problem associated with using the D_{ij} or the D_{ij}^* is their large number—$n(k + 1)$ of each. Of course, these values can be more quickly and effectively examined graphically than in numerical tables. We can, for example, construct an index plot of the D_{ij}^*s for each coefficient, $j = 0, 1, \ldots, k$ (see below for an example). A more informative, if more complex, alternative is to construct a scatterplot matrix of the D_{ij}^* with index plots (or some other univariate display) on the diagonal.[13] Nevertheless, it is useful to have a single summary index of the influence of each observation on the least-squares fit.

   Cook (1977) has proposed measuring the "distance" between the B_j and the corresponding $B_{j(-i)}$ by calculating the F-statistic for the "hypothesis" that $\beta_j = B_{j(-i)}$, for $j = 0, 1, \ldots, k$. This statistic is recalculated for each observation $i = 1, \ldots, n$. The resulting values should not literally be interpreted as F-tests—Cook's approach merely exploits an *analogy* to testing to produce a measure of distance that is independent of the scales of the X variables. Cook's statistic can be written (and simply calculated) as

$$D_i = \frac{E_i'^2}{k + 1} \times \frac{h_i}{1 - h_i}$$

In effect, the first term in the formula for Cook's D is a measure of discrepancy, and the second is a measure of leverage. We look for values of D_i that stand out from the rest.

> Observations that combine high leverage with a large studentized residual exert substantial *influence* on the regression coefficients. Cook's D statistic provides a summary index of influence on the coefficients.

Belsley et al. (1980) have suggested the very similar measure[14]

$$\text{DFFITS}_i = E_i^* \sqrt{\frac{h_i}{1 - h_i}}$$

Except for unusual data configurations, Cook's $D_i \approx \text{DFFITS}_i^2 / (k + 1)$.

---

[13]This interesting display was suggested to me by Michael Friendly of York University.
[14]Other global measures of influence are available; see Chatterjee and Hadi (1988, chap. 4) for a comparative treatment.

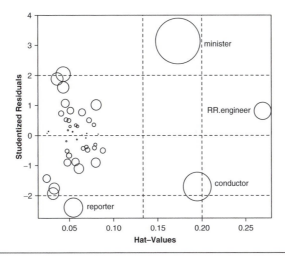

Figure 11.5 "Bubble plot" of Cook's Ds, studentized residuals, and hat-values, for Duncan's regression of occupational prestige on income and education. Each point is plotted as a circle with area proportional to D. Horizontal reference lines are drawn at studentized residuals of 0 and ± 2; vertical reference lines are drawn at hat-values of $2\bar{h}$ and $3\bar{h}$ (see Section 11.5 on numerical cutoffs for diagnostic statistics). Several observations are identified on the plot: *Ministers* and *conductors* have large hat-values and relatively large residuals; *reporters* have a relatively large negative residual but a small hat-value; *railroad engineers* have a large hat-value but a small residual.

Because all the deletion statistics depend on the hat-values and residuals, a graphical alternative to either of these general influence measures is to plot the E_i^* against the h_i and to look for observations for which both are big. A slightly more sophisticated (and more informative) version of this plot displays circles of area proportional to Cook's D instead of points (see Figure 11.5). We can follow up by examining the D_{ij} or D_{ij}^* for the observations with the largest few D_i, $|\text{DFFITS}_i|$, or a combination of large h_i and $|E_i^*|$.

For Davis's regression of reported weight on measured weight, all the indices of influence point to the obviously discrepant 12th observation:

$$\text{Cook's } D_{12} = 85.9 \text{ (next largest, } D_{21} = 0.065)$$
$$\text{DFFITS}_{12} = -38.4 \text{ (next largest, } \text{DFFITS}_{50} = 0.512)$$
$$\text{DFBETAS}_{0, 12} = \text{DFBETAS}_{1, 12} = 0$$
$$\text{DFBETAS}_{2, 12} = 20.0, \text{DFBETAS}_{3, 12} = -24.8$$

Note that the outlying observation 12, which is for a female subject, has no impact on the male intercept B_0 (i.e., A) and slope B_1, but does exert considerable influence on the dummy-variable coefficient B_2 and the interaction coefficient B_3.

Turning our attention to Duncan's occupational prestige regression, Figure 11.5 shows a "bubble plot" of studentized residuals by hat-values, with the areas of the circles proportional to the Cook's distances of the observations. Several noteworthy observations are identified on the plot: *ministers* and *conductors*, who combine relatively high leverage with relatively large studentized residuals; *railroad engineers*, who have very high leverage but a small studentized residual; and *reporters*, who have a relatively large (negative) residual but lower leverage. Index plots of D_{ij}^* for the income and education coefficients in the regression appear in Figure 11.6: *Ministers* and

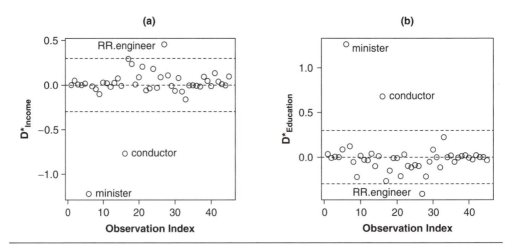

Figure 11.6 Index plots of D_{ij}^* for the (a) income and (b) education coefficients in Duncan's occupational prestige regression. The horizontal lines in the graphs are drawn at $D^* = 0$ and the rule-of-thumb cutoffs $\pm 2/\sqrt{n}$ (see Section 11.5).The observations *ministers* and *conductors* stand out. *Railroad engineers* are beyond the cutoffs for both coefficients but do not stand out from the other observations to the same degree.

conductors serve to decrease the income coefficient and increase the education coefficient—in the case of *ministers* by more than one standard error.

11.4.1 Influence on Standard Errors

In developing the concept of influence in regression, I have focused on changes in regression coefficients. Other regression outputs are also subject to influence, however. One important regression output is the set of coefficient sampling variances and covariances, which capture the precision of estimation in regression.

Recall, for example, Figure 11.1(c) on page 242, in which a high-leverage observation exerts no influence on the regression coefficients because it is in line with the rest of the data. Recall, as well, that the standard error of the least-squares slope in simple regression is[15]

$$\text{SE}(B) = \frac{S_E}{\sqrt{\sum (X_i - \overline{X})^2}}$$

By increasing the variance of X, therefore, a high-leverage but in-line observation serves to decrease $\text{SE}(B)$ even though it does not influence the regression coefficients A and B. Depending on the context, such an observation may be considered beneficial—because it increases the precision of estimation—or it may cause us to exaggerate our confidence in the estimate B.

In multiple regression, we can examine the impact of deleting each observation in turn on the size of the joint confidence region for the regression coefficients.[16] The size of the joint confidence region is analogous to the length of a confidence interval for an individual regression coefficient, which, in turn, is proportional to the standard error of the coefficient. The squared length of a confidence interval is, therefore, proportional to the sampling variance of the coefficient, and,

---

[15] See Chapter 6.
[16] See Section 9.4.4 for a discussion of joint confidence regions.

analogously, the squared size of a joint confidence region is proportional to the "generalized variance" of a set of coefficients.

An influence measure proposed by Belsley et al. (1980) closely approximates the squared ratio of volumes of the deleted and full-data confidence regions for the regression coefficients:[17]

$$\text{COVRATIO}_i = \frac{1}{(1 - h_i) \left(\dfrac{n - k - 2 + E_i^{*2}}{n - k - 1} \right)^{k+1}}$$

Observations that *increase* the precision of estimation have values of COVRATIO that are larger than 1; those that *decrease* the precision of estimation have values smaller than 1. Look for values of COVRATIO, therefore, that differ considerably from 1.

As was true of measures of influence on the regression coefficients, both the hat-value and the (studentized) residual figure in COVRATIO. A large hat-value produces a large COVRATIO, however, even when—indeed, especially when—the studentized residual is small because a high-leverage in-line observation improves the precision of estimation. In contrast, a discrepant, low-leverage observation might not change the coefficients much, but it decreases the precision of estimation by increasing the estimated error variance; such an observation, with small h_i and large E_i^*, produces a COVRATIO$_i$ well below 1.

For Davis's regression of reported weight on measured weight, sex, and their interaction, by far the most extreme value is COVRATIO$_{12} = 0.0103$. The 12th observation, therefore, *decreases* the precision of estimation by a factor of $1/0.0103 \approx 100$. In this instance, a very large leverage, $h_{12} = 0.714$, is more than offset by a massive residual, $E_{12}^* = -24.3$.

In Duncan's occupational prestige regression, the smallest and largest values are COVRATIO$_{\text{minister}} = 0.682$ and COVRATIO$_{\text{railroad engineer}} = 1.402$. Thus, the discrepant, relatively high-leverage observation *minister* decreases the precision of estimation, while the in-line, high-leverage observation *railroad engineer* increases it.

11.4.2   Influence on Collinearity

Other characteristics of a regression analysis can also be influenced by individual observations, including the degree of collinearity among the explanatory variables.[18] I will not address this issue in any detail, but the following points may prove helpful:[19]

- Influence on collinearity is one of the factors reflected in influence on coefficient standard errors. Measures such as COVRATIO, however, also reflect influence on the error variance and on the variation of the Xs. Moreover, COVRATIO and similar measures examine the sampling variances and covariances of *all* the regression coefficients, including the regression constant, while a consideration of collinearity generally excludes the constant. Nevertheless, our concern for collinearity reflects its impact on the precision of estimation, which is precisely what is addressed by COVRATIO.
- Collinearity-influential points are those that either induce or weaken correlations among the Xs. Such points usually—but not always—have large hat-values. Conversely, points with large hat-values often influence collinearity.

---

[17] Alternative, similar measures have been suggested by several authors. Chatterjee and Hadi (1988, Chapter 4) provide a comparative discussion.

[18] See Chapter 13 for a general treatment of collinearity.

[19] See Chatterjee and Hadi (1988, chaps. 4 and 5) for more information about influence on collinearity.

- Individual points that induce collinearity are obviously problematic. More subtly, points that weaken collinearity also merit examination because they may cause us to be overly confident in our results.
- It is frequently possible to detect collinearity-influential points by plotting explanatory variables against each other, as in a scatterplot matrix or a three-dimensional rotating plot. This approach may fail, however, if the collinear relations in question involve more than two or three explanatory variables at a time.

11.5   Numerical Cutoffs for Diagnostic Statistics

I have deliberately refrained from suggesting specific numerical criteria for identifying noteworthy observations on the basis of measures of leverage and influence: I believe that it is generally more effective to examine the distributions of these quantities directly to locate unusual values. For studentized residuals, the hypothesis-testing and insurance approaches provide numerical cutoffs, but even these criteria are no substitute for graphical examination of the residuals.

Still, numerical cutoffs can be of some use, as long as they are not given too much weight and especially when they are employed to enhance graphical displays: A line can be drawn on a graph at the value of a numerical cutoff, and observations that exceed the cutoff can be identified individually.[20]

Cutoffs for a diagnostic statistic may be derived from statistical theory, or they may result from examination of the sample distribution of the statistic. Cutoffs may be absolute, or they may be adjusted for sample size.[21] For some diagnostic statistics, such as measures of influence, absolute cutoffs are unlikely to identify noteworthy observations in large samples. This characteristic reflects the ability of large samples to absorb discrepant data without markedly changing the results, but it is still often of interest to identify *relatively* influential points, even if no observation has strong *absolute* influence, because unusual data may prove to be substantively interesting.

The cutoffs presented below are, as explained briefly here, derived from statistical theory. An alternative and universally applicable data-based criterion is simply to examine the most extreme (e.g., 5% of) values of a diagnostic statistic.

11.5.1   Hat-Values

Belsley et al. (1980) suggest that hat-values exceeding about twice the average $\overline{h} = (k + 1)/n$ are noteworthy. This size-adjusted cutoff was derived as an approximation identifying the most extreme 5% of cases when the Xs are multivariate normal, and the number of regressors k and degrees of freedom for error $n - k - 1$ are relatively large. The cutoff is nevertheless recommended by these authors as a rough general guide even when the regressors are not normally distributed. In small samples, using $2 \times \overline{h}$ tends to nominate too many points for examination, and $3 \times \overline{h}$ can be used instead.[22]

11.5.2   Studentized Residuals

Beyond the issues of "statistical significance" and estimator robustness and efficiency discussed above, it sometimes helps to call attention to residuals that are relatively large. Recall that, under

---

[20]See, for example, Figures 11.4 (page 246) and 11.5 (page 251).

[21]See Belsley et al. (1980, Chapter 2) for further discussion of these distinctions.

[22]See Chatterjee and Hadi (1988, Chapter 4) for a discussion of alternative cutoffs for hat-values.

ideal conditions, about 5% of studentized residuals are outside the range $|E_i^*| \leq 2$. It is, therefore, reasonable, for example, to draw lines at ± 2 on a display of studentized residuals to draw attention to observations outside this range.

11.5.3 Measures of Influence

Many cutoffs have been suggested for various measures of influence. A few are presented here:

- *Standardized change in regression coefficients.* The D_{ij}^* are scaled by standard errors, and, consequently, $|D_{ij}^*| > 1$ or 2 suggests itself as an absolute cutoff. As explained above, however, this criterion is unlikely to nominate observations in large samples. Belsley et al. (1980) propose the size-adjusted cutoff $2/\sqrt{n}$ for identifying noteworthy D_{ij}^*'s.
- *Cook's D and DFFITS.* Several numerical cutoffs have been recommended for Cook's D and for DFFITS—exploiting the analogy between D and an F-statistic, for example. Chatterjee and Hadi (1988) suggest the size-adjusted cutoff[23]

$$|\text{DFFITS}_i| > 2\sqrt{\frac{k+1}{n-k-1}}$$

Because of the approximate relationship between DFFITS and Cook's D, it is simple to translate this criterion into

$$D_i > \frac{4}{n-k-1}$$

Absolute cutoffs for D, such as $D_i > 1$, risk missing relatively influential data.
- *COVRATIO.* Belsley et al. (1980) suggest the size-adjusted cutoff

$$|\text{COVRATIO}_i - 1| > \frac{3(k+1)}{n}$$

11.6 Joint Influence

As illustrated in Figure 11.7, subsets of observations can be *jointly influential* or can offset each other's influence. *Influential subsets* or *multiple outliers* can often be identified by applying single-observation diagnostics, such as Cook's D and studentized residuals, sequentially. It can be important, however, to refit the model after deleting each point because the presence of a single influential value can dramatically affect the fit at other points. Still, the sequential approach is not always successful.

11.6.1 Added-Variable Plots

Although it is possible to generalize deletion statistics to subsets of several points, the very large number of subsets usually renders this approach impractical.[24] An attractive alternative is

---

[23] Also see Cook (1977), Belsley et al. (1980), and Velleman and Welsch (1981).

[24]*Cook and Weisberg (1980), for example, extend the D statistic to a subset of p observations indexed by the vector subscript $\mathbf{i} = (i_1, i_2, \ldots, i_p)'$:

$$D_{\mathbf{i}} = \frac{\mathbf{d_i'}(\mathbf{X'X})\mathbf{d_i}}{(k+1)S_E^2}$$

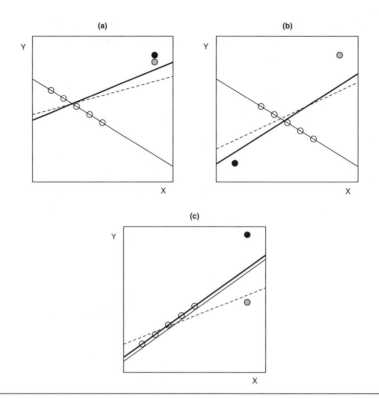

Figure 11.7   Jointly influential data in simple regression. In each graph, the heavier solid line gives
the least-squares regression for all of the data; the broken line gives the regression
with the black circle deleted; and the lighter solid line gives the regression with both
the black circle and the gray circle deleted. (a) Jointly influential observations located
close to one another: Deletion of both observations has a much greater impact than
deletion of only one. (b) Jointly influential observations located on opposite sides of
the data. (c) Observations that offset one another: The regression with both
observations deleted is the same as for the whole data set (the two lines are separated
slightly for visual effect).

to employ graphical methods, and an especially useful influence graph is the *added-variable plot*
(also called a *partial-regression plot* or a *partial-regression leverage plot*).

Let $Y_i^{(1)}$ represent the residuals from the least-squares regression of Y on all the Xs with the
exception of X_1—that is, the residuals from the fitted regression equation

$$Y_i = A^{(1)} + B_2^{(1)} X_{i2} + \cdots + B_k^{(1)} X_{ik} + Y_i^{(1)}$$

The parenthetical superscript (1) indicates the omission of X_1 from the right-hand side of the
regression equation. Likewise, $X_i^{(1)}$ is the residual from the least-squares regression of X_1 on all
the other Xs:

$$X_{i1} = C^{(1)} + D_2^{(1)} X_{i2} + \cdots + D_k^{(1)} X_{ik} + X_i^{(1)}$$

where $\mathbf{d_i} = \mathbf{b} - \mathbf{b_{(-i)}}$ gives the impact on the regression coefficients of deleting the subset $\mathbf{i}$. See Belsley et al. (1980,
chap. 2) and Chatterjee and Hadi (1988) for further discussions of deletion diagnostics based on subsets of observations.
There are, however, $n!/[p!(n-p)!]$ subsets of size p—typically a prohibitively large number, even for modest values of p.

This notation emphasizes the interpretation of the residuals $Y^{(1)}$ and $X^{(1)}$ as the parts of Y and X_1 that remain when the effects of $X_2, \ldots, X_k$ are "removed."

The residuals $Y^{(1)}$ and $X^{(1)}$ have the following interesting properties:

1. The slope from the least-squares regression of $Y^{(1)}$ on $X^{(1)}$ is simply the least-squares slope B_1 from the *full* multiple regression.

2. The residuals from the simple regression of $Y^{(1)}$ on $X^{(1)}$ are the same as those from the full regression; that is,

$$Y_i^{(1)} = B_1 X_i^{(1)} + E_i \tag{11.6}$$

   No constant is required here because both $Y^{(1)}$ and $X^{(1)}$ are least-squares residuals and therefore have means of 0, forcing the regression through the origin.

3. The variation of $X^{(1)}$ is the *conditional variation* of X_1 holding the other Xs constant and, as a consequence, the standard error of B_1 in the auxiliary simple regression (Equation 11.6),

$$\mathrm{SE}(B_1) = \frac{S_E}{\sqrt{\sum X_i^{(1)2}}}$$

   is the same as the *multiple-regression* standard error of B_1.[25] Unless X_1 is uncorrelated with the other Xs, its conditional variation is smaller than its *marginal variation* $\sum (X_{i1} - \overline{X}_1)^2$—much smaller, if X_1 is strongly collinear with the other Xs.

Plotting $Y^{(1)}$ against $X^{(1)}$ permits us to examine the leverage and influence of the observations on B_1. Because of properties 1–3, this plot also provides a visual impression of the precision of the estimate B_1. Similar added-variable plots can be constructed for the other regressors:[26]

$$\text{Plot } Y^{(j)} \text{ versus } X^{(j)} \text{ for each } j = 1, \ldots, k$$

> Subsets of observations can be jointly influential. Added-variable plots are useful for detecting joint influence on the regression coefficients. The added-variable plot for the regressor X_j is formed using the residuals from the least-squares regressions of X_j and Y on all the other Xs.

Illustrative added-variable plots are shown in Figure 11.8, using data from Duncan's regression of occupational prestige on the income and educational levels of 45 U.S. occupations. Recall (from Chapter 5) that Duncan's regression yields the following least-squares fit:

$$\widehat{\text{Prestige}} = -6.06 + 0.599 \times \text{Income} + 0.546 \times \text{Education}$$
$$\qquad\quad (4.27) \quad (0.120) \qquad\qquad\quad (0.098)$$
$$R^2 = 0.83 \quad S_E = 13.4$$

---

[25] There is slight slippage here with respect to the degrees of freedom for error: S_E is from the multiple regression, with $n - k - 1$ degrees of freedom for error. We need not subtract the mean of $X_i^{(1)}$ to calculate the standard error of the slope because the mean of these residuals is already 0.

[26] We can also construct an added-variable plot for the intercept A, by regressing the "constant regressor" $X_0 = 1$ and Y on X_1 through X_k, with no constant in these regression equations.

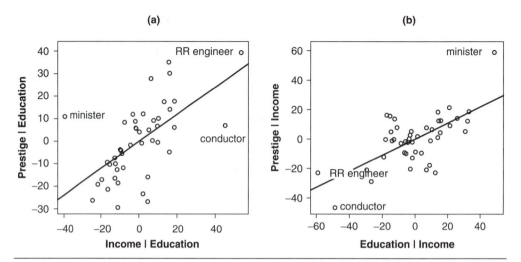

Figure 11.8   Added-variable plots for Duncan's regression of occupational prestige on the
(a) income and (b) education levels of 45 U.S. occupations in 1950. Three unusual
observations, *ministers*, *conductors*, and *railroad engineers*, are identified on the
plots. The added-variable plot for the intercept *A* is not shown.

The added-variable plot for income in Figure 11.8(a) reveals three observations that exert substantial leverage on the income coefficient. Two of these observations serve to decrease the income slope: *ministers*, whose income is unusually low given the educational level of the occupation; and *railroad conductors*, whose income is unusually high given education. The third occupation, *railroad engineers*, is above the fitted regression, but is not as discrepant; it, too, has relatively high income given education. Remember that the horizontal variable in this added-variable plot is the residual from the regression of income on education, and thus values far from 0 in this direction are for occupations with incomes that are unusually high or low given their levels of education.

The added-variable plot for education in Figure 11.8(b) shows that the same three observations have relatively high leverage on the education coefficient: *Ministers* and *railroad conductors* tend to increase the education slope, while *railroad engineers* appear to be closer in line with the rest of the data. Recall that our attention was also called to these occupations when we examined the individual-observation diagnostic statistics: hat-values, studentized residuals, Cook's distances, and so on.

Deleting *ministers* and *conductors* produces the fitted regression

$$\widehat{\text{Prestige}} = -6.41 + 0.867 \times \text{Income} + 0.332 \times \text{Education}$$
$$(3.65) \quad (0.122) \quad\quad\quad (0.099)$$
$$R^2 = 0.88 \quad S_E = 11.4$$

which, as expected from the added-variable plots, has a larger income slope and smaller education slope than the original regression. The coefficient standard errors are likely optimistic, however, because relative outliers have been trimmed away. Deleting *railroad engineers*, along with *ministers* and *conductors*, further increases the income slope and decreases the education slope, but the change is not dramatic: $B_{\text{Income}} = 0.931$, $B_{\text{Education}} = 0.285$.

Added-variable plots can be straightforwardly extended to pairs of regressors in a model with more than two Xs. We can, for example, regress each of X_1, X_2, and Y on the remaining regressors, $X_3, \ldots, X_k$, obtaining residuals $X_{i1}^{(12)}$, $X_{i2}^{(12)}$, and $Y_i^{(12)}$. We then plot $Y^{(12)}$ against $X_1^{(12)}$ and

$X_2^{(12)}$ to produce a dynamic three-dimensional scatterplot on which the partial-regression plane can be displayed.[27]

11.6.2 Forward Search

Atkinson and Riani (2000) suggest a fundamentally different approach, termed a *forward search*, for locating multiple unusual observations: They begin by fitting a regression model to a small subset of the data that is almost surely free of outliers and then proceed to add observations one at a time to this subset, refitting the model at each step and monitoring regression outputs such as coefficients, *t*-statistics, residuals, hat-values, and Cook's distances.

To implement the forward search, Atkinson and Riani begin with a robust-regression fit to the data, employing a method that is highly resistant to outliers.[28] Residuals from this resistant fit are computed, and (in a model with $k+1$ regression coefficients) the $k+1$ observations with the smallest residuals are selected. The least-squares regression coefficients are then computed for the initial subset of observations, and residuals from this least-squares fit are computed for all n observations. Because there are equal numbers of observations and parameters at the first step, the residuals for the $k+1$ observations employed to obtain the initial fit are necessarily 0.[29] The additional observation with the next smallest residual is added to the subset, the least-squares regression coefficients are recomputed for the resulting $k+2$ observations, and new residuals are found from the updated fit. Suppose, at any step, that there are m observations in the subset used to compute the current fit: The $m+1$ observations used in the subsequent step are those with the smallest residuals from the current fit; usually, but not necessarily, these will include the m observations used to determine the current least-squares fit.

Figure 11.9 applies the forward search to Duncan's occupational prestige regression, monitoring the trajectory of the two slope coefficients as observations are added to an initial subset of $k+1 = 3$ occupations. It is clear from this graph that although the income and education coefficients are nearly identical to one another in the least-squares fit to all 45 observations (at the far right),[30] this result depends on the presence of just two observations, which enter in the last two steps of the forward search. It should come as no surprise that these observations are *conductors* and *ministers*. In this instance, therefore, the jointly influential observations were also revealed by more conventional, and less computationally intensive, methods.

> Atkinson and Riani's forward search adds observations successively to an initial small subset that is almost surely uncontaminated by unusual data. By monitoring outputs such as regression coefficients, this strategy can reveal unusual groups of observations that are missed by more conventional methods.

---

[27] See Cook and Weisberg (1989) for a discussion of three-dimensional added-variable plots. An alternative, two-dimensional extension of added-variable plots to subsets of coefficients is described in Section 11.8.4.

[28] The method that they employ, *least median of squares* (or *LMS*) regression, is similar in its properties to *least-trimmed-squares (LTS)* regression, which is described in Chapter 19 on robust regression.

[29] Care must be taken that the initial subset of $k+1$ observations is not perfectly collinear.

[30] Because both income and education are percentages (of, recall, relatively high-income earners and high-school graduates), it makes at least superficial sense to compare their coefficients in this manner.

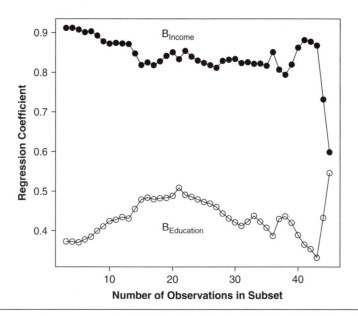

Figure 11.9   Forward-search trajectories of the coefficients for income and education in Duncan's occupational prestige regression.

11.7   Should Unusual Data Be Discarded?

The discussion thus far in this chapter has implicitly assumed that outlying and influential data are simply discarded. Although problematic data should not be ignored, they also should not be deleted automatically and without reflection:

- It is important to investigate *why* an observation is unusual. Truly "bad" data (e.g., an error in data entry as in Davis's regression) can often be corrected or, if correction is not possible, thrown away. When a discrepant data point is correct, we may be able to understand why the observation is unusual. For Duncan's regression, for example, it makes sense that ministers enjoy prestige not accounted for by the income and educational levels of the occupation. In a case like this, we may choose to deal separately with an outlying observation.
- Alternatively, outliers or influential data may motivate model respecification. For example, the pattern of outlying data may suggest the introduction of additional explanatory variables. If, in Duncan's regression, we can identify a variable that produces the unusually high prestige of ministers (net of their income and education), and if we can measure that variable for other observations, then the variable could be added to the regression. In some instances, transformation of the response variable or of an explanatory variable may draw apparent outliers toward the rest of the data, by rendering the error distribution more symmetric or by eliminating nonlinearity. We must, however, be careful to avoid "overfitting" the data—permitting a small portion of the data to determine the form of the model.[31]
- Except in clear-cut cases, we are justifiably reluctant to delete observations or to respecify the model to accommodate unusual data. Some researchers reasonably adopt alternative estimation strategies, such as robust regression, which continuously down-weights outlying data rather than simply discarding them. Because these methods assign zero or very small

---

[31] See Chapter 22.

weight to highly discrepant data, however, the result is generally not very different from careful application of least squares, and, indeed, robust-regression weights can be used to identify outliers.[32]

- Finally, in large samples, unusual data substantially alter the results only in extreme instances. Identifying unusual observations in a large sample, therefore, should be regarded more as an opportunity to learn something about the data not captured by the model that we have fit, rather than as an occasion to re-estimate the model with the unusual observations removed.

Outlying and influential data should not be ignored, but they also should not simply be deleted without investigation. "Bad" data can often be corrected. "Good" observations that are unusual may provide insight into the structure of the data and may motivate respecification of the statistical model used to summarize the data.

11.8 Some Statistical Details*

11.8.1 Hat-Values and the Hat-Matrix

Recall, from Chapter 9, the matrix form of the general linear model, $\mathbf{y} = \mathbf{X}\boldsymbol{\beta} + \boldsymbol{\varepsilon}$. Recall, as well, that the fitted model is given by $\mathbf{y} = \mathbf{X}\mathbf{b} + \mathbf{e}$, in which the vector of least-squares estimates is $\mathbf{b} = (\mathbf{X}'\mathbf{X})^{-1}\mathbf{X}'\mathbf{y}$.

The least-squares fitted values are therefore a linear function of the observed response-variable values:

$$\widehat{\mathbf{y}} = \mathbf{X}\mathbf{b} = \mathbf{X}(\mathbf{X}'\mathbf{X})^{-1}\mathbf{X}'\mathbf{y} = \mathbf{H}\mathbf{y}$$

Here, $\mathbf{H} = \mathbf{X}(\mathbf{X}'\mathbf{X})^{-1}\mathbf{X}'$ is the *hat-matrix*, so named because it transforms $\mathbf{y}$ into $\widehat{\mathbf{y}}$. The hat-matrix is symmetric ($\mathbf{H} = \mathbf{H}'$) and idempotent ($\mathbf{H}^2 = \mathbf{H}$), as can easily be verified.[33] Consequently, the diagonal entries of the hat-matrix $h_i \equiv h_{ii}$, which we called the *hat-values*, are

$$h_i \equiv \mathbf{h}_i'\mathbf{h}_i = \sum_{j=1}^{n} h_{ij}^2 = h_i^2 + \sum_{j \neq i} h_{ij}^2 \tag{11.7}$$

where (because of symmetry) the elements of $\mathbf{h}_i$ comprise both the ith row and the ith column of $\mathbf{H}$.

Equation 11.7 implies that $0 \leq h_i \leq 1$. If the model matrix $\mathbf{X}$ includes the constant regressor $\mathbf{1}_n$, then $1/n \leq h_i$. Because $\mathbf{H}$ is a projection matrix,[34] projecting $\mathbf{y}$ orthogonally onto the $(k+1)$-dimensional subspace spanned by the columns of $\mathbf{X}$, it follows that $\sum h_i = k + 1$, and thus $\overline{h} = (k+1)/n$ (as stated in Section 11.2).

I mentioned as well that when there are several explanatory variables in the model, the leverage h_i of the ith observation is directly related to the distance of this observation from the center of the explanatory-variable scatter. To demonstrate this property of the hat-values, it is convenient

---

[32]See Chapter 19 on robust regression.
[33]See Exercise 11.2.
[34]See Chapter 10 for the vector geometry of linear models.

to rewrite the fitted model with all variables in mean-deviation form: $\mathbf{y}^* = \mathbf{X}^*\mathbf{b}_1 + \mathbf{e}$, where $\mathbf{y}^* \equiv \{Y_i - \overline{Y}\}$ is the "centered" response-variable vector; $\mathbf{X}^* \equiv \{X_{ij} - \overline{X}_j\}$ contains the centered explanatory variables, but no constant regressor, which is no longer required; and $\mathbf{b}_1$ is the vector of least-squares slopes (suppressing the regression intercept). Then the hat-value for the ith observation is

$$h_i^* = \mathbf{h}_i^{*\prime}\mathbf{h}_i^* = \mathbf{x}_i^{*\prime}(\mathbf{X}^{*\prime}\mathbf{X}^*)^{-1}\mathbf{x}_i^* = h_i - \frac{1}{n}$$

where $\mathbf{x}_i^{*\prime} = [X_{i1} - \overline{X}_1, \ldots, X_{ik} - \overline{X}_k]$ is the ith row of $\mathbf{X}^*$ (and $\mathbf{x}_i^*$ is the ith row of $\mathbf{X}^*$ written as a column vector).

As Weisberg (1985, p. 112) has pointed out, $(n-1)h_i^*$ is the *generalized* or *Mahalanobis distance* between $\mathbf{x}_i'$ and $\overline{\mathbf{x}}'$, where $\overline{\mathbf{x}}' = [\overline{X}_1, \ldots, \overline{X}_k]$ is the mean vector or *centroid* of the explanatory variables. The Mahalanobis distances, and hence the hat-values, do not change if the explanatory variables are rescaled. Indeed, the Mahalanobis distances and hat-values are invariant with respect to any nonsingular linear transformation of $\mathbf{X}$.

11.8.2   The Distribution of the Least-Squares Residuals

The least-squares residuals are given by

$$\begin{aligned}
\mathbf{e} &= \mathbf{y} - \widehat{\mathbf{y}} \\
&= (\mathbf{X}\beta + \varepsilon) - \mathbf{X}(\mathbf{X}'\mathbf{X})^{-1}\mathbf{X}'(\mathbf{X}\beta + \varepsilon) \\
&= (\mathbf{I} - \mathbf{H})\varepsilon
\end{aligned}$$

Thus,

$$E(\mathbf{e}) = (\mathbf{I} - \mathbf{H})E(\varepsilon) = (\mathbf{I} - \mathbf{H})\mathbf{0} = \mathbf{0}$$

and

$$V(\mathbf{e}) = (\mathbf{I} - \mathbf{H})V(\mathbf{e})(\mathbf{I} - \mathbf{H})' = \sigma_\varepsilon^2(\mathbf{I} - \mathbf{H})$$

because $\mathbf{I} - \mathbf{H}$, like $\mathbf{H}$ itself, is symmetric and idempotent. The matrix $\mathbf{I} - \mathbf{H}$ is not diagonal, and therefore the residuals are generally correlated, even when the errors are (as assumed here) independent. The diagonal entries of $\mathbf{I} - \mathbf{H}$ generally differ from one another, and so the residuals generally have different variances (as stated in Section 11.3):[35] $V(E_i) = \sigma_\varepsilon^2(1 - h_i)$.

11.8.3   Deletion Diagnostics

Let $\mathbf{b}_{(-i)}$ denote the vector of least-squares regression coefficients calculated with the ith observation omitted. Then $\mathbf{d}_i \equiv \mathbf{b} - \mathbf{b}_{(-i)}$ represents the influence of observation i on the regression coefficients. The influence vector $\mathbf{d}_i$ can be calculated efficiently as[36]

$$\mathbf{d}_i = (\mathbf{X}'\mathbf{X})^{-1}\mathbf{x}_i \frac{E_i}{1 - h_i} \tag{11.8}$$

where $\mathbf{x}_i'$ is the ith row of the model matrix $\mathbf{X}$ (and $\mathbf{x}_i$ is the ith row written as a column vector).

---

[35] Balanced ANOVA models are an exception: Here, all the hat-values are equal. See Exercise 11.3.
[36] See Exercise 11.4.

Cook's D_i is the F-statistic for testing the "hypothesis" that $\beta = \mathbf{b}_{(-i)}$:

$$D_i = \frac{(\mathbf{b} - \mathbf{b}_{(-i)})'\mathbf{X}'\mathbf{X}(\mathbf{b} - \mathbf{b}_{(-i)})}{(k+1)S_E^2}$$

$$= \frac{(\widehat{\mathbf{y}} - \widehat{\mathbf{y}}_{(-i)})'(\widehat{\mathbf{y}} - \widehat{\mathbf{y}}_{(-i)})}{(k+1)S_E^2}$$

An alternative interpretation of D_i, therefore, is that it measures the aggregate influence of observation i on the fitted values $\widehat{\mathbf{y}}$. This is why Belsley et al. (1980) call their similar statistic "DFFITS." Using Equation 11.8,

$$D_i = \frac{E_i^2}{S_E^2(k+1)} \times \frac{h_i}{(1-h_i)^2}$$

$$= \frac{E_i'^2}{k+1} \times \frac{h_i}{1-h_i}$$

which is the formula for Cook's D given in Section 11.4.

11.8.4 Added-Variable Plots and Leverage Plots

In vector form, the fitted multiple-regression model is

$$\mathbf{y} = A\mathbf{1}_n + B_1\mathbf{x}_1 + B_2\mathbf{x}_2 + \cdots + B_k\mathbf{x}_k + \mathbf{e} \qquad (11.9)$$
$$= \widehat{\mathbf{y}} + \mathbf{e}$$

where the fitted-value vector $\widehat{\mathbf{y}}$ is the orthogonal projection of $\mathbf{y}$ onto the subspace spanned by the regressors $\mathbf{1}_n, \mathbf{x}_1, \mathbf{x}_2, \ldots, \mathbf{x}_k$.[37] Let $\mathbf{y}^{(1)}$ and $\mathbf{x}^{(1)}$ be the projections of $\mathbf{y}$ and $\mathbf{x}_1$, respectively, onto the orthogonal complement of the subspace spanned by $\mathbf{1}_n$ and $\mathbf{x}_2, \ldots, \mathbf{x}_k$ (i.e., the residual vectors from the least-squares regressions of Y and X_1 on the other Xs). Then, by the geometry of projections, the orthogonal projection of $\mathbf{y}^{(1)}$ onto $\mathbf{x}^{(1)}$ is $B_1\mathbf{x}^{(1)}$, and $\mathbf{y}^{(1)} - B_1\mathbf{x}^{(1)} = \mathbf{e}$, the residual vector from the overall least-squares regression, given in Equation 11.9.[38]

Sall (1990) suggests the following generalization of added-variable plots, which he terms *leverage plots*: Consider the general linear hypothesis[39]

$$H_0: \underset{(q \times k+1)}{\mathbf{L}} \underset{(k+1 \times 1)}{\beta} = \underset{(q \times 1)}{\mathbf{0}} \qquad (11.10)$$

For example, in the regression of occupational prestige (Y) on education (X_1), income (X_2), and type of occupation (represented by the dummy regressors D_1 and D_2),

$$Y = \alpha + \beta_1 X_1 + \beta_2 X_2 + \gamma_1 D_1 + \gamma_2 D_2 + \varepsilon$$

the hypothesis matrix

$$\mathbf{L} = \begin{bmatrix} 0 & 0 & 0 & 1 & 0 \\ 0 & 0 & 0 & 0 & 1 \end{bmatrix}$$

is used to test the hypothesis $H_0: \gamma_1 = \gamma_2 = 0$ that there is no effect of type of occupation.

---

[37] See Chapter 10.
[38] See Exercises 11.5 and 11.6.
[39] See Section 9.4.3.

The residuals for the full model, unconstrained by the hypothesis in Equation 11.10, are the usual least-squares residuals, $\mathbf{e} = \mathbf{y} - \mathbf{Xb}$. The estimated regression coefficients under the hypothesis are[40]

$$\mathbf{b}_0 = \mathbf{b} - (\mathbf{X'X})^{-1}\mathbf{L'u}$$

and the residuals constrained by the hypothesis are given by

$$\mathbf{e}_0 = \mathbf{e} + \mathbf{X}(\mathbf{X'X})^{-1}\mathbf{L'u}$$

where

$$\mathbf{u} \equiv [\mathbf{L}(\mathbf{X'X})^{-1}\mathbf{L'}]^{-1}\mathbf{Lb}$$

Thus, the incremental sum of squares for H_0 is[41]

$$||\mathbf{e}_0 - \mathbf{e}||^2 = \mathbf{b'L'}[\mathbf{L}(\mathbf{X'X})^{-1}\mathbf{L'}]^{-1}\mathbf{Lb}$$

The leverage plot is a scatterplot with

$$\mathbf{v}_x \equiv \mathbf{X}(\mathbf{X'X})^{-1}\mathbf{L'u}$$

on the horizontal axis, and

$$\mathbf{v}_y \equiv \mathbf{v}_x + \mathbf{e}$$

on the vertical axis. The leverage plot, so defined, has the following properties:

- The residuals around the horizontal line at $V_y = 0$ are the constrained least-squares residuals E_{0i} under the hypothesis H_0.
- The least-squares line fit to the leverage plot has an intercept of 0 and a slope of 1; the residuals around this line are the unconstrained least-squares residuals, E_i. The incremental sum of squares for H_0 is thus the regression sum of squares for the line.
- When the hypothesis matrix $\mathbf{L}$ is formulated with a single row to test the coefficient of an individual regressor, the leverage plot specializes to the usual added-variable plot, with the horizontal axis rescaled so that the least-squares intercept is 0 and the slope 1.

Leverage plots, however, have the following disquieting property, which limits their usefulness: Even when an observation strongly influences the regression coefficients in a hypothesis, it may not influence the sum of squares for the hypothesis. For example, removing a particular observation might increase a formerly small regression coefficient and decrease a formerly large one, so that the F-statistic for the hypothesis that both coefficients are zero is unaltered.

Exercises

Exercise 11.1. *Show that, in simple-regression analysis, the hat-value is

$$h_i = \frac{1}{n} + \frac{(X_i - \overline{X})^2}{\sum_{j=1}^{n}(X_j - \overline{X})^2}$$

[*Hint*: Evaluate $\mathbf{x}'_i(\mathbf{X'X})^{-1}\mathbf{x}_i$ for $\mathbf{x}'_i = (1, X_i)$.]

---

[40]For this and other results pertaining to leverage plots, see Sall (1990).
[41]See Exercise 11.7.

Exercise 11.2. *Show that the hat-matrix $\mathbf{H} = \mathbf{X}(\mathbf{X}'\mathbf{X})^{-1}\mathbf{X}'$ is symmetric ($\mathbf{H} = \mathbf{H}'$) and idempotent ($\mathbf{H}^2 = \mathbf{H}$).

Exercise 11.3. *Show that in a one-way ANOVA with equal numbers of observations in the several groups, all the hat-values are equal to each other. By extension, this result implies that the hat-values in any balanced ANOVA are equal. Why?

Exercise 11.4. *Using Duncan's regression of occupational prestige on the educational and income levels of occupations, verify that the influence vector for the deletion of *ministers* on the regression coefficients, $\mathbf{d}_i = \mathbf{b} - \mathbf{b}_{(-i)}$, can be written as

$$\mathbf{d}_i = (\mathbf{X}'\mathbf{X})^{-1}\mathbf{x}_i \frac{E_i}{1 - h_i}$$

where $\mathbf{x}_i$ is the ith row of the model matrix $\mathbf{X}$ (i.e., the row for *ministers*) written as a column. [A much more difficult problem is to show that this formula works in general; see, e.g., Belsley, et al. (1980, pp. 69–83) or Velleman and Welsch (1981).]

Exercise 11.5. *Consider the two-explanatory-variable linear-regression model, with variables written as vectors in mean-deviation form (as in Section 10.5): $\mathbf{y}^* = B_1\mathbf{x}_1^* + B_2\mathbf{x}_2^* + \mathbf{e}$. Let $\mathbf{x}^{(1)}$ and $\mathbf{y}^{(1)}$ represent the residual vectors from the regression (i.e., orthogonal projection) of $\mathbf{x}_1^*$ and $\mathbf{y}^*$, respectively, on $\mathbf{x}_2^*$. Drawing the three-dimensional diagram of the subspace spanned by $\mathbf{x}_1^*$, $\mathbf{x}_2^*$, and $\mathbf{y}^*$, prove geometrically that the coefficient for the orthogonal projection of $\mathbf{y}^{(1)}$ onto $\mathbf{x}^{(1)}$ is B_1.

Exercise 11.6. *Extending the previous exercise, now consider the more general model $\mathbf{y}^* = B_1\mathbf{x}_1^* + B_2\mathbf{x}_2^* + \cdots + B_k\mathbf{x}_k^* + \mathbf{e}$. Let $\mathbf{x}^{(1)}$ and $\mathbf{y}^{(1)}$ represent the residual vectors from the projections of $\mathbf{x}_1^*$ and $\mathbf{y}^*$, respectively, onto the subspace spanned by $\mathbf{x}_2^*, \ldots, \mathbf{x}_k^*$. Prove that the coefficient for the orthogonal projection of $\mathbf{y}^{(1)}$ onto $\mathbf{x}^{(1)}$ is B_1.

Exercise 11.7. *Show that the incremental sum of squares for the general linear hypothesis H_0: $\mathbf{L}\boldsymbol{\beta} = \mathbf{0}$ can be written as

$$||\mathbf{e}_0 - \mathbf{e}||^2 = \mathbf{b}'\mathbf{L}'[\mathbf{L}(\mathbf{X}'\mathbf{X})^{-1}\mathbf{L}']^{-1}\mathbf{L}\mathbf{b}$$

[*Hint*: $||\mathbf{e}_0 - \mathbf{e}||^2 = (\mathbf{e}_0 - \mathbf{e})'(\mathbf{e}_0 - \mathbf{e})$.]

Summary

- Unusual data are problematic in linear models fit by least squares because they can substantially influence the results of the analysis and because they may indicate that the model fails to capture important features of the data.
- Observations with unusual combinations of explanatory-variable values have high *leverage* in a least-squares regression. The hat-values h_i provide a measure of leverage. A rough cutoff for noteworthy hat-values is $h_i > 2\overline{h} = 2(k + 1)/n$.
- A regression *outlier* is an observation with an unusual response-variable value given its combination of explanatory-variable values. The studentized residuals E_i^* can be used to identify outliers, through graphical examination, a Bonferroni test for the largest absolute E_i^*, or Anscombe's insurance analogy. If the model is correct (and there are no "bad" observations), then each studentized residual follows a t-distribution with $n - k - 2$ degrees of freedom.

- Observations that combine high leverage with a large studentized residual exert substantial *influence* on the regression coefficients. Cook's D statistic provides a summary index of influence on the coefficients. A rough cutoff for noteworthy values of D is $D_i > 4/(n-k-1)$.
- It is also possible to investigate the influence of individual observations on other regression "outputs," such as coefficient standard errors and collinearity.
- Subsets of observations can be jointly influential. Added-variable plots are useful for detecting joint influence on the regression coefficients. The added-variable plot for the regressor X_j is formed using the residuals from the least-squares regressions of X_j and Y on all the other Xs.
- Atkinson and Riani's forward search adds observations successively to an initial small subset that is almost surely uncontaminated by unusual data. By monitoring outputs such as regression coefficients, this strategy can reveal unusual groups of observations that are missed by more conventional methods.
- Outlying and influential data should not be ignored, but they also should not simply be deleted without investigation. "Bad" data can often be corrected. "Good" observations that are unusual may provide insight into the structure of the data and may motivate respecification of the statistical model used to summarize the data.

Recommended Reading

There is a large journal literature on methods for identifying unusual and influential data. Fortunately, there are several texts that present this literature in a more digestible form:[42]

- Although it is now more than two decades old, Cook and Weisberg (1982) is, in my opinion, still the best book-length presentation of methods for assessing leverage, outliers, and influence. There are also good discussions of other problems, such as nonlinearity and transformations of the response and explanatory variables.
- Chatterjee and Hadi (1988) is a thorough text dealing primarily with influential data and collinearity; other problems—such as nonlinearity and nonconstant error variance—are treated briefly.
- Belsley, Kuh, and Welsch (1980) is a seminal text that discusses influential data and the detection of collinearity.[43]
- Barnett and Lewis (1994) present an encyclopedic survey of methods for outlier detection, including methods for detecting outliers in linear models.
- Atkinson and Riani (2000) describe in detail methods for detecting influential data based on a "forward search"; these methods were presented briefly in Section 11.6.2.

---

[42] Also see the recommended readings given at the end of the following chapter.

[43] I believe that Belsley et al.'s (1980) approach to diagnosing collinearity is fundamentally flawed—see the discussion of collinearity in Chapter 13.

12

Diagnosing Non-Normality, Nonconstant Error Variance, and Nonlinearity

C hapters 11, 12, and 13 show how to detect and correct problems with linear models that have been fit to data. The previous chapter focused on problems with specific observations. The current chapter and the next deal with more general problems with the specification of the model.

The first three sections of this chapter take up the problems of non-normally distributed errors, nonconstant error variance, and nonlinearity. The treatment here stresses simple graphical methods for detecting these problems, along with transformations of the data to correct problems that are detected.

Subsequent sections describe tests of nonconstant error variance and nonlinearity for discrete explanatory variables; diagnostic methods based on embedding the usual linear model in a more general nonlinear model that incorporates transformations as parameters; and diagnostics that seek to detect the underlying dimensionality of the regression.

To illustrate the methods described in this chapter, I will primarily use data drawn from the 1994 wave of Statistics Canada's Survey of Labour and Income Dynamics (SLID). The SLID data set includes 3,997 employed individuals who were between 16 and 65 years of age and who resided in Ontario.[1] Regressing the composite hourly wage rate (i.e., the wage rate computed from all sources of employment, in dollars per hour) on a dummy variable for sex (code 1 for males), education (in years), and age (also in years) produces the following results:

$$\widehat{\text{Wages}} = -8.124 + 3.474 \times \text{Male} \quad + 0.2613 \times \text{Age}$$
$$(0.599) \quad (0.2070) \quad\quad (0.0087)$$
$$+ \ 0.9296 \times \text{Education}$$
$$(0.0343)$$

$$R^2 = .3074$$

(12.1)

The coefficient standard errors, in parentheses below the coefficients, reveal that all the regression coefficients are precisely estimated (and highly statistically significant), as is to be expected in a sample of this size. The regression also accounts for more than 30% of the variation in hourly wages.

Although we will get quite a bit of mileage from this example, it is somewhat artificial: (1) A careful data analyst (using the methods for examining and transforming data introduced in Chapters 3 and 4) would not specify the model in this form. Indeed, on substantive grounds, we should not expect linear relationships between wages and age and, possibly, between wages and

---

[1] I assumed that individuals for whom the composite hourly wage rate is missing are not employed. There are, in addition, 150 people who are missing data on education and who are excluded from the analysis reported here.

education.[2] (2) We should entertain the obvious possibility that the effects of age and education on income may be different for men and women (i.e., that sex may interact with age and education), a possibility that we will pursue later in the chapter. (3) A moderately large sample such as this presents the opportunity to introduce additional explanatory variables into the analysis.

12.1 Non-Normally Distributed Errors

The assumption of normally distributed errors is almost always arbitrary. Nevertheless, the central-limit theorem assures that, under very broad conditions, inference based on the least-squares estimator is approximately valid in all but small samples. Why, then, should we be concerned about non-normal errors?

- Although the *validity* of least-squares estimation is robust—the levels of tests and the coverage of confidence intervals are approximately correct in large samples even when the assumption of normality is violated—the *efficiency* of least squares is not robust: Statistical theory assures us that the least-squares estimator is the most efficient unbiased estimator only when the errors are normal. For some types of error distributions, however, particularly those with heavy tails, the efficiency of least-squares estimation decreases markedly. In these cases, the least-squares estimator becomes much less efficient than robust estimators (or least-squares augmented by diagnostics).[3] To a great extent, heavy-tailed error distributions are problematic because they give rise to outliers, a problem that I addressed in the previous chapter.

  A commonly quoted justification of least-squares estimation—called the Gauss-Markov theorem—states that the least-squares coefficients are the most efficient unbiased estimators that are *linear* functions of the observations Y_i. This result depends on the assumptions of linearity, constant error variance, and independence but does not require the assumption of normality.[4] Although the restriction to linear estimators produces simple formulas for coefficient standard errors, it is not compelling in the light of the vulnerability of least squares to heavy-tailed error distributions.

- Highly skewed error distributions, aside from their propensity to generate outliers in the direction of the skew, compromise the interpretation of the least-squares fit. This fit is a conditional mean (of Y given the Xs), and the mean is not a good measure of the center of a highly skewed distribution. Consequently, we may prefer to transform the data to produce a symmetric error distribution.

- A multimodal error distribution suggests the omission of one or more discrete explanatory variables that divide the data naturally into groups. An examination of the distribution of the residuals may, therefore, motivate respecification of the model.

Although there are tests for non-normal errors, I will instead describe graphical methods for examining the distribution of the residuals, employing univariate displays introduced in Chapter 3.[5] These methods are more useful than tests for pinpointing the nature of the problem and for suggesting solutions.

One such graphical display is the quantile-comparison plot. We typically compare the sample distribution of the studentized residuals, E_i^*, with the quantiles of the unit-normal distribution,

---

[2]Unfortunately, in my experience, careful data analysis is far from the norm, and it is not hard to find examples of egregiously misspecified regressions with large R^2s that satisfied the people who performed them.

[3]Robust estimation is discussed in Chapter 19.

[4]A proof of the Gauss-Markov theorem appears in Section 9.3.2.

[5]See the discussion of Box-Cox transformations in Section 12.5.1, however.

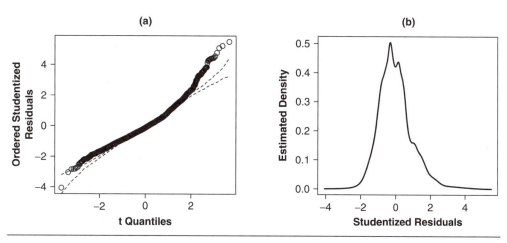

Figure 12.1 (a) Quantile-comparison plot and (b) kernel-density estimate for the studentized residuals from the SLID regression. The broken lines in the quantile-comparison plot represent a pointwise 95% simulated confidence envelope (described in Section 12.1.1).

$N(0, 1)$, or with those of the t-distribution for $n - k - 2$ degrees of freedom. Unless n is small, of course, the normal and t-distributions are nearly identical. We choose to plot *studentized* residuals because they have equal variances and are t-distributed, but, in larger samples, standardized or raw residuals will convey much the same impression.

Even if the model is correct, however, the studentized residuals are not an *independent* random sample from t_{n-k-2}: Different residuals are correlated with one another.[6] These correlations depend on the configuration of the X values, but they are generally negligible unless the sample size is small. Furthermore, at the cost of some computation, it is possible to adjust for the dependencies among the residuals in interpreting a quantile-comparison plot.[7]

The quantile-comparison plot is especially effective in displaying the tail behavior of the residuals: Outliers, skewness, heavy tails, or light tails all show up clearly. Other univariate graphical displays effectively supplement the quantile-comparison plot. In large samples, a histogram with many bars conveys a good impression of the shape of the residual distribution and generally reveals multiple modes more clearly than does the quantile-comparison plot. In smaller samples, a more stable impression is formed by smoothing the histogram of the residuals with a nonparametric density estimator (which is also a reasonable display in large samples).

Figure 12.1 shows the distribution of the studentized residuals from the SLID regression of Equation 12.1. The broken lines in the quantile-comparison plot [Figure 12.1(a)] represent a pointwise 95% confidence envelope computed under the assumption that the errors are normally distributed (according to the method described in Section 12.1.1). The window-width for the kernel density estimate [Figure 12.1(b)] is 3/4 of the "optimal" value for normally distributed data and was selected by visual trial and error. It is clear from both graphs that the residual distribution is positively skewed. The density estimate suggests, in addition, that there may be more than one mode to the distribution.

A positive skew in the residuals can usually be corrected by moving the *response variable* down the ladder of powers and roots. Trial and error suggests that the log transformation of wages

---

[6]* Different residuals are correlated because the off-diagonal entries of the hat-matrix (i.e., h_{ij} for $i \neq j$) are generally nonzero; see Section 11.8.

[7] See Section 12.1.1.

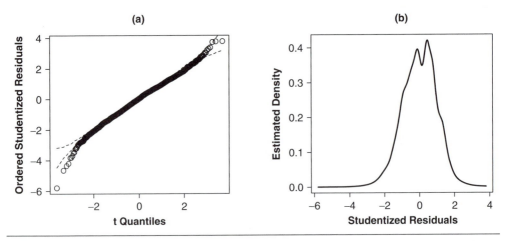

Figure 12.2   (a) Quantile-comparison plot and (b) kernel-density estimate for the studentized
residuals from the SLID regression with wages log-transformed.

renders the distribution of the residuals much more symmetric, as shown in Figure 12.2. The
residuals from the transformed regression appear to be heavy-tailed, a characteristic that in a
small sample would lead us to worry about the efficiency of the least-squares estimator.[8]

A cube-root transformation (i.e., the 1/3 power, not shown) does an even better job (reducing the
long left tail of the residual distribution in Figure 12.2), but because it produces very similar results
in the regression, I prefer the more easily interpreted log transformation. The fitted regression
equation using the log (base 2) of wages is as follows:

$$\widehat{\log_2 \text{Wages}} = \begin{array}{l} 1.585 \\ (0.055) \end{array} + \begin{array}{l} 0.3239 \times \text{Male} \\ (0.0189) \end{array} + \begin{array}{l} 0.02619 \times \text{Age} \\ (0.00079) \end{array}$$

$$+ \begin{array}{l} 0.08061 \times \text{Education} \\ (0.00313) \end{array} \qquad (12.2)$$

$$R^2 = 0.3213$$

We will return to the interpretation of the regression with the log-transformed response after we
fix some other problems with the SLID model.[9]

> Heavy-tailed errors threaten the efficiency of least-squares estimation; skewed and mul-
> timodal errors compromise the interpretation of the least-squares fit. Non-normality can
> often be detected by examining the distribution of the least-squares residuals and frequently
> can be corrected by transforming the data.

---

[8]Heavy-tailed error distributions suggest robust estimation, as described in Chapter 19, but in a sample this large, robust
regression produces essentially the same results as least squares.

[9]For the present, recall that increasing $\log_2$ wages by 1 implies doubling wages; more generally, adding x to $\log_2$ wages
multiplies wages by 2^x.

12.1.1   Confidence Envelopes by Simulated Sampling*

Atkinson (1985) has suggested the following procedure for constructing an approximate confidence "envelope" in a residual quantile-comparison plot, taking into account the correlational structure of the explanatory variables. Atkinson's procedure employs *simulated sampling* and uses the assumption of normally distributed errors.[10]

1. Fit the regression model as usual, obtaining fitted values $\widehat{Y}_i$ and the estimated regression standard error S_E.

2. Construct m samples, each consisting of n simulated Y values; for the jth such sample, the simulated value for observation i is

$$Y_{ij}^s = \widehat{Y}_i + S_E Z_{ij}$$

where Z_{ij} is a random draw from the unit-normal distribution. In other words, we sample from a "population" in which the expectation of Y_i is $\widehat{Y}_i$; the true standard deviation of the errors is S_E; and the errors are normally distributed.

3. Regress the n simulated observations for sample j on the Xs in the original sample, obtaining simulated studentized residuals, $E_{1j}^*, E_{2j}^*, \ldots, E_{nj}^*$. Because this regression employs the original X values, the simulated studentized residuals reflect the correlational structure of the Xs.

4. Order the studentized residuals for sample j from smallest to largest, as required by a quantile-comparison plot: $E_{(1)j}^*, E_{(2)j}^*, \ldots, E_{(n)j}^*$.

5. To construct an estimated $(100 - a)\%$ confidence interval for $E_{(i)}^*$ (the ith ordered studentized residual), find the $a/2$ and $1 - a/2$ empirical quantiles of the m simulated values $E_{(i)1}^*$, $E_{(i)2}^*, \ldots, E_{(i)m}^*$. For example, if $m = 20$ and $a = .05$, then the smallest and largest of the $E_{(1)j}^*$ provide a 95% confidence interval for $E_{(1)}^*$: $[E_{(1)(1)}^*, E_{(1)(20)}^*]$.[11] The confidence limits for the n ordered studentized residuals are graphed as a confidence envelope on the quantile-comparison plot, along with the studentized residuals themselves.

A weakness of Atkinson's procedure is that the probability of *some* studentized residual straying outside the confidence limits by chance is greater than a, which is the probability that an *individual* studentized residual falls outside its confidence interval. Because the joint distribution of the studentized residuals is complicated, however, to construct a correct joint-confidence envelope would require even more calculation. As well, in small samples, where there are few residual degrees of freedom, even radical departures from normally distributed errors can give rise to apparently normally distributed residuals; Andrews (1979) presents an example of this phenomenon, which he terms "supernormality."

---

[10]The notion of simulated sampling from a population constructed from the observed data is the basis of "bootstrapping," discussed in Chapter 21. Atkinson's procedure described here is an application of the *parametric bootstrap*.

[11]Selecting the smallest and largest of the 20 simulated values corresponds to our simple convention that the proportion of the data below the jth of m order statistics is $(j - 1/2)/m$. Here, $(1 - 1/2)/20 = .025$ and $(20 - 1/2)/20 = .975$, defining 95% confidence limits. Atkinson uses a slightly different convention. To estimate the confidence limits more accurately, it helps to make m larger and perhaps to use a more sophisticated version of the bootstrap (see Chapter 21). The envelopes in Figures 12.1(a) and 12.2(a) are based on $m = 100$ replications.

12.2   Nonconstant Error Variance

As we know, one of the assumptions of the regression model is that the variation of the response variable around the regression surface—the error variance—is everywhere the same:

$$V(\varepsilon) = V(Y|x_1, \ldots, x_k) = \sigma_\varepsilon^2$$

Nonconstant error variance is often termed *heteroscedasticity*; similarly, *constant* error variance is termed *homoscedasticity*. Although the least-squares estimator is unbiased and consistent even when the error variance is not constant, the efficiency of the least-squares estimator is impaired, and the usual formulas for coefficient standard errors are inaccurate—the degree of the problem depending on the degree to which error variances differ, the sample size, and the configuration of the X values in the regression. In this section, I will describe graphical methods for detecting nonconstant error variances, and methods for dealing with the problem when it is detected.[12]

12.2.1   Residual Plots

Because the regression surface is k-dimensional and embedded in a space of $k+1$ dimensions, it is generally impractical to assess the assumption of constant error variance by direct graphical examination of the data when k is larger than 1 or 2. Nevertheless, it is common for error variance to increase as the expectation of Y grows larger, or there may be a systematic relationship between error variance and a particular X. The former situation can often be detected by plotting residuals against fitted values, and the latter by plotting residuals against each X.[13]

Plotting residuals against Y (as opposed to $\widehat{Y}$) is generally unsatisfactory because the plot is "tilted": $Y = \widehat{Y} + E$, and consequently the linear correlation between the *observed response* Y and the residuals E is $\sqrt{1 - R^2}$.[14] In contrast, the least-squares fit ensures that the correlation between the *fitted values* $\widehat{Y}$ and E is precisely 0, producing a plot that is much easier to examine for evidence of non-constant spread.

Because the least-squares *residuals* have unequal variances even when the assumption of constant *error* variance is correct, it is preferable to plot studentized residuals against fitted values. A pattern of changing spread is often more easily discerned in a plot of absolute studentized residuals, $|E_i^*|$, or squared studentized residuals, E_i^{*2}, against $\widehat{Y}$. Finally, if the values of $\widehat{Y}$ are all positive, then we can plot $\log |E_i^*|$ (log spread) against $\log \widehat{Y}$ (log level). A line, with slope b fit to this plot, suggests the variance-stabilizing transformation $Y^{(p)}$, with $p = 1 - b$.[15]

Figure 12.3 shows a plot of studentized residuals against fitted values and a spread-level plot of studentized residuals for the SLID regression of Equation 12.1 (page 267). It is apparent from both graphs that the residual spread tends to increase with the level of the response, suggesting transforming the response *down* the ladder of powers and roots. The slope of the line fit to the spread-level plot in Figure 12.3(b) is $b = 0.9994$, corresponding to the power transformation $1 - 0.9994 = 0.0006 \approx 0$ (i.e., the log transformation).[16]

---

[12]Tests for heteroscedasticity are discussed in Section 12.4 on discrete data and in Section 12.5 on maximum-likelihood methods.

[13]These displays are not infallible, however: See Cook (1994), and the discussion in Section 12.6.

[14]See Exercise 12.1.

[15]This is an application of Tukey's rule for selecting a transformation, introduced in Section 4.4. Other analytic methods for choosing a variance-stabilizing transformation are discussed in Section 12.5.

[16]The line in Figure 12.3(b) was fit by M estimation using the Huber weight function—a method of robust regression described in Chapter 19. In this example, however, nearly the same results are provided by least-squares, for which $b = 0.9579$. Note that the plots in Figures 12.3(a) and 12.4 (a) suggest that there is some unmodeled nonlinearity, an issue to which we will turn in Section 12.3.

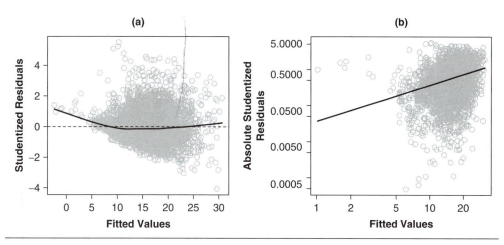

Figure 12.3 (a) Plot of studentized residuals versus fitted values and (b) spread-level plot for studentized residuals. The solid line in the panel (a) is fit by lowess, with a span of 0.4. The line in panel (b) is produced by robust linear regression. The points are plotted in gray to avoid obscuring the lines.

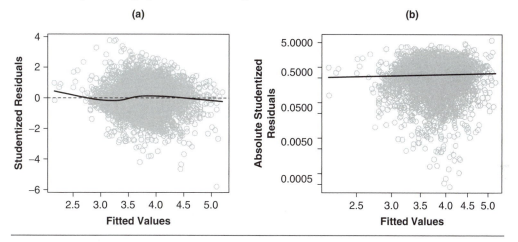

Figure 12.4 (a) Plot of studentized residuals versus fitted values and (b) spread-level plot for studentized residuals following log transformation of wages in the SLID regression.

In the previous section, the log transformation of wages made the distribution of the studentized residuals more symmetric. The same transformation nearly stabilizes the residual variance, as illustrated in diagnostic plots shown in Figure 12.4. This outcome is not surprising because the heavy right tail of the residual distribution and nonconstant spread are both common consequences of the lower bound of 0 for the response variable.

Transforming Y changes the shape of the error distribution, but it also alters the shape of the regression of Y on the Xs. At times, eliminating nonconstant spread also makes the relationship of Y to the Xs more nearly linear, but this is not a necessary consequence of stabilizing the error variance, and it is important to check for nonlinearity following transformation of the response variable. Of course, because there is generally no reason to suppose that the regression is linear *prior* to transforming Y, we should check for nonlinearity in any event.[17]

---

[17] See Section 12.3.

Nonconstant residual spread sometimes is symptomatic of the omission of important effects from the model. Suppose, for example, that there is an omitted categorical explanatory variable, such as urban versus rural residence, that interacts with education in affecting wages; in particular, suppose that the education slope, although positive in both urban and rural areas, is steeper in urban areas. Then the omission of urban/rural residence and its interaction with education could produce a fan-shaped residual plot even if the errors from the correct model have constant variance.[18] The detection of this type of specification error requires insight into the process generating the data and cannot rely on diagnostics alone.

12.2.2   Weighted-Least-Squares Estimation*

Weighted-least-squares (WLS) regression provides an alternative approach to estimation in the presence of nonconstant error variance. Suppose that the errors from the linear regression model $\mathbf{y} = \mathbf{X}\beta + \varepsilon$ are independent and normally distributed, with zero means but *different* variances: $\varepsilon_i \sim N(0, \sigma_i^2)$. Suppose further that the variances of the errors are known up to a constant of proportionality σ_ε^2, so that $\sigma_i^2 = \sigma_\varepsilon^2 / w_i^2$. Then, the likelihood for the model is[19]

$$L(\beta, \sigma_\varepsilon^2) = \frac{1}{(2\pi)^{n/2}|\Sigma|^{1/2}} \exp\left[-\frac{1}{2}(\mathbf{y} - \mathbf{X}\beta)'\Sigma^{-1}(\mathbf{y} - \mathbf{X}\beta) \right]$$

where Σ is the covariance matrix of the errors,

$$\Sigma = \sigma_\varepsilon^2 \times \mathrm{diag}\{1/w_1^2, \dots, 1/w_n^2\} \equiv \sigma_\varepsilon^2 \times \mathbf{W}^{-1}$$

The maximum-likelihood estimators of β and σ_ε^2 are then

$$\widehat{\beta} = (\mathbf{X}'\mathbf{W}\mathbf{X})^{-1}\mathbf{X}'\mathbf{W}\mathbf{y}$$

$$\widehat{\sigma}_\varepsilon^2 = \frac{\sum (w_i E_i)^2}{n}$$

where the residuals are defined in the usual manner as the difference between the observed response and the fitted values, $\mathbf{e} = \{E_i\} = \mathbf{y} - \mathbf{X}\widehat{\beta}$. This procedure is equivalent to minimizing the *weighted sum of squares* $\sum w_i^2 E_i^2$, according greater weight to observations with smaller variance—hence the term *weighted least squares*. The estimated asymptotic covariance matrix of $\widehat{\beta}$ is given by

$$\widehat{V}(\widehat{\beta}) = \widehat{\sigma}_\varepsilon^2 (\mathbf{X}'\mathbf{W}\mathbf{X})^{-1}$$

In practice, we would need to estimate the weights w_i or know that the error variance is systematically related to some observable variable. In the first instance, for example, we could use the residuals from a preliminary *ordinary-least-squares* (OLS) regression to obtain estimates of the error variance within different subsets of observations, formed by partitioning the data according to one or more categorical variables. Basing the weights on a preliminary estimate of error variances can, however, seriously bias the estimated covariance matrix $\widehat{V}(\widehat{\beta})$, because the sampling error in the estimates should reflect the additional source of uncertainty.[20]

In the second instance, suppose that inspection of a residual plot for the preliminary OLS fit suggests that the magnitude of the errors is proportional to the first explanatory variable, X_1.

---

[18]See Exercise 12.2 for an illustration of this phenomenon.

[19]See Exercise 12.3 for this and other results pertaining to weighted-least-squares estimation; also see the discussion of generalized least squares in Section 16.1.

[20]In this case, it is probably better to obtain an honest estimate of the coefficient covariance matrix from the bootstrap, described in Chapter 21, or to estimate the within-group variances simultaneously with the regression parameters.

We can then use $1/X_{i1}$ as the weights w_i. Dividing both sides of the regression equation by X_{i1} produces

$$\frac{Y_i}{X_{i1}} = \alpha \frac{1}{X_{i1}} + \beta_1 + \beta_2 \frac{X_{i2}}{X_{i1}} + \cdots + \beta_k \frac{X_{ik}}{X_{i1}} + \frac{\varepsilon_i}{X_{i1}} \qquad (12.3)$$

Because the standard deviations of the errors are proportional to X_1, the "new" errors $\varepsilon_i' \equiv \varepsilon_i/X_{i1}$ have constant variance, and Equation 12.3 can be estimated by OLS regression of Y/X_1 on $1/X_1$, $X_2/X_1, \ldots, X_k/X_1$. Note that the constant from this regression estimates β_1, while the coefficient of $1/X_1$ estimates α; the remaining coefficients are straightforward.

12.2.3 Correcting OLS Standard Errors for Nonconstant Variance*

The covariance matrix of the OLS estimator is

$$V(\mathbf{b}) = (\mathbf{X}'\mathbf{X})^{-1}\mathbf{X}'V(\mathbf{y})\mathbf{X}(\mathbf{X}'\mathbf{X})^{-1} \qquad (12.4)$$

Under the standard assumptions, including the assumption of constant error variance, $V(\mathbf{y}) = \sigma_\varepsilon^2 \mathbf{I}_n$, Equation 12.4 simplifies to the usual formula, $V(\mathbf{b}) = \sigma_\varepsilon^2 (\mathbf{X}'\mathbf{X})^{-1}$. If, however, the errors are heteroscedastic but independent, then $\mathbf{\Sigma} \equiv V(\mathbf{y}) = \text{diag}\{\sigma_1^2, \ldots, \sigma_n^2\}$, and

$$V(\mathbf{b}) = (\mathbf{X}'\mathbf{X})^{-1}\mathbf{X}'\mathbf{\Sigma}\mathbf{X}(\mathbf{X}'\mathbf{X})^{-1}$$

Because $E(\varepsilon_i) = 0$, the variance of the ith error is $\sigma_i^2 = E(\varepsilon_i^2)$, which suggests the possibility of estimating $V(\mathbf{b})$ by

$$\widetilde{V}(\mathbf{b}) = (\mathbf{X}'\mathbf{X})^{-1}\mathbf{X}'\widehat{\mathbf{\Sigma}}\mathbf{X}(\mathbf{X}'\mathbf{X})^{-1} \qquad (12.5)$$

with $\widehat{\mathbf{\Sigma}} = \text{diag}\{E_1^2, \ldots, E_n^2\}$, where E_i is the OLS residual for observation i. White (1980) shows that Equation 12.5 provides a consistent estimator of $V(\mathbf{b})$.[21]

Subsequent work has suggested small modifications to White's coefficient-variance estimator, and in particular simulation studies by Long and Ervin (2000) support the use of

$$\widetilde{V}^*(\mathbf{b}) = (\mathbf{X}'\mathbf{X})^{-1}\mathbf{X}'\widehat{\mathbf{\Sigma}}^*\mathbf{X}(\mathbf{X}'\mathbf{X})^{-1} \qquad (12.6)$$

where $\widehat{\mathbf{\Sigma}}^* = \text{diag}\{E_i^2/(1-h_i)^2\}$ and h_i is the hat-value associated with observation i.[22] In large samples, where individual hat-values are almost surely very small, the distinction between the coefficient-variance estimators in Equations 12.5 and 12.6 essentially disappears.

For the original SLID regression model in Equation 12.1 (on page 267), coefficient standard errors computed by the usual formula, by White's approach (in Equation 12.5), and by the modification to White's approach (in Equation 12.6) are as follows:

---

[21]White's coefficient-variance estimator is sometimes called a *sandwich estimator* because the matrix $\mathbf{X}'\widehat{\mathbf{\Sigma}}\mathbf{X}$ is "sandwiched between" the two occurences of $(\mathbf{X}'\mathbf{X})^{-1}$ in Equation 12.5.

[22]See Sections 11.2 and 11.8 for a discussion of hat-values. Long and Ervin call the coefficient-variance estimator in Equation 12.6 "HC3" for "heteroscedasticity-consistent" estimator number 3 — one of several such estimators considered in their paper.

	Standard Error of Coefficient		
Coefficient	Traditional OLS	White-Adjusted	Modified White-Adjusted
Constant	0.5990	0.6358	0.6370
Male	0.2070	0.2071	0.2074
Age	0.008664	0.008808	0.008821
Education	0.03426	0.03847	0.03854

In this instance, therefore, the adjusted standard errors are very close to the usual OLS standard errors—despite the strong evidence that we uncovered of nonconstant error variance.

An advantage of White's approach for coping with heteroscedasticity is that knowledge of the *pattern* of nonconstant error variance (e.g., increased variance with the level of Y or with an X) is not required. If, however, the heteroscedasticity problem is severe, and the corrected coefficient standard errors therefore are considerably larger than those produced by the usual formula, then discovering the pattern of nonconstant variance and taking account of it—by a transformation or WLS estimation—offers the possibility of more efficient estimation. In any event, as the next section shows, unequal error variance is usually worth correcting only when the problem is severe.

12.2.4 How Nonconstant Error Variance Affects the OLS Estimator*

The impact of nonconstant error variance on the efficiency of the OLS estimator and on the validity of least-squares inference depends on several factors, including the sample size, the degree of variation in the σ_i^2, the configuration of the X values, and the relationship between the error variance and the Xs. It is therefore not possible to develop wholly general conclusions concerning the harm produced by heteroscedasticity, but the following simple case is nevertheless instructive.

Suppose that $Y_i = \alpha + \beta X_i + \varepsilon_i$, where the errors are independent and normally distributed, with zero means but with different standard deviations proportional to X, so that $\sigma_i = \sigma_\varepsilon X_i$ (where all of the $X_i > 0$). Then the OLS estimator B is less efficient than the WLS estimator $\widehat{\beta}$, which, under these circumstances, is the most efficient unbiased estimator of β.[23]

Formulas for the sampling variances of B and $\widehat{\beta}$ are easily derived.[24] The efficiency of the OLS estimator relative to the optimal WLS estimator is given by $V(\widehat{\beta})/V(B)$, and the relative precision of the OLS estimator is the square root of this ratio, that is, $\mathrm{SD}(\widehat{\beta})/\mathrm{SD}(B)$.

Now suppose that X is uniformly distributed over the interval $[x_0, ax_0]$, where both x_0 and a are positive numbers, so that a is the ratio of the largest to the smallest value of X (and, consequently, of the largest to the smallest σ_i). The relative precision of the OLS estimator stabilizes quickly as the sample size grows, and exceeds 90% when $a = 2$, and 85% when $a = 3$, even when n is as small as 20. For $a = 10$, the penalty for using OLS is greater, but even here the relative precision of OLS exceeds 65% for $n \geq 20$.

The validity of statistical inferences based on OLS estimation is even less sensitive to common patterns of non-constant error variance. Here, we need to compare the expectation of the usual estimator of $V(B)$, which is typically biased when the error variance is not constant, with the true sampling variance of B. The square root of $E[\widehat{V}(B)]/V(B)$ expresses the result in relative standard-deviation terms. For the illustration, where the standard deviation of the errors is

---

[23] This property of the WLS estimator requires the assumption of normality. Without normal errors, the WLS estimator is still the most efficient *linear* unbiased estimator—an extension of the Gauss-Markov theorem. See Exercise 12.4.

[24] See Exercise 12.5 for this and other results described in this section.

proportional to X, and where X is uniformly distributed, this ratio is 98% when $a = 2$; 97% when $a = 3$; and 93% when $a = 10$, all for $n \geq 20$.

The results in this section suggest that nonconstant error variance is a serious problem only when the magnitude (i.e., the standard deviation) of the errors varies by more than a factor of about 3—that is, when the largest error variance is more than about 10 times the smallest. Because there are other distributions of the Xs for which the deleterious effects of heteroscedasticity can be more severe, a safer rule of thumb is to worry about nonconstant error variance when the magnitude of the errors varies by more than a factor of about 2—or, equivalently, when the ratio of largest to smallest error variance exceeds 4. One cautious approach is always to compare (modified) White-adjusted coefficient standard errors with the usual standard errors, preferring the former (or, if the pattern is known, correcting for nonconstant error variance) when the two disagree.

> It is common for the variance of the errors to increase with the level of the response variable. This pattern of nonconstant error variance ("heteroscedasticity") can often be detected in a plot of residuals against fitted values. Strategies for dealing with nonconstant error variance include transformation of the response variable to stabilize the variance; the substitution of weighted-least-squares estimation for ordinary least squares; and the correction of coefficient standard errors for heteroscedasticity. A rough rule is that nonconstant error variance seriously degrades the least-squares estimator only when the ratio of the largest to smallest variance is about 10 or more (or, more conservatively, about 4 or more).

12.3 Nonlinearity

The assumption that the average error, $E(\varepsilon)$, is everywhere 0 implies that the specified regression surface accurately reflects the dependency of the conditional average value of Y on the Xs. Conversely, violating the assumption of linearity implies that the model fails to capture the systematic pattern of relationship between the response and explanatory variables. The term *nonlinearity*, therefore, is not used in the narrow sense here, although it includes the possibility that a partial relationship assumed to be linear is, in fact, nonlinear: If, for example, two explanatory variables specified to have additive effects instead interact, then the average error is not 0 for all combinations of X values, constituting nonlinearity in the broader sense.

If nonlinearity, in the broad sense, is slight, then the fitted model can be a useful approximation even though the regression surface $E(Y|X_1, \ldots X_k)$ is not captured precisely. In other instances, however, the model can be seriously misleading.

The regression surface is generally high dimensional, even after accounting for regressors (such as dummy variables, interactions, and polynomial terms) that are functions of a smaller number of fundamental explanatory variables.[25] As in the case of nonconstant error variance, therefore, it is necessary to focus on particular patterns of departure from linearity. The graphical diagnostics discussed in this section are two-dimensional (and three-dimensional) projections of the $(k + 1)$-dimensional point cloud of observations $\{Y_i, X_{i1}, \ldots, X_{ik}\}$.

---

[25]Polynomial regression—for example, the model $Y = \alpha + \beta_1 X + \beta_2 X^2 + \varepsilon$—is discussed in Section 17.1. In this simple quadratic model, there are two regressors (X and X^2) but only one explanatory variable (X).

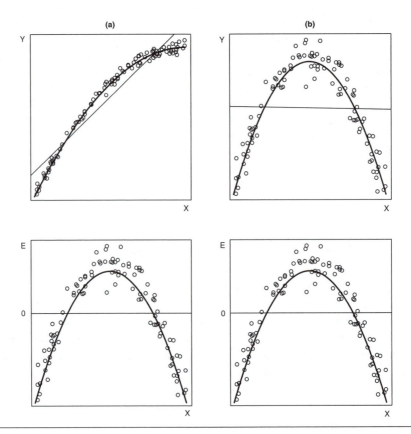

Figure 12.5   The residual plots of E versus X (in the lower panels) are identical, even though the regression of Y on X in (a) is monotone while that in (b) is nonmonotone.

12.3.1   Component-Plus-Residual Plots

Although it is useful in multiple regression to plot Y against each X (e.g., in one row of a scatterplot matrix), these plots often do not tell the whole story—and can be misleading—because our interest centers on the *partial* relationship between Y and each X ("controlling" for the other Xs), not on the *marginal* relationship between Y and an individual X ("ignoring" the other Xs). Residual-based plots are consequently more promising for detecting nonlinearity in multiple regression.

Plotting residuals or studentized residuals against each X, perhaps augmented by a nonparametric-regression smoother, is frequently helpful for detecting departures from linearity. As Figure 12.5 illustrates, however, simple residual plots cannot distinguish between monotone and nonmonotone nonlinearity. This distinction is lost in the residual plots because the least-squares fit ensures that the residuals are linearly uncorrelated with each X. The distinction is important because monotone nonlinearity frequently can be "corrected" by simple transformations.[26] In Figure 12.5, for example, case (a) might be modeled by $Y = \alpha + \beta\sqrt{X} + \varepsilon$, while case (b) cannot be linearized by a power transformation of X and might instead be dealt with by the quadratic regression, $Y = \alpha + \beta_1 X + \beta_2 X^2 + \varepsilon$.[27]

---

[26]Recall the material in Section 4.3 on linearizing transformations.

[27]Case (b) could, however, be accommodated by a more complex transformation of X, of the form $Y = \alpha + \beta(X - \gamma)^\lambda + \varepsilon$.

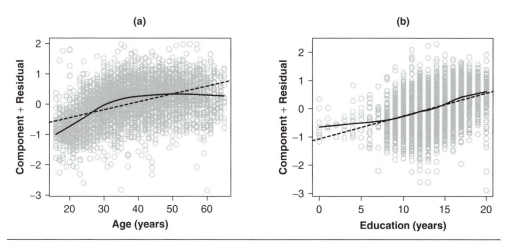

Figure 12.6 Component-plus-residual plots for age and education in the SLID regression of log wages on these variables and sex. The solid lines are for lowess smooths with spans of 0.4, and the broken lines are for linear-least-squares fits.

In contrast to simple residual plots, added-variable plots, introduced in the previous chapter for detecting influential data, can reveal nonlinearity and suggest whether a relationship is monotone. These plots are not always useful for locating a transformation, however: The added-variable plot adjusts X_j for the other Xs, but it is the *unadjusted* X_j that is transformed in respecifying the model. Moreover, as Cook (1998, sect. 14.5) shows, added-variable plots are biased toward linearity when the correlations among the explanatory variables are large. *Component-plus-residual plots*, also called *partial-residual plots*, are often an effective alternative. Component-plus-residual plots are not as suitable as added-variable plots for revealing leverage and influence, however.

Define the *partial residual* for the jth explanatory variable as

$$E_i^{(j)} = E_i + B_j X_{ij}$$

In words, add back the linear component of the partial relationship between Y and X_j to the least-squares residuals, which may include an unmodeled nonlinear component. Then plot $E^{(j)}$ versus X_j. By construction, the multiple-regression coefficient B_j is the slope of the simple linear regression of $E^{(j)}$ on X_j, but nonlinearity may be apparent in the plot as well. Again, a nonparametric-regression smoother may help in interpreting the plot.

Figure 12.6 shows component-plus-residual plots for age and education in the SLID regression of log wages on these variables and sex (Equation 12.2 on page 270). Both plots look nonlinear: It is not entirely clear whether the partial relationship of log wages to age is monotone, simply tending to level off at the higher ages, or whether it is nonmonotone, turning back down at the far right. In the former event, we should be able to linearize the relationship by moving age *down* the ladder of powers because the bulge points to the left. In the latter event, a quadratic partial regression might work. In contrast, the partial relationship of log wages to education is clearly monotone, and the departure from linearity is not great—except at the lowest levels of education, where data are sparse; we should be able to linearize this partial relationship by moving education *up* the ladder of powers, because the bulge points to the right.

In the illustration, γ could be taken as $\overline{X}$, and λ as 2. More generally, γ and λ could be estimated from the data, for example, by nonlinear least squares (as described in Section 17.4). I will not pursue this approach here because there are other obstacles to estimating this more general transformation (see, e.g., Exercise 4.3).

Trial and error experimentation suggests that the quadratic specification for age works better, producing the following fit to the data:[28]

$$\widehat{\log_2 \text{Wages}} = \underset{(0.0834)}{0.5725} + \underset{(0.0180)}{0.3195 \times \text{Male}} + \underset{(0.0046)}{0.1198 \times \text{Age}}$$
$$- \underset{(0.000059)}{0.001230 \times \text{Age}^2} + \underset{(0.000113)}{0.002605 \times \text{Education}^2} \qquad (12.7)$$
$$R^2 = .3892$$

I will consider the interpretation of this model shortly, but first let us examine component-plus-residual plots for the new fit. Because the model is now nonlinear in both age and education, there are two ways to proceed:

1. We can plot partial residuals for each of age and education against the corresponding explanatory variable. In the case of age, the partial residuals are computed as

$$E_i^{(\text{Age})} = 0.1198 \times \text{Age}_i - 0.001230 \times \text{Age}_i^2 + E_i \qquad (12.8)$$

and for education,

$$E_i^{(\text{Education})} = 0.002605 \times \text{Education}_i^2 + E_i \qquad (12.9)$$

The corresponding component-plus-residual plots are shown in the upper panels of Figure 12.7. The solid lines in these graphs are the *partial fits* (i.e., the components) for the two explanatory variables,

$$\widehat{Y}_i^{(\text{Age})} = 0.1198 \times \text{Age}_i - 0.001230 \times \text{Age}_i^2$$
$$\widehat{Y}_i^{(\text{Education})} = 0.002605 \times \text{Education}_i^2 \qquad (12.10)$$

The broken lines are lowess smooths, computed with span $= 0.4$. We look for the components to be close to the lowess smooths.

2. We can plot the partial residuals (as defined in Equations 12.8 and 12.9) against the partial fits (Equation 12.10) for the two variables. These plots are in the two lower panels of Figure 12.7. Here, the solid lines are least-squares lines, and, as before, the broken lines are lowess smooths. We look for the lowess smooths to be close to the least-squares lines.

It is apparent from the component-plus-residual plots in Figure 12.7 that the respecified model has done a good job of capturing the nonlinearity in the partial relationships of log wages with age and education—except possibly at the very highest ages, where the quadratic fit for age may exaggerate the down-turn in wages.

To this point, then, we have log-transformed wages to make the distribution of the residuals more symmetric and to stabilize the error variance, and we have fit a quadratic regression in age and power-transformed education to linearize the relationship of log wages to these variables. The result is the fitted model in Equation 12.7. Two of its characteristics make this model difficult to interpret:

1. The transformations of wages and education move these variables from their familiar scales (i.e., dollars per hour and years, respectively).

---

[28] See Exercise 12.7 for the alternative of transforming age.

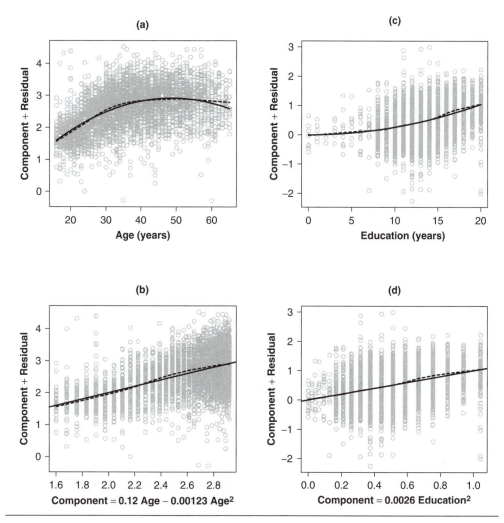

Figure 12.7   Component-plus-residual plots for age [panels (a) and (b)] and education [panels (c) and (d)] in the respecified model fit to the SLID data. In panels (a) and (c), partial residuals for age and education are plotted against the corresponding explanatory variable, with the component for the explanatory variable graphed as a solid line. In panels (b) and (d), the partial residuals are plotted against each component, and the solid line is a least-squares line. In all four panels, the broken line represents a lowess smooth with a span of 0.4.

2. Because the linear term in age is marginal to the squared term, the two terms are not separately interpretable. More precisely, the coefficient of the linear term, 0.1198, is the slope of the regression surface in the direction of age at age 0—clearly not a meaningful quantity— and twice the coefficient of the squared term in age, $2 \times (-0.001230) = -0.002460$, is the *change* in the age slope per year of age; the slope consequently declines with age and eventually becomes negative.[29]

---

[29] * The slope of the partial fit for age is the derivative $d(0.1198 \times \text{Age} - 0.001230 \times \text{Age}^2)/d\text{Age} = 0.1198 - 0.002460\text{Age}$. These points are developed in more detail in the discussion of polynomial regression in Section 17.1.

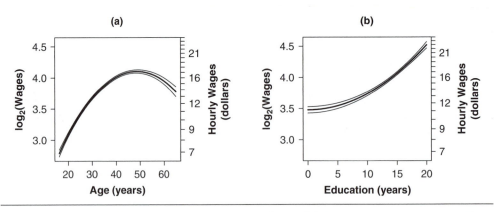

Figure 12.8   Effect displays for age and education in the model in Equation 12.7 (page 280). The lighter lines give 95% pointwise confidence envelopes around the fits.

Interpretation is therefore greatly facilitated by graphing the partial regressions, using the effect-display framework developed in Chapters 7 and 8. Effect displays for age and education appear in Figure 12.8. In the effect display for age, for example, education and the dummy regressor for sex are set to their average values (which, in the latter case, represents the proportion of men in the SLID data set). The effects are graphed on the log-wages scale employed in the model, but I show wages in dollars on the axis at the right of each panel. An alternative would be to graph the effects directly on the dollar scale. The 95% pointwise confidence envelopes around the effects show that they are precisely estimated.[30]

12.3.2   Component-Plus-Residual Plots for Models With Interactions

Traditionally, component-plus-residual plots are applied to additive terms in a linear model, but these displays can be adapted to models with interactions. Suppose, for example, that we augment the SLID regression model with interactions between sex and age and between sex and education, retaining (at least tentatively) the quadratic specification of the age effect and the square of education. Estimated coefficients and standard errors for the new model are in Table 12.1. The R^2 for this model is .4029. The two interactions are highly statistically significant by incremental F-tests: For the interaction of sex with age, we have $F_0 = 31.33$, with 2 and 3,989 degrees of freedom, for which $p \ll .0001$; and for the interaction of sex with education, we have $F_0 = 28.26$ with 1 and 3,989 degrees of freedom, for which $p \ll .0001$ as well.[31]

The complex structure of the model makes it difficult to interpret directly from the coefficients: For example, the coefficient for the sex dummy variable is the log-income advantage of men at age 0 and education 0. Effect displays for the high-order terms in the model, shown in Figure 12.9, are straightforward, however: At average education, men's and women's average income is similar at the lowest ages, but men's income initially rises more rapidly and then falls off more rapidly at the highest ages. Likewise, at average age, men's income advantage is greatest at the lowest levels of education and the advantage declines, while average income itself rises, as education goes up.

To construct component-plus-residual plots for this model, we can divide the data by sex and, for each sex, plot partial residuals against the partial fit. The results, shown in Figures 12.10

---

[30]I could have shown an effect display for sex as well, but this effect is readily ascertained directly from the coefficient: Holding age and education constant, men earn on average $2^{0.3195} = 1.248$ times as much as (i.e., 25% more than) women.

[31]The latter test could be computed from the t-value obtained by dividing the Male×Education^2 coefficient by its standard error.

Table 12.1   Coefficients for the Regression of Log Wages on Sex, Age, Education, and the Interactions Between Sex and Age and Between Sex and Education

Coefficient	Estimate	Standard Error
Constant	0.8607	0.1155
Male	−0.3133	0.1641
Age	0.1024	0.0064
Age^2	−0.001072	0.000083
$Education^2$	−0.003230	0.000166
Male×Age	−0.03694	0.00910
Male×Age^2	−0.0003392	0.0001171
Male×$Education^2$	−0.001198	0.000225

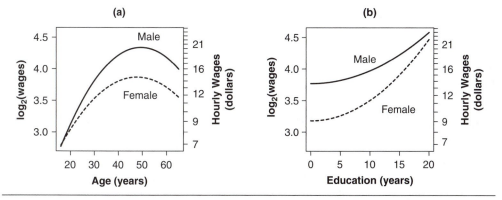

Figure 12.9   Effect displays for (a) the interaction between sex and age and (b) the interaction between sex and education, in the model summarized in Table 12.1.

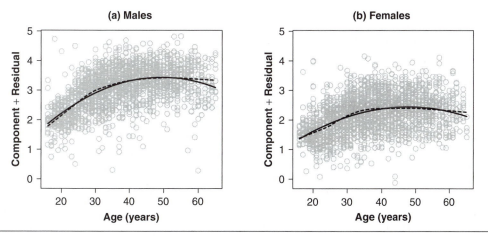

Figure 12.10   Component-plus-residual plots for the sex-by-age interaction. The solid lines give the partial fit (i.e., the component), while the broken lines are for a lowess smooth with a span of 0.4.

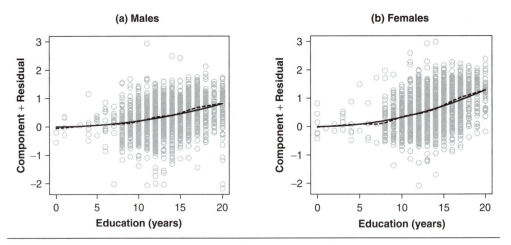

Figure 12.11   Component-plus-residual plots for the sex-by-education interaction.

and 12.11, suggest that the model fits the data adequately (although the quadratic specification for age may exaggerate the decline in income at the highest ages).

12.3.3   When Do Component-Plus-Residual Plots Work?

Circumstances under which regression plots, including component-plus-residual plots, are informative about the structure of data are an active area of statistical research.[32] It is unreasonable to expect that lower-dimensional displays can always uncover structure in a higher-dimensional problem. We may, for example, discern an interaction between two explanatory variables in a three-dimensional scatterplot, but it is not possible to do so in two separate two-dimensional plots, one for each explanatory variable.

It is important, therefore, to understand when graphical displays work and why they sometimes fail: First, understanding the circumstances under which a plot is effective may help us to produce those circumstances. Second, understanding why plots succeed and why they fail may help us to construct more effective displays. Both of these aspects will be developed below.

To provide a point of departure for this discussion, imagine that the following model accurately describes the data:

$$Y_i = \alpha + f(X_{i1}) + \beta_2 X_{i2} + \cdots + \beta_k X_{ik} + \varepsilon_i \qquad (12.11)$$

That is, the partial relationship between Y and X_1 is (potentially) nonlinear, characterized by the function $f(X_1)$, while the other explanatory variables, $X_2, \ldots, X_k$, enter the model linearly.

We do not know in advance the shape of the function $f(X_1)$ and indeed do not know that the partial relationship between Y and X_1 is nonlinear. Instead of fitting the true model (Equation 12.11) to the data, therefore, we fit the "working model":

$$Y_i = \alpha' + \beta_1' X_{i1} + \beta_2' X_{i2} + \cdots + \beta_k' X_{ik} + \varepsilon_i'$$

The primes indicate that the estimated coefficients for this model do not, in general, estimate the corresponding parameters of the true model (Equation 12.11), nor is the "error" of the working model the same as the error of the true model.

---

[32] Much of this work is due to Cook and his colleagues; see, in particular, Cook (1993), on which the current section is based, and Cook (1994). Cook and Weisberg (1994, 1999) provide an accessible summary.

Suppose, now, that we construct a component-plus-residual plot for X_1 in the working model. The partial residuals estimate

$$\varepsilon_i^{(1)} = \beta_1' X_{i1} + \varepsilon_i' \tag{12.12}$$

What we would really like to estimate, however, is $f(X_{i1}) + \varepsilon_i$, which, apart from random error, will tell us the partial relationship between Y and X_1. Cook (1993) shows that $\varepsilon_i^{(1)} = f(X_{i1}) + \varepsilon_i$, as desired, under either of two circumstances:

1. The function $f(X_1)$ is linear after all, in which case the population analogs of the partial residuals in Equation 12.12 are appropriately linearly related to X_1.

2. The *other* explanatory variables $X_2, \ldots, X_k$ are each linearly related to X_1. That is,

$$E(X_{ij}) = \alpha_{j1} + \beta_{j1} X_{i1} \quad \text{for } j = 2, \ldots, k \tag{12.13}$$

If, in contrast, there are *nonlinear* relationships between the other Xs and X_1, then the component-plus-residual plot for X_1 may not reflect the true partial regression $f(X_1)$.[33]

The second result suggests a practical procedure for improving the chances that component-plus-residual plots will provide accurate evidence of nonlinearity: If possible, transform the explanatory variables to linearize the relationships among them (using, e.g., the unconditional Box-Cox procedure described in Section 4.6). Evidence suggests that weak nonlinearity is not especially problematic, but strong nonlinear relationships among the explanatory variables can invalidate the component-plus-residual plot as a useful diagnostic display.[34]

Mallows (1986) has suggested a variation on the component-plus-residual plot that sometimes reveals nonlinearity more clearly. I will focus on X_1, but the spirit of Mallows's suggestion is to draw a plot for each X in turn. First, construct a working model with a quadratic term in X_1 along with the usual linear term:

$$Y_i = \alpha' + \beta_1' X_{i1} + \gamma_1 X_{i1}^2 + \beta_2' X_{i2} + \cdots + \beta_k' X_{ik} + \varepsilon_i'$$

Then, after fitting the working model, form the "augmented" partial residual

$$E_i'^{(1)} = E_i' + B_1' X_{i1} + C_1 X_{i1}^2$$

Note that B_1' generally differs from the regression coefficient for X_1 in the original model, which does not include the squared term. Finally, plot $E'^{(1)}$ versus X_1.

The circumstances under which the augmented partial residuals accurately capture the true partial-regression function $f(X_1)$ are closely analogous to the linear case (see Cook, 1993); either

1. the function $f(X_1)$ is a quadratic in X_1[35] or

2. the regressions of the other explanatory variables on X_1 are quadratic:

$$E(X_{ij}) = \alpha_{j1} + \beta_{j1} X_{i1} + \gamma_{j1} X_{i1}^2 \quad \text{for } j = 2, \ldots, k \tag{12.14}$$

---

[33]Note that each of the other Xs is regressed on X_1, *not* vice versa.
[34]See Exercise 12.6.
[35]This condition covers a linear partial relationship as well—i.e., where $\gamma_1 = 0$.

This is a potentially useful result if we cannot transform away nonlinearity among the explanatory variables—as is the case, for example, when the relationships among the explanatory variables are not monotone.

Mallows's approach can be generalized to higher-order polynomials.

The premise of this discussion, expressed in Equation 12.11, is that Y is a nonlinear function of X_1 but linearly related to the other Xs. In real applications of component-plus-residual plots, however, it is quite possible that there is more than one nonlinear partial relationship, and we typically wish to examine each explanatory variable in turn. Suppose, for example, that the relationship between Y and X_1 is linear; that the relationship between Y and X_2 is nonlinear; and that X_1 and X_2 are correlated. The component-plus-residual plot for X_1 can, in this situation, show apparent nonlinearity—sometimes termed a "leakage" effect. If more than one component-plus-residual plot shows evidence of nonlinearity, it may, therefore, be advisable to refit the model and reconstruct the component-plus-residual plots after correcting the most dramatic instance of nonlinearity.[36]

Applied to the SLID regression of log wages on sex, age, and education, Mallows's augmented component-plus-residual plots look very much like traditional component-plus-residual plots.[37]

Simple forms of nonlinearity can often be detected in component-plus-residual plots. Once detected, nonlinearity can frequently be accommodated by variable transformations or by altering the form of the model (to include a quadratic term in an explanatory variable, for example). Component-plus-residual plots reliably reflect nonlinearity when there are not strong nonlinear relationships among the explanatory variables in a regression.

CERES Plots*

Cook (1993) provides a still more general procedure, which he calls CERES (for "Combining conditional Expectations and RESiduals"): Let

$$\widehat{X}_{ij} = \widehat{g}_{j1}(X_{i1})$$

represent the estimated regression of X_j on X_1, for $j = 2, \ldots, k$. These regressions may be linear (as in Equation 12.13), quadratic (as in Equation 12.14), or they may be nonparametric. Of course, the functions $\widehat{g}_{j1}(X_1)$ will generally be different for different X_js. Once the regression functions for the other explanatory variables are found, form the working model

$$Y_i = \alpha'' + \beta_2'' X_{i2} + \cdots + \beta_k'' X_{ik} + \gamma_{12}\widehat{X}_{i2} + \cdots + \gamma_{1k}\widehat{X}_{ik} + \varepsilon_i''$$

The residuals from this model are then combined with the estimates of the γs,

$$E_i''^{(1)} = E_i'' + C_{12}\widehat{X}_{i2} + \cdots + C_{1k}\widehat{X}_{ik}$$

and plotted against X_1.

CERES plots for the SLID regression of log wages on sex, age, and education are very similar to traditional component-plus-residual plots.[38]

---

[36]An iterative formalization of this procedure provides a basis for fitting nonparametric additive regression models, discussed in Section 18.2.2.

[37]See Exercise 12.8.

[38]See Exercise 12.8.

12.4 Discrete Data

As explained in Chapter 3, discrete explanatory and response variables often lead to plots that are difficult to interpret, a problem that can be partially rectified by "jittering" the plotted points.[39] A discrete *response* variable also violates the assumption that the errors in a linear model are normally distributed. This problem, like that of a limited response variable (i.e., one that is bounded below or above), is only serious in extreme cases—for example, when there are very few response categories or where a large proportion of the data is in a small number of categories, conditional on the values of the explanatory variables. In these cases, it is best to use statistical models for categorical response variables.[40]

Discrete *explanatory* variables, in contrast, are perfectly consistent with the general linear model, which makes no distributional assumptions about the Xs, other than independence between the Xs and the errors. Indeed, because it partitions the data into groups, a discrete X (or combination of Xs) facilitates straightforward tests of nonlinearity and nonconstant error variance.

12.4.1 Testing for Nonlinearity ("Lack of Fit")

Recall the data on vocabulary and education from the U.S. General Social Survey, introduced in Chapter 3. Years of education in this data set range between 0 and 20. Suppose that we model the relationship between vocabulary score and education in two ways:

1. Fit a linear regression of vocabulary on education:

$$Y_i = \alpha + \beta X_i + \varepsilon_i \tag{12.15}$$

2. Model education with a set of dummy regressors. There are 21 distinct values of education, yielding 20 dummy regressors (treating 0 years of education as the baseline category):

$$Y_i = \alpha' + \gamma_1 D_{i1} + \gamma_2 D_{i2} + \cdots + \gamma_{20} D_{i,20} + \varepsilon_i' \tag{12.16}$$

Figure 12.12 contrasts these two models visually, showing the mean vocabulary score at each level of education (corresponding to Equation 12.16) and the least-squares regression line (corresponding to Equation 12.15). The area of the points representing the means is proportional to the number of observations at each educational level.

Contrasting the two models produces a test for nonlinearity because the model in Equation 12.15, specifying a linear relationship between vocabulary and education, is a special case of the model given in Equation 12.16, which can capture *any* pattern of relationship between $E(Y)$ and X. The resulting incremental F-test for nonlinearity appears in Table 12.2. There is, therefore, very strong evidence of a departure from linearity. Nevertheless, the linear regression of vocabulary on education accounts for almost all the variation among the means: The R^2 for the linear regression is $25,340/101,436 = 0.2498$, and for the more general dummy regression, $R^2 = 26,099/101,436 = 0.2573$. In such as large sample, with more than 20,000 observations, even this relatively small difference is statistically significant. Nevertheless, the departure from linearity in Figure 12.12 makes some substantive sense: Discounting the means at very low levels of education where there is little data, there are small jumps in average vocabulary scores at 12 and 16 years of education—corresponding to graduation from high school and university.

---

[39] See Section 3.2.
[40] See Chapter 14.

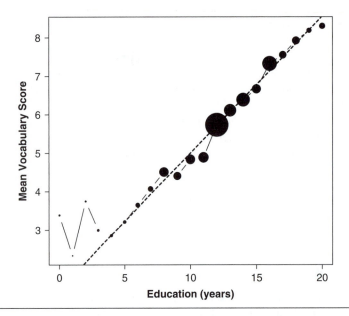

Figure 12.12   Mean vocabulary score by years of education. The size of the points is proportional to the number of observations at each educational level. The broken line is for the least-squares regression of vocabulary on education.

Table 12.2   Analysis of Variance for Vocabulary-Test Scores, Showing the Incremental F-Test for Nonlinearity of the Relationship Between Vocabulary and Education

Source	SS	df	F	p
Education				
(Model 12.16)	26,099	20	374.44	≪.0001
Linear				
(Model 12.15)	25,340	1	7,270.99	≪.0001
Nonlinear				
("lack of fit")	759	19	11.46	≪.0001
Error				
("pure error")	75,337	21,617		
Total	101,436	21,637		

The incremental F-test for nonlinearity can easily be extended to a discrete explanatory variable—say X_1—in a multiple-regression model. Here, we need to contrast the general model

$$Y_i = \alpha + \gamma_1 D_{i1} + \cdots + \gamma_{m-1} D_{i,\,m-1} + \beta_2 X_{i2} + \cdots + \beta_k X_{ik} + \varepsilon_i$$

with the model specifying a linear effect of X_1

$$Y_i = \alpha + \beta_1 X_{i1} + \beta_2 X_{i2} + \cdots + \beta_k X_{ik} + \varepsilon_i$$

where $D_1, \ldots, D_{m-1}$ are dummy regressors constructed to represent the m distinct values of X_1.

Consider, by way of illustration, the additive model that we fit in the previous section to the SLID data (Equation 12.7 on page 280), regressing log wages on sex, a second-degree polynomial in age, and the square of education. Does this specification adequately capture the shape of the partial regressions of log wages on age and education? Because both age and education are discrete, we can fit a model that treats age and education as factors, with 50 and 21 levels respectively. We contrast this larger model with two null models: one that treats age as a second-order polynomial, and the other that includes the square of education, producing the following regression sums of squares and degrees of freedom:

Model	RegSS	df
Sex, Age (as factor), Education (as factor)	855.64	70
Sex, Age (as quadratic), Education (as factor)	827.02	23
Sex, Age (as factor), Education^2	847.53	51

The residual sum of squares for the full model is RSS = 1249.10 on 3,926 degrees of freedom, and consequently incremental F-tests for lack of fit are

$$\text{Age: } F_0 = \frac{\frac{855.64-827.02}{70-23}}{\frac{1249.10}{3926}} = 1.91, df = 47, 3926, \ p = .0002$$

$$\text{Education: } F_0 = \frac{\frac{855.64-847.53}{70-51}}{\frac{1249.10}{3926}} = 1.34, \ df = 19, 3926, \ p = .15$$

The lack of fit from the specified partial relationship of log wages to age is statistically significant, while the lack of fit for education is not. Even in the case of age, however, the lack of fit is substantively trivial: For the full model $R^2 = .4065$, and for the model treating age as a second-degree polynomial $R^2 = .3929$. That this difference of less than 0.5% in explained variation is statistically significant is testimony to the power of the test in a moderately large sample.

A slightly more elaborate example uses the model for the SLID data in Table 12.1 (in the previous section, on page 283). This model specifies a regression of log wages on sex, a quadratic for age, and the square of education, but also permits interactions between sex and age and between sex and education. To test for lack of fit, we contrast the following models:

Model	RegSS	df
Sex, Age (as factor), Education (as factor), with interactions	903.10	138
Sex, Age (as quadratic), Education (as factor), with interactions	858.72	44
Sex, Age (as factor), Education^2, with interactions	893.14	101

These models, especially the full model in which both age and education are treated as factors, have many parameters to estimate, but with nearly 4,000 observations we can spend many degrees of freedom on the model and still have plenty left to estimate the error variance: The residual sum of squares for the full model is RSS = 1201.64 on 3,858 degrees of freedom. Incremental F-tests for lack of fit are as follows:

Age (and its interaction with Sex):

$$F_0 = \frac{\frac{903.10-858.72}{138-44}}{\frac{1201.64}{3858}} = 1.51, df = 94, 3858, \ p = .0011$$

Education (and its interaction with Sex):

$$F_0 = \frac{\frac{903.10-893.14}{138-101}}{\frac{1201.64}{3858}} = 0.86, df = 37, 3858, \ p = .70$$

Thus, as in the preceding example, there is a small but statistically significant lack of fit entailed by using a quadratic for age (the R^2 for the full model is .4291, versus .4080 for the much more parsimonious model with a quadratic in age); and there is no evidence of lack of fit using the square of education in the regression.[41]

Another approach to testing for nonlinearity exploits the fact that a polynomial of degree $m - 1$ can perfectly capture the relationship between Y and a discrete X with m categories, regardless of the specific form of this relationship. We remove one term at a time from the model

$$Y_i = \alpha + \beta_1 X_i + \beta_2 X_i^2 + \cdots + \beta_{m-1} X_i^{m-1} + \varepsilon_i$$

beginning with X^{m-1}. If the decrement in the regression sum of squares is nonsignificant (by an incremental F-test on 1 degree of freedom), then we proceed to remove X^{m-2}, and so on.[42] This approach has the potential advantage of parsimony because we may well require more than one term (i.e., a linear relationship) but fewer than $m - 1$ terms (i.e., a relationship of arbitrary form). High-degree polynomials, however, are usually difficult to interpret.[43]

12.4.2   Testing for Nonconstant Error Variance

A discrete X (or combination of Xs) partitions the data into m groups (as in analysis of variance). Let Y_{ij} denote the ith of n_j response-variable scores in group j. If the error variance is constant across groups, then the within-group sample variances

$$S_j^2 = \frac{\sum_{i=1}^{n_j}(Y_{ij} - \overline{Y}_j)^2}{n_j - 1}$$

should be similar. Tests that examine the S_j^2 directly, such as Bartlett's (1937) classic (and commonly employed) test, do not maintain their validity well when the distribution of the errors is non-normal.

Many alternative tests have been proposed. In a large-scale simulation study, Conover, Johnson, and Johnson (1981) found that the following simple F-test (called "Levene's test") is both robust and powerful: Calculate the values

$$Z_{ij} \equiv |Y_{ij} - \widetilde{Y}_j|$$

---

[41] We could, in principle, go further in testing for lack of fit, specifying a model that divides the data by combinations of levels of sex, age, and education, and comparing this model with our current model for the SLID data. We run into the "curse of dimensionality," however (see Section 2.2 and Chapter 18): There are $2 \times 50 \times 21 = 2, 100$ combinations of values of the three explanatory variables, and "only" about 4,000 observations in the data set.

[42] As usual, the estimate of error variance in the denominator of these F-tests is taken from the full model with all $m - 1$ terms.

[43] *There is a further, technical difficulty with this procedure: The several powers of X are usually highly correlated, sometimes to the point that least-squares calculations break down. A solution is to orthogonalize the power regressors prior to fitting the model. See the discussion of polynomial regression in Section 17.1.

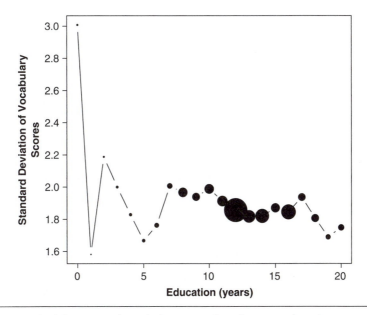

Figure 12.13   Standard deviation of vocabulary scores by education. The relative size of the points
is proportional to the number of respondents at each level of education.

where $\widetilde{Y}_j$ is the median response-variable value in group j. Then perform a one-way analysis of
variance of the Z_{ij} over the m groups. If the error variance is not constant across the groups, then
the group means $\overline{Z}_j$ will tend to differ, producing a large value of the F-test statistic.[44]

For the vocabulary data, for example, where education partitions the 21,638 observations into
$m = 21$ groups, this test gives $F_0 = 4.26$, with 20 and 21,617 degrees of freedom, for which
$p \ll .0001$. There is, therefore, strong evidence of nonconstant spread in vocabulary across the
categories of education, though, as revealed in Figure 12.13, the within-group standard deviations
are not very different (discounting the small numbers of individuals with very low levels of
education).[45]

> Discrete explanatory variables divide the data into groups. A simple incremental F-test for
> nonlinearity compares the sum of squares accounted for by the linear regression of Y on X
> with the sum of squares accounted for by differences in the group means. Likewise, tests
> of non-constant variance can be based on comparisons of spread in the different groups.

12.5 Maximum-Likelihood Methods*

A statistically sophisticated approach to selecting a transformation of Y or an X is to embed
the usual linear model in a more general nonlinear model that contains a parameter for the

---

[44]This test ironically exploits the robustness of the validity of the F-test in one-way ANOVA. (The irony lies in the
common use of tests of constant variance as a preliminary to tests of differences in means.)

[45]The tendency of the standard deviations to decline slightly with increasing education is likely due to a "ceiling" effect—at
higher levels of education, the vocabulary scores push toward the upper boundary of 10.

transformation. If several variables are potentially to be transformed, or if the transformation is complex, then there may be several such parameters.[46]

Suppose that the transformation is indexed by a single parameter λ (e.g., the power transformation $Y \rightarrow Y^\lambda$), and that we can write down the likelihood for the model as a function of the transformation parameter and the usual regression parameters: $L(\lambda, \alpha, \beta_1, \ldots, \beta_k, \sigma_\varepsilon^2)$.[47] Maximizing the likelihood yields the maximum-likelihood estimate of λ along with the MLEs of the other parameters. Now suppose that $\lambda = \lambda_0$ represents *no* transformation (e.g., $\lambda_0 = 1$ for the power transformation Y^λ). A likelihood-ratio test, Wald test, or score test of H_0: $\lambda = \lambda_0$ assesses the evidence that a transformation is required.

A disadvantage of the likelihood-ratio and Wald tests in this context is that they require finding the MLE, which usually necessitates iteration (i.e., a repetitive process of successively closer approximations). In contrast, the slope of the log likelihood at λ_0—on which the score test depends—generally can be assessed or approximated without iteration and therefore is faster to compute.

Often, the score test can be formulated as the t-statistic for a new regressor, called a *constructed variable*, to be added to the linear model. An added-variable plot for the constructed variable then can reveal whether one or a small group of observations is unduly influential in determining the transformation or, alternatively, whether evidence for the transformation is spread throughout the data.

12.5.1 Box-Cox Transformation of Y

Box and Cox (1964) suggested a power transformation of Y with the object of normalizing the error distribution, stabilizing the error variance, and straightening the relationship of Y to the Xs.[48] The general Box-Cox model is

$$Y_i^{(\lambda)} = \alpha + \beta_1 X_{i1} + \cdots + \beta_k X_{ik} + \varepsilon_i$$

where the errors ε_i are independently $N(0, \sigma_\varepsilon^2)$, and

$$Y_i^{(\lambda)} = \begin{cases} \dfrac{Y_i^\lambda - 1}{\lambda} & \text{for } \lambda \neq 0 \\[2ex] \log_e Y_i & \text{for } \lambda = 0 \end{cases}$$

Note that all the Y_i must be positive.[49]

For a particular choice of λ, the conditional maximized log likelihood is[50]

$$\log_e L(\alpha, \beta_1, \ldots, \beta_k, \sigma_\varepsilon^2 | \lambda) = -\frac{n}{2}(1 + \log_e 2\pi)$$

$$-\frac{n}{2} \log_e \widehat{\sigma}_\varepsilon^2(\lambda) + (\lambda - 1) \sum_{i=1}^{n} \log_e Y_i$$

---

[46] Models of this type are fundamentally nonlinear and can be treated by the general methods of Chapter 17 as well as by the methods described in the present section.

[47] See Appendix D for a general introduction to maximum-likelihood estimation.

[48] Subsequent work (Hernandez and Johnson, 1980) showed that Box and Cox's method principally serves to normalize the error distribution.

[49] Strictly speaking, the requirement that the Y_i are positive precludes the possibility that they are normally distributed (because the normal distribution is unbounded), but this is not a serious practical difficulty unless many Y values stack up near 0.

[50] See Exercise 12.9.

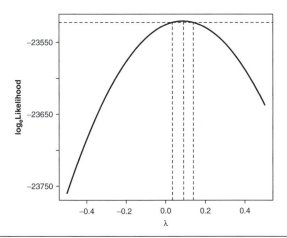

Figure 12.14 Box-Cox transformations for the SLID regression of wages on sex, age, and education. The maximized log likelihood is plotted against the transformation parameter λ. The intersection of the line near the top of the graph with the profile log-likelihood curve marks off a 95% confidence interval for λ. The maximum of the log likelihood corresponds to the MLE of λ.

where $\widehat{\sigma}_\varepsilon^2(\lambda) = \sum E_i^2(\lambda)/n$ and where the $E_i(\lambda)$ are the residuals from the least-squares regression of $Y^{(\lambda)}$ on the Xs. The least-squares coefficients from this regression are the maximum-likelihood estimates of α and the βs, conditional on the value of λ.

A simple procedure for finding the maximum-likelihood estimator $\widehat{\lambda}$, then, is to evaluate the maximized $\log_e L$ (called the *profile log likelihood*) for a range of values of λ, say between -2 and $+2$. If this range turns out not to contain the maximum of the log likelihood, then the range can be expanded. To test H_0: $\lambda = 1$, calculate the likelihood-ratio statistic

$$G_0^2 = -2[\log_e L(\lambda = 1) - \log_e L(\lambda = \widehat{\lambda})]$$

which is asymptotically distributed as χ^2 with one degree of freedom under H_0. Alternatively (but equivalently), a 95% confidence interval for λ includes those values for which

$$\log_e L(\lambda) > \log_e L(\lambda = \widehat{\lambda}) - 1.92$$

The number 1.92 comes from $\frac{1}{2} \times \chi_{1,.05}^2 = \frac{1}{2} \times 1.96^2$.

Figure 12.14 shows a plot of the profile log likelihood against λ for the original SLID regression of composite hourly wages on sex, age, and education (Equation 12.1 on page 267). In constructing this graph, I have "zeroed in" on the maximum-likelihood estimate of λ: I originally plotted the profile log likelihood over the wider range $\lambda = -2$ to $\lambda = 2$. The maximum-likelihood estimate of λ is $\widehat{\lambda} = 0.09$, and a 95% confidence interval, marked out by the intersection of the line near the top of the graph with the profile log likelihood, runs from 0.04 to 0.13. Recall that we previously employed a log transformation for these data (i.e., $\lambda = 0$) to make the residual distribution more nearly normal and to stabilize the error variance. Although $\lambda = 0$ is outside the confidence interval, it represents essentially the same transformation of wages as $\lambda = 0.09$ (indeed, the correlation between log wages and wages$^{0.09}$ is 0.9996). I prefer the log transformation for interpretability.

Atkinson (1985) proposed an approximate score test for the Box-Cox model, based on the constructed variable

$$G_i = Y_i \left[\log_e\left(\frac{Y_i}{\widetilde{Y}}\right) - 1 \right]$$

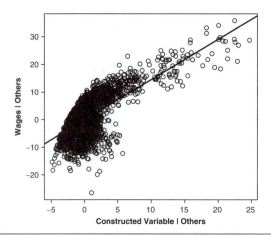

Figure 12.15 Constructed-variable plot for the Box-Cox transformation of wages in the SLID regression. The least-squares line is shown on the plot.

where $\widetilde{Y}$ is the *geometric mean* of Y:[51]

$$\widetilde{Y} \equiv (Y_1 \times Y_2 \times \cdots \times Y_n)^{1/n}$$

This constructed variable is obtained by a linear approximation to the Box-Cox transformation $Y^{(\lambda)}$ evaluated at $\lambda = 1$. The augmented regression, including the constructed variable, is then

$$Y_i = \alpha' + \beta'_1 X_{i1} + \cdots + \beta'_k X_{ik} + \phi G_i + \varepsilon'_i$$

The t-test of H_0: $\phi = 0$, that is, $t_0 = \widehat{\phi}/\mathrm{SE}(\widehat{\phi})$, assesses the need for a transformation. The quantities $\widehat{\phi}$ and $\mathrm{SE}(\widehat{\phi})$ are obtained from the least-squares regression of Y on $X_1, \ldots, X_k$ and G. An estimate of λ (though not the MLE) is given by $\widehat{\lambda} = 1 - \widehat{\phi}$; and the partial-regression plot for the constructed variable G shows influence and leverage on $\widehat{\phi}$ and hence on the choice of λ.

Atkinson's constructed-variable plot for the SLID regression is shown in Figure 12.15. Although the trend in the plot is not altogether linear, it appears that evidence for the transformation of Y is spread generally through the data and does not depend unduly on a small number of observations. The coefficient of the constructed variable in the regression is $\widehat{\phi} = 1.454$, with $\mathrm{SE}(\widehat{\phi}) = 0.026$, providing overwhelmingly strong evidence of the need to transform Y. The suggested transformation, $\widehat{\lambda} = 1 - 1.454 = -0.454$, is far from the MLE.

12.5.2 Box-Tidwell Transformation of the *X*s

Now, consider the model

$$Y_i = \alpha + \beta_1 X_{i1}^{\gamma_1} + \cdots + \beta_k X_{ik}^{\gamma_k} + \varepsilon_i$$

where the errors are independently distributed as $\varepsilon_i \sim N(0, \sigma_\varepsilon^2)$ and all the X_{ij} are positive. The parameters of this model—$\alpha, \beta_1, \ldots, \beta_k, \gamma_1, \ldots, \gamma_k$, and σ_ε^2—could be estimated by general nonlinear least squares, but Box and Tidwell (1962) suggest instead a computationally more efficient procedure that also yields a constructed-variable diagnostic:[52]

---

[51]It is more practical to compute the geometric mean as $\widetilde{Y} = \exp[(\sum \log_e Y_i)/n]$.

[52]Nonlinear least-squares regression is described in Section 17.4.

1. Regress Y on $X_1, \ldots, X_k$, obtaining $A, B_1, \ldots, B_k$.

2. Regress Y on $X_1, \ldots, X_k$ and the constructed variables $X_1 \log_e X_1, \ldots, X_k \log_e X_k$, obtaining $A', B'_1, \ldots, B'_k$ and $D_1, \ldots, D_k$. Because of the presence of the constructed variables in this second regression, in general $A \neq A'$ and $B_j \neq B'_j$. As in the Box-Cox model, the constructed variables result from a linear approximation to $X_j^{\gamma_j}$ evaluated at $\gamma_j = 1$.[53]

3. The constructed variable $X_j \log_e X_j$ can be used to assess the need for a transformation of X_j by testing the null hypothesis $H_0: \delta_j = 0$, where δ_j is the population coefficient of $X_j \log_e X_j$ in Step 2. Partial-regression plots for the constructed variables are useful for assessing leverage and influence on the decision to transform the Xs.

4. A preliminary estimate of the transformation parameter γ_j (not the MLE) is given by

$$\tilde{\gamma}_j = 1 + \frac{D_j}{B_j}$$

Recall that B_j is from the *initial* (i.e., Step 1) regression (not from Step 2).

This procedure can be iterated through Steps 1, 2, and 4 until the estimates of the transformation parameters stabilize, yielding the MLEs $\hat{\gamma}_j$.

By way of example, I will work with the SLID regression of log wages on sex, education, and age. The dummy regressor for sex is not a candidate for transformation, of course, but I will consider power transformations of age and education. Recall that we were initially undecided about whether to model the age effect as a quadratic or as a transformation down the ladder of powers and roots. To make power transformations of age more effective, I use a negative start of 15 (recall that age ranges from 16 to 65).

The coefficients of $(\text{Age} - 15) \times \log_e(\text{Age} - 15)$ and $\text{Education} \times \log_e \text{Education}$ in the step-2 augmented model are, respectively, $D_{\text{Age}} = -0.04699$ with $\text{SE}(D_{\text{Age}}) = 0.00231$, and $D_{\text{Education}} = 0.05612$ with $\text{SE}(D_{\text{Education}}) = 0.01254$. Although both score tests are, consequently, statistically significant, there is much stronger evidence of the need to transform age than education.

The first-step estimates of the transformation parameters are

$$\tilde{\gamma}_{\text{Age}} = 1 + \frac{D_{\text{Age}}}{B_{\text{Age}}} = 1 + \frac{-0.04699}{0.02619} = -0.79$$

$$\tilde{\gamma}_{\text{Education}} = 1 + \frac{D_{\text{Education}}}{B_{\text{Education}}} = 1 + \frac{0.05612}{0.08061} = 1.69$$

The fully iterated MLEs of the transformation parameters are $\hat{\gamma}_{\text{Age}} = 0.051$ and $\hat{\gamma}_{\text{Education}} = 1.89$—very close to the log transformation of started-age and the square of education.

Constructed-variable plots for the transformation of age and education, shown in Figure 12.16, suggest that evidence for the transformation of age is spread throughout the data but that there are some high-leverage, and hence potentially influential, observations determining the transformation of education. Accordingly, I proceeded to remove observations for which the education constructed variable exceeds 1 and found that when I did this, I obtained a similar estimate of the transformation parameter for education ($\hat{\gamma}_{\text{Education}} = 2.40$).

---

[53] See Exercise 12.10.

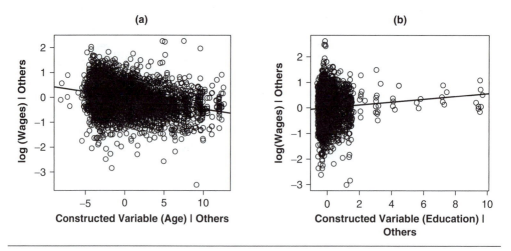

Figure 12.16　Constructed-variable plots for the Box-Tidwell transformation of (a) age and (b) education in the SLID regression of log wages on sex, age, and education.

> A statistically sophisticated general approach to selecting a transformation of Y or an X is to embed the linear-regression model in a more general model that contains a parameter for the transformation. The Box-Cox procedure selects a power transformation of Y to normalize the errors. The Box-Tidwell procedure selects power transformations of the Xs to linearize the regression of Y on the Xs. In both cases, "constructed-variable" plots help us to decide whether individual observations are unduly influential in determining the transformation parameters.

12.5.3　Nonconstant Error Variance Revisited

Breusch and Pagan (1979) developed a score test for heteroscedasticity based on the specification

$$\sigma_i^2 \equiv V(\varepsilon_i) = g(\gamma_0 + \gamma_1 Z_{i1} + \cdots + \gamma_p Z_{ip})$$

where $Z_1, \ldots, Z_p$ are known variables and where the function $g(\cdot)$ is quite general (and need not be explicitly specified). The same test was independently derived by Cook and Weisberg (1983). The score statistic for the hypothesis that the σ_i^2 are all the same, which is equivalent to H_0: $\gamma_1 = \cdots = \gamma_p = 0$, can be formulated as an auxiliary-regression problem.

Let $U_i \equiv E_i^2 / \widehat{\sigma}_\varepsilon^2$, where $\widehat{\sigma}_\varepsilon^2 = \sum E_i^2 / n$ is the MLE of the error variance.[54] The U_i are a type of standardized squared residuals. Regress U on the Zs:

$$U_i = \eta_0 + \eta_1 Z_{i1} + \cdots + \eta_p Z_{ip} + \omega_i \qquad (12.17)$$

Breusch and Pagan (1979) show that the score statistic

$$S_0^2 = \frac{\sum (\widehat{U}_i - \overline{U})^2}{2}$$

---

[54] Note the division by n rather than by $n-1$ in $\widehat{\sigma}_\varepsilon^2$. See Section 9.3.3 on maximum-likelihood estimation of the linear model.

is asymptotically distributed as χ^2 with p degrees of freedom under the null hypothesis of constant error variance. Here, the $\widehat{U}_i$ are fitted values from the regression of U on the Zs, and thus S_0^2 is half the regression sum of squares from fitting Equation 12.17.

To apply this result, it is, of course, necessary to select Zs, the choice of which depends on the suspected pattern of nonconstant error variance. If several patterns are suspected, then several score tests can be performed. Employing $X_1, \ldots, X_k$ in the auxiliary regression (Equation 12.17), for example, permits detection of a tendency of the error variance to increase with the values of one or more of the explanatory variables in the main regression.

Likewise, Cook and Weisberg (1983) suggest regressing U on the fitted values from the main regression (i.e., fitting the auxiliary regression $U_i = \eta_0 + \eta_1 \widehat{Y}_i + \omega_i$), producing a one-degree-of-freedom score test to detect the common tendency of the error variance to increase with the level of the response variable. When the error variance follows this pattern, the auxiliary regression of U on $\widehat{Y}$ provides a more powerful test than the more general regression of U on the Xs. A similar, but more complex, procedure was described by Anscombe (1961), who suggests correcting detected heteroscedasticity by transforming Y to $Y^{(\widetilde{\lambda})}$ with $\widetilde{\lambda} = 1 - \frac{1}{2}\widehat{\eta}_1 \overline{Y}$.

Finally, White (1980) proposed a score test based on a comparison of his heteroscedasticity-corrected estimator of coefficient sampling variance with the usual estimator of coefficient variance.[55] If the two estimators are sufficiently different, then doubt is cast on the assumption of constant error variance. White's test can be implemented as an auxiliary regression of the squared residuals from the main regression, E_i^2, on all the Xs together with all the squares and pairwise products of the Xs. Thus, for $k = 2$ explanatory variables in the main regression, we would fit the model

$$E_i^2 = \delta_0 + \delta_1 X_{i1} + \delta_2 X_{i2} + \delta_{11} X_{i1}^2 + \delta_{22} X_{i2}^2 + \delta_{12} X_{i1} X_{i2} + \upsilon_i$$

In general, there will be $p = k(k+3)/2$ terms in the auxiliary regression, plus the constant. The score statistic for testing the null hypothesis of constant error variance is $S_0^2 = nR^2$, where R^2 is the squared multiple correlation from the auxiliary regression. Under the null hypothesis, S_0^2 follows an asymptotic χ^2 distribution with p degrees of freedom.

Because all these score tests are potentially sensitive to violations of model assumptions other than constant error variance, it is important, in practice, to supplement the tests with graphical diagnostics, as suggested by Cook and Weisberg (1983). When there are several Zs, a simple diagnostic is to plot U_i against $\widehat{U}_i$, the fitted values from the auxiliary regression. We can also construct added-variable plots for the Zs in the auxiliary regression. When U_i is regressed on $\widehat{Y}_i$, these plots convey essentially the same information as the plot of studentized residuals against fitted values proposed in Section 12.2.

Simple score tests are available to determine the need for a transformation and to test for nonconstant error variance.

Applied to the initial SLID regression of wages on sex, age, and education, an auxiliary regression of U on $\widehat{Y}$ yields $\widehat{U} = -0.3449 + 0.08652\widehat{Y}$, and $S_0^2 = 567.66/2 = 283.83$ on 1 degree of freedom. There is, consequently, very strong evidence that the error variance increases with the level of the response variable. The suggested variance-stabilizing transformation using Anscombe's rule is $\widetilde{\lambda} = 1 - \frac{1}{2}(0.08652)(15.545) = 0.33$. Compare this value with those produced

---

[55]White's coefficient-variance estimator is described in Section 12.2.3.

by the Box-Cox model ($\widehat{\lambda} = 0.09$, in Section 12.5.1) and by trial and error ($\lambda = 0$, i.e., the log transformation, in Section 12.2).

An auxiliary regression of U on the explanatory variables in the main regression yields $S_0^2 = 579.08/2 = 289.54$ on $k = 3$ degrees of freedom and thus also provides strong evidence against constant error variance. The score statistic for the more general test is not much larger than that for the regression of U on $\widehat{Y}$, implying that the pattern of nonconstant error variance is indeed for the spread of the errors to increase with the level of Y.

To perform White's test, I regressed the squared residuals from the initial SLID model on the dummy regressor for sex, age, education, the squares of age and education, and the pairwise products of the variables. It does not, of course, make sense to square the dummy regressor for sex. The resulting regression produced an R^2 of .03646, and thus a score statistic of $S_0^2 = 3997 \times 0.03646 = 145.97$ on $p = 6$ degrees of freedom, which also provides very strong evidence of nonconstant error variance.

12.6 Structural Dimension

In discussing the use and potential failure of component-plus-residual plots as a diagnostic for nonlinearity, I explained that it is unreasonable to expect that a collection of two- or three-dimensional graphs can, in every instance, adequately capture the dependence of Y on the Xs: The surface representing this dependence lies, after all, in a space of $k + 1$ dimensions. Relying primarily on Cook (1994), I will now briefly consider the geometric notion of dimension in regression analysis, along with the implications of this notion for diagnosing problems with regression models that have been fit to data.[56] The *structural dimension* of a regression problem corresponds to the dimensionality of the smallest subspace of the Xs required to represent the dependency of Y on the Xs.

Let us initially suppose that the distribution of Y is completely *independent* of the explanatory variables $X_1, \ldots, X_k$. Then, in Cook and Weisberg's (1994) terminology, an "ideal summary" of the data is simply the univariate, unconditional distribution of Y—represented, say, by the density function $p(y)$. In a sample, we could compute a density estimate, a histogram, or some other univariate display. In this case, the structural dimension of the data is 0.

Now suppose that Y depends on the Xs only through the linear regression

$$Y = \alpha + \beta_1 X_1 + \cdots + \beta_k X_k + \varepsilon$$

where $E(\varepsilon) = 0$ and the distribution of the error is independent of the Xs. Then the expectation of Y conditional on the Xs is a linear function of the Xs:

$$E(Y|x_1, \ldots, x_k) = \alpha + \beta_1 x_1 + \cdots + \beta_k x_k$$

A plot of Y against $\alpha + \beta_1 X_1 + \cdots + \beta_k X_k$, therefore, constitutes an ideal summary of the data. This two-dimensional plot shows the systematic component of Y in an edge-on view of the regression hyperplane and also shows the conditional variation of Y around the hyperplane (i.e., the variation of the errors). Because the subspace spanned by the linear combination $\alpha + \beta_1 X_1 + \cdots + \beta_k X_k$ is one dimensional, the structural dimension of the data is 1. In a sample, the ideal summary is a two-dimensional scatterplot of Y_i against $\widehat{Y}_i = A + B_1 X_{i1} + \cdots + B_k X_{ik}$; the regression line in this plot is an edge-on view of the fitted least-squares surface.

---

[56] An extended discussion of structural dimension, at a more elementary level than Cook (1994), may be found in Cook and Weisberg (1994, 1999).

The structural dimension of the data can be 1 even if the regression is *nonlinear* or if the errors are not identically distributed, as long as the expectation of Y and the distribution of the errors depend only on a single linear combination of the Xs—that is, a subspace of dimension 1. The structural dimension is 1, for example, if

$$E(Y|x_1, \ldots, x_k) = f(\alpha + \beta_1 x_1 + \cdots + \beta_k x_k) \tag{12.18}$$

and

$$V(Y|x_1, \ldots, x_k) = g(\alpha + \beta_1 x_1 + \cdots + \beta_k x_k) \tag{12.19}$$

where the mean function $f(\cdot)$ and the variance function $g(\cdot)$, though generally different functions, depend on the *same* linear function of the Xs. In this case, a plot of Y against $\alpha + \beta_1 X_1 + \cdots + \beta_k X_k$ is still an ideal summary of the data, showing the nonlinear dependency of the expectation of Y on the Xs, along with the pattern of nonconstant error variance.

Similarly, we hope to see these features of the data in a sample plot of Y against $\widehat{Y}$ from the *linear* regression of Y on the Xs (even though the linear regression does not itself capture the dependency of Y on the Xs). It turns out, however, that the plot of Y against $\widehat{Y}$ can fail to reflect the mean and variance functions accurately if the Xs themselves are not linearly related—even when the true structural dimension is 1 (i.e., when Equations 12.18 and 12.19 hold).[57] This, then, is another context in which linearly related explanatory variables are desirable.[58] Linearly related explanatory variables are not required here if the true regression is linear—something that, however, we are typically not in a position to know prior to examining the data.

The structural dimension of a regression is the dimensionality of the smallest subspace of the explanatory variables required, along with the response variable, to represent the dependence of Y on the Xs. When Y is completely independent of the Xs, the structural dimension is 0, and an ideal summary of the data is simply the unconditional distribution of Y. When the linear-regression model holds—or when the conditional expectation and variance of Y are functions of a single linear combination of the Xs—the structural dimension is 1.

The structural dimension of the data exceeds 1 if Equations 12.18 and 12.19 do not both hold. If, for example, the mean function depends on one linear combination of the Xs,

$$E(Y|x_1, \ldots, x_k) = f(\alpha + \beta_1 x_1 + \cdots + \beta_k x_k)$$

and the variance function on a *different* linear combination

$$V(Y|x_1, \ldots, x_k) = g(\gamma + \delta_1 x_1 + \cdots + \delta_k x_k)$$

then the structural dimension is 2.

---

[57] See Exercise 12.11.

[58] The requirement of linearity here is, in fact, stronger than pairwise linear relationships among the Xs: The regression of any linear function of the Xs on any set of linear functions of the Xs must be linear. If the Xs are multivariate normal, then this condition is necessarily satisfied (although it may be satisfied even if the Xs are not normal). It is not possible to check for linearity in this strict sense when there are more than two or three Xs, but there is some evidence that checking pairs—and perhaps triples—of Xs is usually sufficient. See Cook and Weisberg (1994). Cf. Section 12.3.3 for the conditions under which component-plus-residual plots are informative.

Correspondingly, if the mean function depends on *two different* linear combinations of the Xs, implying interaction among the Xs,

$$E(Y|x_1, \ldots, x_k) = f(\alpha + \beta_1 x_1 + \cdots + \beta_k x_k, \gamma + \delta_1 x_1 + \cdots + \delta_k x_k)$$

while the errors are independent of the Xs, then the structural dimension is also 2. When the structural dimension is 2, a plot of Y against $\widehat{Y}$ (from the linear regression of Y on the Xs) is necessarily incomplete.

These observations are interesting, but their practical import—beyond the advantage of linearly related regressors—is unclear: Short of modeling the regression of Y on the Xs nonparametrically, we can never be sure that we have captured all the structure of the data in a lower-dimensional subspace of the explanatory variables.

There is, however, a further result that *does* have direct practical application: Suppose that the explanatory variables are linearly related and that there is one-dimensional structure. Then the *inverse regressions* of each of the explanatory variables on the response variable have the following character:

$$E(X_j|y) = \mu_j + \eta_j m(y)$$
$$V(X_j|y) \approx \sigma_j^2 + \eta_j^2 v(y) \tag{12.20}$$

Equation 12.20 has two special features that are useful in checking whether one-dimensional structure is reasonable for a set of data:[59]

1. Most important, the functions $m(\cdot)$ and $v(\cdot)$, through which the means and variances of the Xs depend on Y, are the same for all the Xs. Consequently, if the scatterplot of X_1 against Y shows a linear relationship, for example, then the scatterplots of each of $X_2, \ldots, X_k$ against Y must also show linear relationships. If one of these relationships is quadratic, in contrast, then the others must be quadratic. Likewise, if the variance of X_1 increases linearly with the level of Y, then the variances of the other Xs must also be linearly related to Y. There is only one exception: The constant η_j can be 0, in which case the mean and variance of the corresponding X_j are *unrelated* to Y.

2. The constant η_j appears in the formula for the conditional mean of X_j, and η_j^2 in the formula for its conditional variance, placing constraints on the patterns of these relationships. If, for example, the mean of X_1 is unrelated to Y, then so should the variance be.

The sample inverse regressions of the Xs on Y can be conveniently examined in the first column of the scatterplot matrix for $\{Y, X_1, \ldots, X_k\}$. An illustrative application is shown in Figure 12.17, for the regression of prestige on education, income, and percent women, for the Canadian occupational prestige data.[60] Here, I have log-transformed income and taken the logit of percent women to make the relationships among the explanatory variables more nearly linear. The inverse-response plots in the first column of the scatterplot matrix show roughly similar patterns, as required for one-dimensional structure.

> If the structural dimension is 1, and if the explanatory variables are linearly related to one another, then the inverse regressions of the explanatory variables on the response variable all have the same general form.

---

[59]Equation 12.20 is the basis for formal dimension-testing methods, such as *sliced inverse regression* (Duan & Li, 1991) and related techniques. See Cook and Weisberg (1994, 1999) for an introductory treatment of dimension testing and for additional references.

[60]This data set was introduced in Chapter 2 and used for an example of multiple regression in Chapter 4.

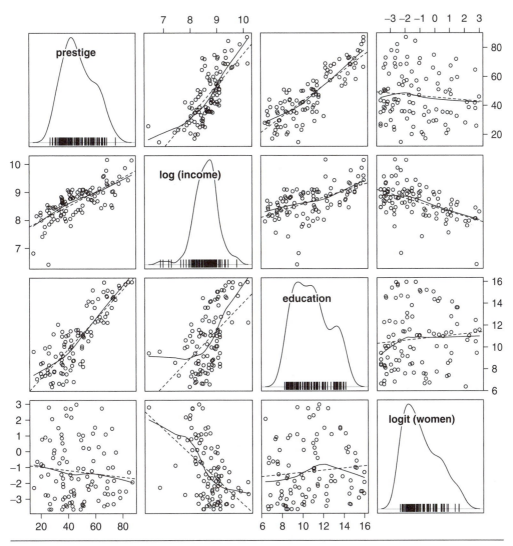

Figure 12.17 Scatterplot matrix for prestige, log of income, education, and logit of percent women in the Canadian occupational prestige data. The inverse response plots are in the first column of the scatterplot matrix. In each panel, the solid line is for a lowess smooth with span 3/4, while the broken line is the least-squares line. Kernel-density estimates are given on the diagonal, with the rug-plot at the bottom of each diagonal panel showing the location of the observations.

Exercises

Exercise 12.1. *Show that the correlation between the least-squares residuals E_i and the response-variable values Y_i is $\sqrt{1 - R^2}$. [*Hint*: Use the geometric vector representation of multiple regression (developed in Chapter 10), examining the plane in which the $\mathbf{e}$, $\mathbf{y}^*$, and $\widehat{\mathbf{y}}^*$ vectors lie.]

Exercise 12.2. Nonconstant variance and specification error: Generate 100 observations according to the following model:

$$Y = 10 + (1 \times X) + (1 \times D) + (2 \times X \times D) + \varepsilon$$

where $\varepsilon \sim N(0, 10^2)$; the values of X are $1, 2, \ldots, 50, 1, 2, \ldots, 50$; the first 50 values of D are 0; and the last 50 values of D are 1. Then regress Y on X alone (i.e., omitting D and XD), $Y = A + BX + E$. Plot the residuals E from this regression against the fitted values $\widehat{Y}$. Is the variance of the residuals constant? How do you account for the pattern in the plot?

Exercise 12.3. *Weighted-least-squares estimation: Suppose that the errors from the linear regression model $\mathbf{y} = \mathbf{X}\boldsymbol{\beta} + \varepsilon$ are independent and normally distributed, but with different variances, $\varepsilon_i \sim N(0, \sigma_i^2)$, and that $\sigma_i^2 = \sigma_\varepsilon^2 / w_i^2$. Show that:

(a) The likelihood for the model is

$$L(\boldsymbol{\beta}, \sigma_\varepsilon^2) = \frac{1}{(2\pi)^{n/2} |\boldsymbol{\Sigma}|^{1/2}} \exp\left[-\frac{1}{2}(\mathbf{y} - \mathbf{X}\boldsymbol{\beta})'\boldsymbol{\Sigma}(\mathbf{y} - \mathbf{X}\boldsymbol{\beta})\right]$$

where

$$\boldsymbol{\Sigma} = \sigma_\varepsilon^2 \times \text{diag}\{1/w_1^2, \ldots, 1/w_n^2\} \equiv \sigma_\varepsilon^2 \times \mathbf{W}^{-1}$$

(b) The maximum-likelihood estimators of $\boldsymbol{\beta}$ and σ_ε^2 are

$$\widehat{\boldsymbol{\beta}} = (\mathbf{X}'\mathbf{W}\mathbf{X})^{-1}\mathbf{X}'\mathbf{W}\mathbf{y}$$

$$\widehat{\sigma}_\varepsilon^2 = \frac{\sum(E_i/w_i)^2}{n}$$

where $\mathbf{e} = \{E_i\} = \mathbf{y} - \mathbf{X}\widehat{\boldsymbol{\beta}}$.

(c) The MLE is equivalent to minimizing the weighted sum of squares $\sum w_i^2 E_i^2$.

(d) The estimated asymptotic covariance matrix of $\widehat{\boldsymbol{\beta}}$ is given by

$$\widehat{V}(\widehat{\boldsymbol{\beta}}) = \widehat{\sigma}_\varepsilon^2 (\mathbf{X}'\mathbf{W}\mathbf{X})^{-1}$$

Exercise 12.4. *Show that when the covariance matrix of the errors is

$$\boldsymbol{\Sigma} = \sigma_\varepsilon^2 \times \text{diag}\{1/w_1^2, \ldots, 1/w_n^2\} \equiv \sigma_\varepsilon^2 \times \mathbf{W}^{-1}$$

the weighted-least-squares estimator

$$\widehat{\boldsymbol{\beta}} = (\mathbf{X}'\mathbf{W}\mathbf{X})^{-1}\mathbf{X}'\mathbf{W}\mathbf{y}$$
$$= \mathbf{M}\mathbf{y}$$

is the minimum-variance linear unbiased estimator of $\boldsymbol{\beta}$. (*Hint*: Adapt the proof of the Gauss-Markov theorem for OLS estimation given in Section 9.3.2.)

Exercise 12.5. *The impact of nonconstant error variance on OLS estimation: Suppose that $Y_i = \alpha + \beta x_i + \varepsilon_i$, with independent errors, $\varepsilon_i \sim N(0, \sigma_i^2)$, and $\sigma_i = \sigma_\varepsilon x_i$. Let B represent the OLS estimator and $\widehat{\beta}$ the WLS estimator of β.

(a) Show that the sampling variance of the OLS estimator is

$$V(B) = \frac{\sum (X_i - \overline{X})^2 \sigma_i^2}{\left[\sum (X_i - \overline{X})^2\right]^2}$$

and that the sampling variance of the WLS estimator is

$$V(\widehat{\beta}) = \frac{\sigma_\varepsilon^2}{\sum w_i^2 (X_i - \widetilde{X})^2}$$

where $\widetilde{X} \equiv (\sum w_i^2 X_i)/(\sum w_i^2)$. (*Hint*: Write each slope estimator as a linear function of the Y_i.)

(b) Now suppose that x is uniformly distributed over the interval $[x_0, ax_0]$, where $x_0 > 0$ and $a > 0$, so that a is the ratio of the largest to the smallest σ_i. The efficiency of the OLS estimator relative to the optimal WLS estimator is $V(\widehat{\beta})/V(B)$, and the relative precision of the OLS estimator is the square root of this ratio, that is, $\text{SD}(\widehat{\beta})/\text{SD}(B)$. Calculate the relative precision of the OLS estimator for all combinations of $a = 2, 3, 5, 10$, and $n = 5$, 10, 20, 50, 100. For example, when $a = 3$ and $n = 10$, you can take the x values as 1, 1.222, 1.444, ..., 2.778, 3. Under what circumstances is the OLS estimator much less precise than the WLS estimator?

(c) The usual variance estimate for the OLS slope (assuming constant error variance) is

$$\widehat{V}(B) = \frac{S_E^2}{\sum (X_i - \overline{X})^2}$$

where $S_E^2 = \sum E_i^2/(n - 2)$. Kmenta (1986, sect. 8.2) shows that the expectation of this variance estimator (under nonconstant error variance σ_i^2) is

$$E[\widehat{V}(B)] = \frac{\overline{\sigma}^2}{\sum (X_i - \overline{X})^2} - \frac{\sum (X_i - \overline{X})^2 (\sigma_i^2 - \overline{\sigma}^2)}{(n - 2)[\sum (X_i - \overline{X})^2]^2}$$

where $\overline{\sigma}^2 \equiv \sum \sigma_i^2/n$. (*Prove this result.) Kmenta also shows that the true variance of the OLS slope estimator, $V(B)$ [derived in part (a)], is generally different from $E[\widehat{V}(B)]$. If $\sqrt{E[\widehat{V}(B)]/V(B)}$ is substantially below 1, then the usual formula for the standard deviation of B will lead us to believe that the OLS estimator is more precise than it really is. Calculate $\sqrt{E[\widehat{V}(B)]/V(B)}$ under the conditions of part (b), for $a = 5, 10, 20, 50$, and $n = 5, 10, 20, 50, 100$. What do you conclude about the robustness of validity of OLS inference with respect to nonconstant error variance?

Exercise 12.6. Experimenting with component-plus-residual plots: Generate random samples of 100 observations according to each of the following schemes. In each case, construct the component-plus-residual plots for X_1 and X_2. Do these plots accurately capture the partial relationships between Y and each of X_1 and X_2? Whenever they appear, ε and δ are $N(0, 1)$ and independent of each other and of the other variables.

(a) Independent Xs and a linear regression: X_1 and X_2 independent and uniformly distributed on the interval $[0, 1]$; $Y = X_1 + X_2 + 0.1\varepsilon$.

(b) Linearly related Xs and a linear regression: X_1 uniformly distributed on the interval $[0, 1]$; $X_2 = X_1 + 0.1\delta$; $Y = X_1 + X_2 + 0.1\varepsilon$.

    (c) Independent Xs and a nonlinear regression on one X: X_1 and X_2 independent and uniformly distributed on the interval $[0, 1]$; $Y = 2(X_1 - 0.5)^2 + X_2 + 0.1\varepsilon$.

    (d) Linearly related Xs and a nonlinear regression on one X: X_1 uniformly distributed on the interval $[0, 1]$; $X_2 = X_1 + 0.1\delta$; $Y = 2(X_1 - 0.5)^2 + X_2 + 0.1\varepsilon$. (Note the "leakage" here from X_1 to X_2.)

    (e) Nonlinearly related Xs and a linear regression: X_1 uniformly distributed on the interval $[0, 1]$; $X_2 = |X_1 - 0.5|$; $Y = X_1 + X_2 + 0.02\varepsilon$.

    (f) Nonlinearly related Xs and a linear regression on one X: X_1 uniformly distributed on the interval $[0, 1]$; $X_2 = |X_1 - 0.5|$; $Y = 2(X_1 - 0.5)^2 + X_2 + 0.02\varepsilon$. (Note how strong a nonlinear relationship between the Xs and how small an error variance in the regression are required for the effects in this example to be noticeable.)

Exercise 12.7. Consider an alternative analysis of the SLID data in which log wages is regressed on sex, transformed education, and transformed age—that is, try to straighten the relationship between log wages and age by a transformation rather than by a quadratic regression. How successful is this approach? *Hint:* Use a negative start, say age -15, prior to transforming age.

Exercise 12.8. Apply Mallows's procedure to construct augmented component-plus-residual plots for the SLID regression of log wages on sex, age, and education. *Then apply Cook's CERES procedure to this regression. Compare the results of these two procedures with each other and with the ordinary component-plus-residual plots in Figure 12.6. Do the more complex procedures give clearer indications of nonlinearity in this case?

Exercise 12.9. *Box-Cox transformations of Y: In matrix form, the Box-Cox regression model given in Section 12.5.1 can be written as

$$\mathbf{y}^{(\lambda)} = \mathbf{X}\boldsymbol{\beta} + \boldsymbol{\varepsilon}$$

    (a) Show that the probability density for the observations is given by

$$p(y) = \frac{1}{(2\pi\sigma_\varepsilon^2)^{n/2}} \exp\left[-\frac{\sum_{i=1}^{n}(Y_i^{(\lambda)} - \mathbf{x}_i'\boldsymbol{\beta})^2}{2\sigma_\varepsilon^2}\right] \prod_{i=1}^{n} Y_i^{\lambda-1}$$

       where $\mathbf{x}_i'$ is the ith row of $\mathbf{X}$. (*Hint*: $Y_i^{\lambda-1}$ is the Jacobian of the transformation from Y_i to ε_i.)

    (b) For a given value of λ, the *conditional* maximum-likelihood estimator of $\boldsymbol{\beta}$ is the least-squares estimator

$$\mathbf{b}_\lambda = (\mathbf{X}'\mathbf{X})^{-1}\mathbf{X}'\mathbf{y}^{(\lambda)}$$

       (Why?) Show that the maximized log likelihood can be written as

$$\log_e L(\alpha, \beta_1, \ldots, \beta_k, \sigma_\varepsilon^2 | \lambda)$$
$$= -\frac{n}{2}(1 + \log_e 2\pi) - \frac{n}{2}\log_e \widehat{\sigma}_\varepsilon^2(\lambda) + (\lambda - 1)\sum_{i=1}^{n}\log_e Y_i$$

    as stated in the text.

Exercise 12.10. *Box-Tidwell transformations of the Xs: Recall the Box-Tidwell model

$$Y_i = \alpha + \beta_1 X_{i1}^{\gamma_1} + \cdots + \beta_k X_{ik}^{\gamma_k} + \varepsilon_i$$

and focus on the first regressor, X_1. Show that the first-order Taylor-series approximation for $X_1^{\gamma_1}$ at $\gamma_1 = 1$ is

$$X_1^{\gamma_1} \approx X_1 + (\gamma_1 - 1)X_1 \log_e X_1$$

providing the basis for the constructed variable $X_1 \log_e X_1$.

Exercise 12.11. *Experimenting with structural dimension: Generate random samples of 100 observations according to each of the following schemes. In each case, fit the linear regression of Y on X_1 and X_2, and plot the values of Y against the resulting fitted values $\widehat{Y}$. Do these plots accurately capture the dependence of Y on X_1 and X_2? To decide this question in each case, it may help (1) to draw graphs of $E(Y|x_1, x_2) = f(\alpha + \beta_1 x_1 + \beta_2 x_2)$ and $V(Y|x_1, x_2) = g(\alpha + \beta_1 x_1 + \beta_2 x_2)$ over the observed range of values for $\alpha + \beta_1 X_1 + \beta_2 X_2$; and (2) to plot a nonparametric-regression smooth in the plot of Y against $\widehat{Y}$. Whenever they appear, ε and δ are $N(0, 1)$ and independent of each other and of the other variables.

(a) Independent Xs, a linear regression, and constant error variance: X_1 and X_2 independent and uniformly distributed on the interval $[0, 1]$; $E(Y|x_1, x_2) = x_1 + x_2$; $V(Y|x_1, x_2) = 0.1\varepsilon$.

(b) Independent Xs, mean and variance of Y dependent on the same linear function of the Xs: X_1 and X_2 independent and uniformly distributed on the interval $[0, 1]$; $E(Y|x_1, x_2) = (x_1 + x_2 - 1)^2$; $V(Y|x_1, x_2) = 0.1 \times |x_1 + x_2 - 1| \times \varepsilon$.

(c) Linearly related Xs, mean and variance of Y dependent on the same linear function of the Xs: X_1 uniformly distributed on the interval $[0, 1]$; $X_2 = X_1 + 0.1\delta$; $E(Y|x_1, x_2) = (x_1 + x_2 - 1)^2$; $V(Y|x_1, x_2) = 0.1 \times |x_1 + x_2 - 1| \times \varepsilon$.

(d) Nonlinearly related Xs, mean and variance of Y dependent on the same linear function of the Xs: X_1 uniformly distributed on the interval $[0, 1]$; $X_2 = |X_1 - 0.5|$; $E(Y|x_1, x_2) = (x_1 + x_2 - 1)^2$; $V(Y|x_1, x_2) = 0.1 \times |x_1 + x_2 - 1| \times \varepsilon$.

Summary _____

- Heavy-tailed errors threaten the efficiency of least-squares estimation; skewed and multi-modal errors compromise the interpretation of the least-squares fit. Non-normality can often be detected by examining the distribution of the least-squares residuals, and frequently can be corrected by transforming the data.

- It is common for the variance of the errors to increase with the level of the response variable. This pattern of nonconstant error variance ("heteroscedasticity") can often be detected in a plot of residuals against fitted values. Strategies for dealing with nonconstant error variance include transformation of the response variable to stabilize the variance; the substitution of weighted-least-squares estimation for ordinary least squares; and the correction of coefficient standard errors for heteroscedasticity. A rough rule is that nonconstant error variance seriously degrades the least-squares estimator only when the ratio of the largest to smallest variance is about 10 or more (or, more conservatively, about 4 or more).

- Simple forms of nonlinearity can often be detected in component-plus-residual plots. Once detected, nonlinearity can frequently be accommodated by variable transformations or by altering the form of the model (to include a quadratic term in an explanatory variable, for example). Component-plus-residual plots reliably reflect nonlinearity when there are not strong nonlinear relationships among the explanatory variables in a regression. More complex versions of these displays, such as augmented component-plus-residual plots and CERES plots, are more robust.

- Discrete explanatory variables divide the data into groups. A simple incremental F-test for nonlinearity compares the sum of squares accounted for by the linear regression of Y on X with the sum of squares accounted for by differences in the group means. Likewise, tests of nonconstant variance can be based on comparisons of spread in the different groups.
- A statistically sophisticated general approach to selecting a transformation of Y or an X is to embed the linear-regression model in a more general model that contains a parameter for the transformation. The Box-Cox procedure selects a power transformation of Y to normalize the errors. The Box-Tidwell procedure selects power transformations of the Xs to linearize the regression of Y on the Xs. In both cases, "constructed-variable" plots help us to decide whether individual observations are unduly influential in determining the transformation parameters.
- Simple score tests are available to determine the need for a transformation and to test for nonconstant error variance.
- The structural dimension of a regression is the dimensionality of the smallest subspace of the explanatory variables required, along with the response variable, to represent the dependence of Y on the Xs. When Y is completely independent of the Xs, the structural dimension is 0, and an ideal summary of the data is simply the unconditional distribution of Y. When the linear-regression model holds—or when the conditional expectation and variance of Y are functions of a single linear combination of the Xs—the structural dimension is 1. If the structural dimension is 1, and if the explanatory variables are linearly related to one another, then the inverse regressions of the explanatory variables on the response variable all have the same general form.

Recommended Reading

Methods for diagnosing problems in regression analysis and for visualizing regression data have been the subject of a great deal of research in statistics. The following texts summarize the current state of the art and include extensive references to the journal literature.

- Cook and Weisberg (1994, 1999) present a lucid and accessible treatment of many of the topics discussed in this chapter. They also describe a freely available computer program written in Lisp-Stat, called Arc, that implements the graphical methods presented in their books (and much more). See Cook (1998) for a more advanced treatment of much the same material. Also see Weisberg (2005) for an accessible account of these methods.
- Cleveland (1993) describes novel graphical methods for regression data, including two-dimensional, three-dimensional, and higher-dimensional displays.
- Atkinson (1985) has written an interesting, if somewhat idiosyncratic, book that stresses the author's important contributions to regression diagnostics. There is, therefore, an emphasis on diagnostics that yield constructed-variable plots. This text includes a strong treatment of transformations, and a discussion of the extension of least-squares diagnostics to generalized linear models (e.g., logistic regression, as described in Chapters 14 and 15[61]).

---

[61] See, in particular, Section 15.4.

13

Collinearity and Its Purported Remedies

A s I have explained, when there is a perfect linear relationship among the regressors in a linear model, the least-squares coefficients are not uniquely defined.[1] A strong, but less-than-perfect, linear relationship among the Xs causes the least-squares coefficients to be unstable: Coefficient standard errors are large, reflecting the imprecision of estimation of the βs; consequently, confidence intervals for the βs are broad, and hypothesis tests have low power. Small changes in the data—even, in extreme cases, due to rounding errors—can greatly alter the least-squares coefficients; and relatively large changes in the coefficients from the least-squares values hardly increase the sum of squared residuals from its minimum (i.e., the least-squares coefficients are not sharply defined).

This chapter describes methods for detecting collinearity and techniques that are often employed for dealing with collinearity when it is present. I would like to make three important points at the outset, however:

1. Except in certain specific contexts—such as time-series regression[2] or regression with aggregated data—collinearity is a comparatively rare problem in social-science applications of linear models. Insufficient variation in explanatory variables, small samples, and large error variance (i.e., weak relationships) are much more frequently the source of imprecision in estimation.

2. Methods that are commonly employed as cures for collinearity—in particular, biased estimation and variable selection—can easily be worse than the disease. A principal goal of this chapter is to explain the substantial limitations of this statistical snake oil.

3. It is not at all obvious that the detection of collinearity in data has practical implications. There are, as mentioned in Point 1, several sources of imprecision in estimation, which can augment or partially offset each other. The standard errors of the regression coefficients are the "bottom line": If the coefficient estimates are sufficiently precise, then the degree of collinearity is irrelevant; if the estimated coefficients are *insufficiently* precise, then knowing that the culprit is collinearity is of use only if the study can be redesigned to decrease the correlations among the Xs. In observational studies, where the Xs are sampled along with Y, it is usually impossible to influence their correlational structure, but it may very well be possible to improve the precision of estimation by increasing the sample size or by decreasing the error variance.[3]

---

[1] See Sections 5.2 and 9.2.

[2] See the example developed below. Chapter 16 describes methods for time-series regression that take account of dependence among the errors.

[3] The error variance can sometimes be decreased by improving the procedures of the study or by introducing additional explanatory variables. The latter remedy may, however, increase collinearity and may change the nature of the research. It may be possible, in some contexts, to increase precision by increasing the variation of the Xs, but only if their values are under the control of the researcher, in which case collinearity could also be reduced. Sometimes, however, researchers may be able to exert indirect control over the variational and correlational structure of the Xs by selecting a research setting judiciously or by designing an advantageous sampling procedure.

13.1 Detecting Collinearity

We have encountered the notion of collinearity at several points, and it is therefore useful to summarize what we know:

- When there is a perfect linear relationship among the Xs,

$$c_1 X_{i1} + c_2 X_{i2} + \cdots + c_k X_{ik} = c_0$$

  where the constants $c_1, c_2, \ldots, c_k$ are not all 0,

  1. the least-squares normal equations do not have a unique solution; and

  2. the sampling variances of the regression coefficients are infinite.

  Perfect collinearity is usually the product of some error in formulating the linear model, such as failing to employ a baseline category in dummy regression.

  *Points 1 and 2 follow from the observation that the matrix $\mathbf{X'X}$ of sums of squares and products is singular. Moreover, because the columns of $\mathbf{X}$ are perfectly collinear, the regressor subspace is of deficient dimension.
- When collinearity is less than perfect:

  1. The sampling variance of the least-squares slope coefficient B_j is

$$V(B_j) = \frac{1}{1 - R_j^2} \times \frac{\sigma_\varepsilon^2}{(n-1)S_j^2}$$

  where R_j^2 is the squared multiple correlation for the regression of X_j on the other Xs, and $S_j^2 = \sum (X_{ij} - \overline{X}_j)^2/(n-1)$ is the variance of X_j. The term $1/(1 - R_j^2)$, called the *variance-inflation factor* (VIF), directly and straightforwardly indicates the impact of collinearity on the precision of B_j. Because the precision of estimation of β_j is most naturally expressed as the width of the confidence interval for this parameter, and because the width of the confidence interval is proportional to the standard deviation of B_j (not its variance), I recommend examining the square root of the VIF in preference to the VIF itself. Figure 13.1 reveals that the linear relationship among the Xs must be very strong before collinearity seriously impairs the precision of estimation: It is not until R_j approaches .9 that the precision of estimation is halved.

  Because of its simplicity and direct interpretation, the VIF (or its square root) is the basic diagnostic for collinearity. It is not, however, applicable to sets of related regressors, such as sets of dummy-variable coefficients, or coefficients for polynomial regressors.[4]

  2. When X_1 is strongly collinear with the other regressors, the residuals $X^{(1)}$ from the regression of X_1 on $X_2, \ldots, X_k$ show little variation—most of the variation in X_1 is accounted for by its regression on the other Xs. The added-variable plot graphs the residuals from the regression of Y on $X_2, \ldots, X_k$ against $X^{(1)}$, converting the multiple regression into a simple regression.[5] Because the explanatory variable in this plot, $X^{(1)}$, is nearly invariant, the slope B_1 is subject to substantial sampling variation.[6]

---

[4]Section 13.1.2 describes a generalization of variance inflation to sets of related regressors.

[5]More precisely, the multiple regression is converted into a sequence of simple regressions, for each X in turn. Added-variable plots are discussed in Section 11.6.1.

[6]See Stine (1995) for a nice graphical interpretation of this point.

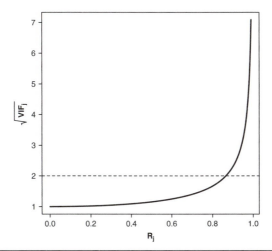

Figure 13.1   Precision of estimation (square root of the variance-inflation factor) of β_j as a function of the multiple correlation R_j between X_j and the other explanatory variables. It is not until the multiple correlation gets very large that the precision of estimation is seriously degraded.

3. *Confidence intervals for individual regression coefficients are projections of the confidence interval generating ellipse. Because this ellipse is the inverse—that is, the rescaled, 90° rotation—of the data ellipse for the explanatory variables, the individual confidence intervals for the coefficients are wide. If the correlations among the Xs are positive, however, then there is considerable information in the data about the *sum* of the regression coefficients, if not about individual coefficients.[7]

> When the regressors in a linear model are perfectly collinear, the least-squares coefficients are not unique. Strong, but less-than-perfect, collinearity substantially increases the sampling variances of the least-squares coefficients and can render them useless as estimators. The variance-inflation factor $\text{VIF}_j = 1/(1 - R_j^2)$ indicates the deleterious impact of collinearity on the precision of the estimate B_j.

Collinearity is sometimes termed *multicollinearity*, which has the virtue of emphasizing that collinear relationships are not limited to strong correlations between *pairs* of explanatory variables.

Figures 13.2 and 13.3 provide further insight into collinearity, illustrating its effect on estimation when there are two explanatory variables in a regression. The black and gray dots in Figure 13.2 represent the data points (the gray dots are below the regression plane), while the white dots represent fitted values lying in the regression plane; the +s show the projection of the data points onto the X_1, X_2 plane. Figure 13.3 shows the sum of squared residuals as a function of the slope coefficients B_1 and B_2. The residual sum of squares is at a minimum, of course, when the Bs are equal to the least-squares estimates; the vertical axis is scaled so that the minimum is at the "floor" of the graphs.[8]

---

[7]See the discussion of joint confidence regions for regression coefficients in Section 9.4.4.
[8]For each pair of slopes B_1 and B_2, the intercept A is chosen to make the residual sum of squares as small as possible.

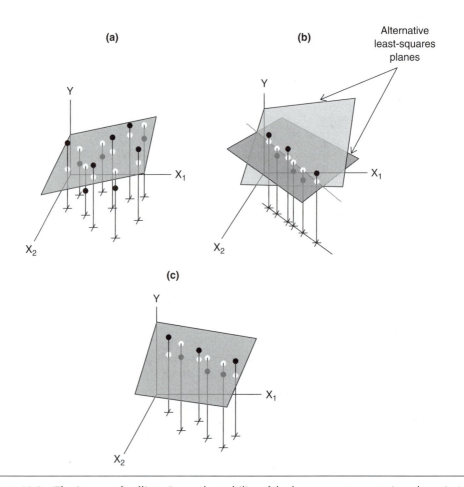

Figure 13.2   The impact of collinearity on the stability of the least-squares regression plane. In (a), the correlation between X_1 and X_2 is small, and the regression plane therefore has a broad base of support. In (b), X_1 and X_2 are perfectly correlated; the least-squares plane is not uniquely defined. In (c), there is a strong, but less-than-perfect, linear relationship between X_1 and X_2; the least-squares plane is uniquely defined, but it is not well supported by the data.

In Figure 13.2(a), the correlation between the explanatory variables X_1 and X_2 is slight, as indicated by the broad scatter of points in the X_1, X_2 plane. The least-squares regression plane, also shown in this figure, therefore has a firm base of support. Correspondingly, Figure 13.3(a) shows that small changes in the regression coefficients are associated with relatively large increases in the residual sum of squares—the sum-of-squares function is like a deep bowl, with steep sides and a well-defined minimum.

In Figure 13.2(b), X_1 and X_2 are perfectly collinear. Because the explanatory-variable observations form a line in the X_1, X_2 plane, the least-squares regression plane, in effect, also reduces to a line. The plane can tip about this line without changing the residual sum of squares, as Figure 13.3(b) reveals: The sum-of-squares function is flat at its minimum along a line defining pairs of values for B_1 and B_2—rather like a sheet of paper with two corners raised—and thus there is an infinite number of pairs of coefficients (B_1, B_2) that yield the minimum RSS.

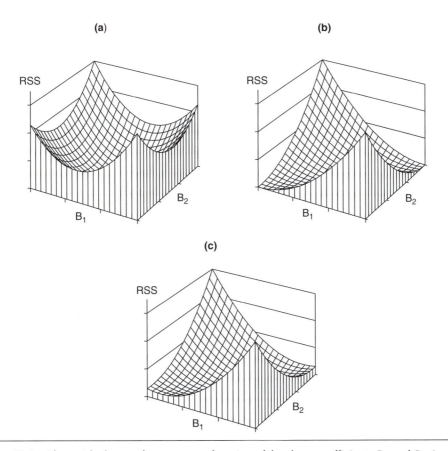

Figure 13.3 The residual sum of squares as a function of the slope coefficients B_1 and B_2. In each graph, the vertical axis is scaled so that the least-squares value of RSS is at the bottom of the axis. When, as in (a), the correlation between the explanatory variables X_1 and X_2 is small, the residual sum of squares has a well-defined minimum, much like a deep bowl. When there is a perfect linear relationship between X_1 and X_2, as in (b), the residual sum of squares is flat at its minimum, above a line in the B_1, B_2 plane: The least-squares values of B_1 and B_2 are not unique. When, as in (c), there is a strong, but less-than-perfect, linear relationship between X_1 and X_2, the residual sum of squares is nearly flat at its minimum, so values of B_1 and B_2 quite different from the least-squares values are associated with residual sums of squares near the minimum.

Finally, in Figure 13.2(c), the linear relationship between X_1 and X_2 is strong, though not perfect. The support afforded to the least-squares plane is tenuous, so that the plane can be tipped without causing large increases in the residual sum of squares, as is apparent in Figure 13.3(c)—the sum-of-squares function is like a shallow bowl with a nearly flat bottom and hence a poorly defined minimum.

Illustrative data on Canadian women's labor-force participation in the postwar period, drawn from B. Fox (1980), are shown in Figure 13.4. These are time-series data, with yearly observations from 1946 through 1975. Fox was interested in determining how women's labor-force participation (measured here as the percentage of adult women in the work force) is related to several factors indicative of the supply of and demand for women's labor. The explanatory variables in the analysis include the total fertility rate (the expected number of births to a cohort of 1,000 women who

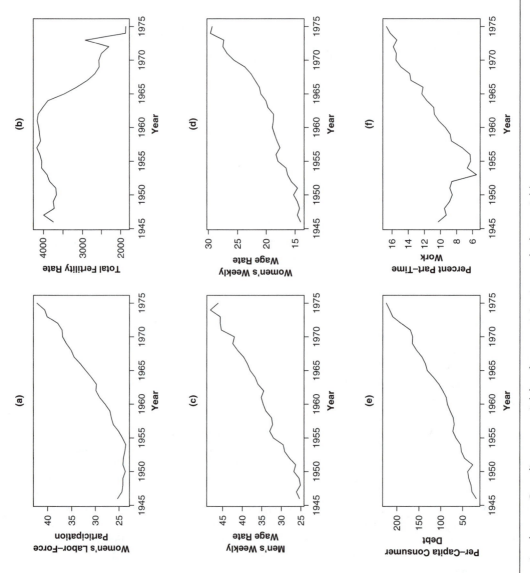

Figure 13.4 Time-series data on Canadian women's labor-force participation and other variables.
SOURCE: B. Fox (1980).

proceed through their child-bearing years at current age-specific fertility rates); men's and women's average weekly wages (expressed in constant 1935 dollars and adjusted for current tax rates); per-capita consumer debt (also in constant dollars); and the prevalence of part-time work (measured as the percentage of the active work force working 34 hours a week or less). Women's wages, consumer debt, and the prevalence of part-time work were expected to affect women's labor-force participation positively, while fertility and men's wages were expected to have negative effects.

The time-series plots in Figure 13.4 do not bode well for the regression of women's labor-force participation on the other variables: Several of the explanatory variables evidence strong linear trends over time and consequently are highly correlated with one another. Moreover, to control for factors that change regularly with time but are not included explicitly in the regression model, the author also included time (years, from 1 to 30) as an explanatory variable.[9] Correlations among the variables in the data set, including time, are given in Table 13.1; some of these correlations are very large. As mentioned previously, time-series regression is a research context in which collinearity problems are common.

The plot of the total fertility rate in Figure 13.4(b) also suggests a possible error in the data: There is an unusual jump in the total fertility rate for 1973. As it turns out, the TFR for this year was misrecorded as 2,931; the correct value is 1,931. This correction is reflected in the analysis reported below.[10]

The results of a least-squares regression of women's labor-force participation on the several explanatory variables proves disappointing despite a very large R^2 of .9935. Table 13.2 shows estimated regression coefficients, standard errors, and p-values for the slope coefficients (for the hypothesis that each coefficient is 0). All the coefficients have the anticipated signs, but some are small (taking into account their units of measurement, of course), and most have very large standard errors despite the large multiple correlation.

Square-root variance-inflation factors for the slope coefficients in the model are as follows:

Fertility	Men's Wages	Women's Wages
3.89	10.67	8.21

Consumer Debt	Part-Time Work	Time
11.47	2.75	9.75

All are large, and most are very large, producing the big standard errors that I noted.

13.1.1 Principal Components*

The method of principal components, introduced early in the 20th century by Karl Pearson and Harold Hotelling, provides a useful representation of the correlational structure of a set of

---

[9]The specification of time as an explanatory variable in a time-series regression is a common (if crude) strategy. As well, the use of time-series data in regression casts doubt on the assumption that errors from different observations are independent because the observation for one period is likely to share unmeasured characteristics with observations from other periods close to it in time. In the present case, however, examination of the least-squares residuals supports the reasonableness of the assumption of independent errors. Time-series regression is taken up at greater depth in Chapter 16.
[10]This example illustrates once again the importance of examining data prior to their analysis. Apparently, I had not learned that lesson sufficiently when I last looked at these data in the 1980s.

Table 13.1   Correlations Among the Variables in B. Fox's Canadian Women's Labor-Force Data

	L	F	M	W	D	P	T
Labor-Force							
Participation	1.0000						
Fertility	−.9011	1.0000					
Men's Wages	.9595	−.8118	1.0000				
Women's Wages	.9674	−.8721	.9830	1.0000			
Consumer Debt	.9819	−.8696	.9861	.9868	1.0000		
Part-Time Work	.9504	−.8961	.8533	.8715	.8875	1.0000	
Time	.9531	−.7786	.9891	.9637	.9805	.8459	1.0000

Table 13.2   Regression of Women's Labor-Force Participation on
Several Explanatory Variables

Coefficient	Estimate	Standard Error	p
Constant	16.80	3.72	
Fertility	−0.000001949	0.0005011	.99
Men's Wages	−0.02919	0.1502	.85
Women's Wages	0.01984	0.1744	.91
Consumer Debt	0.06397	0.01850	.0021
Part-Time Work	0.6566	0.0821	≪.0001
Time	0.004452	0.1107	.97

variables. I will describe the method briefly here, with particular reference to its application to collinearity in regression; more complete accounts can be obtained from texts on multivariate statistics (e.g., Morrison, 2005, chap. 8). Because the material in this section is relatively complex, the section includes a summary; you may, on first reading, wish to pass lightly over most of the section and refer primarily to the summary, and to the two-variable case, which is treated immediately prior to the summary.[11]

We begin with the vectors of standardized regressors, $z_1, z_2, \ldots, z_k$. Because vectors have length equal to the square root of their sum of squared elements, each z_j has length $\sqrt{n-1}$. As we will see, the *principal components* $w_1, w_2, \ldots, w_p$ provide an orthogonal basis for the regressor subspace.[12] The first principal component, w_1, is oriented so as to account for maximum collective variation in the z_j; the second principal component, w_2, is orthogonal to w_1 and—under this restriction of orthogonality—is oriented to account for maximum remaining variation in the z_j; the third component, w_3, is orthogonal to w_1 and w_2; and so on. Each principal component is scaled so that its variance is equal to the combined regressor variance for which it accounts.

There are as many principal components as there are linearly independent regressors: $p \equiv$ rank(Z_X), where $Z_X \equiv [z_1, z_2, \ldots, z_k]$. Although the method of principal components is more general, I will assume throughout most of this discussion that the regressors are not *perfectly* collinear and, consequently, that $p = k$.

---

[11] Appendix B on matrices, linear algebra, and vector geometry provides background for this section.
[12] It is also possible to find principal components of the *unstandardized* regressors $x_1, x_2, \ldots, x_k$, but these are not generally interpretable unless all the Xs are measured on the same scale.

Because the principal components lie in the regressor subspace, each is a linear combination of the regressors. Thus, the first principal component can be written as

$$\underset{(n \times 1)}{\mathbf{w}_1} = A_{11}\mathbf{z}_1 + A_{21}\mathbf{z}_2 + \cdots + A_{k1}\mathbf{z}_k$$

$$= \underset{(n \times k)(k \times 1)}{\mathbf{Z}_X \quad \mathbf{a}_1}$$

The variance of the first component is

$$S_{W_1}^2 = \frac{1}{n-1}\mathbf{w}_1'\mathbf{w}_1 = \frac{1}{n-1}\mathbf{a}_1'\mathbf{Z}_X'\mathbf{Z}_X\mathbf{a}_1 = \mathbf{a}_1'\mathbf{R}_{XX}\mathbf{a}_1$$

where $\mathbf{R}_{XX} \equiv [1/(n-1)]\mathbf{Z}_X'\mathbf{Z}_X$ is the correlation matrix of the regressors.

We want to maximize $S_{W_1}^2$, but, to make maximization meaningful, it is necessary to constrain the coefficients $\mathbf{a}_1$. In the absence of a constraint, $S_{W_1}^2$ can be made arbitrarily large simply by picking large coefficients. The normalizing constraint

$$\mathbf{a}_1'\mathbf{a}_1 = 1 \tag{13.1}$$

proves convenient, but any constraint of this general form would do.[13]

We can maximize $S_{W_1}^2$ subject to the restriction of Equation 13.1 by employing a Lagrange multiplier L_1, defining[14]

$$F_1 \equiv \mathbf{a}_1'\mathbf{R}_{XX}\mathbf{a}_1 - L_1(\mathbf{a}_1'\mathbf{a}_1 - 1)$$

Then, differentiating this equation with respect to $\mathbf{a}_1$ and L_1,

$$\frac{\partial F_1}{\partial \mathbf{a}_1} = 2\mathbf{R}_{XX}\mathbf{a}_1 - 2L_1\mathbf{a}_1$$

$$\frac{\partial F_1}{\partial L_1} = -(\mathbf{a}_1'\mathbf{a}_1 - 1)$$

Setting the partial derivatives to 0 produces the equations

$$(\mathbf{R}_{XX} - L_1\mathbf{I}_k)\mathbf{a}_1 = \mathbf{0}$$

$$\mathbf{a}_1'\mathbf{a}_1 = 1 \tag{13.2}$$

The first line of Equation 13.2 has nontrivial solutions for $\mathbf{a}_1$ only when $(\mathbf{R}_{XX} - L_1\mathbf{I}_k)$ is singular—that is, when $|\mathbf{R}_{XX} - L_1\mathbf{I}_k| = 0$. The multiplier L_1, therefore, is an eigenvalue of $\mathbf{R}_{XX}$, and $\mathbf{a}_1$ is the corresponding eigenvector, scaled so that $\mathbf{a}_1'\mathbf{a}_1 = 1$.

There are, however, k solutions to Equation 13.2, corresponding to the k eigenvalue-eigenvector pairs of $\mathbf{R}_{XX}$, so we must decide which solution to choose. From the first line of Equation 13.2, we have $\mathbf{R}_{XX}\mathbf{a}_1 = L_1\mathbf{a}_1$. Consequently,

$$S_{W_1}^2 = \mathbf{a}_1'\mathbf{R}_{XX}\mathbf{a}_1 = L_1\mathbf{a}_1'\mathbf{a}_1 = L_1$$

Because our purpose is to *maximize* $S_{W_1}^2$ (subject to the constraint on $\mathbf{a}_1$), we must select the *largest* eigenvalue of $\mathbf{R}_{XX}$ to define the first principal component.

---

[13]Normalizing the coefficients so that $\mathbf{a}_1'\mathbf{a}_1 = 1$ causes the variance of the first principal component to be equal to the combined variance of the standardized regressors accounted for by this component, as will become clear presently.

[14]See Appendix C on calculus for an explanation of the method of Lagrange multipliers for constrained optimization.

The second principal component is derived similarly, under the further restriction that it is orthogonal to the first; the third that it is orthogonal to the first two; and so on.[15] It turns out that the second principal component corresponds to the second-largest eigenvalue of $\mathbf{R}_{XX}$, the third to the third-largest eigenvalue, et cetera. We order the eigenvalues of $\mathbf{R}_{XX}$ so that[16]

$$L_1 \geq L_2 \geq \cdots \geq L_k > 0$$

The matrix of principal-component coefficients

$$\underset{(k \times k)}{\mathbf{A}} \equiv [\mathbf{a}_1, \mathbf{a}_2, \ldots, \mathbf{a}_k]$$

contains normalized eigenvectors of $\mathbf{R}_{XX}$. This matrix is, therefore, orthonormal: $\mathbf{A}'\mathbf{A} = \mathbf{A}\mathbf{A}' = \mathbf{I}_k$.

The principal components

$$\underset{(n \times k)}{\mathbf{W}} = \underset{(n \times k)(k \times k)}{\mathbf{Z}_X \ \mathbf{A}} \tag{13.3}$$

have covariance matrix

$$\frac{1}{n-1}\mathbf{W}'\mathbf{W} = \frac{1}{n-1}\mathbf{A}'\mathbf{Z}_X'\mathbf{Z}_X\mathbf{A}$$
$$= \mathbf{A}'\mathbf{R}_{XX}\mathbf{A} = \mathbf{A}'\mathbf{A}\mathbf{L} = \mathbf{L}$$

where $\mathbf{L} \equiv \text{diag}[L_1, L_2, \ldots, L_k]$ is the diagonal matrix of eigenvalues of $\mathbf{R}_{XX}$; the covariance matrix $\mathbf{W}$ of the principal components is, therefore, orthogonal, as required. Furthermore,

$$\text{trace}(\mathbf{L}) = \sum_{j=1}^{k} L_j = k = \text{trace}(\mathbf{R}_{XX})$$

and thus the principal components partition the combined variance of the standardized variables $Z_1, Z_2, \ldots, Z_k$.

Solving Equation 13.3 for $\mathbf{Z}_X$ produces

$$\mathbf{Z}_X = \mathbf{W}\mathbf{A}^{-1} = \mathbf{W}\mathbf{A}'$$

and, consequently,

$$\mathbf{R}_{XX} = \frac{1}{n-1}\mathbf{Z}_X'\mathbf{Z}_X = \frac{1}{n-1}\mathbf{A}\mathbf{W}'\mathbf{W}\mathbf{A}' = \mathbf{A}\mathbf{L}\mathbf{A}'$$

Finally,

$$\mathbf{R}_{XX}^{-1} = (\mathbf{A}')^{-1}\mathbf{L}^{-1}\mathbf{A}^{-1} = \mathbf{A}\mathbf{L}^{-1}\mathbf{A}' \tag{13.4}$$

We will use this result presently in our investigation of collinearity.

---

[15]See Exercise 13.1.

[16]Recall that we are assuming that $\mathbf{R}_{XX}$ is of full rank, and hence none of its eigenvalues is 0. It is possible, but unlikely, that two or more eigenvalues of $\mathbf{R}_{XX}$ are equal. In this event, the orientation of the principal components corresponding to the equal eigenvalues is not unique, although the subspace spanned by these components—and for which they constitute a basis—is unique.

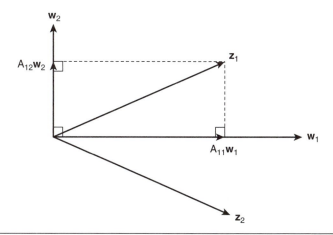

Figure 13.5   Vector geometry of principal components for two positively correlated standardized variables z_1 and z_2.

Two Variables

The vector geometry of principal components is illustrated for two variables in Figure 13.5. The symmetry of this figure is peculiar to the two-dimensional case. The length of each principal-component vector is the square root of the sum of squared orthogonal projections of z_1 and z_2 on the component. The direction of w_1 is chosen to maximize the combined length of these projections and hence to maximize the length of w_1. Because the subspace spanned by z_1 and z_2 is two dimensional, w_2 is simply chosen to be orthogonal to w_1. Note that $\|w_j\|^2 = L_j(n-1)$.[17]

It is clear from the figure that as the correlation between Z_1 and Z_2 increases, the first principal component grows at the expense of the second; thus, L_1 gets larger and L_2 smaller. If, alternatively, z_1 and z_2 are orthogonal, then $\|w_1\| = \|w_2\| = \sqrt{n-1}$ and $L_1 = L_2 = 1$.

The algebra of the two-variable case is also quite simple. The eigenvalues of R_{XX} are the solutions of the characteristic equation

$$\begin{vmatrix} 1-L & r_{12} \\ r_{12} & 1-L \end{vmatrix} = 0$$

that is,

$$(1-L)^2 - r_{12}^2 = L^2 - 2L + 1 - r_{12}^2 = 0$$

Using the quadratic formula to find the roots of the characteristic equation yields

$$L_1 = 1 + \sqrt{r_{12}^2}$$

$$L_2 = 1 - \sqrt{r_{12}^2} \tag{13.5}$$

And so, consistent with the geometry of Figure 13.5, as the magnitude of the correlation between the two variables increases, the variation attributed to the first principal component also grows. If

---

[17]There is a small subtlety here: The subspace spanned by each component is one dimensional, and the length of each component is fixed by the corresponding eigenvalue, but these factors determine the orientation of the component only up to a rotation of 180°—that is, a change in sign.

r_{12} is positive, then solving for $\mathbf{A}$ from the relation $\mathbf{R}_{XX}\mathbf{A} = \mathbf{LA}$ under the restriction $\mathbf{A}'\mathbf{A} = \mathbf{I}_2$ gives[18]

$$
\mathbf{A} =
\begin{bmatrix}
\dfrac{\sqrt{2}}{2} & \dfrac{\sqrt{2}}{2} \\[2mm]
\dfrac{\sqrt{2}}{2} & -\dfrac{\sqrt{2}}{2}
\end{bmatrix}
\tag{13.6}
$$

The generalization to k standardized regressors is straightforward: If the variables are orthogonal, then all $L_j = 1$ and all $\|\mathbf{w}_j\| = \sqrt{n-1}$. As collinearities among the variables increase, some eigenvalues become large while others grow small. Small eigenvalues and the corresponding short principal components represent dimensions along which the regressor subspace has (nearly) collapsed. Perfect collinearities are associated with eigenvalues of 0.

The Data Ellipsoid

The principal components have an interesting interpretation in terms of the standard data ellipsoid for the Zs.[19] The data ellipsoid is given by the equation

$$
\mathbf{z}'\mathbf{R}_{XX}^{-1}\mathbf{z} = 1
$$

where $\mathbf{z} \equiv (Z_1, \ldots, Z_k)'$ is a vector of values for the k standardized regressors. Because the variables are standardized, the data ellipsoid is centered at the origin, and the shadow of the ellipsoid on each axis is of length 2 (i.e., 2 standard deviations). It can be shown that the principal components correspond to the principal axes of the data ellipsoid, and, furthermore, that the half-length of each axis is equal to the square root of the corresponding eigenvalue L_j of $\mathbf{R}_{XX}$.[20] These properties are depicted in Figure 13.6 for $k = 2$. When the variables are uncorrelated, the data ellipse becomes circular, and each axis has a half-length of 1.

Summary

- The principal components of the k standardized regressors $\mathbf{Z}_X$ are a new set of k variables derived from $\mathbf{Z}_X$ by a linear transformation: $\mathbf{W} = \mathbf{Z}_X\mathbf{A}$, where $\mathbf{A}$ is the $(k \times k)$ transformation matrix.
- The transformation $\mathbf{A}$ is selected so that the columns of $\mathbf{W}$ are orthogonal—that is, the principal components are uncorrelated. In addition, $\mathbf{A}$ is constructed so that the first component accounts for maximum variance in the Zs; the second for maximum variance under the constraint that it is orthogonal to the first; and so on. Each principal component is scaled so that its variance is equal to the variance in the Zs for which it accounts. The principal components therefore partition the variance of the Zs.
- The transformation matrix $\mathbf{A}$ contains (by columns) normalized eigenvectors of $\mathbf{R}_{XX}$, the correlation matrix of the regressors. The columns of $\mathbf{A}$ are ordered by their corresponding eigenvalues: The first column corresponds to the largest eigenvalue, and the last column to the smallest. The eigenvalue L_j associated with the jth component represents the variance attributable to that component.

---

[18]Exercise 13.2 derives the solution for $r_{12} < 0$.

[19]The standard data ellipsoid was introduced in Section 9.4.4.

[20]See Exercise 13.3. These relations also hold for *unstandardized* variables. That is, the principal components calculated from the covariance matrix $\mathbf{S}_{XX}$ give the principal axes of the standard data ellipsoid $(\mathbf{x} - \bar{\mathbf{x}})'\mathbf{S}_{XX}^{-1}(\mathbf{x} - \bar{\mathbf{x}})$; and the half-length of the jth principal axis of this ellipsoid is equal to the square root of the jth eigenvalue of $\mathbf{S}_{XX}$.

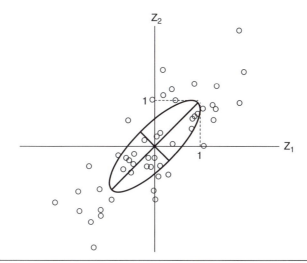

Figure 13.6   The principal components for two standardized variables Z_1 and Z_2 are the principal axes of the standard data ellipse $\mathbf{z}'\mathbf{R}_{XX}^{-1}\mathbf{z} = 1$. The first eigenvalue L_1 of $\mathbf{R}_{XX}$ gives the half-length of the major axis of the ellipse; the second eigenvalue L_2 gives the half-length of the minor axis. In this illustration, the two variables are correlated $r_{12} = .8$, so L_1 is large and L_2 is small.

- If there are perfect collinearities in $\mathbf{Z}_X$, then some eigenvalues of $\mathbf{R}_{XX}$ will be 0, and there will be fewer than k principal components, the number of components corresponding to $\operatorname{rank}(\mathbf{Z}_X) = \operatorname{rank}(\mathbf{R}_{XX})$. Near collinearities are associated with small eigenvalues and correspondingly short principal components.

> Principal components can be used to explicate the correlational structure of the explanatory variables in regression. The principal components are a derived set of variables that form an orthogonal basis for the subspace of the standardized Xs. The first principal component spans the one-dimensional subspace that accounts for maximum variation in the standardized Xs. The second principal component accounts for maximum variation in the standardized Xs, under the constraint that it is orthogonal to the first. The other principal components are similarly defined; unless the Xs are perfectly collinear, there are as many principal components as there are Xs. Each principal component is scaled to have variance equal to the collective variance in the standardized Xs for which it accounts. Collinear relations among the explanatory variables, therefore, correspond to very short principal components, which represent dimensions along which the regressor subspace has nearly collapsed.

A principal-components analysis for the explanatory variables in B. Fox's Canadian women's labor-force regression is summarized in Table 13.3. The first two principal components account for almost 98% of the variation in the six variables.

The principal-components analysis is graphed in Figure 13.7. Here, the variables—including the two principal components—are standardized to common length, and the variables are projected orthogonally onto the subspace spanned by the first two principal components. Because the first

Table 13.3 Principal-Components Analysis for the Explanatory Variables in B. Fox's Regression

| | *Principal Component* | | | | | |
Variable	W_1	W_2	W_3	W_4	W_5	W_6
Fertility	0.3849	0.6676	0.5424	0.2518	−0.1966	−0.0093
Men's Wages	−0.4159	0.3421	−0.0223	0.1571	0.7055	−0.4326
Women's Wages	−0.4196	0.1523	−0.2658	0.7292	−0.2791	0.3472
Consumer Debt	−0.4220	0.1591	−0.0975	−0.2757	−0.6188	−0.5728
Part-Time Work	−0.3946	−0.4693	0.7746	0.1520	−0.0252	−0.0175
Time	−0.4112	0.4106	0.1583	−0.5301	0.0465	0.5951
Eigenvalue	5.5310	0.3288	0.1101	0.0185	0.0071	0.0045
Cumulative percentage	92.18	97.66	99.50	99.81	99.93	100.00

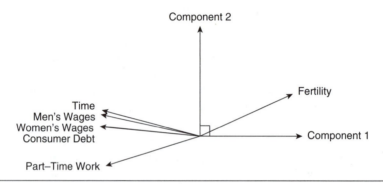

Figure 13.7 Orthogonal projections of the six explanatory variables onto the subspace spanned
by the first two principal components. All the variables, including the components,
are standardized to common length. The projections of the vectors for women's
wages and consumer debt are nearly coincident (the two vectors are essentially on
top of one another).

two components account for almost all the variation in the variables, the vectors for the variables
lie very close to this subspace. Consequently, the projections of the vectors are almost as long as
the vectors themselves, and the cosines of the angles between the projected vectors closely approximate the correlations between the variables. The projected vectors for women's wages and consumer debt are nearly coincident, reflecting the near-perfect correlation between the two variables.

It is clear that the explanatory variables divide into two subsets: time, men's wages, women's
wages, and consumer debt (which are all highly positively correlated) in one subset; fertility and
part-time work (which are strongly negatively correlated) in the other. Correlations *between* the
two sets of variables are also quite high. In effect, the subspace of the explanatory variables has
collapsed into two dimensions.

Diagnosing Collinearity

I explained earlier that the sampling variance of the regression coefficient B_j is

$$V(B_j) = \frac{\sigma_\varepsilon^2}{(n-1)S_j^2} \times \frac{1}{1 - R_j^2}$$

It can be shown that $\text{VIF}_j = 1/(1 - R_j^2)$ is the jth diagonal entry of $\mathbf{R}_{XX}^{-1}$ (see Theil, 1971, p. 166). Using Equation 13.4, the variance inflation factors can be expressed as functions of the eigenvalues of $\mathbf{R}_{XX}$ and the principal components; specifically,

$$\text{VIF}_j = \sum_{l=1}^{k} \frac{A_{jl}^2}{L_l}$$

Thus, it is the small eigenvalues that contribute to large sampling variance, but only for those regressors that have large coefficients associated with the corresponding short principal components. This result is sensible, for small eigenvalues, and their short components correspond to collinear relations among the regressors; regressors with large coefficients for these components are the regressors implicated in the collinearities (see below).

The relative size of the eigenvalues serves as an indicator of the degree of collinearity present in the data. The square root of the ratio of the largest to smallest eigenvalue, $K \equiv \sqrt{L_1/L_k}$, called the *condition number*, is a commonly employed standardized index of the global instability of the least-squares regression coefficients: A large condition number (say, 10 or more) indicates that relatively small changes in the data tend to produce large changes in the least-squares solution. In this event, $\mathbf{R}_{XX}$ is said to be *ill conditioned*.

It is instructive to examine the condition number in the simplified context of the two-regressor model. From Equation 13.5,

$$K = \sqrt{\frac{L_1}{L_2}} = \sqrt{\frac{1 + \sqrt{r_{12}^2}}{1 - \sqrt{r_{12}^2}}}$$

and thus $K = 10$ corresponds to $r_{12}^2 = .9608$, for which $\text{VIF} = 26$ (and $\sqrt{\text{VIF}} \approx 5$).

Belsley, Kuh, and Welsh (1980, chap. 3) define a *condition index* $K_j \equiv \sqrt{L_1/L_j}$ for each principal component of $\mathbf{R}_{XX}$.[21] Then, the number of large condition indices points to the number of different collinear relations among the regressors.

The condition indices for B. Fox's Canadian women's labor-force regression, reported in Table 13.2 on page 314, are as follows:

K_1	K_2	K_3	K_4	K_5	K_6
1.00	4.10	7.09	17.27	27.99	35.11

The last three condition indices are therefore very large, suggesting an unstable regression.

---

[21]Primarily for computational accuracy, Belsley et al. (1980, chap. 3) develop diagnostic methods for collinearity in terms of the *singular-value decomposition* of the regressor matrix, scaled so that each variable has a sum of squares of 1. I employ an equivalent eigenvalue-eigenvector approach because of its conceptual simplicity and broader familiarity. The eigenvectors of $\mathbf{R}_{XX}$, it turns out, are the squares of the singular values of $(1/\sqrt{n-1})\mathbf{Z}_X$. Indeed, the condition number K defined here is actually the condition number of $(1/\sqrt{n-1})\mathbf{Z}_X$ (and hence of $\mathbf{Z}_X$). Information on the singular-value decomposition and its role in linear-model analysis can be found in Belsley et al. (1980, chap. 3) and in Mandel (1982).

A more substantial difference between my approach and that of Belsley et al. is that they base their analysis not on the correlation matrix of the Xs, but rather on $\tilde{\mathbf{X}}'\tilde{\mathbf{X}}$, where $\tilde{\mathbf{X}}$ is the regressor matrix, including the constant regressor, with columns normed to unit length. Consider an explanatory variable that is uncorrelated with the others, but that has scores that are far from 0. Belsley et al. would say that this explanatory variable is "collinear with the constant regressor." This seems to me a corruption of the notion of collinearity, which deals fundamentally with the inability to separate the effects of highly correlated explanatory variables and should not change with linear transformations of individual explanatory variables. See Belsley (1984) and the associated commentary for various points of view on this issue.

Chatterjee and Price (1991, chap. 7) employ the principal-component coefficients to estimate near collinearities: A component $\mathbf{w}_l$ associated with a very small eigenvalue $L_l \approx 0$ is itself approximately equal to the zero vector; consequently,

$$A_{1l}\mathbf{z}_1 + A_{2l}\mathbf{z}_2 + \cdots + A_{kl}\mathbf{0}_k \approx \mathbf{0}$$

and we can use the large A_{jl}s to specify a linear combination of the Zs that is approximately equal to 0.[22]

13.1.2   Generalized Variance Inflation*

The methods for detecting collinearity described thus far are not fully applicable to models that include related sets of regressors, such as dummy regressors constructed from a polytomous categorical variable or polynomial regressors. The reasoning underlying this qualification is subtle but can be illuminated by appealing to the vector representation of linear models.[23]

The correlations among a set of dummy regressors are affected by the choice of baseline category. Similarly, the correlations among a set of polynomial regressors in an explanatory variable X are affected by adding a constant to the X values. Neither of these changes alters the fit of the model to the data, however, so neither is fundamental. It is, indeed, always possible to select an orthogonal basis for the dummy-regressor or polynomial-regressor subspace (although such a basis does not employ dummy variables or simple powers of X). What is at issue is the subspace itself and not the arbitrarily chosen basis for it.[24]

We are not concerned, therefore, with the "artificial" collinearity among dummy regressors or polynomial regressors in the same set. We are instead interested in the relationships between the subspaces generated to represent the effects of *different* explanatory variables. As a consequence, we can legitimately employ variance-inflation factors to examine the impact of collinearity on the coefficients of numerical regressors, or on any single-degree-of-freedom effects, even when sets of dummy regressors or polynomial regressors are present in the model.

Fox and Monette (1992) generalize the notion of variance inflation to sets of related regressors. Rewrite the linear model as

$$\underset{(n\times 1)}{\mathbf{y}} = \alpha \underset{(n\times 1)}{\mathbf{1}} + \underset{(n\times p)}{\mathbf{X}_1}\underset{(p\times 1)}{\boldsymbol{\beta}_1} + \underset{(n\times k-p)}{\mathbf{X}_2}\underset{(k-p\times 1)}{\boldsymbol{\beta}_2} + \underset{(n\times 1)}{\boldsymbol{\varepsilon}}$$

where the p regressors of interest (e.g., a set of dummy regressors) are in $\mathbf{X}_1$, while the remaining $k - p$ regressors (with the exception of the constant) are in $\mathbf{X}_2$. Fox and Monette (1992) show that the squared ratio of the size (i.e., area, volume, or hyper-volume) of the joint confidence region for $\boldsymbol{\beta}_1$ to the size of the same region for orthogonal but otherwise similar data is

$$\mathrm{GVIF}_1 = \frac{\det \mathbf{R}_{11} \det \mathbf{R}_{22}}{\det \mathbf{R}}$$

Here, $\mathbf{R}_{11}$ is the correlation matrix for $\mathbf{X}_1$; $\mathbf{R}_{22}$ is the correlation matrix for $\mathbf{X}_2$; and $\mathbf{R}$ is the matrix of correlations among all the variables. The *generalized variance-inflation factor* (GVIF) is independent of the bases selected for the subspaces spanned by the columns of $\mathbf{X}_1$ and $\mathbf{X}_2$. If $\mathbf{X}_1$ contains only one column, then the GVIF reduces to the familiar variance inflation factor.

---

[22]See Exercise 13.4 for an application to B. Fox's regression.

[23]The vector geometry of linear models is developed in Chapter 10.

[24]A specific basis may be a poor computational choice, however, if it produces numerically unstable results. Consequently, researchers are sometimes advised to pick a category with many cases to serve as the baseline for a set of dummy regressors or to subtract the mean from X prior to constructing polynomial regressors; the latter procedure is called *centering*. Neither of these practices fundamentally alters the model but may lead to more accurate calculations.

To make generalized variance-inflation factors comparable across dimensions, Fox and Monette suggest reporting $\text{GVIF}^{p/2}$—analogous to reporting $\sqrt{\text{VIF}}$ for a single coefficient.

> The notion of variance inflation can be extended to sets of related regressors, such as dummy regressors and polynomial regressors, by considering the size of the joint confidence region for the related coefficients.

13.2 Coping With Collinearity: No Quick Fix _____

Consider the regression of a response variable Y on two explanatory variables X_1 and X_2: When X_1 and X_2 are strongly collinear, the data contain little information about the impact of X_1 on Y holding X_2 constant statistically because there is little variation in X_1 when X_2 is fixed. (Of course, the same is true for X_2 fixing X_1.) Because B_1 estimates the partial effect of X_1 controlling for X_2, this estimate is imprecise.

Although there are several strategies for dealing with collinear data, none magically extracts nonexistent information from the data. Rather, the research problem is redefined, often subtly and implicitly. Sometimes the redefinition is reasonable; usually it is not. The ideal solution to the problem of collinearity is to collect new data in such a manner that the problem is avoided—for example, by experimental manipulation of the Xs, or through a research setting (or sampling procedure) in which the explanatory variables of interest are not strongly related. Unfortunately, these solutions are rarely practical. Several less adequate strategies for coping with collinear data are briefly described in this section.

13.2.1 Model Respecification

Although collinearity is a data problem, not (necessarily) a deficiency of the model, one approach to the problem is to respecify the model. Perhaps, after further thought, several regressors in the model can be conceptualized as alternative indicators of the same underlying construct. Then these measures can be combined in some manner, or one can be chosen to represent the others. In this context, high correlations among the Xs in question indicate high reliability—a fact to be celebrated, not lamented. Imagine, for example, an international analysis of factors influencing infant mortality, in which gross national product per capita, energy use per capita, and televisions per capita are among the explanatory variables and are highly correlated. A researcher may choose to treat these variables as indicators of the general level of economic development.

Alternatively, we can reconsider whether we really need to control for X_2 (for example) in examining the relationship of Y to X_1. Generally, though, respecification of this variety is possible only where the original model was poorly thought out or where the researcher is willing to abandon some of the goals of the research. For example, suppose that in a time-series regression examining determinants of married women's labor-force participation, collinearity makes it impossible to separate the effects of men's and women's wage levels. There may be good theoretical reason to want to know the effect of women's wage level on their labor-force participation, holding men's wage level constant, but the data are simply uninformative about this question. It may still be of interest, however, to determine the partial relationship between *general* wage level and women's labor-force participation, controlling for other explanatory variables in the analysis.[25]

---

[25]In the example developed in this chapter, however, men's and women's wages are not only highly correlated with each other but with other variables (such as time) as well.

13.2.2 Variable Selection

A common, but usually misguided, approach to collinearity is variable selection, where some procedure is employed to reduce the regressors in the model to a less highly correlated set.[26] *Forward-selection* methods add explanatory variables to the model one at a time. At each step, the variable that yields the largest increment in R^2 is selected. The procedure stops, for example, when the increment is smaller than a preset criterion.[27] *Backward-elimination* methods are similar, except that the procedure starts with the full model and deletes variables one at a time. *Forward/backward*—or *stepwise*—methods combine the two approaches, allowing variables to enter or leave at each step. Often the term *stepwise regression* is used for all these variations.

These methods frequently are abused by naive researchers who seek to interpret the order of entry of variables into the regression equation as an index of their "importance." This practice is potentially misleading: For example, suppose that there are two highly correlated explanatory variables that have nearly identical large correlations with Y; only one of these explanatory variables will enter the regression equation because the other can contribute little additional information. A small modification to the data, or a new sample, could easily reverse the result.

A technical objection to stepwise methods is that they can fail to turn up the optimal subset of regressors of a given size (i.e., the subset that maximizes R^2). Advances in computer power and in computing procedures make it feasible to examine all subsets of regressors even when k is quite large.[28] Aside from optimizing the selection criterion, subset techniques also have the advantage of revealing alternative, nearly equivalent models and thus avoid the misleading appearance of producing a uniquely "correct" result.[29]

Figure 13.8 shows the result of applying an all-subset method of variable selection to the Canadian women's labor-force regression. For each subset size of $p = 1$ to 6 explanatory variables, up to 10 "best" models are displayed.[30] The criterion of model quality employed in this graph is the *Bayesian Information Criterion* (or BIC): Smaller values indicate a better-fitting model. Unlike the R^2, which never declines when an additional variable is added to the model, the BIC "penalizes" the fit for the number of parameters in the model and therefore can prefer a smaller model to a larger one.[31] According to the BIC, the best model includes the two explanatory variables consumer debt and part-time work.[32] There are several models with three explanatory variables that are slightly worse than the best model of size two but that are essentially indistinguishable from each other; the same is true for models with four and five explanatory variables.[33]

In applying variable selection, it is essential to keep the following caveats in mind:

- Most important, variable selection results in a respecified model that usually does not address the research questions that were originally posed. In particular, if the original model is

---

[26] Variable selection methods are discussed in a more general context and in greater detail in Chapter 22.

[27] Often, the stopping criterion is calibrated by the incremental F for adding a variable to the model or by using an index of model quality, such as those discussed in Chapter 22.

[28] For k explanatory variables, the number of subsets, excluding the null subset with no predictors, is $2^k - 1$. See Exercise 13.5.

[29] There are algorithms available to find the optimal subset of a given size without examining all possible subsets (see, e.g., Furnival & Wilson, 1974). When the data are highly collinear, however, the optimal subset of a given size may be only trivially "better" than many of its competitors.

[30] The numbers of distinct subsets of one to six explanatory variables are 6, 15, 20, 15, 6, and 1, consecutively.

[31] See Chapter 22 for a discussion of the BIC and other model-selection criteria.

[32] *Not surprisingly, this best subset of size 2 includes one variable from each of the two highly correlated subsets that were identified in the principal-components analysis of the preceding section; these are also the two explanatory variables whose coefficients are statistically significant in the initial regression.

[33] Raftery (1995) suggests that a difference in BIC less than 2 provides "weak" evidence for the superiority of one model relative to another; similarly, a difference between 2 and 6 provides "positive" evidence, between 6 and 10 "strong" evidence, and greater than 10 "very strong" evidence for the relative superiority of a model. In the current application, the difference in BIC between the best-fitting models of size 2 and 3 is 3.3. Again, see Chapter 22 for a more extensive discussion of the BIC.

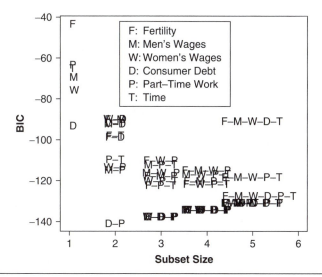

Figure 13.8   Variable selection for B. Fox's Canadian women's labor-force regression. Up to the
10 "best" subsets of each size are shown, using the BIC model-selection criterion.

correctly specified, and if the included and omitted variables are correlated, then coefficient
estimates following variable selection are biased.[34] Consequently, these methods are most
useful for pure prediction problems, in which the values of the regressors for the data to be
predicted will be within the configuration of X values for which selection was employed. In
this case, it is possible to get good estimates of $E(Y)$ even though the regression coefficients
themselves are biased. If, however, the X values for a new observation differ greatly from
those used to obtain the estimates, then the predicted Y can be badly biased.

- When regressors occur in sets (e.g., of dummy variables), then these sets should generally
  be kept together during selection. Likewise, when there are hierarchical relations among
  regressors, these relations should be respected: For example, an interaction regressor should
  not appear in a model that does not contain the main effects marginal to the interaction.

- Because variable selection optimizes the fit of the model to the sample data, coefficient
  standard errors calculated following explanatory-variable selection—and hence confidence
  intervals and hypothesis tests—almost surely overstate the precision of results. There is,
  therefore, a very considerable risk of capitalizing on chance characteristics of the sample.[35]

- As discussed in Chapter 22, variable selection has applications to statistical modeling even
  when collinearity is not an issue. For example, it is generally not problematic to eliminate
  regressors that have small, precisely estimated coefficients, thus producing a more parsimonious model. Indeed, in a very large sample, we may feel justified in deleting regressors
  with trivially small but "statistically significant" coefficients.

13.2.3   Biased Estimation

Still another general approach to collinear data is biased estimation. The essential idea here
is to trade a small amount of bias in the coefficient estimates for a large reduction in coefficient
sampling variance. The hoped-for result is a smaller mean-squared error of estimation of the βs

---

[34] See Sections 6.3, 9.7, and 13.2.5.

[35] This issue is pursued in Chapter 22 on model selection.

than is provided by the least-squares estimates. By far the most common biased estimation method is *ridge regression* (due to Hoerl & Kennard, 1970a, 1970b).

Like variable selection, biased estimation is not a magical panacea for collinearity. Ridge regression involves the arbitrary selection of a "ridge constant," which controls the extent to which ridge estimates differ from the least-squares estimates: The larger the ridge constant, the greater the bias and the smaller the variance of the ridge estimator. Unfortunately, but as one might expect, to pick an optimal ridge constant—or even a good one—generally requires knowledge about the unknown βs that we are trying to estimate. My principal reason for mentioning biased estimation here is to caution against its routine use.

Ridge Regression*

The ridge-regression estimator for the *standardized* regression coefficients is given by

$$\mathbf{b}_d^* \equiv (\mathbf{R}_{XX} + d\mathbf{I}_k)^{-1}\mathbf{r}_{Xy} \tag{13.7}$$

where $\mathbf{R}_{XX}$ is the correlation matrix for the explanatory variables; $\mathbf{r}_{Xy}$ is the vector of correlations between the explanatory variables and the response; and $d \geq 0$ is a scalar constant. When $d = 0$, the ridge and least-squares estimators coincide: $\mathbf{b}_0^* = \mathbf{b}^* = \mathbf{R}_{XX}^{-1}\mathbf{r}_{Xy}$. When the data are collinear, some off-diagonal entries of $\mathbf{R}_{XX}$ are generally large, making this matrix ill conditioned. Heuristically, the ridge-regression method improves the conditioning of $\mathbf{R}_{XX}$ by inflating its diagonal entries.

Although the least-squares estimator $\mathbf{b}^*$ is unbiased, its entries tend to be too large in absolute value, a tendency that is magnified as collinearity increases. In practice, researchers working with collinear data often compute wildly large regression coefficients. The ridge estimator may be thought of as a "shrunken" version of the least-squares estimator, correcting the tendency of the latter to produce coefficients that are too far from 0.

The ridge estimator of Equation 13.7 can be rewritten as[36]

$$\mathbf{b}_d^* = \mathbf{U}\mathbf{b}^* \tag{13.8}$$

where $\mathbf{U} \equiv (\mathbf{I}_k + d\mathbf{R}_{XX}^{-1})^{-1}$. As d increases, the entries of $\mathbf{U}$ tend to grow smaller, and, therefore, $\mathbf{b}_d^*$ is driven toward $\mathbf{0}$. Hoerl and Kennard (1970a) show that for any value of $d > 0$, the squared length of the ridge estimator is less than that of the least-squares estimator: $\mathbf{b}_d^{*\prime}\mathbf{b}_d^* < \mathbf{b}^{*\prime}\mathbf{b}^*$.

The expected value of the ridge estimator can be determined from its relation to the least-squares estimator, given in Equation 13.8; treating the X values, and hence $\mathbf{R}_{XX}$ and $\mathbf{U}$, as fixed,

$$E(\mathbf{b}_d^*) = \mathbf{U}E(\mathbf{b}^*) = \mathbf{U}\beta^*$$

The bias of $\mathbf{b}_d^*$ is, therefore,

$$\text{bias}(\mathbf{b}_d^*) \equiv E(\mathbf{b}_d^*) - \beta^* = (\mathbf{U} - \mathbf{I}_k)\beta^*$$

and because the departure of $\mathbf{U}$ from $\mathbf{I}_k$ increases with d, the bias of the ridge estimator is an increasing function of d.

The variance of the ridge estimator is also simply derived:[37]

$$V(\mathbf{b}_d^*) = \frac{\sigma_\varepsilon^{*2}}{n-1}(\mathbf{R}_{XX} + d\mathbf{I}_k)^{-1}\mathbf{R}_{XX}(\mathbf{R}_{XX} + d\mathbf{I}_k)^{-1} \tag{13.9}$$

---

[36]See Exercise 13.7.
[37]See Exercise 13.8.

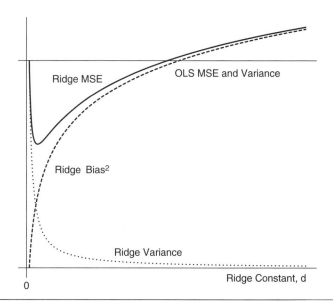

Figure 13.9 Trade-off of bias and against variance for the ridge-regression estimator. The horizontal line gives the variance of the least-squares (OLS) estimator; because the OLS estimator is unbiased, its variance and mean-squared error are the same. The broken line shows the squared bias of the ridge estimator as a function of the ridge constant d. The dotted line shows the variance of the ridge estimator. The mean-squared error (MSE) of the ridge estimator, given by the heavier solid line, is the sum of its variance and squared bias. For some values of d, the MSE error of the ridge estimator is below the variance of the OLS estimator.

where σ_ε^{*2} is the error variance for the standardized regression. As d increases, the inverted term $(\mathbf{R}_{XX} + d\mathbf{I}_k)^{-1}$ is increasingly dominated by $d\mathbf{I}_k$. The sampling variance of the ridge estimator, therefore, is a decreasing function of d. This result is intuitively reasonable because the estimator itself is driven toward $\mathbf{0}$.

The mean-squared error of the ridge estimator is the sum of its squared bias and sampling variance. Hoerl and Kennard (1970a) prove that it is always possible to choose a positive value of the ridge constant d so that the mean-squared error of the ridge estimator is less than the mean-squared error of the least-squares estimator. These ideas are illustrated heuristically in Figure 13.9. As mentioned, however, the optimal value of d depends on the unknown population regression coefficients.

The central problem in applying ridge regression is to find a value of d for which the trade-off of bias against variance is favorable. In deriving the properties of the ridge estimator, I treated d as fixed. If d is determined from the data, however, it becomes a random variable, casting doubt on the conceptual basis for the ridge estimator. A number of methods have been proposed for selecting d. Some of these are rough and qualitative, while others incorporate specific formulas or procedures for estimating the optimal value of d. All these methods, however, have only ad hoc justifications.[38]

There have been many random-sampling simulation experiments exploring the properties of ridge estimation along with other methods meant to cope with collinear data. While these studies are by no means unanimous in their conclusions, the ridge estimator often performs well in comparison with least-squares estimation and in comparison with other biased-estimation methods.

---

[38]Exercise 13.9 describes a qualitative method proposed by Hoerl and Kennard in their 1970 papers.

On the basis of evidence from simulation experiments, it would, however, be misleading to recommend a particular procedure for selecting the ridge constant d, and, indeed, the dependence of the optimal value of d on the unknown regression parameters makes it unlikely that there is a generally best way of finding d. Several authors critical of ridge regression (e.g., Draper & Smith, 1998, p. 395) have noted that simulations supporting the method generally incorporate restrictions on parameter values especially suited to ridge regression.[39]

Because the ridge estimator is biased, standard errors based on Equation 13.9 cannot be used in the normal manner for statistical inferences concerning the population regression coefficients. Indeed, as Obenchain (1977) has pointed out, under the assumptions of the linear model, confidence intervals centered at the least-squares estimates paradoxically retain their optimal properties regardless of the degree of collinearity: In particular, they are the *shortest* possible intervals at the stated level of confidence (Scheffé, 1959, chap. 2). An interval centered at the ridge estimate of a regression coefficient is, therefore, *wider* than the corresponding least-squares interval, even if the ridge estimator has smaller mean-squared error than the least-squares estimator.

13.2.4   Prior Information About the Regression Coefficients

A final approach to estimation with collinear data is to introduce additional prior information (i.e., relevant information external to the data at hand) that reduces the ambiguity produced by collinearity. There are several different ways in which prior information can be brought to bear on a regression, including Bayesian analysis,[40] but I will present a very simple case to illustrate the general point. More complex methods are beyond the scope of this discussion and are, in any event, difficult to apply in practice.[41]

Suppose that we wish to estimate the model

$$Y = \alpha + \beta_1 X_1 + \beta_2 X_2 + \beta_3 X_3 + \varepsilon$$

where Y is savings, X_1 is income from wages and salaries, X_2 is dividend income from stocks, and X_3 is interest income. Imagine that we have trouble estimating β_2 and β_3 because X_2 and X_3 are highly correlated in our data. Suppose further that we have reason to believe that $\beta_2 = \beta_3$, and denote the common quantity β_*. If X_2 and X_3 were *not* so highly correlated, then we could reasonably test this belief as a hypothesis. In the current situation, we can fit the model

$$Y = \alpha + \beta_1 X_1 + \beta_*(X_2 + X_3) + \varepsilon$$

incorporating our belief in the equality of β_2 and β_3 in the specification of the model and thus eliminating the collinearity problem (along with the possibility of testing the belief that the two coefficients are equal).[42]

---

[39] See Section 13.2.5. Simulation studies of ridge regression and other biased estimation methods are too numerous to cite individually here. References to and comments on this literature can be found in many sources, including Draper and Van Nostrand (1979), Vinod (1978), and Hocking (1976). Vinod and Ullah (1981) present an extensive treatment of ridge regression and related methods.

[40] Bayesian inference is introduced in Appendix D on probability and estimation.

[41] See, for example, Belsley et al. (1980, pp. 193–204) and Theil (1971, pp. 346–352).

[42] To test H_0: $\beta_2 = \beta_3$ simply entails contrasting the two models (see Exercise 6.7). In the present context, however, where X_2 and X_3 are very highly correlated, this test has virtually no power: If the second model is wrong, then we cannot, as a practical matter, detect it. We need either to accept the second model on theoretical grounds or to admit that we cannot estimate β_2 and β_3.

13.2.5   Some Comparisons

Although I have presented them separately, the several approaches to collinear data have much in common:

- Model respecification can involve variable selection, and variable selection, in effect, respecifies the model.
- Variable selection implicitly constrains the coefficients of deleted regressors to 0.
- Variable selection produces biased coefficient estimates if the deleted variables have nonzero βs and are correlated with the included variables (as they will be for collinear data).[43] As in ridge regression and similar biased estimation methods, we might hope that the trade-off of bias against variance is favorable, and that, therefore, the mean-squared error of the regression estimates is smaller following variable selection than before. Because the bias and hence the mean-squared error depend on the unknown regression coefficients, however, we have no assurance that this will be the case. Even if the coefficients obtained following selection have smaller mean-squared error, their superiority can easily be due to the very large variance of the least-squares estimates when collinearity is high than to acceptably small bias.
- Certain types of prior information (as in the hypothetical example presented in the previous section) result in a respecified model.
- It can be demonstrated that biased-estimation methods like ridge regression place prior constraints on the values of the βs. Ridge regression imposes the restriction $\sum_{j=1}^{k} B_j^{*2} \leq c$, where c is a decreasing function of the ridge constant d; the ridge estimator finds least-squares coefficients subject to this constraint (Draper & Smith, 1998, pp. 392–393). In effect, large absolute standardized coefficients are ruled out a priori, but the specific constraint is imposed indirectly through the choice of d.

The primary lesson to be drawn from these remarks is that mechanical model selection and modification procedures disguise the substantive implications of modeling decisions. Consequently, these methods generally cannot compensate for weaknesses in the data, and are no substitute for judgment and thought.

Several methods have been proposed for dealing with collinear data. Although these methods are sometimes useful, none can be recommended generally: When the Xs are highly collinear, the data contain little information about the partial relationship between each X and Y, controlling for the other Xs. To resolve the intrinsic ambiguity of collinear data, it is necessary either to introduce information external to the data or to redefine the research question asked of the data. Neither of these general approaches should be undertaken mechanically. Methods that are commonly (and, more often than not, unjustifiably) employed with collinear data include model respecification; variable selection (stepwise and subset methods); biased estimation (e.g., ridge regression); and the introduction of additional prior information. Comparison of the several methods shows that they have more in common than it appears at first sight.

---

[43]Bias due to the omission of explanatory variables is discussed in a general context in Sections 6.3 and 9.7.

Exercises

Exercise 13.1. *The *second* principal component is

$$
\begin{aligned}
\underset{(n\times1)}{\mathbf{w}_1} &= A_{12}\mathbf{z}_1 + A_{22}\mathbf{z}_2 + \cdots + A_{k2}\mathbf{z}_k \\
&= \underset{(n\times k)(k\times1)}{\mathbf{Z}_X\ \mathbf{a}_2}
\end{aligned}
$$

with variance

$$
S_{W_2}^2 = \mathbf{a}_2'\mathbf{R}_{XX}\mathbf{a}_2
$$

We need to maximize this variance subject to the *normalizing constraint* $\mathbf{a}_2'\mathbf{a}_2 = 1$ and the *orthogonality constraint* $\mathbf{w}_1'\mathbf{w}_2 = 0$. Show that the orthogonality constraint is equivalent to $\mathbf{a}_1'\mathbf{a}_2 = 0$. Then, using *two* Lagrange multipliers, one for the normalizing constraint and the other for the orthogonality constraint, show that $\mathbf{a}_2$ is an eigenvector corresponding to the second-largest eigenvalue of $\mathbf{R}_{XX}$. Explain how this procedure can be extended to derive the remaining $k-2$ principal components.

Exercise 13.2. *Find the matrix $\mathbf{A}$ of principal-component coefficients when $k=2$ and r_{12} is *negative*. (Cf. Equation 13.6 on page 318.)

Exercise 13.3. *Show that when $k=2$, the principal components of $\mathbf{R}_{XX}$ correspond to the principal axes of the data ellipse for the standardized regressors Z_1 and Z_2; show that the half-length of each axis is equal to the square root of the corresponding eigenvalue of $\mathbf{R}_{XX}$. Now extend this reasoning to the principal axes of the data ellipsoid for the standardized regressors when $k>2$.

Exercise 13.4. *Use the principal-components analysis of the explanatory variables in B. Fox's time-series regression, given in Table 13.3, to estimate the nearly collinear relationships among the variables corresponding to small principal components. Which variables appear to be involved in each nearly collinear relationship?

Exercise 13.5. Why are there $2^k - 1$ distinct subsets of k explanatory variables? Evaluate this quantity for $k = 2, 3, \ldots, 15$.

Exercise 13.6. Apply the backward, forward, and forward/backward stepwise regression methods to B. Fox's Canadian women's labor-force participation data. Compare the results of these procedures with those shown in Figure 13.8, based on the application of the BIC to all subsets of predictors.

Exercise 13.7. *Show that the ridge-regression estimator of the standardized regression coefficients,

$$
\mathbf{b}_d^* = (\mathbf{R}_{XX} + d\mathbf{I}_k)^{-1}\mathbf{r}_{Xy}
$$

can be written as a linear transformation $\mathbf{b}_d^* = \mathbf{U}\mathbf{b}^*$ of the usual least-squares estimator $\mathbf{b}^* = \mathbf{R}_{XX}^{-1}\mathbf{r}_{Xy}$, where the transformation matrix is $\mathbf{U} \equiv \left(\mathbf{I}_k + d\mathbf{R}_{XX}^{-1}\right)^{-1}$.

Exercise 13.8. *Show that the variance of the ridge estimator is

$$
V(\mathbf{b}_d^*) = \frac{\sigma_\varepsilon^{*2}}{n-1}(\mathbf{R}_{XX} + d\mathbf{I}_k)^{-1}\mathbf{R}_{XX}(\mathbf{R}_{XX} + d\mathbf{I}_k)^{-1}
$$

[*Hint*: Express the ridge estimator as a linear transformation of the standardized response variable, $\mathbf{b}_d^* = (\mathbf{R}_{XX} + d\mathbf{I}_k)^{-1}[1/(n-1)]\mathbf{Z}_X'\mathbf{z}_y.$]

Exercise 13.9. *Finding the ridge constant d: Hoerl and Kennard suggest plotting the entries in $\mathbf{b}_d^*$ against values of d ranging between 0 and 1. The resulting graph, called a *ridge trace*, both furnishes a visual representation of the instability due to collinearity and (ostensibly) provides a basis for selecting a value of d. When the data are collinear, we generally observe dramatic changes in regression coefficients as d is gradually increased from 0. As d is increased further, the coefficients eventually stabilize and then are driven slowly toward $\mathbf{0}$. The estimated error variance, S_E^{*2}, which is minimized at the least-squares solution ($d = 0$), rises slowly with increasing d. Hoerl and Kennard recommend choosing d so that the regression coefficients are stabilized and the error variance is not unreasonably inflated from its minimum value. (A number of other methods have been suggested for selecting d, but none avoids the fundamental difficulty of ridge regression—that good values of d depend on the unknown βs.) Construct a ridge trace, including the regression standard error S_E^*, for B. Fox's Canadian women's labor-force participation data. Use this information to select a value of the ridge constant d, and compare the resulting ridge estimates of the regression parameters with the least-squares estimates. Make this comparison for both standardized and unstandardized coefficients. In applying ridge regression to these data, B. Fox selected $d = 0.05$.

Summary

- When the regressors in a linear model are perfectly collinear, the least-squares coefficients are not unique. Strong, but less-than-perfect, collinearity substantially increases the sampling variances of the least-squares coefficients and can render them useless as estimators.
- The sampling variance of the least-squares slope coefficient B_j is

$$V(B_j) = \frac{1}{1 - R_j^2} \times \frac{\sigma_\varepsilon^2}{(n - 1)S_j^2}$$

  where R_j^2 is the squared multiple correlation for the regression of X_j on the other Xs, and $S_j^2 = \sum(X_{ij} - \overline{X}_j)^2/(n - 1)$ is the variance of X_j. The variance-inflation factor $\text{VIF}_j = 1/(1 - R_j^2)$ indicates the deleterious impact of collinearity on the precision of the estimate B_j. The notion of variance inflation can be extended to sets of related regressors, such as dummy regressors and polynomial regressors, by considering the size of the joint confidence region for the related coefficients.
- Principal components can be used to explicate the correlational structure of the explanatory variables in regression. The principal components are a derived set of variables that form an orthogonal basis for the subspace of the standardized Xs. The first principal component spans the one-dimensional subspace that accounts for maximum variation in the standardized Xs. The second principal component accounts for maximum variation in the standardized Xs, under the constraint that it is orthogonal to the first. The other principal components are similarly defined; unless the Xs are perfectly collinear, there are as many principal components as there are Xs. Each principal component is scaled to have variance equal to the collective variance in the standardized Xs for which it accounts. Collinear relations among the explanatory variables, therefore, correspond to very short principal components, which represent dimensions along which the regressor subspace has nearly collapsed.
- Several methods have been proposed for dealing with collinear data. Although these methods are sometimes useful, none can be recommended generally: When the Xs are highly collinear, the data contain little information about the partial relationship between each X

and Y, controlling for the other Xs. To resolve the intrinsic ambiguity of collinear data, it is necessary either to introduce information external to the data or to redefine the research question asked of the data (or, as is usually impractical, to collect more informative data). Neither of these general approaches should be undertaken mechanically. Methods that are commonly (and, more often than not, unjustifiably) employed with collinear data include model respecification; variable selection (stepwise and subset methods); biased estimation (e.g., ridge regression); and the introduction of additional prior information. Comparison of the several methods shows that they have more in common than it appears at first sight.

PART IV

Generalized Linear Models

14

Logit and Probit Models for Categorical Response Variables

T his chapter and the next deal with generalized linear models—the extension of linear models to variables that have specific non-normal conditional distributions:

- Rather than dive directly into generalized linear models in their full generality, the current chapter takes up linear logit and probit models for categorical response variables. Beginning with this most-important special case allows for a gentler introduction to the topic, I believe. As well, I develop some models for categorical data that are not subsumed by the generalized linear model described in the next chapter.
- Chapter 15 is devoted to the generalized linear model, which has as special cases the linear models of Part II of the text and the dichotomous logit and probit models of the current chapter. Chapter 15 focuses on generalized linear models for count data and develops diagnostic methods for generalized linear models that parallel many of the diagnostics for linear models fit by least-squares, introduced in Part III.

All the statistical models described in previous chapters are for quantitative response variables. It is unnecessary to document the prevalence of qualitative/categorical data in the social sciences. In developing the general linear model, I introduced qualitative *explanatory* variables through the device of coding dummy-variable regressors.[1] There is no reason that qualitative variables should not also appear as response variables, affected by other variables, both qualitative and quantitative.

This chapter deals primarily with logit models for qualitative and ordered-categorical response variables, although related probit models are also briefly considered. The first section of the chapter describes logit and probit models for dichotomous response variables. The second section develops similar statistical models for polytomous response variables, including ordered categories. The third and final section discusses the application of logit models to contingency tables, where the explanatory variables, as well as the response, are categorical.

14.1 Models for Dichotomous Data

Logit and probit models express a qualitative response variable as a function of several explanatory variables, much in the manner of the general linear model. To understand why these models are required, let us begin by examining a representative problem, attempting to apply linear regression to it. The difficulties that are encountered point the way to more satisfactory statistical models for qualitative data.

---

[1] See Chapter 7.

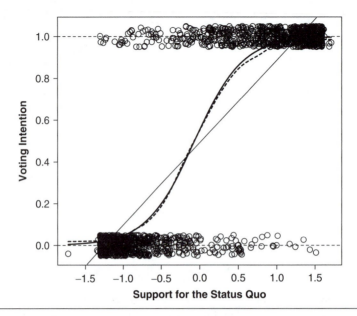

Figure 14.1   Scatterplot of voting intention (1 represents *yes*, 0 represents *no*) by a scale of support
for the status quo, for a sample of Chilean voters surveyed prior to the 1988
plebiscite. The points are jittered vertically to minimize overplotting. The solid
straight line shows the linear least-squares fit; the solid curved line shows the fit of
the logistic-regression model (described in the next section); the broken line
represents a nonparametric kernel regression with a span of 0.4.

In September 1988, 15 years after the coup of 1973, the people of Chile voted in a plebiscite
to decide the future of the military government headed by General Augusto Pinochet. A *yes* vote
would yield eight more years of military rule; a *no* vote would set in motion a process to return
the country to civilian government. Of course, the *no* side won the plebiscite, by a clear if not
overwhelming margin.

Six months before the plebiscite, the independent research center FLACSO/Chile conducted
a national survey of 2,700 randomly selected Chilean voters.[2] Of these individuals, 868 said that
they were planning to vote *yes*, and 889 said that they were planning to vote *no*. Of the remainder,
558 said that they were undecided, 187 said that they planned to abstain, and 168 did not answer
the question. I will look here only at those who expressed a preference.[3]

Figure 14.1 plots voting intention against a measure of support for the status quo. As seems
natural, voting intention appears as a dummy variable, coded 1 for *yes*, 0 for *no*. As we will see
presently, this coding makes sense in the context of a dichotomous response variable. Because
many points would otherwise be overplotted, voting intention is jittered in the graph (although
not in the calculations that follow). Support for the status quo is a scale formed from a number of

----

[2]FLACSO is an acronym for La Facultad Latino-americano des Ciensias Sociales, a respected institution that conducts
social research and trains graduate students in several Latin-American countries. During the Chilean military dictatorship,
FLACSO/Chile was associated with the opposition to the military government. I worked on the analysis of the survey
described here as part of a joint project between FLACSO in Santiago, Chile, and the Centre for Research on Latin
America and the Caribbean at York University, Toronto.

[3]It is, of course, difficult to know how to interpret ambiguous responses such as "undecided." It is tempting to infer that
respondents were afraid to state their opinions, but there is other evidence from the survey that this is not the case. Few
respondents, for example, uniformly refused to answer sensitive political questions, and the survey interviewers reported
little resistance to the survey.

questions about political, social, and economic policies: High scores represent general support for the policies of the miliary regime. (For the moment, disregard the lines plotted in this figure.)

We are used to thinking of a regression as a conditional average. Does this interpretation make sense when the response variable is dichotomous? After all, an average between 0 and 1 represents a "score" for the dummy response variable that cannot be realized by any individual. In the population, the conditional average $E(Y|x_i)$ is simply the proportion of 1s among those individuals who share the value x_i for the explanatory variable—the conditional probability π_i of sampling a *yes* in this group; that is,

$$\pi_i \equiv \Pr(Y_i) \equiv \Pr(Y = 1 | X = x_i)$$

and, thus,

$$E(Y|x_i) = \pi_i(1) + (1 - \pi_i)(0) = \pi_i \tag{14.1}$$

If X is discrete, then in a sample we can calculate the conditional proportion for Y at each value of X. The collection of these conditional proportions represents the sample nonparametric regression of the dichotomous Y on X. In the present example, X is continuous, but we can nevertheless resort to strategies such as local averaging, as illustrated in Figure 14.1.[4] At low levels of support for the status quo, the conditional proportion of *yes* responses is close to 0; at high levels, it is close to 1; and in between, the nonparametric regression curve smoothly approaches 0 and 1 in a gentle S-shaped pattern.

14.1.1 The Linear-Probability Model

Although nonparametric regression works here, it would be useful to capture the dependency of Y on X as a simple function. To do so will be especially helpful when we introduce additional explanatory variables. As a first effort, let us try linear regression with the usual assumptions:

$$Y_i = \alpha + \beta X_i + \varepsilon_i \tag{14.2}$$

where $\varepsilon_i \sim N(0, \sigma_\varepsilon^2)$, and ε_i and ε_j are independent for $i \neq j$. If X is random, then we assume that it is independent of ε.

Under Equation 14.2, $E(Y_i) = \alpha + \beta X_i$, and so, from Equation 14.1,

$$\pi_i = \alpha + \beta X_i$$

For this reason, the linear-regression model applied to a dummy response variable is called the *linear-probability model*. This model is untenable, but its failure will point the way toward more adequate specifications:

- Because Y_i can take on only the values 0 and 1, the error ε_i is dichotomous as well—and, hence, is not normally distributed, as assumed: If $Y_i = 1$, which occurs with probability π_i, then

$$\varepsilon_i = 1 - E(Y_i) = 1 - (\alpha + \beta X_i) = 1 - \pi_i$$

---

[4]The nonparametric-regression line in Figure 14.1 was fit by kernel regression—a method based on locally weighted averaging, which is similar to locally weighted regression (lowess, which was introduced in Chapter 2 for smoothing scatterplots). Unlike lowess, however, the kernel estimator of a proportion cannot be outside the interval from 0 to 1. Both the kernel-regression estimator and other nonparametric-regression methods that are more appropriate for a dichotomous response are described in Chapter 18. The span for the kernel regression (i.e., the fraction of the data included in each local average) is 0.4.

Alternatively, if $Y_i = 0$, which occurs with probability $1 - \pi_i$, then

$$\varepsilon_i = 0 - E(Y_i) = 0 - (\alpha + \beta X_i) = 0 - \pi_i = -\pi_i$$

Because of the central-limit theorem, however, the assumption of normality is not critical to least-squares estimation of the normal-probability model, as long as the sample size is sufficiently large.

- The variance of ε cannot be constant, as we can readily demonstrate: If the assumption of linearity holds over the range of the data, then $E(\varepsilon_i) = 0$. Using the relations just noted,

$$V(\varepsilon_i) = \pi_i(1 - \pi_i)^2 + (1 - \pi_i)(-\pi_i)^2 = \pi_i(1 - \pi_i)$$

The heteroscedasticity of the errors bodes ill for ordinary-least-squares estimation of the linear probability model, but only if the probabilities π_i get close to 0 or 1.[5] Goldberger (1964, pp. 248–250) has proposed a correction for heteroscedasticity employing weighted least squares.[6] Because the variances $V(\varepsilon_i)$ depend on the π_i, however, which, in turn, are functions of the unknown parameters α and β, we require preliminary estimates of the parameters to define weights. Goldberger obtains ad hoc estimates from a preliminary OLS regression; that is, he takes $\widehat{V}(\varepsilon_i) = \widehat{Y}_i(1 - \widehat{Y}_i)$. The fitted values from an OLS regression are not constrained to the interval $[0, 1]$, and so some of these "variances" may be negative.

- This last remark suggests the most serious problem with the linear-probability model: The assumption that $E(\varepsilon_i) = 0$—that is, the assumption of linearity—is only tenable over a limited range of X values. If the range of the Xs is sufficiently broad, then the linear specification cannot confine π to the unit interval $[0, 1]$. It makes no sense, of course, to interpret a number outside the unit interval as a probability. This difficulty is illustrated in Figure 14.1, in which the least-squares line fit to the Chilean plebiscite data produces fitted probabilities below 0 at low levels and above 1 at high levels of support for the status quo.

Dummy *regressor* variables do not cause comparable difficulties because the general linear model makes no distributional assumptions about the regressors (other than independence from the errors). Nevertheless, for values of π not too close to 0 or 1, the linear-probability model estimated by least squares frequently provides results similar to those produced by the more generally adequate methods described in the remainder of this chapter.

> It is problematic to apply least-squares linear regression to a dichotomous response variable: The errors cannot be normally distributed and cannot have constant variance. Even more fundamentally, the linear specification does not confine the probability for the response to the unit interval.

One solution to the problems of the linear-probability model—though not a good general solution—is simply to constrain π to the unit interval while retaining the linear relationship between π and X within this interval:

$$\pi = \begin{cases} 0 & \text{for } 0 > \alpha + \beta X \\ \alpha + \beta X & \text{for } 0 \le \alpha + \beta X \le 1 \\ 1 & \text{for } \alpha + \beta X > 1 \end{cases} \tag{14.3}$$

---

[5]See Exercise 14.1. Remember, however, that it is the *conditional probability*, not the *marginal probability*, of Y that is at issue: The overall proportion of 1s can be near .5 (as in the Chilean plebiscite data), and yet the conditional proportion can still get very close to 0 or 1.

[6]See Section 12.2.2 for a discussion of weighted-least-squares estimation.

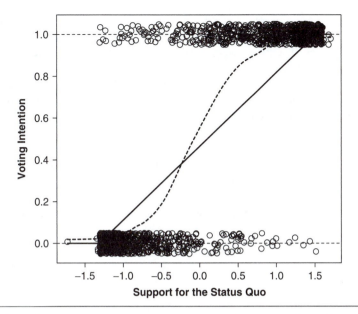

Figure 14.2   The solid line shows the constrained linear-probability model, fit by maximum likelihood to the Chilean plebiscite data. The broken line is for a nonparametric kernel regression with a span of 0.4.

Figure 14.2 shows the fit of this model to the Chilean plebiscite data, with the parameters α and β estimated by maximum likelihood. Although this *constrained linear-probability model* cannot be dismissed on logical grounds, the model has certain unattractive features: Most importantly, the abrupt changes in slope at $\pi = 0$ and $\pi = 1$ are usually unreasonable. A smoother relationship between π and X (as characterizes the nonparametric regression in Figure 14.1) is more generally sensible. Moreover, numerical instability can make the constrained linear-probability model difficult to fit to data, and the statistical properties of estimators of the model are hard to derive because of the discontinuities in the slope.[7]

14.1.2   Transformations of π: Logit and Probit Models

A central difficulty of the unconstrained linear-probability model is its inability to ensure that π stays between 0 and 1. What we require to correct this problem is a positive monotone (i.e., nondecreasing) function that maps the *linear predictor* $\eta = \alpha + \beta X$ into the unit interval. A transformation of this type will allow us to retain the fundamentally linear structure of the model while avoiding the contradiction of probabilities below 0 or above 1. Any cumulative probability distribution function (CDF) meets this requirement.[8] That is, we can respecify the model as

$$\pi_i = P(\eta_i) = P(\alpha + \beta X_i) \tag{14.4}$$

---

[7]*Consider the strong constraints that the data place on the maximum-likelihood estimators of α and β: If, as in the illustration, $\widehat{\beta} > 0$, then the rightmost observation for which $Y = 0$ can have an X value no larger than $(1 - \widehat{\alpha})/\widehat{\beta}$, which is the point at which the estimated regression line hits $\widehat{\pi} = 1$, because any 0 to the right of this point would produce a 0 likelihood. Similarly, the leftmost observation for which $Y = 1$ can have an X value no smaller than $-\widehat{\alpha}/\widehat{\beta}$, the point at which the regression line hits $\widehat{\pi} = 0$. As the sample size grows, these extreme values will tend to to move, respectively, to the right and left, making $\widehat{\beta}$ smaller.

[8]See Appendix D on probability and estimation.

where the CDF $P(\cdot)$ is selected in advance, and α and β are then parameters to be estimated.

If we choose $P(\cdot)$ as the cumulative rectangular distribution, for example, then we obtain the constrained linear-probability model (Equation 14.3).[9] An a priori reasonable $P(\cdot)$ should be both smooth and symmetric and should approach $\pi = 0$ and $\pi = 1$ as asymptotes.[10] Moreover, it is advantageous if $P(\cdot)$ is strictly increasing, for then the transformation (Equation 14.4) is one to one, permitting us to rewrite the model as

$$P^{-1}(\pi_i) = \eta_i = \alpha + \beta X_i \tag{14.5}$$

where $P^{-1}(\cdot)$ is the inverse of the CDF $P(\cdot)$ (i.e., the quantile function for the distribution).[11] Thus, we have a linear model (Equation 14.5) for a transformation of π, or—equivalently—a nonlinear model (Equation 14.4) for π itself.

The transformation $P(\cdot)$ is often chosen as the CDF of the unit-normal distribution, $N(0, 1)$,

$$\Phi(z) = \frac{1}{\sqrt{2\pi}} \int_{-\infty}^{z} \exp\left(-\frac{1}{2}Z^2\right) dZ \tag{14.6}$$

or, even more commonly, of the *logistic distribution*

$$\Lambda(z) = \frac{1}{1 + e^{-z}} \tag{14.7}$$

In these equations, $\pi \approx 3.141$ and $e \approx 2.718$ are the familiar mathematical constants.[12]

- Using the normal distribution $\Phi(\cdot)$ yields the *linear probit model*:

$$\pi_i = \Phi(\alpha + \beta X_i)$$
$$= \frac{1}{\sqrt{2\pi}} \int_{-\infty}^{\alpha + \beta X_i} \exp\left(-\frac{1}{2}Z^2\right) dZ$$

- Using the logistic distribution $\Lambda(\cdot)$ produces the *linear logistic-regression* or *linear logit model*:

$$\pi_i = \Lambda(\alpha + \beta X_i)$$
$$= \frac{1}{1 + \exp[-(\alpha + \beta X_i)]} \tag{14.8}$$

Once their variances are equated—the logistic distribution has variance $\pi^2/3$—the logit and probit transformations are so similar that it is not possible, in practice, to distinguish between them without a great deal of data, as is apparent in Figure 14.3. It is also clear from this graph that both functions are nearly linear over much of their range, say between about $\pi = .2$ and $\pi = .8$. This is why the linear-probability model produces results similar to the logit and probit models, except for extreme values of π_i.

---

[9]See Exercise 14.2.

[10]This is not to say, however, that $P(\cdot)$ needs to be symmetric in every case, just that symmetric $P(\cdot)$s are more appropriate *in general*. For an example of an asymmetric choice of $P(\cdot)$, see the discussion of the complementary log-log transformation in Chapter 15.

[11]If, alternatively, the CDF levels off (as is the case, e.g., for the rectangular distribution), then the inverse of the CDF does not exist.

[12]A note to the reader for whom calculus is unfamiliar: An integral, represented by the symbol $\int$ in Equation 14.6, represents the area under a curve, here the area between $Z = -\infty$ and $Z = z$ under the curve given by the function $\exp\left(-\frac{1}{2}Z^2\right)$. The constant $1/\sqrt{2\pi}$ insures that the total area under the normal density function "integrates" (i.e., adds up) to 1.

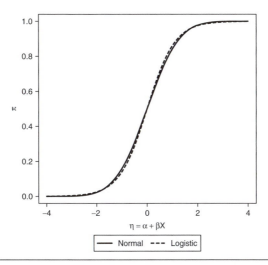

Figure 14.3 Once their variances are equated, the cumulative logistic and cumulative normal distributions—used here to transform $\eta = \alpha + \beta X$ to the unit interval—are virtually indistinguishable.

Despite their essential similarity, there are two practical advantages of the logit model compared to the probit model:

1. The equation of the logistic CDF (Equation 14.7) is very simple, while the normal CDF (Equation 14.6) involves an unevaluated integral. This difference is trivial for dichotomous data because very good closed-form approximations to the normal CDF are available, but for polytomous data, where we will require the *multivariate* logistic or normal distribution, the disadvantage of the probit model is somewhat more acute.[13]

2. The inverse linearizing transformation for the logit model, $\Lambda^{-1}(\pi)$, is directly interpretable as a *log-odds*, while the inverse transformation for the probit model, the quantile function of the standard-normal distribution, $\Phi^{-1}(\pi)$, does not have a direct interpretation. Rearranging Equation 14.8, we get

$$\frac{\pi_i}{1 - \pi_i} = \exp(\alpha + \beta X_i) \qquad (14.9)$$

The ratio $\pi_i/(1 - \pi_i)$ is the *odds* that $Y_i = 1$ (e.g., the odds of voting *yes*), an expression of relative chances familiar from gambling (at least to those who engage in this vice). Unlike the probability scale, odds are unbounded above (though bounded below by 0). Taking the log of both sides of Equation 14.9 produces

$$\log_e \frac{\pi_i}{1 - \pi_i} = \alpha + \beta X_i$$

The inverse transformation $\Lambda^{-1}(\pi) = \log_e[\pi/(1 - \pi)]$, called the *logit* of π, is therefore the log of the odds that Y is 1 rather than 0. As the following table shows, if the odds are "even"—that is, equal to 1, corresponding to $\pi = .5$—then the logit is 0. The logit is symmetric around 0, and unbounded both above and below, making the logit a good candidate for the response variable in a linear-like model.

---

[13] See Section 14.2.1.

Probability π	Odds $\dfrac{\pi}{1-\pi}$	Logit $\log_e \dfrac{\pi}{1-\pi}$
.01	1/99 = 0.0101	−4.60
.05	5/95 = 0.0526	−2.94
.10	1/9 = 0.1111	−2.20
.30	3/7 = 0.4286	−0.85
.50	5/5 = 1	0.00
.70	7/3 = 2.3333	0.85
.90	9/1 = 9	2.20
.95	95/5 = 19	2.94
.99	99/1 = 99	4.60

The logit model is a linear, additive model for the log odds, but (from Equation 14.9) it is also a multiplicative model for the odds:

$$\frac{\pi_i}{1-\pi_i} = \exp(\alpha + \beta X_i) = \exp(\alpha)\exp(\beta X_i)$$
$$= e^\alpha \left(e^\beta\right)^{X_i}$$

So, increasing X by 1 changes the logit by β and multiplies the odds by e^β. For example, if $\beta = 2$, then increasing X by 1 increases the odds by a factor of $e^2 \approx 2.718^2 = 7.389$.[14]

Still another way of understanding the parameter β in the logit model is to consider the slope of the relationship between π and X, given by Equation 14.8. Because this relationship is nonlinear, the slope is not constant; the slope is $\beta\pi(1-\pi)$ and hence is at a maximum when $\pi = \frac{1}{2}$, where the slope is $\beta\frac{1}{2}(1-\frac{1}{2}) = \beta/4$, as illustrated in the following table:[15]

π	$\beta\pi(1-\pi)$
.01	$\beta \times .0099$
.05	$\beta \times .0475$
.10	$\beta \times .09$
.20	$\beta \times .16$
.50	$\beta \times .25$
.80	$\beta \times .16$
.90	$\beta \times .09$
.95	$\beta \times .0475$
.99	$\beta \times .0099$

Notice that the slope of the relationship between π and X does not change very much between $\pi = .2$ and $\pi = .8$, reflecting the near linearity of the logistic curve in this range.

The least-squares line fit to the Chilean plebiscite data in Figure 14.1, for example, has the equation

$$\widehat{\pi}_{\text{yes}} = 0.492 + 0.394 \times \text{Status quo} \tag{14.10}$$

---

[14]The exponentiated coefficient e^β is sometimes called an "odds ratio" because it represents the ratio of the odds of response at two X values, with the X value in the numerator one unit larger than that in the denominator.
[15]See Exercise 14.3.

As I have pointed out, this line is a poor summary of the data. The logistic-regression model, fit by the method of maximum likelihood (to be developed presently), has the equation

$$\log_e \frac{\widehat{\pi}_{\text{yes}}}{\widehat{\pi}_{\text{no}}} = 0.215 + 3.21 \times \text{Status quo}$$

As is apparent from Figure 14.1, the logit model produces a much more adequate summary of the data, one that is very close to the nonparametric regression. Increasing support for the status quo by one unit multiplies the odds of voting *yes* by $e^{3.21} = 24.8$. Put alternatively, the slope of the relationship between the fitted probability of voting *yes* and support for the status quo at $\widehat{\pi}_{\text{yes}} = .5$ is $3.21/4 = 0.80$. Compare this value with the slope ($B = 0.39$) from the linear least-squares regression in Equation 14.10.[16]

14.1.3 An Unobserved-Variable Formulation

An alternative derivation of the logit or probit model posits an underlying regression for a continuous but unobservable response variable ξ (representing, e.g., the "propensity" to vote *yes*), scaled so that

$$Y_i = \begin{cases} 0 & \text{when } \xi_i \leq 0 \\ 1 & \text{when } \xi_i > 0 \end{cases} \qquad (14.11)$$

That is, when ξ crosses 0, the observed discrete response Y changes from *no* to *yes*. The latent variable ξ is assumed to be a linear function of the explanatory variable X and the (usual) unobservable error variable ε:

$$\xi_i = \alpha + \beta X_i - \varepsilon_i \qquad (14.12)$$

(It is notationally convenient here—but otherwise inconsequential—to *subtract* the error ε.) We want to estimate the parameters α and β, but cannot proceed by least-squares regression of ξ on X because the latent response variable (unlike Y) is not observed.

Using Equations 14.11 and 14.12,

$$\pi_i \equiv \Pr(Y_i = 1) = \Pr(\xi_i > 0) = \Pr(\alpha + \beta X_i - \varepsilon_i > 0)$$
$$= \Pr(\varepsilon_i < \alpha + \beta X_i)$$

If the errors are independently distributed according to the unit-normal distribution, $\varepsilon_i \sim N(0, 1)$, then

$$\pi_i = \Pr(\varepsilon_i < \alpha + \beta X_i) = \Phi(\alpha + \beta X_i)$$

which is the probit model.[17] Alternatively, if the ε_i follow the similar logistic distribution, then we get the logit model

$$\pi_i = \Pr(\varepsilon_i < \alpha + \beta X_i) = \Lambda(\alpha + \beta X_i)$$

---

[16]As I have explained, the slope for the logit model is not constant: It is steepest at $\pi = .5$ and flattens out as π approaches 0 and 1. The linear probability model, therefore, will agree more closely with the logit model when the response probabilities do not (as here) attain extreme values.

[17]The variance of the errors is set conveniently to 1. This choice is legitimate because we have not yet fixed the unit of measurement of the latent variable ξ. The location of the ξ scale was implicitly fixed by setting 0 as the point at which the observable response changes from *no* to *yes*. You may be uncomfortable assuming that the errors for an unobservable response variable are normally distributed, because we cannot check the assumption by examining residuals, for example. In fact, in most instances we can ensure that the error distribution has any form we please by transforming ξ to make the assumption true. We cannot, however, simultaneously ensure that the true regression is linear. If the latent-variable regression is not linear, then the probit model will not adequately capture the relationship between the dichotomous Y and X.

We will have occasion to return to the unobserved-variable formulation of logit and probit models when we consider models for ordinal categorical data.[18]

14.1.4   Logit and Probit Models for Multiple Regression

Generalizing the logit and probit models to several explanatory variables is straightforward. All we require is a linear predictor (η_i in Equation 14.13) that is a function of several regressors. For the logit model,

$$\pi_i = \Lambda(\eta_i) = \Lambda(\alpha + \beta_1 X_{i1} + \beta_2 X_{i2} + \cdots + \beta_k X_{ik}) \qquad (14.13)$$

$$= \frac{1}{1 + \exp[-(\alpha + \beta_1 X_{i1} + \beta_2 X_{i2} + \cdots + \beta_k X_{ik})]}$$

or, equivalently,

$$\log_e \frac{\pi_i}{1 - \pi_i} = \alpha + \beta_1 X_{i1} + \beta_2 X_{i2} + \cdots + \beta_k X_{ik}$$

For the probit model,

$$\pi_i = \Phi(\eta_i) = \Phi(\alpha + \beta_1 X_{i1} + \beta_2 X_{i2} + \cdots + \beta_k X_{ik})$$

Moreover, the Xs can be as general as in the general linear model, including, for example:

- quantitative explanatory variables;
- transformations of quantitative explanatory variables;
- polynomial regressors formed from quantitative explanatory variables;
- dummy regressors representing qualitative explanatory variables; and
- interaction regressors.

Interpretation of the partial-regression coefficients in the general linear logit model (Equation 14.13) is similar to the interpretation of the slope in the logit simple-regression model, with the additional provision of holding other explanatory variables in the model constant. For example, expressing the model in terms of odds,

$$\frac{\pi_i}{1 - \pi_i} = \exp(\alpha + \beta_1 X_{i1} + \cdots + \beta_k X_{ik})$$

$$= e^\alpha \left(e^{\beta_1}\right)^{X_{i1}} \cdots \left(e^{\beta_k}\right)^{X_{ik}}$$

Thus, e^{β_j} is the multiplicative effect on the odds of increasing X_j by 1, holding the other Xs constant. Similarly, $\beta_j/4$ is the slope of the logistic regression surface in the direction of X_j at $\pi = .5$.

> More adequate specifications than the linear probability model transform the linear predictor $\eta_i = \alpha + \beta_1 X_{i1} + \cdots + \beta_k X_{ik}$ smoothly to the unit interval, using a cumulative probability distribution function $P(\cdot)$. Two such specifications are the probit and the logit models, which use the normal and logistic CDFs, respectively. Although these models are very similar, the logit model is simpler to interpret because it can be written as a linear model for the log odds: $\log_e[\pi_i/(1 - \pi_i)] = \alpha + \beta_1 X_{i1} + \cdots + \beta_k X_{ik}$.

---

[18]See Section 14.2.3.

The general linear logit and probit models can be fit to data by the method of maximum likelihood. I will concentrate here on outlining maximum-likelihood estimation for the logit model. Details are given in the next section.

Recall that the response variable Y_i takes on the two values 1 and 0 with probabilities π_i and $1 - \pi_i$, respectively. Using a mathematical "trick," the probability distribution for Y_i can be compactly represented as a single equation:[19]

$$p(y_i) \equiv \Pr(Y_i = y_i) = \pi_i^{y_i}(1 - \pi_i)^{1-y_i}$$

where y_i can be 0 or 1.

Now consider a particular sample of n independent observations, $y_1, y_2, \dots, y_n$ (comprising a specific sequence of 0s and 1s). Because the observations are independent, the joint probability for the data is the product of the marginal probabilities:

$$p(y_1, y_2, \dots, y_n) = p(y_1)p(y_2) \cdots p(y_n) \qquad (14.14)$$

$$= \prod_{i=1}^{n} p(y_i)$$

$$= \prod_{i=1}^{n} \pi_i^{y_i}(1 - \pi_i)^{1-y_i}$$

$$= \prod_{i=1}^{n} \left(\frac{\pi_i}{1 - \pi_i}\right)^{y_i} (1 - \pi_i)$$

From the general logit model (Equation 14.13),

$$\frac{\pi_i}{1 - \pi_i} = \exp(\alpha + \beta_1 X_{i1} + \cdots + \beta_k X_{ik})$$

and (after some manipulation)[20]

$$1 - \pi_i = \frac{1}{1 + \exp(\alpha + \beta_1 X_{i1} + \cdots + \beta_k X_{ik})}$$

Substituting these results into Equation 14.14 expresses the probability of the data in terms of the parameters of the logit model:

$$p(y_1, y_2, \dots, y_n)$$
$$= \prod_{i=1}^{n} [\exp(\alpha + \beta_1 X_{i1} + \cdots + \beta_k X_{ik})]^{y_i} \left(\frac{1}{1 + \exp(\alpha + \beta_1 X_{i1} + \cdots + \beta_k X_{ik})}\right)$$

Thinking of this equation as a function of the parameters, and treating the data $(y_1, y_2, \dots, y_n)$ as fixed, produces the likelihood function, $L(\alpha, \beta_1, \dots, \beta_k)$. The values of $\alpha, \beta_1, \dots, \beta_k$ that maximize $L(\alpha, \beta_1, \dots, \beta_k)$ are the maximum-likelihood estimates $A, B_1, \dots, B_k$.

Hypothesis tests and confidence intervals follow from general procedures for statistical inference in maximum-likelihood estimation.[21] For an individual coefficient, it is most convenient to test the hypothesis $H_0: \beta_j = \beta_j^{(0)}$ by calculating the Wald statistic

$$Z_0 = \frac{B_j - \beta_j^{(0)}}{SE(B_j)}$$

---

[19] See Exercise 14.4.
[20] See Exercise 14.5.
[21] These general procedures are discussed in Appendix D on probability and estimation.

where $SE(B_j)$ is the asymptotic (i.e., large-sample) standard error of B_j. To test the most common hypothesis, H_0: $\beta_j = 0$, we simply divide the estimated coefficient by its standard error to compute $Z_0 = B_j/SE(B_j)$; these tests are analogous to t-tests for individual coefficients in the general linear model. The test statistic Z_0 follows an asymptotic standard-normal distribution under the null hypothesis, an approximation that is usually reasonably accurate unless the sample size is small.[22] Similarly, an asymptotic $100(1 - a)\%$ confidence interval for β_j is given by

$$\beta_j = B_j \pm z_{a/2}SE(B_j)$$

where $z_{a/2}$ is the value from $Z \sim N(0, 1)$ with probability $a/2$ to the right. Wald tests and joint confidence regions for several coefficients can be formulated from the estimated asymptotic variances and covariances of the coefficients.[23]

It is also possible to formulate a likelihood-ratio test for the hypothesis that several coefficients are simultaneously 0, H_0: $\beta_1 = \cdots = \beta_q = 0$. We proceed, as in least-squares regression, by fitting two models to the data: the full model (model 1),

$$\text{logit}\,(\pi) = \alpha + \beta_1 X_1 + \cdots + \beta_q X_q + \beta_{q+1} X_{q+1} + \cdots + \beta_k X_k$$

and the null model (model 0),

$$\begin{aligned} \text{logit}\,(\pi) &= \alpha + 0X_1 + \cdots + 0X_q + \beta_{q+1} X_{q+1} + \cdots + \beta_k X_k \\ &= \alpha + \beta_{q+1} X_{q+1} + \cdots + \beta_k X_k \end{aligned}$$

Fitting each model produces a maximized likelihood: L_1 for the full model, L_0 for the null model. Because the null model is a specialization of the full model, $L_1 \geq L_0$. The generalized likelihood-ratio test statistic for the null hypothesis is

$$G_0^2 = 2(\log_e L_1 - \log_e L_0)$$

Under the null hypothesis, this test statistic has an asymptotic chi-square distribution with q degrees of freedom.

By extension, a test of the omnibus null hypothesis H_0: $\beta_1 = \cdots = \beta_k = 0$ is obtained by specifying a null model that includes only the regression constant, $\text{logit}\,(\pi) = \alpha$. At the other extreme, the likelihood-ratio test can, of course, be applied to a *single* coefficient, H_0: $\beta_j = 0$, and this test can be inverted to provide a confidence interval for β_j: For example, the 95% confidence interval for β_j includes all values β_j' for which the hypothesis H_0: $\beta_j = \beta_j'$ is acceptable at the .05 level—that is, all values of β_j' for which $2(\log_e L_1 - \log_e L_0) \leq \chi^2_{.05,1} = 3.84$, where $\log_e L_1$ is (as before) the maximized log likelihood for the full model, and $\log_e L_0$ is the maximized log likelihood for a model in which β_j is constrained to the value β_j'.

An analog to the multiple-correlation coefficient can also be obtained from the log likelihood. The maximized log likelihood for the fitted model can be written as[24]

$$\log_e L = \sum_{i=1}^{n} \left[y_i \log_e P_i + (1 - y_i) \log_e (1 - P_i) \right]$$

---

[22] Under certain circumstances, however, tests and confidence intervals based on the Wald statistic can break down in logistic regression (see Hauck & Donner, 1977). Tests and confidence intervals based on the likelihood-ratio statistic, described immediately below, are more reliable, though more time-consuming to compute.

[23] See Section 14.1.5.

[24] See Exercise 14.6.

where P_i is the fitted probability that $Y_i = 1$,[25] that is,

$$P_i = \frac{1}{1 + \exp[-(A + B_1 X_{i1} + \cdots + B_k X_{ik})]}$$

Thus, if the fitted model can perfectly predict the Y values ($P_i = 1$ whenever $y_i = 1$, and $P_i = 0$ whenever $y_i = 0$), then $\log_e L = 0$ (i.e., the maximized likelihood is $L = 1$).[26] To the extent that predictions are less than perfect, $\log_e L < 0$ (and $0 < L < 1$).

By comparing $\log_e L_0$ for the model containing only the constant to $\log_e L_1$ for the full model, we can measure the degree to which using the explanatory variables improves the predictability of Y. The quantity $G^2 \equiv -2 \log_e L$, called the *residual deviance* under the model, is a generalization of the residual sum of squares for a linear model.[27] Thus,

$$R^2 \equiv 1 - \frac{G_1^2}{G_0^2}$$
$$= 1 - \frac{\log_e L_1}{\log_e L_0}$$

is analogous to R^2 for a linear model.[28]

> The dichotomous logit model can be fit to data by the method of maximum likelihood. Wald tests and likelihood-ratio tests for the coefficients of the model parallel t-tests and incremental F-tests for the general linear model. The deviance for the model, defined as $G^2 = -2 \times$ the maximized log likelihood, is analogous to the residual sum of squares for a linear model.

To illustrate logistic regression, I turn once again to the 1994 wave of the Statistics Canada Survey of Labour and Income Dynamics (the "SLID").[29] Confining our attention to married women between the ages of 20 and 35, I examine how the labor-force participation of these women (defined as working outside the home at some point during the year of the survey) is related to several explanatory variables:

- the region of the country in which the woman resides;
- the presence of children between 0 and 4 years of age in the household, coded as absent or present;
- the presence of children between 5 and 9 years of age;
- the presence of children between 10 and 14 years of age;
- family after-tax income, excluding the woman's own income (if any);[30] and
- education, defined as number of years of schooling.

---

[25]Of course, in a particular sample, y_i is either 0 or 1, so we can interpret this fitted probability as the estimated population proportion of individuals sharing the ith person's characteristics for whom Y is 1. Other interpretations are also possible, but this is the most straightforward.

[26]Because, for the logit model, π never quite reaches 0 or 1, the predictions cannot be perfect, but they can approach perfection in the limit.

[27]See Exercise 14.7 and Chapter 15 on generalized linear models.

[28]For alternative R^2 measures for logit and probit models, see, for example, Veall and Zimmermann (1996).

[29]The SLID was introduced in Chapter 2.

[30]I excluded from the analysis two women for whom this variable is negative.

Table 14.1   Distributions of Variables in the SLID Data Set

Variable	Summary
Labor-Force Participation	Yes, 79%
Region (R)	Atlantic, 23%; Quebec, 13; Ontario, 30; Prairies, 26; BC, 8
Children 0–4 (K04)	Yes, 53%
Children 5–9 (K59)	Yes, 44%
Children 10–14 (K1014)	Yes, 22%
Family Income (I, $1,000s)	5-number summary: 0, 18.6, 26.7, 35.1, 131.1
Education (E, years)	5-number summary: 0, 12, 13, 15, 20

The SLID data set includes 1,936 women with valid data on these variables. Some information about the distribution of the variables appears in Table 14.1. Recall that the five-number summary includes the minimum, first quartile, median, third quartile, and maximum of a variable.

In modeling these data, I want to allow for the possibility of interaction between presence of children and each of family income and education in determining women's labor-force participation. Table 14.2 shows the residual deviances and number of parameters for each of a series of models fit to the SLID data. These models are formulated so that likelihood-ratio tests of terms in the full model can be computed by taking differences in the residual deviances for the models, in conformity with the principle of marginality. The residual deviances are the building blocks of likelihood-ratio tests, much as residual sums of squares are the building blocks of incremental F-tests in linear models. The tests themselves, with an indication of the models contrasted for each test, appear in an *analysis-of-deviance* table in Table 14.3, closely analogous to an ANOVA table for a linear model.

It is clear from the likelihood-ratio tests in Table 14.3 that none of the interactions approach statistical significance. Presence of children four years old and younger and education have very highly statistically significant coefficients; the terms for region, children 5 to 9 years old, and family income are also statistically significant, while that for children 10 through 14 is not.

Estimated coefficients and standard errors for a summary model including the statistically significant terms are given in Table 14.4. The Atlantic provinces are the baseline category for the region effects in this model. The column of the table labelled e^{B_j} represents multiplicative effects on the odds scale. Thus, for example, holding the other explanatory variables constant, having children 0 to 4 years old in the household reduces the *odds* of labor-force participation by $100(1 - 0.379) = 62.1\%$; and increasing education by 1 year increases the odds of labor-force participation by $100(1.246 - 1) = 24.6\%$. As explained, as long as a coefficient is not too large, we can also express effects on the probability scale near $\pi = .5$ by dividing the coefficient by 4: For example (and again, holding other explanatory variables constant), if the probability of labor-force participation is near .5 with children 0 to 4 absent, the presence of children of this age decreases the probability by approximately $0.9702/4 = 0.243$ or 24.3%, while an additional year of education increases the probability by approximately $0.2197/4 = .0549$ or 5.5%.

Still another strategy for interpreting a logit model is to graph the high-order terms in the model, producing effect displays, much as we did for linear models.[31] The final model for the SLID labor-force participation data in Table 14.4 has a simple structure in that there are no interactions or polynomial terms. Nevertheless, it helps to see how each explanatory variable influences the probability of the response holding other explanatory variables to their average

---

[31] See the discussion of effect displays for linear models in Sections 7.3.4 and 8.3.2. Details of effect displays for logit models are developed in a more general context in the next chapter (Section 15.3.4).

Table 14.2 Models Fit to the SLID Labor-Force Participation Data

Model	Terms in the Model	Number of Parameters	Residual Deviance
0	C	1	1988.084
1	C, R, K04, K59, K1014, I, E, K04×I, K59×I, K1014×I, K04×E, K59×E, K1014×E	16	1807.376
2	Model 1 − K04×I	15	1807.378
3	Model 1 − K59×I	15	1808.600
4	Model 1 − K1014×I	15	1807.834
5	Model 1 − K04×E	15	1807.407
6	Model 1 − K59×E	15	1807.734
7	Model 1 − K1014×E	15	1807.938
8	Model 1 − R	12	1824.681
9	C, R, K04, K59, K1014, I, E, K59×I, K1014×I, K59×E, K1014×E	14	1807.408
10	Model 9 − K04	13	1866.689
11	C, R, K04, K59, K1014, I, E, K04×I, K1014×I, K04×E, K1014×E	14	1809.268
12	Model 11 − K59	13	1819.273
13	C, R, K04, K59, K1014, I, E, K04×I, K59×I, K04×E, K59×E	14	1808.310
14	Model 13 − K1014	13	1808.548
15	C, R, K04, K59, K1014, I, E, K04×E, K59×E, K1014×E	13	1808.854
16	Model 15 − I	12	1817.995
17	C, R, K04, K59, K1014, I, E, K04×I, K59×I, K1014×I	13	1808.428
18	Model 17 − E	12	1889.223

NOTE: "C" represents the regression constant; codes for other variables in the model are given in Table 14.1.

Table 14.3 Analysis of Deviance Table for the SLID Labor-Force Participation Logit Model

Term	Models Contrasted	df	G_0^2	p
Region (R)	8-1	4	17.305	.0017
Children 0–4 (K04)	10-9	1	59.281	≪.0001
Children 5–9 (K59)	12-11	1	10.005	.0016
Children 10–14 (K1014)	14-12	1	0.238	.63
Family Income (I)	16-15	1	9.141	.0025
Education (E)	18-17	1	80.795	≪.0001
K04×I	2-1	1	0.002	.97
K59×I	3-1	1	1.224	.29
K1014×I	4-1	1	0.458	.50
K04×E	5-1	1	0.031	.86
K59×E	6-1	1	0.358	.55
K1014×E	7-1	1	0.562	.45

Table 14.4　Estimates for a Final Model Fit to the SLID
Labor-Force Participation Data

Coefficient	Estimate (B_j)	Standard Error	e^{B_j}
Constant	−0.3763	0.3398	
Region: Quebec	−0.5469	0.1899	0.579
Region: Ontario	0.1038	0.1670	1.109
Region: Prairies	0.0742	0.1695	1.077
Region: BC	0.3760	0.2577	1.456
Children 0–4	−0.9702	0.1254	0.379
Children 5–9	−0.3971	0.1187	0.672
Family income ($1,000s)	−0.0127	0.0041	0.987
Education (years)	0.2197	0.0250	1.246
Residual deviance	1810.444		

values. In Figure 14.4, I plot the terms in the model on the logit scale (given by the left-hand axis in each graph), preserving the linear structure of the model, but I also show corresponding fitted probabilities of labor-force participation (on the right-hand axis)—a more familiar scale on which to interpret the results.

We should not forget that the logit model fit to the SLID data is a parametric model, assuming linear partial relationships (on the logit scale) between labor-force participation and the two quantitative explanatory variables, family income and education. There is no more reason to believe that relationships are necessarily linear in logit models than in linear least-squares regression. I will take up diagnostics, including nonlinearity diagnostics, for logit models and other generalized linear models in the next chapter.[32]

Woes of Logistic-Regression Coefficients

Just as the least-squares surface flattens out at its minimum when the Xs are collinear, the likelihood surface for a logistic regression flattens out at its maximum in the presence of collinearity, so that the maximum-likelihood estimates of the coefficients of the model are not uniquely defined. Likewise, strong, but less-than-perfect, collinearity causes the coefficients to be imprecisely estimated.

Paradoxically, problems for estimation can also occur in logit models when the explanatory variables are very strong predictors of the dichotomous response. One such circumstance, illustrated in Figure 14.5, is *separability*. When there is a single X, the data are separable if the "failures" (0s) and "successes" (1s) fail to overlap [as in Figure 14.5(a)]. In this case, the maximum-likelihood estimate of the slope coefficient β is infinite (either $-\infty$ or $+\infty$, depending on the direction of the relationship between X and Y), and the estimate of the intercept α is not unique. When there are two Xs, the data are separable if there is a line in the $\{X_1, X_2\}$ plane that separates successes from failures [as in Figure 14.5(b)]. For three Xs, the data are separable if there is a separating plane in the three-dimensional space of the Xs; and the generalization to any number of Xs is a separating hyperplane—that is, a linear surface of dimension $k - 1$ in the k-dimensional X space.

---

[32] See Section 15.4.

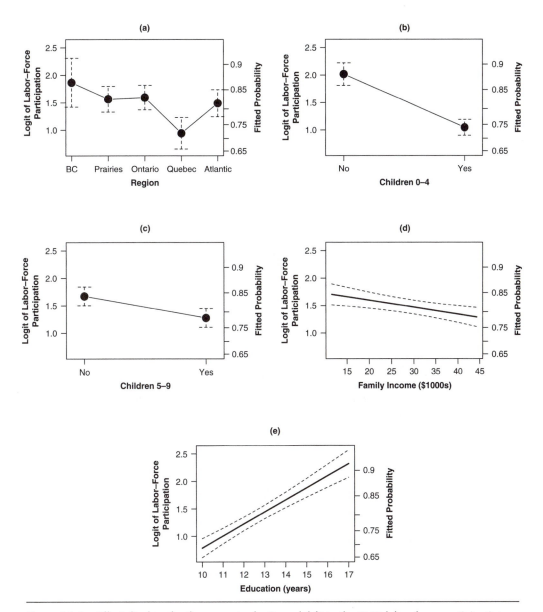

Figure 14.4 Effect displays for the summary logit model fit to the SLID labor-force participation data. The error bars and envelopes give pointwise 95% confidence intervals around the estimated effects. The plots for family income and education range between the 10th and 90th percentiles of these variables.

Still another circumstance that yields infinite coefficients is that of data in which some of the responses become perfectly predictable even in the absence of complete separability. For example, if at one level of a factor all observations are successes, the estimated probability of success for an observation at this level is 1, and the odds of success are $1/0 = \infty$.

Statistical software may or may not detect these problems for estimation. The problems may manifest themselves in failure of the software to converge to a solution, in wildly large estimated coefficients, or in very large coefficient standard errors.

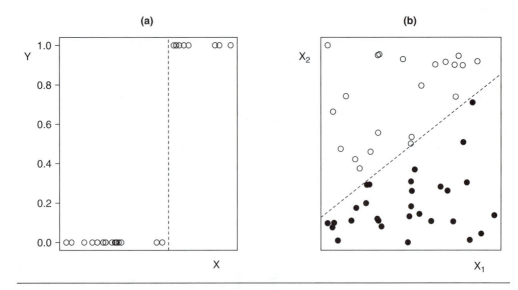

Figure 14.5 Separability in logistic regression: (a) with one explanatory variable, X; (b) with two explanatory variables, X_1 and X_2. In panel *(b)*, the solid dots represent observations for which $Y = 1$, and the hollow dots observations for which $Y = 0$.

14.1.5   Estimating the Linear Logit Model*

In this section, I will develop the details of maximum-likelihood estimation for the general linear logit model (Equation 14.13 on page 344). It is convenient to rewrite the model in vector form as

$$\pi_i = \frac{1}{1 + \exp(-\mathbf{x}_i'\beta)}$$

where $\mathbf{x}_i' \equiv (1, X_{i1}, \ldots, X_{ik})$ is the ith row of the model matrix $\mathbf{X}$, and $\beta \equiv (\alpha, \beta_1, \ldots, \beta_k)'$ is the parameter vector. The probability of the data conditional on $\mathbf{X}$ is, therefore,

$$p(y_1, \ldots, y_n | \mathbf{X}) = \prod_{i=1}^{n} [\exp(\mathbf{x}_i'\beta)]^{y_i} \left[\frac{1}{1 + \exp(\mathbf{x}_i'\beta)} \right]$$

and the log-likelihood function is

$$\log_e L(\beta) = \sum_{i=1}^{n} Y_i \mathbf{x}_i'\beta - \sum_{i=1}^{n} \log_e [1 + \exp(\mathbf{x}_i'\beta)]$$

The partial derivatives of the log likelihood with respect to β are

$$\frac{\partial \log_e L(\beta)}{\partial \beta} = \sum_{i=1}^{n} Y_i \mathbf{x}_i - \sum_{i=1}^{n} \left[\frac{\exp(\mathbf{x}_i'\beta)}{1 + \exp(\mathbf{x}_i'\beta)} \right] \mathbf{x}_i$$

$$= \sum_{i=1}^{n} Y_i \mathbf{x}_i - \sum_{i=1}^{n} \left[\frac{1}{1 + \exp(-\mathbf{x}_i'\beta)} \right] \mathbf{x}_i \qquad (14.15)$$

Setting the vector of partial derivatives to $\mathbf{0}$ to maximize the likelihood yields estimating equations

$$\sum_{i=1}^{n} \left[\frac{1}{1 + \exp(-\mathbf{x}_i'\mathbf{b})} \right] \mathbf{x}_i = \sum_{i=1}^{n} Y_i \mathbf{x}_i \tag{14.16}$$

where $\mathbf{b} = (A, B_1, \ldots, B_k)'$ is the vector of maximum-likelihood estimates.

The estimating equations (Equation 14.16) have the following intuitive justification:

$$P_i \equiv \frac{1}{1 + \exp(-\mathbf{x}_i'\mathbf{b})}$$

is the *fitted* probability for observation i (i.e., the estimated value of π_i). The estimating equations, therefore, set the "fitted sum" $\sum P_i \mathbf{x}_i$ equal to the corresponding observed sum $\sum Y_i \mathbf{x}_i$. In matrix form, we can write the estimating equations as $\mathbf{X}'\mathbf{p} = \mathbf{X}'\mathbf{y}$, where $\mathbf{p} = (P_1, \ldots, P_n)'$ is the vector of fitted values. Note the essential similarity to the least-squares estimating equations $\mathbf{X}'\mathbf{X}\mathbf{b} = \mathbf{X}'\mathbf{y}$, which can be written $\mathbf{X}'\widehat{\mathbf{y}} = \mathbf{X}'\mathbf{y}$.

Because $\mathbf{b}$ is a maximum-likelihood estimator, its estimated asymptotic covariance matrix can be obtained from the inverse of the information matrix[33]

$$\mathcal{J}(\beta) = -E\left[\frac{\partial^2 \log_e L(\beta)}{\partial\beta\,\partial\beta'} \right]$$

evaluated at $\beta = \mathbf{b}$. Differentiating Equation 14.15 and making the appropriate substitutions,[34]

$$\widehat{\mathcal{V}}(\mathbf{b}) = \sum_{i=1}^{n} \left\{ \frac{\exp(-\mathbf{x}_i'\mathbf{b})}{[1 + \exp(-\mathbf{x}_i'\mathbf{b})]^2} \mathbf{x}_i \mathbf{x}_i' \right\}^{-1}$$

$$= \left[\sum_{i=1}^{n} P_i(1 - P_i)\mathbf{x}_i\mathbf{x}_i' \right]^{-1}$$

$$= (\mathbf{X}'\mathbf{V}\mathbf{X})^{-1}$$

where $\mathbf{V} \equiv \text{diag}\{P_i(1 - P_i)\}$ contains the estimated variances of the Y_is. The square roots of the diagonal entries of $\widehat{\mathcal{V}}(\mathbf{b})$ are the asymptotic standard errors, which can be used, as described in the previous section, for inferences about individual parameters of the logit model.

As for the linear model estimated by least squares, general linear hypotheses about the parameters of the logit model can be formulated as $H_0: \mathbf{L}\beta = \mathbf{c}$, where $\mathbf{L}$ is a $(q \times k + 1)$ hypothesis matrix of rank $q \leq k + 1$ and $\mathbf{c}$ is a $q \times 1$ vector of fixed elements, typically 0.[35] Then the Wald statistic

$$Z_0^2 = (\mathbf{L}\mathbf{b} - \mathbf{c})'\left[\mathbf{L}\widehat{\mathcal{V}}(\mathbf{b})\mathbf{L}'\right]^{-1}(\mathbf{L}\mathbf{b} - \mathbf{c})$$

follows an asymptotic chi-square distribution with q degrees of freedom under the hypothesis H_0. For example, to test the omnibus hypothesis $H_0: \beta_1 = \cdots = \beta_k = 0$, we take

$$\mathop{\mathbf{L}}_{(k \times k+1)} = \begin{bmatrix} 0 & 1 & 0 & \cdots & 0 \\ 0 & 0 & 1 & \cdots & 0 \\ \vdots & \vdots & \vdots & \ddots & \vdots \\ 0 & 0 & 0 & \cdots & 1 \end{bmatrix} = [\mathop{\mathbf{0}}_{(k \times 1)}, \mathbf{I}_k]$$

and $\mathbf{c} = \mathop{\mathbf{0}}_{(k \times 1)}$.

---

[33] See Appendix D on probability and estimation.

[34] See Exercise 14.8.

[35] See Section 9.4.3.

Likewise, the asymptotic $100(1 - a)\%$ joint confidence region for a subset of q parameters β_1 takes the form

$$(\mathbf{b}_1 - \beta_1)' \mathbf{V}_{11}^{-1} (\mathbf{b}_1 - \beta_1) \leq \chi_{q,a}^2$$

Here, $\mathbf{V}_{11}$ is the $(q \times q)$ submatrix of $\widehat{V}(\mathbf{b})$ that pertains to the estimates $\mathbf{b}_1$, and $\chi_{q,a}^2$ is the critical value of the chi-square distribution for q degrees of freedom with probability a to the right.

Unlike the normal equations for a linear model, the logit-model estimating equations (Equation 14.16) are nonlinear functions of $\mathbf{b}$ and, therefore, require iterative solution. One common approach to solving the estimating equations is the *Newton-Raphson method*, which can be described as follows:[36]

1. Select initial estimates $\mathbf{b}_0$; a simple choice is $\mathbf{b}_0 = \mathbf{0}$.

2. At each iteration $l + 1$, compute new estimates

$$\mathbf{b}_{l+1} = \mathbf{b}_l + (\mathbf{X}'\mathbf{V}_l\mathbf{X})^{-1}\mathbf{X}'(\mathbf{y} - \mathbf{p}_l) \qquad (14.17)$$

   where $\mathbf{p}_l \equiv \{1/[1 + \exp(-\mathbf{x}_i'\mathbf{b}_l)]\}$ is the vector of fitted values from the previous iteration and $\mathbf{V}_l \equiv \text{diag}\{P_{li}(1 - P_{li})\}$.

3. Iterations continue until $\mathbf{b}_{l+1} \approx \mathbf{b}_l$ to the desired degree of accuracy.
   When convergence takes place,

$$(\mathbf{X}'\mathbf{V}_l\mathbf{X})^{-1}\mathbf{X}'(\mathbf{y} - \mathbf{p}_l) \approx \mathbf{0}$$

   and thus the estimating equations $\mathbf{X}'\mathbf{p} = \mathbf{X}'\mathbf{y}$ are approximately satisfied. Conversely, if the fitted sums $\mathbf{X}'\mathbf{p}_l$ are very different from the observed sums $\mathbf{X}'\mathbf{y}$, then there will be a large adjustment in $\mathbf{b}$ at the next iteration. The Newton-Raphson procedure conveniently produces the estimated asymptotic covariance matrix of the coefficients $\widehat{V}(\mathbf{b}) = (\mathbf{X}'\mathbf{V}\mathbf{X})^{-1}$ as a by-product.

Suppose, now, that we have obtained complete convergence of the Newton-Raphson procedure to the maximum-likelihood estimator $\mathbf{b}$. From Equation 14.17, we have

$$\mathbf{b} = \mathbf{b} + (\mathbf{X}'\mathbf{V}\mathbf{X})^{-1}\mathbf{X}'(\mathbf{y} - \mathbf{p})$$

which we can rewrite as

$$\mathbf{b} = (\mathbf{X}'\mathbf{V}\mathbf{X})^{-1}\mathbf{X}'\mathbf{V}\mathbf{y}^*$$

where[37]

$$\mathbf{y}^* \equiv \mathbf{X}\mathbf{b} + \mathbf{V}^{-1}(\mathbf{y} - \mathbf{p})$$

These formulas suggest an analogy between maximum-likelihood estimation of the linear logit model and weighted-least-squares regression. The analogy is the basis of an alternative method for calculating the maximum-likelihood estimates called *iterative weighted least squares* (IWLS):[38]

---

[36]This approach was first applied by R. A. Fisher, in the context of a probit model, and is sometimes termed *Fisher scoring* in his honor.

[37]See Exercise 14.9.

[38]This method is also called *iteratively reweighted least squares* (IRLS). See Section 12.2.2 for an explanation of weighted-least-squares estimation. In fact, the IWLS algorithm is an alternative implementation of the Newton-Raphson method and leads to the same history of iterations.

1. As before, select arbitrary initial values $\mathbf{b}_0$.

2. At each iteration l, calculate fitted values $\mathbf{p}_l \equiv \{1/[1 + \exp(-\mathbf{x}_i'\mathbf{b}_l)]\}$, the variance matrix $\mathbf{V}_l \equiv \text{diag}\{P_{li}(1 - P_{li})\}$, and the "pseudoresponse variable" $\mathbf{y}_l^* \equiv \mathbf{X}\mathbf{b}_l + \mathbf{V}_l^{-1}(\mathbf{y} - \mathbf{p}_l)$.

3. Calculate updated estimates by weighted-least-squares regression of the pseudoresponse on the Xs, using the current variance matrix for weights:

$$\mathbf{b}_{l+1} = (\mathbf{X}'\mathbf{V}_l\mathbf{X})^{-1}\mathbf{X}'\mathbf{V}_l\mathbf{y}_l^*$$

4. Repeat Steps 2 and 3 until the coefficients converge.

14.2 Models for Polytomous Data

A limitation of the logit and probit models of the previous section is that they apply only to dichotomous response variables. In the Chilean plebiscite data, for example, many of the voters surveyed indicated that they were undecided, and some said that they planned to abstain or refused to reveal their voting intentions. Polytomous data of this sort are common, and it is desirable to model them in a natural manner—not simply to ignore some of the categories (e.g., restricting attention to those who responded *yes* or *no*) or to combine categories arbitrarily to produce a dichotomy.

In this section, I will describe three general approaches to modeling polytomous data:[39]

1. modeling the polytomy directly as a set of unordered categories, using a generalization of the dichotomous logit model;

2. constructing a set of nested dichotomies from the polytomy, fitting an independent logit or probit model to each dichotomy; and

3. extending the unobserved-variable interpretation of the dichotomous logit and probit models to ordered polytomies.

14.2.1 The Polytomous Logit Model

It is possible to generalize the dichotomous logit model to a polytomy by employing the multivariate logistic distribution. This approach has the advantage of treating the categories of the polytomy in a nonarbitrary, symmetric manner (but the disadvantage that the analysis is relatively complex).[40]

Suppose that the response variable Y can take on any of m qualitative values, which, for convenience, we number $1, 2, \ldots, m$. To anticipate the example employed in this section, a voter in the 2001 British election voted for (1) the Labour Party, (2) the Conservative Party, or (3) the Liberal Democrats. Although the categories of Y are numbered, we do not, in general, attribute ordinal properties to these numbers: They are simply category *labels*. Let π_{ij} denote the probability that the ith observation falls in the jth category of the response variable; that is, $\pi_{ij} \equiv \Pr(Y_i = j)$, for $j = 1, \ldots, m$.

---

[39] Additional statistical models for polytomous data are described, for example, in Agresti (2002).

[40] A similar probit model based on the multivariate-normal distribution is somewhat more difficult to estimate because of the necessity of evaluating a multivariate integral, but is sometimes preferred to the polytomous logit model developed in this section (see Exercise 14.12).

We have available k regressors, $X_1, \ldots, X_k$, on which the π_{ij} depend. More specifically, suppose that this dependence can be modeled using the *multivariate logistic distribution*:

$$\pi_{ij} = \frac{\exp(\gamma_{0j} + \gamma_{1j}X_{i1} + \cdots + \gamma_{kj}X_{ik})}{1 + \sum_{l=1}^{m-1} \exp(\gamma_{0l} + \gamma_{1l}X_{i1} + \cdots + \gamma_{kl}X_{ik})} \quad \text{for } j = 1, \ldots, m-1 \qquad (14.18)$$

$$\pi_{im} = 1 - \sum_{j=1}^{m-1} \pi_{ij} \quad \text{(for category } m)$$

This model is sometimes called the *multinomial logit model*.[41] There is, then, one set of parameters, $\gamma_{0j}, \gamma_{1j}, \ldots, \gamma_{kj}$, for each response category but the last. The last category (i.e., category m) functions as a type of baseline. The use of a baseline category is one way of avoiding redundant parameters because of the restriction, reflected in the second part of Equation 14.18, that the response category probabilities for each observation must sum to 1:[42]

$$\sum_{j=1}^{m} \pi_{ij} = 1$$

The denominator of π_{ij} in the first line of Equation 14.18 imposes this restriction.

Some algebraic manipulation of Equation 14.18 produces[43]

$$\log_e \frac{\pi_{ij}}{\pi_{im}} = \gamma_{0j} + \gamma_{1j}X_{i1} + \cdots + \gamma_{kj}X_{ik} \quad \text{for } j = 1, \ldots, m-1$$

The regression coefficients, therefore, represent effects on the log-odds of membership in category j versus the baseline category. It is also possible to form the log-odds of membership in *any* pair of categories j and j' (other than category m):

$$\log_e \frac{\pi_{ij}}{\pi_{ij'}} = \log_e \left(\frac{\pi_{ij}/\pi_{im}}{\pi_{ij'}/\pi_{im}} \right) \qquad (14.19)$$

$$= \log_e \frac{\pi_{ij}}{\pi_{im}} - \log_e \frac{\pi_{ij'}}{\pi_{im}}$$

$$= (\gamma_{0j} - \gamma_{0j'}) + (\gamma_{1j} - \gamma_{1j'})X_{i1} + \cdots + (\gamma_{kj} - \gamma_{kj'})X_{ik}$$

Thus, the regression coefficients for the logit between any pair of categories are the *differences* between corresponding coefficients for the two categories.

---

[41] I prefer to reserve the term *multinomial logit model* for a version of the model that can accommodate counts for the several categories of the response variable in a contingency table formed by discrete explanatory variables. I make a similar distinction between *binary* and *binomial* logit models, with the former term applied to individual observations and the latter to counts of "successes" and "failures" for a dichotomous response. See the discussion of the application of logit models to contingency tables in Section 14.3.

[42] An alternative is to treat the categories symmetrically:

$$\pi_{ij} = \frac{\exp(\gamma_{0j} + \gamma_{1j}X_{i1} + \cdots + \gamma_{kj}X_{ik})}{\sum_{l=1}^{m} \exp(\gamma_{0l} + \gamma_{1l}X_{i1} + \cdots + \gamma_{kl}X_{ik})}$$

but to impose a linear restriction—analogous to a sigma constraint in an ANOVA model (see Chapter 8)—on the parameters of the model. This approach produces somewhat more difficult computations, however, and has no real advantages. Although the choice of baseline category is essentially arbitrary and inconsequential, if one of the response categories represents a natural point of comparison, one might as well use it as the baseline.

[43] See Exercise 14.10.

To gain further insight into the polytomous logit model, suppose that the model is specialized to a dichotomous response variable. Then, $m = 2$, and

$$\log_e \frac{\pi_{i1}}{\pi_{i2}} = \log_e \frac{\pi_{i1}}{1 - \pi_{i1}} = \gamma_{01} + \gamma_{11} X_{i1} + \cdots + \gamma_{k1} X_{ik}$$

When it is applied to a dichotomy, the polytomous logit model is, therefore, identical to the dichotomous logit model of the previous section.

The following example is adapted from work by Andersen, Heath, and Sinnott (2002) on the 2001 British election, using data from the final wave of the 1997–2001 British Election Panel Study (BEPS) (also see Fox & Andersen, 2006). The central issue addressed in the data analysis is the potential interaction between respondents' political knowledge and political attitudes in determining their vote. The response variable, vote, has three categories: Labour, Conservative, and Liberal Democrat; individuals who voted for smaller parties are excluded from the analysis. There are several explanatory variables:

- Attitude toward European integration, an 11-point scale, with high scores representing a negative attitude (so-called Euro-scepticism).
- Knowledge of the platforms of the three parties on the issue of European integration, with integer scores ranging from 0 through 3. (Labour and the Liberal Democrats supported European integration, the Conservatives were opposed.)
- Other variables included in the model primarily as "controls"—age, gender, perceptions of national and household economic conditions, and ratings of the three party leaders.

The coefficients of a polytomous logit model fit to the BEPS data are shown, along with their standard errors, in Table 14.5. This model differs from those I have described previously in this text in that it includes the product of two quantitative explanatory variables, representing the *linear-by-linear interaction* between these variables:[44] Focusing on the Conservative/Liberal-Democrat logit, for example, when political knowledge is 0, the slope for attitude toward European integration ("Europe") is -0.068. With each unit increase in political knowledge, the slope for Europe increases by 0.183, thus becoming increasingly positive. This result is sensible: Those with more knowledge of the parties' positions are more likely to vote in conformity with their own position on the issue. By the same token, at low levels of Europe, the slope for political knowledge is negative, but it increases by 0.183 with each unit increase in Europe. By a Wald test, this interaction coefficient is highly statistically significant, with $Z = 0.183/0.028 = 6.53$, for which $p \ll .0001$.

An analysis-of-deviance table for the model appears in Table 14.6. Note that each term has two degrees of freedom, representing the two coefficients for the term, one for the Labour/Liberal-Democrat logit and the other for the Conservative/Liberal-Democrat logit. All the terms in the model are highly statistically significant, with the exception of gender and perception of household economic position.

Although we can therefore try to understand the fitted model by examining its coefficients, there are two obstacles to doing so: (1) As explained, the interaction between political knowledge and attitude toward European integration requires that we perform mental gymnastics to combine the estimated coefficient for the interaction with the coefficients for the "main-effect" regressors that are marginal to the interaction. (2) The structure of the polytomous logit model, which is for log-odds of pairs of categories (each category versus the baseline Liberal-Democrat category), makes it difficult to formulate a general understanding of the results.

---

[44]For more on models of this form, see Section 17.1 on polynomial regression.

Table 14.5 Polytomous Logit Model Fit to the BEPS Data

Coefficient	Labour/Liberal Democrat	
	Estimate	Standard Error
Constant	−0.155	0.612
Age	−0.005	0.005
Gender (male)	0.021	0.144
Perception of Economy	0.377	0.091
Perception of Household Economic Position	0.171	0.082
Evaluation of Blair (Labour leader)	0.546	0.071
Evaluation of Hague (Conservative leader)	−0.088	0.064
Evaluation of Kennedy (Liberal Democrat leader)	−0.416	0.072
Attitude Toward European Integration	−0.070	0.040
Political Knowledge	−0.502	0.155
Europe × Knowledge	0.024	0.021

Coefficient	Conservative/Liberal Democrat	
	Estimate	Standard Error
Constant	0.718	0.734
Age	0.015	0.006
Gender (male)	−0.091	0.178
Perception of Economy	−0.145	0.110
Perception of Household Economic Position	−0.008	0.101
Evaluation of Blair (Labour leader)	−0.278	0.079
Evaluation of Hague (Conservative leader)	0.781	0.079
Evaluation of Kennedy (Liberal Democrat leader)	−0.656	0.086
Attitude Toward European Integration	−0.068	0.049
Political Knowledge	−1.160	0.219
Europe × Knowledge	0.183	0.028

Table 14.6 Analysis of Deviance for the Polytomous Logit Model Fit to the BEPS Data

Source	df	G_0^2	p
Age	2	13.87	.0009
Gender	2	0.45	.78
Perception of Economy	2	30.60	≪.0001
Perception of Household Economic Position	2	5.65	.059
Evaluation of Blair	2	135.37	≪.0001
Evaluation of Hague	2	166.77	≪.0001
Evaluation of Kennedy	2	68.88	≪.0001
Attitude Toward European Integration	2	78.03	≪.0001
Political Knowledge	2	55.57	≪.0001
Europe × Knowledge	2	50.80	≪.0001

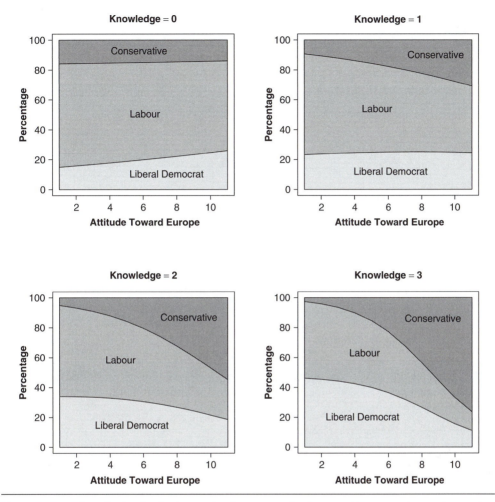

Figure 14.6 Effect display for the interaction between attitude toward European integration and political knowledge in the polytomous logit model for vote in the 2001 British election.

Once more, a graphical representation of the fitted model can greatly aid in its interpretation. An effect plot for the interaction of attitude toward European integration with political knowledge is shown in Figure 14.6. The strategy for constructing this plot is the usual one, adapted to the polytomous logit model: Compute the fitted probability of membership in each of the three categories of the response variable, letting Europe and knowledge range in combination over their values, while the other explanatory variables are fixed to average values. It is apparent that as political knowledge increases, vote conforms more closely to the respondent's attitude toward European integration.

*Details of Estimation**

To fit the polytomous logit model given in Equation 14.18 (on page 356) to data, we may again invoke the method of maximum likelihood. Recall that each Y_i takes on its possible values $1, 2, \ldots, m$ with probabilities $\pi_{i1}, \pi_{i2}, \ldots, \pi_{im}$. Following Nerlove and Press (1973), let us define indicator variables $W_{i1}, \ldots, W_{im}$ so that $W_{ij} = 1$ if $Y_i = j$, and $W_{ij} = 0$ if $Y_i \neq j$; thus,

$$p(y_i) = \pi_{i1}^{w_{i1}} \, \pi_{i2}^{w_{i2}} \, \cdots \pi_{im}^{w_{im}}$$

$$= \prod_{j=1}^{m} \pi_{ij}^{w_{ij}}$$

If the observations are sampled independently, then their joint probability distribution is given by

$$p(y_1, \ldots, y_n) = p(y_1) \times \cdots \times p(y_n)$$

$$= \prod_{i=1}^{n} \prod_{j=1}^{m} \pi_{ij}^{w_{ij}}$$

For compactness, define the following vectors:

$$\mathbf{x}_i' \equiv (1, X_{i1}, \ldots, X_{ik})$$

$$\boldsymbol{\gamma}_j \equiv (\gamma_{0j}, \gamma_{1j}, \ldots, \gamma_{kj})'$$

and the model matrix

$$\underset{(n \times k+1)}{\mathbf{X}} \equiv \begin{bmatrix} \mathbf{x}_1' \\ \mathbf{x}_2' \\ \vdots \\ \mathbf{x}_n' \end{bmatrix}$$

It is convenient to impose the restriction $\sum_{j=1}^{m} \pi_{ij} = 1$ by setting $\boldsymbol{\gamma}_m = \mathbf{0}$ (making category m the baseline, as explained previously). Then, employing Equation 14.18,

$$p(y_1, \ldots, y_n | \mathbf{X}) = \prod_{i=1}^{n} \prod_{j=1}^{m} \left[\frac{\exp(\mathbf{x}_i' \boldsymbol{\gamma}_j)}{1 + \sum_{l=1}^{m-1} \exp(\mathbf{x}_i' \boldsymbol{\gamma}_l)} \right]^{w_{ij}} \tag{14.20}$$

and the log likelihood is

$$\log_e L(\boldsymbol{\gamma}_1, \ldots, \boldsymbol{\gamma}_{m-1}) = \sum_{i=1}^{n} \sum_{j=1}^{m} W_{ij} \left\{ \mathbf{x}_i' \boldsymbol{\gamma}_j - \log_e \left[1 + \sum_{l=1}^{m-1} \exp(\mathbf{x}_i' \boldsymbol{\gamma}_l) \right] \right\}$$

$$= \sum_{i=1}^{n} \sum_{j=1}^{m-1} W_{ij} \mathbf{x}_i' \boldsymbol{\gamma}_j - \sum_{i=1}^{n} \log_e \left[1 + \sum_{l=1}^{m-1} \exp(\mathbf{x}_i' \boldsymbol{\gamma}_l) \right]$$

because $\sum_{j=1}^{m} W_{ij} = 1$ and $\boldsymbol{\gamma}_m = \mathbf{0}$; setting $\boldsymbol{\gamma}_m = \mathbf{0}$ accounts for the 1 in the denominator of Equation 14.20 because $\exp(\mathbf{x}_i' \mathbf{0}) = 1$.

Differentiating the log likelihood with respect to the parameters, and setting the partial derivatives to $\mathbf{0}$, produces the nonlinear estimating equations:[45]

$$\sum_{i=1}^{n} W_{ij} \mathbf{x}_i = \sum_{i=1}^{n} \mathbf{x}_i \frac{\exp(\mathbf{x}_i' \mathbf{c}_j)}{1 + \sum_{l=1}^{m-1} \exp(\mathbf{x}_i' \mathbf{c}_l)} \quad \text{for } j = 1, \ldots, m-1 \tag{14.21}$$

$$= \sum_{i=1}^{n} P_{ij} \mathbf{x}_i$$

---

[45] See Exercise 14.11.

where $\mathbf{c}_j \equiv \widehat{\gamma}_j$ are the maximum-likelihood estimators of the regression coefficients, and the

$$P_{ij} \equiv \frac{\exp(\mathbf{x}_i' \mathbf{c}_j)}{1 + \sum_{l=1}^{m-1} \exp(\mathbf{x}_i' \mathbf{c}_l)}$$

are the fitted probabilities. As in the dichotomous logit model, the maximum-likelihood estimator sets observed sums equal to fitted sums. The estimating equations (Equation 14.21) are nonlinear and, therefore, require iterative solution.

Let us stack up all the parameters in a large vector:

$$\underset{[(m-1)(k+1) \times 1]}{\gamma} \equiv \begin{bmatrix} \gamma_1 \\ \vdots \\ \gamma_{m-1} \end{bmatrix}$$

The information matrix is[46]

$$\underset{[(m-1)(k+1) \times (m-1)(k+1)]}{\mathcal{J}(\gamma)} = \begin{bmatrix} \mathcal{J}_{11} & \mathcal{J}_{12} & \cdots & \mathcal{J}_{1,\,m-1} \\ \mathcal{J}_{21} & \mathcal{J}_{22} & \cdots & \mathcal{J}_{2,\,m-1} \\ \vdots & \vdots & \ddots & \vdots \\ \mathcal{J}_{m-1,\,1} & \mathcal{J}_{m-1,\,2} & \cdots & \mathcal{J}_{m-1,\,m-1} \end{bmatrix}$$

where

$$\underset{[(k+1) \times (k+1)]}{\mathcal{J}_{jj}} = -E\left[\frac{\partial^2 \log_e L(\gamma)}{\partial \gamma_j \partial \gamma_j'}\right] \tag{14.22}$$

$$= \sum_{i=1}^{n} \frac{\mathbf{x}_i \mathbf{x}_i' \exp(\mathbf{x}_i' \gamma_j)[1 + \sum_{l=1}^{m-1} \exp(\mathbf{x}_i' \gamma_l) - \exp(\mathbf{x}_i' \gamma_j)]}{[1 + \sum_{l=1}^{m-1} \exp(\mathbf{x}_i' \gamma_l)]^2}$$

and

$$\underset{[(k+1) \times (k+1)]}{\mathcal{J}_{jj'}} = -E\left[\frac{\partial^2 \log_e L(\gamma)}{\partial \gamma_j \partial \gamma_{j'}'}\right] \tag{14.23}$$

$$= -\sum_{i=1}^{n} \frac{\mathbf{x}_i \mathbf{x}_i' \exp[\mathbf{x}_i'(\gamma_{j'} + \gamma_j)]}{[1 + \sum_{l=1}^{m-1} \exp(\mathbf{x}_i' \gamma_l)]^2}$$

The estimated asymptotic covariance matrix of

$$\mathbf{c} \equiv \begin{bmatrix} \mathbf{c}_1 \\ \vdots \\ \mathbf{c}_{m-1} \end{bmatrix}$$

is obtained from the inverse of the information matrix, replacing γ with $\mathbf{c}$.

14.2.2   Nested Dichotomies

Perhaps the simplest approach to polytomous data—because it employs the already-familiar dichotomous logit or probit model—is to fit separate models to each of a set of dichotomies derived

---

[46]See Exercise 14.11.

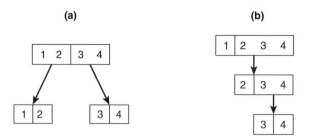

Figure 14.7   Alternative sets of nested dichotomies [(a) and (b)] for a four-category polytomous
response variable.

from the polytomy. These dichotomies are constructed so that the likelihood for the polytomous response variable is the product of the likelihoods for the dichotomies—that is, the models are statistically independent even though they are fitted to data from the same sample. The likelihood is separable in this manner if the set of dichotomies is *nested*.[47] Although the system of nested dichotomies constitutes a model for the polytomy, and although this model often yields fitted probabilities that are very similar to those associated with the polytomous logit model of the previous section, the two models are not equivalent.

A nested set of $m - 1$ dichotomies is produced from an m-category polytomy by successive binary partitions of the categories of the polytomy. Two examples for a four-category variable are shown in Figure 14.7. In part (a) of this figure, the dichotomies are $\{12, 34\}$ (i.e., the combination of Categories 1 and 2 vs. the combination of Categories 3 and 4); $\{1, 2\}$ (Category 1 vs. Category 2); and $\{3, 4\}$ (Category 3 vs. Category 4). In part (b), the nested dichotomies are $\{1, 234\}$, $\{2, 34\}$, and $\{3, 4\}$. This simple—and abstract—example illustrates a key property of nested dichotomies: The set of nested dichotomies selected to represent a polytomy is *not* unique. Because the results of the analysis and their interpretation depend on the set of nested dichotomies that is selected, this approach to polytomous data is reasonable only when a particular choice of dichotomies is substantively compelling. If the dichotomies are purely arbitrary, or if alternative sets of dichotomies are equally reasonable and interesting, then nested dichotomies should probably not be used to analyze the data.

Nested dichotomies are an especially attractive approach when the categories of the polytomy represent ordered progress through the stages of a process. Imagine, for example, that the categories in Figure 14.7(b) represent adults' attained level of education: (1) less than high school; (2) high-school graduate; (3) some postsecondary; (4) postsecondary degree. Because individuals normally progress through these categories in sequence, the dichotomy $\{1, 234\}$ represents the completion of high school; $\{2, 34\}$ the continuation to postsecondary education, conditional on high school graduation; and $\{3, 4\}$ the completion of a degree conditional on undertaking a postsecondary education.[48]

*Why Nested Dichotomies Are Independent**

For simplicity, I will demonstrate the independence of the nested dichotomies $\{12, 3\}$ and $\{1, 2\}$. By repeated application, this result applies generally to any system of nested dichotomies. Let W_{i1}, W_{i2}, and W_{i3} be dummy variables indicating whether the polytomous response variable

---

[47]A proof of this property of nested dichotomies will be given presently.
[48]Fienberg (1980, pp. 110–116) terms ratios of odds formed from these nested dichotomies *continuation ratios*. An example employing nested dichotomies for educational attainment is developed in the data-analysis exercises for this chapter.

Y_i is 1, 2, or 3. For example, $W_{i1} = 1$ if $Y_i = 1$, and 0 otherwise. Let Y_i' be a dummy variable representing the first dichotomy, $\{12, 3\}$: That is, $Y_i' = 1$ when $Y_i = 1$ or 2, and $Y_i' = 0$ when $Y_i = 3$. Likewise, let Y_i'' be a dummy variable representing the second dichotomy, $\{1, 2\}$: $Y_i'' = 1$ when $Y_i = 1$, and $Y_i'' = 0$ when $Y_i = 2$; Y_i'' is *undefined* when $Y_i = 3$. We need to show that $p(y_i) = p(y_i')p(y_i'')$. [To form this product, we adopt the convention that $p(y_i'') \equiv 1$ when $Y_i = 3$.]

The probability distribution of Y_i' is given by

$$p(y_i') = (\pi_{i1} + \pi_{i2})^{y_i'}\, \pi_{i3}^{1-y_i'} \tag{14.24}$$
$$= (\pi_{i1} + \pi_{i2})^{w_{i1}+w_{i2}}\, \pi_{i3}^{w_{i3}}$$

where $\pi_{ij} \equiv \Pr(Y_i = j)$ for $j = 1, 2, 3$. To derive the probability distribution of Y_i'', note that

$$\Pr(Y_i'' = 1) = \Pr(Y_i = 1 | Y_i \neq 3) = \frac{\pi_{i1}}{\pi_{i1} + \pi_{i2}}$$
$$\Pr(Y_i'' = 0) = \Pr(Y_i = 2 | Y_i \neq 3) = \frac{\pi_{i2}}{\pi_{i1} + \pi_{i2}}$$

and, thus,

$$p(y_i'') = \left(\frac{\pi_{i1}}{\pi_{i1} + \pi_{i2}}\right)^{y_i''} \left(\frac{\pi_{i2}}{\pi_{i1} + \pi_{i2}}\right)^{1-y_i''} \tag{14.25}$$
$$= \left(\frac{\pi_{i1}}{\pi_{i1} + \pi_{i2}}\right)^{w_{i1}} \left(\frac{\pi_{i2}}{\pi_{i1} + \pi_{i2}}\right)^{w_{i2}}$$

Multiplying Equation 14.24 by Equation 14.25 produces

$$p(y_i')p(y_i'') = \pi_{i1}^{w_{i1}} \pi_{i2}^{w_{i2}} \pi_{i3}^{w_{i3}} = p(y_i)$$

which is the required result.

Because the dichotomies Y' and Y'' are independent, it is legitimate to combine models for these dichotomies to form a model for the polytomy Y. Likewise, we can sum likelihood-ratio or Wald test statistics for the two dichotomies.

14.2.3   Ordered Logit and Probit Models

Imagine (as in Section 14.1.3) that there is a latent (i.e., unobservable) variable ξ that is a linear function of the Xs plus a random error:

$$\xi_i = \alpha + \beta_1 X_{i1} + \cdots + \beta_k X_{ik} + \varepsilon_i$$

Now, however, suppose that instead of dividing ξ into two regions to produce a dichotomous response, ξ is dissected by $m - 1$ *thresholds* (i.e., boundaries) into m regions. Denoting the thresholds by $\alpha_1 < \alpha_2 < \cdots < \alpha_{m-1}$, and the resulting response by Y, we observe

$$Y_i = \begin{cases} 1 & \text{if } \xi_i \leq \alpha_1 \\ 2 & \text{if } \alpha_1 < \xi_i \leq \alpha_2 \\ \vdots & \\ m - 1 & \text{if } \alpha_{m-2} < \xi_i \leq \alpha_{m-1} \\ m & \text{if } \alpha_{m-1} < \xi_i \end{cases} \tag{14.26}$$

Figure 14.8   The thresholds $\alpha_1 < \alpha_2 < \cdots < \alpha_{m-1}$ divide the latent continuum ξ into m regions, corresponding to the values of the observable variable Y.

The thresholds, regions, and corresponding values of ξ and Y are represented graphically in Figure 14.8. Note that the thresholds are not in general uniformly spaced.

Using Equation 14.26, we can determine the cumulative probability distribution of Y:

$$
\begin{aligned}
\Pr(Y_i \leq j) &= \Pr(\xi_i \leq \alpha_j) \\
&= \Pr(\alpha + \beta_1 X_{i1} + \cdots + \beta_k X_{ik} + \varepsilon_i \leq \alpha_j) \\
&= \Pr(\varepsilon_i \leq \alpha_j - \alpha - \beta_1 X_{i1} - \cdots - \beta_k X_{ik})
\end{aligned}
$$

If the errors ε_i are independently distributed according to the standard normal distribution, then we obtain the ordered probit model.[49] If the errors follow the similar logistic distribution, then we get the ordered logit model. In the latter event,

$$
\begin{aligned}
\text{logit}\,[\Pr(Y_i \leq j)] &= \log_e \frac{\Pr(Y_i \leq j)}{\Pr(Y_i > j)} \\
&= \alpha_j - \alpha - \beta_1 X_{i1} - \cdots - \beta_k X_{ik}
\end{aligned}
$$

Equivalently,

$$
\begin{aligned}
\text{logit}\,[\Pr(Y_i > j)] &= \log_e \frac{\Pr(Y_i > j)}{\Pr(Y_i \leq j)} \\
&= (\alpha - \alpha_j) + \beta_1 X_{i1} + \cdots + \beta_k X_{ik}
\end{aligned}
\tag{14.27}
$$

for $j = 1, 2, \ldots, m - 1$.

The logits in Equation 14.27 are for cumulative categories—at each point contrasting categories above category j with category j and below. The slopes for each of these regression equations are identical; the equations differ only in their intercepts. The logistic-regression surfaces are, therefore, horizontally parallel to each other, as illustrated in Figure 14.9 for $m = 4$ response categories and a single X. (For the more general case, just replace X by the linear predictor $\eta = \beta_1 X_1 + \cdots + \beta_k X_k$.)

Put another way, for a fixed set of Xs, any two different cumulative log-odds (i.e., logits)—say, at categories j and j'—differ only by the constant $(\alpha_{j'} - \alpha_j)$. The odds, therefore, are *proportional* to one another; that is,

$$
\frac{\text{odds}_j}{\text{odds}_{j'}} = \exp\left(\text{logit}_j - \text{logit}_{j'}\right) = \exp(\alpha_{j'} - \alpha_j) = \frac{e^{\alpha_{j'}}}{e^{\alpha_j}}
$$

where, for example, $\text{odds}_j \equiv \Pr(Y_i > j)$ and $\text{logit}_j \equiv \text{logit}\,[\Pr(Y_i > j)]$. For this reason, Equation 14.27 is called the *proportional-odds logit model*.

There are $(k + 1) + (m - 1) = k + m$ parameters to estimate in the proportional-odds model, including the regression coefficients $\alpha, \beta_1, \ldots, \beta_k$ and the category thresholds $\alpha_1, \ldots, \alpha_{m-1}$.

---

[49] As in the dichotomous case, we conveniently fix the error variance to 1 to set the scale of the latent variable ξ. The resulting ordered probit model does not have the proportional-odds property described below.

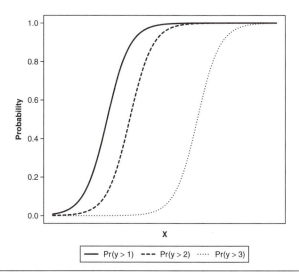

Figure 14.9   The proportional-odds model for four response categories and a single explanatory variable *X*. The logistic regression curves are horizontally parallel.

SOURCE: Adapted from Agresti (1990, fig. 9.1), *Categorical Data Analysis.* Copyright ©1990 John Wiley & Sons, Inc. Reprinted by permission of John Wiley & Sons, Inc.

Note, however, that there is an extra parameter in the regression equations (Equation 14.27) because each equation has its own constant, $-\alpha_j$, along with the common constant α. A simple solution is to set $\alpha = 0$ (and to absorb the negative sign into α_j), producing[50]

$$\text{logit}\,[\Pr(Y_i > j)] = \alpha_j + \beta_1 X_{i1} + \cdots + \beta_k X_{ik} \qquad (14.28)$$

In this parametrization, the intercepts α_j are the *negatives* of the category thresholds.

Figure 14.10 illustrates the proportional-odds model for $m = 4$ response categories and a single X. The conditional distribution of the latent variable ξ is shown for two representative values of the explanatory variable, x_1 [where $\Pr(Y > 3) = \Pr(Y = 4)$ is about .2] and x_2 [where $\Pr(Y = 4)$ is about .98]. McCullagh (1980) explains how Equation 14.27 can be fit by the method of maximum likelihood (and discusses alternatives to the proportional-odds model).

To illustrate the use of the proportional-odds model, I draw on data from the World Values Survey (WVS) of 1995–1997 (European Values Study Group and World Values Survey Association, 2000).[51] Although the WVS collects data in many countries, to provide a manageable example, I will restrict attention to only four: Australia, Sweden, Norway, and the United States. The combined sample size for these four countries is 5,381. The response variable in the analysis is the answer to the question "Do you think that what the government is doing for people in poverty is about the right amount, too much, or too little?" There are, therefore, three ordered categories: *too little, about right, too much.* There are several explanatory variables: gender (represented by a dummy variable coded 1 for *men* and 0 for *women*); whether or not the respondent belonged to a religion (coded 1 for *yes,* 0 for *no*); whether or not the respondent had a university degree (coded 1 for *yes* and 0 for *no*); age (in years, ranging from 18 to 87); and country (entered into the

---

[50]Setting $\alpha = 0$ implicitly establishes the origin of the latent variable ξ (just as fixing the error variance establishes its unit of measurement). An alternative would be to fix one of the thresholds to 0. These choices are arbitrary and inconsequential.

[51]This illustration is adapted from Fox and Andersen (2006).

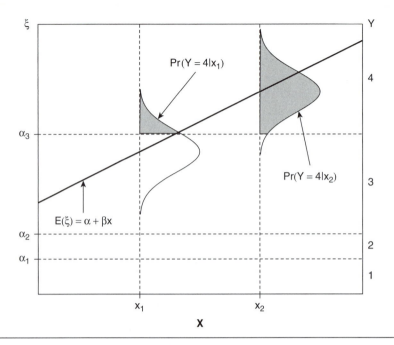

Figure 14.10   The proportional-odds model for four response categories and a single explanatory variable X. The latent response variable ξ has a linear regression on X. The latent continuum ξ and thresholds α_j appear at the left of the graph, the observable response Y at the right. The conditional logistic distribution of the latent variable is shown for two values of the explanatory variable, x_1 and x_2. The shaded area in each distribution gives the conditional probability that $Y = 4$.

SOURCE: Adapted from Agresti (1990, fig. 9.2), *Categorical Data Analysis.* Copyright ©1990 John Wiley & Sons, Inc. Reprinted by permission of John Wiley & Sons, Inc.

model as a set of three dummy regressors, with *Australia* as the baseline category). Preliminary analysis of the data suggested a roughly linear age effect.

Table 14.7 shows the analysis of deviance for an initial model fit to the data incorporating interactions between country and each of the other explanatory variables. As usual, the likelihood-ratio tests in the table are computed by contrasting the deviances for alternative models, with and without the terms in question. These tests were formulated in conformity with the principle of marginality. So, for example, the test for the country-by-age interaction was computed by dropping this term from the full model, and the test for the country main effect was computed by dropping the dummy regressors for country from a model that includes only main effects.

With the exception of the interaction between country and gender, all these interactions prove to be statistically significant. Estimated coefficients and their standard errors for a final model, removing the nonsignificant interaction between country and gender, appear in Table 14.8. This table also shows the estimated thresholds between response categories, which are, as explained, the negatives of the intercepts of the proportional-odds model.

Interpretation of the estimated coefficients for the proportional-odds model in Table 14.8 is complicated by the interactions in the model and by the multiple-category response. I will use the interaction between age and country to illustrate: We can see that the age slope is positive in the baseline country of Australia (suggesting that sympathy for the poor declines with age in Australia) and that this slope is nearly zero in Norway, smaller in Sweden than in Australia, and

Table 14.7 Analysis of Deviance Table for the Proportional-Odds Model Fit to the World Values Survey Data

Source	df	G_0^2	p
Country	3	250.881	≪.0001
Gender	1	10.749	.0010
Religion	1	4.132	.042
Education	1	4.284	.038
Age	1	49.950	≪.0001
Country × Gender	3	3.049	.38
Country × Religion	3	21.143	<.0001
Country × Education	3	12.861	.0049
Country × Age	3	17.529	.0005

Table 14.8 Estimated Proportional-Odds Model Fit to the World Values Survey Data

Coefficient	Estimate	Standard Error
Gender (Men)	0.1744	0.0532
Country (Norway)	0.1516	0.3355
Country (Sweden)	−1.2237	0.5821
Country (United States)	1.2225	0.3068
Religion (Yes)	0.0255	0.1120
Education (Degree)	−0.1282	0.1676
Age	0.0153	0.0026
Country (Norway) × Religion	−0.2456	0.2153
Country (Sweden) × Religion	−0.9031	0.5125
Country (United States) × Religion	0.5706	0.1733
Country (Norway) × Education	0.0524	0.2080
Country (Sweden) × Education	0.6359	0.2141
Country (United States) × Education	0.3103	0.2063
Country (Norway) × Age	−0.0156	0.0044
Country (Sweden) × Age	−0.0090	0.0047
Country (United States) × Age	0.0008	0.0040
Thresholds		
$-\widehat{\alpha}_1$ (Too Little| About Right)	0.7699	0.1491
$-\widehat{\alpha}_2$ (About Right | Too Much)	2.5372	0.1537

very slightly larger in the United States than in Australia, but a more detailed understanding of the age-by-country interaction is hard to discern from the coefficients alone. Figures 14.11 and 14.12 show alternative effect displays of the age-by-country interaction. The strategy for constructing these displays is the usual one—compute fitted values under the model letting age and country range over their values while other explanatory variables (i.e., gender, religion, and education) are held to average values. Figure 14.11 plots the fitted probabilities of response (as percentages) by age for each country; Figure 14.12 plots the fitted value of the latent response variable by age for each country, and shows the intercategory thresholds.

The proportional-odds model of Equation 14.28 (on page 365) constrains corresponding slopes for the $m - 1$ cumulative logits to be equal. By relaxing this strong constraint, and fitting a model to the cumulative logits that permits different slopes along with different intercepts, we can test the proportional-odds assumption:

$$\text{logit}\,[\Pr(Y_i > j)] = \alpha_j + \beta_{j1} X_{i1} + \cdots + \beta_{jk} X_{ik}, \text{ for } j = 1, \ldots, m - 1 \qquad (14.29)$$

Like the polytomous logit model of Equation 14.18 (on page 356), this new model has $(m - 1)$ $(k + 1)$ parameters, but the two models are for *different* sets of logits. The deviances and numbers of parameters for the three models fit to the World Values Survey data are as follows:

Model	Residual Deviance	Number of Parameters
Proportional-Odds Model (Equation 14.28)	10,350.12	18
Cumulative Logits, Unconstrained Slopes (Equation 14.29)	9,961.63	34
Polytomous Logit Model (Equation 14.18)	9,961.26	34

The likelihood-ratio statistic for testing the assumption of proportional odds is therefore $G_0^2 = 10,350.12 - 9,961.63 = 388.49$, on $34 - 18 = 16$ degrees of freedom. This test statistic is highly statistically significant, leading us to reject the proportional-odds assumption for these data. Note that the deviance for the model that relaxes the proportional-odds assumption is nearly identical to the deviance for the polytomous logit model. This is typically the case, in my experience.[52]

14.2.4   Comparison of the Three Approaches

> Several approaches can be taken to modeling polytomous data, including (1) modeling the polytomy directly using a logit model based on the multivariate logistic distribution; (2) constructing a set of $m - 1$ nested dichotomies to represent the m categories of the polytomy; and (3) fitting the proportional-odds model to a polytomous response variable with ordered categories.

The three approaches to modeling polytomous data—the polytomous logit model, logit models for nested dichotomies, and the proportional-odds model—address different sets of log-odds, corresponding to different dichotomies constructed from the polytomy. Consider, for example, the ordered polytomy $\{1, 2, 3, 4\}$—representing, say, four ordered educational categories:

- Treating Category 4 as the baseline, the coefficients of the polytomous logit model apply *directly* to the dichotomies $\{1, 4\}$, $\{2, 4\}$, and $\{3, 4\}$ and *indirectly* to any pair of categories.

---

[52]Consequently, if you are working with software that does not compute the unconstrained-slopes model for cumulative logits, it is generally safe to use the polytomous logit model to formulate an approximate likelihood-ratio test for proportional odds. There is also a score test and a Wald test for the proportional-odds assumption (discussed, e.g., in Long, 1997, sect. 5.5).

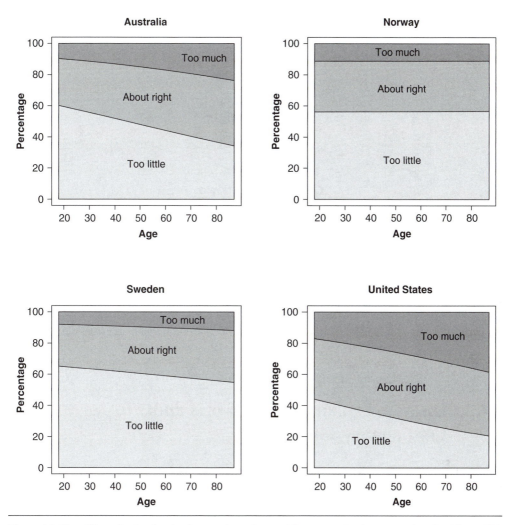

Figure 14.11 Effect display for the interaction of age with country in the proportional-odds model fit to the World Values Survey data. The response variable is assessment of government action for people in poverty.

- Forming continuation dichotomies (one of several possibilities), the nested-dichotomies approach models {1, 234}, {2, 34}, and {3, 4}.
- The proportional-odds model applies to the cumulative dichotomies {1, 234}, {12, 34}, and {123, 4}, imposing the restriction that only the intercepts of the three regression equations differ.

Which of these models is most appropriate depends partly on the structure of the data and partly on our interest in them. If it fits well, the proportional-odds model would generally be preferred for an ordered response on grounds of parsimony, but this model imposes strong structure on the data and may not fit well. Nested dichotomies should only be used if the particular choice of dichotomies makes compelling substantive sense for the data at hand. The implication, then, is that of these three models, the polytomous logit model has the greatest general range of application.[53]

---

[53] But see Exercise 14.12.

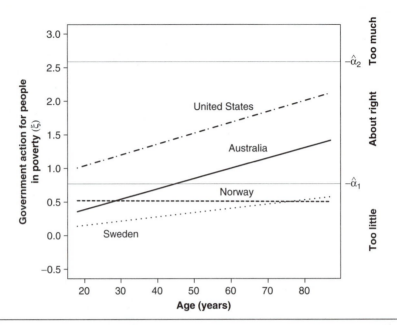

Figure 14.12   Alternative effect display for the proportional-odds model fit to the World Value
Survey data, showing fitted values of the latent response. Intercategory thresholds
and the corresponding response categories are given at the right of the graph and by
the lighter horizontal lines.

14.3   Discrete Explanatory Variables and Contingency Tables

When the explanatory variables—as well as the response—are discrete, the joint sample distribution of the variables defines a contingency table of counts: Each cell of the table records the number of observations possessing a particular combination of characteristics. An example, drawn from *The American Voter* (Campbell, Converse, Miller, & Stokes, 1960), a classical study of electoral behavior, appears in Table 14.9. This table, based on data from sample surveys conducted during the 1956 U.S. presidential election campaign and after the election, relates voting turnout in the election to strength of partisan preference (classified as weak, medium, or strong) and perceived closeness of the election (one-sided or close).

The last column of Table 14.9 gives the *empirical logit* for the response variable,

$$\log_e \frac{\text{Proportion voting}}{\text{Proportion not voting}}$$

for each of the six combinations of categories of the explanatory variables.[54] For example,

$$\text{logit (voted} \mid \text{one-sided, weak preference)} = \log_e \frac{91/130}{39/130} = \log_e \frac{91}{39} = 0.847$$

[54]This calculation will fail if there is a 0 frequency in the table because, in this event, the proportion voting or not voting for some combination of explanatory-variable values will be 0. A simple remedy is to add 0.5 to each of the cell frequencies. Adding 0.5 to each count also serves to reduce the bias of the sample logit as an estimator of the corresponding population logit. See Cox and Snell (1989, pp. 31–32).

Table 14.9   Voter Turnout by Perceived Closeness of the Election and Intensity of Partisan Preference, for the 1956 U.S. Presidential Election

Perceived Closeness	Intensity of Preference	Turnout		Logit
		Voted	Did Not Vote	$\log_e \dfrac{\text{Voted}}{\text{Did Not Vote}}$
One-sided	Weak	91	39	0.847
	Medium	121	49	0.904
	Strong	64	24	0.981
Close	Weak	214	87	0.900
	Medium	284	76	1.318
	Strong	201	25	2.084

NOTE: Frequency counts are shown in the body of the table.

Because the conditional proportions voting and not voting share the same denominator, the empirical logit can also be written as

$$\log_e \frac{\text{Number voting}}{\text{Number not voting}}$$

The empirical logits from Table 14.9 are graphed in Figure 14.13, much in the manner of profiles of cell means for a two-way ANOVA.[55] Perceived closeness of the election and intensity of preference appear to interact in affecting turnout: Turnout increases with increasing intensity of preference, but only if the election is perceived to be close. Those with medium or strong preference who perceive the election to be close are more likely to vote than those who perceive the election to be one-sided; this difference is greater among those with strong partisan preference than those with medium partisan preference.

The methods of this chapter are fully appropriate for tabular data. When, as in Table 14.9, the explanatory variables are qualitative or ordinal, it is natural to use logit or probit models that are analogous to ANOVA models. Treating perceived closeness of the election as the "row" factor and intensity of partisan preference as the "column" factor, for example, yields the model

$$\text{logit } \pi_{jk} = \mu + \alpha_j + \beta_k + \gamma_{jk} \tag{14.30}$$

where

- π_{jk} is the conditional probability of voting in combination of categories j of perceived closeness and k of preference (i.e., in cell jk of the explanatory-variable table);
- μ is the general level of turnout in the population;
- α_j is the main effect on turnout of membership in the jth category of perceived closeness;
- β_k is the main effect on turnout of membership in the kth category of preference; and
- γ_{jk} is the interaction effect on turnout of simultaneous membership in categories j of perceived closeness and k of preference.

---

[55] See Section 8.2.1.

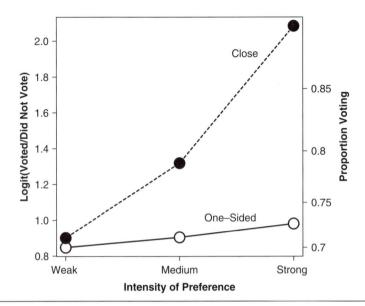

Figure 14.13   Empirical logits for voter turnout by intensity of partisan preference and perceived closeness of the election, for the 1956 U.S. presidential election.

> When all the variables—explanatory as well as response—are discrete, their joint distribution defines a contingency table of frequency counts. It is natural to employ logit models that are analogous to ANOVA models to analyze contingency tables.

Under the usual sigma constraints, Equation 14.30 leads to deviation-coded regressors, as in ANOVA. Adapting the SS($\cdot$) notation of Chapter 8,[56] likelihood-ratio tests for main effects and interactions can then be constructed in close analogy to the incremental F-tests for the two-way ANOVA model. Residual deviances under several models for the *American Voter* data are shown in Table 14.3, and the analysis-of-deviance table for these data is given in Table 14.11. The log-likelihood-ratio statistic for testing H_0: all $\gamma_{jk} = 0$, for example, is

$$G_0^2(\gamma | \alpha, \beta) = G^2(\alpha, \beta) - G^2(\alpha, \beta, \gamma)$$
$$= 1363.552 - 1356.434$$
$$= 7.118$$

with $6 - 4 = 2$ degrees of freedom, for which $p = .028$. The interaction discerned in Figure 14.13 is, therefore, statistically significant, but not overwhelmingly so.

14.3.1   The Binomial Logit Model*

Although the models for dichotomous and polytomous response variables described in this chapter can be directly applied to tabular data, there is some advantage in reformulating these models to take direct account of the replication of combinations of explanatory-variable values.

---

[56]In Chapter 8, we used SS($\cdot$) to denote the *regression* sum of squares for a model including certain terms. Because the deviance is analogous to the *residual* sum of squares, we need to take differences of deviances in the opposite order.

Table 14.10 Residual Deviances for Models Fit to the *American Voter* Data. Terms: α, Perceived Closeness; β, Intensity of Preference; γ, Closeness × Preference Interaction

Model	Terms	$k+1$	Deviance: G^2
1	α, β, γ	6	1356.434
2	α, β	4	1363.552
3	α, γ	4	1368.042
4	β, γ	5	1368.554
5	α	2	1382.658
6	β	3	1371.838

NOTE: The column labeled $k+1$ gives the number of parameters in the model, including the constant μ.

Table 14.11 Analysis-of-Deviance Table for the *American Voter* Data

Source	Models Contrasted	df	G_0^2	p
Perceived closeness		1		
$\alpha \mid \beta$	6−2		8.286	.0040
$\alpha \mid \beta, \gamma$	4−1		12.120	.0005
Intensity of preference		2		
$\beta \mid \alpha$	5−2		19.106	<.0001
$\beta \mid \alpha, \gamma$	3−1		11.608	.0030
Closeness × Preference		2		
$\gamma \mid \alpha, \beta$	2−1		7.118	.028

NOTE: The table shows alternative likelihood-ratio tests for the main effects of perceived closeness of the election and intensity of partisan preference.

In analyzing dichotomous data, for example, we previously treated each observation individually, so the dummy response variable Y_i takes on either the value 0 or the value 1.

Suppose, instead, that we group all the n_i observations that share the specific combination of explanatory-variable values $\mathbf{x}_i' = [x_{i1}, x_{i2}, \ldots, x_{ik}]$. Let Y_i count the number of these observations that fall in the first of the two categories of the response variable; we arbitrarily term these observations *successes*. The count Y_i can take on any integer value between 0 and n_i. Let m denote the number of *distinct combinations* of the explanatory variables (e.g., $m = 6$ in Table 14.9 on page 371).

As in our previous development of the dichotomous logit model, let π_i represent $\Pr(\text{success} \mid \mathbf{x}_i)$. Then the success count Y_i follows the binomial distribution:

$$p(y_i) = \binom{n_i}{y_i} \pi_i^{y_i} (1 - \pi_i)^{n_i - y_i} \tag{14.31}$$

$$= \binom{n_i}{y_i} \left(\frac{\pi_i}{1 - \pi_i} \right)^{y_i} (1 - \pi_i)^{n_i}$$

To distinguish grouped dichotomous data from ungrouped data, I will refer to the former as *binomial data* and the latter as *binary data*.[57]

---

[57]Binary data can be thought of as a limiting case of binomial data, for which all $n_i = 1$.

Suppose, next, that the dependence of the response probabilities π_i on the explanatory variables is well described by the logit model

$$\log_e \frac{\pi_i}{1 - \pi_i} = \mathbf{x}_i' \boldsymbol{\beta}$$

Substituting this model into Equation 14.31, the likelihood for the parameters is

$$L(\boldsymbol{\beta}) = \prod_{i=1}^{m} \binom{n_i}{y_i} [\exp(\mathbf{x}_i'\boldsymbol{\beta})]^{y_i} \left(\frac{1}{1 + \exp(\mathbf{x}_i'\boldsymbol{\beta})} \right)^{n_i}$$

Maximizing the likelihood leads to precisely the same maximum-likelihood estimates, coefficient standard errors, and statistical tests as the binary logit model of Section 14.1.5.[58] The binomial logit model nevertheless has the following advantages:

- Because we deal with m binomial observations rather than the larger $n = \sum_{i=1}^{m} n_i$ binary observations, computations for the binomial logit model are more efficient, especially when the n_i are large.
- The overall residual deviance for the binomial logit model, $-2\log_e L(\mathbf{b})$, implicitly contrasts the model with a *saturated* model that has one parameter for each of the m combinations of explanatory-variable values (e.g., the full two-way "ANOVA" model with main effects and interactions fit in the previous section to the *American Voter* data). The saturated model necessarily recovers the m empirical logits perfectly and, consequently, has a likelihood of 1 and a log likelihood of 0. The residual deviance for a less-than-saturated model, therefore, provides a likelihood-ratio test, on $m - k - 1$ degrees of freedom, of the hypothesis that the functional form of the model is correct.[59] In contrast, the residual deviance for the binary logit model cannot be used for a statistical test because the residual degrees of freedom $n - k - 1$ (unlike $m - k - 1$) grow as the sample size n grows.
- As long as the frequencies n_i are not very small, many diagnostics are much better behaved for the cells of the binomial logit model than for individual binary observations. For example, the individual components of the deviance for the binomial logit model,

$$G_i \equiv \pm \sqrt{-2\left[Y_i \log_e \frac{n_i P_i}{Y_i} + (n_i - Y_i) \log_e \frac{n_i(1 - P_i)}{n_i - Y_i} \right]}$$

  can be compared with the unit-normal distribution to locate outlying cells. Here $P_i = 1/[1 + \exp(-\mathbf{x}_i'\mathbf{b})]$ is the fitted probability of "success" for cell i, and, therefore, $\widehat{Y}_i = n_i P_i$ is the expected number of "successes" in this cell. The sign of G_i is selected to agree with that of the simple cell residual, $E_i = Y_i - \widehat{Y}_i$.[60]

> Although the binary logit model can be applied to tables in which the response variable is dichotomous, it is also possible to use the equivalent binomial logit model; the binomial logit model is based on the frequency counts of "successes" and "failures" for each combination of explanatory-variable values. When it is applicable, the binomial logit model offers several advantages, including efficient computation, a test of the fit of the model based on its residual deviance, and better-behaved diagnostics.

---

[58] See Exercise 14.13.

[59] This test is analogous to the test for "lack of fit" in a linear model with a discrete explanatory variable described in Section 12.4.

[60] Diagnostics for logit models and other generalized linear models are discussed in Section 15.4.

Polytomous data can be handled in a similar manner, employing the multinomial distribution.[61] Consequently, all the logit and probit models discussed in this chapter have generalizations to data in which there are repeated observations for combinations of values of the explanatory variables. For example, the *multinomial logit model* generalizes the polytomous logit model of Equation 14.18 (on page 356); indeed, even when it is fit to individual observations, the polytomous logit model is often called the "multinomial logit model" (as I previously mentioned).[62]

Exercises

Exercise 14.1. Nonconstant error variance in the linear-probability model: Make a table showing the variance of the error $V(\varepsilon) = \pi(1 - \pi)$ for the following values of π:

$$.001, \ .01, \ .05, \ .1, \ .3, \ .5., \ .7, \ .9, \ .95, \ .99, \ .999$$

When is the heteroscedasticity problem serious?

Exercise 14.2. Show that using the cumulative rectangular distribution as $P(\cdot)$ in the general model

$$\pi_i = P(\eta_i) = P(\alpha + \beta X_i)$$

produces the constrained linear-probability model. (See Section 14.1.2.)

Exercise 14.3. *Show that the slope of the logistic-regression curve, $\pi = 1/\left[1 + e^{-(\alpha+\beta X)}\right]$, can be written as $\beta\pi(1 - \pi)$. (*Hint*: Differentiate π with respect to X, and then substitute for expressions that equal π and $1 - \pi$.)

Exercise 14.4. Substitute first $y_i = 0$ and then $y_i = 1$ into the expression

$$p(y_i) \equiv \Pr(Y_i = y_i) = \pi_i^{y_i}(1 - \pi_i)^{1-y_i}$$

to show that this equation captures $p(0) = 1 - \pi_i$ and $p(1) = \pi_i$.

Exercise 14.5. *Show that, for the logit multiple-regression model,

$$\pi_i = \frac{1}{1 + \exp[-(\alpha + \beta_1 X_{i1} + \beta_2 X_{i2} + \cdots + \beta_k X_{ik})]}$$

the probability that $Y_i = 0$ can be written as

$$1 - \pi_i = \frac{1}{1 + \exp(\alpha + \beta_1 X_{i1} + \cdots + \beta_k X_{ik})}$$

Exercise 14.6. *Show that the maximized likelihood for the fitted logit model can be written as

$$\log_e L = \sum_{i=1}^{n} \left[y_i \log_e P_i + (1 - y_i) \log_e(1 - P_i)\right]$$

---

[61] See Exercise 14.14.

[62] As in the case of binary data, we can think of individual polytomous observations as multinomial observations in which all the total counts are $n_i = 1$.

where

$$P_i = \frac{1}{1 + \exp[-(A + B_1 X_{i1} + \cdots + B_k X_{ik})]}$$

is the fitted probability that $Y_i = 1$. [*Hint*: Use $p(y_i) = \pi_i^{y_i}(1 - \pi_i)^{1-y_i}$.]

Exercise 14.7. *Residual deviance in least-squares regression: The log likelihood for the linear regression model with normal errors can be written as

$$\log_e L(\alpha, \beta_1, \ldots, \beta_k, \sigma_\varepsilon^2) = -\frac{n}{2} \log_e \left(2\pi\sigma_\varepsilon^2\right) - \frac{\sum_{i=1}^n \varepsilon_i^2}{2\sigma_\varepsilon^2}$$

where $\varepsilon_i = Y_i - (\alpha + \beta_1 X_{i1} + \cdots + \beta_k X_{ik})$ (see Section 9.3.3). Let l represent the maximized log likelihood, treated as a function of the regression coefficients $\alpha, \beta_1, \ldots, \beta_k$ but not of the error variance σ_ε^2, which is regarded as a "nuisance parameter." Let $l' = -(n/2)\log_e(2\pi\sigma_\varepsilon^2)$ represent the log likelihood for a model that fits the data perfectly (i.e., for which all $\varepsilon_i = 0$). Then the residual deviance is defined as $-2\sigma_\varepsilon^2(l - l')$. Show that, by this definition, the residual deviance for the normal linear model is just the residual sum of squares. (For the logit model, there is no nuisance parameter, and $l' = 0$; the residual deviance for this model is, therefore, $-2\log_e L$, as stated in the text. See Chapter 15 for further discussion of the deviance.)

Exercise 14.8. *Evaluate the information matrix for the logit model,

$$\mathcal{J}(\beta) = -E\left[\frac{\partial^2 \log_e L(\beta)}{\partial \beta \, \partial \beta'}\right]$$

and show that the estimated asymptotic covariance matrix of the coefficients is

$$\widehat{\mathcal{V}}(\mathbf{b}) = \left[\sum_{i=1}^n \frac{\exp(-\mathbf{x}_i'\mathbf{b})}{[1 + \exp(-\mathbf{x}_i'\mathbf{b})]^2}\mathbf{x}_i\mathbf{x}_i'\right]^{-1}$$

Exercise 14.9. *Show that the maximum-likelihood estimator for the logit model can be written as

$$\mathbf{b} = (\mathbf{X}'\mathbf{V}\mathbf{X})^{-1}\mathbf{X}'\mathbf{V}\mathbf{y}^*$$

where

$$\mathbf{y}^* \equiv \mathbf{X}\mathbf{b} + \mathbf{V}^{-1}(\mathbf{y} - \mathbf{p})$$

(*Hint*: Simply multiply out the equation.)

Exercise 14.10. *Show that the polytomous logit model of Equation 14.18 (page 356) can be written in the form

$$\log_e \frac{\pi_{ij}}{\pi_{im}} = \gamma_{0j} + \gamma_{1j}X_{i1} + \cdots + \gamma_{kj}X_{ik} \quad \text{for } j = 1, \ldots, m - 1$$

Exercise 14.11. *Derive the estimating equations (Equation 14.21 on page 360) and the information matrix (Equations 14.22 and 14.23) for the polytomous logit model.

Exercise 14.12. Independence From Irrelevant Alternatives: In the polytomous logit model discussed in Section 14.2.1, the logit for a particular pair of categories depends on the coefficients for those categories but not on those for other categories in the model. Show that this is the case. (*Hint*: See Equation 14.2.1.) In the context of a discrete-choice model (e.g., Greene, 2003, chap. 21; or Alvarez & Nagler, 1998), this property can be interpreted to mean that the relative odds for a pair of categories is independent of the other categories in the choice set. Why is this often an implausible assumption? (*Hint:* Consider a multiparty election in a jurisdiction, such as Canada or the U.K., where some parties field candidates in only part of the country, or what happens to the electoral map when a new party is formed.) For this reason, models such as the polytomous probit model that *do not* assume independence from irrelevant alternatives are sometimes preferred.

Exercise 14.13. *Derive the maximum-likelihood estimating equations for the binomial logit model. Show that this model produces the same estimated coefficients as the dichotomous (binary) logit model of Section 15.1. (*Hint*: Compare the log likelihood for the binomial model with the log likelihood for the binary model; by separating individual observations sharing a common set of X values, show that the former log likelihood is equal to the latter, except for a constant factor. This constant is irrelevant because it does not influence the maximum-likelihood estimator; moreover, the constant disappears in likelihood-ratio tests.)

Exercise 14.14. *Use the multinomial distribution (see Appendix D) to specify a polytomous logit model for discrete explanatory variables (analogous to the binomial logit model), where combinations of explanatory-variable values are replicated. Derive the likelihood under the model, and the maximum-likelihood estimating equations.

Summary _____

- It is problematic to apply least-squares linear regression to a dichotomous response variable: The errors cannot be normally distributed and cannot have constant variance. Even more fundamentally, the linear specification does not confine the probability for the response to the unit interval.
- More adequate specifications transform the linear predictor $\eta_i = \alpha + \beta_1 X_{i1} + \cdots + \beta_k X_{ik}$ smoothly to the unit interval, using a cumulative probability distribution function $P(\cdot)$. Two such specifications are the probit and the logit models, which use the normal and logistic CDFs, respectively. Although these models are very similar, the logit model is simpler to interpret because it can be written as a linear model for the log-odds:

$$\log_e \frac{\pi_i}{1 - \pi_i} = \alpha + \beta_1 X_{i1} + \cdots + \beta_k X_{ik}$$

- The dichotomous logit model can be fit to data by the method of maximum likelihood. Wald tests and likelihood-ratio tests for the coefficients of the model parallel t-tests and incremental F-tests for the general linear model. The residual deviance for the model, defined as $G^2 = -2 \times$ the maximized log likelihood, is analogous to the residual sum of squares for a linear model.
- Several approaches can be taken to modeling polytomous data, including:

  1. modeling the polytomy directly using a logit model based on the multivariate logistic distribution;

  2. constructing a set of $m - 1$ nested dichotomies to represent the m categories of the polytomy; and

3. fitting the proportional-odds model to a polytomous response variable with ordered categories.

- When all the variables—explanatory as well as response—are discrete, their joint distribution defines a contingency table of frequency counts. It is natural to employ logit models that are analogous to ANOVA models to analyze contingency tables. Although the binary logit model can be applied to tables in which the response variable is dichotomous, it is also possible to use the equivalent binomial logit model; the binomial logit model is based on the frequency counts of "successes" and "failures" for each combination of explanatory-variable values. When it is applicable, the binomial logit model offers several advantages, including efficient computation, a test of the fit of the model based on its residual deviance, and better-behaved diagnostics. There are analogous logit and probit models, such as the multinomial logit model, for polytomous responses.

Recommended Reading

The topics introduced in this chapter could easily be expanded to fill several books, and there is a large literature—both in journals and texts—dealing with logit and related models for categorical response variables, and with the analysis of contingency tables.[63]

- Agresti (2002) presents an excellent and comprehensive overview of statistical methods for qualitative data. The emphasis is on logit and log-linear models for contingency tables, but there is some consideration of logistic regression models and other topics. Also see Agresti (1996) for a briefer and lower-level treatment of much of this material.
- Fienberg's (1980) widely read text on the analysis of contingency tables provides an accessible and lucid introduction to log-linear models and related subjects, such as logit models and models for ordered categories.
- The second edition of Cox and Snell's (1989) classic text concentrates on logit models for dichotomous data but also includes some discussion of polytomous nominal and ordinal data.
- Collett (2003) also focuses on the binary and binomial logit models. The book is noteworthy for its extensive review of diagnostic methods for logit models.
- Greene (2003, chap. 21) includes a broad treatment of models for categorical responses from the point of view of "discrete choice models" in econometrics.
- Long (1997) and Powers and Xie (2000) both present high-quality, accessible expositions for social scientists of statistical models for categorical data.

---

[63] Also see the references on generalized linear models given at the end of the next chapter, which briefly describes log-linear models for contingency tables.

15

Generalized Linear Models

D ue originally to Nelder and Wedderburn (1972), generalized linear models are a remarkable synthesis and extension of familiar regression models such as the linear models described in Part II of this text and the logit and probit models described in the preceding chapter. The current chapter begins with a consideration of the general structure and range of application of generalized linear models; proceeds to examine in greater detail generalized linear models for count data, including contingency tables; briefly sketches the statistical theory underlying generalized linear models; and concludes with the extension of regression diagnostics to generalized linear models.

The unstarred sections of this chapter are perhaps more difficult than the unstarred material in preceding chapters. Generalized linear models have become so central to effective statistical data analysis, however, that it is worth the additional effort required to acquire a basic understanding of the subject.

15.1   The Structure of Generalized Linear Models

A *generalized linear model* (or GLM[1]) consists of three components:

1. A *random component*, specifying the conditional distribution of the response variable, Y_i (for the ith of n independently sampled observations), given the values of the explanatory variables in the model. In Nelder and Wedderburn's original formulation, the distribution of Y_i is a member of an *exponential family*, such as the Gaussian (normal), binomial, Poisson, gamma, or inverse-Gaussian families of distributions. Subsequent work, however, has extended GLMs to multivariate exponential families (such as the multinomial distribution), to certain non-exponential families (such as the two-parameter negative-binomial distribution), and to some situations in which the distribution of Y_i is not specified completely. Most of these ideas are developed later in the chapter.

2. A *linear predictor*—that is a linear function of regressors

$$\eta_i = \alpha + \beta_1 X_{i1} + \beta_2 X_{i2} + \cdots + \beta_k X_{ik}$$

As in the linear model, and in the logit and probit models of Chapter 14, the regressors X_{ij} are prespecified functions of the explanatory variables and therefore may include quantitative explanatory variables, transformations of quantitative explanatory variables, polynomial regressors, dummy regressors, interactions, and so on. Indeed, one of the advantages of GLMs is that the structure of the linear predictor is the familiar structure of a linear model.

3. A smooth and invertible linearizing *link function* $g(\cdot)$, which transforms the expectation of the response variable, $\mu_i \equiv E(Y_i)$, to the linear predictor:

$$g(\mu_i) = \eta_i = \alpha + \beta_1 X_{i1} + \beta_2 X_{i2} + \cdots + \beta_k X_{ik}$$

---

[1]Some authors use the acronym "GLM" to refer to the "*general* linear model"—that is, the linear regression model with normal errors described in Part II of the text—and instead employ "GLIM" to denote *generalized* linear models (which is also the name of a computer program used to fit GLMs).

Table 15.1   Some Common Link Functions and Their Inverses

Link	$\eta_i = g(\mu_i)$	$\mu_i = g^{-1}(\eta_i)$
Identity	μ_i	η_i
Log	$\log_e \mu_i$	e^{η_i}
Inverse	μ_i^{-1}	η_i^{-1}
Inverse-square	μ_i^{-2}	$\eta_i^{-1/2}$
Square-root	$\sqrt{\mu_i}$	η_i^2
Logit	$\log_e \dfrac{\mu_i}{1 - \mu_i}$	$\dfrac{1}{1 + e^{-\eta_i}}$
Probit	$\Phi^{-1}(\mu_i)$	$\Phi(\eta_i)$
Log-log	$-\log_e[-\log_e(\mu_i)]$	$\exp[-\exp(-\eta_i)]$
Complementary log-log	$\log_e[-\log_e(1-\mu_i)]$	$1-\exp[-\exp(\eta_i)]$

NOTE: μ_i is the expected value of the response; η_i is the linear predictor; and $\Phi(\cdot)$ is the cumulative distribution function of the standard-normal distribution.

Because the link function is invertible, we can also write

$$\mu_i = g^{-1}(\eta_i) = g^{-1}(\alpha + \beta_1 X_{i1} + \beta_2 X_{i2} + \cdots + \beta_k X_{ik})$$

and, thus, the GLM may be thought of as a linear model for a transformation of the expected response or as a nonlinear regression model for the response. The inverse link $g^{-1}(\cdot)$ is also called the *mean function*. Commonly employed link functions and their inverses are shown in Table 15.1. Note that the *identity link* simply returns its argument unaltered, $\eta_i = g(\mu_i) = \mu_i$, and thus $\mu_i = g^{-1}(\eta_i) = \eta_i$.

The last four link functions in Table 15.1 are for binomial data, where Y_i represents the observed proportion of "successes" in n_i independent binary trials; thus, Y_i can take on any of the values $0, 1/n_i, 2/n_i, \ldots, (n_i - 1)/n_i, 1$. Recall from Chapter 15 that binomial data also encompass binary data, where all the observations represent $n_i = 1$ trial, and consequently Y_i is either 0 or 1. The expectation of the response $\mu_i = E(Y_i)$ is then the probability of success, which we symbolized by π_i in the previous chapter. The logit, probit, log-log, and complementary log-log links are graphed in Figure 15.1. In contrast to the logit and probit links (which, as we noted previously, are nearly indistinguishable once the variances of the underlying normal and logistic distributions are equated), the log-log and complementary log-log links approach the asymptotes of 0 and 1 asymmetrically.[2]

Beyond the general desire to select a link function that renders the regression of Y on the Xs linear, a promising link will remove restrictions on the range of the expected response. This is a familiar idea from the logit and probit models discussed in Chapter 14, where the object was to model the probability of "success," represented by μ_i in our current general notation. As a probability, μ_i is confined to the unit interval [0,1]. The logit and probit links map this interval to the entire real line, from $-\infty$ to $+\infty$. Similarly, if the response Y is a count, taking on only non-negative integer values, $0, 1, 2, \ldots$, and consequently μ_i is an expected count, which (though not necessarily an integer) is also non-negative, the log link maps μ_i to the whole real line. This is not to say that the choice of link function is entirely determined by the range of the response variable.

---

[2]Because the log-log link can be obtained from the complementary log-log link by exchanging the definitions of "success" and "failure," it is common for statistical software to provide only one of the two—typically, the complementary log-log link.

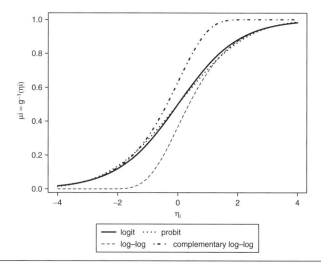

Figure 15.1   Logit, probit, log-log, and complementary log-log links for binomial data. The variances of the normal and logistic distributions have been equated to facilitate the comparison of the logit and probit links [by graphing the cumulative distribution function of $N(0, \pi^2/3)$ for the probit link].

A generalized linear model (or GLM) consists of three components:

1. A random component, specifying the conditional distribution of the response variable, Y_i (for the ith of n independently sampled observations), given the values of the explanatory variables in the model. In the initial formulation of GLMs, the distribution of Y_i was a member of an exponential family, such as the Gaussian, binomial, Poisson, gamma, or inverse-Gaussian families of distributions.

2. A linear predictor—that is a linear function of regressors,

$$\eta_i = \alpha + \beta_1 X_{i1} + \beta_2 X_{i2} + \cdots + \beta_k X_{ik}$$

3. A smooth and invertible linearizing link function $g(\cdot)$, which transforms the expectation of the response variable, $\mu_i = E(Y_i)$, to the linear predictor:

$$g(\mu_i) = \eta_i = \alpha + \beta_1 X_{i1} + \beta_2 X_{i2} + \cdots + \beta_k X_{ik}$$

A convenient property of distributions in the exponential families is that the conditional variance of Y_i is a function of its mean μ_i [say, $v(\mu_i)$] and, possibly, a *dispersion parameter* ϕ. The variance functions for the commonly used exponential families appear in Table 15.2. The conditional variance of the response in the Gaussian family is a constant, ϕ, which is simply alternative notation for what we previously termed the error variance, σ_ε^2. In the binomial and Poisson families, the dispersion parameter is set to the fixed value $\phi = 1$.

Table 15.2 also shows the range of variation of the response variable in each family, and the so-called *canonical* (or *"natural"*) *link function* associated with each family. The canonical link

Table 15.2   Canonical Link, Response Range, and Conditional
Variance Function for Exponential Families

Family	Canonical Link	Range of Y_i	$V(Y_i \mid \eta_i)$
Gaussian	Identity	$(-\infty, +\infty)$	ϕ
Binomial	Logit	$\dfrac{0,1,...,n_i}{n_i}$	$\dfrac{\mu_i(1 - \mu_i)}{n_i}$
Poisson	Log	$0,1,2,...$	μ_i
Gamma	Inverse	$(0,\infty)$	$\phi\mu_i^2$
Inverse-Gaussian	Inverse-square	$(0,\infty)$	$\phi\mu_i^3$

NOTE: ϕ is the dispersion parameter, η_i is the linear predictor, and μ_i is the expectation of Y_i (the response). In the binomial family, n_i is the number of trials.

simplifies the GLM,[3] but other link functions may be used as well. Indeed, one of the strengths of the GLM paradigm—in contrast to transformations of the response variable in linear regression—is that the choice of linearizing transformation is partly separated from the distribution of the response, and the same transformation does not have to both normalize the distribution of Y and make its regression on the Xs linear.[4] The specific links that may be used vary from one family to another and also—to a certain extent—from one software implementation of GLMs to another. For example, it would not be promising to use the identity, log, inverse, inverse-square, or square-root links with binomial data, nor would it be sensible to use the logit, probit, log-log, or complementary log-log link with nonbinomial data.

I assume that the reader is generally familiar with the Gaussian and binomial families and simply give their distributions here for reference. The Poisson, gamma, and inverse-Gaussian distributions are perhaps less familiar, and so I provide some more detail:[5]

- The Gaussian distribution with mean μ and variance σ^2 has density function

$$p(y) = \frac{1}{\sigma\sqrt{2\pi}} \exp\left[\frac{(y - \mu)^2}{2\sigma^2}\right] \tag{15.1}$$

- The binomial distribution for the proportion Y of successes in n independent binary trials with probability of success μ has probability function

$$p(y) = \binom{n}{ny}\mu^{ny}(1 - \mu)^{n(1-y)} \tag{15.2}$$

---

[3]This point is pursued in Section 15.3.

[4]There is also this more subtle difference: When we transform Y and regress the transformed response on the Xs, we are modeling the expectation of the transformed response,

$$E[g(Y_i)] = \alpha + \beta_1 x_{i1} + \beta_2 x_{i2} + \cdots + \beta_k x_{ik}$$

In a GLM, in contrast, we model the transformed expectation of the response,

$$g[E(Y_i)] = \alpha + \beta_1 x_{i1} + \beta_2 x_{i2} + \cdots + \beta_k x_{ik}$$

While similar in spirit, this is not quite the same thing when (as is true except for the identity link) the link function $g(\cdot)$ is nonlinear.

[5]The various distributions used in this chapter are described in a general context in Appendix D on probability and estimation.

Here, ny is the observed *number* of successes in the n trials, and $n(1 - y)$ is the number of failures; and

$$\binom{n}{ny} = \frac{n!}{(ny)![n(1 - y)]!}$$

is the binomial coefficient.

- The Poisson distributions are a discrete family with probability function indexed by the *rate parameter* $\mu > 0$:

$$p(y) = \mu^y \times \frac{e^{-\mu}}{y!} \text{ for } y = 0, 1, 2, \ldots$$

The expectation and variance of a Poisson random variable are both equal to μ. Poisson distributions for several values of the parameter μ are graphed in Figure 15.2. As we will see in Section 15.2, the Poisson distribution is useful for modeling count data. As μ increases, the Poisson distribution grows more symmetric and is eventually well approximated by a normal distribution.

- The gamma distributions are a continuous family with probability-density function indexed by the *scale parameter* $\omega > 0$ and *shape parameter* $\psi > 0$:

$$p(y) = \left(\frac{y}{\omega}\right)^{\psi-1} \times \frac{\exp\left(\frac{-y}{\omega}\right)}{\omega\Gamma(\psi)} \text{ for } y > 0 \tag{15.3}$$

where $\Gamma(\cdot)$ is the gamma function.[6] The expectation and variance of the gamma distribution are, respectively, $E(Y) = \omega\psi$ and $V(Y) = \omega^2\psi$. In the context of a generalized linear model, where, for the gamma family, $V(Y) = \phi\mu^2$ (recall Table 15.2 on page 382), the dispersion parameter is simply the inverse of the shape parameter, $\phi = 1/\psi$. As the names of the parameters suggest, the scale parameter in the gamma family influences the spread (and, incidentally, the location) but not the shape of the distribution, while the shape parameter controls the skewness of the distribution. Figure 15.3 shows gamma distributions for scale $\omega = 1$ and several values of the shape parameter ψ. (Altering the scale parameter would change only the labelling of the horizontal axis in the graph.) As the shape parameter gets larger, the distribution grows more symmetric. The gamma distribution is useful for modeling a positive continuous response variable, where the conditional variance of the response grows with its mean but where the *coefficient of variation* of the response, $SD(Y)/\mu$, is constant.

- The inverse-Gaussian distributions are another continuous family indexed by two parameters, μ and λ, with density function

$$p(y) = \sqrt{\frac{\lambda}{2\pi y^3}} \exp\left[-\frac{\lambda(y - \mu)^2}{2y\mu^2}\right] \text{ for } y > 0$$

The expectation and variance of Y are $E(Y) = \mu$ and $V(Y) = \mu^3/\lambda$. In the context of a GLM, where, for the inverse-Gaussian family, $V(Y) = \phi\mu^3$ (as recorded in Table 15.2

---

[6]* The gamma function is defined as

$$\Gamma(x) = \int_0^\infty e^{-z}z^{x-1}dz$$

and may be thought of as a continuous generalization of the factorial function in that when x is a non-negative integer, $x! = \Gamma(x + 1)$.

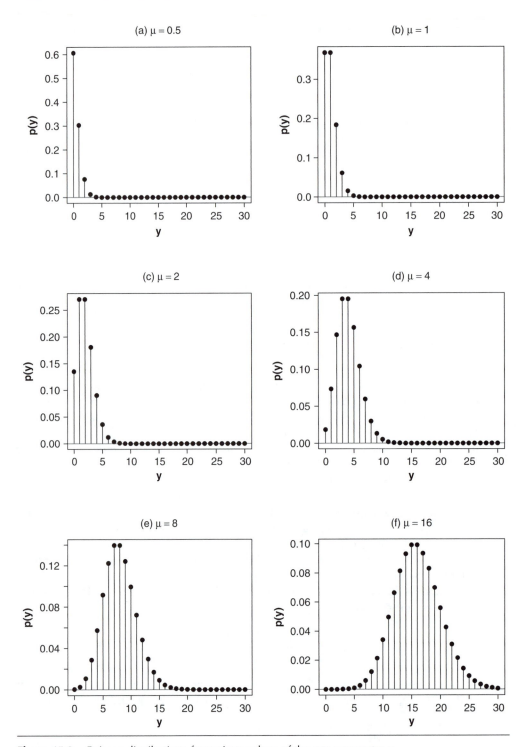

Figure 15.2   Poisson distributions for various values of the rate parameter μ.

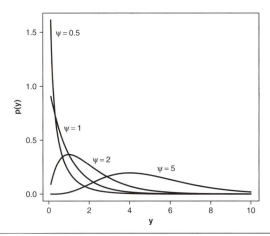

Figure 15.3   Several gamma distributions for scale $\omega = 1$ and various values of the shape parameter ψ.

on page 382), λ is the inverse of the dispersion parameter ϕ. Like the gamma distribution, therefore, the variance of the inverse-Gaussian distribution increases with its mean, but at a more rapid rate. Skewness also increases with the value of μ and decreases with λ. Figure 15.4 shows several inverse-Gaussian distributions.

A convenient property of distributions in the exponential families is that the conditional variance of Y_i is a function of its mean μ_i and, possibly, a dispersion parameter ϕ. In addition to the familiar Gaussian and binomial families (the latter for proportions), the Poisson family is useful for modeling count data, and the gamma and inverse-Gaussian families for modeling positive continuous data, where the conditional variance of Y increases with its expectation.

15.1.1   Estimating and Testing GLMs

GLMs are fit to data by the method of maximum likelihood, providing not only estimates of the regression coefficients but also estimated asymptotic (i.e., large-sample) standard errors of the coefficients.[7] To test the null hypothesis H_0: $\beta_j = \beta_j^{(0)}$ we can compute the Wald statistic $Z_0 = \left(B_j - \beta_j^{(0)}\right)/\text{SE}(B_j)$, where $\text{SE}(B_j)$ is the asymptotic standard error of the estimated coefficient B_j. Under the null hypothesis, Z_0 follows a standard normal distribution.[8]

As explained, some of the exponential families on which GLMs are based include an unknown dispersion parameter ϕ. Although this parameter can, in principle, be estimated by maximum likelihood as well, it is more common to use a "method of moments" estimator, which I will denote $\widetilde{\phi}$.[9]

---

[7]Details are provided in Section 15.3.2. The method of maximum likelihood is introduced in Appendix D on probability and estimation.

[8]Wald tests and F-tests of more general linear hypotheses are described in Section 15.3.3.

[9]Again, see Section 15.3.2.

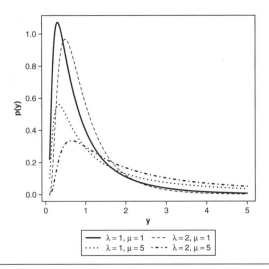

Figure 15.4   Inverse-Gaussian distributions for several combinations of values of the mean μ and inverse-dispersion λ.

As is familiar from the preceding chapter on logit and probit models, the ANOVA for linear models has a close analog in the *analysis of deviance* for GLMs. In the current more general context, the *residual deviance* for a GLM is

$$D_m \equiv 2(\log_e L_s - \log_e L_m)$$

where L_m is the maximized likelihood under the model in question and L_s is the maximized likelihood under a *saturated model*, which dedicates one parameter to each observation and consequently fits the data as closely as possible. The residual deviance is analogous to (and, indeed, is a generalization of) the residual sum of squares for a linear model.

In GLMs for which the dispersion parameter is fixed to 1 (i.e., binomial and Poisson GLMs), the likelihood-ratio test statistic is simply the difference in the residual deviances for nested models. Suppose that Model 0, with $k_0 + 1$ coefficients, is nested within Model 1, with $k_1 + 1$ coefficients (where, then, $k_0 < k_1$); most commonly, Model 0 would simply omit some of the regressors in model 1. We test the null hypothesis that the restrictions on Model 1 represented by Model 0 are correct by computing the likelihood-ratio test statistic

$$G_0^2 = D_0 - D_1$$

Under the hypothesis, G_0^2 is asymptotically distributed as chi-square with $k_1 - k_0$ degrees of freedom.

Likelihood-ratio tests can be turned around to provide confidence intervals for coefficients; as mentioned in Section 14.1.4 in connection with logit and probit models, tests and intervals based on the likelihood-ratio statistic tend to be more reliable than those based on the Wald statistic. For example, the 95% confidence interval for β_j includes all values β_j' for which the hypothesis H_0: $\beta_j = \beta_j'$ is acceptable at the .05 level—that is, all values of β_j' for which $2(\log_e L_1 - \log_e L_0) \leq \chi_{.05,1}^2 = 3.84$, where $\log_e L_1$ is the maximized log likelihood for the full model, and $\log_e L_0$ is the maximized log likelihood for a model in which β_j is constrained to the value β_j'. This procedure is computationally intensive because it required "profiling" the likelihood—refitting the model for various fixed values β_j' of β_j.

For GLMs in which there is a dispersion parameter to estimate (Gaussian, gamma, and inverse-Gaussian GLMs), we can instead compare nested models by an F-test,

$$F_0 = \frac{\dfrac{D_0 - D_1}{k_1 - k_0}}{\widetilde{\phi}}$$

where the estimated dispersion $\widetilde{\phi}$, analogous to the estimated error variance for a linear model, is taken from the *largest* model fit to the data (which is not necessarily Model 1). If the largest model has $k + 1$ coefficients, then, under the hypothesis that the restrictions on Model 1 represented by Model 0 are correct, F_0 follows an F-distribution with $k_1 - k_0$ and $n - k - 1$ degrees of freedom. Applied to a Gaussian GLM, this is simply the familiar incremental F-test. The residual deviance divided by the estimated dispersion, $D^* \equiv D/\widetilde{\phi}$, is called the *scaled deviance*.[10]

As we did for logit and probit models,[11] we can base a GLM analog of the squared multiple correlation on the residual deviance: Let D_0 be the residual deviance for the model including only the regression constant α—termed the *null deviance*—and D_1 the residual deviance for the model in question. Then,

$$R^2 \equiv 1 - \frac{D_1}{D_0}$$

represents the proportion of the null deviance accounted for by the model.

GLMs are fit to data by the method of maximum likelihood, providing not only estimates of the regression coefficients but also estimated asymptotic standard errors of the coefficients.

The ANOVA for linear models has an analog in the analysis of deviance for GLMs. The residual deviance for a GLM is $D_m = 2(\log_e L_s - \log_e L_m)$, where L_m is the maximized likelihood under the model in question and L_s is the maximized likelihood under a saturated model. The residual deviance is analogous to the residual sum of squares for a linear model.

In GLMs for which the dispersion parameter is fixed to 1 (binomial and Poisson GLMs), the likelihood-ratio test statistic is the difference in the residual deviances for nested models. For GLMs in which there is a dispersion parameter to estimate (Gaussian, gamma, and inverse-Gaussian GLMs), we can instead compare nested models by an incremental F-test.

15.2 Generalized Linear Models for Counts

The basic GLM for count data is the Poisson model with log link. Consider, by way of example, Michael Ornstein's data on interlocking directorates among 248 dominant Canadian firms, previously discussed in Chapters 3 and 4. The number of interlocks for each firm is the number of ties

---

[10]Usage is not entirely uniform here, and either of the residual deviance or the scaled deviance is often simply termed "the deviance."

[11]See Section 14.1.4.

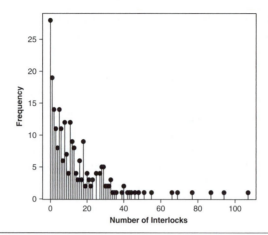

Figure 15.5   The distribution of number of interlocks among 248 dominant Canadian
corporations.

that a firm maintained by virtue of its board members and top executives also serving as board
members or executives of other firms in the data set. Ornstein was interested in the regression
of number of interlocks on other characteristics of the firms—specifically, on their assets (measured in billions of dollars), nation of control (Canada, the United States, the United Kingdom,
or another country), and the principal sector of operation of the firm (10 categories, including
banking, other financial institutions, heavy manufacturing, etc.).

Examining the distribution of number of interlocks (Figure 15.5) reveals that the variable
is highly positively skewed, and that there are many zero counts. Although the conditional
distribution of interlocks given the explanatory variables could differ from its marginal distribution, the extent to which the marginal distribution of interlocks departs from symmetry bodes ill for least-squares regression. Moreover, no transformation will spread out the
zeroes.[12]

The results of the Poisson regression of number of interlocks on assets, nation of control, and
sector are summarized in Table 15.3. I set the *United States* as the baseline category for nation of
control, and *Construction* as the baseline category for sector—these are the categories with the
smallest fitted numbers of interlocks controlling for the other variables in the regression, and the
dummy-regressor coefficients are therefore all positive.

The residual deviance for this model is $D(\text{Assets, Nation, Sector}) = 1887.402$ on $n - k - 1 =$
$248 - 13 - 1 = 234$ degrees of freedom. Deleting each explanatory variable in turn from the
model produces the following residual deviances and degrees of freedom:

Explanatory Variables	Residual Deviance	df
Nation, Sector	2278.298	235
Assets, Sector	2216.345	237
Assets, Nation	2248.861	243

[12]Ornstein (1976) in fact performed a linear least-squares regression for these data, though one with a slightly different
specification from that given here. He cannot be faulted for having done so, however, inasmuch as Poisson regression
models—and, with the exception of loglinear models for contingency tables, other specialized models for counts—were
not typically in sociologists' statistical toolkit at the time.

Table 15.3   Estimated Coefficients for the Poisson Regression of Number
of Interlocks on Assets, Nation of Control, and Sector, for
Ornstein's Canadian Interlocking-Directorate Data

Coefficient	Estimate	Standard Error
Constant	0.8791	0.2101
Assets	0.02085	0.00120
Nation of Control (baseline: United States)		
Canada	0.8259	0.0490
Other	0.6627	0.0755
United Kingdom	0.2488	0.0919
Sector (Baseline: Construction)		
Wood and paper	1.331	0.213
Transport	1.297	0.214
Other financial	1.297	0.211
Mining, metals	1.241	0.209
Holding companies	0.8280	0.2329
Merchandising	0.7973	0.2182
Heavy manufacturing	0.6722	0.2133
Agriculture, food, light industry	0.6196	0.2120
Banking	0.2104	0.2537

Taking differences between these deviances and the residual deviance for the full model yields
the following analysis-of-deviance table:

Source	G_0^2	df	p
Assets	390.90	1	$\ll$.0001
Nation	328.94	3	$\ll$.0001
Sector	361.46	9	$\ll$.0001

All the terms in the model are therefore highly statistically significant.

Because the model uses the log link, we can interpret the exponentiated coefficients (i.e., the e^{B_j}) as multiplicative effects on the expected number of interlocks. Thus, for example, holding nation of control and sector constant, increasing assets by 1 billion dollars (the unit of the assets variable) multiplies the estimated expected number of interlocks by $e^{0.02085} = 1.021$—that is, an increase of just over 2%. Similarly, the estimated expected number of interlocks is $e^{0.8259} = 2.283$ times as high in a Canadian-controlled firm as in a comparable U.S.-controlled firm.

As mentioned, the residual deviance for the full model fit to Ornstein's data is $D_1 = 1887.402$; the deviance for a model fitting only the constant (i.e., the null deviance) is $D_0 = 3737.010$. Consequently, $R^2 = 1 - 1887.402/3737.010 = .495$, revealing that the model accounts for nearly half the deviance in number of interlocks.

The Poisson-regression model is a nonlinear model for the expected response, and I therefore find it generally simpler to interpret the model graphically using effect displays than to examine the estimated coefficients directly. The principles of construction of effect displays for GLMs are essentially the same as for linear models and for logit and probit models:[13] We usually construct one display for each high-order term in the model, allowing the explanatory variables in that

---

[13] See Section 15.3.4 for details.

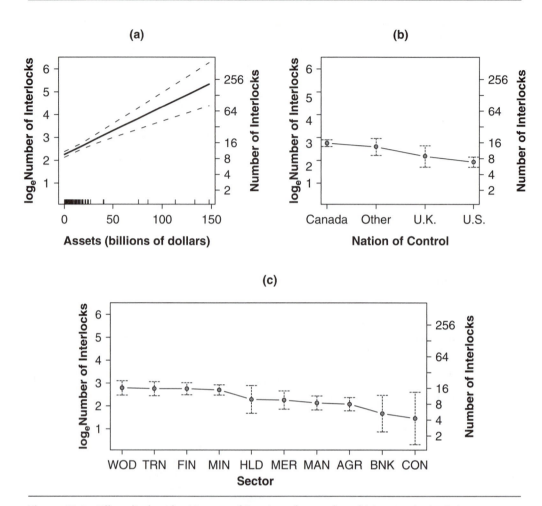

Figure 15.6   Effect displays for (a) assets, (b) nation of control, and (c) sector in the Poisson regression for Ornstein's interlocking-directorate data. The broken lines and error bars give 95% confidence intervals around the fitted effects (computed using the quasi-Poisson model described below). A "rug-plot" at the bottom of panel (a) shows the distribution of assets.

term to range over their values, while holding other explanatory variables in the model to typical values. In a GLM, it is advantageous to plot effects on the scale of the estimated linear predictor, $\widehat{\eta}$, a procedure that preserves the linear structure of the model. In a Poisson model with the log link, the linear predictor is on the log-count scale. We can, however, make the display easier to interpret by relabeling the vertical axis in the scale of the expected response, $\widehat{\mu}$, most informatively by providing a second vertical axis on the right-hand side of the plot. For a Poisson model, the expected response is a count.

Effect displays for the terms in Ornstein's Poisson regression are shown in Figure 15.6. This model has an especially simple structure because each high-order term is a main effect—there are no interactions in the model. The effect display for assets shows a one-dimensional scatterplot (a "rug-plot") for this variable at the bottom of the graph, revealing that the distribution of assets is highly skewed to the right. Skewness produces some high-leverage observations and suggests the possibility of a nonlinear effect for assets, points that I pursue later in the chapter.[14]

15.2.1   Models for Overdispersed Count Data

The residual deviance for the Poisson regression model fit to the interlocking-directorate data, $D = 1887.4$, is much larger than the 234 residual degrees of freedom for the model. If the Poisson model fits the data reasonably, we would expect the residual deviance to be roughly equal to the residual degrees of freedom.[15] That the residual deviance is so large suggests that the conditional variation of the expected number of interlocks exceeds the variation of a Poisson-distributed variable, for which the variance equals the mean. This common occurrence in the analysis of count data is termed *overdispersion*.[16] Indeed, overdispersion is so common in regression models for count data, and its consequences are potentially so severe, that models such as the quasi-Poisson and negative-binomial GLMs discussed in this section should be employed as a matter of course.

The Quasi-Poisson Model

A simple remedy for overdispersed count data is to introduce a dispersion parameter into the Poisson model, so that the conditional variance of the response is now $V(Y_i|\eta_i) = \phi\mu_i$. If $\phi > 1$, therefore, the conditional variance of Y increases more rapidly than its mean. There is no exponential family corresponding to this specification, and the resulting GLM does not imply a specific probability distribution for the response variable. Rather, the model specifies the conditional mean and variance of Y_i directly. Because the model does not give a probability distribution for Y_i, it cannot be estimated by maximum likelihood. Nevertheless, the usual procedure for maximum-likelihood estimation of a GLM yields the so-called *quasi-likelihood* estimators of the regression coefficients, which share many of the properties of maximum-likelihood estimators.[17]

As it turns out, the quasi-likelihood estimates of the regression coefficients are identical to the ML estimates for the Poisson model. The estimated coefficient standard errors differ, however: If $\widetilde{\phi}$ is the estimated dispersion for the model, then the coefficient standard errors for the *quasi-Poisson model* are $\widetilde{\phi}^{1/2}$ times those for the Poisson model. In the event of overdispersion, therefore, where $\widetilde{\phi} > 1$, the effect of introducing a dispersion parameter and obtaining quasi-likelihood estimates is (realistically) to inflate the coefficient standard errors. Likewise, F-tests for terms in the model will reflect the estimated dispersion parameter, producing smaller test statistics and larger p-values.

As explained in the following section, we use a method-of-moments estimator for the dispersion parameter. In the quasi-Poisson model, the dispersion estimator takes the form

$$\widetilde{\phi} = \frac{1}{n - k - 1} \sum \frac{(Y_i - \widehat{\mu}_i)^2}{\widehat{\mu}_i}$$

---

[14]See Section 15.4 on diagnostics for GLMs.

[15]That is, the ratio of the residual deviance to degrees of freedom can be taken as an estimate of the dispersion parameter ϕ, which, in a Poisson model, is fixed to 1. It should be noted, however, that this deviance-based estimator of the dispersion can perform poorly. A generally preferable "method of moments" estimator is given in Section 15.3.

[16]Although it is much less common, it is also possible for count data to be *underdispersed*—that is, for the conditional variation of the response to be *less than* the mean. The remedy for underdispsered count data is the same as for overdispersed data; for example, we can fit a quasi-Poisson model with a dispersion parameter, as described immediately below.

[17]See Section 15.3.2.

where $\widehat{\mu}_i = g^{-1}(\widehat{\eta}_i)$ is the fitted expectation of Y_i. Applied to Ornstein's interlocking-directorate regression, for example, we get $\widetilde{\phi} = 7.9435$, and, therefore, the standard errors of the regression coefficients for the Poisson model in Table 15.3 are each multiplied by $\sqrt{7.9435} = 2.818$.

I note in passing that there is a similar *quasi-binomial model* for over-dispersed proportions, replacing the fixed dispersion parameter of 1 in the binomial distribution with a dispersion parameter ϕ to be estimated from the data. Overdispersed binomial data can arise, for example, when different individuals who share the same values of the explanatory variables nevertheless differ in their probability μ of success, a situation that is termed *unmodelled heterogeneity*. Similarly, overdispersion can occur when binomial observations are not independent, as required by the binomial distribution—for example, when each binomial observation is for related individuals, such as members of a family.

The Negative-Binomial Model

There are several routes to models for counts based on the negative-binomial distribution (see, e.g., Long, 1997, sect. 8.3; McCullagh & Nelder, 1989, sect. 6.2.3). One approach (following McCullagh & Nelder, 1989, p. 233) is to adopt a Poisson model for the count Y_i but to suppose that the expected count μ_i^* is itself an unobservable random variable that is gamma-distributed with mean μ_i and constant scale parameter ω (implying that the the gamma shape parameter is $\psi_i = \mu_i/\omega$ [18]). Then the observed count Y_i follows a *negative-binomial distribution*,[19]

$$p(y_i) = \frac{\Gamma(y_i + \omega)}{y!\Gamma(\omega)} \times \frac{\mu_i^{y_i}\omega^\omega}{(\mu_i + \omega)^{\mu_i+\omega}} \tag{15.4}$$

with expected value $E(Y_i) = \mu_i$ and variance $V(Y_i) = \mu_i + \mu_i^2/\omega$. Unless the parameter ω is large, therefore, the variance of Y increases more rapidly with the mean than the variance of a Poisson variable. Making the expected value of Y_i a random variable incorporates additional variation among observed counts for observations that share the same values of the explanatory variables and consequently have the same linear predictor η_i.

With the gamma scale parameter ω fixed to a known value, the negative-binomial distribution is an exponential family (in the sense of Equation 15.15 in Section 15.3.1), and a GLM based on this distribution can be fit by iterated weighted least squares (as developed in the next section). If instead—and is typically the case—the value of ω is unknown, and must therefore be estimated from the data, standard methods for GLMs based on exponential families do not apply. We can, however, obtain estimates of both the regression coefficients and ω by the method of maximum likelihood. Applied to Ornstein's interlocking-directorate regression, and using the log link, the negative-binomial GLM produces results very similar to those of the quasi-Poisson model (as the reader may wish to verify). The estimated scale parameter for the negative-binomial model is $\widehat{\omega} = 1.312$, with standard error $\text{SE}(\widehat{\omega}) = 0.143$; we have, therefore, strong evidence that the conditional variance of the number of interlocks increases more rapidly than its expected value.[20]

Zero-Inflated Poisson Regression

A particular kind of overdispersion obtains when there are more zeroes in the data than is consistent with a Poisson (or negative-binomial) distribution, a situation that can arise when only certain members of the population are "at risk" of a nonzero count. Imagine, for example, that

---

[18] See Equation 15.3 on page 383.
[19] A simpler form of the negative-binomial distribution is given in Appendix D on probability and estimation.
[20] See Exercise 15.1 for a test of overdispersion based on the negative-binomial GLM.

we are interested in modeling the number of children born to a woman. We might expect that this number is a partial function of such explanatory variables as marital status, age, ethnicity, religion, and contraceptive use. It is also likely, however, that some women (or their partners) are infertile and are distinct from fertile women who, though at risk for bearing children, happen to have none. If we knew which women are infertile, we could simply exclude them from the analysis, but let us suppose that this is not the case. To reiterate, there are two sources of zeroes in the data that cannot be perfectly distinguished: women who cannot bear children and those who can but have none.

Several statistical models have been proposed for count data with an excess of zeroes, including the *zero-inflated Poisson regression* (or *ZIP*) *model*, due to Lambert (1992). The ZIP model consists of two components: (1) A binary logistic-regression model for membership in the *latent class* of individuals for whom the response variable is necessarily 0 (e.g., infertile individuals)[21] and (2) a Poisson-regression model for the latent class of individuals for whom the response may be 0 or a positive count (e.g., fertile women).[22]

Let π_i represent the probability that the response Y_i for the ith individual is necessarily 0. Then

$$\log_e \frac{\pi_i}{1 - \pi_i} = \gamma_0 + \gamma_1 z_{i1} + \gamma_2 z_{i2} + \cdots + \gamma_p z_{ip} \tag{15.5}$$

where the z_{ij} are regressors for predicting membership in the first latent class; and

$$\log_e \mu_i = \alpha + \beta_1 x_{i1} + \beta_2 x_{i2} + \cdots + \beta_k x_{ik} \tag{15.6}$$

$$p(y_i | x_1, \ldots, x_k) = \frac{\mu_i^{y_i} e^{-\mu_i}}{y_i!} \text{ for } y_i = 0, 1, 2, \ldots$$

where $\mu_i \equiv E(Y_i)$ is the expected count for an individual in the second latent class, and the x_{ij} are regressors for the Poisson submodel. In applications, the two sets of regressors—the Xs and the Zs—are often the same, but this is not necessarily the case. Indeed, a particularly simple special case arises when the logistic submodel is $\log_e \pi_i/(1 - \pi_i) = \gamma_0$, a constant, implying that the probability of membership in the first latent class is identical for all observations.

The probability of observing a 0 count is

$$p(0) \equiv \Pr(Y_i = 0) = \pi_i + (1 - \pi_i)e^{-\mu_i}$$

and the probability of observing any particular nonzero count y_i is

$$p(y_i) = (1 - \pi_i) \times \frac{\mu_i^{y_i} e^{-\mu_i}}{y_i!}$$

The conditional expectation and variance of Y_i are

$$E(Y_i) = (1 - \pi_i)\mu_i$$
$$V(Y_i) = (1 - \pi_i)\mu_i(1 + \pi_i \mu_i)$$

with $V(Y_i) > E(Y_i)$ for $\pi_i > 0$ [unlike a pure Poisson distribution, for which $V(Y_i) = E(Y_i) = \mu_i$].[23]

---

[21] See Section 14.1 for a discussion of logistic regression.

[22] Although this form of the zero-inflated count model is the most common, Lambert (1992) also suggested the use of other binary GLMs for membership in the zero latent class (i.e., probit, log-log, and complementary log-log models) and the alternative use of the negative-binomial distribution for the count submodel (see Exercise 15.2).

[23] See Exercise 15.2.

*Estimation of the ZIP model would be simple if we knew to which latent class each observation belongs, but, as I have pointed out, that is not true. Instead, we must maximize the somewhat more complex combined log likelihood for the two components of the ZIP model:[24]

$$\log_e L(\beta, \gamma) = \sum_{y_i=0} \log_e \left\{ \exp\left(\mathbf{z}_i'\gamma\right) + \exp\left[-\exp(\mathbf{x}_i'\beta)\right]\right\} + \sum_{y_i>0} \left[y_i \mathbf{x}_i'\beta - \exp(\mathbf{x}_i'\beta)\right] \quad (15.7)$$

$$- \sum_{i=1}^{n} \log_e \left[1 + \exp(\mathbf{z}_i'\gamma)\right] - \sum_{y_i>0} \log_e(y_i!)$$

where $\mathbf{z}_i' \equiv [1, z_{i1}, \ldots, z_{ip}]$, $\mathbf{x}_i' \equiv [1, x_{i1}, \ldots, x_{ik}]$, $\gamma \equiv [\gamma_0, \gamma_1, \ldots, \gamma_p]'$, and $\beta \equiv [\alpha, \beta_1, \ldots, \beta_k]'$.

The basic GLM for count data is the Poisson model with log link. Frequently, however, when the response variable is a count, its conditional variance increases more rapidly than its mean, producing a condition termed overdispersion, and invalidating the use of the Poisson distribution. The quasi-Poisson GLM adds a dispersion parameter to handle overdispersed count data; this model can be estimated by the method of quasi-likelihood. A similar model is based on the negative-binomial distribution, which is not an exponential family. Negative-binomial GLMs can nevertheless be estimated by maximum likelihood. The zero-inflated Poisson regression model may be appropriate when there are more zeroes in the data than is consistent with a Poisson distribution.

15.2.2   Loglinear Models for Contingency Tables

The joint distribution of several categorical variables defines a *contingency table*. As discussed in the preceding chapter,[25] if one of the variables in a contingency table is treated as the response variable, we can fit a logit or probit model (that is, for a dichotomous response, a binomial GLM) to the table. *Loglinear models*, in contrast, which are models for the associations among the variables in a contingency table, treat the variables symmetrically—they do not distinguish one variable as the response. There is, however, a relationship between loglinear models and logit models that I will develop later in this section. As we will see as well, loglinear models have the formal structure of two-way and higher-way ANOVA models[26] and can be fit to data by Poisson regression.

Loglinear models for contingency tables have many specialized applications in the social sciences—for example to "square" tables, such as mobility tables, where the variables in the table have the same categories. The treatment of loglinear models in this section merely scratches the surface.[27]

---

[24] See Exercise 15.2.
[25] See Section 14.3.
[26] See Sections 8.2 and 8.3.
[27] More extensive accounts are available in many sources, including Agresti (2002), Fienberg (1980), and Powers and Xie (2000).

Table 15.4   Voter Turnout by Intensity of Partisan Preference, for the 1956 U.S. Presidential Election

	Voter Turnout		
Intensity of Preference	*Voted*	*Did Not Vote*	*Total*
Weak	305	126	431
Medium	405	125	530
Strong	265	49	314
Total	975	300	1275

Table 15.5   General Two-Way Frequency Table

	Variable C				
Variable R	1	2	$\cdots$	c	*Total*
1	Y_{11}	Y_{12}	$\cdots$	Y_{1c}	Y_{1+}
2	Y_{21}	Y_{22}	$\cdots$	Y_{2c}	Y_{2+}
$\vdots$	$\vdots$	$\vdots$		$\vdots$	$\vdots$
r	Y_{r1}	Y_{r2}	$\cdots$	Y_{rc}	Y_{r+}
Total	Y_{+1}	Y_{+2}	$\cdots$	Y_{+c}	n

Two-Way Tables

I will examine contingency tables for two variables in some detail, for this is the simplest case, and the key results that I establish here extend straightforwardly to tables of higher dimension. Consider the illustrative *two-way table* shown in Table 15.4, constructed from data reported in the *American Voter* (Campbell, Converse, Miller, & Stokes, 1960), introduced in the previous chapter.[28] The table relates intensity of partisan preference to voting turnout in the 1956 U.S. presidential election. To anticipate my analysis, the data indicate that voting turnout is positively associated with intensity of partisan preference.

More generally, two categorical variables with r and c categories, respectively, define an $r \times c$ contingency table, as shown in Table 15.5, where Y_{ij} is the *observed frequency count* in the i, j th cell of the table. I use a "+" to represent summation over a subscript; thus $Y_{i+} \equiv \sum_{j=1}^{c} Y_{ij}$ is the *marginal frequency* in the ith row; $Y_{+j} \equiv \sum_{i=1}^{r} Y_{ij}$ is the marginal frequency in the jth column; and $n = Y_{++} \equiv \sum_{i=1}^{r} \sum_{j=1}^{c} Y_{ij}$ is the number of observations in the sample.

I assume that the n observations in Table 15.5 are independently sampled from a population with proportion π_{ij} in cell i, j, and therefore that the probability of sampling an individual observation in this cell is π_{ij}. Marginal probability distributions π_{i+} and π_{+j} may be defined as above; note that $\pi_{++} = 1$. If the row and column variables are statistically independent in the population, then the joint probability π_{ij} is the product of the marginal probabilities for all i and j: $\pi_{ij} = \pi_{i+}\pi_{+j}$.

Because the observed frequencies Y_{ij} result from drawing a random sample, they are random variables that generally take on different values in different samples. The *expected frequency* in

---

[28]Table 14.9 (page 371) examined the relationship of voter turnout to intensity of partisan preference *and* perceived closeness of the election. The current example collapses the table for these three variables over the categories of perceived closeness to examine the *marginal table* for turnout and preference. I return below to the analysis of the full three-way table.

cell i, j is $\mu_{ij} \equiv E(Y_{ij}) = n\pi_{ij}$. If the variables are independent, then we have $\mu_{ij} = n\pi_{i+}\pi_{+j}$. Moreover, because $\mu_{i+} = \sum_{j=1}^{c} n\pi_{ij} = n\pi_{i+}$ and $\mu_{+j} = \sum_{i=1}^{r} n\pi_{ij} = n\pi_{+j}$, we may write $\mu_{ij} = \mu_{i+}\mu_{+j}/n$. Taking the log of both sides of this last equation produces

$$\eta_{ij} \equiv \log_e \mu_{ij} = \log_e \mu_{i+} + \log_e \mu_{+j} - \log_e n \tag{15.8}$$

That is, under independence, the log expected frequencies η_{ij} depend additively on the logs of the row marginal expected frequencies, the column marginal expected frequencies, and the sample size. As Fienberg (1980, pp. 13–14) points out, Equation 15.8 is reminiscent of a main-effects two-way ANOVA model, where $-\log_e n$ plays the role of the constant, $\log_e \mu_{i+}$ and $\log_e \mu_{+j}$ are analogous to "main-effect" parameters, and η_{ij} appears in place of the response-variable mean. If we impose ANOVA-like sigma constraints on the model, we may reparametrize Equation 15.8 as follows:

$$\eta_{ij} = \mu + \alpha_i + \beta_j \tag{15.9}$$

where $\alpha_+ \equiv \sum \alpha_i = 0$ and $\beta_+ \equiv \sum \beta_j = 0$. Equation 15.9 is the *loglinear model for independence* in the two-way table. Solving for the parameters of the model, we obtain

$$\mu = \frac{\eta_{++}}{rc} \tag{15.10}$$

$$\alpha_i = \frac{\eta_{i+}}{c} - \mu$$

$$\beta_j = \frac{\eta_{+j}}{r} - \mu$$

It is important to stress that although the loglinear model is *formally* similar to an ANOVA model, the *meaning* of the two models differs importantly: In analysis of variance, the α_i and β_j are main-effect parameters, specifying the partial relationship of the (quantitative) response variable to each explanatory variable. The loglinear model in Equation 15.9, in contrast, does not distinguish a response variable, and, because it is a model for independence, specifies that the row and column variables in the contingency table are *unrelated*; for this model, the α_i and β_j merely express the relationship of the log expected cell frequencies to the row and column marginals. The model for independence describes rc expected frequencies in terms of

$$1 + (r - 1) + (c - 1) = r + c - 1$$

independent parameters.

By analogy to the two-way ANOVA model, we can add parameters to extend the loglinear model to data for which the row and column classifications are not independent in the population but rather are related in an arbitrary manner:

$$\eta_{ij} = \mu + \alpha_i + \beta_j + \gamma_{ij} \tag{15.11}$$

where $\alpha_+ = \beta_+ = \gamma_{i+} = \gamma_{+j} = 0$ for all i and j. As before, we may write the parameters of the model in terms of the log expected counts η_{ij}. Indeed, the solution for μ, α_i, and β_j are the same as in Equation 15.10, and

$$\gamma_{ij} = \eta_{ij} - \mu - \alpha_i - \beta_j$$

By analogy to the ANOVA model, the γ_{ij} in the loglinear model are often called "interactions," but this usage is potentially confusing. I will therefore instead refer to the γ_{ij} as *association parameters* because they represent deviations from independence.

Under the model in Equation 15.11, called the *saturated model* for the two-way table, the number of independent parameters is equal to the number of cells in the table,

$$1 + (r - 1) + (c - 1) + (r - 1)(c - 1) = rc$$

The model is therefore capable of capturing *any* pattern of association in a two-way table.

Remarkably, maximum-likelihood estimates for the parameters of a loglinear model (that is, in the present case, either the model for independence in Equation 15.9 or the saturated model in Equation 15.11) may be obtained by treating the observed cell counts Y_{ij} as the response variable in a Poisson GLM; the log expected counts η_{ij} are then just the linear predictor for the GLM, as the notation suggests.[29]

The constraint that all $\gamma_{ij} = 0$ imposed by the model of independence can be tested by a likelihood-ratio test, contrasting the model of independence (Equation 15.9) with the more general model (Equation 15.11). Because the latter is a saturated model, its residual deviance is necessarily 0, and the likelihood-ratio statistic for the hypothesis of independence H_0: $\gamma_{ij} = 0$ is simply the residual deviance for the independence model, which has $(r - 1)(c - 1)$ residual degrees of freedom. Applied to the illustrative two-way table for the *American Voter* data, we get $G_0^2 = 19.428$ with $(3 - 1)(2 - 1) = 2$ degrees of freedom, for which $p < .0001$, suggesting that there is strong evidence that intensity of preference and turnout are related.[30]

Maximum-likelihood estimates of the parameters of the saturated loglinear model are shown in Table 15.6. It is clear from the estimated association parameters $\widehat{\gamma}_{ij}$ that turning out to vote, $j = 1$, increases with partisan preference (and, of course, that *not* turning out to vote, $j = 2$, decreases with preference).

Three-Way Tables

The saturated loglinear model for a three-way ($a \times b \times c$) table for variables A, B, and C is defined in analogy to the three-way ANOVA model, although, as in the case of two-way tables, the meaning of the parameters is different:

$$\eta_{ijk} = \mu + \alpha_{A(i)} + \alpha_{B(j)} + \alpha_{C(k)} + \alpha_{AB(ij)} + \alpha_{AC(ik)} + \alpha_{BC(jk)} + \alpha_{ABC(ijk)} \qquad (15.12)$$

---

[29]* The reason that this result is remarkable is that a direct route to a likelihood function for the loglinear model leads to the multinomial distribution (discussed in Appendix D on probability and estimation), not to the Poisson distribution. That is, selecting n independent observations from a population characterized by cell probabilities π_{ij} results in cell counts following the multinomial distribution,

$$p(y_{11}, \ldots, y_{rc}) = \frac{n!}{\prod\limits_{i=1}^{r}\prod\limits_{j=1}^{c} y_{ij}!} \prod_{i=1}^{r}\prod_{j=1}^{c} \pi_{ij}^{n_{ij}}$$

$$= \frac{n!}{\prod\limits_{i=1}^{r}\prod\limits_{j=1}^{c} y_{ij}!} \prod_{i=1}^{r}\prod_{j=1}^{c} \left(\frac{\mu_{ij}}{n}\right)^{n_{ij}}$$

Noting that the expected counts μ_{ij} are functions of the parameters of the loglinear model leads to the multinomial likelihood function for the model. It turns out that maximizing this multinomial likelihood is equivalent to maximizing the likelihood for the Poisson GLM described in the text (see, e.g., Fienberg, 1980, app. II).

[30]This test is very similar to the usual Pearson chi-square test for independence in a two-way table. See Exercise 15.3 for details, and for an alternative formula for calculating the likelihood-ratio test statistic G_0^2 directly from the observed frequencies, Y_{ij}, and estimated expected frequencies under independence, $\widehat{\mu}_{ij}$.

Table 15.6   Estimated Parameters for the Saturated
Loglinear Model Fit in Table 15.4

i	$\widehat{\gamma}_{ij}$		$\widehat{\alpha}_i$
	$j=1$	$j=2$	
1	−0.183	0.183	0.135
2	−0.037	0.037	0.273
3	0.219	−0.219	−0.408
$\widehat{\beta}_j$	0.625	−0.625	$\widehat{\mu} = 5.143$

with sigma constraints specifying that each set of parameters sums to zero over each subscript; for example $\alpha_{1(+)} = \alpha_{12(i+)} = \alpha_{123(ij+)} = 0$. Given these constraints, we may solve for the parameters in terms of the log expected counts, with the solution following the usual ANOVA pattern; for example,

$$\mu = \frac{\eta_{+++}}{abc}$$
$$\alpha_{A(i)} = \frac{\eta_{i++}}{bc} - \mu$$
$$\alpha_{AB(ij)} = \frac{\eta_{ij+}}{c} - \mu - \alpha_{A(i)} - \alpha_{B(j)}$$
$$\alpha_{ABC(ijk)} = \eta_{ijk} - \mu - \alpha_{A(i)} - \alpha_{B(j)} - \alpha_{C(k)} - \alpha_{AB(ij)} - \alpha_{AC(ik)} - \alpha_{BC(jk)}$$

The presence of the three-way term α_{ABC} in the model implies that the relationship between any pair of variables (say, A and B) depends on the category of the third variable (say, C).[31]

Other loglinear models are defined by suppressing certain terms in the saturated model, that is, by setting parameters to zero. In specifying a restricted loglinear model, we will be guided by the principle of marginality:[32] Whenever a high-order term is included in the model, its lower-order relatives are included as well. Loglinear models of this type are often called *hierarchical*. Nonhierarchical loglinear models may be suitable for special applications, but they are not sensible in general (see Fienberg, 1980). According to the principle of marginality, for example, if α_{AB} appears in the model, so do α_A and α_B.

- If we set all of $\alpha_{ABC}, \alpha_{AB}, \alpha_{AC}$, and α_{BC} to zero, we produce the model of mutual independence, implying that the variables in the three-way table are completely unrelated:
$$\eta_{ijk} = \mu + \alpha_{A(i)} + \alpha_{B(j)} + \alpha_{C(k)}$$

- Setting $\alpha_{ABC}, \alpha_{AC}$, and α_{BC} to zero yields the model
$$\eta_{ijk} = \mu + \alpha_{A(i)} + \alpha_{B(j)} + \alpha_{C(k)} + \alpha_{AB(ij)}$$

which specifies (1) that variables A and B are related, controlling for (i.e., within categories of) variable C; (2) that this partial relationship is constant across the categories of variable C; and (3) that variable C is independent of variables A and B taken jointly—that is, if we form the two-way table with rows given by combinations of categories of A and B, and columns given by C, the two variables in this table are independent. Note that there are two other models of this sort: one in which α_{AC} is nonzero and another in which α_{BC} is nonzero.

---

[31] Here and below I use the shorthand notation α_{ABC} to represent the whole set of $\alpha_{ABC(ijk)}$, and similarly for the other terms in the model.

[32] See Section 7.3.2.

Table 15.7   Voter Turnout by Perceived Closeness of the Election and Intensity of Partisan Preference, for the 1956 U.S. Presidential Election

		(C) Turnout	
(A) Perceived Closeness	(B) Intensity of Preference	Voted	Did Not Vote
One-sided	Weak	91	39
	Medium	121	49
	Strong	64	24
Close	Weak	214	87
	Medium	284	76
	Strong	201	25

- A third type of model has *two* nonzero two-way terms; for example, setting α_{ABC} and α_{BC} to zero, we obtain

$$\eta_{ijk} = \mu + \alpha_{A(i)} + \alpha_{B(j)} + \alpha_{C(k)} + \alpha_{AB(ij)} + \alpha_{AC(ik)}$$

This model implies that (1) variables A and B have a constant partial relationship across the categories of variable C; (2) variables A and C have a constant partial relationship across the categories of variable B; and (3) variables B and C are independent within categories of variable A. Again, there are two other models of this type.

- Finally, consider the model that sets only the three-way term α_{ABC} to zero:

$$\eta_{ijk} = \mu + \alpha_{A(i)} + \alpha_{B(j)} + \alpha_{C(k)} + \alpha_{AB(ij)} + \alpha_{AC(ik)} + \alpha_{BC(jk)}$$

This model specifies that each pair of variables (e.g., A and B) has a constant partial association across the categories of the remaining variable (e.g., C).

These descriptions are relatively complicated because the loglinear models are models of association among variables. As we will see presently, however, if one of the variables in a table is taken as the response variable, then the loglinear model is equivalent to a logit model with a simpler interpretation.

Table 15.7 shows a three-way table cross-classifying voter turnout by perceived closeness of the election and intensity of partisan preference, elaborating the two-way table for the *American Voter* data presented earlier in Table 15.4.[33] I have fit all hierarchical loglinear models to this three-way table, displaying the results in Table 15.8. Here I employ a compact notation for the high-order terms in each fitted model: For example, AB represents the two-way term α_{AB} and implies that the lower-order relatives of this term—μ, α_A, and α_B—are also in the model. As in the loglinear model for a two-way table, the saturated model has a residual deviance of 0, and consequently the likelihood-ratio statistic to test any model against the saturated model (within which all of the other models are nested, and which is the last model shown) is simply the residual deviance for the unsaturated model.

The first model in Table 15.8 is the model of complete independence, and it fits the data very poorly. At the other end, the model with high-order terms AB, AC, and BC, which may be used to test the hypothesis of no three-way association, H_0: all $\alpha_{ABC(ijk)} = 0$, also has a statistically significant likelihood-ratio test statistic (though not overwhelmingly so), suggesting that the association between any pair of variables in the contingency tables varies over the levels of the remaining variable.

---

[33]This table was also discussed in Chapter 14 (see Table 14.9 on page 371).

Table 15.8 Hierarchical Loglinear Models Fit to Table 15.7

High-Order Terms	Residual Degrees of Freedom General	Table 15.7	G_0^2	p
A,B,C	$(a-1)(b-1)+(a-1)(c-1)(b-1)(c-1)$ $+(a-1)(b-1)(c-1)$	7	36.39	$\ll.0001$
AB,C	$(a-1)(c-1)+(b-1)(c-1)+(a-1)(b-1)(c-1)$	5	34.83	$\ll.0001$
AC,B	$(a-1)(b-1)+(b-1)(c-1)+(a-1)(b-1)(c-1)$	5	16.96	.0046
A,BC	$(a-1)(b-1)+(a-1)(c-1)+(a-1)(b-1)(c-1)$	6	27.78	.0001
AB,AC	$(b-1)(c-1)+(a-1)(b-1)(c-1)$	3	15.40	.0015
AB,BC	$(a-1)(c-1)+(a-1)(b-1)(c-1)$	4	26.22	<.0001
AC,BC	$(a-1)(b-1)+(a-1)(b-1)(c-1)$	4	8.35	.079
AB,AC,BC	$(a-1)(b-1)(c-1)$	2	7.12	.028
ABC	0	0	0.0	—

NOTE: The column labeled G_0^2 is the likelihood-ratio statistic for testing each model against the saturated model.

This approach generalizes to contingency tables of any dimension, although the interpretation of high-order association terms can become complicated.

Loglinear Models and Logit Models

As I explained, the loglinear model for a contingency table is a model for association among the variables in the table; the variables are treated symmetrically, and none is distinguished as the response variable. When one of the variables in a contingency table is regarded as the response, however, the loglinear model for the table implies a logit model (identical to the logit model for a contingency table developed in Chapter 14), the parameters of which bear a simple relationship to the parameters of the loglinear model for the table.

For example, it is natural to regard voter turnout in Table 15.7 as a dichotomous response variable, potentially affected by perceived closeness of the election and by intensity of partisan preference. Indeed, this is precisely what we did previously when we analyzed this table using a logit model.[34] With this example in mind, let us return to the saturated loglinear model for the three-way table (repeating Equation 15.12):

$$\eta_{ijk} = \mu + \alpha_{A(i)} + \alpha_{B(j)} + \alpha_{C(k)} + \alpha_{AB(ij)} + \alpha_{AC(ik)} + \alpha_{BC(jk)} + \alpha_{ABC(ijk)}$$

For convenience, I suppose that the response variable is variable C, as in the illustration. Let Ω_{ij} symbolize the response-variable logit within categories i, j of the two explanatory variables; that is,

$$\Omega_{ij} = \log_e \frac{\pi_{ij1}}{\pi_{ij2}} = \log_e \frac{n\pi_{ij1}}{n\pi_{ij2}} = \log_e \frac{\mu_{ij1}}{\mu_{ij2}}$$

$$= \eta_{ij1} - \eta_{ij2}$$

Then, from the saturated loglinear model for η_{ijk},

$$\Omega_{ij} = \left[\alpha_{C(1)} - \alpha_{C(2)}\right] + \left[\alpha_{AC(i1)} - \alpha_{AC(i2)}\right]$$
$$+ \left[\alpha_{BC(j1)} - \alpha_{BC(j2)}\right] + \left[\alpha_{ABC(ij1)} - \alpha_{ABC(ij2)}\right] \tag{15.13}$$

---

[34]See Section 14.3.

Noting that the first bracketed term in Equation 15.13 does not depend on the explanatory variables, that the second depends only upon variable A, and so forth, let us rewrite this equation in the following manner:

$$\Omega_{ij} = \omega + \omega_{A(i)} + \omega_{B(j)} + \omega_{AB(ij)} \tag{15.14}$$

where, because of the sigma constraints on the αs,

$$\omega \equiv \alpha_{C(1)} - \alpha_{C(2)} = 2\alpha_{C(1)}$$
$$\omega_{A(i)} \equiv \alpha_{AC(i1)} - \alpha_{AC(i2)} = 2\alpha_{AC(i1)}$$
$$\omega_{B(j)} \equiv \alpha_{BC(j1)} - \alpha_{BC(j2)} = 2\alpha_{BC(j1)}$$
$$\omega_{AB(ij)} \equiv \alpha_{ABC(ij1)} - \alpha_{ABC(ij2)} = 2\alpha_{ABC(ij1)}$$

Furthermore, because they are defined as twice the αs, the ωs are also constrained to sum to zero over any subscript:

$$\omega_{A(+)} = \omega_{B(+)} = \omega_{AB(i+)} = \omega_{AB(+j)} = 0, \text{ for all } i \text{ and } j$$

Note that the loglinear-model parameters for the association of the *explanatory* variables A and B do not appear in Equation 15.13. This equation (or, equivalently, Equation 15.14), the saturated logit model for the table, therefore shows how the response-variable log-odds depend on the explanatory variables and their interactions. In light of the constraints that they satisfy, the ωs are interpretable as ANOVA-like effect parameters, and indeed we have returned to the binomial logit model for a contingency table introduced in the previous chapter: Note, for example, that the likelihood-ratio test for the three-way term in the loglinear model for the *American Voter* data (given in the penultimate line of Table 15.8) is identical to the likelihood-ratio test for the interaction between closeness and preference in the logit model fit to these data (see Table 14.11 on page 373).

A similar argument may also be pursued with respect to *any* unsaturated loglinear model for the three-way table: Each such model implies a model for the response-variable logits. Because, however, our purpose is to examine the effects of the explanatory variables on the response, and not to explore the association *between* the explanatory variables, we generally include α_{AB} and its lower-order relatives in *any* model that we fit, thereby treating the association (if any) between variables A and B as given. Furthermore, a similar argument to the one developed here can be applied to a table of any dimension that has a response variable, and to a response variable with more than two categories. In the latter event, the loglinear model is equivalent to a *multinomial logit* model for the table, and in any event, we would generally include in the loglinear model a term of dimension one less than the table corresponding to all associations among the explanatory variables.

Loglinear models for contingency tables bear a formal resemblance to analysis-of-variance models and can be fit to data as Poisson generalized linear models with a log link. The loglinear model for a contingency table, however, treats the variables in the table symmetrically—none of the variables is distinguished as a response variable—and consequently the parameters of the model represent the associations among the variables, not the effects of explanatory variables on a response. When one of the variables is construed as the response, the loglinear model reduces to a binomial or multinomial logit model.

15.3   Statistical Theory for Generalized Linear Models*

In this section, I revisit with greater rigor and more detail many of the points raised in the preceding sections.[35]

15.3.1   Exponential Families

As much else in modern statistics, the insight that many of the most important distributions in statistics could be expressed in the following common "linear-exponential" form was due to R. A. Fisher:

$$p(y; \theta, \phi) = \exp\left[\frac{y\theta - b(\theta)}{a(\phi)} + c(y, \phi)\right] \qquad (15.15)$$

where

- $p(y; \theta, \phi)$ is the probability function for the discrete random variable Y, or the probability-density function for continuous Y.
- $a(\cdot), b(\cdot)$, and $c(\cdot)$ are known functions that vary from one exponential family to another (see below for examples).
- $\theta = g_c(\mu)$, the *canonical parameter* for the exponential family in question, is a function of the expectation $\mu \equiv E(Y)$ of Y; moreover, the *canonical link function* $g_c(\cdot)$ does not depend on ϕ.
- $\phi > 0$ is a *dispersion parameter*, which, in some families, takes on a fixed, known value, while in other families it is an unknown parameter to be estimated from the data along with θ.

Consider, for example, the normal or Gaussian distribution with mean μ and variance σ^2, the density function for which is given in Equation 15.1 (on page 382). To put the normal distribution in the form of Equation 15.15 requires some heroic algebraic manipulation, eventually producing[36]

$$p(y; \theta, \phi) = \exp\left\{\frac{y\theta - \theta^2/2}{\phi} - \frac{1}{2}\left[\frac{y^2}{\phi} + \log_e(2\pi\phi)\right]\right\}$$

with $\theta = g_c(\mu) = \mu$; $\phi = \sigma^2$; $a(\phi) = \phi$; $b(\theta) = \theta^2/2$; and $c(y, \phi) = -\frac{1}{2}\left[y^2/\phi + \log_e(2\pi\phi)\right]$.

Now consider the binomial distribution in Equation 15.2 (page 382), where Y is the proportion of "successes" in n independent binary trials, and μ is the probability of success on an individual trial. Written after more algebraic gymnastics as an exponential family,[37]

$$p(y; \theta, \phi) = \exp\left[\frac{y\theta - \log_e(1 + e^\theta)}{1/n} + \log_e\binom{n}{ny}\right]$$

with $\theta = g_c(\mu) = \log_e[\mu/(1 - \mu)]$; $\phi = 1$; $a(\phi) = 1/n$; $b(\theta) = \log_e(1 + e^\theta)$; and $c(y, \phi) = \log_e\binom{n}{ny}$.

Similarly, the Poisson, gamma, and inverse-Gaussian families can all be put into the form of Equation 15.15, using the results given in Table 15.9.[38]

---

[35]The exposition here owes a debt to Chapter 2 of McCullagh and Nelder (1989), which has become the standard source on GLMs, and to the remarkably lucid and insightful briefer treatment of the topic by Firth (1991).

[36]See Exercise 15.4.

[37]See Exercise 15.5.

[38]See Exercise 15.6.

Table 15.9   Functions $a(\cdot)$, $b(\cdot)$, and $c(\cdot)$ for Constructing the Exponential Families

Family	$a(\phi)$	$b(\theta)$	$c(y, \phi)$
Gaussian	ϕ	$\theta^2/2$	$-\frac{1}{2}\left[y^2/\phi + \log_e(2\pi\phi)\right]$
Binomial	$1/n$	$\log_e(1+e^\theta)$	$\log_e\binom{n}{ny}$
Poisson	1	e^θ	$-\log_e y!$
Gamma	ϕ	$-\log_e(-\theta)$	$\phi^{-2}\log_e(y/\phi)-\log_e y-\log_e\Gamma(\phi^{-1})$
Inverse-Gaussian	ϕ	$-\sqrt{-2\theta}$	$-\frac{1}{2}\left[\log_e(\pi\phi y^3) + 1/(\phi y)\right]$

NOTE: In this table, n is the number of binomial observations, and $\Gamma(\cdot)$ is the gamma function.

The advantage of expressing diverse families of distributions in the common exponential form is that general properties of exponential families can then be applied to the individual cases. For example, it is true in general that

$$b'(\theta) \equiv \frac{db(\theta)}{d\theta} = \mu$$

and that

$$V(Y) = a(\phi)b''(\theta) = a(\phi)\frac{d^2b(\theta)}{d\theta^2} = a(\phi)v(\mu)$$

leading to the results in Table 15.2 (on page 382).[39] Note that $b'(\cdot)$ is the inverse of the canonical link function. For example, for the normal distribution,

$$b'(\theta) = \frac{d(\theta^2/2)}{d\theta} = \theta = \mu$$

$$a(\phi)b''(\theta) = \phi \times 1 = \sigma^2$$

$$v(\mu) = 1$$

and for the binomial distribution,

$$b'(\theta) = \frac{d[\log_e(1 + e^\theta)]}{d\theta} = \frac{e^\theta}{1 + e^\theta} = \frac{1}{1 + e^{-\theta}} = \mu$$

$$a(\phi)b''(\theta) = \frac{1}{n} \times \left[\frac{e^\theta}{1 + e^\theta} - \left(\frac{e^\theta}{1 + e^\theta}\right)^2\right] = \frac{\mu(1 - \mu)}{n}$$

$$v(\mu) = \mu(1 - \mu)$$

The Gaussian, binomial, Poisson, gamma, and inverse-Gaussian distributions can all be written in the common linear-exponential form:

$$p(y; \theta, \phi) = \exp\left[\frac{y\theta - b(\theta)}{a(\phi)} + c(y, \phi)\right]$$

(Continued)

---

[39] See Exercise 15.7.

(Continued)

where $a(\cdot)$, $b(\cdot)$, and $c(\cdot)$ are known functions that vary from one exponential family to another; $\theta = g_c(\mu)$ is the canonical parameter for the exponential family in question; $g_c(\cdot)$ is the canonical link function; and $\phi > 0$ is a dispersion parameter, which takes on a fixed, known value in some families. It is generally the case that $\mu = E(Y) = b'(\theta)$ and that $V(Y) = a(\phi)b''(\theta)$.

15.3.2 Maximum-Likelihood Estimation of Generalized Linear Models

The log likelihood for an individual observation Y_i follows directly from Equation 15.15 (page 402):

$$\log_e L(\theta_i, \phi; Y_i) = \frac{y_i \theta_i - b(\theta_i)}{a_i(\phi)} + c(Y_i, \phi)$$

For n independent observations, we have

$$\log_e L(\boldsymbol{\theta}, \phi; \mathbf{y}) = \sum_{i=1}^{n} \frac{Y_i \theta_i - b(\theta_i)}{a_i(\phi)} + c(Y_i, \phi) \tag{15.16}$$

where $\boldsymbol{\theta} \equiv \{\theta_i\}$ and $\mathbf{y} \equiv \{Y_i\}$.

Suppose that a GLM uses the link function $g(\cdot)$, so that[40]

$$g(\mu_i) = \eta_i = \beta_0 + \beta_1 X_{i1} + \beta_2 X_{i2} + \cdots + \beta_k X_{ik}$$

The model therefore expresses the expected values of the n observations in terms of a much smaller number of regression parameters. To get estimating equations for the regression parameters, we have to differentiate the log likelihood with respect to each coefficient in turn. Let l_i represent the ith component of the log likelihood. Then, by the chain rule,

$$\frac{\partial l_i}{\partial \beta_j} = \frac{\partial l_i}{\partial \theta_i} \times \frac{d\theta_i}{d\mu_i} \times \frac{d\mu_i}{d\eta_i} \times \frac{\partial \eta_i}{\partial \beta_j} \text{ for } j = 0, 1, \ldots, k \tag{15.17}$$

After some work, we can rewrite Equation 15.17 as[41]

$$\frac{\partial l_i}{\partial \beta_j} = \frac{y_i - \mu_i}{a_i(\phi)v(\mu_i)} \times \frac{d\mu_i}{d\eta_i} \times x_{ij}$$

Summing over observations, and setting the sum to zero, produces the maximum-likelihood estimating equations for the GLM,

$$\sum_{i=1}^{n} \frac{Y_i - \mu_i}{a_i v(\mu_i)} \times \frac{d\mu_i}{d\eta_i} \times x_{ij} = 0, \text{ for } j = 0, 1, \ldots, k \tag{15.18}$$

where $a_i \equiv a_i(\phi)/\phi$ does not depend upon the dispersion parameter, which is constant across observations. For example, in a Gaussian GLM, $a_i = 1$, while in a binomial GLM, $a_i = 1/n_i$.

---

[40]It is notationally convenient here to write β_0 for the regression constant α.
[41]See Exercise 15.8.

Further simplification can be achieved when $g(\cdot)$ is the canonical link. In this case, the maximum-likelihood estimating equations become

$$\sum_{i=1}^{n} \frac{Y_i x_{ij}}{a_i} = \sum_{i=1}^{n} \frac{\mu_i x_{ij}}{a_i}$$

setting the "observed sum" on the left of the equation to the "expected sum" on the right. We noted this pattern in the estimating equations for logistic-regression models in the previous chapter.[42] Nevertheless, even here the estimating equations are (except in the case of the Gaussian family paired with the identify link) nonlinear functions of the regression parameters and generally require iterative methods for their solution.

Iterative Weighted Least Squares

Let

$$Z_i \equiv \eta_i + (Y_i - \mu_i)\frac{d\eta_i}{d\mu_i}$$
$$= \eta_i + (Y_i - \mu_i)g'(\mu_i)$$

Then

$$E(Z_i) = \eta_i = \beta_0 + \beta_1 X_{i1} + \beta_2 X_{i2} + \cdots + \beta_k X_{ik}$$

and

$$V(Z_i) = \left[g'(\mu_i)\right]^2 a_i v(\mu_i)$$

If, therefore, we could compute the Z_i, we would be able to fit the model by weighted least-squares regression of Z on the Xs, using the inverses of the $V(Z_i)$ as weights.[43] Of course, this is not the case because we do not know the values of the μ_i and η_i, which, indeed, depend on the regression coefficients that we wish to estimate—that is, the argument is essentially circular. This observation suggested to Nelder and Wedderburn (1972) the possibility of estimating GLMs by *iterative weighted least-squares* (IWLS), cleverly turning the circularity into an iterative procedure:

1. Start with initial estimates of the $\widehat{\mu}_i$ and the $\widehat{\eta}_i = g(\widehat{\mu}_i)$, denoted $\widehat{\mu}_i^{(0)}$ and $\widehat{\eta}_i^{(0)}$. A simple choice is to set $\widehat{\mu}_i^{(0)} = Y_i$.[44]

2. At each iteration l, compute the *working response variable* Z using the values of $\widehat{\mu}$ and $\widehat{\eta}$ from the preceding iteration,

$$Z_i^{(l-1)} = \eta_i^{(l-1)} + \left(Y_i - \mu_i^{(l-1)}\right) g'\left(\mu_i^{(l-1)}\right)$$

---

[42] See Sections 14.1.5 and 14.2.1.

[43] See Section 12.2.2 for a general discussion of weighted least squares.

[44] In certain settings, starting with $\widehat{\mu}_i^{(0)} = Y_i$ can cause computational difficulties. For example, in a binomial GLM, some of the observed proportions may be 0 or 1—indeed, for binary data, this will be true for *all* the observations—requiring us to divide by 0 or to take the log of 0. The solution is to adjust the starting values, which are in any event not critical, to protect against this possibility. For a binomial GLM, where $Y_i = 0$, we can take $\widehat{\mu}_i^{(0)} = 0.5/n_i$, and where $Y_i = 1$, we can take $\widehat{\mu}_i^{(0)} = (n_i - 0.5)/n_i$. For binary data, then, all the $\widehat{\mu}_i^{(0)}$ are 0.5.

along with weights

$$W_i^{(l-1)} = \frac{1}{\left[g'\left(\mu_i^{(l-1)}\right)\right]^2 a_i v\left(\mu_i^{(l-1)}\right)}$$

3. Fit a weighted least-squares regression of $Z^{(l-1)}$ on the Xs, using the $W^{(l-1)}$ as weights. That is, compute

$$\mathbf{b}^{(l)} = \left(\mathbf{X}'\mathbf{W}^{(l-1)}\mathbf{X}\right)^{-1}\mathbf{X}'\mathbf{W}^{(l-1)}\mathbf{z}^{(l-1)}$$

where $\underset{(k+1\times 1)}{\mathbf{b}^{(l)}}$ is the vector of regression coefficients at the current iteration; $\underset{(n\times k+1)}{\mathbf{X}}$ is (as usual) the model matrix; $\underset{(n\times n)}{\mathbf{W}^{(l-1)}} \equiv \mathrm{diag}\left\{W_i^{(l-1)}\right\}$ is the diagonal weight matrix; and $\underset{(n\times 1)}{\mathbf{z}^{(l-1)}} \equiv \left\{Z_i^{(l-1)}\right\}$ is the working-response vector.

4. Repeat Steps 2 and 3 until the regression coefficients stabilize, at which point $\mathbf{b}$ converges to the maximum-likelihood estimates of the βs.

Applied to the canonical link, IWLS is equivalent to the Newton-Raphson method (as we discovered for a logit model in the previous chapter); more generally, IWLS implements Fisher's "method of scoring."

Estimating the Dispersion Parameter

Note that we do not require an estimate of the dispersion parameter to estimate the regression coefficients in a GLM. Although it is in principle possible to estimate ϕ by maximum likelihood as well, this is rarely done. Instead, recall that $V(Y_i) = \phi a_i v(\mu_i)$. Solving for the dispersion parameter, we get $\phi = V(Y_i)/a_i v(\mu_i)$, suggesting the *method of moments* estimator

$$\tilde{\phi} = \frac{1}{n-k-1}\sum\frac{(Y_i - \widehat{\mu}_i)^2}{a_i v(\widehat{\mu}_i)} \tag{15.19}$$

The estimated asymptotic covariance matrix of the coefficients is then obtained from the last IWLS iteration as

$$\widehat{\mathcal{V}}(\mathbf{b}) = \tilde{\phi}\left(\mathbf{X}'\mathbf{W}\mathbf{X}\right)^{-1}$$

Because the maximum-likelihood estimator $\mathbf{b}$ is asymptotically normally distributed, $\widehat{\mathcal{V}}(\mathbf{b})$ may be used as the basis for Wald tests of the regression parameters.

The maximum-likelihood estimating equations for generalized linear models take the common form

$$\sum_{i=1}^{n}\frac{Y_i - \mu_i}{a_i v(\mu_i)} \times \frac{d\mu_i}{d\eta_i} \times x_{ij} = 0, \text{ for } j = 0, 1, \ldots, k$$

These equations are generally nonlinear and therefore have no general closed-form solution, but they can be solved by iterated weighted least squares (IWLS). The estimating equations for the coefficients do not involve the dispersion parameter, which (for models in which the dispersion is not fixed) then can be estimated as

$$\widetilde{\phi} = \frac{1}{n-k-1} \sum \frac{(Y_i - \widehat{\mu}_i)^2}{a_i v(\widehat{\mu}_i)}$$

The estimated asymptotic covariance matrix of the coefficients is

$$\widehat{\mathcal{V}}(\mathbf{b}) = \widetilde{\phi} \left(\mathbf{X}'\mathbf{W}\mathbf{X} \right)^{-1}$$

where **b** is the vector of estimated coefficients and **W** is a diagonal matrix of weights from the last IWLS iteration.

Quasi-Likelihood Estimation

The argument leading to IWLS estimation rests only on the linearity of the relationship between $\eta = g(\mu)$ and the Xs, and on the assumption that $V(Y)$ depends in a particular manner on a dispersion parameter and μ. As long as we can express the transformed mean of Y as a linear function of the Xs, and can write down a variance function for Y (expressing the conditional variance of Y as a function of its mean and a dispersion parameter), we can apply the "maximum-likelihood" estimating equations (Equation 15.18 on page 404) and obtain estimates by IWLS—even without committing ourselves to a particular conditional distribution for Y.

This is the method of *quasi-likelihood estimation*, introduced by Wedderburn (1974), and it has been shown to retain many of the properties of maximum-likelihood estimation: Although the quasi-likelihood estimator may not be maximally asymptotically efficient, it is consistent and has the same asymptotic distribution as the maximum-likelihood estimator of a GLM in an exponential family.[45] We can think of quasi-likelihood estimation of GLMs as analogous to least-squares estimation of linear regression models with potentially non-normal errors: Recall that as long as the relationship between Y and the Xs is linear, the error variance is constant, and the observations are independently sampled, the theory underlying OLS estimation applies—although the OLS estimator may no longer be maximally efficient.[46]

The maximum-likelihood estimating equations, and IWLS estimation, can be applied whenever we can express the transformed mean of Y as a linear function of the Xs, and can write the conditional variance of Y as a function of its mean and (possibly) a dispersion parameter—even when we do not specify a particular conditional distribution for Y. The resulting quasi-likelihood estimator shares many of the properties of maximum-likelihood estimators.

---

[45] See, for example, McCullagh and Nelder (1989, chap. 9) and McCullagh (1991).
[46] See Chapter 9.

15.3.3   Hypothesis Tests

Analysis of Deviance

Originally (in Equation 15.16 on page 404), I wrote the log likelihood for a GLM as a function $\log_e L(\boldsymbol{\theta}, \phi; \mathbf{y})$ of the canonical parameters $\boldsymbol{\theta}$ for the observations. Because $\mu_i = g_c^{-1}(\theta_i)$, for the canonical link $g_c(\cdot)$, we can equally well think of the log likelihood as a function of the expected response, and therefore can write the maximized log likelihood as $\log_e L(\widehat{\boldsymbol{\mu}}, \phi; \mathbf{y})$. If we then dedicate a parameter to each observation, so that $\widehat{\mu}_i = Y_i$ (e.g., by removing the constant from the regression model and defining a dummy regressor for each observation), the log likelihood becomes $\log_e L(\mathbf{y}, \phi; \mathbf{y})$. The *residual deviance* under the initial model is twice the difference in these log likelihoods:

$$D(\mathbf{y}; \widehat{\boldsymbol{\mu}}) \equiv 2[\log_e L(\mathbf{y}, \phi; \mathbf{y}) - \log_e L(\widehat{\boldsymbol{\mu}}, \phi; \mathbf{y})] \tag{15.20}$$

$$= 2 \sum_{i=1}^{n} [\log_e L(Y_i, \phi; Y_i) - \log_e L(\widehat{\mu}_i, \phi; Y_i)]$$

$$= 2 \sum_{i=1}^{n} \frac{Y_i [g(Y_i) - g(\widehat{\mu}_i)] - b [g(Y_i)] + b [g(\widehat{\mu}_i)]}{a_i}$$

Dividing the residual deviance by the estimated dispersion parameter produces the *scaled deviance*, $D^*(\mathbf{y}; \widehat{\boldsymbol{\mu}}) \equiv D(\mathbf{y}; \widehat{\boldsymbol{\mu}})/\widehat{\phi}$. As explained in Section 15.1.1, deviances are the building blocks of likelihood-ratio and F-tests for GLMs.

Applying Equation 15.20 to the Gaussian distribution, where $g_c(\cdot)$ is the identity link, $a_i = 1$, and $b(\theta) = \theta^2/2$, produces (after some simplification)

$$D(\mathbf{y}; \widehat{\boldsymbol{\mu}}) = \sum (Y_i - \widehat{\mu})^2$$

that is, the residual sum of squares for the model. Similarly, applying Equation 15.20 to the binomial distribution, where $g_c(\cdot)$ is the logit link, $a_i = n_i$, and $b(\theta) = \log_e(1 + e^\theta)$, we get (after quite a bit of simplification)[47]

$$D(\mathbf{y}; \widehat{\boldsymbol{\mu}}) = 2 \sum n_i \left[Y_i \log_e \frac{Y_i}{\widehat{\mu}_i} + (1 - Y_i) \log_e \frac{1 - Y_i}{1 - \widehat{\mu}_i} \right]$$

The residual deviance for a model is twice the difference in the log likelihoods for the saturated model, which dedicates one parameter to each observation, and the model in question:

$$D(\mathbf{y}; \widehat{\boldsymbol{\mu}}) \equiv 2[\log_e L(\mathbf{y}, \phi; \mathbf{y}) - \log_e L(\widehat{\boldsymbol{\mu}}, \phi; \mathbf{y})]$$

$$= 2 \sum_{i=1}^{n} \frac{Y_i [g(Y_i) - g(\widehat{\mu}_i)] - b [g(Y_i)] + b [g(\widehat{\mu}_i)]}{a_i}$$

Dividing the residual deviance by the estimated dispersion parameter produces the scaled deviance, $D^*(\mathbf{y}; \widehat{\boldsymbol{\mu}}) \equiv D(\mathbf{y}; \widehat{\boldsymbol{\mu}})/\widehat{\phi}$.

---

[47]See Exercise 15.9, which also develops formulas for the deviance in Poisson, gamma, and inverse-Gaussian models.

Testing General Linear Hypotheses

As was the case for linear models,[48] we can formulate a test for the general linear hypothesis

$$H_0: \underset{(q \times k+1)}{\mathbf{L}} \underset{(k+1 \times 1)}{\boldsymbol{\beta}} = \underset{(q \times 1)}{\mathbf{c}}$$

where the hypothesis matrix $\mathbf{L}$ and right-hand-side vector $\mathbf{c}$ contain pre-specified constants; usually, $\mathbf{c} = \mathbf{0}$. For a GLM, the Wald statistic

$$Z_0^2 = (\mathbf{Lb} - \mathbf{c})' \, [\mathbf{L}\widehat{\mathcal{V}}(\mathbf{b})\,\mathbf{L}']^{-1} \, (\mathbf{Lb} - \mathbf{c})$$

follows an asymptotic chi-square distribution with q degrees of freedom under the hypothesis. The simplest application of this result is to the Wald statistic $Z_0 = B_j/\mathrm{SE}(B_j)$, testing that an individual regression coefficient is zero. Here, Z_0 follows a standard-normal distribution under H_0: $\beta_j = 0$ (or, equivalently, Z_0^2 follows a chi-square distribution with one degree of freedom).

Alternatively, when the dispersion parameter is estimated from the data, we can calculate the test statistic

$$F_0 = \frac{(\mathbf{Lb} - \mathbf{c})' \, [\mathbf{L}\widehat{\mathcal{V}}(\mathbf{b})\,\mathbf{L}']^{-1} \, (\mathbf{Lb} - \mathbf{c})}{q}$$

which is distributed as $F_{q,n-k-1}$ under H_0. Applied to an individual coefficient, $t_0 = \pm\sqrt{F_0} = B_j/\mathrm{SE}(B_j)$ produces a t-test on $n - k - 1$ degrees of freedom.

To test the general linear hypothesis H_0: $\mathbf{L}\boldsymbol{\beta} = \mathbf{c}$, where the hypothesis matrix $\mathbf{L}$ has q rows, we can compute the Wald chi-square test statistic $Z_0^2 = (\mathbf{Lb} - \mathbf{c})' \, [\mathbf{L}\widehat{\mathcal{V}}(\mathbf{b})\mathbf{L}']^{-1}$ $(\mathbf{Lb} - \mathbf{c})$, with q degrees of freedom. Alternatively, if the dispersion parameter is estimated from the data, we can compute the F-test statistic $F_0 = (\mathbf{Lb} - \mathbf{c})' \, [\mathbf{L}\widehat{\mathcal{V}}(\mathbf{b})\mathbf{L}']^{-1}$ $(\mathbf{Lb} - \mathbf{c})\,/q$ on q and $n - k - 1$ degrees of freedom.

Testing Nonlinear Hypotheses

It is occasionally of interest to test a hypothesis or construct a confidence interval for a *nonlinear* function of the parameters of a linear or generalized linear model. If the nonlinear function in question is a differentiable function of the regression coefficients, then an approximate asymptotic standard error may be obtained by the *delta method*.[49]

Suppose that we are interested in the function

$$\gamma \equiv f(\boldsymbol{\beta}) = f(\beta_0, \beta_1, \ldots, \beta_k)$$

where, for notational convenience, I have used β_0 to denote the regression constant. The function $f(\boldsymbol{\beta})$ need not use *all* the regression coefficients (see the example below). The

---

[48] See Section 9.4.4.

[49] The delta method (Rao, 1973) is described in Appendix D on probability and estimation. The method employs a first-order (i.e., linear) Taylor-series approximation to the nonlinear function. The delta method is appropriate here because the maximum-likelihood (or quasi-likelihood) estimates of the coefficients of a GLM are asymptotically normally distributed. Indeed, the procedure described in this section is applicable *whenever* the parameters of a regression model are normally distributed and can therefore be applied in a wide variety of contexts—such as to the nonlinear regression models described in Chapter 17. In small samples, however, the delta-method approximation to the standard error may not be adequate, and the bootstrapping procedures described in Chapter 21 will usually provide more reliable results.

maximum-likelihood estimator of γ is simply $\widehat{\gamma} = f(\widehat{\beta})$ (which, as an MLE, is also asymptotically normal), and the approximate sampling variance of $\widehat{\gamma}$ is then

$$\widehat{\mathcal{V}}(\widehat{\gamma}) \approx \sum_{j=0}^{k} \sum_{j'=0}^{k} v_{jj'} \times \frac{\partial \widehat{\gamma}}{\partial \widehat{\beta}_j} \times \frac{\partial \widehat{\gamma}}{\partial \widehat{\beta}_{j'}}$$

where $v_{jj'}$ is the j, j'th element of the estimated asymptotic covariance matrix of the coefficients, $\widehat{\mathcal{V}}(\widehat{\beta})$.

To illustrate the application of this result, imagine that we are interested in determining the maximum or minimum value of a quadratic partial regression.[50] Focusing on the partial relationship between the response variable and a particular X, we have an equation of the form

$$E(Y) = \cdots + \beta_1 X + \beta_2 X^2 + \cdots$$

Differentiating this equation with respect to X, we get

$$\frac{dE(Y)}{dX} = \beta_1 + 2\beta_2 X$$

Setting the derivative to 0 and solving for X produces the value at which the function reseaches a minimum (if β_2 is positive) or a maximum (if β_2 is negative),

$$X = -\frac{\beta_1}{2\beta_2}$$

which is a nonlinear function of the regression coefficients β_1 and β_2.

For example, in Section 12.3.1, using data from the Canadian Survey of Labour and Income Dynamics (the "SLID"), I fit a least-squares regression of log wage rate on a quadratic in age, a dummy regressor for sex, and the square of education, obtaining (repeating, and slightly rearranging, Equation 12.7 on page 280):

$$\begin{aligned}
\widehat{\log_2 \text{Wages}} = {} & 0.5725 && + && 0.1198 \times \text{Age} && - && 0.001230 \times \text{Age}^2 \\
& (0.0834) && && (0.0046) && && (0.000059) \\
& && && + && 0.3195 \times \text{Male} + 0.002605 \times \text{Education}^2 \\
& && && && (0.0180) && (0.000113) \\
& R^2 = .3892
\end{aligned}$$

Imagine that we are interested in the age $\gamma \equiv -\beta_1/(2\beta_2)$ at which wages are at a maximum, holding sex and education constant. The necessary derivatives are

$$\frac{\partial \widehat{\gamma}}{\partial B_1} = -\frac{1}{2B_2} = -\frac{1}{2(-0.001230)} = 406.5$$

$$\frac{\partial \widehat{\gamma}}{\partial B_2} = \frac{B_1}{2B_2^2} = \frac{0.1198}{2(-0.001230)^2} = 39{,}593$$

Our point estimate of γ is

$$\widehat{\gamma} = -\frac{B_1}{2B_2} = -\frac{0.1198}{2 \times 0.001230} = 48.70 \text{ years}$$

---

[50]See Section 17.1 for a discussion of polynomial regression. The application of the delta method to finding the minimum or maximum of a quadratic curve is suggested by Weisberg (2005, sect. 6.1.2).

The estimated sampling variance of the age coefficient is $\widehat{V}(B_1) = 2.115 \times 10^{-5}$, and of the coefficient of age-squared, $\widehat{V}(B_2) = 3.502 \times 10^{-9}$; the estimated sampling covariance for the two coefficients is $\widehat{C}(B_1, B_2) = -2.685 \times 10^{-7}$. The approximate estimated variance of $\widehat{\gamma}$ is then

$$\widehat{\mathcal{V}}(\widehat{\gamma}) \approx \left(2.115 \times 10^{-5}\right) \times 406.5^2 - \left(2.685 \times 10^{-7}\right) \times 406.5 \times 39,593$$

$$- \left(2.685 \times 10^{-7}\right) \times 406.5 \times 39,593 + \left(3.502 \times 10^{-9}\right) \times 39,593^2$$

$$= 0.3419$$

Consequently, the approximate standard error of $\widehat{\gamma}$ is $\text{SE}(\widehat{\gamma}) \approx \sqrt{0.3419} = 0.5847$, and an approximate 95% confidence interval for the age at which income is highest on average is $\gamma = 48.70 \pm 1.96(0.5847) = (47.55, 49.85)$.

The delta method may be used to approximate the standard error of a nonlinear function of regression coefficients in a GLM. If $\gamma \equiv f(\beta_0, \beta_1, \ldots, \beta_k)$, then

$$\widehat{\mathcal{V}}(\widehat{\gamma}) \approx \sum_{j=0}^{k} \sum_{j'=0}^{k} v_{jj'} \frac{\partial \widehat{\gamma}}{\partial \widehat{\beta}_j} \frac{\partial \widehat{\gamma}}{\partial \widehat{\beta}_{j'}}$$

15.3.4 Effect Displays

Let us write the GLM in matrix form, with linear predictor

$$\underset{(n \times 1)}{\boldsymbol{\eta}} = \underset{(n \times k+1)}{\mathbf{X}} \underset{(k+1 \times 1)}{\boldsymbol{\beta}}$$

and link function $g(\boldsymbol{\mu}) = \boldsymbol{\eta}$, where $\boldsymbol{\mu}$ is the expectation of the response vector $\mathbf{y}$. As described in Section 15.3.2, we compute the maximum-likelihood estimate $\mathbf{b}$ of $\boldsymbol{\beta}$, along with the estimated asymptotic covariance matrix $\widehat{\mathcal{V}}(\mathbf{b})$ of $\mathbf{b}$.

Let the rows of $\mathbf{X}^*$ include regressors corresponding to all combinations of values of explanatory variables appearing in a high-order term of the model (or, for a continuous explanatory variable, values spanning the range of the variable), along with typical values of the remaining regressors. The structure of $\mathbf{X}^*$ with respect to interactions, for example, is the same as that of the model matrix $\mathbf{X}$. Then the fitted values $\widehat{\boldsymbol{\eta}}^* = \mathbf{X}^*\mathbf{b}$ represent the high-order term in question, and a table or graph of these values—or, alternatively, of the fitted values transformed to the scale of the response variable, $g^{-1}(\widehat{\boldsymbol{\eta}}^*)$—is an effect display. The standard errors of $\widehat{\boldsymbol{\eta}}^*$, available as the square-root diagonal entries of $\mathbf{X}^*\widehat{\mathcal{V}}(\mathbf{b})\mathbf{X}^{*\prime}$, may be used to compute pointwise confidence intervals for the effects, the end-points of which may then also be transformed to the scale of the response.

For example, for the Poisson regression model fit to Ornstein interlocking-directorate data, the effect display for assets in Figure 15.6(a) (page 390) is constructed by letting assets range between its minimum value of 0.062 and maximum of 147.670 billion dollars, fixing the dummy variables for nation of control and sector to their sample means—that is, to the observed proportions of the data in each of the corresponding categories of nation and sector. As noted previously, this is an especially simple example, because the model includes no interactions. The model was fit with the log link, and so the estimated effects, which in general are on the scale of the linear predictor, are on the log-count scale; the right-hand axis of the graph shows the corresponding count scale, which is the scale of the response variable.

> Effect displays for GLMs are based on the fitted values $\widehat{\boldsymbol{\eta}}^* = \mathbf{X}^*\mathbf{b}$, representing a high-order term in the model; that is, $\mathbf{X}^*$ has the same general structure as the model matrix $\mathbf{X}$, with the explanatory variables in the high-term order ranging over their values in the data while other explanatory variables are set to typical values. The standard errors of $\widehat{\boldsymbol{\eta}}^*$, given by the square-root diagonal entries of $\mathbf{X}^*\widehat{\mathcal{V}}(\mathbf{b})\mathbf{X}^{*\prime}$, may be used to compute pointwise confidence intervals for the effects.

15.4   Diagnostics for Generalized Linear Models

Most of the diagnostics for linear models presented in Chapters 11 and 12 extend relatively straightforwardly to GLMs. These extensions typically take advantage of the computation of maximum-likelihood and quasi-likelihood estimates for GLMs by iterated weighted least squares, as described in Section 15.3.2. The final weighted-least-squares fit linearizes the model and provides a quadratic approximation to the log likelihood. Approximate diagnostics are then either based directly on the WLS solution or are derived from statistics easily calculated from this solution. Seminal work on the extension of linear least-squares diagnostics to GLMs was done by Pregibon (1981), Landwehr, Pregibon, and Shoemaker (1984), Wang (1985, 1987), and Williams (1987). In my experience, and with the possible exception of added-variable plots for non-Gaussian GLMs, these extended diagnostics typically work reasonably well.

15.4.1   Outlier, Leverage, and Influence Diagnostics

Hat-Values

Hat-values, h_i, for a GLM can be taken directly from the final iteration of the IWLS procedure for fitting the model,[51] and have the usual interpretation—except that, unlike in a linear model, the hat-values in a GLM depend on the response variable Y as well as on the configuration of the Xs.

Residuals

Several kinds of residuals can be defined for GLMs:

- Most straightforwardly (but least usefully), *response residuals* are simply the differences between the observed response and its estimated expected value: $Y_i - \widehat{\mu}_i$, where

$$\widehat{\mu}_i = g^{-1}(\widehat{\eta}_i) = g^{-1}(A + B_1 X_{i1} + B_2 X_{i2} + \cdots + B_k X_{ik})$$

- *Working residuals* are the residuals from the final WLS fit. These may be used to define partial residuals for component-plus-residual plots (see below).

---

[51]* The hat-matrix is

$$\mathbf{H} = \mathbf{W}^{1/2}\mathbf{X}(\mathbf{X}'\mathbf{W}\mathbf{X})^{-1}\mathbf{X}'\mathbf{W}^{1/2}$$

where $\mathbf{W}$ is the weight matrix from the final IWLS iteration.

- *Pearson residuals* are casewise components of the *Pearson goodness-of-fit statistic* for the model:[52]

$$\frac{\widetilde{\phi}^{1/2}(Y_i - \widehat{\mu}_i)}{\sqrt{\widehat{V}(Y_i|\eta_i)}}$$

where $\widetilde{\phi}$ is the estimated dispersion parameter for the model (Equation 15.19 on page 406) and $V(y_i|\eta_i)$ is the conditional variance of the response (given in Table 15.2 on page 382).

- *Standardized Pearson residuals* correct for the conditional response variation and for the differential leverage of the observations:

$$R_{Pi} \equiv \frac{Y_i - \widehat{\mu}_i}{\sqrt{\widehat{V}(Y_i|\eta_i)(1 - h_i)}}$$

- *Deviance residuals*, G_i, are the square-roots of the casewise components of the residual deviance (Equation 15.20 on page 408), attaching the sign of the corresponding response residual.

- *Standardized deviance residuals* are

$$R_{Gi} \equiv \frac{G_i}{\sqrt{\widetilde{\phi}(1 - h_i)}}$$

- Several different approximations to studentized residuals have been proposed. To calculate exact studentized residuals would require literally refitting the model deleting each observation in turn and noting the decline in the deviance; this procedure, of course, is computationally unattractive. Williams suggests the approximation

$$E_i^* \equiv \sqrt{(1 - h_i)R_{Gi}^2 + h_i R_{Pi}^2}$$

where, once again, the sign is taken from the response residual. A Bonferroni outlier test using the standard normal distribution may be based on the largest absolute studentized residual.

Influence Measures

An approximation to Cook's distance influence measure, due to Williams (1987), is

$$D_i \equiv \frac{R_{Pi}^2}{k+1} \times \frac{h_i}{1 - h_i}$$

Approximate values of influence measures for individual coefficients, DFBETA$_{ij}$ and DFBETAS$_{ij}$, may be obtained directly from the final iteration of the IWLS procedure.

Wang (1985) suggests an extension of added-variable plots to GLMs that works as follows: Suppose that the focal regressor is X_j. Refit the model with X_j removed, extracting the working residuals from this fit. Then regress X_j on the other Xs by WLS, using the weights from the last IWLS step, obtaining residuals. Finally, plot the working residuals from the first regression against the residuals for X_j from the second regression.

---

[52]The Pearson statistic, an alternative to the deviance for measuring the fit of the model to the data, is the sum of squared Pearson residuals.

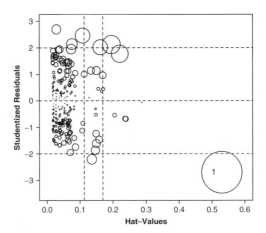

Figure 15.7   Hat-values, studentized residuals, and Cook's distances from the quasi-Poisson regression for Ornstein's interlocking-directorate data. The areas of the circles are proportional to the Cook's distances for the observations. Horizontal lines are drawn at −2, 0, and 2 on the studentized-residual scale, vertical lines at twice and three times the average hat-value.

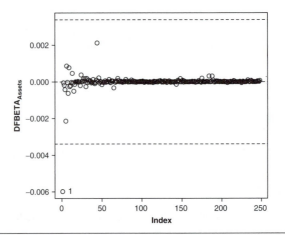

Figure 15.8   Index plot of DFBETA for the assets coefficient. The horizontal lines are drawn at 0 and $\pm \text{SE}(B_{\text{Assets}})$.

Figure 15.7 shows hat-values, studentized residuals, and Cook's distances for the quasi-Poisson model fit to Ornstein's interlocking directorate data. One observation—Number 1, the corporation with the largest assets—stands out by combining a very large hat-value with the biggest absolute studentized residual.[53] This point is not a statistically significant outlier, however (indeed, the Bonferroni p-value for the largest studentized residual exceeds 1). As shown in the DFBETA plot in Figure 15.8, Observation 1 makes the coefficient of assets substantially smaller than it would otherwise be (recall that the coefficient for assets is 0.02085). [54] In this case, the approximate DFBETA is quite accurate: If Observation 1 is deleted, the assets coefficient increases to 0.02602.

---

[53]Unfortunately, the data source does not include the names of the firms, but Observation 1 is the largest of the Canadian banks, which, in the 1970s, was (I believe) the Royal Bank of Canada.

[54]I invite the reader to plot the DFBETA values for the other coefficients in the model.

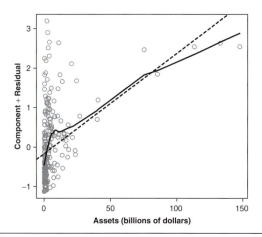

Figure 15.9   Component-plus-residual plot for assets in the interlocking-directorate quasi-Poisson
regression. The broken line shows the least-squares fit to the partial residuals; the
solid line is for a nonrobust lowess smooth with a span of 0.9.

Before concluding that Observation 1 requires special treatment, however, consider the check for
nonlinearity in the next section.

15.4.2   Nonlinearity Diagnostics

Component-plus-residual and CERES plots also extend straightforwardly to GLMs. Nonparametric smoothing of the resulting scatterplots can be important to interpretation, especially in
models for binary response variables, where the discreteness of the response makes the plots difficult to examine. Similar (if typically less extreme) effects can occur for binomial and count data.

Component-plus-residual and CERES plots use the linearized model from the last step of the IWLS
fit. For example, the partial residual for X_j adds the working residual to $B_j X_{ij}$; the component-plus-
residual plot then graphs the partial residual against X_j. In smoothing a component-plus-residual
plot for a non-Gaussian GLM, it is generally preferable to use a nonrobust smoother.

A component-plus-residual plot for assets in the quasi-Poisson regression for the interlocking-
directorate data is shown in Figure 15.9. Assets is so highly positively skewed that the plot is
different to examine, but it is nevertheless apparent that the partial relationship between number
of interlocks and assets is nonlinear, with a much steeper slope at the left than at the right. Because
the bulge points to the left, we can try to straighten this relationship by transforming assets down
the ladder of power and roots. Trial and error suggests the log transformation of assets, after which
a component-plus-residual plot for the modified model (Figure 15.10) is unremarkable.

Box-Tidwell constructed-variable plots[55] also extend straightforwardly to GLMs: When considering the transformation of X_j, simply add the constructed variable $X_j \log_e X_j$ to the model
and examine the added-variable plot for the constructed variable. Applied to assets in Ornstein's
quasi-Poisson regression, this procedure produces the constructed-variable plot in Figure 15.11,
which suggests that evidence for the transformation is spread throughout the data. The coefficient
for assets $\times \log_e$ assets in the constructed-variable regression is -0.02177 with a standard error
of 0.00371; the Wald-test statistic $Z_0 = -0.02177/0.00371 = -5.874$ therefore indicates strong
evidence for the transformation of assets. By comparing the coefficient of assets in the *original*

---

[55] See Section 12.5.2.

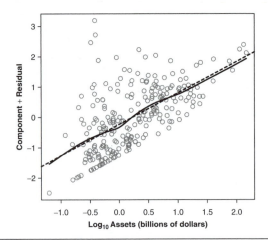

Figure 15.10   Component-plus-residual plot following the log-transformation of assets. The lowess fit is for a span of 0.6.

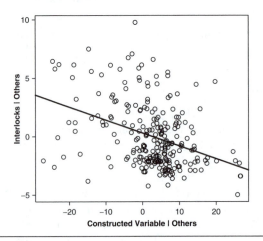

Figure 15.11   Constructed variable plot for the transformation of assets in the interlocking-directorate quasi-Poisson regression.

quasi-Poisson regression (0.02085) with the coefficient of the constructed variable, we get the suggested power transformation

$$\tilde{\lambda} = 1 + \frac{-0.02177}{0.02085} = -0.044$$

that is, essentially the log-transformation, $\lambda = 0$.

Finally, it is worth noting the relationship between the problems of influence and nonlinearity in this example: Observation 1 was influential in the original regression because its very large assets gave it high leverage and because unmodelled nonlinearity put the observation below the erroneously linear fit for assets, pulling the regression surface towards it. Log-transforming assets fixes both these problems.

Alternative effect displays for assets in the transformed model are shown in Figure 15.12. Panel (a) in this figure graphs assets on its "natural" scale; on this scale, of course, the fitted partial relationship between log-interlocks and assets is nonlinear. Panel (b) uses a log scale for assets, rendering the partial relationship linear.

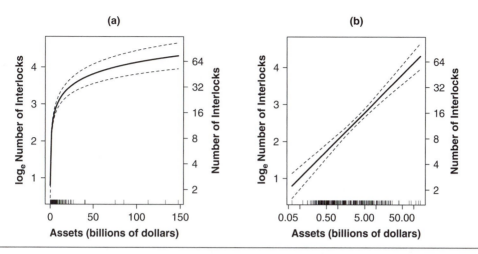

Figure 15.12   Effect displays for assets in the quasi-Poisson regression model in which assets has been log-transformed. Panel (a) plots assets on its "natural" scale, while panel (b) uses a log scale for assets. Rug plots for assets appear at the bottom of the graphs. The broken lines give pointwise 95% confidence intervals around the estimated effect.

Most of the standard diagnostics for linear models extend relatively straightforwardly to GLMs. These extensions typically take advantage of the computation of maximum-likelihood and quasi-likelihood estimates for GLMs by iterated weighted least squares. Such diagnostics include studentized residuals, hat-values, Cook's distances, DFBETA and DFBETAS, added-variable plots, component-plus-residual plots, and the constructed-variable plot for transforming an explanatory variable.

Exercises

Exercise 15.1.   Testing overdisperison: Let $\delta \equiv 1/\omega$ represent the inverse of the scale parameter for the negative-binomial regression model (see Equation 15.4 on page 392). When $\delta = 0$, the negative-binomial model reduces to the Poisson regression model (why?), and consequently a test of H_0: $\delta = 0$ against the one-sided alternative hypothesis H_a: $\delta > 0$ is a test of overdispersion. A Wald test of this hypothesis is straightforward, simply dividing $\widehat{\delta}$ by its standard error. We can also compute a likelihood-ratio test contrasting the deviance under the more specific Poisson regression model with that under the more general negative-binomial model. Because the negative-binomial model has one additional parameter, we refer the likelihood-ratio test statistic to a chi-square distribution with one degree of freedom; as Cameron and Trivedi (1998, p. 78) explain, however, the usual right-tailed p-value obtained from the chi-square distribution must be halved. Apply this likelihood-ratio test for overdispersion to Ornstein's interlocking-directorate regression.

Exercise 15.2.   *Zero-inflated count regression models:

(a) Show that the mean and variance of the response variable Y_i in the zero-inflated Poisson (ZIP) regression model, given in Equations 15.5 and 15.6 on page 393, are

$$E(Y_i) = (1 - \pi_i)\mu_i$$
$$V(Y_i) = (1 - \pi_i)\mu_i(1 + \pi_i\mu_i)$$

(*Hint*: Recall that there are two sources of zeroes: observations in the first latent class, whose value of Y_i is *necessarily* 0, and observations in the second latent class, whose value *may be* zero. Probability of membership in the first class is π_i, and in the second $1 - \pi_i$.) Show that $V(Y_i) > E(Y_i)$ when $\pi_i > 0$.

(b) Derive the log likelihood for the ZIP model, given in Equation 15.7 (page 394).

(c) The *zero-inflated negative-binomial* (ZINB) *regression model* substitutes a negative-binomial GLM for the Poisson-regression submodel of Equation 15.6 on page 393:

$$\log_e \mu_i = \alpha + \beta_1 x_{i1} + \beta_2 x_{i2} + \cdots + \beta_k x_{ik}$$

$$p(y_i | x_1, \ldots, x_k) = \frac{\Gamma(y_i + \omega)}{y!\Gamma(\omega)} \times \frac{\mu_i^{y_i}\omega^\omega}{(\mu_i + \omega)^{\mu_i + \omega}}$$

Show that $E(Y_i) = (1 - \pi_i)\mu_i$ (as in the ZIP model) and that

$$V(Y_i) = (1 - \pi_i)\mu_i[1 + \mu_i(\pi_i + 1/\omega)]$$

When $\pi_i > 0$, the conditional variance is greater in the ZINB model than in the standard negative-binomial GLM, $V(Y_i) = \mu_i + \mu_i^2/\omega$; why? Derive the log likelihood for the ZINB model. [*Hint*: Simply substitute the negative-binomial GLM for the Poisson-regression submodel in Equation 15.7 (page 394)].

Exercise 15.3. The usual Pearson chi-square statistic for testing for independence in a two-way contingency table is

$$X_0^2 = \sum_{i=1}^r \sum_{j=1}^c \frac{(Y_{ij} - \widehat{\mu}_{ij})^2}{\widehat{\mu}_{ij}}$$

where the Y_{ij} are the observed frequencies in the table, and the $\widehat{\mu}_{ij}$ are the estimated expected frequencies under independence. The estimated expected frequencies can be computed from the maximum-likelihood estimates for the loglinear model of independence, or they can be computed directly as $\widehat{\mu}_{ij} = Y_{i+}Y_{+j}/n$. The likelihood-ratio statistic for testing for independence can also be computed from the estimated expected counts as

$$G_0^2 = 2 \sum_{i=1}^r \sum_{j=1}^c Y_{ij} \log_e \frac{Y_{ij}}{\widehat{\mu}_{ij}}$$

Both test statistics have $(r - 1)(c - 1)$ degrees of freedom. The two tests are asymptotically equivalent, and usually produce similar results. Applying these formulas to the two-way table for voter turnout and intensity of partisan preference in Table 15.4 (page 395), compute both test statistics, verifying that the direct formula for G_0^2 produces the same result as given in the text.

Exercise 15.4. *Show that the normal distribution can be written in exponential form as

$$p(y; \theta, \phi) = \exp\left\{\frac{y\theta - \theta^2/2}{\phi} - \frac{1}{2}\left[\frac{y^2}{\phi} + \log_e(2\pi\phi)\right]\right\}$$

where $\theta = g_c(\mu) = \mu$; $\phi = \sigma^2$; $a(\phi) = \phi$; $b(\theta) = \theta^2/2$; and $c(y, \phi) = -\frac{1}{2}\left[y^2/\phi + \log_e(2\pi\phi)\right]$.

Exercise 15.5. *Show that the binomial distribution can be written in exponential form as

$$p(y; \theta, \phi) = \exp\left[\frac{y\theta - \log_e(1 + e^{\theta})}{1/n} + \log_e\binom{n}{ny}\right]$$

where $\theta = g_c(\mu) = \log_e[\mu/(1 - \mu)]$; $\phi = 1$; $a(\phi) = 1/n$; $b(\theta) = \log_e(1 + e^{\theta})$; and $c(y, \phi) = \log_e\binom{n}{ny}$.

Exercise 15.6. *Using the results given in Table 15.9 (on page 403), verify that the Poisson, gamma, and inverse-Gaussian families can all be written in the common exponential form

$$p(y; \theta, \phi) = \exp\left[\frac{y\theta - b(\theta)}{a(\phi)} + c(y, \phi)\right]$$

Exercise 15.7. *Using the general result that the conditional variance of a distribution in an exponential family is

$$V(Y) = a(\phi)\frac{d^2b(\theta)}{d\theta^2}$$

and the values of $a(\cdot)$ and $b(\cdot)$ given in Table 15.9 (on page 403), verify that the variances of the Gaussian, binomial, Poisson, gamma, and inverse-Gaussian families are, consecutively, ϕ, $\mu(1 - \mu)/n$, μ, $\phi\mu^2$, and $\phi\mu^3$.

Exercise 15.8. *Show that the derivative of the log likelihood for an individual observation with respect to the regression coefficients in a GLM can be written as

$$\frac{\partial l_i}{\partial \beta_j} = \frac{y_i - \mu_i}{a_i(\phi)v(\mu_i)} \times \frac{d\mu_i}{d\eta_i} \times x_{ij}, \text{ for } j = 0, 1, \ldots, k$$

(See Equation 15.17 on page 404.)

Exercise 15.9. *Using the general expression for the residual deviance,

$$D(\mathbf{y}; \widehat{\mu}) = 2\sum_{i=1}^{n}\frac{Y_i\left[g(Y_i) - g(\widehat{\mu}_i)\right] - b\left[g(Y_i)\right] + b\left[g(\widehat{\mu}_i)\right]}{a_i}$$

show that the deviances for the several exponential families can be written in the following forms:

Family	Residual Deviance
Gaussian	$\sum(Y_i - \widehat{\mu}_i)^2$
Binomial	$2\sum\left[n_iY_i\log_e\frac{Y_i}{\widehat{\mu}_i} + n_i(1 - Y_i)\log_e\frac{1 - Y_i}{1 - \widehat{\mu}_i}\right]$
Poisson	$2\sum\left[Y_i\log_e\frac{Y_i}{\widehat{\mu}_i} - (Y_i - \widehat{\mu}_i)\right]$
Gamma	$2\sum\left[-\log_e\frac{Y_i}{\widehat{\mu}_i} + \frac{Y_i - \widehat{\mu}_i}{\widehat{\mu}_i}\right]$
Inverse-Gaussian	$\sum\frac{(Y_i - \widehat{\mu}_i)^2}{Y_i\widehat{\mu}_i^2}$

Exercise 15.10. *Using the SLID data, Table 12.1 in Section 12.3.2 (on page 283) reports the results of a regression of log wages on sex, the square of education, a quadratic in age, and interactions between sex and education-squared, and between sex and the quadratic for age.

(a) Estimate the age γ_1 at which women attain on average their highest level of wages, controlling for education. Use the delta method to estimate the standard error of $\widehat{\gamma}_1$. *Note:* You will need to refit the model to obtain the covariance matrix for the estimated regression coefficients.

(b) Estimate the age γ_2 at which men attain on average their highest level of wages, controlling for education. Use the delta method to estimate the standard error of $\widehat{\gamma}_2$.

(c) Let $\gamma_3 \equiv \gamma_1 - \gamma_2$, the difference between the ages at which men and women attain their highest wage levels. Compute $\widehat{\gamma}_3$. Use the delta method to find the standard error of $\widehat{\gamma}_3$ and then test the null hypothesis H_0: $\gamma_3 = 0$.

Exercise 15.11. Coefficient quasi-variances: Coefficient quasi-variances for dummy-variable regressors were introduced in Section 7.2.1. Recall that the object is to approximate the standard errors for pairwise *differences* between categories,

$$\text{SE}(C_j - C_{j'}) = \sqrt{\widehat{V}(C_j) + \widehat{V}(C_{j'}) - 2 \times \widehat{C}(C_j, C_{j'})}$$

where C_j and $C_{j'}$ are two dummy-variable coefficients for an m-category polytomous explanatory variable; $\widehat{V}(C_j)$ is the estimated sampling variance of C_j; and $\widehat{C}(C_j, C_{j'})$ is the estimated sampling covariance of C_j and $C_{j'}$. By convention, we take C_m (the coefficient of the baseline category) and its standard error, $\text{SE}(C_m)$, to be 0. We seek coefficient quasi-variances $\widetilde{V}(C_j)$, so that

$$\text{SE}(C_j - C_{j'}) \approx \sqrt{\widetilde{V}(C_j) + \widetilde{V}(C_{j'})}$$

for all pairs of coefficients C_j and $C_{j'}$, by minimizing the total log relative error of approximation, $\sum_{j < j'} \left[\log(\text{RE}_{jj'})\right]^2$, where

$$\text{RE}_{jj'} \equiv \frac{\widetilde{V}(C_j - C_{j'})}{\widehat{V}(C_j - C_{j'})} = \frac{\widetilde{V}(C_j) + \widetilde{V}(C_{j'})}{\widehat{V}(C_j) + \widehat{V}(C_j) - 2 \times \widehat{C}(C_j, C_{j'})}$$

Firth (2003) cleverly suggests implementing this criterion by fitting a GLM in which the response variable is $Y_{jj'} \equiv \log_e[\widehat{V}(C_j - C_{j'})]$ for all unique pairs of categories j and j'; the linear predictor is $\eta_{jj'} \equiv \beta_j + \beta_{j'}$; the link function is the exponential link, $g(\mu) = \exp(\mu)$ (which is, note, *not* one of the common links in Table 15.1); and the variance function is constant, $V(Y|\eta) = \phi$. The quasi-likelihood estimates of the coefficients β_j are the quasi-variances $\widetilde{V}(C_j)$. For example, for the Canadian occupational prestige regression described in Section 7.2.1, where the dummy variables pertain to type of occupation (professional and managerial, white collar, or blue collar), we have

Pair (j,j')	$Y_{jj'} = \log_e[\widehat{V}(C_j - C_{j'})]$
Professional, White Collar	$\log_e(2.771^2) = 2.038$
Professional, Blue Collar	$\log_e(3.867^2) = 2.705$
White Collar, Blue Collar	$\log_e(2.514^2) = 1.844$

and model matrix

$$\mathbf{X} = \begin{bmatrix} (\beta_1) & (\beta_2) & (\beta_3) \\ 1 & 1 & 0 \\ 1 & 0 & 1 \\ 0 & 1 & 1 \end{bmatrix}$$

With three unique pairs and three coefficients, we should get a perfect fit: As I mentioned in Section 7.2.1, when there are only three categories, the quasi-variances perfectly recover the estimated variances for pairwise differences in coefficients. Demonstrate that this is the case by fitting the GLM. Some additional comments:

- The computation outlined here is the basis of Firth's `qvcalc` package (described in Firth, 2003) for the R statistical programming environment.
- The computation of quasi-variances applies not only to dummy regressors in linear models but to all models with a linear predictor for which coefficients and their estimated covariance matrix are available—for example, the GLMs described in this chapter.
- Quasi-variances may be used to approximate the standard error for any linear combination of dummy-variable coefficients, not just for pairwise differences.
- Having found the quasi-variance approximations to a set of standard errors, we can then compute and report the (typically small) maximum relative error of these approximations. Firth and De Menezes (2004) give more general results for the maximum relative error for *any* contrast of coefficients.

Summary

- A generalized linear model (or GLM) consists of three components:

  1. A random component, specifying the conditional distribution of the response variable, Y_i (for the ith of n independently sampled observations), given the values of the explanatory variables in the model. In the initial formulation of GLMs, the distribution of Y_i was a member of an exponential family, such as the Gaussian (normal), binomial, Poisson, gamma, or inverse-Gaussian families of distributions.

  2. A linear predictor—that is a linear function of regressors,

  $$\eta_i = \alpha + \beta_1 X_{i1} + \beta_2 X_{i2} + \cdots + \beta_{ik} X_k$$

  3. A smooth and invertible linearizing link function $g(\cdot)$, which transforms the expectation of the response variable, $\mu_i \equiv E(Y_i)$, to the linear predictor:

  $$g(\mu_i) = \eta_i = \alpha + \beta_1 X_{i1} + \beta_2 X_{i2} + \cdots + \beta_{ik} X_k$$

- A convenient property of distributions in the exponential families is that the conditional variance of Y_i is a function of its mean μ_i and, possibly, a dispersion parameter ϕ. In addition to the familiar Gaussian and binomial families (the latter for proportions), the Poisson family is useful for modeling count data, and the gamma and inverse-Gaussian families for modeling positive continuous data, where the conditional variance of Y increases with its expectation.
- GLMs are fit to data by the method of maximum likelihood, providing not only estimates of the regression coefficients but also estimated asymptotic standard errors of the coefficients.

- The ANOVA for linear models has an analog in the analysis of deviance for GLMs. The residual deviance for a GLM is $D_m \equiv 2(\log_e L_s - \log_e L_m)$, where L_m is the maximized likelihood under the model in question, and L_s is the maximized likelihood under a saturated model. The residual deviance is analogous to the residual sum of squares for a linear model.
- In GLMs for which the dispersion parameter is fixed to 1 (binomial and Poisson GLMs), the likelihood-ratio test statistic is the difference in the residual deviances for nested models. For GLMs in which there is a dispersion parameter to estimate (Gaussian, gamma, and inverse-Gaussian GLMs), we can instead compare nested models by an incremental F-test.
- The basic GLM for count data is the Poisson model with log link. Frequently, however, when the response variable is a count, its conditional variance increases more rapidly than its mean, producing a condition termed overdispersion and invalidating the use of the Poisson distribution. The quasi-Poisson GLM adds a dispersion parameter to handle overdispersed count data; this model can be estimated by the method of quasi-likelihood. A similar model is based on the negative-binomial distribution, which is not an exponential family. Negative-binomial GLMs can nevertheless be estimated by maximum likelihood. The zero-inflated Poisson regression model may be appropriate when there are more zeroes in the data than is consistent with a Poisson distribution.
- Loglinear models for contingency tables bear a formal resemblance to ANOVA models and can be fit to data as Poisson GLMs with a log link. The loglinear model for a contingency table, however, treats the variables in the table symmetrically—none of the variables is distinguished as a response variable—and consequently the parameters of the model represent the associations among the variables, not the effects of explanatory variables on a response. When one of the variables is construed as the response, the loglinear model reduces to a binomial or multinomial logit model.
- The Gaussian, binomial, Poisson, gamma, and inverse-Gaussian distributions can all be written in the common linear-exponential form:

$$p(y; \theta, \phi) = \exp\left[\frac{y\theta - b(\theta)}{a(\phi)} + c(y, \phi)\right]$$

where $a(\cdot)$, $b(\cdot)$, and $c(\cdot)$ are known functions that vary from one exponential family to another; $\theta = g_c(\mu)$ is the canonical parameter for the exponential family in question; $g_c(\cdot)$ is the canonical link function; and $\phi > 0$ is a dispersion parameter, which takes on a fixed, known value in some families. It is generally the case that $\mu = E(Y) = b'(\theta)$ and that $V(Y) = a(\phi)b''(\theta)$.
- The maximum-likelihood estimating equations for generalized linear models take the common form

$$\sum_{i=1}^{n} \frac{Y_i - \mu_i}{a_i v(\mu_i)} \times \frac{d\mu_i}{d\eta_i} \times x_{ij} = 0, \text{ for } j = 0, 1, \ldots, k$$

These equations are generally nonlinear and therefore have no general closed-form solution, but they can be solved by iterated weighted least squares (IWLS). The estimating equations for the coefficients do not involve the dispersion parameter, which (for models in which the dispersion is not fixed) then can be estimated as

$$\widetilde{\phi} = \frac{1}{n - k - 1} \sum \frac{(Y_i - \widehat{\mu}_i)^2}{a_i v(\widehat{\mu}_i)}$$

The estimated asymptotic covariance matrix of the coefficients is

$$\widehat{\mathcal{V}}(\mathbf{b}) = \widetilde{\phi} \left(\mathbf{X'WX}\right)^{-1}$$

where **b** is the vector of estimated coefficients and **W** is a diagonal matrix of weights from the last IWLS iteration.

- The maximum-likelihood estimating equations, and IWLS estimation, can be applied whenever we can express the transformed mean of Y as a linear function of the Xs and can write the conditional variance of Y as a function of its mean and (possibly) a dispersion parameter—even when we do not specify a particular conditional distribution for Y. The resulting quasi-likelihood estimator shares many of the properties of maximum-likelihood estimators.

- The residual deviance for a model is twice the difference in the log likelihoods for the saturated model, which dedicates one parameter to each observation, and the model in question:

$$D(\mathbf{y}; \widehat{\mu}) \equiv 2[\log_e L(\mathbf{y}, \phi; \mathbf{y}) - \log_e L(\widehat{\mu}, \phi; \mathbf{y})]$$

$$= 2 \sum_{i=1}^{n} \frac{Y_i [g(Y_i) - g(\widehat{\mu}_i)] - b [g(Y_i)] + b [g(\widehat{\mu}_i)]}{a_i}$$

Dividing the residual deviance by the estimated dispersion parameter produces the scaled deviance, $D^*(\mathbf{y}; \widehat{\mu}) \equiv D(\mathbf{y}; \widehat{\mu})/\widetilde{\phi}$.

- To test the general linear hypothesis H_0: $\mathbf{L}\beta = \mathbf{c}$, where the hypothesis matrix $\mathbf{L}$ has q rows, we can compute the Wald chi-square test statistic

$$Z_0^2 = (\mathbf{Lb} - \mathbf{c})' [\mathbf{L}\widehat{\mathcal{V}}(\mathbf{b}) \mathbf{L}']^{-1} (\mathbf{Lb} - \mathbf{c})$$

with q degrees of freedom. Alternatively, if the dispersion parameter is estimated from the data, we can compute the F-test statistic

$$F_0 = \frac{(\mathbf{Lb} - \mathbf{c})' [\mathbf{L}\widehat{\mathcal{V}}(\mathbf{b}) \mathbf{L}']^{-1} (\mathbf{Lb} - \mathbf{c})}{q}$$

on q and $n - k - 1$ degrees of freedom.

- The delta method may be used to approximate the standard error of a nonlinear function of regression coefficients in a GLM. If $\gamma \equiv f(\beta_0, \beta_1, \ldots, \beta_k)$, then

$$\widehat{\mathcal{V}}(\widehat{\gamma}) \approx \sum_{j=0}^{k} \sum_{j'=0}^{k} v_{jj'} \times \frac{\partial \widehat{\gamma}}{\partial \widehat{\beta}_j} \times \frac{\partial \widehat{\gamma}}{\partial \widehat{\beta}_{j'}}$$

- Effect displays for GLMs are based on the fitted values $\widehat{\eta}^* = \mathbf{X}^* \mathbf{b}$, representing a high-order term in the model; that is, $\mathbf{X}^*$ has the same general structure as the model matrix $\mathbf{X}$, with the explanatory variables in the high-term order ranging over their values in the data, while other explanatory variables are set to typical values. The standard errors of $\widehat{\eta}^*$, given by the square-root diagonal entries of $\mathbf{X}^*\widehat{\mathcal{V}}(\mathbf{b})\mathbf{X}^{*'}$, may be used to compute pointwise confidence intervals for the effects.

- Most of the standard diagnostics for linear models extend relatively straightforwardly to GLMs. These extensions typically take advantage of the computation of maximum-likelihood and quasi-likelihood estimates for GLMs by iterated weighted least squares. Such diagnostics include studentized residuals, hat-values, Cook's distances, DFBETA and DFBETAS, added-variable plots, component-plus-residual plots, and the constructed-variable plot for transforming an explanatory variable.

Recommended Reading

- McCullagh and Nelder (1989), the "bible" of GLMs, is a rich and interesting—if generally difficult—text.
- Dobson (2001) presents a much briefer overview of generalized linear models at a more moderate level of statistical sophistication.
- Aitkin, Francis, and Hinde's (2005) text, geared to the statistical computer package GLIM for fitting GLMs, is still more accessible.
- A chapter by Firth (1991) is the best brief treatment of generalized linear models that I have read.
- Long (1997) includes an excellent presentation of regression models for count data (though not from the point of view of GLMs); an even more extensive treatment may be found in Cameron and Trivedi (1998).

PART V

Extending Linear and
Generalized Linear Models

16

Time-Series Regression and Generalized Least Squares*

This part of the book introduces several important extensions of linear least-squares regression and generalized linear models:

- The current chapter describes the application of linear regression models to time-series data in which the errors are correlated over time rather than independent.
- Nonlinear regression, the subject of Chapter 17, fits a specific nonlinear function of the explanatory variables by least squares.
- Chapter 18 develops nonparametric regression analysis, introduced in Chapter 2, which does not assume a specific functional form relating the response variable to the explanatory variables (as do traditional linear, generalized linear, and nonlinear regression models).
- Chapter 19 takes up robust regression analysis, which employs criteria for fitting a linear model that are not as sensitive as least squares to unusual data.

Taken together, the methods in the first four chapters of Part V considerably expand the range of application of regression analysis.

The standard linear model of Chapters 5 through 10 assumes independently distributed errors. The assumption of independence is rarely (if ever) quite right, but it is often a reasonable approximation. When the observations comprise a *time series*, however, dependencies among the errors can be very strong.

In time-series data, a single unit of observation (person, organization, nation, etc.) is tracked over many time periods or points of time.[1] These time periods or time points are usually evenly spaced, at least approximately, and I will assume here that this is the case. Economic statistics for Canada, for example, are reported on a daily, monthly, quarterly, and yearly basis. Crime statistics, likewise, are reported on a yearly basis. Later in this section, we will use yearly time series for the period 1931 to 1968 to examine the relationship between Canadian women's crime rates and fertility, women's labor-force participation, women's participation in higher education, and men's crime rates.

It is not generally reasonable to suppose that the errors in a time-series regression are independent: After all, time periods that are close to one another are more likely to be similar than time periods that are relatively remote. This similarity may well extend to the errors, which represent (most importantly) the omitted causes of the response variable. Although the time dependence among the errors may turn out to be negligible, it is unwise to assume a priori that this is the case.

---

[1]Temperature, for example, may be recorded at evenly spaced time points. Gross national product is cumulated over the period of a year. Most social data are collected in time periods rather than at time points.

> In time-series data, a single individual is tracked over many time periods or points of time. It is not generally reasonable to suppose that the errors in a time-series regression are independent.

16.1 Generalized Least-Squares Estimation

I will first address dependencies among the errors in a very general context. Consider the usual linear model,

$$\underset{(n\times1)}{\mathbf{y}} = \underset{(n\times k+1)}{\mathbf{X}} \underset{(k+1\times1)}{\beta} + \underset{(n\times1)}{\varepsilon}$$

Rather than assuming that the errors are independently distributed, however, let us instead assume that

$$\varepsilon \sim N_n(\mathbf{0}, \Sigma_{\varepsilon\varepsilon})$$

where the order-n matrix $\Sigma_{\varepsilon\varepsilon}$ is symmetric and positive definite. Nonzero off-diagonal entries in the covariance matrix $\Sigma_{\varepsilon\varepsilon}$ correspond to correlated errors.[2]

> To capture serial dependence among the errors in the regression model $\mathbf{y} = \mathbf{X}\beta + \varepsilon$, we drop the assumption that the errors are independent of one another; instead, we assume that $\varepsilon \sim N_n(\mathbf{0}, \Sigma_{\varepsilon\varepsilon})$, where nonzero off-diagonal entries in the error covariance matrix $\Sigma_{\varepsilon\varepsilon}$ correspond to correlated errors.

Let us assume unrealistically (and only temporarily) that we know $\Sigma_{\varepsilon\varepsilon}$. Then the log-likelihood for the model is[3]

$$\log_e L(\beta) = -\frac{n}{2}\log_e 2\pi - \frac{1}{2}\log_e(\det \Sigma_{\varepsilon\varepsilon}) - \frac{1}{2}(\mathbf{y} - \mathbf{X}\beta)'\Sigma_{\varepsilon\varepsilon}^{-1}(\mathbf{y} - \mathbf{X}\beta) \tag{16.1}$$

It is clear that the log-likelihood is maximized when the *generalized sum of squares* $(\mathbf{y} - \mathbf{X}\beta)'\Sigma_{\varepsilon\varepsilon}^{-1}(\mathbf{y} - \mathbf{X}\beta)$ is minimized.[4] Differentiating the generalized sum of squares with respect to β, setting the partial derivatives to $\mathbf{0}$, and solving for β produces the *generalized least-squares (GLS) estimator*

$$\mathbf{b}_{GLS} = (\mathbf{X}'\Sigma_{\varepsilon\varepsilon}^{-1}\mathbf{X})^{-1}\mathbf{X}'\Sigma_{\varepsilon\varepsilon}^{-1}\mathbf{y} \tag{16.2}$$

It is simple to show that the GLS estimator is unbiased, $E(\mathbf{b}_{GLS}) = \beta$; that its sampling variance is

$$V(\mathbf{b}_{GLS}) = (\mathbf{X}'\Sigma_{\varepsilon\varepsilon}^{-1}\mathbf{X})^{-1}$$

---

[2] Because of the assumption of normality, dependence implies correlation. Like the standard linear model with independent errors, however, most of the results of this section do not require the assumption of normality. Note that unequal *diagonal* entries of $\Sigma_{\varepsilon\varepsilon}$ correspond to unequal error variances, a problem discussed in Section 12.2. Indeed, weighted least-squares regression (Section 12.2.2) is a special case of generalized least-squares estimation, where $\Sigma_{\varepsilon\varepsilon}$ is a diagonal matrix.

[3] See Exercise 16.1 for this and other results described in this section.

[4] Recall that $\Sigma_{\varepsilon\varepsilon}$ is assumed to be known.

and that, by an extension of the Gauss-Markov theorem, $\mathbf{b}_{GLS}$ is the minimum-variance linear unbiased estimator of β.[5] None of these results (with the exception of the one establishing the GLS estimator as the ML estimator) requires the assumption of normality.

Here is another way of thinking about the GLS estimator: Let $\boldsymbol{\Gamma}_{(n \times n)}$ be a "square-root" of $\boldsymbol{\Sigma}_{\varepsilon\varepsilon}^{-1}$, in the sense that $\boldsymbol{\Gamma}'\boldsymbol{\Gamma} = \boldsymbol{\Sigma}_{\varepsilon\varepsilon}^{-1}$.[6] From Equation 16.2,

$$\mathbf{b}_{GLS} = (\mathbf{X}'\boldsymbol{\Gamma}'\boldsymbol{\Gamma}\mathbf{X})^{-1}\mathbf{X}'\boldsymbol{\Gamma}'\boldsymbol{\Gamma}\mathbf{y}$$
$$= (\mathbf{X}^{*\prime}\mathbf{X}^*)^{-1}\mathbf{X}^{*\prime}\mathbf{y}^*$$

where $\mathbf{X}^* \equiv \boldsymbol{\Gamma}\mathbf{X}$ and $\mathbf{y}^* \equiv \boldsymbol{\Gamma}\mathbf{y}$. Thus, the GLS estimator is the *ordinary-least-squares (OLS)* estimator for the regression of $\mathbf{y}^*$ on $\mathbf{X}^*$—that is, following the linear transformation of $\mathbf{y}$ and $\mathbf{X}$ using the transformation matrix $\boldsymbol{\Gamma}$.

If the error covariance matrix $\boldsymbol{\Sigma}_{\varepsilon\varepsilon}$ is known, then the maximum-likelihood (ML) estimator of β is the generalized least-squares estimator $\mathbf{b}_{GLS} = (\mathbf{X}'\boldsymbol{\Sigma}_{\varepsilon\varepsilon}^{-1}\mathbf{X})^{-1}\mathbf{X}'\boldsymbol{\Sigma}_{\varepsilon\varepsilon}^{-1}\mathbf{y}$. The sampling variance-covariance matrix of $\mathbf{b}_{GLS}$ is $V(\mathbf{b}_{GLS}) = (\mathbf{X}'\boldsymbol{\Sigma}_{\varepsilon\varepsilon}^{-1}\mathbf{X})^{-1}$. The generalized least-squares estimator can also be expressed as the OLS estimator $(\mathbf{X}^{*\prime}\mathbf{X}^*)^{-1}\mathbf{X}^{*\prime}\mathbf{y}^*$ for the transformed variables $\mathbf{X}^* \equiv \boldsymbol{\Gamma}\mathbf{X}$ and $\mathbf{y}^* \equiv \boldsymbol{\Gamma}\mathbf{y}$, where the transformation matrix $\boldsymbol{\Gamma}$ is a square root of $\boldsymbol{\Sigma}_{\varepsilon\varepsilon}^{-1}$.

16.2 Serially Correlated Errors

I have, thus far, left the covariance matrix of the errors $\boldsymbol{\Sigma}_{\varepsilon\varepsilon}$ very general: Because of its symmetry, there are $n(n+1)/2$ distinct elements in $\boldsymbol{\Sigma}_{\varepsilon\varepsilon}$. Without further assumptions concerning the structure of this matrix, we cannot hope to estimate its elements from only n observations if—as is always the case in real applications of time-series regression—$\boldsymbol{\Sigma}_{\varepsilon\varepsilon}$ is not known.

Suppose, however, that the process generating the errors is *stationary*. Stationarity means that the errors all have the same expectation (which, indeed, we have already assumed to be 0); that the errors have a common variance (σ_ε^2); and that the covariance of two errors depends only on their separation in time. Let ε_t denote the error for time period t, and ε_{t+s} the error for time period $t + s$ (where s is an integer—positive, negative, or 0). Stationarity implies that, for any t, the covariance between ε_t and ε_{t+s} is

$$C(\varepsilon_t, \varepsilon_{t+s}) = E(\varepsilon_t \varepsilon_{t+s}) = \sigma_\varepsilon^2 \rho_s = C(\varepsilon_t, \varepsilon_{t-s})$$

where ρ_s, called the *autocorrelation* (or *serial correlation*) at lag s, is the correlation between two errors separated by $|s|$ time periods.

The error covariance matrix, then, has the following pattern:

$$\boldsymbol{\Sigma}_{\varepsilon\varepsilon} = \sigma_\varepsilon^2 \begin{bmatrix} 1 & \rho_1 & \rho_2 & \cdots & \rho_{n-1} \\ \rho_1 & 1 & \rho_1 & \cdots & \rho_{n-2} \\ \rho_2 & \rho_1 & 1 & \cdots & \rho_{n-3} \\ \vdots & \vdots & \vdots & \ddots & \vdots \\ \rho_{n-1} & \rho_{n-2} & \rho_{n-3} & \cdots & 1 \end{bmatrix} = \sigma_\varepsilon^2 \mathbf{P} \tag{16.3}$$

---

[5]The Gauss-Markov theorem is discussed in Section 9.3.2 in the context of ordinary-least-squares regression.

[6]Because $\boldsymbol{\Sigma}_{\varepsilon\varepsilon}^{-1}$ is nonsingular, it is always possible to find a square-root matrix, although the square-root is not in general unique.

The situation is much improved, but it is not good enough: There are now n distinct parameters to estimate in $\Sigma_{\varepsilon\varepsilon}$—that is, σ_ε^2 and $\rho_1, \ldots, \rho_{n-1}$—still too many.

> When, more realistically, the error covariance matrix $\Sigma_{\varepsilon\varepsilon}$ is unknown, we need to estimate its contents along with the regression coefficients β. Without restricting its form, however, $\Sigma_{\varepsilon\varepsilon}$ contains too many distinct elements to estimate directly. Assuming that the errors are generated by a stationary time-series process reduces the number of independent parameters in $\Sigma_{\varepsilon\varepsilon}$ to n, including the error variance σ_ε^2 and the autocorrelations at various lags, $\rho_1, \ldots, \rho_{n-1}$.

16.2.1   The First-Order Autoregressive Process

To proceed, we need to specify a stationary process for the errors that depends on fewer parameters. The process that is by far most commonly used in practice is the *first-order autoregressive process*, abbreviated *AR(1)*:

$$\varepsilon_t = \rho\varepsilon_{t-1} + v_t \tag{16.4}$$

where the error in time period t depends directly only on the error in the previous time period, ε_{t-1}, and on a random contemporaneous "shock" v_t. Unlike the regression errors ε_t, we will assume that the random shocks v_t are independent of each other (and of εs from earlier time periods), and that $v_t \sim N(0, \sigma_v^2)$. Serial correlation in the regression errors, therefore, is wholly generated by the partial dependence of each error on the error of the previous time period. Because of its importance in applications and its simplicity, I will describe the AR(1) process in some detail.

For Equation 16.4 to specify a stationary process, it is necessary that $|\rho| < 1$. Otherwise, the errors will tend to grow without bound. If the process is stationary, and if all errors have zero expectations and common variance, then

$$\sigma_\varepsilon^2 \equiv V(\varepsilon_t) = E(\varepsilon_t^2)$$
$$= V(\varepsilon_{t-1}) = E(\varepsilon_{t-1}^2)$$

Squaring both sides of Equation 16.4 and taking expectations,

$$E(\varepsilon_t^2) = \rho^2 E(\varepsilon_{t-1}^2) + E(v_t^2) + 2\rho E(\varepsilon_{t-1}v_t)$$
$$\sigma_\varepsilon^2 = \rho^2 \sigma_\varepsilon^2 + \sigma_v^2$$

because $E(\varepsilon_{t-1}v_t) = C(\varepsilon_{t-1}, v_t) = 0$. Solving for the variance of the regression errors yields

$$\sigma_\varepsilon^2 = \frac{\sigma_v^2}{1 - \rho^2}$$

It is also a simple matter to find the autocorrelation at lag s. For example, at lag 1, we have the *autocovariance*

$$C(\varepsilon_t, \varepsilon_{t-1}) = E(\varepsilon_t\varepsilon_{t-1})$$
$$= E[(\rho\varepsilon_{t-1} + v_t)\varepsilon_{t-1}]$$
$$= \rho\sigma_\varepsilon^2$$

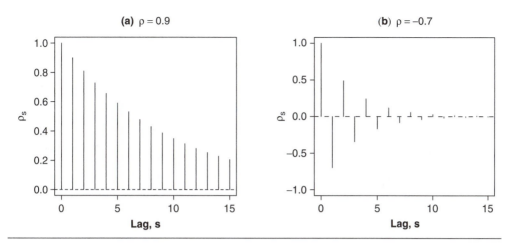

Figure 16.1 Theoretical autocorrelations ρ_s for the first-order autoregressive process $\varepsilon_t = \rho\varepsilon_{t-1} + v_t$, with (a) $\rho = .9$ and (b) $\rho = -.7$.

So the autocorrelation at lag 1 is just

$$
\begin{aligned}
\rho_1 &= \frac{C(\varepsilon_t, \varepsilon_{t-1})}{\sqrt{V(\varepsilon_t) \times V(\varepsilon_{t-1})}} \\
&= \frac{\rho\sigma_\varepsilon^2}{\sigma_\varepsilon^2} \\
&= \rho
\end{aligned}
$$

Likewise, at lag 2,

$$
\begin{aligned}
C(\varepsilon_t, \varepsilon_{t-2}) &= E(\varepsilon_t\varepsilon_{t-2}) \\
&= E\{[\rho(\rho\varepsilon_{t-2} + v_{t-1}) + v_t]\varepsilon_{t-2}\} \\
&= \rho^2\sigma_\varepsilon^2
\end{aligned}
$$

and, therefore, $\rho_2 = \rho^2$.

More generally, for the first-order autoregressive process, $\rho_s = \rho^s$, and because $|\rho| < 1$, the autocorrelations of the errors decay exponentially toward 0 as the lag s gets larger. This behavior is apparent in the examples in Figure 16.1, which shows AR(1) *autocorrelation functions* for $\rho = .9$ and $\rho = -.7$. Note that the autocorrelation at lag 0 is $\rho_0 = 1$.

To reduce the number of parameters in $\Sigma_{\varepsilon\varepsilon}$ further, we can adopt a specific time-series model for the errors. The most commonly employed such model is the first-order autoregressive process $\varepsilon_t = \rho\varepsilon_{t-1} + v_t$, where $|\rho| < 1$ and the random shocks v_t are independently distributed as $N(0, \sigma_v^2)$. Under this specification, two errors, ε_t and ε_{t+s}, separated by s time periods have autocovariance $\rho^s\sigma_\varepsilon^2$ and autocorrelation ρ^s. The variance of the regression errors is $\sigma_\varepsilon^2 = \sigma_v^2/(1 - \rho^2)$.

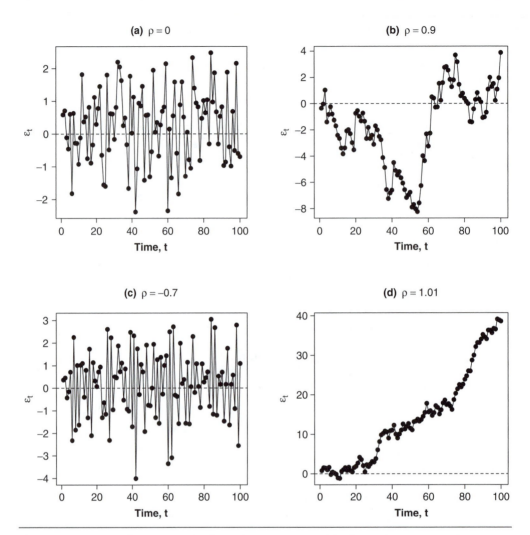

Figure 16.2 Four realizations, each of sample size $n=100$, of the first-order autoregressive process $\varepsilon_t = \rho\varepsilon_{t-1} + \nu_t$: (a) $\rho=0$ ("white noise"), (b) $\rho=.9$, (c) $\rho=-.7$, and (d) $\rho=1.01$ (a nonstationary process). In each case, $\nu_t \sim N(0,1)$.

Some "realizations" of time series generated by Equation 16.4, with $\nu_t \sim N(0, 1)$, are shown in Figure 16.2. In Figure 16.2(a), $\rho = 0$, and, consequently, the ε_t are uncorrelated, a time-series process sometimes termed *white noise*. In Figure 16.2(b), $\rho = .9$; note how values of the series close to one another tend to be similar. In Figure 16.2(c), $\rho = -.7$; note here how the series tends to bounce from negative to positive values. Negatively autocorrelated series are not common in the social sciences. Finally, Figure 16.2(d) illustrates a nonstationary process, with $\rho = 1.01$.

Figure 16.2(b) also provides some intuitive insight into the problems for estimation posed by autocorrelated errors:

- Because errors that are close in time are likely to be similar, there is much less information in a highly autocorrelated time series than in an independent random sample of the same size. It is, for example, often unproductive to proliferate observations by using more closely spaced time periods (e.g., monthly or quarterly rather than yearly data[7]). To do so will likely increase the autocorrelation of the errors.[8]

- Over a relatively short period of time, a highly autocorrelated series is likely to rise or to fall—that is, show a positive or negative trend. This is true even though the series is stationary and, therefore, will eventually return to its expectation of 0. If, for example, our sample consisted only of the first 50 observations in Figure 16.2(b), then there would be a negative trend in the errors; if our sample consisted of observations 60 to 75, then there would be a positive trend.

  Because explanatory variables in a time-series regression also often manifest directional trends, a rise or fall in the errors of a short time series can induce a correlation between an explanatory variable and the errors *for this specific sample*. It is important, however, to understand that there is no implication that the OLS estimates are biased because of correlation between the explanatory variables and the errors: Over many samples, there will sometimes be negative correlations between the errors and the explanatory variables, sometimes positive correlations, and sometimes virtually no correlation. The correlations—sometimes negative, sometimes positive—that occur in specific samples can markedly increase the *variance* of the OLS estimator, however.[9]

- Finally, because the OLS estimator forces zero *sample* correlations between the explanatory variables and the residuals (as opposed to the unobserved errors), the sampling variances of the OLS coefficients may be grossly underestimated by $S_E^2(\mathbf{X'X})^{-1}$. Recall that in a short series, highly autocorrelated errors will often manifest a trend in a *particular* sample.

16.2.2 Higher-Order Autoregressive Processes

The AR(1) process is the simplest member of the family of autoregressive processes. In the pth-order autoregressive process [abbreviated AR(p)], ε_t depends on the previous p errors and a random shock ν_t:

$$\varepsilon_t = \phi_1\varepsilon_{t-1} + \phi_2\varepsilon_{t-2} + \cdots + \phi_p\varepsilon_{t-p} + \nu_t \tag{16.5}$$

(where I use ϕ rather than ρ because the autoregressive coefficients are no longer correlations).

It is rare in time-series regression to go beyond $p = 2$, that is, the AR(2) process,

$$\varepsilon_t = \phi_1\varepsilon_{t-1} + \phi_2\varepsilon_{t-2} + \nu_t \tag{16.6}$$

---

[7]Monthly or quarterly data also raise the possibility of "seasonal" effects. One simple approach to seasonal effects is to include dummy regressors for months or quarters. Likewise, dummy regressors for days of the week might be appropriate for some daily time series. More sophisticated approaches to seasonal effects are described in most texts on time-series analysis, such as Harvey (1990, sec. 7.6), and Judge, Griffiths, Hill, Lütkepohl, and Lee (1985, secs. 7.2.4 and 7.7.2).

[8]This point is nicely illustrated by considering the sampling variance of the sample mean $\overline{Y}$. From elementary statistics, we know that the variance of $\overline{Y}$ in an independent random sample of size n is σ^2/n, where σ^2 is the population variance. If instead we sample observations from a first-order autoregressive process with parameter ρ, the variance of $\overline{Y}$ is

$$\frac{\sigma^2}{n} \times \frac{1+\rho}{1-\rho}$$

The sampling variance of $\overline{Y}$ is, therefore, much larger than σ^2/n when the autocorrelation ρ is close to 1. Put another way, the "effective" number of observations is $n(1-\rho)/(1+\rho)$ rather than n. I am grateful to Robert Stine of the University of Pennsylvania for suggesting this illustration.

[9]The effect of autocorrelated errors on OLS estimation is explored in Exercise 16.3.

For this process to be stationary, the roots β of the quadratic equation

$$1 - \phi_1\beta - \phi_2\beta^2 = 0$$

most both have modulus exceeding 1.[10]

Multiplying Equation 16.6 through by ε_{t-1} and taking expectations produces

$$C(\varepsilon_t, \varepsilon_{t-1}) = \phi_1 E(\varepsilon_{t-1}^2) + \phi_2 E(\varepsilon_{t-1}\varepsilon_{t-2})$$
$$= \phi_1\sigma_\varepsilon^2 + \phi_2 C(\varepsilon_t, \varepsilon_{t-1})$$

because $E(\varepsilon_{t-1}^2) = \sigma_\varepsilon^2$ and $E(\varepsilon_{t-1}\varepsilon_{t-2}) = C(\varepsilon_{t-1}, \varepsilon_{t-2}) = C(\varepsilon_t, \varepsilon_{t-1})$. Solving for the autocovariance,

$$\sigma_1 \equiv C(\varepsilon_t, \varepsilon_{t-1}) = \frac{\phi_1}{1 - \phi_2}\sigma_\varepsilon^2$$

Similarly, for $s > 1$,

$$\sigma_s \equiv C(\varepsilon_t, \varepsilon_{t-s}) = \phi_1 E(\varepsilon_{t-1,t-s}) + \phi_2 E(\varepsilon_{t-2}\varepsilon_{t-s})$$
$$= \phi_1\sigma_{s-1} + \phi_2\sigma_{s-2}$$

and thus we can find the autocovariances recursively. For example, for $j = 2$,

$$\sigma_2 = \phi_1\sigma_1 + \phi_2\sigma_0$$
$$= \phi_1\sigma_1 + \phi_2\sigma_\varepsilon^2$$

(where $\sigma_0 = \sigma_\varepsilon^2$); and for $j = 3$,

$$\sigma_3 = \phi_1\sigma_2 + \phi_2\sigma_1$$

Autocorrelations for the AR(2) process follow upon division of the autocovariances by σ_ε^2:

$$\text{lag } 0: \quad \rho_0 = 1$$
$$\text{lag } 1: \quad \rho_1 = \frac{\phi_1}{1 - \phi_2}$$
$$\text{lag } 2: \quad \rho_2 = \phi_1\rho_1 + \phi_2$$
$$\text{lag } 3: \quad \rho_3 = \phi_1\rho_2 + \phi_2\rho_1$$
$$\text{lag } j > 3: \quad \rho_j = \phi_1\rho_{j-1} + \phi_2\rho_{j-2}$$

If the process is stationary, then these autocorrelations decay towards 0, although the pattern of decay may be more or less complex depending upon the values and signs of the autoregressive parameters ϕ_1 and ϕ_2. Two examples appear in Figure 16.3.

16.2.3 Moving-Average and Autoregressive-Moving-Average Processes

Although autoregressive processes are the most frequently employed in time-series regression, *moving-average* (MA) and combined *autoregressive-moving-average* (ARMA) processes sometimes can provide simplification. That is, a low-order MA or ARMA process may represent the data as well as a much higher-order AR process.

---

[10]In general, the roots can be complex numbers, of the form $\beta = \beta_1 + \beta_2 i$. The modulus of β is $\sqrt{\beta_1^2 + \beta_2^2}$. This stationarity condition generalizes to higher-order AR processes; see, for example, Chatfield (2003, sec. 3.2). For an example, see Exercise 16.7.

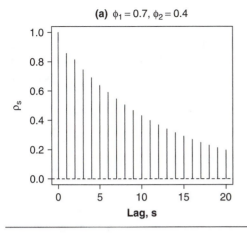

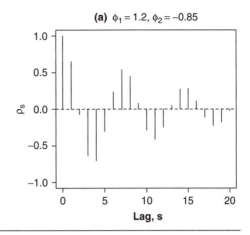

Figure 16.3   Theoretical autocorrelations ρ_s for the AR(2) process $\varepsilon_t = \phi_1 \varepsilon_{t-1} + \phi_2 \varepsilon_{t-2} + v_t$, with (a) $\phi_1 = 0.7$, $\phi_2 = 0.4$, and (b) $\phi_1 = 1.2$, $\phi_2 = -0.85$.

In the order-q moving-average process [MA(q)], the error at time t depends on the random shock at time t and on the shocks in the previous q time periods:[11]

$$\varepsilon_t = v_t + \theta_1 v_{t-1} + \theta_2 v_{t-2} + \cdots + \theta_q v_{t-q}$$

It is unusual to specify $q > 2$. Applying the same tools that we used to analyze AR processes,[12] we find that the MA(1) process

$$\varepsilon_t = v_t + \theta v_{t-1}$$

has autocorrelations

$$\rho_1 = \frac{\theta}{1 + \theta^2}$$
$$\rho_s = 0, \text{ for } s > 1$$

For the MA(2) process,

$$\varepsilon_t = v_t + \theta_1 v_{t-1} + \theta_2 v_{t-2}$$

we have,

$$\rho_1 = \frac{\theta_1 + \theta_1 \theta_2}{1 + \theta_1^2 + \theta_2^2}$$
$$\rho_2 = \frac{\theta_2}{1 + \theta_1^2 + \theta_2^2}$$
$$\rho_s = 0, \text{ for } s > 2$$

More generally, in the MA(q) process, $\rho_s = 0$ for $s > q$.

---

[11]It is common to write the MA(q) model as

$$\varepsilon_t = v_t - \theta_1 v_{t-1} - \theta_2 v_{t-2} - \cdots - \theta_q v_{t-q}$$

that is, *subtracting*, rather than adding the terms $\theta_s v_{t-s}$, and therefore reversing the signs of the MA parameters θ_s. I believe that the notation that I employ is slightly easier to follow. A similar point applies to the MA terms in ARMA(p, q) models, described below.

[12]See Exercise 16.2.

MA processes are stationary without restrictions on the parameters θ_s, but for there to be a one-to-one correspondence between an MA(q) process and a particular autocorrelation function, it is necessary that the process satisfy a condition termed *invertibility*. This condition is closely analogous to the condition for stationarity on the parameters of an AR process, as described above. In particular, for an MA(1) process, we require that $|\theta| < 1$; and for an MA(2) process, we require that the roots of the equation

$$1 + \theta_1 \beta + \theta_2 \beta^2 = 0$$

both have modulus larger than 1.

As its name implies, the autoregressive-moving-average process ARMA(p, q) combines autoregressive and MA components:

$$\varepsilon_t = \phi_1 \varepsilon_{t-1} + \phi_2 \varepsilon_{t-2} + \cdots + \phi_p \varepsilon_{t-p} + v_t + \theta_1 v_{t-1} + \theta_2 v_{t-2} + \cdots + \theta_q v_{t-q}$$

These more general ARMA processes are capable of parsimoniously modeling a wider variety of patterns of autocorrelation, but it is rare to go beyond ARMA(1, 1),[13]

$$\varepsilon_t = \phi \varepsilon_{t-1} + v_t + \theta v_{t-1}$$

This process is stationary if $|\phi| < 1$, and invertible if $|\theta| < 1$.

The autocorrelations for the ARMA(1, 1) process are[14]

$$\rho_1 = \frac{(1 + \phi\theta)(\phi + \theta)}{1 + \theta^2 + 2\phi\theta}$$

$$\rho_s = \phi\rho_{s-1}, \text{ for } s > 1$$

The autocorrelations, consequently, decay exponentially as the lag s grows. Some examples are shown in Figure 16.4.

Higher-order autoregressive processes, moving-average processes, and mixed autoregressive-moving-average processes can be used to model more complex forms of serial dependence in the errors.

16.2.4 Partial Autocorrelations

Let ρ_s^* represent the partial correlation between ε_s and ε_{t-s} "controlling for" $\varepsilon_{t-1}, \ldots,$ ε_{t-s+1}.[15] Suppose that ε_t follows an AR(s) process (as given in Equation 16.5 on page 433). Multiplying through successively by $\varepsilon_{t-1}, \varepsilon_{t-2}, \ldots, \varepsilon_{t-s}$, taking expectations, and dividing by the variance σ_ε^2 produces the so-called *Yule-Walker equations*:

$$
\begin{aligned}
\rho_1 &= \phi_1 &+ \phi_2\rho_1 &+ \cdots + \phi_s\rho_{s-1} \\
\rho_2 &= \phi_1\rho_1 &+ \phi_2 &+ \cdots + \phi_s\rho_{s-2} \\
&\vdots \\
\rho_s &= \phi_1\rho_{s-1} &+ \phi_2\rho_{s-2} &+ \cdots + \phi_s
\end{aligned}
\tag{16.7}
$$

---

[13] For further details, see, for example, Judge et al. (1985, chaps. 7 and 8) and Chatfield (2003, sec. 3.4).

[14] See Exercise 16.2.

[15] Partial correlations were introduced in Exercise 5.8.

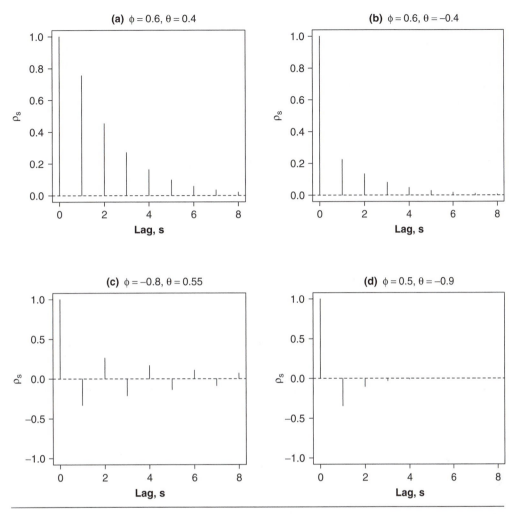

Figure 16.4 Theoretical autocorrelations for the ARMA(1, 1) process, with (a) $\phi = 0.6$, $\theta = 0.4$; (b) $\phi = 0.6$, $\theta = -0.4$; (c) $\phi = -0.8$, $\theta = 0.55$; and (d) $\phi = 0.5$, $\theta = -0.9$.

or, in matrix form, $\rho = \mathbf{P}\phi$. Solving for the autoregressive parameters in terms of the autocorrelations yields $\phi = \mathbf{P}^{-1}\rho$. The *partial autocorrelation* ρ_s^* is the last autoregressive coefficient, ϕ_s. Setting s in turn to the values $1, 2, \ldots$, and forming and solving the resulting sets of Yule-Walker equations, produces the partial autocorrelations $\rho_1^*, \rho_2^*, \ldots$. It is apparent from this mode of computation that for an AR(p) process, $\rho_s^* = 0$ for $s > p$.

The partial autocorrelations can also be computed for MA and ARMA processes, but rather than falling abruptly to 0, the partial autocorrelations decay exponentially in a more or less complex pattern depending on the order and signs of the coefficients of the MA or ARMA process. Put another way, the partial autocorrelations of an MA process behave much like the autocorrelations of an AR process. Indeed, this link between MA and AR processes is more than superficial: An MA process may be represented as an AR process of infinite order, and vice versa.[16]

---

[16] See, for example, Chatfield (2003, sec. 3.4).

> The partial autocorrelations of an AR(p) process fall abruptly to 0 after lag p; those of MA and ARMA processes decay towards 0 in a pattern determined by the coefficients of the process. The distinctive features of the autocorrelation and partial-autocorrelation functions of AR, MA, and ARMA processes may be used to help select a process to model a particular time series.

16.3 GLS Estimation With Autocorrelated Errors

If the errors follow a first-order autoregressive process, then the covariance matrix of the regression errors, given in general form in Equation 16.3 (page 429), takes the relatively simple form

$$\Sigma_{\varepsilon\varepsilon}(\rho, \sigma_v^2) = \frac{\sigma_v^2}{1 - \rho^2} \begin{bmatrix} 1 & \rho & \rho^2 & \cdots & \rho^{n-1} \\ \rho & 1 & \rho & \cdots & \rho^{n-2} \\ \rho^2 & \rho & 1 & \cdots & \rho^{n-3} \\ \vdots & \vdots & \vdots & \ddots & \vdots \\ \rho^{n-1} & \rho^{n-2} & \rho^{n-3} & \cdots & 1 \end{bmatrix} \tag{16.8}$$

As the notation implies, the error covariance matrix depends on *only two* parameters: ρ and σ_v^2—or, alternatively, on ρ and $\sigma_\varepsilon^2 = \sigma_v^2/(1 - \rho^2)$. If we knew the values of these parameters, then we could form $\Sigma_{\varepsilon\varepsilon}$ and proceed directly to GLS estimation.

Recall that GLS estimation can be realized as OLS following a transformation of $\mathbf{y}$ and $\mathbf{X}$. In the present case (ignoring a constant factor), the transformation matrix is[17]

$$\Gamma = \begin{bmatrix} \sqrt{1 - \rho^2} & 0 & 0 & \cdots & 0 & 0 \\ -\rho & 1 & 0 & \cdots & 0 & 0 \\ 0 & -\rho & 1 & \cdots & 0 & 0 \\ \vdots & \vdots & \vdots & \ddots & \vdots & \vdots \\ 0 & 0 & 0 & \cdots & -\rho & 1 \end{bmatrix}$$

Then the transformed variables are

$$\mathbf{y}^* = \Gamma\mathbf{y} = \begin{bmatrix} \sqrt{1 - \rho^2}Y_1 \\ Y_2 - \rho Y_1 \\ \vdots \\ Y_n - \rho Y_{n-1} \end{bmatrix} \tag{16.9}$$

and

$$\mathbf{X}^* = \Gamma\mathbf{X} = \begin{bmatrix} \sqrt{1 - \rho^2} & \sqrt{1 - \rho^2}X_{11} & \cdots & \sqrt{1 - \rho^2}X_{1k} \\ 1 - \rho & X_{21} - \rho X_{11} & \cdots & X_{2k} - \rho X_{1k} \\ \vdots & \vdots & & \vdots \\ 1 - \rho & X_{n1} - \rho X_{n-1, 1} & \cdots & X_{nk} - \rho X_{n-1, k} \end{bmatrix} \tag{16.10}$$

where the first column of $\mathbf{X}^*$ is the transformed constant regressor.

---

[17] See Exercise 16.4.

Note that, except for the first observation, $Y_t^* = Y_t - \rho Y_{t-1}$ and $X_{tj}^* = X_{tj} - \rho X_{t-1,j}$. These transformations have the following intuitive interpretation: Write out the regression equation in scalar form as

$$Y_t = \alpha + \beta_1 X_{t1} + \cdots + \beta_k X_{tk} + \varepsilon_t \tag{16.11}$$
$$= \alpha + \beta_1 X_{t1} + \cdots + \beta_k X_{tk} + \rho \varepsilon_{t-1} + v_t$$

For the previous observation ($t - 1$), we have, similarly,

$$Y_{t-1} = \alpha + \beta_1 X_{t-1,1} + \cdots + \beta_k X_{t-1,k} + \varepsilon_{t-1} \tag{16.12}$$

Multiplying Equation 16.12 through by ρ and subtracting the result from Equation 16.11 produces

$$Y_t - \rho Y_{t-1} = \alpha(1 - \rho) + \beta_1(X_{t1} - \rho X_{t-1,1}) \tag{16.13}$$
$$+ \cdots + \beta_k(X_{tk} - \rho X_{t-1,k}) + v_t$$
$$Y_t^* = \alpha 1^* + \beta_1 X_{t1}^* + \cdots + \beta_k X_{tk}^* + v_t \quad \text{for } t = 2, \ldots, n$$

Because the errors in Equation 16.13 are the v_t, which are independent of each other and of the X^*s, the transformed equation can legitimately be fit by OLS regression. The only slippage here is that the first observation is lost, for there are no data at $t - 1 = 1 - 1 = 0$. Applying OLS to Equation 16.13 is, therefore, not quite the same as GLS.

Qualitatively similar, but more complex, results apply to higher-order AR processes, and to MA and ARMA processes for the errors.

16.3.1 Empirical GLS Estimation

All of this presupposes that we know the value of the error autocorrelation ρ. In practice, of course, we need to estimate ρ along with the regression parameters $\alpha, \beta_1, \ldots, \beta_k$ and the variance of the random shocks σ_v^2 (or, alternatively, the variance of the regression errors σ_ε^2). One approach to this problem is first to estimate ρ. Then, using the estimate (say $\hat{\rho}$) as if ρ were known, we can calculate GLS estimates and their standard errors—either directly or, equivalently, by OLS following transformation of **y** and **X**. This approach is called *empirical generalized least squares (EGLS)*.

An especially simple option is to base the estimate of ρ on the lag-1 sample autocorrelation of the residuals from the OLS regression of **y** on **X**:[18]

$$r_1 = \frac{\sum_{t=2}^{n} E_t E_{t-1}}{\sum_{t=1}^{n} E_t^2} \tag{16.14}$$

where the E_t are the OLS residuals. Note that the sum in the numerator of Equation 16.14 is over observations $t = 2, \ldots, n$ (because E_{t-1}—i.e., E_0—is unavailable for $t = 1$). Using $\hat{\rho} = r_1$ in Equations 16.9 and 16.10 produces transformed variables from which to calculate the EGLS estimates by OLS regression. The variance of the residuals from this OLS regression estimates σ_v^2.

This procedure can be extended to more complex processes for the errors.[19]

---

[18] Although there are other methods to obtain a preliminary estimate of ρ, none holds a particular advantage. For details, see, for example, Judge et al. (1985, sec. 8.2.1).

[19] See, for example, Judge et al. (1985, sec 8.2).

16.3.2 Maximum-Likelihood Estimation

It is preferable to estimate all of the parameters—ρ, σ_v^2, and β—directly and simultaneously, by maximum likelihood, thereby acknowledging the additional uncertainty produced by having to estimate the parameters of the error process—uncertainty that is ignored by the EGLS estimator. We just have to think of the log-likelihood as a function of all of the parameters (adapting Equation 16.1 on page 428):

$$\log_e L(\beta, \rho, \sigma_v^2) = -\frac{n}{2}\log_e 2\pi - \frac{1}{2}\log_e(\det \Sigma_{\varepsilon\varepsilon}) - \frac{1}{2}(\mathbf{y} - \mathbf{X}\beta)'\Sigma_{\varepsilon\varepsilon}^{-1}(\mathbf{y} - \mathbf{X}\beta)$$

where $\Sigma_{\varepsilon\varepsilon}$ for AR(1) errors is determined by the parameters ρ and σ_v^2 according to Equation 16.8 (page 438). This approach is, moreover, quite general, because *any* AR, MA, or ARMA process provides an expression for $\Sigma_{\varepsilon\varepsilon}$ as a function of the parameters of the error process. An illustrative application using an AR(2) process for the errors is described in the next section.

> To apply GLS estimation to a regression model with AR(1) errors, we can first estimate the autocorrelation of the errors from the sample autocorrelation of the OLS residuals: $\widehat{\rho} = r_1 = \left(\sum_{t=2}^n E_t E_{t-1}\right) / \left(\sum_{t=1}^n E_t^2\right)$. We can then use $\widehat{\rho}$ to form an estimate of the correlation matrix of the errors or to transform $\mathbf{y}$ and $\mathbf{X}$. Except for the first observation, these transformations take a very simple form: $Y_t^* = Y_t - \widehat{\rho} Y_{t-1}$ and $X_{tj}^* = X_{tj} - \widehat{\rho} X_{t-1,j}$. This procedure is called empirical GLS estimation. Empirical GLS can be extended to more complex time-series models for the errors. A better approach, however, is to estimate the parameters of the error process along with the regression coefficients by the method of maximum likelihood.

16.4 Diagnosing Serially Correlated Errors

We need to ask whether the data support the hypothesis that the errors are serially correlated, because, in the absence of serially correlated errors, we can legitimately employ OLS estimation. As usual, our key to the behavior of the unobservable errors is the least-squares residuals.[20]

Figure 16.5, based on data from Fox and Hartnagel (1979), shows a yearly time-series plot of the female indictable-offense conviction rate (FCR) per 100,000 Canadian women aged 15 years and above, for the period 1931 to 1968.[21] The conviction rate rose from the mid-1930s until 1940, then declined until the mid-1950s, and subsequently rose again.

Fox and Hartnagel were interested in relating variations in women's crime rates to changes in their position within Canadian society. To this end, they regressed women's conviction rate on the following explanatory variables:

- The *total fertility rate (TFR)*—the number of births to an imaginary cohort of 1000 women who live through their child-bearing years at current age-specific fertility rates.
- *Women's labor-force participation rate (LFPR)* per 1000 population.

---

[20]Cf., the discussion of diagnostics in Chapters 11 and 12.

[21]Because the basis for reporting convictions changed in 1949, the data for the period 1950 to 1968 have been adjusted. The adjustment used here is very slightly different from the one employed by Fox and Hartnagel (1979). Indictable offenses are relatively serious crimes. I am grateful to Timothy Hartnagel of the University of Alberta for helping me to assemble the data for this example.

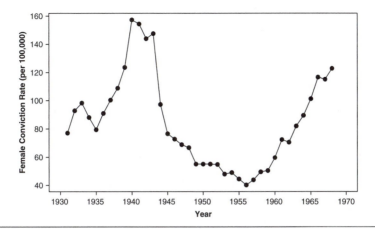

Figure 16.5 Canadian women's indictable-offense conviction rate per 100,000 population, for the period 1931 to 1968.

- *Women's postsecondary-degree rate (PSDR)* per 10,000 population.
- *Men's indictable-offense conviction rate (MCR)* per 100,000 population. This explanatory variable was meant to represent factors affecting women's conviction rate that are not specifically included in the model.

The results from the OLS regression of women's conviction rate on these explanatory variables are as follows (with standard errors in parentheses below the estimated coefficients):

$$\widehat{\text{FCR}} = \begin{array}{l} 127.6 \ \ - \ \ 0.04657 \times \text{TFR} \ \ + \ \ 0.2534 \times \text{LFPR} \\ (59.9) \quad\ (0.00803) \qquad\qquad (0.1152) \\ \qquad\qquad - \ \ 0.2120 \times \text{PSDR} \ + \ \ 0.05911 \times \text{MCR} \\ \qquad\qquad (0.2115) \qquad\qquad (0.04515) \end{array}$$

(16.15)

$$R^2 = .6948$$

The coefficients are not estimated very precisely—after all, the data set is quite small—and those for PSDR and MCR are not statistically significantly different from zero.[22]

A useful next step is to plot the residuals against time, as is done for Fox and Hartnagel's regression in Figure 16.6. It is clear from this graph that the residuals are positively autocorrelated, but another problem is apparent as well: The model is not doing a very good job during the Second World War, accounting neither for the jump in female crime at the beginning of the war, nor for its subsequent decline.

After examining the OLS residuals, we can calculate sample autocorrelations for the residuals:

$$r_s = \frac{\sum_{t=s+1}^{n} E_t E_{t-s}}{\sum_{t=1}^{n} E_t^2}$$

for lags $s = 1, 2, \ldots, m$, where the maximum lag m should be no larger than about $n/4$. We can also compute sample partial autocorrelations, r_s^* at various lags, using the sample analogs of the Yule-Walker equations (given in Equation 16.7 on page 436). If the residuals were independently distributed (which, recall, they are not—even when the errors are independent[23]), then the standard

---

[22]Exercise 16.7 addresses the adequacy of the model.
[23]See Section 11.8.2.

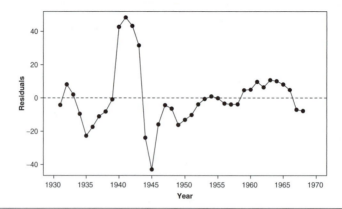

Figure 16.6   Time-series plot of residuals from the OLS regression of female conviction rate on several explanatory variables.

error of each r_s and r_s^* would be approximately $1/\sqrt{n}$, and the autocorrelations and partial autocorrelations would be asymptotically normally distributed.[24]

The pattern of the sample autocorrelations and partial autocorrelations of the residuals can help us to identify a time-series process to use in modeling serial dependency among the errors. If the errors follow a first-order autoregressive process, for example, then the residual correlations should (roughly) decay exponentially toward 0, and only the first partial autocorrelation should be large.

Graphs of the residual autocorrelations and partial autocorrelations (called *correlograms*) for the OLS regression using Fox and Hartnagel's data are shown in Figure 16.7. As a rough guide to the "statistical significance" of the residual autocorrelations and partial autocorrelations, I have placed reference lines in the correlograms at $\pm 2/\sqrt{n}$.[25] The pattern is clearly indicative of an AR(2) process, with a positive autoregressive coefficient at lag 1 and negative coefficient at lag 2.

Because simple tests for autocorrelation based on the r_s and r_s^* are, at best, rough, more precise methods have been proposed. The most popular approach to testing for autocorrelated errors is due to Durbin and Watson (1950, 1951). Durbin and Watson's test statistic is based on the assumption that the errors follow a first-order autoregressive process, and tests the null hypothesis that the autoregressive parameter ρ is 0:[26]

$$D \equiv \frac{\sum_{t=2}^{n}(E_t - E_{t-1})^2}{\sum_{t=1}^{n} E_t^2}$$

When n is large, $D \approx 2(1 - r_1)$.[27] If the null hypothesis is correct, therefore, we expect to observe values of D close to 2; if the null hypothesis is wrong, and the errors are *positively autocorrelated* (i.e., $\rho > 0$), then we expect to observe values of D that are substantially *smaller than* 2. The range of D values is 0 to 4. Although it is applied more broadly, the Durbin-Watson test is most powerful when the true error-generating process is AR(1).

The sampling distribution of the Durbin-Watson statistic is complex and, unfortunately, depends on the configuration of the explanatory variables. Durbin and Watson initially calculated critical values of D for two extreme scenarios: the X configuration producing the smallest

---

[24] See, for example, Chatfield (2003, sec. 4.1).

[25] A further reason for caution in interpreting the correlogram is that there are many sample autocorrelations which are themselves correlated, creating a problem of simultaneous inference.

[26] The Durbin-Watson statistic can be generalized to lags $s > 1$: $D_s \equiv \sum_{t=s+1}^{n}(E_t - E_{t-s})^2 / \sum_{t=1}^{n} E_t^2$. For this and other tests of autocorrelated errors see, for example, Judge et al. (1985, sec 8.4).

[27] See Exercise 16.6.

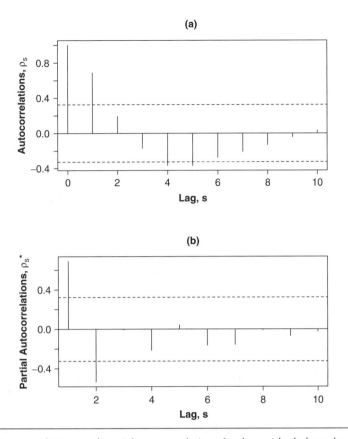

Figure 16.7 Autocorrelations and partial autocorrelations for the residuals from the OLS regression of female conviction rate on several explanatory variables.

critical value, and the X configuration producing the largest critical value. This approach leads to an extensive set of tables (because different critical values are required for different combinations of sample size n and number of explanatory variables k), and to ambiguous results if—as is common—the observed value of D falls between the two extreme critical values.[28]

Modern statistical software for time-series regression, however, typically calculates a p-value for D based on the X values in the sample at hand. For Fox and Hartnagel's regression, for example, $D = 0.617$, for which the two-sided p-value is much less than .0001, strongly supporting the conclusion that the errors are autocorrelated.

Reestimating Fox and Hartnagel's model by ML, assuming AR(2) errors, produces the following estimates and coefficient standard errors:

$$\widehat{\text{FCR}} = \underset{(59.47)}{83.34} \quad - \underset{(0.00928)}{0.03999} \times \text{TFR} \quad + \underset{(0.1120)}{0.2876} \times \text{LFPR}$$
$$- \underset{(0.2066)}{0.2098} \times \text{PSDR} \quad + \underset{(0.03501)}{0.07569} \times \text{MCR} \qquad (16.16)$$
$$\widehat{\phi}_1 = 1.068$$
$$\widehat{\phi}_2 = -0.5507$$

---

[28]Tables of critical values of D were published by Durbin and Watson (1951), and are widely reproduced (e.g., in Harvey, 1990, pp. 362–363).

With the exception of the regression constant,[29] neither the coefficients nor their standard errors change much from the OLS results in Equation 16.15.

The following table compares the maximized log-likelihood for three nested models, in which the error process is $AR(p)$, with p set successively to 2 through 0 [where $AR(0)$ corresponds to the initial OLS regression]:

p	log-likelihood
2	-144.71
1	-149.21
0	-163.50

Because these models are nested, comparing adjacent lines of the table produces likelihood-ratio tests of the hypotheses $H_0^{(2)}$: $\phi_2 = 0$ and $H_0^{(1)}$: $\phi_1 = 0 \mid \phi_2 = 0$. The chi-square test statistics, each on one degree of freedom, are $G_2^2 = 2(149.21 - 144.71) = 9.00$ and $G_1^2 = 2(163.50 - 149.21) = 28.58$, for which the p-values are, respectively, .0027 and $\ll$ .0001, strongly supporting the inclusion of ϕ_1 and ϕ_2 in the model.

To diagnose serial correlation in the errors, we can examine correlograms of the OLS residuals, calculating the sample autocorrelations $r_s = \left(\sum_{t=s+1}^{n} E_t E_{t-s} \right) / \left(\sum_{t=1}^{n} E_t^2 \right)$ and partial autocorrelations r_s^* for a number of lags $s = 1, 2, \dots, m$. If, for example, the serial dependence of the residuals is well described by a first-order autoregressive process, then the autocorrelations should decay exponentially toward 0, and partial autocorrelations after the first should be negligible. The Durbin-Watson statistic $D \equiv \left[\sum_{t=2}^{n} (E_t - E_{t-1})^2 \right] / \left(\sum_{t=1}^{n} E_t^2 \right) \approx 2(1 - r_1)$ can be used to test for serial correlation of the errors.

16.5 Concluding Remarks

It is tempting to conclude that the theoretical advantage of GLS regression should mandate its use, especially if the residuals are significantly autocorrelated, but there are several factors that suggest caution:[30]

- The extent to which GLS estimation is more efficient than OLS estimation, and the extent to which the usual formula for OLS standard errors produces misleading results, depend on a number of complex factors, including the process generating the errors, the degree of autocorrelation of the errors, and the distribution of the explanatory-variable values.[31]
- When the errors are highly autocorrelated and follow a first-order autoregressive process, and when explanatory-variable values manifest a linear trend, the advantage of GLS estimation can be strongly dependent on retaining the first observation (i.e., using the transformation $\sqrt{1 - \rho^2}$ of the first observation).[32] Precisely in these circumstances, the first observation

---

[29]The constant is very imprecisely estimated: After all, setting all of the explanatory variables to 0 extrapolates the regression far beyond the observed range of the data.

[30]For an elaboration of some of these points, see, for example, the discussion in Judge et al. (1985, chap. 8).

[31]See Exercise 16.3.

[32]See Exercise 16.3.

can become influential in the transformed regression, however. The comfort that we derive from GLS may therefore be tenuous. It is, consequently, useful to examine influential-data diagnostics for the *transformed* equation.[33] This point extends to other error processes.

- Many of the properties of GLS, EGLS, and ML estimators depend on asymptotic results, but time-series data sets are usually quite small.[34] Moreover, long time series raise the possibility that regression relationships—for example, the slope associated with a particular explanatory variable—may themselves change over time. There is no *generally* satisfactory method for detecting such changes, although it may help to plot residuals against time.[35]
- The performance of a method like GLS estimation may depend crucially on getting the error-generating process right. If the process is not AR(1), for example, basing estimation on this process may cause more harm than good. Real social processes do not, in any event, unfold according to AR, MA, or ARMA processes which, at best, produce reasonable descriptive summaries. We have to be careful not to construe time-series regression models too literally.

Three further cautionary notes are in order:

- Because time-series data often manifest strong trends, the explanatory variables in a time-series regression can be strongly collinear. This problem can be exacerbated when time itself (i.e., the regressor $X_t = t$) is included in the regression to capture a linear trend. The general rationale for employing time as a regressor is to control statistically for omitted factors that change smoothly with time and that are correlated with the explanatory variables included in the model.
- The models discussed in this chapter assume *contemporaneous* effects. That is, all of the variables in the model are measured at time t. It is sometimes reasonable to suppose, however, that the effect of an explanatory variable (say, X_1) will occur after an interval of time has elapsed, for example, after one time period. The time-series regression model would then take the form

$$Y_t = \alpha + \beta_1 X_{t-1, 1} + \beta_2 X_{t2} + \cdots + \beta_k X_{tk} + \varepsilon_t$$

Aside from the loss of the first observation (because $X_{t-1,1}$ is typically unavailable when $t = 1$ and hence $t - 1 = 0$), specifications of this form pose no new problems. If, however, we do not know in advance that the effect of X_1 is lagged some specific number of time periods, and rather want to consider effects at several lags, then autocorrelation of X_1 can induce serious collinearity. Special techniques of estimation (called "distributed lags"[36]) exist to deal with this situation, but these methods require that we know in advance something about the form of the lagged effects of X_1 on Y.
- Finally, the methods of this chapter are generally inappropriate (in the presence of autocorrelated errors) when the *response variable* appears as a lagged effect on the right-hand side of the model,[37] as in

$$Y_t = \alpha + \beta Y_{t-1} + \beta_1 X_{t1} + \cdots + \beta_k X_{tk} + \varepsilon_t$$

---

[33] See Chapter 11.

[34] Bootstrapping, discussed in Chapter 21, can prove helpful in this context.

[35] This is not to say, however, that there are *no* methods for detecting changes in regression coefficients over time; see, e.g., Brown, Durbin, and Evans (1975).

[36] See, for example, the discussion of distributed lags in Judge et al. (1985, chaps. 9 and 10).

[37] See, for example, Harvey (1990, chap. 8) for a discussion of regression with a lagged response on the right-hand side of the model.

> There are several practical and theoretical difficulties that limit the effectiveness and range
> of application of EGLS and ML estimation of time-series regression models.

Exercises

Exercise 16.1. *Generalized least squares: For the linear model $\mathbf{y} = \mathbf{X}\boldsymbol{\beta} + \boldsymbol{\varepsilon}$ with $\boldsymbol{\varepsilon} \sim N_n(\mathbf{0}, \boldsymbol{\Sigma}_{\varepsilon\varepsilon})$, where the error covariance matrix $\boldsymbol{\Sigma}_{\varepsilon\varepsilon}$ is known:

(a) Show that the log-likelihood for the model is

$$\log_e L(\boldsymbol{\beta}) = -\frac{n}{2}\log_e 2\pi - \frac{1}{2}\log_e(\det \boldsymbol{\Sigma}_{\varepsilon\varepsilon}) - \frac{1}{2}(\mathbf{y} - \mathbf{X}\boldsymbol{\beta})'\boldsymbol{\Sigma}_{\varepsilon\varepsilon}^{-1}(\mathbf{y} - \mathbf{X}\boldsymbol{\beta})$$

(*Hint*: Use the formula for the multivariate normal distribution.)

(b) Show that the ML estimator of $\boldsymbol{\beta}$ is

$$\mathbf{b}_{\text{GLS}} = (\mathbf{X}'\boldsymbol{\Sigma}_{\varepsilon\varepsilon}^{-1}\mathbf{X})^{-1}\mathbf{X}'\boldsymbol{\Sigma}_{\varepsilon\varepsilon}^{-1}\mathbf{y}$$

and that its sampling variance is

$$V(\mathbf{b}_{\text{GLS}}) = (\mathbf{X}'\boldsymbol{\Sigma}_{\varepsilon\varepsilon}^{-1}\mathbf{X})^{-1}$$

(c) Prove the Gauss-Markov theorem for the GLS estimator. That is, show that under the assumptions $E(\boldsymbol{\varepsilon}) = \mathbf{0}$ and $V(\boldsymbol{\varepsilon}) = \boldsymbol{\Sigma}_{\varepsilon\varepsilon}$, $\mathbf{b}_{\text{GLS}}$ is the minimum-variance linear unbiased estimator of $\boldsymbol{\beta}$. (*Hints*: See Section 9.3.2, and Exercise 12.4 on page 302.)

Exercise 16.2. *Autocorrelations for MA and ARMA processes:

(a) Show that the MA(1) process $\varepsilon_t = v_t + \theta v_{t-1}$ has autocorrelations

$$\rho_1 = \frac{\theta}{1 + \theta^2}$$
$$\rho_s = 0, \text{ for } s > 1$$

(b) Show that the MA(2) process $\varepsilon_t = v_t + \theta_1 v_{t-1} + \theta_2 v_{t-2}$ has autocorrelations

$$\rho_1 = \frac{\theta_1 + \theta_1\theta_2}{1 + \theta_1^2 + \theta_2^2}$$
$$\rho_2 = \frac{\theta_2}{1 + \theta_1^2 + \theta_2^2}$$
$$\rho_s = 0, \text{ for } s > 2$$

(c) Show that the ARMA(1, 1) process $\varepsilon_t = \phi\varepsilon_{t-1} + v_t + \theta v_{t-1}$ has autocorrelations

$$\rho_1 = \frac{(1 + \phi\theta)(\phi + \theta)}{1 + \theta^2 + 2\phi\theta}$$
$$\rho_s = \phi\rho_{s-1}, \text{ for } s > 1$$

(*Hint:* To find the autocovariance at lag 1, multiply through the equation for the process by ε_{t-1} and take expectations. Divide by the variance of ε_t to get ρ_1. Repeat this procedure for other lags.)

Exercise 16.3. Autocorrelated errors and OLS estimation: Assume that $\mathbf{y} = \mathbf{X}\beta + \varepsilon$ and that the errors follow an AR(1) process, $\varepsilon_t = \rho\varepsilon_{t-1} + v_t$, where $v_t \sim N(0, \sigma_v^2)$.

(a) Show that the OLS estimator $\mathbf{b} = (\mathbf{X'X})^{-1}\mathbf{X'y}$ is unbiased despite the autocorrelation of the errors. [*Hint:* Recall the proof that $E(\mathbf{b}) = \beta$ from Section 9.3.1.]

(b) Show that the variance of the OLS estimator is

$$V(\mathbf{b}) = (\mathbf{X'X})^{-1}\mathbf{X'}\Sigma_{\varepsilon\varepsilon}\mathbf{X}(\mathbf{X'X})^{-1}$$

where $\Sigma_{\varepsilon\varepsilon}$ is given by Equation 16.8 (page 438).

(c) Suppose that we fit the simple-regression model $Y_t = \alpha + \beta x_t + \varepsilon_t$; that the x values are $1, 2, \ldots, 10$; that the errors follow an AR(1) process; and that the variance of the random shocks v_t is 1. [Recall that the variance of the errors is $\sigma_\varepsilon^2 = \sigma_v^2/(1 - \rho^2)$.] Calculate (1) the *true* sampling variance of the OLS estimator; (2) the sampling variance of the OLS estimator according to the usual formula, $\sigma_\varepsilon^2(\mathbf{X'X})^{-1}$, appropriate when the errors are independent; and (3) the sampling variance of the GLS estimator, using the formula

$$V(\mathbf{b}_{\text{GLS}}) = (\mathbf{X'}\Sigma_{\varepsilon\varepsilon}^{-1}\mathbf{X})^{-1}$$

Pay particular attention to the sampling variance of the estimators of the slope β. What do you conclude from these calculations? Perform the calculations assuming successively that $\rho = 0$, $\rho = .5$, and $\rho = .9$.

(d) *Now suppose that the first observation is dropped, and that we perform the regression in (c) using $t = 2, \ldots, 10$. Working with the transformed scores $x_t^* = x_t - \rho x_{t-1}$, and again employing the three different values of ρ, find the sampling variance of the resulting estimator of β. How does the efficiency of this estimator compare to that of the true GLS estimator? With the OLS estimator? What would happen if there were many more observations?

(e) Repeat (c) [and (d)], but with $x_t = (t - 5)^2$ for $t = 1, 2, \ldots, 9$.

Exercise 16.4. *Show that the appropriate GLS transformation matrix for AR(1) errors is

$$\Gamma = \begin{bmatrix} \sqrt{1 - \rho^2} & 0 & 0 & \cdots & 0 & 0 \\ -\rho & 1 & 0 & \cdots & 0 & 0 \\ 0 & -\rho & 1 & \cdots & 0 & 0 \\ \vdots & \vdots & \vdots & \ddots & \vdots & \vdots \\ 0 & 0 & 0 & \cdots & -\rho & 1 \end{bmatrix}$$

[*Hints:* First show that

$$\frac{1}{1 - \rho^2} \begin{bmatrix} 1 & -\rho & 0 & \cdots & 0 & 0 \\ -\rho & 1 + \rho^2 & -\rho & \cdots & 0 & 0 \\ 0 & -\rho & 1 + \rho^2 & \cdots & 0 & 0 \\ \vdots & \vdots & \vdots & \ddots & \vdots & \vdots \\ 0 & 0 & 0 & \cdots & 1 + \rho^2 & -\rho \\ 0 & 0 & 0 & \cdots & -\rho & 1 \end{bmatrix}$$

is the inverse of

$$\mathbf{P} = \begin{bmatrix} 1 & \rho & \rho^2 & \cdots & \rho^{n-1} \\ \rho & 1 & \rho & \cdots & \rho^{n-2} \\ \rho^2 & \rho & 1 & \cdots & \rho^{n-3} \\ \vdots & \vdots & \vdots & \ddots & \vdots \\ \rho^{n-1} & \rho^{n-2} & \rho^{n-3} & \cdots & 1 \end{bmatrix}$$

Then show that $\mathbf{P}^{-1} = [1/(1-\rho^2)]\mathbf{\Gamma}'\mathbf{\Gamma}$. The constant $1/(1-\rho^2)$ can be ignored in forming the square-root matrix $\mathbf{\Gamma}$. Why?]

Exercise 16.5. *Maximum-likelihood estimation with AR(1) errors: Assume that $\mathbf{y} = \mathbf{X}\boldsymbol{\beta} + \boldsymbol{\varepsilon}$ and that the errors follow an AR(1) process, but that the autoregressive parameter ρ and the variance of the random shocks σ_v^2 are unknown. Show that the log-likelihood under this model can be written in the following form:

$$\log_e L(\boldsymbol{\beta}, \rho, \sigma_v^2) = -\frac{n}{2}\log_e 2\pi - \frac{n}{2}\log_e \sigma_v^2 + \frac{1}{2}\log_e(1-\rho^2)$$
$$- \frac{1}{2\sigma_v^2}(\mathbf{y}^* - \mathbf{X}^*\boldsymbol{\beta})'(\mathbf{y}^* - \mathbf{X}^*\boldsymbol{\beta})$$

where $\mathbf{y}^* = \mathbf{\Gamma}\mathbf{y}$ and $\mathbf{X}^* = \mathbf{\Gamma}\mathbf{X}$. [*Hints*: Start with Equation 16.1 (on page 428) for the log-likelihood of the general model with error covariance matrix $\mathbf{\Sigma}_{\varepsilon\varepsilon}$. Then use $\mathbf{\Sigma}_{\varepsilon\varepsilon} = (1/\sigma_v^2)\mathbf{\Gamma}'\mathbf{\Gamma}$, noting that $\det\mathbf{\Sigma}_{\varepsilon\varepsilon} = (1/\sigma_v^2)^n(\det\mathbf{\Gamma})^2$ and that $\det\mathbf{\Gamma} = \sqrt{1-\rho^2}$.]

Exercise 16.6. Show that when n is large, the Durbin-Watson statistic D is approximately equal to $2(1-r_1)$, where r_1 is the lag-one autocorrelation of the OLS residuals. (*Hint:* When n is large, $\sum_{t=1}^{n} E_t^2 \approx \sum_{t=2}^{n} E_t^2 \approx \sum_{t=2}^{n} E_{t-1}^2$.)

Exercise 16.7. With reference to Fox and Hartnagel's regression of Canadian women's conviction rates on several explanatory variables:

(a) Use regression diagnostics, as described in Part III of the text, to explore the adequacy of the preliminary OLS regression fit to these data (Equation 16.15 on page 441). If you detect any problems, try to correct them, and then repeat the subsequent analysis of the data.
(b) Show that the estimated parameters of the AR(2) process fit to the errors, $\widehat{\phi}_1 = 1.068$ and $\widehat{\phi}_2 = -0.5507$ (see Equation 16.16 on page 443), correspond to a stationary time-series process. (*Hint:* Use the quadratic formula to solve the equation $1 - 1.068\beta + 0.5507\beta^2 = 0$, and verify that both roots have modulus greater than 1.)
(c) Reestimate Fox and Hartnagel's regression with AR(2) errors by EGLS, comparing your results with those produced by the method of maximum likelihood (in Equation 16.16). Obtain estimates of the error autoregressive parameters ϕ_1 and ϕ_2 by solving the Yule-Walker equations (see Equation 16.7 on page 436)

$$\begin{aligned} r_1 &= \widehat{\phi}_1 + \widehat{\phi}_2 r_1 \\ r_2 &= \widehat{\phi}_1 r_1 + \widehat{\phi}_2 \end{aligned}$$

where r_1 and r_2 are the lag-1 and lag-2 sample autocorrelations of the OLS residuals.

Summary

- In time-series data, a single individual is tracked over many time periods or points of time. It is not generally reasonable to suppose that the errors in a time-series regression are independent.
- To capture serial dependence among the errors in the regression model $\mathbf{y} = \mathbf{X}\boldsymbol{\beta} + \boldsymbol{\varepsilon}$, we drop the assumption that the errors are independent of one another; instead, we assume that $\boldsymbol{\varepsilon} \sim N_n(\mathbf{0}, \boldsymbol{\Sigma}_{\varepsilon\varepsilon})$, where nonzero off-diagonal entries in the error covariance matrix $\boldsymbol{\Sigma}_{\varepsilon\varepsilon}$ correspond to correlated errors.
- If the error covariance matrix $\boldsymbol{\Sigma}_{\varepsilon\varepsilon}$ is known, then the maximum-likelihood estimator of $\boldsymbol{\beta}$ is the generalized least-squares estimator

$$\mathbf{b}_{\text{GLS}} = (\mathbf{X}'\boldsymbol{\Sigma}_{\varepsilon\varepsilon}^{-1}\mathbf{X})^{-1}\mathbf{X}'\boldsymbol{\Sigma}_{\varepsilon\varepsilon}^{-1}\mathbf{y}$$

The sampling variance-covariance matrix of $\mathbf{b}_{\text{GLS}}$ is

$$V(\mathbf{b}_{\text{GLS}}) = (\mathbf{X}'\boldsymbol{\Sigma}_{\varepsilon\varepsilon}^{-1}\mathbf{X})^{-1}$$

The generalized least-squares estimator can also be expressed as the OLS estimator $(\mathbf{X}^{*\prime}\mathbf{X}^*)^{-1}\mathbf{X}^{*\prime}\mathbf{y}^*$ for the transformed variables $\mathbf{X}^* \equiv \boldsymbol{\Gamma}\mathbf{X}$ and $\mathbf{y}^* \equiv \boldsymbol{\Gamma}\mathbf{y}$, where the transformation matrix $\boldsymbol{\Gamma}$ is a square root of $\boldsymbol{\Sigma}_{\varepsilon\varepsilon}^{-1}$.
- When, more realistically, the error covariance matrix $\boldsymbol{\Sigma}_{\varepsilon\varepsilon}$ is unknown, we need to estimate its contents along with the regression coefficients $\boldsymbol{\beta}$. Without restricting its form, however, $\boldsymbol{\Sigma}_{\varepsilon\varepsilon}$ contains too many distinct elements to estimate directly. Assuming that the errors are generated by a stationary time-series process reduces the number of independent parameters in $\boldsymbol{\Sigma}_{\varepsilon\varepsilon}$ to n, including the error variance σ_ε^2 and the autocorrelations at various lags, $\rho_1, \ldots, \rho_{n-1}$.
- To reduce the number of parameters in $\boldsymbol{\Sigma}_{\varepsilon\varepsilon}$ further, we can adopt a specific time-series model for the errors. The most commonly employed such model is the first-order autoregressive process $\varepsilon_t = \rho\varepsilon_{t-1} + v_t$, where $|\rho| < 1$ and the random shocks v_t are independently distributed as $N(0, \sigma_v^2)$. Under this specification, two errors, ε_t and ε_{t+s}, separated by s time periods have autocovariance $\rho^s\sigma_\varepsilon^2$ and autocorrelation ρ^s. The variance of the regression errors is $\sigma_\varepsilon^2 = \sigma_v^2/(1 - \rho^2)$.
- Higher-order autoregressive processes, moving-average processes, and mixed autoregressive-moving-average processes can be used to model more complex forms of serial dependence in the errors.
- The partial autocorrelations of an AR(p) process fall abruptly to 0 after lag p; those of MA and ARMA processes decay towards 0 in a pattern determined by the coefficients of the process. The distinctive features of the autocorrelation and partial-autocorrelation functions of AR, MA, and ARMA processes may be used to help select a process to model a particular time series.
- To apply GLS estimation to a regression model with AR(1) errors, we can first estimate the autocorrelation of the errors from the sample autocorrelation of the OLS residuals:

$$\widehat{\rho} = r_1 = \frac{\sum_{t=2}^n E_t E_{t-1}}{\sum_{t=1}^n E_t^2}$$

We can then use $\widehat{\rho}$ to form an estimate of the correlation matrix of the errors or to transform $\mathbf{y}$ and $\mathbf{X}$. Except for the first observation, these transformations take a very simple form: $Y_t^* = Y_t - \widehat{\rho}Y_{t-1}$ and $X_{tj}^* = X_{tj} - \widehat{\rho}X_{t-1,\,j}$. This procedure is called empirical GLS estimation. Empirical GLS can be extended to more complex time-series models for the errors. A better approach, however, is to estimate the parameters of the error process along with the regression coefficients by the method of maximum likelihood.

- To diagnose serial correlation in the errors, we can examine correlograms of the OLS residuals, calculating the autocorrelations

$$r_s = \frac{\sum_{t=s+1}^{n} E_t E_{t-s}}{\sum_{t=1}^{n} E_t^2}$$

and partial autocorrelations r_s^* for a number of lags $s = 1, 2, \ldots, m$. If, for example, the serial dependence of the residuals is well described by a first-order autoregressive process, then the autocorrelations should decay exponentially toward 0, and partial autocorrelations after the first should be negligible. The Durbin-Watson statistic

$$D \equiv \frac{\sum_{t=2}^{n}(E_t - E_{t-1})^2}{\sum_{t=1}^{n} E_t^2} \approx 2(1 - r_1)$$

can be used to test for serial correlation of the errors.

- There are several practical and theoretical difficulties that limit the effectiveness and range of application of EGLS and ML estimation of time-series regression models.

Recommended Reading

- Time-series analysis—including, but not restricted to, time-series regression—is a deep and rich topic, well beyond the scope of the discussion in this chapter. A good, relatively brief, general introduction to the subject may be found in Chatfield (2003).
- Most econometric texts include some treatment of time-series regression. The emphasis is typically on a formal understanding of statistical models and methods of estimation rather than on the use of these techniques in data analysis. Wonnacott and Wonnacott (1979), for example, present an insightful, relatively elementary treatment of time-series regression and generalized least squares. Judge et al.'s (1985) presentation of the subject is more encyclopedic, with many references to the literature. An extensive treatment also appears in Harvey (1990). Greene (2003, Chapters 10, 11, and 20) includes a good overview of GLS estimation, regression with autocorrelated errors, and time-series models more generally.

17

Nonlinear Regression

A s I have explained, there is a distinction between explanatory variables and regressors.[1] The general linear model is linear in the regressors but not necessarily in the explanatory variables that generate these regressors.

In analysis of variance, for example, the explanatory variables are qualitative and do not appear directly in the model; a single polytomous explanatory variable gives rise to several dummy regressors. Likewise, in polynomial regression, a single quantitative explanatory variable generates several regressors (e.g., linear, quadratic, and cubic terms). Interaction regressors are functions of two or more explanatory variables. We can also transform the *response* variable prior to formulating the linear model.

In its least restrictive form, then, we can write the general linear model as

$$f(Y_i) = \beta_0 f_0(\mathbf{x}_i') + \beta_1 f_1(\mathbf{x}_i') + \cdots + \beta_p f_p(\mathbf{x}_i') + \varepsilon_i$$
$$Y_i' = \beta_0 X_{i0}' + \beta_1 X_{i1}' + \cdots + \beta_p X_{ip}' + \varepsilon_i$$

where

- Y_i is the response variable for the ith observation;
- $\mathbf{x}_i' = (X_{i1}, \ldots, X_{ik})$ is a vector of k (not necessarily quantitative) explanatory variables;[2]
- $\beta_0, \beta_1, \ldots, \beta_p$ are parameters to estimate;
- the ε_i are independent and normally distributed errors, with zero expectations and constant variance; and
- the functions $f(\cdot), f_0(\cdot), \ldots, f_p(\cdot)$ do not involve unknown parameters.

For the least-squares estimates of the βs to be unique, the regressors $X_0', \ldots, X_p'$ cannot be perfectly collinear. If, as is usually the case, the model includes the constant regressor, then $X_{i0}' \equiv f_0(\mathbf{x}_i') = 1$. An X_j' can be a function of more than one explanatory variable, encompassing models such as

$$Y = \beta_0 + \beta_1 X_1 + \beta_2 X_2 + \beta_3 X_1^2 + \beta_4 X_2^2 + \beta_5 X_1 X_2 + \varepsilon \qquad (17.1)$$

In an application, the functions $f(\cdot), f_0(\cdot), \ldots, f_p(\cdot)$ may be suggested by prior theoretical considerations, or by examination of the data, as when we transform an explanatory variable to linearize its relationship to Y.

> Nonlinear regression models that are linear in the parameters, for example the quadratic regression model $Y = \beta_0 + \beta_1 X_1 + \beta_2 X_2 + \beta_3 X_1^2 + \beta_4 X_2^2 + \beta_5 X_1 X_2 + \varepsilon$, can be fit by linear least squares.

---

[1] See Chapters 7 and 8.
[2] If you are not familiar with vector notation, simply think of $\mathbf{x}_i'$ as a *list* of the explanatory variables for the ith observation.

17.1   Polynomial Regression

Polynomial regression is an important form of nonlinear regression that is accommodated by the general linear model. We have already seen how a quadratic function can be employed to model a ∪-shaped (or ∩-shaped) relationship.[3] Similarly, a cubic function can be used to model a relationship in which the direction of curvature changes. More generally, a polynomial of order p can have $p - 1$ "bends." Polynomials of degree greater than three are rarely employed in data analysis, however.

Polynomial regressors are especially useful when a quantitative explanatory variable is discrete. As we know,[4] we can capture any—potentially nonlinear—partial relationship between Y and X_j by constructing $m - 1$ dummy regressors to represent the m distinct values of X_j. The powers X_j, $X_j^2, \ldots, X_j^{m-1}$ can be thought of as an alternative coding of the discrete variable X_j, providing the same fit to the data as the dummy regressors (in the same sense as dummy-coding and deviation-coding are equivalent).[5]

We can then "step down" through the powers X_j^{m-1}, $X_j^{m-2}, \ldots, X_j^2$, X_j^1, testing the contribution of each term to the model, omitting the term if it proves unnecessary, and refitting the model. We stop dropping terms when one proves to be important. Thus, if the model includes a cubic term, it will also generally include the lower-order quadratic and linear terms.[6] Even if the relationship between Y and X_j is nonlinear, it is usually possible to represent this relationship with a polynomial of degree less than $m - 1$.[7]

Polynomials in two or more explanatory variables can be used to model interactions between quantitative explanatory variables. Consider, for example, the full quadratic model for two explanatory variables given in Equation 17.1 above. As illustrated in Figure 17.1(a), this model represents a curved surface relating $E(Y)$ to X_1 and X_2. Of course, certain specific characteristics of the regression surface—such as direction of curvature and monotonicity—depend on the parameters of the model and on the range of values for X_1 and X_2.[8] The partial relationships of Y to each of X_1 and X_2 are apparent in the lines drawn on the regression surfaces in Figure 17.1:

- For the full quadratic of Equation 17.1, shown in panel (a), the partial-regression lines are curved, and each quadratic partial relationship changes with the value of the other explanatory variable. Hence, X_1 and X_2 interact in their effect on Y.
- Panel (b) represents the equation

$$E(Y) = \beta_0 + \beta_1 X_1 + \beta_2 X_2 + \beta_3 X_1 X_2$$

  Here, the partial relationships are *linear*, but the partial relationship between Y and each X changes with the value of the other X, inducing a bend in the regression surface, representing the interaction between the two explanatory variables.
- The regression equation

$$E(Y) = \beta_0 + \beta_1 X_1 + \beta_2 X_2 + \beta_3 X_1^2 + \beta_4 X_2^2$$

---

[3] See, for example, the nonlinear partial relationship between log wages and education in the Canadian Survey of Labour and Income Dynamics data, discussed in Section 12.3.

[4] See Section 12.4.

[5] See Section 8.1. *Put another way, the powers $X_j, X_j^2, \ldots, X_j^{m-1}$ provide an alternative—and hence equivalent—basis for the subspace spanned by the dummy regressors.

[6] This is an application of the principle of marginality, introduced in Section 7.3.2. If, in a polynomial in X of order p, all lower-order terms are included, the fit of the model is invariant with respect to linear transformations of X—produced, for example, by subtracting the mean from each value, $X_i - \overline{X}$ (i.e., centering X). If lower-order terms are omitted, however, this invariance does not hold.

[7] Also see Exercise 17.2 for a discussion of *orthogonal* polynomial contrasts.

[8] See Exercise 17.3.

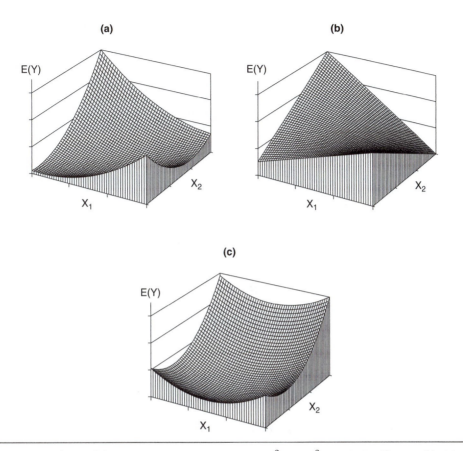

Figure 17.1   The model $E(Y) = \beta_0 + \beta_1 X_1 + \beta_2 X_2 + \beta_3 X_1^2 + \beta_4 X_2^2 + \beta_5 X_1 X_2$, illustrated in (a), represents a curved surface in which the *quadratic* partial relationship of Y to X_1 changes with the value of X_2 (and the quadratic partial relationship of Y to X_2 changes with the value of X_1). The model $E(Y) = \beta_0 + \beta_1 X_1 + \beta_2 X_2 + \beta_3 X_1 X_2$ in (b) represents a curved surface in which the slope of the *linear* partial relationship of Y to X_1 changes with the value of X_2 (and the slope of the linear partial relationship of Y to X_2 changes with the value of X_1). The model $E(Y) = \beta_0 + \beta_1 X_1 + \beta_2 X_2 + \beta_3 X_1^2 + \beta_4 X_2^2$ in (c) represents a curved surface in which the *quadratic* partial relationship of Y to X_1 is the same at different levels of X_2 (and the quadratic partial relationship of Y to X_2 is the same at different levels of X_1).

is illustrated in panel (c). Here, the partial relationships are nonlinear, but, for example, the quadratic partial relationship of Y to X_1 does not depend on the value at which X_2 is "held constant," reflecting the absence of interaction between the two explanatory variables.

To illustrate quadratic regression, and also to make the point that the method is applicable to *any* statistical model with a linear predictor, I will develop an application in logistic regression, taken from research by Cowles and Davis (1987) on volunteering for psychological experiments. The response variable in the study is dichotomous: whether or not each of 1421 subjects volunteered to participate in an experiment.[9]

---

[9]These data were used in Fox (1987). I am grateful to Michael Cowles and Caroline Davis of York University for making the data available.

Table 17.1   Cowles and Davis's Logistic Regression for Volunteering

Coefficient	Estimate	Standard Error
Constant	−2.358	0.501
Sex (Male)	−0.2471	0.1116
Neuroticism	0.1108	0.0376
Extraversion	0.1668	0.0377
Neuroticism × Extraversion	−0.008552	0.002934

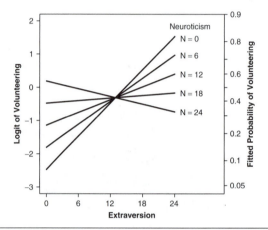

Figure 17.2   Fitted logit and probability of volunteering as a function of neuroticism and extraversion, from Cowles and Davis's logistic regression of volunteering on sex, neuroticism, extraversion, and the product of neuroticism and extraversion. To construct this effect display, the dummy regressor for sex was set to 0.45, which is the proportion of men in the data set.

The authors modeled the data in a logistic regression of volunteering on the factor sex, the personality dimensions neuroticism and extraversion, and the product of neuroticism and extraversion. The personality variables each can take on integer values between 0 and 24. Preliminary work suggests that sex does not interact with the personality dimensions and that squared terms in neuroticism and extraversion are not needed,[10] producing the estimated coefficients and standard errors in Table 17.1.

An effect display for the neuoticism-by-extraversion interaction is shown in Figure 17.2, setting the dummy regressor for sex to 0.45—the proportion of men in the data set (the dummy variable for sex is coded 1 for men and 0 for women). The graph shows the relationship between volunteering and extraversion at representative values of neuroticism. At low levels of neuroticism, volunteering rises with extraversion; this relationship becomes weaker as neuroticism grows, and at the highest level of neuroticism, the relationship between volunteering and extraversion is negative. Because the fitted values are plotted on the logit scale, the partial regression lines relating volunteering to extraversion are straight [and are produced by slicing the regression surface in the direction of extraversion; cf., Figure 17.1(b)]; note that the lines meet at a point—a characteristic of a model of this structure.[11]

---

[10]See Exercise 17.4.
[11]See Exercise 17.5.

17.1.1   A Closer Look at Quadratic Surfaces*

The essential structure of nonlinear models is often clarified by differentiating the model with respect to each explanatory variable.[12] Differentiating the equation for the full quadratic model (repeating Equation 17.1),

$$Y = \beta_0 + \beta_1 X_1 + \beta_2 X_2 + \beta_3 X_1^2 + \beta_4 X_2^2 + \beta_5 X_1 X_2 + \varepsilon$$

produces

$$\frac{\partial E(Y)}{\partial X_1} = \beta_1 + 2\beta_3 X_1 + \beta_5 X_2$$

$$\frac{\partial E(Y)}{\partial X_2} = \beta_2 + 2\beta_4 X_2 + \beta_5 X_1$$

The slope of the partial relationship between Y and X_1, therefore, depends not only on the level of X_1, but also on the specific value at which X_2 is held constant—indicating that X_1 and X_2 interact in affecting Y. Moreover, the shape of the partial relationship between Y and X_1 is quadratic, fixing the value of X_2. Because of the symmetry of the model, similar statements apply to the partial relationship between Y and X_2, holding X_1 constant.

In contrast, although the model

$$Y = \beta_0 + \beta_1 X_1 + \beta_2 X_2 + \beta_3 X_1 X_2 + \varepsilon$$

also represents a curved surface [an illustration appears in Figure 17.1(b)], the *slices* of this surface in the direction of each explanatory variable, holding the other constant, are, as I noted, linear:

$$\frac{\partial E(Y)}{\partial X_1} = \beta_1 + \beta_3 X_2$$

$$\frac{\partial E(Y)}{\partial X_2} = \beta_2 + \beta_3 X_1$$

Thus, for example, the slope of the relationship between Y and X_1 is different *at different levels* of X_2, but *at each fixed level* of X_2, the relationship between Y and X_1 is linear.

Finally, the model

$$Y = \beta_0 + \beta_1 X_1 + \beta_2 X_2 + \beta_3 X_1^2 + \beta_4 X_2^2 + \varepsilon$$

[illustrated in Figure 17.1(c)] represents a curved surface in which the quadratic partial relationship between Y and each of the explanatory variables is invariant across the levels of the other explanatory variable:

$$\frac{\partial E(Y)}{\partial X_1} = \beta_1 + 2\beta_3 X_1$$

$$\frac{\partial E(Y)}{\partial X_2} = \beta_2 + 2\beta_4 X_2$$

17.2   Piece-Wise Polynomials and Regression Splines _____

A potential problem with polynomial-regression fits is that they can be highly nonlocal: Data in one region, including outlying values, can seriously affect the fit in another region. Moreover, polynomials are inappropriate for regressions that approach an asymptote. As illustrated in Figure 17.3,

----

[12] See Exercise 17.1.

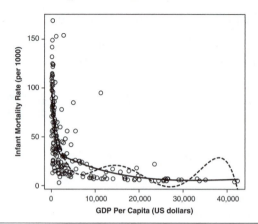

Figure 17.3   Infant-mortality rate by GDP per capita. The broken line is for an order-5 polynomial
fit by least-squares; the solid line is for a natural regression spline with 6 degrees of
freedom, also fit by least-squares.

these problems can be especially acute with high-degree polynomials: Here, I have fit a fifth-degree polynomial to the UN infant-mortality data.[13] The other regression curve drawn on this plot is for a natural regression spline (described later in this section) with 6 degrees of freedom—the same number of degrees of freedom as for the polynomial. It is clear that the regression spline does a much better job of following the pattern of the data.

As an alternative to a global polynomial regression, we can partition the data into bins, fitting a different polynomial regression in each bin—a generalization of the idea of binning and averaging (described in Chapter 2). Indeed, as shown in Figure 17.4(a), binning and averaging can be thought of as fitting a degree-zero polynomial in each bin. The data in this graph, and in the other panels of Figure 17.4, were artificially generated.[14]

In Figure 17.4(b), a least-squares line—that is, a degree-one polynomial—is fit in each bin. Finally, in Figure 17.4(c), a line is fit in each bin, but the lines are constrained to be continuous at the bin boundaries. Continuity can be imposed by fitting the model[15]

$$Y_i = \alpha + \beta_1 X_{i1} + \beta_2 X_{i2} + \beta_3 X_{i3} + \varepsilon_i$$

where $X_{i1} \equiv X_i$;

$$X_{i2} \equiv \begin{cases} 0 & \text{for } X_i \leq k_1 \\ X_i - k_1 & \text{for } X_i > k_1 \end{cases}$$

and

$$X_{i3} \equiv \begin{cases} 0 & \text{for } X_i \leq k_2 \\ X_i - k_2 & \text{for } X_i > k_2 \end{cases}$$

The points at which the lines join, at $X = k_1$ and $X = k_2$, are called *knots*.

---

[13]These data were introduced in Chapter 3. In Section 4.3, we discovered that the relationship between infant mortality and GDP can be rendered nearly linear by log-transforming both variables. The regression-spline fit in Figure 17.3 is reasonably similar to the lowess fit in Figure 3.13 (on page 41).

[14]The data were generated according to the regression equation $Y = \frac{1}{5}X + \cos(X + 1) + \varepsilon$, where $\cos(X + 1)$ is evaluated with X measured in radians, and where the errors were sampled from $N(0, 10^2)$. The 50 X values were drawn from a uniform distribution on the interval [0,10]. This example was inspired by a similar one in Hastie, Tibshirani, and Friedman (2001, pp. 118–119).

[15]See Exercise 17.6 for this and other results in this section.

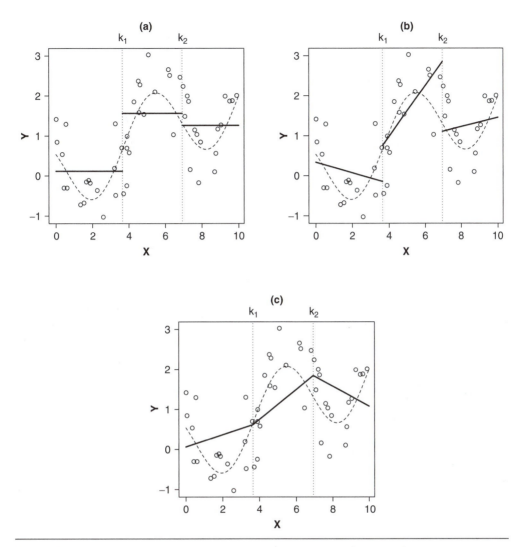

Figure 17.4   (a) Piece-wise constant, (b) piece-wise discontinuous-linear, and (c) piece-wise
continuous-linear fits to artificially generated data. The data are binned at the values
$X = k_1$ and $X = k_2$. The broken line in each graph is the "true" regression function
used to generate the data.

This approach can be generalized to higher-order polynomials, as illustrated for cubic polynomials in Figure 17.5 (using the same artificial data as in Figure 17.4). In panel (a), a separate
cubic is fit to each bin, and consequently the fit is discontinuous at the bin boundaries. In panel
(b), the cubics are constrained to join at the knots, by fitting the regression

$$Y_i = \alpha + \beta_{11} X_{i1} + \beta_{12} X_{i1}^2 + \beta_{13} X_{i1}^3 + \beta_{21} X_{i2} + \beta_{22} X_{i2}^2 + \beta_{23} X_{i2}^3$$
$$+ \beta_{31} X_{i3} + \beta_{32} X_{i3}^2 + \beta_{33} X_{i3}^3 + \varepsilon_i$$

where X_1, X_2, and X_3 are defined as above. In Figure 17.5(c), the cubic regressions are further
constrained to have equal slopes at the knots, by omitting the second and third linear terms from
the model:

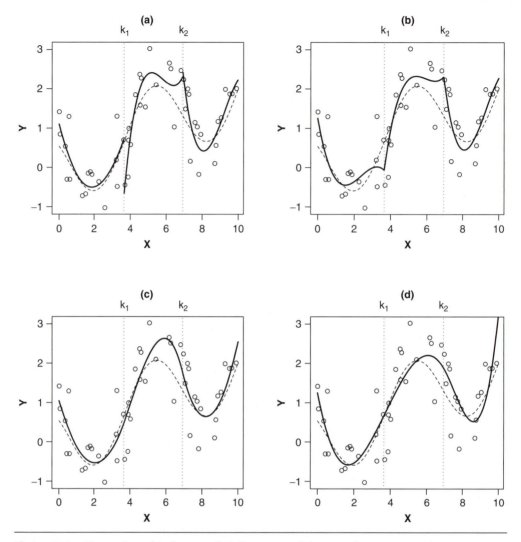

Figure 17.5 Piece-wise cubic fits to artificially generated data: (a) discontinuous; (b) continuous; (c) continuous with continuous slopes; (d) continuous with continuous slopes and curvature. The broken line in each graph is the "true" regression function used to generate the data.

$$Y_i = \alpha + \beta_{11}X_{i1} + \beta_{12}X_{i1}^2 + \beta_{13}X_{i1}^3 + \beta_{22}X_{i2}^2 + \beta_{23}X_{i2}^3 + \beta_{32}X_{i3}^2 + \beta_{33}X_{i3}^3 + \varepsilon_i$$

Finally, in Figure 17.5(d), not only the slopes but also the curvature of the regressions are matched at the knots, fitting the equation[16]

$$Y_i = \alpha + \beta_{11}X_{i1} + \beta_{12}X_{i1}^2 + \beta_{13}X_{i1}^3 + \beta_{23}X_{i2}^3 + \beta_{33}X_{i3}^3 + \varepsilon_i \tag{17.2}$$

Note that as the regression curve is progressively constrained in this manner, it grows smoother.

---

[16]*The slope is the first derivative of the regression function, while the curvature depends upon the second derivative. Thus, not only the regression curve, but also its first and second derivatives are continuous at the knots in Figure 17.5(d).

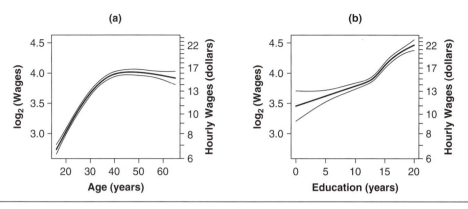

Figure 17.6   Effect displays for age and education in the regression of log wages on these variables and sex. Age and education are represented by natural splines, each with $k = 4$ knots. The lighter lines give point-wise 95% confidence envelopes around the fits.

Equation 17.2 is called a *cubic regression spline*.[17] More generally, if we fit a cubic regression spline with k knots, dividing the data into $k + 1$ bins, the resulting regression model uses $k + 4$ degrees of freedom (i.e., has $k + 4$ parameters): one for the constant, three for the linear, quadratic, and cubic terms in the first bin, and k for the additional cubic terms, one for each remaining bin. In practice, the regressors in the generalization of Equation 17.2 can become highly correlated, and it is therefore advantageous to fit the model with an alternative, but equivalent, set of less correlated regressors.[18]

I have yet to address how to select the number and placement of the knots in fitting a regression spline to data. This is a key point, because with the values of the knots fixed, a regression spline is a linear model, and as such provides a fully parametric fit to the data. The issue is less critical, however, than it may appear: It almost always suffices to use four or five knots, and to distribute the knots at evenly spaced quantiles of the explanatory variable: Thus, for example, four knots divide the data into five bins, and can be placed at the 20th, 40th, 60th, and 80th percentiles of X. Moreover, this strategy extends in a straightforward manner to *multiple* regression analysis, where individual quantitative explanatory variables in the model can be represented by regression splines.

Cubic regression splines can behave erratically near the boundaries of the data. A simple fix is to constrain the regression function to be linear at and beyond the left and right boundaries. These additional constraints produce what is termed a *natural cubic regression spline*; the boundary constraints account for two degrees of freedom, and therefore with k knots, a natural regression spline uses only $k + 2$ degrees of freedom, counting the regression constant.[19]

An illustration, using data from the Canadian Survey of Labour and Income Dynamics, is shown in Figure 17.6. The effect displays in this graph are for the regression of log wages on years of education, years of age, and a dummy regressor for sex (the effect of which is not shown).

---

[17]A *spline* is a flexible tool used in drafting to draw smooth, continuous curves. *Spline functions* in mathematics are piece-wise continuous and smooth polynomials traditionally used for interpolation.

[18]*In the language of Chapters 9 and 10, we select a different basis for the subspace spanned by the cubic-regression-spline regressors. The *B-spline* basis is frequently used in practice; the details are beyond this discussion, but see, for example, Hastie et al., 2001, pp. 160–161.

[19]The natural cubic regression spline can be written as a regression equation in much the same manner as the cubic regression spline of Equation 17.2. The formulation of the regressors is complicated, however; see Hastie et al. (2001, sec. 5.2.1).

Age and education are modeled using natural splines, each with $k = 4$ knots (and, hence, 5 degrees of freedom each, *not* counting the regression constant).[20]

Spline regression models are a bridge between the linear and generalized linear models of Parts II and IV of the text and the nonparametric regression models to be discussed in Chapter 18: Regression splines fit comfortably into the *parametric* linear-predictor toolbox of linear and generalized linear models; yet, like nonparametric-regression models, they are flexible and therefore can conform to local characteristics of the data.

> Regression splines are piece-wise cubic polynomials that are continuous at join-points, called knots, and that are constrained to have equal slopes and curvature on either side of a knot. Though fully parametric, regression splines generally do a good job of responding to local aspects of the data, and can be incorporated as building-blocks into linear and generalized linear models.

17.3   Transformable Nonlinearity

As explained in the previous section, linear statistical models effectively encompass models that are linear in the parameters, even if they are nonlinear in the variables. The forms of nonlinear relationships that can be expressed as linear models are, therefore, very diverse. In certain circumstances, however, theory dictates that we fit models that are nonlinear in their parameters. This is a relatively rare necessity in the social sciences, primarily because our theories are seldom mathematically concrete, although nonlinear models arise in some areas of demography, economics, and psychology, and occasionally in sociology, political science, and other social sciences.

Some models that are nonlinear in the parameters can be transformed into linear models, and, consequently, can be fit to data by linear least squares. A model of this type is the so-called "gravity model" of migration, employed in human geography (see Abler, Adams, & Gould, 1971, pp. 221–233). Let Y_{ij} represent the number of migrants moving from city i to city j; let D_{ij} represent the geographical distance between these cities; and let P_i and P_j represent their respective populations.

The gravity model of migration is built in rough analogy to the Newtonian formula for gravitational attraction between two objects, where population plays the role of mass and migration the role of gravity. The analogy is loose, in part because gravitational attraction is *symmetric*, while there are *two* migration streams of generally *different* sizes between a pair of cities: one from city i to city j, and the other from j to i.

The gravity model is given by the equation

$$Y_{ij} = \alpha \frac{P_i^\beta P_j^\gamma}{D_{ij}^\delta} \varepsilon_{ij} \tag{17.3}$$

$$= \widetilde{Y}_{ij} \varepsilon_{ij}$$

where α, β, γ, and δ are unknown parameters to be estimated from the data; and ε_{ij} is a necessarily positive multiplicative error term that reflects the imperfect determination of migration by distance and population size. When ε_{ij} is 1, Y_{ij} is equal to its "predicted" value $\widetilde{Y}_{ij}$, given by the systematic

---

[20]Compare these effect displays with those in Figure 12.8 (page 282), where I used a quadratic specification for the age effect and squared education to linearize the regression.

part of the model; when ε_{ij} is less than 1, Y_{ij} is smaller than $\widetilde{Y}_{ij}$; and when ε_{ij} is greater than 1, Y_{ij} exceeds $\widetilde{Y}_{ij}$.[21] I will say more about the error presently.

Although the gravity model (Equation 17.3) is nonlinear in its parameters, it can be transformed into a linear equation by taking logs:[22]

$$\log Y_{ij} = \log \alpha + \beta \log P_i + \gamma \log P_j - \delta \log D_{ij} + \log \varepsilon_{ij} \tag{17.4}$$
$$Y'_{ij} = \alpha' + \beta P'_i + \gamma P'_j + \delta D'_{ij} + \varepsilon'_{ij}$$

where

$$\alpha' \equiv \log \alpha$$
$$P'_i \equiv \log P_i$$
$$P'_j \equiv \log P_j$$
$$D'_{ij} \equiv - \log D_{ij}$$
$$\varepsilon'_{ij} \equiv \log \varepsilon_{ij}$$

If we can make the usual linear-model assumptions about the transformed errors ε'_{ij}, then we are justified in fitting the transformed model (Equation 17.4) by linear least squares. In the gravity model, it is probably unrealistic to assume that the transformed errors are independent, because individual cities are involved in many different migration streams. A particularly attractive city, for example, might have positive errors for each of its in-migration streams and negative errors for each of its out-migration streams.[23]

Our ability to linearize the model given in Equation 17.3 by a log transformation depends on the multiplicative errors in this model. The multiplicative error specifies that the general magnitude of the difference between Y_{ij} and $\widetilde{Y}_{ij}$ is proportional to the size of the latter: The model tends to make larger absolute errors in predicting large migration streams than in predicting small ones. This assumption appears reasonable here. In most cases, we would prefer to specify a form of error—additive or multiplicative—that leads to a simple statistical analysis—supposing, of course, that the specification is sensible. A subsequent analysis of residuals permits us to subject these assumptions to scrutiny.

Another form of multiplicative model is

$$Y_i = \alpha \exp(\beta_1 X_{i1}) \exp(\beta_2 X_{i2}) \cdots \exp(\beta_k X_{ik}) \varepsilon_i \tag{17.5}$$
$$= \alpha \exp(\beta_1 X_{i1} + \beta_2 X_{i2} + \cdots + \beta_k X_{ik}) \varepsilon_i$$

Taking logs produces the linear equation

$$Y'_i = \alpha' + \beta_1 X_{i1} + \beta_2 X_{i2} + \cdots + \beta_k X_{ik} + \varepsilon'_i$$

with

$$Y'_i \equiv \log_e Y_i$$

$$\alpha' \equiv \log_e \alpha$$

$$\varepsilon'_i \equiv \log_e \varepsilon_i$$

---

[21]Because of the multiplicative form of the gravity model, $\widetilde{Y}_{ij}$ is not $E(Y_{ij})$—hence the use of the term "predicted" rather than "expected" value.

[22]The log transformation requires that $Y_{ij}, \alpha, P_i, P_j, D_{ij}$, and ε_{ij} are all positive, as is the case for the gravity model of migration.

[23]See Exercise 17.7 for an illustrative application of the gravity model.

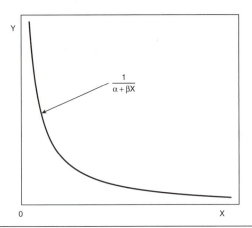

Figure 17.7   The model $Y = 1/(\alpha + \beta X_i + \varepsilon_i)$, for $X > 0$ and $\beta > 0$.

In Equation 17.5, the impact on Y of increasing X_j by one unit is proportional to the level of Y. The effect of rescaling Y by taking logs is to eliminate interaction among the Xs. A similar result is, at times, achievable empirically through other power transformations of Y.[24]

> Some nonlinear models can be rendered linear by a transformation. For example, the multiplicative gravity model of migration,
>
> $$Y_{ij} = \alpha \frac{P_i^\beta P_j^\gamma}{D_{ij}^\delta} \varepsilon_{ij}$$
>
> (where Y_{ij} is the number of migrants moving from location i to location j; P_i is the population at location i; D_{ij} is the distance separating the two locations; and ε_{ij} is a multiplicative error term), can be linearized by taking logs.

Multiplicative models provide the most common instance of transformable nonlinearity, but there are also other models to which this approach is applicable. Consider, for example, the model

$$Y_i = \frac{1}{\alpha + \beta X_i + \varepsilon_i} \tag{17.6}$$

where ε_i is a random error satisfying the standard assumptions. Then, if we take $Y_i' \equiv 1/Y_i$, we can rewrite the model as the linear equation $Y_i' = \alpha + \beta X_i + \varepsilon_i$. This model is illustrated in Figure 17.7 (for a positive β and positive values of X).[25]

---

[24]The use of power transformations to promote additivity was pioneered by Tukey (1949); also see, for example, Emerson and Hoaglin (1983).
[25]The graph shows the systematic part of the model, $\widetilde{Y} = 1/(\alpha + \beta X)$, but because the transformation of Y that linearizes the model is not a linear transformation, the curve does not give the expectation of Y.

17.4 Nonlinear Least Squares* _____

Models that are nonlinear in the parameters and that cannot be rendered linear by a transformation are called *essentially nonlinear*. The *general nonlinear model* is given by the equation

$$Y_i = f \underset{(p \times 1)}{(\boldsymbol{\beta}}, \underset{(1 \times k)}{\mathbf{x}_i')} + \varepsilon_i \tag{17.7}$$

in which

- Y_i is the response-variable value for the ith of n observations;
- $\boldsymbol{\beta}$ is a vector of p parameters to be estimated from the data;
- $\mathbf{x}_i'$ is a row vector of scores for observation i on the k explanatory variables (some of which may be qualitative); and
- ε_i is the error for the ith observation.

It is convenient to write the model in matrix form for the full sample of n observations as

$$\underset{(n \times 1)}{\mathbf{y}} = \mathbf{f} \underset{(p \times 1)}{(\boldsymbol{\beta}}, \underset{(n \times k)}{\mathbf{X})} + \underset{(n \times 1)}{\boldsymbol{\varepsilon}}$$

I will assume, as in the general linear model, that $\boldsymbol{\varepsilon} \sim N_n(\mathbf{0}, \sigma_\varepsilon^2 \mathbf{I}_n)$.[26]

An illustrative essentially nonlinear model is the logistic population-growth model (Shryock, Siegel, & Associates, 1973, pp. 382–385):

$$Y_i = \frac{\beta_1}{1 + \exp(\beta_2 + \beta_3 X_i)} + \varepsilon_i \tag{17.8}$$

where Y_i is population size, and X_i is time; for equally spaced observations, it is conventional to take $X_i = i - 1$, and so $X = 0, 1, 2, \ldots$. Because the logistic growth model is fit to time-series data, the assumption of independent errors is problematic: It may well be the case that the errors are *autocorrelated*—that is, that errors close in time tend to be similar.[27] The additive form of the error is also questionable here, for errors may well grow larger in magnitude as population size increases.[28] Despite these potential difficulties, the logistic population-growth model can provide a useful, if gross and preliminary, representation of the data.

Under the assumption of independent and normally distributed errors, with zero expectations and common variance, the general nonlinear model (Equation 17.7) has likelihood

$$L(\boldsymbol{\beta}, \sigma_\varepsilon^2) = \frac{1}{(2\pi\sigma_\varepsilon^2)^{n/2}} \exp\left\{ -\frac{\sum_{i=1}^n [Y_i - f(\boldsymbol{\beta}, \mathbf{x}_i')]^2}{2\sigma_\varepsilon^2} \right\}$$

$$= \frac{1}{(2\pi\sigma_\varepsilon^2)^{n/2}} \exp\left[-\frac{1}{2\sigma_\varepsilon^2} S(\boldsymbol{\beta}) \right]$$

where $S(\boldsymbol{\beta})$ is the sum-of-squares function

$$S(\boldsymbol{\beta}) \equiv \sum_{i=1}^n [Y_i - f(\boldsymbol{\beta}, \mathbf{x}_i')]^2$$

---

[26] For multiplicative errors, we can put the model in the form of Equation 17.7 by taking logs.
[27] See the discussion of time-series regression in Chapter 16.
[28] See Exercise 17.9.

As for the general linear model, we therefore maximize the likelihood by minimizing the sum of squared errors $S(\beta)$.

To derive estimating equations for the nonlinear model, we need to differentiate $S(\beta)$, obtaining

$$\frac{\partial S(\beta)}{\partial \beta} = -2 \sum \left[Y_i - f(\beta, \mathbf{x}_i') \right] \frac{\partial f(\beta, \mathbf{x}_i')}{\partial \beta}$$

Setting these partial derivatives to $\mathbf{0}$, and replacing the unknown parameters β with the estimator $\mathbf{b}$, produces the *nonlinear least-squares* estimating equations. It is convenient to write the estimating equations in matrix form as

$$[\mathbf{F}(\mathbf{b}, \mathbf{X})]' \left[\mathbf{y} - \mathbf{f}(\mathbf{b}, \mathbf{x}) \right] = \mathbf{0} \tag{17.9}$$

where $\underset{(n \times p)}{\mathbf{F}} (\mathbf{b}, \mathbf{X})$ is the matrix of derivatives, with i, jth entry

$$F_{ij} \equiv \frac{\partial f(\mathbf{b}, \mathbf{x}_i')}{\partial B_j}$$

The solution $\mathbf{b}$ of Equation 17.9 is the maximum-likelihood estimate of β. If there is more than one root to the estimating equations, then we choose the solution associated with the smallest residual sum of squares $S(\mathbf{b})$.

Nonlinear models of the form $Y_i = f(\beta, \mathbf{x}_i') + \varepsilon_i$ can be estimated by nonlinear least squares, finding the value of $\mathbf{b}$ that minimizes $S(\mathbf{b}) = \sum_{i=1}^{n} [Y_i - f(\mathbf{b}, \mathbf{x}_i')]^2$.

17.4.1 Minimizing the Residual Sum of Squares

Because the estimating equations (Equation 17.9) arising from a nonlinear model are, in general, themselves nonlinear, their solution is often difficult. It is, for this reason, unusual to obtain nonlinear least-squares estimates by explicitly solving the estimating equations. Instead, it is more common to work directly with the sum-of-squares function.

There are several practical methods for obtaining nonlinear least-squares estimates. I will pursue in some detail a technique called *steepest descent*. Although the method of steepest descent usually performs poorly relative to alternative procedures, the rationale of the method is simple. Furthermore, many general aspects of nonlinear least-squares calculations can be explained clearly for the steepest-descent procedure. Because of the practical limitations of steepest descent, however, I will also briefly describe two superior procedures—the *Gauss-Newton method* and the *Marquardt method*—without developing their rationales.[29]

The method of steepest descent, like other methods for calculating nonlinear least-squares estimates, begins with a vector $\mathbf{b}^{(0)}$ of initial estimates. These initial estimates can be obtained in a variety of ways. We can, for example, choose p "typical" observations, substitute their values into the model given in Equation 17.7 (page 463), and solve the resulting system of p nonlinear equations for the p parameters.

Alternatively, we can select a set of reasonable trial values for each parameter, find the residual sum of squares for every combination of trial values, and pick as initial estimates the combination

---

[29] See the recommended readings at the end of the chapter for details.

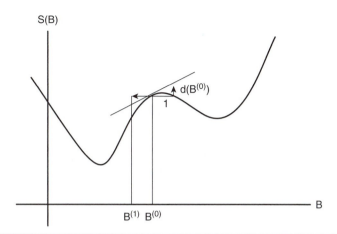

Figure 17.8 The method of steepest descent for one estimated parameter, B. Because the slope of the sum-of-squares function $S(B)$ is positive above the initial estimate $B^{(0)}$, the first step is to the *left*, to $B^{(1)}$.

associated with the smallest residual sum of squares. It is sometimes possible to choose initial estimates on the basis of prior research, hypothesis, or substantive knowledge of the process being modeled.

It is unfortunate that the choice of starting values for the parameter estimates may prove consequential: Iterative methods such as steepest descent generally converge to a solution more quickly for initial values that are close to the final values; and, even more importantly, the sum-of-squares function $S(\mathbf{b})$ may have local minima different from the global minimum (as illustrated in Figure 17.8).

Let us denote the *gradient* (i.e., derivative) vector for the sum-of-squares function as

$$\mathbf{d}(\mathbf{b}) = \frac{\partial S(\mathbf{b})}{\partial \mathbf{b}}$$

The vector $\mathbf{d}(\mathbf{b}^{(0)})$ gives the direction of maximum *increase* of the sum-of-squares function from the initial point $\{\mathbf{b}^{(0)}, S(\mathbf{b}^{(0)})\}$; the *negative* of this vector, $-\mathbf{d}(\mathbf{b}^{(0)})$, therefore, gives the *direction of steepest descent*. Figure 17.8 illustrates these relations for the simple case of one parameter, where we can move either left or right from the initial estimate $B^{(0)}$.

If we move in the direction of steepest descent, then we can find a new estimated parameter vector

$$\mathbf{b}^{(1)} = \mathbf{b}^{(0)} - M_0 \mathbf{d}(\mathbf{b}^{(0)})$$

for which $S(\mathbf{b}^{(1)}) < S(\mathbf{b}^{(0)})$: Because $S(\mathbf{b})$ is, by definition, decreasing in the direction of steepest descent, unless we are already at a minimum we can *always* choose a number M_0 small enough to improve the residual sum of squares. We can, for instance, first try $M_0 = 1$; if this choice does not lead to a decrease in $S(\mathbf{b})$, then we can take $M_0 = \frac{1}{2}$; and so on.

Our new estimate $\mathbf{b}^{(1)}$ can subsequently be improved in the same manner, by finding

$$\mathbf{b}^{(2)} = \mathbf{b}^{(1)} - M_1 \mathbf{d}(\mathbf{b}^{(1)})$$

so that $S(\mathbf{b}^{(2)}) < S(\mathbf{b}^{(1)})$. This procedure continues iteratively until it converges on a solution $\mathbf{b}$—that is, until the changes in $S(\mathbf{b}^{(l)})$ and $\mathbf{b}^{(l)}$ from one iteration to the next are negligible. In practice, however, the method of steepest descent often converges painfully slowly, and at times falls prey to other computational difficulties.

At each iteration, we need to compute the gradient vector $\mathbf{d}(\mathbf{b})$ for the current value of $\mathbf{b} = \mathbf{b}^{(l)}$. From our previous work in this section, we have

$$-\mathbf{d}(\mathbf{b}) = 2[\mathbf{F}(\mathbf{b}, \mathbf{X})]'[\mathbf{y} - \mathbf{f}(\mathbf{b}, \mathbf{x})]$$

$$= 2\sum_{i=1}^{n} \left[\frac{\partial f(\mathbf{b}, \mathbf{x}_i')}{\partial \mathbf{b}} \right] [Y_i - f(\mathbf{b}, \mathbf{x}_i')] \tag{17.10}$$

The partial derivatives $\partial f(\mathbf{b}, \mathbf{x}_i')/\partial B_j$ either can be supplied analytically (which is generally preferable) or can be evaluated numerically [i.e., approximated by finding the slope of $f(\mathbf{b}, \mathbf{x}_i')$ in a small interval around the current value of B_j]. For example, for the logistic growth model (Equation 17.8 on page 463) discussed earlier in this section, the analytic derivatives are

$$\frac{\partial f(\mathbf{b}, X_i)}{\partial B_1} = [1 + \exp(B_2 + B_3 X_i)]^{-1}$$

$$\frac{\partial f(\mathbf{b}, X_i)}{\partial B_2} = -B_1[1 + \exp(B_2 + B_3 X_i)]^{-2} \exp(B_2 + B_3 X_i)$$

$$\frac{\partial f(\mathbf{b}, X_i)}{\partial B_3} = -B_1[1 + \exp(B_2 + B_3 X_i)]^{-2} \exp(B_2 + B_3 X_i) X_i$$

In the method of steepest descent, we take

$$\mathbf{b}^{(l+1)} = \mathbf{b}^{(l)} + M_l \mathbf{F}_l' \mathbf{e}^{(l)}$$

where $\mathbf{F}_l \equiv \mathbf{F}(\mathbf{b}^{(l)}, \mathbf{X})$ and $\mathbf{e}^{(l)} = \mathbf{y} - \mathbf{f}(\mathbf{b}^{(l)}, \mathbf{X})$ (and the constant 2 in Equation 17.10 is absorbed into M_l). The Gauss-Newton method, in contrast, calculates

$$\mathbf{b}^{(l+1)} = \mathbf{b}^{(l)} + M_l (\mathbf{F}_l' \mathbf{F}_l)^{-1} \mathbf{F}_l' \mathbf{e}^{(l)}$$

As for steepest descent, the step-size M_l is selected so that $S(\mathbf{b}^{(l+1)}) < S(\mathbf{b}^{(l)})$; we first try $M_l = 1$, then $M_l = \frac{1}{2}$, and so on. The direction chosen in the Gauss-Newton procedure is based on a first-order Taylor-series expansion of $S(\mathbf{b})$ around $S(\mathbf{b}^{(l)})$.

In the Marquardt procedure,

$$\mathbf{b}^{(l+1)} = \mathbf{b}^{(l)} + (\mathbf{F}_l' \mathbf{F}_l + M_l \mathbf{I}_p)^{-1} \mathbf{F}_l' \mathbf{e}^{(l)}$$

Initially, M_0 is set to some small number, such as 10^{-8}. If $S(\mathbf{b}^{(l+1)}) < S(\mathbf{b}^{(l)})$, then we accept the new value of $\mathbf{b}^{(l+1)}$ and proceed to the next iteration, with $M_{l+1} = M_l/10$; if, however, $S(\mathbf{b}^{(l+1)}) > S(\mathbf{b}^{(l)})$, then we increase M_l by a factor of 10 and try again. When M is small, the Marquardt procedure is similar to Gauss-Newton; as M grows larger, Marquardt approaches steepest descent. Marquardt's method is thus an adaptive compromise between the other two approaches.

Estimated asymptotic sampling covariances for the parameter estimates can be obtained by the maximum-likelihood approach and are given by[30]

$$\widehat{V}(\mathbf{b}) = S_E^2 \left\{ [\mathbf{F}(\mathbf{b}, \mathbf{X})]' \, \mathbf{F}(\mathbf{b}, \mathbf{X}) \right\}^{-1} \tag{17.11}$$

We can estimate the error variance from the residuals $\mathbf{e} = \mathbf{y} - \mathbf{f}(\mathbf{b}, \mathbf{X})$, according to the formula[31]

$$S_E^2 = \frac{\mathbf{e}'\mathbf{e}}{n - p}$$

---

[30] See Bard (1974, pp. 176–179).

[31] Alternatively, we can use the maximum-likelihood estimator of the error variance, without the correction for "degrees of freedom," $\widehat{\sigma}_\varepsilon^2 = \mathbf{e}'\mathbf{e}/n$.

Table 17.2 Population of the United States, in Millions, 1790–2000.

Year	Population	Year	Population
1790	3.929	1900	75.995
1800	5.308	1910	91.972
1810	7.240	1920	105.711
1820	9.638	1930	122.775
1830	12.866	1940	131.669
1840	17.069	1950	150.697
1850	23.192	1960	179.323
1860	31.443	1970	203.302
1870	39.818	1980	226.542
1880	50.156	1990	248.718
1890	62.948	2000	281.425

SOURCE: United States (2006).

Note the similarity of Equation 17.11 to the familiar linear least-squares result, $\widehat{V}(\mathbf{b}) = S_E^2(\mathbf{X}'\mathbf{X})^{-1}$. Indeed, $\mathbf{F}(\mathbf{b}, \mathbf{X}) = \mathbf{X}$ for the linear model $\mathbf{y} = \mathbf{X}\beta + \varepsilon$.

Iterative methods for finding the nonlinear least-squares estimates include the method of steepest descent and, more practically, the Gauss-Newton and Marquardt methods. Estimated asymptotic covariances for the coefficients are given by

$$\widehat{V}(\mathbf{b}) = S_E^2 \left\{ [\mathbf{F}(\mathbf{b}, \mathbf{X})]' \, \mathbf{F}(\mathbf{b}, \mathbf{X}) \right\}^{-1}$$

where $\mathbf{F}(\mathbf{b}, \mathbf{X})$ is the matrix of derivatives, with i, jth entry $\partial f(\mathbf{b}, \mathbf{x}_i')/\partial B_j$, and $S_E^2 = \sum E_i^2/(n - p)$ is the estimated error variance.

17.4.2 An Illustration: U.S. Population Growth

Decennial population data for the United States appear in Table 17.2 for the period from 1790 to 2000; the data are plotted in Figure 17.9(a). Let us fit the logistic growth model (Equation 17.8 on page 463) to these data using nonlinear least squares.

The parameter β_1 of the logistic growth model gives the asymptote that expected population approaches as time increases. In 2000, when $Y = 281.425$ (million), population did not appear to be near an asymptote;[32] so as not to extrapolate too far beyond the data, I will arbitrarily set $B_1^{(0)} = 350$. At time $X_1 = 0$, we have

$$Y_1 = \frac{\beta_1}{1 + \exp(\beta_2 + \beta_3 0)} + \varepsilon_1 \tag{17.12}$$

---

[32]That population in 2000 did not appear to be near an asymptote suggests that we might not need to fit an asymptotic growth model to the data; see Exercise 17.10.

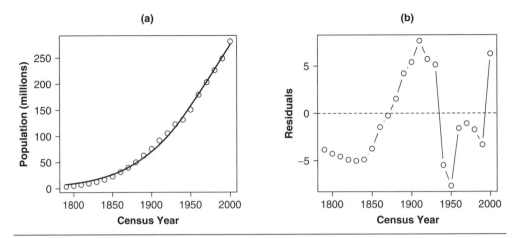

Figure 17.9   Panel (a) shows the population of the United States from 1790 through 2000; the line
represents the fitted logistic growth model. Residuals from the logistic growth model
are plotted against time in panel (b).

Ignoring the error, using $B_1^{(0)} = 350$, and substituting the observed value of $Y_1 = 3.929$ into
Equation 17.12, we get $\exp(B_2^{(0)}) = (350/3.929) - 1$, or $B_2^{(0)} = \log_e 88.081 = 4.478 \approx 4.5$. At
time $X_2 = 1$,

$$Y_2 = \frac{\beta_1}{1 + \exp(\beta_2 + \beta_3 1)} + \varepsilon_2$$

Again ignoring the error, and making appropriate substitutions, $\exp(4.5 + B_3^{(0)}) = (350/
5.308) - 1$, or $B_3^{(0)} = \log_e 64.938 - 4.5 = -0.327 \approx -0.3$.

The Gauss-Newton iterations based on these start values are shown in Table 17.3. Asymptotic
standard errors for the coefficients also appear in this table, and indicate that (with the exception
of the population asymptote β_1) the parameters are estimated precisely. Although the logistic
model captures the major trend in U. S. population growth, the residuals from the least-squares
fit [plotted against time in Figure 17.9(b)] suggest that the error variance is not constant and that
the residuals are autocorrelated.[33] Note as well the large drop in the residual for 1940, and the
large increase for 1960 (when Alaska and Hawaii were first included in the population count),
and again in 2000.

An example of an essentially nonlinear model, which requires nonlinear least squares, is
the logistic population-growth model

$$Y_i = \frac{\beta_1}{1 + \exp(\beta_2 + \beta_3 X_i)} + \varepsilon_i$$

where Y_i is population size, and X_i is time.

---

[33]See Exercise 17.8.

Table 17.3 Gauss-Newton Iterations for the Logistic Growth Model Fit to the U.S. Population Data

| Iteration | Residual Sum of Squares | Coefficients | | |
		B_1	B_2	B_3
0	13,365.12	350.0	4.5	−0.3
1	1,993.82	371.77	3.7730	−0.21383
⋮				
6	455.58	445.52	4.0335	−0.21490
Final	455.58	445.52	4.0335	−0.21490
	Standard error	36.05	0.0674	0.01002

NOTE: Asymptotic standard errors are given below the final coefficient estimates.

Exercises

Exercise 17.1. *Interpreting effects in nonlinear models (based on Stolzenberg, 1979): For simplicity, disregard the error and let Y represent the systematic part of the response variable. Suppose that Y is a function of two explanatory variables, $Y = f(X_1, X_2)$.

- The *metric effect* of X_1 on Y is defined as the partial derivative $\partial Y/\partial X_1$.
- The *effect of proportional change* in X_1 on Y is defined as $X_1(\partial Y/\partial X_1)$.
- The *instantaneous rate of return* of Y with respect to X_1 is $(\partial Y/\partial X_1)/Y$.
- The *point elasticity* of Y with respect to X_1 is $(\partial Y/\partial X_1)(X_1/Y)$.

Find each of these four measures of the effect of X_1 in each of the following models. Which measure yields the simplest result in each case? How can the several measures be interpreted? How would you fit each model to data, assuming convenient forms for the errors [e.g., additive errors for models (a), (b), and (c)]?

(a) $Y = \alpha + \beta_1 X_1 + \beta_2 X_2$.
(b) $Y = \alpha + \beta_1 X_1 + \beta_2 X_1^2 + \beta_3 X_2$.
(c) $Y = \alpha + \beta_1 X_1 + \beta_2 X_2 + \beta_3 X_1 X_2$.
(d) $Y = \exp(\alpha + \beta_1 X_1 + \beta_2 X_2)$.
(e) $Y = \alpha X_1^{\beta_1} X_2^{\beta_2}$.

Exercise 17.2. *Orthogonal polynomial contrasts: The polynomial regressors $X, X^2, \ldots, X^{m-1}$ generated to represent a quantitative, discrete X with values $1, 2, \ldots, m$ are substantially correlated. It is convenient (but by no means essential) to remove these correlations. Suppose that there are equal numbers of observations in the different levels of X, so that it suffices to make the columns of the row basis of the model matrix for X orthogonal. Working with the row basis, begin by subtracting the mean from X, calling the result X^*. *Centering* X in this manner makes X^* orthogonal to the constant regressor **1**. (Why?) X^2 can be made orthogonal to the constant and X^* by projecting the X^2 vector onto the subspace generated by **1** and X^*; call the residual from this projection X^{*2}. The remaining columns $X^{*3}, \ldots, X^{*m-1}$ of the new row basis are formed in a similar manner, each orthogonal to the preceding ones.

(a) Show that the orthogonal polynomial contrasts $\mathbf{1}$, X^*, ..., X^{*m-1} span the same subspace as the original polynomial regressors $\mathbf{1}$, X, ..., X^{m-1}.

(b) Show that the incremental sum of squares for each orthogonal contrast X^*, X^{*2}, ..., X^{*m-1} is the same as the step-down sum of squares for the corresponding regressor among the original (correlated) polynomial terms, X^{m-1}, ..., X^2, X. (*Hint*: Remember that X^*, X^{*2}, ..., X^{*m-1} are uncorrelated.)

(c) What then is the advantage of orthogonal polynomial contrasts?

(d) Can the same approach be applied to a continuous quantitative explanatory variable—defining, for example, a quadratic component that is orthogonal to the linear component, and a cubic component orthogonal to both the linear and quadratic components?

Exercise 17.3. Working with the full quadratic regression model

$$E(Y) = \beta_0 + \beta_1 X_1 + \beta_2 X_2 + \beta_3 X_1^2 + \beta_4 X_2^2 + \beta_5 X_1 X_2$$

and a three-dimensional graphics program, draw pictures of the regression surface (similar to Figure 17.1 on page 453) for various values of the parameters β_1, ..., β_5 and various values of the explanatory variables X_1 and X_2. You will derive a better impression of the flexibility of this model if you experiment freely, but the following suggestions may prove useful:

- Try both positive and negative values of the parameters.
- Try cases in which there are both positive and negative Xs, as well as cases in which the Xs are all positive.
- Try setting some of the parameters to 0.

Exercise 17.4. Cowles and Davis's logistic regression of volunteering on sex, neuroticism, extraversion, and the product of neuroticism and extraversion is discussed in Section 17.1. Show that (*a*) interactions between sex and the other factors, and (*b*) squared terms in neuroticism and extraversion, are not required in this model.

Exercise 17.5. *Show that in the model

$$E(Y) = \beta_0 + \beta_1 X_1 + \beta_2 X_2 + \beta_3 X_1 X_2$$

the lines for the regression of Y on X_1 at various fixed values of X_2 all cross at a point (as in Figure 17.2 for Cowles and Davis's logistic regression).

Exercise 17.6. *Properties of piece-wise fits and regression splines:

(a) For the regression equation

$$Y_i = \alpha + \beta_1 X_{i1} + \beta_2 X_{i2} + \beta_3 X_{i3} + \varepsilon_i$$

where $X_{i1} \equiv X_i$;

$$X_{i2} \equiv \begin{cases} 0 & \text{for } X_i \leq k_1 \\ X_i - k_1 & \text{for } X_i > k_1 \end{cases}$$

and

$$X_{i3} \equiv \begin{cases} 0 & \text{for } X_i \leq k_2 \\ X_i - k_2 & \text{for } X_i > k_2 \end{cases}$$

show that the regression lines in the three bins are continuous (i.e., join at knots on the bin boundaries at $X = k_1$ and $X = k_2$).

(b) Similarly, show that the cubics in the regression equation

$$Y_i = \alpha + \beta_{11} X_{i1} + \beta_{12} X_{i1}^2 + \beta_{13} X_{i1}^3 + \beta_{21} X_{i2} + \beta_{22} X_{i2}^2 + \beta_{23} X_{i2}^3$$
$$+ \beta_{31} X_{i3} + \beta_{32} X_{i3}^2 + \beta_{33} X_{i3}^3 + \varepsilon_i$$

are continuous; that the cubics in the regression equation

$$Y_i = \alpha + \beta_{11} X_{i1} + \beta_{12} X_{i1}^2 + \beta_{13} X_{i1}^3 + \beta_{22} X_{i2}^2 + \beta_{23} X_{i2}^3 + \beta_{32} X_{i3}^2 + \beta_{33} X_{i3}^3 + \varepsilon_i$$

are both continuous and have continuous slopes at the knots; and that the cubics in the regression-spline equation

$$Y_i = \alpha + \beta_{11} X_{i1} + \beta_{12} X_{i1}^2 + \beta_{13} X_{i1}^3 + \beta_{23} X_{i2}^3 + \beta_{33} X_{i3}^3 + \varepsilon_i$$

join at the knots, have continuous slopes, and have continuous curvature.

Exercise 17.7. Table 17.4 reports interprovincial migration in Canada for the period 1966 to 1971. Also shown in this table are the 1966 and 1971 provincial populations. Table 17.5 gives road distances among the major cities in the 10 provinces. Averaging the 1966 and 1971 population figures, fit the gravity model of migration (Equation 17.3 on page 460) to the interprovincial migration data. Display the residuals from the fitted model in a 10×10 table. Can you account for the pattern of residuals? How might the model be modified to provide a more satisfactory fit to the data? (Why can't we simply use dummy regressors to incorporate province effects for the source and destination provinces?)

Exercise 17.8. Calculate the autocorrelation for the residuals from the logistic growth model fit to the U. S. population data in Section 17.4.2. Recalling the discussion of autocorrelated errors in *linear* regression (in Chapter 16), does autocorrelation appear to be a serious problem here?

Exercise 17.9. Using nonlinear least squares, refit the logistic growth model to the U.S. population data (given in Table 17.2) assuming multiplicative rather than additive errors:

$$Y_i = \frac{\beta_1}{1 + \exp(\beta_2 + \beta_3 X_i)} \varepsilon_i$$

Which form of the model appears more adequate for these data?

Exercise 17.10. As mentioned in Section 17.4.2, the population of the United States in the year 2000 did not seem to be near an asymptote. As an alternative to the logistic growth model, we might entertain the exponential growth model for the period 1790 to 2000; assuming multiplicative errors, this model takes the form

$$Y_i = \alpha \exp(\beta X_i) \varepsilon_i$$

where, as in the text, Y_i is population, and $X_i = 0, 1, \ldots, 21$ is time. Because of the multiplicative errors, this model can be transformed to linearity by taking the log of both sides:

$$\log_e Y_i = \alpha' + \beta X_i + \varepsilon_i'$$

where $\alpha' \equiv \log_e \alpha$ and $\varepsilon_i' \equiv \log_e \varepsilon_i$. Fit the exponential growth model to the data by linear least-squares regression and graph the fit as in Figure 17.9. (*Hint*: transform the fitted values back to the original population scale as $\exp(\widehat{Y}_i)$]. Plot fitted values for the exponential growth model against those for the logistic growth model. Which model appears to do a better job of representing the data?

Table 17.4 Canadian Interprovincial Migration and Population for the Period 1966–1971

1971 Residence	1966 Residence									
	NL	PE	NS	NB	QC	ON	MB	SK	AB	BC
Newfoundland		255	2,380	1,140	2,145	6,295	215	185	425	425
Prince Edward Island	340		1,975	1,310	755	3,060	400	95	185	330
Nova Scotia	3,340	2,185		8,310	6,090	18,805	1,825	840	2,000	2,490
New Brunswick	1,740	1,335	7,635		9,315	12,455	1,405	480	1,130	1,195
Quebec	2,235	635	4,350	7,905		48,370	4,630	1,515	3,305	4,740
Ontario	17,860	3,570	25,730	18,550	99,430		23,785	11,805	17,655	21,205
Manitoba	680	265	1,655	1,355	4,330	18,245		16,365	7,190	6,310
Saskatchewan	280	125	620	495	1,570	6,845	9,425		10,580	6,090
Alberta	805	505	3,300	2,150	7,750	23,550	17,410	41,910		27,765
British Columbia	1,455	600	6,075	3,115	16,740	47,395	26,910	29,920	58,915	
1966 Population	493,396	108,535	756,039	616,788	5,780,845	6,960,870	963,066	955,344	1,463,203	1,873,674
1971 Population	522,104	111,641	788,960	534,557	6,027,764	7,703,106	988,247	926,242	1,627,874	2,184,621

SOURCES: Canada (1971, Vol. 1, Part 2, Table 32; 1972, p. 1369).

Table 17.5 Road Distances in Miles Among Major Canadian Cities

City	NL	PE	NS	NB	QC	ON	MB	SK	AB	BC
St. John's, NL	0	924	952	1119	1641	1996	3159	3542	4059	4838
Charlottetown, PE	924	0	164	252	774	1129	2293	2675	3192	3972
Halifax, NS	952	164	0	310	832	1187	2351	2733	3250	4029
Fredericton, NB	1119	252	310	0	522	877	2041	2423	2940	3719
Montreal, QC	1641	774	832	522	0	355	1519	1901	2418	3197
Toronto, ON	1996	1129	1187	877	355	0	1380	1763	2281	3059
Winnipeg, MB	3159	2293	2351	2041	1519	1380	0	382	899	1679
Regina, SK	3542	2675	2733	2423	1901	1763	382	0	517	1297
Edmonton, AB	4059	3192	3250	2940	2418	2281	899	517	0	987
Vancouver, BC	4838	3972	4029	3719	3197	3059	1679	1297	987	0

SOURCE: Canada (1962).

Exercise 17.11. Recall the Box-Tidwell regression model,

$$Y_i = \alpha + \beta_1 X_{i1}^{\gamma_1} + \cdots + \beta_k X_{ik}^{\gamma_k} + \varepsilon_i$$

In Section 12.5.2, I described a procedure for fitting the Box-Tidwell model that relies on constructed variables. I applied this procedure to data from the Canadian Survey of Labour and Income Dynamics to fit the model

$$\log_2 \text{wages} = \alpha + \beta_1 \text{age}^{\gamma_1} + \beta_2 \text{education}^{\gamma_1} + \beta_3 \text{male} + \varepsilon$$

where *male* is a dummy regressor coded 1 for men and 0 for women. Fit this model to the data by general nonlinear least squares. Are there any advantages to using general nonlinear least squares in place of Box and Tidwell's procedure? Any disadvantages? Can the two approaches be combined?

Summary

- Nonlinear regression models that are linear in the parameters, for example, the quadratic regression model

$$Y = \beta_0 + \beta_1 X_1 + \beta_2 X_2 + \beta_3 X_1^2 + \beta_4 X_2^2 + \beta_5 X_1 X_2 + \varepsilon$$

  can be fit by linear least squares.
- Regression splines are piece-wise cubic polynomials that are continuous at join-points, called knots, and that are constrained to have equal slopes and curvature on either side of a knot. Though fully parametric, regression splines generally do a good job of responding to local aspects of the data, and can be incorporated as building-blocks into linear and generalized linear models.
- Some nonlinear models can be rendered linear by a transformation. For example, the multiplicative gravity model of migration,

$$Y_{ij} = \alpha \frac{P_i^\beta P_j^\gamma}{D_{ij}^\delta} \varepsilon_{ij}$$

  (where Y_{ij} is the number of migrants moving from location i to location j; P_i is the population at location i; D_{ij} is the distance separating the two locations; and ε_{ij} is a multiplicative error term), can be linearized by taking logs.
- More generally, nonlinear models of the form $Y_i = f(\boldsymbol{\beta}, \mathbf{x}_i') + \varepsilon_i$ (in which $\boldsymbol{\beta}$ is a vector of p parameters to be estimated, and $\mathbf{x}_i'$ is a vector of explanatory-variable values) can be estimated by nonlinear least squares, finding the value of $\mathbf{b}$ that minimizes

$$S(\mathbf{b}) = \sum_{i=1}^n E_i^2 = \sum_{i=1}^n \left[Y_i - f(\mathbf{b}, \mathbf{x}_i') \right]^2$$

- Iterative methods for finding the nonlinear least-squares estimates include the method of steepest descent and, more practically, the Gauss-Newton and Marquardt methods. Estimated asymptotic covariances for the coefficients are given by

$$\widehat{V}(\mathbf{b}) = S_E^2 \left\{ [\mathbf{F}(\mathbf{b}, \mathbf{X})]' \, \mathbf{F}(\mathbf{b}, \mathbf{X}) \right\}^{-1}$$

  where $\mathbf{F}(\mathbf{b}, \mathbf{X})$ is the matrix of derivatives, with i, jth entry $\partial f(\mathbf{b}, \mathbf{x}_i')/\partial B_j$, and $S_E^2 = \sum E_i^2/(n-p)$ is the estimated error variance.

- An example of an essentially nonlinear model, which requires nonlinear least squares, is the logistic population-growth model,

$$Y_i = \frac{\beta_1}{1 + \exp(\beta_2 + \beta_3 X_i)} + \varepsilon_i$$

where Y_i is population size and X_i is time.

Recommended Reading

- Hastie et al. (2001, chap. 5) provide a rigorous treatment of regression splines, explaining their relationship to smoothing splines for nonparametric regression.[34] Regression splines also figure prominently in Harrell (2001).
- Further discussion of nonlinear least squares can be found in many sources, including Gallant (1975), Draper and Smith (1998, chap. 24), Greene (2003, chap. 9), Bard (1974), and Bates and Watts (1988) in rough order of increasing detail and difficulty.
- Draper and Smith (1998, chaps. 12 and 22) also discuss polynomial and orthogonal-polynomial regression models.

---

[34]Nonparametric regression is taken up in the next chapter.

Nonparametric Regression

T he essential idea of *nonparametric-regression analysis* was introduced in Chapter 2: to examine the conditional distribution of the response variable—or some aspect of that distribution, such as its center—as a function of one or more explanatory variables, without assuming in advance what form that function takes. This chapter elaborates that simple idea, developing methods of nonparametric simple and multiple regression for quantitative response variables, along with generalized nonparametric-regression models for categorical responses, for count data, and for non-normal quantitative response variables. Taken together, these methods provide a more flexible alternative to the *parametric* linear, generalized linear, and nonlinear regression models described in the earlier chapters of the book.

18.1 Nonparametric Simple Regression: Scatterplot Smoothing

This section presents several methods of nonparametric simple regression: kernel regression; local-polynomial regression, which generalizes kernel regression; and smoothing splines. Because kernel regression and local-polynomial regression are mathematically simpler than smoothing splines, I will emphasize these methods in developing some of the statistical theory underlying nonparametric regression.

Nonparametric simple regression is useful in its own right, and for its extension to and use in nonparametric multiple-regression and additive-regression models. A principal application of nonparametric simple regression is to examining the relationship between two quantitative variables in a scatterplot, and these methods are therefore often called "scatterplot smoothers." Indeed, in the preceding chapters, I have often used the lowess local-regression smoother to facilitate the interpretation of scatterplots.

18.1.1 Kernel Regression

Kernel regression generalizes the simple local-averaging method of nonparametric regression described in Chapter 2.[1] Suppose that we wish to estimate the regression function $Y = f(x) + \varepsilon$ at a particular value of the explanatory variable, $X = x_0$. As in linear and nonlinear regression models, we will assume that the error ε is normally and independently distributed with an expectation of 0 and constant variance σ_ε^2.[2] As well, although the regression function $f(\cdot)$ is left unspecified, we will assume that it is smooth and continuous.[3]

---

[1] See Section 2.3. It would be useful to reread that section now, and generally to review the material in Chapter 2.

[2] For simplicity of exposition, I will treat the explanatory variables in this chapter as fixed rather than random. As in linear regression, this stipulation can be relaxed by assuming that the errors are independent of the explanatory variables. See Chapter 6 and Section 9.6.

[3] This assumption of smoothness is common to *all* of the methods of nonparametric regression considered in the chapter. There are methods of nonparametric regression that can, for example, deal with discontinuities (such

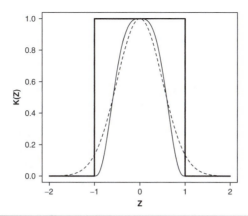

Figure 18.1 Tricube (light solid line), normal (broken line) and rectangular (heavy solid line) kernel functions. The normal kernel is rescaled to facilitate comparison.

The basic idea of kernel regression is that in estimating $f(x_0)$ it is desirable to give greater weight to observations that are close to the focal x_0 and less weight to those that are remote. Let $z_i \equiv (x_i - x_0)/h$ denote the scaled, signed distance between the X value for the ith observation and the focal x_0. As I will explain shortly, the scale factor h, called the *bandwidth* of the kernel estimator, plays a role similar to the window width of a local average, and controls the smoothness of the kernel estimator.

We need a *kernel function* $K(z)$ that attaches greatest weight to observations that are close to the focal x_0, and then falls off symmetrically and smoothly as $|z|$ grows.[4] Given these characteristics, the specific choice of a kernel function is not critical. Having calculated weights $w_i = K[(x_i - x_0)/h]$, we proceed to compute a fitted value at x_0 by weighted local averaging of the Y values:

$$\widehat{f}(x_0) = \widehat{Y}|x_0 = \frac{\sum_{i=1}^{n} w_i Y_i}{\sum_{i=1}^{n} w_i}$$

Two popular choices of kernel functions, illustrated in Figure 18.1, are the *Gaussian* or *normal kernel* and the *tricube kernel*:

- The Gaussian kernel is simply the standard-normal density function,

$$K_N(z) = \frac{1}{\sqrt{2\pi}} e^{-z^2/2}$$

Here, the bandwidth h is the standard deviation of a normal distribution centered at x_0. Observations at distances greater than $2h$ from the focal value therefore receive nearly zero weight, because the normal density is small beyond two standard deviations from the mean.

- The tricube kernel is

$$K_T(z) = \begin{cases} (1 - |z|^3)^3 & \text{for } |z| < 1 \\ 0 & \text{for } |z| \geq 1 \end{cases}$$

For the tricube kernel, h is the half-width of a window centered at the focal x_0. Observations that fall outside of the window receive zero weight.

---

as wavelet regression—see, e.g., Nason and Silverman, 2000), but they are beyond the scope of the current discussion.

[4]Kernel functions were introduced in Section 3.1.2 in connection with nonparametric density estimation, which may be thought of as a univariate analog of kernel and local-polynomial regression.

- Using a *rectangular kernel* (also shown in Figure 18.1)

$$K_R(z) = \begin{cases} 1 & \text{for } |z| < 1 \\ 0 & \text{for } |z| \geq 1 \end{cases}$$

gives equal weight to each observation in a window of half-width h centered at x_0, and zero weight to observations outside of this window, producing an *unweighted* local average.[5]

I have implicitly assumed that the bandwidth h is *fixed*, but the kernel estimator is easily adapted to *nearest-neighbor* bandwidths, which include a constant number or proportion of the data. The adaptation is simplest for kernel functions, like the tricube kernel, that fall to 0: Simply adjust $h(x)$ so that a constant number of observations m are included in the window. The fraction m/n is called the *span* of the kernel smoother. It is common to evaluate the kernel estimator either at a number of values evenly distributed across the range of X or at the ordered observations $x_{(i)}$.

Nearest-neighbor kernel estimation is illustrated in Figure 18.2 for the relationship between the prestige and income levels of 102 Canadian occupations in 1971.[6] Panel (a) shows a neighborhood containing 40 observations centered on the 80th ordered X value. Panel (b) shows the tricube weight function defined on the window; the bandwidth $h[x_{(80)}]$ is selected so that the window accommodates the 40 nearest neighbors of the focal $x_{(80)}$. Thus, the span of the smoother is $40/102 \approx 0.4$. Panel (c) shows the locally weighted average, $\widehat{Y}_{(80)} = \widehat{Y}|x_{(80)}$; note that this is the fitted value associated with $x_{(80)}$, *not* the 80th ordered fitted value. Finally, panel (d) connects the fitted values above the $x_{(i)}$ to obtain the kernel estimate of the regression of prestige on income. In comparison to the local–average regression (Figure 2.8 on page 22), the kernel estimate is smoother, but it still exhibits artificial flattening at the boundaries (called *boundary bias*). Varying the span of the kernel estimator controls the smoothness of the estimated regression function: Larger spans produce smoother results. A simple approach to selecting the span is to pick the smallest value that produces an acceptably smooth fit to the data.[7]

Kernel regression estimates the regression function at a focal value x_0 of the explanatory variable by weighted local averaging of Y:

$$\widehat{f}(x_0) = \widehat{Y}|x_0 = \frac{\sum_{i=1}^{n} w_i Y_i}{\sum_{i=1}^{n} w_i}$$

The weights are provided by a kernel function, $w_i = K[(x_i - x_0)/h]$, which takes on its largest value at $K(0)$ and falls symmetrically toward 0 as $|(x_i - x_0)/h|$ grows. Observations close to the focal x_0 therefore receive greatest weight. The kernel estimator is evaluated at representative focal values of X or at the ordered X values, $x_{(i)}$. The bandwidth h of the kernel estimator can be fixed, or can be adjusted to include a fixed proportion of the data, called the span of the kernel estimate. The larger the span, the smoother the kernel regression.

---

[5]This is the local-averaging estimator described in Section 2.3.

[6]The Canadian occupational prestige data set was introduced in Chapter 2.

[7]Choice of bandwidth or span is discussed in more detail in connection with local polynomial regression in the next section. See Exercise 18.1 for the effect on the kernel estimator of varying the span in the regression of occupational prestige on income.

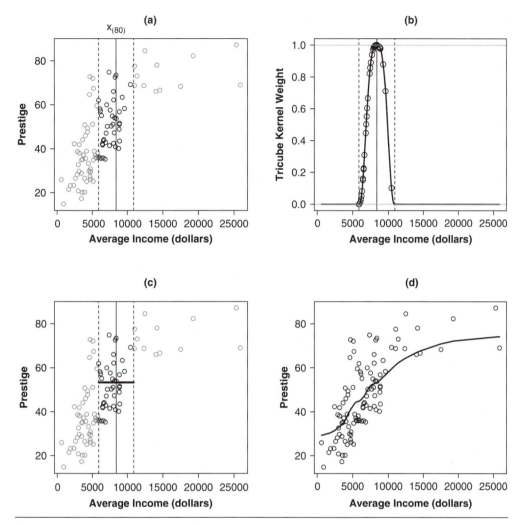

Figure 18.2 The kernel estimator applied to the Canadian occupational prestige data: (a) a window containing the $m = 40$ nearest X neighbors of the focal value $x_{(80)}$; (b) the tricube weight function and weights for observations within the window; (c) the weighted average $\widehat{Y}_{(80)}$ of the Y values in the window; (d) the nonparametric regression line connecting the locally weighted averages centered at each $x_{(i)}$.

18.1.2 Local-Polynomial Regression

Local-polynomial regression corrects some of the deficiencies of kernel estimation. It provides a generally adequate method of nonparametric regression that extends straightforwardly to multiple regression, additive regression, and generalized nonparametric regression (as described later in this chapter).

We are familiar with polynomial regression,[8] where a pth-degree polynomial in an explanatory variable X,

$$Y_i = \alpha + \beta_1 x_i + \beta_2 x_i^2 + \cdots + \beta_p x_i^p + \varepsilon_i$$

---

[8]See Section 17.1.

is fit to data; $p = 1$ corresponds to a linear fit, $p = 2$ to a quadratic fit, and so on. Fitting a constant (i.e., the mean) corresponds to $p = 0$.

Local-polynomial regression extends kernel estimation to a polynomial fit at the focal value x_0, using local kernel weights, $w_i = K[(x_i - x_0)/h]$. The resulting weighted least-squares (WLS) regression[9] fits the equation

$$Y_i = A + B_1(x_i - x_0) + B_2(x_i - x_0)^2 + \cdots + B_p(x_i - x_0)^p + E_i$$

to minimize the weighted residual sum of squares, $\sum_{i=1}^{n} w_i E_i^2$. Once the WLS solution is obtained, the fitted value at the focal x_0 is just $\widehat{Y}|x_0 = A$. As in kernel regression, this procedure is repeated for representative focal values of X, or at the observations x_i.

Also as in kernel regression, we can employ a fixed bandwidth or adjust the bandwidth to include a fixed proportion—or span—of nearest neighbors to the focal value x_0. Nearest-neighbor local-polynomial regression is often called *lowess* (an acronym for *lo*cally *w*eighted *s*catterplot *s*moother, sometimes rendered as *loess*, for *lo*cal regr*ess*ion)—a term with which we are already familiar.

Selecting $p = 1$ produces a local-linear fit, the most common case. The "tilt" of the local-linear fit promises reduced bias in comparison to the kernel estimator of the previous section, which corresponds to $p = 0$. This advantage is most apparent at the boundaries, where the kernel estimator tends to flatten. The values $p = 2$ or $p = 3$, local quadratic or cubic fits, produce more flexible regressions. Greater flexibility has the potential to reduce bias further, but flexibility also entails the cost of greater variation. There is, it turns out, a theoretical advantage to odd-order local polynomials, so $p = 1$ is generally preferred to $p = 0$, and $p = 3$ to $p = 2$. These issues are explored below.

Figure 18.3 illustrates the computation of a local-linear-regression fit to the Canadian occupational prestige data, using the tricube kernel function and nearest-neighbor bandwidths. Panel (a) shows a window accommodating the 40 nearest neighbors of the focal value $x_{(80)}$, corresponding to a span of $40/102 \approx 0.4$. Panel (b) shows the tricube weight function defined on this window. The locally weighted linear fit appears in panel (c). Fitted values calculated at each observed X value are connected in panel (d). There is no flattening of the fitted regression function at the boundaries, as there was for kernel estimation (cf., Figure 18.2 on page 479).

Local-polynomial regression extends kernel estimation to a polynomial fit at the focal value x_0, using local kernel weights, $w_i = K[(x_i - x_0)/h]$. The resulting WLS regression fits the equation

$$Y_i = A + B_1(x_i - x_0) + B_2(x_i - x_0)^2 + \cdots + B_p(x_i - x_0)^p + E_i$$

to minimize the weighted residual sum of squares, $\sum_{i=1}^{n} w_i E_i^2$. The fitted value at the focal x_0 is just $\widehat{Y}|x_0 = A$. This procedure is repeated for representative focal values of X, or at the observations x_i. We can employ a fixed bandwidth or adjust the bandwidth for a fixed span. Nearest-neighbor local-polynomial regression is often called lowess (or loess).

---

[9]Weighted-least-squares regression is developed in Section 12.2.2. Centering at x_0, by employing $x_i - x_0$, is convenient (but inessential) in that the fitted value at x_0 is then simply the intercept A (see below).

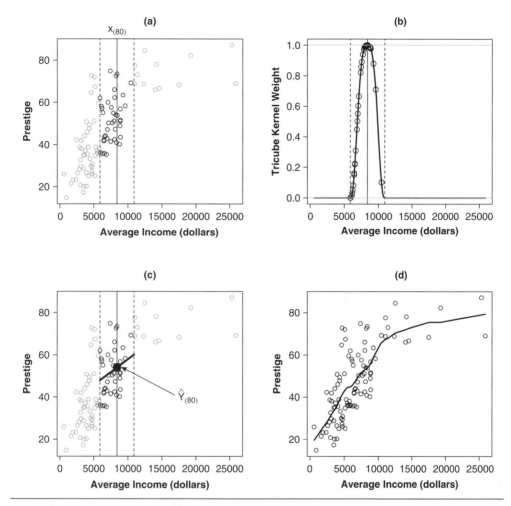

Figure 18.3   Nearest-neighbor local linear regression of prestige on income. The window in (a) includes the $m = 40$ nearest neighbors of the focal value $x_{(80)}$. The tricube weights for this window are shown in (b), and the locally weighted least-squares line in (c), producing the fitted value $\widehat{Y}_{(80)}$. Fitted values for all the observations are connected in (d) to produce the nonparametric local-polynomial regression line.

Selecting the Span

I will assume nearest-neighbor bandwidths, so bandwidth choice is equivalent to selecting the span of the local-regression smoother. I will also assume a locally linear fit. The methods of this section generalize in an obvious manner to fixed-bandwidth and higher-order polynomial smoothers.

A generally effective approach to selecting the span is guided trial and error. The span $s = 0.5$ is often a good point of departure. If the fitted regression looks too rough, then try increasing the span; if it looks smooth, then see if the span can be decreased without making the fit too rough. We want the *smallest* value of s that provides a smooth fit.

The terms "smooth" and "rough" are admittedly subjective, and a sense of what I mean here is probably best conveyed by example. An illustration, for the Canadian occupational prestige data, appears in Figure 18.4. For these data, selecting $s = 0.5$ or $s = 0.7$ appears to provide a reasonable compromise between smoothness and fidelity to the data.

More sophisticated methods for selecting the span will be described presently.[10] The visual approach usually works very well, however, and visual trial and error should be performed even if more sophisticated approaches are used to provide an initial value of s.

> A generally effective visual approach to selecting the span in local-polynomial regression is guided trial and error. The span $s = 0.5$ is often a good point of departure. If the fitted regression looks too rough, then try increasing the span; if it looks smooth, then see if the span can be decreased without making the fit too rough. We want the smallest value of s that provides a smooth fit.

Statistical Issues in Local Regression*

I will again assume local-linear regression. The results in this section extend to local-polynomial fits of higher degree, but the linear case is simpler.

Figure 18.5 demonstrates why the locally linear estimator has a bias advantage in comparison to the kernel estimator. In both panels (a) and (b), the true regression function (given by the heavy line) is linear in the neighborhood of the focal value x_0.

- In panel (a), the X values in the window are symmetrically distributed around the focal x_0 at the center of the window. As a consequence, the weighted average $\overline{\mu}$ of the Ys in the window (or, indeed, the simple average of the Ys in the window) provides an unbiased estimate of $\mu|x_0 \equiv E(Y|x_0)$; the local regression line *also* provides an unbiased estimate of $\mu|x_0$ because it estimates the true local regression function.
- In panel (b), in contrast, there are relatively more observations at the right of the window. Because the true regression function has a positive slope in the window, $\overline{\mu}$ exceeds $\mu|x_0$— that is, the kernel estimator is biased. The local-linear regression, however, *still* estimates the true regression function and therefore provides an unbiased estimate of $\mu|x_0$. The boundaries are regions in which the observations are asymmetrically distributed around the focal x_0, accounting for the boundary bias of the kernel estimator, but the point is more general.

Of course, if the true regression in the window is *nonlinear*, then both the kernel estimate and the locally linear estimate will usually be biased, if to varying degrees.[11] The conclusion to be drawn from these pictures is that *the bias of the kernel estimate depends on the distribution of X values, while the bias of the locally linear estimate does not*. Because the locally linear estimate can adapt to a "tilt" in the true regression function, it generally has smaller bias when the X values are unevenly distributed and at the boundaries of the data. Because the kernel and locally linear estimators have the same asymptotic variance, the smaller bias of the locally linear estimator translates into smaller mean-squared error.

These conclusions generalize to local-polynomial regressions of even degree p and odd degree $p + 1$ (e.g., $p = 2$ and $p + 1 = 3$): Asymptotically, the bias of the odd member of the pair is independent of the distribution of X values, while the bias of the even member is not. The bias of the odd member of the pair is generally smaller than that of the even member, while the variance

---

[10]Also see Exercise 18.2.

[11]It is possible that $\overline{\mu} = \mu|x_0$ by good fortune, but this is an unusual occurrence.

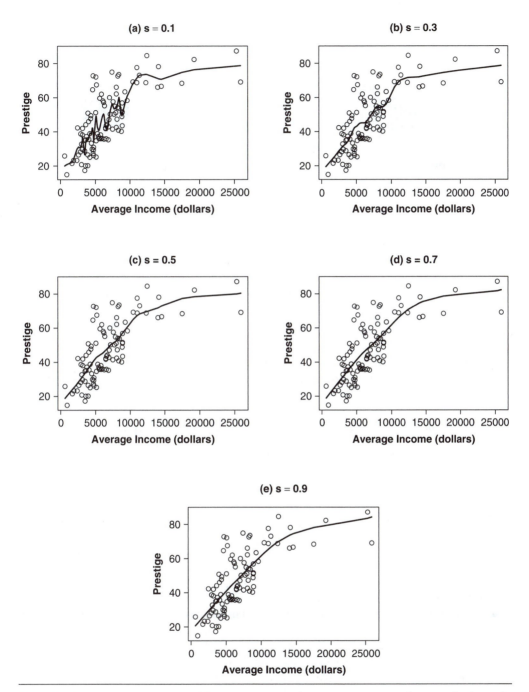

Figure 18.4   Nearest-neighbor local linear regression of prestige on income, for several values of the span *s*. The value *s* = 0.5 or 0.7 appears to reasonably balance smoothness with fidelity to the data.

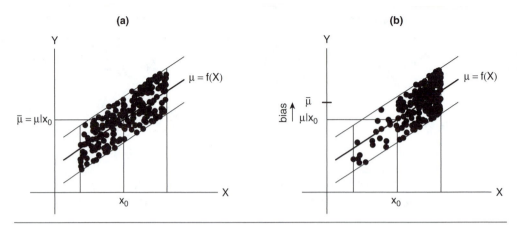

Figure 18.5   (a) When the relationship is linear in the neighborhood of the focal x_0, and the observations are symmetrically distributed around x_0, both the kernel estimator (which estimates $\overline{\mu}$) and the local-linear estimator (which, because the relationship is linear in the window, directly estimates $\mu|x_0$) are unbiased. (b) When the regression is linear in the neighborhood, but the observations are *not* symmetrically distributed around x_0, the local-linear estimator is *still* unbiased, but the kernel estimator is biased.

is the same. Asymptotically, therefore, the odd member of the pair (e.g., the local cubic estimator) has a smaller mean-squared error than the even member (e.g., the local quadratic estimator).

*A Closer Look at the Bandwidth of the Local-Regression Smoother**

As the bandwidth h of the local-regression estimator decreases, the bias of the estimator decreases and its variance increases. Suppose that we evaluate the local regression at the focal value x_0:

- At one extreme, $h = 0$ and only observations with X values *exactly equal to x_0* contribute to the local fit. In this case, it is not possible to fit a unique local regression line, but we could still find the fitted value at x_0 as the average Y value for $X = x_0$; if there are no tied values of x_0, then the fit is exact, $\widehat{Y}_0 = Y_0$, and the local-regression estimator simply joins the points in the scatterplot. Because $E(Y|x_0) = \mu|x_0$, the bias of the estimator is 0; its variance—equal to the conditional variance σ_ε^2 of an individual observation—is large, however.
- At the other extreme, $h = \infty$. Then, the scaled distances of explanatory-variable values x_i from the focal x_0, that is, $x_i = (x_i - x_0)/h$, are all 0, and the weights $w_i = K(z_i)$ are all equal to the maximum (e.g., 1 for the tricube kernel function). With equal weights for all the observations, the fit is no longer local. In effect, we fit a global least-squares line to the data. Now the bias is large (unless, of course, the true regression *really is* globally linear), but the sample-to-sample variance of the fit is small.

The bottom line is the mean-squared error of the estimator,

$$\text{MSE}(\widehat{Y}|x_0) \equiv E[(\widehat{Y}|x_0 - \mu|x_0)^2]$$
$$= E\left\{[\widehat{Y}|x_0 - E(\widehat{Y}|x_0)]^2\right\} + [E(\widehat{Y}|x_0) - \mu|x_0]^2$$

which is the sum of variance and squared bias. We seek the bandwidth h^* at x_0 that minimizes the MSE, providing an optimal trade-off of bias against variance (see below). Of course, we need to repeat this process at each focal value of X for which $f(x) = \mu|x$ is to be estimated, adjusting the bandwidth as necessary to minimize MSE.

The expectation and variance of the local-linear smoother at the focal value x_0 are

$$E(\widehat{Y}|x_0) \approx f(x_0) + \frac{h^2}{2} s_K^2 f''(x_0) \qquad (18.1)$$

$$V(\widehat{Y}|x_0) \approx \frac{\sigma_\varepsilon^2 a_K^2}{nhp_X(x_0)}$$

where (as before)

- $\widehat{Y}|x_0 \equiv \widehat{f}(x_0)$ is the fitted value at $X = x_0$;
- $\sigma_\varepsilon^2 = V(\varepsilon)$ is the variance of the errors, that is, the conditional (constant) variance of Y around the true regression function;
- h is the bandwidth;
- n is the sample size;

and

- $f''(x_0)$ is the second derivative of the true regression function at the focal x_0 (indicative of the curvature of the regression function, that is, the rapidity with which the slope of the regression function is changing at x_0);
- $p_X(x_0)$ is the probability density for the distribution of X at x_0 (large values of which, therefore, indicate an x_0 near which many observations will be made);[12]
- s_K^2 and a_K^2 are positive constants that depend on the kernel function.[13]

The bias at x_0 is

$$\text{bias}(\widehat{Y}|x_0) \equiv E(\widehat{Y}|x_0) - f(x_0) \approx \frac{h^2}{2} s_K^2 f''(x_0)$$

The bias of the estimator is large, therefore, when the bandwidth h and curvature $f''(x_0)$ of the regression function are large. In contrast, the variance of the estimator (from Equation 18.1) is large when the error variance σ_ε^2 is large, when the sample size n is small, when the bandwidth h is small, and where data are sparse [i.e., $p_X(x_0)$ is small].[14]

Because making h larger increases the bias but decreases the variance, bias and variance, as usual, work at cross-purposes. The value of h that minimizes the MSE—the sum of squared bias and variance—at x_0 is

---

[12]In contrast to the rest of the presentation, here the explanatory variable X is treated as a random variable.

[13]These formulas are derived in Bowman and Azzalini (1997: pp. 72–73). The two constants are:

$$s_K^2 = \int z^2 K(z) dZ$$

$$a_K^2 = \int [K(z)]^2 dZ$$

If the kernel $K(z)$ is a probability density function symmetric around 0, such as the standard-normal distribution, then s_K^2 is the variance of this distribution. For the standard-normal kernel, for example, $s_K^2 = 1$ and $a_K^2 = 0.282$. For the tricube kernel (which is *not* a density function), $s_K^2 = 1/6$ and $a_K^2 = 0.949$.

[14]The expected effective sample size contributing to the estimate at $x = x_0$ is proportional to $nhp_X(x_0)$, the denominator of the variance.

$$h^*(x_0) = \left[\frac{a_K^2}{s_K^4} \times \frac{\sigma_\varepsilon^2}{np_X(x_0) \left[f''(x_0) \right]^2} \right]^{\frac{1}{5}} \tag{18.2}$$

Note that where the curvature $f''(x_0)$ is 0, the optimal bandwidth $h^*(x_0)$ is infinite, suggesting a globally linear fit to the data.[15] Nearest-neighbor bandwidths, which employ a fixed span, adjust for the factor $np_X(x_0)$ but do not take account of the local curvature of the regression function.

To assess the overall accuracy of the nearest-neighbor local-regression estimator, we need some way of cumulating mean-squared error over observed X values. One way of doing so is to calculate the *average squared error* (ASE):

$$\text{ASE}(s) = \frac{\sum_{i=1}^n [\widehat{Y}_i(s) - \mu_i]^2}{n} \tag{18.3}$$

where $\mu_i \equiv E(Y|x_i)$ is the "true" expected value of the response for the ith observation, and $\widehat{Y}_i(s)$ is the ith fitted value for span s. Some points to note are the following:

- The squared error is evaluated at the observed X values and then averaged over the n observations.
- The ASE is calculated for a *particular* set of data, not as an expectation with respect to repeated sampling.[16]
- To calculate the ASE requires knowledge of the true regression function, and the ASE therefore cannot be used in practice to select the span. The cross-validation function, described in the next section, estimates the ASE.

The bias and variance of the local-linear estimator at the focal value x_0 are both a function of the bandwidth h, as well as of properties of the data and the kernel function:

$$\text{bias}(\widehat{Y}|x_0) \approx \frac{h^2}{2} s_K^2 f''(x_0)$$

$$V(\widehat{Y}|x_0) \approx \frac{\sigma_\varepsilon^2 a_K^2}{nhp_X(x_0)}$$

where s_K^2 and a_K^2 are constants that depend on the kernel function; $f''(x_0)$ is the second derivative ("curvature") of the regression function at x_0; and $p_X(x_0)$ is the probability-density of X values at x_0. We would ideally like to choose the value of h at each focal value that minimizes the mean-squared error of estimation—that is, the sum of squared bias and variance.

Selecting the Span by Cross-Validation

A conceptually appealing, but complex, approach to bandwidth selection is formally to estimate the optimal bandwidth h^*. We either need to estimate $h^*(x_0)$ for each value x_0 of X at which $\widehat{Y}|x$

---

[15] See Exercise 18.4 for an illustration of these points.
[16] See Exercise 18.5 for an illustration.

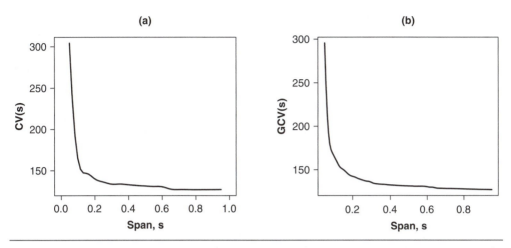

Figure 18.6 (a) Cross-validation function and (b) generalized cross-validation function for the local-linear regression of prestige on income.

is to be evaluated, or to estimate an optimal average value to be used with the fixed-bandwidth estimator. A similar approach is applicable to the nearest-neighbor local-regression estimator.[17]

A simpler approach, applicable to both the fixed-bandwidth and the nearest-neighbor estimators, is to estimate the optimal bandwidth or span by *cross-validation*.[18] I will consider the nearest-neighbor estimator; the development for the fixed-bandwidth estimator is similar. In cross-validation, we evaluate the regression function at the observations x_i.

The key idea in cross-validation is to *omit* the ith observation from the local regression at the focal value x_i. We denote the resulting estimate of $E(Y|x_i)$ as $\widehat{Y}_{-i}|x_i$. Omitting the ith observation makes the fitted value $\widehat{Y}_{-i}|x_i$ *independent of* the observed value Y_i.

The *cross-validation function* is

$$\mathrm{CV}(s) \equiv \frac{\sum_{i=1}^{n}\left[\widehat{Y}_{-i}(s) - Y_i\right]^2}{n}$$

where $\widehat{Y}_{-i}(s)$ is $\widehat{Y}_{-i}|x_i$ for span s. The object is to find the value of s that minimizes $\mathrm{CV}(s)$. In practice, we can compute $\mathrm{CV}(s)$ for a range of values of s.

Figure 18.6(a) shows $\mathrm{CV}(s)$ for the regression of occupational prestige on income. In this case, the cross-validation function provides little specific help in selecting the span, suggesting simply that s should be relatively large. Compare this with the value $s \approx .6$ that we arrived at by visual trial and error.

The cross-validation function $\mathrm{CV}(s)$ can be costly to compute because it requires refitting the model n times for each candidate value of the span s.[19] For this reason, approximations have

---

[17]* The so-called plug-in estimate of h^* proceeds by estimating its components—σ_ε^2, $f''(x_0)$, and $p_X(x_0)$; we need not estimate the other quantities in Equation 18.2 (on page 486), because the sample size n is known, and the constants a_K^2 and s_K^4 can be calculated from the kernel function. Estimating σ_ε^2 and $f''(x_0)$ requires a preliminary estimate of the regression function.

[18] The more general use of cross-validation for model selection is discussed in Chapter 22.

[19] In the current context, we typically want to evaluate the local regression at each observation anyway, but computational short-cuts (such as interpolation for closely spaced values of X) make the point valid. Moreover, the computational burden imposed by cross-validation extends to other contexts as well.

been proposed, one of which is termed *generalized cross-validation*, abbreviated *GCV* (Wahba, 1985).[20] In the present context, the GCV criterion is

$$\text{GCV}(s) \equiv \frac{n \times \text{RSS}(s)}{[df_{\text{res}}(s)]^2} \tag{18.4}$$

where $\text{RSS}(s)$ is the residual sum of squares and $df_{\text{res}}(s)$ the "equivalent" residual degrees of freedom for the local-regression model with span s.[21] The GCV function for the example appears in Figure 18.6(b). In this case, $\text{GCV}(s)$ provides an excellent approximation to $\text{CV}(s)$.

The cross-validation function

$$\text{CV}(s) = \frac{\sum_{i=1}^{n} \left[\widehat{Y}_{-i}(s) - Y_i \right]^2}{n}$$

can be used to select the span s in local-polynomial regression, picking s to minimize $\text{CV}(s)$. The fitted value at each observation $\widehat{Y}_{-i}(s)$ is computed from a local regression that omits that observation. Because the cross-validation function $\text{CV}(s)$ can be costly to compute, approximations such as generalized cross-validation have been proposed. The GCV criterion is

$$\text{GCV}(s) = \frac{n \times \text{RSS}(s)}{[df_{\text{res}}(s)]^2}$$

where $\text{RSS}(s)$ is the residual sum of squares and $df_{\text{res}}(s)$ the "equivalent" residual degrees of freedom for the local-regression smoother with span s.

A Closer Look at Cross-Validation* The cross-validation function is a kind of estimate of the mean (i.e., expected) ASE at the observed Xs,[22]

$$\text{MASE}(s) \equiv E \left\{ \frac{\sum_{i=1}^{n} \left[\widehat{Y}_i(s) - \mu_i \right]^2}{n} \right\}$$

Because of the independence of $\widehat{Y}_{-i}$ and Y_i, the expectation of $\text{CV}(s)$ is

$$E[\text{CV}(s)] = \frac{\sum_{i=1}^{n} E \left[\widehat{Y}_{-i}(s) - Y_i \right]^2}{n}$$
$$\approx \text{MASE}(s) + \sigma_\varepsilon^2$$

The substitution of Y_i for μ_i increases the expectation of $\text{CV}(s)$ by σ_ε^2; but because σ_ε^2 is a constant, the value of s that minimizes $E[\text{CV}(s)]$ is (approximately) the value that minimizes $\text{MASE}(s)$.

---

[20]The GCV criterion also exhibits a desirable invariance property that the CV criterion does not share. See, for example, Wood (2006, sect. 4.5.3).

[21]See below (page 493ff) for an explanation of degrees of freedom in local-polynomial regression.

[22]Alternatively, rather than averaging over the observed X values we could integrate over the probability-density of X, producing the mean integrated square error (MISE):

$$\text{MISE}(s) = \int \left\{ E[\widehat{Y}|x(s)] - \mu|x \right\} p(x) dX$$

We can think of MASE as a discrete version of MISE.

To understand why it is important in this context to omit the ith observation in calculating the fit at the ith observation, consider what would happen were we not to do this. Then, setting the span to zero would minimize the estimated MASE, because (in the absence of tied X values) the local-regression estimator simply interpolates the observed data: The fitted and observed values are equal, and $\widehat{\text{MASE}}(0) = 0$.

Although cross-validation is often a useful method for selecting the span in local-polynomial regression, it should be appreciated that $\text{CV}(s)$ is only an estimate, and is therefore subject to sampling variation. Particularly in small samples, this variability can be substantial. Moreover, the approximations to the expectation and variance of the local-regression estimator in Equation 18.1 (page 485) are asymptotic, and in small samples $\text{CV}(s)$ often tends to provide values of s that are too small.

Statistical Inference for Local-Polynomial Regression

In parametric regression—for example, linear least-squares regression—the central objects of estimation are the regression coefficients. Statistical inference naturally focuses on these coefficients, typically taking the form of confidence intervals or hypothesis tests.[23] In nonparametric regression, in contrast, there are *no* regression coefficients. Instead, the central object of estimation is the regression function, and inference focuses on the regression function *directly*.

Many applications of simple nonparametric regression have as their goal visual smoothing of a scatterplot. In these instances, statistical inference is at best of secondary interest. Inference becomes more prominent in nonparametric multiple regression.[24]

This section takes up several aspects of statistical inference for local-polynomial regression with one explanatory variable. I start by explaining how to construct an approximate confidence envelope for the regression function. Then, I present a simple approach to hypothesis testing, based on an analogy to procedures for testing hypotheses in linear least-squares regression. The statistical theory behind these relatively simple methods is subsequently examined.

A general caveat concerns the selection of the span s: Because s is typically selected on examination of the data—either visually or by employing a criterion such as CV or GCV—the validity of classical statistical inference is compromised. The methods of this section are therefore best regarded as rough guides.[25]

Confidence Envelopes Consider the local-polynomial estimate $\widehat{f}(x) = \widehat{Y}|x$ of the regression function $f(x)$. For notational convenience, I assume that the regression function is evaluated at the observed X values, $x_1, x_2, \ldots, x_n$, although the line of reasoning to be developed here is more general.

The fitted value $\widehat{Y}_i = \widehat{Y}|x_i$ results from a locally weighted least-squares regression of Y on X. This fitted value is therefore a weighted sum of the observations:[26]

$$\widehat{Y}_i = \sum_{j=1}^{n} s_{ij} Y_j \tag{18.5}$$

where the weights s_{ij} are functions of the X values. For the tricube weight function, for example, s_{ij} is 0 for any observations outside the neighborhood of the focal x_i. Because (by assumption)

---

[23] See Chapter 6.

[24] See Section 18.2.

[25] Issues of model selection are addressed more generally in Chapter 22.

[26] See the starred material in this section for this and other results.

the Y_is are independently distributed, with common conditional variance $V(Y|X = x_i) = V(Y_i) = \sigma_\varepsilon^2$, the sampling variance of the fitted value $\widehat{Y}_i$ is

$$V(\widehat{Y}_i) = \sigma_\varepsilon^2 \sum_{j=1}^{n} s_{ij}^2$$

To apply this result, we require an estimate of σ_ε^2. In linear least-squares simple regression, we estimate the error variance as

$$S_E^2 = \frac{\sum E_i^2}{n-2}$$

where $E_i = Y_i - \widehat{Y}_i$ is the residual for observation i, and $n-2$ is the degrees of freedom associated with the residual sum of squares. We "lose" two degrees of freedom as a consequence of estimating the two regression parameters—the intercept α and the slope β.[27]

We can calculate residuals in nonparametric regression in the same manner—that is, $E_i = Y_i - \widehat{Y}_i$, where, of course, the fitted value $\widehat{Y}_i$ is from the nonparametric regression. To complete the analogy, we require the *equivalent number of parameters* or *equivalent degrees of freedom* for the model, df_{mod}, from which we can obtain the equivalent residual degrees of freedom, $df_{\text{res}} = n - df_{\text{mod}}$. Then, the estimated error variance is

$$S_E^2 = \frac{\sum E_i^2}{df_{\text{res}}}$$

and the estimated variance of the fitted value $\widehat{Y}_i$ is

$$\widehat{V}(\widehat{Y}_i) = S_E^2 \sum_{j=1}^{n} s_{ij}^2 \tag{18.6}$$

Assuming normally distributed errors, or a sufficiently large sample, a 95% confidence interval for $E(Y|x_i) = f(x_i)$ is approximately

$$\widehat{Y}_i \pm 2\sqrt{\widehat{V}(\widehat{Y}_i)} \tag{18.7}$$

Putting the confidence intervals together for $X = x_1, x_2, \ldots, x_n$ produces a pointwise 95% confidence band or confidence envelope for the regression function.

An example, employing the local-linear regression of prestige on income in the Canadian occupational prestige data (with span $s = 0.6$), appears in Figure 18.7. Here, $df_{\text{mod}} = 5.006$, and $S_E^2 = 12,004.72/(102 - 5.006) = 123.77$. The nonparametric-regression smooth therefore uses the equivalent of about five parameters—roughly the same as a fourth-degree polynomial. The fit to the data, however, can differ substantially from that of fourth-degree polynomial, which is much less sensitive to local characteristics of the regression function.[28]

Although this procedure for constructing a confidence band has the virtue of simplicity, it is not quite correct, due to the bias in $\widehat{Y}|x$ as an estimate of $E(Y|x)$. If we have chosen the span and degree of the local-polynomial estimator judiciously, however, the bias should be small. Bias in $\widehat{Y}|x$ has the following consequences:

- S_E^2 is biased upward, tending to overstate the error variance, and making the confidence interval too wide.[29]

---

[27] See Section 18.2.

[28] See Exercise 18.7.

[29] Bowman and Azzalini (1997, sect. 4.3) consider alternative approaches to estimating the error variance σ_ε^2.

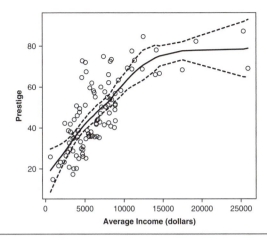

Figure 18.7   Local-linear regression of occupational prestige on income, showing an approximate pointwise 95% confidence envelope. The span of the smoother is $s = 0.6$.

- The confidence interval is on average centered in the wrong location.

These errors tend to offset each other. Because $\widehat{Y}|x$ is biased, it is more accurate to describe the envelope around the sample regression constructed according to Equation 18.7 as a "variability band" rather than as a confidence band.[30]

The fitted values in a local-polynomial regression are linear functions of the observations, $\widehat{Y}_i = \sum_{j=1}^{n} s_{ij} Y_j$. Estimating the error variance as $S_E^2 = \sum E_i^2 / df_{\text{res}}$, where df_{res} is the equivalent residual degrees of freedom for the model, the estimated variance of a fitted value is $\widehat{V}(\widehat{Y}_i) = S_E^2 \sum_{j=1}^{n} s_{ij}^2$. An approximate 95% pointwise confidence band around the regression curve evaluated at the fitted values may be formed as $\widehat{Y}_i \pm 2\sqrt{\widehat{V}(\widehat{Y}_i)}$.

Hypothesis Tests   In linear least-squares regression, F-tests of hypotheses are formulated by comparing alternative nested models. To say that two models are nested means that one, the more specific model, is a special case of the other, more general model.[31] For example, in linear least-squares simple regression, the F-statistic

$$F_0 = \frac{\text{TSS} - \text{RSS}}{\frac{\text{RSS}}{n-2}}$$

with 1 and $n - 2$ degrees of freedom tests the hypothesis of no linear relationship between Y and X. Here, the total sum of squares, $\text{TSS} = \sum (Y_i - \overline{Y})^2$, is the variation in Y associated with the null model of no relationship, $Y_i = \alpha + \varepsilon_i$; and the residual sum of squares, $\text{RSS} = \sum (Y_i - \widehat{Y}_i)^2$, represents the variation in Y conditional on the linear relationship between Y and X, based on residuals from the model $Y_i = \alpha + \beta x_i + \varepsilon_i$. Because the null model is a special case of the linear model, with $\beta = 0$, the two models are nested.

---

[30]We could, moreover, make the same point about confidence intervals for fitted values in *linear* least-squares regression, when the assumption of linearity is not exactly correct. Indeed, the bias in estimates of $E(Y|x)$ is likely to be *less* in nonparametric regression than in linear regression.

[31]See Section 6.2.2.

An analogous, but more general, F-test of no relationship for the nonparametric-regression model is

$$F_0 = \frac{\frac{\text{TSS}-\text{RSS}}{df_{\text{mod}}-1}}{\frac{\text{RSS}}{df_{\text{res}}}} \tag{18.8}$$

with $df_{\text{mod}} - 1$ and $df_{\text{res}} = n - df_{\text{mod}}$ degrees of freedom. Here RSS is the residual sum of squares for the nonparametric-regression model. Applied to the local-linear regression of prestige on income, where $n = 102$, $\text{TSS} = 29,895.43$, $\text{RSS} = 12,004.72$, and $df_{\text{mod}} = 5.006$, we have

$$F_0 = \frac{\frac{29,895.43-12,004.72}{5.006-1}}{\frac{12,004.72}{102-5.006}} = 36.08$$

with $5.006 - 1 = 4.006$ and $102 - 5.006 = 96.994$ degrees of freedom. The resulting p-value is much smaller than .0001, casting strong doubt on the null hypothesis of no relationship between prestige and income of occupations.

A test of nonlinearity is simply constructed by contrasting the nonparametric-regression model with the linear simple-regression model.[32] The models are properly nested because a linear relationship is a special case of a general, potentially nonlinear, relationship. Denoting the residual sum of squares from the linear model as RSS_0 and the residual sum of squares from the more general nonparametric-regression model as RSS_1, we have

$$F_0 = \frac{\frac{\text{RSS}_0-\text{RSS}_1}{df_{\text{mod}}-2}}{\frac{\text{RSS}_1}{df_{\text{res}}}}$$

with $df_{\text{mod}} - 2$ and $df_{\text{res}} = n - df_{\text{mod}}$ degrees of freedom. This test is constructed according to the rule that the most general model—here the nonparametric-regression model—is employed for estimating the error variance in the denominator of the F-statistic, $S_E^2 = \text{RSS}_1/df_{\text{res}}$. For the regression of occupational prestige on income, $\text{RSS}_0 = 14,616.17$, $\text{RSS}_1 = 12,004.72$, and $df_{\text{mod}} = 5.006$; thus

$$F_0 = \frac{\frac{14,616.17-12,004.72}{5.006-2}}{\frac{12,004.72}{102-5.006}} = 7.02$$

with $5.006 - 2 = 3.006$ and $102 - 5.006 = 96.994$ degrees of freedom. The corresponding p-value, .0003, suggests that the relationship between the two variables is significantly nonlinear.

Approximate incremental F-tests for hypotheses in local-polynomial regression are formulated by contrasting nested models, in analogy to similar tests for linear models fit by least-squares. For example, to test the hypothesis of no relationship in the nonparametric-regression model, we can compute the F-test statistic

$$F_0 = \frac{\frac{\text{TSS}-\text{RSS}}{df_{\text{mod}}-1}}{\frac{\text{RSS}}{df_{\text{res}}}}$$

where df_{mod} and $df_{\text{res}} = n - df_{\text{mod}}$ are respectively the equivalent degrees of freedom for the regression model and for error, and RSS is the residual sum of squares for the model.

---

[32]Cf. the test for "lack of fit" described in Section 12.4.

Similarly, to test for nonlinearity, we can contrast the fitted nonparametric-regression model with a linear model, computing

$$F_0 = \frac{\frac{RSS_0 - RSS_1}{df_{mod} - 2}}{\frac{RSS_1}{df_{res}}}$$

where RSS_0 is the residual sum of squares for the linear regression and RSS_1 the residual sum of squares for the more general nonparametric regression.

Degrees of Freedom* As noted, the fitted values $\widehat{Y}_i$ in local-polynomial regression are weighted sums of the observed Y values (repeating Equation 18.5 on page 489):

$$\widehat{Y}_i = \sum_{j=1}^{n} s_{ij} Y_j$$

Let us collect the weights s_{ij} into the *smoother matrix*

$$\underset{(n \times n)}{\mathbf{S}} \equiv \begin{bmatrix} s_{11} & s_{12} & \cdots & s_{1i} & \cdots & s_{1n} \\ s_{21} & s_{22} & \cdots & s_{2i} & \cdots & s_{2n} \\ \vdots & \vdots & \ddots & \vdots & & \vdots \\ s_{i1} & s_{i2} & \cdots & s_{ii} & \cdots & s_{in} \\ \vdots & \vdots & & \vdots & \ddots & \vdots \\ s_{n1} & s_{n2} & \cdots & s_{ni} & \cdots & s_{nn} \end{bmatrix}$$

Then,

$$\underset{(n \times 1)}{\widehat{\mathbf{y}}} = \mathbf{S} \underset{(n \times 1)}{\mathbf{y}}$$

where $\widehat{\mathbf{y}} = [\widehat{y}_1, \widehat{y}_2, \ldots, \widehat{y}_n]'$ is the vector of fitted values, and $\mathbf{y} = [y_1, y_2, \ldots, y_n]'$ is the vector of observed response values.

The covariance matrix of the fitted values is

$$V(\widehat{\mathbf{y}}) = \mathbf{S}V(\mathbf{y})\mathbf{S}' = \sigma_\varepsilon^2 \mathbf{S}\mathbf{S}' \tag{18.9}$$

This result follows from the assumptions that the conditional variance of Y_i is constant (σ_ε^2) and that the observations are independent, implying that $V(\mathbf{y}) = \sigma_\varepsilon^2 \mathbf{I}_n$. Equation 18.6 (page 490) for the variance of $\widehat{Y}_i$ is just an expansion of the ith diagonal entry of $V(\widehat{\mathbf{y}})$.

The smoother matrix $\mathbf{S}$ is analogous to the hat-matrix $\mathbf{H} \equiv \mathbf{X}(\mathbf{X}'\mathbf{X})^{-1}\mathbf{X}'$ in linear least-squares regression, where $\mathbf{X}$ is the model matrix for the linear model.[33] The residuals in linear least-squares regression are

$$\mathbf{e} = \mathbf{y} - \widehat{\mathbf{y}} = (\mathbf{I}_n - \mathbf{H})\mathbf{y}$$

The corresponding expression in local regression is

$$\mathbf{e} = \mathbf{y} - \widehat{\mathbf{y}} = (\mathbf{I}_n - \mathbf{S})\mathbf{y}$$

---

[33] See Section 11.8.

To determine the smoother matrix $\mathbf{S}$, recall that $\widehat{Y}_i$ results from a locally weighted polynomial regression of Y on X:

$$Y_j = A_i + B_{1i}(x_j - x_i) + B_{2i}(x_j - x_i)^2 + \cdots + B_{pi}(x_j - x_i)^P + E_{ji}$$

where the weights $w_{ji} = K[(x_j - x_i)/h]$ decline with distance from the focal x_i. The local-regression coefficients are chosen to minimize $\sum_{j=1}^{n} w_{ji} E_{ji}^2$. The fitted value $\widehat{Y}_i$ is just the regression constant A_i. In matrix form, the local regression is

$$\mathbf{y} = \mathbf{X}_i \mathbf{b}_i + \mathbf{e}_i$$

The model matrix $\mathbf{X}_i$ contains the regressors in the local-regression equation (including an initial column of 1s for the constant), and the coefficient vector $\mathbf{b}_i$ contains the regression coefficients.

Define the diagonal matrix $\mathbf{W}_i \equiv \text{diag}\{\sqrt{w_{ji}}\}$ of square-root kernel weights. Then, the local-regression coefficients are

$$\mathbf{b}_i = (\mathbf{X}_i' \mathbf{W}_i \mathbf{X}_i)^{-1} \mathbf{X}_i' \mathbf{W}_i \mathbf{y}$$

and the ith row of the smoother matrix is the first row of $(\mathbf{X}_i' \mathbf{W}_i \mathbf{X}_i)^{-1} \mathbf{X}_i' \mathbf{W}_i$ (i.e., the row that determines the constant, $A_i = \widehat{Y}_i$). To construct $\mathbf{S}$ we need to repeat this procedure for $i = 1, 2, \ldots, n$.

In linear least-squares regression, the degrees of freedom for the model can be defined in a variety of equivalent ways. Most directly, assuming that the model matrix $\mathbf{X}$ is of full column rank, the degrees of freedom for the model are equal to the number of regressors $k + 1$ (including the regression intercept). The degrees of freedom for the model are also equal to the following:

- the rank and trace of the hat matrix, $\mathbf{H}$;
- the trace of $\mathbf{HH}'$;
- the trace of $2\mathbf{H} - \mathbf{HH}'$.

These alternative expressions follow from the fact that the hat-matrix is symmetric and idempotent—that is, $\mathbf{H} = \mathbf{H}'$ and $\mathbf{H} = \mathbf{HH}$. The degrees of freedom for error in least-squares linear regression are

$$df_{\text{res}} = \text{rank}(\mathbf{I}_n - \mathbf{H}) = \text{trace}(\mathbf{I}_n - \mathbf{H}) = n - \text{trace}(\mathbf{H}) = n - k - 1$$

because $\mathbf{I}_n - \mathbf{H}$ projects $\mathbf{y}$ onto the orthogonal complement of the column space of $\mathbf{X}$ to obtain the residuals: $\mathbf{e} = (\mathbf{I}_n - \mathbf{H})\mathbf{y}$.[34]

Analogous degrees of freedom for the local-regression model are obtained by substituting the smoother matrix $\mathbf{S}$ for the hat-matrix $\mathbf{H}$. The analogy is not perfect, however, and in general $\text{trace}(\mathbf{S}) \neq \text{trace}(\mathbf{SS}') \neq \text{trace}(2\mathbf{S} - \mathbf{SS}')$.

- Defining $df_{\text{mod}} = \text{trace}(\mathbf{S})$ is an attractive choice because it is easy to calculate.
- In a linear model, the degrees of freedom for the model are equal to the sum of variances of the fitted values divided by the error variance,

$$\frac{\sum_{i=1}^{n} V(\widehat{Y}_i)}{\sigma_{\varepsilon}^2} = k + 1$$

In the current context (from Equation 18.9),

$$\frac{\sum_{i=1}^{n} V(\widehat{Y}_i)}{\sigma_{\varepsilon}^2} = \text{trace}(\mathbf{SS}')$$

motivating the definition, $df_{\text{mod}} = \text{trace}(\mathbf{SS}')$.

---

[34]The vector geometry of linear least-squares regression is developed in Chapter 10.

- The expectation of the residual sum of squares in local-polynomial regression is[35]

$$E(\text{RSS}) = \sigma_\varepsilon^2[n - \text{trace}(2\mathbf{S} - \mathbf{S}\mathbf{S}')] + \text{bias}^2$$

where $\text{bias}^2 = \sum_{i=1}^{n}[E(\widehat{Y}_i) - f(x_i)]^2$ is the cumulative bias in the local regression evaluated at the observed X values. If the bias is negligible, then $\text{RSS}/[n - \text{trace}(2\mathbf{S} - \mathbf{S}\mathbf{S}')]$ is an estimator of the error variance σ_ε^2, suggesting that $n - \text{trace}(2\mathbf{S} - \mathbf{S}\mathbf{S}')$ is a suitable definition of the degrees of freedom for error and that $df_{\text{mod}} = \text{trace}(2\mathbf{S} - \mathbf{S}\mathbf{S}')$. This last definition is possibly the most attractive theoretically, but it is relatively difficult to compute.[36]

> The smoother matrix $\mathbf{S}$ in nonparametric local-polynomial regression plays a role analogous to the hat-matrix $\mathbf{H}$ in linear least-squares regression. Like the hat-matrix, the smoother matrix linearly transforms the observations into the fitted values: $\widehat{\mathbf{y}} = \mathbf{S}\mathbf{y}$. Pursuing this analogy, the equivalent degrees of freedom for the nonparametric-regression model can variously be defined as $df_{\text{mod}} = \text{trace}(\mathbf{S})$, $\text{trace}(\mathbf{S}\mathbf{S}')$, or $\text{trace}(2\mathbf{S} - \mathbf{S}\mathbf{S}')$.

18.1.3   Smoothing Splines*

In contrast with regression splines—which are *parametric* regression models[37]—*smoothing splines* arise as the solution to the following *nonparametric*-regression problem: Find the function $\widehat{f}(x)$ with two continuous derivatives that minimizes the *penalized sum of squares*,

$$\text{SS}^*(h) = \sum_{i=1}^{n}[Y_i - f(x_i)]^2 + h \int_{x_{\min}}^{x_{\max}}\left[f''(x)\right]^2 dx \qquad (18.10)$$

where h is a smoothing constant, analogous to the bandwidth of a kernel or local-polynomial estimator.

- The first term in Equation 18.10 is the residual sum of squares.
- The second term is a *roughness penalty,* which is large when the integrated second derivative of the regression function $f''(x)$ is large—that is, when $f(x)$ is rough. The endpoints of the integral enclose the data: $x_{\min} < x_{(1)}$ and $x_{\max} > x_{(n)}$.
- At one extreme, if the smoothing constant is set at $h = 0$ (and if all the X values are distinct), then $\widehat{f}(x)$ simply interpolates the data.
- At the other extreme, if h is very large, then $\widehat{f}$ will be selected so that $\widehat{f}''(x)$ is everywhere 0, which implies a *globally linear* least-squares fit to the data.

It turns out, surprisingly and elegantly, that the function $\widehat{f}(x)$ that minimizes Equation 18.10 is a natural cubic spline with knots at the distinct observed values of X. Although this result

---

[35]See Hastie and Tibshirani (1990, sects. 3.4–3.5).

[36]Hastie and Tibshirani (1990, sect. 3.5) demonstrate a simple relationship between $\text{trace}(2\mathbf{S} - \mathbf{S}\mathbf{S}')$ and $\text{trace}(\mathbf{S})$ that allows the latter to be used to approximate the former. The software used for most of the examples in the current chapter (the gam package for R: Hastie and Tibshirani, 1990; Hastie, 1992) takes this approach. Further discussion of these issues may be found in Hastie and Tibshirani (1990, sect. 3.5) and in Cleveland, Grosse, and Shyu (1992, sect. 8.4.1). Hastie and Tibshirani (1990, sects. 3.8–3.9) show how incremental F-tests can be made more precise by adjusting the degrees of freedom used in finding p-values. Similar procedures can be applied to improve the performance of confidence bands for the regression curve, using the t-distribution in the calculation of margins of error.

[37]See Section 17.2.

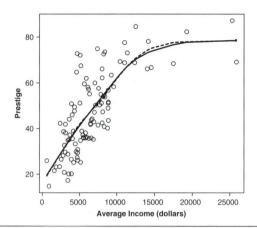

Figure 18.8   Nonparametric regression of occupational prestige on income, using a smoothing
spline (solid line) and local-linear regression (broken line), both with five equivalent
parameters.

seems to imply that n parameters are required (when all X values are distinct), the roughness
penalty imposes additional constraints on the solution, typically reducing the equivalent number
of parameters for the smoothing spline considerably, and preventing $\widehat{f}(x)$ from interpolating the
data. Indeed, it is common practice to select the smoothing constant h *indirectly* by setting the
equivalent number of parameters for the smoother.

An illustration, for the regression of occupational prestige on income, appears in Figure 18.8,
comparing a smoothing spline with a local-linear fit employing the same equivalent number of
parameters (degrees of freedom). The two fits are nearly identical.

Precisely the same considerations arise in the selection of h for smoothing splines as in the
selection of the bandwidth or span for local-polynomial smoothers: We can proceed, for example,
by visual trial and error, or by cross-validation or generalized cross-validation.

Smoothing splines offer certain small advantages in comparison to local-polynomial
smoothers. Both smoothers are linear, in the sense that they can be written in the form $\widehat{\mathbf{y}} = \mathbf{Sy}$
for a suitably defined smoother matrix $\mathbf{S}$. The smoother matrix for smoothing splines is slightly
better behaved, however, and if smoothing splines are employed as building blocks of an additive
regression model, then the backfitting algorithm that can be used to fit this model is guaranteed
to converge, a property that does not hold for the local-polynomial smoother.[38] On the negative
side, smoothing splines are more difficult to generalize to multiple regression.[39]

18.2   Nonparametric Multiple Regression

18.2.1   Local-Polynomial Multiple Regression

Local-polynomial regression extends straightforwardly from simple to multiple regression.
The method also has an intuitively appealing rationale, and it is relatively simple to implement.
Moreover, local-polynomial regression generalizes easily to binary and other non-normal data.[40]

---

[38] Additive regression models and the backfitting algorithm are described in Section 18.2.2.

[39] This is not to say that spline-based methods for multiple regression are either impossible or unattractive, just that their
development is relatively complex. See, for example, Green and Silverman (1994) or Wood (2006).

[40] See Section 18.3.

Kernel Weights in Multiple Regression

As a formal matter, it is simple to extend the local-polynomial estimator to several explanatory variables. To obtain a fitted value $\widehat{Y}|\mathbf{x}$ at the focal point $\mathbf{x}_0 = (x_{01}, x_{02}, \ldots, x_{0k})'$ in the space of the explanatory variables, we perform a weighted-least-squares polynomial regression of Y on the Xs, emphasizing observations close to the focal point.[41]

- A local-linear fit therefore takes the following form:

$$Y_i = A + B_1(x_{i1} - x_{01}) + B_2(x_{i2} - x_{02}) + \cdots + B_k(x_{ik} - x_{0k}) + E_i$$

- For $k = 2$ explanatory variables, a local-quadratic fit takes the form

$$Y_i = A + B_1(x_{i1} - x_{01}) + B_2(x_{i2} - x_{02}) + B_{11}(x_{i1} - x_{01})^2 + B_{22}(x_{i2} - x_{02})^2$$
$$+ B_{12}(x_{i1} - x_{01})(x_{i2} - x_{02}) + E_i$$

including linear, quadratic, and cross-product terms for the Xs. When there are several explanatory variables, the number of terms in the local-quadratic regression grows large. As a consequence, we will not consider cubic or higher-order polynomials, which contain even more terms.

In either the linear or quadratic case, we find local-regression coefficients by minimizing the weighted residual sum of squares $\sum_{i=1}^{n} w_i E_i^2$ for suitably defined weights w_i. The fitted value at the focal point in the X space is then the regression constant, $\widehat{Y}|\mathbf{x}_0 = A$.

Figure 18.9 shows the scatterplot for two variables, X_1 and X_2, sampled from a bivariate-normal distribution with means $\mu_1 = \mu_2 = 20$, standard deviations $\sigma_1 = 8$ and $\sigma_2 = 4$, and covariance $\sigma_{12} = 25$ [producing the correlation $\rho_{12} = 25/(8 \times 4) = .78$]. As illustrated in this figure, there are two straightforward ways to extend kernel weighting to local-polynomial multiple regression:

1. Calculate *marginal weights* separately for each X, and then take the product of the marginal weights. That is, for the jth explanatory variable and observation i, calculate the marginal kernel weight

$$w_{ij} = K\left(\frac{x_{ij} - x_{0j}}{h_j}\right)$$

where x_{0j} is the focal value for explanatory variable X_j, and h_j is the marginal bandwidth for this variable. As in local-polynomial simple regression, we can use a fixed bandwidth or we can adjust the bandwidth to include a constant number of nearest neighbors of x_{0j}. Having found marginal weights for the k explanatory variables, the final weight attributed to observation i in the local regression is their product:

$$w_i = w_{i1}w_{i2}\cdots w_{ik}$$

Product-marginal weights define a rectangular neighborhood around the focal $\mathbf{x}_0$. Figure 18.9(a) shows such a neighborhood for the artificially generated data.[42]

---

[41] If you are unfamiliar with vector notation, think of $\mathbf{x}$ simply as the collection of values of the explanatory variables.
[42] The explanatory variables in Figure 18.9(a) are standardized for comparability with the other parts of the figure (see below). Standardization does not affect the product-marginal weights.

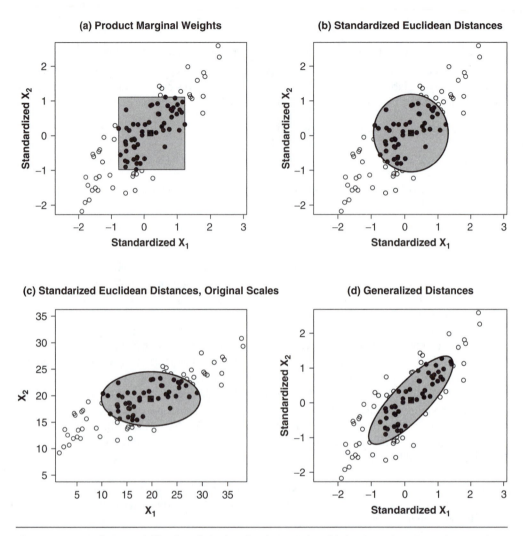

Figure 18.9   Defining neighborhoods for local-polynomial multiple regression: In each case, the
focal point is marked by a black square at the center of the bivariate window.
(a) Product-marginal weights, each for span = 0.7; (b) standardized Euclidean
distances, span = 0.5; (c) standardized Euclidean distances plotted on the
unstandardized scales for the two variables; (d) generalized distances, span = 0.5.

2. Measure the distance $D(\mathbf{x}_i, \mathbf{x}_0)$ in the X space between the explanatory-variable values $\mathbf{x}_i$
for observation i and the focal $\mathbf{x}_0$. Then, kernel weights can be calculated directly from
these distances,

$$w_i = K\left[\frac{D(\mathbf{x}_i, \mathbf{x}_0)}{h}\right]$$

As before, the bandwidth h can either be fixed or adjusted to include a constant number
of nearest neighbors of the focal point. There is, however, more than one way to define
distances between points in the X space:

- *Simple Euclidean distance*:

$$D_E(\mathbf{x}_i, \mathbf{x}_0) = \sqrt{\sum_{j=1}^{k}(x_{ij} - x_{0j})^2}$$

  Euclidean distances only make sense when the Xs are measured in the same units, and even in this case, we may prefer another approach. An obvious application of Euclidean distance is to spatially distributed data, where the two explanatory variables X_1 and X_2 represent coordinates on a map, and the regression surface traces how the average value of Y changes spatially.
- *Scaled Euclidean distance*: Scaled distances adjust each X by a measure of dispersion to make values of the explanatory variables roughly comparable. We could use a robust measure of spread, such as the median absolute deviation from the median or the interquartile range, but the standard deviation is typically used. It is also common to center the Xs by subtracting the mean from each value; centering does not affect distances, however. The first step, then, is to standardize the Xs,

$$z_{ij} = \frac{x_{ij} - \overline{x}_j}{s_j}$$

  where $\overline{x}_j$ and s_j are respectively the mean and standard deviation of X_j. The scaled Euclidean distance between an observation $\mathbf{x}_i$ and the focal point $\mathbf{x}_0$ is

$$D_S(\mathbf{x}_i, \mathbf{x}_0) = \sqrt{\sum_{j=1}^{k}(z_{ij} - z_{0j})^2}$$

  This is the most common approach to defining distances.

  For two Xs, scaled Euclidean distances generate a circular neighborhood around the focal point in the standardized X space [see Figure 18.9(b)]. Plotted in the original, *unscaled* X space, the neighborhood is elliptical, with axes parallel to the X_1 and X_2 axes [Figure 18.9(c)].
- *Generalized distance*: *Generalized distances adjust not only for the dispersion of the Xs but also for their correlational structure:

$$D_G(\mathbf{x}_i, \mathbf{x}_0) = \sqrt{(\mathbf{x}_i - \mathbf{x}_0)'\mathbf{V}^{-1}(\mathbf{x}_i - \mathbf{x}_0)}$$

  where $\mathbf{V}$ is the covariance matrix of the Xs, perhaps estimated robustly.[43] Figure 18.9(d) illustrates generalized distances for $k = 2$ explanatory variables. Here, the neighborhood around the focal point is elliptical, with axes reflecting the correlation between the Xs.

As mentioned, simple Euclidean distances do not make sense unless the explanatory variables are on the same scale. Beyond that point, the choice of product marginal weights, weights based on scaled Euclidean distances, or weights based on generalized distances usually does not make a great deal of difference.

---

[43]Methods such as M estimation, to be introduced in Chapter 19 on robust regression, can be adapted to estimate the mean vector and covariance matrix for a vector of variables.

Generalizing local-polynomial regression to multiple regression is conceptually and computationally straightforward. For example, to obtain the fitted value for a local-linear regression at the focal point $\mathbf{x}_0 = (x_{01}, x_{02}, \ldots, x_{0k})'$ in the space of the explanatory variables, we perform a weighted-least-squares regression of Y on the Xs,

$$Y_i = A + B_1(x_{i1} - x_{01}) + B_2(x_{i2} - x_{02}) + \cdots + B_k(x_{ik} - x_{0k}) + E_i$$

emphasizing observations close to the focal point by minimizing the weighted residual sum of squares, $\sum_{i=1}^{n} w_i E_i^2$. The fitted value at the focal point in the X space is then $\widehat{Y}|\mathbf{x}_0 = A$. The weights w_i can be computed in several ways, including by multiplying marginal kernel weights for the several explanatory variables, or by basing kernel weights on one or another measure of distance between the focal $\mathbf{x}_0$ and the observed X values, $\mathbf{x}_i$. Given a distance measure $D(\mathbf{x}_i, \mathbf{x}_0)$, the kernel weights are calculated as $w_i = K[D(\mathbf{x}_i, \mathbf{x}_0)/h]$.

Span Selection, Statistical Inference, and Order Selection

Methods of span selection for local-polynomial multiple regression are essentially the same as the methods for simple regression discussed in Section 18.1.2; they are, briefly:

- *Visual Trial and Error:* We can vary the span and examine the resulting regression surface, balancing smoothness against detail. We seek the smallest span that produces a smooth regression surface.
- *Cross-Validation:* For a given span s, we fit the model omitting each observation in turn, obtaining a fitted value $\widehat{Y}_{-i}(s) = \widehat{Y}|\mathbf{x}_i$ at the omitted observation. Then, we select the span that minimizes the cross-validation function

$$\mathrm{CV}(s) = \frac{\sum_{i=1}^{n}\left[\widehat{Y}_{-i}(s) - Y_i\right]^2}{n}$$

or the generalized cross-validation function

$$\mathrm{GCV}(s) = \frac{n \times \mathrm{RSS}(s)}{[df_{\mathrm{res}}(s)]^2}$$

It is, in addition, possible to derive an expression for the mean-square error of estimation in local-polynomial multiple regression.[44] One could in principle proceed to estimate the MSE, and to select the span that minimizes the estimate. As far as I know, this more complex approach has not been implemented for multiple regression.

Inference for local-polynomial multiple regression also closely parallels local-polynomial simple regression. At each observation $\mathbf{x}_i$, the fitted value $\widehat{Y}_i = \widehat{Y}|\mathbf{x}_i$ results from a weighted-least-squares regression, and is therefore a linear function of the response,

$$\widehat{Y}_i = \sum_{j=1}^{n} s_{ij} Y_j$$

- *Degrees of Freedom:* *As in local-polynomial simple regression, equivalent degrees of freedom for the model come from the smoother matrix $\mathbf{S}$, where

---

[44] See Fan and Gijbels (1996, sect. 7.8), and Simonoff (1996, sect. 5.7) for the local-linear case.

$$\underset{(n\times 1)}{\widehat{\mathbf{y}}} = \underset{(n\times n)}{\mathbf{S}}\ \underset{(n\times 1)}{\mathbf{y}}$$

and are variously defined as $df_{\text{mod}} = \text{trace}(\mathbf{S})$, $\text{trace}(\mathbf{SS}')$, or $\text{trace}(2\mathbf{S} - \mathbf{SS}')$.

- *Error Variance:* The error variance σ_ε^2 can be estimated as

$$S_E^2 = \frac{\sum E_i^2}{df_{\text{res}}}$$

  where the $E_i = Y_i - \widehat{Y}_i$ are the residuals from the model, and $df_{\text{res}} = n - df_{\text{mod}}$.

- *Confidence Intervals:* The estimated variance of the fitted value $\widehat{Y}_i$ at $\mathbf{x}_i$ is

$$\widehat{V}(\widehat{Y}_i) = S_E^2 \sum_{j=1}^{n} s_{ij}^2$$

  Then, an approximate 95% confidence interval for the population regression surface above $\mathbf{x}_i$ is

$$\widehat{Y}_i \pm 2\sqrt{\widehat{V}(\widehat{Y}_i)}$$

- *Hypothesis Tests:* Incremental F-tests can be formulated by fitting alternative models to the data and comparing residual sums of squares and degrees of freedom. For example, to test for the effect of a particular explanatory variable X_j, we can omit the variable from the model, taking care to adjust the span to reflect the reduced dimensionality of the regression problem.[45] Let RSS_1 represent the residual sum of squares for the full model, which has df_1 equivalent degrees of freedom, and RSS_0 represent the residual sum of squares for the model omitting the jth explanatory variable, which has df_0 degrees of freedom. Then, under the null hypothesis that Y has no partial relationship to X_j,

$$F_0 = \frac{\frac{\text{RSS}_0 - \text{RSS}_1}{df_1 - df_0}}{\frac{\text{RSS}_1}{df_{\text{res}}}}$$

  follows an approximate F-distribution with $df_1 - df_0$ and $df_{\text{res}} = n - df_1$ degrees of freedom. In general, and as usual, we use the most complete model fit to the data for the error-variance estimate in the denominator of the incremental F-statistic.

As explained previously, because of proliferation of terms, it is typical to consider only local-linear (order 1) and quadratic (order 2) regressions. A local-quadratic fit is indicated if the curvature of the regression surface changes too quickly to be captured adequately by the local-linear estimator. To a certain extent, however, the order of the local regressions can be traded off against their span, because a local-linear regression can be made more flexible by reducing the span. To decide between the local linear and quadratic fits, we can compare them visually, or we can perform an incremental F-test of the hypothesis that the additional terms in the local quadratic model are necessary.

---

[45]That is, if the span for the multiple regression is s and there are k explanatory variables, then (by appealing, e.g., to product-marginal weighting) the "span per explanatory variable" is $\sqrt[k]{s}$. Therefore, if one X is dropped from the model, the span should be adjusted to $s^{(k-1)/k}$. For example, for $k = 2$ and $s = 0.25$, on dropping one X from the model, the adjusted span becomes $0.25^{1/2} = 0.5$.

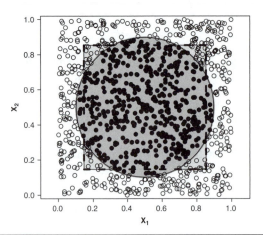

Figure 18.10   The "curse of dimensionality": 1,000 observations for independent, uniformly distributed random variables X_1 and X_2. The 500 nearest neighbors of the focal point $\mathbf{x}_0 = (0.5, 0.5)'$ are highlighted, along with the circle (of diameter ≈ 0.8) that encloses them. Also shown is the square centered on $\mathbf{x}_0$ (with sides $= \sqrt{1/2}$) enclosing about half the data.

Methods for selecting the span in local-polynomial multiple regression are much the same as in local-polynomial simple regression: We can proceed visually by trial and error, or apply a criterion such as $CV(s)$ or $GCV(s)$. Similarly, approximate pointwise confidence limits for the fitted regression can be calculated as in local-polynomial simple regression, as can incremental F-tests comparing nested models.

Obstacles to Nonparametric Multiple Regression

Although, as a formal matter, it is therefore simple to extend local-polynomial estimation to multiple regression, there are two flies in the ointment:

1. *The "curse of dimensionality"*:[46]   As the number of explanatory variables increases, the number of points "near" a focal point tends to decline rapidly. To include a fixed number of observations in the local fit as the number of Xs grows therefore requires making the neighborhood around the focal point less and less local. A general assumption of local-polynomial regression is that observations close in the X space to the focal $\mathbf{x}_0$ are informative about $f(\mathbf{x}_0)$; increasing the size of the neighborhood around the focal point therefore potentially decreases the quality of the estimate of $f(\mathbf{x}_0)$, by inflating the bias of the estimate.

   The problem is illustrated in Figure 18.10 for $k = 2$ explanatory variables. This figure represents a "best-case" scenario, where the Xs are independent and uniformly distributed. As we have seen, neighborhoods constructed by product-marginal weighting correspond to rectangular (here, square) regions in the graph. Neighborhoods defined by distance from a focal point correspond to circular (more generally, if the distances are scaled, elliptical)

---

[46]The curse of dimesionality was introduced in Section 2.2.

regions in the graph. To include half the observations in a square neighborhood centered on a focal $\mathbf{x}_0$, we need to define marginal neighborhoods for each of X_1 and X_2 that include roughly $\sqrt{1/2} \approx 0.71$ of the data; for $k = 10$ explanatory variables, the marginal neighborhoods corresponding to a hyper-cube that encloses half the observations would each include about $\sqrt[10]{1/2} \approx 0.93$ of the data. A circular neighborhood in two dimensions enclosing half the data has diameter $2\sqrt{0.5/\pi} \approx 0.8$ along each axis; the diameter of the hyper-sphere enclosing half the data also grows with dimensionality, but the formula is too complicated to warrant presentation here.

2. *Difficulties of interpretation*: Because nonparametric regression does not provide an equation relating the average response to the explanatory variables, we must display the response surface graphically. This is no problem, of course, when there is only one X, because the scatterplot relating Y to X is two-dimensional, and the regression "surface" is just a curve. When there are two Xs, the scatterplot is three-dimensional, and the regression surface is two-dimensional. Here, we can represent the regression surface in an isometric or perspective plot, as a contour plot, or by slicing the surface. These strategies are illustrated in the example developed immediately below. As I will explain, there are obstacles to extending graphical displays of the regression surface beyond two or three explanatory variables.

These problems motivate the additive regression model, described in Section 18.2.2.

> The curse of dimensionality and the difficulty of visualizing high-dimensional surfaces limit the practical application of unrestricted nonparametric multiple regression when there are more than a very small number of explanatory variables.

An Illustration: Data from the Survey of Labour and Income Dynamics

To illustrate local-polynomial multiple regression, I return to data from the Statistics Canada Survey of Labour and Income Dynamics, regressing the log (base 2) of the $n = 3997$ respondents' composite hourly wage rate on their age and years of education.[47] I selected a span of 0.25 for a local-linear regression after examining the generalized cross-validation criterion.[48] Figures 18.11 to 18.14 show three graphical representations of the local-linear fit:

- Figure 18.11 is a *perspective plot* (perspective projection) of the fitted regression surface. I find it relatively easy to visualize the general relationship of wages to age and education, but hard to make precise visual judgments: I can see that at fixed levels of age, wages generally rise with education (though not at the youngest age levels—see below); likewise, wages first rise and then fall somewhat with age at fixed levels of education. But it is difficult to discern, for example, the fitted value of log-wages for a 40-year-old individual with 10 years of education. Perspective plots are even more effective when they can be dynamically rotated on a computer, allowing us to view the regression surface from different angles, and conveying a greater sense of depth.

- Figure 18.12 is a *contour plot* of the data, showing "iso-log-wages" lines for combinations of values of age and education. I find it difficult to visualize the regression surface from a

---

[47]We previously encountered these data in Chapter 12, where I dealt with nonlinearity in the regression of log-wages on age and education by specifying a quadratic in age and transforming education; and in Chapter 17, where I fit regression splines in the two explanatory variables.

[48]The GCV criterion is lowest between about $s = 0.1$ and $s = 0.2$, and rises very gradually thereafter. Using, for example, $s = 0.15$ produces a regression surface that looks rough, so I opted for somewhat more smoothing.

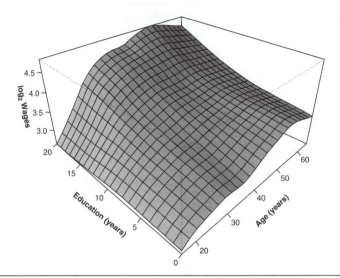

Figure 18.11 Perspective plot for the local-linear regression of log-wages on age and education. The span of the local regression is $s = 0.25$.

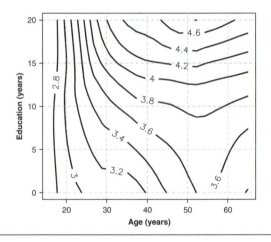

Figure 18.12 Contour plot for the local-linear regression of log-wages on age and education.

contour plot (perhaps hikers and mountain climbers do better), but it is relatively easy to see, for example, that our hypothetical 40-year-old with 10 years of education has fitted log-wages of about 3.8 (i.e., $2^{3.8} = \$13.93$ per hour).

- Figure 18.13 is a *conditioning plot* or "*coplot*,"[49] showing the fitted relationship between log-wages and age for several levels of education. The levels at which education is "held constant" are given in each panel of the figure, which shows the fit at a particular level of education. The lines in the panels of the coplot are lines on the regression surface in the direction of income (fixing education) in Figure 18.11, but displayed two-dimensionally. The broken lines in Figure 18.13 give pointwise 95% confidence envelopes around the fitted regression surface. The confidence envelopes are wide where data are sparse—for

---

[49]See Section 3.3.4.

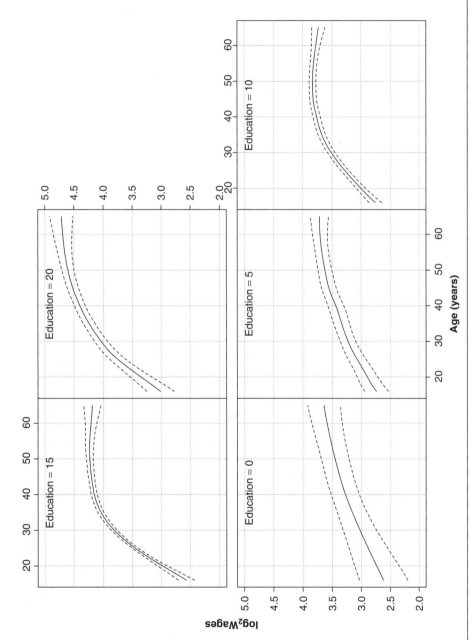

Figure 18.13 Conditioning plot showing the relationship between log-wages and age for various levels of education. The broken lines give a pointwise 95% confidence envelope around the fit.

example, for 0 years of education. That the shape of the partial relationship of log-wages to age varies somewhat with education is indicative of interaction between age and education in affecting income. Figure 18.14 shows a similar coplot displaying the fitted relationship between log-wages and education controlling for age. Note that at age 16, the higher levels of education are not possible (a point that could also have been made with respect to the preceding coplot), making the fit in this region a meaningless extrapolation beyond the data. It is useful to display both coplots because both partial relationships are of interest. Again, a small amount of interaction between education and age is apparent in the fit (after all, interaction is a symmetric concept). As well, the degree of nonlinearity in the partial relationships of log-wages to education at fixed age levels appears slight in most of the partial plots.

Is log-wages significantly related to both age and education? We can answer this question by dropping each explanatory variable in turn and noting the increase in the residual sum of squares. Because the span for the local-linear multiple-regression fit is $s = 0.25$, the corresponding simple-regression models use spans of $s = \sqrt{0.25} = 0.5$:[50]

Model	df_{mod}	RSS
Age and Education	18.6	1348.592
Age (alone)	4.3	1547.237
Education (alone)	4.9	1880.918

(18.11)

F-tests for age and education are as follows:

$$F_{\text{Age|Education}} = \frac{\frac{1880.918 - 1348.592}{18.6 - 4.9}}{\frac{1348.592}{3997 - 18.6}} = 114.63$$

$$F_{\text{Education|Age}} = \frac{\frac{1547.237 - 1348.592}{18.6 - 4.3}}{\frac{1348.592}{3997 - 18.6}} = 40.98$$

$F_{\text{Age| Education}}$, for example, is to be read as the incremental F-statistic for age "after" education. These F-statistics have, respectively, 13.7 and 3978.4 degrees of freedom, and 14.3 and 3978.4 degrees of freedom. Both p-values are close to 0, supporting the partial relationship of log-wages to both age and education.

Extension of these displays beyond two or three explanatory variables presents difficulties:

- Perspective plots and contour plots cannot easily be generalized to more than two explanatory variables: Although three-dimensional contour plots can be constructed, they are very difficult to understand, in my opinion, and higher-dimensional contour plots are out of the question.
- One can draw two-dimensional perspective or contour plots for two explanatory variables at fixed combinations of values of other explanatory variables, but the resulting displays are usually confusing.

---

[50]The heuristic here is as follows: In product-marginal kernel weighting of uniformly distributed data, marginal spans of 0.5 produce a neighborhood including roughly $0.5^2 = 0.25$ of the data. This rough reasoning is also supported by the degrees of freedom for the models in the table in Equation 18.11: The model with the age effect and an intercept has 4.3 degrees of freedom, and the model with the education effect and an intercept has 4.9 degrees of freedom. Therefore, a comparable model that allows age and education to interact should have roughly $4.3 \times 4.9 = 21.1$ degrees of freedom—close to the 18.6 degrees of freedom for the local-linear multiple regression with span 0.25.

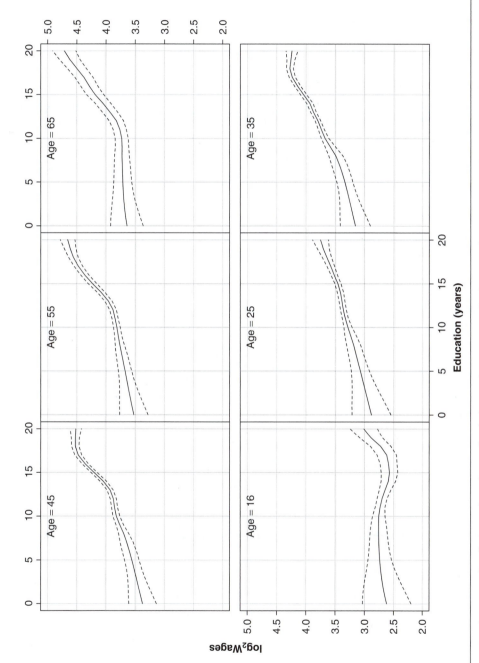

Figure 18.14 Conditioning plot showing the relationship between log-wages and education for various levels of age. The broken lines give a pointwise 95% confidence envelope around the fit.

- Coplots can be usefully constructed for three explanatory variables by arranging combinations of values of two of the variables in a rectangular array, and focusing on the fitted relationship of the response to the third explanatory variable. A complete set of coplots rotates the role of the third variable, producing three such displays.
- Coplots can in principle be extended to *any* number of explanatory variables by focusing on each variable in turn, but the resulting proliferation of graphs quickly gets unwieldy.

> When there are two explanatory variables, the fitted nonparametric-regression surface can be visualized in a three-dimensional perspective plot, in a contour plot, or in coplots for each explanatory variable at fixed levels of the other variable. Coplots can be generalized to three or more explanatory variables, but quickly become unwieldy.

18.2.2   Additive Regression Models

In unrestricted nonparametric multiple regression, we model the conditional average value of Y as a general, smooth function of several Xs,

$$E(Y|x_1, x_2, \ldots, x_k) = f(x_1, x_2, \ldots, x_k)$$

In linear-regression analysis, in contrast, the average value of the response variable is modeled as a linear function of the explanatory variables,

$$E(Y|x_1, x_2, \ldots, x_k) = \alpha + \beta_1 x_1 + \beta_2 x_2 + \cdots + \beta_k x_k$$

Like the linear model, the *additive regression model* specifies that the average value of Y is the sum of separate terms for each explanatory variable, but these terms are merely assumed to be smooth functions of the Xs:

$$E(Y|x_1, x_2, \ldots, x_k) = \alpha + f_1(x_1) + f_2(x_2) + \cdots + f_k(x_k)$$

Because it excludes interactions among the Xs, the additive regression model is more restrictive than the general nonparametric-regression model but more flexible than the standard linear-regression model.

An advantage of the additive regression model in comparison to the general nonparametric-regression model is that the additive model reduces to a series of two-dimensional partial-regression problems. This is true both in the computational sense and, even more importantly, with respect to interpretation:

- Because each partial-regression problem is two-dimensional, we can estimate the partial relationship between Y and X_j by using a suitable scatterplot smoother, such as local-polynomial regression or a smoothing spline. We need somehow to remove the effects of the other explanatory variables, however—we cannot simply smooth the marginal scatterplot of Y on X_j *ignoring* the other Xs. Details are given later in this section.
- A two-dimensional plot suffices to examine the estimated partial-regression function $\widehat{f_j}$ relating Y to X_j holding the other Xs constant. Interpretation of additive regression models is therefore relatively simple—assuming that the additive model adequately captures the dependence of Y on the Xs.

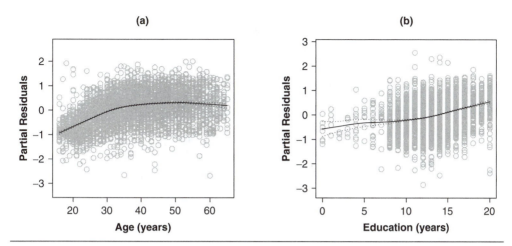

Figure 18.15   Plots of the estimated partial-regression functions for the additive regression of log-wages on (a) age and (b) education. Each partial regression uses a local-linear smoother with span $s = 0.5$. The points in the graphs represent partial residuals for each explanatory variable. The broken lines give pointwise 95% confidence envelopes for the partial fits.

The additive regression model

$$E(Y|x_1, x_2, ..., x_k) = \alpha + f_1(x_1) + f_2(x_2) + \cdots + f_k(x_k)$$

expresses the average value of the response variable as the sum of smooth functions of several explanatory variables. The additive model is therefore more restrictive than the general nonparametric-regression model but more flexible than the linear-regression model.

Figure 18.15 shows estimated partial-regression functions for the additive regression of log-wages on age and education in the SLID data. Each partial-regression function was fit by a nearest-neighbor local-linear smoother, using span $s = 0.5$. The points in each graph are *partial residuals* for the corresponding explanatory variable, removing the effect of the other explanatory variable. The broken lines mark off pointwise 95% confidence envelopes for the partial fits (both of which are very precisely estimated in this moderately large data set).

The component-plus-residual plot, which graphs partial residuals against an explanatory variable, is a standard diagnostic for nonlinearity in regression.[51] The additive model extends the notion of partial residuals by subtracting the potentially *nonlinear* fits for the other Xs from the response; for example, for X_1,

$$E_{i[1]} = Y_i - A - \widehat{f}_2(x_{i2}) - \cdots - \widehat{f}_k(x_{ik})$$

---

[51] See Section 12.3.1 for a discussion of component-plus-residual plots. The notation for partial residuals here differs from that used in Section 12.3.1, however, by denoting the explanatory variable in question by a bracketed subscript rather than a parenthetical superscript. In the development of additive regression below, I will use a parenthetical superscript for an iteration counter.

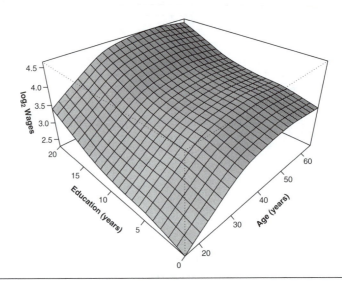

Figure 18.16 Perspective plot of the fitted additive regression of log-wages on age and education.

Then, $E_{[1]}$ is smoothed against X_1 to estimate f_1. (To apply this idea, we need an estimate A of α and estimates of the *other* partial-regression functions, f_2 through f_k—see below.)

Figure 18.16 is a three-dimensional perspective plot of the fitted additive-regression surface relating log-wages to age and education. Slices of this surface in the direction of age (i.e., holding education constant at various values) are all parallel; likewise slices in the direction of education (holding age constant) are parallel: This is the essence of the additive model, ruling out interaction between the explanatory variables. Because all the slices in a given direction are parallel, we need only view *one* of them edge-on, as in Figure 18.15. Compare the additive-regression surface with the fit of the unrestricted nonparametric-regression model in Figure 18.11 (on page 504).

Is anything lost in moving from the general nonparametric-regression model to the more restrictive additive model? Residual sums of squares and equivalent numbers of parameters (degrees of freedom) for the two models are as follows:

Model	df_{mod}	RSS
General	18.6	1348.592
Additive	8.2	1377.801

An approximate F-test comparing the two models is

$$F_0 = \frac{\frac{1377.801 - 1348.592}{18.6 - 8.2}}{\frac{1348.592}{3997 - 18.6}} = 8.29$$

with 10.4 and 3978.4 degrees of freedom, for which $p \ll .0001$. There is, therefore, strong evidence of lack of fit for the additive model; nevertheless, the additive model may be a reasonable, if simplified, summary of the data: The proportion of variation accounted for by the additive model is only slightly smaller than for the general model,

$$\text{General:} \quad R^2 = 1 - \frac{1348.592}{2104.738} = 0.3593$$

$$\text{Additive:} \quad R^2 = 1 - \frac{1377.801}{2104.738} = 0.3454$$

where 2104.738 is the total sum of squares for log-wages.[52]

To test the contribution of each explanatory variable to the additive model, we compare the full additive model with models omitting each variable in turn:

Model	df_{mod}	RSS
Additive	8.2	1377.801
Age (alone)	4.3	1547.237
Education (alone)	4.9	1880.918

Then,

$$F_{\text{Age}|\text{Education}} = \frac{\frac{1880.918 - 1377.801}{8.2 - 4.9}}{\frac{1348.592}{3997 - 18.6}} = 449.76$$

$$F_{\text{Education}|\text{Age}} = \frac{\frac{1547.237 - 1377.801}{8.2 - 4.3}}{\frac{1348.592}{3997 - 18.6}} = 128.16$$

with, respectively, 3.3 and 3978.4, and 3.9 and 3978.4 degrees of freedom; both F-statistics have p-values close to 0. Because there are only two explanatory variables, the second and third models in the table are the same as we employed to test the contribution of each explanatory variable to the *general* nonparametric-regression model (see the table in Equation 18.11 on page 506). The error-variance estimate in the denominator of the F-statistic is based on the largest model that we fit to the data—the general nonparametric-regression model of the preceding section.

Fitting the Additive Regression Model

For simplicity, consider the case of two explanatory variables, as in the regression of log-wages on age and education; the generalization to several explanatory variables is immediate (as is described subsequently):

$$Y_i = \alpha + f_1(x_{i1}) + f_2(x_{i2}) + \varepsilon_i$$

Suppose, unrealistically, that the partial-regression function f_2 is known, but that f_1 is not. Rearranging the regression equation,

$$Y_i - f_2(x_{i2}) = \alpha + f_1(x_{i1}) + \varepsilon_i$$

So smoothing $Y_i - f_2(x_{i2})$ against x_{i1} will produce an estimate of $\alpha + f_1(x_{i1})$.

The regression constant α is a bit of a nuisance here. We could absorb α into one of the partial-regression functions. Or—somewhat more gracefully—we could force the partial-regression

---

[52]Issues of model selection are discussed in a general context in Chapter 22.

functions evaluated at the observed x_{ij}s to sum to 0; in this case, α becomes the unconditional expectation of Y, estimated by $\overline{Y}$. Then, we estimate f_1 by smoothing $Y_i - \overline{Y} - f_2(x_{i2})$ against x_{i1}. Of course, in a real application, neither f_1 nor f_2 is known.

1. Let us start, then, with preliminary estimates of the partial-regression functions, denoted $\widehat{f}_1^{(0)}$ and $\widehat{f}_2^{(0)}$, based on the *linear* least-squares regression of Y on the Xs:

$$Y_i - \overline{Y} = B_1(x_{i1} - \overline{x}_1) + B_2(x_{i2} - \overline{x}_2) + E_i$$

[The parenthetical superscript (0) indicates that these are "step 0" estimates in an iterative (repetitive) process of estimation.] Then,

$$\widehat{f}_1^{(0)}(x_{i1}) = B_1(x_{i2} - \overline{x}_2)$$
$$\widehat{f}_2^{(0)}(x_{i2}) = B_2(x_{i2} - \overline{x}_2)$$

Expressing the variables as deviations from their means insures that the partial-regression functions sum to 0.

2. Form the partial residual

$$\begin{aligned} E_{i[1]}^{(1)} &= Y_i - \overline{Y} - B_2(x_{i2} - \overline{x}_2) \\ &= E_i + B_1(x_{i1} - \overline{x}_1) \end{aligned}$$

which removes from Y its linear relationship to X_2, but retains the linear relationship between Y and X_1, possibly along with a nonlinear relationship in the least-squares residuals E_i.[53] Smoothing $E_{i[1]}^{(1)}$ against X_{i1} provides a new estimate $\widehat{f}_1^{(1)}$ of f_1. [The parenthetical superscript (1) in $e_{i[1]}^{(1)}$ and $\widehat{f}_1^{(1)}$ indicates that these quantities pertain to iteration 1; the bracketed subscript [1] in $e_{i[1]}^{(1)}$ indicates that these are the partial residuals for the *first* explanatory variable, X_1.]

3. Using the updated estimate $\widehat{f}_1^{(1)}$, form partial residuals for X_2:

$$E_{i[2]}^{(1)} = Y_i - \overline{Y} - \widehat{f}_1^{(1)}(x_{i1})$$

Smoothing $E_{i[2]}^{(1)}$ against x_{i2} yields a new estimate $\widehat{f}_2^{(1)}$ of f_2.

4. The new estimate $\widehat{f}_2^{(1)}$, in turn, is used to calculate updated partial residuals $E_{i[1]}^{(2)}$ for X_1, which, when smoothed against x_{i1}, produce the updated estimate $\widehat{f}_1^{(2)}$ of f_1. This iterative process, called *backfitting*, continues until the estimated partial-regression functions stabilize.

> The additive regression model can be fit to data by the method of backfitting, which iteratively smooths the partial residuals for each explanatory variable using current estimates of the regression functions for other explanatory variables.

---

[53] These are simply the familiar partial residuals used for component-plus-residual plots in linear regression (described in Section 12.3.1).

Some Statistical Details*

More on Backfitting Backfitting implicitly solves the following set of estimating equations:

$$
\underbrace{\begin{bmatrix}
1 & \mathbf{0}'_n & \mathbf{0}'_n & \cdots & \mathbf{0}'_n \\
\mathbf{0}_n & \mathbf{I}_n & \mathbf{S}_1 & \cdots & \mathbf{S}_1 \\
\mathbf{0}_n & \mathbf{S}_2 & \mathbf{I}_n & \cdots & \mathbf{S}_2 \\
\cdot & \cdot & \cdot & \cdot & \cdot \\
\cdot & \cdot & \cdot & \cdot & \cdot \\
\cdot & \cdot & \cdot & \cdot & \cdot \\
\mathbf{0}_n & \mathbf{S}_k & \mathbf{S}_k & \cdots & \mathbf{I}_n
\end{bmatrix}}_{\substack{\mathbf{S} \\ [(kn+1)\times(kn+1)]}}
\underbrace{\begin{bmatrix}
A \\
\widehat{\mathbf{f}}_1 \\
\widehat{\mathbf{f}}_2 \\
\cdot \\
\cdot \\
\cdot \\
\widehat{\mathbf{f}}_k
\end{bmatrix}}_{\substack{\widehat{\mathbf{f}} \\ [(kn+1)\times1]}}
=
\underbrace{\begin{bmatrix}
\frac{1}{n}\mathbf{1}'_n\mathbf{y} \\
\mathbf{S}_1\mathbf{y} \\
\mathbf{S}_2\mathbf{y} \\
\cdot \\
\cdot \\
\cdot \\
\mathbf{S}_k\mathbf{y}
\end{bmatrix}}_{\substack{\mathbf{Q} \\ [(kn+1)\times n]}}\underbrace{\vphantom{\begin{bmatrix}\cdot\\\cdot\end{bmatrix}}\mathbf{y}}_{(n\times1)}
\tag{18.12}
$$

where

- A is the estimate of the regression intercept, α.
- $\mathbf{0}_n$ is an $n \times 1$ column-vector of 0s, and thus $\mathbf{0}'_n$ is a $1 \times n$ row-vector of 0s.
- $\mathbf{1}_n$ is an $n \times 1$ vector of 1s.
- $\mathbf{I}_n$ is the order-n identity matrix.
- $\mathbf{S}_j$ is the smoother matrix for the jth explanatory variable.[54]
- $\widehat{\mathbf{f}}_j = \{\widehat{f}_j(x_{ij})\}$ is the $n \times 1$ vector of partial-regression estimates for the jth explanatory variable, evaluated at the observed values, x_{ij}.

The first estimating equation simply specifies that $A = \frac{1}{n}\mathbf{1}'_n\mathbf{y} = \overline{Y}$. The remaining matrix equations, composing the rows of Equation 18.12, are each of the form

$$
\widehat{\mathbf{f}}_j + \mathbf{S}_j \sum_{r \neq j} \widehat{\mathbf{f}}_r = \mathbf{S}_j\mathbf{y}
$$

Solving for $\widehat{\mathbf{f}}_j$, the fitted partial-regression function is the smoothed partial residual:

$$
\widehat{\mathbf{f}}_j = \mathbf{S}_j \left(\mathbf{y} - \sum_{r \neq j} \widehat{\mathbf{f}}_r \right)
$$

The estimating equations in Equation 18.12 are a system of $kn + 1$ linear equations in an equal number of unknowns. As long as the composite smoother matrix $\mathbf{S}$ is non-singular—which would normally be the case—these equations have the explicit solution

$$
\widehat{\mathbf{f}} = \mathbf{S}^{-1}\mathbf{Q}\mathbf{y} = \mathbf{R}\mathbf{y}
\tag{18.13}
$$

(defining $\mathbf{R} \equiv \mathbf{S}^{-1}\mathbf{Q}$). The size of this system of equations, however, makes it impractical to solve it directly by inverting $\mathbf{S}$. Backfitting is a practical, iterative procedure for solving the estimating equations.

Statistical Inference It is apparent from Equation 18.13 that the fitted partial-regression functions are linear functions of the response variable. Focusing on the fit for the jth explanatory variable, therefore,

$$
V(\widehat{\mathbf{f}}_j) = \mathbf{R}_j V(\mathbf{y})\mathbf{R}'_j = \sigma_\varepsilon^2 \mathbf{R}_j\mathbf{R}'_j
$$

where $\mathbf{R}_j$ comprises the rows of $\mathbf{R}$ that produce $\widehat{\mathbf{f}}_j$.

---

[54]The smoother matrix was introduced on page 493.

To apply this result, we require an estimate of the error variance (to be addressed presently). A more immediate obstacle is that we must compute $\mathbf{R}_j$, which is difficult to obtain directly. Notice that $\mathbf{R}_j$, which takes into account relationships among the Xs, is different from the smoother matrix $\mathbf{S}_j$, which depends *only* on the jth X. A simple expedient, which works reasonably well if the explanatory variables are not strongly related, is simply to use $\mathbf{S}_j$ in place of $\mathbf{R}_j$. To construct a confidence envelope for the fit, we require only the *variances* of the elements of $\widehat{\mathbf{f}}_j$, which, in turn depend only on the *diagonal* entries of $\mathbf{S}_j$, and so the burden of computation is not onerous.[55]

To estimate the error variance σ_ε^2, we need the degrees of freedom for error. Any of the approaches described previously could be adapted here,[56] substituting the matrix $\mathbf{R}$ from the solution of the estimating equations for the smoother matrix $\mathbf{S}$. For example, working from the expectation of the residual sum of squares produces

$$df_{\text{res}} = n - \text{trace}(2\mathbf{R} - \mathbf{R}\mathbf{R}')$$

Then, the estimated error variance is $S_E^2 = \text{RSS}/(n - df_{\text{res}})$.

Because, as mentioned, finding $\mathbf{R}$ is computationally demanding, a simpler, if rougher, solution is to take the degrees of freedom for each explanatory variable as $df_j = \text{trace}(2\mathbf{S}_j - \mathbf{S}_j\mathbf{S}_j') - 1$ or even as $df_j = \text{trace}(\mathbf{S}_j) - 1$. Then, define $df_{\text{res}} = n - \sum_{j=1}^{k} df_j - 1$. Note that one is subtracted from the degrees of freedom for each explanatory variable because of the constraint that the partial-regression function for the variable sums to zero; and one is subtracted from the residual degrees of freedom to account for the constant α in the model.

F-tests for the contributions of the several explanatory variables are based on incremental sums of squares and differences in degrees of freedom. The incremental sum of squares for X_j is easily found:

$$\text{SS}_j = \text{RSS}_{-j} - \text{RSS}$$

where RSS is the residual sum of squares for the full model, and RSS_{-j} is the residual sum of squares for the model deleting the jth explanatory variable. The degrees of freedom for the effect of X_j are then

$$df_j = \text{trace}(2\mathbf{R} - \mathbf{R}\mathbf{R}') - \text{trace}(2\mathbf{R}_{-j} - \mathbf{R}_{-j}\mathbf{R}_{-j}')$$

where $\mathbf{R}_{-j}$ comes from the solution of the estimating equations in the *absence* of variable j. Alternatively, df_j can be approximated, as above.

Semiparametric Models and Models With Interactions

This section develops two straightforward relatives of additive regression models:

1. *Semiparametric models* are additive regression models in which some terms enter nonparametrically while others enter linearly. These models are therefore hybrids of the additive regression model and the linear regression model.

2. Models in which some of the explanatory variables are permitted to interact, for example in pair-wise fashion.

It is also possible to combine these strategies, so that some terms enter linearly, others additively, and still others are permitted to interact.

---

[55] Hastie and Tibshirani (1990, sect. 5.4.4) suggest a more sophisticated procedure to calculate the $\mathbf{R}_j$.
[56] See Section 18.1.2.

The semiparametric regression model is written

$$Y_i = \alpha + \beta_1 x_{i1} + \cdots + \beta_r x_{ir} + f_{r+1}(x_{i,r+1}) + \cdots + f_k(x_{ik}) + \varepsilon_i$$

where the errors ε_i are, as usual, assumed to be independently and normally distributed with constant variance. The first r regressors, therefore, enter the model linearly, while the partial relationships of Y to the remaining $k - r$ explanatory variables are simply assumed to be smooth. The semiparametric model can be estimated by backfitting. At each iteration, all of the linear terms can be estimated in a single step: Form partial residuals that remove the current estimates of the nonparametric terms, and then regress these partial residuals on $X_1, ..., X_r$ to obtain updated estimates of the βs.

The semiparametric model is applicable whenever there is reason to believe that one or more Xs enter the regression linearly:

- In rare instances, there may be prior reasons for believing that this is the case, or examination of the data might suggest a linear relationship, perhaps after transforming an X.[57]
- More commonly, if some of the Xs are dummy regressors—representing the effects of one or more categorical explanatory variables—then it is natural to enter the dummy regressors as linear terms.[58]
- Finally, we can test for nonlinearity by contrasting two models, one of which treats an explanatory variable nonparametrically and the other linearly. For example, to test for nonlinearity in the partial relationship between Y and X_1, we contrast the additive model

$$Y_i = \alpha + f_1(x_{i1}) + f_2(x_{i2}) + \cdots + f_k(x_{ik}) + \varepsilon_i$$

with the semiparametric model

$$Y_i = \alpha + \beta_1 x_{i1} + f_2(x_{i2}) + \cdots + f_k(x_{ik}) + \varepsilon_i$$

To illustrate this last procedure, let us return to the SLID data, fitting three models for the regression of log-income on age and education:

	Model	df_{mod}	RSS
1	Additive	8.2	1377.801
2	Age linear	5.9	1523.883
3	Education linear	5.3	1390.481

Model 1 is the additive regression model (fit previously); model 2 is a semiparametric model containing a linear term for age and a nonparametric term for education; model 3 is a semiparametric model with a linear term for education and a nonparametric term for age.

Contrasting models 1 and 2 produces a test for nonlinearity in the partial relationship of log-income to age—that is, a test of the null hypothesis that this partial relationship is linear; contrasting models 1 and 3 produces a test for nonlinearity in the relationship of log-income to education:

---

[57]Transformations for linearity are discussed in Chapters 4 and 12.
[58]Dummy regressors are introduced in Chapter 7.

$$F_{\text{Age(nonlinear)}} = \frac{\frac{1523.883 - 1377.801}{8.2 - 5.9}}{\frac{1348.592}{3997 - 18.6}} = 187.37$$

$$F_{\text{Education(nonlinear)}} = \frac{\frac{1390.481 - 1377.801}{8.2 - 5.3}}{\frac{1348.592}{3997 - 18.6}} = 12.90$$

The first of these F-test statistics has 2.3 and 3978.4 degrees of freedom, for which $p \approx 0$; the second has 2.9 and 3978.4 degrees of freedom, for which $p \ll .0001$. Once again, the estimated error variance in the denominator of these F-statistics comes from the general nonparametric-regression model, which is the largest model that we have entertained. There is, therefore, reliable evidence of nonlinearity in both partial relationships, but the nonlinearity in the partial relationship of log-wages to education is not great, as we can see in Figure 18.15 (page 509) and by comparing the proportion of variation accounted for by the three models:

$$\text{Additive:} \qquad R^2 = 1 - \frac{1377.801}{2104.738} = 0.3454$$

$$\text{Age linear:} \qquad R^2 = 1 - \frac{1523.883}{2104.738} = 0.2760$$

$$\text{Education linear:} \quad R^2 = 1 - \frac{1390.481}{2104.738} = 0.3394$$

While semiparametric regression models make the additive model more restrictive, incorporating interactions makes the model more flexible. For example, the following model permits interaction (nonadditivity) in the partial relationship of Y to X_1 and X_2:

$$Y_i = \alpha + f_{12}(x_{i1}, x_{i2}) + f_3(x_{i3}) + \cdots + f_k(x_{ik}) + \varepsilon_i$$

Once again, this model can be estimated by backfitting, employing a *multiple-regression* smoother (such as local-polynomial multiple regression) to estimate f_{12}. Contrasting this model with the more restrictive additive model produces an incremental F-test for the interaction between X_1 and X_2. This strategy can, in principle, be extended to models with higher-order interactions—for example, $f_{123}(x_{i1}, x_{i2}, x_{i3})$—but the curse of dimensionality and difficulty of interpretation limit the utility of such models.

Semiparametric models are additive regression models in which some terms enter non-parametrically while others enter linearly:

$$Y_i = \alpha + \beta_1 x_{i1} + \cdots + \beta_r x_{ir} + f_{r+1}(x_{i,r+1}) + \cdots + f_k(x_{ik}) + \varepsilon_i$$

Linear terms may be used, for example, to incorporate dummy regressors in the model. Interactions may be included in an otherwise additive regression model by employing a multiple-regression smoother for interacting explanatory variables, such as X_1 and X_2 in the model

$$Y_i = \alpha + f_{12}(x_{i1}, x_{i2}) + f_3(x_{i3}) + \cdots + f_k(x_{ik}) + \varepsilon_i$$

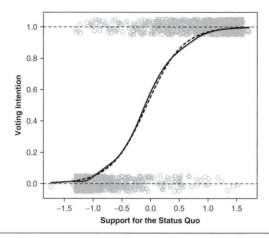

Figure 18.17 Scatterplot of voting intention in the Chilean plebiscite (1 = *yes*, 0 = *no*) by support for the status quo. The points are vertically jittered to minimize overplotting. The broken line shows the fit of a linear logistic regression; the solid line shows the fit of a local-linear logistic regression with a span of 0.3.

18.3 Generalized Nonparametric Regression

Generalized nonparametric regression bears the same relationship to the nonparametric-regression models discussed previously in the chapter that generalized linear models bear to linear models,[59] expanding the range of application of nonparametric regression to a wide variety of response variables. I consider two kinds of generalized nonparametric-regression models in this section: unconstrained generalized nonparametric regression fit by local-likelihood estimation, an extension of the local-polynomial regression models described in Sections 18.1.2 and 18.2.1; and generalized additive models, which are extensions of the additive regression models described in Section 18.2.2.

18.3.1 Local Likelihood Estimation*

Figure 18.17 illustrates generalized regression (and, incidentally, shows why scatterplot smoothing is particularly helpful for dichotomous responses). This graph displays data from a survey conducted prior to the 1989 Chilean plebiscite, where the response variable represents voting intention (1 = *yes*, 0 = *no*), and the explanatory variable is a scale indicating support for the status quo (i.e., the policies of the military government of Augusto Pinochet, who was then in power).[60]

The points in Figure 18.17 are "jittered" vertically to minimize overplotting. The summary curves on the graph, however, are fit to the unjittered data. Two fitted regressions are shown:

1. The broken line shows the linear logistic regression of voting intention on support for the status quo. The relationship appears to be positive, as expected. Fitted values between 0 and 1 are interpretable as the estimated proportion of *yes* voters at various levels of support for the status quo.

---

[59]Generalized linear models are the subject of Part IV of the text.

[60]A *yes* vote was a vote to extend military rule in Chile. The Chilean plebiscite data were introduced in Section 14.1.

2. The solid line shows a local-linear logistic regression of the kind to be described in this section. The fit in this case is very similar to that of the linear logistic regression, lending credibility to the latter.

Generalized linear models are typically estimated by the method of maximum likelihood.[61] The log-likelihood for these models takes the general form

$$\log_e L = \sum_{i=1}^{n} l(\mu_i, \phi; Y_i)$$

where the Y_i are the observations on the response variable; ϕ is a dispersion parameter (which takes on fixed values for some generalized linear models, such as binomial and Poisson-regression models, where $\phi = 1$); and

$$\mu_i \equiv E(Y_i) = g^{-1}(\alpha + \beta_1 x_{i1} + \beta_2 x_{i2} + \cdots + \beta_k x_{ik})$$

Here, $g^{-1}(\cdot)$ is the inverse of the link function. For example, for a binary logistic-regression model, the components of the log-likelihood are

$$l(\mu_i; Y_i) = Y_i \log_e \mu_i + (1 - Y_i) \log_e(1 - \mu_i)$$

and the expected value of Y is

$$\mu_i = g^{-1}(\alpha + \beta_1 x_{i1} + \beta_2 x_{i2} + \cdots + \beta_k x_{ik})$$
$$= \frac{1}{1 + \exp[-(\alpha + \beta_1 x_{i1} + \beta_2 x_{i2} + \cdots + \beta_k x_{ik})]}$$

The maximum-likelihood estimates of the parameters are the values $\widehat{\alpha}, \widehat{\beta}_1, \ldots, \widehat{\beta}_k$ that maximize $\log_e L$.

In *local-polynomial generalized nonparametric regression*, we estimate the regression function at some set of focal values of the explanatory variables. For simplicity, suppose that there is one X, that the response variable is dichotomous, and that we want to estimate $\mu|x_0$ at the focal value x_0. We can perform a logistic polynomial regression of the form

$$\log_e \frac{\mu_i}{1 - \mu_i} = \alpha + \beta_1(x_i - x_0) + \beta_2(x_i - x_0)^2 + \cdots + \beta_p(x_i - x_0)^p$$

maximizing the *weighted log-likelihood*

$$\log_e L_w = \sum_{i=1}^{n} w_i l(\mu_i; Y_i)$$

where the $w_i = K[(x_i - x_0)/h]$ are kernel weights. Then, $\widehat{\mu}|x_0 = g^{-1}(\widehat{\alpha})$.

To trace the estimated regression curve, as in Figure 18.17, we repeat this procedure for representative values of X or at the observed x_i. As in local-polynomial least-squares regression, the window half-width h can either be fixed, or can be adjusted to include a fixed number of nearest neighbors of the focal x_0.

Other characteristics of local-polynomial regression generalize readily as well. For example, as in a generalized linear model, the residual deviance under a generalized local-regression model

---

[61] See Chapters 14 and 15. You may wish to review this material prior to proceeding.

is twice the difference between the log-likelihood for a saturated model that fits the response perfectly and for the model in question:[62]

$$D(\mathbf{y}; \widehat{\boldsymbol{\mu}}) \equiv 2[\log_e L(\mathbf{y}, \phi; \mathbf{y}) - \log_e L(\widehat{\boldsymbol{\mu}}, \phi; \mathbf{y})]$$

where $\mathbf{y} \equiv \{Y_i\}$ is the response vector, and $\widehat{\boldsymbol{\mu}} \equiv \{\widehat{\mu}_i\}$ is the vector of fitted values—that is, the local generalized regression evaluated at the observed X values. Note that this log-likelihood is *not* the weighted likelihood used to get individual fitted values but is rather based on those fitted values.

Approximate hypothesis tests can be formulated from the deviance and equivalent degrees of freedom (obtaining the latter, e.g., from the trace of $\mathbf{SS}'$), much as in a generalized linear model. Similarly, the GCV criterion (Equation 18.4 on page 488) becomes

$$\text{GCV}(s) \equiv \frac{n \times D(s)}{[df_{\text{res}}(s)]^2} \tag{18.14}$$

where D is the deviance and s is the span of the local generalized-regression smoother.[63]

Applied to the Chilean plebiscite data, the GCV criterion suggested a span of 0.13, which produced a fitted regression curve that looked too rough. I adjusted the span visually to $s = 0.3$. The deviance and equivalent degrees of freedom associated with the local logistic-regression model for $s = 0.3$ are, respectively, $D = 746.33$ and $df_{\text{mod}} = 6.2$. The deviance and degrees of freedom for the *linear* logistic-regression model, in comparison, are $D = 752.59$ and $df_{\text{mod}} = 2$. A likelihood-ratio chi-square test for lack of fit in the linear logistic-regression model is therefore $G_0^2 = 752.59 - 746.33 = 6.26$ on $6.2 - 2 = 4.2$ degrees of freedom, for which $p = .20$, suggesting that this model fits the data adequately.

The extension of this approach to multiple regression is straightforward, although the curse of dimensionality and the difficulty of interpreting higher-dimensional fits are no less a problem than in local least-squares regression.

> The method of local likelihood can be used to fit generalized local-polynomial nonparametric-regression models, where, as in generalized linear models, the conditional distribution of the response variable can be a member of an exponential family—such as a binomial or Poisson distribution. Statistical inference can then be based on the deviance and equivalent degrees of freedom for the model, formulating likelihood-ratio chi-square or F-tests as in a generalized linear model. Other aspects of local-polynomial nonparametric regression also generalize readily, such as the selection of the span by generalized cross-validation.

18.3.2   Generalized Additive Models

The *generalized additive model* (or *GAM*) replaces the parametric terms in the generalized linear model with smooth terms in the explanatory variables:

$$\eta_i = \alpha + f_1(x_{i1}) + f_2(x_{i2}) + \cdots + f_k(x_{ik})$$

---

[62] See Section 15.3.2.

[63] In generalized regression models for distributional families in which the dispersion is fixed, such as the binomial or Poisson families, an alternative is to minimize the *Un-Biased Risk Estimator* (*UBRE*) criterion. See Wood (2006, sect. 4.5).

where the *additive predictor* η_i plays a role analogous to the linear predictor in a generalized linear model. Local likelihood (described in the preceding section), however, cannot be easily employed to estimate the generalized additive model. An alternative is to adapt the method of *iterated weighted least squares (IWLS)*, which is typically used to obtain maximum-likelihood estimates for generalized linear models.[64]

To keep the level of difficulty relatively low, I will focus on binary logistic regression. Results for other generalized regression models follow a similar pattern. To estimate the additive logistic-regression model,

$$\log_e \frac{\mu_i}{1 - \mu_i} = \alpha + f_1(x_{i1}) + f_2(x_{i2}) + \cdots + f_k(x_{ik})$$

IWLS estimation can be combined with backfitting (introduced in Section 18.2.2):

1. Pick starting values of the regression constant and the partial-regression functions, such as

$$\alpha^{(0)} = \log_e \frac{\sum Y_i}{n - \sum Y_i}$$

$$\text{all } f_j^{(0)}(x_{ij}) = 0$$

2. Using these initial values, calculate working-response values,

$$Z_i^{(0)} = \eta_i^{(0)} + \frac{Y_i - \mu_i^{(0)}}{\mu_i^{(0)} \left(1 - \mu_i^{(0)} \right)}$$

and weights,

$$W_i^{(0)} = \mu_i^{(0)} \left(1 - \mu_i^{(0)} \right)$$

using the additive predictor (in place of the linear predictor of a generalized linear model):

$$\eta_i^{(0)} = \alpha^{(0)} + f_1^{(0)}(x_{i1}) + f_2^{(0)}(x_{i2}) + \cdots + f_k^{(0)}(x_{ik})$$

$$\mu_i^{(0)} = \frac{1}{1 + \exp\left(-\eta_i^{(0)} \right)}$$

3. Find new values $\alpha^{(1)}$ and $f_1^{(1)}, \ldots, f_k^{(1)}$ by applying the backfitting procedure to the weighted additive regression of $Z^{(0)}$ on the Xs, using the $W_i^{(0)}$ as weights.

4. Return to step 2 to compute new working-response values and weights based on the updated values $\alpha^{(1)}$ and $f_1^{(1)}, \ldots, f_k^{(1)}$. Repeat this procedure until the estimates stabilize, producing $\widehat{\alpha}$ and $\widehat{f_1}, \ldots, \widehat{f_k}$.

Notice that this estimation procedure is *doubly* iterative, because each backfitting step (step 3) requires iteration.

---

[64]See Section 15.3.2. For a different approach to estimating GAMs, see Wood (2000).

Statistical Inference

Once again, I will concentrate on binary logistic regression, with similar results applying to other generalized additive models.

After the IWLS-backfitting procedure converges, the fitted values on the scale of the additive predictor η can be written as linear functions of the working-response values,

$$\widehat{\eta}_i = r_{i1}Z_1 + r_{i2}Z_2 + \cdots + r_{in}Z_n = \sum_{j=1}^{n} r_{ij}Z_j$$

The working response Z_j has estimated asymptotic variance $1/[\widehat{\mu}_j(1-\widehat{\mu}_j)]$, and because the observations are asymptotically independent, the estimated asymptotic variance of $\widehat{\eta}_i$ is[65]

$$\widehat{\mathcal{V}}(\widehat{\eta}_i) = \sum_{j=1}^{n} \frac{r_{ij}^2}{\widehat{\mu}_j(1-\widehat{\mu}_j)}$$

An approximate pointwise 95% confidence band for the fitted regression surface follows as

$$\widehat{\eta}_i \pm 2\sqrt{\widehat{\mathcal{V}}(\widehat{\eta}_i)}$$

If desired, the endpoints of the confidence band can be transformed to the probability scale by using the inverse of the logit link, $\mu = 1/[1+\exp(-\eta)]$. Approximate confidence bands can also be constructed for the individual partial-regression functions, f_j.

The deviance for a generalized additive model can be calculated in the usual manner; for a binary logit model, this is

$$D(\boldsymbol{\mu}; \mathbf{y}) = -2\sum_{i=1}^{n}[Y_i \log_e \widehat{\mu}_i + (1-Y_i)\log_e(1-\widehat{\mu}_i)]$$

with degrees of freedom equal to n minus the equivalent number of parameters in the model.

The generalized additive model (or GAM) replaces the parametric terms in the generalized linear model with smooth terms in the explanatory variables:

$$\eta_i = \alpha + f_1(x_{i1}) + f_2(x_{i2}) + \cdots + f_k(x_{ik})$$

where the additive predictor η_i plays the same role as the linear predictor in a generalized linear model. GAMs can be fit to data by combining the backfitting algorithm used for additive regression models with the iterated weight-least-squares algorithm for fitting generalized linear models. Approximate pointwise confidence intervals around the fitted regression surface and statistical tests based on the deviance of the fitted model follow in a straightforward manner.

---

[65]There are complications here: The working response is itself a function of the fitted values,

$$Z_i = \widehat{\eta}_i + \frac{Y_i - \widehat{\mu}_i}{\widehat{\mu}_i(1-\widehat{\mu}_i)}$$

and, unlike in the additive regression model, the coefficients r_{ij} for transforming the working response depend on the observed Y_is. The results given here hold aymptotically, however. See Hastie and Tibshirani (1990, sect. 6.8.2).

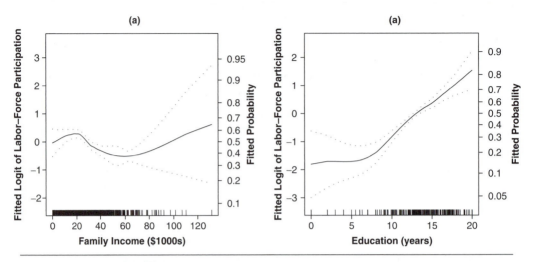

Figure 18.18   Partial plots for family income and education in the generalized semiparametric
regression of young married women's labor-force participation on region, presence
of children 0 to 4 years, presence of children 5 to 9 years, family income, and
education. The dotted lines in each plot give approximate pointwise 95% confidence
envelopes around the fit. The rug-plot at the bottom of each graph shows the
distribution of the corresponding explanatory variable.

An Illustration: Labor-Force Participation in the SLID

To illustrate generalized additive modeling, I will examine young married women's labor-force
participation using data from the Canadian Survey of Labour and Income Dynamics (SLID).[66] The
response variable is dichotomous: Whether or not the woman worked outside the home at some
point during the year preceding the survey. The explanatory variables include a factor representing
region (Atlantic Canada, Quebec, Ontario, the prairie provinces, and British Columbia); factors
representing the presence in the woman's household of children between zero and 4 years of
age, and between 5 and 9 years of age; the woman's after-tax family income excluding her own
income; and the woman's years of education.

I fit a semiparametric generalized additive model to these data, including dummy regressors
for region and the two presence-of-children factors, and local-linear terms for family income
and education, choosing the span for each of these terms by simultaneous generalized cross-
validation. That is, I performed a "grid search" over combinations of values of the spans for these
two explanatory variables, selecting the combination of spans—as it turned out, $s = 0.7$ in both
cases—that together minimize the GCV criterion (given in Equation 18.14 on page 519). The
resulting model uses the equivalent of 3.4 degrees of freedom for the family income effect and
2.9 degrees of freedom for the education effect. The coefficients for the region and presence-of-
children terms are similar to those of a linear logistic regression fit to these data (see Table 14.4
on page 350), and so are not given here.

Partial plots for family income and education are shown in Figure 18.18. Even discounting the
rise at the right—where the very small number of observations (see the rug-plot at the bottom of
the graph) is reflected in very broad confidence limits—the partial plot for family income in panel
(a) of this figure suggests some nonlinearity, with labor-force participation first rising slightly and

---

[66]This example was used to illustrate linear logistic regression in Section 14.1.4, where the data are described in more
detail.

then falling with family income. Similarly discounting the region at the left of panel (b), where data are sparse, the partial plot suggests modest nonlinearity in the partial relationship between labor-force participation and education.

To test these impressions, I fit three models to the data: the initial semiparametric generalized additive model just described, and two other semiparametric models in which income and education, in turn, enter linearly, producing the following equivalent degrees of freedom and deviances:

	Model	df_{mod}	Residual Deviance
1	Initial model	13.3	1787.007
2	Income linear	10.9	1800.406
3	Education linear	11.4	1797.112

Likelihood-ratio chi-square tests for nonlinearity in the family income and education effects are as follows:

$$G^2_{\text{Income(nonlinear)}} = 1800.406 - 1787.007 = 13.40$$

$$G^2_{\text{Education(nonlinear)}} = 1797.112 - 1787.007 = 10.11$$

on, respectively, 2.4 and 1.9 degrees of freedom, for which $p = .0020$ and $p = .010$. Both tests are therefore statistically significant, but there is stronger evidence of nonlinearity in the relationship between labor-force participation and family income.

Exercises

Exercise 18.1. Vary the span of the kernel estimator for the regression of prestige on income in the Canadian occupational prestige data. Does $s = 0.4$ appear to be a reasonable choice?

Exercise 18.2. Selecting the span by smoothing residuals: A complementary visual approach to selecting the span in local-polynomial regression is to find the residuals from the fit from the local regression, $E_i = Y_i - \widehat{Y}_i$, and to smooth the residuals against the x_i. If the data have been oversmoothed, then there will be a systematic relationship between the average residual and X; if the fit does not over-smooth the data, then the average residual will be approximately 0 regardless of the value of X. We seek the *largest* value of s that yields residuals that are unrelated to X. Apply this approach to the regression of prestige on income in the Canadian occupational prestige data by smoothing the residuals from local-linear regressions with various spans. An examination of the scatterplots in Figure 18.4 suggested picking $s \approx 0.6$. Is this choice supported by smoothing the residuals?

Exercise 18.3. Comparing the kernel and local-linear estimators: To illustrate the reduced bias of the local-linear estimator in comparison to the kernel estimator, generate $n = 100$ observations of artificial data according to the cubic regression equation

$$Y = 100 - 5\left(\frac{x}{10} - 5\right) + \left(\frac{x}{10} - 5\right)^3 + \varepsilon \tag{18.15}$$

where the X values are sampled from the uniform distribution $X \sim U(0, 100)$, and the errors are sampled from the normal distribution $\varepsilon \sim N(0, 20^2)$. Draw a scatterplot of the data showing the true regression line $E(Y) = 100 - 5(x/10 - 5) + (x/10 - 5)^3$. Then, use both kernel regression and local-linear regression to estimate the regression of Y on X, in each case adjusting the span to produce a smooth regression curve. Which estimator has less bias? Why?[67] Save the data from this exercise, or generate the data in a manner that can be replicated.

Exercise 18.4. *Bias, variance, and MSE as a function of bandwidth: Consider the artificial regression function introduced in the preceding exercise. Using Equation 18.1 (page 485), write down expressions for the expected value and variance of the local-linear estimator as a function of the bandwidth h of the estimator. Employing these results, compute the variance, bias, and mean-squared error of the local-linear estimator at the focal value $x_0 = 10$ as a function of h, allowing h to range between 1 and 20. What value of h produces the smallest MSE? Does this agree with the optimal bandwidth $h^*(10)$ from Equation 18.2? Then, using Equation 18.2, graph the optimal bandwidth $h^*(x_0)$ as a function of the focal value x_0, allowing x_0 to range between 0 and 100. Relate the resulting function to the regression function.

Exercise 18.5. *Employing the artificial data generated in Exercise 18.3, use Equation 18.3 (on page 486) to compute the average squared error (ASE) of the local-linear regression estimator for various spans between $s = 0.05$ and $s = 0.95$, drawing a graph of ASE(s) versus s. What span produces the smallest ASE? Does this confirm your visual selection of the span of the local-linear estimator in Exercise 18.3?

Exercise 18.6. *Continuing with the artificial data from Exercise 18.3, graph the cross-validation function CV(s) and generalized cross-validation function GCV(s) as a function of span, letting the span range between $s = 0.05$ and $s = 0.95$.

(a) Compare the shape of CV(s) with the average squared error ASE(s) function from the preceding exercise. Are the shapes similar?
(b) Now compare the level of CV(s) to that of ASE(s). Are the levels different? Why?
(c) Does GCV(s) do a good job of approximating CV(s)?
(d) Do CV(s) and GCV(s) provide useful guidance for selecting the span in this problem?

Exercise 18.7. Comparing polynomial and local regression:

(a) The local-linear regression of prestige on income with span $s = 0.6$ (in Figure 18.7 on page 491) has 5.006 equivalent degrees of freedom, very close to the number of degrees of freedom for a global fourth-order polynomial. Fit a fourth-order polynomial to these data and compare the resulting regression curve with the local-linear regression.
(b) Now, consider the local-linear regression of infant mortality on GDP per capita for 193 nations shown in Figure 3.13 (page 41), which is for a span of $s = 0.5$ and which has 5.9 equivalent degrees of freedom. Fit a fifth-order polynomial to these data and compare the fitted regression curve to the local-linear regression.
(c) What do you conclude from these two examples?

Exercise 18.8. Equivalent kernels: One way of comparing linear smoothers like local-polynomial estimators and smoothing splines is to think of them as variants of the kernel estimator, where fitted values arise as weighted averages of observed response values. This approach is illustrated in Figure 18.19, which shows *equivalent kernel weights* at two focal X values in

---

[67] I am using the term "bias" slightly loosely here, because we are examining the performance of each of these estimators for a *particular* sample, rather than averaged over *all* samples, but the point is nevertheless valid.

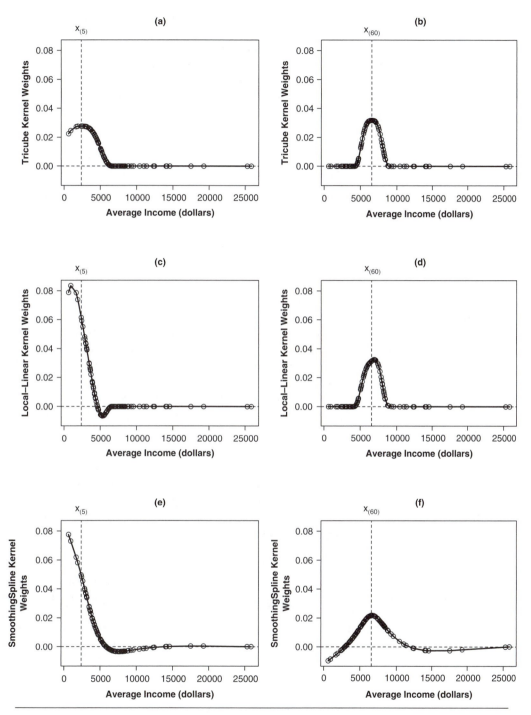

Figure 18.19 Equivalent kernels for three nonparametric estimators of the regression of occupational prestige on income: (a) and (b) nearest-neighbor tricube kernel estimator, with span $= 0.6$; (c) and (d) nearest-neighbor local-linear estimator, with span $= 0.6$ (five equivalent parameters); (e) and (f) smoothing spline, with five equivalent parameters. The focal point, marked at the top of each graph, is $x_{(5)}$ in (a), (c), and (e), and $x_{(60)}$ in (b), (d), and (f).

the Canadian occupational prestige data: One value, $x_{(5)}$, is near the boundary of the data; the other, $x_{(60)}$, is closer to the middle of the data. The figure shows tricube-kernel weights [panels (a) and (b)], along with the equivalent kernel weights for the local-linear estimator with span $= 0.6$ (or five equivalent parameters) [panels (c) and (d)], and the smoothing spline with five equivalent parameters [in panels (e) and (f)]. Compare and contrast the equivalent kernel weights for the three estimators. Are there any properties of the equivalent kernels for the local-linear and smoothing-spline estimators that you find surprising?

Summary

- Kernel regression estimates the regression function at a focal value x_0 of the explanatory variable by weighted local averaging of Y:

$$\widehat{f}(x_0) = \widehat{Y}|x_0 = \frac{\sum_{i=1}^{n} w_i Y_i}{\sum_{i=1}^{n} w_i}$$

  The weights are provided by a kernel function, $w_i = K[(x_i - x_0)/h]$, which takes on its largest value at $K(0)$ and falls symmetrically toward 0 as $|(x_i - x_0)/h|$ grows. Observations close to the focal x_0 therefore receive greatest weight. The kernel estimator is evaluated at representative focal values of X or at the ordered X values, $x_{(i)}$. The bandwidth h of the kernel estimator can be fixed, or can be adjusted to include a fixed proportion of the data, called the span of the kernel estimate. The larger the span, the smoother the kernel regression.

- Local-polynomial regression extends kernel estimation to a polynomial fit at the focal value x_0, using local kernel weights, $w_i = K[(x_i - x_0)/h]$. The resulting WLS regression fits the equation

$$Y_i = A + B_1(x_i - x_0) + B_2(x_i - x_0)^2 + \cdots + B_p(x_i - x_0)^p + E_i$$

  to minimize the weighted residual sum of squares, $\sum_{i=1}^{n} w_i E_i^2$. The fitted value at the focal x_0 is just $\widehat{Y}|x_0 = A$. This procedure is repeated for representative focal values of X, or at the observations x_i. We can employ a fixed bandwidth or adjust the bandwidth for a fixed span. Nearest-neighbor local-polynomial regression is often called lowess (or loess).

- A generally effective visual approach to selecting the span in local-polynomial regression is guided trial and error. The span $s = 0.5$ is often a good point of departure. If the fitted regression looks too rough, then try increasing the span; if it looks smooth, then see if the span can be decreased without making the fit too rough. We want the smallest value of s that provides a smooth fit.

- The bias and variance of the local-linear estimator at the focal value x_0 are both a function of the bandwidth h, as well as of properties of the data and the kernel function:

$$\text{bias}(\widehat{Y}|x_0) \approx \frac{h^2}{2} s_K^2 f''(x_0)$$

$$V(\widehat{Y}|x_0) \approx \frac{\sigma_\varepsilon^2 a_K^2}{nh p_X(x_0)}$$

  where s_K^2 and a_K^2 are constants that depend on the kernel function; $f''(x_0)$ is the second derivative ("curvature") of the regression function at x_0; and $p_X(x_0)$ is the probability-density of X values at x_0. We would ideally like to choose the value of h at each focal value that minimizes the mean-squared error of estimation—that is, the sum of squared bias and variance.

- The cross-validation function

$$CV(s) = \frac{\sum_{i=1}^{n} \left[\widehat{Y}_{-i}(s) - Y_i \right]^2}{n}$$

can be used to select the span s in local-polynomial regression, picking s to minimize $CV(s)$. The fitted value at each observation $\widehat{Y}_{-i}(s)$ is computed from a local regression that omits that observation. Because the cross-validation function $CV(s)$ can be costly to compute, approximations such as generalized cross-validation have been proposed. The GCV criterion is

$$GCV(s) = \frac{n \times RSS(s)}{[df_{res}(s)]^2}$$

where $RSS(s)$ is the residual sum of squares and $df_{res}(s)$ the "equivalent" residual degrees of freedom for the local-regression smoother with span s.

- The fitted values in a local-polynomial regression are linear functions of the observations, $\widehat{Y}_i = \sum_{j=1}^{n} s_{ij} Y_j$. Estimating the error variance as $S_E^2 = \sum E_i^2 / df_{res}$, where df_{res} is the equivalent residual degrees of freedom for the model, the estimated variance of a fitted value is $\widehat{V}(\widehat{Y}_i) = S_E^2 \sum_{j=1}^{n} s_{ij}^2$. An approximate 95% pointwise confidence band around the regression curve evaluated at the fitted values may be formed as $\widehat{Y}_i \pm 2\sqrt{\widehat{V}(\widehat{Y}_i)}$.

- Approximate incremental F-tests for hypotheses in local-polynomial regression are formulated by contrasting nested models, in analogy to similar tests for linear models fit by least-squares. For example, to test the hypothesis of no relationship in the nonparametric-regression model, we can compute the F-test statistic

$$F_0 = \frac{\frac{TSS-RSS}{df_{mod}-1}}{\frac{RSS}{df_{res}}}$$

where df_{mod} and $df_{res} = n - df_{mod}$ are respectively the equivalent degrees of freedom for the regression model and for error, and RSS is the residual sum of squares for the model. Similarly, to test for nonlinearity, we can contrast the fitted nonparametric-regression model with a linear model, computing

$$F_0 = \frac{\frac{RSS_0-RSS_1}{df_{mod}-2}}{\frac{RSS_1}{df_{res}}}$$

where RSS_0 is the residual sum of squares for the linear regression and RSS_1 the residual sum of squares for the more general nonparametric regression.

- The smoother matrix $\mathbf{S}$ in nonparametric local-polynomial regression plays a role analogous to the hat-matrix $\mathbf{H}$ in linear least-squares regression. Like the hat-matrix, the smoother matrix linearly transforms the observations into the fitted values: $\widehat{\mathbf{y}} = \mathbf{Sy}$. Pursuing this analogy, the equivalent degrees of freedom for the nonparametric-regression model can variously be defined as $df_{mod} = \text{trace}(\mathbf{S})$, $\text{trace}(\mathbf{SS}')$, or $\text{trace}(2\mathbf{S} - \mathbf{SS}')$.

- Generalizing local-polynomial regression to multiple regression is conceptually and computationally straightforward. For example, to obtain the fitted value for a local-linear regression at the focal point $\mathbf{x}_0 = (x_{01}, x_{02}, ..., x_{0k})'$ in the space of the explanatory variables, we perform a weighted-least-squares regression of Y on the Xs,

$$Y_i = A + B_1(x_{i1} - x_{01}) + B_2(x_{i2} - x_{02}) + \cdots + B_k(x_{ik} - x_{0k}) + E_i$$

emphasizing observations close to the focal point by minimizing the weighted residual sum of squares, $\sum_{i=1}^{n} w_i E_i^2$. The fitted value at the focal point in the X space is then $\widehat{Y}|\mathbf{x}_0 = A$. The weights w_i can be computed in several ways, including by multiplying marginal kernel weights for the several explanatory variables, or by basing kernel weights on one or another measure of distance between the focal $\mathbf{x}_0$ and the observed X values, $\mathbf{x}_i$. Given a distance measure $D(\mathbf{x}_i, \mathbf{x}_0)$, the kernel weights are calculated as $w_i = K\left[D(\mathbf{x}_i, \mathbf{x}_0)/h\right]$.

- Methods for selecting the span in local-polynomial multiple regression are much the same as in local-polynomial simple regression: We can proceed visually by trial and error, or apply a criterion such as $\text{CV}(s)$ or $\text{GCV}(s)$. Similarly, approximate pointwise confidence limits for the fitted regression can be calculated as in local-polynomial simple regression, as can incremental F-tests comparing nested models.

- The curse of dimensionality and the difficulty of visualizing high-dimensional surfaces limit the practical application of unrestricted nonparametric multiple regression when there are more than a very small number of explanatory variables.

- When there are two explanatory variables, the fitted nonparametric-regression surface can be visualized in a three-dimensional perspective plot, in a contour plot, or in coplots for each explanatory variable at fixed levels of the other variable. Coplots can be generalized to three or more explanatory variables, but quickly become unwieldy.

- The additive regression model

$$E(Y|x_1, x_2, ..., x_k) = \alpha + f_1(x_1) + f_2(x_2) + \cdots + f_k(x_k)$$

expresses the average value of the response variable as the sum of smooth functions of several explanatory variables. The additive model is therefore more restrictive than the general nonparametric-regression model but more flexible than the linear-regression model.

- The additive regression model can be fit to data by the method of backfitting, which iteratively smooths the partial residuals for each explanatory variable using current estimates of the regression functions for other explanatory variables.

- Semiparametric models are additive regression models in which some terms enter nonparametrically while others enter linearly:

$$Y_i = \alpha + \beta_1 x_{i1} + \cdots + \beta_r x_{ir} + f_{r+1}(x_{i,r+1}) + \cdots + f_k(x_{ik}) + \varepsilon_i$$

Linear terms may be used, for example, to incorporate dummy regressors in the model. Interactions may be included in an otherwise additive regression model by employing a multiple-regression smoother for interacting explanatory variables, such as X_1 and X_2 in the model

$$Y_i = \alpha + f_{12}(x_{i1}, x_{i2}) + f_3(x_{i3}) + \cdots + f_k(x_{ik}) + \varepsilon_i$$

- The method of local likelihood can be used to fit generalized local-polynomial nonparametric-regression models, where, as in generalized linear models, the conditional distribution of the response variable can be a member of an exponential family—such as a binomial or Poisson distribution. Statistical inference can then be based on the deviance and equivalent degrees of freedom for the model, formulating likelihood-ratio chi-square or F-tests as in a generalized linear model. Other aspects of local-polynomial nonparametric regression also generalize readily, such as the selection of the span by generalized cross-validation.

- The generalized additive model (or GAM) replaces the parametric terms in the generalized linear model with smooth terms in the explanatory variables:

$$\eta_i = \alpha + f_1(x_{i1}) + f_2(x_{i2}) + \cdots + f_k(x_{ik})$$

where the additive predictor η_i plays the same role as the linear predictor in a generalized linear model. GAMs can be fit to data by combining the backfitting algorithm used for additive regression models with the iterated weight-least-squares algorithm for fitting generalized linear models. Approximate pointwise confidence intervals around the fitted regression surface and statistical tests based on the deviance of the fitted model follow in a straightforward manner.

Recommended Reading

There are many fine sources on nonparametric regression and smoothing.

- Hastie and Tibshirani's (1990) text on generalized additive models includes a wealth of valuable material. Most of the book is leisurely paced and broadly accessible, with many effective examples. As a preliminary to generalized additive models, Hastie and Tibshirani include a fine treatment of scatterplot smoothing.
- Wood (2006) also presents an excellent and wide-ranging treatment of generalized additive models that stresses smoothing splines and automatic selection of smoothing parameters.
- A briefer presentation by Hastie of generalized additive models appears in an edited book (Chambers & Hastie, 1992) on statistical modeling in the S computing environment (implemented in R and S-PLUS). This book also includes a paper by Cleveland, Grosse, and Shyu on local regression models.
- Cleveland's (1993) text on data visualization presents information on local regression in two and more dimensions.
- Härdle (1991) gives an overview of nonparametric regression, stressing kernel smoothers for bivariate scatterplots.
- Additional details may be found in Fan and Gijbels (1996), Simonoff (1996), and Bowman and Azzalini (1997).
- Much of the exposition in the current chapter was adapted from Fox (2000a, 2000b), which presents the topic in greater detail (and which omits some newer material).

19

Robust Regression*

T he efficiency of least-squares regression is seriously impaired by heavy-tailed error distributions; in particular, least squares is vulnerable to outlying observations at high-leverage points.[1] One response to this problem is to employ diagnostics for high-leverage, influential, and outlying data; if unusual data are discovered, then these can be corrected, removed, or otherwise accommodated.

Robust estimation is an alternative approach to outliers and the heavy-tailed error distributions that tend to generate them. Properly formulated, robust estimators are almost as efficient as least squares when the error distribution is normal and much more efficient when the errors are heavy tailed. Robust estimators hold their efficiency well because they are resistant to outliers. Rather than simply discarding discrepant data, however, robust estimation (as we will see) down-weights them.

Much of the chapter is devoted to a particular strategy of robust estimation, termed *M estimation*, due originally to Huber (1964). I also describe two other approaches to robust estimation: *bounded-influence regression* and *quantile regression*. Finally, I briefly present robust estimators for generalized linear models.

19.1 *M* Estimation

19.1.1 Estimating Location

Although our proper interest is in robust estimation of linear models, it is helpful to narrow our focus initially to a simpler setting: robust estimation of *location*—that is, estimation of the center of a distribution. Let us, then, begin our exploration of robust estimation with the minimal linear model

$$Y_i = \mu + \varepsilon_i$$

where the observations Y_i are independently sampled from some symmetric distribution with center μ (and hence the errors ε_i are independently and symmetrically distributed around 0).[2]

If the distribution from which the observations are drawn is normal, then the sample mean $\widehat{\mu} = \overline{Y}$ is the maximally efficient estimator of μ, producing the fitted model

$$Y_i = \overline{Y} + E_i$$

The mean minimizes the least-squares *objective function*:

$$\sum_{i=1}^{n} \rho_{LS}(E_i) = \sum_{i=1}^{n} \rho_{LS}(Y_i - \widehat{\mu}) \equiv \sum_{i=1}^{n}(Y_i - \widehat{\mu})^2$$

---

[1] See Chapter 11.

[2] In the *absence* of symmetry, what we mean by the center of the distribution becomes ambiguous.

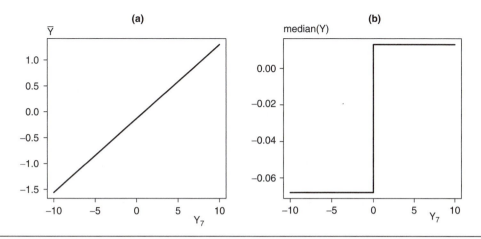

Figure 19.1 The influence functions for the mean (a) and median (b) for the sample $Y_1 = -0.068$, $Y_2 = -1.282$, $Y_3 = 0.013$, $Y_4 = 0.141$, $Y_5 = -0.980$, $Y_6 = 1.263$. The influence function for the median is bounded, while that for the mean is not. Note that the vertical axes for the two graphs have different scales.

The mean, however, is very sensitive to outliers, as is simply demonstrated: I drew a sample of six observations from the standard-normal distribution, obtaining

$$Y_1 = -0.068 \qquad Y_2 = -1.282 \qquad Y_3 = 0.013$$
$$Y_4 = 0.141 \qquad Y_5 = -0.980 \qquad Y_6 = 1.263$$

The mean of these six values is $\overline{Y} = -0.152$. Now, imagine adding a seventh observation, Y_7, allowing it to take on all possible values from -10 to $+10$ (or, with greater imagination, from $-\infty$ to $+\infty$). The result, called the *influence function* of the mean, is graphed in Figure 19.1(a). It is apparent from this figure that as the discrepant seventh observation grows more extreme, the sample mean chases it.

The shape of the influence function for the mean follows from the derivative of the least-squares objective function with respect to E:

$$\psi_{\text{LS}}(E) \equiv \rho'_{\text{LS}}(E) = 2E$$

Influence, therefore, is proportional to the residual E. It is convenient to redefine the least-squares objective function as $\rho_{\text{LS}}(E) \equiv \frac{1}{2} E^2$, so that $\psi_{\text{LS}}(E) = E$.

Now consider the sample median as an estimator of μ. The median minimizes the *least-absolute-values* (LAV) objective function:[3]

$$\sum_{i=1}^{n} \rho_{\text{LAV}}(E_i) = \sum_{i=1}^{n} \rho_{\text{LAV}}(Y_i - \widehat{\mu}) \equiv \sum_{i=1}^{n} |Y_i - \widehat{\mu}|$$

As a result, the median is much more resistant than the mean to outliers. The influence function of the median for the illustrative sample is shown in Figure 19.1(b). In contrast to the mean, the influence of a discrepant observation on the median is *bounded*. Once again, the derivative of the objective function gives the shape of the influence function:[4]

---

[3] See Exercise 19.1.
[4] Strictly speaking, the derivative of ρ_{LAV} is undefined at $E = 0$, but setting $\psi_{\text{LAV}}(0) \equiv 0$ is convenient.

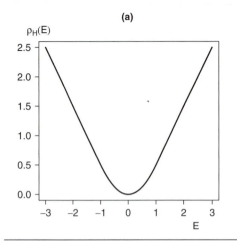
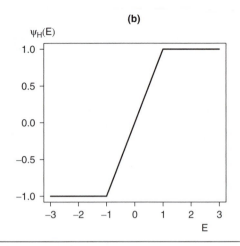

Figure 19.2   Huber objective function ρ_H (a) and "influence function" ψ_H (b). To calibrate these graphs, the tuning constant is set to $k = 1$. (See the text for a discussion of the tuning constant).

$$\psi_{\mathrm{LAV}}(E) \equiv \rho'_{\mathrm{LAV}}(E) = \begin{cases} 1 & \text{for } E > 0 \\ 0 & \text{for } E = 0 \\ -1 & \text{for } E < 0 \end{cases}$$

Although the median is more resistant than the mean to outliers, it is less efficient than the mean if the distribution of Y is normal. When $Y \sim N(\mu, \sigma^2)$, the sampling variance of the mean is σ^2/n, while the variance of the median is $\pi\sigma^2/2n$: That is, $\pi/2 \approx 1.57$ times as large as for the mean. Other objective functions combine resistance to outliers with greater robustness of efficiency. Estimators that can be expressed as minimizing an objective function $\sum_{i=1}^{n} \rho(E)$ are called *M estimators*.[5]

Two common choices of objective functions are the *Huber* and Tukey's *biweight* (or *bisquare*) functions:

- The Huber objective function is a compromise between least squares and least absolute values, behaving like least squares in the center and like least absolute values in the tails:

$$\rho_H(E) \equiv \begin{cases} \frac{1}{2}E^2 & \text{for } |E| \leq k \\ k|E| - \frac{1}{2}k^2 & \text{for } |E| > k \end{cases}$$

The Huber objective function ρ_H and its derivative, the influence function ψ_H, are graphed in Figure 19.2:[6]

$$\psi_H(E) = \begin{cases} k & \text{for } E > k \\ E & \text{for } |E| \leq k \\ -k & \text{for } E < -k \end{cases}$$

The value k, which defines the center and tails, is called a *tuning constant*.

---

[5]Estimators that can be written in this form can be thought of as generalizations of maximum likelihood estimators, hence the term M estimator. The maximum-likelihood estimator is produced by taking $\rho_{\mathrm{ML}}(y - \mu) \equiv -\log_e p(y - \mu)$ for an appropriate probability or probability density function $p(\cdot)$.

[6]My terminology here is loose, but convenient: Strictly speaking, the ψ-function is not the influence function, but it has the same shape as the influence function.

It is most natural to express the tuning constant as a multiple of the *scale* (i.e., the spread) of the variable Y, that is, to take $k = cS$, where S is a measure of scale. The sample standard deviation is a poor measure of scale in this context because it is even more affected than the mean by outliers. A common robust measure of scale is the *median absolute deviation* (MAD):

$$\text{MAD} \equiv \text{median}\left|Y_i - \widehat{\mu}\right|$$

The estimate $\widehat{\mu}$ can be taken, at least initially, as the median value of Y. We can then define $S \equiv \text{MAD}/0.6745$, which ensures that S estimates the standard deviation σ when the population is normal. Using $k = 1.345S$ (i.e., $1.345/0.6745 \approx 2$ MADs) produces 95% efficiency relative to the sample mean when the population is normal, along with considerable resistance to outliers when it is not. A smaller tuning constant can be employed for more resistance.

- The biweight (or bisquare) objective function levels off at very large residuals:[7]

$$\rho_{\text{BW}}(E) \equiv \begin{cases} \dfrac{k^2}{6}\left\{1 - \left[1 - \left(\dfrac{E}{k}\right)^2\right]^3\right\} & \text{for } |E| \leq k \\[2ex] \dfrac{k^2}{6} & \text{for } |E| > k \end{cases}$$

The influence function for the biweight estimator, therefore, "redescends" to 0, *completely discounting* observations that are sufficiently discrepant:

$$\psi_{\text{BW}}(E) = \begin{cases} E\left[1 - \left(\dfrac{E}{k}\right)^2\right]^2 & \text{for } |E| \leq k \\[2ex] 0 & \text{for } |E| > k \end{cases}$$

The functions ρ_{BW} and ψ_{BW} are graphed in Figure 19.3. Using $k = 4.685S$ (i.e., $4.685/0.6745 \approx 7$ MADs) produces 95% efficiency when sampling from a normal population.

Robust M estimators of location, for the parameter μ in the simple model $Y_i = \mu + \varepsilon_i$, minimize the objective function $\sum_{i=1}^{n} \rho(E_i) = \sum_{i=1}^{n} \rho(Y_i - \widehat{\mu})$, selecting $\rho(\cdot)$ so that the estimator is relatively unaffected by outlying values. Two common choices of objective function are the Huber and the bisquare. The sensitivity of an M estimator to individual observations is expressed by the influence function of the estimator, which has the same shape as the derivative of the objective function, $\psi(E) \equiv \rho'(E)$.

Calculation of M estimators usually requires an iterative procedure (although iteration is not necessary for the mean and median, which, as we have seen, fit into the M estimation framework). An estimating equation for $\widehat{\mu}$ is obtained by setting the derivative of the objective function (with respect to $\widehat{\mu}$) to 0, obtaining

$$\sum_{i=1}^{n} \psi\left(Y_i - \widehat{\mu}\right) = 0 \tag{19.1}$$

---

[7]The term bisquare applies literally to the ψ-function and to the weight function (hence biweight) to be introduced presently—not to the objective function.

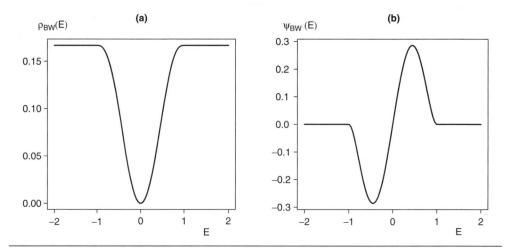

Figure 19.3   Biweight objective function ρ_{BW} (a) and "influence function" ψ_{BW} (b). To calibrate these graphs, the tuning constant is set to $k = 1$. The influence function "redescends" to 0 when $|E|$ is large.

There are several general approaches to solving Equation 19.1; probably the most straightforward, and the simplest to implement computationally, is to re-weight the mean iteratively—a special case of *iterative weighted least squares (IWLS)*:[8]

1. Define the *weight function* $w(E) \equiv \psi(E)/E$. Then, the estimating equation becomes

$$\sum_{i=1}^{n} (Y_i - \widehat{\mu}) \, w_i = 0 \tag{19.2}$$

   where

$$w_i \equiv w\,(Y_i - \widehat{\mu})$$

   The solution of Equation 19.2 is the weighted mean

$$\widehat{\mu} = \frac{\sum w_i Y_i}{\sum w_i}$$

   The weight functions corresponding to the least-squares, LAV, Huber, and bisquare objective functions are shown in Table 19.1 and graphed in Figure 19.4. The least-squares weight function accords equal weight to each observation, while the bisquare gives 0 weight to observations that are sufficiently outlying; the LAV and Huber weight functions descend toward 0 but never quite reach it.

2. Select an initial estimate $\widehat{\mu}^{(0)}$, such as the median of the Y values.[9] Using $\widehat{\mu}^{(0)}$, calculate an initial estimate of scale $S^{(0)}$ and initial weights $w_i^{(0)} = w(Y_i - \widehat{\mu}^{(0)})$. Set the iteration counter $l = 0$. The scale is required to calculate the tuning constant $k = cS$ (for prespecified c).

3. At each iteration l, calculate $\widehat{\mu}^{(l)} = \sum w_i^{(l-1)} Y_i / \sum w_i^{(l-1)}$. Stop when the change in $\widehat{\mu}^{(l)}$ is negligible from one iteration to the next.

---

[8]In Chapter 15, we employed IWLS estimation for generalized linear models. The method is also called *iteratively reweighted least squares (IRLS)*.

[9]Because the estimating equation for redescending M estimators, such as the bisquare, can have more than one root, the selection of an initial estimate might be consequential.

Table 19.1   Weight Functions $w(E) = \psi(E)/E$ for Several *M* Estimators

Estimator	Weight Function $w(E)$	
Least squares	1	
Least absolute values	$1/|E|$	(for $E \neq 0$)
Huber	1	for $|E| \leq k$
	$k/|E|$	for $|E| > k$
Bisquare (biweight)	$\left[1 - \left(\dfrac{E}{k}\right)^2\right]^2$	for $|E| \leq k$
	0	for $|E| > k$

An estimating equation for $\widehat{\mu}$ is obtained by setting the derivative of the objective function (with respect to $\widehat{\mu}$) to 0, obtaining $\sum_{i=1}^{n} \psi(Y_i - \widehat{\mu}) = 0$. The simplest procedure for solving this estimating equation is by iteratively reweighted means. Defining the weight function as $w(E) \equiv \psi(E)/E$, the estimating equation becomes $\sum_{i=1}^{n} (Y_i - \widehat{\mu}) w_i = 0$, from which $\widehat{\mu} = \sum w_i Y_i / \sum w_i$. Starting with an initial estimate $\widehat{\mu}^{(0)}$, initial weights are calculated, and the value of $\widehat{\mu}$ is updated. This procedure continues iteratively until the value of $\widehat{\mu}$ converges.

19.1.2   *M* Estimation in Regression

With the exception of one significant caveat, to be addressed in the next section, the generalization of *M* estimators to regression is immediate. We now wish to estimate the linear model

$$Y_i = \alpha + \beta_1 X_{i1} + \cdots + \beta_k X_{ik} + \varepsilon_i$$
$$= \underset{(1 \times k+1)(k+1 \times 1)}{\mathbf{x}_i' \quad \boldsymbol{\beta}} + \varepsilon_i$$

The estimated model is

$$Y_i = A + B_1 X_{i1} + \cdots + B_k X_{ik} + E_i$$
$$= \mathbf{x}_i' \mathbf{b} + E_i$$

The general *M* estimator minimizes the objective function

$$\sum_{i=1}^{n} \rho(E_i) = \sum_{i=1}^{n} \rho(Y_i - \mathbf{x}_i' \mathbf{b})$$

Differentiating the objective function and setting the derivative to **0** produces

$$\sum_{i=1}^{n} \psi(Y_i - \mathbf{x}_i' \mathbf{b}) \mathbf{x}_i = \mathbf{0} \tag{19.3}$$

which is a system of $k + 1$ estimating equations in the $k + 1$ elements of **b**.

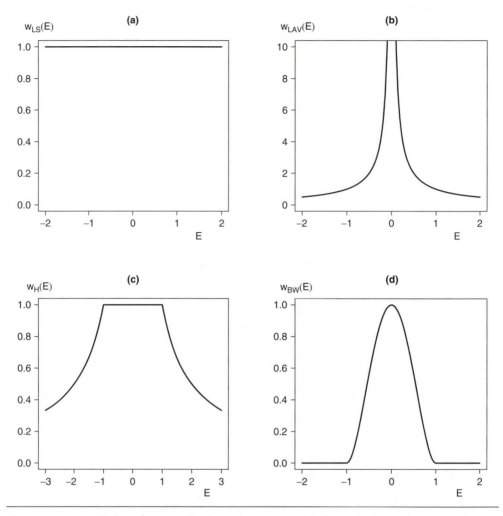

Figure 19.4   Weight functions $w(E)$ for the (a) least-squares, (b) least-absolute-values, (c) Huber, and (d) biweight estimators. The tuning constants for the Huber and biweight estimators are taken as $k = 1$. Note that the vertical axis in the graph for the LAV estimator and the horizontal axis in the graph for the Huber estimator are different from the others.

M estimation for the regression model $Y_i = \mathbf{x}_i'\beta + \varepsilon_i$ is a direct extension of M estimation of location: We seek to minimize an objective function of the regression residuals, $\sum_{i=1}^{n} \rho(E_i) = \sum_{i=1}^{n} \rho(Y_i - \mathbf{x}_i'\mathbf{b})$. Differentiating the objective function and setting the derivatives to 0 produces the estimating equations $\sum_{i=1}^{n} \psi(Y_i - \mathbf{x}_i'\mathbf{b})\mathbf{x}_i = \mathbf{0}$.

Using the weight function $w(E) \equiv \psi(E)/E$ and letting $w_i \equiv w(E_i)$, the estimating equations become

$$\sum_{i=1}^{n} w_i(Y_i - \mathbf{x}_i'\mathbf{b})\mathbf{x}_i = \mathbf{0}$$

The solution to these estimating equations minimizes the weighted sum of squares $\sum w_i E_i^2$.[10] Because the weights depend on the residuals, the estimated coefficients depend on the weights, and the residuals depend on the estimated coefficients, an iterative solution is required. The IWLS algorithm for regression is as follows:

1. Select initial estimates $\mathbf{b}^{(0)}$ and set the iteration counter $l = 0$. Using the initial estimates, find residuals $E_i^{(0)} = Y_i - \mathbf{x}_i'\mathbf{b}^{(0)}$, and from these, calculate the estimated scale of the residuals $S^{(0)}$ and the weights $w_i^{(0)} = w(E_i^{(0)})$.

2. At each iteration l, solve the estimating equations using the current weights, minimizing $\sum w_i^{(l-1)} E_i^2$ to obtain $\mathbf{b}^{(l)}$. The solution is conveniently expressed as

$$\mathbf{b}^{(l)} = (\mathbf{X}'\mathbf{W}\mathbf{X})^{-1}\mathbf{X}'\mathbf{W}\mathbf{y}$$

where the model matrix $\underset{(n \times k+1)}{\mathbf{X}}$ has $\mathbf{x}_i'$ as its ith row, and $\underset{(n \times n)}{\mathbf{W}} \equiv \text{diag}\{w_i^{(l-1)}\}$. Continue until $\mathbf{b}^{(l)} - \mathbf{b}^{(l-1)} \approx \mathbf{0}$.[11]

Using the weight function, the estimating equations can be written as

$$\sum_{i=1}^{n} w_i(Y_i - \mathbf{x}_i'\mathbf{b})\mathbf{x}_i' = \mathbf{0}$$

The solution of the estimating equations then follows by weighted least squares:

$$\mathbf{b} = (\mathbf{X}'\mathbf{W}\mathbf{X})^{-1}\mathbf{X}'\mathbf{W}\mathbf{y}$$

where $\mathbf{W}$ is the diagonal matrix of weights. The method of iterated weighted least squares starts with initial estimates $\mathbf{b}^{(0)}$, calculates initial residuals from these estimates, and calculates initial weights from the residuals. The weights are used to update the parameter estimates, and the procedure is iterated until it converges.

The asymptotic covariance matrix of the *M* estimator is given by

$$\mathcal{V}(\mathbf{b}) = \frac{E(\psi^2)}{[E(\psi')]^2}(\mathbf{X}'\mathbf{X})^{-1}$$

Using $\sum [\psi(E_i)]^2 / n$ to estimate $E(\psi^2)$ and $\left[\sum \psi'(E_i)/n\right]^2$ to estimate $[E(\psi')]^2$ produces the estimated asymptotic covariance matrix $\widehat{\mathcal{V}}(\mathbf{b})$. Research suggests, however, that these sampling variances are not to be trusted unless the sample size is large.[12]

---

[10] See the discussion of weighted-least-squares regression in Section 12.2.2.

[11] As in the location problem, it is possible that the estimating equations for a redescending estimator have more than one root. If you use the bisquare estimator, for example, it is prudent to pick a good start value, such as provided by the Huber estimator.

[12] See Li (1985, pp. 300–301). For an alternative approach that may have better small-sample properties, see Street, Carroll, and Ruppert (1988). Also see the discussion of bootstrap methods in Chapter 21.

Table 19.2 *M* Estimates for Duncan's Regression of
Occupational Prestige on Income and
Education for 45 U.S. Occupations

	Coefficient		
Estimator	*Constant*	*Income*	*Education*
Least squares	−6.065	0.5987	0.5458
Least squares*	−6.409	0.8674	0.3322
Least absolute values	−6.408	0.7477	0.4587
Huber	−7.111	0.7014	0.4854
Bisquare (biweight)	−7.412	0.7902	0.4186

NOTE: The estimator marked "Least squares" omits ministers
and railroad conductors

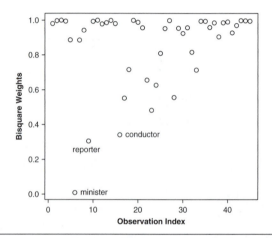

Figure 19.5   Final weights for the bisquare estimator applied to Duncan's regression of
occupational prestige on income and education.

To illustrate *M* estimation, recall Duncan's regression of occupational prestige on income and education. In our previous analysis of these data, we discovered two influential observations: *ministers* and *railroad conductors*.[13] Another observation, *reporters*, has a relatively large residual but is not influential; still another observation, *railroad engineers*, is at a high-leverage point but is not discrepant. Table 19.2 summarizes the results of estimating Duncan's regression using four *M* estimators, including ordinary least squares. (The least-squares estimates obtained after deleting *ministers* and *railroad conductors* are also shown for comparison.) The three robust estimators produce quite similar results, with a larger income coefficient and smaller education coefficient than least squares. The redescending bisquare estimator is most different from least squares (and most similar to least squares after removing the two discrepant observations).

Figure 19.5 shows the final weights for the bisquare estimator applied to Duncan's data. *Ministers*, *railroad conductors*, and *reporters* have very small weights. Rather than simply regarding

[13]See Chapter 11.

robust regression as a procedure for automatically down-weighting outliers, the method can often be used effectively, as here, to identify outlying observations.

19.2 Bounded-Influence Regression

The flies in the ointment of M estimation in regression are high-leverage outliers. In the location problem, M estimators such as the Huber and the bisquare bound the influence of individual discrepant observations; but this is not the case in regression—if we admit the possibility of X values with high leverage. High-leverage observations can force small residuals even when these observations depart from the pattern of the rest of the data.[14]

A key concept in assessing influence is the *breakdown point* of an estimator: The breakdown point is the fraction of arbitrarily "bad" data that the estimator can tolerate without being affected to an arbitrarily large extent. In the location problem, for example, the mean has a breakdown point of 0, because a *single* bad observation can change the mean by an arbitrary amount. The median, in contrast, has a breakdown point of 50%, because fully half the data can be bad without causing the median to become completely unstuck.[15] It is disquieting that in regression analysis *all* M estimators have breakdown points of 0.

There are regression estimators, however, that have breakdown points of nearly 50%. One such *bounded-influence* estimator is *least-trimmed-squares* (LTS) regression.[16]

Return to the fitted regression model $Y_i = \mathbf{x}'_i \mathbf{b} + E_i$, ordering the squared residuals from smallest to largest:[17] $(E^2)_{(1)}, (E^2)_{(2)}, \ldots, (E^2)_{(n)}$. Then, select $\mathbf{b}$ to minimize the sum of the smaller "half" of the squared residuals—that is,

$$\sum_{i=1}^{m}(E^2)_{(i)} \tag{19.4}$$

for $m = \lfloor (n + k + 2)/2 \rfloor$ (where the "floor" brackets indicate rounding down to the next smallest integer).

The LTS criterion is easily stated, but the LTS estimate is not so easily computed. One approach is to consider all subsets of observations of size $k + 1$ for which the vectors $\mathbf{x}'_i$ are distinct. Let the $k + 1 \times k + 1$ model matrix for a particular such subset be represented as $\mathbf{X}^*$. Because the rows of $\mathbf{X}^*$ are all different, it is almost surely the case that the matrix $\mathbf{X}^*$ is of full rank, and we can compute the regression coefficients for this subset as $\mathbf{b}^* = \mathbf{X}^{*-1}\mathbf{y}^*$ (where $\mathbf{y}^*$ contains the corresponding entries of the response vector).[18] For each such subset, we compute the LTS criterion in Equation 19.4 and take as the LTS estimator $\mathbf{b}_{\text{LTS}}$ the value of $\mathbf{b}^*$ that minimizes this criterion.

If there are no repeated rows in the model matrix $\mathbf{X}$, then the number of subsets of observations of size $k + 1$ is

$$\binom{n}{k + 1} = \frac{n!}{(n - k - 1)!(k + 1)!}$$

which is a very large number unless n is small. Even with highly efficient computational methods, it quickly becomes impractical, therefore, to find the LTS estimator by this approach. But we

---

[14] For an illustration of this phenomenon, see Exercise 19.3.

[15] See Exercise 19.2.

[16] The LTS estimator, the MM estimator introduced below, and other bounded-influence estimators in regression are described in detail by Rousseeuw and Leroy (1987).

[17] Lest the notation appear confusing, note that it is the *squared* residuals E_i^2 that are ordered from smallest to largest, *not* the residuals E_i themselves.

[18] See Exercise 19.4.

can compute a close approximation to $\mathbf{b}_{\text{LTS}}$ by randomly sampling many (but not unmanageably many) subsets of observations and minimizing the LTS criterion over the sampled subsets.

In the case of Duncan's occupational prestige regression, it is feasible to compute *all* subsets of size $k + 1 = 3$ of the $n = 45$ observations, of which there are

$$\binom{45}{3} = \frac{45!}{42!3!} = 14,190$$

The LTS estimates, it turns out, are similar to the bisquare estimates given in the previous section (Table 19.2 on page 538):

$$\widehat{\text{Prestige}} = -5.764 + 0.8023 \times \text{Income} + 0.4098 \times \text{Education}$$

Unlike the M estimator of location, the M estimator in regression is vulnerable to high-leverage observations. Bounded-influence estimators limit the impact of high-leverage observations. One such bounded-influence estimator is LTS, which selects the regression coefficients to minimize the smaller "half" of the squared residuals, $\sum_{i=1}^{m}(E^2)_{(i)}$ (where $m = \lfloor (n + k + 2)/2 \rfloor$). The LTS estimator can be computed by calculating the regression coefficients for all subsets of observations of size $k + 1$ and selecting the regression coefficients from the subset that minimizes the LTS criterion. If there are too many such subsets, then a manageable number can be sampled randomly.

LTS and other bounded-influence estimators are not a panacea for linear-model estimation, because they can give unreasonable results for some data configurations.[19] As well, the LTS estimator has much lower efficiency than the M estimators that we considered if the errors are in fact normal.

The latter problem can be addressed by combining bounded-influence estimation with M estimation, producing a so-called MM estimator, which retains the high breakdown point of the bounded-influence estimator and the high efficiency under normality of the M estimator. The MM estimator uses a bounded-influence estimator for start values in the computation of an M estimate and also to estimate the scale of the errors. For example, starting with the LTS estimator of the Duncan regression and following with the bisquare estimator yields the MM estimates

$$\widehat{\text{Prestige}} = -7.490 + 0.8391 \times \text{Income} + 0.3935 \times \text{Education}$$

The MM estimator combines the high breakdown point of bounded-influence regression with the high efficiency of M estimation for normally distributed errors. The MM estimator uses start values and a scale estimate obtained from a preliminary bounded-influence regression.

19.3 Quantile Regression

Quantile regression, due to Koenker and Bassett (1978), is a conceptually straightforward generalization of LAV regression. As I have noted, LAV regression estimates the conditional median

---

[19]See Stefanski (1991).

(i.e., 50th percentile) of the response variable as a function of the explanatory variables. Quantile regression extends this approach to estimating other conditional quantiles of the response, such as the quartiles.

The LAV criterion in linear regression is written most directly as

$$\sum_{i=1}^{n} \rho_{\text{LAV}}(Y_i - \mathbf{x}_i'\mathbf{b}) \equiv \sum_{i=1}^{n} |Y_i - \mathbf{x}_i'\mathbf{b}|$$

The LAV estimator, $\mathbf{b}_{\text{LAV}}$, is the value of $\mathbf{b}$ that minimizes this criterion. An equivalent expression, the motivation for which will become clear presently, is

$$\sum_{i=1}^{n} \rho_{\text{LAV}}(Y_i - \mathbf{x}_i'\mathbf{b}) = 0.5 \times \sum_{i:\,(Y_i-\mathbf{x}_i'\mathbf{b})<0} |Y_i - \mathbf{x}_i'\mathbf{b}| + 0.5 \times \sum_{i:\,(Y_i-\mathbf{x}_i'\mathbf{b})>0} |Y_i - \mathbf{x}_i'\mathbf{b}|$$

that is, the LAV criterion consists of two components: The first component includes observations producing negative residuals and the second, observations producing positive residuals; residuals in these two classes are weighted *equally*.

Koenker and Bassett show that estimating the conditional q quantile (where $0 < q < 1$) is equivalent to minimizing

$$\sum_{i=1}^{n} \rho_q(Y_i - \mathbf{x}_i'\mathbf{b}) = q \times \sum_{i:\,(Y_i-\mathbf{x}_i'\mathbf{b})<0} |Y_i - \mathbf{x}_i'\mathbf{b}| + (1-q) \times \sum_{i:\,(Y_i-\mathbf{x}_i'\mathbf{b})>0} |Y_i - \mathbf{x}_i'\mathbf{b}|$$

(i.e., a sum of *differentially weighted* negative and positive residuals) and that, furthermore, finding the value $\mathbf{b} = \mathbf{b}_q$ that minimizes this criterion is a straightforward linear programming problem.[20] They proceed to derive the asymptotic covariance matrix of the estimated quantile regression coefficients as[21]

$$V(\mathbf{b}_q) = \sigma_q^2(\mathbf{X}'\mathbf{X})^{-1}$$

where

$$\sigma_q^2 \equiv \frac{q(1-q)}{p[P^{-1}(q)]}$$

where $p(\cdot)$ is the probability density function for the error distribution and $P^{-1}(\cdot)$ is the quantile function for the errors (supposing, as may not be the case, that the errors are identically distributed). Thus, $p[P^{-1}(q)]$ is the density at the q quantile of the error distribution.[22] Note that σ_q^2 plays the same role as the error variance σ_ε^2 does in the formula for the covariance matrix of the least-squares estimates.[23] In applications, σ_q^2 is estimated from the distribution of the residuals.

---

[20]Linear programming is a common type of optimization problem, for which there are well-understood and efficient methods. See, for example, Gass (2003).

[21]Koenker and Bassett (1978) also give exact finite-sample results, but these are too computationally demanding to prove useful in practice. An alternative to using the asymptotic standard errors is to base inference for quantile regression on the bootstrap, as described in Chapter 21.

[22]See the formula for the standard error of an order statistic given in Section 3.1.3.

[23]See Section 9.3.1.

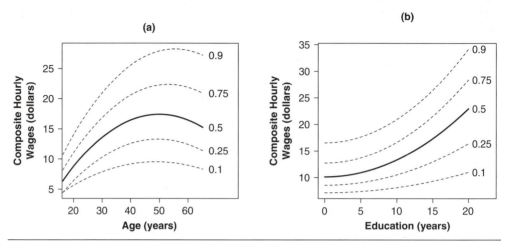

Figure 19.6   Effect displays for (a) age and (b) education in the quantile regression of wages on
these variables and sex in the SLID data. In each case, the conditional .1, .25, .5, .75,
and .9 quantiles are estimated. To construct each effect display, the other quantitative
explanatory variable is set to its median value in the data, and the dummy regressor
for sex is set to 0.5.

Quantile regression estimates a linear model for the conditional quantile q of the response
variable by minimizing the criterion

$$\sum_{i=1}^{n} \rho_q(Y_i - \mathbf{x}_i'\mathbf{b}) = \sum_{i:\,(Y_i - \mathbf{x}_i'\mathbf{b}) < 0} q \times |Y_i - \mathbf{x}_i'\mathbf{b}| + \sum_{i:\,(Y_i - \mathbf{x}_i'\mathbf{b}) > 0} (1-q) \times |Y_i - \mathbf{x}_i'\mathbf{b}|$$

The asymptotic covariance matrix of the quantile regression estimator $\mathbf{b}_q$ is $V(\mathbf{b}_q) =$
$\sigma_q^2 (\mathbf{X}'\mathbf{X})^{-1}$, where $\sigma_q^2 \equiv q(1-q)/\{p[P^{-1}(q)]\}$ and $p[P^{-1}(q)]$ is the density at the q
quantile of the error distribution.

Figure 19.6 illustrates quantile regression by applying it to data from the Canadian Survey of
Labour and Income Dynamics (SLID). I previously fit a model in which the log of the composite
hourly wage rate for individuals in the sample was regressed on a dummy variable for sex, a
quadratic in age, and the square of education.[24] For example, the estimated regression equation
for the conditional median (i.e., the .5 quantile) is

$$\widehat{\text{Median Wages}} = \quad -13.44 + 3.066 \times \text{Male} \quad + 0.9564 \times \text{Age}$$
$$\quad (0.69) \quad (0.216) \quad\quad\quad (0.0485)$$
$$- 0.009567 \times \text{Age}^2 + 0.03213 \times \text{Education}^2$$
$$(0.000679) \quad\quad\quad (0.00157)$$

---

[24] See Section 12.3. There is, however, a subtle change here: We were careful on log-transforming wages to make sure
that the form in which age and education entered the model adequately captured the dependence of the conditional mean
response on these explanatory variables. Because the log transformation is not linear, a quadratic in age and the square of
education may not be appropriate for the conditional median of *untransformed* wages. I could, of course, compute instead
the quantile regression for *log*-wages (and I invite the reader to do so), but I wanted to illustrate how quantile regression
can reveal asymmetry and nonconstant spread in the conditional distribution of the response.

Asymptotic standard errors are in parentheses below the coefficients. Note in Figure 19.6 how the regression quantiles spread apart at higher values of age and education, where the median level of wages is relatively high, and how, for the most part, the conditional distribution of wages is positively skewed, with the upper quantiles more spread out than the lower ones. These characteristics, recall, motivated the log-transformation of wages in least-squares regressions for these data.

Quantile regression is an attractive method not only because of its robustness relative to least squares but because of its simple interpretation and because of its focus on the *whole* conditional distribution of the response. Moreover, quantile regression extends naturally beyond linear models, for example, to nonlinear regression and to nonparametric regression.[25]

19.4 Robust Estimation of Generalized Linear Models

The maximum likelihood or quasi-likelihood estimating equations for a generalized linear model can be written as

$$\sum_{i=1}^{n} \frac{1}{a_i} (Y_i - \mu_i) \underset{(k+1 \times 1)}{\mathbf{x}_i} = \underset{(k+1 \times 1)}{\mathbf{0}} \tag{19.5}$$

where Y_i is the response variable for the ith of n observations, $\mu_i = g^{-1}(\mathbf{x}_i'\boldsymbol{\beta})$ is the conditional expectation of the response given the values of the regressors $\mathbf{x}_i'$ for observation i, $\boldsymbol{\beta}$ is the parameter vector of $k + 1$ regression coefficients to be estimated, and $g^{-1}(\cdot)$ is the inverse of the link function (i.e., the mean function) for the model. The constants a_i depend on the distributional family used to model the response; for example, for the Gaussian family $a_i = 1$, while for the binomial family $a_i = 1/n_i$ (the inverse of the number of binomial trials).[26] Because it depends directly on the difference between the observed and fitted response, the maximum likelihood or quasi-likelihood estimator based on these estimating equations is generally not robust.

Cantoni and Rochetti (2001) suggest replacing Equation 19.5 by estimating equations of the form

$$\sum_{i=1}^{n} \psi(Y_i, \mu_i) = \mathbf{0} \tag{19.6}$$

where $\psi(\cdot)$ is selected to produce high resistance to outliers. Equation 19.6 is a generalization of the estimating equations for M estimators in linear regression (Equation 19.3 on page 535). Bounded influence is achieved by down-weighting high-leverage observations: The weights employed are the product of (1) weights measuring the discrepancy between the observed and fitted response and (2) weights accounting for the leverage of the observations.[27] The details are beyond the scope of this presentation and are developed in Cantoni and Rochetti's paper.

Because the response variable in a binomial generalized linear model is bounded by 0 and 1, it is rare (but not impossible) to find highly influential observations in a logit or probit regression.

---

[25] See Koenker (2005) for an extensive treatment of the subject.

[26] See Section 15.3.

[27] A simple choice of leverage-based weights is $\sqrt{1 - h_i}$, where h_i is the hat-value for the ith observation (see Section 11.2). A higher breakdown point can be achieved, however, by using a robust covariance matrix for the Xs to judge the unusualness of observations in the X-space; using a robust covariance matrix is not sensible when the model matrix includes dummy regressors or other contrasts. Applied to *linear* regression, bounded-influence estimators using weights based on the product of leverage and discrepancy are called *GM* (*generalized-M*) *estimators* (see Rousseeuw & Leroy, 1987, chap. 1).

GLMs for count data and for non-normal continuous responses are another matter, and robust estimation for these models is potentially useful. My limited experience with Cantoni and Rochetti's estimator, however, suggests that it is not entirely reliable for detecting and discounting influential data.[28]

> Robust bounded-influence estimators for generalized linear models can be obtained by replacing the usual maximum likelihood or quasi-likelihood estimating equations for GLMs by $\sum_{i=1}^{n} \psi(Y_i, \mu_i) = \mathbf{0}$, where $\psi(\cdot)$ is selected to produce high resistance to outliers. Bounded influence is achieved by downweighting observations that have large residuals or large leverage.

19.5 Concluding Remarks

A final caution concerning robust regression: Robust estimation is not a substitute for close examination of the data. Although robust estimators can cope with heavy-tailed error distributions and outliers, they cannot correct nonlinearity, for example. Indeed, one use of robust estimation is to employ it as a routine diagnostic for unusual data in small- to medium-size samples, comparing the results obtained for a robust estimator with those of least-squares regression and investigating when the two estimators produce substantially different estimates (see, e.g., the discussion of the final weights for the Duncan regression displayed in Figure 19.5 on page 538).

As I have pointed out with respect to quantile regression, robust estimators can be extended to other settings. For example, it is a simple matter, and indeed common, to employ M estimator "robustness weights" in local-polynomial nonparametric regression, multiplying these weights by the neighborhood weights for the usual local-polynomial estimator, thereby rendering the local-polynomial estimator resistant to outliers.[29]

Exercises

Exercise 19.1. *Prove that the median minimizes the least-absolute-values objective function:

$$\sum_{i=1}^{n} \rho_{\text{LAV}}(E_i) = \sum_{i=1}^{n} |Y_i - \widehat{\mu}|$$

Exercise 19.2. Breakdown: Consider the contrived data set

$$Y_1 = -0.068 \quad Y_2 = -1.282 \quad Y_3 = 0.013 \quad Y_4 = 0.141$$
$$Y_5 = -0.980$$

(an adaptation of the data used to construct Figure 19.1). Show that more than two values must be changed to influence the median of the five values to an arbitrary degree. (Try, e.g., to make the

---

[28] See, for example, Exercise 19.5.
[29] See Chapter 18.

first two values progressively and simultaneously larger, graphing the median of the altered data set against the common value of Y_1 and Y_2; then, do the same for the first three observations.)

Exercise 19.3. The following contrived data set (discussed in Chapter 3) is from Anscombe (1973):

X	Y
10	7.46
8	6.77
13	12.74
9	7.11
11	7.81
14	8.84
6	6.08
4	5.39
12	8.15
7	6.42
5	5.73

(a) Graph the data and confirm that the third observation is an outlier. Find the least-squares regression of Y on X, and plot the least-squares line on the graph.

(b) Fit a robust regression to the data using the bisquare or Huber M estimator. Plot the fitted regression line on the graph. Is the robust regression affected by the outlier?

(c) Omitting the third observation $\{13, 12.74\}$, the line through the rest of the data has the equation $Y = 4 + 0.345X$, and the residual of the third observation from this line is 4.24. (Verify these facts.) Generate equally discrepant observations at X values of 23 and 33 by substituting these values successively into the equation $Y = 4 + 0.345X + 4.24$. Call the resulting Y values Y_3' and Y_3''. Redo parts (a) and (b), replacing the third observation with the point $\{23, Y_3'\}$. Then, replace the third observation with the point $\{33, Y_3''\}$. What happens?

(d) Repeat part (c) using the LTS bounded-influence estimator. Do it again with the MM estimator.

Exercise 19.4. Computing the LTS estimator: Why is it almost surely the case that the $(k + 1) \times (k + 1)$ matrix $\mathbf{X}^*$, with rows selected from among those of the complete model matrix $\mathbf{X}$, is of full rank when all its rows are different? (Put another way, how is it possible that $\mathbf{X}^*$ would *not* be of full rank?) Thinking in terms of the $(k + 1)$-dimensional scatterplot of Y against $X_1, \ldots, X_k$, what does the hyperplane defined by $\mathbf{b}^* = \mathbf{X}^{*-1}\mathbf{y}^*$ represent?

Exercise 19.5. In Chapter 15, I fit a Poisson regression of number of interlocks on assets, nation of control, and sector for Ornstein's Canadian interlocking-directorate data. The results from this regression are given in Table 15.3 (page 389). Influential-data diagnostics (see, e.g., Figure 15.7 on page 414) suggest that the first observation in the data set is quite influential; in particular, the coefficient of assets changes considerably when the first observtion is removed. Perform a robust Poisson regression for this model. How do the results compare to removing the first observation from the data set? (Recall, however, that the influence of the first observation depends on unmodeled nonlinearity in the relationship between interlocks and assets—a problem that I ultimately addressed in Chapter 15 by log-transforming assets.)

Summary

- Robust M estimators of location, for the parameter μ in the simple model $Y_i = \mu + \varepsilon_i$, minimize the objective function

$$\sum_{i=1}^{n} \rho(E_i) = \sum_{i=1}^{n} \rho(Y_i - \widehat{\mu})$$

selecting $\rho(\cdot)$ so that the estimator is relatively unaffected by outlying values. Two common choices of objective function are the Huber and the bisquare.

- The sensitivity of an M estimator to individual observations is expressed by the influence function of the estimator, which has the same shape as the derivative of the objective function, $\psi(E) \equiv \rho'(E)$.

- An estimating equation for $\widehat{\mu}$ is obtained by setting the derivative of the objective function (with respect to $\widehat{\mu}$) to 0, obtaining $\sum_{i=1}^{n} \psi\,(Y_i - \widehat{\mu}) = 0$. The simplest procedure for solving this estimating equation is by iteratively reweighted means. Defining the weight function as $w(E) \equiv \psi(E)/E$, the estimating equation becomes $\sum_{i=1}^{n} (Y_i - \widehat{\mu})\, w_i = 0$, from which $\widehat{\mu} = \sum w_i Y_i / \sum w_i$. Starting with an initial estimate $\widehat{\mu}^{(0)}$, initial weights are calculated, and the value of $\widehat{\mu}$ is updated. This procedure continues iteratively until the value of $\widehat{\mu}$ converges.

- M estimation for the regression model $Y_i = \mathbf{x}_i'\beta + \varepsilon_i$ is a direct extension of M estimation of location: We seek to minimize an objective function of the regression residuals:

$$\sum_{i=1}^{n} \rho(E_i) = \sum_{i=1}^{n} \rho(Y_i - \mathbf{x}_i'\mathbf{b})$$

Differentiating the objective function and setting the derivatives to 0 produces the estimating equations

$$\sum_{i=1}^{n} \psi\,(Y_i - \mathbf{x}_i'\mathbf{b})\mathbf{x}_i' = \mathbf{0}$$

- Using the weight function, the estimating equations can be written as

$$\sum_{i=1}^{n} w_i (Y_i - \mathbf{x}_i'\mathbf{b})\mathbf{x}_i' = \mathbf{0}$$

The solution of the estimating equations then follows by weighted least squares:

$$\mathbf{b} = (\mathbf{X}'\mathbf{W}\mathbf{X})^{-1}\mathbf{X}'\mathbf{W}\mathbf{y}$$

where $\mathbf{W}$ is the diagonal matrix of weights. The method of iterated weighted least squares starts with initial estimates $\mathbf{b}^{(0)}$, calculates initial residuals from these estimates, and calculates initial weights from the residuals. The weights are used to update the parameter estimates, and the procedure is iterated until it converges.

- Unlike the M estimator of location, the M estimator in regression is vulnerable to high-leverage observations. Bounded-influence estimators limit the effect of high-leverage observations. One such bounded-influence estimator is LTS, which selects the regression coefficients to minimize the smaller "half" of the squared residuals $\sum_{i=1}^{m} (E^2)_{(i)}$ (where

$m = \lfloor (n + k + 2)/2 \rfloor$). The LTS estimator can be computed by calculating the regression coefficients for all subsets of observations of size $k + 1$ and selecting the regression coefficients from the subset that minimizes the LTS criterion. If there are too many such subsets, then a manageable number can be sampled randomly.

- The MM estimator combines the high breakdown point of bounded-influence regression with the high efficiency of M estimation for normally distributed errors. The MM estimator uses start values and a scale estimate obtained from a preliminary bounded-influence regression.

- Quantile regression estimates a linear model for the conditional quantile q of the response variable by minimizing the criterion

$$\sum_{i=1}^{n} \rho_q (Y_i - \mathbf{x}_i' \mathbf{b}) = \sum_{i: (Y_i - \mathbf{x}_i' \mathbf{b}) < 0} q \times |Y_i - \mathbf{x}_i' \mathbf{b}| + \sum_{i: (Y_i - \mathbf{x}_i' \mathbf{b}) > 0} (1 - q) \times |Y_i - \mathbf{x}_i' \mathbf{b}|$$

The asymptotic covariance matrix of the quantile regression estimator $\mathbf{b}_q$ is $V(\mathbf{b}_q) = \sigma_q^2 (\mathbf{X}' \mathbf{X})^{-1}$, where $\sigma_q^2 \equiv q(1 - q)/\{p[P^{-1}(q)]\}$, and $p[P^{-1}(q)]$ is the density at the q quantile of the error distribution.

- Robust bounded-influence estimators for generalized linear models can be obtained by replacing the usual maximum-likelihood or quasi-likelihood estimating equations for GLMs by $\sum_{i=1}^{n} \psi(Y_i, \mu_i) = \mathbf{0}$, where $\psi(\cdot)$ is selected to produce high resistance to outliers. Bounded influence is achieved by downweighting observations that have large residuals or large leverage.

Recommended Reading

- In a volume on robust and exploratory methods, edited by Hoaglin, Mosteller, and Tukey (1983), Goodall presents a high-quality, readable treatment of M estimators of location.
- A fine paper by Li on M estimators for regression appears in a companion volume (Hoaglin, Mosteller, & Tukey, 1985).
- Another good source on M estimators is Wu (1985).
- Rousseeuw and Leroy's (1987) book on robust regression and outlier detection emphasizes bounded-influence, high-breakdown estimators.
- Andersen (2007) presents a broad and largely accessible overview of methods of robust regression, including a discussion of robust estimation for generalized linear models.

20

Missing Data in Regression Models

$\mathbf{M}$ issing data are a regrettably common feature of data sets in the social sciences. Despite this fact, almost all statistical methods in widespread use, including the methods introduced in the previous chapters of this book, assume that the data in hand are complete.

The current chapter provides a basic introduction to modern methods for handling missing data. The first section of the chapter draws some basic distinctions concerning the processes that generate missing data. The second section briefly describes traditional methods for coping with missing data and explains why they are problematic. The third section shows how the method of maximum likelihood (ML) can be used to estimate the parameters of statistical models in the presence of missing data. The fourth section introduces multiple imputation of missing data—a general, flexible, and convenient method for dealing with missing data that can perform well in certain circumstances. The final section of the chapter introduces methods for handling selection bias and censored data, which are special kinds of missing data.

Data may be missing for a variety of reasons:

- In survey research, for example, certain respondents may be unreachable or may refuse to participate in the survey, giving rise to *global* or *unit nonresponse*.
- Alternatively, again in survey research, some respondents may not know the answers to specific questions or may refuse to respond to them, giving rise to *item nonresponse*.
- Missing data may also be produced by errors in data collection—as when an interviewer fails to ask a question of a survey respondent—or in data processing.
- In some cases, missing data are built into the design of a study, as when particular questions in a survey are asked only of a random subset of respondents.
- It is sometimes the case that data values in a study are *censored*. The most common example of censored data occurs in *survival analysis* (also called *event-history analysis*, *duration analysis,* or *failure-time analysis*), which concerns the timing of events. In a prototypical biomedical application, subjects in a clinical trial are followed for a fixed period of time, and their survival times are recorded at their deaths. Some subjects, however, happily live beyond the termination of the study, and their survival times are therefore censored. Survival analysis is beyond the scope of this book,[1] but censored data can occur in other contexts as well—as, for example, in an exam with a fixed number of questions where it is not possible to score fewer than zero nor more than the total number of questions correct.

Missing data, in the sense that is developed in this chapter, should be distinguished from data that are *conditionally undefined*. A survey respondent who has no children, for example, cannot report their ages. Conditionally undefined data do not threaten the representativeness of a sample as truly missing data do. Sometimes, however, the distinction between missing and conditionally undefined data is not entirely clear-cut: Voters in a postelection survey who did not vote cannot be asked for whom they voted, but they could be (and may not have been) asked whether and for

---

[1]There are many texts on survival analysis. For example, see Allison (1984) for a brief introduction to survival analysis or Hosmer and Lemeshow (1999) for a more extensive treatment.

whom they had a preference. Similarly, some respondents asked to state an opinion on an issue may not have an opinion. Are these data missing or simply nonexistent?

It is important to realize at the outset that there is no magic cure for missing data, and it is generally impossible to proceed in a principled manner without making at least partly unverifiable assumptions about the process that gives rise to the missing information. As King Lear said, "Nothing will come of nothing" (though he applied this insight unwisely).

20.1 Missing Data Basics

Rubin (1976) introduced some key distinctions concerning missing data.[2] Let the matrix $\underset{(n \times p)}{\mathbf{X}}$ represent the complete data for a sample of n observations on p variables.[3] Some of the entries of $\mathbf{X}$, denoted by $\mathbf{X}_{\mathrm{mis}}$ are missing, and the remaining entries, $\mathbf{X}_{\mathrm{obs}}$, are observed.[4]

- Missing data are said to be *missing completely at random (MCAR)* if the missing data (and hence the observed data) can be regarded as a simple random sample of the complete data. Put alternatively, the probability that a data value is missing, termed *missingness*, is unrelated to the data value itself or to any other value, missing or observed, in the data set.
- If, however, missingness is related to the observed data but—conditioning on the observed data—not to the missing data, then data are said to be *missing at random (MAR)*. In a survey, for example, certain individuals may refuse to report their income, and these people may even differ systematically in income from the sample as a whole. Nevertheless, if the observations are independently sampled, so that one respondent's decision to withhold information about income is independent of others' responses, and if, *conditional on* the information that the respondent does provide (e.g., education, occupation), failure to provide information on income is independent of income itself, then the data are MAR. MCAR is a stronger condition—and a special case—of MAR.
- Finally, if missingness is related to the missing values themselves—that is, if the probability that a data value is missing depends on missing data (including, and indeed usually, the data value itself), even when the information in the observed data is taken into account—then, missing data are said to be *missing not at random (MNAR)*. For example, if conditional on all the observed data, individuals with higher incomes are more likely than others to withhold information about their incomes, then the missing income data are MNAR.

These distinctions are important because they affect the manner in which missing data can be properly handled. In particular, if the data are MCAR or MAR, then it is not necessary to model the process that generates the missing data to accommodate the missing data. When data are MCAR or MAR, the "mechanism" that produces the missing data is therefore *ignorable*. In contrast, when data are MNAR, the missing-data mechanism is *nonignorable*, and it becomes necessary to model this mechanism to deal with the missing data in a valid manner.

Except in some special situations, it is not possible to know whether data are MCAR, MAR, or MNAR. We may be able to show that missingness on some variable in a data set is related to observed data on one or more other variables, in which case we can rule out MCAR; but the

---

[2] Although Rubin's terminology is potentially confusing, it is in common use and has guided most subsequent work on missing data by statisticians. It would therefore be a mistake, I think, to introduce different terms for these concepts.

[3] If you are unfamiliar with matrix notation, simply think of the matrix $\mathbf{X}$ as a rectangular table of data, with the observations given by the n rows of the table and the variables by the p columns.

[4] Despite the notation, $\mathbf{X}_{\mathrm{mis}}$ and $\mathbf{X}_{\mathrm{obs}}$ are not really matrices; they are, rather, subsets of the complete data matrix $\mathbf{X}$. Together, $\mathbf{X}_{\mathrm{mis}}$ and $\mathbf{X}_{\mathrm{obs}}$ comprise $\mathbf{X}$.

converse is not the case—that is, demonstrating that missingness in a variable is not related to observed data in other variables does not *prove* that the missing data are MCAR (because, e.g., nonrespondents in a survey may be differentiated from respondents in some *unobserved* manner). If, on the other hand, a survey question is asked of a random subset of respondents, then data are MCAR by design of the study.

> Missing data are missing completely at random (MCAR) if the missing data can be regarded as a simple random sample of the complete data. If missingness is related to the observed data but not to the missing data (conditional on the observed data), then data are missing at random (MAR). If missingness is related to the missing values themselves, even when the information in the observed data is taken into account, then data are missing not at random (MNAR). When data are MCAR or MAR, the process that produces missing data is ignorable, in the sense that valid methods exist to deal with the missing data without explicitly modeling the process that generates them. In contrast, when data are MNAR, the process producing missing data is nonignorable and must be modeled. Except in special situations, it is not possible to know whether data are MCAR, MAR, or MNAR.

20.1.1   An Illustration

To clarify these distinctions, let us consider the following example (adapted from Little & Rubin, 1990): We have a data set with $n = 250$ observations and two variables. The first variable, X_1, is completely observed, but some of the observations on X_2 are missing. This pattern—where one variable has missing data and all others (in this instance, *one* other variable) are completely observed—is called *univariate missing data*. Univariate missing data are especially easy to handle. For example, while general patterns of missing data may require iterative techniques (as described later in this chapter), univariate missing data do not. Nevertheless, we will get a great deal of mileage out of this simple example.

For concreteness, suppose that the complete data are sampled from a bivariate-normal distribution with means $\mu_1 = 10$, $\mu_2 = 20$, variances $\sigma_1^2 = 9$, $\sigma_2^2 = 16$, and covariance $\sigma_{12} = 8$.[5] The population correlation between X_1 and X_2 is therefore $\rho_{12} = 8/\sqrt{9 \times 16} = 2/3$; the slope for the regression of X_1 on X_2 is $\beta_{12} = 8/16 = 1/2$; and the slope for the regression of X_2 on X_1 is $\beta_{21} = 8/9 \approx 0.889$.

Consider the following three mechanisms for generating missing data in the sample of 250 observations:

1. One hundred of the observations on X_2 are selected at random and set to missing. This situation is illustrated in Figure 20.1(a), where the data points represented by black circles are fully observed, and those represented by gray circles are missing X_2. Here, the missing values of X_2 are MCAR, and the subset of valid observations is a simple random sample of the full data set.

2. In Figure 20.1(b), an observation's missingness on X_2 is related to its (observed) value of X_1:

---

[5]The bivariate-normal distribution is described in Appendix D on probability and estimation.

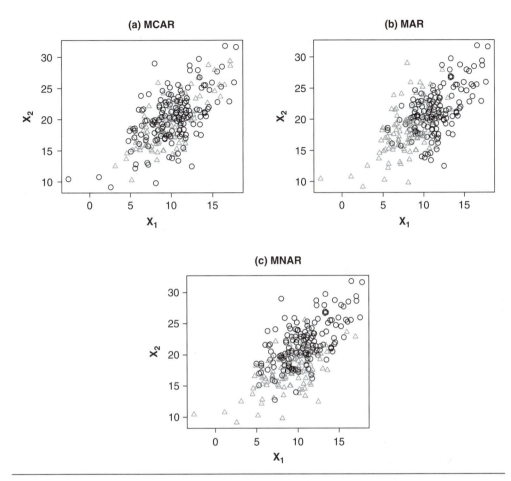

Figure 20.1   The 250 observations in each scatterplot were sampled from a bivariate normal distribution; in each case, the observations shown as gray triangles have missing data on X_2. In panel (a) the 100 observations with missing data were sampled at random, and the missing data on X_2 are therefore missing completely at random (MCAR). In (b) the probability that an observation has a missing value on X_2 is related to its value on X_1, and so the missing data on X_2 are missing at random (MAR). In (c) the probability that an observation has a missing value on X_2 is related to its value on X_2, and so the missing data on X_2 are missing not at random (MNAR).

$$\Pr(X_{i2} \text{ is missing}) = \frac{1}{1 + \exp\left[\frac{1}{2} + \frac{2}{3}(X_{i1} - 10)\right]} \tag{20.1}$$

We recognize Equation 20.1 as a logistic-regression equation, with the probability that X_2 is missing declining as X_1 grows larger. The regression coefficients were calibrated so that approximately 100 observations will have missing data on X_2 (and for the sample in Figure 20.1(b), there are, as it turned out, 109 missing values produced by simulating the missing-data-generating process). X_1 and X_2 are positively correlated, and consequently, there are relatively fewer small values of X_2 in the observed data than in the complete data; moreover, if we look only at the observations with valid data on *both X_1 and X_2*, this subset of observations also has relatively few small values of X_1. Because X_1, recall, is fully observed, the missing data on X_2 are MAR.

3. In Figure 20.1(c), an observation's missingness on X_2 is related to the (potentially unobserved) value of X_2 itself:

$$\Pr(X_{i2} \text{ is missing}) = \frac{1}{1 + \exp\left[\frac{1}{2} + \frac{1}{2}(X_{i2} - 20)\right]} \qquad (20.2)$$

For our data set, the simulation of this process produced exactly 100 observations with missing data on X_2. Here, too, and indeed more directly, there are relatively few small values of X_2 (and, incidentally, if we exclude the observations with missing data on X_2, of X_1 also). Because missingness on X_2 depends directly on the value of X_2, the missing data are MNAR.

As mentioned, except in those relatively rare instances where missing data are built into the design of a study, it is not possible to verify from the data whether they are MCAR or even MAR—that is, whether the missing-data mechanism is ignorable. Indeed, it is fair to say that missing data are almost always MNAR. Nevertheless, if we can argue plausibly that the departure from MAR is likely small, then dealing with missing data becomes a much more tractable problem. Furthermore, unless we are willing to discard the data, we have to proceed in *some* manner. Rather than requiring perfection, which is probably unattainable, we may have to settle for a solution that simply gets us closer to the truth.

20.2   Traditional Approaches to Missing Data

In evaluating missing-data methods, there are three general questions to answer:

1. Does the method provide *consistent estimates* of population parameters, or does it introduce systematic biases into the results?

2. Does the method provide *valid statistical inferences*, or are confidence intervals and p-values distorted?

3. Does the method use the observed data *efficiently* or does it profligately discard information?

The answers to these questions depend partly on the methods themselves, partly on the nature of the process generating missing data, and partly on the statistics of interest.

There are many ad hoc methods that have been proposed for dealing with missing data; I will briefly describe several of the most common here and will explain why, in which respects, and under what circumstances, they are problematic. This discussion is far from complete, however: For example, I have omitted discussion of methods based on reweighting the data.[6]

Complete-case analysis (also called *list-wise* or *case-wise deletion* of missing data), probably the most widely used approach, simply ignores observations with any missing data on the variables included in the analysis. Complete-case analysis has its advantages: It is simple to implement; it provides consistent estimates and valid inferences when the data are missing completely at random; and it provides consistent estimates of regression coefficients and valid inferences when missingness on all the variables in a regression does not depend on the response variable (even

---

[6] As a general matter, relatively simple weighting schemes can reduce bias in estimates, but do not provide valid inferences. See, for example, Little and Rubin (2002, sec. 3.3).

if data are not MCAR). Because it discards some valid data, however, complete-case analysis generally does not use the information in the data efficiently. This problem can become acute when there are many variables, each with some missing data. For example, suppose each of 10 variables is missing 5% of observations and that missingness in different variables is independent.[7] Then, we would expect only $100 \times .95^{10} \approx 60\%$ of the observations to be completely observed. Furthermore, when data are MAR or MNAR, complete-case analysis usually provides biased results and invalid inferences.

Available-case analysis (also called *pair-wise deletion* of missing data) uses all nonmissing observations to compute each statistic of interest. In a least-squares regression analysis, for example, the regression coefficients can be calculated from the means, variances, and covariances of the variables (or, equivalently, from their means, variances, and correlations). To apply available-case analysis to least-square regression, each mean is calculated from all observations with valid data for a variable and the covariance of two variables from all observations that have valid data for both.[8] Available case analysis appears to use more information than complete-case analysis, but in certain instances this is an illusion: That is, estimators based on available cases can be *less* efficient than those based on complete cases.[9] Moreover, by basing different statistics on different subsets of the data, available-case analysis can lead to nonsensical results, such as covariances that are inconsistent with one another or correlations outside the range from -1 to $+1$.[10] Finally, except in simple applications, such as linear least-squares regression, it is not obvious how to apply the available-case approach.

Several methods attempt to fill in missing data, replacing missing values with plausible *imputed* values. The resulting completed data set is then analyzed using standard methods. One such approach, termed *unconditional mean imputation* (or *mean substitution*) replaces each missing value with the mean of the observed data for the variable in question. Although mean imputation preserves the means of variables, it makes their distributions less variable and tends to weaken relationships between variables. One consequence is that mean imputation generally yields biased regression coefficients and invalid inferences even when data are MCAR. In addition, by treating the missing data as if they were observed, mean imputation exaggerates the effective size of the data set, further distorting statistical inference—a deficiency that it shares with other simple imputation methods.

A more sophisticated approach, called *conditional-mean imputation*, replaces missing data with predicted values obtained, for example, from a regression equation (in which case the method is also called *regression imputation*). Using available data, we regress each variable with missing data on other variables in the data set; the resulting regression equation is used to produce predicted values that replace the missing data.[11] A problem with regression imputation is that the imputed observations tend to be less variable than real data because they lack residual variation; another problem is that we have failed to account for uncertainty in the estimation of the regression coefficients used to obtain the imputed values. The first of these problems can be addressed, for example, by adding a randomly sampled residual to each filled-in value. The second problem

---

[7]This is not a generally realistic assumption: Missingness on different variables is probably positively associated, producing a result not quite as dismal as the one described here. The general point is valid, however: With many variables subject to missing data, there are typically many fewer complete cases than valid observations on individual variables.

[8]This description is slightly ambiguous: In computing the covariance, for example, do we use the means for each variable computed from all valid data for that variable or (as is more common and as I have done in the example reported below) recompute the means for each pair using observations with valid data for both variables in the pair?

[9]An example is estimating the difference between the means of two highly correlated variables (as in a paired t-test): See Little and Rubin (1990, pp. 378–380).

[10]See Exercise 20.1.

[11]Because the predictor variables in each of these auxiliary regressions may themselves have missing data, the implementation of regression imputation can be complicated, requiring us to fit different regression equations for different patterns of missing information. The basic idea, however, is straightforward.

Table 20.1   Parameter Estimates Obtained by Several Methods of Handling Missing Data Under Different Conditions

	μ_1	μ_2	σ_1^2	σ_2^2	σ_{12}	ρ_{12}	β_{12}	β_{21}
Parameter	10.000	20.000	9.000	16.000	8.000	.667	0.500	0.889
Complete data (n = 250)								
Estimates	10.002	19.976	9.432	16.731	8.114	.646	0.485	0.860
MCAR data set								
Complete cases	10.210	20.400	9.768	17.114	7.673	.593	0.448	0.785
Available cases	10.002	20.400	9.432	17.114	7.673	.604	0.448	0.813
Mean imputation	10.002	20.400	9.432	10.241	4.591	.467	0.448	0.487
Regression imputation	10.002	20.237	9.432	12.454	7.409	.683	0.595	0.785
Maximum likelihood	10.002	20.237	9.394	16.809	7.379	.587	0.439	0.785
Multiple imputation	10.002	20.269	9.432	16.754	7.415	.590	0.443	0.786
MAR data set								
Complete cases	11.615	21.349	6.291	14.247	5.456	.576	0.383	0.867
Available cases	10.002	21.349	9.432	14.247	5.456	.508	0.383	0.578
Mean imputation	10.002	21.385	9.432	8.010	3.068	.353	0.383	0.325
Regression imputation	10.002	19.950	9.432	12.443	8.179	.755	0.657	0.867
Maximum likelihood	10.002	20.000	9.394	17.044	8.103	.640	0.475	0.863
Multiple imputation	10.002	19.914	9.432	17.493	8.342	.649	0.477	0.884
MNAR data set								
Complete cases	10.811	21.833	8.238	12.823	6.389	.622	0.498	0.776
Available cases	10.002	21.833	9.432	12.823	6.389	.581	0.498	0.677
Mean imputation	10.002	21.833	9.432	7.673	3.823	.449	0.498	0.405
Regression imputation	10.002	21.206	9.432	10.381	7.315	.739	0.705	0.776
Maximum likelihood	10.002	17.891	9.394	9.840	5.421	.564	0.551	0.577
Multiple imputation	10.002	21.257	9.432	13.167	7.154	.642	0.543	0.758

NOTES: The data were sampled from a bivariate-normal distribution with means, variances, and covariance as shown. The ML and multiple-imputation methods are described later in the chapter.

leads naturally to Bayesian multiple imputation of missing values, described below.[12] Regression imputation improves on unconditional mean imputation, but it is far from a perfect technique, generally providing biased estimates and invalid inferences even for missing data that are MCAR.

I applied several methods of handling missing data to the artificial data sets graphed in Figure 20.1 (page 551) and described in the preceding section. The results are shown in Table 20.1. Recall that the data for this example were sampled from a bivariate normal distribution (with parameters shown at the top of the table). Statistics for the complete data set of $n = 250$ observations are also shown (near the top of the table). Some of the results—for example, the equivalence of complete-case analysis, available-case analysis, and mean imputation for the slope coefficient B_{12} of the regression of X_1 (the completely observed variable) on X_2—are peculiar to univariate missing data.[13] Other characteristics are more general, such as the reasonable results produced

---

[12]See Section 20.4.
[13]See Exercise 20.2.

Table 20.2   Mean Parameter Estimates and Confidence-Interval Coverage for a Simulation Experiment With Data Missing at Random (MAR)

Parameter	Complete Cases	Mean Imputation	Regression Imputation	Multiple Imputation
Mean parameter estimate (RMSE)				
$\mu_1 = 10$	11.476	10.001	10.001	10.001
	(1.489)	(0.189)	(0.189)	(0.189)
$\mu_2 = 20$	21.222	21.322	20.008	20.008
	(1.355)	(1.355)	(0.326)	(0.344)
$\beta_{12} = 0.5$	0.391	0.391	0.645	0.498
	(0.117)	(0.117)	(0.151)	(0.041)
$\beta_{21} = 0.889$	0.891	0.353	0.891	0.890
	(0.100)	(0.538)	(0.100)	(0.106)
Confidence-interval coverage (mean interval width)				
μ_1	0	.951	.951	.951
	(0.792)	(0.750)	(0.750)	(0.746)
μ_2	.005	0	.823	.947
	(1.194)	(0.711)	(0.881)	(1.451)
β_{12}	.304	.629	.037	.955
	(0.174)	(0.246)	(0.140)	(0.175)
β_{21}	.953	0	.661	.939
	(0.396)	(0.220)	(0.191)	(0.463)

NOTES: The root-mean-square error (RMSE) of the parameter estimates is shown in parentheses below the mean estimates; the mean width of the confidence intervals is shown in parentheses below the coverage. Confidence intervals were constructed at a nominal level of .95.

by complete-case analysis when missingness does not depend on the response variable (i.e., for the coefficient β_{12} when data are MCAR, or, for this example, MNAR, and for the coefficient β_{21} when, again for this example, data are MAR). Note that ML estimation and multiple imputation are the only methods that provide uniformly good results for *all* parameters in *both* the MCAR and MAR data sets.

To illustrate further the properties of the various missing-data methods, I conducted a small simulation study, drawing 1,000 samples from the bivariate-normal distribution described above, producing from each sample a data set in which missing data were MAR, and applying complete-case analysis, unconditional-mean imputation, regression imputation, and Bayesian multiple imputation to each data set. The results are given in Table 20.2.[14] To simplify the table, I have not shown results for available-case analysis nor for ML estimation (which produces results similar to those for multiple imputation). In addition, I have focussed on the means and regression coefficients, which are the parameters that are usually of most direct interest.

Table 20.2 shows not only the average parameter estimates for each method (in the upper panel), which are useful for assessing bias, but also the RMSE of each estimator (i.e., the square root of the mean-square error, expressing the efficiency of the estimator), and (in the lower panel) the coverage and average interval width of nominally 95% confidence intervals for each method. If a confidence interval is valid, then the coverage should be close to .95. The results generally support the observations that I made above, and in particular, the only method that does uniformly

---

[14]Similar but more extensive simulations appear in Schafer and Graham (2002). Also see Exercise 20.3.

well for all parameters—producing unbiased estimates, valid confidence intervals, and relatively efficient estimates—is multiple imputation.

> Traditional methods of handling missing data include complete-case analysis, available-case analysis, and unconditional and conditional mean imputation. Complete-case analysis produces consistent estimates and valid statistical inferences when data are MCAR (and in certain other special circumstances), but even in this advantageous situation, it does not use information in the sample efficiently. The other traditional methods suffer from more serious problems.

20.3 Maximum-Likelihood Estimation for Data Missing at Random*

The method of ML can be applied to parameter estimation in the presence of missing data. Doing so requires making assumptions about the distribution of the complete data and about the process producing missing data. If the assumptions hold, then the resulting ML estimates have their usual optimal properties, such as consistency and asymptotic efficiency.[15]

Let $p(\mathbf{X}; \theta) = p(\mathbf{X}_{obs}, \mathbf{X}_{mis}; \theta)$ represent the joint probability density for the complete data $\mathbf{X}$, which as before, is composed of observed and missing components denoted, respectively, as $\mathbf{X}_{obs}$ and $\mathbf{X}_{mis}$. The vector θ contains the unknown parameters on which the complete-data distribution depends. For example, if the variables in $\mathbf{X}$ are multivariately normally distributed (a case that I will examine presently), then θ includes the population means and covariances among the variables.

In a seminal paper on statistical methods for missing data—the same paper in which he introduced distinctions among data that are MCAR, MAR, and MNAR—Rubin (1976) showed that the MLs estimate $\widehat{\theta}$ of θ can be obtained from the marginal distribution of the observed data, *if data are missing at random*. In the general case that I am considering here, we can find the marginal distribution for the observed data by integrating over the missing data, producing

$$p(\mathbf{X}_{obs}; \theta) = \int p(\mathbf{X}_{obs}, \mathbf{X}_{mis}; \theta) d\mathbf{X}_{mis}$$

Although it may be difficult to apply this result directly, simplification is possible in certain cases. Moreover, as I will explain shortly, it is, as a practical matter, possible to find $\widehat{\theta}$ in the general case by iterative techniques.[16] As usual, the likelihood function $L(\theta; \mathbf{X}_{obs})$ is the same as the probability density function for the data but treats the observed data as fixed and the unknown parameters as variable. Once we have found the ML parameter estimates $\widehat{\theta}$, we can proceed with statistical inference in the usual manner; for example, we can compute likelihood-ratio tests of nested models and construct Wald tests or confidence intervals for the elements of θ based on estimated asymptotic variances for $\widehat{\theta}$ obtained from the inverse of the observed information matrix

$$\mathcal{I}(\theta; \mathbf{X}_{obs}) = -\frac{\partial^2 \log_e L(\theta; \mathbf{X}_{obs})}{\partial \theta \partial \theta'}$$

---

[15]For a general introduction to the method of ML, see Appendix D on probability and estimation.
[16]See Section 20.3.1 on the expectation maximization (EM) algorithm.

Consider, for example, bivariately normally distributed variables X_1 and X_2; as in the previous section, X_1 is completely observed in a sample of n observations, but X_2 has $m < n$ observations missing at random, which for notational convenience, I will take as the first m observations.[17] Then, from the univariate normal distribution,

$$p_1(x_{i1}; \mu_1, \sigma_1^2) = \frac{1}{\sigma_1\sqrt{2\pi}} \exp\left[-\frac{(x_{i1} - \mu_1)^2}{2\sigma_1^2}\right]$$

is the marginal probability density for observation i on variable X_1; and, from the bivariate-normal distribution,

$$p_{12}(x_{i1}, x_{i2}; \mu_1, \mu_2, \sigma_1^2, \sigma_2^2, \sigma_{12}) = \frac{1}{2\pi\sqrt{\det \boldsymbol{\Sigma}}} \exp\left[-\frac{1}{2}(\mathbf{x}_i - \boldsymbol{\mu})' \boldsymbol{\Sigma}^{-1} (\mathbf{x}_i - \boldsymbol{\mu})\right] \quad (20.3)$$

is the joint probability density for observation i on variables X_1 and X_2. In Equation 20.3, $\mathbf{x}_i \equiv (x_{i1}, x_{i2})'$ is a vector giving a pair of values for X_{i1} and X_{i2}; $\boldsymbol{\mu} \equiv (\mu_1, \mu_2)'$ is the vector of means for the two variables; and

$$\boldsymbol{\Sigma} \equiv \begin{bmatrix} \sigma_1^2 & \sigma_{12} \\ \sigma_{12} & \sigma_2^2 \end{bmatrix}$$

is their covariance matrix. Using results in Little and Rubin (1990, pp. 382–383; 2002, chap. 7), the log-likelihood for the observed data is

$$\log_e L(\mu_1, \mu_2, \sigma_1^2, \sigma_2^2, \sigma_{12}) = \sum_{i=1}^{m} \log_e p_1(x_{i1}; \mu_1, \sigma_1^2)$$

$$+ \sum_{i=m+1}^{n} \log_e p_{12}(x_{i1}, x_{i2}; \mu_1, \mu_2, \sigma_1^2, \sigma_2^2, \sigma_{12}) \quad (20.4)$$

The log-likelihood in Equation 20.4 can easily be maximized numerically, but there is also a simple analytic solution. The statistics

$$\overline{X}_1^* \equiv \frac{\sum_{i=m+1}^{n} X_{i1}}{n - m} \quad (20.5)$$

$$\overline{X}_2^* \equiv \frac{\sum_{i=m+1}^{n} X_{i2}}{n - m}$$

$$S_1^{2*} \equiv \frac{\sum_{i=m+1}^{n} \left(X_{i1} - \overline{X}_1^*\right)^2}{n - m}$$

$$S_2^{2*} \equiv \frac{\sum_{i=m+1}^{n} \left(X_{i2} - \overline{X}_2^*\right)^2}{n - m}$$

$$S_{12}^* \equiv \frac{\sum_{i=m+1}^{n} \left(X_{i1} - \overline{X}_1^*\right)\left(X_{i2} - \overline{X}_2^*\right)}{n - m}$$

---

[17]This is the univariate pattern of missing data employed in the examples of the preceding sections.

are the means, variances, and covariance for the two variables computed from the $n - m$ complete cases, and

$$\overline{X}_1 \equiv \frac{\sum_{i=1}^n X_{i1}}{n}$$

$$S_1^2 \equiv \frac{\sum_{i=1}^n \left(X_{i1} - \overline{X}_1\right)^2}{n}$$

are the mean and variance of X_1 computed from all n available cases.[18] The ML estimators of the parameters of the bivariate-normal model are

$$\widehat{\mu}_1 = \overline{X}_1 \tag{20.6}$$

$$\widehat{\mu}_2 = \overline{X}_2^* + \frac{S_{12}^*}{S_1^{2*}} \left(\overline{X}_1 - \overline{X}_1^*\right)$$

$$\widehat{\sigma}_1^2 = S_1^2$$

$$\widehat{\sigma}_2^2 = S_2^{2*} + \left(\frac{S_{12}^*}{S_1^{2*}}\right)^2 \left(S_1^2 - S_1^{2*}\right)$$

$$\widehat{\sigma}_{12} = S_{12}^* \left(\frac{S_1^2}{S_1^{2*}}\right)$$

Note that the ML estimates combine information from the complete-case and available-case statistics.[19]

> The method of ML can be applied to parameter estimation in the presence of missing data. If the assumptions made concerning the distribution of the complete data and the process generating missing data hold, then ML estimates have their usual optimal properties, such as consistency and asymptotic efficiency. When data are MAR, the ML estimate $\widehat{\theta}$ of the parameters θ of the complete-data distribution can be obtained from the marginal distribution of the observed data, integrating over the missing data:
>
> $$p(\mathbf{X}_{\text{obs}}; \theta) = \int p(\mathbf{X}_{\text{obs}}, \mathbf{X}_{\text{mis}}; \theta) d\mathbf{X}_{\text{mis}}$$
>
> Although it may be difficult to apply this result directly, simplification is possible in certain cases. Once we have found the ML parameter estimates, we can proceed with statistical inference in the usual manner, for example, computing likelihood-ratio tests of nested models and constructing Wald tests or confidence intervals.

20.3.1   The EM Algorithm

Arbitrary patterns of missing data do not yield simple expressions for the log-likelihood (such as in Equation 20.4 on page 557 for a univariate missing-data pattern in bivariate-normal data)

---

[18]Note that the denominators for the variances and covariance are the number of observations, $n - m$ or n, rather than degrees of freedom $n - m - 1$ or $n - 1$. Recall that ML estimators of variance are biased but consistent. (See Appendix D on probability and estimation.)

[19]See Exercise 20.4 for further interpretation of the ML estimators in Equation 20.6.

nor closed-form equations for the ML estimates (such as in Equation 20.6). The *expectation-maximization (EM)* algorithm, due to Dempster, Laird, and Rubin (1977), is a general iterative method for finding ML estimates in the presence of arbitrary patterns missing data. Although the EM algorithm is broadly applicable, generally easy to implement, and effective, it has the disadvantage that it does not produce the information matrix and therefore does not yield standard errors for the estimated parameters. The version of the EM algorithm that I will describe here is for ignorable missing data (and is adapted from Little & Rubin, 2002, chaps. 8 and 11). The algorithm can also be applied to problems for which data are MNAR and hence are nonignorable.[20]

As before, let $\mathbf{X}$ represent the complete data, composed of the observed data $\mathbf{X}_{obs}$ and the missing data $\mathbf{X}_{mis}$. The likelihood based on the complete data is $L(\boldsymbol{\theta}; \mathbf{X})$, where recall, $\boldsymbol{\theta}$ contains the parameters for the distribution of $\mathbf{X}$. Let $\boldsymbol{\theta}^{(l)}$ represent the parameter estimates at the lth iteration of the EM algorithm. Starting values $\boldsymbol{\theta}^{(0)}$ may be obtained from the complete cases, for example. Each iteration of the EM algorithm comprises two steps: an *E (expectation) step* and an *M (maximization) step*. Hence the name "EM."

- In the E step, we find the expectation of the complete-data log-likelihood, integrating over the missing data, given the observed data and the current estimates of the parameters:

$$E\left[\log_e L(\boldsymbol{\theta}; \mathbf{X})|\boldsymbol{\theta}^{(l)}\right] = \int \log_e L(\boldsymbol{\theta}; \mathbf{X}) p\left(\mathbf{X}_{mis}|\mathbf{X}_{obs}, \boldsymbol{\theta}^{(l)}\right) d\mathbf{X}_{mis}$$

- In the M step, we find the values $\boldsymbol{\theta}^{(l+1)}$ of $\boldsymbol{\theta}$ that maximize the expected log-likelihood $E\left[\log_e L(\boldsymbol{\theta}; \mathbf{X})|\boldsymbol{\theta}^{(l)}\right]$; these are the parameter estimates for the next iteration.

When the parameter values stop changing from one iteration to the next (to an acceptable tolerance), they converge to the ML estimates $\widehat{\boldsymbol{\theta}}$.

Suppose, for example, that the complete data $\mathbf{X}$, consisting of n observations on p variables, is multivariately normally distributed, with mean vector $\boldsymbol{\mu}$ and covariance matrix $\boldsymbol{\Sigma}$. The sums and sums of squares and cross-products of the variables are a set of sufficient statistics for these parameters:

$$T_j \equiv \sum_{i=1}^{n} X_{ij} \text{ for } j = 1, \ldots, p$$

$$T_{jj'} \equiv \sum_{i=1}^{n} X_{ij} X_{ij'} \text{ for } j, j' = 1, \ldots, p$$

Had we access to the complete data, then the ML estimates of the parameters could be computed from the sufficient statistics:

$$\widehat{\mu}_j = \frac{T_j}{n}$$

$$\widehat{\sigma}_{jj'} = \frac{T_{jj'}}{n} - \widehat{\mu}_j \widehat{\mu}_{j'}$$

(where the estimated variance of X_j is $\widehat{\sigma}_j^2 = \widehat{\sigma}_{jj}$).

Now, imagine that some of the data in $\mathbf{X}$ are MAR but in an arbitrary pattern. Then, in the E step we find expected sums and sums of products by filling in the missing data with their conditional expected values, given the observed data and current estimates of the parameters. That is,

---

[20]See, for example, Little and Rubin (2002, chap. 15).

$$E\left(T_j|\mathbf{X}_{\text{obs}}, \boldsymbol{\mu}^{(l-1)}, \boldsymbol{\Sigma}^{(l-1)}\right) = \sum_{i=1}^{n} X_{ij}^{(l)}$$

$$E\left(T_{jj'}|\mathbf{X}_{\text{obs}}, \boldsymbol{\mu}^{(l-1)}, \boldsymbol{\Sigma}^{(l-1)}\right) = \sum_{i=1}^{n} \left(X_{ij}^{(l)} X_{ij'}^{(l)} + C_{ijj'}^{(l)}\right)$$

where

$$X_{ij}^{(l)} = \begin{cases} X_{ij} & \text{if } X_{ij} \text{ is observed} \\ E\left(X_{ij}|\mathbf{X}_{\text{obs}}, \boldsymbol{\mu}^{(l-1)}, \boldsymbol{\Sigma}^{(l-1)}\right) & \text{if } X_{ij} \text{ is missing} \end{cases}$$

and

$$C_{ijj'}^{(l)} = \begin{cases} 0 & \text{if } \textit{either } X_{ij} \text{ or } X_{ij'} \text{ is observed} \\ C\left(X_{ij}, X_{ij'}|\mathbf{X}_{\text{obs}}, \boldsymbol{\mu}^{(l-1)}, \boldsymbol{\Sigma}^{(l-1)}\right) & \text{if } \textit{both } X_{ij} \text{ and } X_{ij'} \text{ are missing} \end{cases} \tag{20.7}$$

Finally, $E\left(X_{ij}|\mathbf{X}_{\text{obs}}, \boldsymbol{\mu}^{(l)}, \boldsymbol{\Sigma}^{(l)}\right)$ is obtained as the fitted value from the regression of X_j on the other Xs, using the current estimates $\boldsymbol{\mu}^{(l)}$ and $\boldsymbol{\Sigma}^{(l)}$ to obtain the regression coefficients; and $C\left(X_{ij}, X_{ij'}|\mathbf{X}_{\text{obs}}, \boldsymbol{\mu}^{(l)}, \boldsymbol{\Sigma}^{(l)}\right)$ is the covariance of the fitted values for X_{ij} and $X_{ij'}$ obtained from the multivariate regression of X_j and $X_{j'}$ on the other Xs, again at current values of the parameters.[21]

Once we have the expected sums and sums of cross-products, the M step is straightforward:

$$\mu_j^{(l)} = \frac{\sum_{i=1}^{n} X_{ij}^{(l)}}{n}$$

$$\sigma_{jj'}^{(l)} = \frac{\sum_{i=1}^{n} \left(X_{ij}^{(l)} X_{ij'}^{(l)} + C_{ijj'}^{(l)}\right)}{n} - \mu_j^{(l)} \mu_{j'}^{(l)}$$

Consider the comparatively simple case of bivariate-normal data where the variable X_1 is completely observed and the first m of n observations on X_2 are missing. Take as starting values the means, variances, and covariance computed from the $n-m$ complete cases (given in Equation 20.5 on page 557). Then, because X_1 is completely observed,

$$E\left(T_1|\mathbf{X}_{\text{obs}}, \boldsymbol{\mu}^{(0)}, \boldsymbol{\Sigma}^{(0)}\right) = \sum_{i=1}^{n} X_{i1} \tag{20.8}$$

$$E\left(T_{11}|\mathbf{X}_{\text{obs}}, \boldsymbol{\mu}^{(0)}, \boldsymbol{\Sigma}^{(0)}\right) = \sum_{i=1}^{n} X_{i1}^2$$

and, for sums involving X_2, which has m missing values,

$$E\left(T_2|\mathbf{X}_{\text{obs}}, \boldsymbol{\mu}^{(0)}, \boldsymbol{\Sigma}^{(0)}\right) = \sum_{i=1}^{m} \widehat{X}_{i2} + \sum_{i=m+1}^{n} X_{i2} \tag{20.9}$$

$$E\left(T_{22}|\mathbf{X}_{\text{obs}}, \boldsymbol{\mu}^{(0)}, \boldsymbol{\Sigma}^{(0)}\right) = \sum_{i=1}^{m} \left(\widehat{X}_{i2}^2 + S_{2|1}^{2(0)}\right) + \sum_{i=m+1}^{n} X_{i2}^2$$

$$E\left(T_{12}|\mathbf{X}_{\text{obs}}, \boldsymbol{\mu}^{(0)}, \boldsymbol{\Sigma}^{(0)}\right) = \sum_{i=1}^{m} \left(X_{i1} \widehat{X}_{i2}^2\right) + \sum_{i=m+1}^{n} X_{i1} X_{i2}$$

---

[21] In multivariate regression there is more than one response variable. In the current context, the role of the response variables is played by X_j and $X_{j'}$. See Section 9.5 and Exercise 20.5.

where $\widehat{X}_{i2}$ is the fitted value from the complete-case regression of X_2 on X_1, and $S_{2|1}^{2(0)}$ is the residual variance from this regression. The M-step estimates computed from these expectations are just the ML estimates previously given in Equation 20.6.[22] That is, in the simple case of monotone missing data, the EM algorithm converges to the ML estimates in a single iteration.

The EM algorithm is a general iterative procedure for finding ML estimates—but not their standard errors—in the presence of arbitrary patterns of missing data. When data are MAR, iteration l of the EM algorithm consists of two steps: (1) In the E (expectation) step, we find the expectation of the complete-data log-likelihood, integrating over the missing data, given the observed data and the current estimates of the parameters:

$$E\left[\log_e L(\boldsymbol{\theta}; \mathbf{X})|\boldsymbol{\theta}^{(l)}\right] = \int \log_e L(\boldsymbol{\theta}; \mathbf{X}) p\left(\mathbf{X}_{\text{mis}}|\mathbf{X}_{\text{obs}}, \boldsymbol{\theta}^{(l)}\right) d\mathbf{X}_{\text{mis}}$$

(2) In the M (maximization) step, we find the values $\boldsymbol{\theta}^{(l+1)}$ of $\boldsymbol{\theta}$ that maximize the expected log-likelihood $E\left[\log_e L(\boldsymbol{\theta}; \mathbf{X})|\boldsymbol{\theta}^{(l)}\right]$; these are the parameter estimates for the next iteration. At convergence, the EM algorithm produces the ML estimates $\widehat{\boldsymbol{\theta}}$ of $\boldsymbol{\theta}$.

20.4 Bayesian Multiple Imputation

Bayesian multiple imputation (abbreviated as *MI*) is a flexible and general method for dealing with data that are MAR. Like ML estimation, multiple imputation begins with a specification of the distribution of the complete data (assumed to be known except for a set of parameters to be estimated from the data).

The essential idea of multiple imputation is to reflect the uncertainty associated with missing data by imputing *several* values for each missing value, each imputed value drawn from the *predictive distribution* of the missing data and, therefore, producing not one but several completed data sets. Standard methods of statistical analysis are then applied in parallel to the completed data sets. Parameters of interest are estimated along with their standard errors for each imputed data set. Estimated parameters are then averaged across completed data sets; standard errors are also combined across imputed data sets, taking into account the variation among the estimates in the several data sets, thereby capturing the added uncertainty due to having to impute the missing data.

A multivariate-normal model for the complete data is both relatively simple and useful in applications. Indeed, because the model assumed to describe the complete data is used just to obtain imputed values for the missing data, it turns out that the method of multiple imputation is usually not terribly sensitive to the assumption of multivariate normality.[23]

Suppose that X_1 and X_2 are bivariately normally distributed and that, as in previously developed examples, there is a univariate pattern of missing data, with X_1 completely observed and m of the n observations on X_2 MAR. For convenience, and again as before, let us order the data so that the missing observations on X_2 are the first m observations. Let $A_{2|1}^*$ and $B_{2|1}^*$ represent the

---

[22] See Exercise 20.6.
[23] See, for example, Schafer (1997, chap. 5). As described in Section 20.4.3, however, there are some pitfalls to be avoided.

intercept and slope for the complete-case least-squares regression of X_2 on X_1.[24] In regression imputation, recall, we replace the missing values with the fitted values

$$\widehat{X}_{i2} = A_{2|1}^* + B_{2|1}^* X_{i1} \qquad (20.10)$$

Recall as well that a defect of this procedure is that it ignores residual variation in X_2 conditional on X_1. A more sophisticated version of regression imputation adds a randomly generated residual to the fitted value, taking the imputed value as $\widehat{X}_{i2} + E_{i2|1}$, where $E_{i2|1}$ is drawn randomly from the normal distribution $N(0, S_{2|1}^{*2})$, and where

$$S_{2|1}^{*2} \equiv \frac{\sum_{i=m+1}^{n}(X_{i2} - \widehat{X}_{i2})^2}{n - m}$$

is the ML estimator of the residual variance of X_2 given X_1 (based on the $n - m$ complete cases).

There is still a problem, however: The fitted values and generated residuals on which the imputations are based fail to take into account the fact that the regression coefficients $A_{2|1}^*$ and $B_{2|1}^*$ and the residual variance $S_{2|1}^{*2}$ are themselves *estimates* that are subject to sampling variation. MI draws values of the regression parameters and the error variance—let us call these values $\widetilde{\alpha}_{2|1}$, $\widetilde{\beta}_{2|1}$, and $\widetilde{\sigma}_{2|1}^2$—from the *posterior distribution* of the parameters, typically assuming a *noninformative prior distribution*.[25]

As Little and Rubin (1990, pp. 386–387) explain, we may proceed as follows:

1. Given a random draw Z^2 from the chi-square distribution with $n - m - 2$ degrees of freedom, find

$$\widetilde{\sigma}_{2|1}^2 \equiv \frac{\sum_{i=m+1}^{n}(X_{i2} - \widehat{X}_{i2})^2}{Z^2}$$

2. With $\widetilde{\sigma}_{2|1}^2$ in hand, draw a random slope $\widetilde{\beta}_{2|1}$ from the normal distribution

$$N\left(B_{2|1}^*, \frac{\widetilde{\sigma}_{2|1}^2}{\left[(n - m)S_1^2 \right]^2} \right)$$

   Here, $S_1^2 \equiv \sum_{i=1}^{n}(X_{i1} - \overline{X}_1)^2/n$ is the ML estimate of the variance of X_1, and $\overline{X}_1 \equiv \sum_{i=1}^{n} X_{i1}/n$ is the ML estimate of the mean of X_1, based on all n cases.

3. Using the previously obtained values of $\widetilde{\sigma}_{2|1}^2$ and $\widetilde{\beta}_{2|1}$, draw a random intercept $\widetilde{\alpha}_{2|1}$ from the normal distribution

$$N\left(\widehat{\mu}_2 - \widetilde{\beta}_{2|1}\overline{X}_1, \frac{\widetilde{\sigma}_{2|1}^2}{(n - m)^2} \right)$$

   where $\widehat{\mu}_2$ is the ML estimate of the mean of X_2 (given in Equation 20.6 on page 558).

4. Finally, replace the missing values in X_2 by

$$\widetilde{X}_{i2} \equiv \widetilde{\alpha}_{2|1} + \widetilde{\beta}_{2|1} X_{i1} + \widetilde{E}_i$$

   where $\widetilde{E}_i$ is sampled from $N(0, \widetilde{\sigma}_{2|1}^2)$.

In multiple imputation, this procedure is repeated g times, producing g completed data sets.

---

[24]The results of the preceding section imply that $A_{2|1}^*$ and $B_{2|1}^*$ are the ML estimators of $\alpha_{2|1}$ and $\beta_{2|1}$. See Exercise 20.6.

[25]Think of the posterior distribution of the parameters as capturing our uncertainty about the values of the parameters. Basic concepts of Bayesian statistical inference, including the notions of prior and posterior distributions, are described in Appendix D on probability and estimation.

More generally, we have a complete data set $\mathbf{X}$ comprising n cases and p multivariately normally distributed variables; some of the entries of $\mathbf{X}$ are MAR in an arbitrary pattern. In this more general case, there is no fully adequate closed-form procedure for sampling from the predictive distribution of the data to impute missing values. Instead, simulation methods must be employed to obtain imputations. Two such methods are data augmentation (described in Schafer, 1997) and importance sampling (described in King, Honaker, Joseph, & Scheve, 2001).[26] Multiple imputation can be extended beyond the multivariate-normal distribution to other models for the complete data, such as the multinomial distribution for a set of categorical variables, and mixed multinomial-normal models for data sets containing both quantitative and categorical data.[27]

20.4.1 Inference for Individual Coefficients

Having obtained g completed data sets, imagine that we have analyzed the data sets in parallel, producing g sets of regression coefficients, $B_0^{(l)}, B_1^{(l)}, \ldots, B_k^{(l)}$ for $l = 1, \ldots, g$ (where, for notational convenience, I have represented the regression constant as B_0). We also find the coefficient standard errors, $\text{SE}(B_0^{(l)}), \text{SE}(B_1^{(l)}), \ldots, \text{SE}(B_k^{(l)})$, computed in the usual manner for each completed data set. Rubin (1987) provides simple rules for combining information across multiple imputations of the missing data, rules that are valid as long as the sample size is sufficiently large for the separate estimates to be approximately normally distributed. The context here is quite general: The regression coefficients and their standard errors might be produced by linear least-squares regression, but they might also be produced by ML estimation of a logistic-regression model, by nonlinear least squares, or by *any* parametric method of regression analysis.

Point estimates of the population regression coefficients are obtained by averaging across imputations:

$$\widetilde{\beta}_j \equiv \frac{\sum_{l=1}^{g} B_j^{(l)}}{g} \tag{20.11}$$

The standard errors of the estimated coefficients are obtained by combining information about within- and between-imputation variation in the coefficients:

$$\widetilde{\text{SE}}(\widetilde{\beta}_j) \equiv \sqrt{V_j^{(W)} + \frac{g+1}{g} V_j^{(B)}} \tag{20.12}$$

where the within-imputation component is

$$V_j^{(W)} \equiv \frac{\sum_{l=1}^{g} \text{SE}^2\left(B_j^{(l)}\right)}{g}$$

---

[26]General descriptions of these methods are beyond the scope of this chapter. Multiple imputation by data augmentation is implemented in Schafer's software, available for SAS, S-PLUS, R, and in stand-alone programs. Multiple imputation by importance sampling is implemented in King's software, available for R and in a stand-alone program. Raghunathan, Lepkowski, Van Hoewyk, and Solenberger (2001) and van Buuren and Oudshoorn (1999) suggest a simpler approach that cycles iteratively through a set of regression equations for the variables containing missing data. The formal properties of this approach have not been established, though it appears to work well in practice. The approach is implemented in the IVEware (imputation and variance estimation) software for SAS, as a stand-alone program and in the MICE (multivariate imputation by chained equations) software for S-PLUS and R, and in a stand-alone program. Access to convenient software for multiple imputation is important because the method is computationally intensive.

[27]See, for example, Schafer (1997, chaps. 7–9).

and the between-imputation component is

$$V_j^{(B)} \equiv \frac{\sum_{l=1}^{g}\left(B_j^{(l)} - \widetilde{\beta}_j\right)^2}{g-1}$$

Inference based on $\widetilde{\beta}_j$ and $\widetilde{\mathrm{SE}}(\widetilde{\beta}_j)$ uses the t-distribution, with degrees of freedom determined by

$$df_j = (g-1)\left(1 + \frac{g}{g+1} \times \frac{V_j^{(W)}}{V_j^{(B)}}\right)^2$$

For example, to construct a 95% confidence interval for β_j,

$$\beta_j = \widetilde{\beta}_j \pm t_{.025,df_j} \widetilde{\mathrm{SE}}(\widetilde{\beta}_j)$$

Let γ_j denote the relative amount of information about the parameter β_j that is missing. This is not quite the same as the fraction of observations that are missing on the explanatory variable X_j because, unless X_j is uncorrelated with the other variables in the data set, there will be information in the data relevant to imputing the missing values and because data missing on one variable influence all the regression estimates. The *estimated rate of missing information* is

$$\widehat{\gamma}_j = \frac{R_j}{R_j + 1} \tag{20.13}$$

where

$$R_j \equiv \frac{g+1}{g} \times \frac{V_j^{(B)}}{V_j^{(W)}}$$

The efficiency of the multiple-imputation estimator relative to the maximally efficient ML estimator—that is, the ratio of sampling variances of the ML estimator to the MI estimator—is $\mathrm{RE}(\widetilde{\beta}_j) = g/(g + \gamma_j)$. If the number of imputations g is infinite, MI is therefore as efficient as ML; but even when the rate of missing information is quite high and the number of imputations modest, the relative efficiency of the MI estimator hardly suffers. Suppose, for example, that $\gamma_j = 0.5$ (a high rate of missing information) and that $g = 5$; then $\mathrm{RE}(\widetilde{\beta}_j) = 5/(5+0.5) = 0.91$. Expressed on the scale of the standard error of $\widetilde{\beta}_j$, which is proportional to the length of the confidence interval for β_j, we have $\sqrt{\mathrm{RE}(\widetilde{\beta}_j)} = 0.95$.[28]

Bayesian multiple imputation (MI) is a flexible and general method for dealing with data that are missing at random. The essential idea of multiple imputation is to reflect the uncertainty associated with missing data by imputing g values for each missing value, drawing each imputed value from the predictive distribution of the missing data (a process that usually requires simulation), and therefore producing not one but g completed data sets. Standard methods of statistical analysis are then applied in parallel to the completed data sets.

---

[28] See Exercise 20.7.

- According to Rubin's rules, MI estimates (e.g., of a population regression coefficient β_j) are obtained by averaging over the imputed data sets:

$$\widetilde{\beta}_j = \frac{\sum_{l=1}^{g} B_j^{(l)}}{g}$$

where $B_j^{(l)}$ is the estimate of β_j from imputed data set l.
- Standard errors of the estimated coefficients are obtained by combining information about within- and between-imputation variation in the coefficients,

$$\widetilde{SE}(\widetilde{\beta}_j) = \sqrt{V_j^{(W)} + \frac{g+1}{g} V_j^{(B)}}$$

where the within-imputation component is

$$V_j^{(W)} = \frac{\sum_{l=1}^{g} SE^2\left(B_j^{(l)}\right)}{g}$$

and the between-imputation component is

$$V_j^{(B)} = \frac{\sum_{l=1}^{g} \left(B_j^{(l)} - \widetilde{\beta}_j\right)^2}{g-1}$$

Here, $SE\left(B_j^{(l)}\right)$ is the standard error of B_j computed in the usual manner for the lth imputed data set.
- Inference based on $\widetilde{\beta}_j$ and $\widetilde{SE}(\widetilde{\beta}_j)$ uses the t-distribution, with degrees of freedom determined by

$$df_j = (g-1)\left(1 + \frac{g}{g+1} \times \frac{V_j^{(W)}}{V_j^{(B)}}\right)^2$$

Inference for several coefficients proceeds in a similar, if more complex, manner.

20.4.2 Inference for Several Coefficients*

The generalization of Rubin's rules to simultaneous tests or confidence regions for several coefficients entails some complications.[29] Suppose that we wish to test the hypothesis $H_0: \beta_1 = \beta_0$, where $\underset{(s \times 1)}{\beta_1}$ is a subset of $s > 1$ of the $k + 1$ elements of the parameter vector β; typically,

---

[29]The results that I give here, and alternative procedures, are explained in greater detail in Rubin (1987, chaps. 3 and 4) and in Schafer (1997, sec. 4.3.3).

this would be the hypothesis H_0: $\beta_1 = \mathbf{0}$. Were it not for the missing data, we could base the hypothesis test on the Wald chi-square statistic,

$$Z_0^2 = (\mathbf{b}_1 - \beta_0)'\widehat{\mathcal{V}}^{-1}(\mathbf{b}_1)(\mathbf{b}_1 - \beta_0)$$

where the vector $\mathbf{b}_1$ contains the estimated coefficients and $\widehat{\mathcal{V}}(\mathbf{b}_1)$ is the estimated asymptotic covariance matrix of $\mathbf{b}_1$.[30]

In the present context, we have estimates for several completed data sets in which the missing data have been imputed, and so we first average the estimates, obtaining

$$\tilde{\beta}_1 \equiv \frac{1}{g} \sum_{l=1}^{g} \mathbf{b}_1^{(l)}$$

Then we compute the between- and within-imputation components of the covariance matrix of these estimates:

$$\mathbf{V}^{(W)} \equiv \frac{1}{g} \sum_{l=1}^{g} \widehat{\mathcal{V}}\left(\mathbf{b}_1^{(g)}\right)$$

$$\mathbf{V}^{(B)} \equiv \frac{1}{g-1} \sum_{l=1}^{g} \left(\mathbf{b}_1^{(g)} - \tilde{\beta}_1\right)\left(\mathbf{b}_1^{(g)} - \tilde{\beta}_1\right)'$$

In analogy to the single-coefficient case, we could compute the total covariance matrix

$$\mathbf{V} \equiv \mathbf{V}^{(W)} + \frac{g+1}{g}\mathbf{V}^{(B)}$$

Basing a test on $\mathbf{V}$, however, turns out to be complicated.

Instead, simplification of the problem leads to the test statistic

$$F_0 \equiv \frac{(\tilde{\beta}_1 - \beta_0)'\left(\mathbf{V}^{(W)}\right)^{-1}(\tilde{\beta}_1 - \beta_0)'}{s(1+R)}$$

where

$$R \equiv \frac{g+1}{g} \times \frac{\text{trace}\left[\mathbf{V}^{(B)}\left(\mathbf{V}^{(W)}\right)^{-1}\right]}{s}$$

The test statistic F_0 follows an approximate F-distribution, with s degrees of freedom in the numerator and denominator degrees of freedom given by

$$df = \begin{cases} 4 + [s(g-1) - 4]\left[1 + \frac{1}{R} \times \frac{s(g-1)-2}{s(g-1)}\right] & \text{when } s(g-1) > 4 \\[4mm] \frac{1}{2}(g-1)(s+1)\left(1 + \frac{1}{R}\right)^2 & \text{when } s(g-1) \leq 4 \end{cases}$$

---

[30]See, for example, the discussion of Wald tests for generalized linear models in Section 15.3.3.

20.4.3 Practical Considerations

Although the multivariate-normal model can prove remarkably useful in providing multiple imputations even when the data are not normally distributed, multiple imputation cannot preserve features of the data that are not represented in the imputation model. How essential it is to preserve particular features of the data depends on the statistical model used to analyze the multiply imputed data sets. It is therefore important in formulating an imputation model to insure that the imputation model is consistent with the intended analysis. The following points should assist in this endeavor:

- *Try to include variables in the imputation model that make the assumption of ignorable missingness reasonable.* Think of imputation as a pure prediction problem, not as a statistical model subject to substantive interpretation. If we are able to do a good job of predicting missing values (and missingness), then the assumption that data are MAR is more credible. Finding variables that are highly correlated with a variable that has missing data, but for which data are available, therefore, will likely improve the quality of imputations, as will variables that are related to missingness. In particular, it is perfectly acceptable, and indeed desirable, to include variables in the imputation model that *are not used* in the subsequent statistical analysis, alongside the variables that are used in the data analysis.[31] There is also nothing wrong with using the variable that is ultimately to be treated as a response to help impute missing data in variables that are to be treated as explanatory variables. To reiterate, the model used for imputation is essentially a prediction model—not a model to be interpreted substantively.
- *If possible, transform variables to approximate normality.*[32] After the imputed data are obtained, the variables can be transformed back to their original scales, if desired, prior to analyzing the completed data sets.
- *Adjust the imputed data to resemble the original data.* For example, imputed values of an integer-valued variable can be rounded to the nearest integer. Ordinal variables can be handled by providing integer codes and then rounding the imputed values to integers. Occasional negative imputed values of a non-negative variable can be set to zero. Imputed values of a 0/1 dummy variable can be set to 0 if less than or equal to 0.5 and to 1 if greater than 0.5. These steps may not be necessary to analyze the imputed data, but they should not hurt in any event.
- *Make sure that the imputation model captures relevant features of the data.* What is relevant depends on the use to which the imputed data will be put. For example, the multivariate-normal distribution ensures that regressions of one variable on others are linear and additive. Using the multivariate-normal distribution for imputations, therefore, will not preserve *nonlinear* relationships and *interactions* among the variables, unless we make special provision for these features of the data.

Suppose, for example, that we are interested in modeling the potential interaction between gender and education in determining income. Because gender is likely completely observed, but there may well be missing data on both education and income, we could divide the data set into two parts based on gender, obtaining multiply imputed data sets separately for each part and combining them in our analysis of the completed data sets. This approach runs into problems, however, if we find it necessary to divide the data set into too many parts or if the categorical variable or variables used to partition the data are themselves not completely observed.

---

[31]See Collins, Schafer, and Kam (2001), who present evidence supporting what they term an *inclusive strategy* for formulating imputation models.

[32]The material in Section 4.2 on transformations for symmetry and in Section 4.6 on Box-Cox transformations for multivariate normality is particularly relevant here.

Allison (2002) suggests forming interaction regressors and polynomial regressors as part of the data set to which the imputation model is applied. The imputed interaction and polynomial regressors are then used in the analysis of the completed data sets. Although such variables are not normally distributed, there is some evidence that multiple imputation based on the multivariate-normal model nevertheless works well in these circumstances.

Although, as explained, the multivariate-normal model can be used to impute a dummy regressor for a dichotomous factor, it is not obvious how to proceed with a polytomous factor. Allison (2002) proposes the following procedure: For an m-category factor, select an arbitrary baseline category (say the last), and code $m - 1$ dummy regressors,[33] including these dummy variables in the multiple-imputation process. From the imputed values for the ith observation in the lth imputation, $D_{i1}^{(l)}, D_{i2}^{(l)}, \ldots, D_{i,m-1}^{(l)}$, compute $D_{im}^{(l)} = 1 - \sum_{j=1}^{m-1} D_{ij}^{(l)}$. Assign the ith observation to the category $(1, 2, \ldots, m)$ for which $D_{ij}^{(l)}$ is largest.

> Multiple imputation based on the multivariate-normal distribution can be remarkably effective in practice, even when the data are not normally distributed. To apply multiple imputation effectively, however, it is important to include variables in the imputation model that make the assumption of ignorable missingness reasonable; to transform variables to approximate normality, if possible; to adjust the imputed data so that they resemble the original data; and to make sure that the imputation model captures features of the data, such as nonlinearities and interactions, to be used in subsequent data analysis.

20.4.4   Example: A Regression Model for Infant Mortality

Figure 20.2 (repeating Figure 3.13 from page 48) shows the relationship between infant mortality (number of infant deaths per 1,000 live births) and gross domestic product per capita (in U.S. dollars) for 193 nations, part of a larger data set of 207 countries compiled by the United Nations. The amount of missing data in Figure 20.2 is therefore relatively small, comprising only about 7% of the cases.

Let us now consider the regression of infant mortality not only on GDP per capita, but also on the percentage of married women practicing contraception and the average number of years of education for women. To linearize the regression, I log-transformed both infant mortality and GDP.[34] A complete-case analysis includes only 62 of the 207 countries and produces the results shown in the upper panel of Table 20.3.

The number of observations with missing data for each of the variables in the analysis is as follows:

Infant Mortality	GDP	Contraception	Female Education
6	10	63	131

There are, however, other variables in the full data set that are highly correlated with contraception and female education, such as the total fertility rate and the illiteracy rate for women. I decided to base imputations on a multivariate-normal model with the four variables in the regression plus the total fertility rate, the expectation of life for women, the percentage of women engaged in

---

[33] See Chapter 7 for a general discussion of dummy-variable regressors.
[34] See Exercise 20.8.

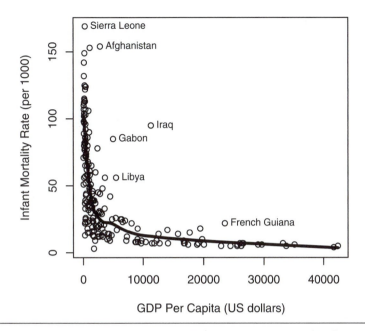

Figure 20.2   Scatterplot for infant mortality and GDP per capita for 193 nations. The line is for a lowess smooth with a span of 1/2. Several nations with high infant mortality for their levels of GDP are identified.

Table 20.3   Estimated Coefficients and Standard Errors for the Regression of Infant Mortality on GDP Per Capita, Percentage Using Contraception, and Average Female Education, for 207 Nations (62 Complete Cases)

	Intercept	*$\log_e$ GDP*	*Contraception*	*Female Education*
Complete-case analysis				
Coefficient, B_j	6.88	−0.294	−0.0113	−0.0770
SE(B_j)	(0.29)	(0.058)	(0.0042)	(0.0338)
Multiple-imputation analysis				
Coefficient, $\widetilde{\beta}_j$	6.57	−0.234	−0.00953	−0.105
$\widetilde{SE}(\widetilde{\beta}_j)$	(0.18)	(0.049)	(0.00294)	(0.033)
Missing Information, $\widehat{\gamma}_j$	0.20	0.61	0.41	0.69

economic activity outside the home, and the illiteracy rate for women. Preliminary examination of the data suggested that the multivariate-normal model could be made more appropriate for the data by transforming several of these variables. In particular—as in the regression model in Table 20.3—I log-transformed infant mortality and GDP. I also took the square-root of the total fertility rate; cubed female expectation of life, after subtracting a start of 35 from each value; and took the 1/4 power of female illiteracy. The resulting data set did not look quite multivariate-normal, but several of the variables were more symmetrically distributed than before.

To get a sense of the possible influence of missing data on conclusions drawn from the data, I computed the complete-case estimates of the means and standard deviations of the four variables

Table 20.4   Means and Standard Deviations of Variables in the Infant-Mortality
Regression, Complete-Case and Maximum-Likelihood Estimates

	$\log_e$ Infant Mortality	$\log_e$ GDP	Contraception	Female Education
	Estimates based on Complete Cases			
Mean	3.041	8.151	50.90	11.30
SD	(1.051)	(1.703)	(23.17)	(3.55)
	Maximum-Likelihood Estimates			
Mean	3.300	7.586	44.36	10.16
SD	(1.022)	(1.682)	(24.01)	(3.51)

to be used in the regression, along with ML estimates, obtained by the EM algorithm applied to the eight variables to be used in the imputation model. These results are given in Table 20.4. As one might expect, the means for the complete cases show lower average infant mortality, higher GDP per capita, higher rates of contraception, and a higher level of female education than the ML estimates assuming ignorable missing data; the two sets of standard deviations, however, are quite similar.

Using Schafer's data-augmentation method and employing the multivariate-normal model, I obtained imputations for 10 completed data sets.[35] Then, applying Equations 20.11, 20.12, and 20.13 (on pages 563–564), I computed the estimated coefficients, standard errors, and estimated rate of missing information for each coefficient, shown in the lower panel of Table 20.3. With the exception of the female-education coefficient, the standard errors from the multiple-imputation analysis are noticeably smaller than those from the complete-case analysis. In addition, the coefficients for GDP and female education differ between the two analyses by about one standard error; the coefficients for contraception, in contrast, are very similar. Finally, the rates of missing information for the three slope coefficients are all large. Because 10 imputations were employed, however, the square-root relative efficiency of the estimated coefficients based on the multiply imputed data is at worst $\sqrt{10/(10 + 0.69)} = 0.97$.

20.5   Selection Bias and Censoring

When missing data are not ignorable (i.e., MNAR), consistent estimation of regression models requires an explicit auxiliary model for the missingness mechanism. Accommodating nonignorable missing data is an intrinsically risky venture because the resulting regression estimates can be very sensitive to the specifics of the model assumed to generate the missing data.

This section introduces two models in wide use for data that are MNAR: Heckman's model to overcome selection bias in regression and the so-called tobit model (and related models) for a censored response variable in regression. Before examining these models, however, it is useful to develop some basic ideas concerning truncated and censored normal distributions.

---

[35] Data augmentation employs a *Markov-chain Monte-Carlo* (*MCMC*) method to sample from the predictive distribution of the data. Using Schafer's norm package for the R statistical computing environment for these computations, I set the number of steps for the data-augmentation algorithm to 20. Technical aspects of the data-augmentation algorithm are discussed in Schafer (1997) and, in less detail, in Allison (2002).

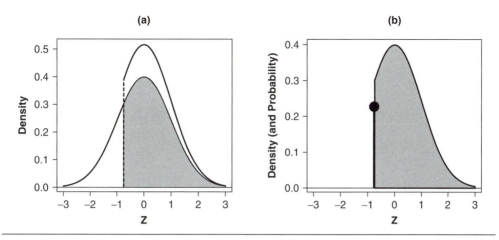

Figure 20.3 (a) Truncated- and (b) censored-normal distributions. In both cases, the underlying distribution is standard-normal, $N(0,1)$. In (a) there are no values of Z observed below $Z = -0.75$, and the remaining density is rescaled (see the upper curve) to an area of 1. In (b) values below -0.75 are set to $Z = -0.75$; the probability of observing this value is represented by the "spike" topped by a circle.

20.5.1 Truncated- and Censored-Normal Distributions

The distinction between *truncation* and *censoring* is illustrated in Figure 20.3. In each case, there is an unobserved variable ξ that follows the standard-normal distribution, $N(0, 1)$. The observed variable Z in panel (a) *truncates* this distribution *on the left* by suppressing all values of ξ below $\xi = -0.75$; that is, there are no observations below the truncation point. The density function $p(z)$ of Z still must enclose an area of 1, and so this density is given by

$$p(z) = \frac{\phi(z)}{1 - \Phi(-0.75)} = \frac{\phi(z)}{\Phi(0.75)} \text{ for } z \geq -0.75$$

where $\phi(\cdot)$ is the density function and $\Phi(\cdot)$ the cumulative distribution function of the standard-normal distribution. In panel (b), where the distribution of ξ is *left-censored* rather than truncated,

$$Z = \begin{cases} -0.75 & \text{for } \xi \leq -0.75 \\ \xi & \text{for } \xi > -0.75 \end{cases}$$

Consequently, $\Pr(Z = -0.75) = \Phi(-0.75)$, that is, the area to the left of -0.75 under the standard-normal density function $\phi(\cdot)$.

It will be useful to have expressions for the mean and variance of a truncated-normal distribution. Suppose now that ξ is normally distributed with an *arbitrary* mean μ and variance σ^2—that is, $\xi \sim N(\mu, \sigma^2)$—and that this distribution is left-truncated at the *threshold* a, giving rise to the observable variable Y. Then, the mean and variance of Y are[36]

$$E(Y) = E(\xi \mid \xi \geq a) = \mu + \sigma m(z_a) \tag{20.14}$$

$$V(Y) = V(\xi \mid \xi \geq a) = \sigma^2 [1 - d(z_a)]$$

---

[36]The derivation of these results, and of some other results in this section, is beyond the level of the text, even in starred material or exercises. See Johnson, Kotz, and Balakrishnan (1994) and Kotz, Balakrishnan, and Johnson (2000).

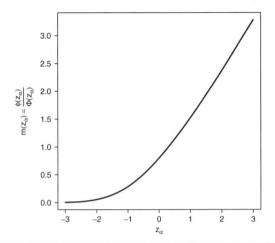

Figure 20.4   The inverse Mills ratio $m(z_\alpha)$ as a function of the standardized threshold z_α.

where

$$z_a \equiv \frac{a - \mu}{\sigma} \tag{20.15}$$

$$m(z_a) \equiv \frac{\phi(z_a)}{1 - \Phi(z_a)} = \frac{\phi(z_a)}{\Phi(-z_a)}$$

$$d(z_a) \equiv m(z_a)\,[m(z_a) - z_a]$$

The quantity $m(z_a)$, called the *inverse Mills ratio*, is a function of the standardized threshold; it will figure prominently in the remainder of this section. As a general matter, the mean of the left-truncated variable Y *exceeds* that of ξ by an amount that depends on the standardized threshold and the standard deviation σ of the untruncated distribution; similarly, the variance of Y is *smaller* than the variance of ξ by a factor dependent on the standardized threshold.[37] The inverse Mills ratio is graphed against z_a in Figure 20.4: As the threshold moves to the right, the relationship between the inverse Mills ratio and z_a becomes more linear.

The expectation and variance of a censored-normal variable follow straightforwardly. Suppose that $\xi \sim N(\mu, \sigma^2)$ is left-censored at $\xi = a$, so that

$$Y = \begin{cases} a & \text{for } \xi \le a \\ \xi & \text{for } \xi > a \end{cases}$$

Then,[38]

$$E(Y) = a\Phi(z_a) + [\mu + \sigma m(z_a)]\,[1 - \Phi(z_a)]$$

$$V(Y) = \sigma^2\,[1 - \Phi(z_a)]\left\{1 - d(z_a) + [z_a - m(z_a)]^2\,\Phi(z_a)\right\} \tag{20.16}$$

A variable can be truncated or censored at the right as well as at the left or can be truncated or censored at both ends simultaneously (the latter is termed *interval censoring*). The analysis of right-censored or interval-censored data is essentially similar to the analysis of left-censored data, making adjustments to the formulas in Equation 20.16.[39]

---

[37] See Exercise 20.9 for the mean and variance of a right-truncated normal variable.
[38] See Exercise 20.10.
[39] See Exercise 20.11.

Finally, suppose that the unobservable variables ξ and ζ follow a bivariate-normal distribution, with means μ_ξ and μ_ζ, variances σ_ξ^2 and σ_ζ^2, and correlation ρ (so that the covariance of ξ and ζ is $\sigma_{\xi\zeta} = \rho\sigma_\xi\sigma_\zeta$). Imagine that, as before, Y is a truncated version of ξ, but now the truncation depends *not* on the value of ξ *itself* but rather on that of ζ, so that $Y = \xi$ when $\zeta \geq a$ and Y is unobserved when $\zeta < a$. This process is called *incidental truncation* or *selection*. The mean and variance for the incidentally truncated variable Y are

$$E(Y) = E(\xi \mid \zeta \geq a) = \mu_\xi + \sigma_\xi \rho m(z_a)$$
$$V(Y) = V(\xi \mid \zeta \geq a) = \sigma_\xi^2 \left[1 - \rho^2 d(z_a) \right] \tag{20.17}$$

where $z_a \equiv (a - \mu_\zeta)/\sigma_\zeta$ and $m(\cdot)$ and $d(\cdot)$ are defined as in Equation 20.15. The effect of incidental truncation depends, therefore, not only on the standardized threshold z_a but also on the correlation ρ between the latent variables ξ and ζ. For example, if these variables are positively correlated, then $E(Y) > E(\xi)$ and $V(Y) < V(\xi)$.

The distribution of a variable is truncated when values below or above a threshold (or outside a particular range) are unobserved. The distribution of a variable is censored when values below or above a threshold (or outside a particular range) are set equal to the threshold. The distribution of a variable is incidentally censored if its value is unobserved when another variable is below or above a threshold (or outside a particular range). Simple formulas exist for the mean and variance of truncated- and censored-normal distributions, and for the mean and variance of an incidentally truncated variable in a bivariate-normal distribution.

20.5.2 Heckman's Selection-Regression Model

The model and methods of estimation described in this section originated with James Heckman (e.g., Heckman, 1974, 1976), whose work on selection bias won him a Nobel Prize in economics. Heckman's selection-regression model consists of two parts:

1. A *regression equation* for a *latent response variable* ξ:

$$\xi_i = \alpha + \beta_1 X_{i1} + \beta_2 X_{i2} + \cdots + \beta_k X_{ik} + \varepsilon_i \tag{20.18}$$
$$= \eta_i + \varepsilon_i$$

2. A *selection equation* that determines whether or not ξ is observed:

$$\zeta_i = \gamma_0 + \gamma_1 Z_{i1} + \gamma_2 Z_{i2} + \cdots + \gamma_p Z_{ip} + \delta_i \tag{20.19}$$
$$= \psi_i + \delta_i$$

where the *observed response variable*

$$Y_i = \begin{cases} \text{missing} & \text{for } \zeta_i \leq 0 \\ \xi_i & \text{for } \zeta_i > 0 \end{cases}$$

The explanatory variables in Equation 20.19 (i.e., the Zs) are intended to predict missingness; they need not be the same as the explanatory variables used in the regression equation of principal interest (Equation 20.18), but in applications there is usually considerable overlap between the Zs and the Xs. The observed response, for example, might represent earnings for married women, which is missing when they are not in the paid labor force; the latent variable would then represent a notional "potential earnings." An example based on this idea is developed below.

It is assumed that the two error variables ε_i and δ_i follow a bivariate-normal distribution with means $E(\varepsilon_i) = E(\delta_i) = 0$, variances $\sigma_\varepsilon^2 \equiv V(\varepsilon_i)$ and $V(\delta_i) = 1$, and correlation $\rho_{\varepsilon\delta}$. Errors for different observations are assumed to be independent. Equation 20.19, together with the assumption that the errors δ are normally distributed, specifies a *probit model* for nonmissingness.[40]

As we will see presently, estimating the regression equation (Equation 20.18) just for complete cases—simply omitting observations for which Y is missing—generally produces inconsistent estimates of the regression coefficients. In addition, because of the correlation of the two error variables, the missing data are not ignorable, and so it would be inappropriate, for example, to generate multiple imputations of the missing values of Y as if they were MAR.

Restricting our attention to the complete cases,

$$E(Y_i \mid \zeta_i > 0) = \eta_i + E(\varepsilon_i \mid \zeta_i > 0)$$
$$= \eta_i + E(\varepsilon_i \mid \delta_i > -\psi_i)$$

The conditional expectation of the error ε_i follows from Equation 20.17 for the incidentally truncated bivariate-normal distribution:[41]

$$E(\varepsilon_i \mid \delta_i > -\psi_i) = \sigma_\varepsilon \rho_{\varepsilon\delta} m\,(-\psi_i)$$

Therefore,

$$E(Y_i \mid \zeta_i > 0) = \eta_i + \sigma_\varepsilon \rho_{\varepsilon\delta} m\,(-\psi_i)$$
$$= \alpha + \beta_1 X_{i1} + \beta_2 X_{i2} + \cdots + \beta_k X_{ik} + \beta_\lambda \lambda_i$$

where $\beta_\lambda \equiv \sigma_\varepsilon \rho_{\varepsilon\delta}$ and $\lambda_i \equiv m\,(-\psi_i)$.

Letting $v_i \equiv Y_i - E(Y_i \mid \zeta_i > 0)$, we can write the regression equation for the complete cases as

$$(Y_i \mid \zeta_i > 0) = \alpha + \beta_1 X_{i1} + \beta_2 X_{i2} + \cdots + \beta_k X_{ik} + \beta_\lambda \lambda_i + v_i$$

Regressing Y on the Xs using only the complete cases omits the explanatory variable λ_i, which is the inverse Mills ratio based on the negative of the linear predictor ψ_i from the selection equation (Equation 20.19). Ignoring the missingness mechanism, therefore, can be conceptualized as a kind of omitted-variable specification error.[42] If the errors from the regression and selection equations are uncorrelated (i.e., $\rho_{\varepsilon\delta} = 0$), then $\beta_\lambda = 0$, and ignoring λ_i is inconsequential. Similarly, if λ_i were uncorrelated with the Xs, then we could ignore it without threatening the consistency of the least-squares estimators of the regression coefficients. Uncorrelation of λ_i and the Xs is unlikely, however: The selection and regression equations typically contain many of the same explanatory variables, and unless the degree of selection is low, the inverse Mills ratio is nearly a linear function of the linear predictor (recall Figure 20.4 on page 572). Indeed, *high* correlation between λ_i and

---

[40]For a general treatment of probit regression, see Section 14.1. Recall that we can arbitrarily set the threshold above which Y is observed and below which it is missing to 0 and the error variance δ to 1, to fix the origin and scale of the latent variable.

[41]See Exercise 20.12.

[42]See Sections 6.3 and 9.7.

the Xs can make consistent estimation of the regression coefficients (by the methods described immediately below) unstable. Note, as well, that the variance of the errors v_i is not constant.[43]

There are two common strategies for estimating Heckman's regression-selection model: direct application of ML estimation and employing an estimate of λ_i as an auxiliary regressor.

- *ML Estimation*:* Let $\boldsymbol{\beta} \equiv (\alpha, \beta_1, \dots, \beta_k)'$ be the vector of regression coefficients in the regression equation (Equation 20.18); let $\boldsymbol{\gamma} \equiv (\gamma_0, \gamma_1, \dots, \gamma_p)'$ be the vector of regression coefficients in the selection equation (Equation 20.19); let $\mathbf{x}_i' \equiv (1, X_{i1}, \dots, X_{ik})$ be the ith row of the model matrix for the regression equation; and let $\mathbf{z}_i' \equiv (1, Z_{i1}, \dots, Z_{ip})$ be the ith row of the model matrix for the selection equation. For notational convenience, order the data so that the missing observations on Y are the first m of n observations. Then the log-likelihood for Heckman's model can be formulated as follows:[44]

$$\log_e L(\boldsymbol{\beta}, \boldsymbol{\gamma}, \sigma_\varepsilon^2, \rho_{\varepsilon\delta}) = \sum_{i=1}^{m} \log_e \Phi\left(\mathbf{z}_i'\boldsymbol{\gamma}\right)$$
$$+ \sum_{i=m+1}^{n} \log_e \left[\frac{1}{\sigma_\varepsilon} \phi\left(\frac{Y_i - \mathbf{x}_i'\boldsymbol{\beta}}{\sigma_\varepsilon}\right) \Phi\left(\frac{\mathbf{z}_i'\boldsymbol{\gamma} + \rho_{\varepsilon\delta}\frac{Y_i - \mathbf{x}_i'\boldsymbol{\beta}}{\sigma_\varepsilon}}{\sqrt{\frac{1-\rho_{\varepsilon\delta}}{\sigma_\varepsilon}}}\right) \right]$$
$$(20.20)$$

This log-likelihood can be maximized numerically.
- *Two-Step Estimation:* Heckman (1979) also proposed a simple and widely used two-step procedure for estimating his regression-selection model.

Step 1: Define the dichotomous response variable

$$W_i = \begin{cases} 1 & \text{if } Y_i \text{ is observed} \\ 0 & \text{if } Y_i \text{ is missing} \end{cases}$$

Perform a probit regression of W_i on the Zs, estimating the γs in the usual manner by ML,[45] and finding fitted values on the probit scale,

$$\widehat{\psi}_i = \widehat{\gamma}_0 + \widehat{\gamma}_1 Z_{i1} + \widehat{\gamma}_2 Z_{i2} + \cdots + \widehat{\gamma}_p Z_{ip}$$

$\widehat{\psi}_i$ is simply the estimated linear predictor from the probit model. For each observation, compute the estimated inverse Mills ratio

$$\widehat{\lambda}_i = m(-\widehat{\psi}_i) = \frac{\phi(-\widehat{\psi}_i)}{1 - \Phi(-\widehat{\psi}_i)} = \frac{\phi(\widehat{\psi}_i)}{\Phi(\widehat{\psi}_i)}$$

Step 2: Use $\widehat{\lambda}$ as an auxiliary regressor in the least-squares regression of Y_i on the Xs for the complete cases,

$$Y_i = \alpha + \beta_1 X_{i1} + \beta_2 X_{i2} + \cdots + \beta_k X_{ik} + \beta_{\widehat{\lambda}}\widehat{\lambda}_i + v_i^*,$$
$$\text{for } i = m+1, \dots, n \qquad (20.21)$$

---

[43]The variance of v_i follows from Equation 20.17 for the variance of an incidentally truncated variable in the bivariate-normal distribution: See Exercise 20.13.
[44]See Exercise 20.14.
[45]As described in Chapters 14 and 15.

This least-squares regression provides consistent estimates of the regression coefficients, α, β_1, β_2, ... , β_k. The heteroscedasticity of the errors, however, requires an adjustment to the usual OLS standard errors.[46]

To illustrate the application of Heckman's selection-regression model, I will return to the Canadian Survey of Labour and Income Dynamics (the SLID),[47] examining the relationship between women's earnings and their education, age, and the region in which they reside, restricting attention to married women between the ages of 18 and 65. Earnings is represented by the women's composite hourly wage rate, which is missing if they are not in the paid labor force. Preliminary examination of the data suggested regressing the log of composite hourly wages on the square of years of education and a quadratic in age, along with four dummy regressors for five regions of Canada (the Atlantic provinces, Quebec, Ontario, the prairie provinces, and British Columbia, taking the Atlantic provinces as the baseline category).

Of the 6,427 women in the sample, 3,936 were in the paid labor force.[48] Because women whose potential earnings are relatively low may very well be less likely to work outside the home, there is a potential for selection bias if we simply ignore the 2,491 women who are not in the labor force, causing us to underestimate the effects of the explanatory variables on (potential) earnings.[49]

I formulated a selection model in which labor-force participation is regressed on region dummy variables; dummy regressors for the presence in the household of children 0–4 and 5–9 years of age; family income less the woman's own income, if any (in thousands of dollars); education (in years); and a quadratic in age (in years). The results are shown in Table 20.5. At the left of the table are ordinary least-squares estimates *ignoring* the selection process. The table also shows two-step and ML estimates for the Heckman model, both for the regression equation and for the selection equation. For the two-step estimation procedure, the selection equation was estimated in a preliminary probit regression.

In this application, the two-step/probit and ML estimates are very similar and are not terribly different from the OLS estimates based on the complete cases. Moreover, the ML estimate of the correlation between the errors of the regression and selection equations is fairly small: $\widehat{\rho}_{\varepsilon\delta} = .320$. The degree of collinearity induced by the introduction of the inverse-Mills-ratio regressor in the second step of the two-step procedure is not serious as shown in Table 20.6, which compares generalized variance inflation factors for the model as estimated by OLS and Heckman's two-step procedure.[50]

---

[46] See Exercise 20.15.

[47] In Chapter 12, I used the SLID for a regression of earnings on sex, age, and education. In Chapter 14, the SLID provided data for a logistic regression of young married women's labor-force participation on region, presence of children, family income, and education.

[48] The complete SLID sample of married women between 18 and 65 years of age consists of 6900 respondents. I omitted the relatively small number of observations (comprising about seven percent of the sample) with missing data on variables other than earnings.

[49] If, however, our goal is to *describe* the regression of earnings on the explanatory variables for those who are in the paid labor force, then an analysis based on women who have earnings should be perfectly fine, as long as we are careful to ensure the descriptive accuracy of the model—for example, by using component-plus-residual plots to check for nonlinearity (see Chapter 12).

[50] Generalized variance-inflation factors (GVIFs), introduced in Section 13.1.2, are appropriate for terms in a model that have more than one degree of freedom, such as the region and age terms in this model. When a term has one degree of freedom, the GVIF reduces to the usual variance inflation factor (VIF, also discussed in Chapter 13). Taking the $1/(2df)$ power of the GVIF makes values roughly comparable across different degrees of freedom. Treating the linear and quadratic components of the age term as a set is important here because otherwise there would be artifactual collinearity induced by the high correlation between Age and Age^2.

Table 20.5 Least-Squares, Heckman Two-Step, and Heckman ML Estimates for the Regression of Women's Composite Hourly Wages on Region, Education, and Age

	OLS		Two-Step/Probit		ML	
	Estimate	SE	Estimate	SE	Estimate	SE
Coefficient	Regression Equation					
Constant	1.10	0.15	0.442	0.227	0.755	0.177
Quebec	0.223	0.031	0.205	0.033	0.214	0.032
Ontario	0.303	0.026	0.332	0.028	0.319	0.027
Prairies	0.126	0.027	0.147	0.029	0.137	0.027
B.C.	0.371	0.036	0.392	0.038	0.382	0.037
Education^2	0.00442	0.00013	0.00492	0.00018	0.00469	0.00014
Age	0.0687	0.0074	0.0917	0.0096	0.0807	0.0081
Age^2	−0.000717	0.000088	−0.00105	0.00012	−0.000892	0.000099
Inv. Mills Ratio			0.361	0.088		
	Selection Equation					
Constant			−1.46	0.30	−1.44	0.30
Quebec			−0.0665	0.0533	−0.0674	0.0533
Ontario			0.193	0.048	0.194	0.048
Prairies			0.117	0.049	0.117	0.049
B.C.			0.145	0.067	0.150	0.067
Children 0–4			−0.414	0.050	−0.439	0.049
Children 5–9			−0.261	0.043	−0.251	0.042
Family Income			−0.00399	0.00097	−0.00475	0.00097
Education			0.0815	0.0061	0.0817	0.0060
Age			0.0878	0.0135	0.0882	0.0134
Age^2			−0.00145	0.00015	−0.00145	0.00015

Table 20.6 Generalized Variance Inflation Factors for Terms in the OLS and Two-Step-Heckman Regression of Log Hourly Wages on Region, Education, and Age

		$GVIF^{1/(2df)}$	
Term	df	OLS Estimates	Heckman Two-Step Estimates
Region	4	1.003	1.024
Education^2	1	1.025	1.402
Age (quadratic)	2	1.012	1.347
Inverse Mills Ratio	1	—	2.202

As is seldom a bad idea, I will leave the last word on Heckman-type adjustments for selection bias to John Tukey (1986), who states[51]

---

[51]Tukey made these comments about a paper delivered by Heckman and Robb (1986) to a symposium on statistical methods for self-selected samples (collected in a volume edited by Wainer, 1986). The models introduced by Heckman and Robb are not the same as Heckman's selection-regression model discussed in this section, but they are similarly motivated and structured.

I think that an important point that we have to come back to at intervals is that knowledge always comes from a combination of data and assumptions. If the assumptions are too important, many of us get unhappy. I think one thing we were told in this last discussion was that all the formal ways that have been found for attacking this problem ended up being very dependent upon these assumptions. Therefore, people like me have to be very uncomfortable about the results. (p. 58)

Heckman's regression model consists of two parts:

1. A regression equation for a latent response variable ξ:

$$\xi_i = \alpha + \beta_1 X_{i1} + \beta_2 X_{i2} + \cdots + \beta_k X_{ik} + \varepsilon_i$$

2. A selection equation that determines whether or not ξ is observed:

$$\zeta_i = \gamma_0 + \gamma_1 Z_{i1} + \gamma_2 Z_{i2} + \cdots + \gamma_p Z_{ip} + \delta_i = \psi_i + \delta_i$$

where the observed response variable

$$Y_i = \begin{cases} \text{missing} & \text{for } \zeta_i \leq 0 \\ \xi_i & \text{for } \zeta_i > 0 \end{cases}$$

It is assumed that the two error variables ε_i and δ_i follow a bivariate-normal distribution with means $E(\varepsilon_i) = E(\delta_i) = 0$, variances $V(\varepsilon_i) = \sigma_\varepsilon^2$ and $V(\delta_i) = 1$, and correlation $\rho_{\varepsilon\delta}$, and that errors for different observations are independent.

Heckman's model can be consistently estimated by ML, or by a two-step procedure. In the first step of the two-step procedure, the selection equation is estimated as a probit model; in the second step, the regression equation is estimated by OLS after incorporating the auxiliary regressor $\widehat{\lambda}_i = \phi(\widehat{\psi}_i)/\Phi(\widehat{\psi}_i)$, where $\widehat{\psi}_i$ is the fitted value from the first-step probit equation, $\phi(\cdot)$ is the density function of the standard-normal distribution, and $\Phi(\cdot)$ is the distribution function of the standard-normal distribution.

20.5.3 Censored-Regression Models

When the response variable Y in a regression is censored, values of Y cannot be observed outside a certain range—say, the interval (a, b). We can detect, however, whether an observation falls below the lower threshold a or above the upper threshold b, and consequently, we have *some* information about the censored values.

Let us assume, in particular, that the *latent response variable* ξ is linearly related to the regressors $X_1, X_2, \ldots, X_k$, so that

$$\xi_i = \alpha + \beta_1 X_{i1} + \beta_2 X_{i2} + \cdots + \beta_k X_{ik} + \varepsilon_i \tag{20.22}$$

and that the other assumptions of the normal regression model hold: $\varepsilon_i \sim N(0, \sigma_\varepsilon^2)$, and $\varepsilon_i, \varepsilon_{i'}$ are independent for $i \neq i'$. We cannot observe ξ directly, however, but instead we collect data on the *censored response variable* Y, where

$$Y_i = \begin{cases} a & \text{for } \xi_i \leq a \\ \xi_i & \text{for } a < \xi_i < b \\ b & \text{for } \xi_i \geq b \end{cases} \tag{20.23}$$

Equations 20.22 and 20.23 define the *censored-regression model*. A model of this type was first proposed by James Tobin (1958), for data censored to the left at 0—that is, for $a = 0$ and $b = \infty$. Left-censored regression models are called *tobit models*, in honor of Tobin (another Nobel Prize winner in economics). The censored-regression model can be estimated by the method of ML.[52]

*Rewriting the regression equation in vector form for compactness as $\xi_i = \mathbf{x}_i'\boldsymbol{\beta} + \varepsilon_i$, the log-likelihood for the censored-regression model in Equations 20.22 and 20.23 is

$$\log_e L(\boldsymbol{\beta}, \sigma_\varepsilon^2) = \sum_{Y_i=a} \log_e \Phi\left(\frac{a - \mathbf{x}_i'\boldsymbol{\beta}}{\sigma_\varepsilon}\right) + \sum_{a < Y_i < b} \log_e \left[\frac{1}{\sigma_\varepsilon}\phi\left(\frac{Y_i - \mathbf{x}_i'\boldsymbol{\beta}}{\sigma_\varepsilon}\right)\right]$$
$$+ \sum_{Y_i=b} \log_e \Phi\left(\frac{\mathbf{x}_i'\boldsymbol{\beta} - b}{\sigma_\varepsilon}\right)$$

Note that the log-likelihood comprises terms for left-censored, fully observed, and right-censored observations.[53]

For an example of censored regression, I turn once again to the Canadian SLID data. We last encountered the SLID in the previous section, where the earnings of married women were regressed on region, education, and age. I employed Heckman's selection-regression model because earnings were unavailable for women who were not in the paid labor force. I will now develop a similar example in which the response variable is hours worked in the year preceding the survey. This variable is left-censored at the value 0, producing a classic tobit regression model.[54] The explanatory variables are region, the presence in the household of children 0–4 and 5–9 years old, family income less the woman's own income (if any), education, and a quadratic in age. The SLID data set includes 6,340 respondents with valid data on the variables employed in this example.

Preliminary examination of the data suggested a square-root transformation of hours worked. This transformation does not, of course, serve to spread out the values of the response variable for the 31% of respondents who reported 0 hours worked—that is, the transformed response for all censored observations is $\sqrt{0} = 0$. OLS and ML tobit estimates for the regression model are shown in Table 20.7. Note that the OLS estimates are consistently smaller in magnitude than the corresponding tobit estimates.[55]

In the censored-regression model, the latent response variable ξ is linearly related to the regressors $X_1, X_2, \ldots, X_k$:

$$\xi_i = \alpha + \beta_1 X_{i1} + \beta_2 X_{i2} + \cdots + \beta_k X_{ik} + \varepsilon_i$$

(Continued)

---

[52] An alternative is to employ Heckman's two-step procedure, described in the preceding section.

[53] Estimation is facilitated by reparametrization. See, for example, Greene (2003, sec. 22.3.3).

[54] The latent response variable therefore represents "propensity" to work outside the home; presumably if that propensity is above the threshold 0, we observe positive hours worked.

[55] See Exercise 20.16.

(Continued)

where $\varepsilon_i \sim N(0, \sigma_\varepsilon^2)$, and $\varepsilon_i, \varepsilon_{i'}$ are independent for $i \neq i'$. We cannot observe ξ directly but instead collect data on the censored response variable Y:

$$Y_i = \begin{cases} a & \text{for } \xi_i \leq a \\ \xi_i & \text{for } a < \xi_i < b \\ b & \text{for } \xi_i \geq b \end{cases}$$

When Y is left-censored at 0 (i.e., $a = 0$ and $b = \infty$), the censored-regression model is called a tobit model in honor of James Tobin. The censored-regression model can be estimated by maximum likelihood.

Table 20.7   OLS and ML Tobit Estimates for the Regression of Square-Root Hours Worked on Several Explanatory Variables

	OLS		Tobit	
Coefficient	Estimate	SE	Estimate	SE
Constant	−20.3	3.8	−58.7	5.4
Quebec	−0.745	0.710	−1.58	1.01
Ontario	3.55	0.63	5.02	0.89
Prairies	3.64	0.65	5.36	0.91
B.C.	2.09	0.88	3.73	1.23
Children 0–4 (present)	−6.56	0.65	−8.63	0.91
Children 5–9 (present)	−5.05	0.56	−6.91	0.79
Family Income ($1000s)	−0.0977	0.0128	−0.139	0.018
Education (years)	1.29	0.08	1.87	0.11
Age (years)	2.32	0.17	3.84	0.25
Age^2	−0.0321	0.0019	−0.0529	0.0028

Exercises

Exercise 20.1. Consider the following contrived data set for the variables X_1, X_2, and X_3, where the question marks indicate missing data:

X_1	X_2	X_3
1	1	?
1	?	1
−1	−1	?
−1	?	−1
?	1	−1
?	−1	1
5	?	?

(a) Using available cases (and recomputing the means and standard deviations for each pair of variables), find the pair-wise correlations among the three variables and explain why the correlations are not consistent with each other.

(b) Compute the correlation between X_1 and X_2 using means and standard deviations computed *separately* from the valid observations for each variable. What do you find?

(c) *Show that the available-case correlation matrix among the variables X_1, X_2, and X_3 is not positive semidefinite.

Exercise 20.2. *In univariate missing data, where there are missing values for only one variable in a data set, some of the apparently distinct methods for handling missing data produce identical results for certain statistics. Consider Table 20.1 on page 554, for example, where data are missing on the variable X_2 but not on X_1. Note that the complete-case, available-case, and mean-imputation estimates of the slope β_{12} for the regression of X_1 on X_2 are identical. Prove that this is no accident. Are there are any other apparent agreements between or among methods in the table? If so, can you determine whether they are coincidences?

Exercise 20.3. *Duplicate the small simulation study reported in Table 20.2 on page 555, comparing several methods of handling univariate missing data that are MAR. Then repeat the study for missing data that are MCAR and for missing data that are MNAR (generated as in Figure 20.1 on page 551). What do you conclude? *Note:* This is not a *conceptually* difficult project, but it is potentially time-consuming; it also requires some programming skills and statistical software that can generate and analyze simulated data.

Exercise 20.4. *Equation 20.6 (on page 558) gives the ML estimators for the parameters μ_1, μ_2, σ_1^2, σ_2^2, and σ_{12} in the bivariate-normal model with some observations on X_2 missing at random but X_1 completely observed. The interpretation of $\widehat{\mu}_1$ and $\widehat{\sigma}_1^2$ is straightforward: They are the available-case mean and variance for X_1. Noting that S_{12}^*/S_1^{2*} is the complete-case slope for the regression of X_2 and X_1, offer interpretations for the other ML estimators.

Exercise 20.5. *Multivariate* linear regression fits the model

$$\underset{(n \times m)}{\mathbf{Y}} = \underset{(n \times k+1)(k+1 \times m)}{\mathbf{X} \quad \mathbf{B}} + \underset{(n \times m)}{\mathbf{E}}$$

where $\mathbf{Y}$ is a matrix of response variables; $\mathbf{X}$ is a model matrix (just as in the *univariate* linear model); $\mathbf{B}$ is a matrix of regression coefficients, one column per response variable; and $\mathbf{E}$ is a matrix of errors. The least-squares estimator of $\mathbf{B}$ is $\widehat{\mathbf{B}} = (\mathbf{X}'\mathbf{X})^{-1}\mathbf{X}'\mathbf{Y}$ (equivalent to what one would get from separate least squares regressions of each Y on the Xs). See Section 9.5 for a discussion of the multivariate linear model.

(a) Show how $\widehat{\mathbf{B}}$ can be computed from the means of the variables, $\widehat{\mu}_Y$ and $\widehat{\mu}_X$, and from their covariances, $\widehat{\boldsymbol{\Sigma}}_{XX}$ and $\widehat{\boldsymbol{\Sigma}}_{XY}$ (among the Xs and between the Xs and Ys, respectively).

(b) The fitted values from the multivariate regression are $\widehat{\mathbf{Y}} = \mathbf{X}\widehat{\mathbf{B}}$. It follows that the fitted values $\widehat{Y}_{ij}$ and $\widehat{Y}_{ij'}$ for the ith observation on response variables j and j' are both linear combinations of the the ith row of the model matrix, $\mathbf{x}'_i$. Use this fact to find an expression for the covariance of $\widehat{Y}_{ij}$ and $\widehat{Y}_{ij'}$.

(c) Show how this result can be used in Equation 20.7 (on page 560), which applies the EM algorithm to multivariate-normal data with missing values.

Exercise 20.6. *Consider once again the case of univariate missing data MAR for two bivariately normal variables, where the first variable, X_1, is completely observed, and m observations (for convenience, the first m) on the second variable, X_2, are missing.

(a) Let $A_{2|1}^*$ and $B_{2|1}^*$ represent the intercept and slope for the complete-case least-squares regression of X_2 on X_1. Show that $A_{2|1}^*$ and $B_{2|1}^*$ are the ML estimators of $\alpha_{2|1}$ and $\beta_{2|1}$. (*Hint*: Use Equation 20.6 giving the ML estimators of μ_1, μ_2, σ_1^2, σ_2^2, and σ_{12}.)

(b) Show that the M step from the first iteration of the EM algorithm (see Equations 20.8 and 20.9 on page 560 for the E step) produces the ML estimates (given in Equation 20.6 on page 558). That is, demonstrate that the EM algorithm converges in a single iteration.

Exercise 20.7. As explained in Section 20.4.1, the efficiency of the multiple-imputation estimator of a coefficient $\widetilde{\beta}_j$ relative to the ML estimator $\widehat{\beta}_j$ is $\mathrm{RE}(\widetilde{\beta}_j) = g/(g + \gamma_j)$, where g is the number of imputations employed and γ_j is the rate of missing information for coefficient β_j. The square root of $\mathrm{RE}(\widetilde{\beta}_j)$ expresses relative efficiency on the coefficient standard-error scale. Compute $\mathrm{RE}(\widetilde{\beta}_j)$ and $\sqrt{RE(\widetilde{\beta}_j)}$ for combinations of values of $g = 1, 2, 3, 5, 10, 20,$ and 100, and $\gamma_j = .05, .1, .2, .5, .9,$ and .99. What do you conclude about the number of imputations required for efficient inference?

Exercise 20.8. Examine the United Nations data on infant mortality and other variables for 207 countries, discussed in Section 20.4.4.

(a) Perform a complete-case linear least-squares regression of infant mortality on GDP per capita, percentage using contraception, and female education. Does it appear reasonable to log-transform infant mortality and GDP to linearize this regression? What about contraception and education?

(b) *Examine a scatterplot matrix (Section 3.3.1) for the variables used in the imputation example. What do you find? Then apply the multivariate Box-Cox procedure described in Section 4.6 to these variables. Remember first to subtract 35 from female expectation of life (why?). Do the results that you obtain support the transformations employed in the text? Apply the transformations and reexamine the data. Do they appear more nearly normal?

Exercise 20.9. Truncated normal distributions:

(a) Suppose that $\xi \sim N(0, 1)$. Using Equation 20.14 (page 571) for the mean and variance of a left-truncated normal distribution, calculate the mean and variance of $\xi \mid \xi > a$ for each of $a = -2, -1, 0, 1,$ and 2.

(b) *Find similar formulas for the mean and variance of a *right*-truncated normal distribution. What happens to the mean and variance as the threshold moves to the left?

Exercise 20.10. *Suppose that $\xi \sim N(\mu, \sigma^2)$ is left-censored at $\xi = a$, so that

$$Y = \begin{cases} a & \text{for } \xi \leq a \\ \xi & \text{for } \xi > a \end{cases}$$

Using Equation 20.14 (on page 571) for the *truncated* normal distribution, show that (repeating Equation 20.16 on page 572)

$$E(Y) = a\Phi(z_a) + [\mu + \sigma m(z_a)][1 - \Phi(z_a)]$$

$$V(Y) = \sigma^2[1 - \Phi(z_a)]\left\{1 - d(z_a) + [z_a - m(z_a)]^2 \Phi(z_a)\right\}$$

Exercise 20.11. *Equation 20.16 (on page 572) gives formulas for the mean and variance of a left-censored normally distributed variable. (These formulas are also shown in the preceding exercise.) Derive similar formulas for (a) a right-censored and (b) an interval-censored normally distributed variable.

Exercise 20.12. *Using Equation 20.17 (page 573) for the incidentally truncated bivariate-normal distribution, show that the expectation of the error ε_i in the Heckman regression model (Equations 20.18 and 20.19 on page 573) conditional on Y being observed is

$$E(\varepsilon_i \mid \zeta_i > 0) = E(\varepsilon_i \mid \delta_i > -\psi_i) = \sigma_\varepsilon \rho_{\varepsilon\delta} m(-\psi_i)$$

Exercise 20.13. *As explained in the text, the Heckman regression model (Equations 20.18 and 20.19, page 573) implies that

$$(Y_i \mid \zeta_i > 0) = \alpha + \beta_1 X_{i1} + \beta_2 X_{i2} + \cdots + \beta_k X_{ik} + \beta_\lambda \lambda_i + \nu_i$$

where $\beta_\lambda \equiv \sigma_\varepsilon \rho_{\varepsilon\delta}$, $\lambda_i \equiv m(-\psi_i)$, and

$$\psi_i = \gamma_0 + \gamma_1 Z_{i1} + \gamma_2 Z_{i2} + \cdots + \gamma_p Z_{ip}$$

Show that the errors ν_i are heteroscedastic, with variance

$$V(\nu_i) = \sigma_\varepsilon^2 \left[1 - \rho_{\varepsilon\delta}^2 \lambda_i(\lambda_i + \psi_i)\right]$$

where σ_ε^2 is the error variance in the regression equation (Equation 20.18), and $\rho_{\varepsilon\delta}$ is the correlation between the errors of the regression and selection equations. (*Hint*: See Equation 20.17 on page 573 for the variance of an incidentally truncated variable in a bivariate-normal distribution.)

Exercise 20.14. *The log-likelihood for the Heckman regression-selection model is given in Equation 20.20 (page 575). Derive this expression. (*Hint*: The first sum in the log-likelihood, for the observations for which Y is missing, is of the log-probability that each such Y_i is missing; the second sum is of the log of the probability density at the observed values of Y_i times the probability that each such value is observed.)

Exercise 20.15. *Explain how White's coefficient-variance estimator (see Section 12.2.3), which is used to correct the covariance matrix of OLS regression coefficients for heteroscedasticity, can be employed to obtain consistent coefficient standard errors for the two-step estimator of Heckman's regression-selection model—the second step of which entails an OLS regression with heteroscedastic errors (Equation 20.21 on page 575). (*Hint*: Refer to Exercise 20.13 for the variance of the errors in the second-step OLS regression.)

Exercise 20.16. Greene (2003 p. 768) remarks that the ML estimates $\widehat{\beta}_j$ of the regression coefficients in a censored-regression model are often approximately equal to the OLS estimates B_j divided by the proportion P of *uncensored* observations; that is, $\widehat{\beta}_j \approx B_j/P$. Does this pattern hold for the hours-worked regression in Table 20.7 (page 580), where $P = .69$?

Summary

- Missing data are missing completely at random (MCAR) if they can be regarded as a simple random sample of the complete data. If missingness is related to the observed data but not to the missing data (conditional on the observed data), then data are missing at random (MAR). If missingness is related to the missing values themselves, even when the information in the observed data is taken into account, then data are missing not at random (MNAR). When data are MCAR or MAR, the process that produces missing data is ignorable, in the sense that valid methods exist to deal with the missing data without explicitly modeling the process that generates them. In contrast, when data are MNAR, the process producing missing data is nonignorable and must be modeled. Except in special situations, it is not possible to know whether data are MCAR, MAR, or MNAR.
- Traditional methods of handling missing data include complete-case analysis, available-case analysis, and unconditional and conditional mean imputation. Complete-case analysis produces consistent estimates and valid statistical inferences when data are MCAR (and in certain other special circumstances); but even in this advantageous situation, it does not use information in the sample efficiently. The other traditional methods suffer from more serious problems.
- The method of maximum likelihood (ML) can be applied to parameter estimation in the presence of missing data. If the assumptions made concerning the distribution of the complete data and the process generating missing data hold, then ML estimates have their usual optimal properties, such as consistency and asymptotic efficiency. When data are MAR, the ML estimate $\widehat{\theta}$ of the parameters θ of the complete-data distribution can be obtained from the marginal distribution of the observed data, by integrating over the missing data,

$$p(\mathbf{X}_{\mathrm{obs}}; \theta) = \int p(\mathbf{X}_{\mathrm{obs}}, \mathbf{X}_{\mathrm{mis}}; \theta) d\mathbf{X}_{\mathrm{mis}}$$

Although it may be difficult to apply this result directly, simplification is possible in certain cases. Once we have found the ML parameter estimates, we can proceed with statistical inference in the usual manner, for example, by computing likelihood-ratio tests of nested models and constructing Wald tests or confidence intervals.
- The EM algorithm is a general iterative procedure for finding ML estimates—but not their standard errors—in the presence of arbitrary patterns of missing data. When data are MAR, iteration l of the EM algorithm consists of two steps: (1) In the E (expectation) step, we find the expectation of the complete-data log-likelihood, integrating over the missing data, given the observed data and the current estimates of the parameters:

$$E\left[\log_e L(\theta; \mathbf{X})|\theta^{(l)}\right] = \int \log_e L(\theta; \mathbf{X}) p\left(\mathbf{X}_{\mathrm{mis}}|\mathbf{X}_{\mathrm{obs}}, \theta^{(l)}\right) d\mathbf{X}_{\mathrm{mis}}$$

(2) In the M (maximization) step, we find the values $\theta^{(l+1)}$ of θ that maximize the expected log-likelihood $E\left[\log_e L(\theta; \mathbf{X})|\theta^{(l)}\right]$; these are the parameter estimates for the next iteration. At convergence, the EM algorithm produces the ML estimates $\widehat{\theta}$ of θ.
- Bayesian multiple imputation (MI) is a flexible and general method for dealing with data that are missing at random. The essential idea of multiple imputation is to reflect the uncertainty associated with missing data by imputing g values for each missing value, drawing each imputed value from the predictive distribution of the missing data (a process that usually requires simulation), and therefore producing not one but g completed data sets. Standard methods of statistical analysis are then applied in parallel to the completed data sets.

– According to Rubin's rules, MI estimates (e.g., of a population regression coefficient β_j) are obtained by averaging over the imputed data sets:

$$\widetilde{\beta}_j = \frac{\sum_{l=1}^{g} B_j^{(l)}}{g}$$

where $B_j^{(l)}$ is the estimate of β_j from imputed data set l.

– Standard errors of the estimated coefficients are obtained by combining information about within- and between-imputation variation in the coefficients,

$$\widetilde{\text{SE}}(\widetilde{\beta}_j) = \sqrt{V_j^{(W)} + \frac{g+1}{g} V_j^{(B)}}$$

where the within-imputation component is

$$V_j^{(W)} = \frac{\sum_{l=1}^{g} \text{SE}^2\left(B_j^{(l)}\right)}{g}$$

and the between-imputation component is

$$V_j^{(B)} = \frac{\sum_{l=1}^{g} \left(B_j^{(l)} - \widetilde{\beta}_j\right)^2}{g-1}$$

Here, $\text{SE}\left(B_j^{(l)}\right)$ is the standard error of B_j computed in the usual manner for the lth imputed data set.

– Inference based on $\widetilde{\beta}_j$ and $\widetilde{\text{SE}}(\widetilde{\beta}_j)$ uses the t-distribution, with degrees of freedom determined by

$$df_j = (g-1)\left(1 + \frac{g}{g+1} \times \frac{V_j^{(W)}}{V_j^{(B)}}\right)^2$$

Inference for several coefficients proceeds in a similar, if more complex, manner.

- Multiple imputation based on the multivariate-normal distribution can be remarkably effective in practice, even when the data are not normally distributed. To apply multiple imputation effectively, however, it is important to include variables in the imputation model that make the assumption of ignorable missingness reasonable; to transform variables to approximate normality, if possible; to adjust the imputed data so that they resemble the original data; and to make sure that the imputation model captures features of the data, such as nonlinearities and interactions, to be used in subsequent data analysis.
- The distribution of a variable is truncated when values below or above a threshold (or outside a particular range) are unobserved. The distribution of a variable is censored when values below or above a threshold (or outside a particular range) are set equal to the threshold. The distribution of a variable is incidentally censored if its value is unobserved when another variable is below or above a threshold (or outside a particular range). Simple formulas exist for the mean and variance of truncated and censored normal distributions and for the mean and variance of an incidentally truncated variable in a bivariate-normal distribution.

- Heckman's regression model consists of two parts:

  1. A regression equation for a latent response variable ξ,

  $$\xi_i = \alpha + \beta_1 X_{i1} + \beta_2 X_{i2} + \cdots + \beta_k X_{ik} + \varepsilon_i$$

  2. A selection equation that determines whether or not ξ is observed,

  $$\zeta_i = \gamma_0 + \gamma_1 Z_{i1} + \gamma_2 Z_{i2} + \cdots + \gamma_p Z_{ip} + \delta_i = \psi_i + \delta_i$$

  where the observed response variable

  $$Y_i = \begin{cases} \text{missing} & \text{for } \zeta_i \leq 0 \\ \xi_i & \text{for } \zeta_i > 0 \end{cases}$$

  It is assumed that the two error variables ε_i and δ_i follow a bivariate-normal distribution with means $E(\varepsilon_i) = E(\delta_i) = 0$, variances $V(\varepsilon_i) = \sigma_\varepsilon^2$ and $V(\delta_i) = 1$, and correlation $\rho_{\varepsilon\delta}$, and that errors for different observations are independent.

  Heckman's model can be consistently estimated by ML, or by a two-step procedure. In the first step of the two-step procedure, the selection equation is estimated as a probit model; in the second step, the regression equation is estimated by OLS after incorporating the auxiliary regressor $\widehat{\lambda}_i = \phi(\widehat{\psi}_i)/\Phi(\widehat{\psi}_i)$, where $\widehat{\psi}_i$ is the fitted value from the first-step probit equation, $\phi(\cdot)$ is the density function of the standard-normal distribution, and $\Phi(\cdot)$ is the distribution function of the standard-normal distribution.

- In the censored-regression model, the latent response variable ξ is linearly related to the regressors $X_1, X_2, \ldots, X_k$:

  $$\xi_i = \alpha + \beta_1 X_{i1} + \beta_2 X_{i2} + \cdots + \beta_k X_{ik} + \varepsilon_i$$

  where $\varepsilon_i \sim N(0, \sigma_\varepsilon^2)$, and $\varepsilon_i, \varepsilon_{i'}$ are independent for $i \neq i'$. We cannot observe ξ directly but instead collect data on the censored response variable Y,

  $$Y_i = \begin{cases} a & \text{for } \xi_i \leq a \\ \xi_i & \text{for } a < \xi_i < b \\ b & \text{for } \xi_i \geq b \end{cases}$$

  When Y is left-censored at 0 (i.e., $a = 0$ and $b = \infty$), the censored-regression model is called a tobit model in honor of James Tobin. The censored-regression model can be estimated by ML.

Recommended Reading

- Little and Rubin (2002), central figures in the recent development of more adequate methods for handling missing data, present a wide-ranging and largely accessible overview of the field. A briefer treatment by the same authors appears in Little and Rubin (1990).
- Another fine, if mathematically more demanding, book on handling missing data is Schafer (1997). Also see the overview paper by Schafer and Graham (2002).
- Allison's (2002) monograph on missing data is clear, comprehensive, and directed to social scientists (as is the paper by King et al., 2001).
- The edited volume by Wainer (1986) on sample-selection issues contrasts the points of view of statisticians and econometricians—in particular in an exchange between John Tukey and James Heckman. Also see the paper by Stolzenberg and Relles (1997) and the review paper by Winship and Mare (1992).

21 Bootstrapping Regression Models

Bootstrapping is a nonparametric approach to statistical inference that substitutes computation for more traditional distributional assumptions and asymptotic results.[1] Bootstrapping offers a number of advantages:

- The bootstrap is quite general, although there are some cases in which it fails.
- Because it does not require distributional assumptions (such as normally distributed errors), the bootstrap can provide more accurate inferences when the data are not well behaved or when the sample size is small.
- It is possible to apply the bootstrap to statistics with sampling distributions that are difficult to derive, even asymptotically.
- It is relatively simple to apply the bootstrap to complex data-collection plans (such as stratified and clustered samples).

21.1 Bootstrapping Basics

My principal aim is to explain how to bootstrap regression models (broadly construed to include generalized linear models, etc.), but the topic is best introduced in a simpler context: Suppose that we draw an independent random sample from a large population.[2] For concreteness and simplicity, imagine that we sample four working, married couples, determining in each case the husband's and wife's income, as recorded in Table 21.1. I will focus on the difference in incomes between husbands and wives, denoted as Y_i for the ith couple.

We want to estimate the mean difference in income between husbands and wives in the population. Please bear with me as I review some basic statistical theory: A point estimate of this population mean difference μ is the sample mean,

$$\overline{Y} = \sum \frac{Y_i}{n} = \frac{6 - 3 + 5 + 3}{4} = 2.75$$

Elementary statistical theory tells us that the standard deviation of the sampling distribution of sample means is $\text{SD}(\overline{Y}) = \sigma/\sqrt{n}$, where σ is the population standard deviation of Y.

If we knew σ, and if Y were normally distributed, then a 95% confidence interval for μ would be

$$\mu = \overline{Y} \pm 1.96 \frac{\sigma}{\sqrt{n}}$$

---

[1]The term *bootstrapping*, coined by Efron (1979), refers to using the sample to learn about the sampling distribution of a statistic without reference to external assumptions—as in "pulling oneself up by one's bootstraps."

[2]In an *independent random sample*, each element of the population can be selected more than once. In a *simple random sample*, in contrast, once an element is selected into the sample, it is removed from the population, so that sampling is done "without replacement." When the population is very large in comparison to the sample (say, at least 10 times as large), the distinction between independent and simple random sampling becomes inconsequential.

Table 21.1   Contrived "Sample" of Four Married Couples, Showing
Husbands' and Wives' Incomes in Thousands of Dollars

Observation	Husband's Income	Wife's Income	Difference Y_i
1	24	18	6
2	14	17	−3
3	40	35	5
4	44	41	3

where $z_{.025} = 1.96$ is the standard normal value with a probability of .025 to the right. If Y is *not* normally distributed in the population, then this result applies asymptotically. Of course, the asymptotics are cold comfort when $n = 4$.

In a real application, we do not know σ. The standard estimator of σ is

$$S = \sqrt{\frac{\sum(Y_i - \overline{Y})^2}{n-1}}$$

from which the standard error of the mean (i.e., the *estimated* standard deviation of $\overline{Y}$) is $\text{SE}(\overline{Y}) = S/\sqrt{n}$. If the population is normally distributed, then we can take account of the added uncertainty associated with estimating the standard deviation of the mean by substituting the heavier-tailed t-distribution for the normal distribution, producing the 95% confidence interval

$$\mu = \overline{Y} \pm t_{n-1,\,.025}\frac{S}{\sqrt{n}}$$

Here, $t_{n-1,\,.025}$ is the critical value of t with $n-1$ degrees of freedom and a right-tail probability of .025.

In the present case, $S = 4.031$, $\text{SE}(\overline{Y}) = 4.031/\sqrt{4} = 2.015$, and $t_{3,\,.025} = 3.182$. The 95% confidence interval for the population mean is thus

$$\mu = 2.75 \pm 3.182 \times 2.015 = 2.75 \pm 6.41$$

or, equivalently,

$$-3.66 < \mu < 9.16$$

As one would expect, this confidence interval—which is based on only four observations—is very wide and includes 0. It is, unfortunately, hard to be sure that the population is reasonably close to normally distributed when we have such a small sample, and so the t-interval may not be valid.[3]

Bootstrapping begins by using the distribution of data values in the sample (here, $Y_1 = 6$, $Y_2 = -3$, $Y_3 = 5$, $Y_4 = 3$) to *estimate* the distribution of Y in the population.[4] That is, we define the random variable Y^* with distribution[5]

---

[3]To say that a confidence interval is "valid" means that it has the stated coverage. That is, a 95% confidence interval is valid if it is constructed according to a procedure that encloses the population mean in 95% of samples.

[4]An alternative would be to resample from a distribution given by a nonparametric density estimate (see, e.g., Silverman & Young, 1987). Typically, however, little if anything is gained by using a more complex estimate of the population distribution. Moreover, the simpler method explained here generalizes more readily to more complex situations in which the population is multivariate or not simply characterized by a distribution.

[5]The asterisks on $p^*(\cdot)$, E^*, and V^* remind us that this probability distribution, expectation, and variance are conditional on the specific sample in hand. Were we to select another sample, the values of Y_1, Y_2, Y_3, and Y_4, would change and—along with them—the probability distribution of Y^*, its expectation, and variance.

y^*	$p^*(y^*)$
6	.25
-3	.25
5	.25
3	.25

Note that

$$E^*(Y^*) = \sum_{\text{all } y^*} y^* p(y^*) = 2.75 = \overline{Y}$$

and

$$V^*(Y^*) = \sum [y^* - E^*(Y^*)]^2 p(y^*)$$
$$= 12.187 = \frac{3}{4}S^2 = \frac{n-1}{n}S^2$$

Thus, the expectation of Y^* is just the sample mean of Y, and the variance of Y^* is [except for the factor $(n-1)/n$, which is trivial in larger samples] the sample variance of Y.

We next mimic sampling from the original population by treating the sample as if it were the population, enumerating all possible samples of size $n = 4$ from the probability distribution of Y^*. In the present case, each *bootstrap sample* selects four values *with replacement* from among the four values of the original sample. There are, therefore, $4^4 = 256$ different bootstrap samples,[6] each selected with probability 1/256. A few of the 256 samples are shown in Table 21.2. Because the four observations in each bootstrap sample are chosen with replacement, particular bootstrap samples usually have repeated observations from the original sample. Indeed, of the illustrative bootstrap samples shown in Table 21.2, only sample 100 does *not* have repeated observations.

Let us denote the bth bootstrap sample[7] as $\mathbf{y}_b^* = [Y_{b1}^*, Y_{b2}^*, Y_{b3}^*, Y_{b4}^*]'$, or more generally, $\mathbf{y}_b^* = [Y_{b1}^*, Y_{b2}^*, \ldots, Y_{bn}^*]'$, where $b = 1, 2, \ldots, n^n$. For each such bootstrap sample, we calculate the mean,

$$\overline{Y}_b^* = \frac{\sum_{i=1}^n Y_{bi}^*}{n}$$

The sampling distribution of the 256 bootstrap means is shown in Figure 21.1.

The mean of the 256 bootstrap sample means is just the original sample mean, $\overline{Y} = 2.75$. The standard deviation of the bootstrap means is

$$SD^*(\overline{Y}^*) = \sqrt{\frac{\sum_{b=1}^{n^n} (\overline{Y}_b^* - \overline{Y})^2}{n^n}}$$
$$= 1.745$$

We divide here by n^n rather than by $n^n - 1$ because the distribution of the $n^n = 256$ bootstrap sample means (Figure 21.1) is known, *not* estimated. The standard deviation of the bootstrap

---

[6]Many of the 256 samples have the same elements but in different order—for example, [6, 3, 5, 3] and [3, 5, 6, 3]. We could enumerate the unique samples without respect to order and find the probability of each, but it is simpler to work with the 256 orderings because each ordering has equal probability.

[7]If vector notation is unfamiliar, then think of $\mathbf{y}_b^*$ simply as a list of the bootstrap observations Y_{bi}^* for sample b.

Table 21.2   A Few of the 256 Bootstrap Samples for the
                 Data Set [6, −3, 5, 3], and the Corresponding
                 Bootstrap Means, $\overline{Y}_b^*$

Bootstrap Sample b	Y_{b1}^*	Y_{b2}^*	Y_{b3}^*	Y_{b4}^*	$\overline{Y}_b^*$
1	6	6	6	6	6.00
2	6	6	6	−3	3.75
3	6	6	6	5	5.75
⋮	⋮				⋮
100	−3	5	6	3	2.75
101	−3	5	−3	6	1.25
⋮	⋮				⋮
255	3	3	3	5	3.50
256	3	3	3	3	3.00

means is nearly equal to the usual standard error of the sample mean; the slight slippage is due to the factor $\sqrt{n/(n-1)}$, which is typically negligible (though not when $n = 4$):[8]

$$SE(\overline{Y}) = \sqrt{\frac{n}{n-1}}SD^*(\overline{Y}^*)$$

$$2.015 = \sqrt{\frac{4}{3}} \times 1.745$$

This precise relationship between the usual formula for the standard error and the bootstrap standard deviation is peculiar to *linear statistics* (i.e., linear functions of the data) like the mean. For the mean, then, the bootstrap standard deviation is just a more complicated way to calculate what we already know, but

- bootstrapping might still provide more accurate confidence intervals, as I will explain presently; and
- bootstrapping can be applied to *nonlinear* statistics for which we do not have standard-error formulas or for which only asymptotic standard errors are available.

Bootstrapping exploits the following central analogy:

> **The population is to the sample**
> **as**
> **the sample is to the bootstrap samples.**

Consequently,

- the *bootstrap observations* Y_{bi}^* are analogous to the *original observations* Y_i;
- the *bootstrap mean* $\overline{Y}_b^*$ is analogous to the *mean of the original sample* $\overline{Y}$;
- the *mean of the original sample* $\overline{Y}$ is analogous to the (unknown) *population mean* μ; and
- the *distribution of the bootstrap sample means* is analogous to the (unknown) *sampling distribution of means* for samples of size n drawn from the original population.

---

[8]See Exercise 21.1.

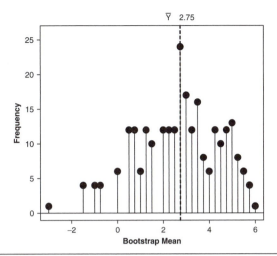

Figure 21.1   Graph of the 256 bootstrap means from the sample [6, −3, 5, 3]. The broken vertical line gives the mean of the original sample, $\overline{Y} = 2.75$, which is also the mean of the 256 bootstrap means.

> Bootstrapping uses the sample data to estimate relevant characteristics of the population. The sampling distribution of a statistic is then constructed empirically by resampling from the sample. The resampling procedure is designed to parallel the process by which sample observations were drawn from the population. For example, if the data represent an independent random sample of size n (or a simple random sample of size n from a much larger population), then each bootstrap sample selects n observations with replacement from the original sample. The key bootstrap analogy is the following: *The population is to the sample as the sample is to the bootstrap samples.*

The bootstrapping calculations that we have undertaken thus far depend on very small sample size, because the number of bootstrap samples (n^n) quickly becomes unmanageable: Even for samples as small as $n = 10$, it is impractical to enumerate all the $10^{10} = 10$ billion bootstrap samples. Consider the "data" shown in Table 21.3, an extension of the previous example. The mean and standard deviation of the differences in income Y are $\overline{Y} = 4.6$ and $S = 5.948$. Thus, the standard error of the sample mean is $\text{SE}(\overline{Y}) = 5.948/\sqrt{10} = 1.881$.

Although we cannot (as a practical matter) enumerate *all* the 10^{10} bootstrap samples, it is easy to draw at random a large number of bootstrap samples. To estimate the standard deviation of a statistic (here, the mean)—that is, to get a bootstrap standard error—100 or 200 bootstrap samples should be more than sufficient. To find a confidence interval, we will need a larger number of bootstrap samples, say 1,000 or 2,000.[9]

A practical bootstrapping procedure, therefore, is as follows:

1. Let r denote the number of *bootstrap replications*—that is, the number of bootstrap samples to be selected.

---

[9]Results presented by Efron and Tibshirani (1993, chap. 19) suggest that basing bootstrap confidence intervals on 1,000 bootstrap samples generally provides accurate results, and using 2,000 bootstrap replications should be very safe.

Table 21.3   Contrived "Sample" of 10 Married Couples, Showing
Husbands' and Wives' Incomes in Thousands of Dollars

Observation	Husband's Income	Wife's Income	Difference Y_i
1	24	18	6
2	14	17	−3
3	40	35	5
4	44	41	3
5	24	18	6
6	19	9	10
7	21	10	11
8	22	30	−8
9	30	23	7
10	24	15	9

2. For each bootstrap sample $b = 1, \ldots, r$, randomly draw n observations $Y_{b1}^*, Y_{b2}^*, \ldots,$ Y_{bn}^* with replacement from among the n sample values, and calculate the bootstrap sample mean,

$$\overline{Y}_b^* = \frac{\sum_{i=1}^n Y_{bi}^*}{n}$$

3. From the r bootstrap samples, *estimate* the standard deviation of the bootstrap means:[10]

$$\mathrm{SE}^*(\overline{Y}^*) = \sqrt{\frac{\sum_{b=1}^r \left(\overline{Y}_b^* - \overline{\overline{Y}}^*\right)^2}{r-1}}$$

where

$$\overline{\overline{Y}}^* \equiv \frac{\sum_{b=1}^r \overline{Y}_b^*}{r}$$

is the mean of the bootstrap means. We can, if we wish, "correct" $\mathrm{SE}^*(\overline{Y}^*)$ for degrees of freedom, multiplying by $\sqrt{n/(n-1)}$.

To illustrate this procedure, I drew $r = 2,000$ bootstrap samples, each of size $n = 10$, from the "data" given in Table 21.3, calculating the mean, $\overline{Y}_b^*$, for each sample. A few of the 2,000 bootstrap replications are shown in Table 21.4, and the distribution of bootstrap means is graphed in Figure 21.2.

We know from statistical theory that were we to enumerate all the 10^{10} bootstrap samples (or, alternatively, to sample infinitely from the population of bootstrap samples), the average bootstrap mean would be $E^*(\overline{Y}^*) = \overline{Y} = 4.6$, and the standard deviation of the bootstrap means would be

---

[10]It is important to distinguish between the "ideal" bootstrap estimate of the standard deviation of the mean, $\mathrm{SD}^*(\overline{Y}^*)$, which is based on *all* n^n bootstrap samples, and the *estimate* of this quantity, $\mathrm{SE}^*(\overline{Y}^*)$, which is based on r randomly selected bootstrap samples. By making r large enough, we seek to ensure that $\mathrm{SE}^*(\overline{Y}^*)$ is close to $\mathrm{SD}^*(\overline{Y}^*)$. Even $\mathrm{SD}^*(\overline{Y}^*) = \mathrm{SE}(\overline{Y})$ is an imperfect estimate of the true standard deviation of the sample mean $\mathrm{SD}(\overline{Y})$, however, because it is based on a *particular sample* of size n drawn from the original population.

Table 21.4   A Few of the $r = 2,000$ Bootstrap Samples Drawn From the Data Set $[6, -3, 5, 3, 6, 10, 11, -8, 7, 9]$ and the Corresponding Bootstrap Means, $\overline{Y}^*_b$

b	Y^*_{b1}	Y^*_{b2}	Y^*_{b3}	Y^*_{b4}	Y^*_{b5}	Y^*_{b6}	Y^*_{b7}	Y^*_{b8}	Y^*_{b9}	Y^*_{b10}	$\overline{Y}^*_b$
1	6	10	6	5	−8	9	9	6	11	3	5.7
2	9	9	7	7	3	3	−3	−3	−8	6	3.0
3	9	−3	6	5	10	6	10	10	10	6	6.9
⋮	⋮										⋮
1999	6	9	6	3	11	6	6	7	3	9	6.6
2000	7	6	7	3	10	6	9	3	10	6	6.7

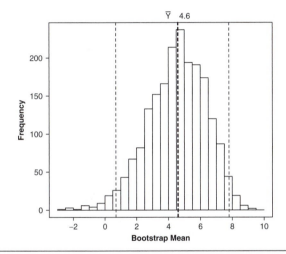

Figure 21.2   Histogram of $r = 2,000$ bootstrap means, produced by resampling from the "sample" $[6, -3, 5, 3, 6, 10, 11, -8, 7, 9]$. The heavier broken vertical line gives the sample mean, $\overline{Y} = 4.6$; the ligher broken vertical lines give the boundaries of the 95% percentile confidence interval for the population mean μ based on the 2,000 bootstrap samples. The procedure for constructing this confidence interval is described in the next section.

$\text{SE}^*(\overline{Y}^*) = \text{SE}(\overline{Y})\sqrt{(n-1)/n} = 1.881\sqrt{9/10} = 1.784$. For the 2,000 bootstrap samples that I selected, $\overline{\overline{Y}}^* = 4.693$ and $\text{SE}(\overline{Y}^*) = 1.750$—both quite close to the theoretical values.

The bootstrapping procedure described in this section can be generalized to derive the empirical sampling distribution for an estimator $\hat{\theta}$ of the parameter θ:

1. Specify the data-collection scheme $\mathcal{S}$ that gives rise to the observed sample when applied to the population:[11]

$$\mathcal{S}(\text{Population}) \Longrightarrow \text{Sample}$$

---

[11] The "population" can be real—the population of working married couples—or hypothetical—the population of conceivable replications of an experiment. What is important in the present context is that the sampling procedure can be described concretely.

The estimator $\widehat{\theta}$ is some function $s(\cdot)$ of the observed sample. In the preceding example, the data-collection procedure is independent random sampling from a large population.

2. Using the observed sample data as a "stand-in" for the population, replicate the data-collection procedure, producing r bootstrap samples:

$$
\mathcal{S}(\text{Sample}) \left\{ \begin{array}{l} \Longrightarrow \quad \text{Bootstrap sample}_1 \\ \Longrightarrow \quad \text{Bootstrap sample}_2 \\ \qquad \vdots \\ \Longrightarrow \quad \text{Bootstrap sample}_r \end{array} \right.
$$

3. For each bootstrap sample, calculate the estimate $\widehat{\theta}_b^* = s(\text{Bootstrap sample}_b)$.

4. Use the distribution of the $\widehat{\theta}_b^*$s to estimate properties of the sampling distribution of $\widehat{\theta}$. For example, the bootstrap standard error of $\widehat{\theta}$ is $\text{SE}^*(\theta^*)$ (i.e., the standard deviation of the r bootstrap replications $\widehat{\theta}_b^*$):[12]

$$
\text{SE}^*(\theta^*) \equiv \sqrt{\frac{\sum_{b=1}^{r}(\widehat{\theta}_b^* - \overline{\theta}^*)^2}{r-1}}
$$

where

$$
\overline{\theta}^* \equiv \frac{\sum_{b=1}^{r}\widehat{\theta}_b^*}{r}
$$

21.2   Bootstrap Confidence Intervals

21.2.1   Normal-Theory Intervals

As I have mentioned, normal-theory confidence intervals for means are based on the t-distribution when the population variance of Y is unknown. Most statistics, including sample means, are asymptotically normally distributed; in large samples we can therefore use the bootstrap standard error, along with the normal distribution, to produce a $100(1-a)\%$ confidence interval for θ based on the estimator $\widehat{\theta}$:

$$
\theta = \widehat{\theta} \pm z_{a/2}\text{SE}^*(\theta^*) \tag{21.1}
$$

In Equation 21.1, $z_{a/2}$ is the standard normal value with probability $a/2$ to the right. This approach will work well if the bootstrap sampling distribution of the estimator is approximately normal, and so it is advisable to examine a normal quantile-comparison plot of the bootstrap distribution.

There is no advantage to calculating normal-theory bootstrap confidence intervals for linear statistics like the mean, because in this case the ideal bootstrap standard deviation of the statistic and the standard error based directly on the sample coincide. Using bootstrap resampling in this setting just makes for extra work and introduces an additional small random component into standard errors.

---

[12]We may want to apply the correction factor $\sqrt{n/(n-1)}$.

Having produced r bootstrap replicates $\widehat{\theta}_b^*$ of an estimator $\widehat{\theta}$, the bootstrap standard error is the standard deviation of the bootstrap replicates: $SE^*(\widehat{\theta}^*) = \sqrt{\sum_{b=1}^r (\widehat{\theta}_b^* - \overline{\theta}^*)^2/(r - 1)}$, where $\overline{\theta}^*$ is the mean of the $\widehat{\theta}_b^*$. In large samples, where we can rely on the normality of $\widehat{\theta}$, a 95% confidence interval for θ is given by $\widehat{\theta} \pm 1.96\, SE^*(\widehat{\theta}^*)$.

21.2.2 Percentile Intervals

Another very simple approach is to use the quantiles of the bootstrap sampling distribution of the estimator to establish the end points of a confidence interval *nonparametrically*. Let $\widehat{\theta}_{(b)}^*$ represent the ordered bootstrap estimates, and suppose that we want to construct a $(100 - a)\%$ confidence interval. If the number of bootstrap replications r is large (as it should be to construct a percentile interval), then the $a/2$ and $1 - a/2$ quantiles of $\widehat{\theta}_b^*$ are approximately $\widehat{\theta}_{(\text{lower})}^*$ and $\widehat{\theta}_{(\text{upper})}^*$, where lower $= ra/2$ and upper $= r(1 - a/2)$. If lower and upper are not integers, then we can interpolate between adjacent ordered values $\widehat{\theta}_{(b)}^*$ or round off to the nearest integer.

A nonparametric confidence interval for θ can be constructed from the quantiles of the bootstrap sampling distribution of $\widehat{\theta}^*$. The 95% percentile interval is $\widehat{\theta}_{(\text{lower})}^* < \theta < \widehat{\theta}_{(\text{upper})}^*$, where the $\widehat{\theta}_{(b)}^*$ are the r ordered bootstrap replicates; lower $= .025 \times r$ and upper $= .975 \times r$.

A 95% confidence interval for the $r = 2,000$ resampled means in Figure 21.2, for example, is constructed as follows:

$$\text{lower} = 2000(.05/2) = 50$$
$$\text{upper} = 2000(1 - .05/2) = 1950$$
$$\overline{Y}_{(50)}^* = 0.7$$
$$\overline{Y}_{(1950)}^* = 7.8$$
$$0.7 < \mu < 7.8$$

The end points of this interval are marked in Figure 21.2. Because of the skew of the bootstrap distribution, the percentile interval is not quite symmetric around $\overline{Y} = 4.6$. By way of comparison, the standard t-interval for the mean of the original sample of 10 observations is

$$\mu = \overline{Y} \pm t_{9,\,.025} SE(\overline{Y})$$
$$= 4.6 \pm 2.262 \times 1.881$$
$$= 4.6 \pm 4.255$$
$$0.345 < \mu < 8.855$$

In this case, the standard interval is a bit wider than the percentile interval, especially at the top.

21.2.3   Improved Bootstrap Intervals

I will briefly describe an adjustment to percentile intervals that improves their accuracy.[13] As before, we want to produce a $100(1 - a)\%$ confidence interval for θ having computed the sample estimate $\widehat{\theta}$ and bootstrap replicates $\widehat{\theta}_b^*$; $b = 1, \ldots, r$. We require $z_{a/2}$, the unit-normal value with probability $a/2$ to the right, and two "correction factors," Z and A, defined in the following manner:

- Calculate

$$
Z \equiv \Phi^{-1} \left[\frac{\overset{r}{\underset{b=1}{\#}} (\widehat{\theta}_b^* < \widehat{\theta})}{r} \right]
$$

   where $\Phi^{-1}(\cdot)$ is the inverse of the standard normal distribution function, and $\#(\widehat{\theta}_b^* < \widehat{\theta})/r$ is the proportion of bootstrap replicates below the estimate $\widehat{\theta}$. If the bootstrap sampling distribution is symmetric and if $\widehat{\theta}$ is unbiased, then this proportion will be close to .5, and the "correction factor" Z will be close to 0.
- Let $\widehat{\theta}_{(-i)}$ represent the value of $\widehat{\theta}$ produced when the ith observation is deleted from the sample;[14] there are n of these quantities. Let $\overline{\theta}$ represent the average of the $\widehat{\theta}_{(-i)}$; that is, $\overline{\theta} \equiv \sum_{i=1}^{n} \widehat{\theta}_{(-i)}/n$. Then calculate

$$
A \equiv \frac{\sum_{i=1}^{n} (\overline{\theta} - \widehat{\theta}_{(-i)})^3}{6[\sum_{i=1}^{n} (\widehat{\theta}_{(-i)} - \overline{\theta})^2]^{3/2}} \tag{21.2}
$$

With the correction factors Z and A in hand, compute

$$
A_1 \equiv \Phi \left[Z + \frac{Z - z_{a/2}}{1 - A(Z - z_{a/2})} \right]
$$

$$
A_2 \equiv \Phi \left[Z + \frac{Z + z_{a/2}}{1 - A(Z + z_{a/2})} \right]
$$

where $\Phi(\cdot)$ is the cumulative standard normal distribution function. Note that when the correction factors Z and A are both 0, $A_1 = \Phi(-z_{a/2}) = a/2$, and $A_2 = \Phi(z_{a/2}) = 1 - a/2$. The values A_1 and A_2 are used to locate the end points of the corrected percentile confidence interval. In particular, the corrected interval is

$$
\widehat{\theta}_{(\text{lower}*)}^* < \theta < \widehat{\theta}_{(\text{upper}*)}^*
$$

where lower* $= rA_1$ and upper* $= rA_2$ (rounding or interpolating as required).

> The lower and upper bounds of percentile confidence intervals can be corrected to improve the accuracy of these intervals.

---

[13]The interval described here is called a "bias-corrected, accelerated" (or BC_a) percentile interval. Details can be found in Efron and Tibshirani (1993, chap. 14); also see Stine (1990) for a discussion of different procedures for constructing bootstrap confidence intervals.

[14]The $\widehat{\theta}_{(-i)}$ are called the *jackknife values* of the statistic $\widehat{\theta}$. The jackknife values can also be used as an alternative to the bootstrap to find a nonparametric confidence interval for θ. See Exercise 21.2.

Applying this procedure to the "data" in Table 21.3, we have $z_{.05/2} = 1.96$ for a 95% confidence interval. There are 926 bootstrapped means below $\overline{Y} = 4.6$, and so $Z = \Phi^{-1}(926/2000) = -0.09288$. The $\overline{Y}_{(-i)}$ are 4.444, 5.444, ... , 4.111; the mean of these values is $\overline{\overline{Y}} = \overline{Y} = 4.6$,[15] and (from Equation 21.2) $A = -0.05630$. Using these correction factors,

$$A_1 = \Phi\left\{-0.09288 + \frac{-0.09288 - 1.96}{1 - [-.05630(-0.09288 - 1.96)]}\right\}$$

$$= \Phi(-2.414) = 0.007889$$

$$A_2 = \Phi\left\{-0.09288 + \frac{-0.09288 + 1.96}{1 - [-.05630(-0.09288 + 1.96)]}\right\}$$

$$= \Phi(1.597) = 0.9449$$

Multiplying by r, we have $2000 \times .0.007889 \approx 16$ and $2000 \times .0.9449 \approx 1890$, from which

$$\overline{Y}^*_{(16)} < \mu < \overline{Y}^*_{(1890)} \tag{21.3}$$

$$-0.4 < \mu < 7.3$$

Unlike the other confidence intervals that we have calculated for the "sample" of 10 differences in income between husbands and wives, the interval given in Equation 21.3 includes 0.

21.3   Bootstrapping Regression Models

The procedures of the previous section can be easily extended to regression models. The most straightforward approach is to collect the response-variable value and regressors for each observation

$$\mathbf{z}'_i \equiv [Y_i, X_{i1}, \ldots, X_{ik}]$$

Then the observations $\mathbf{z}'_1, \mathbf{z}'_2, \ldots, \mathbf{z}'_n$ can be resampled, and the regression estimator computed for each of the resulting bootstrap samples, $\mathbf{z}^{*\prime}_{b1}, \mathbf{z}^{*\prime}_{b2}, \ldots, \mathbf{z}^{*\prime}_{bn}$, producing r sets of bootstrap regression coefficients, $\mathbf{b}^*_b = [A^*_b, B^*_{b1}, \ldots, B^*_{bk}]'$. The methods of the previous section can be applied to compute standard errors or confidence intervals for the regression estimates.

Directly resampling the observations $\mathbf{z}'_i$ implicitly treats the regressors $X_1, \ldots, X_k$ as *random* rather than *fixed*. We may want to treat the Xs as fixed (if, e.g., the data derive from an experimental design). In the case of linear regression, for example,

1. Estimate the regression coefficients $A, B_1, \ldots, B_k$ for the original sample, and calculate the fitted value and residual for each observation:

$$\widehat{Y}_i = A + B_1 x_{i1} + \cdots + B_k x_{ik}$$

$$E_i = Y_i - \widehat{Y}_i$$

2. Select bootstrap samples of the *residuals*, $\mathbf{e}^*_b = [E^*_{b1}, E^*_{b2}, \ldots, E^*_{bn}]'$, and from these, calculate bootstrapped Y values, $\mathbf{y}^*_b = [Y^*_{b1}, Y^*_{b2}, \ldots, Y^*_{bn}]'$, where $Y^*_{bi} = \widehat{Y}_i + E^*_{bi}$.

---

[15]The average of the jackknifed estimates is not, in general, the same as the estimate calculated for the full sample, but this *is* the case for the jackknifed sample means. See Exercise 21.2.

3. Regress the bootstrapped Y values on the *fixed* X values to obtain bootstrap regression coefficients.

   *If, for example, estimates are calculated by least-squares regression, then $\mathbf{b}_b^* = (\mathbf{X}'\mathbf{X})^{-1}\mathbf{X}'\mathbf{y}_b^*$ for $b = 1, \ldots, r$.

4. The resampled $\mathbf{b}_b^* = [A_b^*, B_{b1}^*, \ldots, B_{bk}^*]'$ can be used in the usual manner to construct bootstrap standard errors and confidence intervals for the regression coefficients.

Bootstrapping with fixed X draws an analogy between the fitted value $\widehat{Y}$ in the sample and the conditional expectation of Y in the population, and between the residual E in the sample and the error ε in the population. Although no assumption is made about the *shape* of the error distribution, the bootstrapping procedure, by constructing the Y_{bi}^* according to the linear model, implicitly assumes that the functional form of the model is correct.

Furthermore, by resampling residuals and randomly reattaching them to fitted values, the procedure implicitly assumes that the errors are *identically distributed*. If, for example, the true errors have nonconstant variance, then this property will *not* be reflected in the resampled residuals. Likewise, the unique impact of a high-leverage outlier will be lost to the resampling.[16]

Regression models and similar statistical models can be bootstrapped by (1) treating the regressors as random and selecting bootstrap samples directly from the observations $\mathbf{z}_i' = [Y_i, X_{i1}, \ldots, X_{ik}]$ or (2) treating the regressors as fixed and resampling from the residuals E_i of the fitted regression model. In the latter instance, bootstrap observations are constructed as $Y_{bi}^* = \widehat{Y}_i + E_{bi}^*$, where the $\widehat{Y}_i$ are the fitted values from the original regression, and the E_{bi}^* are the resampled residuals for the bth bootstrap sample. In each bootstrap sample, the Y_{bi}^* are then regressed on the original Xs. A disadvantage of fixed-X resampling is that the procedure implicitly assumes that the functional form of the regression model fit to the data is correct and that the errors are identically distributed.

To illustrate bootstrapping regression coefficients, I will use Duncan's regression of occupational prestige on the income and educational levels of 45 U.S. occupations.[17] The Huber M estimator applied to Duncan's regression produces the following fit, with asymptotic standard errors shown in parentheses beneath each coefficient:[18]

$$\widehat{\text{Prestige}} = \underset{(3.588)}{-7.289} + \underset{(0.1005)}{0.7104} \ \text{Income} + \underset{(0.0825)}{0.4819} \ \text{Education}$$

Using random resampling, I drew $r = 2,000$ bootstrap samples, calculating the Huber estimator for each bootstrap sample. The results of this computationally intensive procedure are summarized in Table 21.5. The distributions of the bootstrapped regression coefficients for income and education are graphed in Figure 21.3(a) and (b), along with the percentile confidence intervals for these coefficients. Figure 21.3(c) shows a scatterplot of the bootstrapped coefficients

---

[16]For these reasons, random-X resampling may be preferable even if the X values are best conceived as fixed. See Exercise 21.3.

[17]These data were discussed in Chapter 19 on robust regression and at several other points in this text.

[18]M estimation is a method of robust regression described in Section 19.1.

Table 21.5 Statistics for $r = 2,000$ Bootstrapped Huber Regressions Applied to Duncan's Occupational Prestige Data

	Coefficient		
	Constant	Income	Education
Average bootstrap estimate	−7.001	0.6903	0.4918
Bootstrap standard error	3.165	0.1798	0.1417
Asymptotic standard error	3.588	0.1005	0.0825
Normal-theory interval	(−13.423,−1.018)	(0.3603,1.0650)	(0.2013,0.7569)
Percentile interval	(−13.150,−0.577)	(0.3205,1.0331)	(0.2030,0.7852)
Adjusted percentile interval	(−12.935,−0.361)	(0.2421,0.9575)	(0.2511,0.8356)

NOTES: Three bootstrap confidence intervals are shown for each coefficient. Asymptotic standard errors are also shown for comparison.

for income and education, which gives a sense of the covariation of the two estimates; it is clear that the income and education coefficients are strongly negatively correlated.[19]

The bootstrap standard errors of the income and education coefficients are much larger than the asymptotic standard errors, underscoring the inadequacy of the latter in small samples. The simple normal-theory confidence intervals based on the bootstrap standard errors (and formed as the estimated coefficients ±1.96 standard errors) are reasonably similar to the percentile intervals for the income and education coefficients; the percentile intervals differ slightly from the adjusted percentile intervals. Comparing the average bootstrap coefficients $\overline{A}^*$, $\overline{B}_1^*$, and $\overline{B}_2^*$ with the corresponding estimates A, B_1, and B_2 suggests that there is little, if any, bias in the Huber estimates.[20]

21.4 Bootstrap Hypothesis Tests*

In addition to providing standard errors and confidence intervals, the bootstrap can also be used to test statistical hypotheses. The application of the bootstrap to hypothesis testing is more or less obvious for individual coefficients because a bootstrap confidence interval can be used to test the hypothesis that the corresponding parameter is equal to any specific value (typically 0 for a regression coefficient).

More generally, let $T \equiv t(\mathbf{z})$ represent a test statistic, written as a function of the sample $\mathbf{z}$. The contents of $\mathbf{z}$ vary by context. In regression analysis, for example, $\mathbf{z}$ is the $n \times k+1$ matrix $[\mathbf{y}, \mathbf{X}]$ containing the response variable and the regressors.

For concreteness, suppose that T is the Wald-like test statistic for the omnibus null hypothesis $H_0: \beta_1 = \cdots = \beta_k = 0$ in a robust regression, calculated using the estimated asymptotic covariance matrix for the regression coefficients. That is, let $\mathbf{V}_{11}$ contain the rows and columns $\underset{(k \times k)}{}$ of the estimated asymptotic covariance matrix $\widehat{\mathcal{V}}(\mathbf{b})$ that pertain to the k slope coefficients $\mathbf{b}_1 = [B_1, \ldots, B_k]'$. We can write the null hypothesis as $H_0: \beta_1 = \mathbf{0}$. Then the test statistic is

$$T = \mathbf{b}_1' \mathbf{V}_{11}^{-1} \mathbf{b}_1$$

---

[19]The negative correlation of the coefficients reflects the *positive* correlation between income and education (see Section 9.4.4). The hint of bimodality in the distribution of the income coefficient suggests the possible presence of influential observations. See the discussion of Duncan's regression in Section 4.6.

[20]For the use of the bootstrap to estimate bias, see Exercise 21.4.

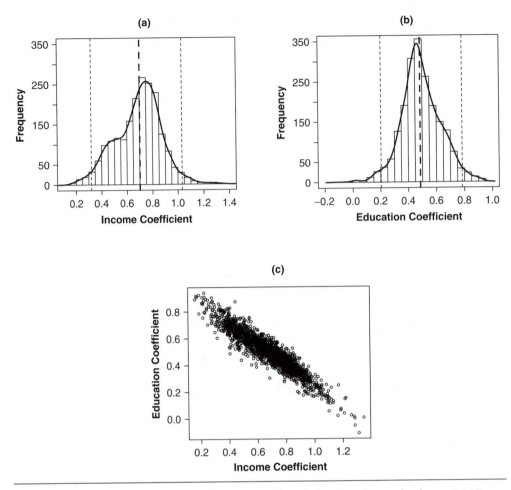

Figure 21.3   Panels (a) and (b) show histograms and kernel density estimates for the $r = 2,000$ bootstrap replicates of the income and education coefficients in Duncan's occupational prestige regression. The regression model was fit by M estimation using the Huber weight function. Panel (c) shows a scatterplot of the income and education coefficients for the 2,000 bootstrap samples.

We could compare the obtained value of this statistic to the quantiles of χ_k^2, but we are loath to do so because we do not trust the asymptotics. We can, instead, construct the sampling distribution of the test statistic nonparametrically, using the bootstrap.

Let $T_b^* \equiv t(\mathbf{z}_b^*)$ represent the test statistic calculated for the bth bootstrap sample, $\mathbf{z}_b^*$. We have to be careful to draw a proper analogy here: Because the original-sample estimates play the role of the regression parameters in the bootstrap "population" (i.e., the original sample), the bootstrap analog of the null hypothesis—to be used with each bootstrap sample—is $H_0: \beta_1 = B_1, \ldots, \beta_k = B_k$. The bootstrapped test statistic is, therefore,

$$T_b^* = (\mathbf{b}_{b1}^* - \mathbf{b}_1)' \mathbf{V}_{b,11}^{*-1} (\mathbf{b}_{b1}^* - \mathbf{b}_1)$$

Having obtained r bootstrap replications of the test statistic, the bootstrap estimate of the p-value for H_0 is simply[21]

$$\widehat{p}^* = \frac{\#_{b=1}^r (T_b^* \geq T)}{r}$$

Note that for this chi-square-like test, the p-value is entirely from the upper tail of the distribution of the bootstrapped test statistics.

> Bootstrap hypothesis tests proceed by constructing an empirical sampling distribution for the test statistic. If T represents the test statistic computed for the original sample, and T_b^* is the test statistic for the bth of r bootstrap samples, then (for a chi-square-like test statistic) the p-value for the test is $\#(T_b^* \geq T)/r$.

21.5 Bootstrapping Complex Sampling Designs

One of the great virtues of the bootstrap is that it can be applied in a natural manner to more complex sampling designs. If, for example, the population is divided into S *strata*, with n_s observations drawn from stratum s, then bootstrap samples can be constructed by resampling n_s observations with replacement from the sth stratum. Likewise, if observations are drawn into the sample in *clusters* rather than individually, then the bootstrap should resample clusters rather than individuals. We can still calculate estimates and test statistics in the usual manner using the bootstrap to assess sampling variation in place of the standard formulas, which are appropriate for independent random samples but not for complex survey samples.

When different observations are selected for the sample with unequal probabilities, it is common to take account of this fact by differentially weighting the observations in inverse proportion to their probability of selection.[22] Thus, for example, in calculating the (weighted) sample mean of a variable Y, we take

$$\overline{Y}^{(w)} = \frac{\sum_{i=1}^n w_i Y_i}{\sum_{i=1}^n w_i}$$

and to calculate the (weighted) correlation of X and Y, we take

$$r_{XY}^{(w)} = \frac{\sum w_i (X_i - \overline{X})(Y_i - \overline{Y})}{\sqrt{[\sum w_i (X_i - \overline{X})^2][\sum w_i (Y_i - \overline{Y})^2]}}$$

Other statistical formulas can be adjusted analogously.[23]

The case weights are often scaled so that $\sum w_i = n$, but simply incorporating the weights in the usual formulas for standard errors does not produce correct results. Once more, the bootstrap

---

[21] There is a subtle point here: We use the sample estimate $\mathbf{b}_1$ in place of the hypothesized parameter $\beta_1^{(0)}$ to calculate the bootstrapped test statistic T_b^* *regardless* of the hypothesis that we are testing—because in the central bootstrap analogy $\mathbf{b}_1$ stands in for β_1 (and the bootstrapped sampling distribution of the test statistic is computed under the assumption that the hypothesis is *true*). See Exercise 21.5 for an application of this test to Duncan's regression.

[22] These "case weights" are to be distinguished from the variance weights used in weighted-least-squares regression (see Section 12.2.2).

[23] See Exercise 21.6.

provides a straightforward solution: Draw bootstrap samples in which the probability of inclusion is proportional to the probability of inclusion in the original sample, and calculate bootstrap replicates of the statistics of interest using the case weights.

The essential "trick" of using the bootstrap in these (and other) instances is to resample from the data in the same way as the original sample was drawn from the population. Statistics are calculated for each bootstrap replication in the same manner as for the original sample.

> The bootstrap can be applied to complex sampling designs (involving, e.g., stratification, clustering, and case-weighting) by resampling from the sample data in the same manner as the original sample was selected from the population.

Social scientists frequently analyze data from complex sampling designs as if they originate from independent random samples (even though there are often non-negligible dependencies among the observations) or employ ad hoc adjustments (e.g., by weighting). A tacit defense of common practice is that to take account of the dependencies in complex sampling designs is too difficult. The bootstrap provides a simple solution.[24]

21.6 Concluding Remarks

If the bootstrap is so simple and of such broad application, why isn't it used more in the social sciences? Beyond the problem of lack of familiarity (which surely can be remedied), there are, I believe, three serious obstacles to increased use of the bootstrap:

1. Common practice—such as relying on asymptotic results in small samples or treating dependent data as if they were independent—usually *understates* sampling variation and makes results look stronger than they really are. Researchers are understandably reluctant to report honest standard errors when the usual calculations indicate greater precision. It is best, however, not to fool yourself, regardless of what you think about fooling others.

2. Although the conceptual basis of the bootstrap is intuitively simple and although the calculations are straightforward, to apply the bootstrap it is necessary to write or find suitable statistical software. There is some bootstrapping software available, but the nature of the bootstrap—which adapts resampling to the data-collection plan and statistics employed in an investigation—apparently precludes full generality and makes it difficult to use traditional statistical computer packages. After all, researchers are not tediously going to draw 2,000 samples from their data unless a computer program can fully automate the process. This impediment is much less acute in programmable statistical computing environments.[25]

3. Even with good software, the bootstrap is computationally intensive. This barrier to bootstrapping is more apparent than real, however. Computational speed is central to the

---

[24] Alternatively, we can use sampling-variance estimates that are appropriate to complex survey samples—a subject that is beyond the scope of this book. See, for example, Skinner, Holt, and Smith (1989).

[25] See, for example, the bootstrapping software for the S (R and S-PLUS) statistical-computing environment described by Efron and Tibshirani (1993, app.) and by Davison and Hinkley (1997, chap. 11). Bootstrapping facilities are also provided in the Stata programming environment.

exploratory stages of data analysis: When the outcome of one of many small steps imme-diately affects the next, rapid results are important. This is why a responsive computing environment is especially useful for regression diagnostics, for example. It is not nearly as important to calculate standard errors and p-values quickly. With powerful, yet relatively inexpensive, desktop computers, there is nothing to preclude the machine from cranking away unattended for a few hours (although that is rarely necessary—a few minutes is more typical). The time and effort involved in a bootstrap calculation are usually small compared with the totality of a research investigation—and are a small price to pay for accurate and realistic inference.

Exercises

Exercise 21.1. *Show that the mean of the n^n bootstrap means is the sample mean

$$E^*(\overline{Y}^*) = \frac{\sum_{b=1}^{n^n} \overline{Y}_b^*}{n^n} = \overline{Y}$$

and that the standard deviation (standard error) of the bootstrap means is

$$SE^*(\overline{Y}^*) = \sqrt{\frac{\sum_{b=1}^{n^n} (\overline{Y}_b^* - \overline{Y})^2}{n^n}} = \frac{S}{\sqrt{n-1}}$$

where $S = \sqrt{\sum_{i=1}^{n} (Y_i - \overline{Y})^2/(n-1)}$ is the sample standard deviation. (*Hint*: Exploit the fact that the mean is a linear function of the observations.)

Exercise 21.2. The jackknife: The "jackknife" (suggested for estimation of standard errors by Tukey, 1958) is an alternative to the bootstrap that requires less computation, but that often does not perform as well and is not quite as general. Efron and Tibshirani (1993, chap. 11) show that the jackknife is an approximation to the bootstrap. Here is a brief description of the jackknife for the estimator $\widehat{\theta}$ of a parameter θ:

1. Divide the sample into m independent groups. In most instances (unless the sample size is very large), we take $m = n$, in which case each observation constitutes a "group." If the data originate from a cluster sample, then the observations in a cluster should be kept together.

2. Recalculate the estimator omitting the jth group, $j = 1, \ldots, m$, denoting the resulting value of the estimator as $\widehat{\theta}_{(-j)}$. The *pseudo-value* associated with the jth group is defined as $\widehat{\theta}_j^* \equiv m\widehat{\theta} - (m-1)\widehat{\theta}_{(-j)}$.

3. The average of the pseudo-values, $\widehat{\theta}^* \equiv (\sum_{j=1}^{m} \widehat{\theta}_j^*)/m$ is the jackknifed estimate of θ. A jackknifed $100(1-a)\%$ confidence interval for θ is given by

$$\theta = \widehat{\theta}^* \pm t_{a/2, m-1} \frac{S^*}{\sqrt{n}}$$

where $t_{a/2, m-1}$ is the critical value of t with probability $a/2$ to the right for $m-1$ degrees of freedom, and $S^* \equiv \sqrt{\sum_{j=1}^{m} (\widehat{\theta}_j^* - \widehat{\theta}^*)^2/(m-1)}$ is the standard deviation of the pseudo-values.

(a) *Show that when the jackknife procedure is applied to the mean with $m = n$, the pseudo-values are just the original observations, $\widehat{\theta}_i^* = Y_i$; the jackknifed estimate $\widehat{\theta}^*$ is, therefore, the sample mean $\overline{Y}$; and the jackknifed confidence interval is the same as the usual t confidence interval.

(b) Demonstrate the results in part (a) numerically for the contrived "data" in Table 21.3. (These results are peculiar to linear statistics like the mean.)

(c) Find jackknifed confidence intervals for the Huber M estimator of Duncan's regression of occupational prestige on income and education. Compare these intervals with the bootstrap and normal-theory intervals given in Table 21.5.

Exercise 21.3. Random versus fixed resampling in regression:

(a) Recall (from Chapter 2), Davis's data on measured and reported weight for 101 women engaged in regular exercise. Bootstrap the least-squares regression of reported weight on measured weight, drawing $r = 1,000$ bootstrap samples using (1) random-X resampling and (2) fixed-X resampling. In each case, plot a histogram (and, if you wish, a density estimate) of the 1,000 bootstrap slopes, and calculate the bootstrap estimate of standard error for the slope. How does the influential outlier in this regression affect random resampling? How does it affect fixed resampling?

(b) Randomly construct a data set of 100 observations according to the regression model $Y_i = 5 + 2x_i + \varepsilon_i$, where $x_i = 1, 2, \ldots, 100$, and the errors are independent (but seriously heteroscedastic), with $\varepsilon_i \sim N(0, x_i^2)$. As in (a), bootstrap the least-squares regression of Y on x, using (1) random resampling and (2) fixed resampling. In each case, plot the bootstrap distribution of the slope coefficient, and calculate the bootstrap estimate of standard error for this coefficient. Compare the results for random and fixed resampling. For a few of the bootstrap samples, plot the least-squares residuals against the fitted values. How do these plots differ for fixed versus random resampling?

(c) Why might random resampling be preferred in these contexts, even if (as is *not* the case for Davis's data) the X values are best conceived as fixed?

Exercise 21.4. Bootstrap estimates of bias: The bootstrap can be used to estimate the bias of an estimator $\widehat{\theta}$ of a parameter θ, simply by comparing the mean of the bootstrap distribution $\overline{\theta}^*$ (which stands in for the expectation of the estimator) with the sample estimate $\widehat{\theta}$ (which stands in for the parameter); that is, $\widehat{\text{bias}} = \overline{\theta}^* - \widehat{\theta}$. (Further discussion and more sophisticated methods are described in Efron and Tibshirani, 1993, chap. 10.) Employ this approach to estimate the bias of the maximum-likelihood estimator of the variance, $\widehat{\sigma}^2 = \sum (Y_i - \overline{Y})^2 / n$, for a sample of $n = 10$ observations drawn from the normal distribution $N(0, 100)$. Use $r = 500$ bootstrap replications. How close is the bootstrap bias estimate to the theoretical value $-\sigma^2 / n = -100/10 = -10$?

Exercise 21.5. *Test the omnibus null hypothesis H_0: $\beta_1 = \beta_2 = 0$ for the Huber M estimator in Duncan's regression of occupational prestige on income and education.

(a) Base the test on the estimated asymptotic covariance matrix of the coefficients.

(b) Use the bootstrap approach described in Section 21.4.

Exercise 21.6. Case weights:

(a) *Show how case weights can be used to "adjust" the usual formulas for the least-squares coefficients and their covariance matrix. How do these case-weighted formulas compare with those for weighted-least-squares regression (discussed in Section 12.2.2)?

(b) Using data from a sample survey that employed disproportional sampling and for which case weights are supplied, estimate a least-squares regression (1) ignoring the case weights; (2) using the case weights to estimate both the regression coefficients and their standard errors (rescaling the case weights, if necessary, so that they sum to the sample size); and (3) using the case weights but estimating coefficient standard errors with the bootstrap. Compare the estimates and standard errors obtained in (1), (2), and (3).

Exercise 21.7. *Bootstrapping time-series regression: Bootstrapping can be adapted to time series regression but, as in the case of fixed-X resampling, the procedure makes strong use of the model fit to the data—in particular, the manner in which serial dependency in the data is modeled. Suppose that the errors in the linear model $\mathbf{y} = \mathbf{X}\boldsymbol{\beta} + \boldsymbol{\varepsilon}$ follow a first-order autoregressive process (see Chapter 16), $\varepsilon_i = \rho\varepsilon_{i-1} + \upsilon_i$; the υ_i are independently and identically distributed with zero expectations and common variance σ_υ^2. Suppose further that we use the method of maximum likelihood to obtain estimates $\widehat{\rho}$ and $\widehat{\boldsymbol{\beta}}$. From the residuals $\mathbf{e} = \mathbf{y} - \mathbf{X}\widehat{\boldsymbol{\beta}}$, we can estimate υ_i as $V_i = E_i - \widehat{\rho}E_{i-1}$ for $i = 2, \ldots, n$; by convention, we take $V_1 = E_1$. Then, for each bootstrap replication, we sample n values with replacement from the V_i; call them V_{b1}^*, $V_{b2}^*, \ldots, V_{bn}^*$. Using these values, we construct residuals $E_{b1}^* = V_{b1}^*$ and $E_{bi}^* = \widehat{\rho}E_{b, i-1}^* + V_{bi}^*$ for $i = 2, \ldots, n$; and from these residuals and the original fitted values $\widehat{Y}_i = \mathbf{x}_i'\widehat{\boldsymbol{\beta}}$, we construct bootstrapped Y values, $Y_{bi}^* = \widehat{Y}_i + E_{bi}^*$. The Y_{bi}^* are used along with the original $\mathbf{x}_i'$ to obtain bootstrap replicates $\widehat{\boldsymbol{\beta}}_b^*$ of the ML coefficient estimates. (Why are the $\mathbf{x}_i'$ treated as fixed?) Employ this procedure to compute standard errors of the coefficient estimates in the time-series regression for the Canadian women's crime-rate data (discussed in Chapter 16), using an AR(1) process for the errors. Compare the bootstrap standard errors with the usual asymptotic standard errors. Which standard errors do you prefer? Why? Then describe a bootstrap procedure for a time-series regression model with AR(2) errors, and apply this procedure to the Canadian women's crime-rate regression.

Summary

- Bootstrapping is a broadly applicable, nonparametric approach to statistical inference that substitutes intensive computation for more traditional distributional assumptions and asymptotic results. The bootstrap can be used to derive accurate standard errors, confidence intervals, and hypothesis tests for most statistics.
- Bootstrapping uses the sample data to estimate relevant characteristics of the population. The sampling distribution of a statistic is then constructed empirically by resampling from the sample. The resampling procedure is designed to parallel the process by which sample observations were drawn from the population. For example, if the data represent an independent random sample of size n (or a simple random sample of size n from a much larger population), then each bootstrap sample selects n observations with replacement from the original sample. The key bootstrap analogy is the following: *The population is to the sample as the sample is to the bootstrap samples.*
- Having produced r bootstrap replicates $\widehat{\theta}_b^*$ of an estimator $\widehat{\theta}$, the bootstrap standard error is the standard deviation of the bootstrap replicates:

$$\text{SE}^*(\widehat{\theta}^*) = \sqrt{\frac{\sum_{b=1}^{r}(\widehat{\theta}_b^* - \overline{\theta}^*)^2}{r - 1}}$$

where $\overline{\theta}^*$ is the mean of the $\widehat{\theta}_b^*$. In large samples, where we can rely on the normality of $\widehat{\theta}$, a 95% confidence interval for θ is given by $\widehat{\theta} \pm 1.96\,\text{SE}^*(\widehat{\theta}^*)$.

- A nonparametric confidence interval for θ can be constructed from the quantiles of the bootstrap sampling distribution of $\widehat{\theta}^*$. The 95% percentile interval is $\widehat{\theta}^*_{(\text{lower})} < \theta < \widehat{\theta}^*_{(\text{upper})}$, where the $\widehat{\theta}^*_{(b)}$ are the r ordered bootstrap replicates; lower $= .025 \times r$ and upper $= .975 \times r$.

- The lower and upper bounds of percentile confidence intervals can be corrected to improve the accuracy of these intervals.

- Regression models can be bootstrapped by (1) treating the regressors as random and selecting bootstrap samples directly from the observations $\mathbf{z}_i' = [Y_i, X_{i1}, \ldots, X_{ik}]$ or (2) treating the regressors as fixed and resampling from the residuals E_i of the fitted regression model. In the latter instance, bootstrap observations are constructed as $Y_{bi}^* = \widehat{Y}_i + E_{bi}^*$, where the $\widehat{Y}_i$ are the fitted values from the original regression, and the E_{bi}^* are the resampled residuals for the bth bootstrap sample. In each bootstrap sample, the Y_{bi}^* are then regressed on the original Xs. A disadvantage of fixed-X resampling is that the procedure implicitly assumes that the regression model fit to the data is correct and that the errors are identically distributed.

- Bootstrap hypothesis tests proceed by constructing an empirical sampling distribution for the test statistic. If T represents the test statistic computed for the original sample and T_b^* is the test statistic for the bth of r bootstrap samples, then (for a chi-square-like test statistic) the p-value for the test is $\#(T_b^* \geq T)/r$.

- The bootstrap can be applied to complex sampling designs (involving, e.g., stratification, clustering, and case weighting) by resampling from the sample data in the same manner as the original sample was selected from the population.

Recommended Reading

Bootstrapping is a rich topic; the presentation in this chapter has stressed computational procedures at the expense of a detailed account of statistical properties and limitations.

- Although Efron and Tibshirani's (1993) book on the bootstrap contains some relatively advanced material, most of the exposition requires only modest statistical background and is eminently readable.

- Davison and Hinkley (1997) is another statistically sophisticated, comprehensive treatment of bootstrapping.

- A briefer source on bootstrapping addressed to social scientists is Stine (1990), which includes a fine discussion of the rationale of bootstrap confidence intervals.

- Young's (1994) paper and the commentary that follows it focus on practical difficulties in applying the bootstrap.

22

Model Selection, Averaging, and Validation

This chapter addresses practical issues in building statistical models. The first section of the chapter discusses criteria for selecting among statistical models—criteria that move beyond hypothesis tests for terms in a model.

The second section deals with an alternative approach, termed model averaging, that combines information from different statistical models fit to the same data.

Model validation, which is described in the third section of the chapter, provides a simple basis for honest statistical inference when—as is typically the case in a careful investigation—we need to examine the data to formulate a descriptively adequate statistical model. In validation, the data are divided at random into two parts: One part is used for data exploration and model formulation (including, possibly, model selection); the second part is used to evaluate the model, thus preserving the integrity of statistical inferences.

22.1 Model Selection

I have touched, in passing, on issues of model selection at several points in the text, often simplifying a model after preliminary statistical hypothesis tests.[1] Issues of model search extend beyond the selection of explanatory variables or terms to include in a regression model to questions such as the removal of outliers and variable transformations. The strategy of basing model selection on hypothesis tests is problematic for a number of reasons (largely familiar from elementary statistics):

- *Simultaneous inference:* If we are testing many terms simultaneously, the probability of rejecting one or more true null hypotheses by chance (i.e., the probability of committing a Type I error) is larger—possibly much larger—than the level of any individual test.[2]
- *The fallacy of affirming the consequent:* Failing to reject a null hypothesis is to be distinguished from demonstrating that the null hypothesis is supported by the data. That is, the power of the test may be weak. It is important to distinguish, therefore, a small coefficient that is precisely estimated (where, e.g., the confidence interval for the coefficient is narrow and includes zero) from a coefficient that is imprecisely estimated (where, e.g., the size of the estimated coefficient may be large, but the confidence interval includes zero). Eliminating an imprecisely estimated term from a model can seriously bias other estimates if the population coefficient is large and the variable in question is strongly related to others in the model.[3]

---

[1] In addition, the Bayesian information criterion (BIC) was used for model selection in Section 13.2.2, and cross-validation and generalized cross-validation were discussed in the context of nonparametric regression in Chapter 18.

[2] See Exercise 22.1.

[3] See the discussions of "specification errors" in Sections 6.3 and 9.7.

- *The impact of large samples on hypothesis tests:* In the social sciences, we would rarely expect a null hypothesis to be *exactly* correct, and given a sufficiently large sample, a false hypothesis—even one that is close to correct—will be rejected with high probability. Thus, we may be led to include terms in a model because they are "statistically significant" even when they are trivially small.
- *Exaggerated precision:* Coefficient standard errors computed after model selection tend to overstate the precision of estimation when terms correlated with those retained in the model are eliminated. Consequently, confidence intervals are artificially narrow and *p*-values artificially small.

There are several general strategies for addressing these concerns:

- *Using alternative model-selection criteria:* One approach—namely, to employ a criterion other than statistical significance to decide questions of model selection—is the principal subject of this section.
- *Compensating for simultaneous inference:* We can seek to compensate for simultaneous inference by employing a Bonferroni adjustment, for example, or by holding back some of our data to validate a statistical model selected by another approach.[4]
- *Avoiding model selection:* Still another strategy, which preserves the integrity of classical statistical inference, is to specify and interpret a maximally complex and flexible model without seeking to simplify it.[5] Although this is a defensible approach, it encounters two general difficulties, in my opinion: (1) We are often not in a position to specify a fully adequate model, even a maximally complex one, prior to examining the data and (2) retaining what prove to be unnecessary terms in a model contradicts a common goal of statistical data analysis, which is permissible simplification (possibly begging the question of what is "permissible").
- *Model averaging:* Rather than selecting a single model and discarding all others, model-averaging techniques seek to account for model uncertainty by weighting contending models according to their relative degree of support from the data.[6]

> It is problematic to use statistical hypothesis tests for model selection. Doing so leads to issues of simultaneous inference; also, it can produce biased results, tends to yield complicated models in large samples, and exaggerates the precision of results.

22.1.1   Model Selection Criteria

Model selection is conceptually simplest when our goal is *prediction*—that is, the development of a regression model that will predict new data as accurately as possible. Although predictive accuracy is a desirable characteristic in any statistical model, most interesting statistical problems in the social sciences are not pure prediction problems, and a more typical objective is to use a statistical model for substantive interpretation, data summary, and explanation.

When our goal is prediction, we need not be concerned about the consequences for interpretation of eliminating an explanatory variable that is highly correlated with one included in the

---

[4]Model validation is the subject of Section 22.3. For an example of the use of Bonferroni adjustment in model selection, see Foster and Stine (2004).

[5]This strategy is advocated, for example, by Harrell (2001).

[6]See Section 22.2.

model, because the excluded variable would typically lend little additional predictive power to the model. This conclusion assumes that the configuration of explanatory variables will be similar in the data for which predictions are desired as in the data used to calibrate the model. Likewise, where the aim is prediction, we need have no qualms about including among the *predictor* variables (note, in this context, not "explanatory" variables) *symptoms* (i.e., effects) of the response variable. Indeed, the inclusion of symptoms as predictors is standard in areas such as differential diagnosis in medicine.

Because of the current expansion of computer power and the availability of very large data sets (e.g., in genomics), model-selection problems in the context of prediction are receiving a great deal of attention in statistics: Once an epithet, "data mining" is now a topic of serious study.[7]

This section describes several criteria that have been suggested for selecting among competing statistical models.[8] I assume that we have n observations on a response variable Y and a set of m contending statistical models $\mathcal{M} = \{M_1, M_2, \ldots, M_m\}$ for Y.

Corrected R^2

The *squared multiple correlation "corrected"* (or *"adjusted"*) *for degrees of freedom* is an intuitively reasonable criterion for comparing linear-regression models with different numbers of parameters.[9] Suppose that model M_j is one of the models under consideration. If M_j has s_j regression coefficients (including the regression constant) and is fit to a data set with n observations, then the corrected R^2 for the model is

$$\widetilde{R}_j^2 \equiv 1 - \frac{S_E^{(j)2}}{S_Y^2}$$

$$= 1 - \frac{n-1}{n-s_j} \times \frac{\text{RSS}_j}{\text{TSS}}$$

where RSS_j is the residual sum of squares under the model, $\text{TSS} = \sum(Y_i - \overline{Y})^2$ is the total sum of squares for the response variable Y, and $S_E^{(j)2} = \text{RSS}_j/(n-s_j)$ is the estimated error variance. Consequently, models with relatively large numbers of parameters are penalized for their lack of parsimony. Beyond this intuitive rationale, however, there is no deep justification for using $\widetilde{R}^2$ as a model-selection criterion.

Mallows's C_p Statistic

One approach to subset selection in least-squares regression is based on the total (normed) mean-squared error (MSE) of estimating the expected values of the response, $E(Y_i)$, from the fitted values, $\widehat{Y}_i$—that is, using the fitted regression to estimate the population regression surface over the observed Xs:

$$\gamma_j \equiv \frac{1}{\sigma_\varepsilon^2} \sum_{i=1}^{n} \text{MSE}\left(\widehat{Y}_i^{(j)}\right) \tag{22.1}$$

$$= \frac{1}{\sigma_\varepsilon^2} \sum_{i=1}^{n} \left\{ V\left(\widehat{Y}_i^{(j)}\right) + \left[E\left(\widehat{Y}_i^{(j)}\right) - E\left(Y_i\right)\right]^2 \right\}$$

---

[7]See, for example, Hastie, Tibshirani, and Friedman (2001).

[8]This presentation is by no means exhaustive. For example, I have omitted a promising new information-theoretic approach described in Stine (2004).

[9]The corrected R^2 was introduced in Section 5.2.3.

where the fitted values $\widehat{Y}_i^{(j)}$ are based on model M_j, which contains $s_j \leq k+1$ regressors (counting the constant, which is always included in the model) and where k is the number of regressors (less the constant) in the largest model under consideration. Using the error in estimating $E(Y)$ as a criterion for model quality is reasonable if the goal is literally to predict Y from the Xs, and if new observations on the Xs for which predictions are required will be similar to those included in the data. An implicit assumption is that the full model, with all $k+1$ regressors, accurately captures the dependence of Y on the Xs.

The term $\left[E\left(\widehat{Y}_i^{(j)}\right) - E\left(Y_i\right)\right]^2$ in Equation 22.1 represents the squared bias of $\widehat{Y}_i^{(j)}$ as an estimator of the population regression surface $E(Y_i)$. When collinear regressors are deleted from the model, for example, the variance of the fitted value, $V\left(\widehat{Y}_i^{(j)}\right)$, will usually decrease, but— depending on the configuration of data points and the true βs for the deleted regressors—bias may be introduced into the fitted values. Because the prediction MSE is the sum of variance and squared bias, the essential question is whether the decrease in variance offsets any increase in bias.

Mallows's C_p statistic (Mallows, 1973) estimates γ_j as

$$C_{p_j} \equiv \frac{\sum E_i^{(j)2}}{S_E^2} + 2s_j - n$$
$$= (k+1-s_j)(F_j - 1) + s_j$$

where the residuals $E_i^{(j)}$ are from model M_j, the error variance estimate S_E^2 is based on the *full* model fit to the data, containing all $k+1$ regressors, and F_j is the incremental F-statistic for testing the hypothesis that the regressors omitted from model M_j have population coefficients of 0.[10] If this hypothesis is true, then $E(F_j) \approx 1$, and thus $E(C_{p_j}) \approx s_j$. A good model, therefore, has C_{p_j} close to or below s_j. As well, minimizing C_p for models of a given size minimizes the sum of squared residuals and thus maximizes R^2. For the full model, C_p necessarily equals $k+1$.

Cross-Validation and Generalized Cross-Validation

We previously encountered cross-validation in Chapter 18 on nonparametric regression as a method for selecting the smoothing parameter in a local-polynomial or smoothing-spline regression model. Cross-validation can be applied more generally to model selection.

As before, suppose that model M_j is one of m models under consideration. In *leave-one-out cross-validation*, we fit the model n times, omitting the ith observation at step i and using the resulting fitted model to obtain a predicted value for the omitted observation, $\widehat{Y}_{-i}^{(j)}$. The *cross-validation criterion* estimates the mean-squared prediction error for model M_j as

$$\text{CV}_j \equiv \frac{\sum_{i=1}^{n}\left(\widehat{Y}_{-i}^{(j)} - Y_i\right)^2}{n} \tag{22.2}$$

We prefer the model with the smallest value of CV_j.[11]

In linear least-squares regression, there are efficient procedures for computing the leave-one-out fitted values $\widehat{Y}_{-i}^{(j)}$ that do not require literally refitting the model.[12] In other cases, however,

---

[10] See Exercise 22.2.

[11] The numerator of $\text{CV}(j)$, that is, $\sum_{i=1}^{n}\left(\widehat{Y}_{-i}^{(j)} - Y_i\right)^2$, is called the *prediction sum of squares* (or *PRESS*).

[12] Recall the discussion of deletion diagnostics in Chapter 11.

leave-one-out cross-validation can be computationally expensive. An alternative is to divide the data into a relatively small number of subsets (e.g., 10) of roughly equal size and to fit the model omitting each subset in turn, obtaining fitted values for all observations in the omitted subset. With p subsets, this method is termed *p-fold cross-validation*. The cross-validation criterion is calculated as in Equation 22.2, using the fitted values from the p omitted subsets. Still another possibility is to approximate CV by the *generalized cross-validation criterion*

$$\text{GCV}_j \equiv \frac{n \times \text{RSS}_j}{df_{\text{res}_j}^2}$$

where RSS_j is the residual sum of squares and $df_{\text{res}_j} = n - s_j$ are the residual degrees of freedom for model M_j—an approach similar to that taken in the adjusted R^2.[13]

The Akaike Information Criterion (AIC) and the Bayesian Information Criterion (BIC)

The *AIC* and the *BIC*, also called *Schwarz's Bayesian criterion* (Schwarz, 1978), are currently the most commonly used model-selection criteria beyond classical hypothesis tests. Both are members of a more general family of *penalized* model-fit statistics (let us call them "*IC"), applicable to regression models fit by maximum likelihood, that take the form

$$\text{*IC}_j = -2\log_e L(\widehat{\boldsymbol{\theta}}_j) + cs_j$$

where $L(\widehat{\boldsymbol{\theta}}_j)$ is the maximized likelihood under model M_j; $\boldsymbol{\theta}_j$ is the vector of parameters of the model,[14] including, for example, regression coefficients and an error-variance or dispersion parameter [and $\widehat{\boldsymbol{\theta}}_j$ is the vector of maximum-likelihood estimates (MLEs) of the parameters]; s_j is the number of parameters in $\boldsymbol{\theta}_j$; and c is a constant that differs from one model-selection criterion to another. The first term, $-2\log_e L(\widehat{\boldsymbol{\theta}}_j)$, is the residual deviance under the model (or differs from the residual deviance by a constant); for a linear model with normal errors, it is simply the residual sum of squares. The *magnitude* of *IC is not generally interpretable, but *differences* between values for different models are of interest, and the model with the smallest *IC is the one that receives most support from the data.

The AIC and BIC are defined as follows:

$$\text{AIC}_j \equiv -2\log_e L(\widehat{\boldsymbol{\theta}}_j) + 2s_j$$
$$\text{BIC}_j \equiv -2\log_e L(\widehat{\boldsymbol{\theta}}_j) + s_j \log_e n$$

For example, in a linear model with normal errors, the MLE of the regression coefficients is the least-squares estimator, and the MLE of the error variance is $\widehat{\sigma}_\varepsilon^{(j)2} = \left(\sum E_i^{(j)2}\right)/n$, where the $E_i^{(j)}$ are the least-squares residuals for model M_j;[15] then,

$$\text{AIC}_j = n\log_e \widehat{\sigma}_\varepsilon^{(j)2} + 2s_j$$
$$\text{BIC}_j = n\log_e \widehat{\sigma}_\varepsilon^{(j)2} + s_j \log_e n$$

---

[13]But see Exercise 22.3.

[14]If you are not familiar with vector notation, simply think of $\boldsymbol{\theta}_j$ as a list of the parameters in the model; for example, in a linear regression model with normal errors, $\boldsymbol{\theta}_j$ contains the regression coefficients, $\alpha^{(j)}, \beta_1^{(j)}, \ldots, \beta_k^{(j)}$ and the error variance $\sigma_\varepsilon^{(j)2}$.

[15]See Section 9.3.3.

The lack-of-parsimony penalty for the BIC grows with the sample size, while that for the AIC does not. The penalty for the BIC is also larger than that for the AIC (when $n \geq 8$), and the BIC therefore tends to nominate models with fewer parameters. Although the AIC and BIC are often justified by vague appeals to parsimony, both statistics are based on deeper statistical considerations, to which I now turn.[16]

Model-selection criteria, some applicable to regression models fit by least-squares and others more general:

- The squared multiple correlation adjusted for degrees of freedom,

$$\widetilde{R}^2 = 1 - \frac{n-1}{n-s} \times \frac{\text{RSS}}{\text{TSS}}$$

where n is the number of observations, s the number of regression coefficients in the model, RSS the residual sum of squares under the model, and TSS the total sum of squares.

- Mallows's C_p statistic,

$$C_p = (k + 1 - s)(F - 1) + s$$

where k is the number of predictors in the full model fit to the data and F is the incremental F-statistic for the hypothesis that the $k + 1 - s$ predictors excluded from the model are zero. A good model has C_p close to or below s.

- The cross-validation criterion,

$$\text{CV} = \frac{\sum_{i=1}^{n} \left(\widehat{Y}_{-i} - Y_i\right)^2}{n}$$

where $\widehat{Y}_{-i}$ is the fitted value for observation i obtained when the model is fit with observation i omitted.

- The generalized cross-validation criterion,

$$\text{GCV} = \frac{n \times \text{RSS}}{df_{\text{res}}^2}$$

where df_{res} is the residual degrees of freedom under the model.

- The Akaike information criterion (AIC),

$$\text{AIC} = -2 \log_e L(\widehat{\boldsymbol{\theta}}) + 2s$$

where $\log_e L(\widehat{\boldsymbol{\theta}})$ is the maximized log-likelihood under the model (and $\boldsymbol{\theta}$ is the parameter vector for the model).

---

[16]The exposition of the AIC is adapted from Burnham and Anderson (2004), and of the BIC from Raftery (1995).

- The Bayesian information criterion (BIC),

$$BIC = -2 \log_e L(\widehat{\boldsymbol{\theta}}) + s \log_e n$$

For both the AIC and the BIC, the model with the smallest value is the one most supported by the data.

A Closer Look at the AIC* Let $p(\mathbf{y})$ represent the "true" probability distribution or density function for the response vector $\mathbf{y}$ in a regression model. The response $\mathbf{y}$ can be quite general—certainly including all the models fit by the method of maximum likelihood in this book.[17] The "true model" generating the data need not be among the models that we are comparing, and, indeed we do not have to commit ourselves to the existence of a true model: The probability distribution of the data could be generated by a complex process that cannot be captured precisely by a statistical model.[18]

Imagine, as before, that we have a set of m statistical models under consideration, each with parameters to be estimated from the data, $\boldsymbol{\theta}_j$ for model M_j, and implying the probability distribution $p_j(\mathbf{y}|\boldsymbol{\theta}_j)$ for the data, which can be thought of as an approximation to the true distribution $p(\mathbf{y})$ of $\mathbf{y}$.[19] The "best" model is the one that provides the most accurate approximation.

Kullback-Leibler information is a measure of the "distance" between two distributions, representing the information "lost" when the second distribution is used to approximate the first. The AIC applies Kullback-Leibler information to the difference between $p(\mathbf{y})$ and each $p_j(\mathbf{y}|\boldsymbol{\theta}_j)$:

$$
\begin{aligned}
J(p, p_j) &\equiv \int_{\text{all } \mathbf{y}} p(\mathbf{y}) \log_e \frac{p(\mathbf{y})}{p_j(\mathbf{y}|\boldsymbol{\theta}_j)} d\mathbf{y} \qquad\qquad (22.3)\\
&= \int_{\text{all } \mathbf{y}} p(\mathbf{y}) \log_e p(\mathbf{y}) d\mathbf{y} - \int_{\text{all } \mathbf{y}} p(\mathbf{y}) \log_e p_j(\mathbf{y}|\boldsymbol{\theta}_j) d\mathbf{y} \\
&= E_p \left[\log_e p(\mathbf{y}) \right] - E_p \left[\log_e p_j(\mathbf{y}|\boldsymbol{\theta}_j) \right] \\
&= \phi - E_p \left[\log_e p_j(\mathbf{y}|\boldsymbol{\theta}_j) \right]
\end{aligned}
$$

The object, then, is to find the model M_j that minimizes the information loss. Note that $\phi \equiv E_p \left[\log_e p(\mathbf{y}) \right]$, in the last line of Equation 22.3, is a constant that does not depend on the model and is therefore irrelevant to model comparisons; the expectation in the term $E_p \left[\log_e p_j(\mathbf{y}|\boldsymbol{\theta}_j) \right]$ is with respect to the *true* probability distribution $p(\mathbf{y})$.

The AIC focuses on the quantity

$$E_{\mathbf{y}} E_{\mathbf{y}^*} \left\{ \log_e p_j \left[\mathbf{y}^* | \widehat{\boldsymbol{\theta}}_j(\mathbf{y}) \right] \right\}$$

Here, $\mathbf{y}^*$ is a notional *second*, independently selected sample of values of the response variable (though, in an application, we have only the sample $\mathbf{y}$); $\widehat{\boldsymbol{\theta}}_j(\mathbf{y})$ is the maximum-likelihood estimator of $\boldsymbol{\theta}_j$ based on the *original* sample $\mathbf{y}$; and the expectation is taken with respect to both samples. The quantity $E_{\mathbf{y}^*} \left\{ \log_e p_j \left[\mathbf{y}^* | \widehat{\boldsymbol{\theta}}_j(\mathbf{y}) \right] \right\}$ is similar to $E_p \left[\log_e p_j(\mathbf{y}|\boldsymbol{\theta}_j) \right]$, substituting the MLE $\widehat{\boldsymbol{\theta}}_j(\mathbf{y})$ for $\boldsymbol{\theta}_j$, and $\log_e p_j \left[\mathbf{y}^* | \widehat{\boldsymbol{\theta}}_j(\mathbf{y}) \right]$ is the new-sample log-likelihood under the model

---

[17]The range of application of the AIC (and the BIC) is wider still—to virtually any class of statistical models fit by maximum likelihood.

[18]This notion is consistent with the view of statistical models presented in Chapter 1.

[19]$p_j(\cdot)$ is subscripted here by the index of the model because we wish to consider the distribution of the data under different models.

M_j evaluated at the MLE for the original sample. The maximized log-likelihood $\log_e L(\widehat{\boldsymbol{\theta}}_j|\mathbf{y}) = \log_e p_j\left[\mathbf{y}|\widehat{\boldsymbol{\theta}}_j(\mathbf{y})\right]$ is an upwardly biased estimate of $E_{\mathbf{y}}E_{\mathbf{y}^*}\left\{\log_e p_j\left[\mathbf{y}^*|\widehat{\boldsymbol{\theta}}_j(\mathbf{y})\right]\right\}$, with asymptotic bias approximately equal to the number of parameters s_j in $\boldsymbol{\theta}_j$. This is an intuitively reasonable result because we expect the *new-sample* (i.e., predicted) log-likelihood $\log_e p_j\left[\mathbf{y}^*|\widehat{\boldsymbol{\theta}}_j(\mathbf{y})\right]$ to be smaller than the maximized log-likelihood $\log_e p_j\left[\mathbf{y}|\widehat{\boldsymbol{\theta}}_j(\mathbf{y})\right]$ for the original sample [for which $\widehat{\boldsymbol{\theta}}_j(\mathbf{y})$ is the optimal value].

For a large sample, and a distribution $p_j(\cdot)$ that is close to $p(\cdot)$, therefore,

$$\widehat{E}_{\widehat{\boldsymbol{\theta}}_j}[J(p, \widehat{p}_j)] \approx \phi - \log_e L(\widehat{\boldsymbol{\theta}}_j|\mathbf{y}) + s_j$$

where $\widehat{E}_{\widehat{\boldsymbol{\theta}}_j}[J(p, \widehat{p}_j)]$ is the estimated expected Kullback-Leibler information loss, and $\widehat{p}_j$ represents $p_j(\cdot|\boldsymbol{\theta}_j)$ evaluated at $\boldsymbol{\theta}_j = \widehat{\boldsymbol{\theta}}_j$. The constant ϕ is not estimable but, as noted, it does not figure in model comparisons. The AIC, therefore, which is used for model comparison, ignores ϕ and is defined as

$$\text{AIC}_j \equiv -2\log_e L(\widehat{\boldsymbol{\theta}}_j|\mathbf{y}) + 2s_j$$

The factor 2 is inessential but puts the AIC on the same scale as the deviance.

An improvement on the AIC, called the *bias-corrected AIC*, or AIC_c, reduces small-sample bias:

$$\text{AIC}_{c_j} \equiv -2\log_e L(\widehat{\boldsymbol{\theta}}_j|\mathbf{y}) + 2s_j + \frac{2s_j(s_j + 1)}{n - s_j - 1} \qquad (22.4)$$

The correction (i.e., the last term in Equation 22.4) gets smaller as the ratio of sample size to number of parameters grows and is negligible when n/s_j is large (say more than about 40). As Burnham and Anderson (2004) suggest, however, one could simply use AIC_c in all cases.

> The AIC is based on the Kullback-Leibler information comparing the true distribution of the data $p(\mathbf{y})$ to the distribution of the data $p_j(\mathbf{y}|\boldsymbol{\theta}_j)$ under a particular model M_j.

A Closer Look at the BIC* The BIC has its origin in Bayesian hypothesis testing, which compares the relative weight of evidence for each of two competing hypotheses. I will broadly sketch the rationale for the BIC here.[20] Suppose, as before, that we are considering a set of m models for the response variable $\mathbf{y}$ and that model M_j has parameter vector $\boldsymbol{\theta}_j$ with s_j elements. The probability or probability density for $\mathbf{y}$ under model M_j given the values of the parameters is $p_j(\mathbf{y}|\boldsymbol{\theta}_j)$. Let $p_j(\boldsymbol{\theta}_j)$ represent the prior distribution for $\boldsymbol{\theta}_j$. Then, the marginal distribution of $\mathbf{y}$ under the model M_j is

$$p_j(\mathbf{y}) = \int_{\text{all } \boldsymbol{\theta}_j} p_j(\mathbf{y}|\boldsymbol{\theta}_j)d\boldsymbol{\theta}_j$$

and the posterior distribution of $\boldsymbol{\theta}_j$ is

$$p_j(\boldsymbol{\theta}_j|\mathbf{y}) = \frac{p_j(\mathbf{y}|\boldsymbol{\theta}_j)p_j(\boldsymbol{\theta}_j)}{p_j(\mathbf{y})}$$

---

[20]This section assumes an acquaintance with the general principles of Bayesian statistical inference, which are described in Appendix D on probability and estimation.

Let us focus initially on two of the models, M_1 and M_2, and assume that one of these is the "correct" model for the data.[21] The posterior probability that M_1 is the correct model is

$$p(M_1|\mathbf{y}) = \frac{p(\mathbf{y}|M_1)p(M_1)}{p(\mathbf{y}|M_1)p(M_1) + p(\mathbf{y}|M_2)p(M_2)}$$

Here, $p(M_j)$ is the prior probability assigned to model M_j, and $p(\mathbf{y}|M_j)$ is the *marginal probability of the data* under model M_j (also called the *predictive probability of the data*):

$$p(\mathbf{y}|M_j) = \int_{\text{all } \boldsymbol{\theta}_j} p_j(\mathbf{y}|\boldsymbol{\theta}_j)p_j(\boldsymbol{\theta}_j)d\boldsymbol{\theta}_j \tag{22.5}$$

A direct formula for $p(M_2|\mathbf{y})$ is similar, but because there are just two models under consideration, it is also the case that $p(M_2|\mathbf{y}) = 1 - p(M_1|\mathbf{y})$.

After observing the data, the relative support for model M_2 versus M_1 is given by the *posterior odds*

$$\frac{p(M_2|\mathbf{y})}{p(M_1|\mathbf{y})} = \frac{p(\mathbf{y}|M_2)}{p(\mathbf{y}|M_1)} \times \frac{p(M_2)}{p(M_1)}$$

The posterior odds are, therefore, the product of two terms: the ratio of marginal probabilities of the data under the competing models, $p(\mathbf{y}|M_2)/p(\mathbf{y}|M_1)$, called the *Bayes factor* for model M_2 versus M_1, and $p(M_2)/p(M_1)$, the ratio of prior probabilities for the models. It seems fair to set equal prior probabilities, $p(M_1) = p(M_2)$,[22] in which case the posterior odds are simply the Bayes factor.

An important point concerning the posterior odds is that there are *two* prior distributions to consider: (1) the prior probabilities $p(M_j)$ for the *models* under consideration and (2) the prior distribution $p_j(\boldsymbol{\theta}_j)$ for the *parameters* in each model, on which the marginal probability of the data under the model depends (Equation 22.5). As mentioned, it seems evenhanded to accord the various models equal prior probability, at least in the absence of a convincing argument to the contrary, but the priors $p_j(\boldsymbol{\theta}_j)$ on the parameters are another question entirely. In *Bayesian estimation*, the importance of the prior distribution on the parameters fades as the sample size grows; thus, unless the sample size is small and there is a sound basis for specific prior beliefs, the argument for so-called noninformative or vague priors can be compelling. This is not the case, however, in *Bayesian hypothesis testing*, where the prior distribution on the parameters of each model affects the marginal probability of the data, and through it the Bayes factor, *even in large samples*.

The BIC is an approximation to the Bayes factor, employing a particular choice of prior distribution on the parameters of each model (see below).[23] It is convenient to introduce the function

$$f(\boldsymbol{\theta}_j) \equiv \log_e \left[p_j(\mathbf{y}|\theta_j)p_j(\boldsymbol{\theta}_j) \right] \tag{22.6}$$

which is the log of the integrand in Equation 22.5. Let $\widetilde{\boldsymbol{\theta}}_j$ represent the value of the parameter vector that maximizes $f(\boldsymbol{\theta}_j)$ for the observed data $\mathbf{y}$. A second-order Taylor-series expansion of $f(\boldsymbol{\theta}_j)$ around $\widetilde{\boldsymbol{\theta}}_j$ is[24]

---

[21]It is possible to develop the BIC by making an argument based on accuracy of out-of-sample prediction without assuming that one of the models is the "true" model for the data. See, for example, Kass and Raftery (1995).

[22]With only two models under consideration, we therefore have $p(M_1) = p(M_2) = 1/2$.

[23]The development here is quite dense, even for starred material; the reader may wish to skip to the key result given in Equation 22.11 (on page 617).

[24]If the sample size is sufficiently large, then higher-order terms in the Taylor expansion should be negligible.

$$f(\theta_j) \approx f(\tilde{\theta}_j) + (\theta_j - \tilde{\theta}_j)' \frac{\partial f(\tilde{\theta}_j)}{\partial \tilde{\theta}_j} + \frac{1}{2}(\theta_j - \tilde{\theta}_j)' \frac{\partial f(\tilde{\theta}_j)}{\partial \tilde{\theta}_j \partial \tilde{\theta}_j'} (\theta_j - \tilde{\theta}_j)$$

$$\approx f(\tilde{\theta}_j) + \frac{1}{2}(\theta_j - \tilde{\theta}_j)' \frac{\partial f(\tilde{\theta}_j)}{\partial \tilde{\theta}_j \partial \tilde{\theta}_j'} (\theta_j - \tilde{\theta}_j)$$

The second term in the expansion vanishes because the first-order partial derivatives $\partial f(\tilde{\theta}_j)/\partial \tilde{\theta}_j$ are $\mathbf{0}$ at the maximum of $f(\theta_j)$. Given sufficient data, we expect $\tilde{\theta}_j$ to be close to θ_j and expect that the likelihood $p_j(\mathbf{y}|\theta_j)$ will decline rapidly as θ_j departs from $\tilde{\theta}_j$. Under these circumstances, the marginal probability of the data (from Equation 22.5) is approximately

$$p(\mathbf{y}|M_j) \approx \exp\left[f(\tilde{\theta}_j)\right] \int \exp\left[\frac{1}{2}(\theta_j - \tilde{\theta}_j)' \frac{\partial^2 f(\tilde{\theta}_j)}{\partial \tilde{\theta}_j \partial \tilde{\theta}_j'} (\theta_j - \tilde{\theta}_j)\right] d\theta_j \qquad (22.7)$$

A clever trick facilitates the evaluation of the integral in Equation 22.7. With the exception of the absence of the multiplicative factor $(2\pi)^{-s_j/2} \left(\det \tilde{\Sigma}\right)^{-1/2}$, where

$$\tilde{\Sigma} \equiv -\left[\frac{\partial^2 f(\tilde{\theta}_j)}{\partial \tilde{\theta}_j \partial \tilde{\theta}_j'}\right]^{-1}$$

the integrand in this equation looks like the formula of the multivariate-normal density, with θ_j playing the role of the vector random variable, $\tilde{\theta}_j$ the role of the mean vector, and $\tilde{\Sigma}$ the role of the covariance matrix;[25] note that this is simply an *analogy* that will help us evaluate the integral in Equation 22.7. Because the multivariate-normal density integrates to 1, the integral evaluates to the inverse of the missing constant, $(2\pi)^{s_j/2} \left(\det \tilde{\Sigma}\right)^{1/2}$. Consequently,

$$p(\mathbf{y}|M_j) \approx \exp\left[f(\tilde{\theta}_j)\right] (2\pi)^{s_j/2} \left(\det \tilde{\Sigma}\right)^{1/2}$$

and (using Equation 22.6)

$$\log_e p(\mathbf{y}|M_j) \approx f(\tilde{\theta}_j) + \frac{s_j}{2} \log_e 2\pi + \frac{1}{2} \log_e \left(\det \tilde{\Sigma}\right) \qquad (22.8)$$

$$\approx \log_e p_j(\mathbf{y}|\tilde{\theta}_j) + \log_e p_j(\tilde{\theta}_j) + \frac{s_j}{2} \log_e 2\pi + \frac{1}{2} \log_e \left(\det \tilde{\Sigma}\right)$$

If the sample size is large, then we would expect the posterior mode $\tilde{\theta}_j$ to be close to the maximum-likelihood estimator $\hat{\theta}_j$ of θ_j. Substituting $\hat{\theta}_j$ for $\tilde{\theta}_j$,

$$\tilde{\Sigma}^{-1} \approx \hat{\Sigma}^{-1} = -\frac{\partial f(\hat{\theta}_j)}{\partial \hat{\theta}_j \partial \hat{\theta}_j'}$$

$$= -n \times E_{\mathbf{y}}\left[\left.\frac{\partial^2 \log_e p(Y|\theta_j)}{\partial \theta_j \partial \theta_j'}\right|\, \theta_j = \hat{\theta}_j\right]$$

$$= n \times \mathcal{I}(\hat{\theta}_j)$$

The matrix

$$\mathcal{I}(\hat{\theta}_j) \equiv -E_{\mathbf{y}}\left[\left.\frac{\partial^2 \log_e p(Y|\theta_j)}{\partial \theta_j \partial \theta_j'}\right|\, \theta_j = \hat{\theta}_j\right]$$

---

[25]See Appendix D on probability and estimation for a discussion of the multivariate-normal distribution.

is the expected Fisher information associated with a single observation Y on the response variable. Noting that in a large sample $\det \widehat{\Sigma} \approx -\left[n^{s_j} \det J(\widehat{\boldsymbol{\theta}}_j)\right]^{-1}$ and substituting this approximation into Equation 22.8 gives

$$\log_e p(\mathbf{y}|M_j) \approx \log_e p_j(\mathbf{y}|\widehat{\boldsymbol{\theta}}_j) + \log_e p_j(\widehat{\boldsymbol{\theta}}_j) + \frac{s_j}{2}\log_e 2\pi - \frac{s_j}{2}\log_e n - \frac{1}{2}\log_e \left[\det J(\widehat{\boldsymbol{\theta}}_j)\right] \tag{22.9}$$

The BIC uses the *unit-information prior distribution* $\boldsymbol{\theta}_j \sim N_{s_j}\left[\widehat{\boldsymbol{\theta}}_j, J(\widehat{\boldsymbol{\theta}}_j)\right]$—quite a diffuse prior centered on the MLE of $\boldsymbol{\theta}_j$; under this prior,[26]

$$\log_e p_j(\widehat{\boldsymbol{\theta}}_j) = -\frac{s_j}{2}\log_e 2\pi + \frac{1}{2}\log_e \left[\det J(\widehat{\boldsymbol{\theta}}_j)\right]$$

Substituting this result into Equation 22.9 produces

$$\log_e p(\mathbf{y}|M_j) \approx \log_e p_j(\mathbf{y}|\widehat{\boldsymbol{\theta}}_j) - \frac{s_j}{2}\log_e n \tag{22.10}$$

On the basis of the preceding work, the log-Bayes factor for model M_2 relative to model M_1 can then be approximated as

$$\log_e \frac{p(\mathbf{y}|M_2)}{p(\mathbf{y}|M_1)} \approx \log_e p_2(\mathbf{y}|\widehat{\boldsymbol{\theta}}_2) - \log_e p_1(\mathbf{y}|\widehat{\boldsymbol{\theta}}_1) - \frac{1}{2}(s_2 - s_1)\log_e n \tag{22.11}$$

Recall that the choice of the unit-information prior to obtain this approximation is not necessarily benign: Different priors produce different Bayes factors.[27] Moreover, several approximations were made in arriving at this result, and for some classes of models, more accurate approximations are available.[28]

The BIC for model M_j is defined as

$$\text{BIC}_j \equiv -2\log_e p_j(\mathbf{y}|\widehat{\boldsymbol{\theta}}_j) + s_j \log_e n$$

Given this definition, twice the log-Bayes factor for any pair of models M_j and $M_{j'}$ is approximated by the difference in their BICs:

$$2 \times \log_e \frac{p(\mathbf{y}|M_j)}{p(\mathbf{y}|M_{j'})} \approx \text{BIC}_{j'} - \text{BIC}_j \tag{22.12}$$

Under the unit-information prior, the difference in BIC therefore expresses the relative support in the data for model M_j versus $M_{j'}$, and the model with the smallest BIC is the one that receives most support from the data. A BIC difference of 0, for example, is equivalent to a Bayes factor of $\exp\left(\frac{1}{2} \times 0\right) = 1$—that is, equal support in the data for the two models; if these are the only models under consideration (and if the prior probabilities for the two models are equal), therefore, we would have posterior probabilities $p(M_2|\mathbf{y}) = p(M_1|\mathbf{y}) = \frac{1}{2}$. Similarly, a BIC of 2 is equivalent to a Bayes factor of $\exp\left(\frac{1}{2} \times 2\right) \approx 2.718$ in favor of model M_2, or $p(M_2|\mathbf{y}) \approx .73$ and $p(M_1|\mathbf{y}) \approx .27$—that is, relatively weak evidence in favor of M_2. Table 22.1, adapted from Raftery (1995), extends these interpretations to various differences in BIC.[29]

---

[26] It is also possible to construe the BIC as an approximation to the Bayes factor under an *unspecified* prior, but then the quality of the approximation can be much worse. See, for example, Raftery (1995).

[27] Burnham and Andersen (2004) show, for example, that the AIC can be derived as an approximation to the log of the Bayes factor using a prior different from the unit-information prior. Consequently, the choice of AIC or BIC as a model-selection criterion cannot simply be construed as a contest between "frequentist" and Bayesian approaches to the problem of model selection.

[28] See, for example, the results given in Raftery (1996) for generalized linear models and the general discussion in Kass and Raftery (1995).

[29] See Exercise 22.4.

Table 22.1   Relative Support for Model M_2 Versus M_1 As a
Function of Differences in BIC

Difference in BIC	Bayes Factor	$p(M_2|\mathbf{y})$	Evidence for M_2
0–2	1–3	.50–.75	"Weak"
2–6	3–20	.75–.95	"Positive"
6–10	20–150	.95–.99	"Strong"
>10	>150	>.99	"Conclusive"

SOURCE: Adapted from Raftery (1995: Table 6).

Like classical testing, then, the BIC is based on the notion of a statistical hypothesis test. What, then, accounts for the difference between the two approaches, and, in particular, why does the BIC tend to prefer more parsimonious models? Part of the difference between the BIC and classical testing lies in the role of prior distributions for the parameters of the models in the formulation of the BIC, but even more fundamentally, the two kinds of tests treat evidence differently. Suppose, for example, that we test model M_2 versus M_1, where M_2 is nested within M_1 (as is the case when M_2 is derived from M_1 by setting certain parameters to zero). In this instance, the classical test is of the null hypothesis that the parameter restrictions on M_1 producing M_2 are correct, against the alternative that they are wrong, and the two models play an *asymmetric* role in the formulation of the test: The *p*-value for the null hypothesis is the probability of obtaining data *as extreme as or more extreme than* the observed data assuming the truth of M_2. In the Bayesian test (to which the BIC is an approximation), the two models play a *symmetric* role, with the Bayes factor weighing the relative strength of evidence for the models *in the observed data*; data more extreme than those observed do not figure in the test, lending greater support to the null hypothesis than it has in the classical test.

The BIC has its basis in Bayesian hypothesis testing, comparing the degree of support in the data for two models. The BIC is an approximation to twice the log of the Bayes factor comparing a particular model to the saturated model, where the Bayes factor is the ratio of the marginal probability of the data under the two models. When the prior probabilities for the two models are the same, the posterior odds for the models are equal to the Bayes factor. Differences in BIC approximate twice the log of the Bayes factor comparing two models to each other. The BIC approximation to the Bayes factor is accurate for a particular choice of prior distribution over the parameters of the models, called the unit-information prior, but may not be accurate for other priors. Differences in BIC of about 6 or more represent strong evidence in favor of the model with the smaller BIC.

22.1.2   An Illustration: Baseball Salaries

To illustrate model selection, I will use data on major-league baseball players' salaries from the 1987 season, excluding pitchers and restricting attention to players who were active during the 1986 season.[30] In addition to the player's name and the team for which he played at the beginning of the 1987 season, the data source also included the player's annual salary (in thousands of

---

[30]The data set originated in a 1988 poster session sponsored by the Statistical Graphics Section of the American Statistical Association and were used, for example, by Friendly (2002) in a paper on graphical display of correlation matrices. The version used here has a number of errors corrected.

dollars) at the start of the 1987 season and information on number of times at bat (AB), number of hits (H), number of home runs (HR), number of runs scored (R), number of runs batted in (RBI), and number of walks (bases on balls, BB), both for the 1986 season and during the player's career; the player's number of put-outs (PO), assists (A), and errors (E) during the 1986 season; the player's position (or positions) in the field during the 1986 season; and the player's number of years in the major leagues.[31]

From these variables, I derived several additional potential predictors of salary: the player's 1986 and career batting average (AVG—i.e., number of hits divided by number of at-bats); 1986 and career on-base percentage (OBP $= 100\times$ [hits + walks]/[at-bats + walks]); and the numbers of at-bats, hits, home runs, runs scored, and runs batted-in recorded per year over the player's career (e.g., number of career home runs divided by number of years in the majors). Rather than create 24 dummy variables for the 25 positions and combinations of positions that appear in the data set, I created four 0/1 dummy variables, coded 1 for players who consistently played second base or shortstop (i.e., middle infielders, MI), catcher (C), center field (CF), or designated hitter (DH). Middle infield, catcher, and center field are generally considered high-skill positions; designated hitters (a role available only in the American League) bat but do not play the field. After 3 years in the major leagues, players are eligible for salary arbitration, and after 6 years they are eligible for free agency (i.e., can negotiate a contract with any team). I consequently created two 0/1 dummy variables, one coded 1 for players with between 3 and 5 years of major-league experience and the other coded 1 for players with 6 or more years in the majors.[32]

Preliminary examination of the data suggested log-transforming salary (the response variable), number of years in the majors, and career at-bats. I also decided to drop one player (Pete Rose) from the data set because of his high leverage in the regressions.[33] These modeling decisions could be made a formal part of the model-selection process, but to do so would further complicate an already complicated example.

The data set to be analyzed includes 262 players and 33 variables. A linear least-squares regression of log-salary on the 32 predictors accounts for most of the variation in the response variable, $R^2 = .861$, but as one might expect, the regression proves difficult to interpret. There are several "statistically significant" regression coefficients (for BB, MI, C, career AB, career H, career R, career BB, and eligibility for free-agency), but the degree of collinearity is very high, with variance-inflation factors topping out at more than 500 (for career H) and a condition number of 133.[34]

Figure 22.1 shows the predictors in the "best" model of each size, selected according to the BIC.[35] Table 22.2 includes all models, regardless of size, within 2 of the minimum BIC, displaying

---

My apologies to readers who are unfamiliar with baseball: Even a superficial explanation of that subtle sport would require more space than the rest of the chapter. I expect that the general sense of the example will be clear even if nuances are missed.

[31] The abbreviations (e.g., AB for at-bats) are standard. There was, in addition, information on the player's team and the division and league (i.e., National or American) in which he played. I decided not to use this information in predicting salary, because I thought that it would weaken interest in the example: One could argue that playing for a high-paying team is a reflection of a player's earning potential.

[32] A disclaimer: This is not a serious investigation of baseball salaries. Such an investigation would take into account additional information about the players' situations, such as whether they were free agents prior to the 1987 season. Moreover, if prediction is the goal, salary in the previous season is obviously relevant. Finally, it was later established that during this period baseball owners colluded to limit the salaries of free agents.

[33] Fans of baseball will find this decision ironic: Pete Rose, baseball's all-time hits leader, was banned for life from the sport because of his gambling activities.

[34] Variance-inflation factors and the condition number are described in Section 13.1. Two of the "significant" predictors— career H and career BB—have unexpectedly negative coefficients.

[35] See Exercise 22.5 for the application of other model-selection criteria to the baseball data.

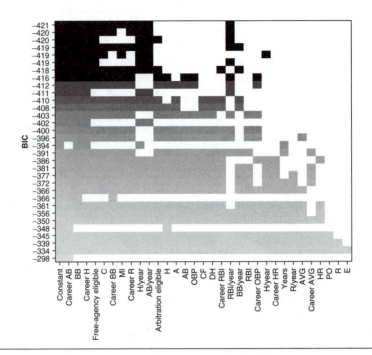

Figure 22.1   BIC for the "best" model of each size fit to the baseball salary data. The models are sorted by BIC, with the lowest BIC at the top; the variables are sorted by the number of models in which they appear. The squares show which variables are included in each model, with darker squares indicating lower values of BIC (i.e., "better" models).

the signs of the coefficients for the predictors in each model, the model R^2, and the difference in BIC compared to the "best" model.[36] An entry of 0 indicates that the corresponding predictor does not appear in the model; only predictors appearing in at least one of the 13 models are shown. The coefficient signs, it turns out, are consistent across models in the table, but not all signs make substantive sense: Why, for example, should number of career hits, which is present in all 13 models, have a negative coefficient, controlling for the other predictors in the models? It is necessary to remind ourselves that the goal here is to select models that produce accurate predictions.

This example is elaborated in the following section.

22.1.3   Comments on Model Selection

I have stressed the point that automatic model-selection methods—stepwise and optimal-subset regression, for example—attend to the predictive adequacy of regression models and are blind to their substantive interpretability. I believe that in most instances researchers would be better served by judiciously selecting the setting within which to conduct an investigation, thinking carefully about the social process under study and the questions to be put to the data, and focusing on a relatively small number of explanatory variables, with the level of detail growing with the sample size.

Model-selection criteria such as the AIC and BIC are not limited to comparing models selected by automatic methods, however, and one of the currently popular applications of the BIC is to

---

[36]Note that some pairs of models (e.g., 1 and 5) with the same number of predictors and the same R^2 have slightly different BIC values. The apparent discrepancy is due to rounding of R^2 to three decimal places.

Table 22.2 The "Best" Models Fit to the Baseball Salary Data According to the BIC

	Model												
Predictor	1	2	3	4	5	6	7	8	9	10	11	12	13
Free-agency eligible	+	+	+	+	+	+	+	+	+	+	+	+	+
H/year	+	+	+	+	+	+	+	+	+	+	+	+	+
AB/year	−	−	−	−	−	−	−	−	−	−	−	−	−
Career H	−	−	−	−	−	−	−	−	−	−	−	−	−
Career AB	+	+	+	+	+	+	+	+	+	+	+	+	+
BB	+	+	+	+	+	+	+	+	+	+	0	+	+
C	+	+	+	0	+	0	+	+	0	+	+	+	0
Career BB	−	−	−	0	−	0	−	−	0	0	−	−	0
Career R	+	+	+	0	+	0	+	+	0	0	−	−	0
RBI/year	+	+	0	+	0	+	+	0	0	0	0	0	+
Career RBI	0	0	+	0	+	+	0	+	+	0	+	+	0
Arbitration	0	0	0	0	0	0	0	0	0	0	0	0	0
BB/year	0	0	0	0	+	0	+	+	+	0	+	+	0
MI	+	0	0	0	0	0	0	0	0	+	0	0	0
HR/year	0	0	0	0	0	0	0	0	0	+	0	0	0
H	0	0	0	0	0	0	0	0	0	0	+	0	0
Number of predictors	11	10	10	8	11	8	12	12	8	9	11	11	7
R^2	.844	.841	.841	.833	.844	.833	.847	.847	.833	.837	.843	.843	.829
$\text{BIC} - \text{BIC}_{min}$	0.00	0.18	0.65	1.01	1.14	1.27	1.29	1.33	1.69	1.71	1.86	1.91	1.96

NOTE: All of the models are within two of the smallest BIC. The table shows the sign of each coefficient; 0 indicates that the predictor is not in the model. Only predictors entering at least one of the models are shown justify the removal of small but "statistically significant" terms in regression models fit to large samples of data. Though largely benign, I believe that this practice slightly misses an essential point: Researchers should feel free to remove "statistically significant" terms from a statistical model based on the substantive judgment that these terms are too small to be of interest. It may be nice that the BIC supports this judgment, but that is by no means essential; and in very large samples, even the BIC may point toward models that are unnecessarily complex for summarizing data cogently.

Although I have drawn a clear distinction between prediction and interpretation, in some cases, the line between the two is blurred. It is common, for example, for interest to center on one or a small number of explanatory variables; other explanatory variables are regarded as statistical "controls"—causally prior variables included in the analysis to avoid spurious results.[37] In this setting, one might be tempted to specify a model in which the explanatory variables of primary interest are *necessarily* included but for which other explanatory variables are selected by an automatic procedure. Unfortunately, this approach is flawed: Control variables that are highly correlated with the focal explanatory variables will likely be excluded from the model, and it is precisely the exclusion of these variables that raises the specter of spuriousness.[38] In most cases, therefore, if simply controlling for *all* the variables thought to be important turns out to be impractical, then the data are probably insufficiently informative to answer the questions posed by the researcher.

> When the focus is on interpretation rather than prediction, researchers should feel free to simplify a statistical model on the basis of substantive considerations, even if that means removing small but "statistically significant" terms from the model. Penalized model-selection criteria, such as the BIC, often provide an unnecessary excuse for doing so.

22.2 Model Averaging*

Model selection, described in the preceding section, implies uncertainty about the "best" statistical model for the data.[39] Often there are several—or even many—models that are roughly equally supported by the data, providing small justification for choosing among them. Uncertainty can arise from other sources as well, such as the selection of transformations of the response or explanatory variables in a regression or the removal of outliers. *Model averaging* seeks to acknowledge model uncertainty explicitly by combining information from competing statistical models rather than discarding all models but one. As I will argue at the end of this section, I believe that model averaging (like model selection) is most sensible when the goal of a statistical investigation is prediction.

---

[37] See the discussion of specification errors in Sections 6.3 and 9.7.

[38] When there is a *binary* explanatory variable of primay interest, an approach based on *propensity scores* can be effective (see, e.g., Rosenbaum and Rubin, 1983). One proceeds by formulating a predictive model, such as a logistic regression model, in which the binary variable appears as the response and the control variables as the predictors. The fitted probabilities from this auxiliary model, the "propensity scores," are then used as an explanatory variable in the main regression analysis. The auxiliary propensity-score regression is a pure prediction problem, and thus, automatic model selection is entirely appropriate.

[39] This section is starred not because of its difficulty but because it depends on starred material in Section 22.1.1.

I will describe an approach to model averaging based on the BIC.[40] As previously explained, under the unit-information prior, the difference in BIC for two competing models—say models M_1 and M_2—approximates twice the log Bayes factor for the two models;[41] using the notation of Section 22.1.1,

$$\mathrm{BIC}_2 - \mathrm{BIC}_1 \approx 2 \times \log_e \frac{p(\mathbf{y}|M_1)}{p(\mathbf{y}|M_2)}$$

Consequently, if the prior probabilities for the two models are equal and if attention is restricted to these models, then the posterior probability for model M_1 is[42]

$$p(M_1|\mathbf{y}) \approx \frac{\exp\left(-\frac{1}{2}\mathrm{BIC}_1\right)}{\exp\left(-\frac{1}{2}\mathrm{BIC}_1\right) + \exp\left(-\frac{1}{2}\mathrm{BIC}_2\right)}$$

The extension to a set of models $\mathcal{M} = \{M_1, M_2, \ldots, M_m\}$ is immediate:

$$p(M_j|\mathbf{y}) \approx p_j \equiv \frac{\exp\left(-\frac{1}{2}\mathrm{BIC}_j\right)}{\sum_{j'=1}^{m} \exp\left(-\frac{1}{2}\mathrm{BIC}_{j'}\right)} \tag{22.13}$$

The approximate posterior probabilities p_j can be used to determine the strength of evidence for including a particular predictor, say X_ℓ, in the model and for estimating model "outputs" such as coefficients and predicted values. The posterior probability that the coefficient β_ℓ of X_ℓ is not zero is

$$\Pr\left(\beta_\ell \neq 0|\mathbf{y}\right) \approx \sum_{j:M_j \in \mathcal{A}_\ell} p_j$$

where $\mathcal{A}_\ell$ is the subset of models $\mathcal{M}$ that include the predictor X_ℓ. Restricting attention to this subset of models, the posterior distribution of β_ℓ assuming that the coefficient is not zero is

$$p\left(\beta_\ell|\mathbf{y}, \beta_\ell \neq 0\right) \approx \sum_{j:M_j \in \mathcal{A}_\ell} p(\beta_\ell|\mathbf{y}, M_j) p_j'$$

where

$$p_j' \equiv \frac{p_j}{\sum_{j':M_{j'} \in \mathcal{A}_\ell} p_{j'}}$$

Likewise, conditional on $\beta_\ell \neq 0$, the posterior mean and variance of β_ℓ can be approximated as

$$E\left(\beta_\ell|\mathbf{y}, \beta_\ell \neq 0\right) \approx \widetilde{\beta}_\ell \equiv \sum_{j:M_j \in \mathcal{A}_\ell} p_j' \widehat{\beta}_\ell^{(j)}$$

$$V\left(\beta_\ell|\mathbf{y}, \beta_\ell \neq 0\right) \approx \sum_{j:M_j \in \mathcal{A}_\ell} p_j' \left[\widehat{V}\left(\widehat{\beta}_\ell^{(j)}\right) + \widehat{\beta}_\ell^{(j)2}\right] - \widetilde{\beta}_\ell^2$$

---

[40]Bayesian model averaging based on the BIC is described in several sources, such as Kass and Raftery (1995), Raftery (1995), and Hoeting, Madigan, Raftery, and Volinsky (1999). The exposition in this section is close to Raftery (1995). There are other approaches to model averaging. See, for example, Exercise 22.6 for model averaging based on the AIC.

[41]See Equation 22.12 on page 617.

[42]See Exercise 22.7.

where $\widehat{\beta}_\ell^{(j)}$ is the MLE of β_ℓ and $\widehat{V}\left(\widehat{\beta}_\ell^{(j)}\right)$ the estimated sampling variance of this coefficient in model M_j.

A practical obstacle to applying these results is the possibly very large number of candidate models in $\mathcal{M}$. For the baseball salary regression, for example, where there are $k = 32$ predictors, the number of models is $m = 2^{32} \approx 4.3 \times 10^9$ or about 4 billion! Most of these models, however, have posterior probabilities very close to zero. To deal with this problem, Madigan and Raftery (1994) suggest excluding from consideration (1) models with BIC more than six units higher than the smallest BIC (i.e., with posterior odds relative to the model most supported by the data of about 1/20 or smaller) and (2) models that have a more probable model nested within them (i.e., models for which eliminating one or more terms produces a model with a smaller BIC). Madigan and Raftery call this rule "Occam's window."[43] Posterior probabilities are computed according to Equation 22.13 but excluding models falling outside the window. Evidence suggests that applying only the first part of the rule tends to produce more accurate predictions; in this case, the window of acceptable models is termed symmetric rather than strict. Efficient methods exist for locating the subset of models in Occam's window without enumerating and fitting all possible models.

22.2.1 Application to the Baseball Salary Data

I applied Bayesian model averaging to the baseball salary regression, with the results given in Table 22.3, using 175 models falling in the symmetric Occam's window that encompasses all models with BIC within 6 of the "best" model. The regression intercept was included in all the models. The best 13 of these models appeared in Table 22.2 (on page 621).

Many variables conventionally used to measure players' performance (such as career batting average and career on-base percentage) have very low probabilities of inclusion in the model. Figure 22.2 shows the posterior distribution of the regression coefficients for the nine predictors that have probability of inclusion in the model greater than .5. The vertical line visible in some of the graphs shows the probability that the corresponding coefficient is zero. Two of the coefficients (for career hits and free-agency eligibility) have clearly bimodal posterior distributions.

22.2.2 Comments on Model Averaging

By combining information from many models and thereby avoiding what is typically the illusion of a single "best" predictive model, model averaging holds out the promise of more accurate predictions. Indeed, one can average *predictions* directly, not just regression coefficients.

Nevertheless, because the meaning of a partial regression coefficient depends on the *other* explanatory variables in the model (what Tukey and Mosteller [1977, especially Chap. 13] termed the "stock" of explanatory variables in the regression), model-averaged regression coefficients can be difficult to interpret. This point is drawn into focus when the distribution of a coefficient across models is bi- or multimodal (as was the case for at least two of the coefficients in Figure 22.2, for example), but the point is more general. Although a proponent of model averaging might well reply that this kind of ambiguity is simply the reflection of model uncertainty, mechanically averaging regression coefficients is not a substitute for thinking about the substantive content of a regression equation.

---

[43]"Occam's razor," due to the English philosopher William of Occam (1285–1329), is an early and famous expression of the principle of parsimony. The principle appeared frequently in Occam's writings, including in the form, "Plurality is not to be assumed without necessity." (See Moody, 1972.)

Table 22.3 Probability of Inclusion in the Model and Posterior Expectation and Standard Deviation if Nonzero for the Predictors in the Baseball Salary Data

Predictor	$Pr(\beta_\ell \neq 0|\mathbf{y})$	$E(\beta_\ell|\mathbf{y},\beta_\ell \neq 0)$	$SD(\beta_\ell|\mathbf{y},\beta_\ell \neq 0)$
Constant	—	−0.586	0.671
Career AB	1.000	0.831	0.129
Career H	1.000	−0.00109	0.00041
Free-agency eligible	1.000	0.403	0.201
AB/year	.985	−0.00717	0.00151
H/year	.985	0.0259	0.0052
BB	.920	0.00659	0.00260
C	.680	0.145	0.120
Career BB	.636	−0.000680	0.000648
Career R	.518	0.000816	0.000884
RBI/year	.450	0.00412	0.00488
Arbitration eligible	.416	0.113	0.155
MI	.408	0.0739	0.1093
Career RBI	.397	0.000424	0.000563
BB/year	.232	0.00267	0.00553
HR/year	.123	0.00220	0.00616
DH	.109	−0.0232	0.0773
A	.089	−0.0000531	0.0001902
R/year	.073	0.000693	0.002741
H	.067	0.000302	0.000188
Career HR	.046	0.0000667	0.0004581
CF	.032	−0.00424	0.02770
AB	.022	−0.0000356	0.0005514
PO	.021	0.00000278	0.00002306
HR	.019	−0.000129	0.001087
R	.015	0.0000713	0.0006055
OBP	.010	−0.000629	0.007083
Career OBP	.009	0.000429	0.005555
RBI	.007	−0.0000111	0.0001894
Career AVG	.007	0.0559	0.6650
E	.004	−0.0000155	0.0003528
AVG	.000	—	—
Years	.000	—	—

The posterior probability for each model M_j in a set of models $\mathcal{M} = \{M_1, M_2, \ldots, M_m\}$ can be approximated using the BIC:

$$p(M_j|\mathbf{y}) \approx p_j = \frac{\exp\left(-\frac{1}{2}\text{BIC}_j\right)}{\sum_{j'=1}^m \exp\left(-\frac{1}{2}\text{BIC}_{j'}\right)}$$

Then, for a model output such as the regression coefficient β_ℓ of the predictor X_ℓ, the posterior probability that β_ℓ is not zero is

(Continued)

(Continued)

$$\Pr\left(\beta_\ell \neq 0|\mathbf{y}\right) \approx \sum_{j:M_j \in \mathcal{A}_\ell} p_j$$

where $\mathcal{A}_\ell$ is the subset of models that include the predictor X_ℓ. Conditional on $\beta_\ell \neq 0$, the posterior mean and variance of β_ℓ are approximately

$$E\left(\beta_\ell|\mathbf{y}, \beta_\ell \neq 0\right) \approx \widetilde{\beta}_\ell = \sum_{j:M_j \in \mathcal{A}_\ell} p'_j \widehat{\beta}_\ell^{(j)}$$

$$V\left(\beta_\ell|\mathbf{y}, \beta_\ell \neq 0\right) \approx \sum_{j:M_j \in \mathcal{A}_\ell} p'_j \left[\widehat{V}\left(\widehat{\beta}_\ell^{(j)}\right) + \widehat{\beta}_\ell^{(j)2}\right] - \widetilde{\beta}_\ell^2$$

where $\widehat{\beta}_\ell^{(j)}$ is the MLE of β_ℓ, $\widehat{V}\left(\widehat{\beta}_\ell^{(j)}\right)$ is the estimated sampling variance of this coefficient in model M_j, and $p'_j = p_j / \sum_{j':M_{j'} \in \mathcal{A}_\ell} p_{j'}$. Because the number of candidate models can be extremely large, there is an advantage to restricting attention only to models with relatively large posterior probabilities, such as those with BIC within 6 of the "best" model; these models are said to fall within "Occam's window." Because the meaning of a partial regression coefficient depends on the other explanatory variables in the model, however, model-averaged regression coefficients can be difficult to interpret.

22.3 Model Validation

In *model validation*, part of the data (called the "training" or "exploratory" subsample) are used to specify a statistical model, which is then evaluated using the other part of the data (the "validation" or "confirmatory" subsample). Cross-validation, already discussed, is an application of this very simple—but powerful—idea, where the roles of training and validation subsamples are interchanged or rotated.[44]

I have stressed the importance of descriptive adequacy in statistical modeling, and—in support of this goal—I have described a variety of methods for screening data and for evaluating and, if necessary, modifying statistical models. This process of data exploration, model fitting, model criticism, and model re-specification is typically iterative, requiring several failed attempts before an adequate description of the data is achieved. In the process, variables may be dropped from the model, terms such as interactions may be incorporated or deleted, variables may be transformed, and unusual data may be corrected, removed, or otherwise accommodated.

The outcome should be a model that more accurately reflects the principal characteristics of the data at hand, but the risk of iterative modeling is that we will capitalize on chance—overfitting the data and overstating the strength of our results. The same risk inheres in the model-selection and model-averaging strategies described in this chapter (although the use of penalized model-selection criteria such as the AIC and BIC at least partly mitigates this risk). It is obviously

---

[44]The term *cross-validation* often is also used for the validation procedure described in the current section, but I believe that it makes more semantic sense to reserve that term for applications in which the roles of training and validation samples are reversed or rotated.

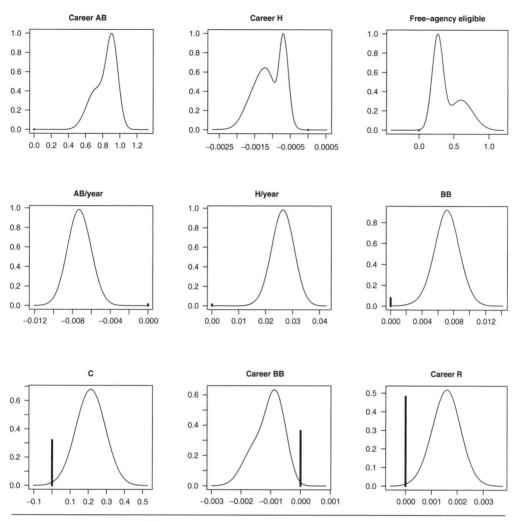

Figure 22.2 Posterior distributions for coefficients in the baseball salary regression. Only coefficients with probability of inclusion in the model exceeding .5 are shown. The vertical line visible in some panels represents the probability that the corresponding coefficient is zero; the vertical axis is scaled so that the highest point of the density curve is the probability that the coefficient is *nonzero*.

problematic to employ the same data both to explore and to validate a statistical model, but the apparent alternative of analyzing data blindly, simply to preserve the "purity" of classical statistical inference, is surely worse.

An ideal solution to this dilemma would be to collect new data with which to validate a model, but this solution is often impractical. Lack of funds or other constraints may preclude the collection of new data; and, in certain circumstances—for example, the examination of historical records—it is impossible even in principle to collect new data.

Model validation simulates the collection of new data by randomly dividing the data that we have in hand into two, possibly equal, parts—the first part to be used for exploration and model formulation, the second for checking the adequacy of the model, formal estimation, and testing.

This is such a simple idea that it hardly requires detailed explanation. Perhaps the only subtle point is that the division of the data into exploratory and validation subsamples can exploit the sampling structure of the data. If, for example, the data are collected in a social survey employing a stratified sample, each stratum can be randomly divided between the two subsamples; of course, methods of analysis appropriate to a stratified sample should be employed.

> When the same data are employed for selecting a statistical model and for drawing statistical inferences based on the model, the integrity of the inferences is compromised. Validation is a general strategy for protecting the accuracy of statistical inference when—as is typically the case—it is not possible to collect new data with which to assess the model. In model validation, the data at hand are divided at random into two subsamples: a training subsample, which is used to select a statistical model for the data, and a validation subsample, which is used for formal statistical inference.

22.3.1   An Illustration: Refugee Appeals

To illustrate model validation, I will present an abbreviated account of some research that I conducted on the Canadian refugee determination process, employing data that were collected and described by Greene and Shaffer (1992).[45] Greene and Shaffer's data pertain to decisions of the Canadian Federal Court of Appeal on cases filed by claimants who were refused refugee status by the Immigration and Refugee Board. The Court either granted or denied leave to appeal the board's decision, and a single judge (rather than the usual tribunal) heard the request for leave to appeal.

During the period of the study, the 10 judges who adjudicated these cases varied widely in the rates with which they approved requests for leave to appeal negative decisions of the Refugee Board—with approval rates ranging from 13% to 56% of cases. The cases were not assigned randomly to judges, however, but rather were heard on a rotating basis. Although it seems unlikely that this procedure would introduce systematic differences into the leave requests processed by different judges, it is conceivable that this is the case. In defending the fairness of the existing procedure, the Crown therefore contended that it was insufficient simply to demonstrate large and statistically significant differences among the rates of approval for the 10 judges.

To determine whether systematic differences among the cases heard by the judges could account for differences in their judgments, I controlled statistically for several factors that—it was suggested—might influence the decisions, including the following:

1. the rate of success of leave applications from the applicant's country;

2. whether or not this country was identified as a "high refugee producing" country;

3. the region of the world in which the applicant's country is located (Latin America, Europe, Africa, the Middle East, or Asia and the Pacific Islands); and

4. the date of the applicant's case.

---

[45] Also see Section 1.2. The analysis of the refugee data reported in the current section uses a larger subset of cases.

Table 22.4 Wald Tests for Terms in the Linear-Logit Model for the Canadian Refugee Data Training and Validation Subsamples

		Subsample					
		Training				Validation	
		Model 1		Model 2		Model 3	
Term	df	Z^2	p	Z^2	p	Z^2	p
Country success	1	14.55	.0001	15.72	.0001	25.64	<.0001
High-refugee country	1	0.09	.77				
Region	4	6.47	.17				
Latin America	1	4.44	.035	4.98	.026	0.58	.45
Time period	4	9.24	.055				
Linear	1	6.46	.011	5.74	.017	0.98	.32
Quadratic	1	1.73	.19				
Cubic	1	0.16	.69				
Quartic	1	0.19	.67				
Judge	9	29.75	.0005	29.67	.0005	37.45	<.0001

NOTE: Z^2 is the Wald test statistic

These explanatory variables were included in a logistic regression, along with dummy variables identifying the judge who heard the case. The response variable was whether or not leave to appeal was granted. Prior to constructing the logistic regression model, the roughly 800 cases meeting the criteria for inclusion in the study were randomly divided into training and validation subsamples. The data in the training subsample were carefully examined, and several variations of the analysis were undertaken. For example, the date of the case was treated both as a quantitative variable with a linear effect and categorically, divided into five quarters (the period of the study was slightly in excess of 1 year).

Wald tests for terms in two of the models fit to the data in the exploratory subsample are shown in Table 22.4.[46] Model 1 contains two explanatory variables—national rate of success and judge—that are highly statistically significant; high-refugee country has a small and nonsignificant coefficient; and the region and time-period effects are relatively small but approach statistical significance. Examination of the region coefficients suggested that applicants from Latin America might be treated differently from those from other regions; likewise, the resolution of time period into orthogonal polynomial components suggested a possible linear effect of time. Model 2 is a final model for the exploratory subsample, incorporating a dummy regressor for Latin America and a linear trend over the five time periods, both of which appear to be statistically significant.

The last columns of Table 22.4 (for Model 3) show the result of refitting Model 2 to the data from the validation subsample. The national rate of success and judge are both still highly statistically significant, but neither the coefficient for Latin America nor the linear time trend proves to be statistically significant. That these latter two coefficients appeared to be statistically significant in the exploratory sub-sample illustrates the risk of selecting and testing a model on the same data. Most notably, however, differences among judges (not shown) are essentially the same before and after controlling for the other explanatory variables in the analysis.

---

[46]Were I to do this analysis now I would prefer likelihood-ratio to Wald tests.

22.3.2   Comments on Model Validation

Like the bootstrap (described in the preceding chapter), model validation is a good, simple, broadly applicable procedure that is rarely used in social research.[47] I believe that researchers resist the idea of dividing their data in half. In very small samples, division of the data is usually not practical. Even in samples of moderate size, however (such as the refugee-appeal data discussed in the previous section), halving the sample size makes it more difficult to find "statistically significant" results.

Yet, if statistical inference is to be more than an incantation spoken over the data, it is necessary to conduct research honestly. This is not to say that procedures of inference cannot be approximate—simplifying abstraction of some sort is unavoidable—but it is easy to introduce substantial errors of inference when the same data are used both to formulate and to test a statistical model.

Model validation is not a panacea for these problems, but it goes a long way toward solving them. Issues such as variable selection and choice of transformation are neatly handled by validation. Problems such as influential data are less easily dealt with, because these problems are particular to specific observations: That we locate an outlier in the training subsample, for example, does not imply that an outlier is present in the validation subsample. The reverse could be true as well, of course. We can, however, use the distribution of residuals in the training subsample to help us decide whether to use a method of estimation in the validation subsample that is resistant to unusual data or to adopt a rule for rejecting outliers.

Exercises

Exercise 22.1. Variable selection with randomly generated "noise" (adapted from Freedman, 1983):

(a) Sampling from the standard normal distribution, independently generate 500 observations for 101 variables. Call the first of these variables the response variable Y and the other variables the predictors $X_1, X_2, \ldots, X_{100}$. Perform a linear least-squares regression of Y on $X_1, X_2, \ldots, X_{100}$. Are any of the individual regression coefficients "statistically significant"? Is the omnibus F-statistic for the regression "statistically significant"? Is this what you expected to observe?

(b) Retain the three predictors in part (a) that have the largest absolute t-values, regressing Y *only* on these variables. Are the individual coefficients "statistically significant"? What about the omnibus F? What happens to the p-values compared to part (a)?

(c) Using any method of variable selection (stepwise regression or subset regression with any criterion), find the "best" model with three explanatory variables. Obtain the individual t-statistics and omnibus F for this model. How do these tests compare to those in part (a)?

(d) Using the methods of model selection discussed in this chapter, find the "best" model for these data. How does that model compare to the true model that generated the data?

(e) Validation: Generate a new set of 500 observations as in part (a), and use that new data set to validate the models that you selected in parts (b), (c), and (d). What do you conclude?

(f) Repeat the entire experiment several times.

---

[47] Barnard (1974, p. 133) put it nicely: "The simple idea of splitting a sample into two and then developing the hypothesis on the basis of one part and testing it on the remainder may perhaps be said to be one of the most seriously neglected ideas in statistics, if we measure the degree of neglect by the ratio of the number of cases where a method could give help to the number where it is actually used."

Exercise 22.2. *Prove that Mallows's C_p statistic,

$$C_{p_j} = \frac{\text{RSS}_j}{S_E^2} + 2s_j - n$$

can also be written

$$C_{p_j} = (k + 1 - s_j)(F_j - 1) + s_j$$

where RSS_j is the residual sum of squares for model M_j; s_j is the number of parameters (including the constant) in model M_j; n is the number of observations; S_E^2 is the usual estimate of error variance for the full model, which has k coefficients (excluding the constant); and F_j is the incremental F-statistic for testing the null hypothesis that the $k + 1 - s_j$ coefficients missing from model M_j are zero.

Exercise 22.3. Both the adjusted R^2,

$$\widetilde{R}^2 = 1 - \frac{n-1}{n-s} \times \frac{\text{RSS}}{\text{TSS}}$$

and the generalized cross-validation criterion

$$\text{GCV} = \frac{n \times \text{RSS}}{(n-s)^2}$$

penalize models that have large numbers of predictors. (Here, n is the number of observations, s the number of parameters in the model, RSS the residual sum of squares under the model, and TSS the total sum of squares.) Do these two criteria necessarily rank a set of models in the same order? That is, if one model has a larger $\widetilde{R}^2$ than another does it necessarily also have a smaller GCV?

Exercise 22.4. Show that the differences in BIC values given in the first column of Table 22.1 (page 618) correspond roughly to the Bayes factors and posterior model probabilities given in columns 2 and 3 of the table.

Exercise 22.5. Perform model selection for the baseball salary regression using a criterion or criteria different from the BIC, examining the "best" model of each size, and the "best" 10 or 15 models regardless of size. Are the models similar to those nominated by the BIC? Why did you obtain these results?

Exercise 22.6. *Burnham and Anderson (2004) suggest the following procedure for model averaging based on the AIC: Let $\text{AIC}_{\min}$ represent the smallest AIC among a set of models $\mathcal{M} = \{M_1, M_2, \ldots, M_m\}$, and let $\text{AIC}_j^* \equiv \text{AIC}_j - \text{AIC}_{\min}$. Then *Akaike model weights* are given by

$$w_j \equiv \frac{\exp\left(-\frac{1}{2}\text{AIC}_j^*\right)}{\sum_{j'=1}^m \exp\left(-\frac{1}{2}\text{AIC}_{j'}^*\right)}$$

Model-averaged regression coefficients and their sampling variances are defined using these weights:

$$\widetilde{\beta}_\ell \equiv \sum_{j=1}^{m} w_j \widehat{\beta}_\ell^{(j)}$$

$$\widetilde{V}\left(\widetilde{\beta}_\ell\right) \equiv \left[\sum_{j=1}^{m} w_j \sqrt{\widehat{V}\left(\widehat{\beta}_\ell^{(j)}\right) + \left(\widehat{\beta}_\ell^{(j)} - \widetilde{\beta}_\ell\right)^2}\right]^2$$

where $\widehat{\beta}_\ell^{(j)}$ is the MLE of β_ℓ and $\widehat{V}\left(\widehat{\beta}_\ell^{(j)}\right)$ is the estimated sampling variance of this coefficient in model M_j.

(a) How does this procedure compare with model averaging based on the BIC, as described in Section 22.2?

(b) Restricting attention to the subset of models with AIC within 6 of the "best" model (i.e., applying the idea of Occam's window to the AIC), find the model-averaged regression coefficients and their estimated variances for the baseball salary regression. Burnham and Anderson indicate that *model averaging* based on the AIC and BIC tends to produce results that are more similar than *model selection* based on the two criteria. Does that hold true here? *Note*: Following Burnham and Anderson, include 0 coefficients (with variances of 0) in the averages.

Exercise 22.7. *Show that when there are only two models M_1 and M_2 under consideration, the approximate posterior probability of the first model is

$$p(M_1|\mathbf{y}) \approx \frac{\exp\left(-\tfrac{1}{2}\mathrm{BIC}_1\right)}{\exp\left(-\tfrac{1}{2}\mathrm{BIC}_1\right) + \exp\left(-\tfrac{1}{2}\mathrm{BIC}_2\right)}$$

Extend this result to the posterior probability of model M_j in the set of models $\mathcal{M} = \{M_1, M_2, \ldots, M_m\}$:

$$p(M_j|\mathbf{y}) \approx \frac{\exp\left(-\tfrac{1}{2}\mathrm{BIC}_j\right)}{\sum_{j'=1}^{m} \exp\left(-\tfrac{1}{2}\mathrm{BIC}_{j'}\right)}$$

Summary

- It is problematic to use statistical hypothesis tests for model selection. Doing so leads to issues of simultaneous inference; it can also produce biased results, tends to yield complicated models in large samples, and exaggerates the precision of results.
- Several criteria are employed for comparing statistical models with differing numbers of parameters, some applicable to regression models fit by least-squares and others more general:
  - The squared multiple correlation adjusted for degrees of freedom,

  $$\widetilde{R}^2 = 1 - \frac{n-1}{n-s} \times \frac{\mathrm{RSS}}{\mathrm{TSS}}$$

where n is the number of observations, s the number of regression coefficients in the model, RSS the residual sum of squares under the model, and TSS the total sum of squares for the response variable.
- Mallows's C_p statistic,

$$C_p = (k + 1 - s)(F - 1) + s$$

where k is the number of predictors in the full model fit to the data and F the incremental F-statistic for the hypothesis that the $k + 1 - s$ predictors excluded from the model are zero. C_p is an estimate of the total MSE of prediction for the model. A good model has C_p close to or below s.
- The cross-validation criterion,

$$\mathrm{CV} = \frac{\sum_{i=1}^{n} \left(\widehat{Y}_{-i} - Y_i\right)^2}{n}$$

where $\widehat{Y}_{-i}$ is the fitted value for observation i obtained when the model is fit with observation i omitted.
- The generalized cross-validation criterion,

$$\mathrm{GCV} = \frac{n \times \mathrm{RSS}}{df_{\mathrm{res}}^2}$$

where df_{res} is the residual degrees of freedom under the model.
- The AIC,

$$\mathrm{AIC} = -2 \log_e L(\widehat{\boldsymbol{\theta}}) + 2s$$

where $\log_e L(\widehat{\boldsymbol{\theta}})$ is the maximized log-likelihood under the model (and $\boldsymbol{\theta}$ is the parameter vector for the model).
- The BIC,

$$\mathrm{BIC} = -2 \log_e L(\widehat{\boldsymbol{\theta}}) + s \log_e n$$

For both the AIC and the BIC, the model with the smallest value is the one most supported by the data.

- The AIC is based on the Kullback-Leibler information comparing the true distribution of the data $p(\mathbf{y})$ to the distribution of the data $p_j(\mathbf{y}|\boldsymbol{\theta}_j)$ under a particular model M_j.
- The BIC has its basis in Bayesian hypothesis testing, comparing the degree of support in the data for two models. The BIC is an approximation to twice the log of the Bayes factor comparing a particular model to the saturated model, where the Bayes factor is the ratio of the marginal probability of the data under the two models. When the prior probabilities for the two models are the same, the posterior odds for the models are equal to the Bayes factor. Differences in BIC approximate twice the log of the Bayes factor comparing two models to each other. The BIC approximation to the Bayes factor is accurate for a particular choice of prior distribution over the parameters of the models, called the unit-information prior, but may not be accurate for other priors. Differences in BIC of about 6 or more represent strong evidence in favor of the model with the smaller BIC.
- When the focus is on interpretation rather than prediction, researchers should feel free to simplify a statistical model on the basis of substantive considerations, even if that means removing small but statistically significant terms from the model. Penalized model-selection criteria, such as the BIC, often provide an unnecessary excuse for doing so.

- The posterior probability for each model M_j in a set of models $\mathcal{M} = \{M_1, M_2, \dots, M_m\}$ can be approximated using the BIC:

$$p(M_j|\mathbf{y}) \approx p_j = \frac{\exp\left(-\frac{1}{2}\text{BIC}_j\right)}{\sum_{j'=1}^{m} \exp\left(-\frac{1}{2}\text{BIC}_{j'}\right)}$$

Then, for a model output such as the regression coefficient β_ℓ of the predictor X_ℓ, the posterior probability that β_ℓ is not zero is

$$\Pr\left(\beta_\ell \neq 0|\mathbf{y}\right) \approx \sum_{j:M_j \in \mathcal{A}_\ell} p_j$$

where $\mathcal{A}_\ell$ is the subset of models that include the predictor X_ℓ. Conditional on $\beta_\ell \neq 0$, the posterior mean and variance of β_ℓ are approximately

$$E\left(\beta_\ell|\mathbf{y}, \beta_\ell \neq 0\right) \approx \tilde{\beta}_\ell = \sum_{j:M_j \in \mathcal{A}_\ell} p'_j \hat{\beta}_\ell^{(j)}$$

$$V\left(\beta_\ell|\mathbf{y}, \beta_\ell \neq 0\right) \approx \sum_{j:M_j \in \mathcal{A}_\ell} p'_j \left[\hat{V}\left(\hat{\beta}_\ell^{(j)}\right) + \hat{\beta}_\ell^{(j)2}\right] - \tilde{\beta}_\ell^2$$

where $\hat{\beta}_\ell^{(j)}$ is the MLE of β_ℓ, $\hat{V}\left(\hat{\beta}_\ell^{(j)}\right)$ is the estimated sampling variance of this coefficient in model M_j, and $p'_j = p_j / \sum_{j':M_{j'} \in \mathcal{A}_\ell} p_{j'}$. Because the number of candidate models can be extremely large, there is an advantage to restricting attention only to models with relatively large posterior probabilities, such as those with BIC within 6 of the best model; these models are said to fall within Occam's window. Because the meaning of a partial regression coefficient depends on the other explanatory variables in the model, however, model-averaged regression coefficients can be difficult to interpret.

- When the same data are employed for selecting a statistical model and for drawing statistical inferences based on the model, the integrity of the inferences is compromised. Validation is a general strategy for protecting the accuracy of statistical inference when—as is typically the case—it is not possible to collect new data with which to assess the model. In model validation, the data at hand are divided at random into two subsamples: a training subsample, which is used to select a statistical model for the data, and a validation subsample, which is used for formal statistical inference.

Recommended Reading

- There is a vast literature in statistics on automatic methods of model selection, most recently under the rubric of "data mining." Hastie, Tibshirani, and Friedmann (2001), all of whom have made important contributions in this area, provide a broad and reasonably up-to-date overview.
- Several interesting papers on model selection appeared in the November 2004 issue of *Sociological Methods and Research* (Volume 33, Number 2). See, in particular, Burnham and Anderson's paper on the AIC, and Stine's paper on information-theoretic methods of model selection.
- Burnham and Anderson (1998) present an extended exposition of the use of the AIC in model selection and its roots in information theory.

- Raftery (1995) provides a largely accessible introduction to the BIC; Kass and Raftery (1995) cover much of the same ground but provide greater statistical detail. These papers also discuss Bayesian model averaging.
- Weakliem (1999) presents a critique of the use of the BIC in model selection; his paper is followed by commentary from several authors, including Raftery.
- Bailey, Harding, and Smith (1989) give an overview of model validation. Some more detail can be found in Mosteller and Tukey (1968, 1977).

Appendix A

Notation

S pecific notation is introduced at various points in the appendices and chapters. Throughout the text, I adhere to the following general conventions, with few exceptions. (Examples are shown in brackets.)

- Known scalar constants (including subscripts) are represented by lowercase italic letters $[a, b, x_i, x_1^*]$.
- Observable scalar random variables are represented by uppercase italic letters $[X, Y_i, B_0']$ or if the names contain more than one character, by Roman letters, the first of which is uppercase [RegSS, RSS$_0$]. Where it is necessary to make the distinction, *specific values* of random variables are represented as constants $[x, y_i, b_0']$.
- Scalar parameters are represented by lowercase Greek letters $[\alpha, \beta, \beta_j^*, \gamma_2]$. (See the Greek alphabet in Table 1.) Their estimators are generally denoted by "corresponding" italic characters $[A, B, B_j^*, C_2]$ or by Greek letters with diacritics $[\widehat{\alpha}, \widehat{\beta}]$.
- Unobservable scalar random variables are also represented by lowercase Greek letters $[\varepsilon_i]$.
- Vectors and matrices are represented by boldface characters—lowercase for vectors $[\mathbf{x}_1, \boldsymbol{\beta}]$ and uppercase for matrices $[\mathbf{X}, \boldsymbol{\Sigma}_{12}]$. Roman letters are used for constants and observable random variables $[\mathbf{y}, \mathbf{x}_1, \mathbf{X}]$. Greek letters are used for parameters and unobservable random variables $[\boldsymbol{\beta}, \boldsymbol{\Sigma}_{12}, \boldsymbol{\varepsilon}]$. It is occasionally convenient to show the order of a vector or matrix below the matrix $[\underset{(n \times 1)}{\boldsymbol{\varepsilon}}, \underset{(n \times k+1)}{\mathbf{X}}]$. The order of an identity matrix is given by a subscript $[\mathbf{I}_n]$. A zero matrix or vector is represented by a boldface 0 $[\mathbf{0}]$; a vector of 1s is represented by a boldface 1, possibly subscripted with its number of elements $[\mathbf{1}_n]$. Vectors are column vectors, unless they are explicitly transposed [column: $\mathbf{x}$; row: $\mathbf{x}'$].
- Diacritics and symbols such as * (asterisk) and ' (prime) are used freely as modifiers to denote alternative forms $[\mathbf{X}^*, \boldsymbol{\beta}', \widetilde{\boldsymbol{\varepsilon}}]$.
- The symbol $\equiv$ can be read as "is defined by" or "is equal to by definition" $[\overline{X} \equiv (\sum X_i)/n]$.
- The symbol $\sim$ means "is distributed as" $[\varepsilon_i \sim N(0, \sigma_\varepsilon^2)]$.
- The symbol $\in$ denotes membership in a set $[1 \in \{1, 2, 3\}]$.
- The operator $E(\ )$ denotes the expectation of a scalar, vector, or matrix random variable $[E(Y_i), E(\boldsymbol{\varepsilon}), E(\mathbf{X})]$.
- The operator $V(\ )$ denotes the variance of a scalar random variable or the variance-covariance matrix of a vector random variable $[V(\varepsilon_i), V(\mathbf{b})]$.
- Estimated variances or variance-covariance matrices are indicated by a circumflex ("hat") placed over the variance operator $[\widehat{V}(\varepsilon_i), \widehat{V}(\mathbf{b})]$.
- The operator $C(\ )$ gives the covariance of two scalar random variables or the covariance matrix of two vector random variables $[C(X, Y), C(\mathbf{x}_i, \boldsymbol{\varepsilon})]$.

Note: Appendixes B, C, and D can be accessed by visiting the book's Web site at www.sagepub.com/fox.

Table 1 The Greek Alphabet With Roman "Equivalents"

Greek Letter			Roman Equivalent	
Lowercase	Uppercase		Phonetic	Other
α	A	alpha	a	
β	B	beta	b	
γ	Γ	gamma	g, n	c
δ	Δ	delta	d	
ε	E	epsilon	e	
ζ	Z	zeta	z	
η	H	eta	e	
θ	Θ	theta	th	
ι	I	iota	i	
κ	K	kappa	k	
λ	Λ	lambda	l	
μ	M	mu	m	
ν	N	nu	n	
ξ	Ξ	xi	x	
o	O	omicron	o	
π	Π	pi	p	
ρ	P	rho	r	
σ	Σ	sigma	s	
τ	T	tau	t	
υ	Υ	upsilon	y, u	
ϕ	Φ	phi	ph	
χ	X	chi	ch	x
ψ	Ψ	psi	ps	
ω	Ω	omega	o	w

- The operators $\mathcal{E}(\ )$ and $\mathcal{V}(\ )$ denote asymptotic expectation and variance, respectively. Their usage is similar to that of $E(\ )$ and $V(\ )$ [$\mathcal{E}(B)$, $\mathcal{V}(\widehat{\beta})$, $\widehat{V}(B)$].
- Probability limits are specified by plim [plim $b = \beta$].
- Standard mathematical functions are shown in lowercase [$\cos W$, trace($\mathbf{A}$)]. The base of the log function is always specified explicitly, unless it is irrelevant [$\log_e L$, $\log_{10} X$]. The exponential function $\exp(x)$ represents e^x.
- The summation sign $\sum$ is used to denote continued addition [$\sum_{i=1}^{n} X_i \equiv X_1 + X_2 + \cdots + X_n$]. Often, the range of the index is suppressed if it is clear from the context [$\sum_i X_i$], and the index may be suppressed as well [$\sum X_i$]. The symbol $\prod$ similarly indicates continued multiplication [$\prod_{i=1}^{n} p(Y_i) \equiv p(Y_1) \times p(Y_2) \times \cdots \times p(Y_n)$]. The symbol # indicates a count [$\#_{i=1}^{n}(T_b^* \geq T)$].
- To avoid awkward and repetitive phrasing in the statement of definitions and results, the words "if" and "when" are understood to mean "if and only if," unless explicitly indicated to the contrary. Terms are generally set in *italics* when they are introduced. ("Two vectors are *orthogonal* if their inner product is 0.")

References

Abler, R., Adams, J. S., & Gould, P. (1971). *Spatial organization: The geographer's view of the world.* Englewood Cliffs, NJ: Prentice Hall.

Achen, C. H. (1982). *Interpreting and using regression.* Beverly Hills, CA: Sage.

Agresti, A. (1996). *An introduction to categorical data analysis.* New York: Wiley.

Agresti, A. (2002). *Categorical data analysis* (2nd ed.). New York: Wiley.

Aitkin, M., Francis, B., & Hinde, J. (2005). *Statistical modeling in GLIM4* (2nd ed.). Oxford, UK: Clarendon Press.

Allison, P. D. (1984). *Event history analysis: Regression for longitudinal event data.* Beverly Hills, CA: Sage.

Allison, P. D. (2002). *Missing data.* Thousand Oaks, CA: Sage.

Alvarez, R. M., & Nagler, J. (1998). When politics and models collide: Estimating models of multiparty elections. *American Journal of Political Science, 42,* 55–96.

Andersen, R. (2007). *Modern methods for robust regression.* Thousand Oaks, CA: Sage.

Andersen, R., Heath, A., & Sinnott, R. (2002). Political knowledge and electoral choice. *British Elections and Parties Review, 12,* 11–27.

Anderson, T. W. (2003). *An Introduction to multivariate statistical analysis* (3rd ed.). New York: Wiley.

Andrews, D. F. (1979). The robustness of residual displays. In R. L. Launer & G. N. Wilkenson (Eds.), *Robustness in statistics* (pp. 19–32). New York: Academic Press.

Andrews, F. M., Morgan, J. N., & Sonquist, J. A. (1973). *Multiple classification analysis: A report on a computer program for multiple regression using categorical predictors* (2nd ed.). Ann Arbor: Institute for Social Research, University of Michigan.

Anscombe, F. J. (1960). Rejection of outliers [with commentary]. *Technometrics, 2,* 123–166.

Anscombe, F. J. (1961). Examination of residuals. *Proceedings of the Fourth Berkeley Symposium on Mathematical Statistics and Probability, 1,* 1–36.

Anscombe, F. J. (1973). Graphs in statistical analysis. *American Statistician, 27,* 17–22.

Anscombe, F. J., & Tukey, J. W. (1963). The examination and analysis of residuals. *Technometrics, 5,* 141–160.

Atkinson, A. C. (1985). *Plots, transformations, and regression: An introduction to graphical methods of diagnostic regression analysis.* Oxford, UK: Clarendon Press.

Atkinson, A., & Riani, M. (2000). *Robust diagnostic regression analysis.* New York: Springer.

Bailey, R. A., Harding, S. A., & Smith, G. L. (1989). Cross-validation. In S. Kotz & N. L. Johnson (Eds.), *Encyclopedia of statistical sciences* (Suppl. Vol., pp. 39–44). New York: Wiley.

Baker, F. B., & Kim, S.-H. (2004) *Item response theory: Parameter estimation techniques* (2nd ed.). New York: Dekker.

Bard, Y. (1974). *Nonlinear parameter estimation.* New York: Academic Press.

Barnard, G. A. (1974). Discussion of Professor Stone's paper. *Journal of the Royal Statistical Society, Series B, 36,* 133–135.

Barnett, V., & Lewis, T. (1994). *Outliers in statistical data* (3rd ed.).New York: Wiley.

Bartlett, M. S. (1937). Properties of sufficiency and statistical tests. *Proceedings of the Royal Society, A, 160,* 268–282.

Bates, D. M., & Watts, D. G. (1988). *Nonlinear regression and its applications.* New York: Wiley.

Becker, R. A., Chambers, J. M., & Wilks, A. R. (1988). *The new S language: A programming environment for data analysis and graphics.* Pacific Grove, CA: Wadsworth.

Beckman, R. J., & Cook, R. D. (1983). Outliers. *Technometrics, 25,* 119–163.

Beckman, R. J., & Trussell, H. J. (1974). The distribution of an arbitrary studentized residual and the effects of updating in multiple regression. *Journal of the American Statistical Association, 69,* 199–201.

Belsley, D. A. (1984). Demeaning condition diagnostics through centering [with commentary]. *American Statistician, 38,* 73–93.

Belsley, D. A., Kuh, E., & Welsch, R. E. (1980). *Regression diagnostics: Identifying influential data and sources of collinearity.* New York: Wiley.

Berk, R. A. (2004). *Regression analysis: A constructive critique.* Thousand Oaks, CA: Sage.

Blau, P. M., & Duncan, O. D. (1967). *The American occupational structure.* New York: Wiley.

Bollen, K. (1989). *Structural equations with latent variables.* New York: Wiley.

Box, G. E. P. (1979) Robustness in the strategy of scientific model building. In R. L. Launer & G. N. Wilkinson (Eds.), *Robustness in statistics* (pp. 201–236). New York: Academic Press.

Box, G. E. P., & Cox, D. R. (1964). An analysis of transformations. *Journal of the Royal Statistical Society, Series B, 26,* 211–252.

Box, G. E. P., & Tidwell, P. W. (1962). Transformation of the independent variables. *Technometrics, 4,* 531–550.

Bowman, A. W., & Azzalini, A. (1997). *Applied smoothing techniques for data analysis: The Kernel approach with S-Plus illustrations.* Oxford, UK: Oxford University Press.

Breusch, T. S., & Pagan, A. R. (1979). A simple test for heteroscedasticity and random coefficient variation. *Econometrica, 47,* 1287–1294.

Brown, R. L., Durbin, J., & Evans, J. M. (1975). Techniques for testing the constancy of regression relationships over time [with discussion]. *Journal of the Royal Statistical Society, Series B, 37,* 149–192.

Burnham, K. P., & Anderson, D. R. (1998). *Model selection and inference: A practical information-theoretical approach.* New York: Springer.

Burnham, K. P., & Anderson, D. R. (2004). Multimodel inference: Understanding AIC and BIC in model selection. *Sociological Methods and Research, 33,* 261–304.

Cameron, A. C, & Trivedi, P. K. (1998). *Regression analysis for count data.* Cambridge, UK: Cambridge University Press.

Campbell, A., Converse, P. E., Miller, W. E., & Stokes, D. E. (1960). *The American voter.* New York: Wiley.

Campbell, D. T., & Stanley, J. C. (1963). *Experimental and quasi-experimental designs for research.* Chicago: Rand McNally.

Canada. (1962). *Major roads (Map).* Ottawa, Ontario, Canada: Department of Mines and Technical Surveys.

Canada. (1971). *Census of Canada.* Ottawa, Ontario, Canada: Statistics Canada.

Cantoni, E., & Ronchetti, E. (2001). Robust inference for generalized linear models. *Journal of the American Statistical Association, 96,* 1022–1030.

Chambers, J. M. (1998). *Programming with data: A guide to the S language.* New York: Springer.

Chambers, J. M., Cleveland, W. S., Kleiner, B., & Tukey, P. A. (1983). *Graphical methods for data analysis.* Belmont, CA: Wadsworth.

Chambers, J. M., & Hastie, T. J. (Eds.). (1992). *Statistical models in S.* Pacific Grove, CA: Wadsworth.

Chatfield, C. (2003). *Analysis of time series: An introduction* (6th ed.). London: Chapman & Hall.

Chatterjee, S., & Hadi, A. S. (1988). *Sensitivity analysis in linear regression.* New York: Wiley.

Chatterjee, S., & Price, B. (1991). *Regression analysis by example* (2nd ed.). New York: Wiley.

Christensen, R. (1976). *Plane answers to complex questions: The theory of linear models* (2nd ed.). New York: Springer.

Cleveland, W. S. (1993). *Visualizing data.* Summit, NJ: Hobart Press.

Cleveland, W. S. (1994). *The elements of graphing data* (rev. ed.). Summit, NJ: Hobart Press.

Cleveland, W. S., Grosse, E., & Shyu, W. M. (1992). Local regression models. In J. M. Chambers & T. J. Hastie (Eds.), *Statistical models in S* (pp. 309–376). Pacific Grove, CA: Wadsworth.

Collett, D. (2003). *Modelling binary data* (2nd ed.). London: Chapman & Hall.

Collins, L. M., Schafer, J. L., & Kam, C.-M. (2001). A comparison of inclusive and restrictive strategies in modern missing data procedures. *Psychological methods, 6,* 330–351.

Conover, W. J., Johnson, M. E., & Johnson, M. M. (1981). A comparative study of tests for homogeneity of variances, with applications to the outer continental shelf bidding data. *Technometrics, 23,* 351–361.

Cook, R. D. (1977). Detection of influential observations in linear regression. *Technometrics, 19,* 15–18.

Cook, R. D. (1993). Exploring partial residual plots. *Technometrics, 35,* 351–362.

Cook, R. D. (1994). On the interpretation of regression plots. *Journal of the American Statistical Association, 89,* 177–189.

Cook, R. D. (1998). *Regression graphics: Ideas for studying regressions through graphics.* New York: Wiley.

Cook, R. D., & Weisberg, S. (1980). Characterizations of an empirical influence function for detecting influential cases in regression. *Technometrics, 22,* 495–508.

Cook, R. D., & Weisberg, S. (1982). *Residuals and influence in regression.* New York: Chapman & Hall.

Cook, R. D., & Weisberg, S. (1983). Diagnostics for heteroscedasticity in regression. *Biometrika, 70,* 1–10.

Cook, R. D., & Weisberg, S. (1989). Regression diagnostics with dynamic graphics [with commentary]. *Technometrics, 31,* 277–311.

Cook, R. D., & Weisberg, S. (1994). *An introduction to regression graphics.* New York: Wiley.

Cook, R. D., & Weisberg, S. (1999). *Applied regression including computing and graphics.* New York: Wiley.

Coombs, C. H., Dawes, R. M., & Tversky, A. (1970). *Mathematical psychology: An elementary introduction.* Englewood Cliffs, NJ: Prentice Hall.

Cox, D. R., & Snell, E. J. (1989). *Analysis of binary data* (2nd ed.). London: Chapman & Hall.

Cowles, M., & Davis, C. (1987). The subject matter of psychology: Volunteers. *British Journal of Social Psychology, 26,* 97–102.

Davis, C. (1990). Body image and weight preoccupation: A comparison between exercising and non-exercising women. *Appetite, 15,* 13–21.

Davison, A. C., & Hinkley, D. V. (1997). *Bootstrap methods and their application.* Cambridge, UK: Cambridge University Press.

Dempster, A. P. (1969). *Elements of continuous multivariate analysis.* Reading, MA: Addison-Wesley.

Dempster, A. P., Laird, N. M., & Rubin, D. B. (1977). Maximum likelihood from incomplete data via the EM algorithm [with discussion]. *Journal of the Royal Statistical Society, Series B, 39,* 1–38.

Dobson, A. J. (2001). *An introduction to generalized linear models* (2nd ed.). London: Chapman & Hall.

Draper, N. R., & Smith, H. (1998). *Applied regression analysis* (3rd ed.). New York: Wiley.

Draper, N. R., & Van Nostrand, R. C. (1979). Ridge regression and James-Stein estimators: Review and comments. *Technometrics, 21,* 451–466.

Duan, N., & Li, K. C. (1991). Slicing regression: A link-free regression method. *Annals of Statistics, 19,* 505–530.

Duncan, O. D. (1961). A socioeconomic index for all occupations. In A. J. Reiss, Jr. (Ed.), *Occupations and social status* (pp. 109–138). New York: Free Press.

Duncan, O. D. (1975). *Introduction to structural equation models.* New York: Academic Press.

Durbin, J., & Watson, G. S. (1950). Testing for serial correlation in least squares regression I. *Biometrika, 37,* 409–428.

Durbin, J., & Watson, G. S. (1951). Testing for serial correlation in least squares regression II. *Biometrika, 38,* 159–178.

Efron, B. (1979). Bootstrap methods: Another look at the jackknife. *Annals of Statistics, 7,* 1–26.

Efron, B., & Tibshirani, R. J. (1993). *An introduction to the bootstrap.* New York: Chapman & Hall.

Emerson, J. D., & Hoaglin, D. C. (1983). Analysis of two-way tables by medians. In D. C. Hoaglin, F. Mosteller, & J. W. Tukey (Eds.), *Understanding robust and exploratory data analysis* (pp. 166–210). New York: Wiley.

European Values Study Group and World Values Survey Association. (2000). *World values surveys and European value surveys, 1981–1984, 1990–1993, and 1995–1997* [computer file]. Ann Arbor, MI: Institute for Social Research [producer], Inter-University Consortium for Political and Social Research [distributor].

Fan, J., & Gijbels, I. (1996). *Local polynomial modelling and its applications.* London: Chapman & Hall.

Fienberg, S. E. (1980). *The analysis of cross-classified categorical data* (2nd ed.). Cambridge: MIT Press.

Firth, D. (1991). Generalized linear models. In D. V. Hinkley, N. Reid, & E. J. Snell (Eds.), *Statistical theory and modelling: In honour of Sir David Cox, FRS* (pp. 55–82). London: Chapman & Hall.

Firth, D. (2003). Overcoming the reference category problem in the presentation of statistical models. In R. M. Stolzenberg (Ed.), *Sociological methodology 2003* (pp. 1–18). Washington, DC: American Sociological Assocation.

Firth, D., & De Menezes, R. X. (2004). Quasi-variances. *Biometrika, 91,* 65–80.

Fisher, R. A. (1925). *Statistical methods for research workers.* Edinburgh, UK: Oliver & Boyd.

Foster, D. P., & Stine, R. A. (2004). Variable selection in data mining: Building a predictive model of bankruptcy. *Journal of the American Statistical Association, 99,* 303–313.

Fox, B. (1980). *Women's domestic labour and their involvement in wage work: Twentieth-century changes in the reproduction of daily life.* Unpublished doctoral dissertation, University of Alberta, Edmonton, Canada.

Fox, J. (1984). *Linear statistical models and related methods: With applications to social research.* New York: Wiley.

Fox, J. (1987). Effect displays for generalized linear models. In C. Clogg (Ed.), *Sociological methodology 1987* (pp. 347–361). Washington, DC: American Sociological Association.

Fox, J. (1991). *Regression diagnostics: An introduction.* Newbury Park, CA: Sage.

Fox, J. (1997). *Applied regression analysis, linear models, and related methods.* Thousand Oaks, CA: Sage.

Fox, J. (2000a) *Multiple and generalized nonparametric regression.* Thousand Oaks, CA: Sage.

Fox, J. (2000b) *Nonparametric simple regression: Smoothing scatterplots.* Thousand Oaks, CA: Sage.

Fox, J. (2000c). Statistical graphics. In E. F. Borgatta & R. J. V. Montgomery (Eds.), *Encyclopedia of sociology* (2nd ed., Vol. 5, pp. 3003–3023). New York: Macmillan.

Fox, J. (2002). *An R and S-PLUS companion to applied regression.* Thousand Oaks, CA: Sage.

Fox, J. (2003). Effect displays in R for generalised linear models. *Journal of Statistical Software, 8*(15), 1–18.

Fox, J., & Andersen, R. (2006). Effect displays for multinomial and proportional-odds logit models. In R. M. Stolzenberg (Ed.), *Sociological methodology 2006.* Washington, DC: American Sociological Assocation.

Fox, J., & Hartnagel, T. F. (1979). Changing social roles and female crime in Canada: A time series analysis. *Canadian Review of Sociology and Anthropology, 16,* 96–104.

Fox, J., & Monette, G. (1992). Generalized collinearity diagnostics. *Journal of the American Statistical Association, 87,* 178–183.

Fox, J., & Suschnigg, C. (1989). A note on gender and the prestige of occupations. *Canadian Journal of Sociology, 14,* 353–360.

Francis, I. (1973). Comparison of several analyses of variance programs. *Journal of the American Statistical Association, 68,* 860–865.

Freedman, D., & Diaconis, P. (1981). On the histogram as a density estimator. *Zeitschrift fur Wahrscheinlichkeitstheorie und verwandte Gebiete, 87,* 453–476.

Freedman, D., Pisani, R., & Purves, R. (1997). *Statistics* (3rd ed.). New York: Norton.

Freedman, D. A. (1983). A note on screening regression equations. *American Statistician, 37,* 152–155.

Freedman, D. A. (1987). As others see us: A case study in path analysis [with commentary]. *Journal of Educational Statistics, 12,* 101–223.

Freedman, J. L. (1975). *Crowding and behavior.* New York: Viking Press.

Friendly, M. (1991). *SAS System for statistical graphics.* Cary, NC: SAS Institute.

Friendly, M. (2002). Corrgrams: Exploratory displays for correlation matrices. *American Statistician, 56,* 316–324.

Friendly, M., & Franklin, P. (1980). Interactive presentation in multitrial free recall. *Memory and Cognition, 8,* 265–270.

Furnival, G. M., & Wilson, R. W. (1974). Regression by leaps and bounds. *Technometrics, 16,* 499–511.

Gallant, A. R. (1975). Nonlinear regression. *American Statistican, 29,* 73–81.

Gass, S. I. (2003). *Linear programming: Methods and applications* (5th ed.). New York: Dover.

Goldberger, A. S. (1973). Structural equation models: An overview. In A. S. Goldberger & O. D. Duncan (Eds.), *Structural equation models in the social sciences* (pp. 1–18). New York: Seminar Press.

Goodall, C. (1983). *M*-estimators of location: An outline of the theory. In D. C. Hoaglin, F. Mosteller, & J. W. Tukey (Eds.), *Understanding robust and exploratory data analysis* (pp. 339–403). New York: Wiley.

Gould, S. J. (1989). *Wonderful life: The burgess shale and the nature of history.* New York: Norton.

Green, P. E., & Carroll, J. D. (1976). *Mathematical tools for applied multivariate analysis.* New York: Academic Press.

Green, P. J., & Silverman, B. W. (1994). *Nonparametric regression and generalized linear models: A roughness penalty approach.* London: Chapman & Hall.

Greene, I., & Shaffer, P. (1992). Leave to appeal and leave to commence judicial review in Canada's refugee-determination system: Is the process fair? *International Journal of Refugee Law, 4,* 71–83.

Greene, W. H. (2003). *Econometric analysis* (5th ed.). Upper Saddle River, NJ: Prentice Hall.

Hand, D. J., & Taylor, C. C. (1987). *Multivariate analysis of variance and repeated measures: A practical approach for behavioural scientists.* London: Chapman & Hall.

Härdle, W. (1991). *Smoothing techniques: With implementation in S.* New York: Springer.

Harrell, F. E., Jr. *Regression modeling strategies: With applications to linear models, logistic regression, and survival analysis.* New York: Springer.

Harvey, A. (1990). *The econometric analysis of time series* (2nd ed.). Cambridge: MIT Press.

Hastie, T., Tibshirani, R., & Friedman, J. (2001). *The elements of statistical learning: Data mining, inference, and prediction.* New York: Springer.

Hastie, T. J. (1992). Generalized additive models. In J. M. Chambers & T. J. Hastie (Eds.), *Statistical models in S* (pp. 249–307). Pacific Grove, CA: Wadsworth.

Hastie, T. J., & Tibshirani, R. J. (1990). *Generalized additive models.* London: Chapman & Hall.

Hauck, W. W., Jr., & Donner, A. (1977). Wald's test as applied to hypotheses in logit analysis. *Journal of the American Statistical Association, 72,* 851–853.

Heckman, J. J. (1974). Shadow prices, market wages, and labor supply. *Econometrica, 42,* 679–693.

Heckman, J. J. (1976). The common structure of statistical models of truncation, sample selection and limited dependent variables and a simple estimator for such models. *Annals of Economic and Social Measurement, 5,* 475–492.

Heckman, J. J. (1979). Sample selection bias as a specification error. *Econometrica, 47,* 153–161.

Heckman, J. J., & Robb, R. (1986). Alternative methods for solving the problem of selection bias in evaluating the impact of treatments on outcomes. In H. Wainer (Ed.) (1986). *Drawing inferences from self-selected samples* (pp. 63–107). New York: Springer.

Hernandez, F., & Johnson, R. A. (1980). The large sample behavior of transformations to normality. *Journal of the American Statistical Association, 75,* 855–861.

Hoaglin, D. C., Mosteller, F., & Tukey, J. W., editors (1983). *Understanding robust and exploratory data analysis.* New York: Wiley.

Hoaglin, D. C., Mosteller, F., & Tukey, J. W. (Eds.). (1985). *Exploring data tables, trends, and shapes.* New York; Wiley.

Hoaglin, D. C., & Welsch, R. E. (1978). The hat matrix in regression and ANOVA. *American Statistician, 32,* 17–22.

Hocking, R. R. (1976). The analysis and selection of variables in linear regression. *Biometrics, 32,* 1–49.

Hocking, R. R. (1985). *The analysis of linear models.* Monterey, CA: Brooks/Cole.

Hocking, R. R., & Speed, F. M. (1975). The full rank analysis of some linear model problems. *Journal of the American Statistical Association, 70,* 706–712.

Hoerl, A. E., & Kennard, R. W. (1970a). Ridge regression: Biased estimation for nonorthogonal problems. *Technometrics, 12,* 55–67.

Hoerl, A. E., & Kennard, R. W. (1970b). Ridge regression: Applications to nonorthogonal problems. *Technometrics, 12,* 69–82.

Hoeting, J. A., Madigan, D., Raftery, A. E., & Volinsky, C. T. (1999). Bayesian model averaging: A tutorial [with discussion]. *Statistical Science, 14,* 382–401; Correction, *15,* 193–195.

Holland, P. W. (1986). Statistics and causal inference [with commentary]. *Journal of the American Statistical Assoication, 81,* 945–970.

Hosmer, D. W., Jr., & Lemeshow, S. (1999). *Applied survival analysis: Regression modeling of time to event data.* New York: Wiley.

Huber, P. J. (1964). Robust estimation of a location parameter. *Annals of Mathematical Statistics, 35,* 73–101.

Ihaka, R., & Gentleman, R. (1996). R: A language for data analysis and graphics. *Journal of Computational and Graphical Statistics, 5,* 299–314.

Jacoby, W. G. (1997). *Statistical graphics for univariate and bivariate data.* Thousand Oaks, CA: Sage.

Jacoby, W. G. (1998). *Statistical graphics for visualizing multivariate data.* Thousand Oaks, CA: Sage.

Johnson, N. L., Kotz, S., & Balakrishnan, N. (1994) *Continuous univariate distributions* (Vol. 1, 2nd ed.). New York: Wiley.

Judge, G. G., Griffiths, W. E., Hill, E. C., Lütkepohl, H., & Lee, T.-C. (1985). *The theory and practice of econometrics* (2nd ed.). New York: Wiley.

Kass, R. E., & Raftery, A. E. (1995). Bayes factors. *Journal of the American Statistical Association, 90,* 773–795.

King, G., Honaker, J., Joseph, A., and Scheve, K. (2001). Analyzing incomplete political science data: An alternative algorithm for multiple imputation. *American Political Science Review, 95,* 49–69.

Kish, L. (1987). *Statistical design for research.* New York: Wiley.

Kmenta, J. (1986). *Elements of econometrics* (2nd ed.). New York: Macmillan.

Koch, G. G., & Gillings, D. B. (1983). Inference, design based vs. model based. In S. Kotz & N. L. Johnson (Eds.), *Encyclopedia of statistical sciences* (Vol. 4, pp. 84–88). New York: Wiley.

Koenker, R. (2005). *Quantile regression.* Cambridge, UK: Cambridge University Press.

Koenker, R., & Bassett, G. (1978). Regression quantiles. *Econometrica, 46,* 33–50.

Kotz, S., Balakrishnan, N., & Johnson, N. L., (1994) *Continuous multivariate distributions: Vol. 1. Models and applications* (2nd ed.). New York: Wiley.

Krzanowski, W. J. (1988). *Principles of multivariate analysis: A user's perspective.* Oxford, UK: Clarendon Press.

Lambert, D. (1992). Zero-inflated Poisson regression, with an application to defects in manufacturing. *Technometrics, 34,* 1–14.

Landwehr, J. M., Pregibon, D., & Shoemaker, A. C. (1980). Some graphical procedures for studying a logistic regression fit. In *Proceedings of the Business and Economic Statistics Section, American Statistical Association* (pp. 15–20). Alexandria, VA: American Statistical Association.

Leinhardt, S. & Wasserman, S. S. (1979). Exploratory data analysis: An introduction to selected methods. In K. F. Schuessler (Ed.), *Sociological methodology 1979* (pp. 311–365). San Francisco: Jossey-Bass.

Li, G. (1985). Robust regression. In Hoaglin, D. C., Mosteller, F., & Tukey, J. W. (Eds.), *Exploring data tables, trends, and shapes* (pp. 281–343). New York: Wiley.

Little, R. J. A., & Rubin, D. B. (1990). The analysis of social science data with missing values. In J. Fox & J. S. Long (Eds.), *Modern methods of data analysis* (pp. 374–409). Newbury Park CA: Sage.

Little, R. J. A., & Rubin, D. B. (2002). *Statistical analysis with missing data* (2nd ed.). New York: Wiley.

Long, J. S. (1997). *Regression models for categorical and limited dependent variables.* Thousand Oaks, CA: Sage.

Long, J. S., & Erwin, L. H. (2000). Using heteroscedasticity consistent standard errors in the linear regression model. *American Statistician, 54,* 217–224.

Madigan, D., & Raftery, A. E. (1994). Model selection and accounting for model uncertainty in graphical models using Occam's window. *Journal of the American Statistical Association, 89,* 1535–1546.

Mallows, C. L. (1973). Some comments on C_p. *Technometrics, 15,* 661–676.

Mallows, C. L. (1986). Augmented partial residuals. *Technometrics, 28,* 313–319.

Mandel, J. (1982). Use of the singular value decomposition in regression analysis. *American Statistician, 36,* 15–24.

Manski, C. (1991). Regression. *Journal of Economic Literature, 29,* 34–50.

McCullagh, P. (1980). Regression models for ordinal data [with commentary]. *Journal of the Royal Statistical Society, B, 42,* 109–142.

McCullagh, P. (1991). Quasi-likelihood and estimating functions. In D. V. Hinkley, N. Reid, & E. J. Snell (Eds.), *Statistical theory and modelling: In honour of Sir David Cox, FRS* (pp. 265–286). London: Chapman & Hall.

McCullagh, P., & Nelder, J. A. (1989). *Generalized linear models* (2nd ed.). London: Chapman & Hall.

Monette, G. (1990). Geometry of multiple regression and 3-D graphics. In J. Fox & J. S. Long (Eds.), *Modern methods of data analysis* (pp. 209–256). Newbury Park, CA: Sage.

Moody, E. A. (1972). William of Ockham. In P. Edwards (Ed.), *The encyclopedia of philosophy* (Vol. 8, pp. 306–317). New York: Macmillan.

Moore, D. S. (1995). *The basic practice of statistics* (4th ed.). New York: Freeman.

Moore, J. C., Jr., & Krupat, E. (1971). Relationship between source status, authoritarianism, and conformity in a social setting. *Sociometry, 34,* 122–134.

Morrison, D. F. (2005). *Multivariate statistical methods* (4th ed.). Belmont, CA: Thomson-Brooks-Cole.

Mosteller, F., & Tukey, J. W. (1968). Data analysis, including statistics. In G. Lindzey & E. Aronson (Eds.), *The handbook of social psychology: Vol. 2. Research methods* (2nd ed., pp. 80–203). Reading, MA: Addison-Wesley.

Mosteller, F., & Tukey, J. W. (1977). *Data analysis and regression.* Reading, MA: Addison-Wesley.

Nason, G. P., & Silverman, B. W. (2000). Wavelets for regression and other statistical problems. In M. G. Schimek (Ed.), *Smoothing and regression: Approaches, computation, and application* (pp. 159–191). New York: Wiley.

National Opinion Research Center (2005). *General Social Survey (GSS).* Retrieved October 31, 2005, from www.gss.norc.org

Nelder, J. A. (1976). Letter to the editor. *American Statistician, 30,* 103.

Nelder, J. A. (1977). A reformulation of linear models [with commentary]. *Journal of the Royal Statistical Society, A, 140,* 48–76.

Nelder, J. A., & Wedderburn, R. W. M. (1972). Generalized linear models. *Journal of the Royal Statistical Society, A, 135,* 370–384.

Nerlove, M., & Press, S. J. (1973). *Univariate and multivariate log-linear and logistic models.* Santa Monica, CA: RAND Corporation.

Obenchain, R. L. (1977). Classical *F*-tests and confidence intervals for ridge regression. *Technometrics, 19,* 429–439.

O'Brien, R. G., & Kaiser, M. K. (1985). MANOVA method for analyzing repeated measures designs: An extensive primer. *Psychological Bulletin 97,* 316–333.

Ornstein, M. D. (1976). The boards and executives of the largest Canadian corporations: Size, composition, and interlocks. *Canadian Journal of Sociology, 1,* 411–437.

Ornstein, M. D. (1983). *Accounting for gender differences in job income in Canada: Results from a 1981 survey.* Ottawa, Ontario, Canada: Labour Canada.

Powers, D. A., & Xie, Y. (2000). *Statistical models for categorical data analysis.* San Diego: Academic Press.

Pregibon, D. (1981). Logistic regression diagnostics. *Annals of Statistics, 9,* 705–724.

Putter, J. (1967). Orthonormal bases of error spaces and their use for investigating the normality and variance of residuals. *Journal of the American Statistical Association, 62,* 1022–1036.

R Development Core Team. (2006). *R: A language and environment for statistical computing.* Vienna: R Foundation for Statistical Computing.

Raftery, A. E. (1995). Bayesian model selection in social research [with discussion]. In P. V. Marsden (Ed.), *Sociological methodology 1995* (pp. 111–195). Washington, DC: American Sociological Association.

Raftery, A. E. (1996). Approximate Bayes factors and accounting for model uncertainty in generalised linear models. *Biometrika, 83,* 251–266.

Raghunathan, T. E., Lepkowski, J. M., Van Hoewyk, J., & Solenberger, P. (2001). A multivariate technique for multiply imputing missing values using a sequence of regression models. *Survey Methodology, 27,* 85–95.

Rao, C. R. (1973). *Linear statistical inference and its applications* (2nd ed.). New York: Wiley.

Rosenbaum, P. R., & Rubin, D. B. (1983). The central role of the propensity score in observational studies for causal effects. *Biometrika, 70,* 41–55.

Rousseeuw, P. J., & Leroy, A. M. (1987). *Robust regression and outlier detection.* New York: Wiley.

Rubin, D. B. (1976). Inference and missing data [with discussion]. *Biometrika, 63,* 581–592.

Rubin, D. B. (1987). *Multiple imputation for nonresponse in surveys.* New York: Wiley.

Rubin, D. B. (2004). Teaching statistical inference for causal effects in experiments and observational studies. *Journal of Educational and Behavioral Statistics, 29,* 343–367.

Sall, J. (1990). Leverage plots for general linear hypotheses. *American Statistician, 44,* 308–315.

Schafer, J. L. (1997). *Analysis of incomplete multivariate data.* London: Chapman & Hall.

Schafer, J. L., & Graham, J. W. (2002). Missing data: Our view of the state of the art. *Psychological Methods, 7,* 147–177.

Scheffé, H. (1959). *The analysis of variance.* New York: Wiley.

Schwarz, G. (1978). Estimating the dimension of a model. *Annals of Statistics, 6,* 461–464.

Searle, S. R. (1971). *Linear models.* New York: Wiley.

Searle, S. R. (1987). *Linear models for unbalanced data.* New York: Wiley.

Searle, S. R., Speed, F. M., & Henderson, H. V. (1981). Some computational and model equivalences in analysis of variance of unequal-subclass-numbers data. *American Statistician, 35,* 16–33.

Searle, S. R., Speed, F. M., & Milliken, G. A. (1980). Population marginal means in the linear model: An alternative to least squares means. *American Statistician, 34,* 216–221.

Seber, G. A. F. (1977). *Linear regression analysis.* New York: Wiley.

Shryock, H. S., Siegel, J. S., & Associates (1973). *The methods and materials of demography* (2 Vols.). Washington, DC: U.S. Bureau of the Census.

Silverman, B. W. (1986). *Density estimation for statistics and data analysis.* London: Chapman & Hall.

Silverman, B. W., & Young, G. A. (1987). The bootstrap: To smooth or not to smooth? *Biometrika, 74,* 469–479.

Simonoff, J. S. (1996). *Smoothing methods in statistics.* New York: Springer.

Simpson, E. H. (1951). The interpretation of interaction in contingency tables. *Journal of the Royal Statistical Society, Series B, 13,* 238–241.

Skinner, C. J., Holt, D., & Smith, T. M. F. (Eds.). (1989). *Analysis of complex surveys.* New York: Wiley.

Speed, F. M., & Hocking, R. R. (1976). The use of the $R(\ )$-notation with unbalanced data. *American Statistician, 30,* 30–33.

Speed, F. M., Hocking, R. R., & Hackney, O. P. (1978). Methods of analysis of linear models with unbalanced data. *Journal of the American Statistical Association, 73,* 105–112.

Speed, F. M., & Monlezun, C. J. (1979). Exact F-tests for the method of unweighted means in a 2^k experiment. *American Statistician, 33,* 15–18.

Spence, I., & Lewandowsky, S. (1990). Graphical perception. In J. Fox & J. S. Long (Eds.), *Modern methods of data analysis* (pp. 13–57). Newbury Park, CA: Sage.

Stefanski, L. A. (1991). A note on high-breakdown estimators. *Statistics and Probability Letters, 11,* 353–358.

Steinhorst, R. K. (1982). Resolving current controversies in analysis of variance. *American Statistician, 36,* 138–139.

Stine, R. (1990). An introduction to bootstrap methods: Examples and ideas. In J. Fox & J. S. Long (Eds.), *Modern methods of data analysis* (pp. 325–373). Newbury Park, CA: Sage.

Stine, R. A. (1995). Graphical interpretation of variance inflation factors. *American Statistician, 49,* 53–56.

Stine, R. A. (2004). Model selection using information theory and the MDL principle. *Sociological Methods and Research, 33,* 230–260.

Stine, R. A., & Fox, J. (Eds.). (1996). *Statistical computing environments for social research.* Thousand Oaks, CA: Sage.

Stolzenberg, R. M. (1979). The measurement and decomposition of causal effects in nonlinear and nonadditive models. In K. F. Schuessler (Ed.), *Sociological methodology 1980* (pp. 459–488). San Francisco: Jossey-Bass.

Stolzenberg, R. M., & Relles, D. A. (1997). Tools for intuition about sample selection bias and its correction. *American Sociological Review, 62,* 494–507.

Stone, M. (1987). *Coordinate-free multivariable statistics: An illustrated geometric progression from Halmos to Gauss and Bayes.* Oxford, UK: Clarendon Press.

Street, J. O., Carroll, R. J., & Ruppert, D. (1988). A note on computing robust regression estimates via iteratively reweighted least squares. *American Statistician, 42,* 152–154.

Theil, H. (1971). *Principles of econometrics.* New York: Wiley.

Thompson, M. E. (1988). Superpopulation models. In S. Kotz & N. L. Johnson (Eds.), *Encyclopedia of statistical sciences* (Vol. 9, pp. 93–99). New York: Wiley.

Tierney, L. (1990). *Lisp-Stat: An object-oriented environment for statistical computing and dynamic graphics*. New York: Wiley.

Tobin, J. (1958). Estimation of relationships for limited dependent variables. *Econometrica, 26,* 24–36.

Torgerson, W. S. (1958). *Theory and methods of scaling*. New York: Wiley.

Tufte, E. R. (1983). *The visual display of quantitative information*. Cheshire, CT: Graphics Press.

Tukey, J. W. (1949). One degree of freedom for non-additivity. *Biometrics, 5,* 232–242.

Tukey, J. W. (1958). Bias and confidence in not quite large samples. *Annals of Mathematical Statistics, 29,* 614.

Tukey, J. W. (1972). Some graphic and semigraphic displays. In T. A. Bancroft (Ed.), *Statistical papers in honor of George W. Snedecor* (pp. 293–316). Ames: Iowa State University Press.

Tukey, J. W. (1977). *Exploratory data analysis*. Reading, MA: Addison-Wesley.

Tukey (1986). Discussion. In H. Wainer (Ed.), *Drawing inferences from self-selected samples* (pp. 58–62). New York: Springer.

United Nations (1998). *Social indicators*. Retrieved June 1, 1998, from www.un.org/Depts/unsd/social/main.htm

United States. (2006). *The 2006 statistical abstract*. Washington, DC: U.S. Bureau of the Census.

van Buuren, S., & Oudshoorn, K. (1999). *Flexible multivariate imputation by MICE*. Leiden, Germany: TNO Preventie en Gezondheid.

Veall, M. R., & Zimmermann, K. F. (1996). Pseudo-R^2 measures for some common limited dependent variable models. *Journal of Economic Surveys, 10,* 241–259.

Velleman, P. F., & Hoaglin, D. C. (1981). *Applications, basics, and computing of exploratory data analysis*. Boston: Duxbury.

Velleman, P. F., & Welsch, R. E. (1981). Efficient computing of regression diagnostics. *American Statistician, 35,* 234–241.

Velilla, S. (1993). A note on the multivariate Box-Cox transformation to normality. *Statistics and Probability Letters, 17,* 259–263.

Vinod, H. D. (1978). A survey of ridge regression and related techniques for improvements over ordinary least squares. *Review of Economics and Statistics, 60,* 121–131.

Vinod, H. D., & Ullah, A. (1981). *Recent advances in regression methods*. New York: Dekker.

Wahba, G. (1985). A comparison of GCV and GML for choosing the smoothing parameter in the generalized spline smoothing problem. *Annals of Statistics, 13,* 1378–1402.

Wainer, H., editor (1986). *Drawing inferences from self-selected samples*. Mahwah, NJ: Erlbaum.

Wang, P. C. (1985). Adding a variable in generalized linear models. *Technometrics, 27,* 273–276.

Wang, P. C. (1987). Residual plots for detecting nonlinearity in generalized linear models. *Technometrics, 29,* 435–438.

Weakliem, D. (1999). A critique of the Bayesian information criterion for model selection [with commentary]. *Sociological Methods and Research, 27,* 359–443.

Wedderburn, R. W. M. (1974). Quasi-likelihood functions, generalized linear models, and the Gauss-Newton method. *Biometrika, 61,* 439–447.

Weisberg, S. (1985). *Applied linear regression* (2nd ed.). New York: Wiley.

Weisberg, S. (2005). *Applied linear regression* (3rd ed.). New York: Wiley.

White, H. (1980). A heteroscedasticity-consistent covariance matrix estimator and a direct test for heteroscedasticity. *Econometrica, 38,* 817–838.

Williams, D. A. (1987). Generalized linear model diagnostics using the deviance and single case deletions. *Applied Statistics, 36,* 181–191.

Winship, C., & Mare, R. D. (1992). Models for sample selection bias. *Annual Review of Sociology, 18,* 327–350.

Wonnacott, R. J., & Wonnacott, T. H. (1979). *Econometrics* (2nd ed.). New York: Wiley.

Wood, S. N. (2006). *Generalized additive models: An introduction with R*. London: Chapman & Hall.

Wu, L. L. (1985). Robust *M*-estimation of location and regression. In N. B. Tuma (Ed.), *Sociological methodology 1985* (pp. 316–388). San Francisco: Jossey-Bass.

Yates, F. (1934). The analysis of multiple classifications with unequal numbers in the different classes. *Journal of the American Statistical Association, 29,* 51–66.

Young, G. A. (1994). Bootstrap: More than a stab in the dark? [with commentary]. *Statistical Science, 9,* 382–415.

Author Index

Abler, A., 460, 638
Achen, C. H., 10, 638
Adams, J. S., 460, 638
Agresti, A., 355, 365–366, 378, 394, 638
Aitkin, M., 10, 424, 638
Allison, P. D., 548, 568, 570, 586, 638
Alvarez, R. M., 377, 638
Andersen, R., 136, 357, 365, 547, 638, 641
Anderson, D. R., 612, 614, 617, 631–632, 634, 639
Anderson, T. W., 219, 638
Andrews, D. F., 271, 638
Andrews, F. M., 167, 638
Anscombe, F. J., 26–28, 248, 265, 297, 545, 638
Atkinson, A. C., 49, 259, 266, 271, 293, 306, 638
Azzalini, A., 485, 490, 529, 639

Bailey, R. A., 635, 638
Baker, F. B., 57, 638
Balakrishnan, N., 571, 643
Bard, Y., 466, 475, 638
Barnard, G. A., 630, 638
Barnett, V., 266, 638
Bartlett, M. S., 290, 638
Bassett, G., 540–541, 643
Bates, D. M., 475, 638
Becker, R. A., 49, 638
Beckman, R. J., 247–248, 639
Belsley, D. A., 250, 253–256, 263, 265–266, 321, 328, 639
Berk, R. A., 7, 10, 639
Blau, P. M., 214–215, 639
Bollen, K., 115, 639
Bowman, A. W., 485, 490, 529, 639
Box, G. E. P., 1, 50, 69–70, 268, 285, 292–294, 296, 298, 304, 306, 474, 567, 639
Breusch, T. S., 296, 639

Brown, R. L., 445, 639
Burnham, K. P., 612, 614, 617, 631–632, 634, 639

Cameron, A. C, 417, 424, 639
Campbell, A., 370, 395, 639
Campbell, D. T., 10, 639
Cantoni, E., 543–544, 639
Carroll, J. D., 238, 642
Carroll, R. J., 537, 645
Chambers, J. M., 49, 529, 638–639
Chatfield, C., 434, 436–437, 442, 450, 639
Chatterjee, S., 250, 253–256, 266, 322, 639
Christensen, R., 238, 639
Cleveland, W. S., 41, 46, 49, 306, 495, 529, 639
Collett, D., 378, 639
Collins, L. M., 567, 639
Conover, W. J., 290, 639
Converse, P. E., 370, 395, 639
Cook, R. D., 56, 46, 49, 73, 248, 250–251, 255, 259, 263, 266, 272, 279, 284–286, 296–298, 300, 304, 306, 639–640
Coombs, C. H., 57, 640
Cowles, M., 453–454, 470, 640
Cox, D. R., 50, 69–70, 268, 285, 292–294, 296, 298, 304, 306, 370, 378, 567, 639–640

Davis, C., 18, 22–23, 45–46, 78, 81–82, 86, 90, 105, 116, 243–245, 248–249, 251, 253, 260, 453–454, 470, 604, 640
Davison, A. C., 602, 606, 640
Dawes, R. M, 57, 640
De Menezes, R. X., 130, 421, 641
Dempster, A. P., 238, 559, 640
Diaconis, P., 30, 641
Dobson, A. J., 424, 640
Donner, A., 346, 642

Draper, N. R., 328–329, 475, 640
Duan, N., 30, 640
Duncan, O. D., 44–45, 47, 57, 88–90, 92–94, 107, 109–110, 115, 117, 147–148, 194, 199, 214–215, 235, 245–246, 248–249, 251–253, 257–260, 538–540, 544, 598–601, 604, 639–640
Durbin, J., 442, 444–445, 448, 450, 639–640

Efron, B., 587, 591, 596, 602–603, 606, 640
Emerson, J. D., 73, 462, 640
Erwin, L. H., 275, 643
Evans, J. M., 445, 639

Fan, J., 500, 529, 640
Fienberg, S. E., 362, 378, 394, 396–397, 640
Firth, D., 130, 402, 420–421, 424, 640–641
Fisher, R. A., 143, 162, 641
Foster, D. P., 608, 641
Fox, B., 311–312, 319–322, 325, 330–331, 641
Fox, J., xviii, 18, 49, 136, 322–323, 357, 365, 440–441, 443, 448, 529, 641, 645
Francis, B., 424,638
Francis, I., 162, 641
Franklin, P., 176–179, 184, 191, 641
Freedman, D. A., 4, 10, 30, 641
Freedman, J. L., 8, 641
Friedman, J., 456, 609, 634, 641–642
Friendly, M., 49, 176–179, 184, 191, 618, 641
Furnival, G. M., 324, 641

Gallant, A. R., 475, 641
Gass, S. I., 541, 641
Gentleman, R., xviii, 643
Gijbels, I., 500, 529, 640
Gillings, D. B., 10, 643
Goldberger, A. S., 110, 641
Goodall, C., 547, 642
Gould, P., 460, 638
Gould, S. J., 10, 641
Graham, J. W., 555, 586, 645
Green, P. E., 238, 642
Green, P. J., 496, 642
Greene, I., 4–5, 628, 642
Greene, W. H., 377–378, 475, 579, 583, 642
Griffiths, W. E., 433, 643
Grosse, E., 495, 529, 639

Hackney, O. P., 163, 645
Hadi, A. S., 250, 253–256, 266, 639
Hand, D. J., 209, 642
Harding, S. A., 635, 638

Härdle, W., 529, 642
Harrell, F. E., Jr., 475, 608, 642
Hartnagel, T. F., 440–441, 443, 448, 641
Harvey, A., 433, 443, 445, 450, 642
Hastie, T. J., 49, 456, 459, 475, 495, 514, 529, 609, 634, 639, 642
Hauck, W. W., Jr., 346, 642
Heath, A., 357, 638
Heckman, J. J., 570, 573, 575–579, 583, 586, 642
Henderson, H. V., 163, 645
Hernandez, F., 292, 642
Hill, E. C., 433, 643
Hinde, J., 424, 638
Hinkley, D. V., 602, 606, 640
Hoaglin, D. C., 49, 72–73, 247, 462, 547, 640, 642, 646
Hocking, R. R., 163, 172, 219, 328, 642, 645
Hoerl, A. E., 326–327, 642
Hoeting, J. A., 623, 642
Holland, P. W., 7, 10, 642
Holt, D., 602, 645
Honaker, J., 563, 643
Hosmer, D. W., Jr., 548, 642
Huber, P. J., 272, 530, 532, 534–536, 538, 545–546, 598–600, 604, 643

Ihaka, R., xviii, 643

Jacoby, W. G., 49, 643
Johnson, M. E., 290, 639
Johnson, M. M., 290, 639
Johnson, N. L., 571, 643
Johnson, R. A., 292, 642
Joseph, A., 563, 643
Judge, G. G., 433, 439, 442, 444–445, 450, 643

Kaiser, M. K., 209, 644
Kam, C. M., 567, 639
Kass, R. E., 615, 617, 623, 635, 643
Kennard, R. W., 326–327, 642
Kim, S. H., 57, 638
King, G., 563, 586, 643
Kish, L., 10, 643
Kleiner, B., 49, 639
Kmenta, J., 303, 643
Koch, G. G., 10, 643
Koenker, R., 540–541, 543, 643
Kotz, S., 571, 643
Krupat, E., 152–154, 160–161, 173–175, 183, 185, 217, 644
Krzanowski,W. J., 219, 643
Kuh, E., 250, 266, 639

Laird, N. M., 559, 640
Lambert, D., 393, 643
Landwehr, J. M., 412, 643
Lee, T. C., 433, 643
Leinhardt, S., 61, 643
Lemeshow, S., 548, 642
Lepkowski, J. M., 563, 644
Leroy, A. M., 543, 547, 644
Lewandowsky, S., 45, 645
Lewis, T., 266, 638
Li, G., 537, 547, 643
Li, K. C., 300, 640
Little, R. J. A., 550, 552–553, 559, 562, 586, 643
Long, J. S., 275, 368, 378, 392, 424, 643
Lütkepohl, H., 433, 643

Madigan, D., 623–624, 642–643
Mallows, C. L., 285–286, 304, 609–610, 633, 643
Mandel, J., 321, 643
Manski, C., 20, 643
Mare, R. D., 586, 646
McCullagh, P., 365, 392, 402, 407, 424, 643
Miller, W. E., 370, 395, 639
Milliken, G. A., 183, 645
Monette, G., 205–206, 219, 322–323, 641, 644
Monlezun, C. J., 163, 645
Moody, E. A., 624, 644
Moore, D. S., xix, 4, 644
Moore, Jr., J. C., 152–154, 160–161, 173–175, 183, 185, 217, 644
Morgan, J. N., 167, 638
Morrison, D. F., 219, 314, 644
Mosteller, F., 49, 58–60, 72–73, 547, 624, 635, 642, 644

Nagler, J., 377, 638
Nason, G. P., 477, 644
Nelder, J. A., 135, 379, 392, 402, 407, 424, 643–644
Nerlove, M., 359, 644

O'Brien, R. G., 209, 644
Obenchain, R. L., 328, 644
Ornstein, M. D., 7, 42–43, 63–64, 387–390, 392, 411, 414–415, 417, 545, 644
Oudshoorn, K., 563, 646

Pagan, A. R., 296, 639
Pisani, R., 4, 641
Powers, D. A., 378, 394, 644
Pregibon, D., 412, 643–644
Press, S. J., 359, 644
Price, B., 322, 639

Purves, R., 4, 641
Putter, J., 231–232, 644

Raftery, A. E., 324, 612, 615, 617–618, 623–624, 635, 642–644
Raghunathan, T. E., 563, 644
Rao, C. R., 196, 209, 219, 409, 644
Relles, D. A., 586, 645
Riani, M., 259, 266, 638
Robb, R., 577, 642
Ronchetti, E., 543–544, 639
Rosenbaum, P. R., 622, 644
Rousseeuw, P. J., 543, 547, 644
Rubin, D. B., 10, 549–550, 552–553, 559, 562, 565, 586, 622, 640, 643–645
Ruppert, D., 537, 645

Sall, J., 263–264, 645
Schafer, J. L., 555, 561, 563, 565, 567, 570, 586, 639, 645
Scheffé, H., 328, 645
Scheve, K., 563, 643
Schwarz, G., 611, 645
Searle, S. R., 163, 172, 183, 219, 645
Seber, G. A. F., 219, 645
Shaffer, P., 4–5, 628, 642
Shoemaker, A. C., 412, 643
Shryock, H. S., 463, 645
Shyu, W. M., 495, 529, 639
Siegel, J. S., 463, 645
Silverman, B. W., 33, 475, 588, 642, 644–645
Simonoff, J. S., 500, 529, 645
Simpson, E. H., 121, 645
Sinnott, R., 357, 638
Skinner, C. J., 602, 645
Smith, G. L., 635, 638
Smith, H., 329, 475, 640
Smith, T. M. F., 602, 645
Snell, E. J., 370, 378, 640
Solenberger, P., 563, 644
Sonquist, J. A., 167, 638
Speed, F. M., 163, 172, 183, 642, 645
Spence, I., 45, 645
Stanley, J. C., 10, 639
Stefanski, L. A., 540, 645
Steinhorst, R. K., 163, 645
Stine, R. A., 49, 308, 596, 606, 608–609, 634, 641, 645
Stokes, D. E., 370, 395, 639
Stolzenberg, R. M., 469, 586, 645
Stone, M., 238, 645
Street, J. O., 537, 645
Suschnigg, C., 18, 641

Taylor, C. C., 209, 642
Theil, H., 232, 321, 328, 645
Thompson, M. E., 10, 646
Tibshirani, R. J., 456, 495, 514, 529, 591, 596,
    602–603, 606, 609, 634, 640, 642
Tidwell, P. W., 294, 296, 304, 306, 474, 639
Tierney, L., 49, 73, 646
Tobin, J., 579–580, 646
Torgerson, W. S., 57, 646
Trivedi, P. K., 417, 424, 639
Trussell, H. J., 247, 639
Tufte, E. R., 27, 49, 646
Tukey, J. W., 29, 37, 40, 49, 51, 58–60, 68,
    72–73, 272, 462, 532, 547, 577, 586, 603,
    624, 635, 638, 642, 644, 646
Tukey, P. A., 49, 639
Tversky, A., 57, 630

Ullah, A., 328, 646

van Buuren, S., 563, 646
Van Hoewyk, J., 563, 644
Van Nostrand, R. C., 328, 640
Veall, M. R., 347, 646
Velilla, S., 70, 646
Velleman, P. E., 49, 72, 255, 265, 646
Vinod, H. D., 328, 646
Volinsky, C. T., 623, 642

Wahba, G., 488, 646
Wainer, H., 577, 586, 646
Wang, P. C., 412–413 , 646
Wasserman, S. S., 61, 643
Watson, G. S., 442, 444, 448, 450, 640
Watts, D. G., 475, 638
Weakliem, D., 635, 646
Wedderburn, R. W. M., 379, 407, 644, 646
Weisberg, S., 46, 49, 73, 255, 259, 266, 284,
    296–298, 300, 306, 410, 640, 646
Welsch, R. E., 92, 247, 250, 255, 265–266, 639,
    642, 646
White, H., 275–276, 297–298, 583, 646
Wilks, A. R., 49, 638
Williams, D. A., 412–413, 646
Wilson, R. W., 324, 641
Winship, C., 586, 646
Wonnacott, R. J., 195–196, 238, 450, 646
Wonnacott, T. H., 195–196, 238, 450, 646
Wood, S. N., 488, 496, 519–520, 529, 646
Wu, L. L., 547, 646

Xie, Y., 378, 394, 644

Yates, F., 162, 647
Young, G. A., 588, 606, 645, 647

Zimmermann, K. F., 347, 646

Subject Index

Adaptive-kernel density estimator, 33–34
Added-variable plots, 255–259, 263
  and collinearity, 308
  for constructed variables, 293–296, 415
  for generalized linear models, 413
Additive regression models, 508–511
  fitting, 511–513
Additive relationships, 120–124, 149–151, 173
Adjusted means, 141, 182–183
  See also Effect displays
Akaike information criterion (AIC), 611–614
  bias-corrected (AIC$_c$), 614
  and model averaging, 631–632
Analysis of covariance (ANCOVA), 173–176
  model for, 174–175
  See also Dummy-variable regression
Analysis of deviance, 348, 357–358, 386, 408
Analysis of variance (ANOVA):
  higher-way, 166–169
  one-way, 143–148, 189
  for regression, 84–85, 92–93, 108, 223, 227
  table, 108, 139, 147, 160, 166
  three-way, 163–166
  two-way, 149–163, 190, 217
  use of, to test constant error variance, 290–291
  vector geometry of, 233–234
AR(1). *See* Autoregressive process, first-order
AR(p). *See* Autoregressive process, higher-order
Arcsine-square-root transformation, 67
ARMA. *See* Autoregressive-moving-average
  process
Assumptions of regression model. *See* Constant
  error variance; Independence; Linearity;
  Normality
Asymptotic standard errors:
  for Box-Cox transformation, 71
  for effect displays, 411
  for generalized linear model, 385, 406

for logit model, 345–346, 353–354, 376
for *M* estimator, 537
for nonlinear functions of parameters, 409–410
for nonlinear least squares, 466
for polytomous logit model, 361
in quantile regression, 541
for weighted least squares, 274, 302
Asymptotic variance-covariance matrix.
  See Asymptotic standard errors
  See also Standard errors; Variance-covariance
  matrix
Attenuation due to measurement error, 114
Autocorrelated errors.
  See Serially correlated errors
Autocorrelation, 429, 431
  partial, 436–437
  of residuals, 439, 441
Autocovariance, 430
Autoregressive process:
  first-order [AR(1)], 430–433, 438–440
  higher-order [AR(p)], 433–434, 436–437, 439
Autoregressive-moving-average (ARMA)
  process, 434, 436–437, 439, 446–447
Average squared error (ASE) of
  local regression, 486
  mean average squared error (MASE), 488

Backfitting, 512–513
Backward elimination, 324
Balanced data in ANOVA,
  161–162, 182–183, 265
Bandwidth in nonparametric
  regression, 478, 486–488
  See also Span; Window
Bartlett's test for constant error variance, 290
Baseline category:
  in dummy regression, 123, 126, 129
  in polytomous logit model, 356

Basis of model matrix in ANOVA, 190, 192
Bayes factor, 615, 623
Bayesian information criterion (BIC),
  324, 611–612, 614–618, 623–624
Best linear unbiased
  estimator (BLUE), 196
  See also Gauss-Markov theorem
Bias:
  bootstrap estimate of, 604
  measurement error and, 114–115
  in nonparametric regression,
    19–24, 482, 484–485
  of ridge estimator, 326–327
  and specification error, 111–112, 120–121
Biased estimation, 325–329
BIC. *See* Bayesian information criterion
Binary vs. binomial data, 373, 380
Binomial distribution, 379, 382–383,
  402–403, 408, 419
Bins, number of, for histogram, 30
Bisquare (biweight) objective and weight
  functions, 533–536
Bivariate-normal distribution.
  See Multivariate-normal distribution
Bonferroni outlier test, 248, 413
Bootstrap:
  advantages of, 587, 602–603
  barriers to use, 602–603
  bias estimate, 604
  central analogy of, 590
  confidence envelope for studentized
    residuals, 271
  confidence intervals, 594–597
  hypothesis tests, 599–601
  for mean, 587–593
  parametric, 271
  procedure, 593–594
  for regression models, 597–598
  standard error, 592, 594
  for survey data, 601–602
  for time-series regression, 605
Boundary bias in nonparametric regression,
  22, 478
Bounded-influence regression, 539–540
Box-Cox transformations.
  See Transformations, Box-Cox
Boxplots, 37–40, 42–43
Box-Tidwell transformations,
  294–296, 304–305, 474
Breakdown point, 539
"Bubble plot" of Cook's D-statistic, 251
"Bulging rule" to select linearizing
  transformation, 58–60

Canonical parameter, 402
Case weights, 601–602, 604–605
Causation, 3–7, 110–112
Censored normal distribution, 571–573, 583
Censored regression, 578–579
Censoring, 548, 571–572
Centering, 200, 332, 452, 469
CERES plots, 286, 415
Clusters in survey sampling, 601
Collinearity, 88, 91, 105–106, 193
  and ANOVA models, 233–234
  detection of, 308–323
  in dummy regression, 127, 144
  estimation in presence of, 323–329
  in Heckman's selection-regression
    model, 376
  influence on, 253–254
  in logistic regression, 350
  in model selection, 610
  in time-series regression, 307, 445
  vector geometry of, 227, 234–235
Comparisons, linear. *See* Contrasts, linear
Complementary log-log link, 380–381
Component-plus-residual plots, 278–282
  augmented, 285–286
  effectiveness of, 284–285, 303–304
  for generalized linear models, 415
  "leakage" in, 286
  for models with interactions, 282–284
Condition index, 321
Condition number, 321
Conditionally undefined data, 548
Conditioning plot (coplot), 46–48, 124–125,
  504–508
Confidence ellipse (and ellipsoid).
  See Confidence regions, joint
  See also Data ellipse, standard
Confidence envelope:
  for nonparametric regression,
    489–491, 501, 504, 506, 521
  for quantile-comparison
    plots, 35–36, 271
Confidence intervals:
  bootstrap, 594–597
  for Box-Cox transformation, 293
  for effect displays, 411
  generating ellipse, 204–206 , 216
  for generalized linear model, 386
  jackknife, 603–604
  for logit models, 345–346
  and missing data, 552, 555–556
  for multiple imputation, 564
  for nonlinear function of parameters, 409

for regression coefficients,
104–107, 116, 199, 216
and ridge regression, 328
and variance-inflation factor, 308–309
Confidence regions, joint, 203–206,
253, 309, 346, 354
Consistency:
of least-squares estimator, 213, 272
and missing data, 552, 556, 570, 574–576
of nonparametric regression, 20–21
of quasi-likelihood estimation, 407
Constant error variance, assumption of,
101, 105, 148, 188
See also Nonconstant error variance
Constructed variables, 293–294, 295–296, 415
Contingency tables:
logit models for, 370–372
loglinear models for, 394–400
Continuation ratios, 362
See also Dichotomies, nested
Contour plot of regression surface, 503–504, 506
Contrasts, linear, in ANOVA, 176–179, 183–185,
191–192, 213–214
Cook's distance (Cook's D),
250–252, 255, 263, 413
Coplot. *See* Conditioning plot
Correlation:
multiple, 93–94, 228
multiple, adjusted for degrees of freedom,
94, 609, 631
multiple, for generalized linear models, 387
multiple, for logit models, 346–347
partial, 98, 235–236
simple, 83–86
vs. slope, 85–86
vs. standard error of regression, 82–83
vector geometry of, 223–224, 228
Correlogram, 442
See also Autocorrelation
Cosine of angle between vectors and
correlation, 223–224
Covariates, 173
COVRATIO, 253, 255
Cross-validation (CV):
generalized (GCV), 488, 611, 631
and model selection, 610–611
to select span in nonparametric regression,
486–489, 500
vs. validation, 626
Cumulative distribution function (CDF),
34–35, 339–340
Curvilinear relationship, 26, 58
See also Nonlinearity

"Curse of dimensionality," 502–503
Cutoffs, relative vs. absolute, for diagnostics, 254

Data craft, 13
Data ellipse (and ellipsoid), standard,
205–207, 245, 318–319
Degrees of freedom:
in ANOVA, 147, 157, 160, 165–166
in dummy regression, 129, 139–140
in estimating the error variance, 231–232
multiple correlation corrected for, 94, 609
in nonparametric regression, 488, 493–495,
500–501, 514
in regression analysis, 82, 92, 108–109, 199
for studentized residuals, 246–247
vector geometry of, 224–226, 230
Delta method, 409–411
Density estimation, 30–33
Design matrix, 188
See also Model matrix
Deviance:
components of, 374
residual, 347, 376, 408, 419, 521
scaled, 387, 408
See also Analysis of deviance
Deviation regressors, 145–146, 158,
164, 175, 189, 372
DFBETA and DFBETAS, 250–251, 262, 413
DFFITS, 250–251, 255
Diagnostic methods. *See* Autocorrelation;
Collinearity; Generalized linear models,
diagnostic methods for; Influential
observations; Leverage of observations;
Nonconstant error variance; Nonlinearity;
Non-normality of errors; Outliers
Dichotomies, nested, 361–363
Dichotomous explanatory variables in dummy
regression, 120–124
Dichotomous response variables.
See Linear-probability model;
Logit models; Probit models
Discrete explanatory variables, 287–291
See also Analysis of variance; Contingency
tables; Dummy-variable regression
Discreteness and residual plots, 415
Dispersion parameter in generalized
linear model, 381, 402
estimation of, 385, 391, 406
Dummy-variable regression:
and analysis of covariance, 173
and analysis of variance, 143–144
collinearity in, 127
for dichotomous explanatory variable, 120–124

interactions in, 131–140
and linear contrasts, 176
model for, 121–122, 132–133
model matrix for, 188
for polytomous explanatory variable, 125–127
and semiparametric regression, 515
and standardized coefficients, 140
and variable selection, 325
Durbin-Watson statistic, 442–443, 448

"Effect" displays:
in analysis of variance, 169–171
in dummy regression, 136–137, 139
following transformations, 282–283
for generalized linear models,
389–391, 411, 416
for logit models, 348, 350–351,
359, 367–370, 454
Elasticity, and log transformations, 62
EM (expectation-maximization) algorithm,
558–561
Empirical cumulative distribution function
(ECDF), 34–35
Empirical vs. structural relations, 110–112
Empty cells in ANOVA, 172–173
Equal cell frequencies in ANOVA,
161–162, 182–183, 265
Equivalent kernels in nonparametric regression,
524–526
Error variance, estimation of:
in linear regression, 104, 106, 198, 231–232
in nonlinear regression, 466
in nonparametric regression, 490, 495, 501, 514
Essential nonlinearity, 463
Estimating equations:
for additive regression model, 513
for generalized linear model, 404–405
for logit models, 353–354, 360
for nonlinear regression model, 464
for robust estimation, 535–536, 543
See also Normal equations
Expected sums of squares, 202
Experimental vs. observational research, 4–6
Exponential families, 379, 402–403
See also Normal (Gaussian) distribution;
Binomial distribution; Poisson
distribution; Gamma distribution;
Inverse-Gaussian distribution
Extra sum of squares. See Incremental sum of
squares

Factors, 120
Fences, to identify outliers, 39–40

Fisher's method of scoring, 406
Fitted values, 23, 78–79, 85–87, 208, 221,
226–227, 230, 244, 261, 411, 477, 480,
489–490, 493–494, 497, 500–501, 521, 581,
609–611
Fitting constants, method of, for ANOVA, 162
Five-number summary, 37
Fixed explanatory variables, 101–102,
105, 597, 604
Forward search, 259–260
Forward selection, 324
F-tests:
in analysis of variance, 144–145, 154–156,
158–160, 165–166
for constant error variance, 290–291
for contrasts, 179
and Cook's D-statistic, 250
in dummy regression, 123, 128–129,
137, 139–140
for general linear hypothesis, 202–203, 409
for generalized linear model, 387, 408–409
and joint confidence regions, 203
and Mallows's C_p-statistic, 610
for multiple imputations, 566
in multiple regression, 107–110, 201–203,
228–231, 491
for nonlinearity (lack of fit), 287–289
for nonparametric regression, 491–493,
501, 510, 514–516
step-down, for polynomial regression, 290, 452

Gamma distribution, 379, 383, 385, 402–403, 419
Gamma function, 383
Gaussian distribution. See Normal distribution
Gaussian (normal) kernel function, 477
Gauss-Markov theorem, 103, 196–197, 268, 429
Gauss-Newton method, for nonlinear least
squares, 464, 466, 468–469
Generalized additive models (GAMs), 519–521
Generalized cross validation (GCV), 488, 611, 631
Generalized least squares (GLS),
428–429, 438–440, 446
bootstrapping, 605
diagnostic methods for, 412–417
empirical (EGLS), 439
limitations of, 445
vs. ordinary least squares, 444–445
See also Weighted least squares
Generalized linear model (GLM), 379–381
robust estimation of, 543–544
saturated, 386
See also Logit models; Poisson regression;
Probit models

Generalized variance, 253
Generalized variance-inflation factor (GVIF),
    322–323
General linear model, 187, 195–196, 451
    multivariate 207–209, 581
    vs. generalized linear model, 379
    See also Analysis of covariance; Analysis of
        variance; Dummy-variable regression;
        Multiple-regression analysis; Polynomial
        regression; Simple-regression analysis
General nonlinear model, 463
Geometric mean, 33
Global (unit) nonresponse, 548
GLS. *See* Generalized least squares
Gravity model of migration, 460–461
Greek alphabet, 637

Hat-matrix, 261–262, 265, 269, 412, 493–494
Hat-values, 244–246, 251, 253–254, 261–262,
    264–265, 275, 412
Heavy-tailed distributions, 16, 36–37,
    268, 530, 544
Heckman's selection-regression model,
    573–576, 583
    cautions concerning, 577–578
Heteroscedasticity. *See* Non-constant error variance;
    See also Constant error variance;
        "White" corrected standard errors
Higher-way ANOVA. *See* Analysis of variance,
    higher-way
Hinges (quartiles), 39, 55
Hinge-spread (interquartile range), 39–40
Histograms, 28–30
    See also Density estimate; Stem-and-leaf
        display
Homoscedasticity. *See* Constant error variance
    See also Non-constant error variance
Hotelling-Lawley trace test statistic, 208
Huber objective and weight functions,
    532, 534–536
Hypothesis tests:
    in ANCOVA, 175–176
    in ANOVA, 144–146, 154–156, 158–160,
        165–166, 180–181
    Bayesian, 614–615
    bootstrap, 599–601
    for Box-Cox transformation, 71, 293
    for Box-Tidwell transformation, 295
    for constant error variance, 290–291, 296–297
    for contrasts, 178–179, 183–184, 191–192
    for difference in means, 180
    in dummy-variable regression, 126–129, 133,
        137, 139–140

    for equality of regression coefficients,
        116, 203, 328
    for general linear hypothesis, 202–203, 209,
        263–264, 353, 409
    for general nonlinear hypothesis, 409–411
    in generalized linear models, 385–387,
        397, 399, 408–411
    impact of large samples on, 608
    for "lack of fit," 287–290
    for linearity, 287–290, 515–516
    in logit models, 345–346, 353
    for multiple imputation, 563–566
    in multivariate linear model, 208–209
    for nonlinear regression, 409–411
    in nonparametric regression, 491–493,
        501, 510, 514–516
    for outliers, 247–248
    for overdispersion, 417
    for regression coefficients, 104, 106–110,
        116, 199–205, 211, 228–229
    for serially correlated errors, 442
    "step down," for polynomial terms, 290, 452
    See also F-tests; Likelihood-ratio test; score
        test; t-tests; Wald tests

Identity link function, 380, 382
Ignorable missing data, 549
Ill conditioning, 321
    See also Collinearity
Incremental sum of squares:
    in ANOVA, 158–160, 162–163, 166, 217
    in dummy regression, 123, 127–129, 137
    for equality of regression coefficients, 116
    for linear hypothesis, 264–265
    for nonlinearity, 287–288
    in nonparametric regression, 492, 501,
        506, 514, 516
    in regression analysis, 109, 201
    vector geometry of, 228–231, 236
    See also F-tests
Incremental sum-of-squares-and-products
    matrix, 208
Independence:
    assumption of, 101, 105
    of nested dichotomies, 362–363
    from irrelevant alternatives, 377
Independent random sample, 15, 587
Index plots, 245
Indicator variables, 121
    for polytomous logit model, 359
    See also Dummy-variable regression
Indirect effect. *See* Intervening variable
Influence function, 531

Influential observations, 26–27, 250–265
Information matrices for logit models,
    353, 361–363, 376
Initial estimates (start values),
    464–465, 537, 540
Interaction effects:
    in ANCOVA, 174–175
    in ANOVA, 150–152, 164, 166–167, 234
    and association parameters in loglinear
        models, 396
    and component-plus-residual plots, 282–284
    disordinal, 151–152
    distinguished from correlation, 132
    in dummy regression, 131–140
    in generalized linear models, 379
    linear-by-linear, 357
    in logit models, 344, 371, 401
    and multiple imputation, 567–568
    in nonparametric regression, 506, 514, 516
    in polynomial regression, 452–453
    and structural dimension, 300
    and variable selection, 325
    See also Effect displays; Marginality,
        principle of
Interquartile range. See Hinge-spread
Intervening variable, 6–7, 112–113
Invariant explanatory variables, 26–27,
    81, 88, 91, 102, 105, 193, 210
Inverse link function, 380, 382
Inverse Mills ratio, 572, 574
Inverse regression, 300
Inverse-Gaussian distribution,
    379, 383–384, 386, 402–403, 419
Inverse-link (mean) function, 380
Inverse-square link function, 380, 382
Invertibility of MA and ARMA
    processes, 436
Irrelevant regressors, 4, 112, 117, 212–213
Item nonreponse, 548
Iteratively weighted (reweighted) least
    squares (IWLS, IRLS), 354–355,
    405–406, 520, 534, 537

Jackknife, 603–604
Joint confidence regions. See Confidence
    regions, joint
Jointly influential observation, 255–259

Kernel smoothing:
    in nonparametric density estimation, 30–33
    in nonparametric regression,
        476-479, 524–526
Kullback-Leibler information, 613

Ladder of powers, 51
    See also Transformations, family of
        powers and roots
Lagged variables, 445
Least-absolute-values (LAV), 79, 531,
    535–536, 540–541
Least squares:
    criterion, 79
    estimators, properties of, 102–104, 106, 194–198
    nonlinear, 463–467
    objective function, 530, 535–536
    vector geometry of, 221–222, 226–227
    See also Generalized least squares; Multiple-
        regression analysis; Ordinary least-squares
        regression; Simple-regression analysis;
        Weighted least squares
Least-trimmed-squares (LTS) regression,
    539–540, 545
Levene's test for constant error variance, 290–291
Leverage of observations. See Hat-values
Leverage plot, 263–264
Likelihood-ratio tests:
    for generalized linear model, 386, 408
    for generalized nonparametric regression,
        522–523
    for independence, 418
    for linear model, 200–201
    for logit models, 346, 372
    for loglinear models, 397, 399
    for overdispersion, 417
    of proportional-odds assumption, 368
    to select transformation, 70–71, 292–293
    See also Analysis of deviance
Linear estimators, 102, 195–196, 268
Linear hypothesis. See Hypothesis tests,
    for general linear hypothesis
Linear model. See General linear model
Linear predictor, 339, 344, 379–380, 411, 453, 460
Linearity:
    assumption of, 15–17, 100–101, 105, 277
    among explanatory variables, 285–286
    See also Nonlinearity
Linear-probability model, 337–3338
    constrained, 338–339
Link function, 379–380
    canonical, 381–382, 402, 405–406
    vs. linearizing transformation of response, 382
    See also Complementary log-log link function;
        Identity link function; Inverse link
        function; Inverse-square link function;
        Log link function; Logit link function;
        Log-log link function; Probit link
        function; Square-root link function

Local averaging, in nonparametric regression, 21–23
Local likelihood estimation, 517–519
Local linear regression. *See* Local polynomial regression
Local polynomial regression, 479–480, 496–503, 544
Loess. *See* Lowess smoother
Log link function, 380, 382, 387
Log odds. *See* Logit
Logarithm, as "zeroth" power, 51–52
Logit (log odds), 66–68, 341–342
  empirical, 370
  link function, 380–382
Logit models:
  binomial, 372–374
  for contingency tables, 370–375, 400–401
  dichotomous, 340–347
  estimation of, 345, 352–355, 359–361, 374, 376–377
  interpretation of, 342, 344
  and loglinear model, 400–401
  multinomial, 356, 375, 377, 401
  for nested dichotomies, 361–363, 368–369
  nonparametric, 517–519
  ordered (proportional-odds), 364–366, 368–369
  polytomous, 355–357, 368–369
  problems with coefficients in, 350–352
  saturated, 374
  unobserved-variable formulation of, 333–334, 363–364
Logistic distribution, 340–341
Logistic population-growth model, 463, 467–468
Logistic regression. *See* Logit models
Loglinear model, 394–400
  relationship to logit model, 400–401
Log-log link function, 380–381
Lowess (loess) smoother, 23, 480
  See also Local polynomial regression
Lurking variable, 112

M estimator:
  of location, 530–535
  in regression, 535. 537, 598–599
MA. *See* Moving-average process
Main effects, 150–151
Mallows's C_p-statistic, 610, 631
MAR. *See* Missing data, missing at random
Marginal means in ANOVA, 149
Marginality, principle of, 135, 152, 159, 163
Marquardt method for nonlinear least squares, 464, 466
MASE. *See* Mean average squared error

Maximum-likelihood estimation:
  of Box-Cox transformation, 68–71, 292–294, 304
  of Box-Tidwell transformation, 294–295
  of constrained linear-probability model, 339
  EM algorithm for, with missing data, 558–561
  of error variance, 200, 296
  of general nonlinear model, 464–466
  of generalized additive models, 520
  and generalized least squares, 428
  of generalized linear model, 385, 404–406
  of Heckman's selection-regression model, 575
  of linear regression model, 103, 106, 116, 197–198, 211
  of logit models, 345, 352–355, 359–361, 373–374, 376–377
  of loglinear models, 397
  with missing data, 556–561
  of multivariate linear model, 208, 217
  with random regressors, 211
  in time series regression, 440, 448
  of transformation parameters, 291–295
  and weighted least squares, 274, 302
  of zero-inflated negative-binomial (ZINB) model, 418
  of zero-inflated Poisson (ZIP) model, 394
MCAR. *See* Missing data, missing completely at random
Mean average squared error (MASE) in local regression, 488
Mean function, 299–300, 380
Mean squares, 108
Mean-deviation form, vector geometry of, 222–223
  See also Centering
"Mean-shift" outlier model, 247
Mean-squared error:
  and biased estimation, 325–326
  and C_p-statistic, 609
  and cross-validation, 610
  of least-squares estimator, 103, 196
  in nonparametric regression, 482, 484–486
  and outlier rejection, 249
  of ridge estimator, 327
Measurement error, 112–115, 117–118
Median, 17, 29, 37, 39, 55, 64, 531–532, 539–541, 544
Median absolute deviation (MAD), 533
Method-of-moments estimator of dispersion parameter, 385, 391, 406
Missing data:
  available-case analysis (pair-wise deletion) of, 553–556
  complete-case analysis (list-wise, case-wise deletion) of, 552–556

conditional mean (regression) imputation of, 553–556

missing at random (MAR), 549–556, 567

missing completely at random (MCAR), 549–551, 553–556

missing not at random (MNAR), 549, 551–556, 570

multiple imputation of, 561–568

unconditional mean imputation of, 553–556

univariate, 550, 581

Missing information, rate of, 564

MM estimator, 540

MNAR. *See* Missing data, missing not at random

Model averaging, 622–624

   based on AIC, 531–632

   comments on, 624

Model matrix, 188–189, 195, 208, 210, 233–234, 411

   row basis of, 190, 192, 213–214, 217

Model respecification and collinearity, 323, 329

Model selection:

   avoiding, 608

   and collinearity, 324, 329

   comments on, 620–621

   criteria for, 608–612

   and fallacy of affirming the consequent, 607

   vs. model averaging, 608

   and simultaneous inference, 607

   See also Akaike information criterion; Bayesian information criterion; Correlation, multiple, adjusted for degrees of freedom; Cross validation; Mallows's C_p statistic; Model averaging

Model validation, 626–628, 630

Modes, multiple, in error distribution, 16, 268

Moving-average process (MA), 434–437, 439, 446–447

Multicollinearity, 309

   See also Collinearity

Multinomial distribution, 375, 379, 397, 563

Multinomial logit model. *See* Logit models, multinomial; Logit models, polytomous

Multiple correlation. *See* Correlation, multiple

Multiple imputation of missing data, 561–568

Multiple outliers, 255

Multiple regression analysis, 86–92, 97–98, 105–110, 187–188, 195–196, 245

   model for, 105

   nonparametric, 496–516

   vs. simple regression analysis, 89

   vector geometry of, 226–231

Multiple-classification analysis (MCA), 167

Multiplicative errors, 460–461

Multivariate linear models, 207–209, 581

Multivariate logistic distribution, 356

Multivariate-normal distribution:

   Box-Cox transformation to, 68–71

   EM algorithm for, 559–561

   and likelihood for linear model, 198

   of errors in linear model, 188, 208

   multiple imputation for, 561–563, 567–568

   and polytomous probit model, 355

   of regression coefficients, 195, 198

   of response in linear model, 188

   singular, of residuals, 231

Negative binomial distribution, 392

Negative-binomial regression model, 392

   zero-inflated (ZINB), 393, 418

Nested dichotomies, 361–363

Newton-Raphson method, 354, 406

Nonconstant error variance or spread, 17,

   and bootstrap, 598

   correction for, 275–276

   detection of, 272–277

   and dummy response variable, 338, 375

   effect on OLS estimator, 276–277, 302–303

   and quantile regression, 542

   and specification error, 274, 302

   tests for, 290–291, 296–298

   transforming, 63–66, 272–273

   and weighted least squares (WLS), 274–275, 302

Nonignorable missing data, 549, 559, 570

Nonlinear least squares, 463–467

Nonlinearity, 17

   and correlation coefficient, 84

   detection of, 277–286, 415–417

   and dummy response variable, 338

   essential, 463

   monotone vs. nonmonotone, 58, 60

   and multiple imputation, 567–568

   tests for, 287–290, 492, 515

   transformable, 460–462

   transformation of, 57–60, 294–295, 415–416

   See also Linearity, assumption of; Nonlinear least squares; Nonparametric regression;

Non-normality of errors:

   detection of, 268–271

   and dummy response variable, 337–338

   See also Normality; Skewness

Nonorthogonal contrasts, 213–214

Nonparametric regression:

   generalized, 517–523

   local averaging, 21–23

   naive, 17–21

obstacles to, 502–503
See also Kernel smoothing; Local polynomial
  regression; Splines, smoothing
Normal (Gaussian) distribution:
  family of, in generalized linear model,
    379, 382, 402–403, 408, 418
  as kernel function, 31–33, 477, 485
  of regression coefficients, 103–104, 106,
    198–199
  to transform probability, 67, 340–341, 343, 364
  See also Censored-normal distribution;
    Multivariate-normal distribution;
    Non-normality of errors; Normality,
    assumption of; Quantile-comparison plots;
    Truncated-normal distribution
Normal equations, 80, 87, 90–91, 97, 193–194, 308
Normality, assumption of, 15–16, 101, 103, 105,
  188, 196, 201, 248, 451, 463, 476, 515, 574,
  578, 587
  See also Non-normality of errors
Normalization, in principal-components
  analysis, 315
Normal-probability plots. *See*
  Quantile-comparison plots
Notation, 636–637

Objective function. *See* Least absolute values;
  Least squares criterion; Huber objective and
  weight functions; Biweight (bisquare)
  objective and weight functions
Observation space, 221
Observational vs. experimental research, 4–6, 9
Occam's window, 624
Odds, 341–342
  posterior, 615
Omnibus null hypothesis, 107–108, 144, 201,
  203, 346, 353
Omitted-variable bias. *See* Specification error
One-way ANOVA. *See* Analysis of variance,
  one-way
Order statistics, 35, 55, 541
Ordinal data, 363–368
Ordinary-least-squares (OLS) regression:
  and generalized-least-squares, 429, 438–439, 444
  for linear-probability model, 337–338
  and nonconstant error variance, 275–277,
    302–303
  vs. ridge estimator, 327
  in time-series regression, 433, 447
  and weighted least squares, 275
  See also Generalized least squares; Least squares;
    Multiple regression analysis; Simple
    regression analysis; Weighted least squares

Orthogonal contrasts, 192, 213
Orthogonal data in ANOVA, 161
Orthogonal (uncorrelated) regressors, 230–231
  in polynomial regression, 469–470
Orthonormal basis for error subspace, 231–232
Outliers, 23, 26, 29, 39–40, 241–244, 246–249,
  530, 538–539
  Anscombe's insurance analogy, 248–249
  multivariate, 245
  See also Unusual data, discarding
Overdispersion, 391–392, 417
Overfitting, 260, 626

Parametric equation, in ANOVA, 190–191, 213, 234
Partial autocorrelation. *See* Autocorrelation,
  partial
Partial correlation. *See* Correlation, partial
Partial regression functions,
  285, 508, 511–514, 520–521
Partial vs. marginal relationship, 278
Partial-regression plots. *See* Added-variable plots;
  Leverage plot
Partial-residual plots.
  See Component-plus-residual plots
Penalized sum of squares, 495
Perspective plot of regression surface,
  503–504, 506
Pillai-Bartlett trace test statistic, 208
Poisson distribution, 379, 383–384, 402–403, 419
  and multinomial distribution, 397
Poisson regression model, 389–391
  zero-inflated (ZIP), 392–394, 417–418
Polynomial regression, 26, 58, 277–278,
  280–282, 290, 322, 410, 451–455, 469–470
  piece-wise, 456–458, 470–471
  See also Local polynomial regression
Polytomous explanatory variables in dummy
  regression, 124–127, 135–136
Polytomous response variables. *See* Logit models;
  Probit models
Prediction in regression, 216, 325, 567, 608–610,
  620–622, 624
Predictive distribution of the data, 562–563, 570
Premium-protection approach to outliers,
  248–249
Principal-components analysis, 313–320, 330
  and diagnosing collinearity, 320–322
Prior cause, common, 112–113
Prior information and collinearity, 328–329
Probit:
  and Heckman's selection-regression model,
    574–575
  link function, 380–381

models, 340, 343–344, 355, 361, 364, 377
transformation, 67–68
Profile log likelihood, 293
Propensity scores, 622
Proportional-odds model, 354–366, 368–369
Pseudoresponse variable in logit model, 355
Pseudo-values in jackknife, 603

Quadratic regression. *See* Polynomial regression
Quadratic surfaces, 453, 455
Quantile function, 34
Quantile regression, 540–541
Quantile-comparison plots, 34–37, 268–271
Quartiles. *See* Hinges
Quasi-binomial models, 392
Quasi-likelihood estimation, 391, 407
Quasi-Poisson regression model, 391–392
Quasi-variances of dummy-variable coefficients, 130, 420–421

Random explanatory variables, 102, 110–112, 210–213, 597, 604
Randomization in experimental design, 4–6
Rectangular kernel function, 479
Reference category. *See* Baseline category
Regression of X on Y, 96–97
Regression toward the mean, 97
Regressors, distinguished from explanatory variables, 122, 451
Residual standard error. *See* Standard error of the regression
Residuals, 2, 78–80, 85–87, 221–222, 226–230
augmented partial, 285–286
deviance, 413
distribution of, 262
in generalized linear models, 412–413, 415
partial, 279, 415
Pearson, 413
plot of, vs. fitted values, 272
quantile-comparison plot for, 268–269, 271
response, 412
standardized, 246–247, 249
standardized deviance, 413
standardized Pearson, 413
studentized, 246–249, 254–255, 269, 413
supernormality of, 271
working, 412
Resistance (to outliers), 79
Restrictions (constraints) on parameters:
in ANCOVA, 174
in ANOVA, 145–146, 155, 164, 189
in logit models for contingency tables, 372
in loglinear models, 396, 398

in polytomous logit model, 356
and ridge regression, 329
sigma, 145–146, 155, 164, 189, 356, 372, 396, 398
Ridge regression, 326–331
Ridge trace, 331
Robust regression. *See* Generalized linear model, robust estimation of; Least-trimmed-squares regression; *M* estimator; *MM* estimator; Quantile regression
Robustness of efficiency and validity, 268
Roy's maximum root test statistic, 208
Rug plot, 32

Sampling variance:
of fitted values, 490
of the generalized-least-squares estimator, 428, 446
of least-squares estimators, 103, 106, 115–116, 196, 198, 214, 276, 308, 320–321, 327, 447
of the mean, 532
of the mean of an AR(1) process, 433
of the median, 532
of a nonlinear function of coefficients, 410
of nonparametric regression, 19, 485
of ridge-regression estimator, 327
of weighted-least-squares estimator, 303
See also Asymptotic standard errors; Standard errors; Variance-covariance matrix
Scatterplot matrices, 44–45, 300–301
Scatterplots, 13–14, 40–42
coded, 45–46
jittering, 41–42
one-dimensional, 32
smoothing, 23, 40–41
three-dimensional, 45–47
vs. vector representation, 220–221
Scheffé intervals, 129, 205
Score test:
of constant error variance, 296–297
of proportional-odds assumption, 368
to select transformation, 292–294
Seasonal effects, 433
Semiparametric regression models, 514–516
Separability in logit models, 350–352
Serially correlated errors, 429–438, 463
diagnosing, 441–444
effect on OLS estimation, 447
estimation with, 438–440
Sigma constraints. *See* Restrictions on parameters, sigma
Simple random sample, 101, 549, 587

Simple regression analysis, 78–82, 100–105
  model for, 100–102, 220
  vector geometry of, 220–226
Simpson's paradox, 121
Skewness, 13, 15–16, 33, 36–37, 41, 65–66,
  268–269, 383, 385
  See also Transformations, to correct skewness
Smoother matrix, 493–494, 496, 500–501,
  513–514
Smoothing. See Density estimation; Lowess
  smoother; Local polynomial regression;
  Scatterplots, smoothing; Splines, smoothing
Span of smoother, 21–24, 478, 480–483,
  486–489, 500–501, 506, 519, 523
  See also Bandwidth; Window
Specification error, 111–112, 116–117, 212–213,
  274, 302, 574
Splines:
  regression, 458–460, 470–471
  smoothing, 495–496
Spread-level plot, 64–66, 272–273
Spurious association, 6–7, 112, 622
Square-root link function, 380
SS notation for ANOVA, 158–163, 166, 217, 236
  adapted to logit models, 372
Standard error(s):
  bootstrap, 591–592, 594, 597–598
  of coefficients in generalized linear models,
    385, 391
  of coefficients in Heckman's selection-
    regression model, 576, 583
  of coefficients in logit models,
    345–346, 351, 353
  of coefficients in regression, 104, 106–107,
    199, 252, 257, 272, 444
  collinearity, impact of, on, 307
  of differences in dummy-variable coefficients,
    129–130, 420–421
  of effect displays, 271, 411
  influence on, 252–253
  of the mean, 588
  and model selection, 608
  from multiple imputations, 563
  for nonlinear function of coefficients, 409–410
  of order statistics, 35
  of the regression, 82–83, 92, 246
  of transformation-parameter estimates, 70
  "White" corrected, 275–277
  See also Asymptotic standard errors;
    Variance-covariance matrix
Standardized regression coefficients,
  94–96, 98, 214
  misuse of, 96, 140

"Start" for power transformation, 53–54, 71–72
Start values, 464–465, 537, 540
Stationary time series, 429–430, 434, 436
Statistical models, limitations of, 1–3
Steepest descent, method of, for nonlinear least
  squares, 464–466
Stem-and-leaf display, 29–30
Stepwise regression, 324, 620
Stratified sampling, 587, 601, 628
Structural dimension, 298–301, 305
Structural-equation models, 3, 115
Studentized residuals. See Residuals, studentized
Subset regression, 324, 330, 609, 620
Sum of squares:
  between-group, 147
  for contrasts, 184, 192
  generalized, 428
  for orthogonal regressors, 230, 235
  penalized, 495
  prediction (PRESS), 610
  raw, 159
  regression (RegSS), 83–85, 92–93, 108–109,
    147, 158, 162, 201–202, 233, 235
  residual (RSS), 80, 83–85, 92–94, 108–109,
    132, 140, 147, 159, 183, 192, 201,
    309–311, 408, 463–466, 488, 490–492,
    495, 500–501, 514, 527, 609, 611, 631
  total (TSS), 83–85, 92–94, 108–109, 140, 147,
    159–160, 166, 491–492, 527, 609, 631
  "Types I, II, and III," 159
  uncorrected total, 225
  vector geometry of, 222–223,
    225, 226–230, 236
  weighted, 274, 302, 480, 497, 537
  within-group, 147
  See also Incremental sum of squares;
    SS notation
Sum-of-squares-and-products (SSP) matrices, 208

Tables. See Contingency tables
Three-way ANOVA. See Analysis of variance,
  three-way
Time-series data, 427
Time-series regression. See Generalized
  least squares
Tobit model, 579
Training subsample, 626
Transformable nonlinearity, 460–462
Transformations:
  arcsine-square-root, 67
  Box-Cox, 50–52, 68–72, 292–294, 304, 567
  Box-Tidwell, 294–296, 304–205, 415, 474
  constructed variables for, 293–296, 415

to correct nonconstant spread,
63–66, 272–273
to correct nonlinearity, 57–63, 278–279
to correct skewness, 54–57, 269–270
family of powers and roots, 50–54
"folded" powers and roots, 68
and generalized least squares, 429, 438–439,
444–445, 447–448
linear, effect of, on regression coefficients,
97, 116
logarithms (logs), 51–52
logit, 66–67
normalizing, *see* Transformations, Box-Cox
of probabilities and proportions, 66–68
probit, 67
Trend in time series, 313, 433, 444–445
Tricube kernel function, 477–481, 484–485,
525–526
Truncated normal distribution,
571–573, 582–583
Truncation, 571–573
t-tests:
for constructed variable, 292, 294
for contrasts in ANOVA, 179, 183–184
for difference of means, 180, 553
in multiple imputation, 564
for regression coefficients, 104, 107, 110, 116,
123, 176, 199, 215, 409
for studentized residuals (outliers),
246–248, 269
Tuning constant, 532–534, 536
Two-way ANOVA. *See* Analysis of
variance, two-way

Unbias of least-squares estimators, 102–103, 106,
110–111, 115, 195–196, 211, 248, 268, 272,
326, 447
Univariate missing data, 550, 581
Unmodelled heterogeneity, 392
Unusual data, discarding, 260–261
See also Influential observations; Leverage of
observations; Outliers

Validation. *See* Cross-validation; Model
validation
Validation subsample, 626
Variable-selection methods in regression.
See Model selection
Variance-covariance matrix:
of errors, 188, 208, 217, 274, 302, 428, 438,
446, 448
of fitted values , 493
of generalized least-squares estimator, 428–429

of generalized linear model coefficients, 406
of least-squares estimator, 195, 199, 275
of logit-model coefficients,
353–354, 361, 376
of *M* estimator coefficients, 537
of principal components, 316
of quantile-regression coefficients, 541
of ridge-regression estimator,
of weighted-least-squares estimator, 274, 302
See also Asymptotic standard errors;
Standard errors
Variance-inflation factors (VIF), 106, 308–309,
321, 323
generalized (GVIF), 322–323, 576
Vector geometry:
of added-variable plots, 263, 265
of analysis of variance, 233–234
of correlation, 223–224, 228
of multiple regression, 226–231, 301, 322
of principal components, 314–317
of simple regression, 220–226

Wald tests:
bootstrapping, 599–601
for generalized linear models, 385, 406, 409
for logit models, 345–346, 353, 363
for overdispersion, 417
for proportional odds, 368
of transformation parameters, 70–71, 292
Weighted least squares (WLS), 274–275,
302–303, 428, 601, 604
estimation of linear probability model, 338
See also Iteratively weighted least squares;
Local polynomial regression; *M* estimator
Weighted squares of means, method of, for
ANOVA, 162
"White" corrected standard errors,
275–277, 297, 583
White noise, 432
Wilks's lambda test statistic, 208
Window:
in density estimation, 31–34
in nonparametric regression,
21–23, 477–482, 484, 498, 518
See also Bandwidth; Span of smoother
Working response, 405

Yule-Walker equations, 436–437

Zero-inflated negative-binomial (ZINB)
regression model, 393, 418
Zero-inflated Poisson (ZIP) regression model,
392–394

Data Set Index

Anscombe's "quartet," 26–28, 545

B. Fox, Canadian women's labor-force time
    series, 311–313, 319–322,
    324–325, 330–331
Baseball salaries, 618–621, 624–625,
    627, 631–632
Blau and Duncan, stratification, 214–215
British Election Panel Study (BEPS), voting,
    357–359

Campbell, et al., *The American Voter,*
    370–373, 395, 397–401
Canadian migration, 471–473
Canadian occupational prestige, 18–20, 24,
    59, 61–62, 66, 69, 91–96, 98, 124–130,
    135–140, 216, 300–301, 420–421, 478–479,
    481, 483, 490–492, 524–526
Chilean plebiscite, 336–339, 342–343,
    355, 516–518
Cowles and Davis, volunteering, 453–454, 470

Davis, height and weight of exercisers, 18–19,
    22–23, 25, 45–46, 78, 81–82, 86, 90, 105,
    116, 243–245, 248–249, 251, 253, 260, 604
Duncan, U.S. occupational prestige, 44–45,
    47, 88–90, 92–94, 107, 109–110, 117,
    147–148, 194, 199–200, 215, 235,
    245–246, 248–249, 251–253, 257–260,
    538–540, 544, 598–601, 604

Fox and Hartnagel, Canadian crime-rates time
    series, 440–444, 448, 605
Friendly and Franklin, memory, 176–179, 184,
    191–192

General Social Survey, vocabulary, 41–42, 46, 48,
    167–171, 287–291
Greene and Shaffer, refugee appeals,
    4–5, 628–629

Moore and Krupat, conformity, 152–154,
    160–161, 173–176, 183, 185, 217

Ornstein, Canadian interlocking
    directorates, 42–43, 63–65, 387–392,
    411, 414–417, 545

Statistics Canada, Survey of Labour and Income
    Dynamics (SLID), 13–15, 267, 269–270,
    272–273, 275–276, 279–284, 294–298,
    347–351, 410–411, 420, 452, 459–460,
    474, 503–507, 509–511, 515–516, 522–523,
    542, 576–577, 579–580

U.S. population, 467–469
United Nations, social indicators, 28–33, 38–41,
    54–57, 61–63, 71, 456, 568–570, 582

World Value Survey (WVS), government action
    on poverty, 365–370

About the Author

John Fox is Professor of Sociology at McMaster University in Hamilton, Ontario, Canada. He was previously Professor of Sociology and of Mathematics and Statistics at York University in Toronto, where he also directed the Statistical Consulting Service at the Institute for Social Research. Professor Fox earned a PhD in Sociology from the University of Michigan in 1972. He has delivered numerous lectures and workshops on statistical topics, at such places as the summer program of the Inter-University Consortium for Political and Social Research and the annual meetings of the American Sociological Association. His recent and current work includes research on statistical methods (for example, work on three-dimensional statistical graphs) and on Canadian society (for example, a study of political polls in the 1995 Quebec sovereignty referendum). He is the author of many articles, in such journals as *Sociological Methodology, The Journal of Computational and Graphical Statistics, The Journal of the American Statistical Association, The Canadian Review of Sociology and Anthropology,* and *The Canadian Journal of Sociology.* He has written several other books, including *Applied Regression Analysis, Linear Models, and Related Methods* (Sage, 1997), *Nonparametric Simple Regression* (Sage, 2000), and *Multiple and Generalized Nonparametric Regression* (Sage, 2000).